UNITED STATES CODE

TITLE 26

INTERNAL REVENUE CODE

&& 1-&& 91 VOLUME 1/7

2022 EDITION

TABLE OF CONTENTS:

4

TITLE 26—INTERNAL REVENUE CODE

ACT AUG. 16, 1954, CH. 736, 68A STAT. 3

The following tables have been prepared as aids in comparing provisions of the Internal Revenue Code of 1954 (redesignated the Internal Revenue Code of 1986 by Pub. L. 99–514, §2, Oct. 22, 1986, 100 Stat. 2095) with provisions of the Internal Revenue Code of 1939. No inferences, implications, or presumptions of legislative construction or intent are to be drawn or made by reason of such tables.

Citations to "R.A." refer to the sections of earlier Revenue Acts.

Table I

1939 Code section number	1986 Code section number
1	Omitted
2	7806(a)
3, 4	Omitted
11	1
12(a), (b)(1), (2)	Omitted
12(b)(3), (c)	1
12(d)	2
12(e)	Omitted
12(f)	1
12(g), 13(a)	Omitted
13(b)	11
13(c)–(f), 14	Omitted
15(a), (b)	11
15(c)	1551
21	63
22(a)	61
22(b)(1)	101
22(b)(2)(A)	72
22(b)(2)(B)	72, 403
22(b)(2)(C)	72
22(b)(3)–(5)	102–104
22(b)(6)	107
22(b)(7)	894
22(b)(8)	115, 526, 892, 893, 911, 912, 933, 943
22(b)(9), (10)	108
22(b)(11)–(14)	109, 111–113
22(b)(15)	621
22(b)(16), (17)	114, 121
22(c)	471
22(d)(1)–(5)	472
22(d)(6)	1321, 6155(a)
22(e)	301(a)
22(f)	1001
22(g)	861, 862, 863, 864
22(h)	Chapter 1, Subchapter G, Part III
22(i)	Omitted
22(j)	76
22(k)	71
22(l)	691
22(m)	73, 6201(c)
22(n)	62
22(o)	75
23	161, 211
23(a)(1)(A), (B)	162
23(a)(1)(C)	263
23(a)(2)	212

26(c)	545, 556
26(d)	535, 545, 601
26(e)	Omitted
26(f)	561, 562, 564
26(g)	565
26(h)	247
26(i)	922
27(a)	561
27(b)	535, 562
27(c)–(i)	562, 564
28	565
31	33
32	32
33	6401
34	Omitted
35	31
41	441, 446
42(a)	451
42(b)–(d)	454
43	461
44	453, 7101
45	482
46	442
47	443, 6011(a)
48	441, 7701
51	6001, 6011(a)
51(a)	6001, 6012(a), 6065(b)
51(b)	6012(b)(1), 6013(a), 6014(b)
51(c)	6012(b)
51(d)	Omitted. See 6064.
51(e)	6065(a)
51(f)	6014(a), (b), 6151(a), (b), 6155(a)
51(g)	6012(b), 6013(b), 6653(a), 6659
52	6012(a), (b), 6062
53	6072, 6081, 6091
54(a)–(b)	6001
54(c)–(e)	Omitted
54(f)	6033(a), 6065(b)
55	6103, 7213(a)
56(a)	6151(a)
56(b)	6152, 6601(c)(2)
56(c)	6161(a), 6162(a), 6165, 7101
56(d)–(f)	Omitted
56(g)	6313
56(h)	Omitted
56(i)	6151(b)
56(j), 57	Omitted
58	6012(b), 6015, 6064, 6065, 6073(a), (c), 6081(a), 6091(b), 6103, 6161(a)
59(a)–(c)	6153
59(d)	6201(b), 6315, 6601(g)
60	6015(g), 6073(b), (d), (e), 6091(b), 6153(b), (d), (e)
61	Omitted
62	7805

113(a)(11), (12)	1051, 1052
113(a)(13)	723, 732
113(a)(14)	1053
113(a)(15)	334
113(a)(16)	1052
113(a)(17)	1082
113(a)(18)	334
113(a)(19)	307
113(a)(20), (21)	373
113(a)(22)	372
113(a)(23)	358
113(b)	1011
113(b)(1), (2)	1016
113(b)(3), (4)	1017, 1018
113(c), (d)	1019, 1020
113(e)	1022
114(a)	167(f)
114(b)(1)	612
114(b)(2)	Omitted
114(b)(3)	613(b)(3)
114(b)(4)	613(b)(4)
115(a)	301, 316
115(b)	301, 316
115(c)	302, 312, 331, 342
115(d), (e)	301
115(f)	305
115(g)(1)	302
115(g)(2)	304
115(g)(3)	303
115(h)	312
115(i)	302, 346
115(j)	301
115(k)	Omitted
115(𝑙), (m)	312
116(a)	911
116(b)	Omitted
116(c)	892
116(d), (e)	115
116(f)	943
116(g)	526
116(h)	893
116(i)	121(a)(17)
116(j), (k)	912
116(𝑙)	933
117(a)	1221, 1222
117(b)	1202
117(c)	1201
117(d)	1211
117(e)(1)	1212
117(e)(2)	Omitted
117(f)	1232
117(g)(1), (2)	1233, 1234
117(g)(3)	1238
117(h)	1223

117(i)	582
117(j)	1231
117(k)	631
117(*l*)	1233
117(m)	341
117(n)	1236
117(*o*), (p)	1239, 1240
118	1091
119(a), (b)	861
119(c), (d)	862
119(e)	861, 862, 863
119(f)	864
120	170
121	583
122	172
123	77
124	Omitted
124A, 124B	168, 169
125	171
126	691
127(a), (b)	Omitted
127(c)(1)–(5)	1331–1335
127(d)	1336
127(e), (f)	1337
128	1346
129, 130	269, 270
130A	421
131(a)	901
131(b)	904
131(c)	905, 6155(a), 7101
131(d), (e)	905
131(f)	902
131(g)	901(c)
131(h)	903
131(i)	905
141	1501–1505, 6071, 6081(a), 6091(b)(2), 6503(a)(2)
142	6012(a), (b), 6065(a)
143(a)	1451
143(b)	1441
143(c)	1461, 6011(a), 6072(a), 6091(b), 6151(a)
143(d), (e)	1462, 1463
143(f)	1464, 6414
143(g)	1461
143(h)	1443, 6151
144	1442, 6151(a)
145	7201, 7202, 7203, 7343
146	443, 6155(a), 6601(a), 6658, 6851, 7101
147	6041(b), (c), 6071, 6081(a), 6091(a)
148	6042, 6043, 6044, 6065(a), 6071, 6081(a), 6091(a)
149	6045, 6065(a), 6071, 6081(a), 6091(a)
150	6071, 6081(a), 6091(a), 7001(a), 7231
151	Omitted
153(a)	6033(b), 6071, 6081(a), 6091(a)
153(b)	6034, 6071, 6081(b), 6091(a)

506(i), (j), 507(a)	Omitted
507(b)	543
508	Omitted
509	531
510	Chapter 1, Subchapter G, Part III
511	6103, 7213(a)
650, 651	1471
722(g)	6105
800	2001, 2101
801, 802	Omitted
810	2001(a), 2011(a), (b)
811	2031(a)
811(a), (b)	2033, 2034
811(c)	2035, 2036, 2037
811(d)(1)	2038(a)(1)
811(d)(2)	2038(a)(2)
811(d)(3)	2038(b)
811(d)(4)	Omitted
811(e)—(g)	2040—2042
811(h)	2044
811(i)	2043(a)
811(j)	2032
811(k), (*l*)	2031(b), 2035
811(m)	Omitted
812	2051
812(a)	Omitted
812(b)	2043(b), 2053, 2054
812(c)	2013
812(d), (e)	Omitted. See 2055, 2056.
813(a)(1)	Omitted
813(a)(2)	2012
813(b)	2011
813(c)	2014
820	6036, 6091(a)
821(a)	6018, 6065(a)
821(b)	6071, 6075(a), 6081(a)
821(c)	6091(b)
821(d)	6001
821(e)	Omitted
822(a)(1)	6151(a)
822(a)(2)	6161(a)(2), 6165, 6503(d), 7101
822(b)	2002
823	6314(b)
824	Omitted
825	2204
826(a)	7404
826(b)—(d)	2205—2207
827(a)	6324(a)(1), 6325(a)(1)
827(b), (c)	6324(a)(2), (3)
828, 840, 841	Omitted
850	2202
851	Omitted
860	2101
861	2102, 2103, 2106

862, 863	2104, 2105
864(a)	6018, 6065(a)
864(b)	6071, 6075(a), 6081(a)
864(c)	6091(b)
865	Omitted
870	6211(a), 6653(c)(1)
871(a)	6212(a), 6213(a)
871(b)	6155(a), 6215(a)
871(c)	6155(a), 6213(c)
871(d), (e)	6213(d), 6214(a)
871(f)	6212(c), 6213(b)
871(g)	6214(c)
871(h)	6161(b)(2), 6165, 6503(d), 7101
871(i)	6155(a), 6653(b), 6659(a)
872(a)	6155(a), 6861(a)
872(b)—(e)	6861(b)—(e)
872(f)	6863(a), (b)(2), 7101
872(g)	6155(a), 6863(b)(1)
872(h)	6863(a), (b)(2)
872(i)	6155(a), 6861(f)
872(j)	6861(g)
873	6404(b)
874(a)	6501(a)
874(b)(1)	6501(c)(1), (3)
874(b)(2)	6502(a)
874(b)(3)	2016, 6071, 6081, 6091, 6155
875	6503(a)(1)
876	Omitted
890	6601(a), (b), (f)(1)
891	6155(a), 6601(a), (d), (f)(1)
892	6601(a), (c)(3)
893	6601(a), (c), (f)
894(a)	6651(a), 6653(a)
894(b)	7201, 7202, 7203, 7207, 7269, 7343
900(a)	6901(a), (b)
900(b), (c)	6901(c), (f)
900(d)	6904, 7421(b)
900(e)	6901(h)
901(a), (b)	6903(a)
901(c)	6903(b)
901(d)	6212(b)
910, 911, 912	6511, 6512(a), (b)
913, 920, 921	Omitted
925	6163(a), 6601(a), (b)
926	6163(a), 7101
927	2015
930(a)	2203
930(b)—(d), 931	Omitted
935	2001, 2052, 2101
936(a)	Omitted
936(b), (c)	2012, 2014
937	6018(a), 7203
938	6103
939	2201

1000(a)	2501
1000(b)	2511(a)
1000(c)	2514
1000(d), (e)	Omitted
1000(f)	2513
1000(g)	Omitted
1001(a), (b)	2502(a), (c)
1001(c)	Omitted
1002	2512(b)
1003	2503
1004(a)(1)–(3)	2521–2523
1004(b), (c)	2522, 2524
1005	2512(a)
1006(a)	6019(a), 6065(a)
1006(b)	6075(b), 6091(b)(1)
1007	6001
1008(a)	2502(d), 6151(a)
1008(b)	6161(a)(1)
1008(c)	Omitted
1008(d)	6313
1008(e)	6314(a)
1009	6324(b), 6325(a)(1)
1010	Omitted
1011	6211(a), 6653(c)(1)
1012(a)	6212(a), 6213(a)
1012(b)	6155(a), 6215(a)
1012(c)	6155(a), 6213(c)
1012(d)	6213(d)
1012(e)	6214(a)
1012(f)	6212(c), 6213(b)
1012(g), (h)	6214(b), (c)
1012(i)	6161(b)(1), 6165, 7101
1012(j)	6212(b)
1013(a)	6155(a), 6861(a)
1013(b)–(e)	6861(b)–(e)
1013(f)	6863(a), (b)(2), 7101
1013(g)	6155(a), 6863(b)(1)
1013(h)	6863(a), (b)(2)
1013(i)	6155(a), 6861(f)
1013(j)	6861(g)
1014	6404(b)
1015(a)	6871
1015(b)	6155(a), 6161(c), 6503(b), 6873(a)
1016	6501, 6502(a)
1017	6503(a)(1)
1018	Omitted
1019	6653, 6659(b)
1020	6601(a), (f)(1)
1021	6155(a), 6601(a), (d), (f)(1)
1022	6601(a), (c)(3)
1023	6601(a), (c)(1), (f)(1)
1024(a)	7201, 7203
1024(b)	7201
1025(a)	6901(a), (b)

1025(b)–(d)	6901(c), (e), (f)
1025(e)	6904, 7421(b)
1025(f)	6901(h)
1025(g)	6901(g)
1026(a)	6903(a)
1026(b)	6903
1026(c)	6903(b)
1027(a)	6402(a)
1027(b)	6511(a), (b)
1027(c), (d)	6512(a), (b)
1028	Omitted
1029	7805(a)
1030(a)	2502(b)
1030(b)	2511(b)
1031	6103
1100, 1101	7441, 7442
1102(a)–(g)	7443(a)–(g)
1103(a)–(d)	7444(a)–(d)
1104–1106	7445–7447
1110, 111	7451, 7453
1112, 1113	7454(a), 7455
1114(a), (b)	7456(a), (c)
1115(a), (b)	7457(a), (b)
1116	7458
1117(a)–(f)	7459(a)–(f)
1117(g)	6155(a), 6659, 6673
1117(h)	Omitted
1118	7460
1119, 1120, 1121	6902, 7461, 7462
1130–1133	7471–7474
1140–1143	7481–7484
1144	Omitted
1145	7101, 7485(a)
1146	7486
1250–1252	1491–1493
1253	1494, 6071, 6081(a), 6091(a), 6151(a)
1400	3101
1401(a), (b)	3102(a), (b)
1401(c)	6205(a), 6413(a)(1)
1401(d)(1), (2)	Omitted
1401(d)(3), (4)	6413(c)(1), (2)
1402	3502
1403	6051(a)
1410	3111
1411	6205(a), 6413(a)
1412	3112
1420(a)	3501
1420(b)	6601(a), (f)(1)
1420(c)	6011(a), 6071, 6081(a), 6091(a), 6302(b)
1420(d)	6313
1420(e)	3122
1421	6205(b), 6413(b)
1422	3503
1423(a)	6802(1)

1423(b), (c)	6803(a)(1), (2)
1424	7509
1425(a)	7209
1425(b)	7208(1)
1426(a)–(e)	3121(a)–(e)
1426(f)	7701(a)(1)
1426(g)–(l)	3121(f)–(k)
1427, 1428	3123, 3124
1429	7805(a), (c)
1430, 1431	Omitted
1432	3125
1500	3201
1501(a), (b)	3202(a), (b)
1501(c)	6205(a)(1), 6413(a)(1)
1502	6205(b), 6413(b)
1503	3502(a)
1510, 1511, 1512	3211, 3212, 3502
1520	3221
1521	6205(a)(1), 6413(a)(1)
1522	6205(b), 6413(b)
1530(a)	3501
1530(b)	6011(a), 6071, 6081(a), 6091(a), 6151(a)
1530(c)	6601(a), (f)(1)
1530(d)	6313
1531	3503
1532(a)–(e)	3231(a)–(e)
1532(f)	7701(a)(9)
1532(g), (h)	3231(f), (g)
1532(i)	7701(a)(1)
1534	3232
1535	7805(a), (c)
1536, 1537	Omitted
1538	3233
1600	3301
1601(a)–(c)	3302
1601(d)	6413(d)
1602	3303
1603	3304
1604(a)	6011(a), 6065, 6071, 6091(b)(1), (2)
1604(b)	6081(a)
1604(c)	6106
1605(a)	3501
1605(b)	6601(a), (f)(1)
1605(c)	6152(a)(3), (b), 6155(a), 6601(c)(2)
1605(d)	6161(a)(1)
1605(e)	6313
1606	3305
1607(a)–(j)	3306(a)–(j)
1607(k)	7701(a)(1)
1607(l)–(o)	3306(k)–(n)
1608	3307
1609	7805(a), (c)
1610	Omitted
1611	3308

1621	3401
1622(a), (b)	3402(a), (b)
1622(c)(1)(A)	Omitted
1622(c)(1)(B), (2)–(5)	3402(c)
1622(d)	3402(d)
1622(e)	3502(b)
1622(f)(1)	6414
1622(f)(2)	6401, 6402
1622(g)–(k)	3402(e)–(i)
1623	3403
1624	3404, 6011(a)
1625(c)	6081(a)
1626(a)	7204
1626(b)	6674
1626(d)	7205
1627	Omitted
1631	6651(a)
1632	3504
1633(a), (b)	6051(a)–(d)
1633(c)	6081(a)
1634(a)	7204
1634(b)	6659, 6674
1635(a)	6501(a)
1635(b)	6501(c)(1), (3)
1635(c)	6501(c)(2)
1635(d)	6502(a)
1635(e)	6501(b)(2)
1635(f), (g)	Omitted
1636(a)(1)	6511(a), (b)(1)
1636(a)(2)	6511(b)(2)
1636(b)	Omitted
1636(c)	6513(c)
1636(d), (e)	Omitted
1650	4001, 4011, 4021, 4471
1651	4031
1652–1655	Omitted
1656(a), (b), (c)	5063(a), (b), (c)
1657–1659	Omitted
1700	4231, 4232, 6011(a)
1701	4233
1702, 1703	4234
1704	4232
1710	4241
1711	4243
1712	4242
1715(a)	4291
1715(b), (c)	6151(a)
1715(d)	6415(b), (c), (d), 6416(a)
1716(a)	6011(a), 6065(a)
1716(b)	6071, 6081(a)
1716(c)	6091(b)(1), (2)
1717	6601(a), (f)(1)
1718(a)	7201, 7203
1718(b)	7201, 7202

1718(c)	6659, 6671(a), 6672
1718(d)	6671(b), 7343
1719	6302(b)
1720	6001
1721—1723	Omitted
1800	4301, 4311, 4321
1801	4311, 4312, 4314, 4315, 4381
1802	4301, 4302, 4304, 4321, 4322, 4323, 4341, 4342, 4343, 4344, 4351, 4352, 4353, 4381
1804	4371, 4372, 4373
1805	4891, 4892, 4894, 4895, 4896, 7701(a)(1)
1807	4451
1808	4303, 4373, 4382
1809	4383, 4454, 4893, 6201(a)(2), 6801(a), (b)
1815	6804
1816	Omitted
1817(a)—(c)	6802(1)—(3)
1818(a)	6803(b)(1), 7101
1818(b)	6803(b)(2)
1819	Omitted
1820	7271(2), (3)
1821(a)(1)	7201, 7203
1821(a)(2)	7201, 7202
1821(a)(3)	6653(e), 6659, 6671(a), 6672
1821(a)(4)	6671(b), 7343
1821(b)(3)	4374, 7270
1821(b)(4)	7201
1822	7208(3), 7271(1)
1823	7303(1)
1823(a)—(c)	7208(2)—(4)
1830	4453
1831	4452, 4455, 7272
1832	4456
1835	6001
1836—1838	Omitted
1850	4286
1851	4291
1852(a)	6011(a), 6065(a), 6071
1852(b)	6091(b)(1), (2)
1853(a), (b)	6151(a)
1853(c)	6601(a), (f)(1)
1854	6415(a), (b), (d)
1855, 1856	Omitted
1857	4287
1858, 1859	Omitted
1900, 1901, 1902	4881, 4883, 4884
1902(a)(1)	6011(a), 6065(a), 6071
1902(a)(2)	6091(b)(1), (2)
1902(a)(3), (b)	6151(a)
1903	4885
1904	Omitted
1905, 1906	4882, 4883
1907	Omitted
1920(a), (b)	4851(a), (b)

1920(c)	4871, 6804
1921	4861
1922	4863
1923	4864
1924	4865
1925	4853, 7492
1926	4854
1927	4862
1928	4872, 6001
1929(a)	7233(1), (2)
1929(b)	7263(b)
1929(c)	7263(a)
1930	4874, 7493
1931	4852, 7701(a)(1)
1932	4873
1933	4876
1934	Omitted
1935	4875
2000(a), (b)	5701(a)
2000(c)(1), (2)	5701(b), (c)
2000(d)	5701(d), (e)
2000(g)(1)—(3)	5707(a)—(c)
2001(a)	5703(a)
2002(b)	5703(d)
2002(c)	5703(a)
2010	5702(b)
2012	5712
2013	5711(a), (b)
2014	5713(a), (b)
2017	5721
2018	5741
2019	5722
2030	5702(e)
2032	5712
2033	5711(a), (b)
2036	5721
2037	5741
2038	5722
2039(a)	5711(a), (b)
2039(b)	5722, 5741
2040	5704(c)
2050	5702(b)(1)
2052	5712
2053	5711(a), (b)
2054	5713(a), (b)
2055	Omitted
2056	5741
2057	Omitted
2058	5732
2059, 2060	5731
2070—2075	Omitted
2100(a), (b)	5723(a)
2100(c)(1)	5723(d)
2100(c)(2)	5723(a)

2324	4815, 6001
2325	4817
2326(a)	7235(a), 7265(a)
2326(b), (c)	7235(b), (c)
2327	4812, 4813, 4816, 4818, 7235(e), 7265(b), (c)
2350	4846
2351	4831, 4832, 6201(a)(2)(A)
2352	4833, 4846, 6001, 7101, 7641
2353, 2354	4834, 4846
2355	4832
2356	4831, 4832
2357	7236, 7266(b)–(f)
2358	7303(2), (4), (5)
2359	Omitted
2360	4835
2361	4832
2362	Omitted
2400	4001, 4003
2401	4011, 4012
2402	4021, 4022
2403(a)	6011(a), 6065(a), 6071, 6081(a), 6091(b)(1), (2)
2403(b)	6151(a), 6601(a), (f)(1)
2403(c)	4051
2404, 2405	4052, 4053
2406	4055, 4056
2407	6416(a), (b)
2408	Omitted
2409	7261
2410, 2411	Omitted
2412	4002, 4003, 4012, 4013
2413	4054
2450	4041
2451(a)	6011(a), 6071, 6081(a), 6091(b)(1), (2), 6151(a)
2451(b)	6151(a), 6601(a), (f)(1)
2452(a)	6416(b)(2)(D)
2452(b)	6416(a)
2453	4055, 6416(b)(2)(A)
2454, 2455	Omitted
2456	4222
2470	4511, 4513
2471	6011(a), 6065(a), 6071, 6081(a), 6091(b)(1), (2)
2472	6151(a)
2473	6417(a)
2474	4513, 6417(b), 7101
2475	6601(a), (f)(1)
2477	4512
2478, 2479	Omitted
2480	7809(a)
2481, 2482	Omitted
2483	7654
2490	4561, 4571, 4581
2491	4561, 4562, 4571, 4572, 4581, 4582
2492	4582, 4602
2493	4601

2494	Omitted
2550	4701, 4771
2550(c)	6302(b)
2551	4702
2552	4703, 4771
2553	4704, 4723
2554	4705
2555	4732, 6001
2555(a)	6065(a)
2555(b)	6071
2555(c)	6065(a), 6071
2555(c)(1)	6081(a), 6091(a)
2556	4773
2557(a)	7237(b)
2557(b)(1)	7237(a)
2557(b)(2)	7201, 7203
2557(b)(3)	7201, 7202
2557(b)(4)	6671(a), 6672
2557(b)(8)	6671(b), 7343
2558	4706, 4733, 7301(a)
2559, 2560	Omitted
2561	4734
2562	4736
2563	4774
2564	4735
2565	Omitted
2567	4711, 4712
2568, 2569	4712, 4713
2569(b)	7101
2569(d)	6001
2569(d)(4)	7641
2570	7238
2571	4714, 7301(a)
2590	4741, 4771
2591	4742
2592	4743, 4771
2593	4744
2594(a)	6001
2595	4773
2596	7237(a)
2597	7491
2598	4745, 7301(a)
2599, 2600	Omitted
2601	4756
2602	4774
2603	4762
2604, 2606	Omitted
2650	4802
2651	4801, 4803
2651(c)(2)	6201(a)(2)(A)
2652(a)	6801(a)
2653	4804
2653(b)	6001, 7641
2653(d)	7101

2654, 2655	4805
2656	7274
2656(a)	7206(4)
2656(b)	7239(a)
2656(c)	7271(1), 7303(6)(B)
2656(d)	7239(b)
2656(f)	7201
2656(g)	7272
2656(h)	7267(d)
2656(i)	7267(c)
2656(j), (k)	7267(a), (b)
2657(a), (b)	7303(6)(B)
2657(c)	7303(6)(A)
2657(d)	7328
2657(e)	7301(c)
2657(f)	7303(6)(B)
2658	Omitted
2659	4803
2660	Omitted
2700	4181, 4182, 4224, 5831
2701	6011(a), 6065(a), 6071, 6081(a), 6091(b)(1), (2)
2702	6151(a)
2703(a)	6416(f)
2704	4216
2705	4225, 6416(e)
2706	6601(a), (f)(1)
2707(a)	6671(a), 6672
2707(b)	7201, 7203
2707(c)	7201, 7202
2707(d)	6671(b), 7343
2708	6302(b)
2709	6001
2710–2712	Omitted
2720–2723	5811–5814
2724	5842, 6001(a)
2725	5843
2726(a)–(c)	5851–5853
2727, 2728	5844, 5845
2729	5861
2730(a), (b)	5862(a), (b)
2731–2733	5846–5848
2733(a)	7701(a)(1)
2734	5821
2734(e)	6071, 6091(a)
2800(a)	5001(a)(9) (Rev. See 5001(a)(8))
2800(a)(1)	5001(a)(1), 5005(a), 5006(a)
2800(a)(1)(A)	5026(a)(1), 5007(a)
2800(a)(1)(B)	5689
2800(a)(2)	5001(a)(2)
2800(a)(3)	5001(a)(3), 5007(b)(2)
2800(a)(4)	5001(a)(4) (Rev. See 5001(a)(10)), 5007(c) (Rev. See 7652, 7805)
2800(a)(5)	5021(a), 5025(b)
2800(a)(6)	5001(a)(5) (Rev. See 5001(a)(4))

2800(b)(2)	5006(c)
2800(c)	5001(b)
2800(d)	5005(b)
2800(e)(1)	5004(a)(1)
2800(e)(2)	5004(a)(2) (Rev. See 5004(b)(2))
2800(e)(3)	5004(a)(3) (Rev. See 5004(b)(3))
2800(e)(4)	5004(a)(4) (Rev. See 5004(b)(4))
2800(f)	5006(d), 5007(b)(1)
2801(b)	5021(b) (Rev. Omitted)
2801(c)(1)	5391
2801(c)(2)	5025(e) (Rev. See 5025(f))
2801(d)	5281 (Rev. See 5201(a))
2801(e)	5025
2801(e)(1)	5272(a) (Rev. See 5173(a), (d)), 5281(a) (Rev. See 5201(a))
2801(e)(2)	5273(a) (Rev. See 5178(a)), 5627 (Rev. See 5687))
2801(e)(3)	5386(b), 5391
2801(e)(4)	5386(a)
2801(e)(5)	5023 (Rev. See 5687)
2801(f)	5628 (Rev. See 5601(a)(10), 5687)
2802(a)	5009(a) (Rev. See 5205(c)(1), (f), 5206(c)), 5010(a) (Rev. See 5205(e))
2802(b)	5010(b) (Rev. See 5205(f))
2802(c)	5027(a) (Rev. See 5061, 5205)
2803(a)	5008(b)(1)(E) (Rev. See 5205(c)(2))
2803(b)	5008(b)(3) (Rev. See 5205(g))
2803(c)	5008(b)(4)
2803(d)	5008(b)(2) (Rev. See 5205(g))
2803(e)	5008(b)(5)
2803(f)	5640 (Rev. See 5613(b))
2803(g)	5642 (Rev. See 5604(a)(1), (4)–(6), (10), (12)–(15), (b))
2804	5211 (Rev. See 5311)
2805(a)	5688(a)
2805(b)	5688(b)
2806(a)(1), (2)	5634 (Rev. See 5601(a)(13), 5615(7))
2806(b)(1)	5645 (Rev. See 7214)
2806(c)	5625 (Rev. See 5612(a))
2806(d)	5639 (Rev. See 5613(a))
2806(e)	5646 (Rev. See Subtitle F)
2806(f)	5626 (Rev. See 5602, 5615(3))
2806(g)	5687 (See 7301, 7302)
2807	5622 (Rev. See 5610)
2808(a)	5212(a) (Rev. See 5204(b))
2809(a)	5002(a) (Rev. See 5002(a)(5))
2809(b)(1)	5002(b)(1) (Rev. See 5002(a)(6)(A))
2809(b)(2)	5002(b)(2) (Rev. See 5002(a)(6)(B))
2809(c)	5002(c) (Rev. See 5002(a)(7))
2809(d)	5002(d) (Rev. See 5002(a)(8))
2810(a)	5174(a) (Rev. See 5179(a), 5505(d)), 5601 (Rev. See 5505(i), 5601(a)(1), 5615(1))
2811	5213(a), 5609
2812(a)	5175(a) (Rev. See 5171(a), 5172, 5271 (Rev. See 5171(a), (c), 5172, 5178(a)(1)(A), (4)(B)–(D)), 5603 (Rev. See 5601(a)(2), (3))
2813(a)	5282 (Rev. See 5201(a), 5202(a), 5204(a), (c), 5205(d), 5206(c),

	5251)
2814(a)(1)	5176(a), (c) (Rev. See 5173(a), (b), 5176(a)), 5177(c) (Rev. See 5173(b)(1), 5551(c)), 5604 (Rev. See 5601(a)(4), (5), 5615(3))
2814(a)(2)	5176(d) (Rev. See 5173(b))
2815(a)	5177(a), 5605 (Rev. See 7214)
2815(b)(1)(A)	5177(b)(1) (Rev. See 5173(b)(1)(A))
2815(b)(1)(B)	5177(b)(2) (Rev. See 5173(b)(1)(B))
2815(b)(1)(C)	5177(b)(3) (Rev. See 5173(b)(1)(C))
2815(b)(1)(D)	5177(b)(4) (Rev. See 5173(b)(3))
2815(c)–(e)	5551(a), (b)(1), (c)
2816(a)	5178 (Rev. See 5171(a), 5172)
2817(a)	5179(a) (Rev. Omitted)
2817(b)	5179(b) (Rev. Omitted)
2818(a)	5105(a)
2818(b)	5602 (Rev. See 5615(2), 5687)
2819	5171 (Rev. See 5178(a)(1)(B), (b), (c)(2), 5505(b), 5601(a)(6)), 5607 (Rev. See 5505(i), 5601(a)(6))
2820(a)	5173(b) (Rev. See 5178(a)(2)(B), 5202(b)), 5192(b) (Rev. See 5202(b)), 5193(a) (Rev. See 5201(a), 5202(f), 5204(a), 5205(b), 5206(a), (c), 5211)
2821	5682
2822(a)	5173(a) (Rev. See 5178(a)(1)(A), (2)(C)), 5618 (Rev. See 5687)
2823(a)	5173(c) (Rev. See 5173(a)(2)(C))
2824	Omitted
2825	5215 (Rev. See 5201(c), 5312(a), (c), 5373(a), 5562)
2826(a)	5196(a) (Rev. See 5203(a)), 5617 (Rev. See 5687)
2827(a)	5196(b) (Rev. See 5203(b)), 5616 (Rev. See 5687)
2828(a)	5196(c) (Rev. See 5203(c)), 5283 (Rev. See 5203(c), (d)), 5615 (Rev. See 5203(c), (e), 5687)
2829(a)	5552 (See 5503, 5505(e))
2830(a)	5196(d) (Rev. See 5203(d)), 5283 (Rev. See 5203(c), (d))
2831	5116(a) (Rev. See 5115), 5180(a), 5274(a) (Rev. See 5180), 5681
2832	5172 (Rev. See 5171(a), 5172, 5173(a), 5178(a)(1)(A), 5601(a)(2), (4))
2833(a)	5606 (Rev. See 5601(a)(4), 5602, 5615(3))
2834	5216(a) (Rev. See 5222(a)(1), (2)(D), 5501, 5502(a), 5503, 5504(a), (b), 5505(a), (c), 5601(a)(7), (8), (9)(A)), 5608(a), (b) (Rev. See 5601(a)(7), (8), (9)(A), (12), 5615(4))
2835	Omitted
2836	5195(a) (Rev. See 5201(c)), 5613 (Rev. See 5687)
2837	Omitted
2838	5192(c) (Rev. See 5202(a), (b)), 5612 (Rev. See 5687)
2839(a)	5196(e) (Rev. See 5203(b), (c)), 5619 (Rev. See 5687)
2840	Omitted
2841(a)	5197(a)(1)(A) (Rev. See 5207(a), (d))
2841(b)	5197(a)(1)(B) (Rev. See 5207(a), (d))
2841(c)	5620 (Rev. See 5603, 5615(5))
2842	5611 (Rev. See 5603)
2843	5610 (Rev. See 5603)
2844(a)	5197(b) (Rev. See 5207(c))
2845	Omitted
2846(a)	5007(e)(1) (Rev. See 5004(b)(1), 5006(a)(3))
2847(a)	5007(e)(2) (Rev. Omitted)
2848	Omitted

2849	5191(a) (Rev. See 5221(a))
2850(a)	5191(a) (Rev. See 5221(a)), 5650 (Rev. See 5601(a)(14), 5615(3))
2851	5682
2852	5624 (Rev. See 5611)
2853(a)	5623 (Rev. See 5609)
2854	5649 (Rev. See 5614)
2855(a)	5285(a) (Rev. See 5207(b))
2856	5629 (Rev. See 5610(a)(10), (11))
2857(a)	5114(a) (Rev. See 5114(a)(1), 5146(a)), 5285(b) (Rev. See 5207(c)), 5621 (Rev. See 5603)
2858	5114(b)
2859	5197(a)(2) (Rev. See 5207(a)), 5621 (Rev. See 5603)
2860	Omitted
2861(a)	5282(b) (Rev. See 5202(a), 5204(a), (c), 5205(d), 5206(c))
2862(a)	5282(c) (Rev. See 5205(d))
2863(a)	5115(a) (Rev. See 5205(d))
2865(a)	5630 (Rev. See 5687)
2866	5010(c) (Rev. See 5205(g)), 5636 (Rev. See 5604(a)(2), (3), (7)–(9), (17), 7301)
2867	5635 (Rev. See 5604(a)(17))
2868	5637 (Rev. See 5604(a)(18))
2869	5638 (Rev. See 5604(a)(19), 5613, 7301, 7302)
2870	5195(b) (Rev. See 5201(c)), 5614 (Rev. See 5687, 7301)
2871	5214(a) (Rev. See 5301(a)), 5641 (Rev. See 5606, 5613, 7301, 7302, 7321–7323)
2872	5231 (Rev. See 5171(a), 5172, 5173(a), 5178(a)(1)(A), (B), (3)(A), (B)), 5241(b) (Rev. See 5202(a), (c), (d))
2873	5231 (Rev. See 5171(a), 5172, 5173(a), 5178(a)(1)(A), (B), (3)(A), (B)), 5241(a) (Rev. See 5201(a), 5202(a), (c))
2874(a)	5252 (Rev. See 5236)
2875	5231 (Rev. See 5171(a), 5172, 5173(a), 5178(a)(1)(A), (B), (3)(A), (B)), 5246(a) (Rev. See 5212)
2876	5631 (Rev. See 5601(a)(12), 5615(6), 5687)
2877(a)	5192(d) (Rev. See 7803; T. 5 §301)
2878(a)	5193(a) (Rev. See 5201(a), 5202(f), 5204(a), 5205(b), 5206(a), (c), 5211)
2878(b)	5009(c), 5193(b) (Rev. See 5206(a), 5214(a)(4))
2878(c)	5193(c) (Rev. See 5206(b))
2878(d)	5193(d) (Rev. See 5204(c))
2879(a)	5242(a) (Rev. See 5211, 5231(a))
2879(b)	5006(a) (Rev. See 5006(a)(1), (2), 5008(c))
2879(c)	5232(a) (Rev. See 5005(c)(1), 5006(a)(2), 5173(a), (c)(1))
2879(d)	5232(a), (c) (Rev. See 5005(c)(1), 5006(a)(2), 5173(a), (c)(1), 5176(a), (b))
2880(a)	5006(b)
2881(a)	5245 (Rev. See 5204(a))
2882(a)	5244 (Rev. See 5213)
2883(a)	5194(a) (Rev. See 5211(a), 5212, 5213)
2883(b)	5194(d) (Rev. See 5214(a))
2883(c)	5194(c) (Rev. See 5241)
2883(d)	5194(e)(1) (Rev. See 5212, 5213)
2883(e)	5025(d), 5194(f) (Rev. See 5005(c)(1), 5212, 5223(a), (d))
2883(f)	5194(g) (Rev. See 5201(a), 5204(a), 5212)
2883(g)	5194(h) (Rev. Omitted)

2884(a)	5250(a) (Rev. See 5205(b))
2885(a)	5247(a) (Rev. See 5175(a), 5206(a), 5214(a)(4))
2885(b)	5009(b) (Rev. See 5205(i)(4)), 5247(b)
2885(d)	5648 (Rev. See 5608)
2886(a)	5247(c)
2887	5012(a) (Rev. See 5009)
2888(a)	5247(d) (Rev. See 5206(a))
2889, 2890	Omitted
2891(a)	5522(a) (Rev. See 5214(a))
2891(b)	5011(a) (Rev. See 5008(a))
2900	5006(a) (Rev. See 5006(a)(1), (2), 5008(c))
2901(a)(1)	5011(a)(1)(A) (Rev. See 5008(a)(1)(A))
2901(a)(2)	5011(a)(1)(B) (Rev. See 5008(a)(1)(B)), 5011(b) (Rev. See 5008(b)(1))
2901(b)	5011(a)(1)(B), (2) (Rev. See 5008(a)(1)(B), (2))
2901(c)	5011(a)(3) (Rev. See 5008(a)(3), (4))
2901(d)	5011(a)(4) (Rev. See 5008(a)(4))
2903(a)	5243(a) (Rev. See 5171, 5172, 5178(a)(3), (4)(A), 5233(a), (b))
2903(b)	5008(a)(1) (Rev. See 5205(a)(1), (3))
2903(c)	5008(a)(2) (Rev. See 5205(a)(3))
2903(d)	5008(a)(3)
2903(e)	5008(a)(4)
2903(f)	5243(d) (Rev. See 5206(c))
2903(g)	5243(c) (Rev. See 5233(c))
2904(a)	5243(a), (b) (Rev. See 5171, 5172, 5178(a)(3), (4)(A), 5202(g), 5233(a), (b))
2905	5243(e) (Rev. See 5175, 5206(c), 5214(a)(4))
2908	5643 (Rev. See 5601(a)(12), 5604(a)(11), (12), (16), 5615(6), 5687)
2909	5644 (Rev. See 5604(a)(4), (5), (10))
2910(a)	5243(b) (Rev. See 5202(g), 5233(b))
2911	5243(f) (Rev. See T. 27 §121)
2912, 2913	5632 (Rev. See 5601(a)(12), 5615(6))
2914(a)	5633 (Rev. See 7214)
2915(a)	5241(c) (Rev. See 7803; T. 5 §301)
2916(a)	5194(b)
3030(a)	5001(a)(9) (Rev. See 5001(a)(8))
3030(a)(1)	5001(a)(5), (9) (Rev. See 5001(a)(4), (8)), 5041(a), 5041(b), 5042(a)(2), 5362, 5368(b)
3030(a)(2)	5022, 5041(b)(4)
3030(b)	5043(b)
3031(a)	5354, 5362, 5373(b)(1), 5373(b)(3), 5391
3032(a)	5373(a), 5382(b)(2)
3033(a)	5373(b)(1)
3034(a), 3035	5366
3036	5025(f) (Rev. See 5025(g)), 5373(a), 5381, 5382(a), (b)(1), (2), 5383(a), (b)(3), (4), 5392
3037(a)	5362, 5373(b)(4)
3038(a)	5362
3039(a)	5370(a)(1)
3040(a)	5351, 5354, 5356, 5368(a), (b), 5369
3041(a)	5043(b), 5368(a)
3042(a)	5192(a) (Rev. See 5202(a)), 5366
3043(a)	5661(a) (See Chapter 68), (b), 5385(b)

3044	5381, 5382, 5383, 5392
3045	5381, 5382, 5384, 5392
3070(a)	5331(a) (Rev. See 5171(a), 5172, 5173(a), (c), 5178(a)(5), 5202(e), 5207(a), (c), (d), 5214(a), 5241, 5242, 5273(b)(1), (2), (d), 5275)
3070(b)	5331(b), (c) (Rev. See 5214(a), 5273(a), (b)(1), (2), (d))
3072	5647 (Rev. See 5273(b)(1), (2), (d), 5601(a)(12), 5607, 5615(6))
3073(a)	5332 (Rev. See 5273(c))
3074(a)	5333 (Rev. See 5243)
3100(a)	5301 (See 5171(a), (b)(1), 5172, 5173(a), (b))
3101(a)	5302 (Rev. See 5171(a), (b)(1), 5172, 5173(a), (c), 5178(a)(3)(A), (B), 5201(a), 5206(a))
3102	5303 (Rev. See 5171(a), (b)(1), 5172, 5173(a), (c), 5178(a)(5), 5241, 5242, 5273(b)(1), (2), (d))
3103	5306 (Rev. See 5025(d), (e)(1), 5103, 5113(a), 5173(c), 5201(a), (c), 5204(c), 5243(a)(1)(A), 5306), 5312(c)
3104(a)	5309 (Rev. See 5222(b)), 5412 (Rev. See 5222(b), 5412)
3105(a)	5305 (Rev. See 5171, 5172, 5173(a), 5178(a)(1)(A), (5), 5201(a), (b), 5207(a), (c), (d), 5211, 5223(a), 5235, 5273(b)(1), (2), (d), 5275, 5312(b))
3106(a)	5307 (Rev. See 5178(a)(2)(A), 5201(a))
3107	5308 (Rev. See 5212, 5223(a))
3108(a)	5310(a) (Rev. See 5214(a), 5241, 5242, 5273(b)(1), (2), (d))
3108(b)	5310(b) (Rev. See 5214(a), 5313)
3108(c)	5310(c) (Rev. See 5214(a))
3108(d)	5310(d) (Rev. See 5272(b))
3109	5310(a) (Rev. See 5214(a), 5241, 5242, 5273(b)(1), (2), (d))
3110	5502 (Rev. Omitted)
3111	5001(a)(6)
3112(a)	5004(b) (Rev. See 5004(a)(1), (b)(1)), 5005(c) (Rev. See 5005(a), (b)(1), (c)(1))
3112(b)	5007(d) (Rev. See 5007(a)(1)), 5689
3113(a)	5011(c)
3114(a)	5304(a) (Rev. See 5171(b)(1), 5271(a), (b), (c), (e)(1), (f), 5272(a))
3114(b)	5304(b) (Rev. See 5271(e))
3114(c)	5304(c) (Rev. See 5271(e))
3114(d)	5304(d)
3115(a)	5686(a) (Rev. See 5687)
3116	5686(b) (Rev. See 5505(i), 5686(a)), 7302
3117(a)	5314 (Rev. See 5557)
3118	5688(d)
3119	5315
3120	5316
3121(a), (c)	5313(a), (b) (Rev. See 5275)
3121(d)	5317(b) (Rev. See 5274)
3122	5317(a)
3123	5318 (Rev. See 5314(a)(2))
3124(a)	5119 (Rev. See 5002(a))
3125(a)	5001(a)(8) (Rev. See 5001(a)(9)), 5007(d) (Rev. See 5007(a)(1)), 5311 (Rev. See 5232)
3125(b)	5310(b) (Rev. See 5214(a), 5313)
3126	Omitted
3150(a)	5051(a)
3150(b)(1)	5054 (Rev. See 5054(a)(1))

3150(b)(2)	5055 (Rev. See 5054(a)(1), (2), (c), (d))
3150(b)(3)	5689
3150(c)	5051(b)
3152	Omitted
3153(b)	5053(a), 5401(b)
3153(c)	5053(b)
3155(a), (b)	5401(a), (b)
3155(c)	5415(a)
3155(f)	5412, 5413, 5675
3156	Omitted
3157(a)	5055 (Rev. See 5054(a)(1), (2), (c), (d))
3158	5402(a), 5411
3159(a)–(c)	5671, 5672, 5673, 5674
3159(e)–(i)	5676(1)–(5)
3159(j)	5674
3160	5052(b)
3170	Omitted
3171(a)	5367, 5555(a) (Rev. See 5207(b)–(d))
3172(a)	5061(b)
3173(a)	5683
3173(b)(1)–(3)	5684 (Rev. See 5687 and Subtitle F)
3173(b)(4)	5690
3173(c)	5685
3173(d)	5688(c)
3174	5064 (Rev. See 5065)
3175	5557 (Rev. See 5560)
3176(a)	5556 (Rev. See 5505(h))
3177(a)	5521(a)
3177(b)	5521(c)(1), (2)
3177(c)	5521(b)
3177(d)(1), (2)	5521(d)(1), (2)
3178	5523
3179(a), (b)	5062(a), (b)
3180	Omitted
3182(a)	5511
3182(b)	5001(a)(7)
3183(a)	5217(a) (Rev. See 5005(c)(1), (2), 5025(d), (e)(2), 5212, 5223(a), 5234(b))
3183(b)	5217(b) (Rev. See 5561)
3183(c)	5217(c) (Rev. Omitted)
3190–3195	Omitted
3206	4821
3207	7235(d), 7264
3208	4822, 4826
3210	4841
3211	7266(a)
3212	4842
3220	4721, 6001, 6151(a)
3221	4722
3222	4772
3223	Omitted
3224	4724
3225	7237(a)
3226	4775

3227	4725
3228	4731, 7343, 7701(a)
3230	4751, 4752, 6151(a)
3231	4753
3232	4772
3233	4754, 6001, 6065(a), 6071, 6081(a), 6091(a)
3234	4755
3235	7237(a)
3236	4775
3237	4756
3238	4761, 7701(a)
3239	Omitted
3250(a)(1)	5111(a)(1) (Rev. See 5111(a))
3250(a)(3)	5111(a)(2) (Rev. See 5112(b))
3250(a)(4)	5113(a)
3250(b)(1)	5121(a)(1) (Rev. See 5121(a))
3250(b)(2)	5122(c) (Rev. See 5121(a)(2))
3250(b)(4)	5121(a)(2) (Rev. See 5122(a), (b))
3250(c)(1)	5091
3250(d)(1)	5111(b)(1) (Rev. See 5111(b))
3250(d)(2)	5111(b)(2) (Rev. See 5112(c))
3250(d)(3)	5091, 5113(b) (Rev. See 5113(a))
3250(e)(1)	5121(b)(1) (Rev. See 5122(b))
3250(e)(2)	5121(b)(2) (Rev. See 5122(b))
3250(e)(3)	5121(c) (Rev. See 5121(c), 5122(c))
3250(e)(4)	5123(a) (Rev. See 5113(a))
3250(f)(1)	5081
3250(g)	5113(c) (Rev. See 5113(a))
3250(h)	5025(g) (Rev. See 5025(h))
3250(i)	5025(h) (Rev. See 5025(i))
3250(j)(1)	5101
3250(j)(3)	5106 (Rev. See 5106(b))
3250(l)(1), (2)	5131(a), (b)
3250(l)(3)—(5)	5132–5134
3251(a)	5113(d)(1) (Rev. See 5113(c)(1))
3251(b)	5113(d)(2) (Rev. See 5113(c)(2))
3251(c)	5123(c) (Rev. See 5113(e))
3252(a)	5124(a)
3252(b)	5124(b) (Rev. See 5146(a))
3252(c)	5124(c) (Rev. See 5146(a))
3252(d)	5692 (Rev. See 5603)
3253	5691 (Rev. See 5607, 5613, 5615, 5661(a), 5671, 5673, 5676(4), 5683, 7301, 7301(a), 7302)
3254(b)	5112(a) (Rev. See 5111(a), 5112(b))
3254(c)(1)	5122(a) (Rev. See 5121(a)(1), 5122(a))
3254(c)(2)	5111 (Rev. See 5111(a), (b), 5112(b), (c))
3254(d)	5052(a), 5092, 5402(a)
3254(e)	5112(b) (Rev. See 5112(c))
3254(f)	5122(b)
3254(g)	5025(c), 5082, 5387(c)
3254(h)	5102
3255(a)	5123(b)(1)
3255(b)	5123(b)(2) (Rev. See 5123(b)(2)(A))
3255(c)	5123(b)(3) (Rev. See 5113(d)(1), (2))

3260	5801(a)
3261(a)	5802
3261(b)	5841
3262	5803
3263(a)	5854(a)
3263(b)	5854(a), (b)
3267	4461, 4462, 4463
3268	4471, 4472, 4473
3270(a)	5141, 7011(a)
3271	4901
3271(a)	5142(a)
3271(b)	5142(b), 6151(a)
3271(c)(1)	5104, 5142(c)
3272(a)	5143(a) (Rev. See Subtitle F), 6011(a), 6065(a), 6071, 6081(a), 6091(b), 6151(a)
3273(a)	5145 (Rev. See 5144), 6801(a)
3273(b)	5146 (Rev. See 6806(a), 7273(a)), 6806(a)
3274	5693 (Rev. See 5692), 7273(a)
3275	5147 (Rev. See 6107), 6107
3276	4906, 5148 (Rev. See 5145)
3277	4902, 5144(a) (Rev. See 5143(a))
3278	4903, 5144(c) (Rev. See 5113(a), 5143(c)(1)—(3))
3279	4904, 5144(b) (Rev. See 5143(b))
3280(a)	4905, 5144 (Rev. See 5113(a) 5143), 7011(b)
3281	6302(b)
3282	5149 (Rev. See 5147), 6302(b)
3283	4907, 5144(e) (Rev. See 5143(e))
3285	4401, 4402, 4404, 4421
3286	6419
3287	4403
3290	4411
3291	4412, 6091(b)
3292	4413, 4903, 4907, 6107
3293	6806(c)
3294	7262, 7273(b)
3297	4422
3298	4423
3300(a)	6801(a)
3300(b)	7208
3300(c)	6808
3301(a)	6801(b), 6804
3301(b)	6808
3303	Omitted
3304(a)—(d)	6805(a)—(d)
3304(e), 3305	Omitted
3310	6331(a)
3310(a)	6011(a), 6071, 6601(c)(4), 6659
3310(b)	6011(a), 6601(c)(4), 6659
3310(c)	6601(a), (f)(1), 6659
3310(d)	6155(a), 6601(f)(1), 6659
3310(e)	6659
3310(f)(1)	6011(a), 6071, 6081(a)
3310(f)(2)	5703(c), 6302(c)
3311	6155(a), 6201(a)(2)(A), 6601(c)(4), 6659

3312(a)	6501(a)
3312(b)	6501(c)(1), (3)
3312(c)	6501(c)(2)
3312(d)	6502(a)
3313	5705(a), 6511(a), (b)(1), (2)
3314	Omitted
3320(a)	7268
3320(b)	Omitted
3321	7206(4)
3321(b)	7301
3321(c)	Omitted
3322	7301(d)
3323(a)(1), (2)	7271(4)
3323(a)(3)	7208(5)
3323(b)	7303(7)
3324(a)–(c)	7341(a)–(c)
3325	7211
3326	7304
3330	6065(a)
3331	5704(b), 7510
3332–3335	Omitted
3350(a), (b)	7652(b)(1), (2)
3351(a)	7653(a)(2)
3351(b), (c)	7653(b), (c)
3360(a)	7652(a)(1)
3360(b)	7101, 7652(a)(2), 7803(c)
3360(c)	7652(a)(3)
3361(a)	7653(a)(1)
3361(b), (c)	7653(b), (c)
3400(a), (c)	4071, 4072, 4073
3400(b), 3401	Omitted
3403	4061, 4062, 4063
3403(e)	6416(c)
3404	4141, 4142, 4143, 4151, 4152
3405	4111, 4112, 4113
3406(a)(1)	4161
3406(a)(2)	Omitted
3406(a)(3)	4121
3406(a)(4)	4171, 4172, 4173
3406(a)(5)	Omitted
3406(a)(6)	4191, 4192
3406(a)(7)–(9)	Omitted
3406(a)(10)	4131
3406(b)	4221
3406(c)	Omitted
3407	4181, 4182, 4224, 5831
3408	4201, 4221
3408(b)	6416(d)
3409(a)	4211
3409(b)	Omitted
3412(a)–(f)	4081, 4082, 4083, 4101, 4102, 7101, 7232
3412(g)	6412(b)
3413	4091, 4092, 4093, 7101
3414, 3415, 3416	Omitted

3420	4521, 4531, 4541, 4551
3422	4521
3423	4531, 4532
3424	4551, 4552, 4553
3425	4541, 4542
3430	4601
3431	Omitted
3440	4217
3441	4216
3442	4220, 4224
3443	6416, 6611
3444, 3445, 3446	4218, 4219, 4223
3447	Omitted
3448(a)	6011(a), 6065(a), 6071, 6081(a), 6091(b), 6151(a)
3448(b)	6151(a), 6601(a), (f)(1)
3449, 3450	Omitted
3451	4222
3453	Omitted
3460	4281, 4282, 4283
3461	6011(a), 6065(a), 6071, 6081, 6091(b), 6151(a)
3462	Omitted
3465	4251, 4252, 4253, 4254
3466	4253, 4292
3467	4291, 6011(a), 6065(a), 6071, 6081(a), 6091(b), 6151(a), 6161(a)
3468	Omitted
3469(a), (b), (c)	4261, 4262
3469(d)	4291, 6011(a), 6065(a), 6071, 6091(b), 6151(a)
3469(e)	6081(a), 6161(a)
3469(f)	4262, 4292
3470	6151(a), 6601(a), (f)
3471	6415, 6416(f)
3472–3474	Omitted
3475(a)	4271, 4272
3475(b)	4272, 4292
3475(c)	4271, 4291, 6011(a), 6065(a), 6071, 6091(b), 6151(a)
3475(d)	6081(a), 6161(a)
3475(e)	4273, 7272
3480	4331, 4361
3481	4331, 4332, 4341, 4342, 4343, 4344, 4351–4353
3482	4361, 4362
3483	4382
3490	4501, 4503
3491	4501, 6011(a), 6071, 6091(b), 6151(a)
3492	4502
3493(a)	6418(b)
3493(b)	6511(e)(2)
3494(a)	6418(a)
3494(b)	6511(e)(1)
3495	6601(a), (f)
3496–3498	Omitted
3500, 3501	4501, 4504
3506	7240
3507	4502, 7701(a)

3508	4501, 6412(d)
3600	7601(a)
3601(a)(1), (2)	7606(a), (b)
3601(b)	7342
3601(c)	7212(a), (b)
3602	Omitted
3603	6001
3604(a)	6046(a), 6071, 6091(a)
3604(b)	6046(b), (c), 6065(a)
3604(c)	7201, 7203
3611(a)(1)	6011(a), 6065(a), 6081(a), 6091(a), (b)(1), (2)
3611(a)(2)	6020(a), 6065(a)
3611(b)	6071
3611(c)	6065(a), 6071, 6091(a), (b)(1), (2)
3612(a), (c)	6020(b)
3612(d)(1)	6651(a)
3612(d)(2)	6653(b)
3612(e)	Omitted
3612(f)	6201(a)(1)
3613	6021
3614	7602, 7605(a)
3615	7605(a)
3615(a)—(c)	7602
3615(d)	7603
3615(e)	7604(b)
3616(a)	7207
3616(b)	7210
3616(c), 3617	Omitted
3630	6101
3631	7605(b)
3632(a)	7622(a)
3632(a)(1)	7602
3632(b)	7622(b)
3633	7402(b)
3633(a)	7604(a)
3633(b)	Omitted
3634	6081(a)
3640	6201(a)
3641	6203
3642	6204
3643	Omitted
3644	6202
3645, 3646	Omitted
3647	6201(a)
3650	7621
3651(a)(1)	6301
3651(a)(2), (b)	Omitted
3652	6302(a)
3653(a), (b)	7421(a), (b)
3654	Omitted
3655(a)	6303(a), 6659
3655(b)	6601(a), (f)(1), 6659
3656(a)(1)	6311(a)
3656(a)(2)(A), (B)	6311(b)(1), (2)

3656(b)(1)	6311(a)
3656(b)(2)	6311(b)(1)
3657	6312(a)
3658	6313
3659(a)	6314(a)
3659(b)	Omitted
3660	6331(a)
3660(a)	6155(a), 6862
3660(b)	6863(a), 7101
3661	7501
3662, 3663	Omitted
3670	6321
3671	6322
3672	7207
3672(a), (b)	6323(a), (d)
3673(a), (b)	6325(a)(1), (2)
3674(a), (b)	6325(b)(1), (2)
3675	6325(c)
3676	7102
3677	Omitted
3678	7403
3679(a)	7424(a)
3679(b)	Omitted
3679(c), (d)	7424(b), (c)
3680	Omitted
3690	6331(a), (b)
3691	6334
3692	6331(a), (b), 6334(c)
3693	6335(e)(2)(E)
3693(a)–(c)	6335(a), (b), (d)
3693(d)	6335(e)(2)(F)
3694	6342(a)
3695(a)	6335(e)(1), (2)(A)
3695(b)	6335(e)(2), 7505(a)
3695(c)	7505(b)
3696	6337(a)
3697(a)–(d)	6339(a)(1)–(4)
3698	Omitted
3700	6331(a), (b)
3701	6335(e)(2)(E)
3701(a)–(c)	6335(a), (b), (d)
3701(d)	6335(e)(1), (2)(A), (B)
3701(e)	6335(e)(1)
3701(f)	6335(e)(2)(D), (F), (3)
3702(a)	6337(a)
3702(b)(1), (2)	6337(b)(1), (2)
3702(c)	6337(c)
3703(a)	6338(c)
3703(b)	6338(a)
3704(a)	6338(c)
3704(b)	6338(b)
3704(c)(1), (2)	6339(b)(1), (2)
3705	Omitted
3706(a), (b)	6340(a)

3706(c)–(e)	Omitted
3706(f)	6340(b)
3707	Omitted
3710(a), (b)	6332(a), (b)
3710(c)	6332(c), 7343
3711	6333
3712	6335(c), 6342(b)
3713, 3714(a)	Omitted
3714(b)	6502(b)
3715	6331(c)
3716	6341
3717	Omitted
3720(a)(1)–(3)	7301(a)–(c)
3720(b)	7321
3720(c)	Omitted
3721, 3722	7322, 7324
3722(a), (b)	7324(1), (2)
3722(c)	7101, 7324(3)
3722(d)	7324(4)
3723(a)–(c)	7323(a)–(c)
3723(d)	Omitted
3724	7101, 7325
3725	6807
3726	7327
3727	Omitted
3740	7401
3742, 3743, 3745	Omitted
3746(a)	7405(a)
3746(b)	6532(b), 7405(b)
3746(c)	Omitted
3746(d)	6602
3747	7406
3748	6531
3760, 3761	7121, 7122
3762	7206(5)
3770(a)(1)	6402(a), 6404(a)
3770(a)(2)	6401(a)
3770(a)(3)	6407
3770(a)(4)	6402(a)
3770(a)(5)	6402(a), 6404(a)
3770(b)	7423
3770(b)(1), (2)	7423(1), (2)
3770(c)	6401(c)
3771(a)	6611(a)
3771(b)(1)	6611(b)(1)
3771(b)(2)	6611(b)(2), (e)
3771(c)	6611(c)
3771(d)	Omitted
3771(e)	6611(f)
3771(f), (g)	Omitted
3772(a)(1)	7422(a)
3772(a)(2), (3)	6532(a)(1), (4)
3772(b)	7422(b)
3772(c)	Omitted

3772(d), (e)	7422(c), (d)
3773	Omitted
3774	6514(a)
3774(b)	6532(a)(2)
3775	6514(b)
3777(a)–(c)	6405(a)–(c)
3778	Omitted
3779(a)	6091(a), 6164(a)
3779(b)	6065(a), 6071, 6081(a), 6164(b)
3779(c)–(g)	6164(c)–(g)
3779(h)	6155(a), 6164(h)
3779(i)	6601(a), (e), (f)(1)
3780(a)	6065(a), (b), 6071, 6091(a), 6411(a)
3780(b)	6411(b)
3780(c)	6213(b)(2)
3781	6164(i), 6411(c)
3790	6406, 6611(g)
3791(a)	6071, 6081(a), 6091(a), (b)(1), (2), 7805(a)
3791(b)	7805(b)
3792	7623
3793	7206(3)
3793(a)(2)	7303(8)
3793(b)	7206(2), 7207
3793(b)(2)	7343
3794	6601(a)
3795(a)–(d)	7506(a)–(d)
3797(a)(1)–(11)	7701(a)(1)–(11)
3797(a)(12)	7701(a)(13)
3797(a)(13)	Omitted
3797(a)(14)–(20)	1465, 7701(a)(14)–(20)
3797(b), (c)	7701(b), (c)
3798	7507
3799	76
3800	7402(a)
3801	1311–1314
3802	7511
3803	7852(a)
3804(a)	7508(a)
3804(b), (c)	Omitted
3804(d)	7508(b)
3804(e)	Omitted
3804(f)	7508(a)
3805	6072(e)
3806	1481
3808	Omitted
3809(a)	7206(1)
3809(b)	6061, 6064
3809(c)	6065(a)
3810	Omitted
3811	7651
3812	6521
3813, 3814	503, 504
3900	7802
3901(a)	6801(a), 7805(c)

3901(b)	7803(b)(2)
3905, 3906, 3910, 3911, 3915, 3916	Omitted
3920, 3921	7803(a)
3930(a)	7801(b)
3930(b)	Omitted
3931, 3932	7801(b), (c)
3940–3942	Omitted
3943	7101, 7803(c)
3944, 3950–3955, 3960–3967	Omitted
3970	7808
3971(a), (b)	7809(a), (b)
3971(b)(1)–(3)	7809(b)(1)–(3)
3975–3978	7803(d)
3990, 3991	Omitted
3992	7101, 7402(d), 7803(c)
3993, 3994	Omitted
3995(c)	7402(d)
3996, 3997	Omitted
4000	7803(a)
4001–4003	Omitted
4010	7101, 7803(c)
4011, 4012	Omitted
4013(a)	5241
4013(b)–(d)	Omitted
4014–4022, 4030–4033	Omitted
4040	7803(b)(1)
4041(a)	7803(a)
4041(b)	Omitted
4042	7402(c)
4043–4046	Omitted
4047(a)(1)	7213(b)
4047(b)	7214(b)
4047(c), (d)	Omitted
4047(e)	7214(a)
4048	7344
5000–5004	8001–8005
5010–5012	8021–8023

Table II

1986 Code section number	1939 Code section number
1	11, 12(b)(3), (c), (f)
2	12(d)
3	400
4	23(aa)(4), 401, 402, 404
5	
11	13, 15, 104(b), 261
12	
21	108
31	35, 322(a)(4)
32	32
33	31
34	
35	25

36	23(aa)(2)
37	
38	
61	22(a)
62	22(n)
63	21
71	22(k)
72	22(b)(2)
73	22(m)
74	
75	22(o)
76	22(j), 3799
77	123
101	22(b)(1)
102	22(b)(3)
103	22(b)(4)
104	22(b)(5)
105	
106	
107	22(b)(6)
108	22(b)(9), (10)
109	22(b)(11)
110	
111	22(b)(12)
112	22(b)(13)
113	22(b)(14)
114	22(b)(16)
115	22(b)(8), 116(d), (e)
116	
117	
118	
119	
120	
121	22(b)(17), 116(i)
141	23(aa)(1)
142	23(aa)(4), (5), 213(d)
143	23(aa)(6)
144	23(aa)(3), (7)
145	
151	25(b)(1)
152	25(b)(3)
153	25(b)(2)
154	
161	23
162	23(a)(1)
163	23(b)
164	23(c), (d)
165	23(e), (f), (g)(1), (2), (3), (4), (h), (i), (k)(2)
166	23(k)
167	23(l), 23(n), 114(a)
168	23(t), 124A
169	23(t), 124B
170	23(o), (q), 120
171	23(v), 125

172	23(s), 122
173	23(bb)
174	
175	
211	23
212	23(a)(2)
213	23(x)
214	
215	23(u)
216	23(z)
217	
241	26
242	26(a)
243	26(b)(1)
244	26(b)(2)
245	26(b)(3)
246	26(b)
247	26(h)
248	
261	24(a)
262	24(a)(1)
263	23(a)(1)(C), 24(a)(2), (3)
264	24(a)(4), (6)
265	23(b), 24(a)(5)
266	24(a)(7)
267	24(b), (c)
268	24(f)
269	129
270	130
271	23(k)(6)
272	
273	24(d)
301	22(e), 115(a), (b), (d), (e), (j)
302	115(c), (g)(1), (i)
303	115(g)(3)
304	115(g)(2)
305	115(f)
306	
307	113(a)(19)
311	
312	115(c), (h), (l), (m), 394(d)
316	115(a), (b)
317	
318	
331	115(c)
332	112(b)(6)
333	112(b)(7)
334	113(a)(15), (18)
336	
337	
338	
341	117(m)
342	115(c)
346	115(i)

351	112(b)(5), (c), (e)
354	112(b)(3)
355	112(b)(3), (11)
356	112(c), (e)
357	112(k)
358	113(a)(6), (23)
361	112(b)(4), (d), (e)
362	113(a)(7), (8)
363	
367	112(i)
368	112(g)(1), (2), (h)
371	112(b)(10), (c), (d), (e), (k), (*l*)
372	113(a)(22)
373	112(b)(9), 113(a)(20), (21)
381	
382	
391	
392	
393	
394	
395	
401	165(a)
402	165(b), (c), (d)
403	22(b)(2)(B)
404	23(p)
421	130A
441	41, 48(a), (b)
442	46
443	47(a), (c), (e), (g); 146(a)
446	41
451	42(a)
452	
453	44
454	42(b), (c), (d)
461	43
462	
471	22(c)
472	22(d)(1)—(5)
481	
482	45
501	101 except (12) and last par.; 165(a), 421
502	Last par. 101
503	3813
504	3814
511	421
512	421(c), (d); 422
513	422(b)
514	423
515	424
521	101(12)(A)
522	101(12)(B)
526	116(g)
531	102(a)
532	102(a)

533	102(b), (c)
534	
535	26(d), 27(b)(2), 102(d)
536	102(f)
537	
541	500
542	501
543	502, 507(b)
544	503
545	26(c), (d); 504, 505
546	505(e)
547	506
551	337
552	331
553	332
554	333
555	334
556	26(c), 335, 336
557	336(d)
561	26(f), 27(a)
562	26(f), 27(b)—(i)
563	504(c)
564	26(f), 27(c)—(i)
565	26(g), 28
581	104(a)
582	23(k)(2), 117(i)
583	121
584	169, second sentence of 170
591	23(r)
592	23(dd)
593	23(k)
594	110
601	26(d)
611	23(m)
612	114(b)(1)
613	114(b)(3), (4)
614	
615	23(ff)
616	23(cc)
621	22(b)(15)
631	117(k)
632	105
641	161
642	162(a), (e), (f); 163, 168, 170, 172
643	162(d)
651	162(b)
652	162(b), 164
661	162(b), (c)
662	162(b), (c), 164
663	162(d)
665	
666	
667	
668	

671	
672	
673	
674	
675	
676	166
677	167
678	
681	162(g)
682	171
683	
691	126
692	154
701	181
702	182, 183, 184, 186, 189
703	183, 189
704	191, 3797(a)(2)
705	
706	188
707	
708	
721	
722	
723	113(a)(13)
731	
732	113(a)(13)
733	
734	
735	
736	
741	
742	
743	
751	
752	
753	
754	
755	
761	3797(a)(2)
771	
801	201(b)
802	201(a)(1)
803	201(c)(1)—(7), (d), (e)
804	202(b)
805	203A(b), (c), (d)
806	202(c)
807	201(a)(2), (3)
821	207(a)
822	207(a)(5), (b)(1), (4), (c), (d), (e), (f)
823	207(b)(2), (3)
831	204(a)
832	204(a)(2), (b)—(f)
841	205
842	206

851	361
852	362(a), (b)(1)—(7)
853	
854	
855	362(b)(8)
861	119(a), (b), (e)
862	119(c), (d), (e)
863	119(e)
864	119(f)
871	211(a), (b), (c)
872	212
873	213, 214
874	215, 216
875	219
876	220
877	221
881	231(a)
882	231(b), (c); 232(a), (b); 233, 234, 235(a)
883	231(d)
884	236(b), 237, 238
891	103
892	116(c)
893	116(h)
894	22(b)(7)
901	131(a), (g)
902	131(f)(1), (2)
903	131(h)
904	131(b)(1)
905	131(c), (d), (e)
911	116(a)
912	116(j), (k)
921	109
922	26(i)
931	251
932	252
933	116(l)
941	262
942	263
943	116(f), 265
1001	111
1002	112(a)
1011	113(b), except (1)—(4)
1012	113(a)
1013	113(a)(1)
1014	113(a)(5)
1015	113(a)(2), (3), (4)
1016	113(b)(1), (2)
1017	113(b)(3)
1018	113(b)(4)
1019	113(c)
1020	113(d)
1021	
1022	113(e)
1031	112(b)(1), (c)(1), (e), 113(a)(6)

1401	480
1402	481
1403	482
1441	143(b)
1442	144
1443	143(h)
1451	143(a)
1461	143(c)
1462	143(d)
1463	143(e)
1464	143(f)
1465	3797(a)(16)
1471	650, 651
1481	3806
1491	1250
1492	1251
1493	1252
1494	1253
1501	141(a)
1502	141(b)
1503	141(c)
1504	141(d), (e), (f), (g)
1505	141(h), (i)
1551	15(c)
1552	
2001	810, 935
2002	822(b)
2011	810, 813(b)
2012	813(a)(2), 936(b)
2013	
2014	813(c), 936(c)
2015	927
2016	874(b)(3)
2031	811(k)
2032	811(j)
2033	811(a)
2034	811(b)
2035	811(c)(1)(A), 811(1)
2036	811(c)(1)(B)
2037	811(c)(1)(C), (c)(2), (3)
2038	811(d)
2039	
2040	811(e)
2041	811(f); 403(d)(2) R.A. 1942; 2, P.L. 635 (80th Cong.)
2042	811(g)
2043	811(i), 812(b)
2044	811(h)
2051	812
2052	935(c)
2053	812(b)
2054	812(b)
2055	812(d)
2056	812(e)
2101	860, 935

2102	861(a)(2)
2103	861(a)
2104	862
2105	863
2106	861
2201	939
2202	850
2203	930(a)
2204	825(a)
2205	826(b)
2206	826(c)
2207	826(d)
2501	1000(a)
2502	1001(a), (b); 1008(a), 1030(a)
2503	1003(a), 1003(b)
2504	
2511	1000(b), 1030(b)
2512	1002, 1005
2513	1000(f)
2514	1000(c); 452(b)(2) R.A. 1942; 2, P.L. 635 (80th Cong.)
2515	
2516	
2521	1004(a)(1)
2522	1004(a)(2), 1004(b)
2523	1004(a)(3)
2524	1004(c)
3101	1400
3102	1401(a), (b)
3111	1410
3112	1412
3121	1426(a)–(e), (g)–(*l*)
3122	1420(e)
3123	1427
3124	1428
3125	1432
3201	1500
3202	1501(a), (b)
3211	1510
3212	1511
3221	1520
3231	1532(a)–(e), (g), (h)
3232	1534
3233	1538
3301	1600
3302	1601(a), (b), (c)
3303	1602
3304	1603
3305	1606
3306	1607(a)–(j), (*l*)–(*o*)
3307	1608
3308	1611
3401	1621
3402	1622(a)–(d), (g)–(k)
3403	1623

3404	1624
3501	1420(a), 1530(a), 1605(a)
3502	1402, 1503, 1512, 1622(e)
3503	1422, 1531
3504	1632
4001	1650, 2400
4002	2412(a)
4003	2400, 2412(b)
4011	1650, 2401
4012	2401, 2412(a)
4013	2412(b)
4021	1650, 2402(a)
4022	2402(a), (b)
4031	1651(a)
4041	2450
4051	2403(c)
4052	2404
4053	2405
4054	2413
4055	2406, 2453
4056	2406
4057	
4061	3403(a), (b), (c)
4062	
4063	3403(c), (d)
4071	3400(a)
4072	3400(c)
4073	3400(a)
4081	3412(a)
4082	3412(b), 3412(c)
4083	3412(a)
4091	3413
4092	3413
4093	3413
4101	3412(d)
4102	3412(e)
4111	3405
4112	3405
4113	3405(b)
4121	3406(a)(3)
4131	3406(a)
4141	3404(a)
4142	3404(b)
4143	3404(a), 3404(b)
4151	3404(d)
4152	3404(d)
4161	3406(a)(1)
4171	3406(a)
4172	3406(a)(4)
4173	3406(a)(4)
4181	2700(a), 3407
4182	2700(b)(2), 3407; 706, P.L. 911 (81st Cong.)
4191	3406(a)(6)
4192	3406(a)(6)

4201	3408(a)
4211	3409(a)
4216	2704, 3441
4217	3440
4218	3444
4219	3445
4220	3442
4221	3406(b), 3408(b)
4222	2456, 3451
4223	3446
4224	2700(b), 3407, 3442(3)
4225	2705
4226	
4231	1700
4232	1700(e), 1704
4233	1701
4234	1702, 1703
4241	1710
4242	1712
4243	1711
4251	3465
4252	3465
4253	3465, 3466(b), (c)
4254	3465
4261	3469
4262	3469(a), (b), (f)
4271	3475(a), (c)
4272	3475(a), (b)
4273	3475(e)
4281	3460(a)
4282	3460(b)
4283	3460(c)
4286	1850
4287	1857
4291	1715(a), 1851, 3467(b), 3469(d), 3475(c)
4292	3466(a), 3469(f), 3475(b)(1)
4293	307 R.A. 1943
4294	
4301	1800, 1802(a)
4302	1802(a)
4303	1808(g)
4304	1802(a)
4305	
4311	1800, 1801
4312	1801
4313	1801
4314	1801
4315	1801
4316	
4321	1800, 1802(b)
4322	1802(b)
4323	1802(b)
4324	
4331	3480, 3481(a)

4332	3481(a)
4333	
4341	1802(b), 3481(a)
4342	1802(b), 3481(a)
4343	1802(c), 3481(b)
4344	1802(b), 3481
4345	
4351	1802(b), 3481(a)
4352	1802(b), 3481(a)
4353	1802(b), 3481(a)
4354	
4361	3480, 3482
4362	3482
4363	
4371	1804(a)–(c)
4372	1804(a)–(d)
4373	1804, 1808(b)
4374	1821(b)(3)
4375	
4381	1801, 1802(a), (b)
4382	1808(a)–(f), except (b), 3483
4383	1809(a)
4401	3285(a), (c), (d)
4402	3285(e)
4403	3287
4404	3285(f)
4405	
4411	3290
4412	3291
4413	3292
4414	
4421	3285(b)
4422	3297
4423	3298
4451	1807
4452	1831(a)
4453	1830
4454	1809(a)
4455	1831(b)
4456	1832
4457	
4461	3267(a)
4462	3267(b)
4463	3267(c)
4471	1650, 3268(a)
4472	3268(a)
4473	3268(a)
4474	
4501	3490(a), 3491(a), 3500, 3508
4502	3492, 3507
4503	3490(b)
4504	3501
4511	2470(a)(1), (2)
4512	2477

4513	2470(a)(2), 2470(b), 2474
4514	
4521	3420, 3422
4531	3420, 3423
4532	3423
4541	3420, 3425
4542	3425
4551	3420, 3424
4552	3424
4553	3424(a)
4561	2490, 2491(a)
4562	2491(a)
4571	2490, 2491(b), 2491(d)
4572	2491(f)
4581	2490, 2491(c)
4582	2491(c), (g), 2492
4591	2306, 2311(a)
4592	2300
4593	2300, 2307
4594	2302
4595	2303, 2404
4596	2302(e)
4597	2303(c)
4601	2493, 3430
4602	2492
4603	
4701	2550(a), (b)
4702	2551(a), (b), (c)
4703	2552(a)
4704	2553
4705	2554
4706	2558(a), (c)
4707	
4711	2567(a)
4712	2567(b), 2568
4713	2569
4714	2571
4715	
4721	3220
4722	3221
4723	2553(a)
4724	3224
4725	3227(a)
4726	
4731	P.L. 240, (83d Cong.); 3228(a)
4732	2555
4733	2558(b)
4734	2561
4735	2564; P.L. 238, (83d Cong.)
4736	2562
4741	2590(a), (b)
4742	2591
4743	2592(a)
4744	2593

4745	2598
4746	
4751	3230(a)
4752	3230(b), (c), (d)
4753	3231
4754	3233
4755	3234
4756	2601, 3237
4757	
4761	3238
4762	2603
4771	2550(c)(1), (2); 2552(b), 2590(c), 2592(b)
4772	3222, 3232
4773	2556, 2595
4774	2563, 2602
4775	3226, 3236
4776	
4801	2651(a), (b)
4802	2650
4803	2651(c), 2659(a)
4804	2653
4805	2654, 2655
4806	
4811	2321(a), (b)
4812	2306, 2327(a)
4813	2305, 2321(c), 2327(a), (d)
4814	2322(b)—(e)
4815	2323(c), 2324
4816	2307, 2327(a)
4817	2325
4818	2311, 2327(a)
4819	
4821	3206
4822	3208
4826	2320, 2322(a), 2323(a), (b); 3208
4831	2351(a), (b); 2356
4832	2351(c), 2355, 2356, 2361
4833	2352(b)—(e)
4834	2353(b), 2354(b), (c)
4835	2360
4836	
4841	3210
4842	3212
4846	2350, 2352(a), 2353(a), 2354(a)
4851	1920(a), (b)
4852	1931
4853	1925
4854	1926
4861	1921
4862	1927
4863	1922
4864	1923
4865	1924
4871	1920(c)

4872	1928
4873	1932
4874	1930
4875	1935
4876	1933
4877	
4881	1900
4882	1905
4883	1901, 1906
4884	1902
4885	1903
4886	
4891	1805
4892	1805
4893	1809(a)
4894	1805
4895	1805
4896	1805
4897	
4901	3271
4902	3277
4903	3278, 3292
4904	3279
4905	3280
4906	3276
4907	3283, 3292
5001	2800(a)(1), (4), (6), (c); 3030(a)(1); 3111; 3125(a); 3182(b)
5002	2809(a), (b)(1), (2), (c), (d)
5003	
5004	2800(e)(1), (2), (3), (4); 3112
5005	2800(a)(1), (d); 3112
5006	2800(a)(1), (b)(2), (f); 2879(b); 2880, 2900(a)
5007	2800(f), (a)(3), (4); 2846(a), 2847(a); 3112(b); 3125(a)
5008	2803(a)—(e), 2903(b)—(e)
5009	2802, 2885, 2878
5010	2802(a), (b); 2866
5011	2891(b), 2901(a), (b), (c), (d); 3113
5012	2887
5021	2800(a)(5), 2801(b)
5022	3030(a)(2)
5023	2801(e)(5)
5024	
5025	2800(a)(5); 2801(c)(2), (e); 2883(e), 3036(a), 3250(h), (i); 3254(g)
5026	2800(a)(1)(A)
5027	2802(c)
5028	
5041	3030(a)(1), (2)
5042	3030(a)(1)
5043	3030(b), 3041
5044	
5045	
5051	3150(a), (c)
5052	3160, 3254

5053	3153(b)(c)
5054	3150(b)(1)
5055	3150(b)(2), 3157(a)
5056	
5057	
5061	3172(a)
5062	3179(a), (b)
5063	1656(a), (b), (c)
5064	3174
5065	
5081	3250(f)(1)
5082	3254(g)
5083	
5084	
5091	3250(c)(1), (d)(3)
5092	3254(d)
5093	
5101	3250(j)(1)
5102	3254(h)
5103	
5104	3271(c)(1)
5105	2818(a)
5106	3250(j)(3)
5111	3250(a)(1), (a)(3), (d)(1), (d)(2); 3254(c)(2)
5112	3254(b), (e)
5113	3250(a)(4), (d)(3), (g); 3251(a), (b)
5114	2857, 2858
5115	2863
5116	2831
5121	3250(b)(1), (b)(4), (e)(1), (2), (3)
5122	3250(b)(2), 3254(c)(1), (f)
5123	3250(e)(4); 3251(c); 3255(a), (b), (c)
5124	3252(a), (b), (c)
5131	3250(l)(1), (2)
5132	3250(l)(3)
5133	3250(l)(4)
5134	3250(l)(5)
5141	3270
5142	3271(a), (b), (c)
5143	3272(a)
5144	3277, 3278, 3279, 3280(a), 3283
5145	3273(a)
5146	3273(b)
5147	3275(a)
5148	3276
5149	3282
5171	2819
5172	2832
5173	2820(a), 2822, 2823
5174	2810
5175	2812
5176	2814(a)(1), (a)(2)
5177	2814(a)(1); 2815(a), (b)(1)(A), (B), (C), (D)
5178	2816

5179	2817(a), (b)
5180	2831
5191	2849, 2850(a)
5192	2820, 2838, 2877, 3042
5193	2820, 2878(a), (b), (c), (d)
5194	2883(a)—(g), 2916
5195	2836, 2870
5196	2826, 2827, 2828, 2830, 2839
5197	2841, 2844, 2859
5211	2804
5212	2808
5213	2811
5214	2871
5215	2825
5216	2834
5217	3183(a), (b), (c)
5231	2872, 2873, 2875
5232	2879(c), (d)
5233	
5241	2872, 2873, 2915, 4013(a)
5242	2879(a)
5243	2903(a), (f), (g); 2904, 2905, 2910, 2911
5244	2882
5245	2881
5246	2875
5247	2885(a), (b), 2886, 2888
5248	
5249	
5250	2884
5251	
5252	2874
5271	2812
5272	2801(e)(1)
5273	2801(e)(2)
5274	2831
5275	
5281	2801(e)(1), (d)
5282	2813, 2861, 2862
5283	2828, 2830
5284	
5285	2855, 2857
5301	3100
5302	3101
5303	3102
5304	3114
5305	3105
5306	3103
5307	3106
5308	3107
5309	3104
5310	3108(a)—(d); 3109, 3125(b)
5311	3125(a)
5312	
5313	3121(a), (c)

5314	3117
5315	3119
5316	3120
5317	3121(d), 3122
5318	3123
5319	3124
5320	
5331	3070(a), (b)
5332	3073
5333	3074
5334	
5351	3040
5352	
5353	
5354	3031(a), 3040
5355	
5356	3040
5357	
5361	
5362	3030(a)(1), 3031(a), 3037, 3038; 19 U.S.C. 81(c), 1309, 1311
5363	
5364	
5365	
5366	3034, 3035, 3042
5367	3171
5368	3030(a)(1), 3040, 3041
5369	3040
5370	3039
5371	
5372	
5373	3031, 3032, 3033, 3036, 3037(a)
5381	3036, 3044(a), 3045
5382	3032, 3036, 3044, 3045
5383	3036, 3044(b), (c)
5384	3045
5385	3043(a)
5386	2801(e)(3), (4)
5387	3254(g)
5388	
5391	2801(c), (e)(3); 3031(a)
5392	3036, 3044(b), 3045
5401	3153(b); 3155(a), (b)
5402	3158, 3254(d)
5403	
5411	3158
5412	3104, 3155(f)
5413	3155(f)
5414	
5415	3155(c)
5416	
5501	
5502	3110
5511	3182(a)
5512	

5521	3177(a), (b), (c), (d)(1)
5522	2891(a)
5523	3178
5551	2815(c), (d), (e)
5552	2829
5553	
5554	
5555	3171
5556	3176
5557	3175
5601	2810
5602	2818
5603	2812
5604	2814
5605	2815(a)
5606	2833
5607	2819
5608	2834
5609	2811
5610	2843
5611	2842
5612	2838
5613	2836
5614	2870
5615	2828
5616	2827
5617	2826
5618	2822
5619	2839
5620	2841
5621	2857(a), 2859
5622	2807
5623	2853
5624	2852
5625	2806(c)
5626	2806(f)
5627	2801(e)(2)
5628	2801(f)
5629	2856
5630	2865
5631	2876
5632	2912, 2913
5633	2914(a)
5634	2806(a)(1)(2)
5635	2867
5636	2866
5637	2868
5638	2869
5639	2806(d)
5640	2803(f)
5641	2871
5642	2803(g)
5643	2908
5644	2909

5645	2806(b)(1)
5646	2806(e)
5647	3072
5648	2885(d)
5649	2854
5650	2850
5661	3043
5662	
5663	
5671	3159
5672	3159
5673	3159
5674	3159
5675	3155(f)
5676	3159(e), (f), (g), (h), (i)
5681	2831
5682	2821, 2851
5683	3173(a)
5684	3173(b)
5685	3173(c)
5686	3115, 3116
5687	2806(g)
5688	2805(a)–(b); 3118, 3173(d), 63 Stat. 377 et seq.
5689	2800(a)(1)(B), 3112(b), 3150(b)(3)
5690	3173(b)(4)
5691	3253
5692	3252
5693	3274
5701	2000
5702	2010, 2030, 2050, 2110
5703	2001, 2002(b), (c), 2194, 3310(f)(2)
5704	2040, 2101, 2111(f); 2130(d); 2135(a)(1), (2), (3); 2197(b); 2130(d)
5705	2137, 2198, 3313
5706	2136
5707	2000(g)(1), (2), (3)
5711	2013, 2033, 2039(a), 2053
5712	2012, 2032, 2052
5713	2014, 2054
5721	2017, 2036
5722	2019, 2038, 2039(b), 2194
5723	2100, 2102, 2103(a)(1), 2111, 2112(a)(1), 2130(a), (b), (c)
5731	2059, 2060
5732	2058
5741	2018, 2037, 2039(b)(1), 2056, 2194
5751	2104(a), 2113, 2170(a)(2)
5752	2103(e), 2112(e)
5753	2190
5761	2156(c), 2161(m)(1), 2180(1)
5762	2130(a), (b), (c); 2151(a), (c); 2155(a), 2156, 2160(a)–(e), (g), (i); 2161(a), (c), (e)–(g); 2162(a)(2), (4), (b); 2170(a)(2), (4), (b); 2171(a), (b)(2); 2172, 2173(a), 2174, 2176(a)(2), (3); 2180(a), (d)–(f)
5763	2155(b), 2160(h), 2161(b), (h), (i)(1), (j)(1), (l)(1), (m)(2);

	2170(b), 2171(a), 2175, 2180(b), (g)(1), (h), (i), (k), (*l*)(1), (2)
5801	3260
5802	3261(a)
5803	3262
5811	2720
5812	2721
5813	2722
5814	2723
5821	2734
5831	2700, 3407
5841	3261(b)
5842	2724
5843	2725
5844	2727
5845	2728
5846	2731
5847	2732
5848	2733
5851	2726(a)
5852	2726(b)
5853	2726(c)
5854	3263
5861	2729
5862	2730
6001	51, 54(a), (b); 821(d), 1007(a), (b); 1720, 1835, 1928(b), 2302, 2303, 2322(c), 2324, 2352, 2555, 2569(d), 2594(a), 2653(b), 2709, 2724, 3220(c), 3233(a), 3603
6011(a)	47(a), 51, 143(c), 215(a), 217, 235, 251(g), 1420(c), 1530(b), 1604(a), 1624, 1700 (c)(2), (d)(2), (e)(2); 1716(a), 1852(a), 1902(a)(1), 2403(a), 2451(a), 2471, 2701, 3272(a), 3310(a), (b), (f)(1), 3448(a), 3461, 3467(b), 3469(d), 3475(c), 3491(a), 3611(a)(1)
6011(b)	
6012(a)	51(a), 52(a), 142(a)(2), (3), (4); 217(b), 235(b)
6012(b)(1)	51(b)(4), (c), (g)(5); 142(a)(1)
6012(b)(2)	51(c), 58(f), 142(a)
6012(b)(3)	52(a)
6012(b)(4)	142(a)
6012(b)(5)	142(b)
6013(a)	51(b)(1), (2), (3), (4), (5)
6013(b)	51(g)(1)—(5)
6014(a)	51(f)(1), (2), (4)
6014(b)	51(b)(1), 51(f)(3)
6015(a)	58(a)
6015(b)	58(c)
6015(c)	58(b)
6015(d)	58(b)
6015(e)	58(d)(2)
6015(f)	58(d)(3)
6015(g)	60(b)
6015(h)	58(a)
6016	
6017	482(a)
6018(a)	821(a)(1), 864(a)(1), 937

6018(b)	821(a)(2), 864(a)(2)
6019(a)	1006(a)
6019(b)	
6020(a)	3611(a)(2)
6020(b)	3612(a), (c)
6020(c)	
6021	3613
6031	187
6032	169(f)
6033(a)	54(f)
6033(b)	153(a)
6033(c)	
6034(a)	153(b)
6034(b)	153(b)
6035(a)	338
6035(b)	339
6036	274(a), 820
6037	
6041(a)	147(b)(2)
6041(b)	147(b)(1)
6041(c)	147(c)
6041(d)	
6042	148(a), (b), (c)
6043	148(d), (e)
6044(a)	148(f)
6044(b)	148(f)
6044(c)	148(f)
6045	149
6046(a)	3604(a)
6046(b)	3604(b)
6046(c)	3604(b)
6046(d)	
6051(a)	1403, 1633(a), (b)
6051(b)	1633(a)
6051(c)	1633(b)
6051(d)	1633(b)
6061	3809(b)
6062	52(a)
6063	187
6064	58(g), 3809(b)
6065(a)	142(a), (b), 148(a), (d), (e); 149, 169(f), 187, 233, 821(a), 864(a), 1006(a), 1604(a), 1716(a), 1852(a), 1902(a)(1), 2403(a), 2471, 2555(a), (c); 2701, 3233(a), 3272(a), 3330, 3448(a), 3461, 3467(b), 3469(d), 3475(c), 3604(b), 3611(a), (c), 3779(b), 3780(a), 3809(c)
6065(b)	51(a), 54(f), 58(b), 215(a), 3780(a)
6071	141(b), 147(a), 148(a), (b), (c), (e); 149, 150, 153(a), (b), 821(b), 864(b), 874(b)(3), 1253(a), 1420(c), 1530(b), 1604(a), 1716(b), 1852(a), 1902(a)(1), 2403(a), 2451(a), 2471, 2555(b), (c), 2701, 2734(e), 3233(a), 3272(a), 3310(a), (f)(1); 3448(a), 3461, 3467(b), 3469(d), 3475(c), 3491(a), 3604(a), 3611(b), (c); 3779(b), 3780(a), 3791(a)
6072(a)	53(a)(1), 143(c)
6072(b)	53(a)
6072(c)	217(a), 235(a)

6072(d)	
6072(e)	3805
6073(a)	58(d)(1)
6073(b)	60(a)
6073(c)	58(d)(2)
6073(d)	60(b)
6073(e)	60(c)
6074(a)	
6074(b)	
6074(c)	
6075(a)	821(b), 864(b)
6075(b)	1006(b)
6081(a)	53(a)(2), 58(e), 141(b), 147(a), 148(a), (b), (c), (e); 149, 150, 153(a), (b); 821(b), 864(b), 874(b)(3), 1253(a), 1420(c), 1530(b), 1604(b), 1625(c), 1633(c), 1716(b), 2403(a), 2451(a), 2471, 2555(c)(1), 2701, 3233(a), 3272(a), 3310(f)(1), 3448(a), 3461, 3467(b), 3469(e), 3475(d), 3611(a)(1), 3634, 3779(b), 3791(a)
6081(b)	
6081(c)	
6091(a)	147(a), 148(b), (c), (d), 149, 150, 153(a), (b), 820, 874(b)(3), 1253(a), 1420(c), 1530(b), 2555(c)(1), 2734(e), 3233(a), 3604(a), 3611(a)(1), (c); 3779(a), 3780(a), 3791(a)
6091(b)(1)	53(b)(1), 58(d)(2), 60(b), 143(c), 821(c), 864(c), 1006(b), 1604(a), 1716(c), 1852(b), 1902(a)(2), 2403(a), 2451(a), 2471, 2701, 3272(a), 3291(a), 3448(a), 3461, 3467(b), 3469(d), 3475(c), 3491(c), 3611(a)(1), (c); 3791(a)
6091(b)(2)	53(b)(2), 141(b), 143(c), 1604(a), 1716(c), 1852(b), 1902(a)(2), 2403(a), 2451(a), 2471, 2701, 3272(a), 3291(a), 3448(a), 3461, 3467(b), 3469(d), 3475(c), 3491(c), 3611(a)(1), (c); 3791(a)
6091(b)(3)	821(c), 864(c)
6091(b)(4)	
6101	3630
6102	
6103(a)	55(a)
6103(b)	55(b)
6103(c)	55(c)
6103(d)	55(d)
6103(e)	58(h)
6103(f)	55(e)
6104	153(c)
6105	722(g)
6106	1604(c)
6107	3275, 3292
6108	63
6109	
6151(a)	56(a), 143(c), (h); 144, 218(a), 236(a), 822(a)(1), 1008(a), 1253(a), 1530(b), 1715(b), (c); 1853(a), (b); 1902(a)(3), (b); 2403(b), 2451(a), (b); 2472, 2702(a), 3220, 3230, 3271(b), 3272(a), 3448(a), (b); 3461, 3467(b), 3469(b), 3470, 3475(c), 3491(a), (c)
6151(b)	51(f)(2), 56(i)
6151(c)	322(b)(4), (e)
6152(a)(1)	56(b)(2)(A)
6152(a)(1)(A)	56(b)(2)(A)

6152(a)(1)(B)	56(b)(2)(B)
6152(a)(2)	56(b)(1)
6152(a)(3)	1605(c)
6152(b)(1)	56(b)(3)(A), 1605(c)
6152(b)(2)	56(b)(3)(B)
6152(c)	272(i)
6152(d)	56(b)(4)
6153(a)	59(a)
6153(b)	60(a)
6153(c)	59(b)
6153(d)	60(b)
6153(e)	60(c)
6153(f)	59(c)
6154	
6155(a)	22(d)(6)(F), 51(f)(2), 131(c), 146(a), 272(b), (c); 273(a), (g), (i); 274(b), 292(a), 871(b), (c), (i); 872(a), (g), (i); 874(b)(3), 891, 1012(b), (c); 1013(a), (g), (i); 1015(b), 1021, 1117(g), 1605(c), 3310(d), 3311, 3660(a), 3779(h)
6155(b)	
6156	
6161(a)(1)	56(c), 58(e), 1008(b), 1605(d), 3467(b), 3469(e), 3475(d)
6161(a)(2)	822(a)(2)
6161(b)(1)	272(j), 1012(i)
6161(b)(2)	871(h)
6161(c)	274(b), 1015(b)
6161(d)	
6162(a)	56(c)(2)
6162(b)	
6163(a)	925, 926
6163(b)	
6164(a)	3779(a)
6164(b)	3779(b)
6164(c)	3779(c)
6164(d)	3779(d)
6164(e)	3779(e)
6164(f)	3779(f)
6164(g)	3779(g)
6164(h)	3779(h)
6164(i)	3781
6165	56(c)(2), 272(j), 822(a)(2), 871(h), 1012(i)
6201(a)	3640, 3647
6201(a)(1)	3612(f)
6201(a)(2)(A)	1809(b)(2), 2351(c)(2), 2651(c)(2), 3311
6201(a)(2)(B)	
6201(a)(3)	
6201(b)	59(d)
6201(c)	22(m)(4)
6201(d)	
6202	3644
6203	3641
6204	3642
6205(a)(1)	1401(c), 1411, 1501(c), 1521
6205(a)(2)	1411
6205(b)	1421, 1502, 1522

6206	
6211(a)	271(a), 870, 1011
6211(b)(1)	271(b)(1)
6211(b)(2)	271(b)(2)
6211(b)(3)	271(b)(3)
6212(a)	272(a), 871(a), 1012(a)
6212(b)(1)	272(k), 1012(j)
6212(b)(2)	272(a)
6212(b)(3)	901(d)
6212(c)(1)	272(f), 871(f), 1012(f)
6212(c)(2)	
6213(a)	272(a), 871(a), 1012(a)
6213(b)(1)	272(f), 871(f), 1012(f)
6213(b)(2)	3780(c)
6213(b)(3)	
6213(c)	272(c), 871(c), 1012(c)
6213(d)	272(d), 871(d), 1012(d)
6213(e)	
6214(a)	272(e), 871(e), 1012(e)
6214(b)	272(g), 1012(g)
6214(c)	272(h), 871(g), 1012(h)
6215(a)	272(b), 871(b), 1012(b)
6215(b)	
6216	
6301	3651(a)(1)
6302(a)	3652
6302(b)	1420(c), 1719, 2550(c), 2708, 3281, 3282
6302(c)	3310(f)(2)
6303(a)	3655(a)
6303(b)	
6304	
6311(a)	3656(a)(1), (b)(1)
6311(b)(1)	3656(a)(2)(A), (b)(2)
6311(b)(2)	3656(a)(2)(B)
6312(a)	3657
6312(b)	
6313	56(g), 1008(d), 1420(d), 1530(d), 1605(e), 3658
6314(a)	1008(e), 3659(a)
6314(b)	823
6314(c)	
6315	59(d)
6316	
6321	3670
6322	3671
6323(a)	3672(a)
6323(a)(1)	3672(a)(1)
6323(a)(2)	3672(a)(2)
6323(a)(3)	3672(a)(3)
6323(b)	
6323(c)	
6323(d)(1)	3672(b)(1)
6323(d)(2)	3672(b)(2)
6323(e)	
6324(a)(1)	827(a)

6324(a)(2)	827(b)
6324(a)(3)	827(c)
6324(b)	1009
6324(c)	
6325(a)(1)	827(a), 1009, 3673(a)
6325(a)(2)	3673(b)
6325(b)(1)	3674(a)
6325(b)(2)	3674(b)
6325(c)	3675
6325(d)	
6326	
6331(a)	3310, 3660, 3690, 3692, 3700
6331(b)	3690, 3692, 3700
6331(c)	3715
6331(d)	
6332(a)	3710(a)
6332(b)	3710(b)
6332(c)	3710(c)
6333	3711
6334(a)	3691(a)
6334(b)	3691(b)
6334(c)	3692
6335(a)	3693(a), 3701(a)
6335(b)	3693(b), 3701(b)
6335(c)	3712
6335(d)	3693(c), 3701(c)
6335(e)(1)	3695(a), 3701(d), (e)
6335(e)(2)	3695(b)
6335(e)(2)(A)	3695(a), 3701(d)
6335(e)(2)(B)	3701(d)
6335(e)(2)(C)	
6335(e)(2)(D)	3701(f)
6335(e)(2)(E)	3693, 3701
6335(e)(2)(F)	3693(d), 3701(f)
6335(e)(3)	3701(f)
6336	
6337(a)	3696, 3702
6337(b)(1)	3702(b)(1)
6337(b)(2)	3702(b)(2)
6337(c)	3702(c)
6338(a)	3703(b)
6338(b)	3704(b)
6338(c)	3703(a), 3704(a)
6339(a)(1)	3697(a)(1)
6339(a)(2)	3697(b)
6339(a)(3)	3697(c)
6339(a)(4)	3697(d)
6339(a)(5)	
6339(b)(1)	3704(c)(1)
6339(b)(2)	3704(c)(2)
6340(a)	3706(a), (b)
6340(b)	3706(f)
6341	3716
6342(a)	3694

6342(b)	3712
6343	
6344	
6401(a)	3770(a)(2)
6401(b)	322(a)(2)
6401(c)	3770(c)
6402(a)	1027(a), 3770(a)(1), (4), (5)
6402(b)	322(a)(3)
6403	321
6404(a)	3770(a)(1), (5)
6404(b)	273(j), 873, 1014
6404(c)	
6405(a)	3777(a)
6405(b)	3777(b)
6405(c)	3777(c)
6406	3790
6407	3770(a)(3)
6411(a)	3780(a)
6411(b)	3780(b)
6411(c)	3781
6412(a)	
6412(b)(1)	3412(g)(1)
6412(b)(2)	3412(g)(2)
6412(c)	
6412(d)	3508
6412(e)	
6413(a)(1)	1401(c), 1411, 1501(c), 1521
6413(a)(2)	1411
6413(b)	1421, 1502, 1522
6413(c)(1)	1401(d)(3)
6413(c)(2)	1401(d)(4)
6413(d)	1601(d)
6414	143(f), 1622(f)(1)
6415(a)	1854(a), 3471(a)
6415(b)	1715(d)(1), (2); 1854(b), (c); 3471(b), (c)
6415(c)	1715(d)(2)
6415(d)	1715(d)(1), 1854(c), 3471(c)
6416(a)	1715(d), 2407(b), 2452(b), 3443(a)(3)(B), (b), (d)
6416(b)(1)	2407(a), 3443(a)(2)
6416(b)(2)(A)	3443(a)(3)(A)(i)
6416(b)(2)(B)	3443(a)(3)(A)(ii)
6416(b)(2)(C)	3443(a)(3)(A)(iii)
6416(b)(2)(D)	2452(a)
6416(b)(2)(E)	3443(a)(3)(A)(iv)
6416(b)(2)(F)	3443(a)(3)(A)(v)
6416(b)(2)(G)	3443(a)(3)(A)(vi)
6416(b)(2)(H)	3443(a)(3)(A)(vii)
6416(b)(3)	3443(a)(1)
6416(c)	3403(e)
6416(d)	3408(b)
6416(e)	2705
6416(f)	2703(a), 3471(b)
6417(a)	2473
6417(b)	2474

6418(a)	3494(a)
6418(b)	3493(a)
6419	3286
6420	
6501(a)	275(a), 874(a), 1016(a), 1635(a), 3312(a)
6501(b)(1)	275(f)
6501(b)(2)	1635(e)
6501(b)(3)	
6501(c)(1)	276(a), 874(b)(1), 1016(b)(1), 1635(b), 3312(b)
6501(c)(2)	1635(c), 3312(c)
6501(c)(3)	276(a), 874(b)(1), 1016(b)(1), 1635(b), 3312(b)
6501(c)(4)	276(b)
6501(c)(5)	
6501(d)	275(b)
6501(e)(1)(A)	275(c)
6501(e)(1)(B)	275(d)(1)
6501(e)(2)	
6501(f)	
6501(g)	
6502(a)	276(c), 874(b)(2), 1016(b)(2), 1635(d), 3312(d)
6502(b)	3714(b)
6503(a)(1)	277, 875, 1017
6503(a)(2)	141(h)
6503(b)	274(b), 1015(b)
6503(c)	
6503(d)	822(a)(2), 871(h)
6503(e)	
6504	
6511(a)	322(b)(1), 910, 1027(b)(1), 1636(a)(1), 3313
6511(b)(1)	322(b)(1), 910, 1027(b)(1), 1636(a)(1), 3313
6511(b)(2)	322(b)(2), 910, 1027(b)(2), 1636(a)(2), 3313
6511(c)	322(b)(3)
6511(d)(1)	322(b)(5)
6511(d)(2)(A)	322(b)(6)
6511(d)(2)(B)	322(g)
6511(d)(3)	
6511(e)(1)	3494(b)
6511(e)(2)	3493(b)
6511(f)	
6512(a)	322(c), 911, 1027(c)
6512(b)	322(d), 912, 1027(d)
6513(a)	322(b)(4)
6513(b)	322(e)
6513(c)	1636(c)
6513(d)	
6514(a)	3774
6514(b)	3775
6515	
6521	3812
6531	3748(a)
6532(a)(1)	3772(a)(2)
6532(a)(2)	3774(b)
6532(a)(3)	
6532(a)(4)	3772(a)(3)

6532(b)	3746(a), (b), (c)
6533	
6601(a)	146(f), 292(a), (c), (d); 294(a)(1), (2), (b), (c); 295, 296, 297, 298, 890(a), (b), 891, 892, 893(a)(1), (2); (b)(1), (2), (3), (4); 925, 1020(a), (b), 1021, 1022, 1023(a)(1), (2); (b)(1), (2), (3), (4), (5), 1420(b), 1530(c), 1605(b), 1717, 1853(c), 2403(b), 2451(b), 2475, 2706, 3310(c), 3448(b), 3470, 3495, 3655(b), 3779(i), 3794
6601(b)	890(a), 925
6601(c)(1)	294(a)(2), 296, 893(a)(2), (b)(3); 1023(a)(2), (b)(3)
6601(c)(2)	56(b), 272(i), 1605(c)
6601(c)(3)	297, 892, 1022
6601(c)(4)	3310(a), (b), 3311
6601(d)	292(a), 891, 1021
6601(e)	292(c), 3779(i)
6601(f)(1)	292(a), 294(b), 295, 296, 298, 890(a), (b), 891, 893(a), (b), 1020(a), (b), 1021, 1023(a), (b), 1420(b), 1530(c), 1605(b), 1717, 1853(c), 2403(b), 2451(b), 2475, 2706, 3310(c), (d), 3448(b), 3470, 3495, 3655(b), 3779(i)
6601(f)(2)	
6601(f)(3)	
6601(g)	59(d)
6601(h)	
6602	3746(d)
6611(a)	3443(c), 3771(a)
6611(b)(1)	3771(b)(1)
6611(b)(2)	3771(b)(2)
6611(c)	3771(c)
6611(d)	322(b)(4), (e); 1636
6611(e)	3771(b)(2)
6611(f)	3771(e)
6611(g)	3790
6612	
6651(a)	291, 894(a), 1631, 3612(d)(1)
6651(b)	
6651(c)	294(d)(1)(A)
6652	
6653(a)	51(g)(6)(A), 293(a), 894(a) 1019(a)
6653(b)	51(g)(6)(B), 293(b), 871(i), 1019(b), 3612(d)(2)
6653(c)(1)	271, 870, 1011
6653(c)(2)	
6653(d)	
6653(e)	1821(a)(3)
6654	294(d)(1)(B)
6655	
6656	
6657	
6658	146(f)
6659	51(g)(6), 291, 293, 871(i), 1019, 1117(g), 1634(b), 1718(c), 1821(a)(3), 3310(a)–(e), 3311, 3655(a)(b)
6671(a)	1718(c), 1821(a)(3), 2557(b)(4), 2707(a)
6671(b)	1718(d), 1821(a)(4), 2557(b)(8), 2707(d)
6672	1718(c), 1821(a)(3), 2557(b)(4), 2707(a)
6673	1117(g)
6674	1634(b)

6801(a)	1809(b)(1), 2652(a), 3273(a), 3300(a), 3901(a)(2)
6801(b)	1809(b)(1), 3301(a)
6802(1)	1423(a), 1817(a)
6802(2)	1817(b)
6802(3)	1817(c)
6803(a)(1)	1423(b)
6803(a)(2)	1423(c)
6803(b)(1)	1818(a)
6803(b)(2)	1818(b)
6804	1815, 1920(c), 3301(a)
6805(a)	3304(a)
6805(b)	3304(b)
6805(c)	3304(c)
6805(d)	3304(d)
6806(a)	3273(b)
6806(b)	
6806(c)	3293
6807	3725
6808	
6851(a)(1)	146(a)(1)
6851(a)(2)	146(a)(2)
6851(b)	
6851(c)	146(d)
6851(d)	146(e)
6851(e)	146(b)
6861(a)	273(a), 872(a), 1013(a)
6861(b)	273(b), 872(b), 1013(b)
6861(c)	273(c), 872(c), 1013(c)
6861(d)	273(d), 872(d), 1013(d)
6861(e)	273(e), 872(e), 1013(e)
6861(f)	273(i), 872(i), 1013(i)
6861(g)	273(k), 872(j), 1013(j)
6861(h)	
6862(a)	3660(a)
6862(b)	
6863(a)	273(f), (h); 872(f), (h); 1013(f), (h); 3660(b)
6863(b)(1)	273(g), 872(g), 1013(g)
6863(b)(2)	273(f), (h); 872(f), (h); 1013(f), (h)
6864	
6871(a)	274(a), 1015(a)
6871(b)	274(a), 1015(a)
6872	274(a)
6873(a)	274(b), 1015(b)
6873(b)	
6901(a)	311(a), 900(a), 1025(a)
6901(b)	311(a), 900(a), 1025(a)
6901(c)	311(b), 900(b), 1025(b)
6901(d)	311(b)(4)
6901(e)	311(c), 1025(c)
6901(f)	311(d), 900(c), 1025(d)
6901(g)	311(e), 1025(g)
6901(h)	311(f), 900(e), 1025(f)
6901(i)	
6902(a)	1119(a)

6902(b)	1119(b)
6903(a)	312(a), 901(a), 1026(a)
6903(b)	312(c), 901(c), 1026(c)
6904	
7001(a)	150
7001(b)	
7011(a)	3270(a)
7011(b)	3280(a)
7012	
7101	44(d), 56(c)(2), 112(b)(6)(D), 131(c), 146(b), 272(j), 273(f), 822(a)(2), 871(h), 872(f), 926, 1012(i), 1013(f), 1145, 1818(a), 2302(e), 2322(e), 2352(e), 2474, 2569(b), 2653(d), 3360(d)(2)(B), 3412(d), 3413, 3660(b), 3722(c), 3724(c), 3943, 3992, 4010, and 6 U.S.C. 15
7102	3676
7103	
7121(a)	3760
7121(b)	3760
7122(a)	3761
7122(b)	3761
7123	
7201	145(a), (b), 153(d), 340, 894(b)(2)(B), (C); 937, 1024(a), (b); 1718(a), (b); 1821(a)(1), (2), (b)(4); 2557(b)(2), (b)(3); 2656(f), 2707(b), 2707(c), 3604(c)
7202	145(b), 894(b)(2)(C), 1718(b), 1821(a)(2), 2557(b)(3), 2707(c)
7203	145(a), 153(d), 340, 894(b)(2)(B), 937, 1024(a), 1718(a), 1821(a)(1), 2557(b)(2), 2707(b), 3604(c)
7204	1634(a)
7205	1626(d)
7206(1)	3809(a)
7206(2)	3793(b)
7206(3)	3793(a)
7206(4)	2656(a), 3321
7206(5)	3762
7207	894(b)(2), 3616(a), 3672, 3793(b)
7208	3300(b)
7208(1)	1425(b)
7208(2)	1823(a)
7208(3)	1822, 1823(b)
7208(4)	1823(c)
7208(5)	3323(a)(3)
7209	1425(a)
7210	3616(b)
7211	3325
7212(a)	3601(c)
7212(b)	3601(c)(2)
7213(a)(1)	55(f)(1)
7213(a)(2)	55(f)(2)
7213(a)(3)	55(f)(3)
7213(b)	4047(a)(1)
7213(c)	
7214(a)	4047(e)
7214(b)	4047
7214(c)	
7231	150

7232	3412(d)
7233(1)	1929(a)(1)
7233(2)	1929(a)(2)
7234(a)	2308(a)
7234(b)	2308(c)
7234(c)	2308(h)
7234(d)(1)	2308(i)(1)
7234(d)(2)(A)	2308(g)(1)
7234(d)(2)(B)	2308(g)(2)
7234(d)(3)	2308(i)(2)
7234(d)(4)	2308(d)
7235(a)	2326(a)
7235(b)	2326(b)
7235(c)	2326(c)
7235(d)	3207(b)
7235(e)	2327
7236	2357(b)
7237(a)	2557(b)(1), 2596, 3225, 3235
7237(b)	2557(a)
7238	2570
7239(a)	2656(b)
7239(b)	2656(d)
7240	3506
7261	2409
7262	3294(a)
7263(a)	1929(c)
7263(b)	1929(b)
7264	3207(a)
7265(a)(1)	2308(b)
7265(a)(2)	2326(a)(2)
7265(b)	2308(e), 2327(a)
7265(c)	2308(j), 2327(a)
7266(a)(1)	3211(a)
7266(a)(2)	3211(b)
7266(a)(3)	3211(c)
7266(b)	2357(a)
7266(c)	2357(c)
7266(d)	2357(d)
7266(e)	2357(e)
7266(f)	2357(f)
7267(a)	2656(j)
7267(b)	2656(k)
7267(c)	2656(i)
7267(d)	2656(h)
7268	3320(a)
7269	894(b)(1)
7270	1821(b)(3)
7271(1)	1822, 2656(c)
7271(2)	1820(b)
7271(3)	1820(a)
7271(4)	3323(a)(1), (2)
7272(a)	1831(c), 2656(g), 3475(e)
7272(b)	
7273(a)	3274

7273(b)	3294(b)
7274	2656
7275	
7301(a)	2558(a), (b); 2571, 2598(a), (b), (c); 3253, 3321(b)(1), 3720(a)(1)
7301(b)	3321(b)(1), 3720(a)(2)
7301(c)	2657(e), 3321(b)(1), 3720(a)(3)
7301(d)	3321(b)(2), 3322
7301(e)	3321(b)(3)
7302	3116
7303(1)	1823
7303(2)	2309(b), 2358(b)
7303(3)	2309(d)
7303(4)	2358(a)
7303(5)	2309(b), 2358(b)
7303(6)(A)	2657(c)
7303(6)(B)	2656(c), 2657(a)(b), (f)
7303(7)	3323(b)
7303(8)	3793(a)(2)
7304	3326
7321	3720(b)
7322	3721
7323(a)	3723(a)
7323(b)	3723(b)
7323(c)	3723(c)
7324	3722
7325	3724
7326	
7327	3726
7328	2657
7329	
7341(a)	3324(a)
7341(b)	3324(b)
7341(c)	3324(c)
7342	3601(b)
7343	145(d), 894(b)(2)(D), 1718(d), 1821(a)(4), 2557(b)(8), 2707(d), 3228, 3710(c), 3793(b)(2)
7344	4048
7401	3740
7402(a)	3800
7402(b)	3633
7402(c)	4042
7402(d)	3992, 3995(c)
7402(e)	
7403(a)	3678(a)
7403(b)	3678(b)
7403(c)	3678(c)
7403(d)	3678(d)
7404	826(a)
7405(a)	3746(a)
7405(b)	3746(b)
7405(c)	
7405(d)	
7406	3747

7407	
7421(a)	3653(a)
7421(b)	3653(b)
7422(a)	3772(a)(1)
7422(b)	3772(b)
7422(c)	3772(d)
7422(d)	3772(e)
7422(e)	
7422(f)	
7423(1)	3770(b)(1)
7423(2)	3770(b)(2)
7424(a)(1)	3679(a)(1)
7424(a)(2)	3679(a)(2)
7424(a)(3)	3679(a)(3)
7424(b)	3679(c)
7424(c)	3679(d)
7425	
7441	1100
7442	1101
7443(a)	1102(a)
7443(b)	1102(b)
7443(c)	1102(c)
7443(d)	1102(d)
7443(e)	1102(e)
7443(f)	1102(f)
7443(g)	1102(g)
7444(a)	1103(a)
7444(b)	1103(b)
7444(c)	1103(c)
7444(d)	1103(d)
7445	1104
7446	1105
7447(a)	1106(a)
7447(b)	1106(b)
7447(c)	1106(c)
7447(d)	1106(d)
7447(e)	1106(e)
7447(f)	1106(f)
7447(g)	1106(g)
7451	1110
7452	504(b), R.A. 1942
7453	1111
7454(a)	1112
7454(b)	
7455	1113
7456(a)	1114
7456(b)	
7456(c)	1114(b)
7457(a)	1115(a)
7457(b)	1115(b)
7458	1116
7459(a)	1117(a)
7459(b)	1117(b)
7459(c)	1117(c)

7459(d)	1117(d)
7459(e)	1117(e)
7459(f)	1117(f)
7459(g)	
7460(a)	1118(a)
7460(b)	1118(b)
7461	1120
7462	1121
7463	
7471(a)	1130(a)
7471(b)	1130(b)
7471(c)	
7472	1131
7473	1132
7474	1133
7481	1140
7482(a)	1141(a)
7482(b)	1141(b)
7482(c)	1141(c)
7483	1142
7484	1143
7485(a)	1145
7485(b)	
7486	1146
7487	
7491	2597
7492	1925(b)
7493	1930
7501(a)	3661
7501(b)	
7502	
7503	
7504	
7505(a)	3695(b)
7505(b)	3695(c)
7506(a)	3795(a)
7506(b)	3795(b)
7506(c)	3795(c)
7506(d)	3795(d)
7507(a)	3798(a)
7507(b)	3798(b)
7507(c)	3798(c)
7507(d)	3798(d)
7508(a)	3804(a)
7508(b)	3804(d)
7509	1424
7510	3331
7511	3802
7601(a)	3600
7601(b)	
7602	3614, 3615(a), (b), (c); 3632(a)(1)
7603	3615(d)
7604(a)	3633(a)
7604(b)	3615(e)

7604(c)	
7605(a)	3614, 3615
7605(b)	3631
7606(a)	3601(a)(1)
7606(b)	3601(a)(2)
7606(c)	
7607	
7621	3650
7622(a)	3632(a)
7622(b)	3632(b)
7623	3792
7641	2302(c), 2322(c), 2352(c), 2569(d)(4), 2653(b)
7651(2)(A)	3811
7652(a)(1)	3360(a)
7652(a)(2)	3360(b)
7652(a)(3)	3360(c)
7652(b)(1)	3350(a)
7652(b)(2)	3350(b)
7653(a)(1)	3361(a)
7653(a)(2)	3351(a)
7653(b)	3351(b), 3361(b)
7653(c)	3351(c), 3361(c)
7653(d)	
7654	2483
7655	
7701(a)(1)	1426(f), 1532(i), 1607(k), 1805, 1931(b), 2733(i), 3228(a), 3238(a), 3507(a), 3797(a)(1)
7701(a)(2)	3797(a)(2)
7701(a)(3)	3797(a)(3)
7701(a)(4)	3797(a)(4)
7701(a)(5)	3797(a)(5)
7701(a)(6)	3797(a)(6)
7701(a)(7)	3797(a)(7)
7701(a)(8)	3797(a)(8)
7701(a)(9)	3797(a)(9)
7701(a)(10)	3797(a)(10)
7701(a)(11)	3797(a)(11)
7701(a)(12)	
7701(a)(13)	3797(a)(12)
7701(a)(14)	3797(a)(14)
7701(a)(15)	3797(a)(15)
7701(a)(16)	3797(a)(16)
7701(a)(17)	3797(a)(17)
7701(a)(18)	3797(a)(18)
7701(a)(19)	3797(a)(19)
7701(a)(20)	3797(a)(20)
7701(a)(21)	
7701(a)(22)	
7701(a)(23)	48(a)
7701(a)(24)	48(b)
7701(a)(25)	48(c)
7701(a)(26)	48(d)
7701(a)(27)	
7701(a)(28)	

7701(b)	3797(b)
7701(c)(1)	3797(c)
7701(c)(2)	
7801(a)	Reorg. Plan No. 26 of 1950
7801(b)	3930(a), 3931
7801(c)	3932
7802	3900
7803(a)	3920, 3921, 4000, 4041(a)
7803(b)(1)	4040
7803(b)(2)	3901(b)
7803(c)	3360(b)(2)(B), 3943, 3992, 4010
7803(d)	3975, 3976, 3977, 3978
7804(a)	616 R.A. 1951
7804(b)	3, P.L. 567 (82d Cong.)
7805(a)	62, 3791(a)
7805(b)	3791(b)
7805(c)	3901(a)(2)
7806(a)	2
7806(b)	Ch. 1, Sec. 6, P.L. 1
7807(a)	
7807(b)	
7808	3970
7809(a)	2480, 3971(a)
7809(b)	3971(b)
7809(b)(1)	3971(b)(1)
7809(b)(2)	3971(b)(2)
7809(b)(3)	3971(b)(3)
7851(a)	*See* 26 U.S.C. 3, 4
7851(b)	*See* 26 U.S.C. 4(b)
7851(c)	*See* 26 U.S.C. 4(c)
7851(d)	*See* 26 U.S.C. 4(d)
7852(a)	3803
7852(b)	*See* 26 U.S.C. 4(a), 5, 7
7852(c)	
7852(d)	108 R.A. 1941; 109 R.A. 1942; 136 R.A. 1943; 214 R.A. 1950; 615 R.A. 1951; *See* 22(b)(7)
8001	5000
8002	5001
8003	5002
8004	5003
8005	5004
8021	5010
8022	5011
8023	5012

An Act to revise the internal revenue laws of the United States

Be it enacted by the Senate and House of Representatives of the United States of America in Congress assembled, That

(a) Citation

(1) The provisions of this Act set forth under the heading "Internal Revenue Title" may be cited as the "Internal Revenue Code of 1986 [formerly I.R.C. 1954]".

(2) The Internal Revenue Code enacted on February 10, 1939, as amended, may be cited as the "Internal Revenue Code of 1939".

(b) Publication

This Act shall be published as volume 68A of the United States Statutes at Large, with a comprehensive table of contents and an appendix; but without an index or marginal references. The date of enactment, bill number, public law number, and chapter number, shall be printed as a headnote.

(c) Cross reference

For saving provisions, effective date provisions, and other related provisions, see chapter 80 (sec. 7801 and following) of the Internal Revenue Code of 1986.

(d) Enactment of Internal Revenue Title into law

The Internal Revenue Title referred to in subsection (a)(1) is as follows: * * *.

(Aug. 16, 1954, ch. 736, 68A Stat. 3; Pub. L. 99–514, §2, Oct. 22, 1986, 100 Stat. 2095.)

EDITORIAL NOTES
AMENDMENTS

1986—Subsecs. (a)(1), (c). Pub. L. 99–514 substituted "Internal Revenue Code of 1986" for "Internal Revenue Code of 1954".

STATUTORY NOTES AND RELATED SUBSIDIARIES
REDESIGNATION OF INTERNAL REVENUE CODE OF 1954; REFERENCES

Pub. L. 99–514, §2, Oct. 22, 1986, 100 Stat. 2095, provided that:

"(a) Redesignation of 1954 Code.—The Internal Revenue Title enacted August 16, 1954, as heretofore, hereby, or hereafter amended, may be cited as the 'Internal Revenue Code of 1986'.

"(b) References in Laws, Etc.—Except when inappropriate, any reference in any law, Executive order, or other document—

"(1) to the Internal Revenue Code of 1954 shall include a reference to the Internal Revenue Code of 1986, and

"(2) to the Internal Revenue Code of 1986 shall include a reference to the provisions of law formerly known as the Internal Revenue Code of 1954."

INTERNAL REVENUE TITLE

Subtitle
A.
Income taxes.
B.
Estate and gift taxes.
C.
Employment taxes.
D.
Miscellaneous excise taxes.
E.
Alcohol, tobacco, and certain other excise taxes.
F.
Procedure and administration.
G.
The Joint Committee on Taxation.
H.
Financing of Presidential election campaigns.
I.
Trust Fund Code.
J.
Coal industry health benefits.[1]

K.
Group health plan requirements.

EDITORIAL NOTES
AMENDMENTS

1997—Pub. L. 105–34, title XV, §1531(b)(3), Aug. 5, 1997, 111 Stat. 1085, added subtitle K heading "Group health plan requirements" and struck out former subtitle K heading "Group health plan portability, access, and renewability requirements".

1996—Pub. L. 104–191, title IV, §401(b), Aug. 21, 1996, 110 Stat. 2082, added subtitle K heading "Group health plan portability, access, and renewability requirements".

1982—Pub. L. 97–248, title III, §§307(b)(2), 308(a), Sept. 3, 1982, 96 Stat. 590, 591, provided that, applicable to payments of interest, dividends, and patronage dividends paid or credited after June 30, 1983, subtitle C heading is amended to read "Employment taxes and collection of income tax at source". Section 102(a), (b) of Pub. L. 98–67, title I, Aug. 5, 1983, 97 Stat. 369, repealed subtitle A (§§301–308) of title III of Pub. L. 97–248 as of the close of June 30, 1983, and provided that the Internal Revenue Code of 1954 [now 1986] [this title] shall be applied and administered (subject to certain exceptions) as if such subtitle A (and the amendments made by such subtitle A) had not been enacted.

1981—Pub. L. 97–119, title I, §103(c)(2), Dec. 29, 1981, 95 Stat. 1638, added subtitle I heading "Trust Fund Code".

1976—Pub. L. 94–455, title XIX, §1907(b)(2), Oct. 4, 1976, 90 Stat. 1836, substituted in subtitle G heading "The Joint Committee on Taxation" for "The Joint Committee on Internal Revenue Taxation".

1974—Pub. L. 93–443, title IV, §408(a), Oct. 15, 1974, 88 Stat. 1297, added subtitle H heading "Financing of Presidential election campaigns".

TABLE OF CONTENTS

This Table of Contents is inserted for the convenience of users and was not enacted as part of the Internal Revenue Code of 1986.

Subtitle A—Income Taxes

Subtitle B—Estate and Gift Taxes

Subtitle C—Employment Taxes

Subtitle D—Miscellaneous Excise Taxes

Subtitle E—Alcohol, Tobacco, and Certain Other Excise Taxes

Subtitle F—Procedure and Administration

7801

Subtitle G—The Joint Committee on Taxation

Subtitle H—Financing of Presidential Election Campaigns

Subtitle I—Trust Fund Code

Subtitle A—Income Taxes

EDITORIAL NOTES

AMENDMENTS

2010—Pub. L. 111–152, title I, §1402(a)(3), Mar. 30, 2010, 124 Stat. 1062, which directed amendment of the "table of chapters for subtitle A of chapter 1 of the Internal Revenue Code of 1986" by adding item for chapter 2A, was executed by adding item for chapter 2A to the table of chapters for this subtitle to reflect the probable intent of Congress.

Pub. L. 111–147, title V, §501(c)(8), Mar. 18, 2010, 124 Stat. 106, which directed amendment of the "table of chapters of the Internal Revenue Code of 1986" by adding item for chapter 4 "at the end", was executed by adding item for chapter 4 after item for chapter 3 in the table of chapters for this subtitle to reflect the probable intent of Congress.

1997—Pub. L. 105–34, title XI, §1131(c)(4), Aug. 5, 1997, 111 Stat. 980, struck out item for chapter 5 "Tax on transfers to avoid income tax".

1990—Pub. L. 101–508, title XI, §11801(b)(11), Nov. 5, 1990, 104 Stat. 1388–522, struck out item for chapter 4 "Rules applicable to recovery of excessive profits on government contracts".

1984—Pub. L. 98–369, div. A, title IV, §474(r)(29)(D), July 18, 1984, 98 Stat. 844, struck out "and tax-free covenant bonds" at end of item for chapter 3.

CHAPTER 1—NORMAL TAXES AND SURTAXES

EDITORIAL NOTES

AMENDMENTS

2018—Pub. L. 115–141, div. U, title IV, §401(a)(1), (d)(4)(A), (5)(A), (6)(A), Mar. 23, 2018, 132 Stat. 1184, 1209-1211, transferred subchapter R to follow subchapter Q and struck out subchapter W "District of Columbia Enterprise Zone", subchapter X "Renewal Communities", and subchapter Y "Short-Term Regional Benefits".

2017—Pub. L. 115–97, title I, §13823(c), Dec. 22, 2017, 131 Stat. 2188, added subchapter Z.

2005—Pub. L. 109–135, title I, §101(b)(4), Dec. 21, 2005, 119 Stat. 2593, substituted "Short-Term Regional Benefits" for "New York Liberty Zone Benefits" in subchapter Y.

2004—Pub. L. 108–357, title II, §248(b)(2), Oct. 22, 2004, 118 Stat. 1457, added subchapter R.

2002—Pub. L. 107–147, title III, §301(c), Mar. 9, 2002, 116 Stat. 40, added subchapter Y.

2000—Pub. L. 106–554, §1(a)(7) [title I, §101(d)], Dec. 21, 2000, 114 Stat. 2763, 2763A-600, added subchapter X.

1997—Pub. L. 105–34, title VII, §701(c), Aug. 5, 1997, 111 Stat. 869, added subchapter W.

1993—Pub. L. 103–66, title XIII, §13301(b), Aug. 10, 1993, 107 Stat. 555, added subchapter U.

1986—Pub. L. 99–514, title XIII, §1303(c)(1), Oct. 22, 1986, 100 Stat. 2658, struck out subchapter U "General stock ownership plans".

1982—Pub. L. 97–354, §5(b), Oct. 19, 1982, 96 Stat. 1697, substituted in subchapter S "Tax treatment of S corporations and their shareholders" for "Election of certain small business corporations as to taxable status".

1980—Pub. L. 96–589, §3(a)(2), Dec. 24, 1980, 94 Stat. 3400, added subchapter V.

1978—Pub. L. 95–600, title VI, §601(c)(1), Nov. 6, 1978, 92 Stat. 2897, added subchapter U.

1966—Pub. L. 89–389, §4(b)(2), Apr. 14, 1966, 80 Stat. 116, struck out subchapter R effective January 1, 1969.

1962—Pub. L. 87–834, §17(b)(4), Oct. 16, 1962, 76 Stat. 1051, added subchapter T.

1960—Pub. L. 86–779, §10(c), Sept. 14, 1960, 74 Stat. 1009, added to subchapter M heading "and real estate investment trusts".

1958—Pub. L. 85–866, title I, §64(d)(1), Sept. 2, 1958, 72 Stat. 1656, added subchapter S.

[1] *Section numbers editorially supplied.*

Subchapter A—Determination of Tax Liability

EDITORIAL NOTES

AMENDMENTS

2017—Pub. L. 115–97, title I, §14401(d)(1), Dec. 22, 2017, 131 Stat. 2233, added part VII.

2014—Pub. L. 113–295, div. A, title II, §221(a)(12)(A), Dec. 19, 2014, 128 Stat. 4038, struck out part VII "Environmental tax".

1989—Pub. L. 101–234, title I, §102(a), Dec. 13, 1989, 103 Stat. 1980, repealed Pub. L. 100–360, §111, and provided that the provisions of law amended by such section are restored or revived as if such section had not been enacted, see 1988 Amendment note below.

1988—Pub. L. 100–360, title I, §111(c), July 1, 1988, 102 Stat. 697, added part VIII "Supplemental medicare premium".

1986—Pub. L. 99–499, title V, §516(b)(5), Oct. 17, 1986, 100 Stat. 1771, added part VII.

1976—Pub. L. 94–455, title XIX, §1901(b)(2), Oct. 4, 1976, 90 Stat. 1792, struck out part V "Tax surcharge".

1969—Pub. L. 91–172, title III, §301(b)(1), Dec. 30, 1969, 83 Stat. 585, added part VI.

1968—Pub. L. 90–364, title I, §102(d), June 28, 1968, 82 Stat. 259, added part V.

[1] *Part heading amended by Pub. L. 99–514 without corresponding amendment of analysis.*

[2] *So in original. Probably should be followed by a period.*

PART I—TAX ON INDIVIDUALS

EDITORIAL NOTES

AMENDMENTS

1976—Pub. L. 94–455, title V, §501(c)(1), Oct. 4, 1976, 90 Stat. 1559, substituted "Tax tables for individuals having taxable income of less than $20,000" for "Optional tax tables for individuals" in item 3 and struck out item 4 relating to rules for optional tax.

1969—Pub. L. 91–172, title VIII, §803(d)(9), Dec. 30, 1969, 83 Stat. 685, substituted "Definitions and special rules" and "Optional tax tables for individuals" for "Tax in case of joint return or return of surviving spouse" and "Optional tax if adjusted gross income is less than $5,000" in items 2 and 3, respectively.

[1] *Section catchline amended by Pub. L. 95–30 without corresponding amendment of analysis.*

§1. Tax imposed

(a) Married individuals filing joint returns and surviving spouses

There is hereby imposed on the taxable income of—

(1) every married individual (as defined in section 7703) who makes a single return jointly with his spouse under section 6013, and

(2) every surviving spouse (as defined in section 2(a)),

a tax determined in accordance with the following table:

If taxable income is:	The tax is:
Not over $36,900	15% of taxable income.

If taxable income is:	The tax is:
Over $36,900 but not over $89,150	$5,535, plus 28% of the excess over $36,900.
Over $89,150 but not over $140,000	$20,165, plus 31% of the excess over $89,150.
Over $140,000 but not over $250,000	$35,928.50, plus 36% of the excess over $140,000.
Over $250,000	$75,528.50, plus 39.6% of the excess over $250,000.

(b) Heads of households

There is hereby imposed on the taxable income of every head of a household (as defined in section 2(b)) a tax determined in accordance with the following table:

If taxable income is:	The tax is:
Not over $29,600	15% of taxable income.
Over $29,600 but not over $76,400	$4,440, plus 28% of the excess over $29,600.
Over $76,400 but not over $127,500	$17,544, plus 31% of the excess over $76,400.
Over $127,500 but not over $250,000	$33,385, plus 36% of the excess over $127,500.
Over $250,000	$77,485, plus 39.6% of the excess over $250,000.

(c) Unmarried individuals (other than surviving spouses and heads of households)

There is hereby imposed on the taxable income of every individual (other than a surviving spouse as defined in section 2(a) or the head of a household as defined in section 2(b)) who is not a married individual (as defined in section 7703) a tax determined in accordance with the following table:

If taxable income is:	The tax is:
Not over $22,100	15% of taxable income.
Over $22,100 but not over $53,500	$3,315, plus 28% of the excess over $22,100.
Over $53,500 but not over $115,000	$12,107, plus 31% of the excess over $53,500.
Over $115,000 but not over $250,000	$31,172, plus 36% of the excess over $115,000.
Over $250,000	$79,772, plus 39.6% of the excess over $250,000.

(d) Married individuals filing separate returns

There is hereby imposed on the taxable income of every married individual (as defined in section 7703) who does not make a single return jointly with his spouse under section 6013, a tax determined in accordance with the following table:

If taxable income is:	The tax is:
Not over $18,450	15% of taxable income.
Over $18,450 but not over $44,575	$2,767.50, plus 28% of the excess over $18,450.
Over $44,575 but not over $70,000	$10,082.50, plus 31% of the excess over $44,575.
Over $70,000 but not over $125,000	$17,964.25, plus 36% of the excess over $70,000.
Over $125,000	$37,764.25, plus 39.6% of the excess over $125,000.

(e) Estates and trusts

There is hereby imposed on the taxable income of—
(1) every estate, and
(2) every trust,

taxable under this subsection a tax determined in accordance with the following table:

If taxable income is:	The tax is:
Not over $1,500	15% of taxable income.
Over $1,500 but not over $3,500	$225, plus 28% of the excess over $1,500.
Over $3,500 but not over $5,500	$785, plus 31% of the excess over $3,500.
Over $5,500 but not over $7,500	$1,405, plus 36% of the excess over $5,500.
Over $7,500	$2,125, plus 39.6% of the excess over $7,500.

(f) Phaseout of marriage penalty in 15-percent bracket; adjustments in tax tables so that inflation will not result in tax increases
(1) In general

Not later than December 15 of 1993, and each subsequent calendar year, the Secretary shall prescribe tables which shall apply in lieu of the tables contained in subsections (a), (b), (c), (d), and (e) with respect to taxable years beginning in the succeeding calendar year.

(2) Method of prescribing tables

The table which under paragraph (1) is to apply in lieu of the table contained in subsection (a), (b), (c), (d), or (e), as the case may be, with respect to taxable years beginning in any calendar year shall be prescribed—

(A) except as provided in paragraph (8), by increasing the minimum and maximum dollar amounts for each bracket for which a tax is imposed under such table by the cost-of-living adjustment for such calendar year, determined—

(i) except as provided in clause (ii), by substituting "1992" for "2016" in paragraph (3)(A)(ii), and

(ii) in the case of adjustments to the dollar amounts at which the 36 percent rate bracket begins or at which the 39.6 percent rate bracket begins, by substituting "1993" for "2016" in paragraph (3)(A)(ii),

(B) by not changing the rate applicable to any rate bracket as adjusted under subparagraph (A), and

(C) by adjusting the amounts setting forth the tax to the extent necessary to reflect the adjustments in the rate brackets.

(3) Cost-of-living adjustment

For purposes of this subsection—

(A) In general

The cost-of-living adjustment for any calendar year is the percentage (if any) by which—

(i) the C-CPI-U for the preceding calendar year, exceeds

(ii) the CPI for calendar year 2016, multiplied by the amount determined under subparagraph (B).

(B) Amount determined

The amount determined under this clause is the amount obtained by dividing—

(i) the C-CPI-U for calendar year 2016, by

(ii) the CPI for calendar year 2016.

(C) Special rule for adjustments with a base year after 2016

For purposes of any provision of this title which provides for the substitution of a year after 2016 for "2016" in subparagraph (A)(ii), subparagraph (A) shall be applied by substituting "the C-CPI-U for calendar year 2016" for "the CPI for calendar year 2016" and all that follows in clause (ii) thereof.

(4) CPI for any calendar year

For purposes of paragraph (3), the CPI for any calendar year is the average of the Consumer Price Index as of the close of the 12-month period ending on August 31 of such calendar year.

(5) Consumer Price Index

For purposes of paragraph (4), the term "Consumer Price Index" means the last Consumer Price Index for all-urban consumers published by the Department of Labor. For purposes of the preceding sentence, the revision of the Consumer Price Index which is most consistent with the Consumer Price Index for calendar year 1986 shall be used.

(6) C-CPI-U

For purposes of this subsection—

(A) In general

The term "C-CPI-U" means the Chained Consumer Price Index for All Urban Consumers (as published by the Bureau of Labor Statistics of the Department of Labor). The values of the Chained Consumer Price Index for All Urban Consumers taken into account for purposes of determining the cost-of-living adjustment for any calendar year under this subsection shall be the latest values so published as of the date on which such Bureau publishes the initial value of the Chained Consumer Price Index for All Urban Consumers for the month of August for the preceding calendar year.

(B) Determination for calendar year

The C-CPI-U for any calendar year is the average of the C-CPI-U as of the close of the 12-month period ending on August 31 of such calendar year.

(7) Rounding

(A) In general

If any increase determined under paragraph (2)(A), section 63(c)(4), section 68(b)(2) or section 151(d)(4) is not a multiple of $50, such increase shall be rounded to the next lowest multiple of $50.

(B) Table for married individuals filing separately

In the case of a married individual filing a separate return, subparagraph (A) (other than with respect to sections 63(c)(4) and 151(d)(4)(A)) shall be applied by substituting "$25" for "$50" each place it appears.

(8) Elimination of marriage penalty in 15-percent bracket

With respect to taxable years beginning after December 31, 2003, in prescribing the tables under paragraph (1)—

(A) the maximum taxable income in the 15-percent rate bracket in the table contained in subsection (a) (and the minimum taxable income in the next higher taxable income bracket in such table) shall be 200 percent of the maximum taxable income in the 15-percent rate bracket in the table contained in subsection (c) (after any other adjustment under this subsection), and

(B) the comparable taxable income amounts in the table contained in subsection (d) shall be ½ of the amounts determined under subparagraph (A).

(g) Certain unearned income of children taxed as if parent's income

(1) In general

In the case of any child to whom this subsection applies, the tax imposed by this section shall be equal to the greater of—

(A) the tax imposed by this section without regard to this subsection, or

(B) the sum of—

(i) the tax which would be imposed by this section if the taxable income of such child for the taxable year were reduced by the net unearned income of such child, plus

(ii) such child's share of the allocable parental tax.

(2) Child to whom subsection applies

This subsection shall apply to any child for any taxable year if—

(A) such child—

(i) has not attained age 18 before the close of the taxable year, or

(ii)(I) has attained age 18 before the close of the taxable year and meets the age requirements of section 152(c)(3) (determined without regard to subparagraph (B) thereof), and

(II) whose earned income (as defined in section 911(d)(2)) for such taxable year does not exceed one-half of the amount of the individual's support (within the meaning of section 152(c)(1)(D) after the application of section 152(f)(5) (without regard to subparagraph (A) thereof)) for such taxable year,

(B) either parent of such child is alive at the close of the taxable year, and

(C) such child does not file a joint return for the taxable year.

(3) Allocable parental tax

For purposes of this subsection—

(A) In general

The term "allocable parental tax" means the excess of—

(i) the tax which would be imposed by this section on the parent's taxable income if such income included the net unearned income of all children of the parent to whom this subsection applies, over

(ii) the tax imposed by this section on the parent without regard to this subsection.

For purposes of clause (i), net unearned income of all children of the parent shall not be taken into account in computing any exclusion, deduction, or credit of the parent.

(B) Child's share

A child's share of any allocable parental tax of a parent shall be equal to an amount which bears the same ratio to the total allocable parental tax as the child's net unearned income bears to the aggregate net unearned income of all children of such parent to whom this subsection applies.

(C) Special rule where parent has different taxable year

Except as provided in regulations, if the parent does not have the same taxable year as the child, the allocable parental tax shall be determined on the basis of the taxable year of the parent ending in the child's taxable year.

(4) Net unearned income

For purposes of this subsection—

(A) In general

The term "net unearned income" means the excess of—

(i) the portion of the adjusted gross income for the taxable year which is not attributable to earned income (as defined in section 911(d)(2)), over

(ii) the sum of—

(I) the amount in effect for the taxable year under section 63(c)(5)(A) (relating to limitation on standard deduction in the case of certain dependents), plus

(II) the greater of the amount described in subclause (I) or, if the child itemizes his deductions for the taxable year, the amount of the itemized deductions allowed by this chapter for the taxable year which are directly connected with the production of the portion of adjusted gross income referred to in clause (i).

(B) Limitation based on taxable income

The amount of the net unearned income for any taxable year shall not exceed the individual's taxable income for such taxable year.

(C) Treatment of distributions from qualified disability trusts

For purposes of this subsection, in the case of any child who is a beneficiary of a qualified disability trust (as defined in section 642(b)(2)(C)(ii)), any amount included in the income of such child under sections 652 and 662 during a taxable year shall be considered earned income of such child for such taxable year.

(5) Special rules for determining parent to whom subsection applies

For purposes of this subsection, the parent whose taxable income shall be taken into account shall be—

(A) in the case of parents who are not married (within the meaning of section 7703), the custodial parent (within the meaning of section 152(e)) of the child, and

(B) in the case of married individuals filing separately, the individual with the greater taxable income.

(6) Providing of parent's TIN

The parent of any child to whom this subsection applies for any taxable year shall provide the TIN of such parent to such child and such child shall include such TIN on the child's return of tax imposed by this section for such taxable year.

(7) Election to claim certain unearned income of child on parent's return

(A) In general

If—

(i) any child to whom this subsection applies has gross income for the taxable year only from interest and dividends (including Alaska Permanent Fund dividends),

(ii) such gross income is more than the amount described in paragraph (4)(A)(ii)(I) and less than 10 times the amount so described,

(iii) no estimated tax payments for such year are made in the name and TIN of such child, and no amount has been deducted and withheld under section 3406, and

(iv) the parent of such child (as determined under paragraph (5)) elects the application of subparagraph (B),

such child shall be treated (other than for purposes of this paragraph) as having no gross income for such year and shall not be required to file a return under section 6012.

(B) Income included on parent's return

In the case of a parent making the election under this paragraph—

(i) the gross income of each child to whom such election applies (to the extent the gross income of such child exceeds twice the amount described in paragraph (4)(A)(ii)(I)) shall be included in such parent's gross income for the taxable year,

(ii) the tax imposed by this section for such year with respect to such parent shall be the amount equal to the sum of—

(I) the amount determined under this section after the application of clause (i), plus

(II) for each such child, 10 percent of the lesser of the amount described in paragraph (4)(A)(ii)(I) or the excess of the gross income of such child over the amount so described, and

(iii) any interest which is an item of tax preference under section 57(a)(5) of the child shall be treated as an item of tax preference of such parent (and not of such child).

(C) Regulations

The Secretary shall prescribe such regulations as may be necessary or appropriate to carry out the purposes of this paragraph.

(h) Maximum capital gains rate

(1) In general

If a taxpayer has a net capital gain for any taxable year, the tax imposed by this section for such taxable year shall not exceed the sum of—

(A) a tax computed at the rates and in the same manner as if this subsection had not been enacted on the greater of—
    (i) taxable income reduced by the net capital gain; or
    (ii) the lesser of—
        (I) the amount of taxable income taxed at a rate below 25 percent; or
        (II) taxable income reduced by the adjusted net capital gain;

(B) 0 percent of so much of the adjusted net capital gain (or, if less, taxable income) as does not exceed the excess (if any) of—
    (i) the amount of taxable income which would (without regard to this paragraph) be taxed at a rate below 25 percent, over
    (ii) the taxable income reduced by the adjusted net capital gain;

(C) 15 percent of the lesser of—
    (i) so much of the adjusted net capital gain (or, if less, taxable income) as exceeds the amount on which a tax is determined under subparagraph (B), or
    (ii) the excess of—
        (I) the amount of taxable income which would (without regard to this paragraph) be taxed at a rate below 39.6 percent, over
        (II) the sum of the amounts on which a tax is determined under subparagraphs (A) and (B),

(D) 20 percent of the adjusted net capital gain (or, if less, taxable income) in excess of the sum of the amounts on which tax is determined under subparagraphs (B) and (C),
    (E) 25 percent of the excess (if any) of—
        (i) the unrecaptured section 1250 gain (or, if less, the net capital gain (determined without regard to paragraph (11))), over
        (ii) the excess (if any) of—
            (I) the sum of the amount on which tax is determined under subparagraph (A) plus the net capital gain, over
            (II) taxable income; and

(F) 28 percent of the amount of taxable income in excess of the sum of the amounts on which tax is determined under the preceding subparagraphs of this paragraph.

(2) Net capital gain taken into account as investment income
For purposes of this subsection, the net capital gain for any taxable year shall be reduced (but not below zero) by the amount which the taxpayer takes into account as investment income under section 163(d)(4)(B)(iii).

(3) Adjusted net capital gain
For purposes of this subsection, the term "adjusted net capital gain" means the sum of—
    (A) net capital gain (determined without regard to paragraph (11)) reduced (but not below zero) by the sum of—
        (i) unrecaptured section 1250 gain, and
        (ii) 28-percent rate gain, plus

    (B) qualified dividend income (as defined in paragraph (11)).

(4) 28-percent rate gain
For purposes of this subsection, the term "28-percent rate gain" means the excess (if any) of—
    (A) the sum of—
        (i) collectibles gain; and
        (ii) section 1202 gain, over

    (B) the sum of—
        (i) collectibles loss;
        (ii) the net short-term capital loss; and
        (iii) the amount of long-term capital loss carried under section 1212(b)(1)(B) to the taxable year.

(5) Collectibles gain and loss
For purposes of this subsection—
(A) In general
The terms "collectibles gain" and "collectibles loss" mean gain or loss (respectively) from the sale or exchange of a collectible (as defined in section 408(m) without regard to paragraph (3) thereof) which is a capital asset held for more than 1 year but only to the extent such gain is taken into account in computing gross income and such loss is taken into account in computing taxable income.
(B) Partnerships, etc.
For purposes of subparagraph (A), any gain from the sale of an interest in a partnership, S corporation, or trust which is attributable to unrealized appreciation in the value of collectibles shall be treated as gain from the sale or exchange of a collectible. Rules similar to the rules of section 751 shall apply for purposes of the preceding sentence.

(6) Unrecaptured section 1250 gain
For purposes of this subsection—
(A) In general
The term "unrecaptured section 1250 gain" means the excess (if any) of—
    (i) the amount of long-term capital gain (not otherwise treated as ordinary income) which would be treated as ordinary income if section 1250(b)(1) included all depreciation and the applicable percentage under section 1250(a) were 100 percent, over
    (ii) the excess (if any) of—
        (I) the amount described in paragraph (4)(B); over
        (II) the amount described in paragraph (4)(A).
(B) Limitation with respect to section 1231 property
The amount described in subparagraph (A)(i) from sales, exchanges, and conversions described in section 1231(a)(3)(A) for any taxable year shall not exceed the net section 1231 gain (as defined in section 1231(c)(3)) for such year.

(7) Section 1202 gain

For purposes of this subsection, the term "section 1202 gain" means the excess of—

(A) the gain which would be excluded from gross income under section 1202 but for the percentage limitation in section 1202(a), over

(B) the gain excluded from gross income under section 1202.

(8) Coordination with recapture of net ordinary losses under section 1231

If any amount is treated as ordinary income under section 1231(c), such amount shall be allocated among the separate categories of net section 1231 gain (as defined in section 1231(c)(3)) in such manner as the Secretary may by forms or regulations prescribe.

(9) Regulations

The Secretary may prescribe such regulations as are appropriate (including regulations requiring reporting) to apply this subsection in the case of sales and exchanges by pass-thru entities and of interests in such entities.

(10) Pass-thru entity defined

For purposes of this subsection, the term "pass-thru entity" means—

(A) a regulated investment company;

(B) a real estate investment trust;

(C) an S corporation;

(D) a partnership;

(E) an estate or trust;

(F) a common trust fund; and

(G) a qualified electing fund (as defined in section 1295).

(11) Dividends taxed as net capital gain

(A) In general

For purposes of this subsection, the term "net capital gain" means net capital gain (determined without regard to this paragraph) increased by qualified dividend income.

(B) Qualified dividend income

For purposes of this paragraph—

(i) In general

The term "qualified dividend income" means dividends received during the taxable year from—

(I) domestic corporations, and

(II) qualified foreign corporations.

(ii) Certain dividends excluded

Such term shall not include—

(I) any dividend from a corporation which for the taxable year of the corporation in which the distribution is made, or the preceding taxable year, is a corporation exempt from tax under section 501 or 521,

(II) any amount allowed as a deduction under section 591 (relating to deduction for dividends paid by mutual savings banks, etc.), and

(III) any dividend described in section 404(k).

(iii) Coordination with section 246(c)

Such term shall not include any dividend on any share of stock—

(I) with respect to which the holding period requirements of section 246(c) are not met (determined by substituting in section 246(c) "60 days" for "45 days" each place it appears and by substituting "121-day period" for "91-day period"), or

(II) to the extent that the taxpayer is under an obligation (whether pursuant to a short sale or otherwise) to make related payments with respect to positions in substantially similar or related property.

(C) Qualified foreign corporations

(i) In general

Except as otherwise provided in this paragraph, the term "qualified foreign corporation" means any foreign corporation if—

(I) such corporation is incorporated in a possession of the United States, or

(II) such corporation is eligible for benefits of a comprehensive income tax treaty with the United States which the Secretary determines is satisfactory for purposes of this paragraph and which includes an exchange of information program.

(ii) Dividends on stock readily tradable on United States securities market

A foreign corporation not otherwise treated as a qualified foreign corporation under clause (i) shall be so treated with respect to any dividend paid by such corporation if the stock with respect to which such dividend is paid is readily tradable on an established securities market in the United States.

(iii) Exclusion of dividends of certain foreign corporations

Such term shall not include—

(I) any foreign corporation which for the taxable year of the corporation in which the dividend was paid, or the preceding taxable year, is a passive foreign investment company (as defined in section 1297), and

(II) any corporation which first becomes a surrogate foreign corporation (as defined in section 7874(a)(2)(B)) after the date of the enactment of this subclause, other than a foreign corporation which is treated as a domestic corporation under section 7874(b).

(iv) Coordination with foreign tax credit limitation

Rules similar to the rules of section 904(b)(2)(B) shall apply with respect to the dividend rate differential under this paragraph.

(D) Special rules

(i) Amounts taken into account as investment income

Qualified dividend income shall not include any amount which the taxpayer takes into account as investment income under section 163(d)(4)(B).

(ii) Extraordinary dividends

If a taxpayer to whom this section applies receives, with respect to any share of stock, qualified dividend income from 1 or more dividends which are extraordinary dividends (within the meaning of section 1059(c)), any loss on the sale or exchange of such share shall, to the extent of such dividends, be treated as long-term capital loss.

(iii) Treatment of dividends from regulated investment companies and real estate investment trusts

A dividend received from a regulated investment company or a real estate investment trust shall be subject to the limitations prescribed in sections 854 and 857.

(i) Rate reductions after 2000

(1) 10-percent rate bracket

(A) In general

In the case of taxable years beginning after December 31, 2000—

(i) the rate of tax under subsections (a), (b), (c), and (d) on taxable income not over the initial bracket amount shall be 10 percent, and

(ii) the 15 percent rate of tax shall apply only to taxable income over the initial bracket amount but not over the maximum dollar amount for the 15-percent rate bracket.

(B) Initial bracket amount

For purposes of this paragraph, the initial bracket amount is—

(i) $14,000 in the case of subsection (a),

(ii) $10,000 in the case of subsection (b), and

(iii) ½ the amount applicable under clause (i) (after adjustment, if any, under subparagraph (C)) in the case of subsections (c) and (d).

(C) Inflation adjustment

In prescribing the tables under subsection (f) which apply with respect to taxable years beginning in calendar years after 2003—

(i) the cost-of-living adjustment shall be determined under subsection (f)(3) by substituting "2002" for "2016" in subparagraph (A)(ii) thereof, and

(ii) the adjustments under clause (i) shall not apply to the amount referred to in subparagraph (B)(iii).

If any amount after adjustment under the preceding sentence is not a multiple of $50, such amount shall be rounded to the next lowest multiple of $50.

(2) 25-, 28-, and 33-percent rate brackets

The tables under subsections (a), (b), (c), (d), and (e) shall be applied—

(A) by substituting "25%" for "28%" each place it appears (before the application of subparagraph (B)),

(B) by substituting "28%" for "31%" each place it appears, and

(C) by substituting "33%" for "36%" each place it appears.

(3) Modifications to income tax brackets for high-income taxpayers

(A) 35-percent rate bracket

In the case of taxable years beginning after December 31, 2012—

(i) the rate of tax under subsections (a), (b), (c), and (d) on a taxpayer's taxable income in the highest rate bracket shall be 35 percent to the extent such income does not exceed an amount equal to the excess of—

(I) the applicable threshold, over

(II) the dollar amount at which such bracket begins, and

(ii) the 39.6 percent rate of tax under such subsections shall apply only to the taxpayer's taxable income in such bracket in excess of the amount to which clause (i) applies.

(B) Applicable threshold

For purposes of this paragraph, the term "applicable threshold" means—

(i) $450,000 in the case of subsection (a),

(ii) $425,000 in the case of subsection (b),

(iii) $400,000 in the case of subsection (c), and

(iv) ½ the amount applicable under clause (i) (after adjustment, if any, under subparagraph (C)) in the case of subsection (d).

(C) Inflation adjustment

For purposes of this paragraph, with respect to taxable years beginning in calendar years after 2013, each of the dollar amounts under clauses (i), (ii), and (iii) of subparagraph (B) shall be adjusted in the same manner as under paragraph (1)(C)(i), except that subsection (f)(3)(A)(ii) shall be applied by substituting "2012" for "2016".

(4) Adjustment of tables

The Secretary shall adjust the tables prescribed under subsection (f) to carry out this subsection.

(j) Modifications for taxable years 2018 through 2025

(1) In general

In the case of a taxable year beginning after December 31, 2017, and before January 1, 2026—

(A) subsection (i) shall not apply, and

(B) this section (other than subsection (i)) shall be applied as provided in paragraphs (2) through (6).

(2) Rate tables

(A) Married individuals filing joint returns and surviving spouses

The following table shall be applied in lieu of the table contained in subsection (a):

If taxable income is:	The tax is:
Not over $19,050	10% of taxable income.
Over $19,050 but not over $77,400	$1,905, plus 12% of the excess over $19,050.
Over $77,400 but not over $165,000	$8,907, plus 22% of the excess over $77,400.
Over $165,000 but not over $315,000	$28,179, plus 24% of the excess over $165,000.
Over $315,000 but not over $400,000	$64,179, plus 32% of the excess over $315,000.
Over $400,000 but not over $600,000	$91,379, plus 35% of the excess over $400,000.
Over $600,000	$161,379, plus 37% of the excess over $600,000.

(B) Heads of households

The following table shall be applied in lieu of the table contained in subsection (b):

If taxable income is:	The tax is:
Not over $13,600	10% of taxable income.
Over $13,600 but not over $51,800	$1,360, plus 12% of the excess over $13,600.
Over $51,800 but not over $82,500	$5,944, plus 22% of the excess over $51,800.
Over $82,500 but not over $157,500	$12,698, plus 24% of the excess over $82,500.
Over $157,500 but not over $200,000	$30,698, plus 32% of the excess over $157,500.
Over $200,000 but not over $500,000	$44,298, plus 35% of the excess over $200,000.
Over $500,000	$149,298, plus 37% of the excess over $500,000.

(C) Unmarried individuals other than surviving spouses and heads of households
The following table shall be applied in lieu of the table contained in subsection (c):

If taxable income is:	The tax is:
Not over $9,525	10% of taxable income.
Over $9,525 but not over $38,700	$952.50, plus 12% of the excess over $9,525.
Over $38,700 but not over $82,500	$4,453.50, plus 22% of the excess over $38,700.
Over $82,500 but not over $157,500	$14,089.50, plus 24% of the excess over $82,500.
Over $157,500 but not over $200,000	$32,089.50, plus 32% of the excess over $157,500.
Over $200,000 but not over $500,000	$45,689.50, plus 35% of the excess over $200,000.
Over $500,000	$150,689.50, plus 37% of the excess over $500,000.

(D) Married individuals filing separate returns
The following table shall be applied in lieu of the table contained in subsection (d):

If taxable income is:	The tax is:
Not over $9,525	10% of taxable income.
Over $9,525 but not over $38,700	$952.50, plus 12% of the excess over $9,525.
Over $38,700 but not over $82,500	$4,453.50, plus 22% of the excess over $38,700.
Over $82,500 but not over $157,500	$14,089.50, plus 24% of the excess over $82,500.
Over $157,500 but not over $200,000	$32,089.50, plus 32% of the excess over $157,500.
Over $200,000 but not over $300,000	$45,689.50, plus 35% of the excess over $200,000.
Over $300,000	$80,689.50, plus 37% of the excess over $300,000.

(E) Estates and trusts
The following table shall be applied in lieu of the table contained in subsection (e):

If taxable income is:	The tax is:
Not over $2,550	10% of taxable income.
Over $2,550 but not over $9,150	$255, plus 24% of the excess over $2,550.
Over $9,150 but not over $12,500	$1,839, plus 35% of the excess over $9,150.
Over $12,500	$3,011.50, plus 37% of the excess over $12,500.

(F) References to rate tables
Any reference in this title to a rate of tax under subsection (c) shall be treated as a reference to the corresponding rate bracket under subparagraph (C) of this paragraph, except that the reference in section 3402(q)(1) to the third lowest rate of tax applicable under subsection (c) shall be treated as a reference to the fourth lowest rate of tax under subparagraph (C).

(3) Adjustments
(A) No adjustment in 2018
The tables contained in paragraph (2) shall apply without adjustment for taxable years beginning after December 31, 2017, and before January 1, 2019.
(B) Subsequent years
For taxable years beginning after December 31, 2018, the Secretary shall prescribe tables which shall apply in lieu of the tables contained in paragraph (2) in the same manner as under paragraphs (1) and (2) of subsection (f) (applied without regard to clauses (i) and (ii) of subsection (f)(2)(A)), except that in prescribing such tables—
(i) subsection (f)(3) shall be applied by substituting "calendar year 2017" for "calendar year 2016" in subparagraph (A)(ii) thereof,
(ii) subsection (f)(7)(B) shall apply to any unmarried individual other than a surviving spouse or head of household, and
(iii) subsection (f)(8) shall not apply.

[(4) Repealed. Pub. L. 116–94, div. O, title V, §501(a), Dec. 20, 2019, 133 Stat. 3180]

(5) Application of current income tax brackets to capital gains brackets

(A) In general

Section 1(h)(1) shall be applied—

(i) by substituting "below the maximum zero rate amount" for "which would (without regard to this paragraph) be taxed at a rate below 25 percent" in subparagraph (B)(i), and

(ii) by substituting "below the maximum 15-percent rate amount" for "which would (without regard to this paragraph) be taxed at a rate below 39.6 percent" in subparagraph (C)(ii)(I).

(B) Maximum amounts defined

For purposes of applying section 1(h) with the modifications described in subparagraph (A)—

(i) Maximum zero rate amount

The maximum zero rate amount shall be—

(I) in the case of a joint return or surviving spouse, $77,200,

(II) in the case of an individual who is a head of household (as defined in section 2(b)), $51,700,

(III) in the case of any other individual (other than an estate or trust), an amount equal to ½ of the amount in effect for the taxable year under subclause (I), and

(IV) in the case of an estate or trust, $2,600.

(ii) Maximum 15-percent rate amount

The maximum 15-percent rate amount shall be—

(I) in the case of a joint return or surviving spouse, $479,000 (½ such amount in the case of a married individual filing a separate return),

(II) in the case of an individual who is the head of a household (as defined in section 2(b)), $452,400,

(III) in the case of any other individual (other than an estate or trust), $425,800, and

(IV) in the case of an estate or trust, $12,700.

(C) Inflation adjustment

In the case of any taxable year beginning after 2018, each of the dollar amounts in clauses (i) and (ii) of subparagraph (B) shall be increased by an amount equal to—

(i) such dollar amount, multiplied by

(ii) the cost-of-living adjustment determined under subsection (f)(3) for the calendar year in which the taxable year begins, determined by substituting "calendar year 2017" for "calendar year 2016" in subparagraph (A)(ii) thereof.

If any increase under this subparagraph is not a multiple of $50, such increase shall be rounded to the next lowest multiple of $50.

(6) Section 15 not to apply

Section 15 shall not apply to any change in a rate of tax by reason of this subsection.

(Aug. 16, 1954, ch. 736, 68A Stat. 5; Pub. L. 88–272, title I, §111, Feb. 26, 1964, 78 Stat. 19; Pub. L. 89–809, title I, §103(a)(2), Nov. 13, 1966, 80 Stat. 1550; Pub. L. 91–172, title VIII, §803(a), Dec. 30, 1969, 83 Stat. 678; Pub. L. 95–30, title I, §101(a), May 23, 1977, 91 Stat. 127; Pub. L. 95–600, title I, §101(a), Nov. 6, 1978, 92 Stat. 2767; Pub. L. 97–34, title I, §§101(a), 104(a), Aug. 13, 1981, 95 Stat. 176, 188; Pub. L. 97–448, title I, §101(a)(3), Jan. 12, 1983, 96 Stat. 2366; Pub. L. 99–514, title I, §101(a), title III, §302(a), title XIV, §1411(a), Oct. 22, 1986, 100 Stat. 2096, 2218, 2714; Pub. L. 100–647, title I, §§1001(a)(3), 1014(e)(1)–(3), (6), (7), title VI, §6006(a), Nov. 10, 1988, 102 Stat. 3349, 3561, 3562, 3686; Pub. L. 101–239, title VII, §§7811(j)(1), 7816(b), 7831(a), Dec. 19, 1989, 103 Stat. 2411, 2420, 2425; Pub. L. 101–508, title XI, §§11101(a)–(c), (d)(1)(A), (2), 11103(c), 11104(b), Nov. 5, 1990, 104 Stat. 1388–403 to 1388-406, 1388-408; Pub. L. 103–66, title XIII, §§13201(a), (b)(3)(A), (B), 13202(a), 13206(d)(2), Aug. 10, 1993, 107 Stat. 457, 459, 461, 467; Pub. L. 104–188, title I, §1704(m)(1), (2), Aug. 20, 1996, 110 Stat. 1882, 1883; Pub. L. 105–34, title III, §311(a), Aug. 5, 1997, 111 Stat. 831; Pub. L. 105–206, title V, §5001(a)(1)–(4), title VI, §§6005(d)(1), 6007(f)(1), July 22, 1998, 112 Stat. 787, 788, 800, 810; Pub. L. 105–277, div. J, title IV, §4002(i)(1), (3), Oct. 21, 1998, 112 Stat. 2681–907, 2681-908; Pub. L. 106–554, §1(a)(7) [title I, §117(b)(1)], Dec. 21, 2000, 114 Stat. 2763, 2763A-604; Pub. L. 107–16, title I, §101(a), (c)(1), (2), title III, §§301(c)(1), 302(a), (b), June 7, 2001, 115 Stat. 41, 43, 54; Pub. L. 108–27, title I, §§102(a), (b)(1), 104(a), (b), 105(a), title III, §§301(a)(1), (2)(A), (b)(1), 302(a), (e)(1), May 28, 2003, 117 Stat. 754, 755, 758, 760, 763; Pub. L. 108–311, title I, §101(c), (d), title IV, §§402(a)(1)–(3), 408(a)(1), (2), Oct. 4, 2004, 118 Stat. 1167, 1168, 1184, 1190; Pub. L. 108–357, title IV, §413(c)(1), Oct. 22, 2004, 118 Stat. 1506; Pub. L. 109–222, title V, §510(a)—(c), May 17, 2006, 120 Stat. 364; Pub. L. 110–28, title VIII, §8241(a), (b), May 25, 2007, 121 Stat. 199; Pub. L. 110–185, title I, §101(f)(2), Feb. 13, 2008, 122 Stat. 617; Pub. L. 112–240, title I, §§101(b)(1), 102(b)(1), (c)(2), Jan. 2, 2013, 126 Stat. 2316, 2318, 2319; Pub. L. 113–295, div. A, title II, §221(a)(1), Dec. 19, 2014, 128 Stat. 4037; Pub. L. 115–97, title I, §§11001(a), 11002(a)–(c), 14223(a), Dec. 22, 2017, 131 Stat. 2054, 2059, 2220; Pub. L. 116–94, div. O, title V, §501(a), Dec. 20, 2019, 133 Stat. 3180.)

INFLATION ADJUSTED ITEMS FOR CERTAIN YEARS

For inflation adjustment of certain items in this section, see Revenue Procedures listed in a table below.

EDITORIAL NOTES
REFERENCES IN TEXT

The date of the enactment of this subclause, referred to in subsec. (h)(11)(C)(iii)(II), is the date of enactment of Pub. L. 115–97, which was approved Dec. 22, 2017.

AMENDMENTS

2019—Subsec. (j)(4). Pub. L. 116–94 struck out par. (4) which related to special rules for certain children with unearned income.

2017—Subsec. (f)(2)(A). Pub. L. 115–97, §11002(c)(1), amended subpar. (A) generally. Prior to amendment, subpar. (A) read as follows: "except as provided in paragraph (8), by increasing the minimum and maximum dollar amounts for each rate bracket for which a tax is imposed under such table by the cost-of-living adjustment for such calendar year,".

Subsec. (f)(3). Pub. L. 115–97, §11002(a), added par. (3) and struck out former par. (3). Prior to amendment, text read as follows: "For purposes of paragraph (2), the cost-of-living adjustment for any calendar year is the percentage (if any) by which—

"(A) the CPI for the preceding calendar year, exceeds

"(B) the CPI for the calendar year 1992."

Subsec. (f)(6), (7). Pub. L. 115–97, §11002(b), added par. (6), redesignated former par. (6) as (7), and struck out former par. (7). Prior to amendment, text of par. (7) read as follows: "In prescribing tables under paragraph (1) which apply to taxable years beginning in a calendar year after 1994, the cost-of-living adjustment used in making adjustments to the dollar amounts at which the 36 percent rate bracket begins or at which the 39.6 percent rate bracket begins shall be determined under paragraph (3) by substituting '1993' for '1992'."

Subsec. (h)(11)(C)(iii). Pub. L. 115–97, §14223(a), substituted "shall not include——" for "shall not include", inserted subcl. (I) designation before "any foreign corporation", and added subcl. (II).

Subsec. (i)(1)(C)(i). Pub. L. 115–97, §11002(c)(2)(A), substituted "for '2016' in subparagraph (A)(ii)" for "for '1992' in subparagraph (B)".

Subsec. (i)(3)(C). Pub. L. 115–97, §11002(c)(2)(B), substituted "subsection (f)(3)(A)(ii) shall be applied by substituting '2012' for '2016' " for "subsection (f)(3)(B) shall be applied by substituting '2012' for '1992' ".

Subsec. (j). Pub. L. 115–97, §11001(a), added subsec. (j).

2014—Subsec. (f)(7). Pub. L. 113–295 amended par. (7) generally. Prior to amendment, text read as follows:

"(A) Calendar year 1994.—In prescribing the tables under paragraph (1) which apply with respect to taxable years beginning in calendar year 1994, the Secretary shall make no adjustment to the dollar amounts at which the 36 percent rate bracket begins or at which the 39.6 percent rate begins under any table contained in subsection (a), (b), (c), (d), or (e).

"(B) Later calendar years.—In prescribing tables under paragraph (1) which apply with respect to taxable years beginning in a calendar year after 1994, the cost-of-living adjustment used in making adjustments to the dollar amounts referred to in subparagraph (A) shall be determined under paragraph (3) by substituting '1993' for '1992'."

2013—Subsec. (h)(1)(B). Pub. L. 112–240, §102(c)(2), substituted "0 percent" for "5 percent (0 percent in the case of taxable years beginning after 2007)" in introductory provisions.

Subsec. (h)(1)(C) to (F). Pub. L. 112–240, §102(b)(1), added subpars. (C) and (D), redesignated former subpars. (D) and (E) as (E) and (F), respectively, and struck out former subpar. (C) which read as follows: "15 percent of the adjusted net capital gain (or, if less, taxable income) in excess of the amount on which a tax is determined under subparagraph (B);".

Subsec. (i)(2). Pub. L. 112–240, §101(b)(1)(A), amended par. (2) generally. Prior to amendment, par. (2) related to reductions in rates after June 30, 2001.

Subsec. (i)(3), (4). Pub. L. 112–240, §101(b)(1)(B), added par. (3) and redesignated former par. (3) as (4).

2008—Subsec. (i)(1)(D). Pub. L. 110–185 struck out heading and text of subpar. (D). Text read as follows: "This paragraph shall not apply to any taxable year to which section 6428 applies."

2007—Subsec. (g). Pub. L. 110–28, §8241(b), struck out "minor" before "children" in heading.

Subsec. (g)(2)(A). Pub. L. 110–28, §8241(a), amended subpar. (A) generally. Prior to amendment, subpar. (A) read as follows: "such child has not attained age 18 before the close of the taxable year,".

2006—Subsec. (g)(2)(A). Pub. L. 109–222, §510(a), substituted "age 18" for "age 14".

Subsec. (g)(2)(C). Pub. L. 109–222, §510(c), added subpar. (C).

Subsec. (g)(4)(C). Pub. L. 109–222, §510(b), added subpar. (C).

2004—Subsec. (f)(8). Pub. L. 108–311, §101(c), amended par. (8) generally, substituting provisions relating to elimination of marriage penalty in 15-percent bracket for provisions relating to phaseout of marriage penalty in 15-percent bracket.

Subsec. (g)(7)(B)(ii)(II). Pub. L. 108–311, §408(a)(1), substituted "10 percent" for "10 percent."

Subsec. (h)(1)(D)(i). Pub. L. 108–311, §402(a)(1), inserted "(determined without regard to paragraph (11))" after "net capital gain".

Subsec. (h)(6)(A)(ii)(I). Pub. L. 108–311, §408(a)(2)(A), substituted "(4)(B)" for "(5)(B)".

Subsec. (h)(6)(A)(ii)(II). Pub. L. 108–311, §408(a)(2)(B), substituted "(4)(A)" for "(5)(A)".

Subsec. (h)(10)(F) to (H). Pub. L. 108–357, §413(c)(1)(A), inserted "and" at end of subpar. (F), redesignated subpar. (H) as (G), and struck out former subpar. (G) which read as follows: "a foreign investment company which is described in section 1246(b)(1) and for which an election is in effect under section 1247; and".

Subsec. (h)(11)(B)(iii)(I). Pub. L. 108–311, §402(a)(2), substituted "substituting in section 246(c)" for "substituting in section 246(c)(1)", "121-day period" for "120-day period", and "91-day period" for "90-day period".

Subsec. (h)(11)(C)(iii). Pub. L. 108–357, §413(c)(1)(B), struck out "a foreign personal holding company (as defined in section 552), a foreign investment company (as defined in section 1246(b)), or" before "a passive foreign investment".

Subsec. (h)(11)(D)(ii). Pub. L. 108–311, §402(a)(3), substituted "a taxpayer to whom this section applies" for "an individual".

Subsec. (i)(1)(B)(i). Pub. L. 108–311, §101(d)(1), struck out "($12,000 in the case of taxable years beginning after December 31, 2004, and before January 1, 2008)" after "$14,000".

Subsec. (i)(1)(C). Pub. L. 108–311, §101(d)(2), reenacted heading without change and amended text generally, substituting provisions relating to inflation adjustment in calendar years after 2003 for such provisions in calendar years after 2000.

2003—Subsec. (f)(8)(A). Pub. L. 108–27, §102(b)(1), substituted "2002" for "2004".

Subsec. (f)(8)(B). Pub. L. 108–27, §102(a), inserted table item relating to years 2003 and 2004.

Subsec. (h)(1)(B). Pub. L. 108–27, §301(a)(1), substituted "5 percent (0 percent in the case of taxable years beginning after 2007)" for "10 percent".

Subsec. (h)(1)(C). Pub. L. 108–27, §301(a)(2)(A), substituted "15 percent" for "20 percent".

Subsec. (h)(2). Pub. L. 108–27, §301(b)(1)(A), (B), redesignated par. (3) as (2) and struck out heading and text of former par. (2). Text read as follows:

"(A) Reduction in 10-percent rate.—In the case of any taxable year beginning after December 31, 2000, the rate under paragraph (1)(B) shall be 8 percent with respect to so much of the amount to which the 10-percent rate would otherwise apply as does not exceed qualified 5-year gain, and 10 percent with respect to the remainder of such amount.

"(B) Reduction in 20-percent rate.—The rate under paragraph (1)(C) shall be 18 percent with respect to so much of the amount to which the 20-percent rate would otherwise apply as does not exceed the lesser of—

"(i) the excess of qualified 5-year gain over the amount of such gain taken into account under subparagraph (A) of this paragraph; or

"(ii) the amount of qualified 5-year gain (determined by taking into account only property the holding period for which begins after December 31, 2000),

and 20 percent with respect to the remainder of such amount. For purposes of determining under the preceding sentence whether the holding period of property begins after December 31, 2000, the holding period of property acquired pursuant to the exercise of an option (or other right or obligation to acquire property) shall include the period such option (or other right or obligation) was held."

Subsec. (h)(3). Pub. L. 108–27, §302(e)(1), amended heading and text of par. (3) generally. Prior to amendment, text read as follows: "For purposes of this subsection, the term 'adjusted net capital gain' means net capital gain reduced (but not below zero) by the sum of—

"(A) unrecaptured section 1250 gain; and

"(B) 28-percent rate gain."

Pub. L. 108–27, §301(b)(1)(B), redesignated par. (4) as (3). Former par. (3) redesignated (2).

Subsec. (h)(4) to (7). Pub. L. 108–27, §301(b)(1)(B), redesignated pars. (5) to (8) as (4) to (7), respectively. Former par. (4) redesignated (3).

Subsec. (h)(8). Pub. L. 108–27, §301(b)(1)(C), redesignated par. (10) as (8). Former par. (8) redesignated (7).

Subsec. (h)(9). Pub. L. 108–27, §301(b)(1)(A), (C), redesignated par. (11) as (9) and struck out heading and text of former par. (9). Text read as follows: "For purposes of this subsection, the term 'qualified 5-year gain' means the aggregate long-term capital gain from property held for more than 5 years. The determination under the preceding sentence shall be made without regard to collectibles gain, gain described in paragraph (7)(A)(i), and section 1202 gain."

Subsec. (h)(10). Pub. L. 108–27, §301(b)(1)(C), redesignated par. (12) as (10). Former par. (10) redesignated (8).

Subsec. (h)(11). Pub. L. 108–27, §302(a), added par. (11).

Pub. L. 108–27, §301(b)(1)(C), redesignated par. (11) as (9).

Subsec. (h)(12). Pub. L. 108–27, §301(b)(1)(C), redesignated par. (12) as (10).

Subsec. (i)(1)(B)(i). Pub. L. 108–27, §104(a), substituted "($12,000 in the case of taxable years beginning after December 31, 2004, and before January 1, 2008)" for "($12,000 in the case of taxable years beginning before January 1, 2008)".

Subsec. (i)(1)(C). Pub. L. 108–27, §104(b), amended heading and text of subpar. (C) generally. Text read as follows: "In prescribing the tables under subsection (f) which apply with respect to taxable years beginning in calendar years after 2000—

"(i) the Secretary shall make no adjustment to the initial bracket amount for any taxable year beginning before January 1, 2009,

"(ii) the cost-of-living adjustment used in making adjustments to the initial bracket amount for any taxable year beginning after December 31, 2008, shall be determined under subsection (f)(3) by substituting '2007' for '1992' in subparagraph (B) thereof, and

"(iii) such adjustment shall not apply to the amount referred to in subparagraph (B)(iii).

If any amount after adjustment under the preceding sentence is not a multiple of $50, such amount shall be rounded to the next lowest multiple of $50."

Subsec. (i)(2). Pub. L. 108–27, §105(a), amended table generally. Prior to amendment, table read as follows:

"In the case of taxable years beginning during calendar year:	The corresponding percentages shall be substituted for the following percentages:			
	28%	31%	36%	39.6%
2001	27.5%	30.5%	35.5%	39.1%
2002 and 2003	27.0%	30.0%	35.0%	38.6%
2004 and 2005	26.0%	29.0%	34.0%	37.6%
2006 and thereafter	25.0%	28.0%	33.0%	35.0%"

2001—Subsec. (f). Pub. L. 107–16, §302(b)(2), substituted "Phaseout of marriage penalty in 15-percent bracket; adjustments" for "Adjustments" in heading.

Subsec. (f)(2)(A). Pub. L. 107–16, §302(b)(1), inserted "except as provided in paragraph (8)," before "by increasing".

Subsec. (f)(6)(B). Pub. L. 107–16, §301(c)(1), substituted "(other than with respect to sections 63(c)(4) and 151(d)(4)(A)) shall be applied" for "(other than with respect to subsection (c)(4) of section 63 (as it applies to subsections (c)(5)(A) and (f) of such section) and section 151(d)(4)(A)) shall be applied".

Subsec. (f)(8). Pub. L. 107–16, §302(a), added par. (8).

Subsec. (g)(7)(B)(ii)(II). Pub. L. 107–16, §101(c)(1), substituted "10 percent." for "15 percent".

Subsec. (h)(1)(A)(ii)(I), (B)(i). Pub. L. 107–16, §101(c)(2)(A), substituted "25 percent" for "28 percent".

Subsec. (h)(13). Pub. L. 107–16, §101(c)(2)(B), struck out par. (13), which set out special rules for determination of 28-percent rate gain, unrecaptured section 1250 gain, pass-thru entities, and charitable remainder trusts.

Subsec. (i). Pub. L. 107–16, §101(a), added subsec. (i).

2000—Subsec.(h)(8). Pub. L. 106–554 substituted "means the excess of—" and subpars. (A) and (B) for "means an amount equal to the gain excluded from gross income under section 1202(a)."

1998—Subsec. (g)(3)(C), (D). Pub. L. 105–206, §6007(f)(1), redesignated subpar. (D) as (C) and struck out heading and text of former subpar. (C). Text read as follows: "If tax is imposed under section 644(a)(1) with respect to the sale or exchange of any property of which the parent was the transferor, for purposes of applying subparagraph (A) to the taxable year of the parent in which such sale or exchange occurs—

"(i) taxable income of the parent shall be increased by the amount treated as included in gross income under section 644(a)(2)(A)(i), and

"(ii) the amount described in subparagraph (A)(ii) shall be increased by the amount of the excess referred to in section 644(a)(2)(A)."

Subsec. (h). Pub. L. 105–206, §6005(d)(1), reenacted subsec. heading without change and amended text of subsec. (h) generally, substituting present provisions comprising pars. (1) to (13) for former similar provisions comprising pars. (1) to (11).

Subsec. (h)(5). Pub. L. 105–206, §5001(a)(1), amended par. (5) generally. Prior to amendment, par. (5) read as follows:

"(5) 28-percent rate gain.—For purposes of this subsection—

"(A) In general.—The term '28-percent rate gain' means the excess (if any) of—

"(i) the sum of—

"(I) the aggregate long-term capital gain from property held for more than 1 year but not more than 18 months;

"(II) collectibles gain; and

"(III) section 1202 gain, over

"(ii) the sum of—

"(I) the aggregate long-term capital loss (not described in subclause (IV)) from property referred to in clause (i)(I);

"(II) collectibles loss;

"(III) the net short-term capital loss; and

"(IV) the amount of long-term capital loss carried under section 1212(b)(1)(B) to the taxable year.

"(B) Special rules.—

"(i) Short sale gains and holding periods.—Rules similar to the rules of section 1233(b) shall apply where the substantially identical property has been held more than 1 year but not more than 18 months; except that, for purposes of such rules—

"(I) section 1233(b)(1) shall be applied by substituting '18 months' for '1 year' each place it appears; and

"(II) the holding period of such property shall be treated as being 1 year on the day before the earlier of the date of the closing of the short sale or the date such property is disposed of.

"(ii) Long-term losses.—Section 1233(d) shall be applied separately by substituting '18 months' for '1 year' each place it appears.

"(iii) Options.—A rule similar to the rule of section 1092(f) shall apply where the stock was held for more than 18 months.

"(iv) Section 1256 contracts.—Amounts treated as long-term capital gain or loss under section 1256(a)(3) shall be treated as attributable to property held for more than 18 months."

Subsec. (h)(6)(A). Pub. L. 105–206, §5001(a)(2), substituted "1 year" for "18 months".

Subsec. (h)(7)(A)(i), (ii). Pub. L. 105–206, §5001(a)(3), amended cls. (i) and (ii) generally. Prior to amendment, cls. (i) and (ii) read as follows:

"(i) the amount of long-term capital gain (not otherwise treated as ordinary income) which would be treated as ordinary income if—

"(I) section 1250(b)(1) included all depreciation and the applicable percentage under section 1250(a) were 100 percent, and

"(II) only gain from property held for more than 18 months were taken into account, over

"(ii) the excess (if any) of—

"(I) the amount described in paragraph (5)(A)(ii), over

"(II) the amount described in paragraph (5)(A)(i)."

Subsec. (h)(13). Pub. L. 105–206, §5001(a)(4), struck out "for periods during 1997" after "Special rules" in par. heading and amended headings and text of subpars. (A) and (B) generally. Prior to amendment, subpars. (A) and (B) read as follows:

"(A) Determination of 28-percent rate gain.—In applying paragraph (5)—

"(i) the amount determined under subclause (I) of paragraph (5)(A)(i) shall include long-term capital gain (not otherwise described in paragraph (5)(A)(i)) which is properly taken into account for the portion of the taxable year before May 7, 1997;

"(ii) the amounts determined under subclause (I) of paragraph (5)(A)(ii) shall include long-term capital loss (not otherwise described in paragraph (5)(A)(ii)) which is properly taken into account for the portion of the taxable year before May 7, 1997; and

"(iii) clauses (i)(I) and (ii)(I) of paragraph (5)(A) shall be applied by not taking into account any gain and loss on property held for more than 1 year but not more than 18 months which is properly taken into account for the portion of the taxable year after May 6, 1997, and before July 29, 1997.

"(B) Other special rules.—

"(i) Determination of unrecaptured section 1250 gain not to include pre-may 7, 1997 gain.—The amount determined under paragraph (7)(A)(i) shall not include gain properly taken into account for the portion of the taxable year before May 7, 1997.

"(ii) Other transitional rules for 18-month holding period.—Paragraphs (6)(A) and (7)(A)(i)(II) shall be applied by substituting '1 year' for '18 months' with respect to gain properly taken into account for the portion of the taxable year after May 6, 1997, and before July 29, 1997."

Subsec. (h)(13)(B). Pub. L. 105–277, §4002(i)(1), substituted "paragraph (7)(A)(i)" for "paragraph (7)(A)" in introductory provisions.

Subsec. (h)(13)(D). Pub. L. 105–277, §4002(i)(3), added subpar. (D).

1997—Subsec. (h). Pub. L. 105–34 amended heading and text of subsec. (h) generally. Prior to amendment, text read as follows: "If a taxpayer has a net capital gain for any taxable year, then the tax imposed by this section shall not exceed the sum of—

"(1) a tax computed at the rates and in the same manner as if this subsection had not been enacted on the greater of—

"(A) taxable income reduced by the amount of the net capital gain, or

"(B) the amount of taxable income taxed at a rate below 28 percent, plus

"(2) a tax of 28 percent of the amount of taxable income in excess of the amount determined under paragraph (1).

For purposes of the preceding sentence, the net capital gain for any taxable year shall be reduced (but not below zero) by the amount which the taxpayer elects to take into account as investment income for the taxable year under section 163(d)(4)(B)(iii)."

1996—Subsec. (g)(7)(A)(ii). Pub. L. 104–188, §1704(m)(1), amended cl. (ii) generally. Prior to amendment, cl. (ii) read as follows: "such gross income is more than $500 and less than $5,000,".

Subsec. (g)(7)(B)(i). Pub. L. 104–188, §1704(m)(2)(A), substituted "twice the amount described in paragraph (4)(A)(ii)(I)" for "$1,000".

Subsec. (g)(7)(B)(ii)(II). Pub. L. 104–188, §1704(m)(2)(B), amended subcl. (II) generally. Prior to amendment, subcl. (II) read as follows: "for each such child, the lesser of $75 or 15 percent of the excess of the gross income of such child over $500, and".

1993—Subsecs. (a) to (e). Pub. L. 103–66, §§13201(a), 13202(a), amended subsecs. (a) to (e) generally, substituting five-tiered tax tables for all categories applicable to tax years after December 31, 1992, for prior three-tiered tax tables.

Subsec. (f)(1). Pub. L. 103–66, §13201(b)(3)(A)(i), substituted "1993" for "1990".

Subsec. (f)(3)(B). Pub. L. 103–66, §13201(b)(3)(A)(ii), substituted "1992" for "1989".

Subsec. (f)(7). Pub. L. 103–66, §13201(b)(3)(B), added par. (7).

Subsec. (h). Pub. L. 103–66, §13206(d)(2), inserted as concluding provision at end "For purposes of the preceding sentence, the net capital gain for any taxable year shall be reduced (but not below zero) by the amount which the taxpayer elects to take into account as investment income for the taxable year under section 163(d)(4)(B)(iii)."

1990—Subsecs. (a) to (e). Pub. L. 101–508, §11101(a), amended subsecs. (a) to (e) generally, substituting three-tiered tax tables for all categories applicable to tax years after Dec. 31, 1990, for prior two-tiered tax tables.

Subsec. (f)(1). Pub. L. 101–508, §11101(d)(1)(A)(i), substituted "1990" for "1988".

Subsec. (f)(3)(B). Pub. L. 101–508, §11101(d)(1)(A)(ii), substituted "1989" for "1987".

Subsec. (f)(6)(A). Pub. L. 101–508, §11104(b)(1), substituted "section 151(d)(4)" for "section 151(d)(3)".

Pub. L. 101–508, §11103(c), inserted reference to section 68(b)(2).

Pub. L. 101–508, §11101(b)(2), struck out "subsection (g)(4)," after "paragraph (2)(A),".

Subsec. (f)(6)(B). Pub. L. 101–508, §11104(b)(2), substituted "section 151(d)(4)(A)" for "section 151(d)(3)".

Subsec. (g). Pub. L. 101–508, §11101(d)(2), redesignated subsec. (i) as (g).

Pub. L. 101–508, §11101(b)(1), struck out subsec. (g) which provided for phaseout of 15-percent rate and personal exemptions.

Subsec. (h). Pub. L. 101–508, §11101(d)(2), redesignated subsec. (j) as (h) and struck out former subsec. (h) which provided tax schedules for taxable years beginning in 1987.

Subsec. (i). Pub. L. 101–508, §11101(d)(2), redesignated subsec. (i) as (g).

Subsec. (j). Pub. L. 101–508, §11101(d)(2), redesignated subsec. (j) as (h).

Pub. L. 101–508, §11101(c), amended subsec. (j) generally. Prior to amendment, subsec. (j) read as follows:

"(1) In general.—If a taxpayer has a net capital gain for any taxable year to which this subsection applies, then the tax imposed by this section shall not exceed the sum of—

"(A) a tax computed at the rates and in the same manner as if this subsection had not been enacted on the greater of—

"(i) the taxable income reduced by the amount of net capital gain, or

"(ii) the amount of taxable income taxed at a rate below 28 percent, plus

"(B) a tax of 28 percent of the amount of taxable income in excess of the amount determined under subparagraph (A), plus

"(C) the amount of increase determined under subsection (g).

"(2) Years to which subsection applies.—This subsection shall apply to—

"(A) any taxable year beginning in 1987, and

"(B) any taxable year beginning after 1987 if the highest rate of tax set forth in subsection (a), (b), (c), (d), or (e) (whichever applies) for such taxable year exceeds 28 percent."

1989—Subsec. (f)(6)(B). Pub. L. 101–239, §7831(a), substituted "subsection (c)(4) of section 63 (as it applies to subsections (c)(5)(A) and (f) of such section) and section 151(d)(3)" for "section 63(c)(4)".

Subsec. (i)(3)(C), (D). Pub. L. 101–239, §7811(j)(1), redesignated subpar. (C), relating to special rule where parent has different taxable year, as (D).

Subsec. (i)(7)(A). Pub. L. 101–239, §7816(b), inserted "(other than for purposes of this paragraph)" after "shall be treated" in concluding provisions.

1988—Subsec. (g)(2). Pub. L. 100–647, §1001(a)(3), inserted provision relating to application of subpar. (B) at end of last sentence.

Subsec. (i)(3)(A). Pub. L. 100–647, §1014(e)(2), substituted "any exclusion, deduction, or credit" for "any deduction or credit".

Subsec. (i)(3)(C). Pub. L. 100–647, §1014(e)(7), added subpar. (C) relating to special rule where parent has different taxable year.

Pub. L. 100–647, §1014(e)(1), added subpar. (C) relating to coordination with section 644.

Subsec. (i)(4)(A)(i). Pub. L. 100–647, §1014(e)(3)(A), substituted "adjusted gross income" for "gross income" and inserted "attributable to" after "which is not".

Subsec. (i)(4)(A)(ii)(II). Pub. L. 100–647, §1014(e)(3)(B)–(D), substituted "his deductions" for "his deduction", "the itemized deductions allowed" for "the deductions allowed", and "adjusted gross income" for "gross income".

Subsec. (i)(5)(A). Pub. L. 100–647, §1014(e)(6), substituted "custodial parent (within the meaning of section 152(e))" for "custodial parent".

Subsec. (i)(7). Pub. L. 100–647, §6006(a), added par. (7).

1986—Subsecs. (a) to (e). Pub. L. 99–514, §101(a), in amending subsecs. (a) to (e) generally, substituted a general tax table for tax tables (1), (2), and (3) in each subsec. applicable to taxable years beginning in 1982, 1983, and after 1983, respectively.

Subsec. (f). Pub. L. 99–514, §101(a), in amending subsec. (f) generally, in par. (1) substituted "1988," for "1984" and struck out "paragraph (3) of" before "subsections", in par. (2) struck out "paragraph (3) of" before "subsection" in introductory provisions, substituted subpars. (A) to (C) for former subpars. (A) to (C) which read as follows:

"(A) by increasing—

"(i) the maximum dollar amount on which no tax is imposed under such table, and

"(ii) the minimum and maximum dollar amounts for each rate bracket for which a tax is imposed under such table,

by the cost-of-living adjustment for such calendar year,

"(B) by not changing the rate applicable to any rate bracket as adjusted under subparagraph (A)(ii), and

"(C) by adjusting the amounts setting forth the tax to the extent necessary to reflect the adjustments in the rate brackets.",

and struck out concluding provisions which read as follows: "If any increase determined under subparagraph (A) is not a multiple of $10, such increase shall be rounded to the nearest multiple of $10 (or if such increase is a multiple of $5, such increase shall be increased to the next highest multiple of $10).", in par. (3)(B) substituted "1987" for "1983", in par. (4) substituted "August 31" for "September 30", in par. (5) inserted requirement that the Consumer Price Index most consistent with such Index for calendar year 1986 be used, and added par. (6).

Subsecs. (g), (h). Pub. L. 99–514, §101(a), in amending section generally, added subsecs. (g) and (h).

Subsec. (i). Pub. L. 99–514, §1411(a), added subsec. (i).

Subsec. (j). Pub. L. 99–514, §302(a), added subsec. (j).

1982—Subsecs. (d), (e). Pub. L. 97–448, §101(a)(3), set out as a note below, provided for amendment of the tables applying to married individuals filing separately or to estates and trusts so as to correct any figure differing by not more than 50 cents from the correct amount under the formula used in constructing such table. Corrections to the tables in subsecs. (d) and (e) appeared in Announcement 83–50 contained in Internal Revenue Bulletin No. 1983–12 of Mar. 21, 1983.

1981—Subsecs. (a) to (e). Pub. L. 97–34, §101(a), generally revised tax tables downward providing for cumulative across-the-board reductions of 23 percent on a three phase schedule under which different new rates were set for taxable years beginning in 1982, for taxable years beginning in 1983, and for taxable years beginning after 1983.

Subsec. (f). Pub. L. 97–34, §104(a), added subsec. (f).

1978—Subsec. (a). Pub. L. 95–600 generally made a downward revision of tax table for married individuals filing joint returns and surviving spouses resulting in a table under which, among other changes, a bottom bracket imposing no tax on taxable income of $3,400 or less was substituted for a bottom bracket imposing no tax on taxable income of $3,200 or less.

Subsec. (b). Pub. L. 95–600 generally made a downward revision of tax table for heads of household resulting in a table under which, among other changes, a bottom bracket imposing no tax on taxable income of $2,300 or less was substituted for a bottom bracket imposing no tax on taxable income of $2,200 or less.

Subsec. (c). Pub. L. 95–600 generally made a downward revision of tax table for unmarried individuals other than surviving spouses and heads of households resulting in a table under which, among other changes, a bottom bracket imposing no tax on taxable income of $2,300 or less was substituted for a bottom bracket imposing no tax on taxable income of $2,200 or less.

Subsec. (d). Pub. L. 95–600 generally made a downward revision of tax tables for married individuals filing separate returns resulting in a table under which, among other changes, a bottom bracket imposing no tax on taxable income of $1,700 or less was substituted for a bottom bracket imposing no tax on taxable income of $1,600 or less.

Subsec. (e). Pub. L. 95–600 generally made a downward revision of tax tables for estates and trusts resulting in a table under which, among other changes, a bottom bracket under which a tax of 14% is imposed on taxable income of $1,050 for a bottom bracket under which a tax of 14% was imposed on taxable income of $500 or less.

1977—Subsec. (a). Pub. L. 95–30 generally made a downward revision of tax table for married individuals filing joint returns and surviving spouses resulting in a table under which, among other changes, a bottom bracket imposing no tax on taxable income of $3,200 or less was substituted for a bottom bracket under which a tax of 14% had been imposed on a taxable income of $1,000 or less.

Subsec. (b). Pub. L. 95–30 generally made a downward revision of tax table for heads of households resulting in a table under which, among other changes, a bottom bracket imposing no tax on taxable income of $2,200 or less was substituted for a bottom bracket under which a tax of 14% had been imposed on a taxable income of $1,000 or less.

Subsec. (c). Pub. L. 95–30 generally made a downward revision of tax table for unmarried individuals other than surviving spouses and heads of households resulting in a table under which, among other changes, a bottom bracket imposing no tax on taxable income of $2,200 or less was substituted for a bottom bracket under which a tax of 14% had been imposed on a taxable income of $500 or less.

Subsec. (d). Pub. L. 95–30 generally made a downward revision of tax table for married individuals filing separate returns resulting in a table under which, among other changes, a bottom bracket imposing no tax on taxable income of $1,600 or less was substituted for a bottom bracket under which a tax of 14% had been imposed on a taxable income of $500 or less. Provisions making table applicable to estates and trusts were struck out. See subsec. (e).

Subsec. (e). Pub. L. 95–30 added subsec. (e) consisting of table formerly contained in subsec. (d) but without any downward revision and limited so as to apply only to estates and trusts.

1969—Subsec. (a). Pub. L. 91–172 substituted a table of rates of tax for married individuals filing joint returns and surviving spouses for the tables of rates of tax on individuals. For rates of taxes on unmarried individuals and married persons filing separate returns, see subsecs. (c) and (d) of this section.

Subsec. (b). Pub. L. 91–172 generally revised rates of tax of heads of household downwards and struck out provisions defining head of household, determination of status, and limitations. For definition of head of household, determination of status, and limitations, see section 2(b) of this title.

Subsec. (c). Pub. L. 91–172 substituted rates of tax on unmarried individuals (other than surviving spouses and heads of household) for special rules explaining the rates of tax imposed under former subsecs. (a) and (b)(1) and prescribing a maximum limit of 87 percent of the taxable year.

Subsec. (d). Pub. L. 91–172 substituted a table of rates of tax for married individuals filing separate returns for provision prescribing the applicability of the rates to non-resident aliens. For applicability of rates of tax to non-resident aliens, see section 2(d) of this title.

Subsec. (e). Pub. L. 91–172 struck out cross reference to section 63. See section 2(e) of this title.

1966—Subsecs. (d), (e). Pub. L. 89–809 added subsec. (d) and redesignated former subsec. (d) as (e).

1964—Pub. L. 88–272 amended section generally by splitting the former first bracket which started at $2,000 into four new brackets, the 14 percent bracket representing a 30 percent reduction, the 15 percent bracket a 25 percent cut, and the 16 percent bracket a 20 percent cut, and reducing all other brackets by cuts averaging about 20 percent and effectuated these cuts in two steps, one in 1964, and one in 1965.

EFFECTIVE DATE OF 2019 AMENDMENT

Pub. L. 116–94, div. O, title V, §501(c), Dec. 20, 2019, 133 Stat. 3181, provided that:

"(1) In general.—Except as otherwise provided in this subsection, the amendment made by subsection (a) [amending this section] shall apply to taxable years beginning after December 31, 2019.

"(2) Coordination with alternative minimum tax.—The amendment made by subsection (b) [amending section 55 of this title] shall apply to taxable years beginning after December 31, 2017.

"(3) Elective retroactive application.—A taxpayer may elect (at such time and in such manner as the Secretary of the Treasury (or the Secretary's designee) may provide) for the amendment made by subsection (a) to also apply to taxable years of the taxpayer which begin in 2018, 2019, or both (as specified by the taxpayer in such election)."

EFFECTIVE DATE OF 2017 AMENDMENT

Pub. L. 115–97, title I, §11001(c), Dec. 22, 2017, 131 Stat. 2059, provided that: "The amendments made by this section [amending this section and section 6695 of this title] shall apply to taxable years beginning after December 31, 2017."

Pub. L. 115–97, title I, §11002(e), Dec. 22, 2017, 131 Stat. 2063, provided that: "The amendments made by this section [amending this section and sections 23, 25A, 25B, 32, 36B, 41, 42, 45R, 55, 59, 62, 63, 68, 125, 132, 135, 137, 146, 147, 151, 162, 179, 213, 219–221, 223, 280F, 408A, 430, 512, 513, 831, 877A, 911, 1274A, 2010, 2032A, 2503, 4161, 4261, 4980I, 5000A, 6039F, 6323, 6334, 6601, 6651, 6652, 6695, 6698, 6699, 6721, 6722, 7345, 7430, 7872, and 9831 of this title] shall apply to taxable years beginning after December 31, 2017."

Pub. L. 115–97, title I, §14223(b), Dec. 22, 2017, 131 Stat. 2221, provided that: "The amendments made by this section [amending this section] shall apply to dividends received after the date of the enactment of this Act [Dec. 22, 2017]."

EFFECTIVE DATE OF 2014 AMENDMENT

Pub. L. 113–295, div. A, title II, §221(b), Dec. 19, 2014, 128 Stat. 4055, provided that:

"(1) General rule.—Except as otherwise provided in subsection (a) [see Tables for classification] or paragraph (2) of this subsection, the amendments made by this section [see Tables for classification] shall take effect on the date of enactment of this Act [Dec. 19, 2014].

"(2) Savings provision.—If—

"(A) any provision amended or repealed by the amendments made by this section applied to—

"(i) any transaction occurring before the date of the enactment of this Act,

"(ii) any property acquired before such date of enactment, or

"(iii) any item of income, loss, deduction, or credit taken into account before such date of enactment, and

"(B) the treatment of such transaction, property, or item under such provision would (without regard to the amendments or repeals made by this section) affect the liability for tax for periods ending after [such] date of enactment, nothing in the amendments or repeals made by this section shall be construed to affect the treatment of such transaction, property, or item for purposes of determining liability for tax for periods ending after such date of enactment."

EFFECTIVE DATE OF 2013 AMENDMENT

Pub. L. 112–240, title I, §101(b)(3), Jan. 2, 2013, 126 Stat. 2317, provided that: "The amendments made by this subsection [amending this section and sections 68 and 151 of this title] shall apply to taxable years beginning after December 31, 2012."

Pub. L. 112–240, title I, §102(d), Jan. 2, 2013, 126 Stat. 2319, provided that:

"(1) In general.—Except as otherwise provided, the amendments made by subsections (b) and (c) [amending this section, sections 55, 531, 541, 1445, and 7518 of this title, and section 53511 of Title 46, Shipping] shall apply to taxable years beginning after December 31, 2012.

"(2) Withholding.—The amendments made by paragraphs (1)(C) and (3) of subsection (c) [amending section 1445 of this title] shall apply to amounts paid on or after January 1, 2013."

EFFECTIVE AND TERMINATION DATES OF 2010 AMENDMENT

Pub. L. 111–148, title X, §10909(c), Mar. 23, 2010, 124 Stat. 1023, as amended by Pub. L. 111–312, title I, §101(b)(1), Dec. 17, 2010, 124 Stat. 3298, provided that: "Each provision of law amended by this section [amending sections 23, 24, 25, 25A, 25B, 26, 30, 30B, 30D, 36C, 137, 904, 1016, 1400C, and 6211 of this title and section 1324 of Title 31, Money and Finance, and renumbering section 23 of this title as section 36C of this title] is amended to read as such provision would read if this section had never been enacted. The amendments made by the preceding sentence shall apply to taxable years beginning after December 31, 2011."

Pub. L. 111–148, title X, §10909(d), Mar. 23, 2010, 124 Stat. 1024, as amended by Pub. L. 111–312, title I, §101(b)(2), Dec. 17, 2010, 124 Stat. 3298, provided that: "Except as provided in subsection (c) [set out as a note above], the amendments made by this section [amending sections 24, 25, 25A, 25B, 26, 30, 30B, 30D, 36C, 137, 904, 1016, 1400C, and 6211 of this title and section 1324 of Title 31, Money and Finance, and renumbering section 23 of this title as section 36C of this title] shall apply to taxable years beginning after December 31, 2009."

EFFECTIVE DATE OF 2007 AMENDMENT

Pub. L. 110–28, title VIII, §8241(c), May 25, 2007, 121 Stat. 199, provided that: "The amendment made by this section [amending this section] shall apply to taxable years beginning after the date of the enactment of this Act [May 25, 2007]."

EFFECTIVE DATE OF 2006 AMENDMENT

Pub. L. 109–222, title V, §510(d), May 17, 2006, 120 Stat. 364, provided that: "The amendment made by this section [amending this section] shall apply to taxable years beginning after December 31, 2005."

EFFECTIVE AND TERMINATION DATES OF 2004 AMENDMENT

Pub. L. 108–357, title IV, §413(d), Oct. 22, 2004, 118 Stat. 1510, provided that:

"(1) In general.—Except as provided in paragraph (2), the amendments made by this section [amending this section and sections 170, 171, 245, 312, 443, 465, 508, 542, 543, 562, 563, 751, 864, 898, 904, 951, 954, 989, 1014, 1016, 1212, 1223, 1248, 1260, 1291, 1294, 4947, 4948, 6103, 6501, and 6679 of this title and repealing sections 551 to 558, 1246, 1247, and 6035 of this title] shall apply to taxable years of foreign corporations beginning after December 31, 2004, and to taxable years of United States shareholders with or within which such taxable years of foreign corporations end.

"(2) Subsection (c)(27).—The amendments made by subsection (c)(27) [amending section 6103 of this title] shall apply to disclosures of return or return information with respect to taxable years beginning after December 31, 2004."

Pub. L. 108–311, title I, §101(e), Oct. 4, 2004, 118 Stat. 1168, provided that: "The amendments made by this section [amending this section and sections 24 and 63 of this title] shall apply to taxable years beginning after December 31, 2003."

Pub. L. 108–311, title I, §105, Oct. 4, 2004, 118 Stat. 1169, provided that: "Each amendment made by this title [amending this section and sections 24, 32, 55, and 63 of this title] shall be subject to title IX of the Economic Growth and Tax Relief Reconciliation Act of 2001 [Pub. L. 107–16, §901, which was repealed by Pub. L. 112–240, title

I, §101(a)(1), Jan. 2, 2013, 126 Stat. 2315, was formerly set out as an Effective and Termination Dates of 2001 Amendment note below] to the same extent and in the same manner as the provision of such Act to which such amendment relates."

Pub. L. 108–311, title IV, §402(b), Oct. 4, 2004, 118 Stat. 1186, provided that: "The amendments made by subsection (a) [amending this section and sections 691, 854, and 857 of this title and provisions set out as a note under this section] shall take effect as if included in section 302 of the Jobs and Growth Tax Relief Reconciliation Act of 2003 [Pub. L. 108–27]."

<h3 style="text-align:center">EFFECTIVE AND TERMINATION DATES OF 2003 AMENDMENT</h3>

Pub. L. 108–27, title I, §102(c), May 28, 2003, 117 Stat. 754, provided that: "The amendments made by this section [amending this section and provisions set out as a note under this section] shall apply to taxable years beginning after December 31, 2002."

Pub. L. 108–27, title I, §104(c), May 28, 2003, 117 Stat. 755, provided that:

"(1) In general.—The amendments made by this section [amending this section] shall apply to taxable years beginning after December 31, 2002.

"(2) Tables for 2003.—The Secretary of the Treasury shall modify each table which has been prescribed under section 1(f) of the Internal Revenue Code of 1986 for taxable years beginning in 2003 and which relates to the amendment made by subsection (a) to reflect such amendment."

Pub. L. 108–27, title I, §105(b), May 28, 2003, 117 Stat. 755, provided that: "The amendment made by this section [amending this section] shall apply to taxable years beginning after December 31, 2002."

Pub. L. 108–27, title I, §107, May 28, 2003, 117 Stat. 755, provided that: "Each amendment made by this title [enacting section 6429 of this title, amending this section and sections 24, 55, and 63 of this title, and amending provisions set out as notes under this section] shall be subject to title IX of the Economic Growth and Tax Relief Reconciliation Act of 2001 [Pub. L. 107–16, §901, which was repealed by Pub. L. 112–240, title I, §101(a)(1), Jan. 2, 2013, 126 Stat. 2315, was formerly set out as an Effective and Termination Dates of 2001 Amendment note below] to the same extent and in the same manner as the provision of such Act to which such amendment relates."

Pub. L. 108–27, title III, §301(d), May 28, 2003, 117 Stat. 760, provided that:

"(1) In general.—Except as otherwise provided by this subsection, the amendments made by this section [amending this section, sections 55, 57, 1445, and 7518 of this title, and section 1177 of Title 46, Appendix, Shipping] shall apply to taxable years ending on or after May 6, 2003.

"(2) Withholding.—The amendment made by subsection (a)(2)(C) [amending section 1445 of this title] shall apply to amounts paid after the date of the enactment of this Act [May 28, 2003].

"(3) Small business stock.—The amendments made by subsection (b)(3) [amending section 57 of this title] shall apply to dispositions on or after May 6, 2003."

Pub. L. 108–27, title III, §302(f), May 28, 2003, 117 Stat. 764, as amended by Pub. L. 108–311, title IV, §402(a)(6), Oct. 4, 2004, 118 Stat. 1185, provided that:

"(1) In general.—Except as provided in paragraph (2), the amendments made by this section [amending this section and sections 163, 301, 306, 338, 467, 531, 541, 584, 702, 854, 857, 1255, and 1257 of this title and repealing section 341 of this title] shall apply to taxable years beginning after December 31, 2002.

"(2) Pass-thru entities.—In the case of a pass-thru entity described in subparagraph (A), (B), (C), (D), (E), or (F) of section 1(h)(10) of the Internal Revenue Code of 1986, as amended by this Act, the amendments made by this section shall apply to taxable years ending after December 31, 2002; except that dividends received by such an entity on or before such date shall not be treated as qualified dividend income (as defined in section 1(h)(11)(B) of such Code, as added by this Act)."

Pub. L. 108–27, title III, §303, May 28, 2003, 117 Stat. 764, as amended by Pub. L. 109–222, title I, §102, May 17, 2006, 120 Stat. 346; Pub. L. 111–312, title I, §102(a), Dec. 17, 2010, 124 Stat. 3298, which provided that all provisions of, and amendments made by, title III of Pub. L. 108–27 would not apply to taxable years beginning after Dec. 31, 2012, and that the Internal Revenue Code of 1986 would be applied and administered to such years as if such provisions and amendments had never been enacted, was repealed by Pub. L. 112–240, title I, §102(a), Jan. 2, 2013, 126 Stat. 2318.

<h3 style="text-align:center">EFFECTIVE AND TERMINATION DATES OF 2001 AMENDMENT</h3>

Pub. L. 111–312, title II, §201(c), Dec. 17, 2010, 124 Stat. 3299, provided that: "Title IX of the Economic Growth and Tax Relief Reconciliation Act of 2001 [Pub. L. 107–16, §901, formerly set out below] (relating to sunset of provisions of such Act) shall not apply to title VII of such Act [Pub. L. 107–16, §701, amending section 55 of this title and enacting provisions set out as a note under section 55 of this title] (relating to alternative minimum tax)."

Pub. L. 109–280, title VIII, §811, Aug. 17, 2006, 120 Stat. 996, provided that: "Title IX of the Economic Growth and Tax Relief Reconciliation Act of 2001 [Pub. L. 107–16, §901, formerly set out below] shall not apply to the provisions of, and amendments made by, subtitles A through F of title VI of such Act [subtitles A to F [§§601–666] of title VI of Pub. L. 107–16, enacting sections 25B, 45E, 402A, and 4980F of this title, amending sections 24, 25, 25B, 26, 38, 39, 72, 132, 196, 219, 401, 402, 403, 404, 408, 408A, 409, 411, 412, 414 to 416, 457, 501, 505, 664, 861, 904, 1400C, 3401, 3405, 4972, 4973, 4975, 4979A, 6047, and 6051 of this title and sections 1003, 1053, 1054, 1082, 1104, and 1108 of Title 29, Labor, enacting provisions set out as notes under sections 24, 38, 72, 132, 219, 401, 402, 403, 404, 408, 409, 411, 412, 414 to 416, 457, 861, 4972, 4975, 4980F, and 7801 of this title and section 1107 of Title 29, and amending provisions set out as notes under section 414 of this title and section 1107 of Title 29] (relating to pension and individual retirement arrangement provisions)."

Pub. L. 109–280, title XIII, §1304(a), Aug. 17, 2006, 120 Stat. 1109, provided that: "Section 901 of the Economic Growth and Tax Relief Reconciliation Act of 2001 [Pub. L. 107–16, formerly set out below] (relating to sunset provisions) shall not apply to section 402 of such Act [amending sections 72, 135, 221, 529, 530, 4973, and 6693 of this title and enacting provisions set out as a note under section 72 of this title] (relating to modifications to qualified tuition programs)."

Pub. L. 107–16, title I, §101(d), June 7, 2001, 115 Stat. 44, provided that:

"(1) In general.—Except as provided in paragraph (2), the amendments made by this section [enacting section 6428 of this title and amending this section and sections 15, 531, 541, 3402, and 3406 of this title] shall apply to taxable years beginning after December 31, 2000.

"(2) Amendments to withholding provisions.—The amendments made by paragraphs (6), (7), (8), (9), (10), and (11) of subsection (c) [amending sections 3402 and 3406 of this title] shall apply to amounts paid after the 60th day after the date of the enactment of this Act [June 7, 2001]. References to income brackets and rates of tax in such paragraphs shall be applied without regard to [former] section 1(i)(1)(D) of the Internal Revenue Code of 1986."

Pub. L. 107–16, title III, §301(d), June 7, 2001, 115 Stat. 54, as amended by Pub. L. 108–27, title I, §103(b), May 28, 2003, 117 Stat. 754, provided that: "The amendments made by this section [amending this section and section 63 of this title] shall apply to taxable years beginning after December 31, 2002."

Pub. L. 107–16, title III, §302(c), June 7, 2001, 115 Stat. 54, as amended by Pub. L. 108–27, title I, §102(b)(2), May 28, 2003, 117 Stat. 754, provided that: "The amendments made by this section [amending this section] shall apply to taxable years beginning after December 31, 2002."

Pub. L. 107–16, title IX, §901, June 7, 2001, 115 Stat. 150, as amended by Pub. L. 107–358, §2, Dec. 17, 2002, 116 Stat. 3015; Pub. L. 111–312, title I, §101(a)(1), Dec. 17, 2010, 124 Stat. 3298, which provided that all provisions of, and amendments made by, Pub. L. 107–16 (except for section 803 thereof (26 U.S.C. note prec. 101)) would not apply to taxable, plan, or limitation years beginning after Dec. 31, 2012, or, in the case of title V of Pub. L. 107–16, to estates of decedents dying, gifts made, or generation skipping transfers, after Dec. 31, 2012, and that the Internal Revenue Code of 1986 and the Employee Retirement Income Security Act of 1974 (29 U.S.C. 1001 et seq.) would be applied and administered to such years, estates, gifts, and transfers as if such provisions and amendments had never been enacted, was repealed by Pub. L. 112–240, title I, §101(a)(1), Jan. 2, 2013, 126 Stat. 2315.

[Pub. L. 112–240, title I, §101(a)(3), Jan. 2, 2013, 126 Stat. 2316, provided that: "The amendments made by this subsection [repealing section 901 of Pub. L. 107–16, formerly set out above, and provisions set out as an Effective and Termination Dates of 2010 Amendment note under section 121 of this title] shall apply to taxable, plan, or limitation years beginning after December 31, 2012, and estates of decedents dying, gifts made, or generation skipping transfers after December 31, 2012."]

<h3 style="text-align:center">EFFECTIVE DATE OF 2000 AMENDMENT</h3>

Pub. L. 106–554, §1(a)(7) [title I, §117(c)], Dec. 21, 2000, 114 Stat. 2763, 2763A-605, provided that: "The amendments made by this section [amending this section and section 1202 of this title] shall apply to stock acquired after the date of the enactment of this Act [Dec. 21, 2000]."

Pub. L. 105–277, div. J, title IV, §4002(k), Oct. 21, 1998, 112 Stat. 2681–908, provided that: "The amendments made by this section [amending this section and sections 408A, 6015, 6103, 6159, 7421, 7443A, and 7491 of this title and amending provisions set out as a note under section 6601 of this title] shall take effect as if included in the provisions of the 1998 Act [Pub. L. 105–206] to which they relate."

Pub. L. 105–206, title V, §5001(b), July 22, 1998, 112 Stat. 788, provided that:

"(1) In general.—Except as provided in paragraph (2), the amendments made by this section [amending this section and sections 1223 and 1235 of this title] shall apply to taxable years ending after December 31, 1997.

"(2) Subsection (a)(5).—The amendments made by subsection (a)(5) [amending sections 1223 and 1235 of this title] shall take effect on January 1, 1998."

Pub. L. 105–206, title VI, §6024, July 22, 1998, 112 Stat. 826, provided that: "Except as otherwise provided in this title [see Tables for classification], the amendments made by this title shall take effect as if included in the provisions of the Taxpayer Relief Act of 1997 [Pub. L. 105–34] to which they relate."

EFFECTIVE DATE OF **1997** AMENDMENT

Pub. L. 105–34, title III, §311(d), Aug. 5, 1997, 111 Stat. 835, provided that:

"(1) In general.—Except as provided in paragraph (2), the amendments made by this section [amending this section, sections 55, 57, 904, 1445, and 7518 of this title, and section 1177 of Title 46, Appendix, Shipping] shall apply to taxable years ending after May 6, 1997.

"(2) Withholding.—The amendment made by subsection (c)(1) [amending section 1445 of this title] shall apply only to amounts paid after the date of the enactment of this Act [Aug. 5, 1997]."

EFFECTIVE DATE OF **1996** AMENDMENT

Pub. L. 104–188, title I, §1704(m)(4), Aug. 20, 1996, 110 Stat. 1883, provided that: "The amendments made by this subsection [amending this section and section 59 of this title] shall apply to taxable years beginning after December 31, 1995."

EFFECTIVE DATE OF **1993** AMENDMENT

Pub. L. 103–66, title XIII, §13201(c), Aug. 10, 1993, 107 Stat. 459, provided that: "The amendments made by this section [amending this section and sections 41, 63, 68, 132, 151, 453A, 513, 531, and 541 of this title] shall apply to taxable years beginning after December 31, 1992."

Pub. L. 103–66, title XIII, §13202(c), Aug. 10, 1993, 107 Stat. 461, provided that: "The amendments made by this section [amending this section and sections 531 and 541 of this title] shall apply to taxable years beginning after December 31, 1992."

Pub. L. 103–66, title XIII, §13206(d)(3), Aug. 10, 1993, 107 Stat. 467, provided that: "The amendments made by this subsection [amending this section and section 163 of this title] shall apply to taxable years beginning after December 31, 1992."

EFFECTIVE DATE OF **1990** AMENDMENT

Pub. L. 101–508, title XI, §11101(e), Nov. 5, 1990, 104 Stat. 1388–405, provided that: "The amendments made by this section [amending this section, sections 32, 41, 59, 63, 135, 151, 513, 691, 904, 6103, and 7518 of this title, and section 1177 of Title 46, Appendix, Shipping] shall apply to taxable years beginning after December 31, 1990."

Pub. L. 101–508, title XI, §11103(e), Nov. 5, 1990, 104 Stat. 1388–407, provided that: "The amendments made by this section [enacting section 68 of this title and amending this section and section 56 of this title] shall apply to taxable years beginning after December 31, 1990."

Pub. L. 101–508, title XI, §11104(c), Nov. 5, 1990, 104 Stat. 1388–408, provided that: "The amendments made by this section [amending this section and section 151 of this title] shall apply to taxable years beginning after December 31, 1990."

EFFECTIVE DATE OF **1989** AMENDMENT

Pub. L. 101–239, title VII, §7817, Dec. 19, 1989, 103 Stat. 2423, provided that: "Except as otherwise provided in this part [part I (§§7811–7817) of subtitle H of title VII of Pub. L. 101–239, see Tables for classification], any amendment made by this part shall take effect as if included in the provision of the 1988 Act [Pub. L. 100–647] to which such amendment relates."

Pub. L. 101–239, title VII, §7831(g), Dec. 19, 1989, 103 Stat. 2427, provided that: "Any amendment made by this section [amending this section and sections 42, 406, 407, and 1250 of this title and provisions set out as notes under sections 141 and 263A of this title] shall take effect as if included in the provision of the Tax Reform Act of 1986 [Pub. L. 99–514] to which such amendment relates."

EFFECTIVE DATE OF **1988** AMENDMENT

Pub. L. 100–647, title I, §1019, Nov. 10, 1988, 102 Stat. 3593, provided that:

"(a) General Rule.—Except as otherwise provided in this title, any amendment made by this title [see Tables for classification], shall take effect as if included in the provision of the Reform Act [Pub. L. 99–514] to which such amendment relates.

"(b) Waiver of Estimated Tax Penalties.—No addition to tax shall be made under section 6654 or 6655 of the 1986 Code for any period before April 16, 1989 (March 16, 1989 in the case of a taxpayer subject to section 6655 of the 1986 Code) with respect to any underpayment to the extent such underpayment was created or increased by any provision of this title or title II [see Tables for classification]."

Pub. L. 100–647, title VI, §6006(b), Nov. 10, 1988, 102 Stat. 3687, provided that: "The amendment made by this section [amending this section] shall apply to taxable years beginning after December 31, 1988."

EFFECTIVE DATE OF **1986** AMENDMENT

Pub. L. 99–514, title I, §151, Oct. 22, 1986, 100 Stat. 2121, provided that:

"(a) General Rule.—Except as otherwise provided in this section, the amendments made by this title [enacting section 67 of this title, amending this section, sections 3, 5, 15, 21, 32, 62, 63, 74, 85, 86, 102, 108, 117, 129, 151, 152, 164, 170, 172, 183, 213, 265, 274, 280A, 402, 441, 443, 527, 541, 613A, 642, 667, 861, 862, 901, 904, 1398, 1441, 2032A, 3121, 3231, 3306, 3401, 3402, 3507, 4941, 4945, 6012 to 6014, 6212, 6504, 6511, and 7871 of this title, and section 409 of Title 42, The Public Health and Welfare, renumbering section 223 of this title as section 220 of this title, repealing sections 24, 221, 222, and 1301 to 1305 of this title, and enacting provisions set out as a note under section 32 of this title] shall apply to taxable years beginning after December 31, 1986.

"(b) Unemployment Compensation.—The amendment made by section 121 [amending section 85 of this title] shall apply to amounts received after December 31, 1986, in taxable years ending after such date.

"(c) Prizes and Awards.—The amendments made by section 122 [amending sections 74, 102, 274, 3121, 3231, 3306, 3401, 4941, and 4945 of this title and section 409 of Title 42, The Public Health and Welfare] shall apply to prizes and awards granted after December 31, 1986.

"(d) Scholarships.—The amendments made by section 123 [amending sections 74, 117, 1441, and 7871 of this title] shall apply to taxable years beginning after December 31, 1986, but only in the case of scholarships and fellowships granted after August 16, 1986.

"(e) Parsonage and Military Housing Allowances.—The amendment made by section 144 [amending section 265 of this title] shall apply to taxable years beginning before, on, or after, December 31, 1986."

Pub. L. 99–514, title III, §302(b), Oct. 22, 1986, 100 Stat. 2218, provided that: "The amendment made by this section [amending this section] shall apply to taxable years beginning after December 31, 1986."

Pub. L. 99–514, title XIV, §1411(c), Oct. 22, 1986, 100 Stat. 2716, provided that: "The amendments made by this section [amending this section and section 6103 of this title] shall apply to taxable years beginning after December 31, 1986."

EFFECTIVE DATE OF **1983** AMENDMENT

Pub. L. 97–448, title I, §109, Jan. 12, 1983, 96 Stat. 2391, provided that: "Except as otherwise provided in this title, any amendment made by this title [see Tables for classification] shall take effect as if it had been included in the provision of the Economic Recovery Tax Act of 1981 [Pub. L. 97–34, Aug. 13, 1981, 95 Stat. 172] to which such amendment relates."

EFFECTIVE DATE OF 1981 AMENDMENT

Pub. L. 97–34, title I, §101(f)(1), Aug. 13, 1981, 95 Stat. 185, as amended by Pub. L. 97–448, title I, §101(a)(1), Jan. 12, 1983, 96 Stat. 2365, provided that: "The amendments made by subsections (a), (c), and (d) [amending this section and sections 3, 21, 55, 541, and 1304 of this title and repealing section 1348 of this title] shall apply to taxable years beginning after December 31, 1981; except that the amendment made by paragraph (3) of subsection (d) [amending section 21 of this title] shall apply to taxable years ending after December 31, 1981."

Pub. L. 97–34, title I, §104(e), Aug. 13, 1981, 95 Stat. 190, provided that: "The amendments made by this section [amending this section and sections 63, 151, 6012, and 6013 of this title] shall apply to taxable years beginning after December 31, 1984."

EFFECTIVE DATE OF 1978 AMENDMENT

Pub. L. 95–600, title I, §101(f)(1), Nov. 6, 1978, 92 Stat. 2770, provided that: "The amendments made by subsections (a), (b), (c), and (d) [amending sections 63, 402, 1302, and 6012 of this title] shall apply to taxable years beginning after December 31, 1978."

EFFECTIVE DATE OF 1977 AMENDMENT

Pub. L. 95–30, title I, §106(a), May 23, 1977, 91 Stat. 141, provided that: "The amendments made by sections 101, 102, and 104 [amending this section and sections 3, 21, 42, 57, 63, 143, 161, 172, 211, 402, 441, 443, 511, 584, 613A, 641, 642, 667, 703, 861, 862, 873, 904, 911, 931, 1034, 1211, 1302, 6012, 6014, 6212, 6504, and 6654 of this title and repealing sections 36, 141, 142, 144, and 145 of this title] shall apply to taxable years beginning after December 31, 1976."

EFFECTIVE DATE OF 1969 AMENDMENT

Pub. L. 91–172, title VIII, §803(f), Dec. 30, 1969, 83 Stat. 685, as amended by Pub. L. 99–514, §2, Oct. 22, 1986, 100 Stat. 2095, provided that: "The amendments made by subsections (a) [amending this section], (b) [amending section 2 of this title], and (d) (other than paragraphs (1) and (8)) [amending sections 5, 511, 632, 641, 1347, and 6015 of this title] shall apply to taxable years beginning after December 31, 1970, except that section 2(c) of the Internal Revenue Code of 1986 [formerly I.R.C. 1954] [section 2(c) of this title], as amended by subsection (b), shall also apply to taxable years beginning after December 31, 1969. The amendments made by subsections (c) [amending section 3 of this title], (d)(1) [amending section 6014 of this title], and (d)(8) [amending section 1304 of this title] shall apply to taxable years beginning after December 31, 1969".

EFFECTIVE DATE OF 1966 AMENDMENT

Pub. L. 89–809, title I, §103(n), Nov. 13, 1966, 80 Stat. 1555, provided that:

"(1) The amendments made by this section (other than the amendments made by subsections (h), (i), and (k)) [enacting section 877 of this title, amending this section and sections 116, 154, 871, 872, 873, 874, 875, 932, 6015, and 7701 of this title, renumbering section 877 as 878, and repealing section 1493 of this title] shall apply with respect to taxable years beginning after December 31, 1966.

"(2) The amendments made by subsection (h) [amending section 1441 of this title] shall apply with respect to payments made in taxable years of recipients beginning after December 31, 1966.

"(3) The amendments made by subsection (i) [amending section 1461 of this title] shall apply with respect to payments occurring after December 31, 1966.

"(4) The amendments made by subsection (k) [amending section 3401 of this title] shall apply with respect to remuneration paid after December 31, 1966."

EFFECTIVE DATE OF 1964 AMENDMENT

Pub. L. 88–272, title I, §131, Feb. 26, 1964, 78 Stat. 30, as amended by Pub. L. 99–514, §2, Oct. 22, 1986, 100 Stat. 2095, provided that: "Except for purposes of section 21 of the Internal Revenue Code of 1986 [formerly I.R.C. 1954] (relating to effect of changes in rates during a taxable year), the amendments made by parts I and II of this title [amending this section and sections 2, 11, 37, 141, 144, 242, 821, 871, 963, 6016, 6074, 6154, 6212, 6504, and 6655 of this title] shall apply with respect to taxable years beginning after December 31, 1963."

SHORT TITLE OF 2020 AMENDMENT

Pub. L. 116–260, div. N, title II, §271(a), Dec. 27, 2020, 134 Stat. 1964, provided that: "This subtitle [subtitle B (§§271–288) of title II of div. N of Pub. L. 116–260, see Tables for classification] may be cited as the 'COVID-related Tax Relief Act of 2020'."

Pub. L. 116–260, div. EE, §1(a), Dec. 27, 2020, 134 Stat. 3038, provided that: "This division [see Tables for classification] may be cited as the 'Taxpayer Certainty and Disaster Tax Relief Act of 2020'."

SHORT TITLE OF 2019 AMENDMENT

Pub. L. 116–94, div. O, §1(a), Dec. 20, 2019, 133 Stat. 3137, provided that: "This Act [div. O of Pub. L. 116–94, see Tables for classification] may be cited as the 'Setting Every Community Up for Retirement Enhancement Act of 2019'."

Pub. L. 116–94, div. P, title XIII, §1301, Dec. 20, 2019, 133 Stat. 3204, provided that: "This title [amending section 4975 of this title and section 1108 of Title 29, Labor, and enacting provisions set out as a note under section 4975 of this title] may be cited as the 'Temporary Relief from Certain ERISA Requirements Act of 2020'."

Pub. L. 116–94, div. Q, §1(a), Dec. 20, 2019, 133 Stat. 3226, provided that: "This division [see Tables for classification] may be cited as the 'Taxpayer Certainty and Disaster Tax Relief Act of 2019'."

Pub. L. 116–25, §1(a), July 1, 2019, 133 Stat. 981, provided that: "This Act [see Tables for classification] may be cited as the 'Taxpayer First Act'."

SHORT TITLE OF 2018 AMENDMENT

Pub. L. 115–250, §1, Sept. 29, 2018, 132 Stat. 3164, provided that: "This Act [amending section 9502 of this title] may be cited as the 'Airport and Airway Extension Act of 2018, Part II'."

Pub. L. 115–141, div. M, title I, §1, Mar. 23, 2018, 132 Stat. 1046, provided that: "This title [amending sections 4081, 4083, 4261, 4271, and 9502 of this title and sections 106, 41742, 41743, 44506, 47104, 47107, 47115, 47124, 47141, and 48101 to 48103 of Title 49, Transportation, and amending provisions set out as a note preceding section 42301 of Title 49 and provisions set out as notes under sections 41731 and 47141 of Title 49] may be cited as the 'Airport and Airway Extension Act of 2018'."

Pub. L. 115–141, div. U, §1(a), Mar. 23, 2018, 132 Stat. 1159, provided that: "This division [see Tables for classification] may be cited as the 'Tax Technical Corrections Act of 2018'."

SHORT TITLE OF 2017 AMENDMENT

Pub. L. 115–63, §1(a), Sept. 29, 2017, 131 Stat. 1168, provided that: "This Act [amending sections 4081, 4083, 4261, 4271, and 9502 of this title, sections 254c–3, 256h, 256i, and 1395iii of Title 42, The Public Health and Welfare, and sections 106, 41742, 41743, 47104, 47107, 47114, 47115, 47124, 47141, 48101 to 48103, and 48114 of Title 49, Transportation, and amending provisions set out as a note under section 1395l of Title 42, provisions set out as a note preceding section 42301 of Title 49, and provisions set out as notes under sections 41731 and 47141 of Title 49] may be cited as the 'Disaster Tax Relief and Airport and Airway Extension Act of 2017'."

SHORT TITLE OF 2016 AMENDMENT

Pub. L. 114–239, §1, Oct. 7, 2016, 130 Stat. 973, provided that: "This Act [amending section 74 of this title and enacting provisions set out as a note under section 74 of this title] may be cited as the 'United States Appreciation for Olympians and Paralympians Act of 2016'."

Pub. L. 114–184, §1, June 30, 2016, 130 Stat. 536, provided that: "This Act [amending sections 6103 and 7213 of this title and enacting provisions set out as a note under section 6103 of this title] may be cited as the 'Recovering Missing Children Act'."

Pub. L. 114–141, §1(a), Mar. 30, 2016, 130 Stat. 322, provided that: "This Act [amending sections 4081, 4083, 4261, 4271, and 9502 of this title and sections 106, 41742, 47104, 47107, 47115, 47124, 47141, and 48101 to 48103 of Title 49, Transportation, and amending provisions set out as a note preceding section 42301 of Title 49 and provisions set out as notes under sections 41731 and 47141 of Title 49] may be cited as the 'Airport and Airway Extension Act of 2016'."

SHORT TITLE OF 2015 AMENDMENT

Pub. L. 114–113, div. Q, §1(a), Dec. 18, 2015, 129 Stat. 3040, provided that: "This division [see Tables for classification] may be cited as the 'Protecting Americans from Tax Hikes Act of 2015'."

Pub. L. 114–74, §1(a), Nov. 2, 2015, 129 Stat. 584, provided that: "This Act [see Tables for classification] may be cited as the 'Bipartisan Budget Act of 2015'."

Pub. L. 114–55, §1(a), Sept. 30, 2015, 129 Stat. 522, provided that: "This Act [amending sections 4081, 4083, 4261, 4271, and 9502 of this title, sections 106, 41742, 47104, 47107, 47115, 47124, 47141, 48101 to 48103, and 48114 of Title 49, Transportation, and section 50905 of Title 51, National and Commercial Space Programs, and amending provisions set out as a note preceding section 42301 of Title 49 and provisions set out as notes under sections 41731 and 47141 of Title 49] may be cited as the 'Airport and Airway Extension Act of 2015'."

Pub. L. 114–26, §1, June 29, 2015, 129 Stat. 319, provided that: "This Act [probably means sections 1 to 3 of Pub. L. 114–26, see Tables for classification] may be cited as the 'Defending Public Safety Employees' Retirement Act'."

Pub. L. 114–14, §1, May 22, 2015, 129 Stat. 198, provided that: "This Act [amending section 104 of this title] may be cited as the 'Don't Tax Our Fallen Public Safety Heroes Act'."

SHORT TITLE OF 2014 AMENDMENT

Pub. L. 113–295, div. A, §1(a), Dec. 19, 2014, 128 Stat. 4010, provided that: "This division [see Tables for classification] may be cited as the 'Tax Increase Prevention Act of 2014'."

Pub. L. 113–295, div. A, title II, §201, Dec. 19, 2014, 128 Stat. 4024, provided that: "This title [see Tables for classification] may be cited as the 'Tax Technical Corrections Act of 2014'."

Pub. L. 113–295, div. B, §1(a), Dec. 19, 2014, 128 Stat. 4056, provided that: "This division [see Tables for classification] may be cited as the 'Stephen Beck, Jr., Achieving a Better Life Experience Act of 2014' or the 'Stephen Beck, Jr., ABLE Act of 2014'."

Pub. L. 113–168, §1, Sept. 26, 2014, 128 Stat. 1883, provided that: "This Act [enacting section 139E of this title and provisions set out as notes under section 139E of this title] may be cited as the 'Tribal General Welfare Exclusion Act of 2014'."

Pub. L. 113–94, §1, Apr. 3, 2014, 128 Stat. 1085, provided that: "This Act [amending sections 9006, 9008, 9009, 9012, and 9037 of this title and sections 282 and 282a of Title 42, The Public Health and Welfare, and enacting provisions set out as a note under section 282a of Title 42] may be cited as the 'Gabriella Miller Kids First Research Act'."

SHORT TITLE OF 2013 AMENDMENT

Pub. L. 112–240, §1(a), Jan. 2, 2013, 126 Stat. 2313, provided that: "This Act [see Tables for classification] may be cited as the 'American Taxpayer Relief Act of 2012'."

SHORT TITLE OF 2012 AMENDMENT

Pub. L. 112–141, div. D, §40001, July 6, 2012, 126 Stat. 844, provided that: "This division [see Tables for classification] may be cited as the 'Highway Investment, Job Creation, and Economic Growth Act of 2012'."

Pub. L. 112–96, §1(a), Feb. 22, 2012, 126 Stat. 156, provided that: "This Act [see Tables for classification] may be cited as the 'Middle Class Tax Relief and Job Creation Act of 2012'."

Pub. L. 112–96, title II, §2001, Feb. 22, 2012, 126 Stat. 159, provided that: "This title [enacting sections 505 and 1111 of Title 42, The Public Health and Welfare, amending sections 3304 and 3306 of this title, section 503 of Title 42, and section 352 of Title 45, Railroads, enacting provisions set out as notes under this section, sections 3304 and 3306 of this title, and sections 503 and 1111 of Title 42, amending provisions set out as notes under section 3304 of this title, and repealing provisions set out as a note under section 3304 of this title] may be cited as the 'Extended Benefits, Reemployment, and Program Integrity Improvement Act'."

Pub. L. 112–96, title II, §2121, Feb. 22, 2012, 126 Stat. 163, provided that: "This subtitle [subtitle B (§§2121–2124) of title II of Pub. L. 112–96, amending section 352 of Title 45, Railroads, and enacting and amending provisions set out as notes under section 3304 of this title] may be cited as the 'Unemployment Benefits Extension Act of 2012'."

Pub. L. 112–96, title II, §2160, Feb. 22, 2012, 126 Stat. 171, provided that: "This subtitle [subtitle D (§§2160–2166) of title II of Pub. L. 112–96, amending sections 3304 and 3306 of this title and section 503 of Title 42, The Public Health and Welfare, enacting provisions set out as notes under sections 3304 and 3306 of this title, and repealing provisions set out as a note under section 3304 of this title] may be cited as the 'Layoff Prevention Act of 2012'."

Pub. L. 112–91, §1, Jan. 31, 2012, 126 Stat. 3, provided that: "This Act [amending sections 4081, 4261, 4271, and 9502 of this title and sections 106, 40117, 41742, 41743, 44302, 44303, 47104, 47107, 47115, 47141, 48101 to 48103, and 49108 of Title 49, Transportation, enacting provisions set out as notes under sections 4081 and 9502 of this title, and amending provisions set out as notes under sections 41731 and 47109 of Title 49] may be cited as the 'Airport and Airway Extension Act of 2012'."

SHORT TITLE OF 2011 AMENDMENT

Pub. L. 112–78, §1(a), Dec. 23, 2011, 125 Stat. 1280, provided that: "This Act [enacting section 4547 of Title 12, Banks and Banking, amending section 645 of Title 2, The Congress, section 1709 of Title 12, sections 1395l, 1395m, 1395w–4, 1396a, 1396r–6, and 1396u–3 of Title 42, The Public Health and Welfare, and section 352 of Title 45, Railroads, enacting provisions set out as notes under sections 1401 and 3304 of this title, section 1709 of Title 12, and section 1395ww of Title 42, and amending provisions set out as notes under sections 1401 and 3304 of this title and sections 1395m, 1395w–4, and 1395ww of Title 42] may be cited as the 'Temporary Payroll Tax Cut Continuation Act of 2011'."

Pub. L. 112–56, title I, §101, Nov. 21, 2011, 125 Stat. 712, provided that: "This title [amending section 3402 of this title and enacting provisions set out as a note under section 3402 of this title] may be cited as the '3% Withholding Repeal and Job Creation Act'."

Pub. L. 112–30, title II, §201, Sept. 16, 2011, 125 Stat. 357, provided that: "This title [amending sections 4081, 4261, 4271 and 9502 of this title and sections 106, 40117, 41742, 41743, 44302, 44303, 47104, 47107, 47115, 47141, 48101 to 48103, and 49108 of Title 49, Transportation, enacting provisions set out as notes under sections 4081 and 9502 of this title, and amending provisions set out as notes under section 41731 and 47109 of Title 49] may be cited as the 'Airport and Airway Extension Act of 2011, Part V'."

Pub. L. 112–27, §1, Aug. 5, 2011, 125 Stat. 270, provided that: "This Act [amending sections 4081, 4261, 4271 and 9502 of this title and sections 40117, 41731, 44302, 44303, 47104, 47107, 47115, 47141, 48103, and 49108 of Title 49, Transportation, enacting provisions set out as notes under sections 4081 and 9502 of this title and section 40117 of Title 49, and amending provisions set out as a note under section 47109 of Title 49] may be cited as the 'Airport and Airway Extension Act of 2011, Part IV'."

Pub. L. 112–21, §1, June 29, 2011, 125 Stat. 233, provided that: "This Act [amending sections 4081, 4261, 4271 and 9502 of this title and sections 40117, 44302, 44303, 47104, 47107, 47115, 47141, 48103, and 49108 of Title 49, Transportation, enacting provisions set out as notes under sections 4081 and 9502 of this title and section 40117 of Title 49, and amending provisions set out as a note under section 47109 of Title 49] may be cited as the 'Airport and Airway Extension Act of 2011, Part III'."

Pub. L. 112–16, §1, May 31, 2011, 125 Stat. 218, provided that: "This Act [amending sections 4081, 4261, 4271, and 9502 of this title and sections 40117, 44302, 44303, 47104, 47107, 47115, 47141, 48103, and 49108 of Title 49, Transportation, enacting provisions set out as notes under sections 4081 and 9502 of this title and section 40117 of Title 49, and amending provisions set out as a note under section 47109 of Title 49] may be cited as the 'Airport and Airway Extension Act of 2011, Part II'."

Pub. L. 112–9, §1, Apr. 14, 2011, 125 Stat. 36, provided that: "This Act [amending sections 36B and 6041 of this title and enacting provisions set out as notes under sections 36B and 6041 of this title] may be cited as the 'Comprehensive 1099 Taxpayer Protection and Repayment of Exchange Subsidy Overpayments Act of 2011'."

Pub. L. 112–7, §1, Mar. 31, 2011, 125 Stat. 31, provided that: "This Act [amending sections 4081, 4261, 4271 and 9502 of this title and sections 40117, 44302, 44303, 47104, 47107, 47115, 47141, 48103, and 49108 of Title 49, Transportation, enacting provisions set out as notes under sections 4081 and 9502 of this title and section 40117 of Title 49, and amending provisions set out as a note under section 47109 of Title 49] may be cited as the 'Airport and Airway Extension Act of 2011'."

SHORT TITLE OF 2010 AMENDMENT

Pub. L. 111–329, §1, Dec. 22, 2010, 124 Stat. 3566, provided that: "This Act [amending sections 4081, 4261, 4271, and 9502 of this title and sections 40117, 44302, 44303, 47104, 47107, 47115, 47141, 48103, and 49108 of Title 49, Transportation, enacting provisions set out as notes under sections 4081 and 9502 of this title and section 40117 of Title 49, and amending provisions set out as a note under section 47109 of Title 49] may be cited as the 'Airport and Airway Extension Act of 2010, Part IV'."

Pub. L. 111–325, §1(a), Dec. 22, 2010, 124 Stat. 3537, provided that: "This Act [amending sections 267, 302, 316, 562, 851, 852, 853, 853A, 854, 855, 860, 871, 1212, and 4982 of this title, repealing section 6697 of this title, and enacting provisions set out as notes under sections 267, 316, 562, 851, 852, 854, 855, 860, 1212, and 4982 of this title] may be cited as the 'Regulated Investment Company Modernization Act of 2010'."

Pub. L. 111–312, §1(a), Dec. 17, 2010, 124 Stat. 3296, provided that: "This Act [see Tables for classification] may be cited as the 'Tax Relief, Unemployment Insurance Reauthorization, and Job Creation Act of 2010'."

Pub. L. 111–249, §1, Sept. 30, 2010, 124 Stat. 2627, provided that: "This Act [amending sections 4081, 4261, 4271, and 9502 of this title and sections 1135, 40117, 41743, 44302, 44303, 44703, 47104, 47107, 47115, 47141, 48103, and 49108 of Title 49, Transportation, enacting provisions set out as notes under sections 4081 and 9502 of this title and sections 1135 and 40117 of Title 49, and amending provisions set out as notes under sections 41731, 44701, and 47109 of Title 49] may be cited as the 'Airport and Airway Extension Act of 2010, Part III'."

Pub. L. 111–240, title II, §2001, Sept. 27, 2010, 124 Stat. 2553, provided that: "This title [amending sections 38 to 40, 55, 72, 162, 168, 179, 195, 280F, 402A, 460, 861, 862, 864, 1202, 1374, 1400L, 1400N, 6041, 6330, 6707A, 6721, and 6722 of this title and enacting provisions set out as notes under sections 38 to 40, 72, 162, 168, 179, 195, 280F, 402A, 460, 861, 1202, 1374, 6041, 6330, 6655, 6662A, 6707A, and 6721 of this title] may be cited as the 'Creating Small Business Jobs Act of 2010'."

Pub. L. 111–237, §1, Aug. 16, 2010, 124 Stat. 2497, provided that: "This Act [amending sections 6201, 6213, 6302, and 6501 of this title and enacting provisions set out as notes under sections 6201, 6302, and 6655 of this title] may be cited as the 'Firearms Excise Tax Improvement Act of 2010'."

Pub. L. 111–226, §1, Aug. 10, 2010, 124 Stat. 2389, provided that: "This Act [enacting section 909 of this title, amending sections 32, 304, 861, 864, 871, 901, 904, 960, 2104, 6012, 6051, 6302, and 6501 of this title and section 1396r–8 of Title 42, The Public Health and Welfare, repealing section 3507 of this title, enacting provisions set out as notes under sections 32, 304, 861, 864, 901, 904, 909, 960, and 6501 of this title and section 1396r–8 of Title 42, and amending provisions set out as a note under section 1396d of Title 42] may be cited as the '_____ Act of _____'. [sic]"

Pub. L. 111–205, §1, July 22, 2010, 124 Stat. 2236, provided that: "This Act [enacting and amending provisions set out as notes under section 3304 of this title] may be cited as the 'Unemployment Compensation Extension Act of 2010'."

Pub. L. 111–198, §1, July 2, 2010, 124 Stat. 1356, provided that: "This Act [amending sections 36, 6103, and 6657 of this title, section 1187 of Title 8, Aliens and Nationality, and section 2131 of Title 22, Foreign Relations and Intercourse, and enacting provisions set out as notes under sections 36, 6103, and 6657 of this title] may be cited as the 'Homebuyer Assistance and Improvement Act of 2010'."

Pub. L. 111–197, §1, July 2, 2010, 124 Stat. 1353, provided that: "This Act [amending sections 4081, 4261, 4271, and 9502 of this title and sections 106, 40117, 44302, 44303, 47104, 47107, 47115, 47141, 48101 to 48103, and 49108 of Title 49, Transportation, enacting provisions set out as notes under sections 4081 and 9502 of this title and section 40117 of Title 49, and amending provisions set out as a note under section 47109 of Title 49] may be cited as the 'Airport and Airway Extension Act of 2010, Part II'."

Pub. L. 111–161, §1, Apr. 30, 2010, 124 Stat. 1126, provided that: "This Act [amending sections 4081, 4261, 4271, and 9502 of this title and sections 106, 40117, 44302, 44303, 47104, 47107, 47115, 47141, 48101 to 48103, and 49108 of Title 49, Transportation, enacting provisions set out as notes under sections 4081 and 9502 of this title and section 40117 of Title 49, and amending provisions set out as a note under section 47109 of Title 49] may be cited as the 'Airport and Airway Extension Act of 2010'."

Pub. L. 111–159, §1, Apr. 26, 2010, 124 Stat. 1123, provided that: "This Act [amending section 5000A of this title and enacting provisions set out as a note under section 5000A of this title] may be cited as the 'TRICARE Affirmation Act'."

Pub. L. 111–157, §1, Apr. 15, 2010, 124 Stat. 1116, provided that: "This Act [amending section 119 of Title 17, Copyrights, sections 1395w–4 and 1396b of Title 42, The Public Health and Welfare, and section 325 of Title 47, Telecommunications, enacting provisions set out as notes under sections 3304 and 6432 of this title and section 1395w–4 of Title 42, and amending provisions set out as notes under sections 3304 and 6432 of this title and section 119 of Title 17] may be cited as the 'Continuing Extension Act of 2010'."

Pub. L. 111–153, §1, Mar. 31, 2010, 124 Stat. 1084, provided that: "This Act [amending sections 4081, 4261, 4271, and 9502 of this title and sections 106, 40117, 44302, 44303, 47104, 47107, 47115, 47141, 48101 to 48103, and 49108 of Title 49, Transportation, enacting provisions set out as notes under sections 4081 and 9502 of this title and section 40117 of Title 49, and amending provisions set out as a note under section 47109 of Title 49] may be cited as the 'Federal Aviation Administration Extension Act of 2010'."

Pub. L. 111–147, §1(a), Mar. 18, 2010, 124 Stat. 71, provided that: "This Act [enacting chapter 4 and section 6038D of this title, amending sections 51, 54F, 149, 163, 165, 179, 643, 679, 864, 871, 881, 1287, 1291, 1298, 3111, 3221, 4701, 6011, 6048, 6229, 6414, 6431, 6501, 6513, 6611, 6662, 6677, 6724, and 9502 to 9504 of this title, section 777c of Title 16, Conservation, sections 405 and 410 of Title 23, Highways, section 3121 of Title 31, Money and Finance, and sections 5305, 5307, 5309, 5311, 5337, 5338, 31104, and 31144 of Title 49, Transportation, enacting provisions set out as notes under sections 38, 51, 54F, 149, 179, 643, 679, 864, 871, 1291, 6011, 6038D, 6048, 6229, 6431, 6655, 6662, 6677, 9502, and 9503 of this title and section 101 of Title 23, and amending provisions set out as notes under section 901 of Title 2, The Congress, sections 402, 403, and 405 of Title 23, and sections 5309, 5310, 5338, 14710, 31100, 31301, and 31309 of Title 49] may be cited as the 'Hiring Incentives to Restore Employment Act'."

Pub. L. 111–144, §1, Mar. 2, 2010, 124 Stat. 42, provided that: "This Act [amending sections 35, 139C, 6432, and 6720C of this title, section 119 of Title 17, Copyrights, sections 1395l and 1395w–4 of Title 42, The Public Health and Welfare, and section 325 of Title 47, Telecommunications, enacting provisions set out as a note under section 6432 of this title, and amending provisions set out as notes under sections 3304 and 6432 of this title and section 119 of Title 17] may be cited as the 'Temporary Extension Act of 2010'."

SHORT TITLE OF 2009 AMENDMENT

Pub. L. 111–116, §1, Dec. 16, 2009, 123 Stat. 3031, provided that: "This Act [amending sections 4081, 4261, 4271, and 9502 of this title and sections 106, 40117, 44302, 44303, 47104, 47107, 47115, 47141, 48101 to 48103, and 49108 of Title 49, Transportation, enacting provisions set out as notes under sections 4081 and

107

9502 of this title and section 40117 of Title 49, and amending provisions set out as a note under section 47109 of Title 49] may be cited as the 'Fiscal Year 2010 Federal Aviation Administration Extension Act, Part II'."

Pub. L. 111–92, §1, Nov. 6, 2009, 123 Stat. 2984, provided that: "This Act [amending sections 36, 56, 132, 172, 810, 864, 1400C, 3301, 6011, 6213, 6698, and 6699 of this title, section 1103 of Title 42, The Public Health and Welfare, and section 352 of Title 45, Railroads, enacting provisions set out as notes under sections 36, 56, 132, 172, 864, 3301, 3304, 6011, 6213, 6655, and 6698 of this title and section 1103 of Title 42, and amending provisions set out as a note under section 3304 of this title] may be cited as the 'Worker, Homeownership, and Business Assistance Act of 2009'."

Pub. L. 111–69, §1, Oct. 1, 2009, 123 Stat. 2054, provided that: "This Act [amending sections 4081, 4261, 4271, and 9502 of this title and sections 106, 40117, 41743, 44302, 44303, 47104, 47107, 47115, 47141, 48101 to 48103, and 49108 of Title 49, Transportation, enacting provisions set out as notes under sections 4081 and 9502 of this title and section 40117 of Title 49, and amending provisions set out as notes under sections 41731 and 47109 of Title 49] may be cited as the 'Fiscal Year 2010 Federal Aviation Administration Extension Act'."

Pub. L. 111–42, title II, §201, July 28, 2009, 123 Stat. 1964, provided that: "This title [enacting provisions set out as a note under section 6655 of this title] may be cited as the 'Corporate Estimated Tax Shift Act of 2009'."

Pub. L. 111–12, §1, Mar. 30, 2009, 123 Stat. 1457, provided that: "This Act [amending sections 4081, 4261, 4271, and 9502 of this title and sections 106, 40117, 44302, 44303, 47104, 47107, 47115, 47141, 48101 to 48103, and 49108 of Title 49, Transportation, enacting provisions set out as notes under sections 4081 and 9502 of this title and section 40117 of Title 49, and amending provisions set out as a note under section 47109 of Title 49] may be cited as the 'Federal Aviation Administration Extension Act of 2009'."

Pub. L. 111–5, §1, Feb. 17, 2009, 123 Stat. 115, provided that: "This Act [see Tables for classification] may be cited as the 'American Recovery and Reinvestment Act of 2009'."

Pub. L. 111–5, div. B, title I, §1000(a), Feb. 17, 2009, 123 Stat. 306, provided that: "This title [see Tables for classification] may be cited as the 'American Recovery and Reinvestment Tax Act of 2009'."

Pub. L. 111–5, div. B, title I, §1899, Feb. 17, 2009, 123 Stat. 423, provided that: "This part [part VI (§§1899–1899L) of subtitle I of title I of div. B of Pub. L. 111–5, amending sections 35, 4980B, 7527, and 9801 of this title, sections 1162, 1181, 2918, and 2919 of Title 29, Labor, and sections 300bb–2 and 300gg of Title 42, The Public Health and Welfare, and enacting provisions set out as notes under sections 35, 4980B, 7527, and 9801 of this title] may be cited as the 'TAA Health Coverage Improvement Act of 2009'."

Pub. L. 111–5, div. B, title II, §2000(a), Feb. 17, 2009, 123 Stat. 436, provided that: "This title [amending sections 603, 604, 607, 1103, 1308, and 1322 of Title 42, The Public Health and Welfare, and section 352 of Title 45, Railroads, enacting provisions set out as notes under sections 3304 and 6428 of this title and sections 603, 607, 655, 1103, and 1308 of Title 42, and amending provisions set out as notes under section 3304 of this title] may be cited as the 'Assistance for Unemployed Workers and Struggling Families Act'."

SHORT TITLE OF 2008 AMENDMENT

Pub. L. 110–449, §1, Nov. 21, 2008, 122 Stat. 5014, provided that: "This Act [enacting and amending provisions set out as notes under section 3304 of this title] may be cited as the 'Unemployment Compensation Extension Act of 2008'."

Pub. L. 110–428, §1, Oct. 15, 2008, 122 Stat. 4839, provided that: "This Act [amending sections 6103 and 7803 of this title and section 376 of Title 28, Judiciary and Judicial Procedure, and enacting provisions set out as notes under sections 6103 and 7207 of this title and section 376 of Title 28] may be cited as the 'Inmate Tax Fraud Prevention Act of 2008'."

Pub. L. 110–343, div. B, §1(a), Oct. 3, 2008, 122 Stat. 3807, provided that: "This division [see Tables for classification] may be cited as the 'Energy Improvement and Extension Act of 2008'."

Pub. L. 110–343, div. C, §1(a), Oct. 3, 2008, 122 Stat. 3861, provided that: "This division [see Tables for classification] may be cited as the 'Tax Extenders and Alternative Minimum Tax Relief Act of 2008'."

Pub. L. 110–343, div. C, title VII, §701, Oct. 3, 2008, 122 Stat. 3912, provided that: "This subtitle [subtitle A (§§701–704) of title VII of div. C of Pub. L. 110–343, amending section 6033 of this title and enacting provisions set out as a note under section 6033 of this title] may be cited as the 'Heartland Disaster Tax Relief Act of 2008'."

Pub. L. 110–330, §1, Sept. 30, 2008, 122 Stat. 3717, provided that: "This Act [amending sections 4081, 4261, 4271, and 9502 of this title and sections 106, 40117, 41743, 44302, 44303, 47104, 47107, 47115, 47141, 48101 to 48103, and 49108 of Title 49, Transportation, enacting provisions set out as notes under sections 4081 and 9502 of this title and section 40117 of Title 49, and amending provisions set out as notes under sections 41731 and 47109 of Title 49] may be cited as the 'Federal Aviation Administration Extension Act of 2008, Part II'."

Pub. L. 110–289, div. C, §3000(a), July 30, 2008, 122 Stat. 2877, provided that: "This division [see Tables for classification] may be cited as the 'Housing Assistance Tax Act of 2008'."

Pub. L. 110–253, §1, June 30, 2008, 122 Stat. 2417, provided that: "This Act [amending sections 4081, 4261, 4271, and 9502 of this title and sections 40117, 44302, 44303, 47104, 47115, 47141, and 48103 of Title 49, Transportation, enacting provisions set out as notes under sections 4081 and 9502 of this title and section 47104 of Title 49, and amending provisions set out as a note under section 47109 of Title 49] may be cited as the 'Federal Aviation Administration Extension Act of 2008'."

Pub. L. 110–245, §1(a), June 17, 2008, 122 Stat. 1624, provided that: "This Act [enacting chapter 15 and sections 45P and 877A of this title, amending sections 32, 38, 72, 121, 125, 134, 143, 219, 280C, 401, 403, 404, 408A, 414, 457, 530, 877, 3121, 3306, 3401, 6039G, 6103, 6428, 6511, 6651, 7701, and 9812 of this title, section 1185a of Title 29, Labor, and sections 300gg–5, 409, 410, 1382a, and 1382b of Title 42, The Public Health and Welfare, and enacting provisions set out as notes under sections 32, 38, 72, 121, 125, 134, 143, 219, 401, 408A, 414, 3121, 3401, 6103, 6428, 6511, and 6651 of this title and section 1382a of Title 42] may be cited as the 'Heroes Earnings Assistance and Relief Tax Act of 2008'."

Pub. L. 110–234, title XV, §15001(a), May 22, 2008, 122 Stat. 1484, and Pub. L. 110–246, §4(a), title XV, §15001(a), June 18, 2008, 122 Stat. 1664, 2246, provided that: "This title [see Tables for classification] may be cited as the 'Heartland, Habitat, Harvest, and Horticulture Act of 2008'."

[Pub. L. 110–234 and Pub. L. 110–246 enacted identical provisions. Pub. L. 110–234 was repealed by section 4(a) of Pub. L. 110–246, set out as a note under section 8701 of Title 7, Agriculture.]

Pub. L. 110–190, §1, Feb. 28, 2008, 122 Stat. 643, provided that: "This Act [amending sections 4081, 4261, 4271, and 9502 of this title and sections 47104 and 48103 of Title 49, Transportation, enacting provisions set out as notes under sections 4081 and 9502 of this title and section 41731 of Title 49, and amending provisions set out as notes under sections 41731 and 47109 of Title 49] may be cited as the 'Airport and Airway Extension Act of 2008'."

Pub. L. 110–185, §1(a), Feb. 13, 2008, 122 Stat. 613, provided that: "This Act [amending this section, sections 168, 179, 1400L, 1400N, 6211, 6213, and 6428 of this title, and section 1324 of Title 31, Money and Finance, and enacting provisions set out as notes under sections 168, 179, and 6428 of this title] may be cited as the 'Economic Stimulus Act of 2008'."

SHORT TITLE OF 2007 AMENDMENT

Pub. L. 110–172, §1(a), Dec. 29, 2007, 121 Stat. 2473, provided that: "This Act [see Tables for classification] may be cited as the 'Tax Technical Corrections Act of 2007'."

Pub. L. 110–166, §1, Dec. 26, 2007, 121 Stat. 2461, provided that: "This Act [amending sections 26 and 55 of this title and enacting provisions set out as notes under sections 26 and 55 of this title] may be cited as the 'Tax Increase Prevention Act of 2007'."

Pub. L. 110–142, §1, Dec. 20, 2007, 121 Stat. 1803, provided that: "This Act [enacting sections 139B and 6699 of this title, amending sections 42, 108, 121, 163, 216, 6103, and 6698 of this title, and enacting provisions set out as notes under sections 42, 108, 121, 139B, 163, 216, 6103, 6655, 6698, and 6699 of this title] may be cited as the 'Mortgage Forgiveness Debt Relief Act of 2007'."

Pub. L. 110–28, title VIII, §8201(a), May 25, 2007, 121 Stat. 190, provided that: "This subtitle [subtitle B (§§8201–8248) of title VIII of Pub. L. 110–28, enacting section 6676 of this title, amending this section, sections 38, 45B, 51, 179, 641, 761, 1361, 1362, 1368, 1400N, 1402, 6060, 6103, 6107, 6l09, 6330, 6404, 6503, 6657, 6694 to 6696, 7407, 7427, 7528, and 7701 of this title, and section 411 of Title 42, The Public Health and Welfare, enacting provisions set out as notes under this section and sections 38, 45B, 51, 179, 641, 761, 1361, 1362, 6060, 6330, 6404, 6657, and 6676 of this title, and amending provisions set out as a note under section 6655 of this title] may be cited as the 'Small Business and Work Opportunity Tax Act of 2007'."

SHORT TITLE OF 2006 AMENDMENT

Pub. L. 109–432, §1(a), Dec. 20, 2006, 120 Stat. 2922, provided that: "This Act [see Tables for classification] may be cited as the 'Tax Relief and Health Care Act of 2006'."

Pub. L. 109–432, div. A, title III, §301, Dec. 20, 2006, 120 Stat. 2948, provided that: "This title [amending sections 106, 223, 408, and 4980G of this title and enacting provisions set out as notes under sections 106, 223, and 4980G of this title] may be cited as the 'Health Opportunity Patient Empowerment Act of 2006'."

Pub. L. 109–227, §1, May 29, 2006, 120 Stat. 385, provided that: "This Act [amending section 219 of this title and enacting provisions set out as notes under section 219 of this title] may be cited as the 'Heroes Earned Retirement Opportunities Act'."

Pub. L. 109–222, §1(a), May 17, 2006, 120 Stat. 345, provided that: "This Act [enacting section 4965 of this title, amending this section and sections 26, 54, 55, 142 to 144, 148, 149, 163, 167, 170, 179, 199, 355, 408A, 468B, 852, 871, 897, 911, 953, 954, 1221, 1355, 1445, 3402, 6011, 6033, 6049, 6159, 6652, 7122, and 7872 of this title, enacting provisions set out as notes under this section and sections 26, 54 to 56, 142, 143, 163, 167, 170, 199, 355, 408A, 468B, 852, 897, 911, 954, 1355, 3402, 4965, 6049, 6159, and 6655 of this title, and amending provisions set out as notes under this section and sections 56 and 114 of this title] may be cited as the 'Tax Increase Prevention and Reconciliation Act of 2005'."

SHORT TITLE OF 2005 AMENDMENT

Pub. L. 109–135, §1(a), Dec. 21, 2005, 119 Stat. 2577, provided that: "This Act [see Tables for classification] may be cited as the 'Gulf Opportunity Zone Act of 2005'."

Pub. L. 109–135, title IV, §401, Dec. 21, 2005, 119 Stat. 2610, provided that: "This subtitle [subtitle A (§§401–413) of title IV of Pub. L. 109–135, see Tables for classification] may be cited as the 'Tax Technical Corrections Act of 2005'."

Pub. L. 109–73, §1(a), Sept. 23, 2005, 119 Stat. 2016, provided that: "This Act [amending sections 170 and 7508 of this title and enacting provisions set out as notes under sections 170 and 7508 of this title] may be cited as the 'Katrina Emergency Tax Relief Act of 2005'."

Pub. L. 109–58, title XIII, §1300(a), Aug. 8, 2005, 119 Stat. 986, provided that: "This title [see Tables for classification] may be cited as the 'Energy Tax Incentives Act of 2005'."

SHORT TITLE OF 2004 AMENDMENT

Pub. L. 108–357, §1(a), Oct. 22, 2004, 118 Stat. 1418, provided that: "This Act [see Tables for classification] may be cited as the 'American Jobs Creation Act of 2004'."

Pub. L. 108–311, §1(a), Oct. 4, 2004, 118 Stat. 1166, provided that: "This Act [see Tables for classification] may be cited as the 'Working Families Tax Relief Act of 2004'."

SHORT TITLE OF 2003 AMENDMENT

Pub. L. 108–121, §1(a), Nov. 11, 2003, 117 Stat. 1335, provided that: "This Act [amending sections 5, 62, 101, 121, 132, 134, 162, 501, 530, 692, 2201, 3121, 3306, 3401, 6013, and 7508 of this title, section 1478 of Title 10, Armed Forces, and section 58c of Title 19, Customs Duties, and enacting provisions set out as notes under sections 5, 62, 101, 121, 132, 134, 501, 530, 2201, and 7508 of this title and section 1478 of Title 10] may be cited as the 'Military Family Tax Relief Act of 2003'."

Pub. L. 108–27, §1(a), May 28, 2003, 117 Stat. 752, provided that: "This Act [enacting section 6429 of this title and section 801 of Title 42, The Public Health and Welfare, amending this section, sections 24, 55, 57, 63, 163, 168, 179, 301, 306, 338, 467, 531, 541, 584, 702, 854, 857, 1255, 1257, 1400L, 1445, and 7518 of this title, and section 1177 of Title 46, Appendix, Shipping, repealing section 341 of this title, enacting provisions set out as notes under this section, sections 24, 55, 63, 168, and 179 of this title, and section 1396d of Title 42, and amending provisions set out as notes under this section] may be cited as the 'Jobs and Growth Tax Relief Reconciliation Act of 2003'."

Pub. L. 108–26, §1, May 28, 2003, 117 Stat. 751, provided that: "This Act [enacting and amending provisions set out as notes under section 3304 of this title] may be cited as the 'Unemployment Compensation Amendments of 2003'."

SHORT TITLE OF 2002 AMENDMENT

Pub. L. 107–358, §1, Dec. 17, 2002, 116 Stat. 3015, provided that: "This Act [amending provisions set out as a note under this section] may be cited as the 'Holocaust Restitution Tax Fairness Act of 2002'."

Pub. L. 107–181, §1, May 20, 2002, 116 Stat. 583, provided that: "This Act [amending section 107 of this title and enacting provisions set out as a note under section 107 of this title] may be cited as the 'Clergy Housing Allowance Clarification Act of 2002'."

Pub. L. 107–147, §1(a), Mar. 9, 2002, 116 Stat. 21, provided that: "This Act [see Tables for classification] may be cited as the 'Job Creation and Worker Assistance Act of 2002'."

Pub. L. 107–134, §1(a), Jan. 23, 2002, 115 Stat. 2427, provided that: This Act [enacting sections 139 and 5891 of this title and section 1148 of Title 29, Labor, amending sections 5, 101, 104, 140, 642, 692, 2011, 2053, 2201, 6013, 6081, 6103, 6105, 6161, 6404, 7213, 7508, and 7508A of this title and section 1302 of Title 29, enacting provisions set out as notes under sections 101, 108, 139, 501, 642, 692, 2011, 5891, 6081, and 6103 of this title, section 401 of Title 42, The Public Health and Welfare, and section 40101 of Title 49, Transportation, and amending provisions set out as a note under section 40101 of Title 49] may be cited as the 'Victims of Terrorism Tax Relief Act of 2001'."

SHORT TITLE OF 2001 AMENDMENT

Pub. L. 107–16, §1(a), June 7, 2001, 115 Stat. 38, provided that: "This Act [see Tables for classification] may be cited as the 'Economic Growth and Tax Relief Reconciliation Act of 2001'."

Pub. L. 107–15, §1, June 5, 2001, 115 Stat. 37, provided that: "This Act [amending provisions set out as a note under section 101 of this title] may be cited as the 'Fallen Hero Survivor Benefit Fairness Act of 2001'."

SHORT TITLE OF 2000 AMENDMENT

Pub. L. 106–573, §1, Dec. 28, 2000, 114 Stat. 3061, provided that: "This Act [amending section 453 of this title and enacting provisions set out as a note under section 453 of this title] may be cited as the 'Installment Tax Correction Act of 2000'."

Pub. L. 106–554, §1(a)(7) [§1(a)], Dec. 21, 2000, 114 Stat. 2763, 2763A-587, provided that: "This Act [H.R. 5662, as enacted by section 1(a)(7) of Pub. L. 106–554, see Tables for classification] may be cited as the 'Community Renewal Tax Relief Act of 2000'."

Pub. L. 106–519, §1(a), Nov. 15, 2000, 114 Stat. 2423, provided that: "This Act [enacting sections 114 and 941 to 943 of this title, amending sections 56, 275, 864, 903 and 999 of this title, and repealing sections 921 to 927 of this title] may be cited as the 'FSC Repeal and Extraterritorial Income Exclusion Act of 2000'."

Pub. L. 106–476, title IV, §4001, Nov. 9, 2000, 114 Stat. 2176, provided that: "This title [enacting sections 1681 to 1681b of Title 19, Customs Duties, amending sections 5704, 5754, and 5761 of this title, and enacting provisions set out as notes under sections 5704 and 5761 of this title and section 1681 of Title 19] may be cited as the 'Imported Cigarette Compliance Act of 2000'."

SHORT TITLE OF 1999 AMENDMENT

Pub. L. 106–170, title V, §500, Dec. 17, 1999, 113 Stat. 1918, provided that: "This title [see Tables for classification] may be cited as the 'Tax Relief Extension Act of 1999'."

SHORT TITLE OF 1998 AMENDMENT

Pub. L. 105–277, div. J, §1000(a), Oct. 21, 1998, 112 Stat. 2681–886, provided that: "This division [§§1000–5301, see Tables for classification] may be cited as the 'Tax and Trade Relief Extension Act of 1998'."

Pub. L. 105–277, div. C, title XV, §1501, Oct. 21, 1998, 112 Stat. 2681–741, provided that: "This title [amending sections 4132 and 9510 of this title and section 300aa–11 of Title 42, The Public Health and Welfare, and enacting provisions set out as notes under sections 4132 and 9510 of this title] may be cited as the 'Vaccine Injury Compensation Program Modification Act'."

Pub. L. 105–206, §1(a), July 22, 1998, 112 Stat. 685, provided that: "This Act [see Tables for classification] may be cited as the 'Internal Revenue Service Restructuring and Reform Act of 1998'."

Pub. L. 105–206, title III, §3000, July 22, 1998, 112 Stat. 726, provided that: "This title [see Tables for classification] may be cited as the 'Taxpayer Bill of Rights 3'."

Pub. L. 105–206, title VI, §6001(a), July 22, 1998, 112 Stat. 790, provided that: "This title [see Tables for classification] may be cited as the 'Tax Technical Corrections Act of 1998'."

Pub. L. 105–178, title IX, §9001(a), June 9, 1998, 112 Stat. 499, provided that: "This title [amending sections 40, 132, 4041, 4051, 4071, 4081, 4091, 4221, 4481 to 4483, 6156, 6412, 6421, 6427, 9503, and 9504 of this title and section 460I–11 of Title 16, Conservation, repealing section 9511 of this title, enacting provisions set out as notes under sections 40, 132, 172, 4041, 6421, and 9503 of this title, and amending provisions set out as a note under section 172 of this title] may be cited as the 'Surface Transportation Revenue Act of 1998'."

SHORT TITLE OF 1997 AMENDMENT

Pub. L. 105–35, §1, Aug. 5, 1997, 111 Stat. 1104, provided that: "This Act [enacting section 7213A of this title, amending sections 7213 and 7431 of this title, and enacting provisions set out as notes under sections 7213 and 7431 of this title] may be cited as the 'Taxpayer Browsing Protection Act'."

Pub. L. 105–34, §1(a), Aug. 5, 1997, 111 Stat. 788, provided that: "This Act [see Tables for classification] may be cited as the 'Taxpayer Relief Act of 1997'."

Pub. L. 105–2, §1(a), Feb. 28, 1997, 111 Stat. 4, provided that: "This Act [amending sections 4041, 4081, 4091, 4261, 4271, and 9502 of this title and enacting provisions set out as notes under sections 4041, 4081, and 4261 of this title] may be cited as the 'Airport and Airway Trust Fund Tax Reinstatement Act of 1997'."

SHORT TITLE OF 1996 AMENDMENT

Pub. L. 104–188, §1(a), Aug. 20, 1996, 110 Stat. 1755, provided that: "This Act [see Tables for classification] may be cited as the 'Small Business Job Protection Act of 1996'."

Pub. L. 104–168, §1(a), July 30, 1996, 110 Stat. 1452, provided that: "This Act [enacting sections 4958, 7434, 7435, and 7524 of this title, amending sections 501, 4955, 4963, 6013, 6033, 6041 to 6042, 6044, 6045, 6049, 6050B, 6050H to 6050K, 6050N, 6103, 6104, 6159, 6201, 6213, 6323, 6334, 6343, 6404, 6503, 6601, 6651, 6652, 6656, 6672, 6685, 7122, 7213, 7422, 7430, 7433, 7454, 7502, 7608, 7609, 7623, 7802, 7805, and 7811 of this title, renumbering sections 7434 and 7435 as sections 7435 and 7436 of this title, enacting provisions set out as notes under sections 501, 4955, 6013, 6033, 6041, 6103, 6104, 6159, 6201, 6311, 6323, 6334, 6404, 6503, 6601, 6651, 6652, 6656, 6672, 7122, 7430, 7433 to 7435, 7524, 7608, 7609, 7623, 7802, 7803, 7805, and 7811 of this title, and amending provisions set out as a note under section 7608 of this title] may be cited as the 'Taxpayer Bill of Rights 2'."

SHORT TITLE OF 1994 AMENDMENT

Pub. L. 103–465, title VII, §750, Dec. 8, 1994, 108 Stat. 5012, provided that: "This subtitle [subtitle F (§§750–781) of title VII of Pub. L. 103–465, enacting sections 1310, 1311, and 1350 of Title 29, Labor, amending sections 401, 404, 411, 412, 415, 417, 4971, and 4972 of this title and sections 1053 to 1056, 1082, 1132, 1301, 1303, 1305, 1306, 1322, 1341, 1342, and 1343 of Title 29, and enacting provisions set out as notes under sections 401, 411, 412, and 4972 of this title and sections 1056, 1082, 1303, 1306, 1310, 1311, 1322, 1341, and 1342 of Title 29] may be cited as the 'Retirement Protection Act of 1994'."

Pub. L. 103–387, §1, Oct. 22, 1994, 108 Stat. 4071, provided that: "This Act [enacting section 3510 of this title, amending sections 3102 and 3121 of this title, section 3701 of Title 31, Money and Finance, and sections 401, 402, 404, 409, 410, and 1383 of Title 42, The Public Health and Welfare, and enacting provisions set out as notes under sections 3102 and 3510 of this title, section 3701 of Title 31, and sections 401, 402, and 1383 of Title 42] may be cited as the 'Social Security Domestic Employment Reform Act of 1994'."

SHORT TITLE OF 1993 AMENDMENT

Pub. L. 103–152, §1, Nov. 24, 1993, 107 Stat. 1516, provided that: "This Act [amending sections 503, 504, 1105, 1108, and 1382j of Title 42, The Public Health and Welfare, enacting provisions set out as notes under section 3304 of this title and sections 503 and 1382j of Title 42, amending provisions set out as notes under section 3304 of this title and section 352 of Title 45, Railroads, and repealing provisions set out as a note under section 3304 of this title] may be cited as the 'Unemployment Compensation Amendments of 1993'."

Pub. L. 103–66, title XIII, §13001(a), Aug. 10, 1993, 107 Stat. 416, provided that: "This chapter [chapter 1 (§§13001–13444) of title XIII of Pub. L. 103–66, see Tables for classification] may be cited as the 'Revenue Reconciliation Act of 1993'."

Pub. L. 103–6, §1, Mar. 4, 1993, 107 Stat. 33, provided that: "This Act [enacting provisions set out as notes under section 3304 of this title, section 31 of Title 2, The Congress, and section 352 of Title 45, Railroads, and amending provisions set out as notes under section 3304 of this title and section 352 of Title 45] may be cited as the 'Emergency Unemployment Compensation Amendments of 1993'."

SHORT TITLE OF 1992 AMENDMENT

Pub. L. 102–486, title XIX, §19141, Oct. 24, 1992, 106 Stat. 3036, provided that: "This subtitle [subtitle C (§§19141–19143) of title XIX of Pub. L. 102–486, enacting sections 9701 to 9722 of this title, amending sections 1231 and 1232 of Title 30, Mineral Lands and Mining, and enacting provisions set out as a note under section 9701 of this title] may be cited as the 'Coal Industry Retiree Health Benefit Act of 1992'."

Pub. L. 102–318, §1, July 3, 1992, 106 Stat. 290, provided that: "This Act [enacting section 1110 of Title 42, The Public Health and Welfare, amending sections 55, 62, 72, 151, 219, 401 to 404, 406 to 408, 411, 414, 415, 457, 691, 871, 877, 1441, 3121, 3304, 3306, 3402, 3405, 4973, 4980A, 6047, 6652, 6655, and 7701 of this title, section 8509 of Title 5, Government Organization and Employees, section 2291 of Title 19, Customs Duties, and sections 502, 503, 1101, 1102, 1104, and 1105 of Title 42, enacting provisions set out as notes under sections 401, 402, 3302, 3304, and 6655 of this title, section 8509 of Title 5, section 2291 of Title 19, and sections 502, 666, 1102, and 1108 of Title 42, and amending provisions set out as notes under section 3304 of this title, sections 502 and 666 of Title 42, and section 352 of Title 45, Railroads] may be cited as the 'Unemployment Compensation Amendments of 1992'."

SHORT TITLE OF 1991 AMENDMENT

Pub. L. 102–240, title VIII, §8001(a), Dec. 18, 1991, 105 Stat. 2203, provided that: "This title [enacting section 9511 of this title, amending sections 4041, 4051, 4071, 4081, 4091, 4221, 4481, 4482, 4483, 6156, 6412, 6420, 6421, 6427, 9503, and 9504 of this title and section 460I–11 of Title 16, Conservation, and enacting provisions set out as notes under section 9503 of this title, section 101 of Title 23, Highways, and section 1601 of former Title 49, Transportation] may be cited as the 'Surface Transportation Revenue Act of 1991'."

Pub. L. 102–227, §1(a), Dec. 11, 1991, 105 Stat. 1686, provided that: "This Act [amending sections 25, 28, 41, 42, 48, 51, 57, 120, 127, 143, 144, 162, 864, and 6655 of this title and enacting provisions set out as notes under sections 25, 28, 42, 51, 120, 127, 143, 144, 162, 864, and 6655 of this title] may be cited as the 'Tax Extension Act of 1991'."

SHORT TITLE OF 1990 AMENDMENT

Pub. L. 101–508, title XI, §11001(a), Nov. 5, 1990, 104 Stat. 1388–400, provided that: "This title [see Tables for classification] may be cited as the 'Revenue Reconciliation Act of 1990'."

SHORT TITLE OF 1989 AMENDMENT

Pub. L. 101–239, title VII, §7001(a), Dec. 19, 1989, 103 Stat. 2301, provided that: "This title [see Tables for classification] may be cited as the 'Revenue Reconciliation Act of 1989'."

Pub. L. 101–239, title VII, §7701, Dec. 19, 1989, 103 Stat. 2388, provided that: "This subtitle [subtitle G (§§7701–7743) of title VII of Pub. L. 101–239, see Tables for classification] may be cited as the 'Improved Penalty Administration and Compliance Tax Act'."

SHORT TITLE OF 1988 AMENDMENT

Pub. L. 100–647, §1(a), Nov. 10, 1988, 102 Stat. 3342, provided that: "This Act [see Tables for classification] may be cited as the 'Technical and Miscellaneous Revenue Act of 1988'."

Pub. L. 100–647, title VI, §6226, Nov. 10, 1988, 102 Stat. 3730, provided that: "This subtitle [subtitle J (§§6226–6247) of title VI of Pub. L. 100–647, enacting sections 6159, 6326, 6712, 7430, 7432, 7433, 7520, 7521, and 7811 of this title, amending sections 6213, 6214, 6331, 6332, 6334, 6335, 6343, 6404, 6512, 6601, 6673, 6863, 7216, 7429, 7481, 7482, 7802, and 7805 of this title and section 504 of Title 5, Government Organization and Employees, renumbering section 6326 as 6327, 7432 as 7433, and 7433 as 7434 of this title, and enacting provisions set out as notes under this section and sections 6159, 6213, 6214, 6326, 6331, 6404, 6512, 6673, 6712, 6863, 7429, 7430, 7432, 7520, 7521, 7605, 7801 to 7803, 7805, and 7811 of this title] may be cited as the 'Omnibus Taxpayer Bill of Rights'."

SHORT TITLE OF 1987 AMENDMENT

Pub. L. 100–223, title IV, §401, Dec. 30, 1987, 101 Stat. 1532, provided that: "This title [enacting section 4283 of this title, amending sections 4041, 4261, 4271, 6427, and 9502 of this title, and enacting provisions set out as notes under sections 4041 and 4261 of this title] may be cited as the 'Airport and Airway Revenue Act of 1987'."

Pub. L. 100–203, title IX, §9302(a), Dec. 22, 1987, 101 Stat. 1330–333, provided that: "This part [part II (§§9302–9346) of subtitle D of part II of Pub. L. 100–203, enacting sections 1085b and 1371 of Title 29, Labor, amending sections 401, 404, 411, 412, 414, and 4971 of this title and sections 1021, 1023, 1024, 1054, 1082 to 1084, 1085a, 1086, 1103, 1107, 1113, 1132, 1201, 1301, 1305 to 1307, 1322, 1341, 1342, 1344, 1349, 1362, 1364, 1367, and 1368 of Title 29, repealing section 1349 of Title 29, and enacting provisions set out as notes under sections 401, 404, 412, and 4971 of this title and sections 1054, 1107, 1132, 1301, 1305, 1322, and 1344 of Title 29] may be cited as the 'Pension Protection Act'."

Pub. L. 100–203, title X, §10000(a), Dec. 22, 1987, 101 Stat. 1330–382, provided that: "This title [see Tables for classification] may be cited as the 'Revenue Act of 1987'."

Pub. L. 100–17, title V, §501, Apr. 2, 1987, 101 Stat. 256, provided that: "This title [amending sections 4041, 4051, 4052, 4071, 4081, 4221, 4481, 4482, 4483, 6156, 6412, 6420, 6421, 6427, and 9503 of this title and section 460I–11 of Title 16, Conservation, and enacting provisions set out as notes under sections 4052 and 4481 of this title] may be cited as the 'Highway Revenue Act of 1987'."

SHORT TITLE OF 1986 AMENDMENT

Pub. L. 99–662, title XIV, §1401, Nov. 17, 1986, 100 Stat. 4266, provided that: "This title [enacting sections 4461, 4462, 9505, and 9506 of this title and section 988a of Title 33, Navigation and Navigable Waters, amending section 4042 of this title and sections 984 and 1804 of Title 33, repealing sections 1801 and 1802 of Title 33, and enacting provisions set out as notes under sections 4042, 4461, 9505, and 9506 of this title and sections 984 and 988 of Title 33] may be cited as the 'Harbor Maintenance Revenue Act of 1986'."

Pub. L. 99–514, §1(a), Oct. 22, 1986, 100 Stat. 2085, provided that: "This Act [see Tables for classification] may be cited as the 'Tax Reform Act of 1986'."

Pub. L. 99–499, title V, §501, Oct. 17, 1986, 100 Stat. 1760, provided that: "This title [enacting sections 59A, 4671, 4672, 9507, and 9508 of this title, amending sections 26, 164, 275, 936, 1561, 4041, 4042, 4081, 4221, 4611, 4612, 4661, 4662, 6154, 6416, 6420, 6421, 6425, 6427, 6655, 9502, 9503, and 9506 of this title and section 9601 of Title 42, The Public Health and Welfare, repealing sections 4681 and 4682 of this title and sections 9631 to 9633, 9641, and 9653 of Title 42, and enacting provisions set out as notes under this section and sections 26, 4041, 4611, 4661, 4671, 4681, 9507, and 9508 of this title] may be cited as the 'Superfund Revenue Act of 1986'."

SHORT TITLE OF 1984 AMENDMENT

Pub. L. 98–369, §1(a), July 18, 1984, 98 Stat. 494, provided that: "This Act [see Tables for classification] may be cited as the 'Deficit Reduction Act of 1984'."

Pub. L. 98–369, div. A (§§5–1082), §5(a), July 18, 1984, 98 Stat. 494, provided that: "This division [see Tables for classification] may be cited as the 'Tax Reform Act of 1984'."

SHORT TITLE OF 1983 AMENDMENT

Pub. L. 98–135, §1, Oct. 24, 1983, 97 Stat. 857, provided that: "This Act [amending section 3306 of this title and sections 1323 and 1397b of Title 42, The Public Health and Welfare, enacting provisions set out as notes under sections 3304 and 3306 of this title and section 1323 of Title 42, and amending provisions set out as notes under section 3304 of this title] may be cited as the 'Federal Supplemental Compensation Amendments of 1983'."

Pub. L. 98–76, title II, §201, Aug. 12, 1983, 97 Stat. 419, provided that: "This title [enacting sections 3321 to 3323 and 6050G of this title, amending sections 72, 86, 105, 3201, 3202, 3211, 3221, 3231, 6157, 6201, 6317, 6513, and 6601 of this title and section 430 of Title 42, The Public Health and Welfare, and enacting provisions set out as notes under sections 72, 105, 3201, 3321, and 6302 of this title and section 231n of Title 45, Railroads] may be cited as the 'Railroad Retirement Revenue Act of 1983'."

Pub. L. 98–67, title I, §101(a), Aug. 5, 1983, 97 Stat. 369, provided that: "This title [enacting sections 3406 and 6705 of this title, amending sections 31, 274, 275, 643, 661, 3402, 3403, 3502, 3507, 6011, 6013, 6015, 6042, 6044, 6049, 6051, 6365, 6401, 6413, 6652, 6653, 6654, 6676, 6678, 6682, 7205, 7215, 7431, 7654, and 7701 of this title, repealing sections 3451 to 3456 of this title, enacting provisions set out as notes under sections 31, 3451, and 6011 of this title, and repealing provisions set out as a note under section 3451 of this title] may be cited as the 'Interest and Dividend Tax Compliance Act of 1983'."

Pub. L. 97–473, title II, §201, Jan. 14, 1983, 96 Stat. 2607, provided that: "This title [enacting section 7871 of this title, amending sections 41, 103, 164, 170, 2055, 2106, 2522, 4227, 4484, 6420, 6421, 6424, 6427, and 7701 of this title, and enacting provisions set out as a note under section 7871 of this title] may be cited as the 'Indian Tribal Governmental Tax Status Act of 1982'."

Pub. L. 97–448, §1(a), Jan. 12, 1983, 96 Stat. 2365, provided that: "This Act [see Tables for classification] may be cited as the 'Technical Corrections Act of 1982'."

Pub. L. 97–424, title V, §501(a), Jan. 6, 1983, 96 Stat. 2168, provided that: "This title [see Tables for classification] may be cited as the 'Highway Revenue Act of 1982'."

SHORT TITLE OF 1982 AMENDMENT

Pub. L. 97–362, §1(a), Oct. 25, 1982, 96 Stat. 1726, provided that: "This Act [amending sections 8509 and 8521 of Title 5, Government Organization and Employees, sections 48, 172, 4401, 4411, 6051, 7447, 7448, 7456, 7459, and 7463 of this title, and section 601 of former Title 46, Shipping, enacting provisions set out as notes under sections 8509 and 8521 of Title 5 and sections 48, 172, 336, 4401, 4411, 6051, 7448, and 7463 of this title, and amending provisions set out as notes under section 2291 of Title 19, Customs Duties, and section 3306 of this title] may be cited as the 'Miscellaneous Revenue Act of 1982'."

Pub. L. 97–354, §1(a), Oct. 19, 1982, 96 Stat. 1669, provided that: "This Act [enacting sections 1361 to 1363, 1366 to 1368, 1371 to 1375, 1377 to 1379, and 6241 to 6245 of this title, amending sections 29, 31, 40, 41, 46, 48, 50A, 50B, 52, 53, 55, 57, 58, 62, 108, 163, 168, 170, 172, 179, 183, 189, 194, 267, 280, 280A, 291, 447, 464, 465, 613A, 992, 1016, 1101, 1212, 1251, 1254, 1256, 3453, 3454, 4992, 4996, 6037, 6042, 6362, and 6661 of this title and section 1108 of Title 29, Labor, omitting section 1376 of this title, and enacting provisions set out as a note under section 1361 of this title] may be cited as the 'Subchapter S Revision Act of 1982'."

Pub. L. 97–248, §1(a), Sept. 3, 1982, 96 Stat. 324, provided that: "This Act [see Tables for classification] may be cited as the 'Tax Equity and Fiscal Responsibility Act of 1982'."

Pub. L. 97–248, title IV, §401, Sept. 3, 1982, 96 Stat. 648, provided that: "This title [enacting sections 6046A and 6221 to 6232 of this title and section 1508 of Title 28, Judiciary and Judicial Procedure, amending sections 702, 6031, 6213, 6216, 6422, 6501, 6504, 6511, 6512, 6515, 6679, 7422, 7451, 7456, 7459, 7482, and 7485 of this title and section 1346 of Title 28, and enacting provisions set out as notes under sections 6031, 6046A, 6221, and 6231 of this title] may be cited as the 'Tax Treatment of Partnership Items Act of 1982'."

Short Title of 1981 Amendment

Pub. L. 97–119, title I, §101(a), Dec. 29, 1981, 95 Stat. 1635, provided that: "This subtitle [subtitle A (§§101–104) of title I of Pub. L. 97–119, enacting sections 9500, 9501, 9601, and 9602 of this title, amending sections 501 and 4121 of this title and sections 902, 925, 932, and 934 of Title 30, Mineral Lands and Mining, repealing section 934a of Title 30, and enacting provisions set out as notes under sections 4121 and 9501 of this title and section 934 of Title 30] may be cited as the 'Black Lung Benefits Revenue Act of 1981'."

Pub. L. 97–34, §1(a), Aug. 13, 1981, 95 Stat. 172, provided that: "This Act [see Tables for classification] may be cited as the 'Economic Recovery Tax Act of 1981'."

Short Title of 1980 Amendment

Pub. L. 96–605, §1(a), Dec. 28, 1980, 94 Stat. 3521, provided that: "This Act [enacting sections 66 and 195 of this title, amending sections 48, 105, 125, 274, 401, 408, 409A, 410, 414, 415, 501, 513, 514, 528, 861, 871, and 2055 of this title, and enacting provisions set out as notes under sections 48, 66, 119, 125, 195, 274, 401, 409A, 414, 415, 501, 513, 514, 528, 861, 871, 2055, 3121, and 7701 of this title] may be cited as the 'Miscellaneous Revenue Act of 1980'."

Pub. L. 96–589, §1(a), Dec. 24, 1980, 94 Stat. 3389, provided that: "This Act [enacting sections 370, 1398, 1399, 6658, and 7464 of this title, redesignating former section 7464 of this title as 7465, amending sections 108, 111, 118, 128, 302, 312, 337, 351, 354, 355, 357, 368, 381, 382, 422, 443, 542, 703, 1017, 1023, 1371, 3302, 6012, 6036, 6103, 6155, 6161, 6212, 6213, 6216, 6326, 6404, 6503, 6512, 6532, 6871, 6872, 6873, 7430, and 7508 of this title, repealing section 1018 of this title, and enacting provisions set out as a note under section 108 of this title] may be cited as the 'Bankruptcy Tax Act of 1980'."

Pub. L. 96–510, title II, §201(a), Dec. 11, 1980, 94 Stat. 2796, provided that: "This title [enacting chapter 38 of this title, sections 9631 to 9641 of Title 42, The Public Health and Welfare, and provisions set out as a note under section 4611 of this title] may be cited as the 'Hazardous Substance Response Revenue Act of 1980'."

Pub. L. 96–499, title XI, §1100, Dec. 5, 1980, 94 Stat. 2660, provided: "This title [enacting sections 103A, 280D, 897, 6039C, and 6429 of this title, amending sections 103, 861, 871, 882, 3121, 3306, 4251, 6652, and 6655 of this title and section 409 of Title 42, The Public Health and Welfare, and enacting provisions set out as notes under sections 1, 103A, 280D, 897, 3121, and 6655 of this title] may be cited as the 'Revenue Adjustments Act of 1980'."

Pub. L. 96–499, title XI, subtitle A (§§1101–1104), §1101, Dec. 5, 1980, 94 Stat. 2660, provided: "This subtitle [enacting section 103A of this title, amending section 103 of this title, and enacting provisions set out as a note under section 103A of this title] may be cited as the 'Mortgage Subsidy Bond Tax Act of 1980'."

Pub. L. 96–499, title XI, §1121, Dec. 5, 1980, 94 Stat. 2682, provided: "This subtitle [subtitle C (§§1121–1125) of title XI of Pub. L. 96–499, enacting sections 897 and 6039C of this title, amending sections 861, 871, 882, and 6652 of this title, and enacting provisions set out as notes under section 897 of this title] may be cited as the 'Foreign Investment in Real Property Tax Act of 1980'."

Pub. L. 96–471, §1(a), Oct. 19, 1980, 94 Stat. 2247, provided: "This Act [enacting sections 453 to 453B of this title, amending sections 311, 336, 337, 381, former section 453, sections 453B, 481, 644, 691, 1038, 1239, and 1255 of this title, and enacting provisions set out as notes under sections 453, 691, and 1038 of this title] may be cited as the 'Installment Sales Revision Act of 1980'."

Pub. L. 96–283, title IV, §401, June 28, 1980, 94 Stat. 582, provided that: "This title [enacting sections 4495 to 4498 of this title and sections 1472, 1473 of Title 30, Mineral Lands and Mining, and enacting provision set out as a note under section 4495 of this title] may be cited as the 'Deep Seabed Hard Mineral Removal Tax Act of 1979'."

Pub. L. 96–223, §1(a) Apr. 2, 1980, 94 Stat. 229, provided that: "This Act [see Tables for classification] may be cited as the 'Crude Oil Windfall Profit Tax Act of 1980'."

Pub. L. 96–222, §1(a), Apr. 1, 1980, 94 Stat. 194, provided that: "This Act [see Tables for classification] may be cited as the 'Technical Corrections Act of 1979'."

Short Title of 1979 Amendment

Pub. L. 96–39, title VIII, §801(a), July 26, 1979, 93 Stat. 273, provided that: "This subtitle [subtitle A (§§801–810) of title VIII of Pub. L. 96–39, amending sections 5001, 5002 to 5008, 5043, 5061, 5064, 5066, 5116, 5171 to 5173, 5175 to 5178, 5180, 5181, 5201 to 5205, 5207, 5211 to 5215, 5221 to 5223, 5231, 5232, 5235, 5241, 5273, 5291, 5301, 5352, 5361 to 5363, 5365, 5381, 5391, 5551, 5601, 5604, 5610, 5612, 5615, 5663, 5681, 5682, and 5691 of this title, repealing sections 5009, 5021 to 5026, 5081 to 5084, 5174, 5233, 5234, 5251, 5252, 5364, and 5521 to 5523 of this title, and enacting provisions set out as notes under sections 5001, 5061, 5171, and 5173 of this title] may be cited as the 'Distilled Spirits Tax Revision Act of 1979'."

Short Title of 1978 Amendment

Pub. L. 95–618, §1(a), Nov. 9, 1978, 92 Stat. 3174, provided that: "This Act [enacting sections 44C, 124, and 4064 of this title, amending sections 39, 46 to 48, 56, 57, 167, 263, 465, 613, 613A, 614, 751, 1016, 1254, 4041, 4063, 4081, 4092, 4093, 4217, 4221, 4222, 4293, 4483, 6096, 6401, 6412, 6416, 6421, 6424, 6427, 6504, and 6675 of this title, redesignating section 124 of this title as section 125, enacting provisions set out as notes under sections 39, 44C, 48, 124, 167, 263, 613, 613A, 4041, 4063, 4064, 4081, 4093, and 4221 of this title, and amending provisions set out as notes under section 57 of this title and section 120 of Title 23, Highways] may be cited as the 'Energy Tax Act of 1978'."

Pub. L. 95–615, §1, Nov. 8, 1978, 92 Stat. 3097, provided that: "This Act [probably meaning sections 1 to 8 of Pub. L. 95–615, amending section 167 of this title, enacting provisions set out as notes under sections 61, 62, and 911 of this title, and amending provisions set out as notes under sections 117, 167, 382, 401, and 911 of this title] may be cited as the 'Tax Treatment Extension Act of 1977'."

Pub. L. 95–615, §201(a), Nov. 8, 1978, 92 Stat. 3098, provided that: "This Act [probably meaning sections 201 to 210 of Pub. L. 95–615, enacting section 913 of this title, amending sections 43, 62, 119, 217, 911, 1034, 1302, 1304, 1402, 3401, 6011, 6012, and 6091 of this title, and enacting provisions set out as notes under sections 61, 401, and 911 of this title] may be cited as the 'Foreign Earned Income Act of 1978'."

Pub. L. 95–600, §1(a), Nov. 6, 1978, 92 Stat. 2763, provided that: "This Act [see Tables for classification] may be cited as the 'Revenue Act of 1978'."

Pub. L. 95–502, title II, §201, Oct. 21, 1978, 92 Stat. 1696, provided that: "This title [enacting section 4042 of this title and sections 1801 to 1804 of Title 33, Navigation and Navigable Waters, amending section 4293 of this title, and enacting provisions set out as notes under section 4042 of this title] may be cited as the 'Inland Waterways Revenue Act of 1978'."

Pub. L. 95–227, §1, Feb. 10, 1978, 92 Stat. 11, provided that: "This Act [enacting sections 192, 4121, and 4951 to 4953 of this title and section 934a of Title 30, Mineral Lands and Mining, amended sections 501, 4218, 4221, 4293, 4946, 6104, 6213, 6405, 6416, 6501, 6503, and 7454 of this title and section 934 of Title 30 and enacted provisions set out as notes under sections 192 and 4121 of this title and section 934 of Title 30] may be cited as the 'Black Lung Benefits Revenue Act of 1977'."

Short Title of 1977 Amendment

Pub. L. 95–30, §1(a), May 23, 1977, 91 Stat. 126, provided that: "This Act [see Tables for classification] may be cited as the 'Tax Reduction and Simplification Act of 1977'."

Pub. L. 95–19, §1, Apr. 12, 1977, 91 Stat. 39, provided that: "This Act [amending section 3304 of this title, enacting provisions set out as notes under sections 3302, 3304, and 3309 of this title, and amending provisions set out as notes under sections 3302, 3304, and 3309 of this title and sections 359 and 360 of Title 2, The Congress] may be cited as the 'Emergency Unemployment Compensation Extension Act of 1977'."

SHORT TITLE OF 1976 AMENDMENT

Pub. L. 94–455, title I, §101, Oct. 4, 1976, 90 Stat. 1525, provided that: "This Act [see Tables for classification] may be cited as the 'Tax Reform Act of 1976'."

Pub. L. 94–452, §1, Oct. 2, 1976, 90 Stat. 1503, provided that: "This Act [enacting section 6158 of this title, amending sections 311, 1101, 1102, 1103, 6151, 6503, and 6601 of this title, and enacting provisions set out as notes under sections 311, 1101, and 6158 of this title] may be cited as the 'Bank Holding Company Tax Act of 1976'."

SHORT TITLE OF 1975 AMENDMENT

Pub. L. 94–164, §1, Dec. 23, 1975, 89 Stat. 970, provided that: "This Act [amending sections 11, 21, 42, 43, 103, 141, 883, 962, 1561, 3402, 6012, 6153, and 6154 of this title and provisions set out as notes under sections 42, 43, and 3402 of this title, and enacting provisions set out as notes under this section and sections 3, 11, 43, 103, and 883 of this title] may be cited as the 'Revenue Adjustment Act of 1975'."

Pub. L. 94–12, §1(a), Mar. 29, 1975, 89 Stat. 26, provided that: "This Act [enacting sections, 42, 43, 44, 613A, 907, 955, and 6428 of this title, amending sections 3, 11, 12, 21, 46, 47, 48, 50A, 50B, 56, 141, 214, 535, 613, 703, 851, 901, 902, 951, 954, 962, 993, 1034, 1561, 3304 note, 3402, 6012, 6096, 6201, and 6401 of this title, repealing sections 955 and 963 of this title, and enacting provisions set out as notes under sections 3, 11, 43, 44, 46, 48, 50A, 214, 410, 535, 613A, 907, 955, 993, 3304, 3402, 6428, and 6611 of this title and section 402 of Title 42, The Public Health and Welfare] may be cited as the 'Tax Reduction Act of 1975'."

SHORT TITLE OF 1973 AMENDMENT

Pub. L. 93–69, title I, §110, July 10, 1973, 87 Stat. 166, provided that: "This title [amending sections 3201, 3202, 3211, and 3221 of this title and sections 228b, 228c, and 228e of Title 45, Railroads, enacting provisions set out as notes under section 3201 of this title and sections 228b, 228c, 228f, and 228o of Title 45, and amending provisions set out as notes under section 228c of Title 45] may be cited as the 'Railroad Retirement Amendments of 1973'."

For short title of Pub. L. 93–17 as the "Interest Equalization Tax Extension Act of 1973", see section 1(a) of Pub. L. 93–17, set out as a note under section 2104 of this title.

SHORT TITLE OF 1972 AMENDMENT

Pub. L. 92–512, title II, §201, Oct. 20, 1972, 86 Stat. 936, provided that: "This title [enacting sections 6361 to 6363 of this title, amending sections 6405 and 7463 of this title, and enacting provisions set out as a note under section 7463 of this title] may be cited as the 'Federal-State Tax Collection Act of 1972'."

SHORT TITLE OF 1971 AMENDMENT

Pub. L. 92–178, §1(a), Dec. 10, 1971, 85 Stat. 497, provided that: "This Act [see Tables for classification] may be cited as the 'Revenue Act of 1971'."

For short title of Pub. L. 92–9 as the "Interest Equalization Tax Extension Act of 1971", see section 1(a) of Pub. L. 92–9, set out as a note under section 861 of this title.

SHORT TITLE OF 1970 AMENDMENT

For short title of Pub. L. 91–614 as the "Excise, Estate, and Gift Tax Adjustment Act of 1970", see section 1 of Pub. L. 91–614, set out as a Short Title note under section 2001 of this title.

SHORT TITLE OF 1969 AMENDMENT

Pub. L. 91–172, §1(a), Dec. 30, 1969, 83 Stat. 487, provided that: "This Act [see Tables for classification] may be cited as the 'Tax Reform Act of 1969'."

For short title of Pub. L. 91–128 as the "Interest Equalization Tax Extension Act of 1969", see section 1(a) of Pub. L. 91–128, set out as a note under section 4182 of this title.

SHORT TITLE OF 1968 AMENDMENT

Pub. L. 90–364, §1(a), June 28, 1968, 82 Stat. 251, provided that: "This Act [enacting sections 51 and 6425 of this title, amending sections 103, 243, 276, 501, 963, 3402, 4061, 4251, 6020, 6154, 6412, 6651, 6655, 7203, 7502, and 7701 of this title and sections 603, 607, and 1396b of Title 42, The Public Health and Welfare, repealing sections 6016, 6074, and 4251 to 4254 of this title, enacting provisions set out as notes under sections 51, 103, 276, 501, 4061, 6154, and 7502 of this title, section 3101 of Title 5, Government Organization and Employees, sections 11 and 757b of former Title 31, Money and Finance, and section 1396b of Title 42, and amending notes under section 1396b of Title 42,] may be cited as the 'Revenue and Expenditure Control Act of 1968'."

SHORT TITLE OF 1967 AMENDMENT

For short title of Pub. L. 90–59 as the "Interest Equalization Tax Extension Act of 1967", see section 1(a) of Pub. L. 90–59, set out as a note under section 6011 of this title.

SHORT TITLE OF 1966 AMENDMENT

For short title of title I of Pub. L. 89–809 as the "Foreign Investors Tax Act of 1966", see section 101 of Pub. L. 89–809, set out as a note under section 861 of this title.

For short title of title III of Pub. L. 89–809 as the "Presidential Election Campaign Fund Act of 1966", see section 301 of Pub. L. 89–809, set out as a Short Title note under section 6096 of this title.

For short title of Pub. L. 89–719 as the "Federal Tax Lien Act of 1966", see section 1(a) of Pub. L. 89–719, set out as a Short Title note under section 6321 of this title.

SHORT TITLE OF 1965 AMENDMENT

Pub. L. 89–44, §1(a), June 21, 1965, 79 Stat. 136, provided that: "This Act [see Tables for classification] may be cited as the 'Excise Tax Reduction Act of 1965'."

SHORT TITLE OF 1964 AMENDMENT

Pub. L. 88–348, §1, June 30, 1964, 78 Stat. 237, provided: "That this Act [amending sections 165, 4061, 4251, 4261, 5001, 5022, 5041, 5051, 5063, 5701, 5707, and 6412 of this title, and provisions set out as notes under sections 165, 4261, and 5701 of this title] may be cited as the 'Excise-Tax Rate Extension Act of 1964'."

Pub. L. 88–272, §2(a), Feb. 26, 1964, 78 Stat 19, provided that: "This Act [see Tables for classification] may be cited as the 'Revenue Act of 1964'."

SHORT TITLE OF 1963 AMENDMENT

Pub. L. 88–52, §1, June 29, 1963, 77 Stat. 72, provided: "That this Act [amending sections 11, 821, 4061, 4251, 4261, 5001, 5022, 5041, 5051, 5063, 5701, 5707, 6412 of this title and provisions set out as notes under sections 4261 and 5701 of this title] may be cited as the 'Tax Rate Extension Act of 1963'."

SHORT TITLE OF 1962 AMENDMENT

Pub. L. 87–834, §1(a), Oct. 16, 1962, 76 Stat. 960, provided that: "This Act [see Tables for classification] may be cited as the 'Revenue Act of 1962'."

For short title of Pub. L. 87–792 as the "Self-Employed Individuals Tax Retirement Act of 1962", see section 1 of Pub. L. 87–792, set out as a note under section 401 of this title.

Pub. L. 87–508, §1, June 28, 1962, 76 Stat. 114, provided: "That this Act [amending sections 11, 821, 4061, 4251 to 4253, 4261 to 4264, 5001, 5002, 5041, 5051, 5063, 5701, 6707, 6412, 6416, and 6421 of this title, enacting provisions set out as notes under section 4261, 6416, and 6421 of this title, and amending provisions set out as a note under section 5701 of this title] may be cited as the 'Tax Rate Extension Act of 1962'."

SHORT TITLE OF 1961 AMENDMENT

Pub. L. 87–72, §1, June 30, 1961, 75 Stat. 193, provided: "That this Act [amending sections 11, 821, 4061, 4251, 4261, 5001, 5022, 5041, 5051, 5063, 5701, 5707, and 6412 of this title and provisions set out as a note under section 5701 of this title] may be cited as the 'Tax Rate Extension Act of 1961'."

Pub. L. 86–75, §1, June 30, 1959, 73 Stat. 157, provided: "That this Act [amending sections 11, 821, 4061, 4251, 4261, 5001, 5022, 5041, 5051, 5063, 5701, 5707 and 6412 of this title and provisions set out as a note under section 5701 of this title] may be cited as the 'Tax Rate Extension Act of 1959'."

Pub. L. 86–69, §1, June 25, 1959, 73 Stat. 112, provided that: "This Act [amending former part I of subchapter L of this chapter and sections 116, 381, 841, 842, 891, 1016, 1201, 1232, 1504, 4371, and 6501 of this title and enacting provisions set out as notes under sections 801, 6072, and 6655 of this title] may be cited as the 'Life Insurance Company Income Tax Act of 1959'."

SHORT TITLE OF 1958 AMENDMENT

Pub. L. 85–866, title I, §1(a), Sept. 2, 1958, 72 Stat. 1606, provided that: "This title [see Tables for classification] may be cited as the 'Technical Amendments Act of 1958'."

Pub. L. 85–866, title II, §201, Sept. 2, 1958, 72 Stat. 1676, provided that: "This title [amending sections 165, 172, 179, 535, 1244, 1551, 6161, 6166, 6503, and 6601 of this title and enacting provisions set out as notes under sections 172, 179, 535, 6161 of this title] may be cited as the 'Small Business Tax Revision Act of 1958'."

For short title of Pub. L. 85–859 as the "Excise Tax Technical Changes Act of 1958", see section 1(a) of Pub. L. 85–859, set out as a Short Title note under section 5001 of this title.

Pub. L. 85–475, §1, June 30, 1958, 72 Stat. 259, provided: "That this Act [amending sections 11, 821, 4061, 4292, 5001, 5022, 5041, 5051, 5063, 5134, 5701, 5707, 6412, 6415, 6416, 7012, and 7272 of this title and repealing sections 4271 to 4273 and 4281 to 4283 of this title] may be cited as the 'Tax Rate Extension Act of 1958'."

SHORT TITLE OF 1957 AMENDMENT

Pub. L. 85–12, §1, Mar. 29, 1957, 71 Stat. 9, provided: "That this Act [amending sections 11, 821, 4061, 5001, 5022, 5041, 5051, 5063, 5134, 5701, 5707, and 6412 of this title] may be cited as the 'Tax Rate Extension Act of 1957'."

SHORT TITLE OF 1956 AMENDMENT

For short title of title II of act June 29, 1956 as the "Highway Revenue Act of 1956", see section 201(a) of act June 29, 1956, set out as a note under section 4041 of this title.

For short title of act Mar. 29, 1956 as the "Tax Rate Extension Act of 1956", see section 1 of act Mar. 29, 1956, set out as a note under section 4041 of this title.

Act Mar. 13, 1956, ch. 83, §1, 70 Stat. 36, provided: "That this Act [enacting section 843 of this title and amending sections 316, 501, 594, 801 to 805, 811 to 813, 816 to 818, 821, 822, 832, 841, 842, 891, 1201, 1504, and 4371 of this title] be cited as the 'Life Insurance Company Tax Act for 1955'."

SHORT TITLE OF 1955 AMENDMENT

For short title of act Mar. 30, 1955 as the "Tax Rate Extension Act of 1955", see section 1 of act Mar. 30, 1955, set out as a note under section 4041 of this title.

PURPOSES AND PRINCIPLES

Pub. L. 111–5, §3, Feb. 17, 2009, 123 Stat. 115, provided that:

"(a) Statement of Purposes.—The purposes of this Act [see Tables for classification] include the following:

"(1) To preserve and create jobs and promote economic recovery.

"(2) To assist those most impacted by the recession.

"(3) To provide investments needed to increase economic efficiency by spurring technological advances in science and health.

"(4) To invest in transportation, environmental protection, and other infrastructure that will provide long-term economic benefits.

"(5) To stabilize State and local government budgets, in order to minimize and avoid reductions in essential services and counterproductive state and local tax increases.

"(b) General Principles Concerning Use of Funds.—The President and the heads of Federal departments and agencies shall manage and expend the funds made available in this Act so as to achieve the purposes specified in subsection (a), including commencing expenditures and activities as quickly as possible consistent with prudent management."

TRANSITIONAL RULES FOR TAXABLE YEARS WHICH INCLUDE MAY 6, 2003

Pub. L. 108–27, title III, §301(c), May 28, 2003, 117 Stat. 759, provided that: "For purposes of applying section 1(h) of the Internal Revenue Code of 1986 in the case of a taxable year which includes May 6, 2003—

"(1) The amount of tax determined under subparagraph (B) of section 1(h)(1) of such Code shall be the sum of—

"(A) 5 percent of the lesser of—

"(i) the net capital gain determined by taking into account only gain or loss properly taken into account for the portion of the taxable year on or after May 6, 2003 (determined without regard to collectibles gain or loss, gain described in section 1(h)(6)(A)(i) of such Code, and section 1202 gain), or

"(ii) the amount on which a tax is determined under such subparagraph (without regard to this subsection),

"(B) 8 percent of the lesser of—

"(i) the qualified 5-year gain (as defined in section 1(h)(9) of the Internal Revenue Code of 1986, as in effect on the day before the date of the enactment of this Act [May 28, 2003]) properly taken into account for the portion of the taxable year before May 6, 2003, or

"(ii) the excess (if any) of—

"(I) the amount on which a tax is determined under such subparagraph (without regard to this subsection), over

"(II) the amount on which a tax is determined under subparagraph (A), plus

"(C) 10 percent of the excess (if any) of—

"(i) the amount on which a tax is determined under such subparagraph (without regard to this subsection), over

"(ii) the sum of the amounts on which a tax is determined under subparagraphs (A) and (B).

"(2) The amount of tax determined under [former] subparagraph (C) of section (1)(h)(1) of such Code shall be the sum of—

"(A) 15 percent of the lesser of—

"(i) the excess (if any) of the amount of net capital gain determined under subparagraph (A)(i) of paragraph (1) of this subsection over the amount on which a tax is determined under subparagraph (A) of paragraph (1) of this subsection, or

"(ii) the amount on which a tax is determined under such subparagraph (C) (without regard to this subsection), plus

"(B) 20 percent of the excess (if any) of—

"(i) the amount on which a tax is determined under such subparagraph (C) (without regard to this subsection), over

"(ii) the amount on which a tax is determined under subparagraph (A) of this paragraph.

"(3) For purposes of applying section 55(b)(3) of such Code, rules similar to the rules of paragraphs (1) and (2) of this subsection shall apply.

"(4) In applying this subsection with respect to any pass-thru entity, the determination of when gains and losses are properly taken into account shall be made at the entity level.

"(5) For purposes of applying section 1(h)(11) of such Code, as added by section 302 of this Act, to this subsection, dividends which are qualified dividend income shall be treated as gain properly taken into account for the portion of the taxable year on or after May 6, 2003.

"(6) Terms used in this subsection which are also used in section 1(h) of such Code shall have the respective meanings that such terms have in such section."

Pub. L. 105–277, div. J, title IV, §4001(b), Oct. 21, 1998, 112 Stat. 2681–906, provided that: "For purposes of applying the amendments made by any title of this division [§§1000–5301, see Tables for classification] other than this title [see Definitions note set out below for classification], the provisions of this title shall be treated as having been enacted immediately before the provisions of such other titles."

Pub. L. 105–206, title VI, §6001(b), July 22, 1998, 112 Stat. 790, provided that: "For purposes of applying the amendments made by any title of this Act other than this title, the provisions of this title [see Tables for classification] shall be treated as having been enacted immediately before the provisions of such other titles."

Pub. L. 105–34, title XVI, §1600, Aug. 5, 1997, 111 Stat. 1086, provided that: "For purposes of applying the amendments made by any title of this Act other than this title, the provisions of this title [see Tables for classification] shall be treated as having been enacted immediately before the provisions of such other titles."

Pub. L. 104–188, title I, §1701, Aug. 20, 1996, 110 Stat. 1868, provided that: "For purposes of applying the amendments made by any subtitle [subtitle A to F (§§1111–1621) and H to J (§§1801–1954) of title I of Pub. L. 104–188, see Tables for classification] of this title other than this subtitle [subtitle G (§§1701–1704) of title I of Pub. L. 104–188, see Tables for classification], the provisions of this subtitle shall be treated as having been enacted immediately before the provisions of such other subtitles."

Pub. L. 101–508, title XI, §11700, Nov. 5, 1990, 104 Stat. 1388–505, provided that: "For purposes of applying the amendments made by any subtitle [subtitles A to F (§§11101–11622) and H and I (§§11801–11901) of title XI of Pub. L. 101–508, see Tables for classification] of this title other than this subtitle [subtitle G (§§11700–11704) of title XI of Pub. L. 101–508, see Tables for classification], the provisions of this subtitle shall be treated as having been enacted immediately before the provisions of such other subtitles."

Pub. L. 101–239, title VII, §7801(b), Dec. 19, 1989, 103 Stat. 2406, provided that: "For purposes of applying the amendments made by any subtitle [subtitles A to G (§§7101–7743) of title VII of Pub. L. 101–239, see Tables for classification] of this title other than this subtitle [subtitle H (§§7801–7894) of title VII of Pub. L. 101–239, see Tables for classification], the provisions of this subtitle shall be treated as having been enacted immediately before the provisions of such other subtitles."

Pub. L. 99–514, title XVIII, §1800, Oct. 22, 1986, 100 Stat. 2784, provided that: "For purposes of applying the amendments made by any title of this Act other than this title, the provisions of this title [see Tables for classification] shall be treated as having been enacted immediately before the provisions of such other titles."

Pub. L. 106–554, §1(a)(7) [title III, §308], Dec. 21, 2000, 114 Stat. 2763, 2763A-636, provided that:

"(a) Determinations by OMB.—As soon as practicable after the date of the enactment of this Act [Dec. 21, 2000], the Director of the Office of Management and Budget shall determine with respect to each applicable Federal benefit program whether the CPI computation error for 1999 has or will result in a shortfall in payments to beneficiaries under such program (as compared to payments that would have been made if the error had not occurred). As soon as practicable after the date of the enactment of this Act, but not later than 60 days after such date, the Director shall direct the head of the Federal agency which administers such program to make a payment or payments that, insofar as the Director finds practicable and feasible—

"(1) are targeted to the amount of the shortfall experienced by individual beneficiaries, and

"(2) compensate for the shortfall.

"(b) Coordination with Federal Agencies.—As soon as practicable after the date of the enactment of this Act [Dec. 21, 2000], each Federal agency that administers an applicable Federal benefit program shall, in accordance with such guidelines as are issued by the Director pursuant to this section, make an initial determination of whether, and the extent to which, the CPI computation error for 1999 has or will result in a shortfall in payments to beneficiaries of an applicable Federal benefit program administered by such agency. Not later than 30 days after such date, the head of such agency shall submit a report to the Director and to each House of the Congress of such determination, together with a complete description of the nature of the shortfall.

"(c) Implementation Pursuant to Agency Reports.—Upon receipt of the report submitted by a Federal agency pursuant to subsection (b), the Director shall review the initial determination of the agency, the agency's description of the nature of the shortfall, and the compensation payments proposed by the agency. Prior to directing payment of such payments pursuant to subsection (a), the Director shall make appropriate adjustments (if any) in the compensation payments proposed by the agency that the Director determines are necessary to comply with the requirements of subsection (a) and transmit to the agency a summary report of the review, indicating any adjustments made by the Director. The agency shall make the compensation payments as directed by the Director pursuant to subsection (a) in accordance with the Director's summary report.

"(d) Income Disregard Under Federal Means-Tested Benefit Programs.—A payment made under this section to compensate for a shortfall in benefits shall, in accordance with guidelines issued by the Director pursuant to this section, be disregarded in determining income under title VIII of the Social Security Act [42 U.S.C. 1001 et seq.] or any applicable Federal benefit program that is means-tested.

"(e) Funding.—Funds otherwise available under each applicable Federal benefit program for making benefit payments under such program are hereby made available for making compensation payments under this section in connection with such program.

"(f) No Judicial Review.—No action taken pursuant to this section shall be subject to judicial review.

"(g) Director's Report.—Not later than April 1, 2001, the Director shall submit to each House of the Congress a report on the activities performed by the Director pursuant to this section.

"(h) Definitions.—For purposes of this section:

"(1) Applicable federal benefit program.—The term 'applicable Federal benefit program' means any program of the Government of the United States providing for regular or periodic payments or cash assistance paid directly to individual beneficiaries, as determined by the Director of the Office of Management and Budget.

"(2) Federal agency.—The term 'Federal agency' means a department, agency, or instrumentality of the Government of the United States.

"(3) CPI computation error for 1999.—The term 'CPI computation error for 1999' means the error in the computation of the Consumer Price Index announced by the Bureau of Labor Statistics on September 28, 2000.

"(i) Tax Provisions.—In the case of taxable years (and other periods) beginning after December 31, 2000, if any Consumer Price Index (as defined in section 1(f)(5) of the Internal Revenue Code of 1986) reflects the CPI computation error for 1999—

"(1) the correct amount of such Index shall (in such manner and to such extent as the Secretary of the Treasury determines to be appropriate) be taken into account for purposes of such Code, and

"(2) tables prescribed under section 1(f) of such Code to reflect such correct amount shall apply in lieu of any tables that were prescribed based on the erroneous amount."

Pub. L. 105–277, div. J, title IV, §4002(i)(2), Oct. 21, 1998, 112 Stat. 2681–907, provided that:

"(2)(A) Subparagraphs (A)(i)(II), (A)(ii)(II), and (B)(ii) of section 1(h)(13) of the 1986 Code shall not apply to any distribution after December 31, 1997, by a regulated investment company or a real estate investment trust with respect to—

"(i) gains and losses recognized directly by such company or trust, and

"(ii) amounts properly taken into account by such company or trust by reason of holding (directly or indirectly) an interest in another such company or trust to the extent that such subparagraphs did not apply to such other company or trust with respect to such amounts.

"(B) Subparagraph (A) shall not apply to any distribution which is treated under section 852(b)(7) or 857(b)(8) of the 1986 Code as received on December 31, 1997.

"(C) For purposes of subparagraph (A), any amount which is includible in gross income of its shareholders under section 852(b)(3)(D) or 857(b)(3)(D) of the 1986 Code after December 31, 1997, shall be treated as distributed after such date.

"(D)(i) For purposes of subparagraph (A), in the case of a qualified partnership with respect to which a regulated investment company meets the holding requirement of clause (iii)—

"(I) the subparagraphs referred to in subparagraph (A) shall not apply to gains and losses recognized directly by such partnership for purposes of determining such company's distributive share of such gains and losses, and

"(II) such company's distributive share of such gains and losses (as so determined) shall be treated as recognized directly by such company.

The preceding sentence shall apply only if the qualified partnership provides the company with written documentation of such distributive share as so determined.

"(ii) For purposes of clause (i), the term 'qualified partnership' means, with respect to a regulated investment company, any partnership if—

"(I) the partnership is an investment company registered under the Investment Company Act of 1940 [15 U.S.C. 80a–1 et seq.],

"(II) the regulated investment company is permitted to invest in such partnership by reason of section 12(d)(1)(E) of such Act [15 U.S.C. 80a–12(d)(1)(E)] or an exemptive order of the Securities and Exchange Commission under such section, and

"(III) the regulated investment company and the partnership have the same taxable year.

"(iii) A regulated investment company meets the holding requirement of this clause with respect to a qualified partnership if (as of January 1, 1998)—

"(I) the value of the interests of the regulated investment company in such partnership is 35 percent or more of the value of such company's total assets, or

"(II) the value of the interests of the regulated investment company in such partnership and all other qualified partnerships is 90 percent or more of the value of such company's total assets."

CAPITAL GAIN DISTRIBUTION BY TRUST

Pub. L. 105–277, div. J, title IV, §4003(b), Oct. 21, 1998, 112 Stat. 2681–909, as amended by Pub. L. 106–554, §1(a)(7) [title III, §312(b)], Dec. 21, 2000, 114 Stat. 2763, 2763A-640, provided that: "In the case of any capital gain distribution made after 1997 by a trust to which section 664 of the 1986 Code applies with respect to amounts properly taken into account by such trust during 1997, paragraphs (5)(A)(i)(I), (5)(A)(ii)(I), (7)(A)(i)(II), and (13)(A) of section 1(h) of the 1986 Code (as in effect for taxable years ending on December 31, 1997) shall not apply."

ELECTION TO RECOGNIZE GAIN ON ASSETS HELD ON JANUARY 1, 2001

Pub. L. 105–34, title III, §311(e), Aug. 5, 1997, 111 Stat. 835, as amended by Pub. L. 106–554, §1(a)(7) [title III, §314(c)], Dec. 21, 2000, 114 Stat. 2763, 2763A-643; Pub. L. 107–147, title IV, §414(a), Mar. 9, 2002, 116 Stat. 54, provided that: "For purposes of the Internal Revenue Code of 1986—

"(1) In general.—A taxpayer other than a corporation may elect to treat—

"(A) any readily tradable stock (which is a capital asset) held by such taxpayer on January 1, 2001, and not sold before the next business day after such date, as having been sold on such next business day for an amount equal to its closing market price on such next business day (and as having been reacquired on such next business day for an amount equal to such closing market price), and

"(B) any other capital asset or property used in the trade or business (as defined in section 1231(b) of the Internal Revenue Code of 1986) held by the taxpayer on January 1, 2001, as having been sold on such date for an amount equal to its fair market value on such date (and as having been reacquired on such date for an amount equal to such fair market value).

"(2) Treatment of gain or loss.—

"(A) Any gain resulting from an election under paragraph (1) shall be treated as received or accrued on the date the asset is treated as sold under paragraph (1) and shall be included in gross income notwithstanding any provision of the Internal Revenue Code of 1986.

"(B) Any loss resulting from an election under paragraph (1) shall not be allowed for any taxable year.

"(3) Election.—An election under paragraph (1) shall be made in such manner as the Secretary of the Treasury or his delegate may prescribe and shall specify the assets for which such election is made. Such an election, once made with respect to any asset, shall be irrevocable. Such an election shall not apply to any asset which is disposed of (in a transaction in which gain or loss is recognized in whole or in part) before the close of the 1-year period beginning on the date that the asset would have been treated as sold under such election.

"(4) Readily tradable stock.—For purposes of this subsection, the term 'readily tradable stock' means any stock which, as of January 1, 2001, is readily tradable on an established securities market or otherwise.

"(5) Disposition of interest in passive activity.—Section 469(g)(1)(A) of the Internal Revenue Code of 1986 shall not apply by reason of an election made under paragraph (1)."

[Pub. L. 107–147, title IV, §414(b), Mar. 9, 2002, 116 Stat. 54, provided that: "The amendments made by this section [amending section 311(e) of Pub. L. 105–34, set out above] shall take effect as if included in section 311 of the Taxpayer Relief Act of 1997 [Pub. L. 105–34]."]

ELECTION TO PAY ADDITIONAL 1993 TAXES IN INSTALLMENTS

Pub. L. 103–66, title XIII, §13201(d), Aug. 10, 1993, 107 Stat. 459, provided that:

"(1) In general.—At the election of the taxpayer, the additional 1993 taxes may be paid in 3 equal installments.

"(2) Dates for paying installments.—In the case of any tax payable in installments by reason of paragraph (1)—

"(A) the first installment shall be paid on or before the due date for the taxpayer's taxable year beginning in calendar year 1993,

"(B) the second installment shall be paid on or before the date 1 year after the date determined under subparagraph (A), and

"(C) the third installment shall be paid on or before the date 2 years after the date determined under subparagraph (A).

For purposes of the preceding sentence, the term 'due date' means the date prescribed for filing the taxpayer's return determined without regard to extensions.

"(3) Extension without interest.—For purposes of section 6601 of the Internal Revenue Code of 1986, the date prescribed for the payment of any tax payable in installments under paragraph (1) shall be determined with regard to the extension under paragraph (1).

"(4) Additional 1993 taxes.—

"(A) In general.—For purposes of this subsection, the term 'additional 1993 taxes' means the excess of—

"(i) the taxpayer's net chapter 1 liability as shown on the taxpayer's return for the taxpayer's taxable year beginning in calendar year 1993, over

"(ii) the amount which would have been the taxpayer's net chapter 1 liability for such taxable year if such liability had been determined using the rates which would have been in effect under section 1 of the Internal Revenue Code of 1986 for taxable years beginning in calendar year 1993 but for the amendments made by this section [amending this section and sections 41, 63, 68, 132, 151, 453A, 513, 531, and 541 of this title] and section 13202 [amending this section and sections 531 and 541 of this title] and such liability had otherwise been determined on the basis of the amounts shown on the taxpayer's return.

"(B) Net chapter 1 liability.—For purposes of subparagraph (A), the term 'net chapter 1 liability' means the liability for tax under chapter 1 of the Internal Revenue Code of 1986 determined—

"(i) after the application of any credit against such tax other than the credits under sections 31 and 34, and

"(ii) before crediting any payment of estimated tax for the taxable year.

"(5) Acceleration of payments.—If the taxpayer does not pay any installment under this section on or before the date prescribed for its payment or if the Secretary of the Treasury or his delegate believes that the collection of any amount payable in installments under this section is in jeopardy, the Secretary shall immediately terminate the extension under paragraph (1) and the whole of the unpaid tax shall be paid on notice and demand from the Secretary.

"(6) Election on return.—An election under paragraph (1) shall be made on the taxpayer's return for the taxpayer's taxable year beginning in calendar year 1993.

"(7) Exception for estates and trusts.—This subsection shall not apply in the case of an estate or trust."

TRANSITIONAL RULE FOR MAXIMUM CAPITAL GAINS RATE

Pub. L. 99–514, title III, §302(c), Oct. 22, 1986, 100 Stat. 2218, which related to long-term capital gain on rights to royalties paid under particular leases and assignments, was repealed by Pub. L. 100–647, title I, §1003(b)(1), Nov. 10, 1988, 102 Stat. 3382.

COORDINATION WITH OTHER PROVISIONS

Pub. L. 99–509, title VIII, §8081, Oct. 21, 1986, 100 Stat. 1965, provided that: "Nothing in any provision of this Act [see Tables for classifications] (other than this title) shall be construed as—

"(1) imposing any tax (or exempting any person or property from any tax),

"(2) establishing any trust fund, or

"(3) authorizing amounts to be expended from any trust fund."

[S.Con.Res. 174, agreed to Oct. 18, 1986, provided: "That, in the enrollment of the bill (H.R. 5300) to provide for reconciliation pursuant to section 2 of the concurrent resolution on the budget for fiscal year 1987, the Clerk of the House of Representatives shall insert at the end of section 8081 of the bill the following: Paragraph (3) shall not apply to any authorization made by title IX of this Act." As a result of clerical error, the sentence was inserted at the end of section 8101 of the bill, and appears at the end of section 8101 of Pub. L. 99–509, 100 Stat. 1967.]

Pub. L. 99–499, title V, §531, Oct. 17, 1986, 100 Stat. 1782, provided that: "Notwithstanding any provision of this Act [see Tables for classifications] not contained in this title [see Short Title of 1986 Amendment note above], any provision of this Act (not contained in this title) which—

"(1) imposes any tax, premium, or fee,

"(2) establishes any trust fund, or

"(3) authorizes amounts to be expended from any trust fund,

shall have no force or effect."

ELIMINATION OF 50-CENT ROUNDING ERRORS

Pub. L. 97–448, title I, §101(a)(3), Jan. 12, 1983, 96 Stat. 2366, as amended by Pub. L. 99–514, §2, Oct. 22, 1986, 100 Stat. 2095, provided that: "If any figure in any table—

"(A) which is set forth in section 1 of the Internal Revenue Code of 1986 [formerly I.R.C. 1954] (as amended by section 101 of the Economic Recovery Tax Act of 1981 [Pub. L. 97–34, title I, §101, Aug. 13, 1981, 95 Stat. 176], and

"(B) which applies to married individuals filing separately or to estates and trusts,

differs by not more than 50 cents from the correct amount under the formula used in constructing such table, such figure is hereby corrected to the correct amount." [See 1982 Amendment note above.]

POLICY WITH RESPECT TO ADDITIONAL TAX REDUCTIONS

Pub. L. 95–600, §3, Nov. 6, 1978, 92 Stat. 2767, provided that: "As a matter of national policy the rate of growth in Federal outlays, adjusted for inflation, should not exceed 1 percent per year between fiscal year 1979 and fiscal year 1983; Federal outlays as a percentage of gross national product should decline to below 21 percent in fiscal year 1980, 20.5 percent in fiscal year 1981, 20 percent in fiscal year 1982 and 19.5 percent in fiscal year 1983; and the Federal budget should be balanced in fiscal years 1982 and 1983. If these conditions are met, it is the intention that the tax-writing committees of Congress will report legislation providing significant tax reductions for individuals to the extent that these tax reductions are justified in the light of prevailing and expected economic conditions."

EFFECTIVE DATE OF CERTAIN DEFINITIONS AND DESIGNATIONS

Pub. L. 94–455, title XIX, §1908, Oct. 4, 1976, 90 Stat. 1836, provided that: "For purposes of any amendment made by any provision of this Act [see Tables for classification] (other than this title)—

"(1) which contains a term the meaning of which is defined in or modified by any provision of this title, and

"(2) which has an effective date earlier than the effective date of the provision of this title defining or modifying such term,

that definition or modification shall be considered to take effect as of such earlier effective date."

CONGRESSIONAL DECLARATION RELATING TO 1975 AMENDMENT

Pub. L. 94–164, §1A, Dec. 23, 1975, 89 Stat. 970, provided that:

"(a) Congress is determined to continue the tax reduction for the first 6 months of 1976 in order to assure continued economic recovery.

"(b) Congress is also determined to continue to control spending levels in order to reduce the national deficit.

"(c) Congress reaffirms its commitments to the procedures established by the Congressional Budget and Impoundment Control Act of 1974 [see Tables for classification of Pub. L. 93–344, July 12, 1974, 88 Stat. 297] under which it has already established a binding spending ceiling for the fiscal year 1976.

"(d) If the Congress adopts a continuation of the tax reduction provided by this Act [see Short Title of 1975 Amendment note above] beyond June 30, 1976, and if economic conditions warrant doing so, Congress shall provide, through the procedures in the Budget Act [Pub. L. 93–344], for reductions in the level of spending in the fiscal year 1977 below what would otherwise occur, equal to any additional reduction in taxes (from the 1974 tax rate levels) provided for the fiscal year 1977: *Provided, however,* That nothing shall preclude the right of the Congress to pass a budget resolution containing a higher or lower expenditure figure if the Congress concludes that this is warranted by economic conditions or unforeseen circumstances."

CONGRESSIONAL DECLARATION RELATING TO 1964 AMENDMENT

Pub. L. 88–272, §1, Feb. 26, 1964, 78 Stat. 19, provided that: "It is the sense of Congress that the tax reduction provided by this Act [see Short Title of 1964 Amendment note above] through stimulation of the economy, will, after a brief transitional period, raise (rather than lower) revenues and that such revenue increases should first be used to eliminate the deficits in the administrative budgets and then to reduce the public debt. To further the objective of obtaining balanced budgets in the near future, Congress by this action, recognizes the importance of taking all reasonable means to restrain Government spending and urges the President to declare his accord with this objective."

INFLATION ADJUSTED ITEMS FOR CERTAIN YEARS

Provisions relating to inflation adjustment of items in sections 1, 23, 24, 25A, 25B, 32, 36B, 42, 45R, 55, 59, 62, 63, 68, 125, 132, 135, 137, 146, 147, 148, 151, 152, 179, 179D, 199A, 213, 219, 220, 221, 223, 408A, 448, 461, 512, 513, 642, 685, 831, 877, 877A, 911, 1274A, 2010, 2032A, 2503, 2523, 2631, 4001, 4003, 4161, 4261, 5000A, 6012, 6013, 6033, 6039F, 6323, 6334, 6601, 6651, 6652, 6695, 6698, 6699, 6721, 6722, 7345, 7430, 7702B, and 9831 of this title for certain years were contained in the following:

2022—Revenue Procedure 2021–45.

2021—Revenue Procedure 2020–45.

2020—Revenue Procedure 2019–44.

2019—Revenue Procedure 2018–57.

2018—Revenue Procedure 2017–58.

2017—Revenue Procedure 2016–55.

2016—Revenue Procedure 2015–53, as modified by Revenue Procedure 2016–11.

2015—Revenue Procedures 2014–61 and 2016–11.
2014—Revenue Procedure 2013–35.
2013—Revenue Procedures 2012–41 and 2013–15.
2012—Revenue Procedure 2011–52, as modified by Revenue Procedure 2013–15.
2011—Revenue Procedures 2010–40 and 2011–12.
2010—Revenue Procedures 2009–50, 2010–24, and 2010–35.
2009—Revenue Procedure 2008–66.
2008—Revenue Procedure 2007–66.
2007—Revenue Procedures 2006–53 and 2007–36.
2006—Revenue Procedure 2005–70.
2005—Revenue Procedure 2004–71.
2004—Revenue Procedure 2003–85.
2003—Revenue Procedure 2002–70.
2002—Revenue Procedure 2001–59.
2001—Revenue Procedure 2001–13.
2000—Revenue Procedure 99–42.
1999—Revenue Procedure 98–61.
1998—Revenue Procedure 97–57.
1997—Revenue Procedure 96–59.
1996—Revenue Procedure 95–53.
1995—Revenue Procedure 94–72.
1994—Revenue Procedure 93–49.
1993—Revenue Procedure 92–102.
1992—Revenue Procedure 91–65.
1991—Revenue Procedure 90–64.
1990—Revenue Procedure 90–7.
1989—Revenue Procedure 88–56.
1986—Revenue Procedure 85–55.
1985—Revenue Procedure 84–79.

DEFINITIONS

Pub. L. 105–277, div. J, title IV, §4001(a), Oct. 21, 1998, 112 Stat. 2681–906, provided that: "For purposes of this title [amending this section, sections 51, 56, 67, 68, 86, 135, 137, 163, 172, 219, 221, 264, 351, 368, 408A, 469, 873, 954, 2001, 2031, 6015, 6103, 6159, 6311, 6404, 6693, 7421, 7443A, 7491, 9503, and 9510 of this title, and sections 401 and 407 of Title 42, The Public Health and Welfare, enacting provisions set out as notes under this section, sections 51, 67, 68, 86, 172, 833, 6103, and 9503 of this title, and section 401 of Title 42, and amending provisions set out as notes under sections 6601 and 7508A of this title]—

"(1) 1986 code.—The term '1986 Code' means the Internal Revenue Code of 1986.
"(2) 1998 act.—The term '1998 Act' means the Internal Revenue Service Restructuring and Reform Act of 1998 (Public Law 105–206) [see Tables for classification].
"(3) 1997 act.—The term '1997 Act' means the Taxpayer Relief Act of 1997 (Public Law 105–34) [see Tables for classification]."

§2. Definitions and special rules

(a) Definition of surviving spouse

(1) In general

For purposes of section 1, the term "surviving spouse" means a taxpayer—
(A) whose spouse died during either of his two taxable years immediately preceding the taxable year, and
(B) who maintains as his home a household which constitutes for the taxable year the principal place of abode (as a member of such household) of a dependent (i) who (within the meaning of section 152, determined without regard to subsections (b)(1), (b)(2), and (d)(1)(B) thereof) is a son, stepson, daughter, or stepdaughter of the taxpayer, and (ii) with respect to whom the taxpayer is entitled to a deduction for the taxable year under section 151.

For purposes of this paragraph, an individual shall be considered as maintaining a household only if over half of the cost of maintaining the household during the taxable year is furnished by such individual.

(2) Limitations

Notwithstanding paragraph (1), for purposes of section 1 a taxpayer shall not be considered to be a surviving spouse—
(A) if the taxpayer has remarried at any time before the close of the taxable year, or
(B) unless, for the taxpayer's taxable year during which his spouse died, a joint return could have been made under the provisions of section 6013 (without regard to subsection (a)(3) thereof).

(3) Special rule where deceased spouse was in missing status

If an individual was in a missing status (within the meaning of section 6013(f)(3)) as a result of service in a combat zone (as determined for purposes of section 112) and if such individual remains in such status until the date referred to in subparagraph (A) or (B), then, for purposes of paragraph (1)(A), the date on which such individual died shall be treated as the earlier of the date determined under subparagraph (A) or the date determined under subparagraph (B):
(A) the date on which the determination is made under section 556 of title 37 of the United States Code or under section 5566 of title 5 of such Code (whichever is applicable) that such individual died while in such missing status, or
(B) except in the case of the combat zone designated for purposes of the Vietnam conflict, the date which is 2 years after the date designated under section 112 as the date of termination of combatant activities in that zone.

(b) Definition of head of household

(1) In general

For purposes of this subtitle, an individual shall be considered a head of a household if, and only if, such individual is not married at the close of his taxable year, is not a surviving spouse (as defined in subsection (a)), and either—
(A) maintains as his home a household which constitutes for more than one-half of such taxable year the principal place of abode, as a member of such household, of—
(i) a qualifying child of the individual (as defined in section 152(c), determined without regard to section 152(e)), but not if such child—

(I) is married at the close of the taxpayer's taxable year, and

(II) is not a dependent of such individual by reason of section 152(b)(2) or 152(b)(3), or both, or

(ii) any other person who is a dependent of the taxpayer, if the taxpayer is entitled to a deduction for the taxable year for such person under section 151, or

(B) maintains a household which constitutes for such taxable year the principal place of abode of the father or mother of the taxpayer, if the taxpayer is entitled to a deduction for the taxable year for such father or mother under section 151.

For purposes of this paragraph, an individual shall be considered as maintaining a household only if over half of the cost of maintaining the household during the taxable year is furnished by such individual.

(2) Determination of status

For purposes of this subsection—

(A) an individual who is legally separated from his spouse under a decree of divorce or of separate maintenance shall not be considered as married;

(B) a taxpayer shall be considered as not married at the close of his taxable year if at any time during the taxable year his spouse is a nonresident alien; and

(C) a taxpayer shall be considered as married at the close of his taxable year if his spouse (other than a spouse described in subparagraph (B)) died during the taxable year.

(3) Limitations

Notwithstanding paragraph (1), for purposes of this subtitle a taxpayer shall not be considered to be a head of a household—

(A) if at any time during the taxable year he is a nonresident alien; or

(B) by reason of an individual who would not be a dependent for the taxable year but for—

(i) subparagraph (H) of section 152(d)(2), or

(ii) paragraph (3) of section 152(d).

(c) Certain married individuals living apart

For purposes of this part, an individual shall be treated as not married at the close of the taxable year if such individual is so treated under the provisions of section 7703(b).

(d) Nonresident aliens

In the case of a nonresident alien individual, the taxes imposed by sections 1 and 55 shall apply only as provided by section 871 or 877.

(e) Cross reference

For definition of taxable income, see section 63.

(Aug. 16, 1954, ch. 736, 68A Stat. 8; Pub. L. 88–272, title I, §112(b), Feb. 26, 1964, 78 Stat. 24; Pub. L. 91–172, title VIII, §803(b), Dec. 30, 1969, 83 Stat. 682; Pub. L. 93–597, §3(b), Jan. 2, 1975, 88 Stat. 1951; Pub. L. 94–455, title XIX, §1901(a)(1), (b)(9), Oct. 4, 1976, 90 Stat. 1764, 1795; Pub. L. 94–569, §3(a), Oct. 20, 1976, 90 Stat. 2699; Pub. L. 97–448, title III, §307(a), Jan. 12, 1983, 96 Stat. 2407; Pub. L. 98–369, div. A, title IV, §423(c)(2), July 18, 1984, 98 Stat. 801; Pub. L. 99–514, title XIII, §1301(j)(10), title XVII, §1708(a)(1), Oct. 22, 1986, 100 Stat. 2658, 2782; Pub. L. 100–647, title I, §1007(g)(13)(A), Nov. 10, 1988, 102 Stat. 3436; Pub. L. 108–311, title II, §§202, 207(1), Oct. 4, 2004, 118 Stat. 1175, 1177; Pub. L. 109–135, title IV, §412(a), Dec. 21, 2005, 119 Stat. 2636.)

EDITORIAL NOTES
AMENDMENTS

2005—Subsec. (b)(2)(C). Pub. L. 109–135 substituted "subparagraph (B)" for "subparagraph (C)".

2004—Subsec. (a)(1)(B)(i). Pub. L. 108–311, §207(1), inserted ", determined without regard to subsections (b)(1), (b)(2), and (d)(1)(B) thereof" after "section 152".

Subsec. (b)(1)(A)(i). Pub. L. 108–311, §202(a), amended cl. (i) generally. Prior to amendment, cl. (i) read as follows: "a son, stepson, daughter, or stepdaughter of the taxpayer, or a descendant of a son or daughter of the taxpayer, but if such son, stepson, daughter, stepdaughter, or descendant is married at the close of the taxpayer's taxable year, only if the taxpayer is entitled to a deduction for the taxable year for such person under section 151 (or would be so entitled but for paragraph (2) or (4) of section 152(e)), or".

Subsec. (b)(2). Pub. L. 108–311, §202(b)(1), redesignated subpars. (B) to (D) as (A) to (C), respectively, and struck out former subpar. (A) which read as follows: "a legally adopted child of a person shall be considered a child of such person by blood;".

Subsec. (b)(3)(B)(i), (ii). Pub. L. 108–311, §202(b)(2), amended cls. (i) and (ii) generally. Prior to amendment, cls. (i) and (ii) read as follows:

"(i) paragraph (9) of section 152(a), or

"(ii) subsection (c) of section 152."

1988—Subsec. (d). Pub. L. 100–647 substituted "the taxes imposed by sections 1 and 55" for "the tax imposed by section 1".

1986—Subsec. (a)(3)(B). Pub. L. 99–514, §1708(a)(1), amended subpar. (B) generally. Prior to amendment, subpar. (B) read as follows: "the date which is—

"(i) December 31, 1982, in the case of service in the combat zone designated for purposes of the Vietnam conflict, or

"(ii) 2 years after the date designated under section 112 as the date of termination of combatant activities in that zone, in the case of any combat zone other than that referred to in clause (i)."

Subsec. (c). Pub. L. 99–514, §1301(j)(10), substituted "section 7703(b)" for "section 143(b)".

1984—Subsec. (b)(1)(A). Pub. L. 98–369, §423(c)(2)(A), substituted "which constitutes for more than one-half of such taxable year" for "which constitutes for such taxable year".

Subsec. (b)(1)(A)(i). Pub. L. 98–369, §423(c)(2)(B), inserted "(or would be so entitled but for paragraph (2) or (4) of section 152(e))".

1983—Subsec. (a)(3)(B)(i). Pub. L. 97–448 substituted "December 31, 1982" for "January 2, 1978".

1976—Subsec. (a)(3)(B). Pub. L. 94–569 substituted "the date which is 2 years after" in provisions preceding cl. (i), substituted "January 2, 1978" for "the date of the enactment of this paragraph" in cl. (i), and substituted "2 years after the date" for "the date" in cl. (ii).

Subsec. (b)(3)(B)(ii). Pub. L. 94–455, §1901(b)(9), redesignated cl. (iii) as (ii) and struck out former cl. (ii) which provided that an individual who was a dependent solely by reason of par. (10) of section 152(a) would not be considered as a head of a household.

Subsec. (c). Pub. L. 94–455, §1901(a)(1), substituted "shall be treated as not married at the close of the taxable year" for "shall not be considered as married".

1975—Subsec. (a)(3). Pub. L. 93–597 added par. (3).

1969—Subsec. (a). Pub. L. 91–172 redesignated subsec. (b) as (a). See sec. 1(a) of this title.

Subsec. (b). Pub. L. 91–172 redesignated provisions of former section 1(b)(2) to (4) of this title as subsec. (b). Former subsec. (b) redesignated (a), with minor changes.

Subsec. (c). Pub. L. 91–172 added subsec. (c).

Subsec. (d). Pub. L. 91–172 redesignated as subsec. (d) provisions of former section 1(d) with minor changes.

Subsec. (e). Pub. L. 91–172 redesignated as subsec. (e) provisions of former section 1(e).

1964—Subsec. (a). Pub. L. 88–272 inserted reference to section 141.

STATUTORY NOTES AND RELATED SUBSIDIARIES

EFFECTIVE DATE OF 2004 AMENDMENT

Pub. L. 108–311, title II, §208, Oct. 4, 2004, 118 Stat. 1178, provided that: "The amendments made by this title [amending this section and sections 21, 24, 25B, 32, 42, 51, 72, 105, 120, 125, 129, 132, 151 to 153, 170, 213, 220, 221, 529, 2032A, 2057, 7701, 7702B, and 7703 of this title] shall apply to taxable years beginning after December 31, 2004."

EFFECTIVE DATE OF 1988 AMENDMENT

Amendment by Pub. L. 100–647 effective, except as otherwise provided, as if included in the provision of the Tax Reform Act of 1986, Pub. L. 99–514, to which such amendment relates, see section 1019(a) of Pub. L. 100–647, set out as a note under section 1 of this title.

EFFECTIVE DATE OF 1986 AMENDMENT

Amendment by section 1301(j)(10) of Pub. L. 99–514 applicable to bonds issued after Aug. 15, 1986, except as otherwise provided, see sections 1311 to 1318 of Pub. L. 99–514, set out as an Effective Date; Transitional Rules note under section 141 of this title.

Pub. L. 99–514, title XVII, §1708(b), Oct. 22, 1986, 100 Stat. 2783, provided that: "The amendments made by this section [amending this section and sections 692, 6013, and 7508 of this title] shall apply to taxable years beginning after December 31, 1982."

EFFECTIVE DATE OF 1984 AMENDMENT

Pub. L. 98–369, div. A, title IV, §423(d), July 18, 1984, 98 Stat. 801, provided that: "The amendments made by this section [amending this section and sections 43, 44A, 105, 143, 152, and 213 of this title] shall apply to taxable years beginning after December 31, 1984."

EFFECTIVE DATE OF 1976 AMENDMENT

Pub. L. 94–455, title XIX, §1901(d), Oct. 4, 1976, 90 Stat. 1803, provided that: "Except as otherwise expressly provided in this section, the amendments made by this section [see Tables for classification] shall apply with respect to taxable years beginning after December 31, 1976. The amendments made by subsections (a)(29) and (b)(10) shall apply with respect to taxable years ending after the date of the enactment of this Act [Oct. 4, 1976]."

EFFECTIVE DATE OF 1975 AMENDMENT

Amendment by Pub. L. 93–597 applicable to taxable years ending on or after Feb. 28, 1961, see section 3(c) of Pub. L. 93–597, set out as a note under section 6013 of this title.

EFFECTIVE DATE OF 1969 AMENDMENT

Amendment by Pub. L. 91–172 applicable to taxable years beginning after Dec. 31, 1970, except that subsec. (c) is applicable to taxable years beginning after Dec. 31, 1969, see section 803(f) of Pub. L. 91–172, set out as a note under section 1 of this title.

EFFECTIVE DATE OF 1964 AMENDMENT

Amendment by Pub. L. 88–272, except for purposes of section 21 of this title, effective with respect to taxable years beginning after Dec. 31, 1963, see section 131 of Pub. L. 88–272, set out as a note under section 1 of this title.

§3. Tax tables for individuals

(a) Imposition of tax table tax

(1) In general

In lieu of the tax imposed by section 1, there is hereby imposed for each taxable year on the taxable income of every individual—

(A) who does not itemize his deductions for the taxable year, and

(B) whose taxable income for such taxable year does not exceed the ceiling amount,

a tax determined under tables, applicable to such taxable year, which shall be prescribed by the Secretary and which shall be in such form as he determines appropriate. In the table so prescribed, the amounts of the tax shall be computed on the basis of the rates prescribed by section 1.

(2) Ceiling amount defined

For purposes of paragraph (1), the term "ceiling amount" means, with respect to any taxpayer, the amount (not less than $20,000) determined by the Secretary for the tax rate category in which such taxpayer falls.

(3) Authority to prescribe tables for taxpayers who itemize deductions

The Secretary may provide that this section shall apply also for any taxable year to individuals who itemize their deductions. Any tables prescribed under the preceding sentence shall be on the basis of taxable income.

(b) Section inapplicable to certain individuals

This section shall not apply to—

(1) an individual making a return under section 443(a)(1) for a period of less than 12 months on account of a change in annual accounting period, and

(2) an estate or trust.

(c) Tax treated as imposed by section 1

For purposes of this title, the tax imposed by this section shall be treated as tax imposed by section 1.

(d) Taxable income

Whenever it is necessary to determine the taxable income of an individual to whom this section applies, the taxable income shall be determined under section 63.

(e) Cross reference

For computation of tax by Secretary, see section 6014.

(Aug. 16, 1954, ch. 736, 68A Stat. 8; Pub. L. 88–272, title III, §301(a), Feb. 26, 1964, 78 Stat. 129; Pub. L. 91–172, title VIII, §803(c), Dec. 30, 1969, 83 Stat. 684; Pub. L. 94–12, title II, §201(c), Mar. 29, 1975, 89 Stat. 29; Pub. L. 94–455, title V, §501(a), Oct. 4, 1976, 90 Stat. 1558; Pub. L. 95–30, title I, §101(b), May 23, 1977, 91 Stat. 131; Pub. L. 95–600, title IV, §401(b)(1), Nov. 6, 1978, 92 Stat. 2867; Pub. L. 95–615, title II, §202(f), as added Pub. L. 96–222, title I, §108(a)(1)(A), Apr. 1, 1980, 94 Stat. 223; Pub. L. 96–222, title I, §108(a)(1)(E), Apr. 1, 1980, 94 Stat. 225; Pub. L. 97–34, title I, §§101(b)(2)(B), (C), (c)(2)(A), 121(c)(3), Aug. 13, 1981, 95 Stat. 183, 197; Pub. L. 99–514, title I, §§102(b), 141(b)(1), Oct. 22, 1986, 100 Stat. 2102, 2117.)

EDITORIAL NOTES

AMENDMENTS

1986—Subsec. (a). Pub. L. 99–514, §102(b), substituted subsec. (a) for former subsec. (a) which read as follows:

"(1) In general.—In lieu of the tax imposed by section 1, there is hereby imposed for each taxable year on the tax table income of every individual whose tax table income for such year does not exceed the ceiling amount, a tax determined under tables, applicable to such taxable year, which shall be prescribed by the Secretary and which shall be in such form as he determines appropriate. In the tables so prescribed, the amounts of tax shall be computed on the basis of the rates prescribed by section 1.

"(2) Ceiling amount defined.—For purposes of paragraph (1), the term 'ceiling amount' means, with respect to any taxpayer, the amount (not less than $20,000) determined by the Secretary for the tax rate category in which such taxpayer falls.

"(3) Certain taxpayers with large number of exemptions.—The Secretary may exclude from the application of this section taxpayers in any tax rate category having more than the number of exemptions for that category determined by the Secretary.

"(4) Tax table income defined.—For purposes of this section, the term 'tax table income' means adjusted gross income—

"(A) reduced by the sum of—

"(i) the excess itemized deductions, and

"(ii) the direct charitable deduction, and

"(B) increased (in the case of an individual to whom section 63(e) applies) by the unused zero bracket amount.

"(5) Section may be applied on the basis of taxable income.—The Secretary may provide that this section shall be applied for any taxable year on the basis of taxable income in lieu of tax table income."

Subsec. (b). Pub. L. 99–514, §141(b)(1), struck out par. (1) which read: "an individual to whom section 1301 (relating to income averaging) applies for the taxable year," and redesignated pars. (2) and (3) as (1) and (2), respectively.

1981—Subsec. (a)(1). Pub. L. 97–34, §101(b)(2)(B), inserted "and which shall be in such form as he determines appropriate" after "Secretary".

Subsec. (a)(4)(A). Pub. L. 97–34, §121(c)(3), substituted "reduced by the sum of (i) the excess itemized deductions, and (ii) the direct charitable deduction" for "reduced by the excess itemized deductions".

Subsec. (a)(5). Pub. L. 97–34, §101(b)(2)(C), added par. (5).

Subsec. (b)(1). Pub. L. 97–34, §101(c)(2)(A), substituted "an individual to whom section 1301 (relating to income averaging) applies for the taxable year" for "an individual to whom (A) section 1301 (relating to income averaging), or (B) section 1348 (relating to maximum rate on personal service income), applies for the taxable year".

1980—Subsec. (b)(1). Pub. L. 96–222, §108(a)(1)(E), redesignated subpars. (B) and (C) as (A) and (B), respectively.

Pub. L. 95–615, §202(f), as added by Pub. L. 96–222, §108(a)(1)(A), struck out subpar. (A) which related to earned income from sources without the United States under section 911 of this title.

1978—Subsec. (b)(1). Pub. L. 95–600 redesignated subpars. (C) and (D) as (B) and (C), respectively, and struck out former subpar. (B) which related to the alternative capital gains tax under section 1201 of this title.

1977—Pub. L. 95–30 struck out "having taxable income of less than $20,000" after "individuals" in section catchline.

Subsec. (a). Pub. L. 95–30 designated existing provisions as par. (1), substituted "tax table income" for "taxable income" and "does not exceed the ceiling amount" for "does not exceed $20,000", and added pars. (2) to (4).

Subsecs. (b) to (e). Pub. L. 95–30 added subsec. (b), redesignated former subsec. (b) as (c), and added subsecs. (d) and (e).

1976—Pub. L. 94–455 designated existing provisions as subsec. (a), substituted provision relating to taxable income for such year does not exceed $20,000 for provision relating to adjusted gross income for such year is less than $15,000 and who has elected for such year to pay the tax imposed by this section, struck out "or his delegate" after "Secretary", "beginning after Dec. 31, 1969" after "each taxable year", struck out provision requiring computation of taxable income by using standard deduction, and added subsec. (b).

1975—Pub. L. 94–12 substituted "$15,000" for "$10,000".

1969—Pub. L. 91–172 raised the individual gross income limit of $5,000 to $10,000 for exercising the option and substituted provision that the tax has to be determined under tables to be prescribed by the Secretary or his delegate for tables of tax rates for single persons, heads of household, married persons filing joint returns, married persons filing separate returns with 10 per cent standard deduction and married persons filing separate returns with minimum standard deduction.

1964—Pub. L. 88–272 substituted optional tax tables covering five categories for taxable years beginning on or after Jan. 1, 1964, and before Jan. 1, 1965, and for years beginning after Dec. 31, 1964, for a single general table.

STATUTORY NOTES AND RELATED SUBSIDIARIES
EFFECTIVE DATE OF 1986 AMENDMENT

Amendment by Pub. L. 99–514 applicable to taxable years beginning after Dec. 31, 1986, see section 151(a) of Pub. L. 99–514, set out as a note under section 1 of this title.

EFFECTIVE DATE OF 1981 AMENDMENT

Amendment by section 101(c)(2)(A) of Pub. L. 97–34 applicable to taxable years beginning after Dec. 31, 1981, see section 101(f)(1) of Pub. L. 97–34, set out as a note under section 1 of this title.

Amendment by section 121(c)(3) of Pub. L. 97–34 applicable to contributions made after Dec. 31, 1981, in taxable years beginning after such date, see section 121(d) of Pub. L. 97–34, set out as a note under section 170 of this title.

EFFECTIVE DATE OF 1980 AMENDMENT

Pub. L. 96–222, title I, §108(a)(2), Apr. 1, 1980, 94 Stat. 225, provided that:

"(A) In general.—Except as provided in subparagraph (B), the amendments made by paragraph (1) [amending this section and sections 119, 911, and 913 of this title] shall take effect as if included in the Foreign Earned Income Act of 1978 [Pub. L. 95–615].

"(B) Paragraph (1)(E).—The amendment made by paragraph (1)(E) [amending this section] shall apply to taxable years beginning after December 31, 1978."

EFFECTIVE DATE OF 1978 AMENDMENT

Pub. L. 95–600, title IV, §401(c), Nov. 6, 1978, 92 Stat. 2867, provided that: "The amendments made by this section [amending this section and sections 5, 871, 911, 1201, and 1304 of this title] shall apply to taxable years beginning after December 31, 1978."

EFFECTIVE DATE OF 1977 AMENDMENT

Amendment by Pub. L. 95–30 applicable to taxable years beginning after Dec. 31, 1976, see section 106(a) of Pub. L. 95–30, set out as a note under section 1 of this title.

EFFECTIVE DATE OF 1976 AMENDMENT

Pub. L. 94–455, title V, §508, Oct. 4, 1976, 90 Stat. 1569, provided that: "Except as otherwise provided, the amendments made by this title [enacting section 44A, amending this section and sections 36, 37, 41, 42, 46, 50A, 104, 144, 213, 217, 904, 1211, 1304, 3402, 6014, and 6096, enacting provisions set out as notes under sections 105, 8022, and repealing sections 4 and 214 of this title] shall apply to taxable years beginning after December 31, 1975."

EFFECTIVE AND TERMINATION DATES OF 1975 AMENDMENT

Pub. L. 94–12, title II, §209(a), Mar. 29, 1975, 89 Stat. 35, as amended by Pub. L. 94–164, §2(e), Dec. 23, 1975, 89 Stat. 972, provided that: "The amendments made by sections 201, 202(a), and 203 [enacting section 42 of this title and amending this section and sections 56, 141, 6012, and 6096 of this title] shall apply to taxable years ending after December 31, 1974. The amendments made by sections 201(a) and 202(a) [amending section 141 of this title] shall cease to apply to taxable years ending after December 31, 1975; those made by sections 201(b), 201(c), and 203 [enacting section 42 of this title and amending this section and sections 56, 6012, and 6096 of this title] shall cease to apply to taxable years ending after December 31, 1976."

EFFECTIVE DATE OF 1969 AMENDMENT

Amendment by Pub. L. 91–172 applicable to taxable years beginning after Dec. 31, 1969, see section 803(f) of Pub. L. 91–172, set out as a note under section 1 of this title.

EFFECTIVE DATE OF 1964 AMENDMENT

Pub. L. 88–272, title III, §301(c), Feb. 26, 1964, 78 Stat. 140, as amended by Pub. L. 99–514, §2, Oct. 22, 1986, 100 Stat. 2095, provided that: "Except for purposes of section 21 of the Internal Revenue Code of 1986 [formerly I.R.C. 1954] (relating to effect of changes in rates during a taxable year), the amendments made by this section [amending this section and sections 4 and 6014 of this title] shall apply to taxable years beginning after December 31, 1963."

[§4. Repealed. Pub. L. 94–455, title V, §501(b)(1), Oct. 4, 1976, 90 Stat. 1558]

Section, acts Aug. 16, 1954, ch. 736, 68A Stat. 10; Feb. 26, 1964, Pub. L. 88–272, title II, §232(f)(1), title III, §301(b)(1), (3), 78 Stat. 111, 140; Dec. 30, 1969, Pub. L. 91–172, title VIII, §802(c)(1)–(3), 83 Stat. 677, 678; Dec. 10, 1971, Pub. L. 92–178, title III, §301(b), 85 Stat. 520, related to rules for optional tax.

STATUTORY NOTES AND RELATED SUBSIDIARIES
EFFECTIVE DATE OF REPEAL

Repeal applicable to taxable years beginning after Dec. 31, 1975, see section 508 of Pub. L. 94–455, set out as an Effective Date of 1976 Amendment note under section 3 of this title.

§5. Cross references relating to tax on individuals

(a) Other rates of tax on individuals, etc.

(1) For rates of tax on nonresident aliens, see section 871.

(2) For doubling of tax on citizens of certain foreign countries, see section 891.

(3) For rate of withholding in the case of nonresident aliens, see section 1441.

(4) For alternative minimum tax, see section 55.

(b) Special limitations on tax

(1) For limitation on tax in case of income of members of Armed Forces, astronauts, and victims of certain terrorist attacks on death, see section 692.

(2) For computation of tax where taxpayer restores substantial amount held under claim of right, see section 1341.

(Aug. 16, 1954, ch. 736, 68A Stat. 10; Pub. L. 88–272, title II, §232(f)(2), Feb. 26, 1964, 78 Stat. 111; Pub. L. 91–172, title III, §301(b)(2), title VIII, §803(d)(6), Dec. 30, 1969, 83 Stat. 585, 684; Pub. L. 94–455, title XIX, §§1901(b)(22)(B), 1951(c)(3)(A), Oct. 4, 1976, 90 Stat. 1798, 1841; Pub. L. 95–600, title IV, §§401(b)(2), 421(e)(1), Nov. 6, 1978, 92 Stat. 2867, 2875; Pub. L. 96–222, title I, §104(a)(4)(H)(vii), Apr. 1, 1980, 94 Stat. 218; Pub. L. 97–248, title II, §201(d)(4), formerly §201(c)(4), Sept. 3, 1982, 96 Stat. 419, renumbered §201(d)(4), Pub. L. 97–448, title III, §306(a)(1)(A)(i), Jan. 12, 1983, 96 Stat. 2400; Pub. L. 99–514, title I, §141(b)(2), title VII, §701(e)(4)(A), Oct. 22, 1986, 100 Stat. 2117, 2343; Pub. L. 107–134, title I, §101(b)(1), Jan. 23, 2002, 115 Stat. 2428; Pub. L. 108–121, title I, §110(a)(2)(A), Nov. 11, 2003, 117 Stat. 1342.)

EDITORIAL NOTES
AMENDMENTS

2003—Subsec. (b)(1). Pub. L. 108–121 inserted ", astronauts," after "Forces".

2002—Subsec. (b)(1). Pub. L. 107–134 inserted "and victims of certain terrorist attacks" before "on death".

1986—Subsec. (a)(4). Pub. L. 99–514, §701(e)(4)(A), amended par. (4) generally, substituting "alternative minimum tax" for "minimum tax for taxpayers other than corporations".

Subsec. (b)(2), (3). Pub. L. 99–514, §141(b)(2), struck out par. (2) which read: "For limitation on tax where an individual chooses the benefits of income averaging, see section 1301." and redesignated former par. (3) as (2).

1982—Subsec. (a)(4). Pub. L. 97–248, §201(d)(4), formerly §201(c)(4), substituted "section 55" for "sections 55 and 56".

1980—Subsec. (a)(4). Pub. L. 96–222 substituted "sections 55 and 56" for "section 55".

1978—Subsec. (a)(3). Pub. L. 95–600, §401(b)(2), redesignated par. (4) as (3). Former par. (3), relating to the alternative tax in the case of capital gains, was struck out.

Subsec. (a)(4), (5). Pub. L. 95–600, §§401(b)(2), 421(e)(1), redesignated par. (5) as (4) and substituted "taxpayers other than corporations, see section 55" for "preferences, see section 56". Former par. (4) redesignated (3).

1976—Subsec. (b). Pub. L. 94–455 redesignated pars. (2), (3), and (4), as (1), (2), (3), respectively, and struck out former par. (1) which referred to section 632 for limitation on tax attributable to sales of oil or gas properties and par. (5) which referred to section 1347 for limitation on tax attributable to claims against the U.S. involving acquisition of property.

1969—Subsec. (a)(5). Pub. L. 91–172, §301(b)(2), added par. (5).

Subsec. (b). Pub. L. 91–172, §803(d)(6), substituted "tax" for "surtax" in pars. (1) and (5).

1964—Subsec. (b). Pub. L. 88–272 redesignated pars. (2), (3), (4), (7) and (8) as pars. (1) to (5), respectively, substituted "where an individual chooses the benefits of income averaging" for "with respect to compensation for longterm services" in par. (3), and struck out former pars. (1), (5) and (6) which referred to tax attributable to receipt of lump sum under annuity, endowment, or life insurance contract, to income from artistic work or inventions, and to back pay, respectively.

STATUTORY NOTES AND RELATED SUBSIDIARIES
EFFECTIVE DATE OF 2003 AMENDMENT

Pub. L. 108–121, title I, §110(a)(4), Nov. 11, 2003, 117 Stat. 1342, provided that: "The amendments made by this subsection [amending this section and sections 692 and 6013 of this title] shall apply with respect to any astronaut whose death occurs after December 31, 2002."

EFFECTIVE DATE OF 2002 AMENDMENT

Amendment by Pub. L. 107–134 applicable to taxable years ending before, on, or after Sept. 11, 2001, with provisions relating to waiver of limitations, see section 101(d) of Pub. L. 107–134, set out as a note under section 692 of this title.

EFFECTIVE DATE OF 1986 AMENDMENT

Amendment by section 141(b)(2) of Pub. L. 99–514 applicable to taxable years beginning after Dec. 31, 1986, see section 151(a) of Pub. L. 99–514, set out as a note under section 1 of this title.

Amendment by section 701(e)(4)(A) of Pub. L. 99–514 applicable to taxable years beginning after Dec. 31, 1986, with certain exceptions and qualifications, see section 701(f) of Pub. L. 99–514, set out as an Effective Date note under section 55 of this title.

EFFECTIVE DATE OF 1982 AMENDMENT

Pub. L. 97–248, title II, §201(e)(1), Sept. 3, 1982, 96 Stat. 421, provided that: "The amendments made by this section [amending this section and sections 46, 53, 55, 56, 57, 58, 173, 174, 511, 616, 617, 897, 901, 936, 1016, 6015, 6362, 6654, and 7701 of this title] shall apply to taxable years beginning after December 31, 1982."

Amendment by Pub. L. 96–222 effective, except as otherwise provided, as if it had been included in the provisions of the Revenue Act of 1978, Pub. L. 95–600, to which such amendment relates, see section 201 of Pub. L. 96–222, set out as a note under section 32 of this title.

Amendment by section 401(b)(2) of Pub. L. 95–600 applicable to taxable years beginning after Dec. 31, 1978, see section 401(c) of Pub. L. 95–600, set out as a note under section 3 of this title.

Pub. L. 95–600, title IV, §421(g), Nov. 6, 1978, 92 Stat. 2877, provided that: "The amendments made by this section [enacting section 55 of this title and amending this section and sections 57, 58, 443, 511, 666, 871, 877, 904, 6015, 6362, and 6654 of this title] shall apply to taxable years beginning after December 31, 1978, except that the amendment made by paragraph (1) of subsection (b) [amending section 57 of this title] shall apply to sales and exchanges made after July 26, 1978, in taxable years ending after such date."

Pub. L. 91–172, title III, §301(c), Dec. 30, 1969, 83 Stat. 586, as amended by Pub. L. 99–514, §2, Oct. 22, 1986, 100 Stat. 2095, provided that: "The amendments made by this section [enacting sections 56 to 58 of this title and amending this section and sections 12, 46, 51, 443, 453, 511, 901, 1373, 1375, 6015, and 6654 of this title] shall apply to taxable years ending after December 31, 1969. In the case of a taxable year beginning in 1969 and ending in 1970, the tax imposed by section 56 of the Internal Revenue Code of 1986 [formerly I.R.C. 1954] (as added by subsection (a)) shall be an amount equal to the tax imposed by such section (determined without regard to this sentence) multiplied by a fraction—

"(1) the numerator of which is the number of days in the taxable year occurring after December 31, 1969, and

"(2) the denominator of which is the number of days in the entire taxable year."

Amendment by section 803(d)(6) of Pub. L. 91–172 applicable to taxable years beginning after Dec. 31, 1970, see section 803(f) of Pub. L. 91–172, set out as a note under section 1 of this title.

Pub. L. 88–272, title II, §232(g), Feb. 26, 1964, 78 Stat. 112, as amended by Pub. L. 99–514, §2, Oct. 22, 1986, 100 Stat. 2095, provided that:

"(1) General rule.—Except as provided in paragraph (2), the amendments made by this section [enacting sections 1301 to 1305, amending this section and sections 4, 72, 144, 402, 403, 6511, and omitting former sections 1301 to 1307 of this title] shall apply with respect to taxable years beginning after December 31, 1963.

"(2) Income from an employment.—If, in a taxable year beginning after December 31, 1963, an individual or partnership receives or accrues compensation from an employment (as defined by section 1301(b) of the Internal Revenue Code of 1986 [formerly I.R.C. 1954] as in effect immediately before the enactment of this Act [Feb. 26, 1964] and the employment began before February 6, 1963, the tax attributable to such compensation may, at the election of the taxpayer, be computed under the provisions of sections 1301 and 1307 of such Code as in effect immediately before the enactment of this Act. If a taxpayer so elects (at such time and in such manner as the Secretary of the Treasury or his delegate by regulations prescribes), he may not choose for such taxable year the benefits provided by part I of subchapter Q of chapter 1 of such Code (relating to income averaging) as amended by this Act and (if he elects to have subsection (e) of such section 1307 apply) section 170(b)(5) of such Code as amended by this Act shall not apply to charitable contributions paid in such taxable year."

For applicability of amendment by section 701(e)(4)(A) of Pub. L. 99–514 notwithstanding any treaty obligation of the United States in effect on Oct. 22, 1986, see section 1012(aa)(2) of Pub. L. 100–647, set out as a note under section 861 of this title.

PART II—TAX ON CORPORATIONS

§11. Tax imposed

(a) Corporations in general

A tax is hereby imposed for each taxable year on the taxable income of every corporation.

(b) Amount of tax

The amount of the tax imposed by subsection (a) shall be 21 percent of taxable income.

(c) Exceptions

Subsection (a) shall not apply to a corporation subject to a tax imposed by—

(1) section 594 (relating to mutual savings banks conducting life insurance business),

(2) subchapter L (sec. 801 and following, relating to insurance companies), or

(3) subchapter M (sec. 851 and following, relating to regulated investment companies and real estate investment trusts).

(d) Foreign corporations

In the case of a foreign corporation, the tax imposed by subsection (a) shall apply only as provided by section 882.

(Aug. 16, 1954, ch. 736, 68A Stat. 11; Mar. 30, 1955, ch. 18, §2, 69 Stat. 14; Mar. 29, 1956, ch. 115, §2, 70 Stat. 66; Pub. L. 85–12, §2, Mar. 29, 1957, 71 Stat. 9; Pub. L. 85–475, §2, June 30, 1958, 72 Stat. 259; Pub. L. 86–75, §2, June 30, 1959, 73 Stat. 157; Pub. L. 86–564, title II, §201, June 30, 1960, 74 Stat. 290; Pub. L. 86–779, §10(d), Sept. 14, 1960, 74 Stat. 1009; Pub. L. 87–72, §2, June 30, 1961, 75 Stat. 193; Pub. L. 87–508, §2, June 28, 1962, 76 Stat. 114; Pub. L. 88–52, §2, June 29, 1963, 77 Stat. 72; Pub. L. 88–272, title I, §121, Feb. 26, 1964, 78 Stat. 25; Pub. L. 89–809, title I, §104(b)(2), Nov. 13, 1966, 80 Stat. 1557; Pub. L. 91–172, title IV, §401(b)(2)(B), Dec. 30, 1969, 83 Stat. 602; Pub. L. 94–12, title III, §303(a), (b), Mar. 29, 1975, 89 Stat. 44; Pub. L. 94–164, §4(a)–(c), Dec. 23, 1975, 89 Stat. 973, 974; Pub. L. 94–455, title IX, §901(a), Oct. 4, 1976, 90 Stat. 1606; Pub. L. 95–30, title II, §201(1), (2), May 23, 1977, 91 Stat. 141; Pub. L. 95–600, title III, §301(a), Nov. 6, 1978, 92 Stat. 2820; Pub. L. 97–34, title II, §231(a), Aug. 13, 1981, 95 Stat. 249; Pub. L. 98–369, div. A, title I, §66(a), July 18, 1984, 98 Stat. 585; Pub. L. 99–514, title VI, §601(a), Oct. 22, 1986, 100 Stat. 2249; Pub. L. 100–203, title X, §10224(a), Dec. 22, 1987, 101 Stat. 1330–412; Pub. L. 100–647, title I, §1007(g)(13)(B), Nov. 10, 1988, 102 Stat. 3436; Pub. L. 103–66, title XIII, §13221(a), (b), Aug. 10, 1993, 107 Stat. 477; Pub. L. 115–97, title I, §§12001(b)(11), 13001(a), Dec. 22, 2017, 131 Stat. 2094, 2096.)

2017—Subsec. (b). Pub. L. 115–97, §13001(a), amended subsec. (b) generally. Prior to amendment, text read as follows:

"(1) In general.—The amount of the tax imposed by subsection (a) shall be the sum of—

"(A) 15 percent of so much of the taxable income as does not exceed $50,000,

"(B) 25 percent of so much of the taxable income as exceeds $50,000 but does not exceed $75,000,

"(C) 34 percent of so much of the taxable income as exceeds $75,000 but does not exceed $10,000,000, and

"(D) 35 percent of so much of the taxable income as exceeds $10,000,000.

In the case of a corporation which has taxable income in excess of $100,000 for any taxable year, the amount of tax determined under the preceding sentence for such taxable year shall be increased by the lesser of (i) 5 percent of such excess, or (ii) $11,750. In the case of a corporation which has taxable income in excess of $15,000,000, the amount of the tax determined under the foregoing provisions of this paragraph shall be increased by an additional amount equal to the lesser of (i) 3 percent of such excess, or (ii) $100,000.

"(2) Certain personal service corporations not eligible for graduated rates.—Notwithstanding paragraph (1), the amount of the tax imposed by subsection (a) on the taxable income of a qualified personal service corporation (as defined in section 448(d)(2)) shall be equal to 35 percent of the taxable income."

Subsec. (d). Pub. L. 115–97, §12001(b)(11), substituted "the tax imposed by subsection (a)" for "the taxes imposed by subsection (a) and section 55".

1993—Subsec. (b)(1). Pub. L. 103–66, §13221(a)(3), inserted at end of closing provisions "In the case of a corporation which has taxable income in excess of $15,000,000, the amount of the tax determined under the foregoing provisions of this paragraph shall be increased by an additional amount equal to the lesser of (i) 3 percent of such excess, or (ii) $100,000."

Subsec. (b)(1)(C), (D). Pub. L. 103–66, §13221(a)(1), (2), added subpars. (C) and (D) and struck out former subpar. (C) which read as follows: "34 percent of so much of the taxable income as exceeds $75,000."

Subsec. (b)(2). Pub. L. 103–66, §13221(b), substituted "35 percent" for "34 percent".

1988—Subsec. (d). Pub. L. 100–647 substituted "the taxes imposed by subsection (a) and section 55" for "the tax imposed by subsection (a)".

1987—Subsec. (b). Pub. L. 100–203 amended subsec. (b) generally. Prior to amendment, subsec. (b) read as follows: "The amount of the tax imposed by subsection (a) shall be the sum of—

"(1) 15 percent of so much of the taxable income as does not exceed $50,000,

"(2) 25 percent of so much of the taxable income as exceeds $50,000 but does not exceed $75,000, and

"(3) 34 percent of so much of the taxable income as exceeds $75,000.

In the case of a corporation which has taxable income in excess of $100,000 for any taxable year, the amount of tax determined under the preceding sentence for such taxable year shall be increased by the lesser of (A) 5 percent of such excess, or (B) $11,750."

1986—Subsec. (b). Pub. L. 99–514 amended subsec. (b) generally. Prior to amendment, subsec. (b) read as follows: "The amount of the tax imposed by subsection (a) shall be the sum of—

"(1) 15 percent (16 percent for taxable years beginning in 1982) of so much of the taxable income as does not exceed $25,000;

"(2) 18 percent (19 percent for taxable years beginning in 1982) of so much of the taxable income as exceeds $25,000 but does not exceed $50,000;

"(3) 30 percent of so much of the taxable income as exceeds $50,000 but does not exceed $75,000;

"(4) 40 percent of so much of the taxable income as exceeds $75,000 but does not exceed $100,000; plus

"(5) 46 percent of so much of the taxable income as exceeds $100,000.

In the case of a corporation with taxable income in excess of $1,000,000 for any taxable year, the amount of tax determined under the preceding sentence for such taxable year shall be increased by the lesser of (A) 5 percent of such excess, or (B) $20,250."

1984—Subsec. (b). Pub. L. 98–369 inserted "In the case of a corporation with taxable income in excess of $1,000,000 for any taxable year, the amount of tax determined under the preceding sentence for such taxable year shall be increased by the lesser of (A) 5 percent of such excess, or (B) $20,250."

1981—Subsec. (b)(1). Pub. L. 97–34, §231(a)(1), substituted "15 percent (16 percent for taxable years beginning in 1982)" for "17 percent".

Subsec. (b)(2). Pub. L. 97–34, §231(a)(2), substituted "18 percent (19 percent for taxable years beginning in 1982)" for "20 percent".

1978—Pub. L. 95–600 reduced corporate tax rates by substituting provisions imposing a five-step tax rate structure on corporate taxable income for provisions using a normal tax and surtax approach to the taxation of corporate taxable income.

1977—Subsec. (b)(1). Pub. L. 95–30, §201(1), substituted "December 31, 1978" for "December 31, 1977".

Subsec. (b)(2). Pub. L. 95–30, §201(1), substituted "January 1, 1979" for "January 1, 1978" in provisions preceding subpar. (A).

Subsec. (d)(1). Pub. L. 95–30, §201(2), substituted "December 31, 1978" for "December 31, 1977".

Subsec. (d)(2). Pub. L. 95–30, §201(2), substituted "January 1, 1979" for "January 1, 1978".

1976—Subsec. (a). Pub. L. 94–455 reenacted subsec. (a) without change.

Subsec. (b). Pub. L. 94–455, among other changes, substituted "December 31, 1977, 22 percent" for "December 31, 1976, 22 percent" and "after December 31, 1974 and before January 1, 1978" for "after December 31, 1974 and before January 1, 1977" and struck out provisions relating to the six-month application of the general rule.

Subsec. (c). Pub. L. 94–455 struck out provisions relating to the special rule for 1976 for calendar year taxpayers.

Subsec. (d). Pub. L. 94–455, among other changes, substituted provisions relating to surtax exemption of $25,000 for a taxable year ending Dec. 31, 1977, or $50,000 for a taxable year ending after Dec. 31, 1974, and before Jan. 1, 1978, for provisions relating to surtax exemption of $50,000 for any taxable year and struck out provisions relating to six-month application of the general rule.

1975—Subsec. (b). Pub. L. 94–164 redesignated existing pars. (1) and (2) as pars. (1)(A) and (1)(B), and in par. (1)(A) as so redesignated substituted "after December 31, 1976" for "before January 1, 1975 or after December 31, 1975", and in par. (1)(B) as so redesignated substituted "January 1, 1977" for "January 1, 1976", and added par. (2).

Pub. L. 94–12, §303(a), reduced the normal tax for a taxable year ending after Dec. 31, 1974, and before Jan. 1, 1976, to 20 percent of so much of the taxable income as does not exceed $25,000 plus 22 percent of so much of the taxable income as exceeds $25,000.

Subsec. (c). Pub. L. 94–164 designated existing provisions as par. (1), struck out special percentages for taxable years beginning before Jan. 1, 1964, and after Dec. 31, 1963 and before Jan. 1, 1965, and added par. (2).

Subsec. (d). Pub. L. 94–164 designated existing provisions as par. (1), substituted "$50,000" for "$25,000", inserted reference to section 1564 of this title, and added par. (2).

Pub. L. 94–12, §303(b), substituted "$50,000" for "$25,000".

1969—Subsec. (d). Pub. L. 91–172 substituted "section 1561 or 1564" for "section 1561".

1966—Subsec. (e)(4). Pub. L. 89–809, §104(b)(2)(A), struck out par. (4) which made reference to section 881(a) (relating to foreign corporations not engaged in business in United States).

Subsec. (f). Pub. L. 89–809, §104(b)(2)(B), added subsec. (f).

1964—Subsec. (b). Pub. L. 88–272 applied the 30 percent tax to years beginning before Jan. 1, 1964 instead of July 1, 1964 in par. (1), and in par. (2), reduced the rate from 25 percent to 22 percent, and applied it to years beginning after Dec. 31, 1963, instead of June 30, 1964.

Subsec. (c). Pub. L. 88–272 increased the percentage from 22 to 28 for taxable years beginning after Dec. 31, 1963, and before Jan. 1, 1965, and to 26 percent for taxable years beginning after Dec. 31, 1964. The surtax exemption previously carried in subsec. (c), is now stated in subsec. (d).

Subsecs. (d), (e). Pub. L. 88–272 added subsec. (d) and redesignated former subsec. (d) as (e).

1963—Subsec. (b). Pub. L. 88–52 substituted "July 1, 1964" for "July 1, 1963" and "June 30, 1964" for "June 30, 1963" wherever appearing.

1962—Subsec. (b). Pub. L. 87–508 substituted "July 1, 1963" for "July 1, 1962" and "June 30, 1963" for "June 30, 1962" wherever appearing.

1961—Subsec. (b). Pub. L. 87–72 substituted "July 1, 1962" for "July 1, 1961" and "June 30, 1962" for "June 30, 1961" wherever appearing.

1960—Subsec. (b). Pub. L. 86–564 substituted "July 1, 1961" for "July 1, 1960" and "June 30, 1961" for "June 30, 1960" wherever appearing.

Subsec. (d)(3). Pub. L. 86–779 inserted "and real estate investment trusts" after "regulated investment companies".

1959—Subsec. (b). Pub. L. 86–75 substituted "July 1, 1960" for "July 1, 1959" and "June 30, 1960" for "June 30, 1959" wherever appearing.

1958—Subsec. (b). Pub. L. 85–475 substituted "July 1, 1959" for "July 1, 1958" and "June 30, 1959" for "June 30, 1958" wherever appearing.

1957—Subsec. (b). Pub. L. 85–12 substituted "July 1, 1958" for "April 1, 1957" and "June 30, 1958" for "March 31, 1957" wherever appearing.

1956—Subsec. (b). Act Mar. 29, 1956, substituted "April 1, 1957" for "April 1, 1956" and "March 31, 1957" for "March 31, 1956" wherever appearing.

1955—Subsec. (b). Act Mar. 30, 1955, substituted "April 1, 1956" for "April 1, 1955" and "March 31, 1956" for "March 31, 1955" wherever appearing.

STATUTORY NOTES AND RELATED SUBSIDIARIES

EFFECTIVE DATE OF 2017 AMENDMENT

Pub. L. 115–97, title I, §12001(c), Dec. 22, 2017, 131 Stat. 2094, provided that: "The amendments made by this section [amending this section and sections 12, 38, 53, 55, 56, 58, 59, 168, 847, 848, 882, 897, 911, 962, 1561, 6425, and 6655 of this title] shall apply to taxable years beginning after December 31, 2017."

Pub. L. 115–97, title I, §13001(c), Dec. 22, 2017, 131 Stat. 2098, provided that:

"(1) In general.—Except as otherwise provided in this subsection, the amendments made by subsections (a) and (b) [amending this section and sections 12, 280C, 453A, 527, 535, 594, 691, 801, 831, 832, 834, 852, 857, 860E, 882, 904, 1374, 1381, 1445, 1446, 1561, 6425, 6655, 7518, and 7874 of this title and repealing sections 1201 and 1551 of this title] shall apply to taxable years beginning after December 31, 2017.

"(2) Withholding.—The amendments made by subsection (b)(3) [amending sections 1445 and 1446 of this title] shall apply to distributions made after December 31, 2017.

"(3) Certain transfers.—The amendments made by subsection (b)(6) [amending section 1561 of this title] shall apply to transfers made after December 31, 2017."

EFFECTIVE DATE OF 1993 AMENDMENT

Pub. L. 103–66, title XIII, §13221(d), Aug. 10, 1993, 107 Stat. 477, provided that: "The amendments made by this section [amending this section and sections 852, 1201, and 1445 of this title] shall apply to taxable years beginning on or after January 1, 1993; except that the amendment made by subsection (c)(3) [amending section 1445 of this title] shall take effect on the date of the enactment of this Act [Aug. 10, 1993]."

EFFECTIVE DATE OF 1988 AMENDMENT

Amendment by Pub. L. 100–647 effective, except as otherwise provided, as if included in the provision of the Tax Reform Act of 1986, Pub. L. 99–514, to which such amendment relates, see section 1019(a) of Pub. L. 100–647, set out as a note under section 1 of this title.

EFFECTIVE DATE OF 1987 AMENDMENT

Pub. L. 100–203, title X, §10224(b), Dec. 22, 1987, 101 Stat. 1330–413, provided that: "The amendment made by subsection (a) [amending this section] shall apply to taxable years beginning after December 31, 1987."

EFFECTIVE DATE OF 1986 AMENDMENT

Pub. L. 99–514, title VI, §601(b), Oct. 22, 1986, 100 Stat. 2249, provided that:

"(1) In general.—The amendment made by subsection (a) [amending this section] shall apply to taxable years beginning on or after July 1, 1987.

"(2) Cross reference.—

"For treatment of taxable years which include July 1, 1987, see section 15 of the Internal Revenue Code of 1986."

EFFECTIVE DATE OF 1984 AMENDMENT

Pub. L. 98–369, div. A, title I, §66(c), July 18, 1984, 98 Stat. 585, as amended by Pub. L. 99–514, §2, Oct. 22, 1986, 100 Stat. 2095, provided that:

"(1) In general.—The amendments made by this section [amending this section and section 1561 of this title] shall apply to taxable years beginning after December 31, 1983.

"(2) Amendments not treated as changed in rate of tax.—The amendments made by this subsection [probably should be "section"] shall not be treated as a change in a rate of tax for purposes of section 21 of the Internal Revenue Code of 1986 [formerly I.R.C. 1954]."

EFFECTIVE DATE OF 1981 AMENDMENT

Pub. L. 97–34, title II, §231(c), Aug. 13, 1981, 95 Stat. 250, provided that: "The amendments made by subsection (a) [amending this section] shall apply to taxable years beginning after December 31, 1981."

EFFECTIVE DATE OF 1978 AMENDMENT

Pub. L. 95–600, title III, §301(c), Nov. 6, 1978, 92 Stat. 2824, provided that: "The amendments made by this section [amending this section and sections 12, 57, 244, 247, 511, 527, 528, 802, 821, 826, 852, 857, 882, 907, 922, 962, 1351, 1551, 1561, 6154, and 6655 of this title] shall apply to taxable years beginning after December 31, 1978."

EFFECTIVE DATE OF 1976 AMENDMENT

Pub. L. 94–455, title IX, §901(d), Oct. 4, 1976, 90 Stat. 1607, provided that: "The amendment made by subsection (a) [amending this section] shall take effect on December 23, 1975. The amendments made by subsection (b) [amending section 821 of this title] shall apply to taxable years ending after December 31, 1974. The amendments made by subsection (c) [amending sections 21, 1561, and 6154 of this title] shall apply to taxable years ending after December 31, 1975."

EFFECTIVE AND TERMINATION DATES OF 1975 AMENDMENT

Pub. L. 94–164, §4(e), Dec. 23, 1975, 89 Stat. 975, provided that: "The amendments made by subsections (b), (c), and (d) [amending this section and sections 21, 962, and 1561 of this title] apply to taxable years beginning after December 31, 1975. The amendment made by subsection (c) [amending this section] ceases to apply for taxable years beginning after December 31, 1976."

Pub. L. 94–12, title III, §305(b)(1), Mar. 29, 1975, 89 Stat. 45, provided that: "The amendments made by section 303 [amending this section and sections 12, 962, and 1561 of this title and enacting provisions set out as a note under this section] shall apply to taxable years ending after December 31, 1974. The amendments made by subsections (b) and (c) of such section [amending this section and sections 12, 962, and 1561 of this title and enacting provisions set out as a note under this section] shall cease to apply for taxable years ending after December 31, 1975."

EFFECTIVE DATE OF 1969 AMENDMENT

Amendment by Pub. L. 91–172 applicable with respect to taxable years beginning after Dec. 31, 1969, see section 401(h)(2) of Pub. L. 91–172, set out as a note under section 1561 of this title.

EFFECTIVE DATE OF 1966 AMENDMENT

Pub. L. 89–809, title I, §104(n), Nov. 13, 1966, 80 Stat. 1563, provided that: "The amendments made by this section (other than subsection (k)) [enacting section 6683 to this title and amending this section and sections 245, 301, 512, 542, 543, 545, 819, 821, 822, 831, 832, 841, 842, 881, 882, 884, 952, 953, 1249, 1442, and

6016 of this title] shall apply with respect to taxable years beginning after December 31, 1966. The amendment made by subsection (k) [amending section 1248(d)(4) of this title] shall apply with respect to sales or exchanges occurring after December 31, 1966."

EFFECTIVE DATE OF 1964 AMENDMENT

Amendment by Pub. L. 88–272, except for purposes of section 21 of this title, effective with respect to taxable years beginning after Dec. 31, 1963, see section 131 of Pub. L. 88–272, set out as a note under section 1 of this title.

EFFECTIVE DATE OF 1960 AMENDMENT

Amendment by Pub. L. 86–779 applicable with respect to taxable years of real estate investment trusts beginning after Dec. 31, 1960, see section 10(k) of Pub. L. 86–779, set out as an Effective Date note under section 856 of this title.

ALLOCATION OF 1975 TAXABLE INCOME AMONG COMPONENT MEMBERS OF CONTROLLED GROUP OF CORPORATIONS

Pub. L. 94–12, title III, §303(c)(1), Mar. 29, 1975, 89 Stat. 44, provided in part that: "In applying subsection (b)(2) of section 11 [former subsec. (b)(2) of this section], the first $25,000 of taxable income and the second $25,000 of taxable income shall each be allocated among the component members of a controlled group of corporations in the same manner as the surtax exemption is allocated."

§12. Cross references relating to tax on corporations

> **(1)** For tax on the unrelated business income of certain charitable and other corporations exempt from tax under this chapter, see section 511.
> **(2)** For accumulated earnings tax and personal holding company tax, see parts I and II of subchapter G (sec. 531 and following).
> **(3)** For doubling of tax on corporations of certain foreign countries, see section 891.
> **(4)** For rate of withholding in case of foreign corporations, see section 1442.

(Aug. 16, 1954, ch. 736, 68A Stat. 11; Pub. L. 88–272, title II, §234(b)(4), Feb. 26, 1964, 78 Stat. 115; Pub. L. 91–172, title III, §301(b)(3), Dec. 30, 1969, 83 Stat. 585; Pub. L. 94–12, title III, §303(c)(2), Mar. 29, 1975, 89 Stat. 44; Pub. L. 95–600, title III, §301(b)(1), Nov. 6, 1978, 92 Stat. 2820; Pub. L. 98–369, div. A, title IV, §474(r)(29)(E), July 18, 1984, 98 Stat. 844; Pub. L. 99–514, title VII, §701(e)(4)(B), Oct. 22, 1986, 100 Stat. 2343; Pub. L. 115–97, title I, §§12001(b)(12), 13001(b)(2)(B), Dec. 22, 2017, 131 Stat. 2094, 2096.)

EDITORIAL NOTES
AMENDMENTS

2017—Pars. (4) to (6). Pub. L. 115–97, §13001(b)(2)(B), redesignated par. (5) as (4) and struck out former pars. (4) and (6) which read as follows:

"(4) For alternative tax in case of capital gains, see section 1201(a).

"(6) For limitation on benefits of graduated rate schedule provided in section 11(b), see section 1551."

Par. (7). Pub. L. 115–97, §12001(b)(12), struck out par. (7) which read as follows: "For alternative minimum tax, see section 55."

1986—Par. (7). Pub. L. 99–514 amended par. (7) generally, substituting "alternative minimum tax" and "55" for "minimum tax for tax preferences" and "56", respectively.

1984—Pars. (6) to (8). Pub. L. 98–369 redesignated pars. (7) and (8) as (6) and (7), respectively. Former par. (6), which referred to section 1451 for withholding of tax on tax-free covenant bonds, was struck out.

1978—Par. (7). Pub. L. 95–600 substituted "benefits of graduated rate schedule provided in section 11(b)" for "the $25,000 exemption from surtax provided in section 11(c)".

1975—Par. (7). Pub. L. 94–12 substituted "$50,000" for "$25,000" for a limited period. See Effective and Termination Dates of 1975 Amendment note set out below.

1969—Par. (8). Pub. L. 91–172 added par. (8).

1964—Par. (8). Pub. L. 88–272 struck out par. (8) which referred to section 1503 for additional tax for corporations filing consolidated returns.

STATUTORY NOTES AND RELATED SUBSIDIARIES
EFFECTIVE DATE OF 2017 AMENDMENT

Amendment by section 12001(b)(12) of Pub. L. 115–97 applicable to taxable years beginning after Dec. 31, 2017, see section 12001(c) of Pub. L. 115–97, set out as a note under section 11 of this title.

Amendment by section 13001(b)(2)(B) of Pub. L. 115–97 applicable to taxable years beginning after Dec. 31, 2017, see section 13001(c)(1) of Pub. L. 115–97, set out as a note under section 11 of this title.

EFFECTIVE DATE OF 1986 AMENDMENT

Amendment by Pub. L. 99–514 applicable to taxable years beginning after Dec. 31, 1986, with certain exceptions and qualifications, see section 701(f) of Pub. L. 99–514, set out as an Effective Date note under section 55 of this title.

EFFECTIVE DATE OF 1984 AMENDMENT

Amendment by Pub. L. 98–369 not applicable with respect to obligations issued before Jan. 1, 1984, see section 475(b) of Pub. L. 98–369, set out as a note under section 33 of this title.

EFFECTIVE DATE OF 1978 AMENDMENT

Amendment by Pub. L. 95–600 applicable to taxable years beginning after Dec. 31, 1978, see section 301(c) of Pub. L. 95–600, set out as a note under section 11 of this title.

EFFECTIVE AND TERMINATION DATES OF 1975 AMENDMENT

Amendment by Pub. L. 94–12 applicable to taxable years ending after Dec. 31, 1974, but to cease to apply for taxable years ending after Dec. 31, 1975, see section 305(b)(1) of Pub. L. 94–12, set out as a note under section 11 of this title.

EFFECTIVE DATE OF 1969 AMENDMENT

Amendment by Pub. L. 91–172 applicable to taxable years ending after Dec. 31, 1969, see section 301(c) of Pub. L. 91–172, set out as a note under section 5 of this title.

EFFECTIVE DATE OF 1964 AMENDMENT

Amendment by Pub. L. 88–272 applicable to taxable years beginning after Dec. 31, 1963, see section 234(c) of Pub. L. 88–272, set out as a note under section 1503 of this title.

APPLICABILITY OF CERTAIN AMENDMENTS BY PUBLIC LAW 99–514 IN RELATION TO TREATY OBLIGATIONS OF UNITED STATES

For applicability of amendment by Pub. L. 99–514 notwithstanding any treaty obligation of the United States in effect on Oct. 22, 1986, see section 1012(aa)(2) of Pub. L. 100–647, set out as a note under section 861 of this title.

PART III—CHANGES IN RATES DURING A TAXABLE YEAR

Sec.
15.
Effect of changes.

1984—Pub. L. 98–369, div. A, title IV, §474(b)(3), July 18, 1984, 98 Stat. 830, substituted "15. Effect of changes" for "21. Effect of changes".

§15. Effect of changes

(a) General rule

If any rate of tax imposed by this chapter changes, and if the taxable year includes the effective date of the change (unless that date is the first day of the taxable year), then—

(1) tentative taxes shall be computed by applying the rate for the period before the effective date of the change, and the rate for the period on and after such date, to the taxable income for the entire taxable year; and

(2) the tax for such taxable year shall be the sum of that proportion of each tentative tax which the number of days in each period bears to the number of days in the entire taxable year.

(b) Repeal of tax

For purposes of subsection (a)—

(1) if a tax is repealed, the repeal shall be considered a change of rate; and

(2) the rate for the period after the repeal shall be zero.

(c) Effective date of change

For purposes of subsections (a) and (b)—

(1) if the rate changes for taxable years "beginning after" or "ending after" a certain date, the following day shall be considered the effective date of the change; and

(2) if a rate changes for taxable years "beginning on or after" a certain date, that date shall be considered the effective date of the change.

(d) Section not to apply to inflation adjustments

This section shall not apply to any change in rates under subsection (f) of section 1 (relating to adjustments in tax tables so that inflation will not result in tax increases).

(e) References to highest rate

If the change referred to in subsection (a) involves a change in the highest rate of tax imposed by section 1 or 11(b), any reference in this chapter to such highest rate (other than in a provision imposing a tax by reference to such rate) shall be treated as a reference to the weighted average of the highest rates before and after the change determined on the basis of the respective portions of the taxable year before the date of the change and on or after the date of the change.

(f) Rate reductions enacted by Economic Growth and Tax Relief Reconciliation Act of 2001

This section shall not apply to any change in rates under subsection (i) of section 1 (relating to rate reductions after 2000).

(Aug. 16, 1954, ch. 736, 68A Stat. 12, §21; Pub. L. 88–272, title I, §132, Feb. 26, 1964, 78 Stat. 30; Pub. L. 91–172, title VIII, §803(e), Dec. 30, 1969, 83 Stat. 685; Pub. L. 92–178, title II, §205, Dec. 10, 1971, 85 Stat. 511; Pub. L. 94–12, title III, §305(b)(2), Mar. 29, 1975, 89 Stat. 45; Pub. L. 94–164, §4(d)(2), Dec. 23, 1975, 89 Stat. 975; Pub. L. 94–455, title IX, §901(c)(2), Oct. 4, 1976, 90 Stat. 1607; Pub. L. 95–30, title I, §101(d)(2), May 23, 1977, 91 Stat. 133; Pub. L. 95–600, title I, §106, Nov. 6, 1978, 92 Stat. 2776; Pub. L. 97–34, title I, §101(d)(3), Aug. 13, 1981, 95 Stat. 184; renumbered §15, Pub. L. 98–369, div. A, title IV, §474(b)(1), July 18, 1984, 98 Stat. 830; Pub. L. 99–514, title I, §101(b), Oct. 22, 1986, 100 Stat. 2099; Pub. L. 100–647, title I, §1006(a), Nov. 10, 1988, 102 Stat. 3393; Pub. L. 107–16, title I, §101(c)(3), June 7, 2001, 115 Stat. 43.)

2001—Subsec. (f). Pub. L. 107–16, §101(c)(3), added subsec. (f).

1988—Subsec. (e). Pub. L. 100–647 added subsec. (e).

1986—Subsec. (d). Pub. L. 99–514 amended subsec. (d) generally, substituting "apply to inflation adjustments" for "apply to section 1 rate changes made by Economic Recovery Tax Act of 1981" in heading and struck out "section 1 attributable to the amendments made by section 101 of the Economic Tax Act of 1981 or" before "subsection (f)" in text.

1984—Pub. L. 98–369 renumbered section 21 of this title as this section.

1981—Subsec. (d). Pub. L. 97–34 substituted provisions that this section shall not apply to any change in rates under section 1 attributable to the amendments made by section 101 of the Economic Recovery Tax Act of 1981 or subsec. (f) of section 1 for provisions that had related to the changes made by section 303(b) of the Tax Reduction Act of 1975 in the surtax exemption.

Subsecs. (e), (f). Pub. L. 97–34 struck out subsecs. (e) and (f) which had related, respectively, to changes made by the Tax Reduction and Simplification Act of 1977 and to changes made by Revenue Act of 1978.

1978—Subsec. (f). Pub. L. 95–600 added subsec. (f).

1977—Subsec. (d). Pub. L. 95–30, §101(d)(2)(A), (B), redesignated subsec. (f) as (d). Former subsec. (d), which directed that, in applying subsec. (a) to a taxable year of an individual which was not a calendar year, each change made by the Tax Reform Act of 1969 in part I or in the application of part IV or V of subchapter B for purposes of the determination of taxable income should be treated as a change in a rate of tax, was struck out.

Subsec. (e). Pub. L. 95–30, §101(d)(2)(A), (C), added subsec. (e). Former subsec. (e), which directed that, in applying subsec. (a) to a taxable year of an individual which was not a calendar year, each change made by the Revenue Act of 1971 in section 141 (relating to the standard deduction) and section 151 (relating to personal exemptions) should be treated as a change in a rate of tax, was struck out.

Subsec. (f). Pub. L. 95–30, §101(d)(2)(B), redesignated subsec. (f) as (d).

1976—Subsec. (f). Pub. L. 94–455 substituted "in the surtax exemption and any change under section 11(d) in the surtax exemption" for "and the change made by section 3(c) of the Revenue Adjustment Act of 1975 in section 11(d) (relating to corporate surtax exemption)".

1975—Subsec. (f). Pub. L. 94–164 inserted reference to change made by section 3(c) of the Revenue Adjustment Act of 1975.

Pub. L. 94–12 added subsec. (f).

1971—Subsec. (e). Pub. L. 92–178 added subsec. (e).

1969—Subsec. (d). Pub. L. 91–172 substituted provisions covering changes made by the Tax Reform Act of 1969 in case of individuals for provisions covering changes made by Revenue Act of 1964.

1964—Subsec. (d). Pub. L. 88–272 amended subsection generally by substituting provisions relating to changes made by the Revenue Act of 1964, for provisions relating to taxable years beginning before Jan. 1, 1954, and ending after Dec. 31, 1953.

Amendment by Pub. L. 107–16 applicable to taxable years beginning after Dec. 31, 2000, see section 101(d)(1) of Pub. L. 107–16, set out as an Effective and Termination Dates of 2001 Amendment note under section 1 of this title.

Amendment by Pub. L. 100–647 effective, except as otherwise provided, as if included in the provision of the Tax Reform Act of 1986, Pub. L. 99–514, to which such amendment relates, see section 1019(a) of Pub. L. 100–647, set out as a note under section 1 of this title.

EFFECTIVE DATE OF 1986 AMENDMENT
Amendment by Pub. L. 99–514 applicable to taxable years beginning after Dec. 31, 1986, see section 151(a) of Pub. L. 99–514, set out as a note under section 1 of this title.

EFFECTIVE DATE OF 1981 AMENDMENT
Amendment by Pub. L. 97–34 applicable to taxable years beginning after Dec. 31, 1981, see section 101(f)(1) of Pub. L. 97–34, set out as a note under section 1 of this title.

EFFECTIVE DATE OF 1977 AMENDMENT
Amendment by Pub. L. 95–30 applicable to taxable years beginning after Dec. 31, 1976, see section 106(a) of Pub. L. 95–30, set out as a note under section 1 of this title.

EFFECTIVE DATE OF 1976 AMENDMENT
Amendment by Pub. L. 94–455 applicable with respect to taxable years ending after Dec. 31, 1975, see section 901(d) of Pub. L. 94–455, set out as a note under section 11 of this title.

EFFECTIVE DATE OF 1975 AMENDMENT
Amendment by Pub. L. 94–164 applicable to taxable years beginning after Dec. 31, 1975, see section 4(e) of Pub. L. 94–164, set out as an Effective and Termination Dates of 1975 Amendments note under section 11 of this title.

EFFECTIVE DATE OF 1964 AMENDMENT
Pub. L. 88–272, title I, §132, Feb. 26, 1964, 78 Stat. 30, provided that the amendment made by that section is effective with respect to taxable years ending after Dec. 31, 1963.

COORDINATION OF 2017 AMENDMENT WITH SECTION 15
This section not to apply to any change in a rate of tax by reason of section 1(j) of this title, as added by Pub. L. 115–97, see section 1(j)(6) of this title.

COORDINATION OF 1997 AMENDMENT WITH SECTION 15
Pub. L. 105–34, title I, §1(c), Aug. 5, 1997, 111 Stat. 788, provided that: "No amendment made by this Act [see Tables for classification] shall be treated as a change in a rate of tax for purposes of section 15 of the Internal Revenue Code of 1986."

COORDINATION OF 1993 AMENDMENT WITH SECTION 15
Pub. L. 103–66, title XIII, §13001(c), Aug. 10, 1993, 107 Stat. 416, provided that: "Except in the case of the amendments made by section 13221 [amending sections 11, 852, 1201, and 1445 of this title] (relating to corporate rate increase), no amendment made by this chapter [chapter 1 (§§13001–13444) of title XIII of Pub. L. 103–66, see Tables for classification] shall be treated as a change in a rate of tax for purposes of section 15 of the Internal Revenue Code of 1986."

COORDINATION OF 1990 AMENDMENT WITH SECTION 15
Pub. L. 101–508, title XI, §11001(c), Nov. 5, 1990, 104 Stat. 1388–400, provided that: "Except as otherwise expressly provided in this title, no amendment made by this title [see Tables for classification] shall be treated as a change in a rate of tax for purposes of section 15 of the Internal Revenue Code of 1986."

COORDINATION OF 1987 AMENDMENT WITH SECTION 15
Pub. L. 100–203, title X, §10000(c), Dec. 22, 1987, 101 Stat. 1330–382, provided that: "No amendment made by this title [see Tables for classification] shall be treated as a change in a rate of tax for purposes [of] section 15 of the Internal Revenue Code of 1986."

COORDINATION OF 1986 AMENDMENT WITH SECTION 15
Pub. L. 99–514, §3(b), Oct. 22, 1986, 100 Stat. 2095, provided that:

"(1) In general.—Except as provided in paragraph (2), for purposes of section 15 of the Internal Revenue Code of 1986, no amendment or repeal made by this Act [see Tables for classification] shall be treated as a change in the rate of a tax imposed by chapter 1 of such Code.

"(2) Exception.—Paragraph (1) shall not apply to the amendment made by section 601 [amending section 11 of this title] (relating to corporate rate reductions)."

PART IV—CREDITS AGAINST TAX

Subpart
A.
Nonrefundable personal credits.
B.
Other credits.
C.
Refundable credits.
D.
Business-related credits.
E.
Rules for computing investment credit.
F.
Rules for computing work opportunity credit.
G.
Credit against regular tax for prior year minimum tax liability.[1]

[H to J.
Repealed.]

EDITORIAL NOTES
AMENDMENTS
2017—Pub. L. 115–97, title I, §13404(a), Dec. 22, 2017, 131 Stat. 2138, struck out items for subparts H "Nonrefundable credit to holders of clean renewable energy bonds", I "Qualified tax credit bonds", and J "Build America bonds".

2009—Pub. L. 111–5, div. B, title I, §1531(c)(6), Feb. 17, 2009, 123 Stat. 360, added item for subpart J.

2008—Pub. L. 110–234, title XV, §15316(c)(5), May 22, 2008, 122 Stat. 1511, and Pub. L. 110–246, title XV, §15316(c)(5), June 18, 2008, 122 Stat. 2273, made identical amendments, adding items for subparts H and I and striking out item for former subpart H "Nonrefundable credit to holders of certain bonds". The amendment by Pub. L. 110–234 was repealed by Pub. L. 110–246, §4(a), June 18, 2008, 122 Stat. 1664.

2005—Pub. L. 109–58, title XIII, §1303(c)(1), Aug. 8, 2005, 119 Stat. 996, added item for subpart H.

1996—Pub. L. 104–188, title I, §§1201(e)(3), 1601(b)(2)(F)(ii), Aug. 20, 1996, 110 Stat. 1772, 1833, substituted "Other credits" for "Foreign tax credit, etc." in item for subpart B and "work opportunity credit" for "targeted jobs credit" in item for subpart F.

1990—Pub. L. 101–508, title XI, §11813(b)(26), Nov. 5, 1990, 104 Stat. 1388–555, substituted "Rules for computing investment credit" for "Rules for computing credit for investment in certain depreciable property" in item for subpart E.

1984—Pub. L. 98–369, div. A, title IV, §§471(a), 474(n)(3), July 18, 1984, 98 Stat. 825, 834, substituted "Nonrefundable personal credits" for "Credits allowable" in item for subpart A, "Foreign tax credit, etc" for "Rules for computing credit for investment in certain depreciable property" in item for subpart B, "Refundable credits" for "Rules for computing credit for expense of work incentive programs" in item for subpart C, and "Business-related credits" for "Rules for computing credit for employment of certain new employees" in item for subpart D, and added items for subparts E and F.

1977—Pub. L. 95–30, title II, §202(d)(1)(B), May 23, 1977, 91 Stat. 147, added subpart D.

1971—Pub. L. 92–178, title VI, §601(c)(1), Dec. 10, 1971, 85 Stat. 557, added subpart C.

¹ *Editorially supplied. Subpart G of part IV added by Pub. L. 99–514 without corresponding amendment of part analysis.*

Subpart A—Nonrefundable Personal Credits

Editorial Notes
Amendments

2018—Pub. L. 115–141, div. U, title I, §101(l)(10), Mar. 23, 2018, 132 Stat. 1165, substituted "American Opportunity and Lifetime Learning credits" for "Hope and Lifetime Learning credits" in item 25A.

2010—Pub. L. 111–148, title X, §10909(b)(2)(O), (c), Mar. 23, 2010, 124 Stat. 1023, as amended by Pub. L. 111–312, title I, §101(b)(1), Dec. 17, 2010, 124 Stat. 3298, temporarily struck out item 23 "Adoption expenses". See Effective and Termination Dates of 2010 Amendment note set out under section 1 of this title.

2005—Pub. L. 109–58, title XIII, §§1333(b)(2), 1335(b)(5), Aug. 8, 2005, 119 Stat. 1030, 1036, added items 25C and 25D.

2001—Pub. L. 107–16, title VI, §618(c), June 7, 2001, 115 Stat. 108, added item 25B.

1998—Pub. L. 105–206, title VI, §6004(a)(1), July 22, 1998, 112 Stat. 792, substituted "Hope and Lifetime Learning credits" for "Higher education tuition and related expenses" in item 25A.

1997—Pub. L. 105–34, title I, §101(d)(3), title II, §201(e), Aug. 5, 1997, 111 Stat. 799, 806, added items 24 and 25A.

1996—Pub. L. 104–188, title I, §1807(c)(6), Aug. 20, 1996, 110 Stat. 1902, added item 23.

1990—Pub. L. 101–508, title XI, §11801(b)(1), Nov. 5, 1990, 104 Stat. 1388–522, struck out item 23 "Residential energy credit".

1986—Pub. L. 99–514, title I, §112(b)(5), Oct. 22, 1986, 100 Stat. 2109, struck out item 24 "Contributions to candidates for public office".

1984—Pub. L. 98–369, div. A, title IV, §§471(b), 612(f), July 18, 1984, 98 Stat. 826, 913, substituted "Nonrefundable Personal Credits" for "Credits Allowable" as subpart A heading, struck out analysis of sections 31 through 45 formerly comprising subpart A, and inserted a new analysis of sections consisting of items 21 (formerly 44A), 22 (formerly 37), 23 (formerly 44C), 24 (formerly 41), and 25 and 26 (newly enacted).

1983—Pub. L. 98–67 repealed amendments made by Pub. L. 97–248. See 1982 Amendment note below.

Pub. L. 98–21, title I, §122(c)(7), Apr. 20, 1983, 97 Stat. 87, inserted "and the permanently and totally disabled" to item 37.

Pub. L. 97–424, title V, §515(b)(6)(D), Jan. 6, 1983, 96 Stat. 2181, substituted "and special fuels" for ", special fuels, and lubricating oil" after "gasoline" in item 39.

Pub. L. 97–414, §4(c)(1), Jan. 4, 1983, 96 Stat. 2056, added item 44H.

1982—Pub. L. 97–248, title III, §§307(b)(3), 308(a), Sept. 3, 1982, 96 Stat. 590, 591, provided that, applicable to payments of interest, dividends, and patronage dividends paid or credited after June 30, 1983, item 31 is amended to read "Tax withheld on wages, interest, dividends, and patronage dividends". Section 102(a), (b) of Pub. L. 98–67, title I, Aug. 5, 1983, 97 Stat. 369, repealed subtitle A (§§301–308) of title III of Pub. L. 97–248 as of the close of June 30, 1983, and provided that the Internal Revenue Code of 1954 [now 1986] [this title] shall be applied and administered (subject to certain exceptions) as if such subtitle A (and the amendments made by such subtitle A) had not been enacted.

1981—Pub. L. 97–34, title II, §221(c)(2), title III, §331(e)(2), Aug. 13, 1981, 95 Stat. 247, 295, added items 44F and 44G.

1980—Pub. L. 96–223, title II, §§231(b)(1), 232(b)(3)(B), Apr. 2, 1980, 94 Stat. 272, 276, added items 44D and 44E.

1978—Pub. L. 95–618, title I, §101(b)(1), Nov. 9, 1978, 92 Stat. 3179, added item 44C.

1977—Pub. L. 95–30, title I, §101(e)(1), title II, §202(d)(1)(A), May 23, 1977, 91 Stat. 134, 147, added item 44B and struck out item 36 "Credit not allowed to individuals taking standard deduction".

1976—Pub. L. 94–455, title IV, §401(a)(2)(D), title V, §§501(c)(2), 503(b)(5), 504(a)(2), title XIX, §1901(b)(1)(Z), Oct. 4, 1976, 90 Stat. 1555, 1559, 1562, 1565, 1792, substituted in item 42 "General tax credit" for "Taxable income credit", struck out in item 36 "pay optional tax or", inserted in item 33 "possession tax credit", substituted in item 37 "Credit of the elderly" for "Retirement income", added item 44A, and struck out item 35 "Partially tax-exempt interest received by individuals".

1975—Pub. L. 94–164, §3(a)(2), Dec. 23, 1975, 89 Stat. 973, substituted "Taxable income credit" for "Credit for personal exemptions" in item 42.

Pub. L. 94–12, title II, §§203(b)(1), 204(c), 208(d)(1), Mar. 29, 1975, 89 Stat. 30, 32, 35, renumbered item 42 as 45 and added item 42 applicable to taxable years ending after Dec. 31, 1974, but to cease to apply to taxable years ending after Dec. 31, 1975, item 43 applicable to taxable years beginning after Dec. 31, 1974, but before Jan. 1, 1976, and item 44.

1971—Pub. L. 92–178, title VI, §601(c)(2), Dec. 10, 1971, 85 Stat. 557, added items 40 and 41, and redesignated former item 40 as 42.

1970—Pub. L. 91–258, title II, §207(d)(10), May 21, 1970, 84 Stat. 249, inserted ", special fuels," after "gasoline" in item 39.

1965—Pub. L. 89–44, title VIII, §809(d)(1), June 21, 1965, 79 Stat. 167, added item 39 and redesignated former item 39 as 40.

1964—Pub. L. 88–272, title II, §201(d)(1), Feb. 26, 1964, 78 Stat. 32, struck out item 34.

1962—Pub. L. 87–834, §2(g)(1), (2), Oct. 16, 1962, 76 Stat. 972, 973, added headings of subparts A and B and item 38, and redesignated former item 38 as 39.

§21. Expenses for household and dependent care services necessary for gainful employment

(a) Allowance of credit

(1) In general

In the case of an individual for which there are 1 or more qualifying individuals (as defined in subsection (b)(1)) with respect to such individual, there shall be allowed as a credit against the tax imposed by this chapter for the taxable year an amount equal to the applicable percentage of the employment-related expenses (as defined in subsection (b)(2)) paid by such individual during the taxable year.

(2) Applicable percentage defined

For purposes of paragraph (1), the term "applicable percentage" means 35 percent reduced (but not below 20 percent) by 1 percentage point for each $2,000 (or fraction thereof) by which the taxpayer's adjusted gross income for the taxable year exceeds $15,000.

(b) Definitions of qualifying individual and employment-related expenses

For purposes of this section—

(1) Qualifying individual

The term "qualifying individual" means—

(A) a dependent of the taxpayer (as defined in section 152(a)(1)) who has not attained age 13,

(B) a dependent of the taxpayer (as defined in section 152, determined without regard to subsections (b)(1), (b)(2), and (d)(1)(B)) who is physically or mentally incapable of caring for himself or herself and who has the same principal place of abode as the taxpayer for more than one-half of such taxable year, or

(C) the spouse of the taxpayer, if the spouse is physically or mentally incapable of caring for himself or herself and who has the same principal place of abode as the taxpayer for more than one-half of such taxable year.

(2) Employment-related expenses

(A) In general

The term "employment-related expenses" means amounts paid for the following expenses, but only if such expenses are incurred to enable the taxpayer to be gainfully employed for any period for which there are 1 or more qualifying individuals with respect to the taxpayer:

(i) expenses for household services, and

(ii) expenses for the care of a qualifying individual.

Such term shall not include any amount paid for services outside the taxpayer's household at a camp where the qualifying individual stays overnight.

(B) Exception

Employment-related expenses described in subparagraph (A) which are incurred for services outside the taxpayer's household shall be taken into account only if incurred for the care of—

(i) a qualifying individual described in paragraph (1)(A), or

(ii) a qualifying individual (not described in paragraph (1)(A)) who regularly spends at least 8 hours each day in the taxpayer's household.

(C) Dependent care centers

Employment-related expenses described in subparagraph (A) which are incurred for services provided outside the taxpayer's household by a dependent care center (as defined in subparagraph (D)) shall be taken into account only if—

(i) such center complies with all applicable laws and regulations of a State or unit of local government, and

(ii) the requirements of subparagraph (B) are met.

(D) Dependent care center defined

For purposes of this paragraph, the term "dependent care center" means any facility which—

(i) provides care for more than six individuals (other than individuals who reside at the facility), and

(ii) receives a fee, payment, or grant for providing services for any of the individuals (regardless of whether such facility is operated for profit).

(c) Dollar limit on amount creditable

The amount of the employment-related expenses incurred during any taxable year which may be taken into account under subsection (a) shall not exceed—

(1) $3,000 if there is 1 qualifying individual with respect to the taxpayer for such taxable year, or

(2) $6,000 if there are 2 or more qualifying individuals with respect to the taxpayer for such taxable year.

The amount determined under paragraph (1) or (2) (whichever is applicable) shall be reduced by the aggregate amount excludable from gross income under section 129 for the taxable year.

(d) Earned income limitation

(1) In general

Except as otherwise provided in this subsection, the amount of the employment-related expenses incurred during any taxable year which may be taken into account under subsection (a) shall not exceed—

(A) in the case of an individual who is not married at the close of such year, such individual's earned income for such year, or

(B) in the case of an individual who is married at the close of such year, the lesser of such individual's earned income or the earned income of his spouse for such year.

(2) Special rule for spouse who is a student or incapable of caring for himself

In the case of a spouse who is a student or a qualifying individual described in subsection (b)(1)(C), for purposes of paragraph (1), such spouse shall be deemed for each month during which such spouse is a full-time student at an educational institution, or is such a qualifying individual, to be gainfully employed and to have earned income of not less than—

(A) $250 if subsection (c)(1) applies for the taxable year, or

(B) $500 if subsection (c)(2) applies for the taxable year.

In the case of any husband and wife, this paragraph shall apply with respect to only one spouse for any one month.

(e) Special rules

For purposes of this section—

(1) Place of abode

An individual shall not be treated as having the same principal place of abode of the taxpayer if at any time during the taxable year of the taxpayer the relationship between the individual and the taxpayer is in violation of local law.

(2) Married couples must file joint return

If the taxpayer is married at the close of the taxable year, the credit shall be allowed under subsection (a) only if the taxpayer and his spouse file a joint return for the taxable year.

(3) Marital status

An individual legally separated from his spouse under a decree of divorce or of separate maintenance shall not be considered as married.

(4) Certain married individuals living apart

If—

(A) an individual who is married and who files a separate return—

(i) maintains as his home a household which constitutes for more than one-half of the taxable year the principal place of abode of a qualifying individual, and

(ii) furnishes over half of the cost of maintaining such household during the taxable year, and

(B) during the last 6 months of such taxable year such individual's spouse is not a member of such household,

such individual shall not be considered as married.

(5) Special dependency test in case of divorced parents, etc.

If—

(A) section 152(e) applies to any child with respect to any calendar year, and

(B) such child is under the age of 13 or is physically or mentally incapable of caring for himself,

in the case of any taxable year beginning in such calendar year, such child shall be treated as a qualifying individual described in subparagraph (A) or (B) of subsection (b)(1) (whichever is appropriate) with respect to the custodial parent (as defined in section 152(e)(4)(A)), and shall not be treated as a qualifying individual with respect to the noncustodial parent.

(6) Payments to related individuals

No credit shall be allowed under subsection (a) for any amount paid by the taxpayer to an individual—

(A) with respect to whom, for the taxable year, a deduction under section 151(c) (relating to deduction for personal exemptions for dependents) is allowable either to the taxpayer or his spouse, or

(B) who is a child of the taxpayer (within the meaning of section 152(f)(1)) who has not attained the age of 19 at the close of the taxable year.

For purposes of this paragraph, the term "taxable year" means the taxable year of the taxpayer in which the service is performed.

(7) Student

The term "student" means an individual who during each of 5 calendar months during the taxable year is a full-time student at an educational organization.

(8) Educational organization

The term "educational organization" means an educational organization described in section 170(b)(1)(A)(ii).

(9) Identifying information required with respect to service provider

No credit shall be allowed under subsection (a) for any amount paid to any person unless—

(A) the name, address, and taxpayer identification number of such person are included on the return claiming the credit, or

(B) if such person is an organization described in section 501(c)(3) and exempt from tax under section 501(a), the name and address of such person are included on the return claiming the credit.

In the case of a failure to provide the information required under the preceding sentence, the preceding sentence shall not apply if it is shown that the taxpayer exercised due diligence in attempting to provide the information so required.

(10) Identifying information required with respect to qualifying individuals

No credit shall be allowed under this section with respect to any qualifying individual unless the TIN of such individual is included on the return claiming the credit.

(f) Regulations

The Secretary shall prescribe such regulations as may be necessary to carry out the purposes of this section.

(g) Special rules for 2021

In the case of any taxable year beginning after December 31, 2020, and before January 1, 2022—

(1) Credit made refundable

If the taxpayer (in the case of a joint return, either spouse) has a principal place of abode in the United States (determined as provided in section 32) for more than one-half of the taxable year, the credit allowed under subsection (a) shall be treated as a credit allowed under subpart C (and not allowed under this subpart).

(2) Increase in dollar limit on amount creditable

Subsection (c) shall be applied—

(A) by substituting "$8,000" for "$3,000" in paragraph (1) thereof, and

(B) by substituting "$16,000" for "$6,000" in paragraph (2) thereof.

(3) Increase in applicable percentage

Subsection (a)(2) shall be applied—

(A) by substituting "50 percent" for "35 percent", and

(B) by substituting "$125,000" for "$15,000".

(4) Application of phaseout to high income individuals

(A) In general

Subsection (a)(2) shall be applied by substituting "the phaseout percentage" for "20 percent".

(B) Phaseout percentage

The term "phaseout percentage" means 20 percent reduced (but not below zero) by 1 percentage point for each $2,000 (or fraction thereof) by which the taxpayer's adjusted gross income for the taxable year exceeds $400,000.

(h) Application of credit in possessions

(1) Payment to possessions with mirror code tax systems

The Secretary shall pay to each possession of the United States with a mirror code tax system amounts equal to the loss (if any) to that possession by reason of the application of this section (determined without regard to this subsection) with respect to taxable years beginning in or with 2021. Such amounts shall be determined by the Secretary based on information provided by the government of the respective possession.

(2) Payments to other possessions

The Secretary shall pay to each possession of the United States which does not have a mirror code tax system amounts estimated by the Secretary as being equal to the aggregate benefits that would have been provided to residents of such possession by reason of this section with respect to taxable years beginning in or with 2021 if a mirror code tax system had been in effect in such possession. The preceding sentence shall not apply unless the respective possession has a plan, which has been approved by the Secretary, under which such possession will promptly distribute such payments to its residents.

(3) Coordination with credit allowed against United States income taxes

In the case of any taxable year beginning in or with 2021, no credit shall be allowed under this section to any individual—

(A) to whom a credit is allowable against taxes imposed by a possession with a mirror code tax system by reason of this section, or

(B) who is eligible for a payment under a plan described in paragraph (2).

(4) Mirror code tax system

For purposes of this subsection, the term "mirror code tax system" means, with respect to any possession of the United States, the income tax system of such possession if the income tax liability of the residents of such possession under such system is determined by reference to the income tax laws of the United States as if such possession were the United States.

(5) Treatment of payments

For purposes of section 1324 of title 31, United States Code, the payments under this subsection shall be treated in the same manner as a refund due from a credit provision referred to in subsection (b)(2) of such section.

(Added Pub. L. 94–455, title V, §504(a)(1), Oct. 4, 1976, 90 Stat. 1563, §44A; amended Pub. L. 95–600, title I, §121(a), Nov. 6, 1978, 92 Stat. 2779; Pub. L. 97–34, title I §124 (a)–(d), Aug. 13, 1981, 95 Stat. 197, 198; Pub. L. 98–21, title I, §122(c)(1), Apr. 20, 1983, 97 Stat. 87; renumbered §21 and amended Pub. L. 98–369, div. A, title IV, §§423(c)(4), 471(c), 474(c), July 18, 1984, 98 Stat. 801, 826, 830; Pub. L. 99–514, title I, §104(b)(1), Oct. 22, 1986, 100 Stat. 2104; Pub. L. 100–203, title X, §10101(a), Dec. 22, 1987, 101 Stat. 1330–384; Pub. L. 100–485, title VII, §703(a)–(c)(1), Oct. 13, 1988, 102 Stat. 2426, 2427; Pub. L. 104–188, title I, §1615(b), Aug. 20, 1996, 110 Stat. 1853; Pub. L. 107–16, title II, §204(a), (b), June 7, 2001, 115 Stat. 49; Pub. L. 107–147, title IV, §418(b), Mar. 9, 2002, 116 Stat. 57; Pub. L. 108–311, title II, §§203, 207(2), (3), Oct. 4, 2004, 118 Stat. 1175, 1177; Pub. L. 109–135, title IV, §404(b), Dec. 21, 2005, 119 Stat. 2634; Pub. L. 110–172, §11(a)(1), Dec. 29, 2007, 121 Stat. 2484; Pub. L. 117–2, title IX, §9631(a), (b), Mar. 11, 2021, 135 Stat. 159.)

EDITORIAL NOTES
PRIOR PROVISIONS

A prior section 21 was renumbered section 15 of this title.

AMENDMENTS

2021—Subsec. (g). Pub. L. 117–2, §9631(a), added subsec. (g).

Subsec. (h). Pub. L. 117–2, §9631(b), added subsec. (h).

2007—Subsec. (e)(5). Pub. L. 110–172 substituted "section 152(e)(4)(A)" for "section 152(e)(3)(A)" in concluding provisions.

2005—Subsec. (b)(1)(B). Pub. L. 109–135 inserted "(as defined in section 152, determined without regard to subsections (b)(1), (b)(2), and (d)(1)(B))" after "dependent of the taxpayer".

2004—Subsec. (a)(1). Pub. L. 108–311, §203(a), substituted "In the case of an individual for which there are 1 or more qualifying individuals (as defined in subsection (b)(1)) with respect to such individual" for "In the case of an individual who maintains a household which includes as a member one or more qualifying individuals (as defined in subsection (b)(1))".

Subsec. (b)(1). Pub. L. 108–311, §203(b), reenacted heading without change and amended text generally. Prior to amendment, text read as follows: "The term 'qualifying individual' means—

"(A) a dependent of the taxpayer who is under the age of 13 and with respect to whom the taxpayer is entitled to a deduction under section 151(c),

"(B) a dependent of the taxpayer who is physically or mentally incapable of caring for himself, or

"(C) the spouse of the taxpayer, if he is physically or mentally incapable of caring for himself."

Subsec. (e)(1). Pub. L. 108–311, §203(c), amended heading and text of par. (1) generally. Prior to amendment, text read as follows: "An individual shall be treated as maintaining a household for any period only if over half the cost of maintaining the household for such period is furnished by such individual (or, if such individual is married during such period, is furnished by such individual and his spouse)."

Subsec. (e)(5). Pub. L. 108–311, §207(2), struck out "paragraph (2) or (4) of" before "section 152(e)" in subpar. (A) and substituted "as defined in section 152(e)(3)(A)" for "within the meaning of section 152(e)(1)" in concluding provisions.

Subsec. (e)(6)(B). Pub. L. 108–311, §207(3), substituted "section 152(f)(1)" for "section 151(c)(3)".

2002—Subsec. (d)(2)(A). Pub. L. 107–147, §418(b)(1), substituted "$250" for "$200".

Subsec. (d)(2)(B). Pub. L. 107–147, §418(b)(2), substituted "$500" for "$400".

2001—Subsec. (a)(2). Pub. L. 107–16, §204(b), substituted "35 percent" for "30 percent" and "$15,000" for "$10,000".

Subsec. (c)(1). Pub. L. 107–16, §204(a)(1), substituted "$3,000" for "$2,400".

Subsec. (c)(2). Pub. L. 107–16, §204(a)(2), substituted "$6,000" for "$4,800".

1996—Subsec. (e)(10). Pub. L. 104–188 added par. (10).

1988—Subsec. (b)(1)(A). Pub. L. 100–485, §703(a), substituted "age of 13" for "age of 15".

Subsec. (c). Pub. L. 100–485, §703(b), inserted at end: "The amount determined under paragraph (1) or (2) (whichever is applicable) shall be reduced by the aggregate amount excludable from gross income under section 129 for the taxable year."

Subsec. (e)(5)(B). Pub. L. 100–485, §703(a), substituted "age of 13" for "age of 15".

Subsec. (e)(9). Pub. L. 100–485, §703(c)(1), added par. (9).

1987—Subsec. (b)(2)(A). Pub. L. 100–203 inserted at end "Such term shall not include any amount paid for services outside the taxpayer's household at a camp where the qualifying individual stays overnight."

1986—Subsecs. (b)(1)(A), (e)(6)(A). Pub. L. 99–514, §104(b)(1)(A), substituted "section 151(c)" for "section 151(e)".

Subsec. (e)(6)(B). Pub. L. 99–514, §104(b)(1)(B), substituted "section 151(c)(3)" for "section 151(e)(3)".

1984—Pub. L. 98–369, §471(c), renumbered section 44A of this title as this section.

Subsec. (a)(1). Pub. L. 98–369, §474(c)(2), (3), substituted "subsection (b)(1)" for "subsection (c)(1)" and "subsection (b)(2)" for "subsection (c)(2)".

Subsec. (b). Pub. L. 98–369, §474(c)(1), redesignated subsec. (c) as (b). Former subsec. (b), which provided that the credit allowed by subsec. (a) could not exceed the amount of the tax imposed by this chapter for the taxable year reduced by the sum of the credits allowable under sections 33, 37, 38, 40, 41, 42, and 44, was struck out.

Subsec. (c). Pub. L. 98–369, §474(c)(1), redesignated subsec. (d) as (c). Former subsec. (c) redesignated (b).

Subsec. (d). Pub. L. 98–369, §474(c)(1), redesignated subsec. (e) as (d). Former subsec. (d) redesignated (c).

Subsec. (d)(2). Pub. L. 98–369, §474(c)(4), substituted "subsection (b)(1)(C)" for "subsection (c)(1)(C)" in introductory provisions.

Subsec. (d)(2)(A). Pub. L. 98–369, §474(c)(5), substituted "subsection (c)(1)" for "subsection (d)(1)".

Subsec. (d)(2)(B). Pub. L. 98–369, §474(c)(6), substituted "subsection (c)(2)" for "subsection (d)(2).

Subsec. (e). Pub. L. 98–369, §474(c)(1), redesignated subsec. (f) as (e). Former subsec. (e) redesignated (d).

Subsec. (e)(5). Pub. L. 98–369, §474(c)(7), substituted "subsection (b)(1)" for "subsection (c)(1)" in provisions following subpar. (B).

Pub. L. 98–369, §423(c)(4), amended par. (5) generally, substituting subpars. (A) and (B) reading:

"(A) paragraph (2) or (4) of section 152(e) applies to any child with respect to any calendar year, and

"(B) such child is under the age of 15 or is physically or mentally incapable of caring for himself,"

for former provisions:

"(A) a child (as defined in section 151(e)(3)) who is under the age of 15 or who is physically or mentally incapable of caring for himself receives over half of his support during the calendar year from his parents who are divorced or legally separated under a decree of divorce or separate maintenance or who are separated under a written separation agreement, and

"(B) such child is in the custody of one or both of his parents for more than one-half of the calendar year."

and substituted in concluding text "(whichever is appropriate) with respect to the custodial parent (within the meaning of section 152(e)(1)), and shall not be treated as a qualifying individual with respect to the noncustodial parent" for ", as the case may be, with respect to that parent who has custody for a longer period during such calendar year than the other parent, and shall not be treated as being a qualifying individual with respect to such other parent."

Subsecs. (f), (g). Pub. L. 98–369, §474(c)(1), redesignated subsecs. (f) and (g) as (e) and (f), respectively.

1983—Subsec. (b)(2). Pub. L. 98–21 substituted "relating to credit for the elderly and the permanently and totally disabled" for "relating to credit for the elderly".

1981—Subsec. (a). Pub. L. 97–34, §124(a), designated existing provisions as par. (1), substituted "the applicable percentage" for "20 percent" in par. (1) as so designated, and added par. (2).

Subsec. (c)(2)(B). Pub. L. 97–34, §124(c), designated existing provisions as cl. (i) and added cl. (ii).

Subsec. (c)(2)(C), (D). Pub. L. 97–34, §124(d), added subpars. (C) and (D).

Subsec. (d)(1). Pub. L. 97–34, §124(b)(1)(A), substituted "$2,400" for "$2,000".

Subsec. (d)(2). Pub. L. 97–34, §124(b)(1)(B), substituted "$4,800" for "$4,000".

Subsec. (e)(2)(A). Pub. L. 97–34, §124(b)(2)(A), substituted "$200" for "$166".

Subsec. (e)(2)(B). Pub. L. 97–34, §124(b)(2)(B), substituted "$400" for "$333".

1978—Subsec. (f)(6). Pub. L. 95–600 substituted provision disallowing a credit for any amount paid by a taxpayer to an individual with respect to whom, for the taxable year, a deduction under section 151(e) is allowable either to the taxpayer or his spouse or who is a child of the taxpayer who has not attained the age of 19 at the close of the taxable year and defining "taxpayer year" for provision disallowing a credit for any amount paid by the taxpayer to an individual bearing a relationship described in section 152(a)(1) through (8), or a dependent described in section 152(a)(9), except that a credit was allowed for an amount paid by a taxpayer to an individual with respect to whom, for the taxable year of the taxpayer in which the service was performed, neither the taxpayer nor his spouse was entitled to a deduction under section 151(e), provided the service constituted employment within the meaning of section 3121(b).

STATUTORY NOTES AND RELATED SUBSIDIARIES

EFFECTIVE DATE OF 2021 AMENDMENT

Pub. L. 117–2, title IX, §9631(d), Mar. 11, 2021, 135 Stat. 160, provided that: "The amendments made by this section [amending this section, section 6211 of this title and section 1324 of Title 31, Money and Finance] shall apply to taxable years beginning after December 31, 2020."

EFFECTIVE DATE OF 2005 AMENDMENT

Pub. L. 109–135, title IV, §404(d), Dec. 21, 2005, 119 Stat. 2634, provided that: "The amendments made by this section [amending this section and sections 152 and 223 of this title] shall take effect as if included in the provisions of the Working Families Tax Relief Act of 2004 [Pub. L. 108–311] to which they relate."

EFFECTIVE DATE OF 2004 AMENDMENT

Amendment by Pub. L. 108–311 applicable to taxable years beginning after Dec. 31, 2004, see section 208 of Pub. L. 108–311, set out as a note under section 2 of this title.

EFFECTIVE DATE OF 2002 AMENDMENT

Pub. L. 107–147, title IV, §418(c), Mar. 9, 2002, 116 Stat. 58, provided that: "The amendments made by this section [amending this section and sections 23 and 137 of this title] shall take effect as if included in the provisions of the Economic Growth and Tax Relief Reconciliation Act of 2001 [Pub. L. 107–16] to which they relate."

EFFECTIVE DATE OF 2001 AMENDMENT

Pub. L. 107–16, title II, §204(c), June 7, 2001, 115 Stat. 50, provided that: "The amendments made by this section [amending this section] shall apply to taxable years beginning after December 31, 2002."

EFFECTIVE DATE OF 1996 AMENDMENT

Pub. L. 104–188, title I, §1615(d), Aug. 20, 1996, 110 Stat. 1853, provided that:

"(1) In general.—The amendments made by this section [amending this section and sections 151, 6109, 6213, and 6724 of this title] shall apply with respect to returns the due date for which (without regard to extensions) is on or after the 30th day after the date of the enactment of this Act [Aug. 20, 1996].

"(2) Special rule for 1995 and 1996.—In the case of returns for taxable years beginning in 1995 or 1996, a taxpayer shall not be required by the amendments made by this section to provide a taxpayer identification number for a child who is born after October 31, 1995, in the case of a taxable year beginning in 1995 or November 30, 1996, in the case of a taxable year beginning in 1996."

EFFECTIVE DATE OF 1988 AMENDMENT

Pub. L. 100–485, title VII, §703(d), Oct. 13, 1988, 102 Stat. 2427, provided that: "The amendments made by this section [amending this section and sections 129 and 6109 of this title] shall apply to taxable years beginning after December 31, 1988."

EFFECTIVE DATE OF 1987 AMENDMENT

Pub. L. 100–203, title X, §10101(b), Dec. 22, 1987, 101 Stat. 1330–384, as amended by Pub. L. 100–647, title II, §2004(a), Nov. 10, 1988, 102 Stat. 3598, provided that:

"(1) In general.—The amendment made by subsection (a) [amending this section] shall apply to expenses paid in taxable years beginning after December 31, 1987.

"(2) Special rule for cafeteria plans.—For purposes of section 125 of the Internal Revenue Code of 1986, a plan shall not be treated as failing to be a cafeteria plan solely because under the plan a participant elected before January 1, 1988, to receive reimbursement under the plan for dependent care assistance for periods after December 31, 1987, and such assistance included reimbursement for expenses at a camp where the dependent stays overnight."

EFFECTIVE DATE OF 1986 AMENDMENT

Amendment by Pub. L. 99–514 applicable to taxable years beginning after Dec. 31, 1986, see section 151(a) of Pub. L. 99–514, set out as a note under section 1 of this title.

EFFECTIVE DATE OF 1984 AMENDMENT

Amendment by section 423(c)(4) of Pub. L. 98–369 applicable to taxable years beginning after Dec. 31, 1984, see section 423(d) of Pub. L. 98–369, set out as a note under section 2 of this title.

Pub. L. 98–369, title IV, §475(a), July 18, 1984, 98 Stat. 847, provided that: "The amendments made by this title [probably means subtitle F (§§471–475) of title IV of Pub. L. 98–369, which enacted sections 25, 38, and 39 of this title, amended this section and sections 12, 15, 22 to 24, 27 to 35, 37, 39 to 41, 44A, 44C to 44H, 45 to 48, 51, 52, 55, 56, 86, 87, 103, 108, 129, 168, 196, 213, 280C, 381, 383, 401, 404, 409, 441, 527, 642, 691, 874, 882, 901, 904, 936, 1016, 1033, 1351, 1366, 1374, 1375, 1441, 1442, 1451, 3507, 6013, 6096, 6201, 6211, 6213, 6362, 6401, 6411, 6420, 6421, 6427, 6501, 6511, 7701, 7871, 9502, and 9503 of this title, repealed sections 38, 40, 44, 44B, 50A, 50B, and 53 of this title, and enacted provisions set out as notes under sections 30, 33, 46, and 48 of this title] shall apply to taxable years beginning after December 31, 1983, and to carrybacks from such years."

EFFECTIVE DATE OF 1983 AMENDMENT

Amendment by Pub. L. 98–21 applicable to taxable years beginning after Dec. 31, 1983, except that if an individual's annuity starting date was deferred under section 105(d)(6) of this title as in effect on the day before Apr. 20, 1983, such deferral shall end on the first day of such individual's first taxable year beginning after Dec. 31, 1983, see section 122(d) of Pub. L. 98–21, set out as a note under section 22 of this title.

EFFECTIVE DATE OF 1981 AMENDMENT

Pub. L. 97–34, title I, §124(f), Aug. 13, 1981, 95 Stat. 201, provided that:

"(1) Except as provided in paragraph (2), the amendments made by this section [amending this section and enacting section 129 of this title] shall apply to taxable years beginning after December 31, 1981.

"(2) The amendments made by subsection (e)(2) [amending sections 3121, 3306, and 3401 of this title and section 409 of Title 42, The Public Health and Welfare] shall apply to remuneration paid after December 31, 1981."

EFFECTIVE DATE OF 1978 AMENDMENT

Pub. L. 95–600, title I, §121(b), Nov. 6, 1978, 92 Stat. 2779, provided that: "The amendment made by subsection (a) [amending this section] shall apply to taxable years beginning after December 31, 1978."

EFFECTIVE DATE

Section applicable to taxable years beginning after Dec. 31, 1975, see section 508 of Pub. L. 94–455, set out as an Effective Date of 1976 Amendment note under section 3 of this title.

PROGRAM TO INCREASE PUBLIC AWARENESS

Pub. L. 101–508, title XI, §11114, Nov. 5, 1990, 104 Stat. 1388–414, provided that: "Not later than the first calendar year following the date of the enactment of this subtitle [Nov. 5, 1990], the Secretary of the Treasury, or the Secretary's delegate, shall establish a taxpayer awareness program to inform the taxpaying public of the availability of the credit for dependent care allowed under section 21 of the Internal Revenue Code of 1986 and the earned income credit and child health insurance under section 32 of such Code. Such public awareness program shall be designed to assure that individuals who may be eligible are informed of the availability of such credit and filing procedures. The Secretary shall use appropriate means of communication to carry out the provisions of this section."

§22. Credit for the elderly and the permanently and totally disabled

(a) General rule

In the case of a qualified individual, there shall be allowed as a credit against the tax imposed by this chapter for the taxable year an amount equal to 15 percent of such individual's section 22 amount for such taxable year.

(b) Qualified individual

For purposes of this section, the term "qualified individual" means any individual—

(1) who has attained age 65 before the close of the taxable year, or

(2) who retired on disability before the close of the taxable year and who, when he retired, was permanently and totally disabled.

(c) Section 22 amount

For purposes of subsection (a)—

(1) In general

An individual's section 22 amount for the taxable year shall be the applicable initial amount determined under paragraph (2), reduced as provided in paragraph (3) and in subsection (d).

(2) Initial amount

(A) In general

Except as provided in subparagraph (B), the initial amount shall be—

(i) $5,000 in the case of a single individual, or a joint return where only one spouse is a qualified individual,

(ii) $7,500 in the case of a joint return where both spouses are qualified individuals, or

(iii) $3,750 in the case of a married individual filing a separate return.

(B) Limitation in case of individuals who have not attained age 65

(i) In general

In the case of a qualified individual who has not attained age 65 before the close of the taxable year, except as provided in clause (ii), the initial amount shall not exceed the disability income for the taxable year.

(ii) Special rules in case of joint return

In the case of a joint return where both spouses are qualified individuals and at least one spouse has not attained age 65 before the close of the taxable year—

(I) if both spouses have not attained age 65 before the close of the taxable year, the initial amount shall not exceed the sum of such spouses' disability income, or

(II) if one spouse has attained age 65 before the close of the taxable year, the initial amount shall not exceed the sum of $5,000 plus the disability income for the taxable year of the spouse who has not attained age 65 before the close of the taxable year.

(iii) Disability income

For purposes of this subparagraph, the term "disability income" means the aggregate amount includable in the gross income of the individual for the taxable year under section 72 or 105(a) to the extent such amount constitutes wages (or payments in lieu of wages) for the period during which the individual is absent from work on account of permanent and total disability.

(3) Reduction

(A) In general

The reduction under this paragraph is an amount equal to the sum of the amounts received by the individual (or, in the case of a joint return, by either spouse) as a pension or annuity or as a disability benefit—

(i) which is excluded from gross income and payable under—

(I) title II of the Social Security Act,

(II) the Railroad Retirement Act of 1974, or

(III) a law administered by the Department of Veterans Affairs, or

(ii) which is excluded from gross income under any provision of law not contained in this title.

No reduction shall be made under clause (i)(III) for any amount described in section 104(a)(4).

(B) Treatment of certain workmen's compensation benefits

For purposes of subparagraph (A), any amount treated as a social security benefit under section 86(d)(3) shall be treated as a disability benefit received under title II of the Social Security Act.

(d) Adjusted gross income limitation

If the adjusted gross income of the taxpayer exceeds—

(1) $7,500 in the case of a single individual,

(2) $10,000 in the case of a joint return, or

(3) $5,000 in the case of a married individual filing a separate return,

the section 22 amount shall be reduced by one-half of the excess of the adjusted gross income over $7,500, $10,000, or $5,000, as the case may be.

(e) Definitions and special rules

For purposes of this section—

(1) Married couple must file joint return

Except in the case of a husband and wife who live apart at all times during the taxable year, if the taxpayer is married at the close of the taxable year, the credit provided by this section shall be allowed only if the taxpayer and his spouse file a joint return for the taxable year.

(2) Marital status

Marital status shall be determined under section 7703.

(3) Permanent and total disability defined

An individual is permanently and totally disabled if he is unable to engage in any substantial gainful activity by reason of any medically determinable physical or mental impairment which can be expected to result in death or which has lasted or can be expected to last for a continuous period of not less than 12 months. An individual shall not be considered to be permanently and totally disabled unless he furnishes proof of the existence thereof in such form and manner, and at such times, as the Secretary may require.

(f) Nonresident alien ineligible for credit

No credit shall be allowed under this section to any nonresident alien.

(Aug. 16, 1954, ch. 736, 68A Stat. 15, §37; Aug. 9, 1955, ch. 659, §1, 69 Stat. 591; Jan. 28, 1956, ch. 17, §1, 70 Stat. 8; Pub. L. 87–792, §7(a), Oct. 10, 1962, 76 Stat. 828; Pub. L. 87–876, §1, Oct. 24, 1962, 76 Stat. 1199; Pub. L. 88–272, title I, §113(a), title II, §§201(d)(3), 202(a), Feb. 26, 1964, 78 Stat. 24, 32, 33; Pub. L. 93–406, title II, §2002(g)(1), Sept. 2, 1974, 88 Stat. 968; Pub. L. 94–455, title V, §503(a), title XIX, §1901(c)(1), Oct. 4, 1976, 90 Stat. 1559, 1803; Pub. L. 95–600, title VII, §§701(a)(1)–(3), 703(j)(11), Nov. 6, 1978, 92 Stat. 2897, 2942; Pub. L. 96–222, title I, §107(a)(1)(E)(i), Apr. 1, 1980, 94 Stat. 222; Pub. L. 97–34, title I, §111(b)(4), Aug. 13, 1981, 95 Stat. 194; Pub. L. 98–21, title I, §122(a), Apr. 20, 1983, 97 Stat. 85; renumbered §22 and amended Pub. L. 98–369, div. A, title IV, §§471(c), 474(d), July 18, 1984, 98 Stat. 826, 830; Pub. L. 99–514, title XIII, §1301(j)(8), Oct. 22, 1986, 100 Stat. 2658; Pub. L. 115–141, div. U, title IV, §401(a)(2)(A), Mar. 23, 2018, 132 Stat. 1184.)

EDITORIAL NOTES

REFERENCES IN TEXT

The Social Security Act, referred to in subsec. (c)(3)(A)(i)(I), (B), is act Aug. 14, 1935, ch. 531, 49 Stat. 620, as amended. Title II of the Social Security Act is classified generally to subchapter II (§401 et seq.) of chapter 7 of Title 42, The Public Health and Welfare. For complete classification of this Act to the Code, see section 1305 of Title 42 and Tables.

The Railroad Retirement Act of 1974, referred to in subsec. (c)(3)(A)(i)(II), is act Aug. 29, 1935, ch. 812, as amended generally by Pub. L. 93–445, title I, §101, Oct. 16, 1974, 88 Stat. 1305, which is classified generally to subchapter IV (§231 et seq.) of chapter 9 of Title 45, Railroads. For further details and complete classification of this Act to the Code, see Codification note set out preceding section 231 of Title 45, section 231t of Title 45, and Tables.

AMENDMENTS

2018—Subsec. (c)(3)(A)(i)(III). Pub. L. 115–141 substituted "Department of Veterans Affairs" for "Veterans' Administration".

1986—Subsec. (e)(2). Pub. L. 99–514 substituted "section 7703" for "section 143".

1984—Pub. L. 98–369, §471(c), renumbered section 37 of this title as this section.

Subsec. (a). Pub. L. 98–369, §474(d)(1), substituted "section 22 amount" for "section 37 amount".

Subsec. (c). Pub. L. 98–369, §474(d)(2), substituted "Section 22 amount" for "Section 37 amount" in heading.

Subsec. (c)(1). Pub. L. 98–369, §474(d)(1), substituted "section 22 amount" for "section 37 amount".

Subsec. (d). Pub. L. 98–369, §474(d)(3), amended subsec. (d) generally, striking out heading "Limitations" and designation "(1)" before "Adjusted gross income limitation" thereby making existing par. (1) the entire subsec. (d), redesignating existing subpars. (A), (B), and (C) as pars. (1), (2), and (3), respectively, and striking out provisions, formerly comprising par. (2), which had limited the amount of the credit allowed by this section for the taxable year to the amount of the tax imposed by this chapter for such taxable year.

1983—Pub. L. 98–21 inserted reference to permanently and totally disabled in section catchline.

Subsec. (a). Pub. L. 98–21 amended subsec. (a) generally, substituting reference to a qualified individual for reference to an individual who has attained the age of 65 before the close of the taxable year.

Subsec. (b). Pub. L. 98–21 in amending section generally added subsec. (b). Former subsec. (b) redesignated (c).

Subsec. (c). Pub. L. 98–21 in amending section generally, redesignated former subsec. (b) as (c) and, in (c) as so redesignated, added par. (2) and struck out former (2), which had provided that the initial amount was $2,500 in the case of a single individual, $2,500 in the case of a joint return where only one spouse was eligible for the credit under subsection (a), $3,750 in the case of a joint return where both spouses were eligible for the credit under subsection (a), or $1,875 in the case of a married individual filing a separate return, redesignated existing provisions as par. (3)(A), inserted "benefit" after "disability" therein, struck out former subpars. (A) to (C), which had specified sources of amounts received under title II of the Social Security Act, under the Railroad Retirement Act of 1935 or 1937, or otherwise excluded from gross income, added cls. (i) and (ii), substituted provision that no reduction would be made under cl. (i)(III) for any amount described in section 104(a)(4) for provision that no reduction would be made under former par. (3) for any amount excluded from gross income under section 72 (relating to annuities), 101 (relating to life insurance proceeds), 104 (relating to compensation for injuries or sickness), 105 (relating to amounts received under accident and health plans), 120 (relating to amounts received under qualified group legal services plans), 402 (relating to taxability of beneficiary of employees' trust), 403 (relating to taxation of employee annuities), or 405 (relating to qualified bond purchase plans), and added subpar. (B). Former subsec. (c) redesignated (d).

Subsec. (d). Pub. L. 98–21 in amending section generally redesignated former subsec. (c) as (d). Former subsec. (d) redesignated (e).

Subsec. (e). Pub. L. 98–21 in amending section generally, redesignated former subsec. (d) as (e) and struck out provision that "joint return" meant the joint return of a husband and wife made under section 6013 and inserted provisions defining permanent and total disability. Former subsec. (e), which provided for an election of prior law with respect to public retirement system income, was struck out.

Subsec. (f). Pub. L. 98–21 reenacted subsec. (f) without change.

1981—Subsec. (e)(9)(B). Pub. L. 97–34 substituted "section 911(d)(2)" for "section 911(b)".

1978—Subsec. (e)(2). Pub. L. 95–600, §701(a)(1), inserted "(and whose gross income includes income described in paragraph (4)(B))" after "who has not attained age 65 before the close of the taxable year".

Subsec. (e)(4)(B). Pub. L. 95–600, §701(a)(2), (3)(B), as amended by Pub. L. 96–222, §107(a)(1)(E)(i), inserted "and who performed the services giving rise to the pension or annuity (or is the spouse of the individual who performed the services)" after "before the close of the taxable year" and substituted reference to paragraph (9)(A) for reference to paragraph (8)(A).

Subsec. (e)(5)(B). Pub. L. 95–600, §701(a)(3)(C), as amended by Pub. L. 96–222, §107(a)(1)(E)(i), substituted reference to paragraph (9)(A) for reference to paragraph (8)(A).

Subsec. (e)(8), (9). Pub. L. 95–600, §701(a)(3)(A), as amended by Pub. L. 96–222, §107(a)(1)(E)(i), added par. (8) and redesignated former par. (8) as (9).

1976—Pub. L. 94–455, §503(a), among other changes, substituted "Credits for the elderly" for "Retirement income" in section catchline and in text substituted provisions permitting taxpayers who have all types of income to be eligible for the tax credit for provisions permitting taxpayers who have only retirement income to be eligible for the tax credit, eliminated provisions requiring taxpayers to earn $600 for the previous ten years for tax credit eligibility and provisions relating variations in treatment of married couples, and inserted provisions broadening coverage of the tax credit relief to low and middle income taxpayers.

Pub. L. 94–455, §1901(c)(1), purported to amend subsec. (f) of this section by striking out "a Territory". The amendment could not be executed in view of the prior general amendment of this section by section 503(a) of Pub. L. 94–455. Section 1901(c)(1) was repealed by section 703(j)(11) of Pub. L. 95–600.

1974—Subsec. (c)(1)(E), (F). Pub. L. 93–406 inserted reference in subpar. (E) to retirement bonds described in section 409 and added subpar. (F).

1964—Subsec. (a). Pub. L. 88–272, §§113(a), 201(d)(3), substituted "an amount equal to 17 percent, in the case of a taxable year beginning in 1964, or 15 percent, in the case of a taxable year beginning after December 31, 1964, of the amount received by such individual as retirement income (as defined in subsection (c) and as limited by subsection (d));" for "an amount equal to the amount received by such individual as retirement income (as defined in subsection (c) and as limited by subsection (d)), multiplied by the rate provided in section 1 for the first $2,000 of taxable income;", and struck out "section 34 (relating to credit for dividends received by individuals)", before "and section 35".

Subsecs. (i), (j). Pub. L. 88–272, §202(a), added subsec. (i) and redesignated former subsec. (i) as (j).

1962—Subsec. (c)(1). Pub. L. 87–792 inserted provisions in subpar. (A) requiring inclusion, in the case of an individual who is, or has been, an employee within the meaning of section 401(c)(1), distributions by a trust described in section 401(a) which is exempt from tax under section 501(a), and added subpar. (E).

Subsec. (d). Pub. L. 87–876 increased the limit on retirement income from $1,200 to $1,524, lowered the age requirement in par. (2)(A) from 65 to 62, and substituted provisions in par. (2)(B) which reduce the amount of retirement income for individuals who reach age 62, by one-half the amount of earned income in excess of $1,200 but not in excess of $1,700, and by the amount received over $1,700, for provisions which reduced such income by the amount earned over $1,200 by persons having reached age 65, and which defined income as in subsec. (g) of this section.

1956—Subsec. (d)(2). Act Jan. 28, 1956, reduced from 75 to 72 the age at which there will be no limitation on earned income and increased from $900 to $1,200 the amount that an individual over 65 can earn without reducing the $1,200 on which the retirement credit is computed.

1955—Subsec. (f). Act Aug. 9, 1955, extended the retirement income tax credit to members of the Armed Forces.

STATUTORY NOTES AND RELATED SUBSIDIARIES

EFFECTIVE DATE OF 1986 AMENDMENT

Amendment by Pub. L. 99–514 applicable to bonds issued after Aug. 15, 1986, except as otherwise provided, see sections 1311 to 1318 of Pub. L. 99–514, set out as an Effective Date; Transitional Rules note under section 141 of this title.

EFFECTIVE DATE OF 1984 AMENDMENT

Amendment by section 474(d) of Pub. L. 98–369 applicable to taxable years beginning after Dec. 31, 1983, and to carrybacks from such years, see section 475(a) of Pub. L. 98–369, set out as a note under section 21 of this title.

EFFECTIVE DATE OF 1983 AMENDMENT

Pub. L. 98–21, title I, §122(d), Apr. 20, 1983, 97 Stat. 87, as amended by Pub. L. 99–514, §2, Oct. 22, 1986, 100 Stat. 2095, provided that:

"(1) In general.—The amendments made by this section [amending sections 37 [now 22], 41 [now 24], 44A [now 21], 46, 53, 85, 105, 128, 403, 415, 904, and 7871 of this title] shall apply to taxable years beginning after December 31, 1983.

"(2) Transitional rule.—If an individual's annuity starting date was deferred under section 105(d)(6) of the Internal Revenue Code of 1986 [formerly I.R.C. 1954] (as in effect on the day before the date of the enactment of this section [Apr. 20, 1983]), such deferral shall end on the first day of such individual's first taxable year beginning after December 31, 1983."

EFFECTIVE DATE OF 1981 AMENDMENT

Amendment by Pub. L. 97–34 applicable with respect to taxable years beginning after Dec. 31, 1981, see section 115 of Pub. L. 97–34, set out as a note under section 911 of this title.

EFFECTIVE DATE OF 1978 AMENDMENT

Pub. L. 95–600, title VII, §701(a)(4), Nov. 6, 1978, 92 Stat. 2898, provided that:

"(A) The amendments made by paragraphs (1) and (2) [amending this section] shall apply to taxable years beginning after December 31, 1975.

"(B) The amendments made by paragraph (3) [amending this section] shall apply to taxable years beginning after December 31, 1977."

EFFECTIVE DATE OF 1976 AMENDMENT

Amendment by Pub. L. 94–455 applicable with respect to taxable years beginning after Dec. 31, 1975, see section 508 of Pub. L. 94–455, set out as a note under section 3 of this title.

EFFECTIVE DATE OF 1974 AMENDMENT

Amendment by Pub. L. 93–406 effective Jan. 1, 1974, see section 2002(i)(2) of Pub. L. 93–406, set out as an Effective Date note under section 4973 of this title.

EFFECTIVE DATE OF 1964 AMENDMENT

Amendment by section 113(a) of Pub. L. 88–272, except for purposes of section 21 [now 15] of this title, effective with respect to taxable years beginning after Dec. 31, 1963, see section 131 of Pub. L. 88–272, set out as a note under section 1 of this title.

Pub. L. 88–272, title II, §201(e), Feb. 26, 1964, 78 Stat. 32, provided that: "The amendments made by subsection (a) [amending section 34 of this title] shall apply with respect to taxable years ending after December 31, 1963. The amendment made by subsection (b) [repealing section 34 of this title] shall apply with respect to taxable years ending after December 31, 1964. The amendment made by subsection (c) [amending section 116 of this title] shall apply with respect to taxable years beginning after December 31, 1963. The amendments made by subsection (d) [amending sections 35, 37 [now 22], 46, 116, 584, 642, 702, 854, 857, 871, 1375, and 6014 of this title] shall apply with respect to dividends received after December 31, 1964, in taxable years ending after such date".

Pub. L. 88–272, title II, §202(b), Feb. 26, 1964, 78 Stat. 33, provided that: "The amendments made by subsection (a) [amending this section] shall apply to taxable years beginning after December 31, 1963."

EFFECTIVE DATE OF 1962 AMENDMENT

Pub. L. 87–876, §2, Oct. 24, 1962, 76 Stat. 1199, provided that: "The amendment made by the first section of this Act [amending this section] shall apply only to taxable years ending after the date of the enactment of this Act [Oct. 24, 1962]."

Pub. L. 87–792, §8, Oct. 10, 1962, 76 Stat. 831, provided that: "The amendments made by this Act [enacting sections 405 and 6047 of this title and amending sections 37 [now 22], 62, 72, 101, 104, 105, 172, 401 to 404, 503, 805, 1361, 2039, 2517, 3306, 3401 and 7207 of this title] shall apply to taxable years beginning after December 31, 1962."

EFFECTIVE DATE OF 1956 AMENDMENT

Act Jan. 28, 1956, ch. 18, §2, 70 Stat. 9, provided that: "The amendment made by the first section of this Act [amending this section] shall apply only with respect to taxable years beginning after December 31, 1955."

EFFECTIVE DATE OF 1955 AMENDMENT

Act Aug. 9, 1955, ch. 659, §2, 69 Stat. 591, provided that: "The amendment made by this Act [amending this section] shall be applicable to taxable years beginning after December 31, 1954."

DETERMINATION OF RETIREMENT INCOME CREDIT UNDER PROVISIONS AS THEY EXISTED PRIOR TO AMENDMENT BY PUB. L. 94–455 ELECTION

Pub. L. 95–30, title IV, §403, May 23, 1977, 91 Stat. 155, as amended by Pub. L. 99–514, §2, Oct. 22, 1986, 100 Stat. 2095, provided that: "A taxpayer may elect (at such time and in such manner as the Secretary of the Treasury or his delegate shall prescribe) to determine the amount of his credit under section 37 [now 22] of the Internal Revenue Code of 1986 [formerly I.R.C. 1954] for his first taxable year beginning in 1976 under the provisions of such section as they existed before the amendment made by section 503 of the Tax Reform Act of 1976 [Pub. L. 94–455]."

§23. Adoption expenses

(a) Allowance of credit

(1) In general

In the case of an individual, there shall be allowed as a credit against the tax imposed by this chapter the amount of the qualified adoption expenses paid or incurred by the taxpayer.

(2) Year credit allowed

The credit under paragraph (1) with respect to any expense shall be allowed—

(A) in the case of any expense paid or incurred before the taxable year in which such adoption becomes final, for the taxable year following the taxable year during which such expense is paid or incurred, and

(B) in the case of an expense paid or incurred during or after the taxable year in which such adoption becomes final, for the taxable year in which such expense is paid or incurred.

(3) $10,000 credit for adoption of child with special needs regardless of expenses

In the case of an adoption of a child with special needs which becomes final during a taxable year, the taxpayer shall be treated as having paid during such year qualified adoption expenses with respect to such adoption in an amount equal to the excess (if any) of $10,000 over the aggregate qualified adoption expenses actually paid or incurred by the taxpayer with respect to such adoption during such taxable year and all prior taxable years.

(b) Limitations

(1) Dollar limitation

The aggregate amount of qualified adoption expenses which may be taken into account under subsection (a) for all taxable years with respect to the adoption of a child by the taxpayer shall not exceed $10,000.

(2) Income limitation

(A) In general

The amount allowable as a credit under subsection (a) for any taxable year (determined without regard to subsection (c)) shall be reduced (but not below zero) by an amount which bears the same ratio to the amount so allowable (determined without regard to this paragraph but with regard to paragraph (1)) as—

(i) the amount (if any) by which the taxpayer's adjusted gross income exceeds $150,000, bears to

(ii) $40,000.

(B) Determination of adjusted gross income

For purposes of subparagraph (A), adjusted gross income shall be determined without regard to sections 911, 931, and 933.

(3) Denial of double benefit

(A) In general

No credit shall be allowed under subsection (a) for any expense for which a deduction or credit is allowed under any other provision of this chapter.

(B) Grants

No credit shall be allowed under subsection (a) for any expense to the extent that funds for such expense are received under any Federal, State, or local program.

(c) Carryforwards of unused credit

(1) In general

If the credit allowable under subsection (a) for any taxable year exceeds the limitation imposed by section 26(a) for such taxable year reduced by the sum of the credits allowable under this subpart (other than this section and section 25D), such excess shall be carried to the succeeding taxable year and added to the credit allowable under subsection (a) for such taxable year.

(2) Limitation

No credit may be carried forward under this subsection to any taxable year following the fifth taxable year after the taxable year in which the credit arose. For purposes of the preceding sentence, credits shall be treated as used on a first-in first-out basis.

(d) Definitions

For purposes of this section—

(1) Qualified adoption expenses

The term "qualified adoption expenses" means reasonable and necessary adoption fees, court costs, attorney fees, and other expenses—

(A) which are directly related to, and the principal purpose of which is for, the legal adoption of an eligible child by the taxpayer,

(B) which are not incurred in violation of State or Federal law or in carrying out any surrogate parenting arrangement,

(C) which are not expenses in connection with the adoption by an individual of a child who is the child of such individual's spouse, and

(D) which are not reimbursed under an employer program or otherwise.

(2) Eligible child

The term "eligible child" means any individual who—

(A) has not attained age 18, or

(B) is physically or mentally incapable of caring for himself.

(3) Child with special needs

The term "child with special needs" means any child if—

(A) a State has determined that the child cannot or should not be returned to the home of his parents,

(B) such State has determined that there exists with respect to the child a specific factor or condition (such as his ethnic background, age, or membership in a minority or sibling group, or the presence of factors such as medical conditions or physical, mental, or emotional handicaps) because of which it is reasonable to conclude that such child cannot be placed with adoptive parents without providing adoption assistance, and

(C) such child is a citizen or resident of the United States (as defined in section 217(h)(3)).

(e) Special rules for foreign adoptions

In the case of an adoption of a child who is not a citizen or resident of the United States (as defined in section 217(h)(3))—

(1) subsection (a) shall not apply to any qualified adoption expense with respect to such adoption unless such adoption becomes final, and

(2) any such expense which is paid or incurred before the taxable year in which such adoption becomes final shall be taken into account under this section as if such expense were paid or incurred during such year.

(f) Filing requirements

(1) Married couples must file joint returns

Rules similar to the rules of paragraphs (2), (3), and (4) of section 21(e) shall apply for purposes of this section.

(2) Taxpayer must include TIN

(A) In general

No credit shall be allowed under this section with respect to any eligible child unless the taxpayer includes (if known) the name, age, and TIN of such child on the return of tax for the taxable year.

(B) Other methods

The Secretary may, in lieu of the information referred to in subparagraph (A), require other information meeting the purposes of subparagraph (A), including identification of an agent assisting with the adoption.

(g) Basis adjustments

For purposes of this subtitle, if a credit is allowed under this section for any expenditure with respect to any property, the increase in the basis of such property which would (but for this subsection) result from such expenditure shall be reduced by the amount of the credit so allowed.

(h) Adjustments for inflation

In the case of a taxable year beginning after December 31, 2002, each of the dollar amounts in subsection (a)(3) and paragraphs (1) and (2)(A)(i) of subsection (b) shall be increased by an amount equal to—

(1) such dollar amount, multiplied by

(2) the cost-of-living adjustment determined under section 1(f)(3) for the calendar year in which the taxable year begins, determined by substituting "calendar year 2001" for "calendar year 2016" in subparagraph (A)(ii) thereof.

If any amount as increased under the preceding sentence is not a multiple of $10, such amount shall be rounded to the nearest multiple of $10.

(i) Regulations

The Secretary shall prescribe such regulations as may be appropriate to carry out this section and section 137, including regulations which treat unmarried individuals who pay or incur qualified adoption expenses with respect to the same child as 1 taxpayer for purposes of applying the dollar amounts in subsections (a)(3) and (b)(1) of this section and in section 137(b)(1).

(Added Pub. L. 104–188, title I, §1807(a), Aug. 20, 1996, 110 Stat. 1899, §23; amended Pub. L. 105–34, title XVI, §1601(h)(2)(A), (B), Aug. 5, 1997, 111 Stat. 1092; Pub. L. 105–206, title VI, §§6008(d)(6), 6018(f)(1), July 22, 1998, 112 Stat. 812, 823; Pub. L. 107–16, title II, §§201(b)(2)(E), 202(a)(1), (b)(1)(A), (2)(A), (c), (d)(1), (e)(1), (f)(1), (2)(A), June 7, 2001, 115 Stat. 46–49; Pub. L. 107–147, title IV, §§411(c)(1)(A)–(E), 418(a)(1), Mar. 9, 2002, 116 Stat. 45, 57; Pub. L. 109–58, title XIII, §1335(b)(1), Aug. 8, 2005, 119 Stat. 1036; Pub. L. 109–135, title IV, §402(i)(3)(A), (4), Dec. 21, 2005, 119 Stat. 2612, 2615; Pub. L. 110–343, div. B, title I, §106(e)(2)(A), Oct. 3, 2008, 122 Stat. 3817; renumbered §36C, amended, and renumbered §23, Pub. L. 111–148, title X, §10909(a)(1), (b)(1), (2)(I), (c), Mar. 23, 2010, 124 Stat. 1021, 1022, 1023; Pub. L. 111–312, title I, §101(b)(1), Dec. 17, 2010, 124 Stat. 3298; Pub. L. 112–240, title I, §104(c)(2)(A), Jan. 2, 2013, 126 Stat. 2321; Pub. L. 115–97, title I, §11002(d)(1)(A), Dec. 22, 2017, 131 Stat. 2060; Pub. L. 115–141, div. U, title IV, §401(d)(4)(B)(i), Mar. 23, 2018, 132 Stat. 1209.)

INFLATION ADJUSTED ITEMS FOR CERTAIN YEARS

For inflation adjustment of certain items in this section, see Revenue Procedures listed in a table under section 1 of this title.

EDITORIAL NOTES
PRIOR PROVISIONS

A prior section 23, added <u>Pub. L. 95–618, title I, §101(a), Nov. 9, 1978, 92 Stat. 3175</u>, §44C; amended <u>Pub. L. 96–223, title II, §§201, 202(a)–(d), 203(a), Apr. 2, 1980, 94 Stat. 256, 258</u>; renumbered §23 and amended <u>Pub. L. 98–369, div. A, title IV, §§471(c), 474(e), title VI, §612(e)(2), July 18, 1984, 98 Stat. 826, 831, 912</u>, related to residential energy credit, prior to repeal by <u>Pub. L. 101–508, title XI, §11801(a)(1), Nov. 5, 1990, 104 Stat. 1388–520</u>.

AMENDMENTS

2018—Subsec. (c)(1). Pub. L. 115–141 substituted "section 25D" for "sections 25D and 1400C".

2017—Subsec. (h)(2). Pub. L. 115–97 substituted "for 'calendar year 2016' in subparagraph (A)(ii)" for "for 'calendar year 1992' in subparagraph (B)".

2013—Subsec. (b)(4). Pub. L. 112–240, §104(c)(2)(A)(i), struck out par. (4). Prior to amendment, text read as follows: "In the case of a taxable year to which section 26(a)(2) does not apply, the credit allowed under subsection (a) for any taxable year shall not exceed the excess of—

"(A) the sum of the regular tax liability (as defined in section 26(b)) plus the tax imposed by section 55, over

"(B) the sum of the credits allowable under this subpart (other than this section and section 25D) and section 27 for the taxable year."

Subsec. (c). Pub. L. 112–240, §104(c)(2)(A)(ii), (iii), added par. (1), redesignated par. (3) as (2), and struck out former pars. (1) and (2) which related to rule for years in which all personal credits allowed against regular and alternative minimum tax and rule for other years, respectively.

2010—Subsec. (a)(3). Pub. L. 111–148, §10909(a)(1)(B), (c), as amended by Pub. L. 111–312, temporarily substituted "$13,170" for "$10,000" in heading and text. See Effective and Termination Dates of 2010 Amendment note below.

Subsec. (b)(1). Pub. L. 111–148, §10909(a)(1)(A), (c), as amended by Pub. L. 111–312, temporarily substituted "$13,170" for "$10,000". See Effective and Termination Dates of 2010 Amendment note below.

Subsec. (b)(4). Pub. L. 111–148, §10909(b)(2)(I)(i), (c), as amended by Pub. L. 111–312, temporarily struck out par. (4). Text read as follows: "In the case of a taxable year to which section 26(a)(2) does not apply, the credit allowed under subsection (a) for any taxable year shall not exceed the excess of—

"(A) the sum of the regular tax liability (as defined in section 26(b)) plus the tax imposed by section 55, over

"(B) the sum of the credits allowable under this subpart (other than this section and section 25D) and section 27 for the taxable year."

See Effective and Termination Dates of 2010 Amendment note below.

Subsec. (c). Pub. L. 111–148, §10909(b)(2)(I)(ii), (c), as amended by Pub. L. 111–312, temporarily struck out subsec. (c) which related to carryforwards of unused credit. See Effective and Termination Dates of 2010 Amendment note below.

Subsec. (h). Pub. L. 111–148, §10909(a)(1)(C), (c), as amended by Pub. L. 111–312, temporarily amended subsec. (h) generally. Prior to amendment, subsec. (h) related to adjustments for inflation. See Effective and Termination Dates of 2010 Amendment note below.

2008—Subsec. (b)(4)(B). Pub. L. 110–343 inserted "and section 25D" after "this section".

2005—Subsec. (b)(4). Pub. L. 109–135, §402(i)(3)(A)(i), substituted "In the case of a taxable year to which section 26(a)(2) does not apply, the credit" for "The credit" in introductory provisions.

Subsec. (c). Pub. L. 109–135, §402(i)(3)(A)(ii), reenacted heading without change and amended text generally. Prior to amendment, text read as follows: "If the credit allowable under subsection (a) for any taxable year exceeds the limitation imposed by subsection (b)(4) for such taxable year, such excess shall be carried to the succeeding taxable year and added to the credit allowable under subsection (a) for such taxable year. No credit may be carried forward under this subsection to any taxable year following the fifth taxable year after the taxable year in which the credit arose. For purposes of the preceding sentence, credits shall be treated as used on a first-in first-out basis."

Pub. L. 109–58, §1335(b)(1), which directed amendment of subsec. (c) by substituting "this section, section 25D, and section 1400C" for "this section and section 1400C", was repealed by Pub. L. 109–135, §402(i)(4). See Effective and Termination Dates of 2005 Amendment notes below.

2002—Subsec. (a)(1). Pub. L. 107–147, §411(c)(1)(A), reenacted heading without change and amended text of par. (1) generally. Prior to amendment, text read as follows: "In the case of an individual, there shall be allowed as a credit against the tax imposed by this chapter—

"(A) in the case of an adoption of a child other than a child with special needs, the amount of the qualified adoption expenses paid or incurred by the taxpayer, and

"(B) in the case of an adoption of a child with special needs, $10,000."

Subsec. (a)(2). Pub. L. 107–147, §411(c)(1)(C), struck out concluding provisions which read as follows: "In the case of the adoption of a child with special needs, the credit allowed under paragraph (1) shall be allowed for the taxable year in which the adoption becomes final."

Subsec. (a)(3). Pub. L. 107–147, §411(c)(1)(B), added par. (3).

Subsec. (b)(1). Pub. L. 107–147, §411(c)(1)(D), substituted "subsection (a)" for "subsection (a)(1)(A)".

Subsec. (h). Pub. L. 107–147, §418(a)(1), substituted "subsection (a)(3)" for "subsection (a)(1)(B)" in introductory provisions and inserted concluding provisions.

Subsec. (i). Pub. L. 107–147, §411(c)(1)(E), substituted "the dollar amounts in subsections (a)(3) and (b)(1)" for "the dollar limitation in subsection (b)(1)".

2001—Subsec. (a)(1). Pub. L. 107–16, §202(a)(1), amended heading and text of par. (1) generally. Prior to amendment, text read as follows: "In the case of an individual, there shall be allowed as a credit against the tax imposed by this chapter the amount of the qualified adoption expenses paid or incurred by the taxpayer."

Subsec. (a)(2). Pub. L. 107–16, §202(c), inserted concluding provisions.

Subsec. (b)(1). Pub. L. 107–16, §202(c)(1)(A), substituted "subsection (a)(1)(A)" for "subsection (a)" and "$10,000" for "$5,000" and struck out "($6,000, in the case of a child with special needs)" before period at end.

Subsec. (b)(2)(A)(i). Pub. L. 107–16, §202(b)(2)(A), substituted "$150,000" for "$75,000".

Subsec. (b)(4). Pub. L. 107–16, §202(f)(1), added par. (4).

Subsec. (c). Pub. L. 107–16, §202(f)(2)(A), substituted "subsection (b)(4)" for "section 26(a)" and struck out "reduced by the sum of the credits allowable under this subpart (other than this section and sections 24 and 1400C)" before ", such excess".

Pub. L. 107–16, §201(b)(2)(E), substituted "and sections 24 and 1400C" for "and section 1400C".

Subsec. (d)(2). Pub. L. 107–16, §202(d)(1), amended heading and text of par. (2) generally. Prior to amendment, text read as follows: "The term 'eligible child' means any individual—

"(A) who—

"(i) has not attained age 18, or

"(ii) is physically or mentally incapable of caring for himself, and

"(B) in the case of qualified adoption expenses paid or incurred after December 31, 2001, who is a child with special needs."

Subsecs. (h), (i). Pub. L. 107–16, §202(e)(1), added subsec. (h) and redesignated former subsec. (h) as (i).

1998—Subsec. (b)(2)(A). Pub. L. 105–206, §6018(f)(1), inserted "(determined without regard to subsection (c))" after "for any taxable year" in introductory provisions.

Subsec. (c). Pub. L. 105–206, §6008(d)(6), inserted "and section 1400C" after "other than this section".

1997—Subsec. (a)(2). Pub. L. 105–34, §1601(h)(2)(A), amended heading and text of par. (2) generally. Prior to amendment, text read as follows: "The credit under paragraph (1) with respect to any expense shall be allowed—

"(A) for the taxable year following the taxable year during which such expense is paid or incurred, or

"(B) in the case of an expense which is paid or incurred during the taxable year in which the adoption becomes final, for such taxable year."

Subsec. (b)(2)(B). Pub. L. 105–34, §1601(h)(2)(B), substituted "determined without regard to sections 911, 931, and 933." for "determined—

"(i) without regard to sections 911, 931, and 933, and

139

"(ii) after the application of sections 86, 135, 137, 219, and 469."

STATUTORY NOTES AND RELATED SUBSIDIARIES

EFFECTIVE DATE OF 2017 AMENDMENT

Amendment by Pub. L. 115–97 applicable to taxable years beginning after Dec. 31, 2017, see section 11002(e) of Pub. L. 115–97, set out as a note under section 1 of this title.

EFFECTIVE DATE OF 2013 AMENDMENT

Pub. L. 112–240, title I, §104(d), Jan. 2, 2013, 126 Stat. 2323, provided that: "The amendments made by this section [amending this section and sections 24, 25, 25A, 25B, 25D, 26, 30, 30B, 30D, 55, 904, and 1400C of this title] shall apply to taxable years beginning after December 31, 2011."

EFFECTIVE AND TERMINATION DATES OF 2010 AMENDMENT

Amendment by Pub. L. 111–148 terminated applicable to taxable years beginning after Dec. 31, 2011, and section is amended to read as if such amendment had never been enacted, see section 10909(c) of Pub. L. 111–148, set out as a note under section 1 of this title.

Amendment by Pub. L. 111–148 applicable to taxable years beginning after Dec. 31, 2009, see section 10909(d) of Pub. L. 111–148, set out as a note under section 1 of this title.

EFFECTIVE AND TERMINATION DATES OF 2008 AMENDMENT

Pub. L. 110–343, div. B, title I, §106(f), Oct. 3, 2008, 122 Stat. 3817, provided that:

"(1) In general.—Except as provided in paragraph (2), the amendments made by this section [amending this section and sections 24, 25B, 25D, 26, and 45 of this title] shall apply to taxable years beginning after December 31, 2007.

"(2) Solar electric property limitation.—The amendments made by subsection (b) [amending section 25D of this title] shall apply to taxable years beginning after December 31, 2008.

"(3) Application of egtrra sunset.—The amendments made by subparagraphs (A) and (B) of subsection (e)(2) [amending this section and section 24 of this title] shall be subject to title IX of the Economic Growth and Tax Relief Reconciliation Act of 2001 [Pub. L. 107–16, §901, which was repealed by Pub. L. 112–240, title I, §101(a)(1), Jan. 2, 2013, 126 Stat. 2315, was formerly set out as an Effective and Termination Dates of 2001 Amendment note under section 1 of this title] in the same manner as the provisions of such Act to which such amendments relate."

EFFECTIVE AND TERMINATION DATES OF 2005 AMENDMENT

Pub. L. 109–135, title IV, §402(i)(3)(H), Dec. 21, 2005, 119 Stat. 2615, provided that: "The amendments made by this paragraph [amending this section and sections 24, 25, 25B, 25D, 904, and 1400C of this title] (and each part thereof) shall be subject to title IX of the Economic Growth and Tax Relief Reconciliation Act of 2001 [Pub. L. 107–16, §901, which was repealed by Pub. L. 112–240, title I, §101(a)(1), Jan. 2, 2013, 126 Stat. 2315, was formerly set out as an Effective and Termination Dates of 2001 Amendment note under section 1 of this title] in the same manner as the provisions of such Act to which such amendment (or part thereof) relates."

Pub. L. 109–135, title IV, §402(i)(4), Dec. 21, 2005, 119 Stat. 2615, struck out Pub. L. 109–58, §1335(b)(1)–(3), and provided in part that: "The Internal Revenue Code of 1986 shall be applied and administered as if the amendments made [by] such paragraphs [amending this section and sections 25 and 1400C of this title] had never been enacted."

Pub. L. 109–135, title IV, §402(m), Dec. 21, 2005, 119 Stat. 2615, provided that:

"(1) In general.—Except as provided in paragraphs (2) and (3), the amendments made by this section [see Tables for classification] shall take effect as if included in the provisions of the Energy Policy Act of 2005 [Pub. L. 109–58] to which they relate.

"(2) Repeal of public utility holding company act of 1935.—The amendments made by subsection (a) [amending sections 121, 246, 247, 1223, 1245, and 1250 of this title and repealing sections 1081 to 1083 of this title] shall not apply with respect to any transaction ordered in compliance with the Public Utility Holding Company Act of 1935 [15 U.S.C. 79 et seq.] before its repeal.

"(3) Coordination of personal credits.—The amendments made by subsection (i)(3) [amending this section and sections 24, 25, 25B, 25D, 904, and 1400C of this title] shall apply to taxable years beginning after December 31, 2005."

Pub. L. 109–58, title XIII, §1335(c), Aug. 8, 2005, 119 Stat. 1036, provided that: "The amendments made by this section [enacting section 25D of this title and amending this section and sections 25, 1016, and 1400C of this title] shall apply to property placed in service after December 31, 2005, in taxable years ending after such date."

EFFECTIVE DATE OF 2002 AMENDMENT

Pub. L. 107–147, title IV, §411(c)(3), Mar. 9, 2002, 116 Stat. 46, provided that: "The amendments made by this subsection [amending this section and section 137 of this title] shall apply to taxable years beginning after December 31, 2002; except that the amendments made by paragraphs (1)(C), (1)(D) [amending this section], and (2)(B) [amending section 137 of this title] shall apply to taxable years beginning after December 31, 2001."

Amendment by section 418(a)(1) of Pub. L. 107–147 effective as if included in the provisions of the Economic Growth and Tax Relief Reconciliation Act of 2001, Pub. L. 107–16, to which such amendment relates, see section 418(c) of Pub. L. 107–147, set out as a note under section 21 of this title.

EFFECTIVE DATE OF 2001 AMENDMENT

Pub. L. 108–311, title III, §312(b)(2), Oct. 4, 2004, 118 Stat. 1181, provided that: "The amendments made by sections 201(b), 202(f), and 618(b) of the Economic Growth and Tax Relief Reconciliation Act of 2001 [Pub. L. 107–16, amending this section and sections 24, 25, 25B, 26, 904, and 1400C of this title] shall not apply to taxable years beginning during 2004 or 2005."

Pub. L. 107–147, title VI, §601(b)(2), Mar. 9, 2002, 116 Stat. 59, provided that: "The amendments made by sections 201(b), 202(f), and 618(b) of the Economic Growth and Tax Relief Reconciliation Act of 2001 [Pub. L. 107–16, amending this section and sections 24, 25, 25B, 26, 904, and 1400C of this title] shall not apply to taxable years beginning during 2002 and 2003."

Amendment by section 201(b)(2)(E) of Pub. L. 107–16 applicable to taxable years beginning after Dec. 31, 2001, see section 201(e)(2) of Pub. L. 107–16, set out as a note under section 24 of this title.

Pub. L. 107–16, title II, §202(g), June 7, 2001, 115 Stat. 49, provided that:

"(1) In general.—Except as provided in paragraph (2), the amendments made by this section [amending this section and sections 24, 26, 137, 904, and 1400C of this title] shall apply to taxable years beginning after December 31, 2001.

"(2) Subsection (a).—The amendments made by subsection (a) [amending this section and section 137 of this title] shall apply to taxable years beginning after December 31, 2002."

EFFECTIVE DATE OF 1998 AMENDMENT

Pub. L. 105–206, title VI, §6018(h), July 22, 1998, 112 Stat. 823, provided that: "The amendments made by this section [amending this section and sections 219, 408, 414, and 679 of this title and amending provisions set out as notes under sections 167 and 4091 of this title] shall take effect as if included in the provisions of the Small Business Job Protection Act of 1996 [Pub. L. 104–188] to which they relate."

Amendment by section 6008(d)(6) of Pub. L. 105–206 effective, except as otherwise provided, as if included in the provisions of the Taxpayer Relief Act of 1997, Pub. L. 105–34, to which such amendment relates, see section 6024 of Pub. L. 105–206, set out as a note under section 1 of this title.

EFFECTIVE DATE OF 1997 AMENDMENT

Pub. L. 105–34, title XVI, §1601(j), Aug. 5, 1997, 111 Stat. 1093, provided that:

"(1) In general.—Except as provided in paragraph (2), the amendments made by this section [amending this section, sections 30A, 52, 55, 137, 401, 403, 404, 408, 414, 512, 529, 593, 641, 679, 860L, 956, 1361, 1374, 4001, 4041, 4092, 4261, 6039D, 6048, 6050R, 6501, 6693, 7701, and 9503 of this title, section 1055 of Title 29, Labor, and provisions set out as notes under sections 529 and 4091 of this title] shall take effect as if included in the provisions of the Small Business Job Protection Act of 1996 [Pub. L. 104–188] to which they relate.

"(2) Certain administrative requirements with respect to certain pension plans.—The amendment made by subsection (d)(2)(D) [amending section 401 of this title] shall apply to calendar years beginning after the date of the enactment of this Act [Aug. 5, 1997]."

EFFECTIVE DATE

Pub. L. 104–188, title I, §1807(e), Aug. 20, 1996, 110 Stat. 1903, provided that: "The amendments made by this section [enacting this section and section 137 of this title, renumbering former section 137 of this title as section 138, and amending sections 25, 86, 135, 219, 469, and 1016 of this title] shall apply to taxable years beginning after December 31, 1996."

SAVINGS PROVISION

Amendment by Pub. L. 115–141 not applicable to certain obligations issued, DC Zone assets acquired, or principal residences acquired before Jan. 1, 2012, see section 401(d)(4)(C) of Pub. L. 115–141, set out as a note under former section 1400 of this title.

Pub. L. 115–141, div. U, title IV, §401(e), Mar. 23, 2018, 132 Stat. 1212, provided that: "If—

"(1) any provision amended or repealed by the amendments made by subsection (b) or (d) [see Tables for classification] applied to—

"(A) any transaction occurring before the date of the enactment of this Act [Mar. 23, 2018],

"(B) any property acquired before such date of enactment, or

"(C) any item of income, loss, deduction, or credit taken into account before such date of enactment, and

"(2) the treatment of such transaction, property, or item under such provision would (without regard to the amendments or repeals made by such subsection) affect the liability for tax for periods ending after such date of enactment,

nothing in the amendments or repeals made by this section [see Tables for classification] shall be construed to affect the treatment of such transaction, property, or item for purposes of determining liability for tax for periods ending after such date of enactment."

EXPENSES PAID OR INCURRED BEFORE 2002

Pub. L. 107–147, title IV, §411(c)(1)(F), Mar. 9, 2002, 116 Stat. 45, provided that: "Expenses paid or incurred during any taxable year beginning before January 1, 2002, may be taken into account in determining the credit under section 23 of the Internal Revenue Code of 1986 only to the extent the aggregate of such expenses does not exceed the applicable limitation under section 23(b)(1) of such Code as in effect on the day before the date of the enactment of the Economic Growth and Tax Relief Reconciliation Act of 2001 [June 7, 2001]."

TAX CREDIT AND GROSS INCOME EXCLUSION STUDY AND REPORT

Pub. L. 104–188, title I, §1807(d), Aug. 20, 1996, 110 Stat. 1903, provided that: "The Secretary of the Treasury shall study the effect on adoptions of the tax credit and gross income exclusion established by the amendments made by this section [enacting this section and section 137 of this title, renumbering former section 137 of this title as section 138, and amending sections 25, 86, 135, 219, 469, and 1016 of this title] and shall submit a report regarding the study to the Committee on Finance of the Senate and the Committee on Ways and Means of the House of Representatives not later than January 1, 2000."

§24. Child tax credit

(a) Allowance of credit

There shall be allowed as a credit against the tax imposed by this chapter for the taxable year with respect to each qualifying child of the taxpayer for which the taxpayer is allowed a deduction under section 151 an amount equal to $1,000.

(b) Limitations

(1) Limitation based on adjusted gross income

The amount of the credit allowable under subsection (a) shall be reduced (but not below zero) by $50 for each $1,000 (or fraction thereof) by which the taxpayer's modified adjusted gross income exceeds the threshold amount. For purposes of the preceding sentence, the term "modified adjusted gross income" means adjusted gross income increased by any amount excluded from gross income under section 911, 931, or 933.

(2) Threshold amount

For purposes of paragraph (1), the term "threshold amount" means—

(A) $110,000 in the case of a joint return,

(B) $75,000 in the case of an individual who is not married, and

(C) $55,000 in the case of a married individual filing a separate return.

For purposes of this paragraph, marital status shall be determined under section 7703.

(c) Qualifying child

For purposes of this section—

(1) In general

The term "qualifying child" means a qualifying child of the taxpayer (as defined in section 152(c)) who has not attained age 17.

(2) Exception for certain noncitizens

The term "qualifying child" shall not include any individual who would not be a dependent if subparagraph (A) of section 152(b)(3) were applied without regard to all that follows "resident of the United States".

(d) Portion of credit refundable

(1) In general

The aggregate credits allowed to a taxpayer under subpart C shall be increased by the lesser of—

(A) the credit which would be allowed under this section without regard to this subsection and the limitation under section 26(a) or

(B) the amount by which the aggregate amount of credits allowed by this subpart (determined without regard to this subsection) would increase if the limitation imposed by section 26(a) were increased by the greater of—

(i) 15 percent of so much of the taxpayer's earned income (within the meaning of section 32) which is taken into account in computing taxable income for the taxable year as exceeds $3,000, or

(ii) in the case of a taxpayer with 3 or more qualifying children, the excess (if any) of—

(I) the taxpayer's social security taxes for the taxable year, over

(II) the credit allowed under section 32 for the taxable year.

The amount of the credit allowed under this subsection shall not be treated as a credit allowed under this subpart and shall reduce the amount of credit otherwise allowable under subsection (a) without regard to section 26(a). For purposes of subparagraph (B), any amount excluded from gross income by reason of section 112 shall be treated as earned income which is taken into account in computing taxable income for the taxable year.

(2) Social security taxes

For purposes of paragraph (1)—

(A) In general

The term "social security taxes" means, with respect to any taxpayer for any taxable year—

(i) the amount of the taxes imposed by sections 3101 and 3201(a) on amounts received by the taxpayer during the calendar year in which the taxable year begins,

(ii) 50 percent of the taxes imposed by section 1401 on the self-employment income of the taxpayer for the taxable year, and

(iii) 50 percent of the taxes imposed by section 3211(a) on amounts received by the taxpayer during the calendar year in which the taxable year begins.

(B) Coordination with special refund of social security taxes

The term "social security taxes" shall not include any taxes to the extent the taxpayer is entitled to a special refund of such taxes under section 6413(c).

(C) Special rule

Any amounts paid pursuant to an agreement under section 3121(l) (relating to agreements entered into by American employers with respect to foreign affiliates) which are equivalent to the taxes referred to in subparagraph (A)(i) shall be treated as taxes referred to in such subparagraph.

(3) Exception for taxpayers excluding foreign earned income

Paragraph (1) shall not apply to any taxpayer for any taxable year if such taxpayer elects to exclude any amount from gross income under section 911 for such taxable year.

(e) Identification requirements

(1) Qualifying child identification requirement

No credit shall be allowed under this section to a taxpayer with respect to any qualifying child unless the taxpayer includes the name and taxpayer identification number of such qualifying child on the return of tax for the taxable year and such taxpayer identification number was issued on or before the due date for filing such return.

(2) Taxpayer identification requirement

No credit shall be allowed under this section if the taxpayer identification number of the taxpayer was issued after the due date for filing the return for the taxable year.

(f) Taxable year must be full taxable year

Except in the case of a taxable year closed by reason of the death of the taxpayer, no credit shall be allowable under this section in the case of a taxable year covering a period of less than 12 months.

(g) Restrictions on taxpayers who improperly claimed credit in prior year

(1) Taxpayers making prior fraudulent or reckless claims

(A) In general

No credit shall be allowed under this section for any taxable year in the disallowance period.

(B) Disallowance period

For purposes of subparagraph (A), the disallowance period is—

(i) the period of 10 taxable years after the most recent taxable year for which there was a final determination that the taxpayer's claim of credit under this section was due to fraud, and

(ii) the period of 2 taxable years after the most recent taxable year for which there was a final determination that the taxpayer's claim of credit under this section was due to reckless or intentional disregard of rules and regulations (but not due to fraud).

(2) Taxpayers making improper prior claims

In the case of a taxpayer who is denied credit under this section for any taxable year as a result of the deficiency procedures under subchapter B of chapter 63, no credit shall be allowed under this section for any subsequent taxable year unless the taxpayer provides such information as the Secretary may require to demonstrate eligibility for such credit.

(h) Special rules for taxable years 2018 through 2025

(1) In general

In the case of a taxable year beginning after December 31, 2017, and before January 1, 2026, this section shall be applied as provided in paragraphs (2) through (7).

(2) Credit amount

Subsection (a) shall be applied by substituting "$2,000" for "$1,000".

(3) Limitation

In lieu of the amount determined under subsection (b)(2), the threshold amount shall be $400,000 in the case of a joint return ($200,000 in any other case).

(4) Partial credit allowed for certain other dependents

(A) In general

The credit determined under subsection (a) (after the application of paragraph (2)) shall be increased by $500 for each dependent of the taxpayer (as defined in section 152) other than a qualifying child described in subsection (c).

(B) Exception for certain noncitizens

Subparagraph (A) shall not apply with respect to any individual who would not be a dependent if subparagraph (A) of section 152(b)(3) were applied without regard to all that follows "resident of the United States".

(C) Certain qualifying children

In the case of any qualifying child with respect to whom a credit is not allowed under this section by reason of paragraph (7), such child shall be treated as a dependent to whom subparagraph (A) applies.

(5) Maximum amount of refundable credit

(A) In general

The amount determined under subsection (d)(1)(A) with respect to any qualifying child shall not exceed $1,400, and such subsection shall be applied without regard to paragraph (4) of this subsection.

(B) Adjustment for inflation

In the case of a taxable year beginning after 2018, the $1,400 amount in subparagraph (A) shall be increased by an amount equal to—

    (i) such dollar amount, multiplied by

    (ii) the cost-of-living adjustment determined under section 1(f)(3) for the calendar year in which the taxable year begins, determined by substituting "2017" for "2016" in subparagraph (A)(ii) thereof.

If any increase under this clause is not a multiple of $100, such increase shall be rounded to the next lowest multiple of $100.

(6) Earned income threshold for refundable credit

Subsection (d)(1)(B)(i) shall be applied by substituting "$2,500" for "$3,000".

(7) Social security number required

No credit shall be allowed under this section to a taxpayer with respect to any qualifying child unless the taxpayer includes the social security number of such child on the return of tax for the taxable year. For purposes of the preceding sentence, the term "social security number" means a social security number issued to an individual by the Social Security Administration, but only if the social security number is issued—

    (A) to a citizen of the United States or pursuant to subclause (I) (or that portion of subclause (III) that relates to subclause (I)) of section 205(c)(2)(B)(i) of the Social Security Act, and

    (B) before the due date for such return.

(i) Special rules for 2021

In the case of any taxable year beginning after December 31, 2020, and before January 1, 2022—

(1) Refundable credit

If the taxpayer (in the case of a joint return, either spouse) has a principal place of abode in the United States (determined as provided in section 32) for more than one-half of the taxable year or is a bona fide resident of Puerto Rico (within the meaning of section 937(a)) for such taxable year—

    (A) subsection (d) shall not apply, and

    (B) so much of the credit determined under subsection (a) (after application of subparagraph (A)) as does not exceed the amount of such credit which would be so determined without regard to subsection (h)(4) shall be allowed under subpart C (and not allowed under this subpart).

(2) 17-year-olds eligible for treatment as qualifying children

This section shall be applied—

    (A) by substituting "age 18" for "age 17" in subsection (c)(1), and

    (B) by substituting "described in subsection (c) (determined after the application of subsection (i)(2)(A))" for "described in subsection (c)" in subsection (h)(4)(A).

(3) Credit amount

Subsection (h)(2) shall not apply and subsection (a) shall be applied by substituting "$3,000 ($3,600 in the case of a qualifying child who has not attained age 6 as of the close of the calendar year in which the taxable year of the taxpayer begins)" for "$1,000".

(4) Reduction of increased credit amount based on modified adjusted gross income

(A) In general

The amount of the credit allowable under subsection (a) (determined without regard to subsection (b)) shall be reduced by $50 for each $1,000 (or fraction thereof) by which the taxpayer's modified adjusted gross income (as defined in subsection (b)) exceeds the applicable threshold amount.

(B) Applicable threshold amount

For purposes of this paragraph, the term "applicable threshold amount" means—

    (i) $150,000, in the case of a joint return or surviving spouse (as defined in section 2(a)) ,[1]

    (ii) $112,500, in the case of a head of household (as defined in section 2(b)), and

    (iii) $75,000, in any other case.

(C) Limitation on reduction

(i) In general

The amount of the reduction under subparagraph (A) shall not exceed the lesser of—

    (I) the applicable credit increase amount, or

    (II) 5 percent of the applicable phaseout threshold range.

(ii) Applicable credit increase amount

For purposes of this subparagraph, the term "applicable credit increase amount" means the excess (if any) of—

    (I) the amount of the credit allowable under this section for the taxable year determined without regard to this paragraph and subsection (b), over

    (II) the amount of such credit as so determined and without regard to paragraph (3).

(iii) Applicable phaseout threshold range

For purposes of this subparagraph, the term "applicable phaseout threshold range" means the excess of—

    (I) the threshold amount applicable to the taxpayer under subsection (b) (determined after the application of subsection (h)(3)), over

    (II) the applicable threshold amount applicable to the taxpayer under this paragraph.

(D) Coordination with limitation on overall credit

Subsection (b) shall be applied by substituting "the credit allowable under subsection (a) (determined after the application of subsection (i)(4)(A))" for "the credit allowable under subsection (a)".

(j) Reconciliation of credit and advance credit

(1) In general

The amount of the credit allowed under this section to any taxpayer for any taxable year shall be reduced (but not below zero) by the aggregate amount of payments made under section 7527A to such taxpayer during such taxable year. Any failure to so reduce the credit shall be treated as arising out of a mathematical or clerical error and assessed according to section 6213(b)(1).

(2) Excess advance payments

(A) In general

If the aggregate amount of payments under section 7527A to the taxpayer during the taxable year exceeds the amount of the credit allowed under this section to such taxpayer for such taxable year (determined without regard to paragraph (1)), the tax imposed by this chapter for such taxable year shall be increased by the amount of such excess. Any failure to so increase the tax shall be treated as arising out of a mathematical or clerical error and assessed according to section 6213(b)(1).

(B) Safe harbor based on modified adjusted gross income

(i) In general

In the case of a taxpayer whose modified adjusted gross income (as defined in subsection (b)) for the taxable year does not exceed 200 percent of the applicable income threshold, the amount of the increase determined under subparagraph (A) with respect to such taxpayer for such taxable year shall be reduced (but not below zero) by the safe harbor amount.

(ii) Phase out of safe harbor amount

In the case of a taxpayer whose modified adjusted gross income (as defined in subsection (b)) for the taxable year exceeds the applicable income threshold, the safe harbor amount otherwise in effect under clause (i) shall be reduced by the amount which bears the same ratio to such amount as such excess bears to the applicable income threshold.

(iii) Applicable income threshold

For purposes of this subparagraph, the term "applicable income threshold" means—

(I) $60,000 in the case of a joint return or surviving spouse (as defined in section 2(a)),

(II) $50,000 in the case of a head of household, and

(III) $40,000 in any other case.

(iv) Safe harbor amount

For purposes of this subparagraph, the term "safe harbor amount" means, with respect to any taxable year, the product of—

(I) $2,000, multiplied by

(II) the excess (if any) of the number of qualified children taken into account in determining the annual advance amount with respect to the taxpayer under section 7527A with respect to months beginning in such taxable year, over the number of qualified children taken into account in determining the credit allowed under this section for such taxable year.

(k) Application of credit in possessions

(1) Mirror code possessions

(A) In general

The Secretary shall pay to each possession of the United States with a mirror code tax system amounts equal to the loss (if any) to that possession by reason of the application of this section (determined without regard to this subsection) with respect to taxable years beginning after 2020. Such amounts shall be determined by the Secretary based on information provided by the government of the respective possession.

(B) Coordination with credit allowed against United States income taxes

No credit shall be allowed under this section for any taxable year to any individual to whom a credit is allowable against taxes imposed by a possession of the United States with a mirror code tax system by reason of the application of this section in such possession for such taxable year.

(C) Mirror code tax system

For purposes of this paragraph, the term "mirror code tax system" means, with respect to any possession of the United States, the income tax system of such possession if the income tax liability of the residents of such possession under such system is determined by reference to the income tax laws of the United States as if such possession were the United States.

(2) Puerto Rico

(A) Application to taxable years in 2021

(i) For application of refundable credit to residents of Puerto Rico, see subsection (i)(1).

(ii) For nonapplication of advance payment to residents of Puerto Rico, see section 7527A(e)(4)(A).

(B) Application to taxable years after 2021

In the case of any bona fide resident of Puerto Rico (within the meaning of section 937(a)) for any taxable year beginning after December 31, 2021—

(i) the credit determined under this section shall be allowable to such resident, and

(ii) subsection (d)(1)(B)(ii) shall be applied without regard to the phrase "in the case of a taxpayer with 3 or more qualifying children".

(3) American Samoa

(A) In general

The Secretary shall pay to American Samoa amounts estimated by the Secretary as being equal to the aggregate benefits that would have been provided to residents of American Samoa by reason of the application of this section for taxable years beginning after 2020 if the provisions of this section had been in effect in American Samoa (applied as if American Samoa were the United States and without regard to the application of this section to bona fide residents of Puerto Rico under subsection (i)(1)).

(B) Distribution requirement

Subparagraph (A) shall not apply unless American Samoa has a plan, which has been approved by the Secretary, under which American Samoa will promptly distribute such payments to its residents.

(C) Coordination with credit allowed against United States income taxes

(i) In general

In the case of a taxable year with respect to which a plan is approved under subparagraph (B), this section (other than this subsection) shall not apply to any individual eligible for a distribution under such plan.

(ii) Application of section in event of absence of approved plan

In the case of a taxable year with respect to which a plan is not approved under subparagraph (B)—

(I) if such taxable year begins in 2021, subsection (i)(1) shall be applied by substituting "bona fide resident of Puerto Rico or American Samoa" for "bona fide resident of Puerto Rico", and

(II) if such taxable year begins after December 31, 2021, rules similar to the rules of paragraph (2)(B) shall apply with respect to bona fide residents of American Samoa (within the meaning of section 937(a)).

(4) Treatment of payments

For purposes of section 1324 of title 31, United States Code, the payments under this subsection shall be treated in the same manner as a refund due from a credit provision referred to in subsection (b)(2) of such section.

(Added Pub. L. 105–34, title I, §101(a), Aug. 5, 1997, 111 Stat. 796; amended Pub. L. 105–206, title VI, §6003(a), July 22, 1998, 112 Stat. 790; Pub. L. 105–277, div. J, title II, §2001(b), Oct. 21, 1998, 112 Stat. 2681–901; Pub. L. 106–170, title V, §501(b)(1), Dec. 17, 1999, 113 Stat. 1919; Pub. L. 107–16, title II, §§201(a)–(b)(2)(C), (c)(1), (2), (d), 202(f)(2)(B), title VI, §618(b)(2)(A), June 7, 2001, 115 Stat. 45–47, 49, 108; Pub. L. 107–90, title II, §204(e)(1), Dec. 21, 2001, 115 Stat. 893; Pub. L. 107–147, title IV, §§411(b), 417(23)(A), Mar. 9, 2002, 116 Stat. 45, 57; Pub. L. 108–27, title I, §101(a), May 28, 2003, 117 Stat. 753; Pub. L. 108–311, title I, §§101(a), 102(a), 104(a), title II, §204, title IV, §408(b)(4), Oct. 4, 2004, 118 Stat. 1167, 1168, 1176, 1192; Pub. L. 109–135, title IV, §402(i)(3)(B), Dec. 21, 2005, 119 Stat. 2613; Pub. L. 110–172, §11(c)(1), Dec. 29, 2007, 121 Stat. 2488; Pub. L. 110–343, div. B, title I, §106(e)(2)(B), title II, §205(d)(1)(A), div. C, title V, §501(a), Oct. 3,

2008, 122 Stat. 3817, 3838, 3876; Pub. L. 110–351, title V, §501(c)(1), Oct. 7, 2008, 122 Stat. 3979; Pub. L. 111–5, div. B, title I, §§1003(a), 1004(b)(1), 1142(b)(1)(A), 1144(b)(1)(A), Feb. 17, 2009, 123 Stat. 313, 314, 330, 332; Pub. L. 111–148, title X, §10909(b)(2)(A), (c), Mar. 23, 2010, 124 Stat. 1023; Pub. L. 111–312, title I, §§101(b)(1), 103(b), Dec. 17, 2010, 124 Stat. 3298, 3299; Pub. L. 112–240, title I, §§103(b), 104(c)(2)(B), Jan. 2, 2013, 126 Stat. 2319, 2321; Pub. L. 113–295, div. A, title II, §209(a), Dec. 19, 2014, 128 Stat. 4028; Pub. L. 114–27, title VIII, §807(a), June 29, 2015, 129 Stat. 418; Pub. L. 114–113, div. Q, title I, §101(a), (b), title II, §§205(a), (b), 208(a)(1), Dec. 18, 2015, 129 Stat. 3044, 3081, 3083; Pub. L. 115–97, title I, §11022(a), Dec. 22, 2017, 131 Stat. 2073; Pub. L. 115–141, div. U, title I, §101(i)(1), title IV, §401(a)(3), Mar. 23, 2018, 132 Stat. 1162, 1184; Pub. L. 117–2, title IX, §§9611(a), (b)(2), 9612(a), Mar. 11, 2021, 135 Stat. 144, 148, 150.)

INFLATION ADJUSTED ITEMS FOR CERTAIN YEARS

For inflation adjustment of certain items in this section, see Revenue Procedures listed in a table under section 1 of this title.

EDITORIAL NOTES
REFERENCES IN TEXT

Section 205(c)(2)(B)(i) of the Social Security Act, referred to in subsec. (h)(7)(A), is classified to section 405(c)(2)(B)(i) of Title 42, The Public Health and Welfare.

PRIOR PROVISIONS

A prior section 24, added Pub. L. 92–178, title VII, §701(a), Dec. 10, 1971, 85 Stat. 560, §41; amended Pub. L. 93–625, §§11(a)–(c), (e), 12(a), Jan. 3, 1975, 88 Stat. 2119, 2120; Pub. L. 94–455, title V, §503(b)(4), title XIX, §§1901(b)(1)(B), (H)(ii), 1906(b)(13)(A), Oct. 4, 1976, 90 Stat. 1562, 1790, 1791, 1834; Pub. L. 95–600, title I, §113(c), Nov. 6, 1978, 92 Stat. 2778; Pub. L. 97–473, title II, §202(b)(1), Jan. 14, 1983, 96 Stat. 2609; Pub. L. 98–21, title I, §122(c)(1), Apr. 20, 1983, 97 Stat. 87; renumbered §24 and amended Pub. L. 98–369, div. A, title IV, §§471(c), 474(f), July 18, 1984, 98 Stat. 826, 831, related to contributions to candidates for public office, prior to repeal by Pub. L. 99–514, title I, §§112(a), 151(a), Oct. 22, 1986, 100 Stat. 2108, 2121, applicable to taxable years beginning after Dec. 31, 1986.

AMENDMENTS

2021—Subsec. (i). Pub. L. 117–2, §9611(a), added subsec. (i).

Subsec. (j). Pub. L. 117–2, §9611(b)(2), added subsec. (j).

Subsec. (k). Pub. L. 117–2, §9612(a), added subsec. (k).

2018—Subsec. (d)(3), (5). Pub. L. 115–141, §401(a)(3), redesignated par. (5) as (3).

Subsec. (e)(2). Pub. L. 115–141, §101(i)(1), substituted "taxpayer identification number" for "identifying number".

2017—Subsec. (h). Pub. L. 115–97 added subsec. (h).

2015—Subsec. (d)(1)(B)(i). Pub. L. 114–113, §101(a), substituted "$3,000" for "$10,000".

Subsec. (d)(3), (4). Pub. L. 114–113, §101(b), struck out pars. (3) and (4) which related to inflation adjustment and special rule for certain years, respectively.

Subsec. (d)(5). Pub. L. 114–27 added par. (5).

Subsec. (e). Pub. L. 114–113, §205(a), (b), substituted "requirements" for "requirement" in subsec. heading, designated existing provisions as par. (1), inserted par. heading and "and such taxpayer identification number was issued on or before the due date for filing such return" before period at end, and added par. (2).

Subsec. (g). Pub. L. 114–113, §208(a)(1), added subsec. (g).

2014—Subsec. (d)(4). Pub. L. 113–295 amended par. (4) generally. The amendment was effective as if included in the provisions of the American Recovery and Reinvestment Tax Act of 2009 (Pub. L. 111–5, div. B, title I) to which the amendment related. As amended by Pub. L. 111–5, §1003(a), par. (4) read as follows: "Special rule for 2009 and 2010.—Notwithstanding paragraph (3), in the case of any taxable year beginning in 2009 or 2010, the dollar amount in effect for such taxable year under paragraph (1)(B)(i) shall be $3,000." See 2009 Amendment and Effective Date of 2014 Amendment notes below.

2013—Subsec. (b)(3). Pub. L. 112–240, §104(c)(2)(B)(i), struck out par. (3). Prior to amendment, text read as follows: "In the case of a taxable year to which section 26(a)(2) does not apply, the credit allowed under subsection (a) for any taxable year shall not exceed the excess of—

"(A) the sum of the regular tax liability (as defined in section 26(b)) plus the tax imposed by section 55, over

"(B) the sum of the credits allowable under this subpart (other than this section and sections 23, 25A(i), 25B, 25D, 30, 30B, and 30D) and section 27 for the taxable year."

Subsec. (d)(1). Pub. L. 112–240, §104(c)(2)(B)(ii)(II), substituted "section 26(a)" for "section 26(a)(2) or subsection (b)(3), as the case may be" in concluding provisions.

Subsec. (d)(1)(A), (B). Pub. L. 112–240, §104(c)(2)(B)(ii)(I), substituted "section 26(a)" for "section 26(a)(2) or subsection (b)(3), as the case may be," in subpar. (A) and in introductory provisions in subpar. (B).

Subsec. (d)(4). Pub. L. 112–240, §103(b), which directed substitution of "for certain years" for "2009, 2010, 2011, and 2012" in heading and "after 2008 and before 2018" for "in 2009, 2010, 2011, or 2012" in text, could not be executed because of the subsequent general amendment of subsec. (d)(4) by Pub. L. 113–295, which was effective as if included in the provisions of the American Recovery and Reinvestment Tax Act of 2009 (Pub. L. 111–5, div. B, title I) to which the amendment related. See 2014 Amendment note above and Effective Date of 2014 Amendment note below.

2010—Subsec. (b)(3)(B). Pub. L. 111–148, §10909(b)(2)(A), (c), as amended by Pub. L. 111–312, §101(b)(1), temporarily struck out "23," before "25A(i),". See Effective and Termination Dates of 2010 Amendment note below.

Subsec. (d)(4). Pub. L. 111–312, §103(b), which directed substitution of "2009, 2010, 2011, and 2012" for "2009 and 2010" in heading and ", 2010, 2011, or 2012" for "or 2010" in text, could not be executed because of the subsequent general amendment of subsec. (d)(4) by Pub. L. 113–295, which was effective as if included in the provisions of the American Recovery and Reinvestment Tax Act of 2009 (Pub. L. 111–5, div. B, title I) to which the amendment related. See 2014 Amendment note above and Effective Date of 2014 Amendment note below.

2009—Subsec. (b)(3)(B). Pub. L. 111–5, §1144(b)(1)(A), inserted "30B," after "30,".

Pub. L. 111–5, §1142(b)(1)(A), inserted "30," after "25D,".

Pub. L. 111–5, §1004(b)(1), inserted "25A(i)," after "23,".

Subsec. (d)(4). Pub. L. 111–5, §1003(a), amended par. (4) generally. Prior to amendment, text read as follows: "Notwithstanding paragraph (3), in the case of any taxable year beginning in 2008, the dollar amount in effect for such taxable year under paragraph (1)(B)(i) shall be $8,500." Par. (4) was subsequently generally amended by Pub. L. 113–295, effective as if included in the provisions of the American Recovery and Reinvestment Tax Act of 2009 (Pub. L. 111–5, div. B, title I) to which the amendment related. See 2014 Amendment note above and Effective Date of 2014 Amendment note below.

2008—Subsec. (a). Pub. L. 110–351 inserted "for which the taxpayer is allowed a deduction under section 151" after "of the taxpayer".

Subsec. (b)(3)(B). Pub. L. 110–343, §205(d)(1)(A), substituted "25D, and 30D" for "and 25D".

Pub. L. 110–343, §106(e)(2)(B), substituted ", 25B, and 25D" for "and 25B".

Subsec. (d)(4). Pub. L. 110–343, §501(a), added par. (4).

2007—Subsec. (d)(1)(B). Pub. L. 110–172, §11(c)(1)(A), substituted "the greater of" for "the excess (if any) of" in introductory provisions.

Subsec. (d)(1)(B)(ii)(II). Pub. L. 110–172, §11(c)(1)(B), substituted "section 32" for "section".

2005—Subsec. (b)(3). Pub. L. 109–135, §402(i)(3)(B)(i), substituted "In the case of a taxable year to which section 26(a)(2) does not apply, the credit" for "The credit" in introductory provisions.

145

Subsec. (d)(1). Pub. L. 109–135, §402(i)(3)(B)(ii), reenacted heading without change and amended text generally. Prior to amendment, text read as follows: "The aggregate credits allowed to a taxpayer under subpart C shall be increased by the lesser of—

"(A) the credit which would be allowed under this section without regard to this subsection and the limitation under subsection (b)(3), or

"(B) the amount by which the amount of credit allowed by this section (determined without regard to this subsection) would increase if the limitation imposed by subsection (b)(3) were increased by the greater of—

"(i) 15 percent of so much of the taxpayer's earned income (within the meaning of section 32) which is taken into account in computing taxable income for the taxable year as exceeds $10,000, or

"(ii) in the case of a taxpayer with 3 or more qualifying children, the excess (if any) of—

"(I) the taxpayer's social security taxes for the taxable year, over

"(II) the credit allowed under section 32 for the taxable year.

The amount of the credit allowed under this subsection shall not be treated as a credit allowed under this subpart and shall reduce the amount of credit otherwise allowable under subsection (a) without regard to subsection (b)(3). For purposes of subparagraph (B), any amount excluded from gross income by reason of section 112 shall be treated as earned income which is taken into account in computing taxable income for the taxable year."

2004—Subsec. (a). Pub. L. 108–311, §101(a), reenacted heading without change and amended text generally, substituting provisions relating to $1,000 per year credit per qualifying child for provisions relating to different credit amounts for calendar years 2003 through 2010 or thereafter.

Subsec. (c)(1). Pub. L. 108–311, §204(a), reenacted heading without change and amended text generally. Prior to amendment, text read as follows: "The term 'qualifying child' means any individual if—

"(A) the taxpayer is allowed a deduction under section 151 with respect to such individual for the taxable year,

"(B) such individual has not attained the age of 17 as of the close of the calendar year in which the taxable year of the taxpayer begins, and

"(C) such individual bears a relationship to the taxpayer described in section 32(c)(3)(B)."

Subsec. (c)(2). Pub. L. 108–311, §204(b), substituted "subparagraph (A) of section 152(b)(3)" for "the first sentence of section 152(b)(3)".

Subsec. (d)(1). Pub. L. 108–311, §104(a), inserted at end of concluding provisions "For purposes of subparagraph (B), any amount excluded from gross income by reason of section 112 shall be treated as earned income which is taken into account in computing taxable income for the taxable year."

Subsec. (d)(1)(B)(i). Pub. L. 108–311, §102(a), struck out "(10 percent in the case of taxable years beginning before January 1, 2005)" after "15 percent".

Subsec. (d)(2)(A)(iii). Pub. L. 108–311, §408(b)(4), amended directory language of Pub. L. 107–90. See 2001 Amendment note below.

2003—Subsec. (a)(2). Pub. L. 108–27 amended table by deleting items relating to calendar years 2001 and 2002 and increasing per child amount from $600 to $1,000 for calendar years 2003 or 2004.

2002—Subsec. (b)(3)(B). Pub. L. 107–147, §417(23)(A), amended directory language of Pub. L. 107–16, §618(b)(2)(A). See 2001 Amendment note below.

Subsec. (d)(1)(B). Pub. L. 107–147, §411(b), substituted "aggregate amount of credits allowed by this subpart" for "amount of credit allowed by this section" in introductory provisions.

2001—Subsec. (a). Pub. L. 107–16, §201(a), amended heading and text of subsec. (a) generally. Prior to amendment, text read as follows: "There shall be allowed as a credit against the tax imposed by this chapter for the taxable year with respect to each qualifying child of the taxpayer an amount equal to $500 ($400 in the case of taxable years beginning in 1998)."

Subsec. (b). Pub. L. 107–16, §201(b)(2)(A), amended heading generally, substituting "Limitations" for "Limitation based on adjusted gross income".

Subsec. (b)(1). Pub. L. 107–16, §201(b)(2)(B), amended heading generally, substituting "Limitation based on adjusted gross income" for "In general".

Subsec. (b)(3). Pub. L. 107–16, §201(b)(1), added par. (3).

Subsec. (b)(3)(B). Pub. L. 107–16, §618(b)(2)(A), as amended by Pub. L. 107–147, §417(23)(A), substituted "sections 23 and 25B" for "section 23".

Pub. L. 107–16, §202(f)(2)(B), substituted "this section and section 23" for "this section".

Subsec. (d). Pub. L. 107–16, §201(c)(1), amended subsec. heading and heading and text of par. (1) generally. Prior to amendment, text read as follows: "In the case of a taxpayer with three or more qualifying children for any taxable year, the aggregate credits allowed under subpart C shall be increased by the lesser of—

"(A) the credit which would be allowed under this section without regard to this subsection and the limitation under section 26(a); or

"(B) the amount by which the aggregate amount of credits allowed by this subpart (without regard to this subsection) would increase if the limitation imposed by section 26(a) were increased by the excess (if any) of—

"(i) the taxpayer's Social Security taxes for the taxable year, over

"(ii) the credit allowed under section 32 (determined without regard to subsection (n)) for the taxable year.

The amount of the credit allowed under this subsection shall not be treated as a credit allowed under this subpart and shall reduce the amount of credit otherwise allowable under subsection (a) without regard to section 26(a)."

Subsec. (d)(1). Pub. L. 107–16, §201(b)(2)(C)(i), substituted "subsection (b)(3)" for "section 26(a)" wherever appearing in subsec. (d), as amended by Pub. L. 107–16, §201(c).

Subsec. (d)(1)(B). Pub. L. 107–16, §201(b)(2)(C)(ii), substituted "amount of credit allowed by this section" for "aggregate amount of credits allowed by this subpart" in subpar. (B) as amended by Pub. L. 107–16, §201(c).

Subsec. (d)(2). Pub. L. 107–16, §201(d), redesignated par. (3) as (2) and struck out heading and text of former par. (2). Text read as follows: "For taxable years beginning after December 31, 2001, the credit determined under this subsection for the taxable year shall be reduced by the excess (if any) of—

"(A) the amount of tax imposed by section 55 (relating to alternative minimum tax) with respect to such taxpayer for such taxable year, over

"(B) the amount of the reduction under section 32(h) with respect to such taxpayer for such taxable year."

Subsec. (d)(2)(A)(iii). Pub. L. 107–90, as amended by Pub. L. 108–311, §408(b)(4), substituted "section 3211(a)" for "section 3211(a)(1)".

Subsec. (d)(3). Pub. L. 107–16, §201(d)(2), redesignated par. (4) as (3). Former par. (3) redesignated (2).

Subsec. (d)(4). Pub. L. 107–16, §201(c)(2), added par. (4). Former par. (4) redesignated (3).

1999—Subsec. (d)(2). Pub. L. 106–170 substituted "2001" for "1998" in introductory provisions.

1998—Subsec. (d)(1). Pub. L. 105–206, §6003(a)(1)(C), added par. (1) and struck out heading and text of former par. (1). Text read as follows: "In the case of a taxpayer with 3 or more qualifying children for any taxable year, the amount of the credit allowed under this section shall be equal to the greater of—

"(A) the amount of the credit allowed under this section (without regard to this subsection and after application of the limitation under section 26), or

"(B) the alternative credit amount determined under paragraph (2)."

Subsec. (d)(2). Pub. L. 105–277 substituted "For taxable years beginning after December 31, 1998, the credit" for "The credit".

Pub. L. 105–206, §6003(a)(1)(C), added par. (2) and struck out heading and text of former par. (2). Text read as follows: "For purposes of this subsection, the alternative credit amount is the amount of the credit which would be allowed under this section if the limitation under paragraph (3) were applied in lieu of the limitation under section 26."

Subsec. (d)(3). Pub. L. 105–206, §6003(a)(1)(A), (B), (2), redesignated par. (5) as (3), substituted "paragraph (1)" for "paragraph (3)" in introductory provisions, and struck out heading and text of former par. (3). Text read as follows: "The limitation under this paragraph for any taxable year is the limitation under section 26 (without regard to this subsection)—

"(A) increased by the taxpayer's social security taxes for such taxable year, and

"(B) reduced by the sum of—

"(i) the credits allowed under this part other than under subpart C or this section, and

"(ii) the credit allowed under section 32 without regard to subsection (m) thereof."

Subsec. (d)(4). Pub. L. 105–206, §6003(a)(1)(A), struck out heading and text of par. (4). Text read as follows: "If the amount of the credit under paragraph (1)(B) exceeds the amount of the credit under paragraph (1)(A), such excess shall be treated as a credit to which subpart C applies. The rule of section 32(h) shall apply to such excess."

Subsec. (d)(5). Pub. L. 105–206, §6003(a)(1)(B), redesignated par. (5) as (3).

STATUTORY NOTES AND RELATED SUBSIDIARIES

EFFECTIVE DATE OF 2021 AMENDMENT

Pub. L. 117–2, title IX, §9611(c)(1), Mar. 11, 2021, 135 Stat. 150, provided that: "The amendments made by this section [enacting section 7527A of this title and amending this section, sections 26, 3402, and 6211 of this title, and section 1324 of Title 31, Money and Finance] shall apply to taxable years beginning after December 31, 2020."

Pub. L. 117–2, title IX, §9612(b), Mar. 11, 2021, 135 Stat. 152, provided that: "The amendments made by this section [amending this section] shall apply to taxable years beginning after December 31, 2020."

EFFECTIVE DATE OF 2018 AMENDMENT

Pub. L. 115–141, div. U, title I, §101(s), Mar. 23, 2018, 132 Stat. 1169, provided that: "The amendments made by this section [see Tables for classification] shall take effect as if included in the provision of the Protecting Americans from Tax Hikes Act of 2015 [Pub. L. 114–113, div. Q] to which they relate."

EFFECTIVE DATE OF 2017 AMENDMENT

Pub. L. 115–97, title I, §11022(b), Dec. 22, 2017, 131 Stat. 2074, provided that: "The amendment made by this section [amending this section] shall apply to taxable years beginning after December 31, 2017."

EFFECTIVE DATE OF 2015 AMENDMENT

Pub. L. 114–113, div. Q, title I, §101(c), Dec. 18, 2015, 129 Stat. 3044, provided that: "The amendments made by this section [amending this section] shall apply to taxable years beginning after the date of the enactment of this Act [Dec. 18, 2015]."

Pub. L. 114–113, div. Q, title II, §205(c), Dec. 18, 2015, 129 Stat. 3081, as amended by Pub. L. 115–141, div. U, title I, §101(i)(2), Mar. 23, 2018, 132 Stat. 1162, provided that: "The amendments made by this section [amending this section] shall apply to any return of tax, and any amendment or supplement to any return of tax, which is filed after the date of the enactment of this Act [Dec. 18, 2015]."

Pub. L. 114–113, div. Q, title II, §208(c), Dec. 18, 2015, 129 Stat. 3084, provided that: "The amendments made by this section [amending this section and sections 25A and 6213 of this title] shall apply to taxable years beginning after December 31, 2015."

Pub. L. 114–27, title VIII, §807(b), June 29, 2015, 129 Stat. 418, provided that: "The amendment made by this section [amending this section] shall apply to taxable years beginning after December 31, 2014."

EFFECTIVE DATE OF 2014 AMENDMENT

Pub. L. 113–295, div. A, title II, §209(k), Dec. 19, 2014, 128 Stat. 4031, provided that: "The amendments made by this section [amending this section, sections 25A, 30, 30D, 35, 38, 45Q, 48, 48C, 164, 853A, and 1016 of this title, and provisions set out as notes under sections 6428 and 6432 of this title] shall take effect as if included in the provisions of the American Recovery and Reinvestment Tax Act of 2009 [Pub. L. 111–5, div. B, title I] to which they relate."

EFFECTIVE DATE OF 2013 AMENDMENT

Pub. L. 112–240, title I, §103(e), Jan. 2, 2013, 126 Stat. 2320, provided that:

"(1) In general.—Except as provided in paragraph (2), the amendments made by this section [amending this section and sections 25A, 32, and 6409 of this title and amending provisions set out as a note under section 25A of this title] shall apply to taxable years beginning after December 31, 2012.

"(2) Rule regarding disregard of refunds.—The amendment made by subsection (d) [amending section 6409 of this title] shall apply to amounts received after December 31, 2012."

Amendment by section 104(c)(2)(B) of Pub. L. 112–240 applicable to taxable years beginning after Dec. 31, 2011, see section 104(d) of Pub. L. 112–240, set out as a note under section 23 of this title.

EFFECTIVE AND TERMINATION DATES OF 2010 AMENDMENT

Pub. L. 111–312, title I, §103(d), Dec. 17, 2010, 124 Stat. 3299, provided that: "The amendments made by this section [amending this section and sections 25A and 32 of this title and amending provisions set out as a note under section 25A of this title] shall apply to taxable years beginning after December 31, 2010."

Amendment by Pub. L. 111–148 terminated applicable to taxable years beginning after Dec. 31, 2011, and section is amended to read as if such amendment had never been enacted, see section 10909(c) of Pub. L. 111–148, set out as a note under section 1 of this title.

Amendment by Pub. L. 111–148 applicable to taxable years beginning after Dec. 31, 2009, see section 10909(d) of Pub. L. 111–148, set out as a note under section 1 of this title.

EFFECTIVE AND TERMINATION DATES OF 2009 AMENDMENT

Pub. L. 111–5, div. B, title I, §1003(b), Feb. 17, 2009, 123 Stat. 313, provided that: "The amendments made by this section [amending this section] shall apply to taxable years beginning after December 31, 2008."

Pub. L. 111–5, div. B, title I, §1004(d), Feb. 17, 2009, 123 Stat. 315, provided that: "The amendments made by this section [amending this section, sections 25 to 25B, 26, 904, 1400C, and 6211 of this title, and section 1324 of Title 31, Money and Finance] shall apply to taxable years beginning after December 31, 2008."

Pub. L. 111–5, div. B, title I, §1004(e), Feb. 17, 2009, 123 Stat. 315, provided that: "The amendment made by subsection (b)(1) [amending this section] shall be subject to title IX of the Economic Growth and Tax Relief Reconciliation Act of 2001 [Pub. L. 107–16, §901, which was repealed by Pub. L. 112–240, title I, §101(a)(1), Jan. 2, 2013, 126 Stat. 2315, was formerly set out as an Effective and Termination Dates of 2001 Amendment note under section 1 of this title] in the same manner as the provision of such Act to which such amendment relates."

Pub. L. 111–5, div. B, title I, §1142(c), Feb. 17, 2009, 123 Stat. 331, provided that: "The amendments made by this section [amending this section and sections 25, 25B, 26, 30, 30B, 30C, 53, 55, 904, 1016, 1400C, and 6501 of this title] shall apply to vehicles acquired after the date of the enactment of this Act [Feb. 17, 2009]."

Pub. L. 111–5, div. B, title I, §1142(e), Feb. 17, 2009, 123 Stat. 331, provided that: "The amendment made by subsection (b)(1)(A) [amending this section] shall be subject to title IX of the Economic Growth and Tax Relief Reconciliation Act of 2001 [Pub. L. 107–16, §901, which was repealed by Pub. L. 112–240, title I, §101(a)(1), Jan. 2, 2013, 126 Stat. 2315, was formerly set out as an Effective and Termination Dates of 2001 Amendment note under section 1 of this title] in the same manner as the provision of such Act to which such amendment relates."

Pub. L. 111–5, div. B, title I, §1144(c), Feb. 17, 2009, 123 Stat. 333, provided that: "The amendments made by this section [amending this section and sections 25, 25B, 26, 30B, 30C, 55, 904, and 1400C of this title] shall apply to taxable years beginning after December 31, 2008."

Pub. L. 111–5, div. B, title I, §1144(d), Feb. 17, 2009, 123 Stat. 333, provided that: "The amendment made by subsection (b)(1)(A) [amending this section] shall be subject to title IX of the Economic Growth and Tax Relief Reconciliation Act of 2001 [Pub. L. 107–16, §901, which was repealed by Pub. L. 112–240, title I, §101(a)(1), Jan.

2, 2013, 126 Stat. 2315, was formerly set out as an Effective and Termination Dates of 2001 Amendment note under section 1 of this title] in the same manner as the provision of such Act to which such amendment relates."

EFFECTIVE AND TERMINATION DATES OF 2008 AMENDMENT

Pub. L. 110–351, title V, §501(d), Oct. 7, 2008, 122 Stat. 3980, provided that: "The amendments made by this section [amending this section and section 152 of this title] shall apply to taxable years beginning after December 31, 2008."

Amendment by section 106(e)(2)(B) of title I of div. B of Pub. L. 110–343 applicable to taxable years beginning after Dec. 31, 2007, and subject to title IX of the Economic Growth and Tax Relief Reconciliation Act of 2001, Pub. L. 107–16, §901, in the same manner as the provisions of such Act to which such amendment relates, see section 106(f)(1), (3) of Pub. L. 110–343, set out as a note under section 23 of this title. Title IX of Pub. L. 107–16 was repealed by Pub. L. 112–240, title I, §101(a)(1), Jan. 2, 2013, 126 Stat. 2315.

Pub. L. 110–343, div. B, title II, §205(e), (f), Oct. 3, 2008, 122 Stat. 3839, provided that:

"(e) Effective Date.—The amendments made by this section [enacting section 30D of this title and amending this section and sections 25, 25B, 26, 30B, 38, 1016, 1400C, and 6501 of this title] shall apply to taxable years beginning after December 31, 2008.

"(f) Application of EGTRRA Sunset.—The amendment made by subsection (d)(1)(A) [amending this section] shall be subject to title IX of the Economic Growth and Tax Relief Reconciliation Act of 2001 [Pub. L. 107–16, §901, which was repealed by Pub. L. 112–240, title I, §101(a)(1), Jan. 2, 2013, 126 Stat. 2315, was formerly set out as an Effective and Termination Dates of 2001 Amendment note under section 1 of this title] in the same manner as the provision of such Act to which such amendment relates."

Pub. L. 110–343, div. C, title V, §501(b), Oct. 3, 2008, 122 Stat. 3876, provided that: "The amendment made by this section [amending this section] shall apply to taxable years beginning after December 31, 2007."

EFFECTIVE DATE OF 2007 AMENDMENT

Pub. L. 110–172, §11(c)(2), Dec. 29, 2007, 121 Stat. 2489, provided that: "The amendments made by this subsection [amending this section] shall take effect as if included in the provisions of the Gulf Opportunity Zone Act of 2005 [Pub. L. 109–135] to which they relate."

EFFECTIVE AND TERMINATION DATES OF 2005 AMENDMENT

Amendment by Pub. L. 109–135 subject to title IX of the Economic Growth and Tax Relief Reconciliation Act of 2001, Pub. L. 107–16, §901, in the same manner as the provisions of such Act to which such amendment relates, see section 402(i)(3)(H) of Pub. L. 109–135, set out as a note under section 23 of this title. Title IX of Pub. L. 107–16 was repealed by Pub. L. 112–240, title I, §101(a)(1), Jan. 2, 2013, 126 Stat. 2315.

Amendment by Pub. L. 109–135 effective as if included in the provisions of the Energy Policy Act of 2005, Pub. L. 109–58, to which it relates and applicable to taxable years beginning after Dec. 31, 2005, see section 402(m) of Pub. L. 109–135, set out as a note under section 23 of this title.

EFFECTIVE AND TERMINATION DATES OF 2004 AMENDMENT

Amendment by section 101(a) of Pub. L. 108–311 applicable to taxable years beginning after Dec. 31, 2003, see section 101(e) of Pub. L. 108–311, set out as a note under section 1 of this title.

Pub. L. 108–311, title I, §102(b), Oct. 4, 2004, 118 Stat. 1168, provided that: "The amendment made by this section [amending this section] shall apply to taxable years beginning after December 31, 2003."

Pub. L. 108–311, title I, §104(c)(1), Oct. 4, 2004, 118 Stat. 1169, provided that: "The amendment made by subsection (a) [amending this section] shall apply to taxable years beginning after December 31, 2003."

Amendment by title I of Pub. L. 108–311 subject to title IX of the Economic Growth and Tax Relief Reconciliation Act of 2001, Pub. L. 107–16, §901, to the same extent and in the same manner as the provisions of such Act to which such amendments relate, see section 105 of Pub. L. 108–311, set out as a note under section 1 of this title. Title IX of Pub. L. 107–16 was repealed by Pub. L. 112–240, title I, §101(a)(1), Jan. 2, 2013, 126 Stat. 2315.

Amendment by section 204 of Pub. L. 108–311 applicable to taxable years beginning after Dec. 31, 2004, see section 208 of Pub. L. 108–311, set out as a note under section 2 of this title.

EFFECTIVE AND TERMINATION DATES OF 2003 AMENDMENT

Pub. L. 108–27, title I, §101(c), May 28, 2003, 117 Stat. 754, provided that:

"(1) In general.—Except as provided in paragraph (2), the amendments made by this section [enacting section 6429 of this title and amending this section] shall apply to taxable years beginning after December 31, 2002.

"(2) Subsection (b).—The amendments made by subsection (b) [enacting section 6429 of this title] shall take effect on the date of the enactment of this Act [May 28, 2003]."

Amendments by title I of Pub. L. 108–27 subject to title IX of the Economic Growth and Tax Relief Reconciliation Act of 2001, Pub. L. 107–16, §901, to the same extent and in the same manner as the provisions of such Act to which such amendments relate, see section 107 of Pub. L. 108–27, set out as a note under section 1 of this title. Title IX of Pub. L. 107–16 was repealed by Pub. L. 112–240, title I, §101(a)(1), Jan. 2, 2013, 126 Stat. 2315.

EFFECTIVE DATE OF 2002 AMENDMENT

Amendment by section 411(b) of Pub. L. 107–147 effective as if included in the provisions of the Economic Growth and Tax Relief Reconciliation Act of 2001, Pub. L. 107–16, to which such amendment relates, see section 411(x) of Pub. L. 107–147, set out as a note under section 25B of this title.

EFFECTIVE DATE OF 2001 AMENDMENT

Amendment by sections 201(b), 202(f), and 618(b) of Pub. L. 107–16 inapplicable to taxable years beginning during 2004 or 2005, see section 312(b)(2) of Pub. L. 108–311, set out as a note under section 23 of this title.

Amendment by sections 201(b), 202(f), and 618(b) of Pub. L. 107–16 inapplicable to taxable years beginning during 2002 and 2003, see section 601(b)(2) of Pub. L. 107–147, set out as a note under section 23 of this title.

Pub. L. 107–90, title II, §204(f), Dec. 21, 2001, 115 Stat. 893, provided that: "The amendments made by this section [enacting subchapter E of chapter 22 of this title and amending this section and sections 72, 3201, 3211, 3221, and 3231 of this title] shall apply to calendar years beginning after December 31, 2001."

Pub. L. 107–16, title II, §201(e), June 7, 2001, 115 Stat. 47, provided that:

"(1) In general.—Except as provided in paragraph (2), the amendments made by this section [amending this section and sections 23, 25, 26, 32, 904, and 1400C of this title] shall apply to taxable years beginning after December 31, 2000.

"(2) Subsection (b).—The amendments made by subsection (b) [amending this section and sections 23, 25, 26, 904, and 1400C of this title] shall apply to taxable years beginning after December 31, 2001."

Amendment by section 202(f)(2)(B) of Pub. L. 107–16 applicable to taxable years beginning after Dec. 31, 2001, see section 202(g)(1) of Pub. L. 107–16, set out as a note under section 23 of this title.

Pub. L. 107–16, title VI, §618(d), June 7, 2001, 115 Stat. 108, provided that: "The amendments made by this section [enacting section 25B of this title and amending this section and sections 25, 25B, 26, 904, and 1400C of this title] shall apply to taxable years beginning after December 31, 2001."

EFFECTIVE DATE OF 1999 AMENDMENT

Pub. L. 106–170, title V, §501(c), Dec. 17, 1999, 113 Stat. 1919, provided that: "The amendments made by this section [amending this section and sections 26 and 904 of this title] shall apply to taxable years beginning after December 31, 1998."

EFFECTIVE DATE OF 1998 AMENDMENT

Pub. L. 105–277, div. J, title II, §2001(c), Oct. 21, 1998, 112 Stat. 2681–901, provided that: "The amendments made by this section [amending this section and section 26 of this title] shall apply to taxable years beginning after December 31, 1997."

Amendment by Pub. L. 105–206 effective, except as otherwise provided, as if included in the provisions of the Taxpayer Relief Act of 1997, Pub. L. 105–34, to which such amendment relates, see section 6024 of Pub. L. 105–206, set out as a note under section 1 of this title.

EFFECTIVE DATE

Pub. L. 105–34, title I, §101(e), Aug. 5, 1997, 111 Stat. 799, provided that: "The amendments made by this section [enacting this section and amending sections 32, 501, and 6213 of this title and section 1324 of Title 31, Money and Finance] shall apply to taxable years beginning after December 31, 1997."

REFUNDS DISREGARDED IN ADMINISTRATION OF FEDERAL AND FEDERALLY ASSISTED PROGRAMS

Pub. L. 107–16, title II, §203, June 7, 2001, 115 Stat. 49, provided that: "Any payment considered to have been made to any individual by reason of section 24 of the Internal Revenue Code of 1986, as amended by section 201, shall not be taken into account as income and shall not be taken into account as resources for the month of receipt and the following month, for purposes of determining the eligibility of such individual or any other individual for benefits or assistance, or the amount or extent of benefits or assistance, under any Federal program or under any State or local program financed in whole or in part with Federal funds."

¹ So in original.

§25. Interest on certain home mortgages

(a) Allowance of credit

(1) In general

There shall be allowed as a credit against the tax imposed by this chapter for the taxable year an amount equal to the product of—

(A) the certificate credit rate, and

(B) the interest paid or accrued by the taxpayer during the taxable year on the remaining principal of the certified indebtedness amount.

(2) Limitation where credit rate exceeds 20 percent

(A) In general

If the certificate credit rate exceeds 20 percent, the amount of the credit allowed to the taxpayer under paragraph (1) for any taxable year shall not exceed $2,000.

(B) Special rule where 2 or more persons hold interests in residence

If 2 or more persons hold interests in any residence, the limitation of subparagraph (A) shall be allocated among such persons in proportion to their respective interests in the residence.

(b) Certificate credit rate; certified indebtedness amount

For purposes of this section—

(1) Certificate credit rate

The term "certificate credit rate" means the rate of the credit allowable by this section which is specified in the mortgage credit certificate.

(2) Certified indebtedness amount

The term "certified indebtedness amount" means the amount of indebtedness which is—

(A) incurred by the taxpayer—

(i) to acquire the principal residence of the taxpayer,

(ii) as a qualified home improvement loan (as defined in section 143(k)(4)) with respect to such residence, or

(iii) as a qualified rehabilitation loan (as defined in section 143(k)(5)) with respect to such residence, and

(B) specified in the mortgage credit certificate.

(c) Mortgage credit certificate; qualified mortgage credit certificate program

For purposes of this section—

(1) Mortgage credit certificate

The term "mortgage credit certificate" means any certificate which—

(A) is issued under a qualified mortgage credit certificate program by the State or political subdivision having the authority to issue a qualified mortgage bond to provide financing on the principal residence of the taxpayer,

(B) is issued to the taxpayer in connection with the acquisition, qualified rehabilitation, or qualified home improvement of the taxpayer's principal residence,

(C) specifies—

(i) the certificate credit rate, and

(ii) the certified indebtedness amount, and

(D) is in such form as the Secretary may prescribe.

(2) Qualified mortgage credit certificate program

(A) In general

The term "qualified mortgage credit certificate program" means any program—

(i) which is established by a State or political subdivision thereof for any calendar year for which it is authorized to issue qualified mortgage bonds,

(ii) under which the issuing authority elects (in such manner and form as the Secretary may prescribe) not to issue an amount of private activity bonds which it may otherwise issue during such calendar year under section 146,

(iii) under which the indebtedness certified by mortgage credit certificates meets the requirements of the following subsections of section 143 (as modified by subparagraph (B) of this paragraph):

(I) subsection (c) (relating to residence requirements),

(II) subsection (d) (relating to 3-year requirement),

(III) subsection (e) (relating to purchase price requirement),

(IV) subsection (f) (relating to income requirements),

(V) subsection (h) (relating to portion of loans required to be placed in targeted areas), and

(VI) paragraph (1) of subsection (i) (relating to other requirements),

(iv) under which no mortgage credit certificate may be issued with respect to any residence any of the financing of which is provided from the proceeds of a qualified mortgage bond or a qualified veterans' mortgage bond,

(v) except to the extent provided in regulations, which is not limited to indebtedness incurred from particular lenders,

(vi) except to the extent provided in regulations, which provides that a mortgage credit certificate is not transferrable, and

(vii) if the issuing authority allocates a block of mortgage credit certificates for use in connection with a particular development, which requires the developer to furnish to the issuing authority and the homebuyer a certificate that the price for the residence is no higher than it would be without the use of a mortgage credit certificate.

Under regulations, rules similar to the rules of subparagraphs (B) and (C) of section 143(a)(2) shall apply to the requirements of this subparagraph.

(B) Modifications of section 143

Under regulations prescribed by the Secretary, in applying section 143 for purposes of subclauses (II), (IV), and (V) of subparagraph (A)(iii)—

(i) each qualified mortgage certificate credit program shall be treated as a separate issue,

(ii) the product determined by multiplying—

(I) the certified indebtedness amount of each mortgage credit certificate issued under such program, by

(II) the certificate credit rate specified in such certificate,

shall be treated as proceeds of such issue and the sum of such products shall be treated as the total proceeds of such issue, and

(iii) paragraph (1) of section 143(d) shall be applied by substituting "100 percent" for "95 percent or more".

Clause (iii) shall not apply if the issuing authority submits a plan to the Secretary for administering the 95-percent requirement of section 143(d)(1) and the Secretary is satisfied that such requirement will be met under such plan.

(d) Determination of certificate credit rate

For purposes of this section—

(1) In general

The certificate credit rate specified in any mortgage credit certificate shall not be less than 10 percent or more than 50 percent.

(2) Aggregate limit on certificate credit rates

(A) In general

In the case of each qualified mortgage credit certificate program, the sum of the products determined by multiplying—

(i) the certified indebtedness amount of each mortgage credit certificate issued under such program, by

(ii) the certificate credit rate with respect to such certificate,

shall not exceed 25 percent of the nonissued bond amount.

(B) Nonissued bond amount

For purposes of subparagraph (A), the term "nonissued bond amount" means, with respect to any qualified mortgage credit certificate program, the amount of qualified mortgage bonds which the issuing authority is otherwise authorized to issue and elects not to issue under subsection (c)(2)(A)(ii).

(e) Special rules and definitions

For purposes of this section—

(1) Carryforward of unused credit

(A) In general

If the credit allowable under subsection (a) for any taxable year exceeds the applicable tax limit for such taxable year, such excess shall be a carryover to each of the 3 succeeding taxable years and, subject to the limitations of subparagraph (B), shall be added to the credit allowable by subsection (a) for such succeeding taxable year.

(B) Limitation

The amount of the unused credit which may be taken into account under subparagraph (A) for any taxable year shall not exceed the amount (if any) by which the applicable tax limit for such taxable year exceeds the sum of—

(i) the credit allowable under subsection (a) for such taxable year determined without regard to this paragraph, and

(ii) the amounts which, by reason of this paragraph, are carried to such taxable year and are attributable to taxable years before the unused credit year.

(C) Applicable tax limit

For purposes of this paragraph, the term "applicable tax limit" means the limitation imposed by section 26(a) for the taxable year reduced by the sum of the credits allowable under this subpart (other than this section and sections 23 and 25D).

(2) Indebtedness not treated as certified where certain requirements not in fact met

Subsection (a) shall not apply to any indebtedness if all the requirements of subsection (c)(1), (d), (e), (f), and (i) of section 143 and clauses (iv), (v), and (vii) of subsection (c)(2)(A), were not in fact met with respect to such indebtedness. Except to the extent provided in regulations, the requirements described in the preceding sentence shall be treated as met if there is a certification, under penalty of perjury, that such requirements are met.

(3) Period for which certificate in effect

(A) In general

Except as provided in subparagraph (B), a mortgage credit certificate shall be treated as in effect with respect to interest attributable to the period—

(i) beginning on the date such certificate is issued, and

(ii) ending on the earlier of the date on which—

(I) the certificate is revoked by the issuing authority, or

(II) the residence to which such certificate relates ceases to be the principal residence of the individual to whom the certificate relates.

(B) Certificate invalid unless indebtedness incurred within certain period

A certificate shall not apply to any indebtedness which is incurred after the close of the second calendar year following the calendar year for which the issuing authority made the applicable election under subsection (c)(2)(A)(ii).

(C) Notice to Secretary when certificate revoked

Any issuing authority which revokes any mortgage credit certificate shall notify the Secretary of such revocation at such time and in such manner as the Secretary shall prescribe by regulations.

(4) Reissuance of mortgage credit certificates

The Secretary may prescribe regulations which allow the administrator of a mortgage credit certificate program to reissue a mortgage credit certificate specifying a certified mortgage indebtedness that replaces the outstanding balance of the certified mortgage indebtedness specified on the original certificate to any taxpayer to whom the original certificate was issued, under such terms and conditions as the Secretary determines are necessary to ensure that the amount of the credit allowable under subsection (a) with respect to such reissued certificate is equal to or less than the amount of credit which would be allowable under subsection (a) with respect to the original certificate for any taxable year ending after such reissuance.

(5) Public notice that certificates will be issued

At least 90 days before any mortgage credit certificate is to be issued after a qualified mortgage credit certificate program, the issuing authority shall provide reasonable public notice of—

(A) the eligibility requirements for such certificate,

(B) the methods by which such certificates are to be issued, and

(C) such other information as the Secretary may require.

(6) Interest paid or accrued to related persons

No credit shall be allowed under subsection (a) for any interest paid or accrued to a person who is a related person to the taxpayer (within the meaning of section 144(a)(3)(A)).

(7) Principal residence

The term "principal residence" has the same meaning as when used in section 121.

(8) Qualified rehabilitation and home improvement

(A) Qualified rehabilitation

The term "qualified rehabilitation" has the meaning given such term by section 143(k)(5)(B).

(B) Qualified home improvement

The term "qualified home improvement" means an alteration, repair, or improvement described in section 143(k)(4).

(9) Qualified mortgage bond

The term "qualified mortgage bond" has the meaning given such term by section 143(a)(1).

(10) Manufactured housing

For purposes of this section, the term "single family residence" includes any manufactured home which has a minimum of 400 square feet of living space and a minimum width in excess of 102 inches and which is of a kind customarily used at a fixed location. Nothing in the preceding sentence shall be construed as providing that such a home will be taken into account in making determinations under section 143.

(f) Reduction in aggregate amount of qualified mortgage bonds which may be issued where certain requirements not met

(1) In general

If for any calendar year any mortgage credit certificate program which satisfies procedural requirements with respect to volume limitations prescribed by the Secretary fails to meet the requirements of paragraph (2) of subsection (d), such requirements shall be treated as satisfied with respect to any certified indebtedness of such program, but the applicable State ceiling under subsection (d) of section 146 for the State in which such program operates shall be reduced by 1.25 times the correction amount with respect to such failure. Such reduction shall be applied to such State ceiling for the calendar year following the calendar year in which the Secretary determines the correction amount with respect to such failure.

(2) Correction amount

(A) In general

For purposes of paragraph (1), the term "correction amount" means an amount equal to the excess credit amount divided by 0.25.

(B) Excess credit amount

(i) In general

For purposes of subparagraph (A)(ii), the term "excess credit amount" means the excess of—

(I) the credit amount for any mortgage credit certificate program, over

(II) the amount which would have been the credit amount for such program had such program met the requirements of paragraph (2) of subsection (d).

(ii) Credit amount

For purposes of clause (i), the term "credit amount" means the sum of the products determined under clauses (i) and (ii) of subsection (d)(2)(A).

(3) Special rule for States having constitutional home rule cities

In the case of a State having one or more constitutional home rule cities (within the meaning of section 146(d)(3)(C)), the reduction in the State ceiling by reason of paragraph (1) shall be allocated to the constitutional home rule city, or to the portion of the State not within such city, whichever caused the reduction.

(4) Exception where certification program

The provisions of this subsection shall not apply in any case in which there is a certification program which is designed to ensure that the requirements of this section are met and which meets such requirements as the Secretary may by regulations prescribe.

(5) Waiver

The Secretary may waive the application of paragraph (1) in any case in which he determines that the failure is due to reasonable cause.

(g) Reporting requirements

Each person who makes a loan which is a certified indebtedness amount under any mortgage credit certificate shall file a report with the Secretary containing—

(1) the name, address, and social security account number of the individual to which the certificate was issued,

(2) the certificate's issuer, date of issue, certified indebtedness amount, and certificate credit rate, and

(3) such other information as the Secretary may require by regulations.

Each person who issues a mortgage credit certificate shall file a report showing such information as the Secretary shall by regulations prescribe. Any such report shall be filed at such time and in such manner as the Secretary may require by regulations.

(h) Regulations; contracts

(1) Regulations

The Secretary shall prescribe such regulations as may be necessary to carry out the purposes of this section, including regulations which may require recipients of mortgage credit certificates to pay a reasonable processing fee to defray the expenses incurred in administering the program.

(2) Contracts

The Secretary is authorized to enter into contracts with any person to provide services in connection with the administration of this section.

(i) Recapture of portion of Federal subsidy from use of mortgage credit certificates

For provisions increasing the tax imposed by this chapter to recapture a portion of the Federal subsidy from the use of mortgage credit certificates, see section 143(m).

(Added Pub. L. 98–369, div. A, title VI, §612(a), July 18, 1984, 98 Stat. 905; amended Pub. L. 99–514, title XIII, §1301(f), title XVIII, §§1862(a)–(d)(1), 1899A(1), Oct. 22, 1986, 100 Stat. 2655, 2883, 2884, 2958; Pub. L. 100–647, title I, §1013(a)(25), (26), title IV, §4005(a)(2), (g)(7), Nov. 10, 1988, 102 Stat. 3543, 3645, 3651; Pub. L. 101–239, title VII, §7104(b), Dec. 19, 1989, 103 Stat. 2305; Pub. L. 101–508, title XI, §11408(b), Nov. 5, 1990, 104 Stat. 1388–477; Pub. L. 102–227, title I, §108(b), Dec. 11, 1991, 105 Stat. 1688; Pub. L. 103–66, title XIII, §13141(b), Aug. 10, 1993, 107 Stat. 436; Pub. L. 104–188, title I, §1807(c)(1), Aug. 20, 1996, 110 Stat. 1902; Pub. L. 105–34, title III, §312(d)(1), Aug. 5, 1997, 111 Stat. 839; Pub. L. 105–206, title VI, §6008(d)(7), July 22, 1998, 112 Stat. 812; Pub. L. 107–16, title II, §201(b)(2)(F), title VI, §618(b)(2)(B), June 7, 2001, 115 Stat. 46, 108; Pub. L. 109–58, title XIII, §1335(b)(2), Aug. 8, 2005, 119 Stat. 1036; Pub. L. 109–135, title IV, §402(i)(3)(C), (4), Dec. 21, 2005, 119 Stat. 2613, 2615; Pub. L. 110–343, div. B, title II, §205(d)(1)(B), Oct. 3, 2008, 122 Stat. 3838; Pub. L. 111–5, div. B, title I, §§1004(b)(2), 1142(b)(1)(B), 1144(b)(1)(B), Feb. 17, 2009, 123 Stat. 314, 330, 332; Pub. L. 111–148, title X, §10909(b)(2)(B), (c), Mar. 23, 2010, 124 Stat. 1023; Pub. L. 111–312, title I, §101(b)(1), Dec. 17, 2010, 124 Stat. 3298; Pub. L. 112–240, title I, §104(c)(2)(C), Jan. 2, 2013, 126 Stat. 2322; Pub. L. 115–141, div. U, title IV, §401(d)(4)(B)(ii), Mar. 23, 2018, 132 Stat. 1209.)

EDITORIAL NOTES
PRIOR PROVISIONS

A prior section 25 was renumbered section 26 of this title.

AMENDMENTS

2018—Subsec. (e)(1)(C). Pub. L. 115–141 substituted "sections 23 and 25D" for "sections 23, 25D, and 1400C".

2013—Subsec. (e)(1)(C). Pub. L. 112–240 amended subpar. (C) generally. Prior to amendment, text read as follows: "For purposes of this paragraph, the term 'applicable tax limit' means—

"(i) in the case of a taxable year to which section 26(a)(2) applies, the limitation imposed by section 26(a)(2) for the taxable year reduced by the sum of the credits allowable under this subpart (other than this section and sections 23, 25D, and 1400C), and

"(ii) in the case of a taxable year to which section 26(a)(2) does not apply, the limitation imposed by section 26(a)(1) for the taxable year reduced by the sum of the credits allowable under this subpart (other than this section and sections 23, 24, 25A(i), 25B, 25D, 30, 30B, 30D, and 1400C)."

2010—Subsec. (e)(1)(C). Pub. L. 111–148, §10909(b)(2)(B), (c), as amended by Pub. L. 111–312, temporarily struck out "23," after "and sections" in cls. (i) and (ii). See Effective and Termination Dates of 2010 Amendment note below.

2009—Subsec. (e)(1)(C)(ii). Pub. L. 111–5, §1144(b)(1)(B), inserted "30B," after "30,".

Pub. L. 111–5, §1142(b)(1)(B), inserted "30," after "25D,".

Pub. L. 111–5, §1004(b)(2), inserted "25A(i)," after "24,".

2008—Subsec. (e)(1)(C)(ii). Pub. L. 110–343 inserted "30D," after "25D,".

2005—Subsec. (e)(1)(C). Pub. L. 109–135, §402(i)(3)(C), reenacted heading without change and amended text generally. Prior to amendment, text read as follows: "For purposes of this paragraph, the term 'applicable tax limit' means the limitation imposed by section 26(a) for the taxable year reduced by the sum of the credits allowable under this subpart (other than this section and sections 23, 24, 25B, and 1400C)."

Pub. L. 109–58, §1335(b)(2), which directed amendment of subpar. (C) by substituting "other than this section, section 23, section 25D, and section 1400C" for "this section and sections 23 and 1400C", was repealed by Pub. L. 109–135, §402(i)(4). See Effective and Termination Dates of 2005 Amendments notes below.

2001—Subsec. (e)(1)(C). Pub. L. 107–16, §618(b)(2)(B), inserted "25B," after "24,".

Pub. L. 107–16, §201(b)(2)(F), inserted ", 24," after "sections 23".

1998—Subsec. (e)(1)(C). Pub. L. 105–206 substituted "sections 23 and 1400C" for "section 23".

1997—Subsec. (e)(7). Pub. L. 105–34 substituted "section 121" for "section 1034".

1996—Subsec. (e)(1)(C). Pub. L. 104–188 inserted "and section 23" after "other than this section".

1993—Subsecs. (h) to (j). Pub. L. 103–66 redesignated subsecs. (i) and (j) as (h) and (i), respectively, and struck out heading and text of former subsec. (h). Text read as follows: "No election may be made under subsection (c)(2)(A)(ii) for any period after June 30, 1992."

1991—Subsec. (h). Pub. L. 102–227 substituted "June 30, 1992" for "December 31, 1991".

1990—Subsec. (h). Pub. L. 101–508 substituted "December 31, 1991" for "September 30, 1990".

1989—Subsec. (h). Pub. L. 101–239 substituted "for any period after September 30, 1990" for "for any calendar year after 1989".

1988—Subsec. (c)(2)(A)(ii). Pub. L. 100–647, §1013(a)(25), amended Pub. L. 99–514, §1301(f)(2)(C)(ii), see 1986 Amendment note below.

Subsec. (h). Pub. L. 100–647, §4005(a)(2), substituted "1989" for "1988".

Pub. L. 100–647, §1013(a)(26), substituted "1988" for "1987".

Subsec. (j). Pub. L. 100–647, §4005(g)(7), added subsec. (j).

1986—Subsec. (a)(1)(B). Pub. L. 99–514, §1862(d)(1), substituted "paid or accrued" for "paid or incurred".

Subsec. (b)(2)(A)(ii). Pub. L. 99–514, §1301(f)(2)(A), substituted "section 143(k)(4)" for "section 103A(I)(6)".

Subsec. (b)(2)(A)(iii). Pub. L. 99–514, §1301(f)(2)(B), substituted "section 143(k)(5)" for "section 103A(I)(7)".

Subsec. (c)(2)(A). Pub. L. 99–514, §1301(f)(2)(E), substituted "section 143(a)(2)" for "section 103A(c)(2)" in provision following cl. (vii).

Pub. L. 99–514, §1862(b), inserted "Under regulations, rules similar to the rules of subparagraphs (B) and (C) of section 103A(c)(2) shall apply to the requirements of this subparagraph."

Subsec. (c)(2)(A)(ii). Pub. L. 99–514, §1301(f)(2)(C)(ii), as amended by Pub. L. 100–647, §1013(a)(25), substituted "private activity bonds which it may otherwise issue during such calendar year under section 146" for "qualified mortgage bonds which it may otherwise issue during such calendar year under section 103A".

Subsec. (c)(2)(A)(iii). Pub. L. 99–514, §1301(f)(2)(C)(i), substituted "section 143" for "section 103A" in introductory provisions, added subcls. (I) to (VI), and struck out former subcls. (I) to (V) which read as follows:

"(I) subsection (d) (relating to residence requirements),

"(II) subsection (e) (relating to 3-year requirement),

"(III) subsection (f) (relating to purchase price requirement),

"(IV) subsection (h) (relating to portion of loans required to be placed in targeted areas), and

"(V) subsection (j), other than paragraph (2) thereof (relating to other requirements),".

Subsec. (c)(2)(A)(iii)(V). Pub. L. 99–514, §1862(a), substituted "subsection (j), other than paragraph (2) thereof" for "paragraph (1) of subsection (j)".

Subsec. (c)(2)(B). Pub. L. 99–514, §1301(f)(2)(C)(i), substituted in heading and introductory provisions "section 143" for "section 103A".

Pub. L. 99–514, §1301(f)(2)(F), inserted in introductory provisions reference to subcl. (V), added cl. (iii) and closing provisions, and struck out former cl. (iii) and closing provisions which read as follows:

"(iii) paragraph (1) of section 103A(e) shall be applied by substituting '100 percent' for '90 percent or more'.

Clause (iii) shall not apply if the issuing authority submits a plan to the Secretary for administering the 90-percent requirement of section 103A(e)(1) and the Secretary is satisfied that such requirement will be met under such plan."

Subsec. (d)(2)(A). Pub. L. 99–514, §1301(f)(1)(A), substituted "25 percent" for "20 percent" in concluding provisions.

Subsec. (d)(3). Pub. L. 99–514, §1301(f)(2)(G), struck out par. (3) "Additional limit in certain cases" which read as follows: "In the case of a qualified mortgage credit certificate program in a State which—

"(A) has a State ceiling (as defined in section 103A(g)(4)) for the year an election is made that exceeds 20 percent of the average annual aggregate principal amount of mortgages executed during the immediately preceding 3 calendar years for single family owner-occupied residences located within the jurisdiction of such State, or

"(B) issued qualified mortgage bonds in an aggregate amount less than $150,000,000 for calendar year 1983,

the certificate credit rate for any mortgage credit certificate shall not exceed 20 percent unless the issuing authority submits a plan to the Secretary to ensure that the weighted average of the certificate credit rates in such mortgage credit certificate program does not exceed 20 percent and the Secretary approves such plan."

Subsec. (e)(1)(B). Pub. L. 99–514, §1862(c), amended subpar. (B) generally. Prior to amendment, subpar. (B) "Limitations" read as follows: "The amount of the unused credit which may be taken into account under subparagraph (A) for any taxable year shall not exceed the amount by which the applicable tax limit for such taxable year exceeds the sum of the amounts which, by reason of this paragraph, are carried to such taxable year and are attributable to taxable years before the unused credit year."

Subsec. (e)(2). Pub. L. 99–514, §1301(f)(2)(H), substituted "subsections (c)(1), (d), (e), (f), and (i) of section 143" for "subsection (d)(1), (e), (f), and (j) of section 103A".

Subsec. (e)(6). Pub. L. 99–514, §1301(f)(2)(I), substituted "section 144(a)(3)(A)" for "section 103(b)(6)(C)(i)".

Subsec. (e)(8)(A). Pub. L. 99–514, §1301(f)(2)(J), substituted "section 143(k)(5)(B)" for "section 103A(l)(7)(B)".

Subsec. (e)(8)(B). Pub. L. 99–514, §1301(f)(2)(K), substituted "section 143(k)(4)" for "section 103A(l)(6)".

Subsec. (e)(9). Pub. L. 99–514, §1301(f)(2)(L), substituted "section 143(a)(1)" for "section 103A(c)(1)".

Subsec. (e)(10). Pub. L. 99–514, §1301(f)(2)(M), substituted "section 143" for "section 103A".

Subsec. (f)(1). Pub. L. 99–514, §1301(f)(2)(N), substituted "subsection (d) of section 146" for "paragraph (4) of section 103A(g)".

Subsec. (f)(2)(A). Pub. L. 99–514, §1301(f)(1)(B), substituted "0.25" for "0.20".

Subsec. (f)(3). Pub. L. 99–514, §1301(f)(2)(O), substituted "section 146(d)(3)(C)" for "section 103A(g)(5)(C)".

Subsec. (f)(4). Pub. L. 99–514, §1899A(1), substituted "ensure" for "insure".

STATUTORY NOTES AND RELATED SUBSIDIARIES
EFFECTIVE DATE OF 2013 AMENDMENT

Amendment by Pub. L. 112–240 applicable to taxable years beginning after Dec. 31, 2011, see section 104(d) of Pub. L. 112–240, set out as a note under section 23 of this title.

EFFECTIVE AND TERMINATION DATES OF 2010 AMENDMENT

Amendment by Pub. L. 111–148 terminated applicable to taxable years beginning after Dec. 31, 2011, and section is amended to read as if such amendment had never been enacted, see section 10909(c) of Pub. L. 111–148, set out as a note under section 1 of this title.

Amendment by Pub. L. 111–148 applicable to taxable years beginning after Dec. 31, 2009, see section 10909(d) of Pub. L. 111–148, set out as a note under section 1 of this title.

EFFECTIVE DATE OF 2009 AMENDMENT

Amendment by section 1004(b)(2) of Pub. L. 111–5 applicable to taxable years beginning after Dec. 31, 2008, see section 1004(d) of Pub. L. 111–5, set out as an Effective and Termination Dates of 2009 Amendment note under section 24 of this title.

Amendment by section 1142(b)(1)(B) of Pub. L. 111–5 applicable to vehicles acquired after Feb. 17, 2009, see section 1142(c) of Pub. L. 111–5, set out as an Effective and Termination Dates of 2009 Amendment note under section 24 of this title.

Amendment by section 1144(b)(1)(B) of Pub. L. 111–5 applicable to taxable years beginning after Dec. 31, 2008, see section 1144(c) of Pub. L. 111–5, set out as an Effective and Termination Dates of 2009 Amendment note under section 24 of this title.

EFFECTIVE DATE OF 2008 AMENDMENT

Amendment by Pub. L. 110–343 applicable to taxable years beginning after Dec. 31, 2008, see section 205(e) of Pub. L. 110–343, set out as an Effective and Termination Dates of 2008 Amendment note under section 24 of this title.

EFFECTIVE AND TERMINATION DATES OF 2005 AMENDMENT

Amendment by section 402(i)(3)(C) of Pub. L. 109–135 subject to title IX of the Economic Growth and Tax Relief Reconciliation Act of 2001, Pub. L. 107–16, §901, in the same manner as the provisions of such Act to which such amendment relates, see section 402(i)(3)(H) of Pub. L. 109–135, set out as a note under section 23 of this title. Title IX of Pub. L. 107–16 was repealed by Pub. L. 112–240, title I, §101(a)(1), Jan. 2, 2013, 126 Stat. 2315.

The Internal Revenue Code of 1986 to be applied and administered as if the amendments made by section 1335(b)(1)–(3) of Pub. L. 109–58 had never been enacted, see section 402(i)(4) of Pub. L. 109–135, set out as a note under section 23 of this title.

Amendments by Pub. L. 109–135 effective as if included in the provisions of the Energy Policy Act of 2005, Pub. L. 109–58, to which they relate, except that amendment by section 402(i)(3)(C) of Pub. L. 109–135 is applicable to taxable years beginning after Dec. 31, 2005, see section 402(m) of Pub. L. 109–135, set out as a note under section 23 of this title.

Amendment by Pub. L. 109–58 applicable to property placed in service after Dec. 31, 2005, in taxable years ending after such date, see section 1335(c) of Pub. L. 109–58, set out as a note under section 23 of this title.

EFFECTIVE DATE OF 2001 AMENDMENT

Amendment by Pub. L. 107–16 inapplicable to taxable years beginning during 2004 or 2005, see section 312(b)(2) of Pub. L. 108–311, set out as a note under section 23 of this title.

Amendment by Pub. L. 107–16 inapplicable to taxable years beginning during 2002 and 2003, see section 601(b)(2) of Pub. L. 107–147, set out as a note under section 23 of this title.

Amendment by section 201(b)(2)(F) of Pub. L. 107–16 applicable to taxable years beginning after Dec. 31, 2001, see section 201(e)(2) of Pub. L. 107–16, set out as a note under section 24 of this title.

Amendment by section 618(b)(2)(B) of Pub. L. 107–16 applicable to taxable years beginning after Dec. 31, 2001, see section 618(d) of Pub. L. 107–16, set out as a note under section 24 of this title.

EFFECTIVE DATE OF 1998 AMENDMENT

Amendment by Pub. L. 105–206 effective, except as otherwise provided, as if included in the provisions of the Taxpayer Relief Act of 1997, Pub. L. 105–34, to which such amendment relates, see section 6024 of Pub. L. 105–206, set out as a note under section 1 of this title.

EFFECTIVE DATE OF 1997 AMENDMENT

Amendment by Pub. L. 105–34 applicable to sales and exchanges after May 6, 1997, with certain exceptions, see section 312(d) of Pub. L. 105–34, set out as a note under section 121 of this title.

EFFECTIVE DATE OF 1996 AMENDMENT

Amendment by Pub. L. 104–188 applicable to taxable years beginning after Dec. 31, 1996, see section 1807(e) of Pub. L. 104–188, set out as an Effective Date note under section 23 of this title.

Pub. L. 103–66, title XIII, §13141(f)(2), Aug. 10, 1993, 107 Stat. 437, provided that: "The amendment made by subsection (b) [amending this section] shall apply to elections for periods after June 30, 1992."

Pub. L. 102–227, title I, §108(c)(2), Dec. 11, 1991, 105 Stat. 1688, provided that: "The amendment made by subsection (b) [amending this section] shall apply to elections for periods after December 31, 1991."

Amendment by Pub. L. 101–508 applicable to elections for periods after Sept. 30, 1990, see section 11408(d)(2) of Pub. L. 101–508, set out as a note under section 143 of this title.

Amendment by section 1013(a)(25), (26) of Pub. L. 100–647 effective, except as otherwise provided, as if included in the provision of the Tax Reform Act of 1986, Pub. L. 99–514, to which such amendment relates, see section 1019(a) of Pub. L. 100–647, set out as a note under section 1 of this title.

Amendment by section 4005(a)(2) of Pub. L. 100–647 applicable to bonds issued, and nonissued bond amounts elected, after Dec. 31, 1988, see section 4005(h)(1) of Pub. L. 100–647, set out as a note under section 143 of this title.

Amendment by section 4005(g)(7) of Pub. L. 100–647 applicable to financing provided, and mortgage credit certificates issued, after Dec. 31, 1990, with certain exceptions, see section 4005(h)(3) of Pub. L. 100–647, set out as a note under section 143 of this title.

Amendment by section 1301(f)(1) of Pub. L. 99–514 applicable to nonissued bond amounts elected after Aug. 15, 1986, and amendment by section 1301(f)(2) of Pub. L. 99–514 applicable to certificates issued with respect to nonissued bond amounts elected after Aug. 15, 1986, see section 1311(b) of Pub. L. 99–514, as amended, set out as an Effective Date; Transitional Rules note under section 141 of this title.

Amendment by section 1862(a)–(d)(1) of Pub. L. 99–514 effective, except as otherwise provided, as if included in the provisions of the Tax Reform Act of 1984, Pub. L. 98–369, div. A, to which such amendment relates, see section 1881 of Pub. L. 99–514, set out as a note under section 48 of this title.

Pub. L. 98–369, div. A, title VI, §612(g), July 18, 1984, 98 Stat. 913, as amended by Pub. L. 99–514, §2, Oct. 22, 1986, 100 Stat. 2095, provided that:

"(1) In general.—Except as otherwise provided in this subsection, the amendments made by this section [enacting this section and section 6708 of this title, redesignating former section 25 as 26, and amending sections 23, 28 to 30, 38, 55, 103A, 163, 168, and 901 of this title] shall apply to interest paid or accrued after December 31, 1984, on indebtedness incurred after December 31, 1984.

"(2) Elections.—The amendments made by this section shall apply to elections under section 25(c)(2)(A)(ii) of the Internal Revenue Code of 1986 [formerly I.R.C. 1954] (as added by this section) for calendar years after 1983."

Amendment by Pub. L. 115–141 not applicable to certain obligations issued, DC Zone assets acquired, or principal residences acquired before Jan. 1, 2012, see section 401(d)(4)(C) of Pub. L. 115–141, set out as a note under former section 1400 of this title.

For provisions that nothing in amendment by Pub. L. 115–141 be construed to affect treatment of certain transactions occurring, property acquired, or items of income, loss, deduction, or credit taken into account prior to Mar. 23, 2018, for purposes of determining liability for tax for periods ending after Mar. 23, 2018, see section 401(e) of Pub. L. 115–141, set out as a note under section 23 of this title.

For provisions directing that if any amendments made by subtitle A or subtitle C of title XI [§§1101–1147 and 1171–1177] or title XVIII [§§1800–1899A] of Pub. L. 99–514 require an amendment to any plan, such plan amendment shall not be required to be made before the first plan year beginning on or after Jan. 1, 1989, see section 1140 of Pub. L. 99–514, as amended, set out as a note under section 401 of this title.

§25A. American Opportunity and Lifetime Learning credits

(a) Allowance of credit

In the case of an individual, there shall be allowed as a credit against the tax imposed by this chapter for the taxable year the amount equal to the sum of—
> (1) the American Opportunity Tax Credit, plus
> (2) the Lifetime Learning Credit.

(b) American Opportunity Tax Credit

(1) Per student credit

In the case of any eligible student for whom an election is in effect under this section for any taxable year, the American Opportunity Tax Credit is an amount equal to the sum of—
> (A) 100 percent of so much of the qualified tuition and related expenses paid by the taxpayer during the taxable year (for education furnished to the eligible student during any academic period beginning in such taxable year) as does not exceed $2,000, plus
> (B) 25 percent of such expenses so paid as exceeds $2,000 but does not exceed $4,000.

(2) Limitations applicable to American Opportunity Tax Credit

(A) Credit allowed only for 4 taxable years

An election to have this section apply with respect to any eligible student for purposes of the American Opportunity Tax Credit under subsection (a)(1) may not be made for any taxable year if such an election (by the taxpayer or any other individual) is in effect with respect to such student for any 4 prior taxable years.

(B) Credit allowed for year only if individual is at least ½ time student for portion of year

The American Opportunity Tax Credit under subsection (a)(1) shall not be allowed for a taxable year with respect to the qualified tuition and related expenses of an individual unless such individual is an eligible student for at least one academic period which begins during such year.

(C) Credit allowed only for first 4 years of postsecondary education

The American Opportunity Tax Credit under subsection (a)(1) shall not be allowed for a taxable year with respect to the qualified tuition and related expenses of an eligible student if the student has completed (before the beginning of such taxable year) the first 4 years of postsecondary education at an eligible educational institution.

(D) Denial of credit if student convicted of a felony drug offense

The American Opportunity Tax Credit under subsection (a)(1) shall not be allowed for qualified tuition and related expenses for the enrollment or attendance of a student for any academic period if such student has been convicted of a Federal or State felony offense consisting of the possession or distribution of a controlled substance before the end of the taxable year with or within which such period ends.

(3) Eligible student

For purposes of this subsection, the term "eligible student" means, with respect to any academic period, a student who—

    (A) meets the requirements of section 484(a)(1) of the Higher Education Act of 1965 (20 U.S.C. 1091(a)(1)), as in effect on the date of the enactment of this section, and

    (B) is carrying at least ½ the normal full-time work load for the course of study the student is pursuing.

(4) Restrictions on taxpayers who improperly claimed American Opportunity Tax Credit in prior years

(A) Taxpayers making prior fraudulent or reckless claims

(i) In general

No American Opportunity Tax Credit shall be allowed under this section for any taxable year in the disallowance period.

(ii) Disallowance period

For purposes of subparagraph (A), the disallowance period is—

    (I) the period of 10 taxable years after the most recent taxable year for which there was a final determination that the taxpayer's claim of the American Opportunity Tax Credit under this section was due to fraud, and

    (II) the period of 2 taxable years after the most recent taxable year for which there was a final determination that the taxpayer's claim of the American Opportunity Tax Credit under this section was due to reckless or intentional disregard of rules and regulations (but not due to fraud).

(B) Taxpayers making improper prior claims

In the case of a taxpayer who is denied the American Opportunity Tax Credit under this section for any taxable year as a result of the deficiency procedures under subchapter B of chapter 63, no American Opportunity Tax Credit shall be allowed under this section for any subsequent taxable year unless the taxpayer provides such information as the Secretary may require to demonstrate eligibility for such credit.

(c) Lifetime Learning Credit

(1) Per taxpayer credit

The Lifetime Learning Credit for any taxpayer for any taxable year is an amount equal to 20 percent of so much of the qualified tuition and related expenses paid by the taxpayer during the taxable year (for education furnished during any academic period beginning in such taxable year) as does not exceed $10,000.

(2) Special rules for determining expenses

(A) Coordination with American Opportunity Tax Credit

The qualified tuition and related expenses with respect to an individual who is an eligible student for whom a [1] American Opportunity Tax Credit under subsection (a)(1) is allowed for the taxable year shall not be taken into account under this subsection.

(B) Expenses eligible for Lifetime Learning Credit

For purposes of paragraph (1), qualified tuition and related expenses shall include expenses described in subsection (f)(1) with respect to any course of instruction at an eligible educational institution to acquire or improve job skills of the individual.

(d) Limitations based on modified adjusted gross income

(1) In general

The American Opportunity Tax Credit and the Lifetime Learning Credit shall each (determined without regard to this paragraph) be reduced (but not below zero) by the amount which bears the same ratio to each such credit (as so determined) as—

    (A) the excess of—

        (i) the taxpayer's modified adjusted gross income for such taxable year, over

        (ii) $80,000 ($160,000 in the case of a joint return), bears to

    (B) $10,000 ($20,000 in the case of a joint return).

(2) Modified adjusted gross income

For purposes of this subsection, the term "modified adjusted gross income" means the adjusted gross income of the taxpayer for the taxable year increased by any amount excluded from gross income under section 911, 931, or 933.

(e) Election not to have section apply

A taxpayer may elect not to have this section apply with respect to the qualified tuition and related expenses of an individual for any taxable year.

(f) Definitions

For purposes of this section—

(1) Qualified tuition and related expenses

(A) In general

The term "qualified tuition and related expenses" means tuition and fees required for the enrollment or attendance of—

    (i) the taxpayer,

    (ii) the taxpayer's spouse, or

    (iii) any dependent of the taxpayer with respect to whom the taxpayer is allowed a deduction under section 151,

at an eligible educational institution for courses of instruction of such individual at such institution.

(B) Exception for education involving sports, etc.

Such term does not include expenses with respect to any course or other education involving sports, games, or hobbies, unless such course or other education is part of the individual's degree program.

(C) Exception for nonacademic fees

Such term does not include student activity fees, athletic fees, insurance expenses, or other expenses unrelated to an individual's academic course of instruction.

(D) Required course materials taken into account for American Opportunity Tax Credit

For purposes of determining the American Opportunity Tax Credit, subparagraph (A) shall be applied by substituting "tuition, fees, and course materials" for "tuition and fees".

(2) Eligible educational institution

The term "eligible educational institution" means an institution—

    (A) which is described in section 481 of the Higher Education Act of 1965 (20 U.S.C. 1088), as in effect on the date of the enactment of this section, and

    (B) which is eligible to participate in a program under title IV of such Act.

(g) Special rules

(1) Identification requirement

(A) In general

No credit shall be allowed under subsection (a) to a taxpayer with respect to the qualified tuition and related expenses of an individual unless the taxpayer includes the name and taxpayer identification number of such individual on the return of tax for the taxable year.

(B) Additional identification requirements with respect to American Opportunity Tax Credit

(i) Student

The requirements of subparagraph (A) shall not be treated as met with respect to the American Opportunity Tax Credit unless the individual's taxpayer identification number was issued on or before the due date for filing the return of tax for the taxable year.

(ii) Taxpayer

No American Opportunity Tax Credit shall be allowed under this section if the taxpayer identification number of the taxpayer was issued after the due date for filing the return for the taxable year.

(iii) Institution

No American Opportunity Tax Credit shall be allowed under this section unless the taxpayer includes the employer identification number of any institution to which qualified tuition and related expenses were paid with respect to the individual.

(2) Adjustment for certain scholarships, etc.

The amount of qualified tuition and related expenses otherwise taken into account under subsection (a) with respect to an individual for an academic period shall be reduced (before the application of subsections (b), (c), and (d)) by the sum of any amounts paid for the benefit of such individual which are allocable to such period as—

(A) a qualified scholarship which is excludable from gross income under section 117,

(B) an educational assistance allowance under chapter 30, 31, 32, 34, or 35 of title 38, United States Code, or under chapter 1606 of title 10, United States Code, and

(C) a payment (other than a gift, bequest, devise, or inheritance within the meaning of section 102(a)) for such individual's educational expenses, or attributable to such individual's enrollment at an eligible educational institution, which is excludable from gross income under any law of the United States.

(3) Treatment of expenses paid by dependent

If a deduction under section 151 with respect to an individual is allowed to another taxpayer for a taxable year beginning in the calendar year in which such individual's taxable year begins—

(A) no credit shall be allowed under subsection (a) to such individual for such individual's taxable year,

(B) qualified tuition and related expenses paid by such individual during such individual's taxable year shall be treated for purposes of this section as paid by such other taxpayer, and

(C) a statement described in paragraph (8) and received by such individual shall be treated as received by the taxpayer.

(4) Treatment of certain prepayments

If qualified tuition and related expenses are paid by the taxpayer during a taxable year for an academic period which begins during the first 3 months following such taxable year, such academic period shall be treated for purposes of this section as beginning during such taxable year.

(5) Denial of double benefit

No credit shall be allowed under this section for any expense for which a deduction is allowed under any other provision of this chapter.

(6) No credit for married individuals filing separate returns

If the taxpayer is a married individual (within the meaning of section 7703), this section shall apply only if the taxpayer and the taxpayer's spouse file a joint return for the taxable year.

(7) Nonresident aliens

If the taxpayer is a nonresident alien individual for any portion of the taxable year, this section shall apply only if such individual is treated as a resident alien of the United States for purposes of this chapter by reason of an election under subsection (g) or (h) of section 6013.

(8) Payee statement requirement

Except as otherwise provided by the Secretary, no credit shall be allowed under this section unless the taxpayer receives a statement furnished under section 6050S(d) which contains all of the information required by paragraph (2) thereof.

[(h) Repealed. Pub. L. 116–260, div. EE, title I, §104(a)(2), Dec. 27, 2020, 134 Stat. 3041]

(i) Portion of American Opportunity Tax Credit made refundable

Forty percent of so much of the credit allowed under subsection (a) as is attributable to the American Opportunity Tax Credit (determined after application of subsection (d) and without regard to this paragraph [2] and section 26(a)) shall be treated as a credit allowable under subpart C (and not allowed under subsection (a)). The preceding sentence shall not apply to any taxpayer for any taxable year if such taxpayer is a child to whom subsection (g) of section 1 applies for such taxable year.

(j) Regulations

The Secretary may prescribe such regulations as may be necessary or appropriate to carry out this section, including regulations providing for a recapture of the credit allowed under this section in cases where there is a refund in a subsequent taxable year of any amount which was taken into account in determining the amount of such credit.

(Added Pub. L. 105–34, title II, §201(a), Aug. 5, 1997, 111 Stat. 799; amended Pub. L. 107–16, title IV, §401(g)(2)(A), June 7, 2001, 115 Stat. 59; Pub. L. 111–5, div. B, title I, §1004(a), Feb. 17, 2009, 123 Stat. 313; Pub. L. 111–148, title X, §10909(b)(2)(C), (c), Mar. 23, 2010, 124 Stat. 1023; Pub. L. 111–312, title I, §§101(b)(1), 103(a)(1), Dec. 17, 2010, 124 Stat. 3298, 3299; Pub. L. 112–240, title I, §§103(a)(1), 104(c)(2)(D), Jan. 2, 2013, 126 Stat. 2319, 2322; Pub. L. 113–295, div. A, title II, §209(b), Dec. 19, 2014, 128 Stat. 4028; Pub. L. 114–27, title VIII, §804(a), June 29, 2015, 129 Stat. 415; Pub. L. 114–113, div. Q, title I, §102(a), title II, §§206(a), 208(a)(2), 211(a), Dec. 18, 2015, 129 Stat. 3044, 3082, 3083, 3085; Pub. L. 115–97, title I, §11002(d)(1)(B), Dec. 22, 2017, 131 Stat. 2060; Pub. L. 115–141, div. U, title I, §101(l)(1)–(9), (11)–(14), title IV, §401(b)(1), Mar. 23, 2018, 132 Stat. 1162–1165, 1201; Pub. L. 116–260, div. EE, title I, §104(a), Dec. 27, 2020, 134 Stat. 3040.)

INFLATION ADJUSTED ITEMS FOR CERTAIN YEARS

For inflation adjustment of certain items in this section, see Revenue Procedures listed in a table under section 1 of this title.

EDITORIAL NOTES
REFERENCES IN TEXT

The date of the enactment of this section, referred to in subsecs. (b)(3)(A) and (f)(2)(A), is the date of enactment of Pub. L. 105–34 which was approved Aug. 5, 1997.

The Higher Education Act of 1965, referred to in subsec. (f)(2)(B), is Pub. L. 89–329, Nov. 8, 1965, 79 Stat. 1219. Title IV of the Act is classified generally to subchapter IV (§1070 et seq.) of chapter 28 of Title 20, Education. For complete classification of this Act to the Code, see Short Title note set out under section 1001 of Title 20 and Tables.

AMENDMENTS

2020—Subsec. (d). Pub. L. 116–260, §104(a)(1), added par. (1), redesignated par. (3) as (2), and struck out former pars. (1) and (2) which provided income limitations for the American Opportunity Tax Credit and Lifetime Learning Credit, respectively.

Subsec. (h). Pub. L. 116–260, §104(a)(2), struck out subsec. (h) which related to inflation adjustments for the Lifetime Learning Credit for taxable years beginning after 2001.

2018—Pub. L. 115–141, §101(l)(14), substituted "American Opportunity Tax Credit" for "Hope Scholarship Credit" wherever appearing in text.

Pub. L. 115–141, §101(l)(9), substituted "American Opportunity" for "Hope" in section catchline.

Subsec. (b). Pub. L. 115–141, §101(l)(11), substituted "American Opportunity Tax Credit" for "Hope Scholarship Credit" in heading.

Subsec. (b)(1)(A). Pub. L. 115–141, §101(l)(1)(A), substituted "$2,000" for "$1,000".

Subsec. (b)(1)(B). Pub. L. 115–141, §101(l)(1)(B), substituted "25 percent" for "50 percent", "$2,000" for "$1,000", and "$4,000" for "the applicable limit".

Subsec. (b)(2). Pub. L. 115–141, §101(l)(12), substituted "American Opportunity Tax Credit" for "Hope Scholarship Credit" in heading.

Subsec. (b)(2)(A), (C). Pub. L. 115–141, §101(l)(2), substituted "4" for "2" in heading and text.

Subsec. (b)(4). Pub. L. 115–141, §101(l)(3), amended par. (4) generally. Prior to amendment, text read as follows: "For purposes of paragraph (1)(B), the applicable limit for any taxable year is an amount equal to 2 times the dollar amount in effect under paragraph (1)(A) for such taxable year."

Subsec. (c)(1). Pub. L. 115–141, §401(b)(1), struck out "($5,000 in the case of taxable years beginning before January 1, 2003)" after "$10,000".

Subsec. (c)(2)(A). Pub. L. 115–141, §101(l)(13), substituted "American Opportunity Tax Credit" for "Hope Scholarship" in heading.

Subsec. (d). Pub. L. 115–141, §101(l)(4), amended subsec. (d) generally. Prior to amendment, subsec. (d) related to limitation based on modified adjusted gross income.

Subsec. (f)(1)(D). Pub. L. 115–141, §101(l)(5), added subpar. (D).

Subsec. (g)(1). Pub. L. 115–141, §101(l)(6), designated existing provisions as subpar. (A), inserted heading, and added subpar. (B).

Subsec. (h). Pub. L. 115–141, §101(l)(7), amended subsec. (h) generally. Prior to amendment, subsec. (h) related to inflation adjustments.

Subsec. (i). Pub. L. 115–141, §101(l)(8), amended subsec. (i) generally. Prior to amendment, subsec. (i) related to the American Opportunity Tax Credit in any taxable year beginning after 2008.

2017—Subsec. (h)(1)(A)(ii), (2)(A)(ii). Pub. L. 115–97 substituted "for 'calendar year 2016' in subparagraph (A)(ii)" for "for 'calendar year 1992' in subparagraph (B)".

2015—Subsec. (g)(3)(C). Pub. L. 114–27, §804(a)(2), added subpar. (C).

Subsec. (g)(8). Pub. L. 114–27, §804(a)(1), added par. (8).

Subsec. (i). Pub. L. 114–113, §102(a), struck out "and before 2018" after "2008" in introductory provisions.

Subsec. (i)(6). Pub. L. 114–113, §206(a)(2), added par. (6).

Pub. L. 114–113, §206(a)(1), struck out par. (6). Text read as follows: "In the case of a taxpayer with respect to whom section 702(a)(1)(B) of the Heartland Disaster Tax Relief Act of 2008 applies for any taxable year, such taxpayer may elect to waive the application of this subsection to such taxpayer for such taxable year."

Subsec. (i)(6)(C). Pub. L. 114–113, §211(a), added subpar. (C).

Subsec. (i)(7). Pub. L. 114–113, §208(a)(2), added par. (7).

2014—Subsec. (i)(3). Pub. L. 113–295 substituted "For purposes of determining the Hope Scholarship Credit, subsection (f)(1)(A) shall be applied" for "Subsection (f)(1)(A) shall be applied".

2013—Subsec. (i). Pub. L. 112–240, §103(a)(1), substituted "after 2008 and before 2018" for "in 2009, 2010, 2011, or 2012" in introductory provisions.

Subsec. (i)(5) to (7). Pub. L. 112–240, §104(c)(2)(D), redesignated pars. (6) and (7) as (5) and (6), respectively, substituted "section 26(a)" for "section 26(a)(2) or paragraph (5), as the case may be" in par. (5), and struck out former par. (5) which related to credit allowed against alternative minimum tax.

2010—Subsec. (i). Pub. L. 111–312, §103(a)(1), substituted ", 2010, 2011, or 2012" for "or 2010" in introductory provisions.

Subsec. (i)(5)(B). Pub. L. 111–148, §10909(b)(2)(C), (c), as amended by Pub. L. 111–312, §101(b)(1), temporarily substituted "25D" for "23, 25D,". See Effective and Termination Dates of 2010 Amendment note below.

2009—Subsecs. (i), (j). Pub. L. 111–5 added subsec. (i) and redesignated former subsec. (i) as (j).

2001—Subsec. (e). Pub. L. 107–16, §401(g)(2)(A), amended heading and text of subsec. (e) generally. Prior to amendment, text read as follows:

"(1) In general.—No credit shall be allowed under subsection (a) for a taxable year with respect to the qualified tuition and related expenses of an individual unless the taxpayer elects to have this section apply with respect to such individual for such year.

"(2) Coordination with exclusions.—An election under this subsection shall not take effect with respect to an individual for any taxable year if any portion of any distribution during such taxable year from an education individual retirement account is excluded from gross income under section 530(d)(2)."

STATUTORY NOTES AND RELATED SUBSIDIARIES

EFFECTIVE DATE OF 2020 AMENDMENT

Pub. L. 116–260, div. EE, title I, §104(c), Dec. 27, 2020, 134 Stat. 3041, provided that: "The amendments made by this section [amending this section and sections 62, 74, 86, 135, 137, 219, 221, and 469 of this title and repealing section 222 of this title] shall apply to taxable years beginning after December 31, 2020."

EFFECTIVE DATE OF 2018 AMENDMENT

Amendment by section 101(l)(1) to (9), (11) to (14) of Pub. L. 115–141 effective as if included in the provision of the Protecting Americans from Tax Hikes Act of 2015, div. Q of Pub. L. 114–113, to which such amendment relates, see section 101(s) of Pub. L. 115–141, set out as a note under section 24 of this title.

EFFECTIVE DATE OF 2017 AMENDMENT

Amendment by Pub. L. 115–97 applicable to taxable years beginning after Dec. 31, 2017, see section 11002(e) of Pub. L. 115–97, set out as a note under section 1 of this title.

EFFECTIVE DATE OF 2015 AMENDMENT

Pub. L. 114–113, div. Q, title I, §102(c), Dec. 18, 2015, 129 Stat. 3044, provided that: "The amendments made by this section [amending this section and provisions set out as a note below] shall apply to taxable years beginning after the date of the enactment of this Act [Dec. 18, 2015]."

Pub. L. 114–113, div. Q, title II, §206(b), Dec. 18, 2015, 129 Stat. 3082, as amended by Pub. L. 115–141, div. U, title I, §101(j), Mar. 23, 2018, 132 Stat. 1162, provided that:

"(1) In general.—The amendment made by subsection (a)(2) [amending this section] shall apply to any return of tax, and any amendment or supplement to any return of tax, which is filed after the date of the enactment of this Act [Dec. 18, 2015].

"(2) Repeal of deadwood.—The amendment made by subsection (a)(1) [amending this section] shall take effect on the date of the enactment of this Act."

Amendment by section 208(a)(2) of Pub. L. 114–113 applicable to taxable years beginning after Dec. 31, 2015, see section 208(c) of Pub. L. 114–113, set out as a note under section 24 of this title.

Pub. L. 114–113, div. Q, title II, §211(c)(1), Dec. 18, 2015, 129 Stat. 3085, provided that: "The amendments made by subsection (a) [amending this section] shall apply to taxable years beginning after December 31, 2015."

Pub. L. 114–27, title VIII, §804(d), June 29, 2015, 129 Stat. 416, provided that: "The amendments made by this section [amending this section and sections 222 and 6050S of this title] shall apply to taxable years beginning after the date of the enactment of this Act [June 29, 2015]."

EFFECTIVE DATE OF 2014 AMENDMENT

Amendment by Pub. L. 113–295 effective as if included in the provisions of the American Recovery and Reinvestment Tax Act of 2009, Pub. L. 111–5, div. B, title I, to which such amendment relates, see section 209(k) of Pub. L. 113–295, set out as a note under section 24 of this title.

EFFECTIVE DATE OF 2013 AMENDMENT

Amendment by section 103(a)(1) of Pub. L. 112–240 applicable to taxable years beginning after Dec. 31, 2012, see section 103(e)(1) of Pub. L. 112–240, set out as a note under section 24 of this title.

Amendment by section 104(c)(2)(D) of Pub. L. 112–240 applicable to taxable years beginning after Dec. 31, 2011, see section 104(d) of Pub. L. 112–240, set out as a note under section 23 of this title.

EFFECTIVE AND TERMINATION DATES OF 2010 AMENDMENT

Amendment by section 103(a)(1) of Pub. L. 111–312 applicable to taxable years beginning after Dec. 31, 2010, see section 103(d) of Pub. L. 111–312, set out as a note under section 24 of this title.

Amendment by Pub. L. 111–148 terminated applicable to taxable years beginning after Dec. 31, 2011, and section is amended to read as if such amendment had never been enacted, see section 10909(c) of Pub. L. 111–148, set out as a note under section 1 of this title.

Amendment by Pub. L. 111–148 applicable to taxable years beginning after Dec. 31, 2009, see section 10909(d) of Pub. L. 111–148, set out as a note under section 1 of this title.

EFFECTIVE DATE OF 2009 AMENDMENT

Amendment by Pub. L. 111–5 applicable to taxable years beginning after Dec. 31, 2008, see section 1004(d) of Pub. L. 111–5, set out as an Effective and Termination Dates of 2009 Amendment note under section 24 of this title.

EFFECTIVE DATE OF 2001 AMENDMENT

Pub. L. 107–16, title IV, §401(h), June 7, 2001, 115 Stat. 60, provided that: "The amendments made by this section [amending this section and sections 135, 530, and 4973 of this title] shall apply to taxable years beginning after December 31, 2001."

EFFECTIVE DATE

Pub. L. 105–34, title II, §201(f), Aug. 5, 1997, 111 Stat. 806, provided that:

"(1) In general.—The amendments made by this section [enacting this section and section 6050S of this title and amending sections 135, 6213, and 6724 of this title] shall apply to expenses paid after December 31, 1997 (in taxable years ending after such date), for education furnished in academic periods beginning after such date.

"(2) Lifetime learning credit.—Section 25A(a)(2) of the Internal Revenue Code of 1986 shall apply to expenses paid after June 30, 1998 (in taxable years ending after such date), for education furnished in academic periods beginning after such dates."

SAVINGS PROVISION

For provisions that nothing in amendment by section 401(b)(1) of Pub. L. 115–141 be construed to affect treatment of certain transactions occurring, property acquired, or items of income, loss, deduction, or credit taken into account prior to Mar. 23, 2018, for purposes of determining liability for tax for periods ending after Mar. 23, 2018, see section 401(e) of Pub. L. 115–141, set out as a note under section 23 of this title.

TREATMENT OF POSSESSIONS

Pub. L. 111–5, div. B, title I, §1004(c), Feb. 17, 2009, 123 Stat. 314, as amended by Pub. L. 111–312, title I, §103(a)(2), Dec. 17, 2010, 124 Stat. 3299; Pub. L. 112–240, title I, §103(a)(2), Jan. 2, 2013, 126 Stat. 2319; Pub. L. 114–113, div. Q, title I, §102(b), Dec. 18, 2015, 129 Stat. 3044, provided that:

"(1) Payments to possessions.—

"(A) Mirror code possession.—The Secretary of the Treasury shall pay to each possession of the United States with a mirror code tax system amounts equal to the loss to that possession by reason of the application of section 25A(i)(6) [now 25A(i)] of the Internal Revenue Code of 1986 (as added by this section) with respect to taxable years beginning after 2008. Such amounts shall be determined by the Secretary of the Treasury based on information provided by the government of the respective possession.

"(B) Other possessions.—The Secretary of the Treasury shall pay to each possession of the United States which does not have a mirror code tax system amounts estimated by the Secretary of the Treasury as being equal to the aggregate benefits that would have been provided to residents of such possession by reason of the application of section 25A(i)(6) [now 25A(i)] of such Code (as so added) for taxable years beginning after 2008 if a mirror code tax system had been in effect in such possession. The preceding sentence shall not apply with respect to any possession of the United States unless such possession has a plan, which has been approved by the Secretary of the Treasury, under which such possession will promptly distribute such payments to the residents of such possession.

"(2) Coordination with credit allowed against united states income taxes.—Section 25A(i)(6) [now 25A(i)] of such Code (as added by this section) shall not apply to a bona fide resident of any possession of the United States.

"(3) Definitions and special rules.—

"(A) Possession of the united states.—For purposes of this subsection, the term 'possession of the United States' includes the Commonwealth of Puerto Rico and the Commonwealth of the Northern Mariana Islands.

"(B) Mirror code tax system.—For purposes of this subsection, the term 'mirror code tax system' means, with respect to any possession of the United States, the income tax system of such possession if the income tax liability of the residents of such possession under such system is determined by reference to the income tax laws of the United States as if such possession were the United States.

"(C) Treatment of payments.—For purposes of section 1324(b)(2) of title 31, United States Code, the payments under this subsection shall be treated in the same manner as a refund due from the credit allowed under section 25A of the Internal Revenue Code of 1986 by reason of subsection (i)(6) [now (i)(5)] of such section (as added by this section)."

[Amendments by Pub. L. 112–240, §103(a)(2), and Pub. L. 114–113, §102(b), were executed as the probable intent of Congress to section 1004(c)(1) of the American Recovery and Reinvestment Tax Act of 2009, set out above, which act is title I of div. B of Pub. L. 111–5, notwithstanding directory language amending section 1004(c)(1) of division B of the American Recovery and Reinvestment Tax Act of 2009.]

¹ So in original. Probably should be "an".
² So in original. Probably should be "this subsection".

§25B. Elective deferrals and IRA contributions by certain individuals

(a) Allowance of credit

In the case of an eligible individual, there shall be allowed as a credit against the tax imposed by this subtitle for the taxable year an amount equal to the applicable percentage of so much of the qualified retirement savings contributions of the eligible individual for the taxable year as do not exceed $2,000.

(b) Applicable percentage

For purposes of this section—

(1) Joint returns

In the case of a joint return, the applicable percentage is—

    (A) if the adjusted gross income of the taxpayer is not over $30,000, 50 percent,

    (B) if the adjusted gross income of the taxpayer is over $30,000 but not over $32,500, 20 percent,

    (C) if the adjusted gross income of the taxpayer is over $32,500 but not over $50,000, 10 percent, and

    (D) if the adjusted gross income of the taxpayer is over $50,000, zero percent.

(2) Other returns

In the case of—

    (A) a head of household, the applicable percentage shall be determined under paragraph (1) except that such paragraph shall be applied by substituting for each dollar amount therein (as adjusted under paragraph (3)) a dollar amount equal to 75 percent of such dollar amount, and

    (B) any taxpayer not described in paragraph (1) or subparagraph (A), the applicable percentage shall be determined under paragraph (1) except that such paragraph shall be applied by substituting for each dollar amount therein (as adjusted under paragraph (3)) a dollar amount equal to 50 percent of such dollar amount.

(3) Inflation adjustment

In the case of any taxable year beginning in a calendar year after 2006, each of the dollar amounts in paragraph (1) shall be increased by an amount equal to—

    (A) such dollar amount, multiplied by

    (B) the cost-of-living adjustment determined under section 1(f)(3) for the calendar year in which the taxable year begins, determined by substituting "calendar year 2005" for "calendar year 2016" in subparagraph (A)(ii) thereof.

Any increase determined under the preceding sentence shall be rounded to the nearest multiple of $500.

(c) Eligible individual

For purposes of this section—

(1) In general

The term "eligible individual" means any individual if such individual has attained the age of 18 as of the close of the taxable year.

(2) Dependents and full-time students not eligible

The term "eligible individual" shall not include—

    (A) any individual with respect to whom a deduction under section 151 is allowed to another taxpayer for a taxable year beginning in the calendar year in which such individual's taxable year begins, and

    (B) any individual who is a student (as defined in section 152(f)(2)).

(d) Qualified retirement savings contributions

For purposes of this section—

(1) In general

The term "qualified retirement savings contributions" means, with respect to any taxable year, the sum of—

    (A) the amount of the qualified retirement contributions (as defined in section 219(e)) made by the eligible individual,

    (B) the amount of—

        (i) any elective deferrals (as defined in section 402(g)(3)) of such individual, and

        (ii) any elective deferral of compensation by such individual under an eligible deferred compensation plan (as defined in section 457(b)) of an eligible employer described in section 457(e)(1)(A),

    (C) the amount of voluntary employee contributions by such individual to any qualified retirement plan (as defined in section 4974(c)), and

    (D) the amount of contributions made before January 1, 2026, by such individual to the ABLE account (within the meaning of section 529A) of which such individual is the designated beneficiary.

(2) Reduction for certain distributions

(A) In general

The qualified retirement savings contributions determined under paragraph (1) shall be reduced (but not below zero) by the aggregate distributions received by the individual during the testing period from any entity of a type to which contributions under paragraph (1) may be made. The preceding sentence shall not apply to the portion of any distribution which is not includible in gross income by reason of a trustee-to-trustee transfer or a rollover distribution.

(B) Testing period

For purposes of subparagraph (A), the testing period, with respect to a taxable year, is the period which includes—

    (i) such taxable year,

    (ii) the 2 preceding taxable years, and

    (iii) the period after such taxable year and before the due date (including extensions) for filing the return of tax for such taxable year.

(C) Excepted distributions

There shall not be taken into account under subparagraph (A)—

    (i) any distribution referred to in section 72(p), 401(k)(8), 401(m)(6), 402(g)(2), 404(k), or 408(d)(4), and

    (ii) any distribution to which section 408A(d)(3) applies.

(D) Treatment of distributions received by spouse of individual

For purposes of determining distributions received by an individual under subparagraph (A) for any taxable year, any distribution received by the spouse of such individual shall be treated as received by such individual if such individual and spouse file a joint return for such taxable year and for the taxable year during which the spouse receives the distribution.

(e) Adjusted gross income

For purposes of this section, adjusted gross income shall be determined without regard to sections 911, 931, and 933.

(f) Investment in the contract

Notwithstanding any other provision of law, a qualified retirement savings contribution shall not fail to be included in determining the investment in the contract for purposes of section 72 by reason of the credit under this section.

(Added and amended Pub. L. 107–16, title VI, §618(a), (b)(1), June 7, 2001, 115 Stat. 106, 108; Pub. L. 107–147, title IV, §§411(m), 417(1), Mar. 9, 2002, 116 Stat. 48, 56; Pub. L. 108–311, title II, §207(4), Oct. 4, 2004, 118 Stat. 1177; Pub. L. 109–135, title IV, §402(i)(3)(D), Dec. 21, 2005, 119 Stat. 2614; Pub. L. 109–280, title VIII, §§812, 833(a), Aug. 17, 2006, 120 Stat. 997, 1003; Pub. L. 110–343, div. B, title I, §106(e)(2)(C), title II, §205(d)(1)(C), Oct. 3, 2008, 122 Stat. 3817, 3838; Pub. L. 111–5, div. B, title I, §§1004(b)(4), 1142(b)(1)(C), 1144(b)(1)(C), Feb. 17, 2009, 123 Stat. 314, 330, 332; Pub. L. 111–148, title X, §10909(b)(2)(D), (c), Mar. 23,

INFLATION ADJUSTED ITEMS FOR CERTAIN YEARS

For inflation adjustment of certain items in this section, see Revenue Procedures listed in a table under section 1 of this title and Revenue Notices listed in a table under section 401 of this title.

EDITORIAL NOTES

AMENDMENTS

2017—Subsec. (b)(3)(B). Pub. L. 115–97, §11002(d)(1)(C), substituted "for 'calendar year 2016' in subparagraph (A)(ii)" for "for 'calendar year 1992' in subparagraph (B)".

Subsec. (d)(1)(D). Pub. L. 115–97, §11024(b), added subpar. (D).

2013—Subsec. (g). Pub. L. 112–240 struck out subsec. (g). Text read as follows: "In the case of a taxable year to which section 26(a)(2) does not apply, the credit allowed under subsection (a) for the taxable year shall not exceed the excess of—

"(1) the sum of the regular tax liability (as defined in section 26(b)) plus the tax imposed by section 55, over

"(2) the sum of the credits allowable under this subpart (other than this section and sections 23, 25A(i), 25D, 30, 30B, and 30D) and section 27 for the taxable year."

2010—Subsec. (g)(2). Pub. L. 111–148, §10909(b)(2)(D), (c), as amended by Pub. L. 111–312, temporarily struck out "23," before "25A(i),". See Effective and Termination Dates of 2010 Amendment note below.

2009—Subsec. (g)(2). Pub. L. 111–5, §1144(b)(1)(C), inserted "30B," after "30,".

Pub. L. 111–5, §1142(b)(1)(C), inserted "30," after "25D,".

Pub. L. 111–5, §1004(b)(4), inserted "25A(i)," after "23,".

2008—Subsec. (g)(2). Pub. L. 110–343, §205(d)(1)(C), substituted ", 25D, and 30D" for "and 25D".

Pub. L. 110–343, §106(e)(2)(C), substituted "sections 23 and 25D" for "section 23".

2006—Subsec. (b). Pub. L. 109–280, §833(a), reenacted heading without change and amended text of subsec. (b) generally, substituting provisions consisting of introductory provisions and pars. (1) to (3) for former provisions consisting of introductory provisions and a table of applicable percentages for amounts of adjusted gross income for a joint return, a head of household, and all other cases.

Subsec. (h). Pub. L. 109–280, §812, struck out heading and text of subsec. (h). Text read as follows: "This section shall not apply to taxable years beginning after December 31, 2006."

2005—Subsec. (g). Pub. L. 109–135 substituted "In the case of a taxable year to which section 26(a)(2) does not apply, the credit" for "The credit" in introductory provisions.

2004—Subsec. (c)(2)(B). Pub. L. 108–311 substituted "152(f)(2)" for "151(c)(4)".

2002—Subsec. (d)(2)(A). Pub. L. 107–147, §411(m), reenacted heading without change and amended text of subpar. (A) generally. Prior to amendment, text read as follows: "The qualified retirement savings contributions determined under paragraph (1) shall be reduced (but not below zero) by the sum of—

"(i) any distribution from a qualified retirement plan (as defined in section 4974(c)), or from an eligible deferred compensation plan (as defined in section 457(b)), received by the individual during the testing period which is includible in gross income, and

"(ii) any distribution from a Roth IRA or a Roth account received by the individual during the testing period which is not a qualified rollover contribution (as defined in section 408A(e)) to a Roth IRA or a rollover under section 402(c)(8)(B) to a Roth account."

Subsecs. (g), (h). Pub. L. 107–147, §417(1), redesignated subsec. (g), relating to termination, as (h).

2001—Subsec. (g). Pub. L. 107–16, §618(b)(1), added subsec. (g) relating to limitation based on amount of tax.

STATUTORY NOTES AND RELATED SUBSIDIARIES

EFFECTIVE DATE OF 2013 AMENDMENT

Amendment by Pub. L. 112–240 applicable to taxable years beginning after Dec. 31, 2011, see section 104(d) of Pub. L. 112–240, set out as a note under section 23 of this title.

EFFECTIVE AND TERMINATION DATES OF 2010 AMENDMENT

Amendment by Pub. L. 111–148 terminated applicable to taxable years beginning after Dec. 31, 2011, and section is amended to read as if such amendment had never been enacted, see section 10909(c) of Pub. L. 111–148, set out as a note under section 1 of this title.

Amendment by Pub. L. 111–148 applicable to taxable years beginning after Dec. 31, 2009, see section 10909(d) of Pub. L. 111–148, set out as a note under section 1 of this title.

EFFECTIVE DATE OF 2017 AMENDMENT

Amendment by section 11002(d)(1)(C) of Pub. L. 115–97 applicable to taxable years beginning after Dec. 31, 2017, see section 11002(e) of Pub. L. 115–97, set out as a note under section 1 of this title.

Pub. L. 115–97, title I, §11024(c), Dec. 22, 2017, 131 Stat. 2076, provided that: "The amendments made by this section [amending this section and section 529A of this title] shall apply to taxable years beginning after the date of the enactment of this Act [Dec. 22, 2017]."

EFFECTIVE DATE OF 2009 AMENDMENT

Amendment by section 1004(b)(4) of Pub. L. 111–5 applicable to taxable years beginning after Dec. 31, 2008, see section 1004(d) of Pub. L. 111–5, set out as an Effective and Termination Dates of 2009 Amendment note under section 24 of this title.

Amendment by section 1142(b)(1)(C) of Pub. L. 111–5 applicable to vehicles acquired after Feb. 17, 2009, see section 1142(c) of Pub. L. 111–5, set out as an Effective and Termination Dates of 2009 Amendment note under section 24 of this title.

Amendment by section 1144(b)(1)(C) of Pub. L. 111–5 applicable to taxable years beginning after Dec. 31, 2008, see section 1144(c) of Pub. L. 111–5, set out as an Effective and Termination Dates of 2009 Amendment note under section 24 of this title.

EFFECTIVE DATE OF 2008 AMENDMENT

Amendment by section 106(e)(2)(C) of Pub. L. 110–343 applicable to taxable years beginning after Dec. 31, 2007, see section 106(f)(1) of Pub. L. 110–343, set out as an Effective and Termination Dates of 2008 Amendment note under section 23 of this title.

Amendment by section 205(d)(1)(C) of Pub. L. 110–343 applicable to taxable years beginning after Dec. 31, 2008, see section 205(e) of Pub. L. 110–343, set out as an Effective and Termination Dates of 2008 Amendment note under section 24 of this title.

EFFECTIVE DATE OF 2006 AMENDMENT

Pub. L. 109–280, title VIII, §833(d), Aug. 17, 2006, 120 Stat. 1004, provided that: "The amendments made by this section [amending this section and sections 219 and 408A of this title] shall apply to taxable years beginning after 2006."

EFFECTIVE AND TERMINATION DATES OF 2005 AMENDMENT

Amendment by Pub. L. 109–135 subject to title IX of the Economic Growth and Tax Relief Reconciliation Act of 2001, Pub. L. 107–16, §901, in the same manner as the provisions of such Act to which such amendment relates, see section 402(i)(3)(H) of Pub. L. 109–135, set out as a note under section 23 of this title. Title IX of Pub. L. 107–16 was repealed by Pub. L. 112–240, title I, §101(a)(1), Jan. 2, 2013, 126 Stat. 2315.

Amendment by Pub. L. 109–135 effective as if included in the provisions of the Energy Policy Act of 2005, Pub. L. 109–58, to which it relates and applicable to taxable years beginning after Dec. 31, 2005, see section 402(m) of Pub. L. 109–135, set out as a note under section 23 of this title.

EFFECTIVE DATE OF 2004 AMENDMENT

Amendment by Pub. L. 108–311 applicable to taxable years beginning after Dec. 31, 2004, see section 208 of Pub. L. 108–311, set out as a note under section 2 of this title.

EFFECTIVE DATE OF 2002 AMENDMENT

Pub. L. 107–147, title IV, §411(x), Mar. 9, 2002, 116 Stat. 53, provided that: "Except as provided in subsection (c) [amending sections 23 and 137 of this title and enacting provisions set out as a note under section 23 of this title], the amendments made by this section [amending this section, sections 23, 24, 38, 45E, 45F, 63, 137, 401 to 404, 408, 409, 412, 414 to 417, 457, 530, 2016, 2101, 2511, 4980F, and 6428 of this title, sections 1003, 1054, 1055, 1082, and 1104 of Title 29, Labor, and provisions set out as notes under sections 38, 415, and 4980F of this title] shall take effect as if included in the provisions of the Economic Growth and Tax Relief Reconciliation Act of 2001 [Pub. L. 107–16] to which they relate."

EFFECTIVE DATE

Amendment by section 618(b)(1) of Pub. L. 107–16 inapplicable to taxable years beginning during 2004 or 2005, see section 312(b)(2) of Pub. L. 108–311, set out as an Effective Date of 2001 Amendment note under section 23 of this title.

Amendment by section 618(b)(1) of Pub. L. 107–16 inapplicable to taxable years beginning during 2002 and 2003, see section 601(b)(2) of Pub. L. 107–147, set out as an Effective Date of 2001 Amendment note under section 23 of this title.

Amendment by section 618(b)(1) of Pub. L. 107–16 applicable to taxable years beginning after Dec. 31, 2001, see section 618(d) of Pub. L. 107–16, set out as an Effective Date of 2001 Amendment note under section 24 of this title.

§25C. Nonbusiness energy property

(a) Allowance of credit

In the case of an individual, there shall be allowed as a credit against the tax imposed by this chapter for the taxable year an amount equal to the sum of—

(1) 10 percent of the amount paid or incurred by the taxpayer for qualified energy efficiency improvements installed during such taxable year, and

(2) the amount of the residential energy property expenditures paid or incurred by the taxpayer during such taxable year.

(b) Limitations

(1) Lifetime limitation

The credit allowed under this section with respect to any taxpayer for any taxable year shall not exceed the excess (if any) of $500 over the aggregate credits allowed under this section with respect to such taxpayer for all prior taxable years ending after December 31, 2005.

(2) Windows

In the case of amounts paid or incurred for components described in subsection (c)(3)(B) by any taxpayer for any taxable year, the credit allowed under this section with respect to such amounts for such year shall not exceed the excess (if any) of $200 over the aggregate credits allowed under this section with respect to such amounts for all prior taxable years ending after December 31, 2005.

(3) Limitation on residential energy property expenditures

The amount of the credit allowed under this section by reason of subsection (a)(2) shall not exceed—

(A) $50 for any advanced main air circulating fan,

(B) $150 for any qualified natural gas, propane, or oil furnace or hot water boiler, and

(C) $300 for any item of energy-efficient building property.

(c) Qualified energy efficiency improvements

For purposes of this section—

(1) In general

The term "qualified energy efficiency improvements" means any energy efficient building envelope component, if—

(A) such component is installed in or on a dwelling unit located in the United States and owned and used by the taxpayer as the taxpayer's principal residence (within the meaning of section 121),

(B) the original use of such component commences with the taxpayer, and

(C) such component reasonably can be expected to remain in use for at least 5 years.

(2) Energy efficient building envelope component

The term "energy efficient building envelope component" means a building envelope component which meets—

(A) applicable Energy Star program requirements, in the case of a roof or roof products,

(B) version 6.0 Energy Star program requirements, in the case of an exterior window, a skylight, or an exterior door, and

(C) the prescriptive criteria for such component established by the 2009 International Energy Conservation Code, as such Code (including supplements) is in effect on the date of the enactment of the American Recovery and Reinvestment Tax Act of 2009, in the case of any other component.

(3) Building envelope component

The term "building envelope component" means—

(A) any insulation material or system which is specifically and primarily designed to reduce the heat loss or gain of a dwelling unit when installed in or on such dwelling unit,

(B) exterior windows (including skylights),

(C) exterior doors, and

(D) any metal roof or asphalt roof installed on a dwelling unit, but only if such roof has appropriate pigmented coatings or cooling granules which are specifically and primarily designed to reduce the heat gain of such dwelling unit.

(4) Manufactured homes included

The term "dwelling unit" includes a manufactured home which conforms to Federal Manufactured Home Construction and Safety Standards (part 3280 of title 24, Code of Federal Regulations).

(d) Residential energy property expenditures

For purposes of this section—

(1) In general

The term "residential energy property expenditures" means expenditures made by the taxpayer for qualified energy property which is—

(A) installed on or in connection with a dwelling unit located in the United States and owned and used by the taxpayer as the taxpayer's principal residence (within the meaning of section 121), and

(B) originally placed in service by the taxpayer.

Such term includes expenditures for labor costs properly allocable to the onsite preparation, assembly, or original installation of the property.

(2) Qualified energy property

(A) In general

The term "qualified energy property" means—

(i) energy-efficient building property,

(ii) a qualified natural gas, propane, or oil furnace or hot water boiler, or

(iii) an advanced main air circulating fan.

(B) Performance and quality standards

Property described under subparagraph (A) shall meet the performance and quality standards, and the certification requirements (if any), which—

(i) have been prescribed by the Secretary by regulations (after consultation with the Secretary of Energy or the Administrator of the Environmental Protection Agency, as appropriate), and

(ii) are in effect at the time of the acquisition of the property, or at the time of the completion of the construction, reconstruction, or erection of the property, as the case may be.

(C) Requirements and standards for air conditioners and heat pumps

The standards and requirements prescribed by the Secretary under subparagraph (B) with respect to the energy efficiency ratio (EER) for central air conditioners and electric heat pumps—

(i) shall require measurements to be based on published data which is tested by manufacturers at 95 degrees Fahrenheit, and

(ii) may be based on the certified data of the Air Conditioning and Refrigeration Institute that are prepared in partnership with the Consortium for Energy Efficiency.

(3) Energy-efficient building property

The term "energy-efficient building property" means—

(A) an electric heat pump water heater which yields a Uniform Energy Factor of at least 2.2 in the standard Department of Energy test procedure,

(B) an electric heat pump which achieves the highest efficiency tier established by the Consortium for Energy Efficiency, as in effect on January 1, 2009,

(C) a central air conditioner which achieves the highest efficiency tier established by the Consortium for Energy Efficiency, as in effect on January 1, 2009, and

(D) a natural gas, propane, or oil water heater which has either a Uniform Energy Factor of at least 0.82 or a thermal efficiency of at least 90 percent.

(4) Qualified natural gas, propane, or oil furnace or hot water boiler

The term "qualified natural gas, propane, or oil furnace or hot water boiler" means a natural gas, propane, or oil furnace or hot water boiler which achieves an annual fuel utilization efficiency rate of not less than 95.

(5) Advanced main air circulating fan

The term "advanced main air circulating fan" means a fan used in a natural gas, propane, or oil furnace and which has an annual electricity use of no more than 2 percent of the total annual energy use of the furnace (as determined in the standard Department of Energy test procedures).

(e) Special rules

For purposes of this section—

(1) Application of rules

Rules similar to the rules under paragraphs (4), (5), (6), (7), and (8) of section 25D(e) shall apply.

(2) Joint ownership of energy items

(A) In general

Any expenditure otherwise qualifying as an expenditure under this section shall not be treated as failing to so qualify merely because such expenditure was made with respect to two or more dwelling units.

(B) Limits applied separately

In the case of any expenditure described in subparagraph (A), the amount of the credit allowable under subsection (a) shall (subject to paragraph (1)) be computed separately with respect to the amount of the expenditure made for each dwelling unit.

(3) Property financed by subsidized energy financing

For purposes of determining the amount of expenditures made by any individual with respect to any property, there shall not be taken into account expenditures which are made from subsidized energy financing (as defined in section 48(a)(4)(C)).

(f) Basis adjustments

For purposes of this subtitle, if a credit is allowed under this section for any expenditure with respect to any property, the increase in the basis of such property which would (but for this subsection) result from such expenditure shall be reduced by the amount of the credit so allowed.

(g) Termination

This section shall not apply with respect to any property placed in service—

(1) after December 31, 2007, and before January 1, 2009, or

(2) after December 31, 2021.

(Added Pub. L. 109–58, title XIII, §1333(a), Aug. 8, 2005, 119 Stat. 1026; amended Pub. L. 109–135, title IV, §412(b), Dec. 21, 2005, 119 Stat. 2636; Pub. L. 110–172, §11(a)(2), Dec. 29, 2007, 121 Stat. 2484; Pub. L. 110–343, div. B, title III, §302(a)–(e), Oct. 3, 2008, 122 Stat. 3844, 3845; Pub. L. 111–5, div. B, title I, §§1103(b)(2)(A), 1121(a)–(e), Feb. 17, 2009, 123 Stat. 320, 322-324; Pub. L. 111–312, title VII, §710(a), (b), Dec. 17, 2010, 124 Stat. 3314; Pub. L. 112–240, title IV, §401(a), Jan. 2, 2013, 126 Stat. 2337; Pub. L. 113–295, div. A, title I, §151(a), Dec. 19, 2014, 128 Stat. 4021; Pub. L. 114–113, div. Q, title I, §181(a), (b), Dec. 18, 2015, 129 Stat. 3072; Pub. L. 115–123, div. D, title I, §40401(a), Feb. 9, 2018, 132 Stat. 148; Pub. L. 115–141, div. U, title IV, §401(a)(4)–(6), Mar. 23, 2018, 132 Stat. 1184; Pub. L. 116–94, div. Q, title I, §123(a), (b), Dec. 20, 2019, 133 Stat. 3231; Pub. L. 116–260, div. EE, title I, §§141(a), 148(b)(3), Dec. 27, 2020, 134 Stat. 3054, 3055.)

EDITORIAL NOTES
REFERENCES IN TEXT

The date of the enactment of the American Recovery and Reinvestment Tax Act of 2009, referred to in subsec. (c)(2)(C), is the date of enactment of title I of div. B of Pub. L. 111–5, which was approved Feb. 17, 2009.

2020—Subsec. (d)(3)(E). Pub. L. 116–260, §148(b)(3)(A), struck out subpar. (E) which read as follows: "a stove which uses the burning of biomass fuel to heat a dwelling unit located in the United States and used as a residence by the taxpayer, or to heat water for use in such a dwelling unit, and which has a thermal efficiency rating of at least 75 percent."

Subsec. (d)(6). Pub. L. 116–260, §148(b)(3)(B), struck out par. (6). Text read as follows: "The term 'biomass fuel' means any plant-derived fuel available on a renewable or recurring basis, including agricultural crops and trees, wood and wood waste and residues (including wood pellets), plants (including aquatic plants), grasses, residues, and fibers."

Subsec. (g)(2). Pub. L. 116–260, §141(a), substituted "December 31, 2021" for "December 31, 2020".

2019—Subsec. (d)(3)(A). Pub. L. 116–94, §123(b)(1), substituted "a Uniform Energy Factor of at least 2.2" for "an energy factor of at least 2.0".

Subsec. (d)(3)(D). Pub. L. 116–94, §123(b)(2), substituted "a Uniform Energy Factor" for "an energy factor".

Subsec. (g)(2). Pub. L. 116–94, §123(a), substituted "December 31, 2020" for "December 31, 2017".

2018—Subsec. (b)(2). Pub. L. 115–141, §401(a)(4), substituted "subsection (c)(3)(B)" for "subsection (c)(2)(B)".

Subsec. (d)(3)(B). Pub. L. 115–141, §401(a)(5)(A), substituted comma for period at end.

Subsec. (d)(3)(D). Pub. L. 115–141, §401(a)(5)(B), substituted ", and" for period at end.

Subsec. (g)(2). Pub. L. 115–141, §401(a)(6), substituted "2017." for "2017..".

Pub. L. 115–123 substituted "December 31, 2017" for "December 31, 2016".

2015—Subsec. (c)(1). Pub. L. 114–113, §181(b)(1), struck out "which meets the prescriptive criteria for such component established by the 2009 International Energy Conservation Code, as such Code (including supplements) is in effect on the date of the enactment of the American Recovery and Reinvestment Tax Act of 2009 (or, in the case of an exterior window, a skylight, an exterior door, a metal roof with appropriate pigmented coatings, or an asphalt roof with appropriate cooling granules, which meet the Energy Star program requirements)" after "envelope component" in introductory provisions.

Subsec. (c)(2) to (4). Pub. L. 114–113, §181(b)(2), added par. (2) and redesignated former pars. (2) and (3) as (3) and (4), respectively.

Subsec. (g)(2). Pub. L. 114–113, §181(a), substituted "December 31, 2016" for "December 31, 2014".

2014—Subsec. (g)(2). Pub. L. 113–295 substituted "December 31, 2014" for "December 31, 2013".

2013—Subsec. (g)(2). Pub. L. 112–240 substituted "December 31, 2013" for "December 31, 2011".

2010—Subsecs. (a), (b). Pub. L. 111–312, §710(b)(1), amended subsecs. (a) and (b) generally. Prior to amendment, subsecs. (a) and (b) read as follows:

"(a) Allowance of credit.—In the case of an individual, there shall be allowed as a credit against the tax imposed by this chapter for the taxable year an amount equal to 30 percent of the sum of—

"(1) the amount paid or incurred by the taxpayer during such taxable year for qualified energy efficiency improvements, and

"(2) the amount of the residential energy property expenditures paid or incurred by the taxpayer during such taxable year.

"(b) Limitation.—The aggregate amount of the credits allowed under this section for taxable years beginning in 2009 and 2010 with respect to any taxpayer shall not exceed $1,500."

Subsec. (c)(1). Pub. L. 111–312, §710(b)(2)(D)(ii), inserted "an exterior window, a skylight, an exterior door," after "in the case of" in introductory provisions.

Pub. L. 111–312, §710(b)(2)(A), in introductory provisions, substituted "2009 International Energy Conservation Code, as such Code (including supplements) is in effect on the date of the enactment of the American Recovery and Reinvestment Tax Act of 2009" for "2000 International Energy Conservation Code, as such Code (including supplements) is in effect on the date of the enactment of this section".

Subsec. (c)(2)(A). Pub. L. 111–312, §710(b)(2)(E), struck out "and meets the prescriptive criteria for such material or system established by the 2009 International Energy Conservation Code, as such Code (including supplements) is in effect on the date of the enactment of the American Recovery and Reinvestment Tax Act of 2009" after "on such dwelling unit".

Subsec. (c)(4). Pub. L. 111–312, §710(b)(2)(D)(i), struck out par. (4). Text read as follows: "Such term shall not include any component described in subparagraph (B) or (C) of paragraph (2) unless such component is equal to or below a U factor of 0.30 and SHGC of 0.30."

Subsec. (d)(2)(A)(ii). Pub. L. 111–312, §710(b)(2)(C)(ii), amended cl. (ii) generally. Prior to amendment, cl. (ii) read as follows: "any qualified natural gas furnace, qualified propane furnace, qualified oil furnace, qualified natural gas hot water boiler, qualified propane hot water boiler, or qualified oil hot water boiler, or".

Subsec. (d)(3)(E). Pub. L. 111–312, §710(b)(2)(B), struck out ", as measured using a lower heating value" after "75 percent".

Subsec. (d)(4). Pub. L. 111–312, §710(b)(2)(C)(i), amended par. (4) generally. Prior to amendment, par. (4) defined the terms "qualified natural gas furnace", "qualified natural gas hot water boiler", "qualified propane furnace", "qualified propane hot water boiler", "qualified oil furnace", and "qualified oil hot water boiler".

Subsec. (e)(3). Pub. L. 111–312, §710(b)(3), added par. (3).

Subsec. (g)(2). Pub. L. 111–312, §710(a), substituted "2011" for "2010".

2009—Subsecs. (a), (b). Pub. L. 111–5, §1121(a), added subsecs. (a) and (b) and struck out former subsecs. (a) and (b) which related to credit equal to the sum of 10 percent of the amount paid for qualified energy efficiency improvements and the amount of energy property expenditures and provided limits on credits and expenditures.

Subsec. (c)(2)(A). Pub. L. 111–5, §1121(d)(2), inserted "and meets the prescriptive criteria for such material or system established by the 2009 International Energy Conservation Code, as such Code (including supplements) is in effect on the date of the enactment of the American Recovery and Reinvestment Tax Act of 2009" after "such dwelling unit".

Subsec. (c)(4). Pub. L. 111–5, §1121(d)(1), added par. (4).

Subsec. (d)(2)(A)(ii). Pub. L. 111–5, §1121(c)(2), amended cl. (ii) generally. Prior to amendment, cl. (ii) read as follows: "a qualified natural gas, propane, or oil furnace or hot water boiler, or".

Subsec. (d)(3)(B). Pub. L. 111–5, §1121(b)(1), amended subpar. (B) generally. Prior to amendment, subpar. (B) read as follows: "an electric heat pump which has a heating seasonal performance factor (HSPF) of at least 9, a seasonal energy efficiency ratio (SEER) of at least 15, and an energy efficiency ratio (EER) of at least 13,".

Subsec. (d)(3)(C). Pub. L. 111–5, §1121(b)(2), substituted "2009" for "2006".

Subsec. (d)(3)(D). Pub. L. 111–5, §1121(b)(3), amended subpar. (D) generally. Prior to amendment, subpar. (D) read as follows: "a natural gas, propane, or oil water heater which has an energy factor of at least 0.80 or a thermal efficiency of at least 90 percent, and".

Subsec. (d)(3)(E). Pub. L. 111–5, §1121(b)(4), inserted ", as measured using a lower heating value" after "75 percent".

Subsec. (d)(4). Pub. L. 111–5, §1121(c)(1), amended par. (4) generally. Prior to amendment, text read as follows: "The term 'qualified natural gas, propane, or oil furnace or hot water boiler' means a natural gas, propane, or oil furnace or hot water boiler which achieves an annual fuel utilization efficiency rate of not less than 95."

Subsec. (e)(1). Pub. L. 111–5, §1103(b)(2)(A), substituted "and (8)" for "(8), and (9)".

Subsec. (g)(2). Pub. L. 111–5, §1121(e), substituted "December 31, 2010" for "December 31, 2009".

2008—Subsec. (c)(1). Pub. L. 110–343, §302(e)(1), in introductory provisions, inserted ", or an asphalt roof with appropriate cooling granules," before "which meet the Energy Star program requirements".

Subsec. (c)(2)(D). Pub. L. 110–343, §302(e)(2), inserted "or asphalt roof" after "metal roof" and "or cooling granules" after "pigmented coatings".

Subsec. (d)(2)(C). Pub. L. 110–343, §302(d)(2), amended heading and text of subpar. (C) generally. Prior to amendment, subpar. (C) related to requirements for standards for central air conditioners, electric heat pumps, and geothermal heat pumps.

Subsec. (d)(3)(C), (D). Pub. L. 110–343, §302(d)(1), redesignated subpars. (D) and (E) as (C) and (D), respectively, and struck out former subpar. (C) which read as follows: "a geothermal heat pump which—

"(i) in the case of a closed loop product, has an energy efficiency ratio (EER) of at least 14.1 and a heating coefficient of performance (COP) of at least 3.3,

"(ii) in the case of an open loop product, has an energy efficiency ratio (EER) of at least 16.2 and a heating coefficient of performance (COP) of at least 3.6, and

"(iii) in the case of a direct expansion (DX) product, has an energy efficiency ratio (EER) of at least 15 and a heating coefficient of performance (COP) of at least 3.5,".

Subsec. (d)(3)(E). Pub. L. 110–343, §302(d)(1), redesignated subpar. (F) as (E). Former subpar. (E) redesignated (D).

Pub. L. 110–343, §302(c), inserted "or a thermal efficiency of at least 90 percent" after "0.80".

Subsec. (d)(3)(F). Pub. L. 110–343, §302(d)(1), redesignated subpar. (F) as (E).

Pub. L. 110–343, §302(b)(1), added subpar. (F).

Subsec. (d)(6). Pub. L. 110–343, §302(b)(2), added par. (6).

Subsec. (g). Pub. L. 110–343, §302(a), substituted "placed in service—" for "placed in service after December 31, 2007" and added pars. (1) and (2).

2007—Subsec. (c)(3). Pub. L. 110–172 substituted "part 3280" for "section 3280".

2005—Subsec. (b)(2). Pub. L. 109–135 substituted "subsection (c)(2)(B)" for "subsection (c)(3)(B)".

STATUTORY NOTES AND RELATED SUBSIDIARIES

EFFECTIVE DATE OF 2020 AMENDMENT

Pub. L. 116–260, div. EE, title I, §141(b), Dec. 27, 2020, 134 Stat. 3054, provided that: "The amendment made by this section [amending this section] shall apply to property placed in service after December 31, 2020."

Pub. L. 116–260, div. EE, title I, §148(c)(2), Dec. 27, 2020, 134 Stat. 3056, provided that: "The amendments made by subsection (b) [amending this section and section 25D of this title] shall apply to expenditures paid or incurred in taxable years beginning after December 31, 2020."

EFFECTIVE DATE OF 2019 AMENDMENT

Pub. L. 116–94, div. Q, title I, §123(c), Dec. 20, 2019, 133 Stat. 3231, provided that: "The amendments made by this section [amending this section] shall apply to property placed in service after December 31, 2017."

EFFECTIVE DATE OF 2018 AMENDMENT

Pub. L. 115–123, div. D, title I, §40401(b), Feb. 9, 2018, 132 Stat. 148, provided that: "The amendment made by this section [amending this section] shall apply to property placed in service after December 31, 2016."

EFFECTIVE DATE OF 2015 AMENDMENT

Pub. L. 114–113, div. Q, title I, §181(c), Dec. 18, 2015, 129 Stat. 3072, provided that:

"(1) Extension.—The amendment made by subsection (a) [amending this section] shall apply to property placed in service after December 31, 2014.

"(2) Modification.—The amendments made by subsection (b) [amending this section] shall apply to property placed in service after December 31, 2015."

EFFECTIVE DATE OF 2014 AMENDMENT

Pub. L. 113–295, div. A, title I, §151(b), Dec. 19, 2014, 128 Stat. 4021, provided that: "The amendment made by this section [amending this section] shall apply to property placed in service after December 31, 2013."

EFFECTIVE DATE OF 2013 AMENDMENT

Pub. L. 112–240, title IV, §401(b), Jan. 2, 2013, 126 Stat. 2337, provided that: "The amendment made by this section [amending this section] shall apply to property placed in service after December 31, 2011."

EFFECTIVE DATE OF 2010 AMENDMENT

Pub. L. 111–312, title VII, §710(c), Dec. 17, 2010, 124 Stat. 3315, provided that: "The amendments made by this section [amending this section] shall apply to property placed in service after December 31, 2010."

EFFECTIVE DATE OF 2009 AMENDMENT

Pub. L. 111–5, div. B, title I, §1103(c), Feb. 17, 2009, 123 Stat. 321, provided that:

"(1) In general.—Except as provided in paragraph (2), the amendment made by this section [amending this section and sections 25D and 48 to 48B of this title] shall apply to periods after December 31, 2008, under rules similar to the rules of section 48(m) of the Internal Revenue Code of 1986 (as in effect on the day before the date of the enactment of the Revenue Reconciliation Act of 1990 [Nov. 5, 1990]).

"(2) Conforming amendments.—The amendments made by subparagraphs (A) and (B) of subsection (b)(2) [amending this section and section 25D of this title] shall apply to taxable years beginning after December 31, 2008."

Pub. L. 111–5, div. B, title I, §1121(f), Feb. 17, 2009, 123 Stat. 324, provided that:

"(1) In general.—Except as provided in paragraph (2), the amendments made by this section [amending this section] shall apply to taxable years beginning after December 31, 2008.

"(2) Efficiency standards.—The amendments made by paragraphs (1), (2), and (3) of subsection (b) and subsections (c) and (d) shall apply to property placed in service after the date of the enactment of this Act [Feb. 17, 2009]."

EFFECTIVE DATE OF 2008 AMENDMENT

Pub. L. 110–343, div. B, title III, §302(f), Oct. 3, 2008, 122 Stat. 3845, provided that:

"(1) In general.—Except as provided in paragraph (2), the amendments made [by] this section [amending this section] shall apply to expenditures made after December 31, 2008.

"(2) Modification of qualified energy efficiency improvements.—The amendments made by subsection (e) [amending this section] shall apply to property placed in service after the date of the enactment of this Act [Oct. 3, 2008]."

EFFECTIVE DATE

Pub. L. 109–58, title XIII, §1333(c), Aug. 8, 2005, 119 Stat. 1030, provided that: "The amendments made by this section [enacting this section and amending section 1016 of this title] shall apply to property placed in service after December 31, 2005."

§25D. Residential energy efficient property

(a) Allowance of credit

In the case of an individual, there shall be allowed as a credit against the tax imposed by this chapter for the taxable year an amount equal to the sum of the applicable percentages of—

(1) the qualified solar electric property expenditures,

(2) the qualified solar water heating property expenditures,

(3) the qualified fuel cell property expenditures,

(4) the qualified small wind energy property expenditures,

(5) the qualified geothermal heat pump property expenditures, and

(6) the qualified biomass fuel property expenditures, and

made by the taxpayer during such year.

(b) Limitations

(1) Maximum credit for fuel cells

In the case of any qualified fuel cell property expenditure, the credit allowed under subsection (a) (determined without regard to subsection (c)) for any taxable year shall not exceed $500 with respect to each half kilowatt of capacity of the qualified fuel cell property (as defined in section 48(c)(1)) to which such expenditure relates.

(2) Certification of solar water heating property

No credit shall be allowed under this section for an item of property described in subsection (d)(1) unless such property is certified for performance by the non-profit Solar Rating Certification Corporation or a comparable entity endorsed by the government of the State in which such property is installed.

(c) Carryforward of unused credit

If the credit allowable under subsection (a) exceeds the limitation imposed by section 26(a) for such taxable year reduced by the sum of the credits allowable under this subpart (other than this section), such excess shall be carried to the succeeding taxable year and added to the credit allowable under subsection (a) for such succeeding taxable year.

(d) Definitions

For purposes of this section—

(1) Qualified solar water heating property expenditure

The term "qualified solar water heating property expenditure" means an expenditure for property to heat water for use in a dwelling unit located in the United States and used as a residence by the taxpayer if at least half of the energy used by such property for such purpose is derived from the sun.

(2) Qualified solar electric property expenditure

The term "qualified solar electric property expenditure" means an expenditure for property which uses solar energy to generate electricity for use in a dwelling unit located in the United States and used as a residence by the taxpayer.

(3) Qualified fuel cell property expenditure

The term "qualified fuel cell property expenditure" means an expenditure for qualified fuel cell property (as defined in section 48(c)(1)) installed on or in connection with a dwelling unit located in the United States and used as a principal residence (within the meaning of section 121) by the taxpayer.

(4) Qualified small wind energy property expenditure

The term "qualified small wind energy property expenditure" means an expenditure for property which uses a wind turbine to generate electricity for use in connection with a dwelling unit located in the United States and used as a residence by the taxpayer.

(5) Qualified geothermal heat pump property expenditure

(A) In general

The term "qualified geothermal heat pump property expenditure" means an expenditure for qualified geothermal heat pump property installed on or in connection with a dwelling unit located in the United States and used as a residence by the taxpayer.

(B) Qualified geothermal heat pump property

The term "qualified geothermal heat pump property" means any equipment which—

(i) uses the ground or ground water as a thermal energy source to heat the dwelling unit referred to in subparagraph (A) or as a thermal energy sink to cool such dwelling unit, and

(ii) meets the requirements of the Energy Star program which are in effect at the time that the expenditure for such equipment is made.

(6) Qualified biomass fuel property expenditure

(A) In general

The term "qualified biomass fuel property expenditure" means an expenditure for property—

(i) which uses the burning of biomass fuel to heat a dwelling unit located in the United States and used as a residence by the taxpayer, or to heat water for use in such a dwelling unit, and

(ii) which has a thermal efficiency rating of at least 75 percent (measured by the higher heating value of the fuel).

(B) Biomass fuel

For purposes of this section, the term "biomass fuel" means any plant-derived fuel available on a renewable or recurring basis.

(e) Special rules

For purposes of this section—

(1) Labor costs

Expenditures for labor costs properly allocable to the onsite preparation, assembly, or original installation of the property described in subsection (d) and for piping or wiring to interconnect such property to the dwelling unit shall be taken into account for purposes of this section.

(2) Solar panels

No expenditure relating to a solar panel or other property installed as a roof (or portion thereof) shall fail to be treated as property described in paragraph (1) or (2) of subsection (d) solely because it constitutes a structural component of the structure on which it is installed.

(3) Swimming pools, etc., used as storage medium

Expenditures which are properly allocable to a swimming pool, hot tub, or any other energy storage medium which has a function other than the function of such storage shall not be taken into account for purposes of this section.

(4) Fuel cell expenditure limitations in case of joint occupancy

In the case of any dwelling unit with respect to which qualified fuel cell property expenditures are made and which is jointly occupied and used during any calendar year as a residence by two or more individuals, the following rules shall apply:

(A) Maximum expenditures for fuel cells

The maximum amount of such expenditures which may be taken into account under subsection (a) by all such individuals with respect to such dwelling unit during such calendar year shall be $1,667 in the case of each half kilowatt of capacity of qualified fuel cell property (as defined in section 48(c)(1)) with respect to which such expenditures relate.

(B) Allocation of expenditures

The expenditures allocated to any individual for the taxable year in which such calendar year ends shall be an amount equal to the lesser of—

(i) the amount of expenditures made by such individual with respect to such dwelling during such calendar year, or

(ii) the maximum amount of such expenditures set forth in subparagraph (A) multiplied by a fraction—

(I) the numerator of which is the amount of such expenditures with respect to such dwelling made by such individual during such calendar year, and

(II) the denominator of which is the total expenditures made by all such individuals with respect to such dwelling during such calendar year.

(5) Tenant-stockholder in cooperative housing corporation

In the case of an individual who is a tenant-stockholder (as defined in section 216) in a cooperative housing corporation (as defined in such section), such individual shall be treated as having made his tenant-stockholder's proportionate share (as defined in section 216(b)(3)) of any expenditures of such corporation.

(6) Condominiums

(A) In general

In the case of an individual who is a member of a condominium management association with respect to a condominium which the individual owns, such individual shall be treated as having made the individual's proportionate share of any expenditures of such association.

(B) Condominium management association

For purposes of this paragraph, the term "condominium management association" means an organization which meets the requirements of paragraph (1) of section 528(c) (other than subparagraph (E) thereof) with respect to a condominium project substantially all of the units of which are used as residences.

(7) Allocation in certain cases

If less than 80 percent of the use of an item is for nonbusiness purposes, only that portion of the expenditures for such item which is properly allocable to use for nonbusiness purposes shall be taken into account.

(8) When expenditure made; amount of expenditure

(A) In general

Except as provided in subparagraph (B), an expenditure with respect to an item shall be treated as made when the original installation of the item is completed.

(B) Expenditures part of building construction

In the case of an expenditure in connection with the construction or reconstruction of a structure, such expenditure shall be treated as made when the original use of the constructed or reconstructed structure by the taxpayer begins.

(f) Basis adjustments

For purposes of this subtitle, if a credit is allowed under this section for any expenditure with respect to any property, the increase in the basis of such property which would (but for this subsection) result from such expenditure shall be reduced by the amount of the credit so allowed.

(g) Applicable percentage

For purposes of subsection (a), the applicable percentage shall be—

(1) in the case of property placed in service after December 31, 2016, and before January 1, 2020, 30 percent,

(2) in the case of property placed in service after December 31, 2019, and before January 1, 2023, 26 percent, and

(3) in the case of property placed in service after December 31, 2022, and before January 1, 2024, 22 percent.

(h) Termination

The credit allowed under this section shall not apply to property placed in service after December 31, 2023.

(Added Pub. L. 109–58, title XIII, §1335(a), Aug. 8, 2005, 119 Stat. 1033; amended Pub. L. 109–135, title IV, §402(i)(1), (2), (3)(E), Dec. 21, 2005, 119 Stat. 2612, 2614; Pub. L. 109–432, div. A, title II, §206, Dec. 20, 2006, 120 Stat. 2945; Pub. L. 110–343, div. B, title I, §106(a)–(c)(3)(A), (c)(4)–(e)(1), Oct. 3, 2008, 122 Stat. 3814–3816; Pub. L. 111–5, div. B, title I, §§1103(b)(2)(B), 1122(a), Feb. 17, 2009, 123 Stat. 320, 324; Pub. L. 112–240, title I, §104(c)(2)(F), Jan. 2, 2013, 126 Stat. 2322; Pub. L. 114–113, div. P, title III, §304(a), Dec. 18, 2015, 129 Stat. 3039; Pub. L. 115–123, div. D, title I, §40402(a), (b), Feb. 9, 2018, 132 Stat. 148; Pub. L. 116–260, div. EE, title I, §148(a)–(b)(2), Dec. 27, 2020, 134 Stat. 3055.)

EDITORIAL NOTES

AMENDMENTS

2020—Subsec. (a)(6). Pub. L. 116–260, §148(b)(1), added par. (6).

Subsec. (d)(6). Pub. L. 116–260, §148(b)(2), added par. (6).

Subsec. (g)(2). Pub. L. 116–260, §148(a)(2)(A), substituted "January 1, 2023" for "January 1, 2021".

Subsec. (g)(3). Pub. L. 116–260, §148(a)(2)(B), substituted "after December 31, 2022, and before January 1, 2024" for "after December 31, 2020, and before January 1, 2022".

Subsec. (h). Pub. L. 116–260, §148(a)(1), substituted "December 31, 2023" for "December 31, 2021".

2018—Subsec. (a). Pub. L. 115–123, §40402(b)(1), substituted "the sum of the applicable percentages of—", pars. (1) to (5), and concluding provisions for "the sum of—

"(1) the applicable percentage of the qualified solar electric property expenditures made by the taxpayer during such year,

"(2) the applicable percentage of the qualified solar water heating property expenditures made by the taxpayer during such year,

"(3) 30 percent of the qualified fuel cell property expenditures made by the taxpayer during such year,

"(4) 30 percent of the qualified small wind energy property expenditures made by the taxpayer during such year, and

"(5) 30 percent of the qualified geothermal heat pump property expenditures made by the taxpayer during such year."

Subsec. (g). Pub. L. 115–123, §40402(b)(2), struck out "paragraphs (1) and (2) of" before "subsection (a)," in introductory provisions.

Subsec. (h). Pub. L. 115–123, §40402(a), substituted "December 31, 2021." for "December 31, 2016 (December 31, 2021, in the case of any qualified solar electric property expenditures and qualified solar water heating property expenditures)."

2015—Subsec. (a)(1), (2). Pub. L. 114–113, §304(a)(1), substituted "the applicable percentage" for "30 percent".

Subsec. (g). Pub. L. 114–113, §304(a)(4), added subsec. (g). Former subsec. (g) redesignated (h).

Pub. L. 114–113, §304(a)(2), inserted "(December 31, 2021, in the case of any qualified solar electric property expenditures and qualified solar water heating property expenditures)" before period at end.

Subsec. (h). Pub. L. 114–113, §304(a)(3), redesignated subsec. (g) as (h).

2013—Subsec. (c). Pub. L. 112–240 amended subsec. (c) generally. Prior to amendment, subsec. (c) related to limitation based on amount of tax and carryforward of unused credit.

2009—Subsec. (b)(1). Pub. L. 111–5, §1122(a)(1), amended par. (1) generally. Prior to amendment, par. (1) related to maximum credit with respect to qualified solar water heating property expenditures, qualified fuel cell property, qualified small wind energy property expenditures, and qualified geothermal heat pump property expenditures.

Subsec. (e)(4). Pub. L. 111–5, §1122(a)(2)(A), added par. heading and introductory provisions and struck out former heading and introductory provisions. Former introductory provisions read as follows: "In the case of any dwelling unit which is jointly occupied and used during any calendar year as a residence by two or more individuals the following rules shall apply:".

Subsec. (e)(4)(A). Pub. L. 111–5, §1122(a)(2)(A), added subpar. (A) and struck out former subpar. (A) which related to maximum amount of expenditures allowed for credit in jointly occupied dwelling units with respect to qualified solar water heating property expenditures, qualified fuel cell property, qualified small wind energy property expenditures, and qualified geothermal heat pump property expenditures.

Subsec. (e)(4)(C). Pub. L. 111–5, §1122(a)(2)(B), struck out subpar. (C) which read as follows: "Subparagraphs (A) and (B) shall be applied separately with respect to expenditures described in paragraphs (1), (2), and (3) of subsection (d)."

Subsec. (e)(9). Pub. L. 111–5, §1103(b)(2)(B), struck out par. (9). Text read as follows: "For purposes of determining the amount of expenditures made by any individual with respect to any dwelling unit, there shall not be taken into account expenditures which are made from subsidized energy financing (as defined in section 48(a)(4)(C))."

2008—Subsec. (a)(4). Pub. L. 110–343, §106(c)(1), added par. (4).

Subsec. (a)(5). Pub. L. 110–343, §106(d)(1), added par. (5).

Subsec. (b)(1). Pub. L. 110–343, §106(b)(1), amended par. (1) as amended by Pub. L. 110–343, §106(c)(2) and (d)(2), by redesignating subpars. (B) to (E) as (A) to (D), respectively, and striking out former subpar. (A) which read as follows: "$2,000 with respect to any qualified solar electric property expenditures,".

Subsec. (b)(1)(D). Pub. L. 110–343, §106(c)(2), added subpar. (D).

Subsec. (b)(1)(E). Pub. L. 110–343, §106(d)(2), added subpar. (E).

Subsec. (c). Pub. L. 110–343, §106(e)(1), amended heading and text of subsec. (c) generally. Prior to amendment, subsec. (c) related to carryforward of unused credit.

Subsec. (d)(4). Pub. L. 110–343, §106(c)(3)(A), added par. (4).

Subsec. (d)(5). Pub. L. 110–343, §106(d)(3), added par. (5).

Subsec. (e)(4)(A). Pub. L. 110–343, §106(b)(2), amended subpar. (A) as amended by Pub. L. 110–343, §106(c)(4) and (d)(4), by redesignating cls. (ii) to (v) as (i) to (iv), respectively, and striking out former cl. (i) which read as follows: "$6,667 in the case of any qualified solar electric property expenditures,".

Subsec. (e)(4)(A)(iv). Pub. L. 110–343, §106(c)(4), added cl. (iv).

Subsec. (e)(4)(A)(v). Pub. L. 110–343, §106(d)(4), added cl. (v).

Subsec. (g). Pub. L. 110–343, §106(a), substituted "December 31, 2016" for "December 31, 2008".

2006—Subsecs. (a)(1), (b)(1)(A). Pub. L. 109–432, §206(b)(1), substituted "solar electric property expenditures" for "photovoltaic property expenditures".

Subsec. (d)(2). Pub. L. 109–432, §206(b)(2), substituted "solar electric property expenditure" for "photovoltaic property expenditure" in heading and text.

Subsec. (e)(4)(A)(i). Pub. L. 109–432, §206(b)(1), substituted "solar electric property expenditures" for "photovoltaic property expenditures".

Subsec. (g). Pub. L. 109–432, §206(a), substituted "2008" for "2007".

2005—Subsec. (b)(1). Pub. L. 109–135, §402(i)(1), inserted "(determined without regard to subsection (c))" after "subsection (a)" in introductory provisions.

Subsec. (c). Pub. L. 109–135, §402(i)(3)(E), reenacted heading without change and amended text generally. Prior to amendment, text read as follows: "If the credit allowable under subsection (a) exceeds the limitation imposed by section 26(a) for such taxable year reduced by the sum of the credits allowable under this subpart (other than this section), such excess shall be carried to the succeeding taxable year and added to the credit allowable under subsection (a) for such succeeding taxable year."

Subsec. (e)(4)(A), (B). Pub. L. 109–135, §402(i)(2), amended subpars. (A) and (B) generally. Prior to amendment, subpars. (A) and (B) read as follows:

"(A) The amount of the credit allowable, under subsection (a) by reason of expenditures (as the case may be) made during such calendar year by any of such individuals with respect to such dwelling unit shall be determined by treating all of such individuals as 1 taxpayer whose taxable year is such calendar year.

"(B) There shall be allowable, with respect to such expenditures to each of such individuals, a credit under subsection (a) for the taxable year in which such calendar year ends in an amount which bears the same ratio to the amount determined under subparagraph (A) as the amount of such expenditures made by such individual during such calendar year bears to the aggregate of such expenditures made by all of such individuals during such calendar year."

STATUTORY NOTES AND RELATED SUBSIDIARIES
EFFECTIVE DATE OF 2020 AMENDMENT

Pub. L. 116–260, div. EE, title I, §148(c)(1), Dec. 27, 2020, 134 Stat. 3056, provided that: "The amendments made by subsection (a) [amending this section] shall apply to property placed in service after December 31, 2020."

Amendment by section 148(b) of Pub. L. 116–260 applicable to expenditures paid or incurred in taxable years beginning after Dec. 31, 2020, see section 148(c)(2) of div. EE of Pub. L. 116–260, set out as a note under section 25C of this title.

EFFECTIVE DATE OF 2018 AMENDMENT

Pub. L. 115–123, div. D, title I, §40402(c), Feb. 9, 2018, 132 Stat. 148, provided that: "The amendment made by this section [amending this section] shall apply to property placed in service after December 31, 2016."

EFFECTIVE DATE OF 2015 AMENDMENT

Pub. L. 114–113, div. P, title III, §304(b), Dec. 18, 2015, 129 Stat. 3040, provided that: "The amendments made by this section [amending this section] shall take effect on January 1, 2017."

EFFECTIVE DATE OF 2013 AMENDMENT

Amendment by Pub. L. 112–240 applicable to taxable years beginning after Dec. 31, 2011, see section 104(d) of Pub. L. 112–240, set out as a note under section 23 of this title.

EFFECTIVE DATE OF 2009 AMENDMENT

Amendment by section 1103(b)(2)(B) of Pub. L. 111–5 applicable to taxable years beginning after Dec. 31, 2008, see section 1103(c)(2) of Pub. L. 111–5, set out as a note under section 25C of this title.

Pub. L. 111–5, div. B, title I, §1122(b), Feb. 17, 2009, 123 Stat. 324, provided that: "The amendments made by this section [amending this section] shall apply to taxable years beginning after December 31, 2008."

EFFECTIVE DATE OF 2008 AMENDMENT

Amendment by Pub. L. 110–343 applicable to taxable years beginning after Dec. 31, 2007, except that amendment by section 106(b) of Pub. L. 110–343 applicable to taxable years beginning after Dec. 31, 2008, see section 106(f)(1), (2) of Pub. L. 110–343, set out as an Effective and Termination Dates of 2008 Amendment note under section 23 of this title.

EFFECTIVE AND TERMINATION DATES OF 2005 AMENDMENT

Amendment by section 402(i)(3)(E) of Pub. L. 109–135 subject to title IX of the Economic Growth and Tax Relief Reconciliation Act of 2001, Pub. L. 107–16, §901, in the same manner as the provisions of such Act to which such amendment relates, see section 402(i)(3)(H) of Pub. L. 109–135, set out as a note under section 23 of this title. Title IX of Pub. L. 107–16 was repealed by Pub. L. 112–240, title I, §101(a)(1), Jan. 2, 2013, 126 Stat. 2315.

Amendments by Pub. L. 109–135 effective as if included in the provisions of the Energy Policy Act of 2005, Pub. L. 109–58, to which they relate, except that amendment by section 402(i)(3)(E) of Pub. L. 109–135 is applicable to taxable years beginning after Dec. 31, 2005, see section 402(m) of Pub. L. 109–135, set out as a note under section 23 of this title.

EFFECTIVE DATE

Section applicable to property placed in service after Dec. 31, 2005, in taxable years ending after such date, see section 1335(c) of Pub. L. 109–58, set out as an Effective and Termination Dates of 2005 Amendments note under section 23 of this title.

§26. Limitation based on tax liability; definition of tax liability

(a) Limitation based on amount of tax

The aggregate amount of credits allowed by this subpart for the taxable year shall not exceed the sum of—
(1) the taxpayer's regular tax liability for the taxable year reduced by the foreign tax credit allowable under section 27, and
(2) the tax imposed by section 55(a) for the taxable year.

(b) Regular tax liability

For purposes of this part—

(1) In general

The term "regular tax liability" means the tax imposed by this chapter for the taxable year.

(2) Exception for certain taxes

For purposes of paragraph (1), any tax imposed by any of the following provisions shall not be treated as tax imposed by this chapter:
(A) section 55 (relating to minimum tax),
(B) section 59A (relating to base erosion and anti-abuse tax),
(C) subsection (m)(5)(B), (q), (t), or (v) of section 72 (relating to additional taxes on certain distributions),
(D) section 143(m) (relating to recapture of proration of Federal subsidy from use of mortgage bonds and mortgage credit certificates),
(E) section 530(d)(4) (relating to additional tax on certain distributions from Coverdell education savings accounts),
(F) section 531 (relating to accumulated earnings tax),
(G) section 541 (relating to personal holding company tax),
(H) section 1351(d)(1) (relating to recoveries of foreign expropriation losses),
(I) section 1374 (relating to tax on certain built-in gains of S corporations),
(J) section 1375 (relating to tax imposed when passive investment income of corporation having subchapter C earnings and profits exceeds 25 percent of gross receipts),
(K) subparagraph (A) of section 7518(g)(6) (relating to nonqualified withdrawals from capital construction funds taxed at highest marginal rate),
(L) sections 871(a) and 881 (relating to certain income of nonresident aliens and foreign corporations),
(M) section 860E(e) (relating to taxes with respect to certain residual interests),
(N) section 884 (relating to branch profits tax),
(O) sections 453(l)(3) and 453A(c) (relating to interest on certain deferred tax liabilities),
[(P) Repealed. Pub. L. 115–141, div. U, title IV, §401(b)(2), Mar. 23, 2018, 132 Stat. 1201.]
(Q) section 220(f)(4) (relating to additional tax on Archer MSA distributions not used for qualified medical expenses),
(R) section 138(c)(2) (relating to penalty for distributions from Medicare Advantage MSA not used for qualified medical expenses if minimum balance not maintained),
(S) sections 106(e)(3)(A)(ii), 223(b)(8)(B)(i)(II), and 408(d)(9)(D)(i)(II) (relating to certain failures to maintain high deductible health plan coverage),
(T) section 170(o)(3)(B) (relating to recapture of certain deductions for fractional gifts),
(U) section 223(f)(4) (relating to additional tax on health savings account distributions not used for qualified medical expenses),
(V) subsections (a)(1)(B)(i) and (b)(4)(A) of section 409A (relating to interest and additional tax with respect to certain deferred compensation),
(W) section 36(f) (relating to recapture of homebuyer credit),
(X) section 457A(c)(1)(B) (relating to determinability of amounts of compensation),
(Y) section 529A(c)(3)(A) (relating to additional tax on ABLE account distributions not used for qualified disability expenses), and
(Z) section 24(j)(2) (relating to excess advance payments).

(c) Tentative minimum tax

For purposes of this part, the term "tentative minimum tax" means the amount determined under section 55(b)(1).

(Added §25, renumbered §26, Pub. L. 98–369, div. A, title IV, §472, title VI, §612(a), July 18, 1984, 98 Stat. 827, 905; amended Pub. L. 99–499, title V, §516(b)(1)(A), Oct. 17, 1986, 100 Stat. 1770; Pub. L. 99–514, title II, §261(c), title VI, §632(c)(1), title VII, §701(c)(1), Oct. 22, 1986, 100 Stat. 2214, 2277, 2340; Pub. L. 100–647, title I, §§1006(t)(16)(C), 1007(g)(1), 1011A(c)(10), 1012(q)(8), title IV, §4005(g)(4), title V, §5012(b)(2), Nov. 10, 1988, 102 Stat. 3425, 3434, 3476, 3524, 3650, 3662; Pub. L. 101–239, title VII, §§7811(c)(1), (2), 7821(a)(4)(A), Dec. 19, 1989, 103 Stat. 2406, 2407, 2424; Pub. L. 104–188, title I, §1621(b)(1), Aug. 20, 1996, 110 Stat. 1866; Pub. L. 105–34, title II, §213(e)(1), title XVI, §1602(a)(1), Aug. 5, 1997, 111 Stat. 817, 1093; Pub. L. 105–277, div. J, title II, §2001(a), Oct. 21, 1998, 112 Stat. 2681–901; Pub. L. 106–170, title V, §501(a), Dec. 17, 1999, 113 Stat. 1918; Pub. L. 106–554, §1(a)(7) [title II, §202(a)(1)], Dec. 21, 2000, 114 Stat. 2763, 2763A–628; Pub. L. 107–16, title II, §§201(b)(2)(D), 202(f)(2)(C), title VI, §618(b)(2)(C), June 7, 2001, 115 Stat. 46, 49, 108; Pub. L. 107–22, §1(b)(2)(A), July 26, 2001, 115 Stat. 197; Pub. L. 107–147, title IV, §§415(a), 417(23)(B), title VI, §601(a), Mar. 9, 2002, 116 Stat. 54, 57, 59; Pub. L. 108–311, title III, §312(a), title IV, §§401(a)(1), 408(a)(5)(A), Oct. 4, 2004, 118 Stat. 1181, 1183, 1191; Pub. L. 109–135, title IV, §§403(hh)(1), 412(c), Dec. 21, 2005, 119 Stat. 2631, 2636; Pub. L. 109–222, title III, §302(a), May 17, 2006, 120 Stat. 353; Pub. L. 110–166, §3(a), Dec. 26, 2007, 121 Stat. 2461; Pub. L. 110–172, §11(a)(3), Dec. 29, 2007, 121 Stat. 2484; Pub. L. 110–289, div. C, title I, §3011(b)(1), July 30, 2008, 122 Stat. 2891; Pub. L. 110–343, div. B, title I, §106(e)(2)(D), title II, §205(d)(1)(D), div. C, title I, §101(a), title VIII, §801(b), Oct. 3, 2008, 122 Stat. 3817, 3839, 3863, 3931; Pub. L. 111–5, div. B, title I, §§1004(b)(3), 1011(a), 1142(b)(1)(D), 1144(b)(1)(D), Feb. 17, 2009, 123 Stat. 314, 319, 330, 332; Pub. L. 111–148, title X, §10909(b)(2)(E), (c), Mar. 23, 2010, 124 Stat. 1023; Pub. L. 111–312, title I, §101(b)(1), title II, §202(a), Dec. 17, 2010, 124 Stat. 3298, 3299; Pub. L. 112–240, title I, §104(c)(1), Jan. 2, 2013, 126 Stat. 2321; Pub. L. 113–295, div. A, title II, §221(a)(12)(B), div. B, title I, §102(e)(1), Dec. 19, 2014, 128 Stat. 4038, 4062; Pub. L. 115–97, title I, §14401(c), Dec. 22, 2017, 131 Stat. 2233; Pub. L. 115–141, div. U, title IV, §401(b)(2), (d)(1)(D)(ii), Mar. 23, 2018, 132 Stat. 1201, 1206; Pub. L. 117–2, title IX, §9611(b)(4)(A), Mar. 11, 2021, 135 Stat. 150.)

EDITORIAL NOTES
AMENDMENTS

2021—Subsec. (b)(2)(Z). Pub. L. 117–2 added subpar. (Z).
2018—Subsec. (a)(1). Pub. L. 115–141, §401(d)(1)(D)(ii), substituted "section 27" for "section 27(a)".
Subsec. (b)(2)(P). Pub. L. 115–141, §401(b)(2), struck out subpar. (P) which read as follows: "section 860K (relating to treatment of transfers of high-yield interests to disqualified holders),".
2017—Subsec. (b)(2)(B). Pub. L. 115–97 added subpar. (B).
2014—Subsec. (b)(2)(B). Pub. L. 113–295, §221(a)(12)(B), struck out subpar. (B) which read as follows: "section 59A (relating to environmental tax),".
Subsec. (b)(2)(Y). Pub. L. 113–295, §102(e)(1), added subpar. (Y).

2013—Subsec. (a). Pub. L. 112–240 amended subsec. (a) generally. Prior to amendment, subsec. (a) related to limitation based on amount of tax with a special rule for taxable years 2000 through 2011.

2010—Subsec. (a)(1). Pub. L. 111–148, §10909(b)(2)(E), (c), as amended by Pub. L. 111–312, §101(b)(1), temporarily struck out "23," before "24," in introductory provisions. See Effective and Termination Dates of 2010 Amendment note below.

Subsec. (a)(2). Pub. L. 111–312, §202(a), substituted "2011" for "2009" in heading and "2009, 2010, or 2011" for "or 2009" in introductory provisions.

2009—Subsec. (a)(1). Pub. L. 111–5, §1144(b)(1)(D), inserted "30B," after "30," in introductory provisions.

Pub. L. 111–5, §1142(b)(1)(D), inserted "30," after "25D," in introductory provisions.

Pub. L. 111–5, §1004(b)(3), inserted "25A(i)," after "24," in introductory provisions.

Subsec. (a)(2). Pub. L. 111–5, §1011(a), substituted "2009" for "2008" in heading and "2008, or 2009" for "or 2008" in introductory provisions.

2008—Subsec. (a)(1). Pub. L. 110–343, §205(d)(1)(D), substituted "25D, and 30D" for "and 25D" in introductory provisions.

Pub. L. 110–343, §106(e)(2)(D), substituted "25B, and 25D" for "and 25B" in introductory provisions.

Subsec. (a)(2). Pub. L. 110–343, §101(a), substituted "2008" for "2007" in heading and "2007, or 2008" for "or 2007" in introductory provisions.

Subsec. (b)(2)(W). Pub. L. 110–289 added subpar. (W).

Subsec. (b)(2)(X). Pub. L. 110–343, §801(b), added subpar. (X).

2007—Subsec. (a)(2). Pub. L. 110–166 substituted "2007" for "2006" in heading and "2006, or 2007" for "or 2006" in introductory provisions.

Subsec. (b)(2)(S) to (V). Pub. L. 110–172 added subpars. (S) and (T) and redesignated former subpars. (S) and (T) as (U) and (V), respectively.

2006—Subsec. (a)(2). Pub. L. 109–222 substituted "2006" for "2005" in heading and "2005, or 2006" for "or 2005" in introductory provisions.

2005—Subsec. (b)(2)(E). Pub. L. 109–135, §412(c), substituted "section 530(d)(4)" for "section 530(d)(3)".

Subsec. (b)(2)(T). Pub. L. 109–135, §403(hh)(1), added subpar. (T).

2004—Subsec. (a)(2). Pub. L. 108–311, §312(a), substituted "rule for taxable years 2000 through 2005" for "rule for 2000, 2001, 2002, and 2003" in heading and "2003, 2004, or 2005" for "or 2003" in text.

Subsec. (b)(2)(R). Pub. L. 108–311, §408(a)(5)(A), substituted "Medicare Advantage MSA" for "Medicare+Choice MSA".

Subsec. (b)(2)(S). Pub. L. 108–311, §401(a)(1), added subpar. (S).

2002—Subsec. (a)(1). Pub. L. 107–147, §417(23)(B), amended directory language of Pub. L. 107–16, §618(b)(2)(C). See 2001 Amendment note below.

Subsec. (a)(2). Pub. L. 107–147, §601(a), substituted "rule for 2000, 2001, 2002, and 2003" for "rule for 2000 and 2001" in heading and "during 2000, 2001, 2002, or 2003," for "during 2000 or 2001," in introductory provisions.

Subsec. (b)(2)(P), (Q). Pub. L. 107–147, §415(a), which directed striking "and" at end of subpar. (P) and substituting ", and" for the period at the end of subpar. (Q), was executed to subpars. (P) and (Q) as redesignated by Pub. L. 105–34, §213(e)(1), to reflect the probable intent of Congress. See 1997 Amendment notes below.

Subsec. (b)(2)(R). Pub. L. 107–147, §415(a), added subpar. (R).

2001—Subsec. (a)(1). Pub. L. 107–16, §618(b)(2)(C), as amended by Pub. L. 107–147, §417(23)(B), substituted ", 24, and 25B" for "and 24" in introductory provisions.

Pub. L. 107–16, §202(f)(2)(C), substituted "sections 23 and 24" for "section 24" in introductory provisions.

Pub. L. 107–16, §201(b)(2)(D), inserted "(other than section 24)" after "this subpart" in introductory provisions.

Subsec. (b)(2)(E). Pub. L. 107–22 substituted "Coverdell education savings" for "education individual retirement".

2000—Subsec. (b)(2)(Q). Pub. L. 106–554 substituted "Archer MSA" for "medical savings account".

1999—Subsec. (a). Pub. L. 106–170 reenacted subsec. heading without change and amended text generally. Prior to amendment, text read as follows: "The aggregate amount of credits allowed by this subpart for the taxable year shall not exceed the excess (if any) of—

"(1) the taxpayer's regular tax liability for the taxable year, over

"(2) the tentative minimum tax for the taxable year (determined without regard to the alternative minimum tax foreign tax credit).

For purposes of paragraph (2), the taxpayer's tentative minimum tax for any taxable year beginning during 1998 shall be treated as being zero."

1998—Subsec. (a). Pub. L. 105–277 inserted concluding provisions.

1997—Subsec. (b)(2)(E) to (O). Pub. L. 105–34, §213(e)(1), added subpar. (E) and redesignated former subpars. (E) to (N) as (F) to (O), respectively. Former subpar. (O) redesignated (P).

Subsec. (b)(2)(P). Pub. L. 105–34, §213(e)(1), redesignated subpar. (P) as (Q).

Pub. L. 105–34, §1602(a)(1), added subpar. (P).

Subsec. (b)(2)(Q). Pub. L. 105–34, §213(e)(1), redesignated subpar. (P) as (Q).

1996—Subsec. (b)(2)(O). Pub. L. 104–188 added subpar. (O).

1989—Subsec. (b)(2)(C), (D). Pub. L. 101–239, §7811(c)(1), amended subpars. (C) and (D) generally. Prior to amendment, subpars. (C) and (D) read as follows:

"(C) subsection (m)(5)(B) (q), or (v) of section 72 (relating to additional tax on certain distributions),

"(D) section 72(t) (relating to 10-percent additional tax on early distributions from qualified retirement plans),".

Subsec. (b)(2)(K). Pub. L. 101–239, §7811(c)(2), added subpar. (K) and struck out former subpar. (K) which was identical.

Subsec. (b)(2)(L), (M). Pub. L. 101–239, §7811(c)(2), added subpars. (L) and (M) and struck out former subpars. (L) and (M) which read as follows:

"(L) section 860E(e) (relating to taxes with respect to certain residual interests), and

"(L) section 884 (relating to branch profits tax), and

"(M) section 143(m) (relating to recapture of portion of federal subsidy from use of mortgage bonds and mortgage credit certificates)."

Subsec. (b)(2)(N). Pub. L. 101–239, §7821(a)(4)(A), which directed amendment of subsec. (b)(2) of this section "as amended by section 11811" by adding subpar. (N), was executed as if it directed amendment of subsec. (b)(2) of this section "as amended by section 7811", to reflect the probable intent of Congress and the renumbering of section 11811 of H.R. 3299 as section 7811 prior to the enactment of H.R. 3299 into law as Pub. L. 101–239.

1988—Subsec. (b)(2)(C). Pub. L. 100–647, §1011A(c)(10)(A), struck out ", (o)(2)," after "subsection (m)(5)(B)".

Pub. L. 100–647, §5012(b)(2), substituted "(q), or (v)" for "or (q)".

Subsec. (b)(2)(D). Pub. L. 100–647, §1011A(c)(10)(B), substituted "72(t) (relating to 10-percent additional tax on early distributions from qualified retirement plans)" for "408(f) (relating to additional tax on income from certain retirement accounts)".

Subsec. (b)(2)(K). Pub. L. 100–647, §1007(g)(1), substituted "corporations)." for "corporations,".

Subsec. (b)(2)(L). Pub. L. 100–647, §1012(q)(8), added subpar. (L) relating to branch profits tax.

Pub. L. 100–647, §1006(t)(16)(C), added subpar. (L) relating to taxes with respect to certain residual interests.

Subsec. (b)(2)(M). Pub. L. 100–647, §4005(g)(4), added subpar. (M).

1986—Subsec. (a). Pub. L. 99–514, §701(c)(1)(A), amended subsec. (a) generally. Prior to amendment, subsec. (a) read as follows: "The aggregate amount of credits allowed by this subpart for the taxable year shall not exceed the taxpayer's tax liability for such taxable year."

Subsec. (b). Pub. L. 99–514, §701(c)(1)(B)(i), (v), substituted "Regular tax liability" for "Tax liability" in heading and "this part" for "this section" in introductory provisions.

Subsec. (b)(1). Pub. L. 99–514, §701(c)(1)(B)(ii), substituted "regular tax liability" for "tax liability".

Subsec. (b)(2). Pub. L. 99–499 added subpar. (B) and redesignated former subpars. (B) to (J) as (C) to (K), respectively.

Pub. L. 99–514, §701(c)(1)(B)(iii), substituted "section 55 (relating to minimum tax)" for "section 56 (relating to corporate minimum tax)" in subpar. (A).

Pub. L. 99–514, §632(c)(1), substituted "certain built-in gains" for "certain capital gains" in subpar. (G).

Pub. L. 99–514, §261(c), added subpar. (I).

Pub. L. 99–514, §701(c)(1)(B)(iv), added subpar. (J).

Subsec. (c). Pub. L. 99–514, §701(c)(1)(C), amended subsec. (c) generally, substituting provisions relating to tentative minimum tax for provisions referring to section 55(c) of this title for similar rule for alternative minimum tax for taxpayers other than corporations.

STATUTORY NOTES AND RELATED SUBSIDIARIES

EFFECTIVE DATE OF 2021 AMENDMENT

Amendment by Pub. L. 117–2 applicable to taxable years beginning after Dec. 31, 2020, see section 9611(c)(1) of Pub. L. 117–2, set out as a note under section 24 of this title.

EFFECTIVE DATE OF 2017 AMENDMENT

Pub. L. 115–97, title I, §14401(e), Dec. 22, 2017, 131 Stat. 2234, provided that: "The amendments made by this section [enacting section 59A of this title and amending this section and sections 882, 6038A, 6425, and 6655 of this title] shall apply to base erosion payments (as defined in section 59A(d) of the Internal Revenue Code of 1986 [26 U.S.C. 59A(d)], as added by this section) paid or accrued in taxable years beginning after December 31, 2017."

EFFECTIVE DATE OF 2014 AMENDMENT

Amendment by section 221(a)(12)(B) of Pub. L. 113–295 effective Dec. 19, 2014, subject to a savings provision, see section 221(b) of div. A of Pub. L. 113–295, set out as a note under section 1 of this title.

Amendment by section 102(e)(1) of Pub. L. 113–295 applicable to taxable years beginning after Dec. 31, 2014, see section 102(f)(1) of div. B of Pub. L. 113–295, set out as a note under section 552a of Title 5, Government Organization and Employees.

EFFECTIVE DATE OF 2013 AMENDMENT

Amendment by Pub. L. 112–240 applicable to taxable years beginning after Dec. 31, 2011, see section 104(d) of Pub. L. 112–240, set out as a note under section 23 of this title.

EFFECTIVE AND TERMINATION DATES OF 2010 AMENDMENT

Pub. L. 111–312, title II, §202(b), Dec. 17, 2010, 124 Stat. 3299, provided that: "The amendments made by this section [amending this section] shall apply to taxable years beginning after December 31, 2009."

Amendment by Pub. L. 111–148 terminated applicable to taxable years beginning after Dec. 31, 2011, and section is amended to read as if such amendment had never been enacted, see section 10909(c) of Pub. L. 111–148, set out as a note under section 1 of this title.

Amendment by Pub. L. 111–148 applicable to taxable years beginning after Dec. 31, 2009, see section 10909(d) of Pub. L. 111–148, set out as a note under section 1 of this title.

EFFECTIVE DATE OF 2009 AMENDMENT

Amendment by section 1004(b)(3) of Pub. L. 111–5 applicable to taxable years beginning after Dec. 31, 2008, see section 1004(d) of Pub. L. 111–5, set out as an Effective and Termination Dates of 2009 Amendment note under section 24 of this title.

Pub. L. 111–5, div. B, title I, §1011(b), Feb. 17, 2009, 123 Stat. 319, provided that: "The amendments made by this section [amending this section] shall apply to taxable years beginning after December 31, 2008."

Amendment by section 1142(b)(1)(D) of Pub. L. 111–5 applicable to vehicles acquired after Feb. 17, 2009, see section 1142(c) of Pub. L. 111–5, set out as an Effective and Termination Dates of 2009 Amendment note under section 24 of this title.

Amendment by section 1144(b)(1)(D) of Pub. L. 111–5 applicable to taxable years beginning after Dec. 31, 2008, see section 1144(c) of Pub. L. 111–5, set out as an Effective and Termination Dates of 2009 Amendment note under section 24 of this title.

EFFECTIVE DATE OF 2008 AMENDMENT

Amendment by section 106(e)(2)(D) of Pub. L. 110–343 applicable to taxable years beginning after Dec. 31, 2007, see section 106(f)(1) of div. B of Pub. L. 110–343, set out as an Effective and Termination Dates of 2008 Amendment note under section 23 of this title.

Amendment by section 205(d)(1)(D) of Pub. L. 110–343 applicable to taxable years beginning after Dec. 31, 2008, see section 205(e) of div. B of Pub. L. 110–343, set out as an Effective and Termination Dates of 2008 Amendment note under section 24 of this title.

Pub. L. 110–343, div. C, title I, §101(b), Oct. 3, 2008, 122 Stat. 3863, provided that: "The amendments made by this section [amending this section] shall apply to taxable years beginning after December 31, 2007."

Amendment by section 801(b) of Pub. L. 110–343 applicable to amounts deferred which are attributable to services performed after Dec. 31, 2008, with certain exceptions, see section 801(d) of div. C of Pub. L. 110–343, set out as an Effective Date note under section 457A of this title.

Pub. L. 110–289, div. C, title I, §3011(c), July 30, 2008, 122 Stat. 2891, provided that: "The amendments made by this section [enacting section 36 of this title, amending this section and section 6211 of this title and section 1324 of Title 31, Money and Finance, and renumbering former section 36 of this title as section 37 of this title] shall apply to residences purchased on or after April 9, 2008, in taxable years ending on or after such date."

EFFECTIVE DATE OF 2007 AMENDMENT

Pub. L. 110–166, §3(b), Dec. 26, 2007, 121 Stat. 2461, provided that: "The amendments made by this section [amending this section] shall apply to taxable years beginning after December 31, 2006."

EFFECTIVE DATE OF 2006 AMENDMENT

Pub. L. 109–222, title III, §302(b), May 17, 2006, 120 Stat. 353, provided that: "The amendments made by this section [amending this section] shall apply to taxable years beginning after December 31, 2005."

EFFECTIVE DATE OF 2005 AMENDMENT

Pub. L. 109–135, title IV, §403(nn), Dec. 21, 2005, 119 Stat. 2632, provided that: "The amendments made by this section [see Tables for classification] shall take effect as if included in the provisions of the American Jobs Creation Act of 2004 [Pub. L. 108–357] to which they relate."

EFFECTIVE DATE OF 2004 AMENDMENT

Pub. L. 108–311, title III, §312(c), Oct. 4, 2004, 118 Stat. 1181, provided that: "The amendments made by this section [amending this section and section 904 of this title] shall apply to taxable years beginning after December 31, 2003."

Pub. L. 108–311, title IV, §401(b), Oct. 4, 2004, 118 Stat. 1183, provided that: "The amendments made by subsection (a) [amending this section and section 35 of this title] shall take effect as if included in section 1201 of the Medicare Prescription Drug, Improvement, and Modernization Act of 2003 [Pub. L. 108–173]."

EFFECTIVE DATE OF 2002 AMENDMENT

Pub. L. 107–147, title IV, §415(b), Mar. 9, 2002, 116 Stat. 54, provided that: "The amendment made by this section [amending this section] shall take effect as if included in section 4006 of the Balanced Budget Act of 1997 [Pub. L. 105–33]."

Pub. L. 107–147, title VI, §601(c), Mar. 9, 2002, 116 Stat. 59, provided that: "The amendments made by this section [amending this section and section 904 of this title] shall apply to taxable years beginning after December 31, 2001."

EFFECTIVE DATE OF 2001 AMENDMENT

Amendment by Pub. L. 107–16 inapplicable to taxable years beginning during 2004 or 2005, see section 312(b)(2) of Pub. L. 108–311, set out as a note under section 23 of this title.

Amendment by Pub. L. 107–16 inapplicable to taxable years beginning during 2002 and 2003, see section 601(b)(2) of Pub. L. 107–147, set out as a note under section 23 of this title.

Pub. L. 107–22, §1(c), July 26, 2001, 115 Stat. 197, provided that: "The amendments made by this section [amending this section and sections 72, 135, 529, 530, 4973, 4975, and 6693 of this title] shall take effect on the date of the enactment of this Act [July 26, 2001]."

Amendment by section 201(b)(2)(D) of Pub. L. 107–16 applicable to taxable years beginning after Dec. 31, 2001, see section 201(e)(2) of Pub. L. 107–16, set out as a note under section 24 of this title.

Amendment by section 202(f)(2)(C) of Pub. L. 107–16 applicable to taxable years beginning after Dec. 31, 2001, see section 202(g)(1) of Pub. L. 107–16, set out as a note under section 23 of this title.

Amendment by section 618(b)(2)(C) of Pub. L. 107–16 applicable to taxable years beginning after Dec. 31, 2001, see section 618(d) of Pub. L. 107–16, set out as a note under section 24 of this title.

EFFECTIVE DATE OF 1999 AMENDMENT

Amendment by Pub. L. 106–170 applicable to taxable years beginning after Dec. 31, 1998, see section 501(c) of Pub. L. 106–170, set out as a note under section 24 of this title.

EFFECTIVE DATE OF 1998 AMENDMENT

Amendment by Pub. L. 105–277 applicable to taxable years beginning after Dec. 31, 1997, see section 2001(c) of Pub. L. 105–277, set out as a note under section 24 of this title.

EFFECTIVE DATE OF 1997 AMENDMENT

Pub. L. 105–34, title II, §213(f), Aug. 5, 1997, 111 Stat. 817, provided that: "The amendments made by this section [enacting section 530 of this title and amending this section and sections 135, 4973, 4975, and 6693 of this title] shall apply to taxable years beginning after December 31, 1997."

Pub. L. 105–34, title XVI, §1602(i), Aug. 5, 1997, 111 Stat. 1096, provided that: "The amendments made by this section [amending this section and sections 162, 220, 264, 877, 2107, 2501, 4975, 6050Q, 6652, 6693, 6724, and 7702B of this title, renumbering section 6039F of this title as section 6039G of this title, and amending provisions set out as a note under section 264 of this title] shall take effect as if included in the provisions of the Health Insurance Portability and Accountability Act of 1996 [Pub. L. 104–191] to which such amendments relate."

EFFECTIVE DATE OF 1996 AMENDMENT

Pub. L. 104–188, title I, §1621(d), Aug. 20, 1996, 110 Stat. 1867, provided that: "The amendments made by this section [enacting sections 860H to 860L of this title and amending this section and sections 56, 382, 582, 856, 860G, 1202, and 7701 of this title] shall take effect on September 1, 1997."

EFFECTIVE DATE OF 1989 AMENDMENT

Amendment by section 7811(c)(1), (2) of Pub. L. 101–239 effective, except as otherwise provided, as if included in the provision of the Technical and Miscellaneous Revenue Act of 1988, Pub. L. 100–647, to which such amendment relates, see section 7817 of Pub. L. 101–239, set out as a note under section 1 of this title.

Pub. L. 101–239, title VII, §7823, Dec. 19, 1989, 103 Stat. 2425, provided that: "Except as otherwise provided in this part [part II (§§7821–7823) of subtitle H of title VII of Pub. L. 101–239, amending this section and sections 453A, 842, 1503, 6427, 6655, 6863, 7519, 7611, 9502, 9503, and 9508 of this title and enacting provisions set out as notes under sections 56 and 7519 of this title], any amendment made by this part shall take effect as if included in the provision of the 1987 Act [Pub. L. 100–203, title X] to which such amendment relates."

EFFECTIVE DATE OF 1988 AMENDMENT

Amendment by section 1006(t)(16)(C) of Pub. L. 100–647 applicable, with certain exceptions, to transfers after Mar. 31, 1988, and to excess inclusions for periods after Mar. 31, 1988, see section 1006(t)(16)(D)(ii)–(iv) of Pub. L. 100–647, set out as a note under section 860E of this title.

Amendment by sections 1007(g)(1), 1011A(c)(10), and 1012(q)(8) of Pub. L. 100–647 effective, except as otherwise provided, as if included in the provision of the Tax Reform Act of 1986, Pub. L. 99–514, to which such amendment relates, see section 1019(a) of Pub. L. 100–647, set out as a note under section 1 of this title.

Amendment by section 4005(g)(4) of Pub. L. 100–647 applicable, with certain exceptions, to financing provided, and mortgage credit certificates issued, after Dec. 31, 1990, see section 4005(h)(3) of Pub. L. 100–647, set out as a note under section 143 of this title.

Amendment by section 5012(b)(2) of Pub. L. 100–647 applicable to contracts entered into on or after June 21, 1988, with special rule where death benefit increases by more than $150,000, certain other material changes taken into account, and certain exchanges permitted, see section 5012(e) of Pub. L. 100–647, set out as an Effective Date note under section 7702A of this title.

EFFECTIVE DATE OF 1986 AMENDMENT

Amendment by section 261(c) of Pub. L. 99–514 applicable to taxable years beginning after Dec. 31, 1986, see section 261(g) of Pub. L. 99–514, set out as an Effective Date note under section 7518 of this title.

Amendment by section 632(c)(1) of Pub. L. 99–514 applicable to taxable years beginning after Dec. 31, 1986, but only in cases where the return for the taxable year is filed pursuant to an S election made after Dec. 31, 1986, see section 633(b) of Pub. L. 99–514, as amended, set out as an Effective Date note under section 336 of this title.

Amendment by section 632(c)(1) of Pub. L. 99–514 not applicable in the case of certain transactions, see section 54(d)(3)(D) of Pub. L. 98–369, as amended, set out as an Effective Date of 1984 Amendment note under section 311 of this title.

Amendment by section 701(c)(1) of Pub. L. 99–514 applicable to taxable years beginning after Dec. 31, 1986, with certain exceptions and qualifications, see section 701(f) of Pub. L. 99–514, set out as an Effective Date note under section 55 of this title.

Pub. L. 99–499, title V, §516(c), Oct. 17, 1986, 100 Stat. 1772, provided that: "The amendments made by this section [enacting section 59A of this title and amending this section and sections 164, 275, 936, 1561, 6154, 6425, and 6655 of this title] shall apply to taxable years beginning after December 31, 1986."

EFFECTIVE DATE

Section applicable to taxable years beginning after Dec. 31, 1983, and to carrybacks from such years, see section 475(a) of Pub. L. 98–369, set out as an Effective Date of 1984 Amendment note under section 21 of this title.

SAVINGS PROVISION

For provisions that nothing in amendment by Pub. L. 115–141 be construed to affect treatment of certain transactions occurring, property acquired, or items of income, loss, deduction, or credit taken into account prior to Mar. 23, 2018, for purposes of determining liability for tax for periods ending after Mar. 23, 2018, see section 401(e) of Pub. L. 115–141, set out as a note under section 23 of this title.

APPLICABILITY OF CERTAIN AMENDMENTS BY PUBLIC LAW 99–514 IN RELATION TO TREATY OBLIGATIONS OF UNITED STATES

For applicability of amendment by section 701(c)(1) of Pub. L. 99–514 notwithstanding any treaty obligation of the United States in effect on Oct. 22, 1986, with provision that for such purposes any amendment by title I of Pub. L. 100–647 be treated as if it had been included in the provision of Pub. L. 99–514 to which such amendment relates, see section 1012(aa)(2), (4) of Pub. L. 100–647, set out as a note under section 861 of this title.

TREATMENT OF TAX IMPOSED UNDER FORMER SECTION 409(c)

Pub. L. 98–369, div. A, title IV, §491(f)(5), July 18, 1984, 98 Stat. 853, as amended by Pub. L. 99–514, §2, Oct. 22, 1986, 100 Stat. 2095, provided that: "For purposes of section 26(b) of the Internal Revenue Code of 1986 [formerly I.R.C. 1954] (as amended by this Act), any tax imposed by section 409(c) of such Code (as in effect before its repeal by this section) shall be treated as a tax imposed by section 408(f) of such Code."

Subpart B—Other Credits

Sec.
27.
Taxes of foreign countries and possessions of the United States.
[28, 29.
Renumbered.]
[30, 30A.
Repealed.]
30B.
Alternative motor vehicle credit.
30C.
Alternative fuel vehicle refueling property credit.
30D.
New qualified plug-in electric drive motor vehicles.

EDITORIAL NOTES
AMENDMENTS

2018—Pub. L. 115–141, div. U, title IV, §401(d)(1)(D)(i), Mar. 23, 2018, 132 Stat. 1206, substituted "Taxes of foreign countries and possessions of the United States" for "Taxes of foreign countries and possessions of the United States; possession tax credit" in item 27.

Pub. L. 115–141, div. U, title IV, §401(d)(1)(B), Mar. 23, 2018, 132 Stat. 1206, which directed amendment of the table of sections for subpart C of part IV of subchapter A of chapter 1 by striking out item 30A "Puerto Rico economic activity credit", was executed to the table of sections for this subpart to reflect the probable intent of Congress.

2014—Pub. L. 113–295, div. A, title II, §221(a)(2)(A), Dec. 19, 2014, 128 Stat. 4037, struck out item 30 "Certain plug-in electric vehicles".

2009—Pub. L. 111–5, div. B, title I, §1142(b)(8), Feb. 17, 2009, 123 Stat. 331, substituted "Certain plug-in electric vehicles" for "Credit for qualified electric vehicles" in item 30.

2008—Pub. L. 110–343, div. B, title II, §205(d)(4), Oct. 3, 2008, 122 Stat. 3839, added item 30D.

2005—Pub. L. 109–135, title IV, §412(e), Dec. 21, 2005, 119 Stat. 2637, substituted "Alternative fuel vehicle refueling property credit" for "Clean-fuel vehicle refueling property credit" in item 30C.

Pub. L. 109–58, title XIII, §§1322(a)(3)(K), 1341(b)(5), 1342(b)(5), Aug. 8, 2005, 119 Stat. 1012, 1049, 1051, struck out item 29 "Credit for producing fuel from a nonconventional source" and added items 30B and 30C.

1997—Pub. L. 105–34, title XVI, §1601(f)(1)(B), Aug. 5, 1997, 111 Stat. 1090, substituted "Puerto Rico" for "Puerto Rican" in item 30A.

1996—Pub. L. 104–188, title I, §§1205(a)(3)(A), 1601(b)(2)(E), (F)(i), Aug. 20, 1996, 110 Stat. 1775, 1833, substituted "Other Credits" for "Foreign Tax Credits, Etc." in subpart heading, struck out item 28 "Clinical testing expenses for certain drugs for rare diseases or conditions", and added item 30A.

1992—Pub. L. 102–486, title XIX, §1913(b)(2)(A), Oct. 24, 1992, 106 Stat. 3020, added item 30.

1986—Pub. L. 99–514, title II, §231(d)(3)(J), Oct. 22, 1986, 100 Stat. 2180, struck out item 30 "Credit for increasing research activities".

1984—Pub. L. 98–369, div. A, title IV, §471(b), July 18, 1984, 98 Stat. 826, added subpart B heading and analysis of sections for subpart B consisting of items 27 (formerly 33), 28 (formerly 44H), 29 (formerly 44D), and 30 (formerly 44F). Former subpart B was redesignated E.

§27. Taxes of foreign countries and possessions of the United States

The amount of taxes imposed by foreign countries and possessions of the United States shall be allowed as a credit against the tax imposed by this chapter to the extent provided in section 901 [1]

(Aug. 16, 1954, ch. 736, 68A Stat. 13, §33; Pub. L. 94–455, title X, §1051(a), Oct. 4, 1976, 90 Stat. 1643; renumbered §27, Pub. L. 98–369, div. A, title IV, §471(c), July 18, 1984, 98 Stat. 826; Pub. L. 115–141, div. U, title IV, §401(d)(1)(A), Mar. 23, 2018, 132 Stat. 1206.)

EDITORIAL NOTES
AMENDMENTS

2018—Pub. L. 115–141 amended section generally. Prior to amendment, section consisted of subsecs. (a) and (b) relating to the foreign tax credit under section 901 and the tax credit under section 936, respectively.

1984—Pub. L. 98–369, §471(c), renumbered section 33 of this title as this section.

1976—Pub. L. 94–455 designated existing provisions as subsec. (a) and added subsec. (b).

STATUTORY NOTES AND RELATED SUBSIDIARIES
EFFECTIVE DATE OF 1976 AMENDMENT

Pub. L. 94–455, title X, §1051(i), Oct. 4, 1976, 90 Stat. 1647, as amended by Pub. L. 99–514, §2, Oct. 22, 1986, 100 Stat. 2095, provided that:

"(1) Except as provided by paragraph (2), the amendments made by this section [enacting section 936 of this title and amending sections 33 [now 27], 48, 116, 243, 246, 861, 901, 904, 931, 1504, and 6091 of this title] shall apply to taxable years beginning after December 31, 1975, except that 'qualified possession source investment income' as defined in [former] section 936(d)(2) of the Internal Revenue Code of 1986 [formerly I.R.C. 1954] shall include income from any source outside the United States if the taxpayer establishes to the satisfaction of the Secretary of the Treasury or his delegate that the income from such sources was earned before October 1, 1976.

"(2) The amendment made by subsection (d)(2) [amending section 901 of this title] shall not apply to any tax imposed by a possession of the United States with respect to the complete liquidation occurring before January 1, 1979, of a corporation to the extent that such tax is attributable to earnings and profits accumulated by such corporation during periods ending before January 1, 1976."

SAVINGS PROVISION

For provisions that nothing in amendment by Pub. L. 115–141 be construed to affect treatment of certain transactions occurring, property acquired, or items of income, loss, deduction, or credit taken into account prior to Mar. 23, 2018, for purposes of determining liability for tax for periods ending after Mar. 23, 2018, see section 401(e) of Pub. L. 115–141, set out as a note under section 23 of this title.

[1] So in original. Probably should be followed by a period.

[§28. Renumbered §45C]

[§29. Renumbered §45K]

[§30. Repealed. Pub. L. 113–295, div. A, title II, §221(a)(2)(A), Dec. 19, 2014, 128 Stat. 4037]

Section, added Pub. L. 102–486, title XIX, §1913(b)(1), Oct. 24, 1992, 106 Stat. 3019; amended Pub. L. 104–188, title I, §§1205(d)(4), 1704(j)(4)(A), Aug. 20, 1996, 110 Stat. 1776, 1881; Pub. L. 107–147, title VI, §602(a), Mar. 9, 2002, 116 Stat. 59; Pub. L. 108–311, title III, §318(a), Oct. 4, 2004, 118 Stat. 1182; Pub. L. 109–58, title XIII, §1322(a)(3)(A), Aug. 8, 2005, 119 Stat. 1011; Pub. L. 111–5, div. B, title I, §1142(a), Feb. 17, 2009, 123 Stat. 328; Pub. L. 111–148, title X, §10909(b)(2)(F), (c), Mar. 23, 2010, 124 Stat. 1023; Pub. L. 111–312, title I, §101(b)(1), Dec. 17, 2010, 124 Stat. 3298; Pub. L. 112–240, title I, §104(c)(2)(G), Jan. 2, 2013, 126 Stat. 2322; Pub. L. 113–295, div. A, title II, §209(f)(2), Dec. 19, 2014, 128 Stat. 4028, related to certain plug-in electric vehicles.

A prior section 30 was renumbered section 41 of this title.

STATUTORY NOTES AND RELATED SUBSIDIARIES

EFFECTIVE DATE OF REPEAL

Repeal effective Dec. 19, 2014, subject to a savings provision, see section 221(b) of Pub. L. 113–295, set out as an Effective Date of 2014 Amendment note under section 1 of this title.

[§30A. Repealed. Pub. L. 115–141, div. U, title IV, §401(d)(1)(B), Mar. 23, 2018, 132 Stat. 1206]

Section, added Pub. L. 104–188, title I, §1601(b)(1), Aug. 20, 1996, 110 Stat. 1830; amended Pub. L. 105–34, title XVI, §1601(f)(1)(A), Aug. 5, 1997, 111 Stat. 1090; Pub. L. 106–554, §1(a)(7) [title III, §311(a)(2)], Dec. 21, 2000, 114 Stat. 2763, 2763A-640; Pub. L. 113–295, div. A, title II, §221(a)(12)(C), Dec. 19, 2014, 128 Stat. 4038, related to Puerto Rico economic activity credit. Repeal was executed to this section, which is in subpart B of part IV of subchapter A of chapter 1, to reflect the probable intent of Congress, notwithstanding directory language of Pub. L. 115–141, which repealed section 30A in subpart C of part IV of subchapter A of chapter 1.

STATUTORY NOTES AND RELATED SUBSIDIARIES

SAVINGS PROVISION

For provisions that nothing in repeal by Pub. L. 115–141 be construed to affect treatment of certain transactions occurring, property acquired, or items of income, loss, deduction, or credit taken into account prior to Mar. 23, 2018, for purposes of determining liability for tax for periods ending after Mar. 23, 2018, see section 401(e) of Pub. L. 115–141, set out as a note under section 23 of this title.

AMERICAN SAMOA ECONOMIC DEVELOPMENT CREDIT

Pub. L. 109–432, div. A, title I, §119, Dec. 20, 2006, 120 Stat. 2942, as amended by Pub. L. 110–343, div. C, title III, §309(a), Oct. 3, 2008, 122 Stat. 3869; Pub. L. 111–312, title VII, §756(a), Dec. 17, 2010, 124 Stat. 3322; Pub. L. 112–240, title I, §330(a), (b), Jan. 2, 2013, 126 Stat. 2335; Pub. L. 113–295, div. A, title I, §141(a), Dec. 19, 2014, 128 Stat. 4020; Pub. L. 114–113, div. Q, title I, §173(a), Dec. 18, 2015, 129 Stat. 3071; Pub. L. 115–123, div. D, title I, §40312(a), Feb. 9, 2018, 132 Stat. 147; Pub. L. 116–94, div. Q, title I, §119(a), (b), Dec. 20, 2019, 133 Stat. 3230; Pub. L. 116–260, div. EE, title I, §139(a), Dec. 27, 2020, 134 Stat. 3054, provided that:

"(a) In General.—For purposes of [former] section 30A of the Internal Revenue Code of 1986, a domestic corporation shall be treated as a qualified domestic corporation to which such section applies if—

"(1) in the case of a taxable year beginning before January 1, 2012, such corporation—

"(A) is an existing credit claimant with respect to American Samoa, and

"(B) elected the application of [former] section 936 of the Internal Revenue Code of 1986 for its last taxable year beginning before January 1, 2006, and

"(2) in the case of a taxable year beginning after December 31, 2011, such corporation meets the requirements of subsection (e).

"(b) Special Rules for Application of Section.—The following rules shall apply in applying [former] section 30A of the Internal Revenue Code of 1986 for purposes of this section:

"(1) Amount of credit.—Notwithstanding section 30A(a)(1) of such Code, the amount of the credit determined under section 30A(a)(1) of such Code for any taxable year shall be the amount determined under section 30A(d) of such Code, except that section 30A(d) shall be applied without regard to paragraph (3) thereof.

"(2) Separate application.—In applying section 30A(a)(3) of such Code in the case of a corporation treated as a qualified domestic corporation by reason of this section, section [former] 30A of such Code (and so much of [former] section 936 of such Code as relates to such [former] section 30A) shall be applied separately with respect to American Samoa.

"(3) Foreign tax credit allowed.—Notwithstanding [former] section 30A(e) of such Code, the provisions of [former] section 936(c) of such Code shall not apply with respect to the credit allowed by reason of this section.

"(c) Definitions.—For purposes of this section, any term which is used in this section which is also used in [former] section 30A or 936 of such Code shall have the same meaning given such term by such [former] section 30A or 936.

"(d) Application of Section.—Notwithstanding [former] section 30A(h) or [former] section 936(j) of such Code, this section (and so much of [former] section 30A and [former] section 936 of such Code as relates to this section) shall apply—

"(1) in the case of a corporation that meets the requirements of subparagraphs (A) and (B) of subsection (a)(1), to the first 16 taxable years of such corporation which begin after December 31, 2006, and before January 1, 2022, and

"(2) in the case of a corporation that does not meet the requirements of subparagraphs (A) and (B) of subsection (a)(1), to the first 10 taxable years of such corporation which begin after December 31, 2011, and before January 1, 2022.

In the case of a corporation described in subsection (a)(2), the Internal Revenue Code of 1986 shall be applied and administered without regard to the amendments made by section 401(d)(1) of the Tax Technical Corrections Act of 2018 [div. U of Pub. L. 115–141, see Tables for classification].

"(e) Qualified Production Activities Income Requirement.—A corporation meets the requirement of this subsection if such corporation has qualified production activities income, as defined in [former] subsection (c) of section 199 of the Internal Revenue Code of 1986 (as in effect before its repeal), determined by substituting 'American Samoa' for 'the United States' each place it appears in paragraphs (3), (4), and (6) of such subsection (c), for the taxable year. References in this subsection to section 199 of the Internal Revenue Code of 1986 shall be treated as references to such section as in effect before its repeal."

[Pub. L. 116–260, div. EE, title I, §139(b), Dec. 27, 2020, 134 Stat. 3054, provided that: "The amendments made by this section [amending section 119 of Pub. L. 109–432, set out above] shall apply to taxable years beginning after December 31, 2020."]

[Pub. L. 116–94, div. Q, title I, §119(c), Dec. 20, 2019, 133 Stat. 3230, provided that: "The amendments made by this section [amending section 119 of Pub. L. 109–432, set out above] shall apply to taxable years beginning after December 31, 2017."]

[Pub. L. 115–123, div. D, title I, §40312(b), Feb. 9, 2018, 132 Stat. 147, provided that: "The amendments made by this section [amending section 119 of Pub. L. 109–432, set out above] shall apply to taxable years beginning after December 31, 2016."]

[Pub. L. 114–113, div. Q, title I, §173(b), Dec. 18, 2015, 129 Stat. 3071, provided that: "The amendments made by this section [amending section 119 of Pub. L. 109–432, set out above] shall apply to taxable years beginning after December 31, 2014."]

[Pub. L. 113–295, div. A, title I, §141(b), Dec. 19, 2014, 128 Stat. 4020, provided that: "The amendments made by this section [amending section 119 of Pub. L. 109–432, set out above] shall apply to taxable years beginning after December 31, 2013."]

[Pub. L. 112–240, title III, §330(c), Jan. 2, 2013, 126 Stat. 2335, provided that: "The amendments made by this section [amending section 119 of Pub. L. 109–432, set out above] shall apply to taxable years beginning after December 31, 2011."]

[Pub. L. 111–312, title VII, §756(b), Dec. 17, 2010, 124 Stat. 3322, provided that: "The amendments made by this section [amending section 119 of Pub. L. 109–432, set out above] shall apply to taxable years beginning after December 31, 2009."]

[Pub. L. 110–343, div. C, title III, §309(b), Oct. 3, 2008, 122 Stat. 3869, provided that: "The amendments made by this section [amending section 119 of Pub. L. 109–432, set out above] shall apply to taxable years beginning after December 31, 2007."]

§30B. Alternative motor vehicle credit

(a) Allowance of credit

There shall be allowed as a credit against the tax imposed by this chapter for the taxable year an amount equal to the sum of—

(1) the new qualified fuel cell motor vehicle credit determined under subsection (b),

(2) the new advanced lean burn technology motor vehicle credit determined under subsection (c),

(3) the new qualified hybrid motor vehicle credit determined under subsection (d),

(4) the new qualified alternative fuel motor vehicle credit determined under subsection (e), and

(5) the plug-in conversion credit determined under subsection (i).

(b) New qualified fuel cell motor vehicle credit

(1) In general

For purposes of subsection (a), the new qualified fuel cell motor vehicle credit determined under this subsection with respect to a new qualified fuel cell motor vehicle placed in service by the taxpayer during the taxable year is—

(A) $8,000 ($4,000 in the case of a vehicle placed in service after December 31, 2009), if such vehicle has a gross vehicle weight rating of not more than 8,500 pounds,

(B) $10,000, if such vehicle has a gross vehicle weight rating of more than 8,500 pounds but not more than 14,000 pounds,

(C) $20,000, if such vehicle has a gross vehicle weight rating of more than 14,000 pounds but not more than 26,000 pounds, and

(D) $40,000, if such vehicle has a gross vehicle weight rating of more than 26,000 pounds.

(2) Increase for fuel efficiency

(A) In general

The amount determined under paragraph (1)(A) with respect to a new qualified fuel cell motor vehicle which is a passenger automobile or light truck shall be increased by—

(i) $1,000, if such vehicle achieves at least 150 percent but less than 175 percent of the 2002 model year city fuel economy,

(ii) $1,500, if such vehicle achieves at least 175 percent but less than 200 percent of the 2002 model year city fuel economy,

(iii) $2,000, if such vehicle achieves at least 200 percent but less than 225 percent of the 2002 model year city fuel economy,

(iv) $2,500, if such vehicle achieves at least 225 percent but less than 250 percent of the 2002 model year city fuel economy,

(v) $3,000, if such vehicle achieves at least 250 percent but less than 275 percent of the 2002 model year city fuel economy,

(vi) $3,500, if such vehicle achieves at least 275 percent but less than 300 percent of the 2002 model year city fuel economy, and

(vii) $4,000, if such vehicle achieves at least 300 percent of the 2002 model year city fuel economy.

(B) 2002 model year city fuel economy

For purposes of subparagraph (A), the 2002 model year city fuel economy with respect to a vehicle shall be determined in accordance with the following tables:

(i) In the case of a passenger automobile:

If vehicle inertia weight class is:	The 2002 model year city fuel economy is:
1,500 or 1,750 lbs	45.2 mpg
2,000 lbs	39.6 mpg
2,250 lbs	35.2 mpg
2,500 lbs	31.7 mpg
2,750 lbs	28.8 mpg
3,000 lbs	26.4 mpg
3,500 lbs	22.6 mpg
4,000 lbs	19.8 mpg
4,500 lbs	17.6 mpg
5,000 lbs	15.9 mpg
5,500 lbs	14.4 mpg
6,000 lbs	13.2 mpg
6,500 lbs	12.2 mpg
7,000 to 8,500 lbs	11.3 mpg.

(ii) In the case of a light truck:

If vehicle inertia weight class is:	The 2002 model year city fuel economy is:
1,500 or 1,750 lbs	39.4 mpg
2,000 lbs	35.2 mpg
2,250 lbs	31.8 mpg

2,500 lbs	29.0 mpg
2,750 lbs	26.8 mpg
3,000 lbs	24.9 mpg
3,500 lbs	21.8 mpg
4,000 lbs	19.4 mpg
4,500 lbs	17.6 mpg
5,000 lbs	16.1 mpg
5,500 lbs	14.8 mpg
6,000 lbs	13.7 mpg
6,500 lbs	12.8 mpg
7,000 to 8,500 lbs	12.1 mpg.

(C) Vehicle inertia weight class

For purposes of subparagraph (B), the term "vehicle inertia weight class" has the same meaning as when defined in regulations prescribed by the Administrator of the Environmental Protection Agency for purposes of the administration of title II of the Clean Air Act (42 U.S.C. 7521 et seq.).

(3) New qualified fuel cell motor vehicle

For purposes of this subsection, the term "new qualified fuel cell motor vehicle" means a motor vehicle—

(A) which is propelled by power derived from 1 or more cells which convert chemical energy directly into electricity by combining oxygen with hydrogen fuel which is stored on board the vehicle in any form and may or may not require reformation prior to use,

(B) which, in the case of a passenger automobile or light truck, has received on or after the date of the enactment of this section a certificate that such vehicle meets or exceeds the Bin 5 Tier II emission level established in regulations prescribed by the Administrator of the Environmental Protection Agency under section 202(i) of the Clean Air Act for that make and model year vehicle,

(C) the original use of which commences with the taxpayer,

(D) which is acquired for use or lease by the taxpayer and not for resale, and

(E) which is made by a manufacturer.

(c) New advanced lean burn technology motor vehicle credit

(1) In general

For purposes of subsection (a), the new advanced lean burn technology motor vehicle credit determined under this subsection for the taxable year is the credit amount determined under paragraph (2) with respect to a new advanced lean burn technology motor vehicle placed in service by the taxpayer during the taxable year.

(2) Credit amount

(A) Fuel economy

(i) In general

The credit amount determined under this paragraph shall be determined in accordance with the following table:

In the case of a vehicle which achieves a fuel economy (expressed as a percentage of the 2002 model year city fuel economy) of—	The credit amount is—
At least 125 percent but less than 150 percent	$400
At least 150 percent but less than 175 percent	$800
At least 175 percent but less than 200 percent	$1,200
At least 200 percent but less than 225 percent	$1,600
At least 225 percent but less than 250 percent	$2,000
At least 250 percent	$2,400.

(ii) 2002 model year city fuel economy

For purposes of clause (i), the 2002 model year city fuel economy with respect to a vehicle shall be determined on a gasoline gallon equivalent basis as determined by the Administrator of the Environmental Protection Agency using the tables provided in subsection (b)(2)(B) with respect to such vehicle.

(B) Conservation credit

The amount determined under subparagraph (A) with respect to a new advanced lean burn technology motor vehicle shall be increased by the conservation credit amount determined in accordance with the following table:

In the case of a vehicle which achieves a lifetime fuel savings (expressed in gallons of gasoline) of—	The conservation credit amount is—
At least 1,200 but less than 1,800	$250
At least 1,800 but less than 2,400	$500
At least 2,400 but less than 3,000	$750
At least 3,000	$1,000.

(3) New advanced lean burn technology motor vehicle

For purposes of this subsection, the term "new advanced lean burn technology motor vehicle" means a passenger automobile or a light truck—

(A) with an internal combustion engine which—

(i) is designed to operate primarily using more air than is necessary for complete combustion of the fuel,

(ii) incorporates direct injection,

(iii) achieves at least 125 percent of the 2002 model year city fuel economy,

(iv) for 2004 and later model vehicles, has received a certificate that such vehicle meets or exceeds—

(I) in the case of a vehicle having a gross vehicle weight rating of 6,000 pounds or less, the Bin 5 Tier II emission standard established in regulations prescribed by the Administrator of the Environmental Protection Agency under section 202(i) of the Clean Air Act for that make and model year vehicle, and

(II) in the case of a vehicle having a gross vehicle weight rating of more than 6,000 pounds but not more than 8,500 pounds, the Bin 8 Tier II emission standard which is so established,

(B) the original use of which commences with the taxpayer,

(C) which is acquired for use or lease by the taxpayer and not for resale, and

(D) which is made by a manufacturer.

(4) Lifetime fuel savings

For purposes of this subsection, the term "lifetime fuel savings" means, in the case of any new advanced lean burn technology motor vehicle, an amount equal to the excess (if any) of—

(A) 120,000 divided by the 2002 model year city fuel economy for the vehicle inertia weight class, over

(B) 120,000 divided by the city fuel economy for such vehicle.

(d) New qualified hybrid motor vehicle credit

(1) In general

For purposes of subsection (a), the new qualified hybrid motor vehicle credit determined under this subsection for the taxable year is the credit amount determined under paragraph (2) with respect to a new qualified hybrid motor vehicle placed in service by the taxpayer during the taxable year.

(2) Credit amount

(A) Credit amount for passenger automobiles and light trucks

In the case of a new qualified hybrid motor vehicle which is a passenger automobile or light truck and which has a gross vehicle weight rating of not more than 8,500 pounds, the amount determined under this paragraph is the sum of the amounts determined under clauses (i) and (ii).

(i) Fuel economy

The amount determined under this clause is the amount which would be determined under subsection (c)(2)(A) if such vehicle were a vehicle referred to in such subsection.

(ii) Conservation credit

The amount determined under this clause is the amount which would be determined under subsection (c)(2)(B) if such vehicle were a vehicle referred to in such subsection.

(B) Credit amount for other motor vehicles

(i) In general

In the case of any new qualified hybrid motor vehicle to which subparagraph (A) does not apply, the amount determined under this paragraph is the amount equal to the applicable percentage of the qualified incremental hybrid cost of the vehicle as certified under clause (v).

(ii) Applicable percentage

For purposes of clause (i), the applicable percentage is—

(I) 20 percent if the vehicle achieves an increase in city fuel economy relative to a comparable vehicle of at least 30 percent but less than 40 percent,

(II) 30 percent if the vehicle achieves such an increase of at least 40 percent but less than 50 percent, and

(III) 40 percent if the vehicle achieves such an increase of at least 50 percent.

(iii) Qualified incremental hybrid cost

For purposes of this subparagraph, the qualified incremental hybrid cost of any vehicle is equal to the amount of the excess of the manufacturer's suggested retail price for such vehicle over such price for a comparable vehicle, to the extent such amount does not exceed—

(I) $7,500, if such vehicle has a gross vehicle weight rating of not more than 14,000 pounds,

(II) $15,000, if such vehicle has a gross vehicle weight rating of more than 14,000 pounds but not more than 26,000 pounds, and

(III) $30,000, if such vehicle has a gross vehicle weight rating of more than 26,000 pounds.

(iv) Comparable vehicle

For purposes of this subparagraph, the term "comparable vehicle" means, with respect to any new qualified hybrid motor vehicle, any vehicle which is powered solely by a gasoline or diesel internal combustion engine and which is comparable in weight, size, and use to such vehicle.

(v) Certification

A certification described in clause (i) shall be made by the manufacturer and shall be determined in accordance with guidance prescribed by the Secretary. Such guidance shall specify procedures and methods for calculating fuel economy savings and incremental hybrid costs.

(3) New qualified hybrid motor vehicle

For purposes of this subsection—

(A) In general

The term "new qualified hybrid motor vehicle" means a motor vehicle—

(i) which draws propulsion energy from onboard sources of stored energy which are both—

(I) an internal combustion or heat engine using consumable fuel, and

(II) a rechargeable energy storage system,

(ii) which, in the case of a vehicle to which paragraph (2)(A) applies, has received a certificate of conformity under the Clean Air Act and meets or exceeds the equivalent qualifying California low emission vehicle standard under section 243(e)(2) of the Clean Air Act for that make and model year, and

(I) in the case of a vehicle having a gross vehicle weight rating of 6,000 pounds or less, the Bin 5 Tier II emission standard established in regulations prescribed by the Administrator of the Environmental Protection Agency under section 202(i) of the Clean Air Act for that make and model year vehicle, and

(II) in the case of a vehicle having a gross vehicle weight rating of more than 6,000 pounds but not more than 8,500 pounds, the Bin 8 Tier II emission standard which is so established,

(iii) which has a maximum available power of at least—
(I) 4 percent in the case of a vehicle to which paragraph (2)(A) applies,
(II) 10 percent in the case of a vehicle which has a gross vehicle weight rating of more than 8,500 pounds and not more than 14,000 pounds, and
(III) 15 percent in the case of a vehicle in excess of 14,000 pounds,

(iv) which, in the case of a vehicle to which paragraph (2)(B) applies, has an internal combustion or heat engine which has received a certificate of conformity under the Clean Air Act as meeting the emission standards set in the regulations prescribed by the Administrator of the Environmental Protection Agency for 2004 through 2007 model year diesel heavy duty engines or ottocycle heavy duty engines, as applicable,
(v) the original use of which commences with the taxpayer,
(vi) which is acquired for use or lease by the taxpayer and not for resale, and
(vii) which is made by a manufacturer.

Such term shall not include any vehicle which is not a passenger automobile or light truck if such vehicle has a gross vehicle weight rating of less than 8,500 pounds.

(B) Consumable fuel

For purposes of subparagraph (A)(i)(I), the term "consumable fuel" means any solid, liquid, or gaseous matter which releases energy when consumed by an auxiliary power unit.

(C) Maximum available power

(i) Certain passenger automobiles and light trucks

In the case of a vehicle to which paragraph (2)(A) applies, the term "maximum available power" means the maximum power available from the rechargeable energy storage system, during a standard 10 second pulse power or equivalent test, divided by such maximum power and the SAE net power of the heat engine.

(ii) Other motor vehicles

In the case of a vehicle to which paragraph (2)(B) applies, the term "maximum available power" means the maximum power available from the rechargeable energy storage system, during a standard 10 second pulse power or equivalent test, divided by the vehicle's total traction power. For purposes of the preceding sentence, the term "total traction power" means the sum of the peak power from the rechargeable energy storage system and the heat engine peak power of the vehicle, except that if such storage system is the sole means by which the vehicle can be driven, the total traction power is the peak power of such storage system.

(D) Exclusion of plug-in vehicles

Any vehicle with respect to which a credit is allowable under section 30D (determined without regard to subsection (c) thereof) shall not be taken into account under this section.

(e) New qualified alternative fuel motor vehicle credit

(1) Allowance of credit

Except as provided in paragraph (5), the new qualified alternative fuel motor vehicle credit determined under this subsection is an amount equal to the applicable percentage of the incremental cost of any new qualified alternative fuel motor vehicle placed in service by the taxpayer during the taxable year.

(2) Applicable percentage

For purposes of paragraph (1), the applicable percentage with respect to any new qualified alternative fuel motor vehicle is—
(A) 50 percent, plus
(B) 30 percent, if such vehicle—
(i) has received a certificate of conformity under the Clean Air Act and meets or exceeds the most stringent standard available for certification under the Clean Air Act for that make and model year vehicle (other than a zero emission standard), or
(ii) has received an order certifying the vehicle as meeting the same requirements as vehicles which may be sold or leased in California and meets or exceeds the most stringent standard available for certification under the State laws of California (enacted in accordance with a waiver granted under section 209(b) of the Clean Air Act) for that make and model year vehicle (other than a zero emission standard).

For purposes of the preceding sentence, in the case of any new qualified alternative fuel motor vehicle which weighs more than 14,000 pounds gross vehicle weight rating, the most stringent standard available shall be such standard available for certification on the date of the enactment of the Energy Tax Incentives Act of 2005.

(3) Incremental cost

For purposes of this subsection, the incremental cost of any new qualified alternative fuel motor vehicle is equal to the amount of the excess of the manufacturer's suggested retail price for such vehicle over such price for a gasoline or diesel fuel motor vehicle of the same model, to the extent such amount does not exceed—
(A) $5,000, if such vehicle has a gross vehicle weight rating of not more than 8,500 pounds,
(B) $10,000, if such vehicle has a gross vehicle weight rating of more than 8,500 pounds but not more than 14,000 pounds,
(C) $25,000, if such vehicle has a gross vehicle weight rating of more than 14,000 pounds but not more than 26,000 pounds, and
(D) $40,000, if such vehicle has a gross vehicle weight rating of more than 26,000 pounds.

(4) New qualified alternative fuel motor vehicle

For purposes of this subsection—

(A) In general

The term "new qualified alternative fuel motor vehicle" means any motor vehicle—
(i) which is only capable of operating on an alternative fuel,
(ii) the original use of which commences with the taxpayer,
(iii) which is acquired by the taxpayer for use or lease, but not for resale, and
(iv) which is made by a manufacturer.

(B) Alternative fuel

The term "alternative fuel" means compressed natural gas, liquefied natural gas, liquefied petroleum gas, hydrogen, and any liquid at least 85 percent of the volume of which consists of methanol.

(5) Credit for mixed-fuel vehicles

(A) In general

In the case of a mixed-fuel vehicle placed in service by the taxpayer during the taxable year, the credit determined under this subsection is an amount equal to—

(i) in the case of a 75/25 mixed-fuel vehicle, 70 percent of the credit which would have been allowed under this subsection if such vehicle was a qualified alternative fuel motor vehicle, and

(ii) in the case of a 90/10 mixed-fuel vehicle, 90 percent of the credit which would have been allowed under this subsection if such vehicle was a qualified alternative fuel motor vehicle.

(B) Mixed-fuel vehicle

For purposes of this subsection, the term "mixed-fuel vehicle" means any motor vehicle described in subparagraph (C) or (D) of paragraph (3), which—

(i) is certified by the manufacturer as being able to perform efficiently in normal operation on a combination of an alternative fuel and a petroleum-based fuel,

(ii) either—

(I) has received a certificate of conformity under the Clean Air Act, or

(II) has received an order certifying the vehicle as meeting the same requirements as vehicles which may be sold or leased in California and meets or exceeds the low emission vehicle standard under section 88.105–94 of title 40, Code of Federal Regulations, for that make and model year vehicle,

(iii) the original use of which commences with the taxpayer,

(iv) which is acquired by the taxpayer for use or lease, but not for resale, and

(v) which is made by a manufacturer.

(C) 75/25 mixed-fuel vehicle

For purposes of this subsection, the term "75/25 mixed-fuel vehicle" means a mixed-fuel vehicle which operates using at least 75 percent alternative fuel and not more than 25 percent petroleum-based fuel.

(D) 90/10 mixed-fuel vehicle

For purposes of this subsection, the term "90/10 mixed-fuel vehicle" means a mixed-fuel vehicle which operates using at least 90 percent alternative fuel and not more than 10 percent petroleum-based fuel.

(f) Limitation on number of new qualified hybrid and advanced lean-burn technology vehicles eligible for credit

(1) In general

In the case of a qualified vehicle sold during the phaseout period, only the applicable percentage of the credit otherwise allowable under subsection (c) or (d) shall be allowed.

(2) Phaseout period

For purposes of this subsection, the phaseout period is the period beginning with the second calendar quarter following the calendar quarter which includes the first date on which the number of qualified vehicles manufactured by the manufacturer of the vehicle referred to in paragraph (1) sold for use in the United States after December 31, 2005, is at least 60,000.

(3) Applicable percentage

For purposes of paragraph (1), the applicable percentage is—

(A) 50 percent for the first 2 calendar quarters of the phaseout period,

(B) 25 percent for the 3d and 4th calendar quarters of the phaseout period, and

(C) 0 percent for each calendar quarter thereafter.

(4) Controlled groups

(A) In general

For purposes of this subsection, all persons treated as a single employer under subsection (a) or (b) of section 52 or subsection (m) or (o) of section 414 shall be treated as a single manufacturer.

(B) Inclusion of foreign corporations

For purposes of subparagraph (A), in applying subsections (a) and (b) of section 52 to this section, section 1563 shall be applied without regard to subsection (b)(2)(C) thereof.

(5) Qualified vehicle

For purposes of this subsection, the term "qualified vehicle" means any new qualified hybrid motor vehicle (described in subsection (d)(2)(A)) and any new advanced lean burn technology motor vehicle.

(g) Application with other credits

(1) Business credit treated as part of general business credit

So much of the credit which would be allowed under subsection (a) for any taxable year (determined without regard to this subsection) that is attributable to property of a character subject to an allowance for depreciation shall be treated as a credit listed in section 38(b) for such taxable year (and not allowed under subsection (a)).

(2) Personal credit

For purposes of this title, the credit allowed under subsection (a) for any taxable year (determined after application of paragraph (1)) shall be treated as a credit allowable under subpart A for such taxable year.

(h) Other definitions and special rules

For purposes of this section—

(1) Motor vehicle

The term "motor vehicle" means any vehicle which is manufactured primarily for use on public streets, roads, and highways (not including a vehicle operated exclusively on a rail or rails) and which has at least 4 wheels.

(2) City fuel economy

The city fuel economy with respect to any vehicle shall be measured in a manner which is substantially similar to the manner city fuel economy is measured in accordance with procedures under part 600 of subchapter Q of chapter I of title 40, Code of Federal Regulations, as in effect on the date of the enactment of this section.

(3) Other terms

The terms "automobile", "passenger automobile", "medium duty passenger vehicle", "light truck", and "manufacturer" have the meanings given such terms in regulations prescribed by the Administrator of the Environmental Protection Agency for purposes of the administration of title II of the Clean Air Act (42 U.S.C. 7521 et seq.).

(4) Reduction in basis

For purposes of this subtitle, the basis of any property for which a credit is allowable under subsection (a) shall be reduced by the amount of such credit so allowed (determined without regard to subsection (g)).

(5) No double benefit

The amount of any deduction or other credit allowable under this chapter—

(A) for any incremental cost taken into account in computing the amount of the credit determined under subsection (e) shall be reduced by the amount of such credit attributable to such cost, and

(B) with respect to a vehicle described under subsection (b) or (c), shall be reduced by the amount of credit allowed under subsection (a) for such vehicle for the taxable year (determined without regard to subsection (g)).

(6) Property used by tax-exempt entity

In the case of a vehicle whose use is described in paragraph (3) or (4) of section 50(b) and which is not subject to a lease, the person who sold such vehicle to the person or entity using such vehicle shall be treated as the taxpayer that placed such vehicle in service, but only if such person clearly discloses to such person or entity in a document the amount of any credit allowable under subsection (a) with respect to such vehicle (determined without regard to subsection (g)). For purposes of subsection (g), property to which this paragraph applies shall be treated as of a character subject to an allowance for depreciation.

(7) Property used outside United States, etc., not qualified

No credit shall be allowable under subsection (a) with respect to any property referred to in section 50(b)(1) or with respect to the portion of the cost of any property taken into account under section 179.

(8) Recapture

The Secretary shall, by regulations, provide for recapturing the benefit of any credit allowable under subsection (a) with respect to any property which ceases to be property eligible for such credit (including recapture in the case of a lease period of less than the economic life of a vehicle), except that no benefit shall be recaptured if such property ceases to be eligible for such credit by reason of conversion to a qualified plug-in electric drive motor vehicle.

(9) Election to not take credit

No credit shall be allowed under subsection (a) for any vehicle if the taxpayer elects to not have this section apply to such vehicle.

(10) Interaction with air quality and motor vehicle safety standards

Unless otherwise provided in this section, a motor vehicle shall not be considered eligible for a credit under this section unless such vehicle is in compliance with—

(A) the applicable provisions of the Clean Air Act for the applicable make and model year of the vehicle (or applicable air quality provisions of State law in the case of a State which has adopted such provision under a waiver under section 209(b) of the Clean Air Act), and

(B) the motor vehicle safety provisions of sections 30101 through 30169 of title 49, United States Code.

(i) Plug-in conversion credit

(1) In general

For purposes of subsection (a), the plug-in conversion credit determined under this subsection with respect to any motor vehicle which is converted to a qualified plug-in electric drive motor vehicle is 10 percent of so much of the cost of the converting such vehicle as does not exceed $40,000.

(2) Qualified plug-in electric drive motor vehicle

For purposes of this subsection, the term "qualified plug-in electric drive motor vehicle" means any new qualified plug-in electric drive motor vehicle (as defined in section 30D, determined without regard to whether such vehicle is made by a manufacturer or whether the original use of such vehicle commences with the taxpayer).

(3) Credit allowed in addition to other credits

The credit allowed under this subsection shall be allowed with respect to a motor vehicle notwithstanding whether a credit has been allowed with respect to such motor vehicle under this section (other than this subsection) in any preceding taxable year.

(4) Termination

This subsection shall not apply to conversions made after December 31, 2011.

(j) Regulations

(1) In general

Except as provided in paragraph (2), the Secretary shall promulgate such regulations as necessary to carry out the provisions of this section.

(2) Coordination in prescription of certain regulations

The Secretary of the Treasury, in coordination with the Secretary of Transportation and the Administrator of the Environmental Protection Agency, shall prescribe such regulations as necessary to determine whether a motor vehicle meets the requirements to be eligible for a credit under this section.

(k) Termination

This section shall not apply to any property purchased after—

(1) in the case of a new qualified fuel cell motor vehicle (as described in subsection (b)), December 31, 2021,

(2) in the case of a new advanced lean burn technology motor vehicle (as described in subsection (c)) or a new qualified hybrid motor vehicle (as described in subsection (d)(2)(A)), December 31, 2010,

(3) in the case of a new qualified hybrid motor vehicle (as described in subsection (d)(2)(B)), December 31, 2009, and

(4) in the case of a new qualified alternative fuel vehicle (as described in subsection (e)), December 31, 2010.

(Added Pub. L. 109–58, title XIII, §1341(a), Aug. 8, 2005, 119 Stat. 1038; amended Pub. L. 109–135, title IV, §§402(j), 412(d), Dec. 21, 2005, 119 Stat. 2615, 2636; Pub. L. 110–343, div. B, title II, §205(b), Oct. 3, 2008, 122 Stat. 3838; Pub. L. 111–5, div. B, title I, §§1141(b)(1), 1142(b)(2), 1143(a)–(c), 1144(a), Feb. 17, 2009, 123 Stat. 328, 330–332; Pub. L. 111–148, title X, §10909(b)(2)(G), (c), Mar. 23, 2010, 124 Stat. 1023; Pub. L. 111–312, title I, §101(b)(1), Dec. 17, 2010, 124 Stat. 3298; Pub. L. 112–240, title I, §104(c)(2)(H), Jan. 2, 2013, 126 Stat. 2322; Pub. L. 113–295, div. A, title II, §§218(a), 220(a), Dec. 19, 2014, 128 Stat. 4035; Pub. L. 114–113, div. Q, title I, §193(a), Dec. 18, 2015, 129 Stat. 3075; Pub. L. 115–123, div. D, title I, §40403(a), Feb. 9, 2018, 132 Stat. 148; Pub. L. 116–94, div. Q, title I, §124(a), Dec. 20, 2019, 133 Stat. 3231; Pub. L. 116–260, div. EE, title I, §142(a), Dec. 27, 2020, 134 Stat. 3054.)

EDITORIAL NOTES
REFERENCES IN TEXT

The Clean Air Act, referred to in text, is act July 14, 1955, ch. 360, 69 Stat. 322, as amended, which is classified generally to chapter 85 (§7401 et seq.) of Title 42, The Public Health and Welfare. Title II of the Act, known as the National Emissions Standards Act, is classified generally to subchapter II (§7521 et seq.) of chapter 85 of Title 42. Sections 202(i), 209(b), and 243(e)(2) of the Act are classified to sections 7521(i), 7543(b), and 7583(e)(2), respectively, of Title 42. For complete classification of this Act to the Code, see Short Title note set out under section 7401 of Title 42 and Tables.

The date of the enactment of this section, referred to in subsecs. (b)(3)(B) and (h)(2), is the date of enactment of Pub. L. 109–58, which was approved Aug. 8, 2005.

The date of the enactment of the Energy Tax Incentives Act of 2005, referred to in subsec. (e)(2), is the date of enactment of title XIII of Pub. L. 109–58, which was approved Aug. 8, 2005.

AMENDMENTS

2020—Subsec. (k)(1). Pub. L. 116–260 substituted "December 31, 2021" for "December 31, 2020".

2019—Subsec. (k)(1). Pub. L. 116–94 substituted "December 31, 2020" for "December 31, 2017".

2018—Subsec. (k)(1). Pub. L. 115–123 substituted "December 31, 2017" for "December 31, 2016".

2015—Subsec. (k)(1). Pub. L. 114–113 substituted "December 31, 2016" for "December 31, 2014".

2014—Subsec. (h)(5)(B). Pub. L. 113–295, §218(a), inserted "(determined without regard to subsection (g))" before period at end.

Subsec. (h)(8). Pub. L. 113–295, §220(a), substituted "vehicle), except that" for "vehicle)., except that".

2013—Subsec. (g)(2). Pub. L. 112–240 amended par. (2) generally. Prior to amendment, par. (2) related to personal credit with a limitation based on amount of tax.

2010—Subsec. (g)(2)(B)(ii). Pub. L. 111–148, §10909(b)(2)(G), (c), as amended by Pub. L. 111–312, temporarily struck out "23," before "25D,". See Effective and Termination Dates of 2010 Amendment note below.

2009—Subsec. (a)(5). Pub. L. 111–5, §1143(b), added par. (5).

Subsec. (d)(3)(D). Pub. L. 111–5, §1141(b)(1), substituted "subsection (c) thereof" for "subsection (d) thereof".

Subsec. (g)(2). Pub. L. 111–5, §1144(a), amended par. (2) generally. Prior to amendment, text read as follows: "The credit allowed under subsection (a) (after the application of paragraph (1)) for any taxable year shall not exceed the excess (if any) of—

"(A) the regular tax liability (as defined in section 26(b)) reduced by the sum of the credits allowable under subpart A and sections 27 and 30, over

"(B) the tentative minimum tax for the taxable year."

Subsec. (h)(1). Pub. L. 111–5, §1142(b)(2), amended par. (1) generally. Prior to amendment, text read as follows: "The term 'motor vehicle' has the meaning given such term by section 30(c)(2)."

Subsec. (h)(8). Pub. L. 111–5, §1143(c), inserted at end ", except that no benefit shall be recaptured if such property ceases to be eligible for such credit by reason of conversion to a qualified plug-in electric drive motor vehicle."

Subsecs. (i) to (k). Pub. L. 111–5, §1143(a), added subsec. (i) and redesignated former subsecs. (i) and (j) as (j) and (k), respectively.

2008—Subsec. (d)(3)(D). Pub. L. 110–343 added subpar. (D).

2005—Subsec. (g)(2)(A). Pub. L. 109–135, §412(d), substituted "regular tax liability (as defined in section 26(b))" for "regular tax".

Subsec. (h)(6). Pub. L. 109–135, §402(j), inserted at end "For purposes of subsection (g), property to which this paragraph applies shall be treated as of a character subject to an allowance for depreciation."

STATUTORY NOTES AND RELATED SUBSIDIARIES

EFFECTIVE DATE OF 2020 AMENDMENT

Pub. L. 116–260, div. EE, title I, §142(b), Dec. 27, 2020, 134 Stat. 3054, provided that: "The amendment made by this section [amending this section] shall apply to property purchased after December 31, 2020."

EFFECTIVE DATE OF 2019 AMENDMENT

Pub. L. 116–94, div. Q, title I, §124(b), Dec. 20, 2019, 133 Stat. 3231, provided that: "The amendment made by this section [amending this section] shall apply to property purchased after December 31, 2017."

EFFECTIVE DATE OF 2018 AMENDMENT

Pub. L. 115–123, div. D, title I, §40403(b), Feb. 9, 2018, 132 Stat. 148, provided that: "The amendment made by this section [amending this section] shall apply to property purchased after December 31, 2016."

EFFECTIVE DATE OF 2015 AMENDMENT

Pub. L. 114–113, div. Q, title I, §193(b), Dec. 18, 2015, 129 Stat. 3076, provided that: "The amendment made by this section [amending this section] shall apply to property purchased after December 31, 2014."

EFFECTIVE DATE OF 2014 AMENDMENT

Pub. L. 113–295, div. A, title II, §218(c), Dec. 19, 2014, 128 Stat. 4035, provided that: "The amendments made by this section [amending this section and section 30C of this title] shall take effect as if included in the provision of the Energy Tax Incentives Act of 2005 [Pub. L. 109–58, title XIII] to which it relates."

EFFECTIVE DATE OF 2013 AMENDMENT

Amendment by Pub. L. 112–240 applicable to taxable years beginning after Dec. 31, 2011, see section 104(d) of Pub. L. 112–240, set out as a note under section 23 of this title.

EFFECTIVE AND TERMINATION DATES OF 2010 AMENDMENT

Amendment by Pub. L. 111–148 terminated applicable to taxable years beginning after Dec. 31, 2011, and section is amended to read as if such amendment had never been enacted, see section 10909(c) of Pub. L. 111–148, set out as a note under section 1 of this title.

Amendment by Pub. L. 111–148 applicable to taxable years beginning after Dec. 31, 2009, see section 10909(d) of Pub. L. 111–148, set out as a note under section 1 of this title.

EFFECTIVE DATE OF 2009 AMENDMENT

Pub. L. 111–5, div. B, title I, §1141(c), Feb. 17, 2009, 123 Stat. 328, provided that: "The amendments made by this section [amending this section and sections 30D, 38, 1016, and 6501 of this title] shall apply to vehicles acquired after December 31, 2009."

Amendment by section 1142(b)(2) of Pub. L. 111–5 applicable to vehicles acquired after Feb. 17, 2009, see section 1142(c) of Pub. L. 111–5, set out as an Effective and Termination Dates of 2009 Amendment note under section 24 of this title.

Pub. L. 111–5, div. B, title I, §1143(d), Feb. 17, 2009, 123 Stat. 332, provided that: "The amendments made by this section [amending this section] shall apply to property placed in service after the date of the enactment of this Act [Feb. 17, 2009]."

Amendment by section 1144(a) of Pub. L. 111–5 applicable to taxable years beginning after Dec. 31, 2008, see section 1144(c) of Pub. L. 111–5, set out as an Effective and Termination Dates of 2009 Amendment note under section 24 of this title.

EFFECTIVE DATE OF 2008 AMENDMENT

Amendment by Pub. L. 110–343 applicable to taxable years beginning after Dec. 31, 2008, see section 205(e) of Pub. L. 110–343, set out as an Effective and Termination Dates of 2008 Amendment note under section 24 of this title.

EFFECTIVE DATE OF 2005 AMENDMENT

Amendment by section 402(j) of Pub. L. 109–135 effective as if included in the provision of the Energy Policy Act of 2005, Pub. L. 109–58, to which such amendment relates, see section 402(m)(1) of Pub. L. 109–135, set out as an Effective and Termination Dates of 2005 Amendments note under section 23 of this title.

EFFECTIVE DATE

Pub. L. 109–58, title XIII, §1341(c), Aug. 8, 2005, 119 Stat. 1049, provided that: "The amendments made by this section [enacting this section and amending sections 38, 55, 1016, and 6501 of this title] shall apply to property placed in service after December 31, 2005, in taxable years ending after such date."

§30C. Alternative fuel vehicle refueling property credit

(a) Credit allowed

There shall be allowed as a credit against the tax imposed by this chapter for the taxable year an amount equal to 30 percent of the cost of any qualified alternative fuel vehicle refueling property placed in service by the taxpayer during the taxable year.

(b) Limitation

The credit allowed under subsection (a) with respect to all qualified alternative fuel vehicle refueling property placed in service by the taxpayer during the taxable year at a location shall not exceed—

(1) $30,000 in the case of a property of a character subject to an allowance for depreciation, and

(2) $1,000 in any other case.

(c) Qualified alternative fuel vehicle refueling property

For purposes of this section, the term "qualified alternative fuel vehicle refueling property" has the same meaning as the term "qualified clean-fuel vehicle refueling property" would have under section 179A if—

(1) paragraph (1) of section 179A(d) did not apply to property installed on property which is used as the principal residence (within the meaning of section 121) of the taxpayer, and

(2) only the following were treated as clean-burning fuels for purposes of section 179A(d):

(A) Any fuel at least 85 percent of the volume of which consists of one or more of the following: ethanol, natural gas, compressed natural gas, liquified natural gas, liquefied petroleum gas, or hydrogen.

(B) Any mixture—

(i) which consists of two or more of the following: biodiesel (as defined in section 40A(d)(1)), diesel fuel (as defined in section 4083(a)(3)), or kerosene, and

(ii) at least 20 percent of the volume of which consists of biodiesel (as so defined) determined without regard to any kerosene in such mixture.

(C) Electricity.

(d) Application with other credits

(1) Business credit treated as part of general business credit

So much of the credit which would be allowed under subsection (a) for any taxable year (determined without regard to this subsection) that is attributable to property of a character subject to an allowance for depreciation shall be treated as a credit listed in section 38(b) for such taxable year (and not allowed under subsection (a)).

(2) Personal credit

The credit allowed under subsection (a) (after the application of paragraph (1)) for any taxable year shall not exceed the excess (if any) of—

(A) the regular tax liability (as defined in section 26(b)) reduced by the sum of the credits allowable under subpart A and section 27, over

(B) the tentative minimum tax for the taxable year.

(e) Special rules

For purposes of this section—

(1) Reduction in basis

For purposes of this subtitle, the basis of any property for which a credit is allowable under subsection (a) shall be reduced by the amount of such credit so allowed (determined without regard to subsection (d)).

(2) Property used by tax-exempt entity

In the case of any qualified alternative fuel vehicle refueling property the use of which is described in paragraph (3) or (4) of section 50(b) and which is not subject to a lease, the person who sold such property to the person or entity using such property shall be treated as the taxpayer that placed such property in service, but only if such person clearly discloses to such person or entity in a document the amount of any credit allowable under subsection (a) with respect to such property (determined without regard to subsection (d)). For purposes of subsection (d), property to which this paragraph applies shall be treated as of a character subject to an allowance for depreciation.

(3) Property used outside United States not qualified

No credit shall be allowable under subsection (a) with respect to any property referred to in section 50(b)(1) or with respect to the portion of the cost of any property taken into account under section 179.

(4) Election not to take credit

No credit shall be allowed under subsection (a) for any property if the taxpayer elects not to have this section apply to such property.

(5) Recapture rules

Rules similar to the rules of section 179A(e)(4) shall apply.

(6) Reference

For purposes of this section, any reference to section 179A shall be treated as a reference to such section as in effect immediately before its repeal.

(f) Regulations

The Secretary shall prescribe such regulations as necessary to carry out the provisions of this section.

(g) Termination

This section shall not apply to any property placed in service after December 31, 2021.

(Added Pub. L. 109–58, title XIII, §1342(a), Aug. 8, 2005, 119 Stat. 1049; amended Pub. L. 109–135, title IV, §§402(k), 412(d), Dec. 21, 2005, 119 Stat. 2615, 2636; Pub. L. 110–172, §6(b), Dec. 29, 2007, 121 Stat. 2479; Pub. L. 110–343, div. B, title II, §207(a), (b), Oct. 3, 2008, 122 Stat. 3839; Pub. L. 111–5, div. B, title I, §§1123(a), 1142(b)(3), 1144(b)(2), Feb. 17, 2009, 123 Stat. 325, 331, 332; Pub. L. 111–312, title VII, §711(a), Dec. 17, 2010, 124 Stat. 3315; Pub. L. 112–240, title IV, §402(a), Jan. 2, 2013, 126 Stat. 2337; Pub. L. 113–295, div. A, title I, §161(a), title II, §§218(b), 221(a)(34)(B), Dec. 19, 2014, 128 Stat. 4023, 4035, 4042; Pub. L. 114–113, div. Q, title I, §182(a), Dec. 18, 2015, 129 Stat. 3072; Pub. L. 115–123, div. D, title I, §40404(a), Feb. 9, 2018, 132 Stat. 148; Pub. L. 115–141, div. U, title IV, §401(b)(3), Mar. 23, 2018, 132 Stat. 1201; Pub. L. 116–94, div. Q, title I, §125(a), Dec. 20, 2019, 133 Stat. 3231; Pub. L. 116–260, div. EE, title I, §143(a), Dec. 27, 2020, 134 Stat. 3054.)

EDITORIAL NOTES

REFERENCES IN TEXT

Section 179A as in effect immediately before its repeal, referred to in subsec. (e)(6), means section 179A of this title as in effect before it was repealed by Pub. L. 113–295, div. A, title II, §221(a)(34)(A), Dec. 19, 2014, 128 Stat. 4042, effective Dec. 19, 2014.

AMENDMENTS

2020—Subsec. (g). Pub. L. 116–260 substituted "December 31, 2021" for "December 31, 2020".

2019—Subsec. (g). Pub. L. 116–94 substituted "December 31, 2020" for "December 31, 2017".

2018—Subsec. (e)(6), (7). Pub. L. 115–141 redesignated par. (7) as (6) and struck out former par. (6) which related to special rule for property placed in service during 2009 and 2010.

Subsec. (g). Pub. L. 115–123 substituted "December 31, 2017" for "December 31, 2016".

2015—Subsec. (g). Pub. L. 114–113 substituted "December 31, 2016" for "December 31, 2014".

2014—Subsec. (e)(1). Pub. L. 113–295, §218(b), amended par. (1) generally. Prior to amendment, text read as follows: "The basis of any property shall be reduced by the portion of the cost of such property taken into account under subsection (a)."

Subsec. (e)(7). Pub. L. 113–295, §221(a)(34)(B), added par. (7).

Subsec. (g). Pub. L. 113–295, §161(a), substituted "placed in service after December 31, 2014." for "placed in service—

"(1) in the case of property relating to hydrogen, after December 31, 2014, and

"(2) in the case of any other property, after December 31, 2013."

2013—Subsec. (g)(2). Pub. L. 112–240 substituted "December 31, 2013" for "December 31, 2011.".

2010—Subsec. (g)(2). Pub. L. 111–312 substituted "December 31, 2011." for "December 31, 2010".

2009—Subsec. (d)(2)(A). Pub. L. 111–5, §1144(b)(2), substituted "section 27" for "sections 27 and 30B".

Pub. L. 111–5, §1142(b)(3), struck out ", 30," before "and 30B".

Subsec. (e)(6). Pub. L. 111–5, §1123(a), added par. (6).

2008—Subsec. (c)(2)(C). Pub. L. 110–343, §207(b), added subpar. (C).

Subsec. (g)(2). Pub. L. 110–343, §207(a), substituted "December 31, 2010" for "December 31, 2009".

2007—Subsec. (b). Pub. L. 110–172, §6(b)(1), reenacted heading without change and amended introductory provisions generally. Prior to amendment, introductory provisions read as follows: "The credit allowed under subsection (a) with respect to any alternative fuel vehicle refueling property shall not exceed—".

Subsec. (c). Pub. L. 110–172, §6(b)(2), reenacted heading without change and amended text generally. Prior to amendment, text read as follows:

"(1) In general.—Except as provided in paragraph (2), the term 'qualified alternative fuel vehicle refueling property' has the meaning given to such term by section 179A(d), but only with respect to any fuel—

"(A) at least 85 percent of the volume of which consists of one or more of the following: ethanol, natural gas, compressed natural gas, liquefied natural gas, liquefied petroleum gas, or hydrogen, or

"(B) any mixture of biodiesel (as defined in section 40A(d)(1)) and diesel fuel (as defined in section 4083(a)(3)), determined without regard to any use of kerosene and containing at least 20 percent biodiesel.

"(2) Residential property.—In the case of any property installed on property which is used as the principal residence (within the meaning of section 121) of the taxpayer, paragraph (1) of section 179A(d) shall not apply."

2005—Subsec. (d)(2)(A). Pub. L. 109–135, §412(d), substituted "regular tax liability (as defined in section 26(b))" for "regular tax".

Subsec. (e)(2). Pub. L. 109–135, §402(k), inserted at end "For purposes of subsection (d), property to which this paragraph applies shall be treated as of a character subject to an allowance for depreciation."

STATUTORY NOTES AND RELATED SUBSIDIARIES

EFFECTIVE DATE OF 2020 AMENDMENT

Pub. L. 116–260, div. EE, title I, §143(b), Dec. 27, 2020, 134 Stat. 3054, provided that: "The amendment made by this section [amending this section] shall apply to property placed in service after December 31, 2020."

EFFECTIVE DATE OF 2019 AMENDMENT

Pub. L. 116–94, div. Q, title I, §125(b), Dec. 20, 2019, 133 Stat. 3231, provided that: "The amendment made by this section [amending this section] shall apply to property placed in service after December 31, 2017."

EFFECTIVE DATE OF 2018 AMENDMENT

Pub. L. 115–123, div. D, title I, §40404(b), Feb. 9, 2018, 132 Stat. 148, provided that: "The amendment made by this section [amending this section] shall apply to property placed in service after December 31, 2016."

EFFECTIVE DATE OF 2015 AMENDMENT

Pub. L. 114–113, div. Q, title I, §182(b), Dec. 18, 2015, 129 Stat. 3072, provided that: "The amendment made by this section [amending this section] shall apply to property placed in service after December 31, 2014."

EFFECTIVE DATE OF 2014 AMENDMENT

Pub. L. 113–295, div. A, title I, §161(b), Dec. 19, 2014, 128 Stat. 4023, provided that: "The amendment made by this section [amending this section] shall apply to property placed in service after December 31, 2013."

Amendment by section 218(b) of Pub. L. 113–295 effective as if included in the provision of the Energy Tax Incentives Act of 2005, Pub. L. 109–58, title XIII, to which such amendment relates, see section 218(c) of Pub. L. 113–295, set out as a note under section 30B of this title.

Amendment by section 221(a)(34)(B) of Pub. L. 113–295 effective Dec. 19, 2014, subject to a savings provision, see section 221(b) of Pub. L. 113–295, set out as a note under section 1 of this title.

EFFECTIVE DATE OF 2013 AMENDMENT

Pub. L. 112–240, title IV, §402(b), Jan. 2, 2013, 126 Stat. 2337, provided that: "The amendment made by this section [amending this section] shall apply to property placed in service after December 31, 2011."

EFFECTIVE DATE OF 2010 AMENDMENT

Pub. L. 111–312, title VII, §711(b), Dec. 17, 2010, 124 Stat. 3315, provided that: "The amendment made by this section [amending this section] shall apply to property placed in service after December 31, 2010."

EFFECTIVE DATE OF 2009 AMENDMENT

Pub. L. 111–5, div. B, title I, §1123(b), Feb. 17, 2009, 123 Stat. 325, provided that: "The amendment made by this section [amending this section] shall apply to taxable years beginning after December 31, 2008."

Amendment by section 1142(b)(3) of Pub. L. 111–5 applicable to vehicles acquired after Feb. 17, 2009, see section 1142(c) of Pub. L. 111–5, set out as an Effective and Termination Dates of 2009 Amendment note under section 24 of this title.

Amendment by section 1144(b)(2) of Pub. L. 111–5 applicable to taxable years beginning after Dec. 31, 2008, see section 1144(c) of Pub. L. 111–5, set out as an Effective and Termination Dates of 2009 Amendment note under section 24 of this title.

EFFECTIVE DATE OF 2008 AMENDMENT

Pub. L. 110–343, div. B, title II, §207(c), Oct. 3, 2008, 122 Stat. 3840, provided that: "The amendments made by this section [amending this section] shall apply to property placed in service after the date of the enactment of this Act [Oct. 3, 2008], in taxable years ending after such date."

EFFECTIVE DATE OF 2007 AMENDMENT

Pub. L. 110–172, §6(e), Dec. 29, 2007, 121 Stat. 2481, provided that:

"(1) In general.—Except as otherwise provided in this subsection, the amendments made by this section [amending this section and sections 41, 45J, 4041, 4042, 4082, and 6430 of this title, and enacting provisions set out as a note under section 6430 of this title] shall take effect as if included in the provisions of the Energy Policy Act of 2005 [Pub. L. 109–58] to which they relate.

"(2) Nonapplication of exemption for off-highway business use.—The amendment made by subsection (d)(3) [amending section 4041 of this title] shall apply to fuel sold for use or used after the date of the enactment of this Act [Dec. 29, 2007].

"(3) Amendment made by the safetea–lu.—The amendment made by subsection (d)(2)(C)(ii) [amending section 4082 of this title] shall take effect as if included in section 11161 of the SAFETEA–LU [Pub. L. 109–59]."

EFFECTIVE DATE OF 2005 AMENDMENT

Amendment by section 402(k) of Pub. L. 109–135 effective as if included in the provision of the Energy Policy Act of 2005, Pub. L. 109–58, to which such amendment relates, see section 402(m)(1) of Pub. L. 109–135, set out as an Effective and Termination Dates of 2005 Amendments note under section 23 of this title.

EFFECTIVE DATE

Pub. L. 109–58, title XIII, §1342(c), Aug. 8, 2005, 119 Stat. 1051, provided that: "The amendments made by this section [enacting this section and amending sections 38, 55, 1016, and 6501 of this title] shall apply to property placed in service after December 31, 2005, in taxable years ending after such date."

SAVINGS PROVISION

For provisions that nothing in amendment by Pub. L. 115–141 be construed to affect treatment of certain transactions occurring, property acquired, or items of income, loss, deduction, or credit taken into account prior to Mar. 23, 2018, for purposes of determining liability for tax for periods ending after Mar. 23, 2018, see section 401(e) of Pub. L. 115–141, set out as a note under section 23 of this title.

§30D. New qualified plug-in electric drive motor vehicles

(a) Allowance of credit

There shall be allowed as a credit against the tax imposed by this chapter for the taxable year an amount equal to the sum of the credit amounts determined under subsection (b) with respect to each new qualified plug-in electric drive motor vehicle placed in service by the taxpayer during the taxable year.

(b) Per vehicle dollar limitation

(1) In general

The amount determined under this subsection with respect to any new qualified plug-in electric drive motor vehicle is the sum of the amounts determined under paragraphs (2) and (3) with respect to such vehicle.

(2) Base amount

The amount determined under this paragraph is $2,500.

(3) Battery capacity

In the case of a vehicle which draws propulsion energy from a battery with not less than 5 kilowatt hours of capacity, the amount determined under this paragraph is $417, plus $417 for each kilowatt hour of capacity in excess of 5 kilowatt hours. The amount determined under this paragraph shall not exceed $5,000.

(c) Application with other credits

(1) Business credit treated as part of general business credit

So much of the credit which would be allowed under subsection (a) for any taxable year (determined without regard to this subsection) that is attributable to property of a character subject to an allowance for depreciation shall be treated as a credit listed in section 38(b) for such taxable year (and not allowed under subsection (a)).

(2) Personal credit

For purposes of this title, the credit allowed under subsection (a) for any taxable year (determined after application of paragraph (1)) shall be treated as a credit allowable under subpart A for such taxable year.

(d) New qualified plug-in electric drive motor vehicle

For purposes of this section—

(1) In general

The term "new qualified plug-in electric drive motor vehicle" means a motor vehicle—

    (A) the original use of which commences with the taxpayer,

    (B) which is acquired for use or lease by the taxpayer and not for resale,

    (C) which is made by a manufacturer,

    (D) which is treated as a motor vehicle for purposes of title II of the Clean Air Act,

    (E) which has a gross vehicle weight rating of less than 14,000 pounds, and

    (F) which is propelled to a significant extent by an electric motor which draws electricity from a battery which—

        (i) has a capacity of not less than 4 kilowatt hours, and

        (ii) is capable of being recharged from an external source of electricity.

(2) Motor vehicle

The term "motor vehicle" means any vehicle which is manufactured primarily for use on public streets, roads, and highways (not including a vehicle operated exclusively on a rail or rails) and which has at least 4 wheels.

(3) Manufacturer

The term "manufacturer" has the meaning given such term in regulations prescribed by the Administrator of the Environmental Protection Agency for purposes of the administration of title II of the Clean Air Act (42 U.S.C. 7521 et seq.).

(4) Battery capacity

The term "capacity" means, with respect to any battery, the quantity of electricity which the battery is capable of storing, expressed in kilowatt hours, as measured from a 100 percent state of charge to a 0 percent state of charge.

(e) Limitation on number of new qualified plug-in electric drive motor vehicles eligible for credit

(1) In general

In the case of a new qualified plug-in electric drive motor vehicle sold during the phaseout period, only the applicable percentage of the credit otherwise allowable under subsection (a) shall be allowed.

(2) Phaseout period

For purposes of this subsection, the phaseout period is the period beginning with the second calendar quarter following the calendar quarter which includes the first date on which the number of new qualified plug-in electric drive motor vehicles manufactured by the manufacturer of the vehicle referred to in paragraph (1) sold for use in the United States after December 31, 2009, is at least 200,000.

(3) Applicable percentage

For purposes of paragraph (1), the applicable percentage is—

(A) 50 percent for the first 2 calendar quarters of the phaseout period,

(B) 25 percent for the 3d and 4th calendar quarters of the phaseout period, and

(C) 0 percent for each calendar quarter thereafter.

(4) Controlled groups

Rules similar to the rules of section 30B(f)(4) shall apply for purposes of this subsection.

(f) Special rules

(1) Basis reduction

For purposes of this subtitle, the basis of any property for which a credit is allowable under subsection (a) shall be reduced by the amount of such credit so allowed (determined without regard to subsection (c)).

(2) No double benefit

The amount of any deduction or other credit allowable under this chapter for a vehicle for which a credit is allowable under subsection (a) shall be reduced by the amount of credit allowed under such subsection for such vehicle (determined without regard to subsection (c)).

(3) Property used by tax-exempt entity

In the case of a vehicle the use of which is described in paragraph (3) or (4) of section 50(b) and which is not subject to a lease, the person who sold such vehicle to the person or entity using such vehicle shall be treated as the taxpayer that placed such vehicle in service, but only if such person clearly discloses to such person or entity in a document the amount of any credit allowable under subsection (a) with respect to such vehicle (determined without regard to subsection (c)). For purposes of subsection (c), property to which this paragraph applies shall be treated as of a character subject to an allowance for depreciation.

(4) Property used outside United States not qualified

No credit shall be allowable under subsection (a) with respect to any property referred to in section 50(b)(1).

(5) Recapture

The Secretary shall, by regulations, provide for recapturing the benefit of any credit allowable under subsection (a) with respect to any property which ceases to be property eligible for such credit.

(6) Election not to take credit

No credit shall be allowed under subsection (a) for any vehicle if the taxpayer elects to not have this section apply to such vehicle.

(7) Interaction with air quality and motor vehicle safety standards

A vehicle shall not be considered eligible for a credit under this section unless such vehicle is in compliance with—

(A) the applicable provisions of the Clean Air Act for the applicable make and model year of the vehicle (or applicable air quality provisions of State law in the case of a State which has adopted such provision under a waiver under section 209(b) of the Clean Air Act), and

(B) the motor vehicle safety provisions of sections 30101 through 30169 of title 49, United States Code.

(g) Credit allowed for 2- and 3-wheeled plug-in electric vehicles

(1) In general

In the case of a qualified 2- or 3-wheeled plug-in electric vehicle—

(A) there shall be allowed as a credit against the tax imposed by this chapter for the taxable year an amount equal to the sum of the applicable amount with respect to each such qualified 2- or 3-wheeled plug-in electric vehicle placed in service by the taxpayer during the taxable year, and

(B) the amount of the credit allowed under subparagraph (A) shall be treated as a credit allowed under subsection (a).

(2) Applicable amount

For purposes of paragraph (1), the applicable amount is an amount equal to the lesser of—

(A) 10 percent of the cost of the qualified 2- or 3-wheeled plug-in electric vehicle, or

(B) $2,500.

(3) Qualified 2- or 3-wheeled plug-in electric vehicle

The term "qualified 2- or 3-wheeled plug-in electric vehicle" means any vehicle which—

(A) has 2 or 3 wheels,

(B) meets the requirements of subparagraphs (A), (B), (C), (E), and (F) of subsection (d)(1) (determined by substituting "2.5 kilowatt hours" for "4 kilowatt hours" in subparagraph (F)(i)),

(C) is manufactured primarily for use on public streets, roads, and highways,

(D) is capable of achieving a speed of 45 miles per hour or greater, and

(E) is acquired—

(i) after December 31, 2011, and before January 1, 2014, or

(ii) in the case of a vehicle that has 2 wheels, after December 31, 2014, and before January 1, 2022.

(Added Pub. L. 110–343, div. B, title II, §205(a), Oct. 3, 2008, 122 Stat. 3835; amended Pub. L. 111–5, div. B, title I, §1141(a), Feb. 17, 2009, 123 Stat. 326; Pub. L. 111–148, title X, §10909(b)(2)(H), (c), Mar. 23, 2010, 124 Stat. 1023; Pub. L. 111–312, title I, §101(b)(1), Dec. 17, 2010, 124 Stat. 3298; Pub. L. 112–240, title I, §104(c)(2)(I), title IV, §403(a), (b), Jan. 2, 2013, 126 Stat. 2322, 2337, 2338; Pub. L. 113–295, div. A, title II, §209(e), Dec. 19, 2014, 128 Stat. 4028; Pub. L. 114–113, div. Q, title I, §183(a), Dec. 18, 2015, 129 Stat. 3072; Pub. L. 115–123, div. D, title I, §40405(a), Feb. 9, 2018, 132 Stat. 148; Pub. L. 116–94, div. Q, title I, §126(a), Dec. 20, 2019, 133 Stat. 3231; Pub. L. 116–260, div. EE, title I, §144(a), Dec. 27, 2020, 134 Stat. 3054.)

EDITORIAL NOTES

REFERENCES IN TEXT

The Clean Air Act, referred to in subsecs. (d)(1)(D), (3), (f)(7)(A), is act July 14, 1955, ch. 360, 69 Stat. 322, which is classified generally to chapter 85 (§7401 et seq.) of Title 42, The Public Health and Welfare. Title II of the Act, known as the National Emissions Standards Act, is classified generally to subchapter II (§7521 et seq.) of chapter 85 of Title 42. Section 209(b) of the Act is classified to section 7543(b) of Title 42. For complete classification of this Act to the Code, see Short Title note set out under section 7401 of Title 42 and Tables.

AMENDMENTS

2020—Subsec. (g)(3)(E)(ii). Pub. L. 116–260 substituted "January 1, 2022" for "January 1, 2021".

2019—Subsec. (g)(3)(E)(ii). Pub. L. 116–94 substituted "January 1, 2021" for "January 1, 2018".

2018—Subsec. (g)(3)(E)(ii). Pub. L. 115–123 substituted "January 1, 2018" for "January 1, 2017".

2015—Subsec. (g)(3)(E). Pub. L. 114–113 substituted "acquired—" for "acquired after December 31, 2011, and before January 1, 2014." and added cls. (i) and (ii).

2014—Subsec. (f)(1), (2). Pub. L. 113–295, §209(e)(1)(A), (B), inserted "(determined without regard to subsection (c))" before period at end.

Subsec. (f)(3). Pub. L. 113–295, §209(e)(2), inserted at end "For purposes of subsection (c), property to which this paragraph applies shall be treated as of a character subject to an allowance for depreciation."

2013—Subsec. (c)(2). Pub. L. 112–240, §104(c)(2)(I), amended par. (2) generally. Prior to amendment, par. (2) related to personal credit with a limitation based on amount of tax.

Subsec. (f)(2). Pub. L. 112–240, §403(b)(1), substituted "vehicle for which a credit is allowable under subsection (a)" for "new qualified plug-in electric drive motor vehicle" and "allowed under such subsection" for "allowed under subsection (a)".

Subsec. (f)(7). Pub. L. 112–240, §403(b)(2), substituted "A vehicle" for "A motor vehicle" in introductory provisions.

Subsec. (g). Pub. L. 112–240, §403(a), added subsec. (g).

2010—Subsec. (c)(2)(B)(ii). Pub. L. 111–148, §10909(b)(2)(H), (c), as amended by Pub. L. 111–312, temporarily substituted "section 25D" for "sections 23 and 25D". See Effective and Termination Dates of 2010 Amendment note below.

2009—Pub. L. 111–5 amended section generally. Prior to amendment, section provided credit with respect to each new qualified plug-in electric drive motor vehicle placed in service and set forth provisions defining "applicable amount" and "new qualified plug-in electric drive motor vehicle" and stating limitations based on vehicle weight, the number of vehicles eligible for credit, and amount of tax liability.

STATUTORY NOTES AND RELATED SUBSIDIARIES
EFFECTIVE DATE OF 2020 AMENDMENT
Pub. L. 116–260, div. EE, title I, §144(b), Dec. 27, 2020, 134 Stat. 3054, provided that: "The amendment made by this section [amending this section] shall apply to vehicles acquired after December 31, 2020."
EFFECTIVE DATE OF 2019 AMENDMENT
Pub. L. 116–94, div. Q, title I, §126(b), Dec. 20, 2019, 133 Stat. 3231, provided that: "The amendment made by this section [amending this section] shall apply to vehicles acquired after December 31, 2017."
EFFECTIVE DATE OF 2018 AMENDMENT
Pub. L. 115–123, div. D, title I, §40405(b), Feb. 9, 2018, 132 Stat. 148, provided that: "The amendment made by this section [amending this section] shall apply to vehicles acquired after December 31, 2016."
EFFECTIVE DATE OF 2015 AMENDMENT
Pub. L. 114–113, div. Q, title I, §183(b), Dec. 18, 2015, 129 Stat. 3073, provided that: "The amendments made by this section [amending this section] shall apply to vehicles acquired after December 31, 2014."
EFFECTIVE DATE OF 2014 AMENDMENT
Amendment by Pub. L. 113–295 effective as if included in the provisions of the American Recovery and Reinvestment Tax Act of 2009, Pub. L. 111–5, div. B, title I, to which such amendment relates, see section 209(k) of Pub. L. 113–295, set out as a note under section 24 of this title.
EFFECTIVE DATE OF 2013 AMENDMENT
Amendment by section 104(c)(2)(I) of Pub. L. 112–240 applicable to taxable years beginning after Dec. 31, 2011, see section 104(d) of Pub. L. 112–240, set out as a note under section 23 of this title.
Pub. L. 112–240, title IV, §403(c), Jan. 2, 2013, 126 Stat. 2338, provided that: "The amendments made by this section [amending this section] shall apply to vehicles acquired after December 31, 2011."
EFFECTIVE AND TERMINATION DATES OF 2010 AMENDMENT
Amendment by Pub. L. 111–148 terminated applicable to taxable years beginning after Dec. 31, 2011, and section is amended to read as if such amendment had never been enacted, see section 10909(c) of Pub. L. 111–148, set out as a note under section 1 of this title.
Amendment by Pub. L. 111–148 applicable to taxable years beginning after Dec. 31, 2009, see section 10909(d) of Pub. L. 111–148, set out as a note under section 1 of this title.
EFFECTIVE DATE OF 2009 AMENDMENT
Amendment by Pub. L. 111–5 applicable to vehicles acquired after Dec. 31, 2009, see section 1141(c) of Pub. L. 111–5, set out as a note under section 30B of this title.
EFFECTIVE DATE
Section applicable to taxable years beginning after Dec. 31, 2008, see section 205(e) of Pub. L. 110–343, set out as an Effective and Termination Dates of 2008 Amendment note under section 24 of this title.

Subpart C—Refundable Credits

EDITORIAL NOTES
AMENDMENTS

2014—Pub. L. 113–295, div. A, title II, §221(a)(5)(A), Dec. 19, 2014, 128 Stat. 4037, struck out item 36A "Making work pay credit".

2010—Pub. L. 111–148, title X, §10909(b)(2)(Q), (c), Mar. 23, 2010, 124 Stat. 1023, as amended by Pub. L. 111–312, title I, §101(b)(1), Dec. 17, 2010, 124 Stat. 3298, temporarily added item 36C "Adoption expenses". See Effective and Termination Dates of 2010 Amendment note set out under section 1 of this title.

Pub. L. 111–148, title I, §1401(d)(2), Mar. 23, 2010, 124 Stat. 220, added item 36B.

2009—Pub. L. 111–5, div. B, title I, §1001(e)(3), Feb. 17, 2009, 123 Stat. 312, added item 36A.

2008—Pub. L. 110–289, div. C, title I, §3011(b)(4), July 30, 2008, 122 Stat. 2891, added item 36 and redesignated former item 36 as 37.

2002—Pub. L. 107–210, div. A, title II, §201(c)(2), Aug. 6, 2002, 116 Stat. 960, which directed amendment of the table of sections for subpart C of part IV of this chapter by adding items 35 and 36 and striking out the last item, was executed to the table of sections for this subpart which is in part IV of subchapter A of this chapter by adding those items and striking out former item 35 "Overpayments of tax" to reflect the probable intent of Congress.

1984—Pub. L. 98–369, div. A, title IV, §471(b), July 18, 1984, 98 Stat. 826, added subpart C heading and analysis of sections for subpart C consisting of items 31, 32 (formerly 43), 33 (formerly 32), 34 (formerly 39), and 35 (formerly 45). Former subpart C, setting out the rules for computing credit for expenses of work incentive programs, was repealed.

§31. Tax withheld on wages

(a) Wage withholding for income tax purposes
(1) In general
The amount withheld as tax under chapter 24 shall be allowed to the recipient of the income as a credit against the tax imposed by this subtitle.

(2) Year of credit
The amount so withheld during any calendar year shall be allowed as a credit for the taxable year beginning in such calendar year. If more than one taxable year begins in a calendar year, such amount shall be allowed as a credit for the last taxable year so beginning.

(b) Credit for special refunds of social security tax
(1) In general
The Secretary may prescribe regulations providing for the crediting against the tax imposed by this subtitle of the amount determined by the taxpayer or the Secretary to be allowable under section 6413(c) as a special refund of tax imposed on wages. The amount allowed as a credit under such regulations shall, for purposes of this subtitle, be considered an amount withheld at source as tax under section 3402.

(2) Year of credit
Any amount to which paragraph (1) applies shall be allowed as a credit for the taxable year beginning in the calendar year during which the wages were received. If more than one taxable year begins in the calendar year, such amount shall be allowed as a credit for the last taxable year so beginning.

(c) Special rule for backup withholding
Any credit allowed by subsection (a) for any amount withheld under section 3406 shall be allowed for the taxable year of the recipient of the income in which the income is received.

(Aug. 16, 1954, ch. 736, 68A Stat. 12; Pub. L. 94–455, title XIX, §1906(b)(13)(D), Oct. 4, 1976, 90 Stat. 1834; Pub. L. 97–248, title III, §§302(a), 308(a), Sept. 3, 1982, 96 Stat. 585, 591; Pub. L. 97–354, §3(i)(4), Oct. 19, 1982, 96 Stat. 1691; Pub. L. 97–448, title III, §306(b)(1), Jan. 12, 1983, 96 Stat. 2405; Pub. L. 98–67, title I, §§102(a), 104(d)(2), Aug. 5, 1983, 97 Stat. 369, 379; Pub. L. 98–369, div. A, title IV, §471(c), title VII, §714(j)(2), July 18, 1984, 98 Stat. 826, 962.)

1984—Subsec. (a)(1). Pub. L. 98–369, §714(j)(2), substituted "as tax under chapter 24" for "under section 3402 as tax on the wages of any individual".

1983—Pub. L. 98–67 added subsec. (c) and repealed amendments made by Pub. L. 97–248. See 1982 Amendment note below.

Pub. L. 97–448 amended subsec. (d) generally. See 1982 Amendment note below.

1982—Pub. L. 97–248, as amended by Pub. L. 97–354 and Pub. L. 97–448, amended section generally, applicable to payments of interest, dividends, and patronage dividends paid or credited after June 30, 1983. Section 102(a), (b) of Pub. L. 98–67, title I, Aug. 5, 1983, 97 Stat. 369, repealed subtitle A (§§301–308) of title III of Pub. L. 97–248 as of the close of June 30, 1983, and provided that the Internal Revenue Code of 1954 [now 1986] [this title] shall be applied and administered (subject to certain exceptions) as if such subtitle A (and the amendments made by such subtitle A) had not been enacted.

1976—Subsec. (b)(1). Pub. L. 94–455 struck out "or his delegate" after "The Secretary" and "(or his delegate)" after "taxpayer or the Secretary".

Pub. L. 98–369, div. A, title VII, §715, July 18, 1984, 98 Stat. 966, provided that: "Any amendment made by this subtitle [subtitle A (§§711–715) of title VII of Pub. L. 98–369, see Tables for classification] shall take effect as if included in the provision of the Tax Equity and Fiscal Responsibility Act of 1982 [Pub. L. 97–248] to which such amendment relates."

Pub. L. 98–67, title I, §110, Aug. 5, 1983, 97 Stat. 384, provided that:

"(a) General Rule.—Except as otherwise provided in this section, the amendments made by this title [enacting sections 3406 and 6705 of this title, amending this section and sections 274, 275, 643, 661, 3402, 3403, 3502, 3507, 6011, 6013, 6015, 6042, 6044, 6049, 6051, 6365, 6401, 6413, 6652, 6653, 6654, 6676, 6678, 6682, 7205, 7215, 7431, 7654, and 7701 of this title, repealing sections 3451 to 3456 of this title, enacting provisions set out as notes under sections 1, 3451, and 6011 of this title, and repealing provisions set out as a note under section 3451 of this title] shall apply with respect to payments made after December 31, 1983.

"(b) Section 102.—The amendments made by section 102 [amending this section and sections 274, 275, 643, 661, 3403, 3502, 3507, 6013, 6015, 6042, 6044, 6049, 6051, 6365, 6401, 6413, 6654, 6682, 7205, 7215, 7654, and 7701 of this title, repealing sections 3451 to 3456 of this title, enacting provisions set out as a note under section 3451 of this title, and repealing provisions set out as a note under section 3451 of this title] shall take effect as of the close of June 30, 1983.

"(c) Sections 104(b) and 107.—The amendments made by sections 104(b) and 107 [amending sections 6682, 7205, and 7431 of this title] shall take effect on the date of the enactment of this Act [Aug. 5, 1983]."

Pub. L. 97–448, title III, §311(d), Jan. 12, 1983, 96 Stat. 2412, provided that: "The amendments made by section 306 [amending this section and sections 48, 55, 263, 291, 312, 338, 401, 501, 1232, 6038A, 6226, 6228, 6679, and 7701 of this title, enacting provisions set out as notes under sections 338 and 1232 of this title, and amending provisions set out as notes under sections 56, 72, 101, 103, 168, 302, 311, 338, 415, 907, and 5701 of this title] shall take effect as if included in the provisions of the Tax Equity and Fiscal Responsibility Act of 1982 [Pub. L. 97–248] to which such amendments relate."

Pub. L. 98–369, div. A, title VII, §701, July 18, 1984, 98 Stat. 942, provided that: "For purposes of applying the amendments made by any title of this Act [see Tables for classification] other than this title, the provisions of this title shall be treated as having been enacted immediately before the provisions of such other titles."

§32. Earned income

(a) Allowance of credit
(1) In general
In the case of an eligible individual, there shall be allowed as a credit against the tax imposed by this subtitle for the taxable year an amount equal to the credit percentage of so much of the taxpayer's earned income for the taxable year as does not exceed the earned income amount.
(2) Limitation
The amount of the credit allowable to a taxpayer under paragraph (1) for any taxable year shall not exceed the excess (if any) of—
(A) the credit percentage of the earned income amount, over
(B) the phaseout percentage of so much of the adjusted gross income (or, if greater, the earned income) of the taxpayer for the taxable year as exceeds the phaseout amount.
(b) Percentages and amounts
For purposes of subsection (a)—
(1) Percentages
The credit percentage and the phaseout percentage shall be determined as follows:

In the case of an eligible individual with:	The credit percentage is:	The phaseout percentage is:
1 qualifying child	34	15.98
2 qualifying children	40	21.06
3 or more qualifying children	45	21.06
No qualifying children	7.65	7.65

(2) Amounts
(A) In general
Subject to subparagraph (B), the earned income amount and the phaseout amount shall be determined as follows:

In the case of an eligible individual with:	The earned income amount is:	The phaseout amount is:
1 qualifying child	$6,330	$11,610
2 or more qualifying children	$8,890	$11,610
No qualifying children	$4,220	$5,280

(B) Joint returns
In the case of a joint return filed by an eligible individual and such individual's spouse, the phaseout amount determined under subparagraph (A) shall be increased by $5,000.
(c) Definitions and special rules
For purposes of this section—
(1) Eligible individual
(A) In general
The term "eligible individual" means—
(i) any individual who has a qualifying child for the taxable year, or
(ii) any other individual who does not have a qualifying child for the taxable year, if—
(I) such individual's principal place of abode is in the United States for more than one-half of such taxable year,
(II) such individual (or, if the individual is married, either the individual or the individual's spouse) has attained age 25 but not attained age 65 before the close of the taxable year, and
(III) such individual is not a dependent for whom a deduction is allowable under section 151 to another taxpayer for any taxable year beginning in the same calendar year as such taxable year.
(B) Qualifying child ineligible
If an individual is the qualifying child of a taxpayer for any taxable year of such taxpayer beginning in a calendar year, such individual shall not be treated as an eligible individual for any taxable year of such individual beginning in such calendar year.
(C) Exception for individual claiming benefits under section 911
The term "eligible individual" does not include any individual who claims the benefits of section 911 (relating to citizens or residents living abroad) for the taxable year.
(D) Limitation on eligibility of nonresident aliens
The term "eligible individual" shall not include any individual who is a nonresident alien individual for any portion of the taxable year unless such individual is treated for such taxable year as a resident of the United States for purposes of this chapter by reason of an election under subsection (g) or (h) of section 6013.
(E) Identification number requirement
No credit shall be allowed under this section to an eligible individual who does not include on the return of tax for the taxable year—
(i) such individual's taxpayer identification number, and
(ii) if the individual is married, the taxpayer identification number of such individual's spouse.
(2) Earned income

(A) The term "earned income" means—

(i) wages, salaries, tips, and other employee compensation, but only if such amounts are includible in gross income for the taxable year, plus

(ii) the amount of the taxpayer's net earnings from self-employment for the taxable year (within the meaning of section 1402(a)), but such net earnings shall be determined with regard to the deduction allowed to the taxpayer by section 164(f).

(B) For purposes of subparagraph (A)—

(i) the earned income of an individual shall be computed without regard to any community property laws,

(ii) no amount received as a pension or annuity shall be taken into account,

(iii) no amount to which section 871(a) applies (relating to income of nonresident alien individuals not connected with United States business) shall be taken into account,

(iv) no amount received for services provided by an individual while the individual is an inmate at a penal institution shall be taken into account,

(v) no amount described in subparagraph (A) received for service performed in work activities as defined in paragraph (4) or (7) of section 407(d) of the Social Security Act to which the taxpayer is assigned under any State program under part A of title IV of such Act shall be taken into account, but only to the extent such amount is subsidized under such State program, and

(vi) a taxpayer may elect to treat amounts excluded from gross income by reason of section 112 as earned income.

(3) Qualifying child

(A) In general

The term "qualifying child" means a qualifying child of the taxpayer (as defined in section 152(c), determined without regard to paragraph (1)(D) thereof and section 152(e)).

(B) Married individual

The term "qualifying child" shall not include an individual who is married as of the close of the taxpayer's taxable year unless the taxpayer is entitled to a deduction under section 151 for such taxable year with respect to such individual (or would be so entitled but for section 152(e)).

(C) Place of abode

For purposes of subparagraph (A), the requirements of section 152(c)(1)(B) shall be met only if the principal place of abode is in the United States.

(D) Identification requirements

(i) In general

A qualifying child shall not be taken into account under subsection (b) unless the taxpayer includes the name, age, and TIN of the qualifying child on the return of tax for the taxable year.

(ii) Other methods

The Secretary may prescribe other methods for providing the information described in clause (i).

(4) Treatment of military personnel stationed outside the United States

For purposes of paragraphs (1)(A)(ii)(I) and (3)(C), the principal place of abode of a member of the Armed Forces of the United States shall be treated as in the United States during any period during which such member is stationed outside the United States while serving on extended active duty with the Armed Forces of the United States. For purposes of the preceding sentence, the term "extended active duty" means any period of active duty pursuant to a call or order to such duty for a period in excess of 90 days or for an indefinite period.

(d) Married individuals

(1) In general

In the case of an individual who is married, this section shall apply only if a joint return is filed for the taxable year under section 6013.

(2) Determination of marital status

For purposes of this section—

(A) In general

Except as provided in subparagraph (B), marital status shall be determined under section 7703(a).

(B) Special rule for separated spouse

An individual shall not be treated as married if such individual—

(i) is married (as determined under section 7703(a)) and does not file a joint return for the taxable year,

(ii) resides with a qualifying child of the individual for more than one-half of such taxable year, and

(iii)(I) during the last 6 months of such taxable year, does not have the same principal place of abode as the individual's spouse, or

(II) has a decree, instrument, or agreement (other than a decree of divorce) described in section 121(d)(3)(C) with respect to the individual's spouse and is not a member of the same household with the individual's spouse by the end of the taxable year.

(e) Taxable year must be full taxable year

Except in the case of a taxable year closed by reason of the death of the taxpayer, no credit shall be allowable under this section in the case of a taxable year covering a period of less than 12 months.

(f) Amount of credit to be determined under tables

(1) In general

The amount of the credit allowed by this section shall be determined under tables prescribed by the Secretary.

(2) Requirements for tables

The tables prescribed under paragraph (1) shall reflect the provisions of subsections (a) and (b) and shall have income brackets of not greater than $50 each—

(A) for earned income between $0 and the amount of earned income at which the credit is phased out under subsection (b), and

(B) for adjusted gross income between the dollar amount at which the phaseout begins under subsection (b) and the amount of adjusted gross income at which the credit is phased out under subsection (b).

[(g) Repealed. Pub. L. 111–226, title II, §219(a)(2), Aug. 10, 2010, 124 Stat. 2403]

[(h) Repealed. Pub. L. 107–16, title III, §303(c), June 7, 2001, 115 Stat. 55]

(i) Denial of credit for individuals having excessive investment income

(1) In general

No credit shall be allowed under subsection (a) for the taxable year if the aggregate amount of disqualified income of the taxpayer for the taxable year exceeds $10,000.

(2) Disqualified income

For purposes of paragraph (1), the term "disqualified income" means—

 (A) interest or dividends to the extent includible in gross income for the taxable year,

 (B) interest received or accrued during the taxable year which is exempt from tax imposed by this chapter,

 (C) the excess (if any) of—

  (i) gross income from rents or royalties not derived in the ordinary course of a trade or business, over

  (ii) the sum of—

   (I) the deductions (other than interest) which are clearly and directly allocable to such gross income, plus

   (II) interest deductions properly allocable to such gross income,

 (D) the capital gain net income (as defined in section 1222) of the taxpayer for such taxable year, and

 (E) the excess (if any) of—

  (i) the aggregate income from all passive activities for the taxable year (determined without regard to any amount included in earned income under subsection (c)(2) or described in a preceding subparagraph), over

  (ii) the aggregate losses from all passive activities for the taxable year (as so determined).

For purposes of subparagraph (E), the term "passive activity" has the meaning given such term by section 469.

(j) Inflation adjustments
(1) In general

In the case of any taxable year beginning after 2015 (2021 in the case of the dollar amount in subsection (i)(1)), each of the dollar amounts in subsections (b)(2) and (i)(1) shall be increased by an amount equal to—

 (A) such dollar amount, multiplied by

 (B) the cost-of-living adjustment determined under section 1(f)(3) for the calendar year in which the taxable year begins, determined by substituting in subparagraph (A)(ii) thereof—

  (i) in the case of amounts in subsection (b)(2)(A), "calendar year 1995" for "calendar year 2016",

  (ii) in the case of the $5,000 amount in subsection (b)(2)(B), "calendar year 2008" for "calendar year 2016", and

  (iii) in the case of the $10,000 amount in subsection (i)(1), "calendar year 2020" for "calendar year 2016".

(2) Rounding
(A) In general

If any dollar amount in subsection (b)(2)(A) (after being increased under subparagraph (B) thereof), after being increased under paragraph (1), is not a multiple of $10, such dollar amount shall be rounded to the nearest multiple of $10.

(B) Disqualified income threshold amount

If the dollar amount in subsection (i)(1), after being increased under paragraph (1), is not a multiple of $50, such amount shall be rounded to the next lowest multiple of $50.

(k) Restrictions on taxpayers who improperly claimed credit in prior year
(1) Taxpayers making prior fraudulent or reckless claims
(A) In general

No credit shall be allowed under this section for any taxable year in the disallowance period.

(B) Disallowance period

For purposes of paragraph (1), the disallowance period is—

 (i) the period of 10 taxable years after the most recent taxable year for which there was a final determination that the taxpayer's claim of credit under this section was due to fraud, and

 (ii) the period of 2 taxable years after the most recent taxable year for which there was a final determination that the taxpayer's claim of credit under this section was due to reckless or intentional disregard of rules and regulations (but not due to fraud).

(2) Taxpayers making improper prior claims

In the case of a taxpayer who is denied credit under this section for any taxable year as a result of the deficiency procedures under subchapter B of chapter 63, no credit shall be allowed under this section for any subsequent taxable year unless the taxpayer provides such information as the Secretary may require to demonstrate eligibility for such credit.

(l) Coordination with certain means-tested programs

For purposes of—

 (1) the United States Housing Act of 1937,

 (2) title V of the Housing Act of 1949,

 (3) section 101 of the Housing and Urban Development Act of 1965,

 (4) sections 221(d)(3), 235, and 236 of the National Housing Act, and

 (5) the Food and Nutrition Act of 2008,

any refund made to an individual (or the spouse of an individual) by reason of this section shall not be treated as income (and shall not be taken into account in determining resources for the month of its receipt and the following month).

(m) Identification numbers

Solely for purposes of subsections (c)(1)(E) and (c)(3)(D), a taxpayer identification number means a social security number issued to an individual by the Social Security Administration (other than a social security number issued pursuant to clause (II) (or that portion of clause (III) that relates to clause (II)) of section 205(c)(2)(B)(i) of the Social Security Act) on or before the due date for filing the return for the taxable year.

(n) Special rules for individuals without qualifying children

In the case of any taxable year beginning after December 31, 2020, and before January 1, 2022—

(1) Decrease in minimum age for credit
(A) In general

Subsection (c)(1)(A)(ii)(II) shall be applied by substituting "the applicable minimum age" for "age 25".

(B) Applicable minimum age

For purposes of this paragraph, the term "applicable minimum age" means—

(i) except as otherwise provided in this subparagraph, age 19,

(ii) in the case of a specified student (other than a qualified former foster youth or a qualified homeless youth), age 24, and

(iii) in the case of a qualified former foster youth or a qualified homeless youth, age 18.

(C) Specified student

For purposes of this paragraph, the term "specified student" means, with respect to any taxable year, an individual who is an eligible student (as defined in section 25A(b)(3)) during at least 5 calendar months during the taxable year.

(D) Qualified former foster youth

For purposes of this paragraph, the term "qualified former foster youth" means an individual who—

(i) on or after the date that such individual attained age 14, was in foster care provided under the supervision or administration of an entity administering (or eligible to administer) a plan under part B or part E of title IV of the Social Security Act (without regard to whether Federal assistance was provided with respect to such child under such part E), and

(ii) provides (in such manner as the Secretary may provide) consent for entities which administer a plan under part B or part E of title IV of the Social Security Act to disclose to the Secretary information related to the status of such individual as a qualified former foster youth.

(E) Qualified homeless youth

For purposes of this paragraph, the term "qualified homeless youth" means, with respect to any taxable year, an individual who certifies, in a manner as provided by the Secretary, that such individual is either an unaccompanied youth who is a homeless child or youth, or is unaccompanied, at risk of homelessness, and self-supporting.

(2) Elimination of maximum age for credit

Subsection (c)(1)(A)(ii)(II) shall be applied without regard to the phrase "but not attained age 65".

(3) Increase in credit and phaseout percentages

The table contained in subsection (b)(1) shall be applied by substituting "15.3" for "7.65" each place it appears therein.

(4) Increase in earned income and phaseout amounts

(A) In general

The table contained in subsection (b)(2)(A) shall be applied—

(i) by substituting "$9,820" for "$4,220", and

(ii) by substituting "$11,610" for "$5,280".

(B) Coordination with inflation adjustment

Subsection (j) shall not apply to any dollar amount specified in this paragraph.

(Added Pub. L. 94–12, title II, §204(a), Mar. 29, 1975, 89 Stat. 30, §43; amended Pub. L. 94–164, §2(c), Dec. 23, 1975, 89 Stat. 971; Pub. L. 94–455, title IV, §401(c)(1)(B), (2), Oct. 4, 1976, 90 Stat. 1557; Pub. L. 95–600, title I, §§104(a)–(e), 105(a), Nov. 6, 1978, 92 Stat. 2772, 2773; Pub. L. 95–615, §202(g)(5), formerly §202(f)(5), Nov. 8, 1978, 92 Stat. 3100, renumbered §202(g)(5) and amended Pub. L. 96–222, title I, §§101(a)(1), (2)(E), 108(a)(1)(A), Apr. 1, 1980, 94 Stat. 194, 195, 223; Pub. L. 97–34, title I, §§111(b)(2), 112(b)(3), Aug. 13, 1981, 95 Stat. 194, 195; Pub. L. 98–21, title I, §124(c)(4)(B), Apr. 20, 1983, 97 Stat. 91; renumbered §32 and amended Pub. L. 98–369, div. A, title IV, §§423(c)(3), 471(c), title X, §1042(a)–(d)(2), July 18, 1984, 98 Stat. 801, 826, 1043; Pub. L. 99–514, title I, §§104(b)(1)(B), 111(a)–(d)(1), title XII, §1272(d)(4), title XIII, §1301(j)(8), Oct. 22, 1986, 100 Stat. 2104, 2107, 2594, 2658; Pub. L. 100–647, title I, §1001(c), 1007(g)(12), Nov. 10, 1988, 102 Stat. 3350, 3436; Pub. L. 101–508, title XI, §§11101(d)(1)(B), 11111(a), (b), (e), Nov. 5, 1990, 104 Stat. 1388–405, 1388-408, 1388-412, 1388-413; Pub. L. 103–66, title XIII, §13131(a)–(d)(1), Aug. 10, 1993, 107 Stat. 433–435; Pub. L. 103–465, title VII, §§721(a), 722(a), 723(a), 742(a), Dec. 8, 1994, 108 Stat. 5002, 5003, 5010; Pub. L. 104–7, §4(a), Apr. 11, 1995, 109 Stat. 95; Pub. L. 104–193, title IV, §451(a), (b), title IX, §§909(a), (b), 910(a), (b), Aug. 22, 1996, 110 Stat. 2276, 2277, 2351, 2352; Pub. L. 105–34, title I, §101(b), title III, §312(d)(2), title X, §1085(a)(1), (b)–(d), Aug. 5, 1997, 111 Stat. 798, 840, 955, 956; Pub. L. 105–206, title VI, §§6003(b), 6010(p)(1), (2), 6021(a), (b), July 22, 1998, 112 Stat. 791, 816, 817, 823, 824; Pub. L. 106–170, title IV, §412(a), Dec. 17, 1999, 113 Stat. 1917; Pub. L. 107–16, title II, §201(c)(3), title III, §303(a)–(f), (h), June 7, 2001, 115 Stat. 47, 55-57; Pub. L. 107–147, title IV, §416(a)(1), Mar. 9, 2002, 116 Stat. 55; Pub. L. 108–311, title I, §104(b), title II, §205, Oct. 4, 2004, 118 Stat. 1169, 1176; Pub. L. 109–135, title III, §302(a), Dec. 21, 2005, 119 Stat. 2608; Pub. L. 109–432, div. A, title I, §106(a), Dec. 20, 2006, 120 Stat. 2938; Pub. L. 110–234, title IV, §4002(b)(1)(B), (2)(O), May 22, 2008, 122 Stat. 1096, 1097; Pub. L. 110–245, title I, §102(a), June 17, 2008, 122 Stat. 1625; Pub. L. 110–246, §4(a), title IV, §4002(b)(1)(B), (2)(O), June 18, 2008, 122 Stat. 1664, 1857, 1858; Pub. L. 111–5, div. B, title I, §1002(a), Feb. 17, 2009, 123 Stat. 312; Pub. L. 111–226, title II, §219(a)(2), Aug. 10, 2010, 124 Stat. 2403; Pub. L. 111–312, title I, §103(c), Dec. 17, 2010, 124 Stat. 3299; Pub. L. 112–240, title I, §103(c), Jan. 2, 2013, 126 Stat. 2319; Pub. L. 113–295, div. A, title II, §§206(a), 221(a)(3), Dec. 19, 2014, 128 Stat. 4027, 4037; Pub. L. 114–113, div. Q, title I, §103(a)–(c), title II, §204(a), Dec. 18, 2015, 129 Stat. 3044, 3045, 3081; Pub. L. 115–97, title I, §11002(d)(1)(D), Dec. 22, 2017, 131 Stat. 2060; Pub. L. 115–141, div. U, title I, §101(a), title IV, §401(b)(4), Mar. 23, 2018, 132 Stat. 1160, 1201; Pub. L. 117–2, title IX, §§9621(a), 9622(a), 9623(a), (b), 9624(a), Mar. 11, 2021, 135 Stat. 152–154.)

INFLATION ADJUSTED ITEMS FOR CERTAIN YEARS

For inflation adjustment of certain items in this section, see Revenue Procedures listed in a table under section 1 of this title.

EDITORIAL NOTES
REFERENCES IN TEXT

The Social Security Act, referred to in subsecs. (c)(2)(B)(v), (m), and (n)(1)(D), is act Aug. 14, 1935, ch. 531, 49 Stat. 620. Parts A, B and E of title IV of the Act are classified generally to parts A (§601 et seq.), B (§620 et seq.), and E (§670 et seq.), respectively, of subchapter IV of chapter 7 of Title 42, The Public Health and Welfare. Sections 205(c)(2)(B)(i) and 407(d)(4), (7) of the Act are classified to sections 405(c)(2)(B)(i) and 607(d)(4), (7), respectively, of Title 42. For complete classification of this Act to the Code, see section 1305 of Title 42 and Tables.

The United States Housing Act of 1937, referred to in subsec. (l)(1), is act Sept. 1, 1937, ch. 896, as revised generally by Pub. L. 93–383, title II, §201(a), Aug. 22, 1974, 88 Stat. 653, which is classified generally to chapter 8 (§1437 et seq.) of Title 42, The Public Health and Welfare. For complete classification of this Act to the Code, see Short Title note under section 1437 of Title 42 and Tables.

The Housing Act of 1949, referred to in subsec. (l)(2), is act July 15, 1949, ch. 338, 63 Stat. 413, as amended. Title V of the Act is classified generally to subchapter III (§1471 et seq.) of chapter 8A of Title 42. For complete classification of this Act to the Code, see Short Title note set out under section 1441 of Title 42 and Tables.

Section 101 of the Housing and Urban Development Act of 1965, referred to in subsec. (l)(3), is section 101 of Pub. L. 89–117, title I, Aug. 10, 1965, 79 Stat. 451, which enacted section 1701s of Title 12, Banks and Banking, and amended sections 1451 and 1465 of Title 42.

Sections 221(d)(3), 235, and 236 of the National Housing Act, referred to in subsec. (l)(4), are classified to sections 1715l(d)(3), 1715z, and 1715z–1, respectively, of Title 12.

The Food and Nutrition Act of 2008, referred to in subsec. (l)(5), is Pub. L. 88–525, Aug. 31, 1964, 78 Stat. 703, which is classified generally to chapter 51 (§2011 et seq.) of Title 7, Agriculture. For complete classification of this Act to the Code, see Short Title note set out under section 2011 of Title 7 and Tables.

CODIFICATION

Pub. L. 110–234 and Pub. L. 110–246 made identical amendments to this section. The amendments by Pub. L. 110–234 were repealed by section 4(a) of Pub. L. 110–246.

PRIOR PROVISIONS

A prior section 32 was renumbered section 33 of this title.

AMENDMENTS

2021—Subsec. (c)(1)(A). Pub. L. 117–2, §9623(b)(1), struck out concluding provisions which read as follows: "For purposes of the preceding sentence, marital status shall be determined under section 7703."

Subsec. (c)(1)(E)(ii). Pub. L. 117–2, §9623(b)(2), struck out "(within the meaning of section 7703)" after "is married".

Subsec. (c)(1)(F). Pub. L. 117–2, §9622(a), struck out heading and text of subpar. (F). Text read as follows: "No credit shall be allowed under this section to any eligible individual who has one or more qualifying children if no qualifying child of such individual is taken into account under subsection (b) by reason of paragraph (3)(D)."

Subsec. (d). Pub. L. 117–2, §9623(a), designated existing provisions as par. (1), inserted heading, and added par. (2).

Subsec. (d)(1). Pub. L. 117–2, §9623(b)(3), struck out "(within the meaning of section 7703)" after "is married".

Subsec. (i)(1). Pub. L. 117–2, §9624(a), substituted "$10,000" for "$2,200".

Subsec. (j)(1). Pub. L. 117–2, §9624(b)(1), inserted "(2021 in the case of the dollar amount in subsection (i)(1))" after "2015" in introductory provisions.

Subsec. (j)(1)(B)(i). Pub. L. 117–2, §9624(b)(2)(A), substituted "subsection (b)(2)(A)" for "subsections (b)(2)(A) and (i)(1)".

Subsec. (j)(1)(B)(iii). Pub. L. 117–2, §9624(b)(2)(B)–(4), added cl. (iii).

Subsec. (n). Pub. L. 117–2, §9621(a), added subsec. (n).

2018—Subsec. (b)(2)(B). Pub. L. 115–141, §101(a)(1), struck out cl. (i) designation and heading and struck out cls. (ii) and (iii) which related to inflation adjustment for taxable years after 2015 and application of rounding provisions in subsec. (j)(2)(A) of this section, respectively.

Subsec. (j)(1). Pub. L. 115–141, §101(a)(2)(A), substituted "after 2015" for "after 1996" in introductory provisions.

Subsec. (j)(1)(B). Pub. L. 115–141, §101(a)(2)(B), inserted "by substituting in subparagraph (A)(ii) thereof" after ", determined" in introductory provisions.

Subsec. (j)(1)(B)(i). Pub. L. 115–141, §101(a)(2)(C), struck out "by substituting" after "(i)(1)," and "in subparagraph (A)(ii) thereof" after " 'calendar year 2016' ".

Subsec. (j)(1)(B)(ii). Pub. L. 115–141, §101(a)(2)(D), substituted "$5,000 amount in subsection (b)(2)(B), 'calendar year 2008' for 'calendar year 2016' " for "$3,000 amount in subsection (b)(2)(B)(iii), by substituting 'calendar year 2007' for 'calendar year 2016' in subparagraph (A)(ii) of such section 1".

Subsec. (l). Pub. L. 115–141, §401(b)(4), struck out ", and any payment made to such individual (or such spouse) by an employer under section 3507," after "reason of this section" in concluding provisions.

2017—Subsecs. (b)(2)(B)(ii)(II), (j)(1)(B)(i), (ii). Pub. L. 115–97 substituted "for 'calendar year 2016' in subparagraph (A)(ii)" for "for 'calendar year 1992' in subparagraph (B)".

2015—Subsec. (b)(1). Pub. L. 114–113, §103(a), amended par. (1) generally. Prior to amendment, par. (1) provided credit and phaseout percentages for eligible individuals with 1, 2 or more, or no qualifying children.

Subsec. (b)(2)(B). Pub. L. 114–113, §103(b), amended subpar. (B) generally. Prior to amendment, text read as follows: "In the case of a joint return filed by an eligible individual and such individual's spouse, the phaseout amount determined under subparagraph (A) shall be increased by $3,000."

Subsec. (b)(3). Pub. L. 114–113, §103(c), struck out par. (3) which provided for increased credit percentage for taxpayers with 3 or more qualifying children and reduction of marriage penalty in taxable years beginning after 2008 and before 2018, with adjustment for inflation.

Subsec. (m). Pub. L. 114–113, §204(a), inserted "on or before the due date for filing the return for the taxable year" before period at end.

2014—Subsec. (b)(1). Pub. L. 113–295, §221(a)(3)(A), struck out subpar. (A) designation, heading "In general", and introductory provisions "In the case of taxable years beginning after 1995:" before the table and struck out subpars. (B) and (C) which related to transitional percentages for 1995 and transitional percentages for 1994, respectively, and realigned margins.

Subsec. (b)(2)(B). Pub. L. 113–295, §221(a)(3)(B), substituted "increased by $3,000." for "increased by—

"(i) $1,000 in the case of taxable years beginning in 2002, 2003, and 2004,

"(ii) $2,000 in the case of taxable years beginning in 2005, 2006, and 2007, and

"(iii) $3,000 in the case of taxable years beginning after 2007."

Subsec. (b)(3)(B)(ii). Pub. L. 113–295, §206(a), substituted "after 2009" for "in 2010" in introductory provisions.

2013—Subsec. (b)(3). Pub. L. 112–240 substituted "for certain years" for "2009, 2010, 2011, and 2012" in heading and "after 2008 and before 2018" for "in 2009, 2010, 2011, or 2012" in introductory provisions.

2010—Subsec. (b)(3). Pub. L. 111–312 substituted "2009, 2010, 2011, and 2012" for "2009 and 2010" in heading and ", 2010, 2011, or 2012" for "or 2010" in introductory provisions.

Subsec. (g). Pub. L. 111–226 struck out subsec. (g). Text read as follows:

"(1) Recapture of excess advance payments.—If any payment is made to the individual by an employer under section 3507 during any calendar year, then the tax imposed by this chapter for the individual's last taxable year beginning in such calendar year shall be increased by the aggregate amount of such payments.

"(2) Reconciliation of payments advanced and credit allowed.—Any increase in tax under paragraph (1) shall not be treated as tax imposed by this chapter for purposes of determining the amount of any credit (other than the credit allowed by subsection (a)) allowable under this part."

2009—Subsec. (b)(3). Pub. L. 111–5 added par. (3).

2008—Subsec. (c)(2)(B)(vi). Pub. L. 110–245 amended cl. (vi) generally. Prior to amendment, cl. (vi) read as follows: "in the case of any taxable year ending—

"(I) after the date of the enactment of this clause, and

"(II) before January 1, 2008,

a taxpayer may elect to treat amounts excluded from gross income by reason of section 112 as earned income."

Subsec. (l)(5). Pub. L. 110–246, §4002(b)(1)(B), (2)(O), substituted "Food and Nutrition Act of 2008" for "Food Stamp Act of 1977".

2006—Subsec. (c)(2)(B)(vi)(II). Pub. L. 109–432 substituted "2008" for "2007".

2005—Subsec. (c)(2)(B)(vi)(II). Pub. L. 109–135 substituted "2007" for "2006".

2004—Subsec. (c)(1)(C) to (G). Pub. L. 108–311, §205(b)(1), redesignated subpars. (D) to (G) as (C) to (F), respectively, and struck out former subpar. (C) which related to 2 or more claiming qualifying child.

Subsec. (c)(2)(B)(vi). Pub. L. 108–311, §104(b), added cl. (vi).

Subsec. (c)(3). Pub. L. 108–311, §205(a), amended par. (3) generally, substituting subpars. (A) to (D) for former subpars. (A) to (E), relating to qualifying child in general, relationship test, age requirements, identification requirements, and place of abode requirements.

Subsec. (c)(4). Pub. L. 108–311, §205(b)(2), substituted "(3)(C)" for "(3)(E)".

Subsec. (m). Pub. L. 108–311, §205(b)(3), substituted "(c)(1)(E)" for "(c)(1)(F)".

2002—Subsec. (g)(2). Pub. L. 107–147 substituted "part" for "subpart".

2001—Subsec. (a)(2)(B). Pub. L. 107–16, §303(d)(1), struck out "modified" before "adjusted gross income".

Subsec. (b)(2). Pub. L. 107–16, §303(a)(1), reenacted par. heading without change, designated existing provisions as subpar. (A), inserted subpar. heading, substituted "Subject to subparagraph (B), the earned" for "The earned", and added subpar. (B).

Subsec. (c)(1)(C). Pub. L. 107–16, §303(f), amended heading and text of subpar. (C) generally. Prior to amendment, text read as follows: "If 2 or more individuals would (but for this subparagraph and after application of subparagraph (B)) be treated as eligible individuals with respect to the same qualifying child for taxable years beginning in the same calendar year, only the individual with the highest modified adjusted gross income for such taxable years shall be treated as an eligible individual with respect to such qualifying child."

Subsec. (c)(2)(A)(i). Pub. L. 107–16, §303(b), inserted ", but only if such amounts are includible in gross income for the taxable year" after "other employee compensation".

Subsec. (c)(3)(A)(ii). Pub. L. 107–16, §303(e)(2)(B), struck out "except as provided in subparagraph (B)(iii)," before "who has".

Subsec. (c)(3)(B)(i). Pub. L. 107–16, §303(e)(1), reenacted heading, introductory provisions, and subcl. (III) of cl. (i) without change and amended subcls. (I) and (II) generally. Prior to amendment, subcls. (I) and (II) read as follows:

"(I) a son or daughter of the taxpayer, or a descendant of either,

"(II) a stepson or stepdaughter of the taxpayer, or."

Subsec. (c)(3)(B)(iii). Pub. L. 107–16, §303(e)(2)(A), reenacted heading without change and amended text generally. Prior to amendment, text read as follows: "For purposes of clause (i)(III), the term 'eligible foster child' means an individual not described in clause (i)(I) or (II) who—

"(I) is a brother, sister, stepbrother, or stepsister of the taxpayer (or a descendant of any such relative) or is placed with the taxpayer by an authorized placement agency,

"(II) the taxpayer cares for as the taxpayer's own child, and

"(III) has the same principal place of abode as the taxpayer for the taxpayer's entire taxable year."

Subsec. (c)(3)(E). Pub. L. 107–16, §303(h), substituted "subparagraph (A)(ii)" for "subparagraphs (A)(ii) and (B)(iii)(II)".

Subsec. (c)(5). Pub. L. 107–16, §303(d)(2)(A), struck out heading and text of par. (5), which defined "modified adjusted gross income" as meaning adjusted gross income without regard to certain described amounts and increased by certain described amounts.

Subsec. (f)(2)(B). Pub. L. 107–16, §303(d)(2)(B), struck out "modified" before "adjusted gross income" in two places.

Subsec. (h). Pub. L. 107–16, §303(c), struck out heading and text of subsec. (h). Text read as follows: "The credit allowed under this section for the taxable year shall be reduced by the amount of tax imposed by section 55 (relating to alternative minimum tax) with respect to such taxpayer for such taxable year."

Subsec. (j)(1)(B). Pub. L. 107–16, §303(a)(2), amended subpar. (B) generally. Prior to amendment, subpar. (B) read as follows: "the cost-of-living adjustment determined under section 1(f)(3) for the calendar year in which the taxable year begins, determined by substituting 'calendar year 1995' for 'calendar year 1992' in subparagraph (B) thereof."

Subsec. (j)(2)(A). Pub. L. 107–16, §303(a)(3), substituted "subsection (b)(2)(A) (after being increased under subparagraph (B) thereof)" for "subsection (b)(2)".

Subsec. (n). Pub. L. 107–16, §201(c)(3), struck out heading and text of subsec. (n), which had increased credit allowable under this section in the case of a taxpayer with respect to whom a child tax credit is allowed under section 24(a), described amount of increase, and set forth provisions relating to coordination with other credits allowable under this part.

1999—Subsec. (c)(3)(B)(iii). Pub. L. 106–170 added subcl. (I) and redesignated former subcls. (I) and (II) as (II) and (III), respectively.

1998—Subsec. (c)(1)(F). Pub. L. 105–206, §6021(a), added introductory provisions and struck out former introductory provisions which read as follows: "The term 'eligible individual' does not include any individual who does not include on the return of tax for the taxable year—".

Subsec. (c)(1)(G). Pub. L. 105–206, §6021(b)(2), added subpar. (G).

Subsec. (c)(2)(B)(v). Pub. L. 105–206, §6010(p)(2), inserted "shall be taken into account" before ", but only".

Subsec. (c)(3)(A)(ii) to (iv). Pub. L. 105–206, §6021(b)(3), inserted "and" at end of cl. (ii), substituted a period for ", and" at end of cl. (iii), and struck out cl. (iv) which read as follows: "with respect to whom the taxpayer meets the identification requirements of subparagraph (D)".

Subsec. (c)(3)(D)(i). Pub. L. 105–206, §6021(b)(1), reenacted heading without change and amended text of cl. (i) generally. Prior to amendment, text read as follows: "The requirements of this subparagraph are met if the taxpayer includes the name, age, and TIN of each qualifying child (without regard to this subparagraph) on the return of tax for the taxable year."

Subsec. (c)(5)(A). Pub. L. 105–206, §6010(p)(1)(A), inserted "and increased by the amounts described in subparagraph (C)" before period at end.

Subsec. (c)(5)(B). Pub. L. 105–206, §6010(p)(1)(B), (C), inserted "or" at end of cl. (iii) and substituted cl. (iv)(III) and concluding provisions for former cls. (iv)(III), (v), (vi), and concluding provisions which read as follows:

"(III) other trades or businesses

"(v) interest received or accrued during the taxable year which is exempt from tax imposed by this chapter, and

"(vi) amounts received as a pension or annuity, and any distributions or payments received from an individual retirement plan, by the taxpayer during the taxable year to the extent not included in gross income.

For purposes of clause (iv), there shall not be taken into account items which are attributable to a trade or business which consists of the performance of services by the taxpayer as an employee. Clause (vi) shall not include any amount which is not includible in gross income by reason of section 402(c), 403(a)(4), 403(b), 408(d)(3), (4), or (5), or 457(e)(10)."

Subsec. (c)(5)(C). Pub. L. 105–206, §6010(p)(1)(C), added subpar. (C).

Subsecs. (m), (n). Pub. L. 105–206, §6003(b), redesignated subsec. (m), relating to supplemental child credit, as (n) and amended text generally. Prior to amendment, text read as follows:

"(1) In general.—In the case of a taxpayer with respect to whom a credit is allowed under section 24 for the taxable year, there shall be allowed as a credit under this section an amount equal to the supplemental child credit (if any) determined for such taxpayer for such taxable year under paragraph (2). Such credit shall be in addition to the credit allowed under subsection (a).

"(2) Supplemental child credit.—For purposes of this subsection, the supplemental child credit is an amount equal to the excess (if any) of—

"(A) the amount determined under section 24(d)(1)(A), over

"(B) the amount determined under section 24(d)(1)(B).

The amounts referred to in subparagraphs (A) and (B) shall be determined as if section 24(d) applied to all taxpayers.

"(3) Coordination with section 24.—The amount of the credit under section 24 shall be reduced by the amount of the credit allowed under this subsection."

1997—Subsec. (c)(2)(B)(v). Pub. L. 105–34, §1085(c), added cl. (v).

Subsec. (c)(4). Pub. L. 105–34, §312(d)(2), struck out "(as defined in section 1034(h)(3))" after "serving on extended active duty" and inserted at end "For purposes of the preceding sentence, the term 'extended active duty' means any period of active duty pursuant to a call or order to such duty for a period in excess of 90 days or for an indefinite period."

Subsec. (c)(5)(B). Pub. L. 105–34, §1085(d)(4), inserted at end of concluding provisions "Clause (vi) shall not include any amount which is not includible in gross income by reason of section 402(c), 403(a)(4), 403(b), 408(d)(3), (4), or (5), or 457(e)(10)."

Subsec. (c)(5)(B)(iv). Pub. L. 105–34, §1085(b), substituted "75 percent" for "50 percent" in introductory provisions.

Subsec. (c)(5)(B)(v), (vi). Pub. L. 105–34, §1085(d)(1)–(3), added cls. (v) and (vi).

Subsec. (k). Pub. L. 105–34, §1085(a)(1), added subsec. (k). Former subsec. (k) redesignated (l).

Subsec. (l). Pub. L. 105–34, §1085(a)(1), redesignated subsec. (k) as (l). Former subsec. (l) redesignated (m).

Subsec. (m). Pub. L. 105–34, §1085(a)(1), redesignated subsec. (l) as (m) relating to identification numbers.

Pub. L. 105–34, §101(b), added subsec. (m) relating to supplemental child credit.

1996—Subsec. (a)(2)(B). Pub. L. 104–193, §910(a), inserted "modified" before "adjusted gross income".

Subsec. (b)(2). Pub. L. 104–193, §909(a)(3), reenacted heading without change and amended text generally. Prior to amendment, text consisted of subpars. (A) and (B) setting out tables for determining the earned income amount for taxable years beginning after 1994 and for taxable years beginning in 1994.

Subsec. (c)(1)(C). Pub. L. 104–193, §910(a), inserted "modified" before "adjusted gross income".

Subsec. (c)(1)(F). Pub. L. 104–193, §451(a), added subpar. (F).

Subsec. (c)(5). Pub. L. 104–193, §910(b), added par. (5).

Subsec. (f)(2)(B). Pub. L. 104–193, §910(a), inserted "modified" before "adjusted gross income" in two places.

Subsec. (i)(1). Pub. L. 104–193, §909(a)(1), substituted "$2,200" for "$2,350".

Subsec. (i)(2). Pub. L. 104–193, §909(b), added subpars. (D) and (E) and concluding provisions.

Subsec. (j). Pub. L. 104–193, §909(a)(2), reenacted heading without change and amended text generally. Prior to amendment, text read as follows:

"(1) In general.—In the case of any taxable year beginning after 1994, each dollar amount contained in subsection (b)(2)(A) shall be increased by an amount equal to—

"(A) such dollar amount, multiplied by

"(B) the cost-of-living adjustment determined under section 1(f)(3), for the calendar year in which the taxable year begins, by substituting 'calendar year 1993' for 'calendar year 1992'.

"(2) Rounding.—If any dollar amount after being increased under paragraph (1) is not a multiple of $10, such dollar amount shall be rounded to the nearest multiple of $10 (or, if such dollar amount is a multiple of $5, such dollar amount shall be increased to the next higher multiple of $10)."

Subsec. (l). Pub. L. 104–193, §451(b), added subsec. (l).

1995—Subsecs. (i) to (k). Pub. L. 104–7 added subsec. (i) and redesignated former subsecs. (i) and (j) as (j) and (k), respectively.

1994—Subsec. (c)(1)(E). Pub. L. 103–465, §722(a), added subpar. (E).

Subsec. (c)(2)(B)(iv). Pub. L. 103–465, §723(a), added cl. (iv).

Subsec. (c)(3)(D)(i). Pub. L. 103–465, §742(a), amended heading and text of cl. (i) generally. Prior to amendment, text read as follows: "The requirements of this subparagraph are met if—

"(I) the taxpayer includes the name and age of each qualifying child (without regard to this subparagraph) on the return of tax for the taxable year, and

"(II) in the case of an individual who has attained the age of 1 year before the close of the taxpayer's taxable year, the taxpayer includes the taxpayer identification number of such individual on such return of tax for such taxable year."

Subsec. (c)(4). Pub. L. 103–465, §721(a), added par. (4).

1993—Subsec. (a). Pub. L. 103–66, §13131(a), amended heading and text of subsec. (a) generally. Prior to amendment, text read as follows: "In the case of an eligible individual, there shall be allowed as a credit against the tax imposed by this subtitle for the taxable year an amount equal to the sum of—

"(1) the basic earned income credit, and

"(2) the health insurance credit."

Subsec. (b). Pub. L. 103–66, §13131(a), substituted "Percentages and amounts" for "Computation of credit" in heading and amended text generally. Prior to amendment, text related to method of computation of both earned income credit and health insurance credit.

Subsec. (c)(1)(A). Pub. L. 103–66, §13131(b), amended heading and text of subpar. (A) generally. Prior to amendment, text read as follows: "The term 'eligible individual' means any individual who has a qualifying child for the taxable year."

Subsec. (c)(3)(D)(ii). Pub. L. 103–66, §13131(d)(1), redesignated cl. (iii) as (ii), substituted "clause (i)" for "clause (i) or (ii)", and struck out heading and text of former cl. (ii). Text read as follows: "In the case of any taxpayer with respect to which the health insurance credit is allowed under subsection (a)(2), the Secretary may require a taxpayer to include an insurance policy number or other adequate evidence of insurance in addition to any information required to be included in clause (i)."

Subsec. (i)(1). Pub. L. 103–66, §13131(c)(1), added par. (1) and struck out text and heading of former par. (1). Text read as follows: "In the case of any taxable year beginning after the applicable calendar year, each dollar amount referred to in paragraph (2)(B) shall be increased by an amount equal to—

"(A) such dollar amount, multiplied by

"(B) the cost-of-living adjustment determined under section 1(f)(3), for the calendar year in which the taxable year begins, by substituting 'calendar year 1984' for 'calendar year 1989' in subparagraph (B) thereof."

Subsec. (i)(2), (3). Pub. L. 103–66, §13131(c), redesignated par. (3) as (2) and struck out former par. (2) which defined terms for purposes of the inflation adjustment in par. (1).

1990—Subsec. (a). Pub. L. 101–508, §11111(a), amended subsec. (a) generally. Prior to amendment, subsec. (a) read as follows: "In the case of an eligible individual, there is allowed as a credit against the tax imposed by this subtitle for the taxable year an amount equal to 14 percent of so much of the earned income for the taxable year as does not exceed $5,714."

Subsec. (b). Pub. L. 101–508, §11111(a), substituted heading for one which read "Limitation" and amended subsec. (b) generally. Prior to amendment, subsec. (b) read as follows: "The amount of the credit allowable to a taxpayer under subsection (a) for any taxable year shall not exceed the excess (if any) of—

"(1) the maximum credit allowable under subsection (a) to any taxpayer, over

"(2) 10 percent of so much of the adjusted gross income (or, if greater, the earned income) of the taxpayer for the taxable year as exceeds $9,000.

In the case of any taxable year beginning in 1987, paragraph (2) shall be applied by substituting '$6,500' for '$9,000'."

Subsec. (c). Pub. L. 101–508, §11111(a), amended subsec. (c) generally, inserting "and special rules" in heading and substituting present provisions for provisions defining "eligible individual" and "earned income".

Subsec. (i)(1)(B). Pub. L. 101–508, §11101(d)(1)(B), substituted "1989" for "1987".

Subsec. (i)(2)(A). Pub. L. 101–508, §11111(e)(1), (2), substituted "clause (i) of subparagraph (B)" for "clause (i) or (ii) of subparagraph (B)" in cl. (i) and "clause (ii)" for "clause (iii)" in cl. (ii).

Subsec. (i)(2)(B). Pub. L. 101–508, §11111(e)(3), amended subpar. (B) generally. Prior to amendment, subpar. (B) read as follows: "The dollar amounts referred to in this subparagraph are—

"(i) the $5,714 amount contained in subsection (a),

"(ii) the $6,500 amount contained in the last sentence of subsection (b), and

"(iii) the $9,000 amount contained in subsection (b)(2)."

Subsec. (j). Pub. L. 101–508, §11111(b), added subsec. (j).

1988—Subsec. (h). Pub. L. 100–647, §1007(g)(12), struck out "for taxpayers other than corporations" after "alternative minimum tax".

Subsec. (i)(3). Pub. L. 100–647, §1001(c), amended par. (3) generally. Prior to amendment, par. (3) read as follows: "If any increase determined under paragraph (1) is not a multiple of $10, such increase shall be rounded to the nearest multiple of $10 (or, if such increase is a multiple of $5, such increase shall be increased to the next higher multiple of $10)."

1986—Subsec. (a). Pub. L. 99–514, §111(a), substituted "14 percent" for "11 percent" and "$5,714" for "$5,000".

Subsec. (b). Pub. L. 99–514, §111(b), amended subsec. (b) generally. Prior to amendment, subsec. (b) read as follows: "The amount of the credit allowable to a taxpayer under subsection (a) for any taxable year shall not exceed the excess (if any) of—

"(1) $550, over

"(2) 122/9 percent of so much of the adjusted gross income (or, if greater, the earned income) of the taxpayer for the taxable year as exceeds $6,500."

Subsec. (c)(1)(A)(i). Pub. L. 99–514, §1301(j)(8), substituted "section 7703" for "section 143".

Pub. L. 99–514, §104(b)(1)(B), substituted "section 151(c)(3)" for "section 151(e)(3)".

Subsec. (c)(1)(C). Pub. L. 99–514, §1272(d)(4), struck out "or 931" after "911" in heading, and amended text generally. Prior to amendment, text read as follows: "The term 'eligible individual' does not include an individual who, for the taxable year, claims the benefits of—

"(i) section 911 (relating to citizens or residents of the United States living abroad),

"(ii) section 931 (relating to income from sources within possessions of the United States)."

Subsec. (d). Pub. L. 99–514, §1301(j)(8), substituted "section 7703" for "section 143".

Subsec. (f)(2)(A), (B). Pub. L. 99–514, §111(d), added subpars. (A) and (B) and struck out former subpars. (A) and (B) which read as follows:

"(A) for earned income between $0 and $11,000, and

"(B) for adjusted gross income between $6,500 and $11,000."

Subsec. (i). Pub. L. 99–514, §111(c), added subsec. (i).

1984—Pub. L. 98–369, §471(c), renumbered section 43 of this title as this section.

Subsec. (a). Pub. L. 98–369, §1042(a), substituted "11 percent" for "10 percent".

Subsec. (b)(1). Pub. L. 98–369, §1042(d)(1), substituted "$550" for "$500".

Subsec. (b)(2). Pub. L. 98–369, §1042(b), substituted "122/9 percent" for "12.5 percent" and "$6,500" for "$6,000".

Subsec. (c)(1)(A)(i). Pub. L. 98–369, §423(c)(3)(A), inserted "or would be so entitled but for paragraph (2) or (4) of section 152(e)".

Subsec. (c)(1)(B). Pub. L. 98–369, §423(c)(3)(B), substituted "as the individual for more than one-half of the taxable year" for "as the individual".

Subsec. (f)(2)(A). Pub. L. 98–369, §1042(d)(2), substituted "between $0 and $11,000" for "between $0 and $10,000".

Subsec. (f)(2)(B). Pub. L. 98–369, §1042(d)(2), substituted "between $6,500 and $11,000" for "between $6,000 and $10,000".

Subsec. (h). Pub. L. 98–369, §1042(c), added subsec. (h).

1983—Subsec. (c)(2)(A)(ii). Pub. L. 98–21 inserted before period at end ", but such net earnings shall be determined with regard to the deduction allowed to the taxpayer by section 164(f)".

1981—Subsec. (c)(1)(C). Pub. L. 97–34 struck out reference to section 913 in heading, substituted "relating to citizens or residents of the United States living abroad" for "relating to income earned by individuals in certain camps outside the United States" in cl. (i), struck out cl. (ii) which made reference to section 913, and redesignated cl. (iii) as (ii).

1980—Subsec. (c)(1)(C). Pub. L. 96–222, §101(a)(1), in heading substituted "who claims benefit of section 911, 913, or 931" for "entitled to exclude income under section 911" and in text substituted "claims the benefits of" for "is entitled to exclude any amounts from gross income under" and inserted reference to section 913 (relating to deduction for certain expenses of living abroad).

Subsecs. (g), (h). Pub. L. 96–222, §101(a)(2)(E), redesignated subsec. (h) as (g).

1978—Subsec. (a). Pub. L. 95–600, §104(a), substituted "subtitle" for "chapter" and "$5,000" for "$4,000".

Subsec. (b). Pub. L. 95–600, §104(b), substituted provision limiting the allowable credit to an amount not to exceed the excess of $500 over 12.5 percent of so much of the adjusted gross income for the taxable year as exceeds $6,000 for provision limiting the allowable credit to an amount reduced by 10 percent of so much of the adjusted gross income for the taxable year as exceeds $4,000.

Subsec. (c)(1). Pub. L. 95–600, §104(e), amended par. (1) generally, substituting in definition of eligible individual one who is married and is entitled to a deduction under section 151 for a child, provided the child has the same principal abode as the individual and the abode is in the United States, is a surviving spouse, or is a head of household, provided the household is in the United States for one who maintains a household in the United States which is the principal abode of that individual and a child of that individual who meets the requirements of section 151(e)(1)(B) or a child of that individual who is disabled within the meaning of section 72(m)(7) and to whom the individual is entitled to claim a deduction under section 151.

Subsec. (c)(1)(C). Pub. L. 95–615, §202(f)(5), which directed the amendment of subsec. (c)(1)(B) by substituting "(relating to income earned by employees in certain camps)" for "(relating to income earned from sources without the United States)", was executed to subsec. (c)(1)(C) to reflect the probable intent of Congress and the general amendment of subsec. (c)(1) by Pub. L. 95–600 which enacted provisions formerly contained in subsec. (c)(1)(B) in subsec. (c)(1)(C).

Subsec. (c)(2)(B). Pub. L. 95–600, §104(d), redesignated cls. (ii) to (iv) as (i) to (iii), respectively. Former cl. (i), which provided that amounts be taken into account only if includible in the gross income of the taxpayer for the taxable year, was struck out.

Subsec. (f). Pub. L. 95–600, §104(c), added subsec. (f).

Subsec. (h). Pub. L. 95–600, §105(a), added subsec. (h).

1976—Subsec. (a). Pub. L. 94–455, §401(c)(1)(B), substituted "is allowed" for "shall be allowed" and struck out provisions relating to the application of the six-month rule.

Subsec. (b). Pub. L. 94–455, §401(c)(1)(B), struck out provisions relating to the application of the six-month rule.

Subsec. (c)(1)(A). Pub. L. 94–455, §401(c)(2), among other changes, substituted "section 44A(f)(1)" for "section 214(b)(3)" and "if such child meets the requirements of section 151(e)(1)(B)" for "with respect to whom he is entitled to claim a deduction under section 151(e)(1)(B)" and inserted reference to a child of that individual who is disabled (within the meaning of section 72(m)(7)) and with respect to whom that individual is entitled to claim a deduction under section 151.

1975—Subsec. (a). Pub. L. 94–164 designated existing provisions as par. (1) and added par. (2).

Subsec. (b). Pub. L. 94–164 designated existing provisions as par. (1) and added par. (2).

STATUTORY NOTES AND RELATED SUBSIDIARIES

EFFECTIVE DATE OF 2021 AMENDMENT

Pub. L. 117–2, title IX, §9621(c), Mar. 11, 2021, 135 Stat. 153, provided that: "The amendment made by this section [amending this section] shall apply to taxable years beginning after December 31, 2020."

Pub. L. 117–2, title IX, §9622(b), Mar. 11, 2021, 135 Stat. 153, provided that: "The amendment made by this section [amending this section] shall apply to taxable years beginning after December 31, 2020."

Pub. L. 117–2, title IX, §9623(c), Mar. 11, 2021, 135 Stat. 154, provided that: "The amendments made by this section [amending this section] shall apply to taxable years beginning after December 31, 2020."

Pub. L. 117–2, title IX, §9624(c), Mar. 11, 2021, 135 Stat. 154, provided that: "The amendments made by this section [amending this section] shall apply to taxable years beginning after December 31, 2020."

EFFECTIVE DATE OF 2018 AMENDMENT

Amendment by section 101(a) of Pub. L. 115–141 effective as if included in the provision of the Protecting Americans from Tax Hikes Act of 2015, div. Q of Pub. L. 114–113, to which such amendment relates, see section 101(s) of Pub. L. 115–141, set out as a note under section 24 of this title.

EFFECTIVE DATE OF 2017 AMENDMENT

Amendment by Pub. L. 115–97 applicable to taxable years beginning after Dec. 31, 2017, see section 11002(e) of Pub. L. 115–97, set out as a note under section 1 of this title.

EFFECTIVE DATE OF 2015 AMENDMENT

Pub. L. 114–113, div. Q, title I, §103(d), Dec. 18, 2015, 129 Stat. 3045, provided that: "The amendments made by this section [amending this section] shall apply to taxable years beginning after December 31, 2015."

Pub. L. 114–113, div. Q, title II, §204(b), Dec. 18, 2015, 129 Stat. 3081, as amended by Pub. L. 115–141, div. U, title I, §101(h), Mar. 23, 2018, 132 Stat. 1162, provided that: "The amendment made by this section [amending this section] shall apply to any return of tax, and any amendment or supplement to any return of tax, which is filed after the date of the enactment of this Act [Dec. 18, 2015]."

EFFECTIVE DATE OF 2014 AMENDMENT

Pub. L. 113–295, div. A, title II, §206(d), Dec. 19, 2014, 128 Stat. 4027, provided that: "The amendments made by this section [amending this section and sections 1397B and 2801 of this title and provisions set out as a note under section 2001 of this title] shall take effect as if included in the provisions of the Tax Relief, Unemployment Insurance Reauthorization, and Job Creation Act of 2010 [Pub. L. 111–312] to which they relate."

Amendment by section 221(a)(3) of Pub. L. 113–295 effective Dec. 19, 2014, subject to a savings provision, see section 221(b) of Pub. L. 113–295, set out as a note under section 1 of this title.

EFFECTIVE DATE OF 2013 AMENDMENT

Amendment by Pub. L. 112–240 applicable to taxable years beginning after Dec. 31, 2012, see section 103(e)(1) of Pub. L. 112–240, set out as a note under section 24 of this title.

EFFECTIVE DATE OF 2010 AMENDMENT

Amendment by Pub. L. 111–312 applicable to taxable years beginning after Dec. 31, 2010, see section 103(d) of Pub. L. 111–312, set out as an Effective and Termination Dates of 2010 Amendment note under section 24 of this title.

Pub. L. 111–226, title II, §219(c), Aug. 10, 2010, 124 Stat. 2403, provided that: "The repeals and amendments made by this section [amending this section and sections 6012, 6051, and 6302 of this title and repealing section 3507 of this title] shall apply to taxable years beginning after December 31, 2010."

EFFECTIVE DATE OF 2009 AMENDMENT

Pub. L. 111–5, div. B, title I, §1002(b), Feb. 17, 2009, 123 Stat. 312, provided that: "The amendments made by this section [amending this section] shall apply to taxable years beginning after December 31, 2008."

EFFECTIVE DATE OF 2008 AMENDMENT

Amendment of this section and repeal of Pub. L. 110–234 by Pub. L. 110–246 effective May 22, 2008, the date of enactment of Pub. L. 110–234, except as otherwise provided, see section 4 of Pub. L. 110–246, set out as an Effective Date note under section 8701 of Title 7, Agriculture.

Amendment by section 4002(b)(1)(B), (2)(O) of Pub. L. 110–246 effective Oct. 1, 2008, see section 4407 of Pub. L. 110–246, set out as a note under section 1161 of Title 2, The Congress.

Pub. L. 110–245, title I, §102(d), June 17, 2008, 122 Stat. 1625, provided that: "The amendments made by this section [amending this section and section 6428 of this title] shall apply to taxable years ending after December 31, 2007."

EFFECTIVE DATE OF 2006 AMENDMENT

Pub. L. 109–432, div. A, title I, §106(b), Dec. 20, 2006, 120 Stat. 2938, provided that: "The amendment made by this section [amending this section] shall apply to taxable years beginning after December 31, 2006."

EFFECTIVE DATE OF 2005 AMENDMENT

Pub. L. 109–135, title III, §302(b), Dec. 21, 2005, 119 Stat. 2608, provided that: "The amendment made by subsection (a) [amending this section] shall apply to taxable years beginning after December 31, 2005."

EFFECTIVE DATE OF 2004 AMENDMENT

Pub. L. 110–245, title I, §102(c), June 17, 2008, 122 Stat. 1625, provided that: "Section 105 of the Working Families Tax Relief Act of 2004 [section 105 of Pub. L. 108–311, set out as a note under section 1 of this title] (relating to application of EGTRRA sunset to this title [probably means title I of Pub. L. 108–311, see Tables for classification]) shall not apply to section 104(b) of such Act [amending this section]."

Pub. L. 108–311, title I, §104(c)(2), Oct. 4, 2004, 118 Stat. 1169, provided that: "The amendments made by subsection (b) [amending this section] shall apply to taxable years ending after the date of the enactment of this Act [Oct. 4, 2004]."

Amendment by section 205 of Pub. L. 108–311 applicable to taxable years beginning after Dec. 31, 2004, see section 208 of Pub. L. 108–311, set out as a note under section 2 of this title.

EFFECTIVE DATE OF 2002 AMENDMENT

Pub. L. 107–147, title IV, §416(a)(2), Mar. 9, 2002, 116 Stat. 55, provided that: "The amendment made by this subsection [amending this section] shall take effect as if included in section 474 of the Tax Reform Act of 1984 [Pub. L. 98–369]."

EFFECTIVE DATE OF 2001 AMENDMENT

Amendment by section 201(c)(3) of Pub. L. 107–16 applicable to taxable years beginning after Dec. 31, 2000, see section 201(e)(1) of Pub. L. 107–16, set out as a note under section 24 of this title.

Pub. L. 107–16, title III, §303(i), June 7, 2001, 115 Stat. 57, provided that:

"(1) In general.—Except as provided in paragraph (2), the amendments made by this section [amending this section and section 6213 of this title] shall apply to taxable years beginning after December 31, 2001.

"(2) Subsection (g).—The amendment made by subsection (g) [amending section 6213 of this title] shall take effect on January 1, 2004."

EFFECTIVE DATE OF 1999 AMENDMENT

Pub. L. 106–170, title IV, §412(b), Dec. 17, 1999, 113 Stat. 1917, provided that: "The amendments made by this section [amending this section] shall apply to taxable years beginning after December 31, 1999."

EFFECTIVE DATE OF 1998 AMENDMENT

Pub. L. 105–206, title VI, §6021(c), July 22, 1998, 112 Stat. 824, provided that:

"(1) Eligible individuals.—The amendment made by subsection (a) [amending this section] shall take effect as if included in the amendments made by section 451 of the Personal Responsibility and Work Opportunity Reconciliation Act of 1996 [Pub. L. 104–193].

"(2) Qualifying children.—The amendments made by subsection (b) [amending this section] shall take effect as if included in the amendments made by section 11111 of Revenue Reconciliation Act of 1990 [Pub. L. 101–508]."

Amendment by sections 6003(b) and 6010(p)(1), (2) of Pub. L. 105–206 effective, except as otherwise provided, as if included in the provisions of the Taxpayer Relief Act of 1997, Pub. L. 105–34, to which such amendment relates, see section 6024 of Pub. L. 105–206, set out as a note under section 1 of this title.

EFFECTIVE DATE OF 1997 AMENDMENT

Amendment by section 101(b) of Pub. L. 105–34 applicable to taxable years beginning after Dec. 31, 1997, see section 101(e) of Pub. L. 105–34, set out as an Effective Date note under section 24 of this title.

Amendment by section 312(d)(2) of Pub. L. 105–34 applicable to sales and exchanges after May 6, 1997, with certain exceptions, see section 312(d) of Pub. L. 105–34, set out as a note under section 121 of this title.

Pub. L. 105–34, title X, §1085(e), Aug. 5, 1997, 111 Stat. 957, provided that:

"(1) The amendments made by subsection (a) [amending this section and sections 6213 and 6695 of this title] shall apply to taxable years beginning after December 31, 1996.

"(2) The amendments made by subsections (b), (c), and (d) [amending this section] shall apply to taxable years beginning after December 31, 1997."

EFFECTIVE DATE OF 1996 AMENDMENT

Pub. L. 104–193, title IV, §451(d), Aug. 22, 1996, 110 Stat. 2277, provided that: "The amendments made by this section [amending this section and section 6213 of this title] shall apply with respect to returns the due date for which (without regard to extensions) is more than 30 days after the date of the enactment of this Act [Aug. 22, 1996]."

Pub. L. 104–193, title IX, §909(c), Aug. 22, 1996, 110 Stat. 2352, provided that:

"(1) In general.—Except as provided in paragraph (2), the amendments made by this section [amending this section] shall apply to taxable years beginning after December 31, 1995.

"(2) Advance payment individuals.—In the case of any individual who on or before June 26, 1996, has in effect an earned income eligibility certificate for the individual's taxable year beginning in 1996, the amendments made by this section shall apply to taxable years beginning after December 31, 1996."

Pub. L. 104–193, title IX, §910(c), Aug. 22, 1996, 110 Stat. 2353, provided that:

"(1) In general.—Except as provided in paragraph (2), the amendments made by this section [amending this section] shall apply to taxable years beginning after December 31, 1995.

"(2) Advance payment individuals.—In the case of any individual who on or before June 26, 1996, has in effect an earned income eligibility certificate for the individual's taxable year beginning in 1996, the amendments made by this section shall apply to taxable years beginning after December 31, 1996."

EFFECTIVE DATE OF 1995 AMENDMENT

Pub. L. 104–7, §4(b), Apr. 11, 1995, 109 Stat. 96, provided that: "The amendments made by this section [amending this section] shall apply to taxable years beginning after December 31, 1995."

EFFECTIVE DATE OF 1994 AMENDMENT

Pub. L. 103–465, title VII, §721(d)(1), Dec. 8, 1994, 108 Stat. 5002, provided that: "The amendment made by subsection (a) [amending this section] shall apply to taxable years beginning after December 31, 1994."

Pub. L. 103–465, title VII, §722(b), Dec. 8, 1994, 108 Stat. 5003, provided that: "The amendment made by subsection (a) [amending this section] shall apply to taxable years beginning after December 31, 1994."

Pub. L. 103–465, title VII, §723(b), Dec. 8, 1994, 108 Stat. 5003, provided that: "The amendment made by subsection (a) [amending this section] shall apply to taxable years beginning after December 31, 1993."

Pub. L. 103–465, title VII, §742(c), Dec. 8, 1994, 108 Stat. 5010, provided that:

"(1) In general.—Except as provided in paragraph (2), the amendments made by this section [amending this section and section 6109 of this title] shall apply to returns for taxable years beginning after December 31, 1994.

"(2) Exception.—The amendments made by this section shall not apply to—

"(A) returns for taxable years beginning in 1995 with respect to individuals who are born after October 31, 1995, and

"(B) returns for taxable years beginning in 1996 with respect to individuals who are born after November 30, 1996."

EFFECTIVE DATE OF 1993 AMENDMENT

Pub. L. 103–66, title XIII, §13131(e), Aug. 10, 1993, 107 Stat. 435, provided that: "The amendments made by this section [amending this section and sections 162, 213, and 3507 of this title] shall apply to taxable years beginning after December 31, 1993."

EFFECTIVE DATE OF 1990 AMENDMENT

Amendment by section 11101(d)(1)(B) of Pub. L. 101–508 applicable to taxable years beginning after Dec. 31, 1990, see section 11101(e) of Pub. L. 101–508, set out as a note under section 1 of this title.

Pub. L. 101–508, title XI, §11111(f), Nov. 5, 1990, 104 Stat. 1388–413, provided that: "The amendments made by this section [amending this section and sections 162, 213, and 3507 of this title] shall apply to taxable years beginning after December 31, 1990."

EFFECTIVE DATE OF 1988 AMENDMENT

Amendment by Pub. L. 100–647 effective, except as otherwise provided, as if included in the provision of the Tax Reform Act of 1986, Pub. L. 99–514, to which such amendment relates, see section 1019(a) of Pub. L. 100–647, set out as a note under section 1 of this title.

EFFECTIVE DATE OF 1986 AMENDMENT

Amendment by sections 104(b)(1)(B) and 111(a)–(d)(1) of Pub. L. 99–514 applicable to taxable years beginning after Dec. 31, 1986, see section 151(a) of Pub. L. 99–514, set out as a note under section 1 of this title.

Amendment by section 1272(d)(4) of Pub. L. 99–514 applicable to taxable years beginning after Dec. 31, 1986, with certain exceptions and qualifications, see section 1277 of Pub. L. 99–514, set out as a note under section 931 of this title.

Amendment by section 1301(j)(8) of Pub. L. 99–514 applicable to bonds issued after Aug. 15, 1986, except as otherwise provided, see sections 1311 to 1318 of Pub. L. 99–514, set out as an Effective Date; Transitional Rules note under section 141 of this title.

EFFECTIVE DATE OF 1984 AMENDMENT

Amendment by section 423(c)(3) of Pub. L. 98–369 applicable to taxable years beginning after Dec. 31, 1984, see section 423(d) of Pub. L. 98–369, set out as a note under section 2 of this title.

Pub. L. 98–369, div. A, title X, §1042(e), July 18, 1984, 98 Stat. 1044, provided that: "The amendments made by this section [amending sections 32 and 3507 of this title] shall apply to taxable years beginning after December 31, 1984."

EFFECTIVE DATE OF 1983 AMENDMENT

Amendment by Pub. L. 98–21 applicable to taxable years beginning after Dec. 31, 1989, see section 124(d)(2) of Pub. L. 98–21, set out as a note under section 1401 of this title.

EFFECTIVE DATE OF 1981 AMENDMENT

Amendment by Pub. L. 97–34 applicable with respect to taxable years beginning after Dec. 31, 1981, see section 115 of Pub. L. 97–34, set out as a note under section 911 of this title.

EFFECTIVE DATE OF 1980 AMENDMENT

Pub. L. 96–222, title I, §101(b)(1)(A), Apr. 1, 1980, 94 Stat. 205, provided that: "The amendment made by subsection (a)(1) [amending this section] shall apply to taxable years beginning after December 31, 1977."

Pub. L. 96–222, title II, §201, Apr. 1, 1980, 94 Stat. 228, provided that: "Except as otherwise provided in title I, any amendment made by title I [see Tables for classification] shall take effect as if it had been included in the provision of the Revenue Act of 1978 [Pub. L. 95–600, see Tables for classification] to which such amendment relates."

EFFECTIVE DATE OF 1978 AMENDMENT

Pub. L. 95–600, title I, §104(f), Nov. 6, 1978, 92 Stat. 2773, provided that: "The amendments made by this section [amending this section] shall apply to taxable years beginning after December 31, 1978."

Pub. L. 95–600, title I, §105(g)(1), Nov. 6, 1978, 92 Stat. 2776, provided that: "The amendments made by subsections (a) and (d) [amending this section and section 6012 of this title] shall apply to taxable years beginning after December 31, 1978."

EFFECTIVE DATE OF 1978 AMENDMENT; ELECTION OF PRIOR LAW

Amendment by Pub. L. 95–615 applicable to taxable years beginning after Dec. 31, 1977, with provision for election of prior law, see section 209 of Pub. L. 95–615, set out as a note under section 911 of this title.

EFFECTIVE AND TERMINATION DATES OF 1976 AMENDMENT

Pub. L. 94–455, title IV, §401(e), Oct. 4, 1976, 90 Stat. 1558, as amended by Pub. L. 95–30, title I, §103(c), May 23, 1977, 91 Stat. 139; Pub. L. 95–600, title I, §103(b), Nov. 6, 1978, 92 Stat. 2771, provided that: "The amendments made by subsection (a) [amending sections 43 [now 32] and 6096 of this title] shall apply to taxable years ending after December 31, 1975, and shall cease to apply to taxable years ending after December 31, 1978. The amendments made by subsection (c) [amending this section] shall apply to taxable years ending after December 31, 1975. The amendments made by subsection (b) [amending sections 141 and 6012 of this title] shall apply to taxable years ending after December 31, 1975. The amendments made by subsection (d) [amending section 3402 of this title] shall apply to wages paid after September 14, 1976."

EFFECTIVE AND TERMINATION DATES OF 1975 AMENDMENT

Pub. L. 94–164, §2(g), Dec. 23, 1975, 89 Stat. 972, as amended by Pub. L. 94–455, §402(b), provided that: "The amendments made by this section [amending sections 43 [now 32], 141, 3402, and 6012 of this title and provisions set out as notes under sections 42 and 43 [now 32] of this title] (other than by subsection (d) [enacting provisions set out as a note under this section]) apply to taxable years ending after December 31, 1975, and before January 1, 1978. Subsection (d) applies to taxable years ending after December 31, 1975."

Pub. L. 94–12, title II, §209(b), Mar. 29, 1975, 89 Stat. 35, as amended by Pub. L. 94–164, §2(f), Dec. 23, 1975, 89 Stat. 972; Pub. L. 94–455, title IV, §401(c)(1)(A), Oct. 4, 1976, 90 Stat. 1557; Pub. L. 95–30, title I, §103(b), May 23, 1977, 91 Stat. 139; Pub. L. 95–600, title I, §103(a), Nov. 6, 1978, 92 Stat. 2771, provided that: "The amendments made by section 204 [enacting this section and amending sections 6201 and 6401 of this title] shall apply to taxable years beginning after December 31, 1974."

SAVINGS PROVISION

For provisions that nothing in amendment by section 401(b)(4) of Pub. L. 115–141 be construed to affect treatment of certain transactions occurring, property acquired, or items of income, loss, deduction, or credit taken into account prior to Mar. 23, 2018, for purposes of determining liability for tax for periods ending after Mar. 23, 2018, see section 401(e) of Pub. L. 115–141, set out as a note under section 23 of this title.

INFORMATION RETURN MATCHING

Pub. L. 117–2, title IX, §9621(b), Mar. 11, 2021, 135 Stat. 153, provided that: "As soon as practicable, the Secretary of the Treasury (or the Secretary's delegate) shall develop and implement procedures to use information returns under section 6050S (relating to returns relating to higher education tuition and related expenses) to check the status of individuals as specified students for purposes of section 32(n)(1)(B)(ii) of the Internal Revenue Code of 1986 (as added by this section)."

TEMPORARY SPECIAL RULE FOR DETERMINING EARNED INCOME FOR PURPOSES OF EARNED INCOME TAX CREDIT

Pub. L. 117–2, title IX, §9626, Mar. 11, 2021, 135 Stat. 157, provided that:

"(a) In General.——If the earned income of the taxpayer for the taxpayer's first taxable year beginning in 2021 is less than the earned income of the taxpayer for the taxpayer's first taxable year beginning in 2019, the credit allowed under section 32 of the Internal Revenue Code of 1986 may, at the election of the taxpayer, be determined by substituting——

"(1) such earned income for the taxpayer's first taxable year beginning in 2019, for

"(2) such earned income for the taxpayer's first taxable year beginning in 2021.

"(b) Earned Income.——

"(1) In general.——For purposes of this section, the term 'earned income' has the meaning given such term under section 32(c) of the Internal Revenue Code of 1986.

"(2) Application to joint returns.——For purposes of subsection (a), in the case of a joint return, the earned income of the taxpayer for the first taxable year beginning in 2019 shall be the sum of the earned income of each spouse for such taxable year.

"(c) Special Rules.——

"(1) Errors treated as mathematical errors.——For purposes of section 6213 of the Internal Revenue Code of 1986, an incorrect use on a return of earned income pursuant to subsection (a) shall be treated as a mathematical or clerical error.

"(2) No effect on determination of gross income, etc.——Except as otherwise provided in this subsection, the Internal Revenue Code of 1986 shall be applied without regard to any substitution under subsection (a).

"(d) Treatment of Certain Possessions.——

"(1) Payments to possessions with mirror code tax systems.——The Secretary of the Treasury shall pay to each possession of the United States which has a mirror code tax system amounts equal to the loss (if any) to that possession by reason of the application of the provisions of this section (other than this subsection) with respect to section 32 of the Internal Revenue Code of 1986. Such amounts shall be determined by the Secretary of the Treasury based on information provided by the government of the respective possession.

"(2) Payments to other possessions.——The Secretary of the Treasury shall pay to each possession of the United States which does not have a mirror code tax system amounts estimated by the Secretary of the Treasury as being equal to the aggregate benefits (if any) that would have been provided to residents of such possession by reason of the provisions of this section (other than this subsection) with respect to section 32 of the Internal Revenue Code of 1986 if a mirror code tax system had been in effect in such possession. The preceding sentence shall not apply unless the respective possession has a plan, which has been approved by the Secretary of the Treasury, under which such possession will promptly distribute such payments to its residents.

"(3) Mirror code tax system.——For purposes of this section, the term 'mirror code tax system' means, with respect to any possession of the United States, the income tax system of such possession if the income tax liability of the residents of such possession under such system is determined by reference to the income tax laws of the United States as if such possession were the United States.

"(4) Treatment of payments.—For purposes of section 1324 of title 31, United States Code, the payments under this section shall be treated in the same manner as a refund due from a credit provision referred to in subsection (b)(2) of such section."

TEMPORARY SPECIAL RULE FOR DETERMINATION OF EARNED INCOME

Pub. L. 116–260, div. EE, title II, §211, Dec. 27, 2020, 134 Stat. 3066, provided that:

"(a) In General.—If the earned income of the taxpayer for the taxpayer's first taxable year beginning in 2020 is less than the earned income of the taxpayer for the preceding taxable year, the credits allowed under sections 24(d) and 32 of the Internal Revenue Code of 1986 may, at the election of the taxpayer, be determined by substituting—

"(1) such earned income for the preceding taxable year, for

"(2) such earned income for the taxpayer's first taxable year beginning in 2020.

"(b) Earned Income.—

"(1) In general.—For purposes of this section, the term 'earned income' has the meaning given such term under section 32(c) of the Internal Revenue Code of 1986.

"(2) Application to joint returns.—For purposes of subsection (a), in the case of a joint return, the earned income of the taxpayer for the preceding taxable year shall be the sum of the earned income of each spouse for such preceding taxable year.

"(c) Special Rules.—

"(1) Errors treated as mathematical error.—For purposes of section 6213 of the Internal Revenue Code of 1986, an incorrect use on a return of earned income pursuant to subsection (a) shall be treated as a mathematical or clerical error.

"(2) No effect on determination of gross income, etc.—Except as otherwise provided in this section, the Internal Revenue Code of 1986 shall be applied without regard to any substitution under subsection (a)."

STUDY ON EARNED INCOME TAX CREDIT CERTIFICATION PROGRAM

Pub. L. 108–199, div. F, title II, §206, Jan. 23, 2004, 118 Stat. 319, provided that:

"(a) Study.—The Internal Revenue Service shall conduct a study, as a part of any program that requires certification (including pre-certification) in order to claim the earned income tax credit under section 32 of the Internal Revenue Code of 1986, on the following matters:

"(1) The costs (in time and money) incurred by the participants in the program.

"(2) The administrative costs incurred by the Internal Revenue Service in operating the program.

"(3) The percentage of individuals included in the program who were not certified for the credit, including the percentage of individuals who were not certified due to—

"(A) ineligibility for the credit; and

"(B) failure to complete the requirements for certification.

"(4) The percentage of individuals to whom paragraph (3)(B) applies who were—

"(A) otherwise eligible for the credit; and

"(B) otherwise ineligible for the credit.

"(5) The percentage of individuals to whom paragraph (3)(B) applies who—

"(A) did not respond to the request for certification; and

"(B) responded to such request but otherwise failed to complete the requirements for certification.

"(6) The reasons—

"(A) for which individuals described in paragraph (5)(A) did not respond to requests for certification; and

"(B) for which individuals described in paragraph (5)(B) had difficulty in completing the requirements for certification.

"(7) The characteristics of those individuals who were denied the credit due to—

"(A) failure to complete the requirements for certification; and

"(B) ineligibility for the credit.

"(8) The impact of the program on non-English speaking participants.

"(9) The impact of the program on homeless and other highly transient individuals.

"(b) Report.—

"(1) Preliminary report.—Not later than July 30, 2004, the Commissioner of the Internal Revenue Service shall submit to Congress a preliminary report on the study conducted under subsection (a).

"(2) Final report.—Not later than June 30, 2005, the Commissioner of the Internal Revenue Service shall submit to Congress a final report detailing the findings of the study conducted under subsection (a)."

PROGRAM TO INCREASE PUBLIC AWARENESS

Secretary of the Treasury, or Secretary's delegate, to establish taxpayer awareness program to inform taxpaying public of availability of earned income credit and child health insurance under this section, see section 11114 of Pub. L. 101–508, set out as a note under section 21 of this title.

EMPLOYEE NOTIFICATION

Pub. L. 99–514, title I, §111(e), Oct. 22, 1986, 100 Stat. 2108, provided that: "The Secretary of the Treasury is directed to require, under regulations, employers to notify any employee who has not had any tax withheld from wages (other than an employee whose wages are exempt from withholding pursuant to section 3402(n) of the Internal Revenue Code of 1986) that such employee may be eligible for a refund because of the earned income credit."

DISREGARD OF REFUND FOR DETERMINATION OF ELIGIBILITY FOR FEDERAL BENEFITS OR ASSISTANCE

Pub. L. 94–164, §2(d), Dec. 23, 1975, 89 Stat. 972, as amended by Pub. L. 94–455, title IV, §402(a), Oct. 4, 1976, 90 Stat. 1558; Pub. L. 95–600, title I, §105(f), Nov. 6, 1978, 92 Stat. 2776; Pub. L. 99–514, §2, Oct. 22, 1986, 100 Stat. 2095, provided that: "Any refund of Federal income taxes made to any individual by reason of section 43 [now 32] of the Internal Revenue Code of 1986 [formerly I.R.C. 1954] (relating to earned income credit), and any payment made by an employer under [former] section 3507 of such Code (relating to advance payment of earned income credit) shall not be taken into account in any year ending before 1980 as income or receipts for purposes of determining the eligibility, for the month in which such refund is made or any month thereafter of such individual or any other individual for benefits or assistance, or the amount or extent of benefits or assistance, under any Federal program or under any State or local program financed in whole or in part with Federal funds, but only if such individual (or the family unit of which he is a member) is a recipient of benefits or assistance under such a program for the month before the month in which such refund is made."

[Pub. L. 95–600, title I, §105(g)(3), Nov. 6, 1978, 92 Stat. 2776, provided that: "Subsection (f) [amending section 2(d) of Pub. L. 94–164, set out above] shall take effect on the date of enactment of this Act [Nov. 6, 1978]."]

§33. Tax withheld at source on nonresident aliens and foreign corporations

There shall be allowed as a credit against the tax imposed by this subtitle the amount of tax withheld at source under subchapter A of chapter 3 (relating to withholding of tax on nonresident aliens and on foreign corporations).

(Aug. 16, 1954, ch. 736, 68A Stat. 13, §32; renumbered §33 and amended Pub. L. 98–369, div. A, title IV, §§471(c), 474(j), July 18, 1984, 98 Stat. 826, 832.)

A prior section 33 was renumbered section 27 of this title.

1984—Pub. L. 98–369, §471(c), renumbered section 32 of this title as this section.

Pub. L. 98–369, §474(j), amended section generally, striking out "and on tax-free covenant bonds" after "foreign corporations" in section catchline, and, in text, substituting "as a credit against the tax imposed by this subtitle" for "as credits against the tax imposed by this chapter", and striking out designation "(1)" before "the amount of tax withheld", and ", and (2) the amount of tax withheld at source under subchapter B of chapter 3 (relating to interest on tax-free covenant bonds)" after "on foreign corporations)".

Pub. L. 98–369, div. A, title IV, §475(b), July 18, 1984, 98 Stat. 847, provided that: "The amendments made by subsections (j) and (r)(29) [amending this section and sections 12, 164, 1441, 1442, 6049, and 7701 of this title and repealing section 1451 of this title] shall not apply with respect to obligations issued before January 1, 1984."

§34. Certain uses of gasoline and special fuels

(a) General rule

There shall be allowed as a credit against the tax imposed by this subtitle for the taxable year an amount equal to the sum of the amounts payable to the taxpayer—

(1) under section 6420 (determined without regard to section 6420(g)),

(2) under section 6421 (determined without regard to section 6421(i)), and

(3) under section 6427 (determined without regard to section 6427(k)).

(b) Exception

Credit shall not be allowed under subsection (a) for any amount payable under section 6421 or 6427, if a claim for such amount is timely filed and, under section 6421(i) or 6427(k), is payable under such section.

(Added Pub. L. 89–44, title VIII, 809(c), June 21, 1965, 79 Stat. 167, §39; amended Pub. L. 91–258, title II, §207(c), May 21, 1970, 84 Stat. 248; Pub. L. 94–455, title XIX, §§1901(a)(3), 1906(b)(8), (9), Oct. 4, 1976, 90 Stat. 1764, 1834; Pub. L. 94–530, §1(c)(1), Oct. 17, 1976, 90 Stat. 2487; Pub. L. 95–599, title V, §505(c)(1), Nov. 6, 1978, 92 Stat. 2760; Pub. L. 95–618, title II, §233(b)(2)(C), Nov. 9, 1978, 92 Stat. 3191; Pub. L. 96–223, title II, §232(d)(4)(A), Apr. 2, 1980, 94 Stat. 278; Pub. L. 97–424, title V, §515(b)(6)(A)–(C), Jan. 6, 1983, 96 Stat. 2181; renumbered §34 and amended Pub. L. 98–369, div. A, title IV, §471(c), title IX, §911(d)(2)(A), July 18, 1984, 98 Stat. 826, 1006; Pub. L. 99–514, title XVII, §1703(e)(2)(F), title XVIII, §1877(a), Oct. 22, 1986, 100 Stat. 2778, 2902; Pub. L. 100–647, title I, §1017(c)(2), Nov. 10, 1988, 102 Stat. 3576; Pub. L. 104–188, title I, §1606(b)(1), Aug. 20, 1996, 110 Stat. 1839; Pub. L. 105–206, title VI, §6023(24)(B), July 22, 1998, 112 Stat. 826; Pub. L. 110–172, §11(a)(4), Dec. 29, 2007, 121 Stat. 2484.)

A prior section 34, acts Aug. 16, 1954, ch. 736, 68A Stat. 13; June 25, 1959, Pub. L. 86–69, §3(a)(1), 73 Stat. 139; Sept. 14, 1960, Pub. L. 86–779, §10(e), 74 Stat. 1009; Feb. 26, 1964, Pub. L. 88–272, title II, §201(a), 78 Stat. 31, related to dividends received by individuals, prior to repeal by Pub. L. 88–272, title II, §201(b), Feb. 26, 1964, 78 Stat. 31, effective with respect to dividends received after Dec. 31, 1964.

2007—Subsec. (a)(1). Pub. L. 110–172, §11(a)(4)(A), struck out "with respect to gasoline used during the taxable year on a farm for farming purposes" before "(determined without regard to section 6420(g))".

Subsec. (a)(2). Pub. L. 110–172, §11(a)(4)(B), which directed striking out "with respect to gasoline used during the taxable year: (A) otherwise than as a fuel in a highway vehicle; or (B) in vehicles while engaged in furnishing certain public passenger land transportation service", was executed by striking out "with respect to gasoline used during the taxable year (A) otherwise than as a fuel in a highway vehicle or (B) in vehicles while engaged in furnishing certain public passenger land transportation service" before "(determined without regard to section 6421(i))", to reflect the probable intent of Congress.

Subsec. (a)(3). Pub. L. 110–172, §11(a)(4)(C), struck out "with respect to fuels used for nontaxable purposes or resold during the taxable year" before "(determined without regard to section 6427(k))".

1998—Subsec. (b). Pub. L. 105–206 substituted "section 6421(i)" for "section 6421(j)".

1996—Subsec. (a)(3). Pub. L. 104–188 amended par. (3) generally. Prior to amendment, par. (3) read as follows: "under section 6427—

"(A) with respect to fuels used for nontaxable purposes or resold, or

"(B) with respect to any qualified diesel-powered highway vehicle purchased (or deemed purchased under section 6427(g)(6)),

during the taxable year (determined without regard to section 6427(k))".

1988—Subsec. (b). Pub. L. 100–647 substituted "section 6421(j) or 6427(k)" for "section 6421(i) or 6427(j)".

1986—Subsec. (a)(3). Pub. L. 99–514, §1877(a), amended par. (3) generally. Prior to amendment, par. (3) read as follows: "under section 6427 with respect to fuels used for nontaxable purposes or resold during the taxable year (determined without regard to section 6427(j))."

Pub. L. 99–514, §1703(e)(2)(F), substituted "6427(k)" for "6427(j)".

1984—Pub. L. 98–369, §471(c), renumbered section 39 of this title as this section.

Subsec. (a)(3). Pub. L. 98–369, §911(d)(2)(A), which directed the amendment of par. (4) by substituting "6427(j)" for "6427(i)" was executed to par. (3) to reflect the probable intent of Congress and the redesignation of par. (4) as (3) by Pub. L. 97–424.

Subsec. (b). Pub. L. 98–369, §911(d)(2)(A), substituted "6427(j)" for "6427(i)".

1983—Pub. L. 97–424, §515(b)(6)(C), substituted "and special fuels" for ", special fuels, and lubricating oil" after "gasoline" in section catchline.

Subsec. (a)(2) to (4). Pub. L. 97–424, §515(b)(6)(A), inserted "and" at end of par. (2), redesignated par. (4) as (3), and struck out former (3) which referred to amounts payable to the taxpayer under section 6424 with respect to lubricating oil used during the taxable year for certain nontaxable purposes (determined without regard to section 6424(f)).

Subsec. (b). Pub. L. 97–424, §515(b)(6)(B)(i), substituted "6421 or 6427" for "6421, 6424, or 6427" after "amount payable under".

Pub. L. 97–424, §515(b)(6)(B)(ii), substituted "6421(i) or 6427(i)" for "6421(i), 6424(f), or 6427(i)" after "and, under".

1980—Subsec. (a)(4). Pub. L. 96–223 substituted "6427(i)" for "6427(h)".

Subsec. (b). Pub. L. 96–223 substituted "6427(i)" for "6427(h)".

1978—Subsec. (a)(3). Pub. L. 95–618 substituted "for certain nontaxable purposes" for "otherwise than in a highway motor vehicle".

Subsec. (a)(4). Pub. L. 95–599 substituted "6427(h)" for "6427(g)".

Subsec. (b). Pub. L. 95–599 substituted "6427(h)" for "6427(g)".

1976—Subsec. (a)(1). Pub. L. 94–455, §1906(b)(8), substituted "6420(g)" for "6420(h)".

Subsec. (a)(3). Pub. L. 94–455, §1906(b)(9), substituted "6424(f)" for "6424(g)".

Subsec. (a)(4). Pub. L. 94–530 substituted "6427(g)" for "6427(f)".

Subsec. (b). Pub. L. 94–530, which directed the amendment of subsec. (c) by substituting "6427(g)" for "6427(f)", was executed to subsec. (b) to reflect the probable intent of Congress and the redesignation of subsec. (c) as (b) by Pub. L. 94–455.

Pub. L. 94–455, §1901(a)(3), redesignated subsec. (c) as (b) and substituted "section 6421(i), 6424(f), or 6427(f), is payable" for "section 6421(i), 6424(g) or 6427(f) is payable". Former subsec. (b), relating to determination of taxpayers first taxable year with respect to tax credit for certain uses of gasoline and lubricating oil, was struck out.

Subsec. (c). Pub. L. 94–455, §1901(a)(3), redesignated subsec. (c) as (b).

1970—Pub. L. 91–258, §207(c)(1), inserted reference to special fuels in section catchline.

Subsec. (a)(4). Pub. L. 91–258, §207(c)(2), added par. (4).

Subsec. (c). Pub. L. 91–258, §207(c)(3), (4), inserted references to sections 6427 and 6427(f), respectively.

STATUTORY NOTES AND RELATED SUBSIDIARIES

EFFECTIVE DATE OF 1998 AMENDMENT

Pub. L. 105–206, title VI, §6023(32), July 22, 1998, 112 Stat. 826, provided that: "The amendments made by this section [amending this section and sections 45A, 59, 72, 142, 501, 512, 543, 871, 1017, 1250, 3121, 3401, 4092, 4221, 4222, 4973, 4975, 6039, 6050R, 6103, 6416, 6421, 6427, 6501, 7434, 7702B, 7872, and 9502 of this title] shall take effect on the date of the enactment of this Act [July 22, 1998]."

EFFECTIVE DATE OF 1996 AMENDMENT

Pub. L. 104–188, title I, §1606(c), Aug. 20, 1996, 110 Stat. 1839, provided that: "The amendments made by this section [amending this section and section 6427 of this title] shall apply to vehicles purchased after the date of the enactment of this Act [Aug. 20, 1996]."

EFFECTIVE DATE OF 1988 AMENDMENT

Amendment by Pub. L. 100–647 effective, except as otherwise provided, as if included in the provision of the Tax Reform Act of 1986, Pub. L. 99–514, to which such amendment relates, see section 1019(a) of Pub. L. 100–647, set out as a note under section 1 of this title.

EFFECTIVE DATE OF 1986 AMENDMENT

Amendment by section 1703(e)(2)(F) of Pub. L. 99–514 applicable to gasoline removed (as defined in section 4082 of this title as amended by section 1703 of Pub. L. 99–514) after Dec. 31, 1987, see section 1703(h) of Pub. L. 99–514 set out as a note under section 4081 of this title.

Amendment by section 1877(a) of Pub. L. 99–514 effective, except as otherwise provided, as if included in the provisions of the Tax Reform Act of 1984, Pub. L. 98–369, div. A, to which such amendment relates, see section 1881 of Pub. L. 99–514, set out as a note under section 48 of this title.

EFFECTIVE DATE OF 1984 AMENDMENT

Amendment by section 911(d)(2)(A) of Pub. L. 98–369 effective Aug. 1, 1984, see section 911(e) of Pub. L. 98–369, set out as a note under section 6427 of this title.

EFFECTIVE DATE OF 1983 AMENDMENT

Pub. L. 97–424, title V, §515(c), Jan. 6, 1983, 96 Stat. 2182, provided that: "The amendments made by this section [amending sections 39 [now 34], 874, 882, 4101, 4102, 4221, 4222, 6201, 6206, 6416, 6421, 6504, 6675, 7210, 7603 to 7605, 7609, and 7610 of this title and repealing sections 4091 to 4094 and 6424 of this title] shall apply with respect to articles sold after the date of the enactment of this Act [Jan. 6, 1983]."

EFFECTIVE DATE OF 1980 AMENDMENT

Amendment by Pub. L. 96–223 effective on Jan. 1, 1979, see section 232(h)(2) of Pub. L. 96–223, set out as a note under section 6427 of this title.

EFFECTIVE DATE OF 1978 AMENDMENT

Pub. L. 95–618, title II, §233(d), Nov. 9, 1978, 92 Stat. 3192, provided that: "The amendments made by this section [amending sections 39 [now 34], 4041, 4221, 4483, 6416, 6421, 6424, 6427, 6504, and 6675 of this title and amending a provision set out as a note under section 120 of Title 23, Highways] shall take effect on the first day of the first calendar month which begins more than 10 days after the date of the enactment of this Act [Nov. 9, 1978]."

Amendment by Pub. L. 95–599 effective Jan. 1, 1979, see section 505(d) of Pub. L. 95–599, set out as a note under section 6427 of this title.

EFFECTIVE DATE OF 1976 AMENDMENTS

Amendment by Pub. L. 94–530 effective on Oct. 1, 1976, see section 1(d) of Pub. L. 94–530, set out as a note under section 4041 of this title.

Amendment by section 1901(a)(3) of Pub. L. 94–455 applicable with respect to taxable years beginning after Dec. 31, 1976, see section 1901(d) of Pub. L. 94–455, set out as a note under section 2 of this title.

Amendment by section 1906(b)(8), (9) of Pub. L. 94–455, to take effect on Feb. 1, 1977, see section 1906(d) of Pub. L. 94–455, set out as a note under section 6013 of this title.

EFFECTIVE DATE OF 1970 AMENDMENT

Amendment by Pub. L. 91–258 applicable with respect to taxable years ending after June 30, 1970, see section 211(b) of Pub. L. 91–258, set out as a note under section 4041 of this title.

EFFECTIVE DATE

Section applicable to taxable years beginning on or after July 1, 1965, see section 809(f) of Pub. L. 89–44, set out as an Effective Date of 1965 Amendment note under section 6420 of this title.

§35. Health insurance costs of eligible individuals

(a) In general

In the case of an individual, there shall be allowed as a credit against the tax imposed by subtitle A an amount equal to 72.5 percent of the amount paid by the taxpayer for coverage of the taxpayer and qualifying family members under qualified health insurance for eligible coverage months beginning in the taxable year.

(b) Eligible coverage month

For purposes of this section—

(1) In general

The term "eligible coverage month" means any month if—

 (A) as of the first day of such month, the taxpayer—

  (i) is an eligible individual,

  (ii) is covered by qualified health insurance, the premium for which is paid by the taxpayer,

  (iii) does not have other specified coverage, and

  (iv) is not imprisoned under Federal, State, or local authority, and

(B) such month begins more than 90 days after the date of the enactment of the Trade Act of 2002, and before January 1, 2022.

(2) Joint returns

In the case of a joint return, the requirements of paragraph (1)(A) shall be treated as met with respect to any month if at least 1 spouse satisfies such requirements.

(c) Eligible individual

For purposes of this section—

(1) In general

The term "eligible individual" means—

(A) an eligible TAA recipient,

(B) an eligible alternative TAA recipient, and

(C) an eligible PBGC pension recipient.

(2) Eligible TAA recipient

(A) In general

Except as provided in subparagraph (B), the term "eligible TAA recipient" means, with respect to any month, any individual who is receiving for any day of such month a trade readjustment allowance under chapter 2 of title II of the Trade Act of 1974 or who would be eligible to receive such allowance if section 231 of such Act were applied without regard to subsection (a)(3)(B) of such section. An individual shall continue to be treated as an eligible TAA recipient during the first month that such individual would otherwise cease to be an eligible TAA recipient by reason of the preceding sentence.

(B) Special rule

In the case of any eligible coverage month beginning after the date of the enactment of this paragraph, the term "eligible TAA recipient" means, with respect to any month, any individual who—

(i) is receiving for any day of such month a trade readjustment allowance under chapter 2 of title II of the Trade Act of 1974,

(ii) would be eligible to receive such allowance except that such individual is in a break in training provided under a training program approved under section 236 of such Act that exceeds the period specified in section 233(e) of such Act, but is within the period for receiving such allowances provided under section 233(a) of such Act, or

(iii) is receiving unemployment compensation (as defined in section 85(b)) for any day of such month and who would be eligible to receive such allowance for such month if section 231 of such Act were applied without regard to subsections (a)(3)(B) and (a)(5) thereof.

An individual shall continue to be treated as an eligible TAA recipient during the first month that such individual would otherwise cease to be an eligible TAA recipient by reason of the preceding sentence.

(3) Eligible alternative TAA recipient

The term "eligible alternative TAA recipient" means, with respect to any month, any individual who—

(A) is a worker described in section 246(a)(3)(B) of the Trade Act of 1974 who is participating in the program established under section 246(a)(1) of such Act, and

(B) is receiving a benefit for such month under section 246(a)(2) of such Act.

An individual shall continue to be treated as an eligible alternative TAA recipient during the first month that such individual would otherwise cease to be an eligible alternative TAA recipient by reason of the preceding sentence.

(4) Eligible PBGC pension recipient

The term "eligible PBGC pension recipient" means, with respect to any month, any individual who—

(A) has attained age 55 as of the first day of such month, and

(B) is receiving a benefit for such month any portion of which is paid by the Pension Benefit Guaranty Corporation under title IV of the Employee Retirement Income Security Act of 1974.

(d) Qualifying family member

For purposes of this section—

(1) In general

The term "qualifying family member" means—

(A) the taxpayer's spouse, and

(B) any dependent of the taxpayer with respect to whom the taxpayer is entitled to a deduction under section 151(c).

Such term does not include any individual who has other specified coverage.

(2) Special dependency test in case of divorced parents, etc.

If section 152(e) applies to any child with respect to any calendar year, in the case of any taxable year beginning in such calendar year, such child shall be treated as described in paragraph (1)(B) with respect to the custodial parent (as defined in section 152(e)(4)(A)) and not with respect to the noncustodial parent.

(e) Qualified health insurance

For purposes of this section—

(1) In general

The term "qualified health insurance" means any of the following:

(A) Coverage under a COBRA continuation provision (as defined in section 9832(d)(1)).

(B) State-based continuation coverage provided by the State under a State law that requires such coverage.

(C) Coverage offered through a qualified State high risk pool (as defined in section 2744(c)(2) of the Public Health Service Act).

(D) Coverage under a health insurance program offered for State employees.

(E) Coverage under a State-based health insurance program that is comparable to the health insurance program offered for State employees.

(F) Coverage through an arrangement entered into by a State and—

(i) a group health plan (including such a plan which is a multiemployer plan as defined in section 3(37) of the Employee Retirement Income Security Act of 1974),

(ii) an issuer of health insurance coverage,

(iii) an administrator, or

(iv) an employer.

(G) Coverage offered through a State arrangement with a private sector health care coverage purchasing pool.

(H) Coverage under a State-operated health plan that does not receive any Federal financial participation.

(I) Coverage under a group health plan that is available through the employment of the eligible individual's spouse.

(J) In the case of any eligible individual and such individual's qualifying family members, coverage under individual health insurance (other than coverage enrolled in through an Exchange established under the Patient Protection and Affordable Care Act). For purposes of this subparagraph, the term "individual health insurance" means any insurance which constitutes medical care offered to individuals other than in connection with a group health plan and does not include Federal- or State-based health insurance coverage.

(K) Coverage under an employee benefit plan funded by a voluntary employees' beneficiary association (as defined in section 501(c)(9)) established pursuant to an order of a bankruptcy court, or by agreement with an authorized representative, as provided in section 1114 of title 11, United States Code.

(2) Requirements for state-based coverage

(A) In general

The term "qualified health insurance" does not include any coverage described in subparagraphs (B) through (H) of paragraph (1) unless the State involved has elected to have such coverage treated as qualified health insurance under this section and such coverage meets the following requirements:

(i) Guaranteed issue

Each qualifying individual is guaranteed enrollment if the individual pays the premium for enrollment or provides a qualified health insurance costs credit eligibility certificate described in section 7527 and pays the remainder of such premium.

(ii) No imposition of preexisting condition exclusion

No pre-existing condition limitations are imposed with respect to any qualifying individual.

(iii) Nondiscriminatory premium

The total premium (as determined without regard to any subsidies) with respect to a qualifying individual may not be greater than the total premium (as so determined) for a similarly situated individual who is not a qualifying individual.

(iv) Same benefits

Benefits under the coverage are the same as (or substantially similar to) the benefits provided to similarly situated individuals who are not qualifying individuals.

(B) Qualifying individual

For purposes of this paragraph, the term "qualifying individual" means—

(i) an eligible individual for whom, as of the date on which the individual seeks to enroll in the coverage described in subparagraphs (B) through (H) of paragraph (1), the aggregate of the periods of creditable coverage (as defined in section 9801(c)) is 3 months or longer and who, with respect to any month, meets the requirements of clauses (iii) and (iv) of subsection (b)(1)(A); and

(ii) the qualifying family members of such eligible individual.

(3) Exception

The term "qualified health insurance" shall not include—

(A) a flexible spending or similar arrangement, and

(B) any insurance if substantially all of its coverage is of excepted benefits described in section 9832(c).

(f) Other specified coverage

For purposes of this section, an individual has other specified coverage for any month if, as of the first day of such month—

(1) Subsidized coverage

(A) In general

Such individual is covered under any insurance which constitutes medical care (except insurance substantially all of the coverage of which is of excepted benefits described in section 9832(c)) under any health plan maintained by any employer (or former employer) of the taxpayer or the taxpayer's spouse and at least 50 percent of the cost of such coverage (determined under section 4980B) is paid or incurred by the employer.

(B) Eligible alternative TAA recipients

In the case of an eligible alternative TAA recipient, such individual is either—

(i) eligible for coverage under any qualified health insurance (other than insurance described in subparagraph (A), (B), or (F) of subsection (e)(1)) under which at least 50 percent of the cost of coverage (determined under section 4980B(f)(4)) is paid or incurred by an employer (or former employer) of the taxpayer or the taxpayer's spouse, or

(ii) covered under any such qualified health insurance under which any portion of the cost of coverage (as so determined) is paid or incurred by an employer (or former employer) of the taxpayer or the taxpayer's spouse.

(C) Treatment of cafeteria plans

For purposes of subparagraphs (A) and (B), the cost of coverage shall be treated as paid or incurred by an employer to the extent the coverage is in lieu of a right to receive cash or other qualified benefits under a cafeteria plan (as defined in section 125(d)).

(2) Coverage under Medicare, Medicaid, or SCHIP

Such individual—

(A) is entitled to benefits under part A of title XVIII of the Social Security Act or is enrolled under part B of such title, or

(B) is enrolled in the program under title XIX or XXI of such Act (other than under section 1928 of such Act).

(3) Certain other coverage

Such individual—

(A) is enrolled in a health benefits plan under chapter 89 of title 5, United States Code, or

(B) is entitled to receive benefits under chapter 55 of title 10, United States Code.

(g) Special rules

(1) Coordination with advance payments of credit

With respect to any taxable year, the amount which would (but for this subsection) be allowed as a credit to the taxpayer under subsection (a) shall be reduced (but not below zero) by the aggregate amount paid on behalf of such taxpayer under section 7527 for months beginning in such taxable year.

(2) Coordination with other deductions

Amounts taken into account under subsection (a) shall not be taken into account in determining any deduction allowed under section 162(l) or 213.

(3) Medical and health savings accounts

Amounts distributed from an Archer MSA (as defined in section 220(d)) or from a health savings account (as defined in section 223(d)) shall not be taken into account under subsection (a).

(4) Denial of credit to dependents

No credit shall be allowed under this section to any individual with respect to whom a deduction under section 151 is allowable to another taxpayer for a taxable year beginning in the calendar year in which such individual's taxable year begins.

(5) Both spouses eligible individuals

The spouse of the taxpayer shall not be treated as a qualifying family member for purposes of subsection (a), if—

(A) the taxpayer is married at the close of the taxable year,

(B) the taxpayer and the taxpayer's spouse are both eligible individuals during the taxable year, and

(C) the taxpayer files a separate return for the taxable year.

(6) Marital status; certain married individuals living apart

Rules similar to the rules of paragraphs (3) and (4) of section 21(e) shall apply for purposes of this section.

(7) Insurance which covers other individuals

For purposes of this section, rules similar to the rules of section 213(d)(6) shall apply with respect to any contract for qualified health insurance under which amounts are payable for coverage of an individual other than the taxpayer and qualifying family members.

(8) Treatment of payments

For purposes of this section—

(A) Payments by Secretary

Payments made by the Secretary on behalf of any individual under section 7527 (relating to advance payment of credit for health insurance costs of eligible individuals) shall be treated as having been made by the taxpayer on the first day of the month for which such payment was made.

(B) Payments by taxpayer

Payments made by the taxpayer for eligible coverage months shall be treated as having been made by the taxpayer on the first day of the month for which such payment was made.

(9) Continuation coverage premium assistance

In the case of an assistance eligible individual who receives premium assistance for continuation coverage under section 9501(a)(1) of the American Rescue Plan Act of 2021 for any month during the taxable year, such individual shall not be treated as an eligible individual, a certified individual, or a qualifying family member for purposes of this section or section 7527 with respect to such month.

(10) Continued qualification of family members after certain events

(A) Medicare eligibility

In the case of any month which would be an eligible coverage month with respect to an eligible individual but for subsection (f)(2)(A), such month shall be treated as an eligible coverage month with respect to such eligible individual solely for purposes of determining the amount of the credit under this section with respect to any qualifying family members of such individual (and any advance payment of such credit under section 7527). This subparagraph shall only apply with respect to the first 24 months after such eligible individual is first entitled to the benefits described in subsection (f)(2)(A).

(B) Divorce

In the case of the finalization of a divorce between an eligible individual and such individual's spouse, such spouse shall be treated as an eligible individual for purposes of this section and section 7527 for a period of 24 months beginning with the date of such finalization, except that the only qualifying family members who may be taken into account with respect to such spouse are those individuals who were qualifying family members immediately before such finalization.

(C) Death

In the case of the death of an eligible individual—

(i) any spouse of such individual (determined at the time of such death) shall be treated as an eligible individual for purposes of this section and section 7527 for a period of 24 months beginning with the date of such death, except that the only qualifying family members who may be taken into account with respect to such spouse are those individuals who were qualifying family members immediately before such death, and

(ii) any individual who was a qualifying family member of the decedent immediately before such death (or, in the case of an individual to whom paragraph (4) applies, the taxpayer to whom the deduction under section 151 is allowable) shall be treated as an eligible individual for purposes of this section and section 7527 for a period of 24 months beginning with the date of such death, except that in determining the amount of such credit only such qualifying family member may be taken into account.

(11) Election

(A) In general

This section shall not apply to any taxpayer for any eligible coverage month unless such taxpayer elects the application of this section for such month.

(B) Timing and applicability of election

Except as the Secretary may provide—

(i) an election to have this section apply for any eligible coverage month in a taxable year shall be made not later than the due date (including extensions) for the return of tax for the taxable year; and

(ii) any election for this section to apply for an eligible coverage month shall apply for all subsequent eligible coverage months in the taxable year and, once made, shall be irrevocable with respect to such months.

(12) Coordination with premium tax credit

(A) In general

An eligible coverage month to which the election under paragraph (11) applies shall not be treated as a coverage month (as defined in section 36B(c)(2)) for purposes of section 36B with respect to the taxpayer.

(B) Coordination with advance payments of premium tax credit

In the case of a taxpayer who makes the election under paragraph (11) with respect to any eligible coverage month in a taxable year or on behalf of whom any advance payment is made under section 7527 with respect to any month in such taxable year—

(i) the tax imposed by this chapter for the taxable year shall be increased by the excess, if any, of—

(I) the sum of any advance payments made on behalf of the taxpayer under section 1412 of the Patient Protection and Affordable Care Act and section 7527 for months during such taxable year, over

(II) the sum of the credits allowed under this section (determined without regard to paragraph (1)) and section 36B (determined without regard to subsection (f)(1) thereof) for such taxable year; and

(ii) section 36B(f)(2) shall not apply with respect to such taxpayer for such taxable year, except that if such taxpayer received any advance payments under section 7527 for any month in such taxable year and is later allowed a credit under section 36B for such taxable year, then section 36B(f)(2)(B) shall be applied by substituting the amount determined under clause (i) for the amount determined under section 36B(f)(2)(A).

(13) Regulations

The Secretary may prescribe such regulations and other guidance as may be necessary or appropriate to carry out this section, section 6050T, and section 7527.
(Added Pub. L. 107–210, div. A, title II, §201(a), Aug. 6, 2002, 116 Stat. 954; amended Pub. L. 108–311, title IV, §401(a)(2), Oct. 4, 2004, 118 Stat. 1183; Pub. L. 110–172, §11(a)(5), Dec. 29, 2007, 121 Stat. 2485; Pub. L. 111–5, div. B, title I, §§1899A(a)(1), 1899C(a), 1899E(a), 1899G(a), title III, §3001(a)(14)(A), Feb. 17, 2009, 123 Stat. 423, 424, 426, 430, 465; Pub. L. 111–144, §3(b)(5)(A), Mar. 2, 2010, 124 Stat. 44; Pub. L. 111–344, title I, §§111(a), 113(a), 115(a), 117(a), Dec. 29, 2010, 124 Stat. 3614–3616; Pub. L. 112–40, title II, §241(a), (b)(1), (3)(A)–(C), Oct. 21, 2011, 125 Stat. 418, 419; Pub. L. 113–295, div. A, title II, §209(j)(3), Dec. 19, 2014, 128 Stat. 4031; Pub. L. 114–27, title IV, §407(a), (b), (d), June 29, 2015, 129 Stat. 381, 382; Pub. L. 116–94, div. Q, title I, §146(a), Dec. 20, 2019, 133 Stat. 3236; Pub. L. 116–260, div. EE, title I, §134(a), Dec. 27, 2020, 134 Stat. 3053; Pub. L. 117–2, title IX, §9501(b)(3)(A), Mar. 11, 2021, 135 Stat. 137.)

EDITORIAL NOTES
REFERENCES IN TEXT

The date of the enactment of the Trade Act of 2002, referred to in subsec. (b)(1)(B), is the date of enactment of Pub. L. 107–210, which was approved Aug. 6, 2002.

The Trade Act of 1974, referred to in subsec. (c)(2), (3), is Pub. L. 93–618, Jan. 3, 1975, 88 Stat. 1978. Chapter 2 of title II of the Act is classified generally to part 2 (§2271 et seq.) of subchapter II of chapter 12 of Title 19, Customs Duties. Sections 231, 233, 236, and 246 of the Act are classified to sections 2291, 2293, 2296, and 2318 of Title 19, respectively. For complete classification of this Act to the Code, see section 2101 of Title 19 and Tables.

The date of the enactment of this paragraph, referred to in subsec. (c)(2)(B), probably means the date of enactment of Pub. L. 111–5, which amended par. (2) generally and which was approved Feb. 17, 2009.

The Employee Retirement Income Security Act of 1974, referred to in subsecs. (c)(4)(B) and (e)(1)(F)(i), is Pub. L. 93–406, Sept. 2, 1974, 88 Stat. 829. Title IV of the Act is classified principally to subchapter III (§1301 et seq.) of chapter 18 of Title 29, Labor. Section 3(37) of the Act is classified to section 1002(37) of Title 29. For complete classification of this Act to the Code, see Short Title note set out under section 1001 of Title 29 and Tables.

Section 2744(c)(2) of the Public Health Service Act, referred to in subsec. (e)(1)(C), is classified to section 300gg–44(c)(2) of Title 42, The Public Health and Welfare.

The Patient Protection and Affordable Care Act, referred to in subsecs. (e)(1)(J) and (g)(12)(B)(i)(I), is Pub. L. 111–148, Mar. 23, 2010, 124 Stat. 119. Section 1412 of the Act is classified to section 18082 of Title 42, The Public Health and Welfare. For complete classification of this Act to the Code, see Short Title note set out under section 18001 of Title 42 and Tables.

The Social Security Act, referred to in subsec. (f)(2), is act Aug. 14, 1935, ch. 531, 49 Stat. 620. Parts A and B of title XVIII of the Act are classified generally to parts A (§1395c et seq.) and B (§1395j et seq.), respectively, of subchapter XVIII of chapter 7 of Title 42, The Public Health and Welfare. Titles XIX and XXI of the Act are classified generally to subchapters XIX (§1396 et seq.) and XXI (§1397aa et seq.), respectively, of chapter 7 of Title 42. Section 1928 of the Act is classified to section 1396s of Title 42. For complete classification of this Act to the Code, see section 1305 of Title 42 and Tables.

Section 9501(a)(1) of the American Rescue Plan Act of 2021, referred to in subsec. (g)(9), is section 9501(a)(1) of Pub. L. 117–2, which is set out in a note under section 4980B of this title.

PRIOR PROVISIONS

A prior section 35 was renumbered section 37 of this title.

Another prior section 35, acts Aug. 16, 1954, ch. 736, 68A Stat. 14; Sept. 2, 1958, Pub. L. 85–866, title I, §41(b), 72 Stat. 1639; Feb. 26, 1964, Pub. L. 88–272, title II, §201(d)(2), 78 Stat. 32, related to partially tax-exempt interest received by individuals, prior to repeal by Pub. L. 94–455, title XIX, §1901(a)(2), Oct. 4, 1976, 90 Stat. 1764, effective with respect to taxable years beginning after Dec. 31, 1976.

AMENDMENTS

2021—Subsec. (g)(9). Pub. L. 117–2 amended par. (9) generally. Prior to amendment, par. (9) related to COBRA premium assistance.

2020—Subsec. (b)(1)(B). Pub. L. 116–260 substituted "January 1, 2022" for "January 1, 2021".

2019—Subsec. (b)(1)(B). Pub. L. 116–94 substituted "January 1, 2021" for "January 1, 2020".

2015—Subsec. (b)(1)(B). Pub. L. 114–27, §407(a), substituted "before January 1, 2020" for "before January 1, 2014".

Subsec. (e)(1)(J). Pub. L. 114–27, §407(d)(2), inserted "(other than coverage enrolled in through an Exchange established under the Patient Protection and Affordable Care Act)" after "under individual health insurance"

Pub. L. 114–27, §407(d)(1), substituted "under individual health insurance. For purposes of" for "under individual health insurance if the eligible individual was covered under individual health insurance during the entire 30-day period that ends on the date that such individual became separated from the employment which qualified such individual for—

"(i) in the case of an eligible TAA recipient, the allowance described in subsection (c)(2),

"(ii) in the case of an eligible alternative TAA recipient, the benefit described in subsection (c)(3)(B), or

"(iii) in the case of any eligible PBGC pension recipient, the benefit described in subsection (c)(4)(B).

For purposes of".

Subsec. (g)(11) to (13). Pub. L. 114–27, §407(b), added pars. (11) and (12) and redesignated former par. (11) as (13).

2014—Subsec. (g)(9) to (11). Pub. L. 113–295, §209(j)(3), amended directory language of Pub. L. 111–5, §3001(a)(14)(A). See 2009 Amendment notes below.

2011—Subsec. (a). Pub. L. 112–40, §241(b)(1), substituted "72.5 percent" for "65 percent (80 percent in the case of eligible coverage months beginning before February 13, 2011)".

Subsec. (b)(1)(B). Pub. L. 112–40, §241(a), inserted ", and before January 1, 2014" after "2002".

Subsec. (c)(2)(B). Pub. L. 112–40, §241(b)(3)(A), struck out "and before February 13, 2011" after "paragraph" in introductory provisions.

Subsec. (e)(1)(K). Pub. L. 112–40, §241(b)(3)(B), substituted "Coverage" for "In the case of eligible coverage months beginning before February 13, 2012, coverage".

Subsec. (g)(10). Pub. L. 112–40, §241(b)(3)(C), which directed amendment of par. (9) relating to continued qualification of family members after certain events by striking out "In the case of eligible coverage months beginning before February 13, 2011—", was executed by striking out such introductory provisions in par. (10) to reflect the probable intent of Congress and the redesignation of par. (9) as (10) by Pub. L. 111–5, §3001(a)(14)(A), as amended by Pub. L. 113–295, §209(j)(3). See 2009 Amendment and Effective Date of 2014 Amendment notes below.

2010—Subsec. (a). Pub. L. 111–344, §111(a), substituted "February 13, 2011" for "January 1, 2011".

Subsec. (c)(2)(B). Pub. L. 111–344, §113(a), substituted "February 13, 2011" for "January 1, 2011" in introductory provisions.

Subsec. (e)(1)(K). Pub. L. 111–344, §117(a), substituted "February 13, 2012" for "January 1, 2011".

Subsec. (g)(9). Pub. L. 111–144 substituted "section 3001(a) of title III of division B of the American Recovery and Reinvestment Act of 2009" for "section 3002(a) of the Health Insurance Assistance for the Unemployed Act of 2009".

Subsec. (g)(10). Pub. L. 111–344, §115(a), which directed amendment of par. (9) relating to continued qualification of family members after certain events by substituting "February 13, 2011" for "January 1, 2011", was executed by making the substitution in introductory provisions of par. (10) to reflect the probable intent of

204

Congress and the redesignation of par. (9) as (10) by Pub. L. 111–5, §3001(a)(14)(A), as amended by Pub. L. 113–295, §209(j)(3). See 2009 Amendment and Effective Date of 2014 Amendment notes below.

2009—Subsec. (a). Pub. L. 111–5, §1899A(a)(1), inserted "(80 percent in the case of eligible coverage months beginning before January 1, 2011)" after "65 percent".

Subsec. (c)(2). Pub. L. 111–5, §1899C(a), amended par. (2) generally. Prior to amendment, text read as follows: "The term 'eligible TAA recipient' means, with respect to any month, any individual who is receiving for any day of such month a trade readjustment allowance under chapter 2 of title II of the Trade Act of 1974 or who would be eligible to receive such allowance if section 231 of such Act were applied without regard to subsection (a)(3)(B) of such section. An individual shall continue to be treated as an eligible TAA recipient during the first month that such individual would otherwise cease to be an eligible TAA recipient by reason of the preceding sentence."

Subsec. (e)(1)(K). Pub. L. 111–5, §1899G(a), added subpar. (K).

Subsec. (g)(9), (10). Pub. L. 111–5, §3001(a)(14)(A), as amended by Pub. L. 113–295, §209(j)(3), added par. (9) relating to COBRA premium assistance and redesignated former par. (9) relating to continued qualification of family members after certain events as (10). Former par. (10) relating to regulations redesignated (11).

Pub. L. 111–5, §1899E(a), added par. (9) relating to continued qualification of family members after certain events and redesignated former par. (9) relating to regulations as (10).

Subsec. (g)(11). Pub. L. 111–5, §3001(a)(14)(A), as amended by Pub. L. 113–295, §209(j)(3), redesignated par. (10) relating to regulations as (11).

2007—Subsec. (d)(2). Pub. L. 110–172 struck out "paragraph (2) or (4) of" before "section 152(e)" and substituted "(as defined in section 152(e)(4)(A))" for "(within the meaning of section 152(e)(1))".

2004—Subsec. (g)(3). Pub. L. 108–311 amended heading and text of par. (3) generally. Prior to amendment, text read as follows: "Amounts distributed from an Archer MSA (as defined in section 220(d)) shall not be taken into account under subsection (a)."

STATUTORY NOTES AND RELATED SUBSIDIARIES

EFFECTIVE DATE OF 2021 AMENDMENT

Pub. L. 117–2, title IX, §9501(b)(3)(B), Mar. 11, 2021, 135 Stat. 137, provided that: "The amendment made by subparagraph (A) [amending this section] shall apply to taxable years ending after the date of the enactment of this Act [Mar. 11, 2021]."

EFFECTIVE DATE OF 2020 AMENDMENT

Pub. L. 116–260, div. EE, title I, §134(b), Dec. 27, 2020, 134 Stat. 3053, provided that: "The amendment made by this section [amending this section] shall apply to months beginning after December 31, 2020."

EFFECTIVE DATE OF 2019 AMENDMENT

Pub. L. 116–94, div. Q, title I, §146(b), Dec. 20, 2019, 133 Stat. 3236, provided that: "The amendment made by this section [amending this section] shall apply to months beginning after December 31, 2019."

EFFECTIVE DATE OF 2015 AMENDMENT

Pub. L. 114–27, title IV, §407(f), June 29, 2015, 129 Stat. 382, provided that:

"(1) In general.—Except as provided in paragraph (2), the amendments made by this section [amending this section and sections 6501 and 7527 of this title] shall apply to coverage months in taxable years beginning after December 31, 2013.

"(2) Plans available on individual market for use of tax credit.—The amendment made by subsection (d)(2) [amending this section] shall apply to coverage months in taxable years beginning after December 31, 2015.

"(3) Transition rule.—Notwithstanding section 35(g)(11)(B)(i) of the Internal Revenue Code of 1986 (as added by this title), an election to apply section 35 of such Code to an eligible coverage month (as defined in section 35(b) of such Code) (and not to claim the credit under section 36B of such Code with respect to such month) in a taxable year beginning after December 31, 2013, and before the date of the enactment of this Act [June 29, 2015]—

"(A) may be made at any time on or after such date of enactment and before the expiration of the 3-year period of limitation prescribed in section 6511(a) with respect to such taxable year; and

"(B) may be made on an amended return."

EFFECTIVE DATE OF 2014 AMENDMENT

Amendment by Pub. L. 113–295 effective as if included in the provisions of the American Recovery and Reinvestment Tax Act of 2009, Pub. L. 111–5, div. B, title I, to which such amendment relates, see section 209(k) of Pub. L. 113–295, set out as a note under section 24 of this title.

EFFECTIVE DATE OF 2011 AMENDMENT

Pub. L. 112–40, title II, §241(c), Oct. 21, 2011, 125 Stat. 419, provided that:

"(1) In general.—Except as otherwise provided in this subsection, the amendments made by this section [amending this section, section 7527 of this title, and former section 2918 of Title 29, Labor] shall apply to coverage months beginning after February 12, 2011.

"(2) Advance payment provisions.—

"(A) The amendment made by subsection (b)(2)(B) [amending section 7527 of this title] shall apply to certificates issued after the date which is 30 days after the date of the enactment of this Act [Oct. 21, 2011].

"(B) The amendment made by subsection (b)(2)(D) [amending section 7527 of this title] shall apply to coverage months beginning after the date which is 30 days after the date of the enactment of this Act."

EFFECTIVE DATE OF 2010 AMENDMENT

Pub. L. 111–344, title I, §111(c), Dec. 29, 2010, 124 Stat. 3615, provided that: "The amendments made by this section [amending this section and section 7527 of this title] shall apply to coverage months beginning after December 31, 2010."

Pub. L. 111–344, title I, §113(b), Dec. 29, 2010, 124 Stat. 3615, provided that: "The amendment made by this section [amending this section] shall apply to coverage months beginning after December 31, 2010."

Pub. L. 111–344, title I, §115(c), Dec. 29, 2010, 124 Stat. 3615, provided that: "The amendment made by this section [amending this section and former section 2918 of Title 29, Labor] shall apply to months beginning after December 31, 2010."

Pub. L. 111–344, title I, §117(b), Dec. 29, 2010, 124 Stat. 3616, provided that: "The amendment made by this section [amending this section] shall apply to coverage months beginning after December 31, 2010."

Pub. L. 111–144, §3(c), Mar. 2, 2010, 124 Stat. 45, provided that: "The amendments made by this section [amending this section, sections 139C, 6432, and 6720C of this title, and provisions set out as a note under section 6432 of this title] shall take effect as if included in the provisions of section 3001 of division B of the American Recovery and Reinvestment Act of 2009 [Pub. L. 111–5, set out below] to which they relate, except that—

"(1) the amendments made by subsection (b)(1) [amending provisions set out as a note under section 6432 of this title] shall apply to periods of coverage beginning after the date of the enactment of this Act [Mar. 2, 2010];

"(2) the amendments made by subsection (b)(2) [amending provisions set out as a note under section 6432 of this title] shall take effect as if included in the amendments made by section 1010 of division B of the Department of Defense Appropriations Act, 2010 [Pub. L. 111–118, amending provisions set out a note under this section]; and

"(3) the amendments made by subsections (b)(3) and (b)(4) [amending provisions set out as a note under section 6432 of this title] shall take effect on the date of the enactment of this Act [Mar. 2, 2010]."

EFFECTIVE DATE OF 2009 AMENDMENT

Except as otherwise provided and subject to certain applicability provisions, amendment by sections 1899A(a)(1), 1899C(a), 1899E(a), and 1899G(a) of Pub. L. 111–5 effective upon the expiration of the 90-day period beginning on Feb. 17, 2009, see section 1891 of Pub. L. 111–5, set out as an Effective and Termination Dates of 2009 Amendment note under section 2271 of Title 19, Customs Duties.

Pub. L. 111–5, div. B, title I, §1899A(b), Feb. 17, 2009, 123 Stat. 424, provided that: "The amendments made by this section [amending this section and section 7527 of this title] shall apply to coverage months beginning on or after the first day of the first month beginning 60 days after the date of the enactment of this Act [Feb. 17, 2009]."

Pub. L. 111–5, div. B, title I, §1899C(b), Feb. 17, 2009, 123 Stat. 425, provided that: "The amendment made by this section [amending this section] shall apply to coverage months beginning after the date of the enactment of this Act [Feb. 17, 2009]."

Pub. L. 111–5, div. B, title I, §1899E(c), Feb. 17, 2009, 123 Stat. 428, provided that: "The amendments made by this section [amending this section and former section 2918 of Title 29, Labor] shall apply to months beginning after December 31, 2009."

Pub. L. 111–5, div. B, title I, §1899G(b), Feb. 17, 2009, 123 Stat. 430, provided that: "The amendments made by this section [amending this section] shall apply to coverage months beginning after the date of the enactment of this Act [Feb. 17, 2009]."

Pub. L. 111–5, div. B, title III, §3001(a)(14)(B), Feb. 17, 2009, 123 Stat. 465, provided that: "The amendment made by subparagraph (A) [amending this section] shall apply to taxable years ending after the date of the enactment of this Act [Feb. 17, 2009]."

EFFECTIVE DATE OF 2004 AMENDMENT

Amendment by Pub. L. 108–311 effective as if included in section 1201 of Pub. L. 108–173, see section 401(b) of Pub. L. 108–311, set out as a note under section 26 of this title.

Pub. L. 107–210, div. A, title II, §201(d), Aug. 6, 2002, 116 Stat. 960, provided that:

"(1) In general.—Except as provided in paragraph (2), the amendments made by this section [enacting this section and section 300gg–45 of Title 42, The Public Health and Welfare, amending section 1324 of Title 31, Money and Finance, and renumbering former section 35 of this title as section 36 of this title] shall apply to taxable years beginning after December 31, 2001.

"(2) State high risk pools.—The amendment made by subsection (b) [enacting section 300gg–45 of Title 42] shall take effect on the date of the enactment of this Act [Aug. 6, 2002]."

Pub. L. 107–210, div. A, title II, §203(f), Aug. 6, 2002, 116 Stat. 972, provided that: "Nothing in this title [enacting this section and sections 6050T and 7527 of this title, and section 300gg–45 of Title 42, The Public Health and Welfare, amending sections 4980B, 6103, 6724, and 7213A of this title, sections 1165, 2862, 2918, and 2919 of Title 29, Labor, section 1324 of Title 31, Money and Finance, and section 300bb–5 of Title 42, renumbering former section 35 of this title as section 36 of this title, and enacting provisions set out as notes under this section and section 6050T of this title] (or the amendments made by this title), other than provisions relating to COBRA continuation coverage and reporting requirements, shall be construed as creating any new mandate on any party regarding health insurance coverage."

Pub. L. 114–27, title IV, §407(g), June 29, 2015, 129 Stat. 383, provided that: "As soon as possible after the date of the enactment of this Act [June 29, 2015], the Secretaries of the Treasury, Health and Human Services, and Labor (or such Secretaries' delegates) and the Director of the Pension Benefit Guaranty Corporation (or the Director's delegate) shall carry out programs of public outreach, including on the Internet, to inform potential eligible individuals (as defined in section 35(c)(1) of the Internal Revenue Code of 1986) of the extension of the credit under section 35 of the Internal Revenue Code of 1986 and the availability of the election to claim such credit retroactively for coverage months beginning after December 31, 2013."

SURVEY AND REPORT ON ENHANCED HEALTH COVERAGE TAX CREDIT PROGRAM

Pub. L. 111–5, div. B, title I, §1899I, Feb. 17, 2009, 123 Stat. 431, provided that:

"(a) Survey.—

"(1) In general.—The Secretary of the Treasury shall conduct a biennial survey of eligible individuals (as defined in section 35(c) of the Internal Revenue Code of 1986) relating to the health coverage tax credit under section 35 of the Internal Revenue Code of 1986 (hereinafter in this section referred to as the 'health coverage tax credit').

"(2) Information obtained.—The survey conducted under subsection (a) shall obtain the following information:

"(A) HCTC participants.—In the case of eligible individuals receiving the health coverage tax credit (including individuals participating in the health coverage tax credit program under section 7527 of such Code, hereinafter in this section referred to as the 'HCTC program')—

"(i) demographic information of such individuals, including income and education levels,

"(ii) satisfaction of such individuals with the enrollment process in the HCTC program,

"(iii) satisfaction of such individuals with available health coverage options under the credit, including level of premiums, benefits, deductibles, cost-sharing requirements, and the adequacy of provider networks, and

"(iv) any other information that the Secretary determines is appropriate.

"(B) Non-HCTC participants.—In the case of eligible individuals not receiving the health coverage tax credit—

"(i) demographic information of each individual, including income and education levels,

"(ii) whether the individual was aware of the health coverage tax credit or the HCTC program,

"(iii) the reasons the individual has not enrolled in the HCTC program, including whether such reasons include the burden of the process of enrollment and the affordability of coverage,

"(iv) whether the individual has health insurance coverage, and, if so, the source of such coverage, and

"(v) any other information that the Secretary determines is appropriate.

"(3) Report.—Not later than December 31 of each year in which a survey is conducted under paragraph (1) (beginning in 2010), the Secretary of the Treasury shall report to the Committee on Finance and the Committee on Health, Education, Labor, and Pensions of the Senate and the Committee on Ways and Means, the Committee on Education and Labor, and the Committee on Energy and Commerce of the House of Representatives the findings of the most recent survey conducted under paragraph (1).

"(b) Report.—Not later than October 1 of each year (beginning in 2010), the Secretary of the Treasury (after consultation with the Secretary of Health and Human Services, and, in the case of the information required under paragraph (7), the Secretary of Labor) shall report to the Committee on Finance and the Committee on Health, Education, Labor, and Pensions of the Senate and the Committee on Ways and Means, the Committee on Education and Labor, and the Committee on Energy and Commerce of the House of Representatives the following information with respect to the most recent taxable year ending before such date:

"(1) In each State and nationally—

"(A) the total number of eligible individuals (as defined in section 35(c) of the Internal Revenue Code of 1986) and the number of eligible individuals receiving the health coverage tax credit,

"(B) the total number of such eligible individuals who receive an advance payment of the health coverage tax credit through the HCTC program,

"(C) the average length of the time period of the participation of eligible individuals in the HCTC program, and

"(D) the total number of participating eligible individuals in the HCTC program who are enrolled in each category of coverage as described in section 35(e)(1) of such Code,

with respect to each category of eligible individuals described in section 35(c)(1) of such Code.

"(2) In each State and nationally, an analysis of—

"(A) the range of monthly health insurance premiums, for self-only coverage and for family coverage, for individuals receiving the health coverage tax credit, and

"(B) the average and median monthly health insurance premiums, for self-only coverage and for family coverage, for individuals receiving the health coverage tax credit,

with respect to each category of coverage as described in section 35(e)(1) of such Code.

"(3) In each State and nationally, an analysis of the following information with respect to the health insurance coverage of individuals receiving the health coverage tax credit who are enrolled in coverage described in subparagraphs (B) through (H) of section 35(e)(1) of such Code:

"(A) Deductible amounts.

"(B) Other out-of-pocket cost-sharing amounts.

"(C) A description of any annual or lifetime limits on coverage or any other significant limits on coverage services, or benefits.

The information required under this paragraph shall be reported with respect to each category of coverage described in such subparagraphs.

"(4) In each State and nationally, the gender and average age of eligible individuals (as defined in section 35(c) of such Code) who receive the health coverage tax credit, in each category of coverage described in section 35(e)(1) of such Code, with respect to each category of eligible individuals described in such section.

"(5) The steps taken by the Secretary of the Treasury to increase the participation rates in the HCTC program among eligible individuals, including outreach and enrollment activities.

"(6) The cost of administering the HCTC program by function, including the cost of subcontractors, and recommendations on ways to reduce administrative costs, including recommended statutory changes.

"(7) The number of States applying for and receiving national emergency grants under [former] section 173(f) of the Workforce Investment Act of 1998 ([former] 29 U.S.C. 2918(f)), the activities funded by such grants on a State-by-State basis, and the time necessary for application approval of such grants."

§36. First-time homebuyer credit

(a) Allowance of credit

In the case of an individual who is a first-time homebuyer of a principal residence in the United States during a taxable year, there shall be allowed as a credit against the tax imposed by this subtitle for such taxable year an amount equal to 10 percent of the purchase price of the residence.

(b) Limitations

(1) Dollar limitation

(A) In general

Except as otherwise provided in this paragraph, the credit allowed under subsection (a) shall not exceed $8,000.

(B) Married individuals filing separately

In the case of a married individual filing a separate return, subparagraph (A) shall be applied by substituting "$4,000" for "$8,000".

(C) Other individuals

If two or more individuals who are not married purchase a principal residence, the amount of the credit allowed under subsection (a) shall be allocated among such individuals in such manner as the Secretary may prescribe, except that the total amount of the credits allowed to all such individuals shall not exceed $8,000.

(D) Special rule for long-time residents of same principal residence

In the case of a taxpayer to whom a credit under subsection (a) is allowed by reason of subsection (c)(6), subparagraphs (A), (B), and (C) shall be applied by substituting "$6,500" for "$8,000" and "$3,250" for "$4,000".

(2) Limitation based on modified adjusted gross income

(A) In general

The amount allowable as a credit under subsection (a) (determined without regard to this paragraph) for the taxable year shall be reduced (but not below zero) by the amount which bears the same ratio to the amount which is so allowable as—

(i) the excess (if any) of—

(I) the taxpayer's modified adjusted gross income for such taxable year, over

(II) $125,000 ($225,000 in the case of a joint return), bears to

(ii) $20,000.

(B) Modified adjusted gross income

For purposes of subparagraph (A), the term "modified adjusted gross income" means the adjusted gross income of the taxpayer for the taxable year increased by any amount excluded from gross income under section 911, 931, or 933.

(3) Limitation based on purchase price

No credit shall be allowed under subsection (a) for the purchase of any residence if the purchase price of such residence exceeds $800,000.

(4) Age limitation

No credit shall be allowed under subsection (a) with respect to the purchase of any residence unless the taxpayer has attained age 18 as of the date of such purchase. In the case of any taxpayer who is married (within the meaning of section 7703), the taxpayer shall be treated as meeting the age requirement of the preceding sentence if the taxpayer or the taxpayer's spouse meets such age requirement.

(c) Definitions

For purposes of this section—

(1) First-time homebuyer

The term "first-time homebuyer" means any individual if such individual (and if married, such individual's spouse) had no present ownership interest in a principal residence during the 3-year period ending on the date of the purchase of the principal residence to which this section applies.

(2) Principal residence

The term "principal residence" has the same meaning as when used in section 121.

(3) Purchase
(A) In general
The term "purchase" means any acquisition, but only if—

(i) the property is not acquired from a person related to the person acquiring such property (or, if married, such individual's spouse), and

(ii) the basis of the property in the hands of the person acquiring such property is not determined—

(I) in whole or in part by reference to the adjusted basis of such property in the hands of the person from whom acquired, or

(II) under section 1014(a) (relating to property acquired from a decedent).

(B) Construction
A residence which is constructed by the taxpayer shall be treated as purchased by the taxpayer on the date the taxpayer first occupies such residence.

(4) Purchase price
The term "purchase price" means the adjusted basis of the principal residence on the date such residence is purchased.

(5) Related persons
A person shall be treated as related to another person if the relationship between such persons would result in the disallowance of losses under section 267 or 707(b) (but, in applying section 267(b) and (c) for purposes of this section, paragraph (4) of section 267(c) shall be treated as providing that the family of an individual shall include only his spouse, ancestors, and lineal descendants).

(6) Exception for long-time residents of same principal residence
In the case of an individual (and, if married, such individual's spouse) who has owned and used the same residence as such individual's principal residence for any 5-consecutive-year period during the 8-year period ending on the date of the purchase of a subsequent principal residence, such individual shall be treated as a first-time homebuyer for purposes of this section with respect to the purchase of such subsequent residence.

(d) Exceptions
No credit under subsection (a) shall be allowed to any taxpayer for any taxable year with respect to the purchase of a residence if—

(1) the taxpayer is a nonresident alien,

(2) the taxpayer disposes of such residence (or such residence ceases to be the principal residence of the taxpayer (and, if married, the taxpayer's spouse)) before the close of such taxable year,

(3) a deduction under section 151 with respect to such taxpayer is allowable to another taxpayer for such taxable year, or

(4) the taxpayer fails to attach to the return of tax for such taxable year a properly executed copy of the settlement statement used to complete such purchase.

(e) Reporting
If the Secretary requires information reporting under section 6045 by a person described in subsection (e)(2) thereof to verify the eligibility of taxpayers for the credit allowable by this section, the exception provided by section 6045(e) shall not apply.

(f) Recapture of credit
(1) In general
Except as otherwise provided in this subsection, if a credit under subsection (a) is allowed to a taxpayer, the tax imposed by this chapter shall be increased by 62/3 percent of the amount of such credit for each taxable year in the recapture period.

(2) Acceleration of recapture
If a taxpayer disposes of the principal residence with respect to which a credit was allowed under subsection (a) (or such residence ceases to be the principal residence of the taxpayer (and, if married, the taxpayer's spouse)) before the end of the recapture period—

(A) the tax imposed by this chapter for the taxable year of such disposition or cessation shall be increased by the excess of the amount of the credit allowed over the amounts of tax imposed by paragraph (1) for preceding taxable years, and

(B) paragraph (1) shall not apply with respect to such credit for such taxable year or any subsequent taxable year.

(3) Limitation based on gain
In the case of the sale of the principal residence to a person who is not related to the taxpayer, the increase in tax determined under paragraph (2) shall not exceed the amount of gain (if any) on such sale. Solely for purposes of the preceding sentence, the adjusted basis of such residence shall be reduced by the amount of the credit allowed under subsection (a) to the extent not previously recaptured under paragraph (1).

(4) Exceptions
(A) Death of taxpayer
Paragraphs (1) and (2) shall not apply to any taxable year ending after the date of the taxpayer's death.

(B) Involuntary conversion
Paragraph (2) shall not apply in the case of a residence which is compulsorily or involuntarily converted (within the meaning of section 1033(a)) if the taxpayer acquires a new principal residence during the 2-year period beginning on the date of the disposition or cessation referred to in paragraph (2). Paragraph (2) shall apply to such new principal residence during the recapture period in the same manner as if such new principal residence were the converted residence.

(C) Transfers between spouses or incident to divorce
In the case of a transfer of a residence to which section 1041(a) applies—

(i) paragraph (2) shall not apply to such transfer, and

(ii) in the case of taxable years ending after such transfer, paragraphs (1) and (2) shall apply to the transferee in the same manner as if such transferee were the transferor (and shall not apply to the transferor).

(D) Waiver of recapture for purchases in 2009 and 2010
In the case of any credit allowed with respect to the purchase of a principal residence after December 31, 2008—

(i) paragraph (1) shall not apply, and

(ii) paragraph (2) shall apply only if the disposition or cessation described in paragraph (2) with respect to such residence occurs during the 36-month period beginning on the date of the purchase of such residence by the taxpayer.

(E) Special rule for members of the armed forces, etc.
(i) In general
In the case of the disposition of a principal residence by an individual (or a cessation referred to in paragraph (2)) after December 31, 2008, in connection with Government orders received by such individual, or such individual's spouse, for qualified official extended duty service—

(I) paragraph (2) and subsection (d)(2) shall not apply to such disposition (or cessation), and

(II) if such residence was acquired before January 1, 2009, paragraph (1) shall not apply to the taxable year in which such disposition (or cessation) occurs or any subsequent taxable year.

(ii) Qualified official extended duty service

For purposes of this section, the term "qualified official extended duty service" means service on qualified official extended duty as—

(I) a member of the uniformed services,

(II) a member of the Foreign Service of the United States, or

(III) an employee of the intelligence community.

(iii) Definitions

Any term used in this subparagraph which is also used in paragraph (9) of section 121(d) shall have the same meaning as when used in such paragraph.

(5) Joint returns

In the case of a credit allowed under subsection (a) with respect to a joint return, half of such credit shall be treated as having been allowed to each individual filing such return for purposes of this subsection.

(6) Return requirement

If the tax imposed by this chapter for the taxable year is increased under this subsection, the taxpayer shall, notwithstanding section 6012, be required to file a return with respect to the taxes imposed under this subtitle.

(7) Recapture period

For purposes of this subsection, the term "recapture period" means the 15 taxable years beginning with the second taxable year following the taxable year in which the purchase of the principal residence for which a credit is allowed under subsection (a) was made.

(g) Election to treat purchase in prior year

In the case of a purchase of a principal residence after December 31, 2008, a taxpayer may elect to treat such purchase as made on December 31 of the calendar year preceding such purchase for purposes of this section (other than subsections (b)(4), (c), (f)(4)(D), and (h)).

(h) Application of section

(1) In general

This section shall only apply to a principal residence purchased by the taxpayer on or after April 9, 2008, and before May 1, 2010.

(2) Exception in case of binding contract

In the case of any taxpayer who enters into a written binding contract before May 1, 2010, to close on the purchase of a principal residence before July 1, 2010, and who purchases such residence before October 1, 2010, paragraph (1) shall be applied by substituting "October 1, 2010" for "May 1, 2010".

(3) Special rule for individuals on qualified official extended duty outside the United States

In the case of any individual who serves on qualified official extended duty service (as defined in section 121(d)(9)(C)(i)) outside the United States for at least 90 days during the period beginning after December 31, 2008, and ending before May 1, 2010, and, if married, such individual's spouse—

(A) paragraphs (1) and (2) shall each be applied by substituting "May 1, 2011" for "May 1, 2010", and

(B) paragraph (2) shall be applied by substituting "July 1, 2011" for "July 1, 2010", and for "October 1, 2010".

(Added Pub. L. 110–289, div. C, title I, §3011(a), July 30, 2008, 122 Stat. 2888; amended Pub. L. 111–5, div. B, title I, §1006(a)–(c), (d)(2), (e), Feb. 17, 2009, 123 Stat. 316, 317; Pub. L. 111–92, §§11(a)–(g), 12(a)–(c), Nov. 6, 2009, 123 Stat. 2989–2992; Pub. L. 111–198, §2(a), (b), July 2, 2010, 124 Stat. 1356.)

EDITORIAL NOTES
PRIOR PROVISIONS

A prior section 36 was renumbered section 37 of this title.

Another prior section 36, acts Aug. 16, 1954, ch. 736, 68A Stat. 15; Oct. 4, 1976, Pub. L. 94–455, title V, §501(b)(2), title X, §1011(c), title XIX, §1901(b)(1)(A), 90 Stat. 1558, 1611, 1790, directed that credits provided by section 32 not be allowed if an individual elects under section 144 to take standard deduction, prior to repeal by Pub. L. 95–30, title I, §§101(d)(3), 106(a), May 23, 1977, 91 Stat. 133, 141, applicable to taxable years beginning after Dec. 31, 1976.

AMENDMENTS

2010—Subsec. (h)(2). Pub. L. 111–198, §2(a), substituted "and who purchases such residence before October 1, 2010, paragraph (1) shall be applied by substituting 'October 1, 2010' " for "paragraph (1) shall be applied by substituting 'July 1, 2010' ".

Subsec. (h)(3)(B). Pub. L. 111–198, §2(b), inserted ", and for 'October 1, 2010' " after "for 'July 1, 2010' ".

2009—Subsec. (b)(1)(A). Pub. L. 111–5, §1006(b)(1), substituted "$8,000" for "$7,500".

Subsec. (b)(1)(B). Pub. L. 111–5, §1006(b), substituted "$4,000" for "$3,750" and "$8,000" for "$7,500".

Subsec. (b)(1)(C). Pub. L. 111–5, §1006(b)(1), substituted "$8,000" for "$7,500".

Subsec. (b)(1)(D). Pub. L. 111–92, §11(c)(1), added subpar. (D).

Subsec. (b)(2)(A)(i)(II). Pub. L. 111–92, §11(c)(2), substituted "$125,000 ($225,000" for "$75,000 ($150,000".

Subsec. (b)(3). Pub. L. 111–92, §11(d), added par. (3).

Subsec. (b)(4). Pub. L. 111–92, §12(a)(1), added par. (4).

Subsec. (c)(3)(A)(i). Pub. L. 111–92, §12(c), inserted "(or, if married, such individual's spouse)" after "person acquiring such property".

Subsec. (c)(6). Pub. L. 111–92, §11(b), added par. (6).

Subsec. (d). Pub. L. 111–5, §1006(d)(2), (e), redesignated pars. (3) and (4) as (1) and (2), respectively, and struck out former pars. (1) and (2) which read as follows:

"(1) a credit under section 1400C (relating to first-time homebuyer in the District of Columbia) is allowable to the taxpayer (or the taxpayer's spouse) for such taxable year or any prior taxable year,

"(2) the residence is financed by the proceeds of a qualified mortgage issue the interest on which is exempt from tax under section 103,".

Subsec. (d)(3). Pub. L. 111–92, §11(g), added par. (3).

Subsec. (d)(4). Pub. L. 111–92, §12(b), added par. (4).

Subsec. (f)(4)(D). Pub. L. 111–92, §11(a)(2), inserted "and 2010" after "2009" in heading and struck out ", and before December 1, 2009" after "December 31, 2008" in introductory provisions.

Pub. L. 111–5, §1006(c)(1), added subpar. (D).

Subsec. (f)(4)(E). Pub. L. 111–92, §11(e), added subpar. (E).

Subsec. (g). Pub. L. 111–92, §12(a)(2), inserted "(b)(4)," before "(c)".

Pub. L. 111–92, §11(a)(3), amended subsec. (g) generally. Prior to amendment, text read as follows: "In the case of a purchase of a principal residence after December 31, 2008, and before December 1, 2009, a taxpayer may elect to treat such purchase as made on December 31, 2008, for purposes of this section (other than subsections (c) and (f)(4)(D))."

Pub. L. 111–5, §1006(a)(2), (c)(2), substituted "December 1, 2009" for "July 1, 2009" and "subsections (c) and (f)(4)(D)" for "subsection (c)".

Subsec. (h). Pub. L. 111–92, §11(a)(1), substituted "May 1, 2010" for "December 1, 2009", designated existing provisions as par. (1), inserted heading, and added par. (2).

Pub. L. 111–5, §1006(a)(1), substituted "December 1, 2009" for "July 1, 2009".

Subsec. (h)(3). Pub. L. 111–92, §11(f), added par. (3).

STATUTORY NOTES AND RELATED SUBSIDIARIES

EFFECTIVE DATE OF 2010 AMENDMENT

Pub. L. 111–198, §2(c), July 2, 2010, 124 Stat. 1356, provided that: "The amendments made by this section [amending this section] shall apply to residences purchased after June 30, 2010."

EFFECTIVE DATE OF 2009 AMENDMENT

Pub. L. 111–92, §11(j)(1)–(3), Nov. 6, 2009, 123 Stat. 2991, provided that:

"(1) In general.——The amendments made by subsections (b), (c), (d), and (g) [amending this section] shall apply to residences purchased after the date of the enactment of this Act [Nov. 6, 2009].

"(2) Extensions.——The amendments made by subsections (a) [amending this section], (f) [amending this section], and (i) [amending section 1400C of this title] shall apply to residences purchased after November 30, 2009.

"(3) Waiver of recapture.——The amendment made by subsection (e) [amending this section] shall apply to dispositions and cessations after December 31, 2008."

Pub. L. 111–92, §12(e), Nov. 6, 2009, 123 Stat. 2992, provided that:

"(1) In general.——Except as otherwise provided in this subsection, the amendments made by this section [amending this section and section 6213 of this title] shall apply to purchases after the date of the enactment of this Act [Nov. 6, 2009].

"(2) Documentation requirement.——The amendments made by subsection (b) [amending this section] shall apply to returns for taxable years ending after the date of the enactment of this Act [Nov. 6, 2009].

"(3) Treatment as mathematical and clerical errors.——The amendments made by subsection (d) [amending section 6213 of this title] shall apply to returns for taxable years ending on or after April 9, 2008."

Pub. L. 111–5, div. B, title I, §1006(f), Feb. 17, 2009, 123 Stat. 317, provided that: "The amendments made by this section [amending this section and section 1400C of this title] shall apply to residences purchased after December 31, 2008."

EFFECTIVE DATE

Section applicable to residences purchased on or after Apr. 9, 2008, in taxable years ending on or after such date, see section 3011(c) of Pub. L. 110–289, set out as an Effective Date of 2008 Amendment note under section 26 of this title.

[§36A. Repealed. Pub. L. 113–295, div. A, title II, §221(a)(5)(A), Dec. 19, 2014, 128 Stat. 4037]

Section, added Pub. L. 111–5, div. B, title I, §1001(a), Feb. 17, 2009, 123 Stat. 309, related to making work pay credit.

STATUTORY NOTES AND RELATED SUBSIDIARIES

EFFECTIVE DATE OF REPEAL

Repeal effective Dec. 19, 2014, subject to a savings provision, see section 221(b) of Pub. L. 113–295, set out as an Effective Date of 2014 Amendment note under section 1 of this title.

TREATMENT OF POSSESSIONS

Pub. L. 111–5, div. B, title I, §1001(b), Feb. 17, 2009, 123 Stat. 310, with respect to taxable years beginning in 2009 and 2010, required the Secretary of the Treasury to pay each possession of the United States with a mirror code tax system amounts equal to the loss to that possession by reason of the making work pay credit and to pay certain possessions without a mirror code tax system amounts estimated as being equal to aggregate benefits that would have been provided to its residents, and provided that, for purposes of section 1324(b)(2) of Title 31, Money and Finance, such payments to possessions would be treated in the same manner as a refund due from the credit formerly allowed under this section.

§36B. Refundable credit for coverage under a qualified health plan

(a) In general

In the case of an applicable taxpayer, there shall be allowed as a credit against the tax imposed by this subtitle for any taxable year an amount equal to the premium assistance credit amount of the taxpayer for the taxable year.

(b) Premium assistance credit amount

For purposes of this section—

(1) In general

The term "premium assistance credit amount" means, with respect to any taxable year, the sum of the premium assistance amounts determined under paragraph (2) with respect to all coverage months of the taxpayer occurring during the taxable year.

(2) Premium assistance amount

The premium assistance amount determined under this subsection with respect to any coverage month is the amount equal to the lesser of—

(A) the monthly premiums for such month for 1 or more qualified health plans offered in the individual market within a State which cover the taxpayer, the taxpayer's spouse, or any dependent (as defined in section 152) of the taxpayer and which were enrolled in through an Exchange established by the State under 1311 [1] of the Patient Protection and Affordable Care Act, or

(B) the excess (if any) of—

(i) the adjusted monthly premium for such month for the applicable second lowest cost silver plan with respect to the taxpayer, over

(ii) an amount equal to 1/12 of the product of the applicable percentage and the taxpayer's household income for the taxable year.

(3) Other terms and rules relating to premium assistance amounts

For purposes of paragraph (2)—

(A) Applicable percentage

(i) In general

Except as provided in clause (ii), the applicable percentage for any taxable year shall be the percentage such that the applicable percentage for any taxpayer whose household income is within an income tier specified in the following table shall increase, on a sliding scale in a linear manner, from the initial premium percentage to the final premium percentage specified in such table for such income tier:

In the case of household income (expressed as a percent of poverty line) within the following income tier:	The initial premium percentage is—	The final premium percentage is—
Up to 133%	2.0%	2.0%
133% up to 150%	3.0%	4.0%

150% up to 200%	4.0%	6.3%
200% up to 250%	6.3%	8.05%
250% up to 300%	8.05%	9.5%
300% up to 400%	9.5%	9.5%.

(ii) Indexing

(I) In general

Subject to subclause (II), in the case of taxable years beginning in any calendar year after 2014, the initial and final applicable percentages under clause (i) (as in effect for the preceding calendar year after application of this clause) shall be adjusted to reflect the excess of the rate of premium growth for the preceding calendar year over the rate of income growth for the preceding calendar year.

(II) Additional adjustment

Except as provided in subclause (III), in the case of any calendar year after 2018, the percentages described in subclause (I) shall, in addition to the adjustment under subclause (I), be adjusted to reflect the excess (if any) of the rate of premium growth estimated under subclause (I) for the preceding calendar year over the rate of growth in the consumer price index for the preceding calendar year.

(III) Failsafe

Subclause (II) shall apply for any calendar year only if the aggregate amount of premium tax credits under this section and cost-sharing reductions under section 1402 of the Patient Protection and Affordable Care Act for the preceding calendar year exceeds an amount equal to 0.504 percent of the gross domestic product for the preceding calendar year.

(iii) Temporary percentages for 2021 and 2022

In the case of a taxable year beginning in 2021 or 2022—

(I) clause (ii) shall not apply for purposes of adjusting premium percentages under this subparagraph, and

(II) the following table shall be applied in lieu of the table contained in clause (i):

In the case of household income (expressed as a percent of poverty line) within the following income tier:	The initial premium percentage is—	The final premium percentage is—
Up to 150.0 percent	0.0	0.0
150.0 percent up to 200.0 percent	0.0	2.0
200.0 percent up to 250.0 percent	2.0	4.0
250.0 percent up to 300.0 percent	4.0	6.0
300.0 percent up to 400.0 percent	6.0	8.5
400.0 percent and higher	8.5	8.5

(B) Applicable second lowest cost silver plan

The applicable second lowest cost silver plan with respect to any applicable taxpayer is the second lowest cost silver plan of the individual market in the rating area in which the taxpayer resides which—

(i) is offered through the same Exchange through which the qualified health plans taken into account under paragraph (2)(A) were offered, and

(ii) provides—

(I) self-only coverage in the case of an applicable taxpayer—

(aa) whose tax for the taxable year is determined under section 1(c) [2] (relating to unmarried individuals other than surviving spouses and heads of households) and who is not allowed a deduction under section 151 for the taxable year with respect to a dependent, or

(bb) who is not described in item (aa) but who purchases only self-only coverage, and

(II) family coverage in the case of any other applicable taxpayer.

If a taxpayer files a joint return and no credit is allowed under this section with respect to 1 of the spouses by reason of subsection (e), the taxpayer shall be treated as described in clause (ii)(I) unless a deduction is allowed under section 151 for the taxable year with respect to a dependent other than either spouse and subsection (e) does not apply to the dependent.

(C) Adjusted monthly premium

The adjusted monthly premium for an applicable second lowest cost silver plan is the monthly premium which would have been charged (for the rating area with respect to which the premiums under paragraph (2)(A) were determined) for the plan if each individual covered under a qualified health plan taken into account under paragraph (2)(A) were covered by such silver plan and the premium was adjusted only for the age of each such individual in the manner allowed under section 2701 of the Public Health Service Act. In the case of a State participating in the wellness discount demonstration project under section 2705(d) of the Public Health Service Act, the adjusted monthly premium shall be determined without regard to any premium discount or rebate under such project.

(D) Additional benefits

If—

(i) a qualified health plan under section 1302(b)(5) of the Patient Protection and Affordable Care Act offers benefits in addition to the essential health benefits required to be provided by the plan, or

(ii) a State requires a qualified health plan under section 1311(d)(3)(B) of such Act to cover benefits in addition to the essential health benefits required to be provided by the plan,

the portion of the premium for the plan properly allocable (under rules prescribed by the Secretary of Health and Human Services) to such additional benefits shall not be taken into account in determining either the monthly premium or the adjusted monthly premium under paragraph (2).

(E) Special rule for pediatric dental coverage

For purposes of determining the amount of any monthly premium, if an individual enrolls in both a qualified health plan and a plan described in section 1311(d)(2)(B)(ii)(I) [2] of the Patient Protection and Affordable Care Act for any plan year, the portion of the premium for the plan described in such section that (under regulations prescribed by the Secretary) is properly allocable to pediatric dental benefits which are included in the essential health benefits required to be provided by a qualified health plan under section 1302(b)(1)(J) of such Act shall be treated as a premium payable for a qualified health plan.

(c) Definition and rules relating to applicable taxpayers, coverage months, and qualified health plan

For purposes of this section—

(1) Applicable taxpayer

(A) In general

The term "applicable taxpayer" means, with respect to any taxable year, a taxpayer whose household income for the taxable year equals or exceeds 100 percent but does not exceed 400 percent of an amount equal to the poverty line for a family of the size involved.

(B) Special rule for certain individuals lawfully present in the United States

If—

(i) a taxpayer has a household income which is not greater than 100 percent of an amount equal to the poverty line for a family of the size involved, and

(ii) the taxpayer is an alien lawfully present in the United States, but is not eligible for the medicaid program under title XIX of the Social Security Act by reason of such alien status,

the taxpayer shall, for purposes of the credit under this section, be treated as an applicable taxpayer with a household income which is equal to 100 percent of the poverty line for a family of the size involved.

(C) Married couples must file joint return

If the taxpayer is married (within the meaning of section 7703) at the close of the taxable year, the taxpayer shall be treated as an applicable taxpayer only if the taxpayer and the taxpayer's spouse file a joint return for the taxable year.

(D) Denial of credit to dependents

No credit shall be allowed under this section to any individual with respect to whom a deduction under section 151 is allowable to another taxpayer for a taxable year beginning in the calendar year in which such individual's taxable year begins.

(E) Temporary rule for 2021 and 2022

In the case of a taxable year beginning in 2021 or 2022, subparagraph (A) shall be applied without regard to "but does not exceed 400 percent".

(2) Coverage month

For purposes of this subsection—

(A) In general

The term "coverage month" means, with respect to an applicable taxpayer, any month if—

(i) as of the first day of such month the taxpayer, the taxpayer's spouse, or any dependent of the taxpayer is covered by a qualified health plan described in subsection (b)(2)(A) that was enrolled in through an Exchange established by the State under section 1311 of the Patient Protection and Affordable Care Act, and

(ii) the premium for coverage under such plan for such month is paid by the taxpayer (or through advance payment of the credit under subsection (a) under section 1412 of the Patient Protection and Affordable Care Act).

(B) Exception for minimum essential coverage

(i) In general

The term "coverage month" shall not include any month with respect to an individual if for such month the individual is eligible for minimum essential coverage other than eligibility for coverage described in section 5000A(f)(1)(C) (relating to coverage in the individual market).

(ii) Minimum essential coverage

The term "minimum essential coverage" has the meaning given such term by section 5000A(f).

(C) Special rule for employer-sponsored minimum essential coverage

For purposes of subparagraph (B)—

(i) Coverage must be affordable

Except as provided in clause (iii), an employee shall not be treated as eligible for minimum essential coverage if such coverage—

(I) consists of an eligible employer-sponsored plan (as defined in section 5000A(f)(2)), and

(II) the employee's required contribution (within the meaning of section 5000A(e)(1)(B)) with respect to the plan exceeds 9.5 percent of the applicable taxpayer's household income.

This clause shall also apply to an individual who is eligible to enroll in the plan by reason of a relationship the individual bears to the employee.

(ii) Coverage must provide minimum value

Except as provided in clause (iii), an employee shall not be treated as eligible for minimum essential coverage if such coverage consists of an eligible employer-sponsored plan (as defined in section 5000A(f)(2)) and the plan's share of the total allowed costs of benefits provided under the plan is less than 60 percent of such costs.

(iii) Employee or family must not be covered under employer plan

Clauses (i) and (ii) shall not apply if the employee (or any individual described in the last sentence of clause (i)) is covered under the eligible employer-sponsored plan or the grandfathered health plan.

(iv) Indexing

In the case of plan years beginning in any calendar year after 2014, the Secretary shall adjust the 9.5 percent under clause (i)(II) in the same manner as the percentages are adjusted under subsection (b)(3)(A)(ii).

(3) Definitions and other rules

(A) Qualified health plan

The term "qualified health plan" has the meaning given such term by section 1301(a) of the Patient Protection and Affordable Care Act, except that such term shall not include a qualified health plan which is a catastrophic plan described in section 1302(e) of such Act.

(B) Grandfathered health plan

The term "grandfathered health plan" has the meaning given such term by section 1251 of the Patient Protection and Affordable Care Act.

(4) Special rules for qualified small employer health reimbursement arrangements

(A) In general

The term "coverage month" shall not include any month with respect to an employee (or any spouse or dependent of such employee) if for such month the employee is provided a qualified small employer health reimbursement arrangement which constitutes affordable coverage.

(B) Denial of double benefit

In the case of any employee who is provided a qualified small employer health reimbursement arrangement for any coverage month (determined without regard to subparagraph (A)), the credit otherwise allowable under subsection (a) to the taxpayer for such month shall be reduced (but not below zero) by the amount described in subparagraph (C)(i)(II) for such month.

(C) Affordable coverage

For purposes of subparagraph (A), a qualified small employer health reimbursement arrangement shall be treated as constituting affordable coverage for a month if—

(i) the excess of—

(I) the amount that would be paid by the employee as the premium for such month for self-only coverage under the second lowest cost silver plan offered in the relevant individual health insurance market, over

(II) 1/12 of the employee's permitted benefit (as defined in section 9831(d)(3)(C) under such arrangement, does not exceed—

(ii) 1/12 of 9.5 percent of the employee's household income.

(D) Qualified small employer health reimbursement arrangement

For purposes of this paragraph, the term "qualified small employer health reimbursement arrangement" has the meaning given such term by section 9831(d)(2).

(E) Coverage for less than entire year

In the case of an employee who is provided a qualified small employer health reimbursement arrangement for less than an entire year, subparagraph (C)(i)(II) shall be applied by substituting "the number of months during the year for which such arrangement was provided" for "12".

(F) Indexing

In the case of plan years beginning in any calendar year after 2014, the Secretary shall adjust the 9.5 percent amount under subparagraph (C)(ii) in the same manner as the percentages are adjusted under subsection (b)(3)(A)(ii).

(d) Terms relating to income and families

For purposes of this section—

(1) Family size

The family size involved with respect to any taxpayer shall be equal to the number of individuals for whom the taxpayer is allowed a deduction under section 151 (relating to allowance of deduction for personal exemptions) for the taxable year.

(2) Household income

(A) Household income

The term "household income" means, with respect to any taxpayer, an amount equal to the sum of—

(i) the modified adjusted gross income of the taxpayer, plus

(ii) the aggregate modified adjusted gross incomes of all other individuals who—

(I) were taken into account in determining the taxpayer's family size under paragraph (1), and

(II) were required to file a return of tax imposed by section 1 for the taxable year.

(B) Modified adjusted gross income

The term "modified adjusted gross income" means adjusted gross income increased by—

(i) any amount excluded from gross income under section 911,

(ii) any amount of interest received or accrued by the taxpayer during the taxable year which is exempt from tax, and

(iii) an amount equal to the portion of the taxpayer's social security benefits (as defined in section 86(d)) which is not included in gross income under section 86 for the taxable year.

(3) Poverty line

(A) In general

The term "poverty line" has the meaning given that term in section 2110(c)(5) of the Social Security Act (42 U.S.C. 1397jj(c)(5)).

(B) Poverty line used

In the case of any qualified health plan offered through an Exchange for coverage during a taxable year beginning in a calendar year, the poverty line used shall be the most recently published poverty line as of the 1st day of the regular enrollment period for coverage during such calendar year.

(e) Rules for individuals not lawfully present

(1) In general

If 1 or more individuals for whom a taxpayer is allowed a deduction under section 151 (relating to allowance of deduction for personal exemptions) for the taxable year (including the taxpayer or his spouse) are individuals who are not lawfully present—

(A) the aggregate amount of premiums otherwise taken into account under clauses (i) and (ii) of subsection (b)(2)(A) shall be reduced by the portion (if any) of such premiums which is attributable to such individuals, and

(B) for purposes of applying this section, the determination as to what percentage a taxpayer's household income bears to the poverty level for a family of the size involved shall be made under one of the following methods:

(i) A method under which—

(I) the taxpayer's family size is determined by not taking such individuals into account, and

(II) the taxpayer's household income is equal to the product of the taxpayer's household income (determined without regard to this subsection) and a fraction—

(aa) the numerator of which is the poverty line for the taxpayer's family size determined after application of subclause (I), and

(bb) the denominator of which is the poverty line for the taxpayer's family size determined without regard to subclause (I).

(ii) A comparable method reaching the same result as the method under clause (i).

(2) Lawfully present

For purposes of this section, an individual shall be treated as lawfully present only if the individual is, and is reasonably expected to be for the entire period of enrollment for which the credit under this section is being claimed, a citizen or national of the United States or an alien lawfully present in the United States.

(3) Secretarial authority

The Secretary of Health and Human Services, in consultation with the Secretary, shall prescribe rules setting forth the methods by which calculations of family size and household income are made for purposes of this subsection. Such rules shall be designed to ensure that the least burden is placed on individuals enrolling in qualified health plans through an Exchange and taxpayers eligible for the credit allowable under this section.

(f) Reconciliation of credit and advance credit

(1) In general

The amount of the credit allowed under this section for any taxable year shall be reduced (but not below zero) by the amount of any advance payment of such credit under section 1412 of the Patient Protection and Affordable Care Act.

(2) Excess advance payments

(A) In general

If the advance payments to a taxpayer under section 1412 of the Patient Protection and Affordable Care Act for a taxable year exceed the credit allowed by this section (determined without regard to paragraph (1)), the tax imposed by this chapter for the taxable year shall be increased by the amount of such excess.

(B) Limitation on increase

(i) In general

In the case of a taxpayer whose household income is less than 400 percent of the poverty line for the size of the family involved for the taxable year, the amount of the increase under subparagraph (A) shall in no event exceed the applicable dollar amount determined in accordance with the following table (one-half of such amount in the case of a taxpayer whose tax is determined under section 1(c) [2] for the taxable year):

If the household income (expressed as a percent of poverty line) is:	The applicable dollar amount is:
Less than 200%	$600
At least 200% but less than 300%	$1,500
At least 300% but less than 400%	$2,500.

(ii) Indexing of amount

In the case of any calendar year beginning after 2014, each of the dollar amounts in the table contained under clause (i) shall be increased by an amount equal to—

(I) such dollar amount, multiplied by

(II) the cost-of-living adjustment determined under section 1(f)(3) for the calendar year, determined by substituting "calendar year 2013" for "calendar year 2016" in subparagraph (A)(ii) thereof.

If the amount of any increase under clause (i) is not a multiple of $50, such increase shall be rounded to the next lowest multiple of $50.

(iii) Temporary modification of limitation on increase

In the case of any taxable year beginning in 2020, for any taxpayer who files for such taxable year an income tax return reconciling any advance payment of the credit under this section, the Secretary shall treat subparagraph (A) as not applying.

(3) Information requirement

Each Exchange (or any person carrying out 1 or more responsibilities of an Exchange under section 1311(f)(3) or 1321(c) of the Patient Protection and Affordable Care Act) shall provide the following information to the Secretary and to the taxpayer with respect to any health plan provided through the Exchange:

(A) The level of coverage described in section 1302(d) of the Patient Protection and Affordable Care Act and the period such coverage was in effect.

(B) The total premium for the coverage without regard to the credit under this section or cost-sharing reductions under section 1402 of such Act.

(C) The aggregate amount of any advance payment of such credit or reductions under section 1412 of such Act.

(D) The name, address, and TIN of the primary insured and the name and TIN of each other individual obtaining coverage under the policy.

(E) Any information provided to the Exchange, including any change of circumstances, necessary to determine eligibility for, and the amount of, such credit.

(F) Information necessary to determine whether a taxpayer has received excess advance payments.

(g) Special rule for individuals who receive unemployment compensation during 2021

(1) In general

For purposes of this section, in the case of a taxpayer who has received, or has been approved to receive, unemployment compensation for any week beginning during 2021, for the taxable year in which such week begins—

(A) such taxpayer shall be treated as an applicable taxpayer, and

(B) there shall not be taken into account any household income of the taxpayer in excess of 133 percent of the poverty line for a family of the size involved.

(2) Unemployment compensation

For purposes of this subsection, the term "unemployment compensation" has the meaning given such term in section 85(b).

(3) Evidence of unemployment compensation

For purposes of this subsection, a taxpayer shall not be treated as having received (or been approved to receive) unemployment compensation for any week unless such taxpayer provides self-attestation of, and such documentation as the Secretary shall prescribe which demonstrates, such receipt or approval.

(4) Clarification of rules remaining applicable

(A) Joint return requirement

Paragraph (1)(A) shall not affect the application of subsection (c)(1)(C).

(B) Household income and affordability [3]

Paragraph (1)(B) shall not apply to any determination of household income for purposes of paragraph (2)(C)(i)(II) or (4)(C)(ii) of subsection (c) [4]

(h) Regulations

The Secretary shall prescribe such regulations as may be necessary to carry out the provisions of this section, including regulations which provide for—

(1) the coordination of the credit allowed under this section with the program for advance payment of the credit under section 1412 of the Patient Protection and Affordable Care Act, and

(2) the application of subsection (f) where the filing status of the taxpayer for a taxable year is different from such status used for determining the advance payment of the credit.

(Added and amended Pub. L. 111–148, title I, §1401(a), title X, §§10105(a)–(c), 10108(h)(1), Mar. 23, 2010, 124 Stat. 213, 906, 914; Pub. L. 111–152, title I, §§1001(a), 1004(a)(1)(A), (2)(A), (c), Mar. 30, 2010, 124 Stat. 1030, 1034, 1035; Pub. L. 111–309, title II, §208(a), (b), Dec. 15, 2010, 124 Stat. 3291, 3292; Pub. L. 112–9, §4(a), Apr. 14, 2011, 125 Stat. 36; Pub. L. 112–10, div. B, title VIII, §1858(b)(1), Apr. 15, 2011, 125 Stat. 168; Pub. L. 112–56, title IV, §401(a), Nov. 21, 2011,

125 Stat. 734; Pub. L. 114–255, div. C, title XVIII, §18001(a)(3), Dec. 13, 2016, 130 Stat. 1341; Pub. L. 115–97, title I, §11002(d)(1)(E), Dec. 22, 2017, 131 Stat. 2060; Pub. L. 117–2, title IX, §§9661(a), (b), 9662(a), 9663(a), Mar. 11, 2021, 135 Stat. 182, 183.)

INFLATION ADJUSTED ITEMS FOR CERTAIN YEARS

For inflation adjustment of certain items in this section, see Revenue Procedures listed in a table under section 1 of this title.

EDITORIAL NOTES
REFERENCES IN TEXT

Sections 1251, 1301, 1302, 1311, 1321, 1402, and 1412 of the Patient Protection and Affordable Care Act, referred to in text, are classified to sections 18011, 18021, 18022, 18031, 18041, 18071, and 18082, respectively, of Title 42, The Public Health and Welfare.

Section 1(c), referred to in subsecs. (b)(3)(B)(ii)(I)(aa) and (f)(2)(B)(i), to be treated, for purposes of the rate of tax, as a reference to the corresponding rate bracket under section 1(j)(2)(C) of this title, see section 1(j)(2)(F) of this title.

Sections 2701 and 2705(d) of the Public Health Service Act, referred to in subsec. (b)(3)(C), are classified to sections 300gg and 300gg–4(d), respectively, of Title 42, The Public Health and Welfare. The reference to section 2705(d) probably should be a reference to section 2705(l), which relates to wellness program demonstration project and is classified to section 300gg–4(l) of Title 42.

Section 1311(d)(2)(B)(ii)(I) of the Patient Protection and Affordable Care Act, referred to in subsec. (b)(3)(E), probably means section 1311(d)(2)(B)(ii) of Pub. L. 111–148, which is classified to section 18031(d)(2)(B)(ii) of Title 42, The Public Health and Welfare, and which does not contain subclauses.

The Social Security Act, referred to in subsec. (c)(1)(B)(ii), is act Aug. 14, 1935, ch. 531, 49 Stat. 620. Title XIX of the Act is classified generally to subchapter XIX (§1396 et seq.) of chapter 7 of Title 42, The Public Health and Welfare. For complete classification of this Act to the Code, see section 1305 of Title 42 and Tables.

AMENDMENTS

2021—Subsec. (b)(3)(A)(iii). Pub. L. 117–2, §9661(a), added cl. (iii).

Subsec. (c)(1)(E). Pub. L. 117–2, §9661(b), added subpar. (E).

Subsec. (f)(2)(B)(iii). Pub. L. 117–2, §9662(a), added cl. (iii).

Subsecs. (g), (h). Pub. L. 117–2, §9663(a), added subsec. (g) and redesignated former subsec. (g) as (h).

2017—Subsec. (f)(2)(B)(ii)(II). Pub. L. 115–97 substituted "for 'calendar year 2016' in subparagraph (A)(ii)" for "for 'calendar year 1992' in subparagraph (B)".

2016—Subsec. (c)(4). Pub. L. 114–255 added par. (4).

2011—Subsec. (c)(2)(D). Pub. L. 112–10 struck out subpar. (D). Prior to amendment, text read as follows: "The term 'coverage month' shall not include any month in which such individual has a free choice voucher provided under section 10108 of the Patient Protection and Affordable Care Act."

Subsec. (d)(2)(B)(iii). Pub. L. 112–56 added cl. (iii).

Subsec. (f)(2)(B)(i). Pub. L. 112–9 amended cl. (i) generally. Prior to amendment, cl. (i) consisted of text and a table limiting increase in amount recovered on reconciliation of health insurance tax credit and advance of that credit for households with income below 500 percent of Federal poverty line.

2010—Subsec. (b)(3)(A)(i). Pub. L. 111–152, §1001(a)(1)(A), substituted "for any taxable year shall be the percentage such that the applicable percentage for any taxpayer whose household income is within an income tier specified in the following table shall increase, on a sliding scale in a linear manner, from the initial premium percentage to the final premium percentage specified in such table for such income tier:" for "with respect to any taxpayer for any taxable year is equal to 2.8 percent, increased by the number of percentage points (not greater than 7) which bears the same ratio to 7 percentage points as—" in introductory provisions, inserted table, and struck out subcls. (I) and (II) which read as follows:

"(I) the taxpayer's household income for the taxable year in excess of 100 percent of the poverty line for a family of the size involved, bears to

"(II) an amount equal to 200 percent of the poverty line for a family of the size involved."

Subsec. (b)(3)(A)(ii). Pub. L. 111–152, §1001(a)(1)(B), added cl. (ii) and struck out former cl. (ii). Text read as follows: "If a taxpayer's household income for the taxable year equals or exceeds 100 percent, but not more than 133 percent, of the poverty line for a family of the size involved, the taxpayer's applicable percentage shall be 2 percent."

Pub. L. 111–148, §10105(a), substituted "equals or exceeds" for "is in excess of".

Subsec. (b)(3)(A)(iii). Pub. L. 111–152, §1001(a)(1)(B), struck out cl. (iii). Text read as follows: "In the case of taxable years beginning in any calendar year after 2014, the Secretary shall adjust the initial and final applicable percentages under clause (i), and the 2 percent under clause (ii), for the calendar year to reflect the excess of the rate of premium growth between the preceding calendar year and 2013 over the rate of income growth for such period."

Subsec. (c)(1)(A). Pub. L. 111–148, §10105(b), inserted "equals or" before "exceeds".

Subsec. (c)(2)(C)(i)(II). Pub. L. 111–152, §1001(a)(2)(A), substituted "9.5 percent" for "9.8 percent".

Subsec. (c)(2)(C)(iv). Pub. L. 111–152, §1001(a)(2), substituted "9.5 percent" for "9.8 percent" and "(b)(3)(A)(ii)" for "(b)(3)(A)(iii)".

Pub. L. 111–148, §10105(c), substituted "subsection (b)(3)(A)(iii)" for "subsection (b)(3)(A)(ii)".

Subsec. (c)(2)(D). Pub. L. 111–148, §10108(h)(1), added subpar. (D).

Subsec. (d)(2)(A)(i), (ii). Pub. L. 111–152, §1004(a)(1)(A), substituted "modified adjusted gross" for "modified gross".

Subsec. (d)(2)(B). Pub. L. 111–152, §1004(a)(2)(A), amended subpar. (B) generally. Prior to amendment, text read as follows: "The term 'modified gross income' means gross income—

"(i) decreased by the amount of any deduction allowable under paragraph (1), (3), (4), or (10) of section 62(a),

"(ii) increased by the amount of interest received or accrued during the taxable year which is exempt from tax imposed by this chapter, and

"(iii) determined without regard to sections 911, 931, and 933."

Subsec. (f)(2)(B). Pub. L. 111–309, §208(a), amended generally subpar. heading and cl. (i). Prior to amendment, text of cl. (i) read as follows: "In the case of an applicable taxpayer whose household income is less than 400 percent of the poverty line for the size of the family involved for the taxable year, the amount of the increase under subparagraph (A) shall in no event exceed $400 ($250 in the case of a taxpayer whose tax is determined under section 1(c) for the taxable year)."

Subsec. (f)(2)(B)(ii). Pub. L. 111–309, §208(b), inserted "in the table contained" after "each of the dollar amounts" in introductory provisions.

Subsec. (f)(3). Pub. L. 111–152, §1004(c), added par. (3).

STATUTORY NOTES AND RELATED SUBSIDIARIES
EFFECTIVE DATE OF 2021 AMENDMENT

Pub. L. 117–2, title IX, §9661(c), Mar. 11, 2021, 135 Stat. 183, provided that: "The amendments made by this section [amending this section] shall apply to taxable years beginning after December 31, 2020."

Pub. L. 117–2, title IX, §9662(b), Mar. 11, 2021, 135 Stat. 183, provided that: "The amendment made by this section [amending this section] shall apply to taxable years beginning after December 31, 2019."

Pub. L. 117–2, title IX, §9663(b), Mar. 11, 2021, 135 Stat. 184, provided that: "The amendments made by this section [amending this section] shall apply to taxable years beginning after December 31, 2020."

EFFECTIVE DATE OF 2017 AMENDMENT

Amendment by Pub. L. 115–97 applicable to taxable years beginning after Dec. 31, 2017, see section 11002(e) of Pub. L. 115–97, set out as a note under section 1 of this title.

EFFECTIVE DATE OF 2016 AMENDMENT

Pub. L. 114–255, div. C, title XVIII, §18001(a)(7), Dec. 13, 2016, 130 Stat. 1343, provided that:

"(A) In general.—Except as otherwise provided in this paragraph, the amendments made by this subsection [amending this section, sections 106, 4980I, 6051, 6652, and 9831 of this title, and section 18081 of Title 42, The Public Health and Welfare] shall apply to years beginning after December 31, 2016.

"(B) Transition relief.—The relief under Treasury Notice 2015–17 shall be treated as applying to any plan year beginning on or before December 31, 2016.

"(C) Coordination with health insurance premium credit.—The amendments made by paragraph (3) [amending this section] shall apply to taxable years beginning after December 31, 2016.

"(D) Employee notice.—

"(i) In general.—The amendments made by paragraph (5) [amending section 6652 of this title] shall apply to notices with respect to years beginning after December 31, 2016.

"(ii) Transition relief.—For purposes of section 6652(o) of the Internal Revenue Code of 1986 (as added by this Act), a person shall not be treated as failing to provide a written notice as required by section 9831(d)(4) of such Code if such notice is so provided not later than 90 days after the date of the enactment of this Act [Dec. 13, 2016].

"(E) W–2 reporting.—The amendments made by paragraph (6)(A) [amending section 6051 of this title] shall apply to calendar years beginning after December 31, 2016.

"(F) Information provided by exchange subsidy applicants.—

"(i) In general.—The amendments made by paragraph (6)(B) [amending section 18081 of Title 42] shall apply to applications for enrollment made after December 31, 2016.

"(ii) Verification.—Verification under section 1411 of the Patient Protection and Affordable Care Act [42 U.S.C. 18081] of information provided under section 1411(b)(3)(B) of such Act shall apply with respect to months beginning after October 2016.

"(iii) Transitional relief.—In the case of an application for enrollment under section 1411(b) of the Patient Protection and Affordable Care Act [42 U.S.C. 18081(b)] made before April 1, 2017, the requirement of section 1411(b)(3)(B) of such Act shall be treated as met if the information described therein is provided not later than 30 days after the date on which the applicant receives the notice described in section 9831(d)(4) of the Internal Revenue Code of 1986."

EFFECTIVE DATE OF 2011 AMENDMENT

Pub. L. 112–56, title IV, §401(b), Nov. 21, 2011, 125 Stat. 734, provided that: "The amendments made by this section [amending this section] shall take effect on the date of the enactment of this Act [Nov. 21, 2011]."

Pub. L. 112–10, div. B, title VIII, §1858(d), Apr. 15, 2011, 125 Stat. 169, provided that: "The amendments made by this section [amending this section, sections 162, 4980H, and 6056 of this title, and section 218b of Title 29, Labor, and repealing section 139D of this title and section 18101 of Title 42, The Public Health and Welfare] shall take effect as if included in the provisions of, and the amendments made by, the provisions of the Patient Protection and Affordable Care Act [Pub. L. 111–148] to which they relate."

Pub. L. 112–9, §4(b), Apr. 14, 2011, 125 Stat. 37, provided that: "The amendment made by this section [amending this section] shall apply to taxable years ending after December 31, 2013."

EFFECTIVE DATE OF 2010 AMENDMENT

Pub. L. 111–309, title II, §208(c), Dec. 15, 2010, 124 Stat. 3292, provided that: "The amendment made by this section [amending this section] shall apply to taxable years beginning after December 31, 2013."

Pub. L. 111–148, title X, §10108(h)(2), Mar. 23, 2010, 124 Stat. 914, provided that: "The amendment made by this subsection [amending this section] shall apply to taxable years beginning after December 31, 2013."

EFFECTIVE DATE

Pub. L. 111–148, title I, §1401(e), Mar. 23, 2010, 124 Stat. 220, provided that: "The amendments made by this section [enacting this section and amending sections 280C and 6211 of this title and section 1324 of Title 31, Money and Finance] shall apply to taxable years ending after December 31, 2013."

SUBSTANTIATION REQUIREMENTS

Pub. L. 114–255, div. C, title XVIII, §18001(a)(8), Dec. 13, 2016, 130 Stat. 1343, provided that: "The Secretary of the Treasury (or his designee) may issue substantiation requirements as necessary to carry out this subsection [amending this section, sections 106, 4980I, 6051, 6652, and 9831 of this title, and section 18081 of Title 42, The Public Health and Welfare, and enacting provisions set out as a note under this section]."

NO IMPACT ON SOCIAL SECURITY TRUST FUNDS

Pub. L. 112–56, title IV, §401(c), Nov. 21, 2011, 125 Stat. 734, provided that:

"(1) Estimate of secretary.—The Secretary of the Treasury, or the Secretary's delegate, shall annually estimate the impact that the amendments made by subsection (a) [amending this section] have on the income and balances of the trust funds established under section 201 of the Social Security Act (42 U.S.C. 401).

"(2) Transfer of funds.—If, under paragraph (1), the Secretary of the Treasury or the Secretary's delegate estimates that such amendments have a negative impact on the income and balances of such trust funds, the Secretary shall transfer, not less frequently than quarterly, from the general fund an amount sufficient so as to ensure that the income and balances of such trust funds are not reduced as a result of such amendments."

¹ So in original. Probably should be preceded by "section".
² See References in Text note below.
³ So in original. Probably should be "affordability".
⁴ So in original. Probably should be followed by a period.

[§36C. Renumbered §23]

§37. Overpayments of tax

For credit against the tax imposed by this subtitle for overpayments of tax, see section 6401.

(Aug. 16, 1954, ch. 736, 68A Stat. 16, §38; renumbered §39, Pub. L. 87–834, §2(a), Oct. 16, 1962, 76 Stat. 962; renumbered §40, Pub. L. 89–44, title VIII, §809(c), June 21, 1965, 79 Stat. 167; renumbered §42, Pub. L. 92–178, title VI, §601(a), Dec. 10, 1971, 85 Stat. 553; renumbered §43, Pub. L. 94–12, title II, §203(a), Mar. 29, 1975, 89 Stat. 29; renumbered §44, Pub. L. 94–12, title II, §204(a), Mar. 29, 1975, 89 Stat. 30; renumbered §45, Pub. L. 94–12, title II, §208(a), Mar. 29, 1975, 89 Stat. 32; renumbered §35, Pub. L. 98–369, div. A, title IV, §471(c), July 18, 1984, 98 Stat. 826; renumbered §36, Pub. L. 107–210, div. A, title II, §201(a), Aug. 6, 2002, 116 Stat. 954; renumbered §37, Pub. L. 110–289, div. C, title I, §3011(a), July 30, 2008, 122 Stat. 2888.)

EDITORIAL NOTES
PRIOR PROVISIONS

A prior section 37 was renumbered section 22 of this title.

Subpart D—Business Related Credits

EDITORIAL NOTES
AMENDMENTS
2019—Pub. L. 116–94, div. O, title I, §105(c), Dec. 20, 2019, 133 Stat. 3148, added item 45T.
2018—Pub. L. 115–141, div. U, title IV, §401(a)(7), (d)(2)(A), Mar. 23, 2018, 132 Stat. 1184, 1208, struck out item 41 "Employee stock ownership credit" and item 45M "Energy efficient appliance credit" and transferred item 45K to appear after item 45J.
2017—Pub. L. 115–97, title I, §13403(d)(3), Dec. 22, 2017, 131 Stat. 2138, added item 45S.
2010—Pub. L. 111–148, title I, §1421(e), Mar. 23, 2010, 124 Stat. 242, added item 45R.

2008—Pub. L. 110–343, div. B, title I, §115(c), Oct. 3, 2008, 122 Stat. 3831, which directed amendment of table of sections for subpart B by adding item 45Q at end, was executed by adding item 45Q at end of table of sections for this subpart to reflect the probable intent of Congress.

Pub. L. 110–245, title I, §111(d), June 17, 2008, 122 Stat. 1635, added item 45P.

Pub. L. 110–234, title XV, §§15321(b)(3)(B), 15343(d), May 22, 2008, 122 Stat. 1513, 1520, and Pub. L. 110–246, title XV, §§15321(b)(3)(B), 15343(d), June 18, 2008, 122 Stat. 2275, 2282, made identical amendments, inserting ", etc.," after "Alcohol" in item 40 and adding item 45O. The amendments by Pub. L. 110–234 were repealed by Pub. L. 110–246, §4(a), June 18, 2008, 122 Stat. 1664.

2006—Pub. L. 109–432, div. A, title IV, §405(d), Dec. 20, 2006, 120 Stat. 2958, added item 45N.

2005—Pub. L. 109–58, title XIII, §§1306(c), 1322(a)(3)(L), 1332(e), 1334(c), 1346(b)(2), Aug. 8, 2005, 119 Stat. 999, 1012, 1026, 1033, 1055, inserted "and renewable diesel" after "Biodiesel" in item 40A and added items 45I to 45M.

2004—Pub. L. 108–357, title II, §245(d), title III, §§302(c)(3), 339(e), 341(d), title VII, §710(b)(3)(B), Oct. 22, 2004, 118 Stat. 1448, 1466, 1484, 1487, 1556, added items 40A and 45G to 45I and inserted ", etc" after "resources" in item 45.

Pub. L. 108–311, title IV, §408(b)(7), Oct. 4, 2004, 118 Stat. 1193, amended directory language of Pub. L. 107–16, §619(c)(3). See 2001 Amendment note below.

2001—Pub. L. 107–16, title VI, §619(c)(3), June 7, 2001, 115 Stat. 110, as amended by Pub. L. 108–311, title IV, §408(b)(7), Oct. 4, 2004, 118 Stat. 1193, added item 45E.

Pub. L. 107–16, title II, §205(b)(2), June 7, 2001, 115 Stat. 53, added item 45F.

2000—Pub. L. 106–554, §1(a)(7) [title I, §121(d)], Dec. 21, 2000, 114 Stat. 2763, 2763A-610, added item 45D.

1996—Pub. L. 104–188, title I, §1205(a)(3)(B), Aug. 20, 1996, 110 Stat. 1775, added item 45C.

1993—Pub. L. 103–66, title XIII, §§13322(e), 13443(c), Aug. 10, 1993, 107 Stat. 563, 569, added items 45A and 45B.

1992—Pub. L. 102–486, title XIX, §1914(d), Oct. 24, 1992, 106 Stat. 3023, added item 45.

1990—Pub. L. 101–508, title XI, §§11511(c)(1), 11611(d), Nov. 5, 1990, 104 Stat. 1388–485, 1388-503, added items 43 and 44.

1986—Pub. L. 99–514, title II, §§231(d)(3)(K), 252(d), Oct. 22, 1986, 100 Stat. 2180, 2205, added item 41 relating to credit for increasing research activities and item 42.

1984—Pub. L. 98–369, div. A, title IV, §471(b), July 18, 1984, 98 Stat. 826, added subpart D heading and analysis of sections for subpart D, consisting of items 38 (new), 39 (new), 40 (formerly 44E), and 41 (formerly 44G). Former subpart D was redesignated F.

§38. General business credit

(a) Allowance of credit

There shall be allowed as a credit against the tax imposed by this chapter for the taxable year an amount equal to the sum of—

(1) the business credit carryforwards carried to such taxable year,

(2) the amount of the current year business credit, plus

(3) the business credit carrybacks carried to such taxable year.

(b) Current year business credit

For purposes of this subpart, the amount of the current year business credit is the sum of the following credits determined for the taxable year:

(1) the investment credit determined under section 46,

(2) the work opportunity credit determined under section 51(a),

(3) the alcohol fuels credit determined under section 40(a),

(4) the research credit determined under section 41(a),

(5) the low-income housing credit determined under section 42(a),

(6) the enhanced oil recovery credit under section 43(a),

(7) in the case of an eligible small business (as defined in section 44(b)), the disabled access credit determined under section 44(a),

(8) the renewable electricity production credit under section 45(a),

(9) the empowerment zone employment credit determined under section 1396(a),

(10) the Indian employment credit as determined under section 45A(a),

(11) the employer social security credit determined under section 45B(a),

(12) the orphan drug credit determined under section 45C(a),

(13) the new markets tax credit determined under section 45D(a),

(14) in the case of an eligible employer (as defined in section 45E(c)), the small employer pension plan startup cost credit determined under section 45E(a),

(15) the employer-provided child care credit determined under section 45F(a),

(16) the railroad track maintenance credit determined under section 45G(a),

(17) the biodiesel fuels credit determined under section 40A(a),

(18) the low sulfur diesel fuel production credit determined under section 45H(a),

(19) the marginal oil and gas well production credit determined under section 45I(a),

(20) the distilled spirits credit determined under section 5011(a),

(21) the advanced nuclear power facility production credit determined under section 45J(a),

(22) the nonconventional source production credit determined under section 45K(a),

(23) the new energy efficient home credit determined under section 45L(a),

(24) the portion of the alternative motor vehicle credit to which section 30B(g)(1) applies,

(25) the portion of the alternative fuel vehicle refueling property credit to which section 30C(d)(1) applies,

(26) the mine rescue team training credit determined under section 45N(a),

(27) in the case of an eligible agricultural business (as defined in section 45O(e)), the agricultural chemicals security credit determined under section 45O(a),

(28) the differential wage payment credit determined under section 45P(a),

(29) the carbon dioxide sequestration credit determined under section 45Q(a),

(30) the portion of the new qualified plug-in electric drive motor vehicle credit to which section 30D(c)(1) applies,

(31) the small employer health insurance credit determined under section 45R,

(32) in the case of an eligible employer (as defined in section 45S(c)), the paid family and medical leave credit determined under section 45S(a), plus

(33) in the case of an eligible employer (as defined in section 45T(c)), the retirement auto-enrollment credit determined under section 45T(a).

(c) Limitation based on amount of tax

(1) In general

The credit allowed under subsection (a) for any taxable year shall not exceed the excess (if any) of the taxpayer's net income tax over the greater of—

(A) the tentative minimum tax for the taxable year, or

(B) 25 percent of so much of the taxpayer's net regular tax liability as exceeds $25,000.

For purposes of the preceding sentence, the term "net income tax" means the sum of the regular tax liability and the tax imposed by section 55, reduced by the credits allowable under subparts A and B of this part, and the term "net regular tax liability" means the regular tax liability reduced by the sum of the credits allowable under subparts A and B of this part.

(2) Empowerment zone employment credit may offset 25 percent of minimum tax

(A) In general

In the case of the empowerment zone employment credit—

(i) this section and section 39 shall be applied separately with respect to such credit, and

(ii) for purposes of applying paragraph (1) to such credit—

(I) 75 percent of the tentative minimum tax shall be substituted for the tentative minimum tax under subparagraph (A) thereof, and

(II) the limitation under paragraph (1) (as modified by subclause (I)) shall be reduced by the credit allowed under subsection (a) for the taxable year (other than the empowerment zone employment credit and the specified credits).

(B) Empowerment zone employment credit

For purposes of this paragraph, the term "empowerment zone employment credit" means the portion of the credit under subsection (a) which is attributable to the credit determined under section 1396 (relating to empowerment zone employment credit).

[(3) Repealed. Pub. L. 115–141, div. U, title IV, §401(d)(6)(B)(iii), Mar. 23, 2018, 132 Stat. 1211]

(4) Special rules for specified credits

(A) In general

In the case of specified credits—

(i) this section and section 39 shall be applied separately with respect to such credits, and

(ii) in applying paragraph (1) to such credits—

(I) the tentative minimum tax shall be treated as being zero, and

(II) the limitation under paragraph (1) (as modified by subclause (I)) shall be reduced by the credit allowed under subsection (a) for the taxable year (other than the specified credits).

(B) Specified credits

For purposes of this subsection, the term "specified credits" means—

(i) for taxable years beginning after December 31, 2004, the credit determined under section 40,

(ii) the credit determined under section 41 for the taxable year with respect to an eligible small business (as defined in paragraph (5)(A) after application of the rules of paragraph (5)(B)),

(iii) the credit determined under section 42 to the extent attributable to buildings placed in service after December 31, 2007,

(iv) the credit determined under section 45 to the extent that such credit is attributable to electricity or refined coal produced—

(I) at a facility which is originally placed in service after the date of the enactment of this paragraph, and

(II) during the 4-year period beginning on the date that such facility was originally placed in service,

(v) the credit determined under section 45 to the extent that such credit is attributable to section 45(e)(10) (relating to Indian coal production facilities),

(vi) the credit determined under section 45B,

(vii) the credit determined under section 45G,

(viii) the credit determined under section 45R,

(ix) the credit determined under section 45S,

(x) the credit determined under section 46 to the extent that such credit is attributable to the energy credit determined under section 48,

(xi) the credit determined under section 46 to the extent that such credit is attributable to the rehabilitation credit under section 47, but only with respect to qualified rehabilitation expenditures properly taken into account for periods after December 31, 2007, and

(xii) the credit determined under section 51.

(5) Rules related to eligible small businesses

(A) Eligible small business

For purposes of this subsection, the term "eligible small business" means, with respect to any taxable year—

(i) a corporation the stock of which is not publicly traded,

(ii) a partnership, or

(iii) a sole proprietorship,

if the average annual gross receipts of such corporation, partnership, or sole proprietorship for the 3-taxable-year period preceding such taxable year does not exceed $50,000,000. For purposes of applying the test under the preceding sentence, rules similar to the rules of paragraphs (2) and (3) of section 448(c) shall apply.

(B) Treatment of partners and S corporation shareholders

For purposes of paragraph (4)(B)(ii), any credit determined under section 41 with respect to a partnership or S corporation shall not be treated as a specified credit by any partner or shareholder unless such partner or shareholder meets the gross receipts test under subparagraph (A) for the taxable year in which such credit is treated as a current year business credit.

(6) Special rules

(A) Married individuals

In the case of a husband or wife who files a separate return, the amount specified under subparagraph (B) of paragraph (1) shall be $12,500 in lieu of $25,000. This subparagraph shall not apply if the spouse of the taxpayer has no business credit carryforward or carryback to, and has no current year business credit for, the taxable year of such spouse which ends within or with the taxpayer's taxable year.

(B) Controlled groups

In the case of a controlled group, the $25,000 amount specified under subparagraph (B) of paragraph (1) shall be reduced for each component member of such group by apportioning $25,000 among the component members of such group in such manner as the Secretary shall by regulations prescribe. For purposes of the preceding sentence, the term "controlled group" has the meaning given to such term by section 1563(a).

(C) Limitations with respect to certain persons

In the case of a person described in subparagraph (A) or (B) of section 46(e)(1) (as in effect on the day before the date of the enactment of the Revenue Reconciliation Act of 1990), the $25,000 amount specified under subparagraph (B) of paragraph (1) shall equal such person's ratable share (as determined under section 46(e)(2) (as so in effect) of such amount.

(D) Estates and trusts

In the case of an estate or trust, the $25,000 amount specified under subparagraph (B) of paragraph (1) shall be reduced to an amount which bears the same ratio to $25,000 as the portion of the income of the estate or trust which is not allocated to beneficiaries bears to the total income of the estate or trust.

(E) Corporations

In the case of a corporation, this subsection shall be applied by treating the corporation as having a tentative minimum tax of zero.

(d) Ordering rules

For purposes of any provision of this title where it is necessary to ascertain the extent to which the credits determined under any section referred to in subsection (b) are used in a taxable year or as a carryback or carryforward—

(1) In general

The order in which such credits are used shall be determined on the basis of the order in which they are listed in subsection (b) as of the close of the taxable year in which the credit is used.

(2) Components of investment credit

The order in which the credits listed in section 46 are used shall be determined on the basis of the order in which such credits are listed in section 46 as of the close of the taxable year in which the credit is used.

(Added and amended Pub. L. 98–369, div. A, title IV, §473, title VI, §612(e)(1), July 18, 1984, 98 Stat. 827, 912; Pub. L. 99–514, title II, §§221(a), 231(d)(1), (3)(B), 252(b), title VII, §701(c)(4), title XI, §1171(b)(1), (2), Oct. 22, 1986, 100 Stat. 2173, 2178, 2179, 2205, 2341, 2513; Pub. L. 100–647, title I, §§1002(e)(8)(A), 1007(g)(2), (8), Nov. 10, 1988, 102 Stat. 3368, 3434, 3435; Pub. L. 101–508, title XI, §§11511(b)(1), 11611(b)(1), 11813(b)(2), Nov. 5, 1990, 104 Stat. 1388–485, 1388-503, 1388-551; Pub. L. 102–486, title XIX, §1914(b), Oct. 24, 1992, 106 Stat. 3023; Pub. L. 103–66, title XIII, §§13302(a)(1), (c)(1), 13322(a), 13443(b)(1), Aug. 10, 1993, 107 Stat. 555, 559, 569; Pub. L. 104–188, title I, §§1201(e)(1), 1205(a)(2), 1702(e)(4), Aug. 20, 1996, 110 Stat. 1772, 1775, 1870; Pub. L. 106–554, §1(a)(7) [title I, §121(b)(1)], Dec. 21, 2000, 114 Stat. 2763, 2763A-609; Pub. L. 107–16, title II, §205(b)(1), title VI, §619(b), June 7, 2001, 115 Stat. 53, 110; Pub. L. 107–147, title III, §301(b)(1), (2), title IV, §411(d)(2), Mar. 9, 2002, 116 Stat. 39, 46; Pub. L. 108–357, title II, §245(c)(1), title III, §§302(b), 339(b), 341(b), title VII, §711(a), (b), Oct. 22, 2004, 118 Stat. 1448, 1465, 1484, 1487, 1557, 1558; Pub. L. 109–58, title XIII, §§1306(b), 1322(a)(2), 1332(b), 1334(b), 1341(b)(1), 1342(b)(1), Aug. 8, 2005, 119 Stat. 999, 1011, 1026, 1033, 1049, 1051; Pub. L. 109–59, title XI, §§11126(b), 11151(d)(1), Aug. 10, 2005, 119 Stat. 1958, 1968; Pub. L. 109–135, title I, §103(b)(1), title II, §201(b)(1), title IV, §412(f), Dec. 21, 2005, 119 Stat. 2595, 2607, 2637; Pub. L. 109–432, div. A, title IV, §405(b), Dec. 20, 2006, 120 Stat. 2957; Pub. L. 110–28, title VIII, §§8214(a), May 25, 2007, 121 Stat. 193; Pub. L. 110–172, §11(a)(6), Dec. 29, 2007, 121 Stat. 2485; Pub. L. 110–234, title XV, §15343(b), May 22, 2008, 122 Stat. 1519; Pub. L. 110–245, title I, §111(b), June 17, 2008, 122 Stat. 1635; Pub. L. 110–246, §4(a), title XV, §15343(b), June 18, 2008, 122 Stat. 1664, 2281; Pub. L. 110–289, div. C, title I, §3022(b), (c), July 30, 2008, 122 Stat. 2894; Pub. L. 110–343, div. B, title I, §§103(b), 115(b), title II, §205(c), div. C, title III, §316(b), Oct. 3, 2008, 122 Stat. 3811, 3831, 3838, 3872; Pub. L. 111–5, div. B, title I, §1141(b)(2), Feb. 17, 2009, 123 Stat. 328; Pub. L. 111–148, title I, §1421(b), (c), Mar. 23, 2010, 124 Stat. 241, 242; Pub. L. 111–240, title II, §2013(a), (c), Sept. 27, 2010, 124 Stat. 2555; Pub. L. 113–295, div. A, title II, §209(f)(1), 220(b), 221(a)(2)(B), (6), Dec. 19, 2014, 128 Stat. 4028, 4035, 4037, 4038; Pub. L. 114–113, div. Q, title I, §§121(b), 186(d)(1), Dec. 18, 2015, 129 Stat. 3049, 3074; Pub. L. 115–97, title I, §§12001(b)(1), 13403(b), (c), Dec. 22, 2017, 131 Stat. 2092, 2137; Pub. L. 115–141, div. U, title IV, §401(a)(8), (b)(5)(A)–(D), (d)(2)(B), (6)(B)(i)–(iii), Mar. 23, 2018, 132 Stat. 1184, 1201, 1208, 1211; Pub. L. 116–94, div. O, title I, §105(b), Dec. 20, 2019, 133 Stat. 3148.)

EDITORIAL NOTES
REFERENCES IN TEXT

The date of the enactment of this paragraph, referred to in subsec. (c)(4)(B)(iv)(I), is the date of enactment of Pub. L. 108–357, which was approved Oct. 22, 2004.

The date of the enactment of the Revenue Reconciliation Act of 1990, referred to in subsec. (c)(6)(C), is the date of enactment of Pub. L. 101–508, which was approved Nov. 5, 1990.

CODIFICATION

Pub. L. 110–234 and Pub. L. 110–246 made identical amendments to this section. The amendments by Pub. L. 110–234 were repealed by section 4(a) of Pub. L. 110–246.

PRIOR PROVISIONS

A prior section 38, added Pub. L. 87–834, §2(a), Oct. 16, 1962, 76 Stat. 962; amended Pub. L. 94–455, title XIX, §1906(b)(13)(A), Oct. 4, 1976, 90 Stat. 1834, related to investment in certain depreciable property, prior to repeal by Pub. L. 98–369, div. A, title IV, §474(m)(1), July 18, 1984, 98 Stat. 833.

Another prior section 38 was renumbered section 37 of this title.

AMENDMENTS

2019—Subsec. (b)(33). Pub. L. 116–94 added par. (33).

2018—Subsec. (b)(24), (25). Pub. L. 115–141, §401(d)(2)(B), redesignated pars. (25) and (26) as (24) and (25), respectively, and struck out former par. (24) which read as follows: "the energy efficient appliance credit determined under section 45M(a),".

Subsec. (b)(26) to (29). Pub. L. 115–141, §401(d)(2)(B), (6)(B)(i), redesignated pars. (31) to (34) first as (30) to (33), and then as (26) to (29), respectively. Former par. (26) redesignated (25), and former pars. (27) to (29) redesignated (26) to (28), respectively, and then struck out.

Pub. L. 115–141, §401(d)(2)(B), (6)(B)(i), redesignated pars. (27) to (30) as (26) to (29), respectively, and then struck them out. Prior to amendment, these four pars. set out credits for the Hurricane Katrina housing credit determined under section 1400P(b), the Hurricane Katrina employee retention credit determined under section 1400R(a), the Hurricane Rita employee retention credit determined under section 1400R(b), and the Hurricane Wilma employee retention credit determined under section 1400R(c).

Subsec. (b)(30) to (32). Pub. L. 115–141, §401(d)(2)(B), (6)(B)(i), redesignated pars. (35) to (37) first as (34) to (36), and then as (30) to (32), respectively. Former par. (30) redesignated (29) and then struck out, and former pars. (31) and (32) first redesignated (30) and (31), then (26) and (27), respectively.

Subsec. (b)(33) to (37). Pub. L. 115–141, §401(a)(8), (d)(2)(B), (6)(B)(i), inserted comma at end of par. (34) and subsequently redesignated pars. (33) to (37) first as (32) to (36), and then as (28) to (32), respectively.

Subsec. (c)(2)(A)(ii)(II). Pub. L. 115–141, §401(d)(6)(B)(ii), struck out ", the New York Liberty Zone business employee credit," after "empowerment zone employment credit".

Pub. L. 115–141, §401(b)(5)(B), struck out "the eligible small business credits," before "and the specified credits".

Subsec. (c)(3). Pub. L. 115–141, §401(d)(6)(B)(iii), struck out par. (3) which related to special rules for New York Liberty Zone business employee credit.

Subsec. (c)(4)(A)(ii)(II). Pub. L. 115–141, §401(b)(5)(C), struck out "the eligible small business credits and" before "the specified credits".

Subsec. (c)(4)(B)(ii). Pub. L. 115–141, §401(b)(5)(D), substituted "as defined in paragraph (5)(A) after application of the rules of paragraph (5)(B))" for "(as defined in paragraph (5)(C), after application of rules similar to the rules of paragraph (5)(D))".

Subsec. (c)(5). Pub. L. 115–141, §401(b)(5)(A)(i), substituted "Rules related to eligible small businesses" for "Special rules for eligible small business credits in 2010" in heading.

Subsec. (c)(5)(A). Pub. L. 115–141, §401(b)(5)(A)(i), (ii), redesignated subpar. (C) as (A) and struck out former subpar. (A) which related to eligible small business credits determined in taxable years beginning in 2010.

Subsec. (c)(5)(B). Pub. L. 115–141, §401(b)(5)(A)(iii), amended subpar. (B) generally. Prior to amendment, text read as follows: "Credits determined with respect to a partnership or S corporation shall not be treated as eligible small business credits by any partner or shareholder unless such partner or shareholder meets the gross receipts test under subparagraph (C) for the taxable year in which such credits are treated as current year business credits."

Pub. L. 115–141, §401(b)(5)(A)(i), (ii), redesignated subpar. (D) as (B) and struck out former subpar. (B) which defined "eligible small business credits".

Subsec. (c)(5)(C), (D). Pub. L. 115–141, §401(b)(5)(A)(ii), redesignated subpars. (C) and (D) as (A) and (B), respectively.

2017—Subsec. (b)(35) to (37). Pub. L. 115–97, §13403(b), struck out "plus" at end of par. (35), substituted ", plus" for period at end of par. (36), and added par. (37).

Subsec. (c)(4)(B)(ix) to (xii). Pub. L. 115–97, §13403(c), added cl. (ix) and redesignated former cls. (ix) to (xi) as (x) to (xii), respectively.

Subsec. (c)(6)(E). Pub. L. 115–97, §12001(b)(1), added subpar. (E).

2015—Subsec. (c)(4)(B)(ii) to (iv). Pub. L. 114–113, §121(b), added cl. (ii) and redesignated former cls. (ii) and (iii) as (iii) and (iv), respectively. Former cl. (iv) redesignated (v).

Subsec. (c)(4)(B)(v) to (x). Pub. L. 114–113, §186(d)(1), added cl. (v) and redesignated former cls. (v) to (ix) as (vi) to (x), respectively. Former cl. (x) redesignated (xi).

Pub. L. 114–113, §121(b), redesignated cls. (iv) to (ix) as (v) to (x), respectively.

Subsec. (c)(4)(B)(xi). Pub. L. 114–113, §186(d)(1), redesignated cl. (x) as (xi).

2014—Subsec. (b)(35) to (37). Pub. L. 113–295, §221(a)(2)(B), inserted "plus" at end of par. (35), redesignated par. (37) as (36), and struck out former par. (36) which read as follows: "the portion of the qualified plug-in electric vehicle credit to which section 30(c)(1) applies, plus".

Pub. L. 113–295, §209(f)(1), struck out "plus" at end of par. (35), added par. (36), and redesignated former par. (36) as (37). Amendment was executed to subsec. (b) as it appeared after amendment by Pub. L. 111–148, §1421(b), to reflect the probable intent of Congress, despite amendment being effective as if included in the enactment of Pub. L. 111–5. See 2010 Amendment and Effective Date of 2014 Amendment notes below.

Subsec. (c)(2)(A). Pub. L. 113–295, §220(b), substituted "credit" for "credit credit" in introductory provisions.

Subsec. (d)(3). Pub. L. 113–295, §221(a)(6), struck out par. (3) which related to ordering of credits no longer listed.

2010—Subsec. (b)(36). Pub. L. 111–148, §1421(b), added par. (36).

Subsec. (c)(2)(A)(ii)(II). Pub. L. 111–240, §2013(c)(1), inserted "the eligible small business credits," after "the New York Liberty Zone business employee credit,".

Subsec. (c)(3)(A)(ii)(II). Pub. L. 111–240, §2013(c)(2), inserted ", the eligible small business credits," after "the New York Liberty Zone business employee credit".

Subsec. (c)(4)(A)(ii)(II). Pub. L. 111–240, §2013(c)(3), inserted "the eligible small business credits and" before "the specified credits".

Subsec. (c)(4)(B)(vi) to (ix). Pub. L. 111–148, §1421(c), added cl. (vi) and redesignated former cls. (vi) to (viii) as (vii) to (ix), respectively.

Subsec. (c)(5), (6). Pub. L. 111–240, §2013(a), added par. (5) and redesignated former par. (5) as (6).

2009—Subsec. (b)(35). Pub. L. 111–5 substituted "30D(c)(1)" for "30D(d)(1)".

2008—Subsec. (b)(32). Pub. L. 110–246, §15343(b), added par. (32).

Subsec. (b)(33). Pub. L. 110–245 added par. (33).

Subsec. (b)(34). Pub. L. 110–343, §115(b), added par. (34).

Subsec. (b)(35). Pub. L. 110–343, §205(c), added par. (35).

Subsec. (c)(4)(B)(ii) to (iv). Pub. L. 110–289, §3022(b), added cl. (ii) and redesignated former cls. (ii) and (iii) as (iii) and (iv), respectively. Former cl. (iv) redesignated (v).

Subsec. (c)(4)(B)(v). Pub. L. 110–343, §316(b)(2), added cl. (v). Former cl. (v) redesignated (vi).

Pub. L. 110–343, §103(b)(1), added cl. (v). Former cl. (v) redesignated (vi).

Pub. L. 110–289, §3022(c), added cl. (v). Former cl. (v) redesignated (vi).

Pub. L. 110–289, §3022(b), redesignated cl. (iv) as (v).

Subsec. (c)(4)(B)(vi). Pub. L. 110–343, §316(b)(1), redesignated cl. (v) as (vi). Former cl. (vi) redesignated (vii).

Pub. L. 110–343, §103(b)(2), substituted "section 46 to the extent that such credit is attributable to the rehabilitation credit under section 47, but only with respect to" for "section 47 to the extent attributable to".

Pub. L. 110–343, §103(b)(1), which directed amendment of subpar. (B) by "redesignating clause (vi) as clause (vi) and (vii), respectively", was executed by redesignating cls. (v) and (vi) as (vi) and (vii), respectively, to reflect the probable intent of Congress.

Pub. L. 110–289, §3022(c), redesignated cl. (v) as (vi).

Subsec. (c)(4)(B)(vii). Pub. L. 110–343, §316(b)(1), redesignated cl. (vi) as (vii). Former cl. (vii) redesignated (viii).

Pub. L. 110–343, §103(b)(1), which directed amendment of subpar. (B) by "redesignating clause (vi) as clause (vi) and (vii), respectively", was executed by redesignating cls. (v) and (vi) as (vi) and (vii), respectively, to reflect the probable intent of Congress.

Subsec. (c)(4)(B)(viii). Pub. L. 110–343, §316(b)(1), redesignated cl. (vii) as (viii).

2007—Subsec. (b)(8), (24). Pub. L. 110–172, §11(a)(6)(A), struck out "and" at end.

Subsec. (b)(30). Pub. L. 110–172, §11(a)(6)(C), inserted "plus" at end.

Pub. L. 110–172, §11(a)(6)(B), struck out "plus" at end.

Subsec. (c)(4)(B)(iii), (iv). Pub. L. 110–28 added cls. (iii) and (iv).

2006—Subsec. (b)(29) to (31). Pub. L. 109–432 struck out "and" at end of par. (29), substituted ", plus" for period at end of par. (30), and added par. (31).

2005—Subsec. (b)(20). Pub. L. 109–59, §11126(b), added par. (20).

Subsec. (b)(21). Pub. L. 109–58, §1306(b), as amended by Pub. L. 109–59, §11151(d)(1), added par. (21).

Subsec. (b)(22). Pub. L. 109–58, §1322(a)(2), added par. (22).

Subsec. (b)(23). Pub. L. 109–58, §1332(b), added par. (23).

Subsec. (b)(24). Pub. L. 109–58, §1342(b)(1), which directed the striking out of "plus" at end, could not be executed because "plus" did not appear at end.

Pub. L. 109–58, §1334(b), added par. (24).

Subsec. (b)(25). Pub. L. 109–58, §1341(b)(1), added par. (25).

Subsec. (b)(26). Pub. L. 109–58, §1342(b)(1), added par. (26).

Subsec. (b)(27). Pub. L. 109–135, §103(b)(1), added par. (27).

Subsec. (b)(28) to (30). Pub. L. 109–135, §201(b)(1), added pars. (28) to (30).

Subsec. (c)(2)(A)(ii)(II). Pub. L. 109–135, §412(f)(1), substituted ", the New York Liberty Zone business employee credit, and the specified credits" for "or the New York Liberty Zone business employee credit or the specified credits".

Subsec. (c)(3)(A)(ii)(II). Pub. L. 109–135, §412(f)(2), substituted "and the specified credits" for "or the specified credits".

Subsec. (c)(4)(B). Pub. L. 109–135, §412(f)(3), substituted "means" for "includes" in introductory provisions and inserted "and" at end of cl. (i).

2004—Subsec. (b)(16). Pub. L. 108–357, §245(c)(1), added par. (16).

Subsec. (b)(17). Pub. L. 108–357, §302(b), added par. (17).

Subsec. (b)(18). Pub. L. 108–357, §339(b), added par. (18).

Subsec. (b)(19). Pub. L. 108–357, §341(b), added par. (19).

Subsec. (c)(2)(A)(ii)(II), (3)(A)(ii)(II). Pub. L. 108–357, §711(b), inserted "or the specified credits" after "employee credit".

Subsec. (c)(4), (5). Pub. L. 108–357, §711(a), added par. (4) and redesignated former par. (4) as (5).

2002—Subsec. (b)(15). Pub. L. 107–147, §411(d)(2), substituted "45F(a)" for "45F".

Subsec. (c)(2)(A)(ii)(II). Pub. L. 107–147, §301(b)(2), inserted "or the New York Liberty Zone business employee credit" after "employment credit".

Subsec. (c)(3), (4). Pub. L. 107–147, §301(b)(1), added par. (3) and redesignated former par. (3) as (4).

2001—Subsec. (b)(12). Pub. L. 107–16, §619(b), struck out "plus" at end.

Subsec. (b)(13). Pub. L. 107–16, §619(b), substituted ", plus" for period at end.

Pub. L. 107–16, §205(b)(1), struck out "plus" at end.

Subsec. (b)(14). Pub. L. 107–16, §619(b), added par. (14).

Pub. L. 107–16, §205(b)(1), substituted ", plus" for period at end.

Subsec. (b)(15). Pub. L. 107–16, §205(b)(1), added par. (15).

2000—Subsec. (b)(13). Pub. L. 106–554 added par. (13).

1996—Subsec. (b)(2). Pub. L. 104–188, §1201(e)(1), substituted "work opportunity credit" for "targeted jobs credit".

Subsec. (b)(12). Pub. L. 104–188, §1205(a)(2), added par. (12).

Subsec. (c)(2)(C). Pub. L. 104–188, §1702(e)(4), amended subpar. (C), as in effect on day before date of enactment of the Revenue Reconciliation Act of 1990 (title XI of Pub. L. 101–508, approved Nov. 5, 1990), by inserting before period at end of first sentence "and without regard to the deduction under section 56(h)".

1993—Subsec. (b)(7). Pub. L. 103–66, §13302(a)(1), struck out "plus" at end.

Subsec. (b)(8). Pub. L. 103–66, §13322(a), which directed amendment of par. (8) by striking "plus" at end, could not be executed because "plus" did not appear at end.

Pub. L. 103–66, §13302(a)(1), substituted ", and" for period at end.

Subsec. (b)(9). Pub. L. 103–66, §13443(b)(1), struck out "plus" at end.

Pub. L. 103–66, §13322(a), substituted ", plus" for period at end.

Pub. L. 103–66, §13302(a)(1), added par. (9).

Subsec. (b)(10). Pub. L. 103–66, §13443(b)(1), substituted ", plus" for period at end.

Pub. L. 103–66, §13322(a), added par. (10).

Subsec. (b)(11). Pub. L. 103–66, §13443(b)(1), added par. (11).

Subsec. (c)(2), (3). Pub. L. 103–66, §13302(c)(1), added par. (2) and redesignated former par. (2) as (3).

1992—Subsec. (b)(6) to (8). Pub. L. 102–486 struck out "plus" at end of par. (6), substituted "; plus" for period at end of par. (7), and added par. (8).

1990—Subsec. (b)(1). Pub. L. 101–508, §11813(b)(2)(A), substituted "section 46" for "section 46(a)".

Subsec. (b)(4). Pub. L. 101–508, §11511(b)(1), struck out "plus" at end.

Subsec. (b)(5). Pub. L. 101–508, §11611(b)(1), struck out "plus" at end.

Pub. L. 101–508, §11511(b)(1), substituted ", plus" for period at end.

Subsec. (b)(6). Pub. L. 101–508, §11611(b)(1), substituted ", plus" for period at end.

Pub. L. 101–508, §11511(b)(1), added par. (6).

Subsec. (b)(7). Pub. L. 101–508, §11611(b)(1), added par. (7).

Subsec. (c)(2). Pub. L. 101–508, §11813(b)(2)(B), redesignated par. (3) as (2) and struck out former par. (2) which permitted an offset of regular investment tax credit against 25 percent of minimum tax.

Subsec. (c)(2)(C). Pub. L. 101–508, §11813(b)(2)(C), inserted "(as in effect on the day before the date of the enactment of the Revenue Reconciliation Act of 1990)" after "46(e)(1)" and "(as so in effect)" after "46(e)(2)".

Subsec. (c)(3). Pub. L. 101–508, §11813(b)(2)(B), redesignated par. (3) as (2).

Subsec. (d). Pub. L. 101–508, §11813(b)(2)(D)(i), substituted "any provision" for "sections 46(f), 47(a), 196(a), and any other provision" in introductory provisions.

Subsec. (d)(2). Pub. L. 101–508, §11813(b)(2)(D)(ii), amended par. (2) generally. Prior to amendment, par. (2) read as follows: "The order in which credits attributable to a percentage referred to in section 46(a) are used shall be determined on the basis of the order in which such percentages are listed in section 46(a) as of the close of the taxable year in which the credit is used."

Subsec. (d)(3)(B). Pub. L. 101–508, §11813(b)(2)(D)(iii), amended subpar. (B) generally. Prior to amendment, subpar. (B) read as follows: "the employee plan percentage (as defined in section 46(a)(2)(E), as in effect on the day before the date of the enactment of the Tax Reform Act of 1984) shall be treated as referred to after section 46(a)(2)."

1988—Subsec. (c). Pub. L. 100–647, §1007(g)(2), amended pars. (1) to (3) generally, substituting pars. (1) and (2) for former pars. (1) to (3), redesignating former par. (4) as (3), and substituting "subparagraph (B) of paragraph (1)" for "subparagraphs (A) and (B) of paragraph (1)" in subpars. (A), (B), (C), and (D).

Pub. L. 100–647, §1007(g)(8), made technical correction to directory language of Pub. L. 99–514, §701(c)(4), see 1986 Amendment note below.

Subsec. (d). Pub. L. 100–647, §1002(e)(8)(A), substituted "Ordering rules" for "Special rules for certain regulated companies" in heading and amended text generally. Prior to amendment, text read as follows: "In the case of any taxpayer to which section 46(f) applies, for purposes of sections 46(f), 47(a), and 196(a) and any other provision of this title where it is necessary to ascertain the extent to which the credits determined under section 40(a), 41(a), 42(a), 46(a), or 51(a) are used in a taxable year or as a carryback or carryforward, the order in which such credits are used shall be determined on the basis of the order in which they are listed in subsection (b)."

1986—Subsec. (b)(4). Pub. L. 99–514, §231(d)(1), added par. (4).

Pub. L. 99–514, §1171(b)(1), struck out former par. (4) which read as follows: "the employee stock ownership credit determined under section 41(a)".

Subsec. (b)(5). Pub. L. 99–514, §252(b)(1), added par. (5).

Subsec. (c). Pub. L. 99–514, §701(c)(4), as amended by Pub. L. 100–647, §1007(g)(8), added pars. (1) to (3), redesignated former par. (3) as (4), and struck out former par. (1) "In general" which provided: "The credit allowed under subsection (a) for any taxable year shall not exceed the sum of—

"(A) so much of the taxpayer's net tax liability for the taxable year as does not exceed $25,000, plus

"(B) 75 percent of so much of the taxpayer's net tax liability for the taxable year as exceeds $25,000."

and former par. (2) "Net tax liability", which provided: "For purposes of paragraph (1), the term 'net tax liability' means the tax liability (as defined in section 26(b)), reduced by the sum of the credits allowable under subparts A and B of this part."

Subsec. (c)(1)(B). Pub. L. 99–514, §221(a), substituted "75 percent" for "85 percent".

Subsec. (d). Pub. L. 99–514, §252(b)(2), inserted "42(a),".

Pub. L. 99–514, §1171(b)(2), substituted "and 196(a)" for "196(a), and 404(i)" and struck out "41(a)," after "40(a)".

Pub. L. 99–514, §231(d)(3)(B), inserted "41(a)," after "40(a),".

1984—Subsec. (c)(2). Pub. L. 98–369, §612(e)(1), substituted "section 26(b)" for "section 25(b)".

STATUTORY NOTES AND RELATED SUBSIDIARIES
EFFECTIVE DATE OF 2019 AMENDMENT

Pub. L. 116–94, div. O, title I, §105(d), Dec. 20, 2019, 133 Stat. 3148, provided that: "The amendments made by this section [enacting section 45T of this title and amending this section] shall apply to taxable years beginning after December 31, 2019."

EFFECTIVE DATE OF 2017 AMENDMENT

Amendment by section 12001(b)(1) of Pub. L. 115–97 applicable to taxable years beginning after Dec. 31, 2017, see section 12001(c) of Pub. L. 115–97, set out as a note under section 11 of this title.

Pub. L. 115–97, title I, §13403(e), Dec. 22, 2017, 131 Stat. 2138, provided that: "The amendments made by this section [enacting section 45S of this title and amending this section and sections 280C and 6501 of this title] shall apply to wages paid in taxable years beginning after December 31, 2017."

EFFECTIVE DATE OF 2015 AMENDMENT

Pub. L. 114–113, div. Q, title I, §121(d), Dec. 18, 2015, 129 Stat. 3052, provided that:

"(1) Extension.——The amendments made by subsection (a) [amending sections 41 and 45C of this title] shall apply to shall apply to [sic] amounts paid or incurred after December 31, 2014.

"(2) Credit allowed against alternative minimum tax in case of eligible small business.——The amendments made by subsection (b) [amending this section] shall apply to credits determined for taxable years beginning after December 31, 2015.

"(3) Treatment of research credit for certain startup companies.——The amendments made by subsection (c) [amending sections 41 and 3111 of this title] shall apply to taxable years beginning after December 31, 2015."

Pub. L. 114–113, div. Q, title I, §186(e)(3), Dec. 18, 2015, 129 Stat. 3074, provided that: "The amendments made by subsection (d) [amending this section and section 45 of this title] shall apply to credits determined for taxable years beginning after December 31, 2015."

EFFECTIVE DATE OF 2014 AMENDMENT

Amendment by section 209(f)(1) of Pub. L. 113–295 effective as if included in the provisions of the American Recovery and Reinvestment Tax Act of 2009, Pub. L. 111–5, div. B, title I, to which such amendment relates, see section 209(k) of Pub. L. 113–295, set out as a note under section 24 of this title.

Amendment by section 221(a)(2)(B), (6) of Pub. L. 113–295 effective Dec. 19, 2014, subject to a savings provision, see section 221(b) of Pub. L. 113–295, set out as a note under section 1 of this title.

EFFECTIVE DATE OF 2010 AMENDMENT

Pub. L. 111–240, title II, §2013(d), Sept. 27, 2010, 124 Stat. 2556, provided that: "The amendments made by subsection (a) [amending this section] shall apply to credits determined in taxable years beginning after December 31, 2009, and to carrybacks of such credits."

Pub. L. 111–148, title I, §1421(f), title X, §10105(e)(4), Mar. 23, 2010, 124 Stat. 242, 907, provided that:

"(1) In general.——The amendments made by this section [enacting section 45R of this title and amending this section and sections 196 and 280C of this title] shall apply to amounts paid or incurred in taxable years beginning after December 31, 2009.

"(2) Minimum tax.——The amendments made by subsection (c) [amending this section] shall apply to credits determined under section 45R of the Internal Revenue Code of 1986 in taxable years beginning after December 31, 2009, and to carrybacks of such credits."

EFFECTIVE DATE OF 2009 AMENDMENT

Amendment by Pub. L. 111–5 applicable to vehicles acquired after Dec. 31, 2009, see section 1141(c) of Pub. L. 111–5, set out as a note under section 30B of this title.

EFFECTIVE DATE OF 2008 AMENDMENT

Amendment by section 103(b) of Pub. L. 110–343 applicable to credits determined under section 46 of this title in taxable years beginning after Oct. 3, 2008, and to carrybacks of such credits, see section 103(f)(1), (2) of Pub. L. 110–343, set out as a note under section 48 of this title.

Pub. L. 110–343, div. B, title I, §115(d), Oct. 3, 2008, 122 Stat. 3831, provided that: "The amendments made by this section [enacting section 45Q of this title and amending this section] shall apply to carbon dioxide captured after the date of the enactment of this Act [Oct. 3, 2008]."

Amendment by section 205(c) of Pub. L. 110–343 applicable to taxable years beginning after Dec. 31, 2008, see section 205(e) of Pub. L. 110–343, set out as an Effective and Termination Dates of 2008 Amendment note under section 24 of this title.

Pub. L. 110–343, div. C, title III, §316(c)(2), Oct. 3, 2008, 122 Stat. 3873, provided that: "The amendments made by subsection (b) [amending this section] shall apply to credits determined under section 45G of the Internal Revenue Code of 1986 in taxable years beginning after December 31, 2007, and to carrybacks of such credits."

Pub. L. 110–289, div. C, title I, §3022(d)(2), (3), July 30, 2008, 122 Stat. 2894, provided that:

"(2) Low income housing credit.——The amendments made by subsection (b) [amending this section] shall apply to credits determined under section 42 of the Internal Revenue Code of 1986 to the extent attributable to buildings placed in service after December 31, 2007.

"(3) Rehabilitation credit.——The amendments made by subsection (c) [amending this section] shall apply to credits determined under section 47 of the Internal Revenue Code of 1986 to the extent attributable to qualified rehabilitation expenditures properly taken into account for periods after December 31, 2007."

Pub. L. 110–245, title I, §111(e), June 17, 2008, 122 Stat. 1635, provided that: "The amendments made by this section [enacting section 45P of this title and amending this section and section 280C of this title] shall apply to amounts paid after the date of the enactment of this Act [June 17, 2008]."

Amendment of this section and repeal of Pub. L. 110–234 by Pub. L. 110–246 effective May 22, 2008, the date of enactment of Pub. L. 110–234, except as otherwise provided, see section 4 of Pub. L. 110–246, set out as an Effective Date note under section 8701 of Title 7, Agriculture.

Pub. L. 110–234, title XV, §15343(e), May 22, 2008, 122 Stat. 1520, and Pub. L. 110–246, §4(a), title XV, §15343(e), June 18, 2008, 122 Stat. 1664, 2282, provided that: "The amendments made by this section [enacting section 45O of this title and amending this section and section 280C of this title] shall apply to amounts paid or incurred after the date of the enactment of this Act [June 18, 2008]."

[Pub. L. 110–234 and Pub. L. 110–246 enacted identical provisions. Pub. L. 110–234 was repealed by section 4(a) of Pub. L. 110–246, set out as a note under section 8701 of Title 7, Agriculture.]

EFFECTIVE DATE OF 2007 AMENDMENT

Pub. L. 110–28, title VIII, §8214(b), May 25, 2007, 121 Stat. 193, provided that: "The amendments made by this section [amending this section] shall apply to credits determined under sections 45B and 51 of the Internal Revenue Code of 1986 in taxable years beginning after December 31, 2006, and to carrybacks of such credits."

EFFECTIVE DATE OF 2006 AMENDMENT

Pub. L. 109–432, div. A, title IV, §405(e), Dec. 20, 2006, 120 Stat. 2958, provided that: "The amendments made by this section [enacting section 45N of this title and amending this section and section 280C of this title] shall apply to taxable years beginning after December 31, 2005."

EFFECTIVE DATE OF 2005 AMENDMENT

Pub. L. 109–59, title XI, §11126(d), Aug. 10, 2005, 119 Stat. 1958, provided that: "The amendments made by this section [enacting section 5011 of this title and amending this section] shall apply to taxable years beginning after September 30, 2005."

Pub. L. 109–59, title XI, §11151(d)(2), Aug. 10, 2005, 119 Stat. 1968, provided that: "If the Energy Policy Act of 2005 [Pub. L. 109–58, see Tables for classification] is enacted before the date of the enactment of this Act [Aug. 10, 2005], for purposes of executing any amendments made by the Energy Policy Act of 2005 to section 38(b) of the Internal Revenue Code of 1986, the amendments made by section 11126(b) of this Act [amending this section] shall be treated as having been executed before such amendments made by the Energy Policy Act of 2005."

Pub. L. 109–59, title XI, §11151(f)(3), Aug. 10, 2005, 119 Stat. 1969, provided that: "The amendments made by subsections (d)(1) and (e)(2) [amending this section and sections 4041 and 6426 of this title] shall take effect as if included in the provision of the Energy Tax Incentives Act of 2005 [Pub. L. 109–58, title XIII] to which they relate."

Pub. L. 109–58, title XIII, §1306(d), Aug. 8, 2005, 119 Stat. 999, provided that: "The amendments made by this section [enacting section 45J of this title and amending this section] shall apply to production in taxable years beginning after the date of the enactment of this Act [Aug. 8, 2005]."

Amendment by section 1322(a)(2) of Pub. L. 109–58 applicable to credits determined under the Internal Revenue Code of 1986 for taxable years ending after Dec. 31, 2005, see section 1322(c)(1) of Pub. L. 109–58, set out as a note under section 45K of this title.

Pub. L. 109–58, title XIII, §1332(f), Aug. 8, 2005, 119 Stat. 1026, provided that: "The amendments made by this section [enacting section 45L of this title and amending this section and sections 196 and 1016 of this title] shall apply to qualified new energy efficient homes acquired after December 31, 2005, in taxable years ending after such date."

Pub. L. 109–58, title XIII, §1334(d), Aug. 8, 2005, 119 Stat. 1033, provided that: "The amendments made by this section [enacting section 45M of this title and amending this section] shall apply to appliances produced after December 31, 2005."

Amendment by section 1341(b)(1) of Pub. L. 109–58 applicable to property placed in service after Dec. 31, 2005, in taxable years ending after such date, see section 1341(c) of Pub. L. 109–58, set out as an Effective Date note under section 30B of this title.

Amendment by section 1342(b)(1) of Pub. L. 109–58 applicable to property placed in service after Dec. 31, 2005, in taxable years ending after such date, see section 1342(c) of Pub. L. 109–58, set out as an Effective Date note under section 30C of this title.

EFFECTIVE DATE OF 2004 AMENDMENT

Pub. L. 108–357, title II, §245(e), Oct. 22, 2004, 118 Stat. 1448, provided that: "The amendments made by this section [enacting section 45G of this title and amending this section and sections 39 and 1016 of this title] shall apply to taxable years beginning after December 31, 2004."

Pub. L. 108–357, title III, §302(d), Oct. 22, 2004, 118 Stat. 1466, provided that: "The amendments made by this section [enacting section 40A of this title and amending this section and sections 87 and 196 of this title] shall apply to fuel produced, and sold or used, after December 31, 2004, in taxable years ending after such date."

Pub. L. 108–357, title III, §339(f), Oct. 22, 2004, 118 Stat. 1485, provided that: "The amendments made by this section [enacting section 45H of this title and amending this section and sections 196, 280C, and 1016 of this title] shall apply to expenses paid or incurred after December 31, 2002, in taxable years ending after such date."

Pub. L. 108–357, title III, §341(e), Oct. 22, 2004, 118 Stat. 1487, provided that: "The amendments made by this section [enacting section 45I of this title and amending this section and section 39 of this title] shall apply to production in taxable years beginning after December 31, 2004."

Pub. L. 108–357, title VII, §711(c), Oct. 22, 2004, 118 Stat. 1558, provided that: "Except as otherwise provided, the amendments made by this section [amending this section] shall apply to taxable years ending after the date of the enactment of this Act [Oct. 22, 2004]."

EFFECTIVE DATE OF 2002 AMENDMENT

Pub. L. 107–147, title III, §301(b)(3), Mar. 9, 2002, 116 Stat. 40, provided that: "The amendments made by this subsection [amending this section] shall apply to taxable years ending after December 31, 2001."

Amendment by section 411(d)(2) of Pub. L. 107–147 effective as if included in the provisions of the Economic Growth and Tax Relief Reconciliation Act of 2001, Pub. L. 107–16, to which such amendment relates, see section 411(x) of Pub. L. 107–147, set out as a note under section 25B of this title.

EFFECTIVE DATE OF 2001 AMENDMENT

Pub. L. 107–16, title II, §205(c), June 7, 2001, 115 Stat. 53, provided that: "The amendments made by this section [enacting section 45F of this title and amending this section and section 1016 of this title] shall apply to taxable years beginning after December 31, 2001."

Pub. L. 107–16, title VI, §619(d), June 7, 2001, 115 Stat. 110, as amended by Pub. L. 107–147, title IV, §411(n)(2), Mar. 9, 2002, 116 Stat. 48, provided that: "The amendments made by this section [enacting section 45E of this title and amending this section and sections 39 and 196 of this title] shall apply to costs paid or incurred in taxable years beginning after December 31, 2001, with respect to qualified employer plans first effective after such date."

EFFECTIVE DATE OF 2000 AMENDMENT

Pub. L. 106–554, §1(a)(7) [title I, §121(e)], Dec. 21, 2000, 114 Stat. 2763, 2763A-610, provided that: "The amendments made by this section [enacting section 45D of this title, amending this section and sections 39 and 196 of this title, and enacting provisions set out as notes under section 45D of this title] shall apply to investments made after December 31, 2000."

EFFECTIVE DATE OF 1996 AMENDMENT

Pub. L. 104–188, title I, §1201(g), Aug. 20, 1996, 110 Stat. 1772, provided that: "The amendments made by this section [amending this section and sections 41, 45A, 51, 196, and 1396 of this title] shall apply to individuals who begin work for the employer after September 30, 1996."

Amendment by section 1205(a)(2) of Pub. L. 104–188 applicable to amounts paid or incurred in taxable years ending after June 30, 1996, see section 1205(e) of Pub. L. 104–188, set out as a note under section 45K of this title.

Pub. L. 104–188, title I, §1702(i), Aug. 20, 1996, 110 Stat. 1875, provided that: "Except as otherwise expressly provided, any amendment made by this section [amending this section, sections 50, 56, 59, 143, 151, 168, 172, 179, 243, 280F, 341, 424, 460, 613A, 805, 832, 861, 897, 1248, 1250, 1367, 1504, 2701, 2702, 2704, 4093, 4975, 5041, 5061, 5354, 6038A, 6302, 6416, 6427, 6501, 6503, 6621, 6724, and 7012 of this title, and provisions set out as a note under section 42 of this title] shall take effect as if included in the provision of the Revenue Reconciliation Act of 1990 [Pub. L. 101–508, title XI] to which such amendment relates."

EFFECTIVE DATE OF 1993 AMENDMENT

Pub. L. 103–66, title XIII, §13303, Aug. 10, 1993, 107 Stat. 556, provided that: "The amendments made by this part [part I (§§13301–13303) of subchapter C of chapter 1 of title XIII of Pub. L. 103–66, enacting sections 1391 to 1394 and 1396 to 1397D of this title and amending this section and sections 39, 51, 196, 280C, and 381 of this title] shall take effect on the date of the enactment of this Act [Aug. 10, 1993]."

Pub. L. 103–66, title XIII, §13322(f), Aug. 10, 1993, 107 Stat. 563, provided that: "The amendments made by this section [enacting section 45A of this title and amending this section and sections 39, 196, and 280C of this title] shall apply to wages paid or incurred after December 31, 1993."

Pub. L. 103–66, title XIII, §13443(d), Aug. 10, 1993, 107 Stat. 569, as amended by Pub. L. 104–188, title I, §1112(a)(2), Aug. 20, 1996, 110 Stat. 1759, provided that: "The amendments made by this section [enacting section 45B of this title and amending this section and section 39 of this title] shall apply with respect to taxes paid after December 31, 1993, with respect to services performed before, on, or after such date."

EFFECTIVE DATE OF 1992 AMENDMENT

Pub. L. 102–486, title XIX, §1914(e), Oct. 24, 1992, 106 Stat. 3023, provided that: "The amendments made by this section [enacting section 45 of this title and amending this section and section 39 of this title] shall apply to taxable years ending after December 31, 1992."

EFFECTIVE DATE OF 1990 AMENDMENT

Amendment by section 11511(b)(1) of Pub. L. 101–508 applicable to costs paid or incurred in taxable years beginning after Dec. 31, 1990, see section 11511(d)(1) of Pub. L. 101–508, set out as an Effective Date note under section 43 of this title.

Pub. L. 101–508, title XI, §11611(e), Nov. 5, 1990, 104 Stat. 1388–503, provided that:

"(1) In general.—Except as provided in paragraph (2), the amendments made by this section [enacting section 44 of this title and amending this section and sections 39 and 190 of this title] shall apply to expenditures paid or incurred after the date of the enactment of this Act [Nov. 5, 1990].

"(2) Subsection (c).—The amendment made by subsection (c) [amending section 190 of this title] shall apply to taxable years beginning after the date of the enactment of this Act."

Amendment by section 11813(b)(2) of Pub. L. 101–508 applicable to property placed in service after Dec. 31, 1990, but not applicable to any transition property (as defined in section 49(e) of this title), any property with respect to which qualified progress expenditures were previously taken into account under section 46(d) of this title, and any property described in section 46(b)(2)(C) of this title, as such sections were in effect on Nov. 4, 1990, see section 11813(c) of Pub. L. 101–508, set out as a note under section 45K of this title.

EFFECTIVE DATE OF 1988 AMENDMENT

Pub. L. 100–647, title I, §1002(e)(8)(C), Nov. 10, 1988, 102 Stat. 3369, provided that: "The amendments made by this paragraph [amending this section and section 49 of this title] shall apply to taxable years beginning after December 31, 1983, and to carrybacks from such years."

Amendment by section 1007(g)(2), (8) of Pub. L. 100–647 effective, except as otherwise provided, as if included in the provision of the Tax Reform Act of 1986, Pub. L. 99–514, to which such amendment relates, see section 1019(a) of Pub. L. 100–647, set out as a note under section 1 of this title.

EFFECTIVE DATE OF 1986 AMENDMENT

Pub. L. 99–514, title II, §221(b), Oct. 22, 1986, 100 Stat. 2173, provided that: "The amendment made by subsection (a) [amending this section] shall apply to taxable years beginning after December 31, 1985."

Amendment by section 231(d)(1), (3)(B) of Pub. L. 99–514 applicable to taxable years beginning after Dec. 31, 1985, see section 231(g) of Pub. L. 99–514, set out as a note under section 41 of this title.

Amendment by section 252(b) of Pub. L. 99–514 applicable to buildings placed in service after Dec. 31, 1986, in taxable years ending after such date, see section 252(e) of Pub. L. 99–514, set out as an Effective Date note under section 42 of this title.

Amendment by section 701(c)(4) of Pub. L. 99–514 applicable to taxable years beginning after Dec. 31, 1986, with certain exceptions and qualifications, see section 701(f) of Pub. L. 99–514, set out as an Effective Date note under section 55 of this title.

Pub. L. 99–514, title XI, §1171(c), Oct. 22, 1986, 100 Stat. 2513, provided that:

"(1) In general.—Except as provided in paragraph (2), the amendments made by this section [amending this section and sections 56, 108, 401, and 404 of this title and repealing sections 41 and 6699 of this title] shall apply to compensation paid or accrued after December 31, 1986, in taxable years ending after such date.

"(2) Sections 404(i) and 6699 to continue to apply to pre-1987 credits.—The provisions of sections 404(i) and 6699 of the Internal Revenue Code of 1986 shall continue to apply with respect to credits under section 41 of such Code attributable to compensation paid or accrued before January 1, 1987 (or under section 38 of such Code with respect to qualified investment before January 1, 1983)."

EFFECTIVE DATE OF 1984 AMENDMENT

Amendment by Pub. L. 98–369 applicable to interest paid or accrued after December 31, 1984, on indebtedness incurred after December 31, 1984, see section 612(g) of Pub. L. 98–369, set out as an Effective Date note under section 25 of this title.

EFFECTIVE DATE

Section applicable to taxable years beginning after Dec. 31, 1983, and to carrybacks from such years, see section 475(a) of Pub. L. 98–369, set out as an Effective Date of 1984 Amendment note under section 21 of this title.

SAVINGS PROVISION

For provisions that amendment made by section 401(d)(6)(B)(i)–(iii) of Pub. L. 115–141 not apply, in the case of certain repeals, to various types of wages, bonds, property, or other items before specific dates, see section 401(d)(6)(C) of Pub. L. 115–141, set out as a note under former section 1400L of this title.

For provisions that nothing in amendment by section 401(b)(5)(A)–(D), (d)(2)(B), (6)(B)(i)–(iii) of Pub. L. 115–141 be construed to affect treatment of certain transactions occurring, property acquired, or items of income, loss, deduction, or credit taken into account prior to Mar. 23, 2018, for purposes of determining liability for tax for periods ending after Mar. 23, 2018, see section 401(e) of Pub. L. 115–141, set out as a note under section 23 of this title.

For provisions that nothing in amendment by section 11813(b)(2) of Pub. L. 101–508 be construed to affect treatment of certain transactions occurring, property acquired, or items of income, loss, deduction, or credit taken into account prior to Nov. 5, 1990, for purposes of determining liability for tax for periods ending after Nov. 5, 1990, see section 11821(b) of Pub. L. 101–508, set out as a note under section 45K of this title.

BUSINESS CREDIT FOR RETENTION OF CERTAIN NEWLY HIRED INDIVIDUALS IN 2010

Pub. L. 111–147, title I, §102, Mar. 18, 2010, 124 Stat. 75, provided that:

"(a) In General.—In the case of any taxable year ending after the date of the enactment of this Act [Mar. 18, 2010], the current year business credit determined under section 38(b) of the Internal Revenue Code of 1986 for such taxable year shall be increased, with respect to each retained worker with respect to which subsection (b)(2) is first satisfied during such taxable year, by the lesser of—

"(1) $1,000, or

"(2) 6.2 percent of the wages (as defined in section 3401(a) [probably means section 3401(a) of the Internal Revenue Code of 1986]) paid by the taxpayer to such retained worker during the 52 consecutive week period referred to in subsection (b)(2).

"(b) Retained Worker.—For purposes of this section, the term 'retained worker' means any qualified individual (as defined in [former] section 3111(d)(3) or [former] section 3221(c)(3) of the Internal Revenue Code of 1986)—

"(1) who was employed by the taxpayer on any date during the taxable year,

"(2) who was so employed by the taxpayer for a period of not less than 52 consecutive weeks, and

"(3) whose wages (as defined in section 3401(a) [probably means section 3401(a) of the Internal Revenue Code of 1986]) for such employment during the last 26 weeks of such period equaled at least 80 percent of such wages for the first 26 weeks of such period.

"(c) Limitation on Carrybacks.—No portion of the unused business credit under section 38 of the Internal Revenue Code of 1986 for any taxable year which is attributable to the increase in the current year business credit under this section may be carried to a taxable year beginning before the date of the enactment of this section [Mar. 18, 2010].

"(d) Treatment of Possessions.—

"(1) Payments to possessions.—

"(A) Mirror code possessions.—The Secretary of the Treasury shall pay to each possession of the United States with a mirror code tax system amounts equal to the loss to that possession by reason of the application of this section (other than this subsection). Such amounts shall be determined by the Secretary of the Treasury based on information provided by the government of the respective possession.

"(B) Other possessions.—The Secretary of the Treasury shall pay to each possession of the United States which does not have a mirror code tax system amounts estimated by the Secretary of the Treasury as being equal to the aggregate benefits that would have been provided to residents of such possession by reason of the application of this section (other than this subsection) if a mirror code tax system had been in effect in such possession. The preceding sentence shall not apply with respect to any possession of the United States unless such possession has a plan, which has been approved by the Secretary of the Treasury, under which such possession will promptly distribute such payments to the residents of such possession.

"(2) Coordination with credit allowed against united states income taxes.—No increase in the credit determined under section 38(b) of the Internal Revenue Code of 1986 against United States income taxes for any taxable year determined under subsection (a) shall be taken into account with respect to any person—

"(A) to whom a credit is allowed against taxes imposed by the possession by reason of this section for such taxable year, or

"(B) who is eligible for a payment under a plan described in paragraph (1)(B) with respect to such taxable year.

"(3) Definitions and special rules.—

"(A) Possession of the united states.—For purposes of this subsection, the term 'possession of the United States' includes the Commonwealth of Puerto Rico and the Commonwealth of the Northern Mariana Islands.

"(B) Mirror code tax system.—For purposes of this subsection, the term 'mirror code tax system' means, with respect to any possession of the United States, the income tax system of such possession if the income tax liability of the residents of such possession under such system is determined by reference to the income tax laws of the United States as if such possession were the United States.

"(C) Treatment of payments.—For purposes of section 1324(b)(2) of title 31, United States Code, rules similar to the rules of section 1001(b)(3)(C) of the American Recovery and Reinvestment Tax Act of 2009 [section 1001(b)(3)(C) of Pub. L. 111–5, formerly set out as a note under section 36A of this title] shall apply."

CREDIT FOR CONTRIBUTIONS TO CERTAIN COMMUNITY DEVELOPMENT CORPORATIONS

Pub. L. 103–66, title XIII, §13311, Aug. 10, 1993, 107 Stat. 556, as amended by Pub. L. 104–188, title I, §1703(n)(13), Aug. 20, 1996, 110 Stat. 1877, provided that:

"(a) In General.—For purposes of section 38 of the Internal Revenue Code of 1986, the current year business credit shall include the credit determined under this section.

"(b) Determination of Credit.—The credit determined under this section for each taxable year in the credit period with respect to any qualified CDC contribution made by the taxpayer is an amount equal to 5 percent of such contribution.

"(c) Credit Period.—For purposes of this section, the credit period with respect to any qualified CDC contribution is the period of 10 taxable years beginning with the taxable year during which such contribution was made.

"(d) Qualified CDC Contribution.—For purposes of this section—

"(1) In general.—The term 'qualified CDC contribution' means any transfer of cash—

"(A) which is made to a selected community development corporation during the 5-year period beginning on the date such corporation was selected for purposes of this section,

"(B) the amount of which is available for use by such corporation for at least 10 years,

"(C) which is to be used by such corporation for qualified low-income assistance within its operational area, and

"(D) which is designated by such corporation for purposes of this section.

"(2) Limitations on amount designated.—The aggregate amount of contributions to a selected community development corporation which may be designated by such corporation shall not exceed $2,000,000.

"(e) Selected Community Development Corporations.—

"(1) In general.—For purposes of this section, the term 'selected community development corporation' means any corporation—

"(A) which is described in section 501(c)(3) of such Code and exempt from tax under section 501(a) of such Code,

"(B) the principal purposes of which include promoting employment of, and business opportunities for, low-income individuals who are residents of the operational area, and

"(C) which is selected by the Secretary of Housing and Urban Development for purposes of this section.

"(2) Only 20 corporations may be selected.—The Secretary of Housing and Urban Development may select 20 corporations for purposes of this section, subject to the availability of eligible corporations. Such selections may be made only before July 1, 1994. At least 8 of the operational areas of the corporations selected must be rural areas (as defined by section 1393(a)(2) of such Code).

"(3) Operational areas must have certain characteristics.—A corporation may be selected for purposes of this section only if its operational area meets the following criteria:

"(A) The area meets the size requirements under section 1392(a)(3).

"(B) The unemployment rate (as determined by the appropriate available data) is not less than the national unemployment rate.

"(C) The median family income of residents of such area does not exceed 80 percent of the median gross income of residents of the jurisdiction of the local government which includes such area.

"(f) Qualified Low-Income Assistance.—For purposes of this section, the term 'qualified low-income assistance' means assistance—

"(1) which is designed to provide employment of, and business opportunities for, low-income individuals who are residents of the operational area of the community development corporation, and

"(2) which is approved by the Secretary of Housing and Urban Development."

APPLICABILITY OF CERTAIN AMENDMENTS BY PUBLIC LAW 99–514 IN RELATION TO TREATY OBLIGATIONS OF UNITED STATES

For applicability of amendment by section 701(c)(4) of Pub. L. 99–514 notwithstanding any treaty obligation of the United States in effect on Oct. 22, 1986, with provision that for such purposes any amendment by title I of Pub. L. 100–647 be treated as if it had been included in the provision of Pub. L. 99–514 to which such amendment relates, see section 1012(aa)(2), (4) of Pub. L. 100–647, set out as a note under section 861 of this title.

EFFECTIVE 15-YEAR CARRYBACK OF EXISTING CARRYFORWARDS OF STEEL COMPANIES

Pub. L. 99–514, title II, §212, Oct. 22, 1986, 100 Stat. 2170, as amended by Pub. L. 100–647, title I, §1002(f), Nov. 10, 1988, 102 Stat. 3369, provided that:

"(a) General Rule.—If a qualified corporation makes an election under this section for its 1st taxable year beginning after December 31, 1986, with respect to any portion of its existing carryforwards, the amount determined under subsection (b) shall be treated as a payment against the tax imposed by chapter 1 of the Internal Revenue Code of 1986 made by such corporation on the last day prescribed by law (without regard to extensions) for filing its return of tax under chapter 1 of such Code for such 1st taxable year.

"(b) Amount.—For purposes of subsection (a), the amount determined under this subsection shall be the lesser of—

"(1) 50 percent of the portion of the corporation's existing carryforwards to which the election under subsection (a) applies, or

"(2) the corporation's net tax liability for the carryback period.

"(c) Corporation Making Election May Not Use Same Amounts Under Section 38.—In the case of a qualified corporation which makes an election under subsection (a), the portion of such corporation's existing carryforwards to which such an election applies shall not be taken into account under section 38 of the Internal Revenue Code of 1986 for any taxable year beginning after December 31, 1986.

"(d) Net Tax Liability for Carryback Period.—For purposes of this section—

"(1) In general.—A corporation's net tax liability for the carryback period is the aggregate of such corporation's net tax liability for taxable years in the carryback period.

"(2) Net tax liability.—The term 'net tax liability' means, with respect to any taxable year, the amount of the tax imposed by chapter 1 of the Internal Revenue Code of 1954 [now 1986] for such taxable year, reduced by the sum of the credits allowable under part IV of subchapter A of such chapter 1 (other than section 34 thereof). For purposes of the preceding sentence, any tax treated as not imposed by chapter 1 of such Code under section 26(b)(2) of such Code shall not be treated as tax imposed by such chapter 1.

"(3) Carryback period.—The term 'carryback period' means the period—

"(A) which begins with the corporation's 15th taxable year preceding the 1st taxable year from which there is an unused credit included in such corporation's existing carryforwards (but in no event shall such period begin before the corporation's 1st taxable year ending after December 31, 1961), and

"(B) which ends with the corporation's last taxable year beginning before January 1, 1986.

"(e) No Recomputation of Minimum Tax, Etc.—Nothing in this section shall be construed to affect—

"(1) the amount of the tax imposed by section 56 of the Internal Revenue Code of 1986, or

"(2) the amount of any credit allowable under such Code,

for any taxable year in the carryback period.

"(f) Reinvestment Requirement.—

"(1) In general.—Any amount determined under this section must be committed to reinvestment in, and modernization of the steel industry through investment in modern plant and equipment, research and development, and other appropriate projects, such as working capital for steel operations and programs for the retraining of steel workers.

"(2) Special rule.—In the case of the LTV Corporation, in lieu of the requirements of paragraph (1)—

"(A) such corporation shall place such refund in a separate account; and

"(B) amounts in such separate account—

"(i) shall only be used by the corporation—

"(I) to purchase an insurance policy which provides that, in the event the corporation becomes involved in a title 11 or similar case (as defined in section 368(a)(3)(A) of the Internal Revenue Code of 1954 [now 1986]), the insurer will provide life and health insurance coverage during the 1-year period beginning on the date when the corporation receives the refund to any individual with respect to whom the corporation would (but for such involvement) have been obligated to provide such coverage the coverage provided by the insurer will be identical to the coverage which the corporation would (but for such involvement) have been obligated to provide, and provides that the payment of insurance premiums will not be required during such 1-year period to keep such policy in force, or

"(II) directly in connection with the trade or business of the corporation in the manufacturer or production of steel; and

"(ii) shall be used (or obligated) for purposes described in clause (i) not later than 3 months after the corporation receives the refund.

"(3) In the case of a qualified corporation, no offset to any refund under this section may be made by reason of any tax imposed by section 4971 of the Internal Revenue Code of 1986 (or any interest or penalty attributable to any such tax), and the date on which any such refund is to be paid shall be determined without regard to such corporation's status under title 11, United States Code.

"(g) Definitions.—For purposes of this section—

"(1) Qualified corporation.—

"(A) In general.—The term 'qualified corporation' means any corporation which is described in section 806(b) of the Steel Import Stabilization Act [19 U.S.C. 2253 note] and a company which was incorporated on February 11, 1983, in Michigan.

"(B) Certain predecessors included.—In the case of any qualified corporation which has carryforward attributable to a predecessor corporation described in such section 806(b), the qualified corporation and the predecessor corporation shall be treated as 1 corporation for purposes of subsections (d) and (e).

"(2) Existing carryforwards.—The term 'existing carryforward' means the aggregate of the amounts which—

"(A) are unused business credit carryforwards to the taxpayer's 1st taxable year beginning after December 31, 1986 (determined without regard to the limitations of section 38(c) and any reduction under section 49 of the Internal Revenue Code of 1986), and

"(B) are attributable to the amount of the regular investment credit determined for periods before January 1, 1986, under section 46(a)(1) of such Code (relating to regular percentage), or any corresponding provision of prior law, determined on the basis that the regular investment credit was used first.

"(3) Special rule for restructuring.—In the case of any corporation, any restructuring shall not limit, increase, or otherwise affect the benefits which would have been available under this section but for such restructuring.

"(h) Tentative Refunds.—Rules similar to the rules of section 6425 of the Internal Revenue Code of 1986 shall apply to any overpayment resulting from the application of this section."

EFFECTIVE 15-YEAR CARRYBACK OF EXISTING CARRYFORWARDS OF QUALIFIED FARMERS

Pub. L. 99–514, title II, §213, Oct. 22, 1986, 100 Stat. 2172, as amended by Pub. L. 100–647, title I, §1002(g), Nov. 10, 1988, 102 Stat. 3369, provided that:

"(a) General Rule.—If a taxpayer who is a qualified farmer makes an election under this section for its 1st taxable year beginning after December 31, 1986, with respect to any portion of its existing carryforwards, the amount determined under subsection (b) shall be treated as a payment against the tax imposed by chapter 1 of the Internal Revenue Code of 1986 made by such taxpayer on the last day prescribed by law (without regard to extensions) for filing its return of tax under chapter 1 of such Code for such 1st taxable year.

"(b) Amount.—For purposes of subsection (a), the amount determined under this subsection shall be equal to the smallest of—

"(1) 50 percent of the portion of the taxpayer's existing carryforwards to which the election under subsection (a) applies,

"(2) the taxpayer's net tax liability for the carryback period (within the meaning of section 212(d) of this Act [set out as a note above]), or

"(3) $750.

"(c) Taxpayer Making Election May Not Use Same Amounts Under Section 38.—In the case of a qualified farmer who makes an election under subsection (a), the portion of such farmer's existing carryforwards to which such an election applies shall not be taken into account under section 38 of the Internal Revenue Code of 1986 for any taxable year beginning after December 31, 1986.

"(d) No Recomputation of Minimum Tax, Etc.—Nothing in this section shall be construed to affect—

"(1) the amount of the tax imposed by section 56 of the Internal Revenue Code of 1954 [now 1986], or

"(2) the amount of any credit allowable under such Code,

for any taxable year in the carryback period (within the meaning of section 212(d)(3) of this Act [set out as a note above]).

"(e) Definitions and Special Rules.—For purposes of this section—

"(1) Qualified farmer.—The term 'qualified farmer' means any taxpayer who, during the 3-taxable year period preceding the taxable year for which an election is made under subsection (a), derived 50 percent or more of the taxpayer's gross income from the trade or business of farming.

"(2) Existing carryforward.—The term 'existing carryforward' means the aggregate of the amounts which—

"(A) are unused business credit carryforwards to the taxpayer's 1st taxable year beginning after December 31, 1986 (determined without regard to the limitations of section 38(c) of the Internal Revenue Code of 1986), and

"(B) are attributable to the amount of the investment credit determined for periods before January 1, 1986, under section 46(a) of such Code (or any corresponding provision of prior law) with respect to section 38 property which was used by the taxpayer in the trade or business of farming, determined on the basis that such credit was used first.

"(3) Farming.—The term 'farming' has the meaning given such term by section 2032A(e)(4) and (5) of such Code."

TREATMENT OF INVESTMENT TAX CREDITS WITH RESPECT TO CERTAIN PUBLIC UTILITIES

For provisions requiring different applications of subsec. (c) of this section to certain public utilities by making substitutions in the percentages of the tentative minimum tax referred to in subsec. (c)(3)(A)(ii), (B), under certain circumstances, see section 701(f)(6) of Pub. L. 99–514, set out as an Effective Date note under section 55 of this title.

PLAN AMENDMENTS NOT REQUIRED UNTIL JANUARY 1, 1989

For provisions directing that if any amendments made by subtitle A or subtitle C of title XI [§§1101–1147 and 1171–1177] or title XVIII [§§1800–1899A] of Pub. L. 99–514 require an amendment to any plan, such plan amendment shall not be required to be made before the first plan year beginning on or after Jan. 1, 1989, see section 1140 of Pub. L. 99–514, as amended, set out as a note under section 401 of this title.

TRANSITION RULES

Pub. L. 99–514, title XI, §1177, Oct. 22, 1986, 100 Stat. 2520, as amended by Pub. L. 100–647, title I, §1011B(l)(1), (2), Nov. 10, 1988, 102 Stat. 3493, provided that:

"(a) Section 1171.—The amendments made by section 1171 [amending this section and sections 56, 108, 401, and 404 of this title and repealing sections 41 and 6699 of this title] shall not apply in the case of a tax credit employee stock ownership plan if—

"(1) such plan was favorably approved on September 23, 1983, by employees, and

"(2) not later than January 11, 1984, the employer of such employees was 100 percent owned by such plan.

"(b) Subtitle Not To Apply to Certain Newspaper.—The amendments made by section 1175 [amending section 401 of this title] shall not apply to any daily newspaper—

"(1) which was first published on December 17, 1855, and which began publication under its current name in 1954, and

"(2) which is published in a constitutional home rule city (within the meaning of section 146(d)(3)(C) of the Internal Revenue Code of 1986) which has a population of less than 2,500,000."

Pub. L. 100–647, title I, §1011B(l)(3), Nov. 10, 1988, 102 Stat. 3493, provided that: "If any newspaper corporation described in section 1177(b) of the Reform Act [section 1177(b) of Pub. L. 99–514, set out above], as amended by this subsection, pays in cash a dividend within 60 days after the date of the enactment of this Act [Nov. 10, 1988] to the corporation's employee stock ownership plans and if a corporate resolution declaring such dividend was adopted before November 30, 1987, and such resolution specifies that such dividend shall be contingent upon passage by the Congress of technical corrections, then such dividend (to the extent the aggregate amount so paid does not exceed $3,500,000) shall be treated as if it had been declared and paid in 1987 for all purposes of the Internal Revenue Code of 1986."

ACCOUNTING FOR INVESTMENT CREDIT IN CERTAIN FINANCIAL REPORTS AND REPORTS TO FEDERAL AGENCIES

Pub. L. 92–178, title I, §101(c), Dec. 10, 1971, 85 Stat. 499, as amended by Pub. L. 98–369, div. A, title IV, §450(a), July 18, 1984, 98 Stat. 818; Pub. L. 99–514, §2, Oct. 22, 1986, 100 Stat. 2095, provided that:

"(1) In general.—It was the intent of Congress in enacting, in the Revenue Act of 1962 [see Short Title of 1962 Amendment note set out under section 1 of this title], the investment credit allowed by section 38 of the Internal Revenue Code of 1986 [formerly I.R.C. 1954], and it is the intent of the Congress in restoring that credit in this Act [section 50 of this title], to provide an incentive for modernization and growth of private industry. Accordingly, notwithstanding any other provision of law, on and after the date of the enactment of this Act [Dec. 10, 1971]—

"(A) no taxpayer shall be required to use, for purposes of financial reports subject to the jurisdiction of any Federal agency or reports made to any Federal agency, any particular method of accounting for the credit allowed by such section 38 [this section], and

"(B) a taxpayer shall disclose, in any such report, the method of accounting for such credit used by him for purposes of such report.

"(2) Exceptions.—Paragraph (1) shall not apply to taxpayers who are subject to the provisions of section 46(e) of the Internal Revenue Code of 1986 (as added by section 105(c) of this Act) or to section 203(e) of the Revenue Act of 1964 (as modified by section 105(e) of this Act) [set out as note below]."

[Pub. L. 98–369, div. A, title IV, §450(b), July 18, 1984, 98 Stat. 818, provided that: "The amendments made by this section [amending this note] shall take effect as if included in the Revenue Act of 1971."]

TREATMENT OF INVESTMENT CREDIT BY FEDERAL REGULATORY AGENCIES

Pub. L. 88–272, title II, §203(e), Feb. 26, 1964, 78 Stat. 35, as amended by Pub. L. 99–514, §2, Oct. 22, 1986, 100 Stat. 2095, provided that: "It was the intent of the Congress in providing an investment credit under section 38 of the Internal Revenue Code of 1986 [formerly I.R.C. 1954] and it is the intent of the Congress in repealing the reduction in basis required by section 48(g) of such Code to provide an incentive for modernization and growth of private industry (including that portion thereof which is regulated). Accordingly, Congress does not intend that any agency or instrumentality of the United States having jurisdiction with respect to a taxpayer shall, without the consent of the taxpayer, use—

"(1) in the case of public utility property (as defined in section 46(c)(3)(B) of the Internal Revenue Code of 1986, more than a proportionate part (determined with reference to the average useful life of the property with respect to which the credit was allowed) of the credit against tax allowed for any taxable year by section 38 of such Code, or

"(2) in the case of any other property, any credit against tax allowed by section 38 of such Code,

to reduce such taxpayer's Federal income taxes for the purpose of establishing the cost of service of the taxpayer or to accomplish a similar result by any other method."

Section 203(e) of Pub. L. 88–272, not applicable to public utility property to which section 46(e) of this title applies, see section 105(e) of Pub. L. 92–178, set out as a note under section 46 of this title.

§39. Carryback and carryforward of unused credits

(a) In general

(1) 1-year carryback and 20-year carryforward

If the sum of the business credit carryforwards to the taxable year plus the amount of the current year business credit for the taxable year exceeds the amount of the limitation imposed by subsection (c) of section 38 for such taxable year (hereinafter in this section referred to as the "unused credit year"), such excess (to the extent attributable to the amount of the current year business credit) shall be—

(A) a business credit carryback to the taxable year preceding the unused credit year, and

(B) a business credit carryforward to each of the 20 taxable years following the unused credit year,

and, subject to the limitations imposed by subsections (b) and (c), shall be taken into account under the provisions of section 38(a) in the manner provided in section 38(a).

(2) Amount carried to each year

(A) Entire amount carried to first year

The entire amount of the unused credit for an unused credit year shall be carried to the earliest of the 21 taxable years to which (by reason of paragraph (1)) such credit may be carried.

(B) Amount carried to other 20 years

The amount of the unused credit for the unused credit year shall be carried to each of the other 20 taxable years to the extent that such unused credit may not be taken into account under section 38(a) for a prior taxable year because of the limitations of subsections (b) and (c).

(3) 5-year carryback for marginal oil and gas well production credit

Notwithstanding subsection (d), in the case of the marginal oil and gas well production credit—

(A) this section shall be applied separately from the business credit (other than the marginal oil and gas well production credit),

(B) paragraph (1) shall be applied by substituting "each of the 5 taxable years" for "the taxable year" in subparagraph (A) thereof, and

(C) paragraph (2) shall be applied—

(i) by substituting "25 taxable years" for "21 taxable years" in subparagraph (A) thereof, and

(ii) by substituting "24 taxable years" for "20 taxable years" in subparagraph (B) thereof.

(b) Limitation on carrybacks

The amount of the unused credit which may be taken into account under section 38(a)(3) for any preceding taxable year shall not exceed the amount by which the limitation imposed by section 38(c) for such taxable year exceeds the sum of—

(1) the amounts determined under paragraphs (1) and (2) of section 38(a) for such taxable year, plus

(2) the amounts which (by reason of this section) are carried back to such taxable year and are attributable to taxable years preceding the unused credit year.

(c) Limitation on carryforwards

The amount of the unused credit which may be taken into account under section 38(a)(1) for any succeeding taxable year shall not exceed the amount by which the limitation imposed by section 38(c) for such taxable year exceeds the sum of the amounts which, by reason of this section, are carried to such taxable year and are attributable to taxable years preceding the unused credit year.

(d) Transitional rule

No portion of the unused business credit for any taxable year which is attributable to a credit specified in section 38(b) or any portion thereof may be carried back to any taxable year before the first taxable year for which such specified credit or such portion is allowable (without regard to subsection (a)).

(Added Pub. L. 98–369, div. A, title IV, §473, July 18, 1984, 98 Stat. 828; amended Pub. L. 99–514, title II, §231(d)(3)(C)(i), title XVIII, §1846, Oct. 22, 1986, 100 Stat. 2179, 2856; Pub. L. 100–647, title I, §1002(I)(26), Nov. 10, 1988, 102 Stat. 3381; Pub. L. 101–508, title XI, §§11511(b)(2), 11611(b)(2), 11801(a)(2), Nov. 5, 1990, 104 Stat. 1388–485, 1388-503, 1388-520; Pub. L. 102–486, title XIX, §1914(c), Oct. 24, 1992, 106 Stat. 3023; Pub. L. 103–66, title XIII, §§13302(a)(2), 13322(d), 13443(b)(2), Aug. 10, 1993, 107 Stat. 555, 563, 569; Pub. L. 104–188, title I, §§1205(c), 1703(n)(1), Aug. 20, 1996, 110 Stat. 1775, 1877; Pub. L. 105–34, title VII, §701(b)(1), title X, §1083(a), Aug. 5, 1997, 111 Stat. 869, 951; Pub. L. 105–206, title VI, §6010(n), July 22, 1998, 112 Stat. 816; Pub. L. 106–554, §1(a)(7) [title I, §121(b)(2)], Dec. 21, 2000, 114 Stat. 2763, 2763A-610; Pub. L. 107–16, title VI, §619(c)(1), June 7, 2001, 115 Stat. 110; Pub. L. 108–357, title II, §245(b)(1), title III, §341(c), Oct. 22, 2004, 118 Stat. 1447, 1487; Pub. L. 109–135, title IV, §412(g), Dec. 21, 2005, 119 Stat. 2637; Pub. L. 111–240, title II, §2012(a), (b), Sept. 27, 2010, 124 Stat. 2554; Pub. L. 115–141, div. U, title IV, §401(b)(5)(E), (F), Mar. 23, 2018, 132 Stat. 1202.)

EDITORIAL NOTES
PRIOR PROVISIONS

A prior section 39 was renumbered section 34 of this title.

Another prior section 39 was renumbered section 37 of this title.

AMENDMENTS

2018—Subsec. (a)(3)(A). Pub. L. 115–141, §401(b)(5)(F), struck out "or the eligible small business credits" after "gas well production credit)".

Subsec. (a)(4). Pub. L. 115–141, §401(b)(5)(E), struck out par. (4) which related to 5-year carryback for eligible small business credits.

2010—Subsec. (a)(3)(A). Pub. L. 111–240, §2012(b), inserted "or the eligible small business credits" after "credit)".

Subsec. (a)(4). Pub. L. 111–240, §2012(a), added par. (4).

2005—Subsec. (a)(1)(A). Pub. L. 109–135, §412(g)(1), substituted "the taxable year" for "each of the 1 taxable years".

Subsec. (a)(3)(B). Pub. L. 109–135, §412(g)(2), amended subpar. (B) generally. Prior to amendment, subpar. (B) read as follows: "paragraph (1) shall be applied by substituting '5 taxable years' for '1 taxable years' in subparagraph (A) thereof, and".

2004—Subsec. (a)(3). Pub. L. 108–357, §341(c), added par. (3).

Subsec. (d). Pub. L. 108–357, §245(b)(1), amended heading and text of subsec. (d) generally, substituting provisions prohibiting carryback of the unused business credit attributable to a credit specified in section 38(b) for provisions prohibiting carryback of the enhanced oil recovery credit before 1991, sections 44, 45A, and 45B credits before their enactments, the renewable electricity production credit before its effective date, the empowerment zone employment credit, section 45C credit before July 1, 1996, DC Zone credits before their effective date, the new markets tax credit before Jan. 1, 2001, and the small employer pension plan startup cost credit before Jan. 1, 2002.

2001—Subsec. (d)(10). Pub. L. 107–16, §619(c)(1), added par. (10).

2000—Subsec. (d)(9). Pub. L. 106–554 added par. (9).

1998—Subsec. (a)(2). Pub. L. 105–206 amended Pub. L. 105–34, §1083(a)(2). See 1997 Amendment note below.

1997—Subsec. (a)(1). Pub. L. 105–34, §1083(a)(1), substituted "1-year" for "3-year" and "20-year" for "15-year" in heading, "1 taxable" for "3 taxable" in subpar. (A), and "20 taxable" for "15 taxable" in subpar. (B).

Subsec. (a)(2). Pub. L. 105–34, §1083(a)(2), as amended by Pub. L. 105–206, §6010(n), in subpar. (A), substituted "21 taxable" for "18 taxable", and in subpar. (B), substituted "20 years" for "17 years" in heading and "20 taxable" for "17 taxable" in text.

Subsec. (d)(8). Pub. L. 105–34, §701(b)(1), added par. (8).

1996—Subsec. (d)(5). Pub. L. 104–188, §1703(n)(1)(A), substituted "45A" for "45" in heading.

Subsec. (d)(6). Pub. L. 104–188, §1703(n)(1)(B), substituted "45B" for "45" in heading.

Subsec. (d)(7). Pub. L. 104–188, §1205(c), added par. (7).

1993—Subsec. (d)(4). Pub. L. 103–66, §13302(a)(2), added par. (4).

Subsec. (d)(5). Pub. L. 103–66, §13322(d), added par. (5).

Subsec. (d)(6). Pub. L. 103–66, §13443(b)(2), added par. (6).

1992—Subsec. (d). Pub. L. 102–486 redesignated par. (5), relating to carryback of enhanced oil recovery credit, as (1), redesignated par. (5), relating to carryback of section 44 credit, as (2), and added par. (3).

1990—Subsec. (d)(1) to (4). Pub. L. 101–508, §11801(a)(2), struck out par. (1) which related to carryforwards from an unused credit year which did not expire before first taxable year beginning after Dec. 31, 1983, par. (2) which related to carrybacks in determining amount allowable as credit including net tax liability, par. (3) which related to similar rules for research credit under section 30, and par. (4) which provided for no carryback of low-income housing credit before 1987.

Subsec. (d)(5). Pub. L. 101–508, §11611(b)(2), added par. (5) relating to carryback of section 44 credit.

Pub. L. 101–508, §11511(b)(2), added par. (5) relating to carryback of enhanced oil recovery credit.

1988—Subsec. (d)(4). Pub. L. 100–647 added par. (4).

1986—Subsec. (d)(1)(A). Pub. L. 99–514, §1846(1), inserted "(as in effect before the enactment of the Tax Reform Act of 1984)".

Subsec. (d)(2)(B). Pub. L. 99–514, §1846(2), substituted "as defined in section 26(b)" for "as so defined in section 25(b)".

Subsec. (d)(3). Pub. L. 99–514, §231(d)(3)(C)(i), added par. (3).

STATUTORY NOTES AND RELATED SUBSIDIARIES

EFFECTIVE DATE OF 2010 AMENDMENT

Pub. L. 111–240, title II, §2012(c), Sept. 27, 2010, 124 Stat. 2554, provided that: "The amendments made by this section [amending this section] shall apply to credits determined in taxable years beginning after December 31, 2009."

EFFECTIVE DATE OF 2004 AMENDMENT

Pub. L. 108–357, title II, §245(b)(2), Oct. 22, 2004, 118 Stat. 1448, provided that: "The amendment made by paragraph (1) [amending this section] shall apply with respect to taxable years ending after December 31, 2003."

Amendment by section 245(b) of Pub. L. 108–357 applicable to taxable years beginning after Dec. 31, 2004, see section 245(e) of Pub. L. 108–357, set out as a note under section 38 of this title.

Amendment by section 341(c) of Pub. L. 108–357 applicable to production in taxable years beginning after Dec. 31, 2004, see section 341(e) of Pub. L. 108–357, set out as a note under section 38 of this title.

EFFECTIVE DATE OF 2001 AMENDMENT

Amendment by Pub. L. 107–16 applicable to costs paid or incurred in taxable years beginning after Dec. 31, 2001, with respect to qualified employer plans first effective after such date, see section 619(d) of Pub. L. 107–16, set out as a note under section 38 of this title.

EFFECTIVE DATE OF 2000 AMENDMENT

Amendment by Pub. L. 106–554 applicable to investments made after Dec. 31, 2000, see §1(a)(7) [title I, §121(e)] of Pub. L. 106–554, set out as a note under section 38 of this title.

EFFECTIVE DATE OF 1998 AMENDMENT

Amendment by Pub. L. 105–206 effective, except as otherwise provided, as if included in the provisions of the Taxpayer Relief Act of 1997, Pub. L. 105–34, to which such amendment relates, see section 6024 of Pub. L. 105–206, set out as a note under section 1 of this title.

EFFECTIVE DATE OF 1997 AMENDMENT

Pub. L. 105–34, title VII, §701(d), Aug. 5, 1997, 111 Stat. 869, provided that: "Except as provided in subsection (c) [amending table of subchapters for this chapter], the amendments made by this section [enacting subchapter W of this chapter and amending this section and section 1016 of this title] shall take effect on the date of the enactment of this Act [Aug. 5, 1997]."

Pub. L. 105–34, title X, §1083(b), Aug. 5, 1997, 111 Stat. 951, provided that: "The amendments made by this section [amending this section] shall apply to credits arising in taxable years beginning after December 31, 1997."

EFFECTIVE DATE OF 1996 AMENDMENT

Amendment by section 1205(c) of Pub. L. 104–188 applicable to amounts paid or incurred in taxable years ending after June 30, 1996, see section 1205(e) of Pub. L. 104–188, set out as a note under section 45K of this title.

Pub. L. 104–188, title I, §1703(o), Aug. 20, 1996, 110 Stat. 1878, provided that: "Any amendment made by this section [amending this section and sections 40, 59, 108, 117, 135, 143, 163, 904, 956A, 958, 1017, 1044, 1201, 1245, 1297, 1394, 1397B, 1561, 4001, 6033, 6427, 6501, 6655, and 9502 of this title, renumbering section 6714 of this title as section 6715, and amending provisions set out as notes under sections 38, 42, 197, and 1258 of this title and section 401 of Title 42, The Public Health and Welfare] shall take effect as if included in the provision of the Revenue Reconciliation Act of 1993 [Pub. L. 103–66, title XIII, ch. I, §§13001–13444] to which such amendment relates."

EFFECTIVE DATE OF 1993 AMENDMENT

Amendment by section 13322(d) of Pub. L. 103–66 applicable to wages paid or incurred after Dec. 31, 1993, see section 13322(f) of Pub. L. 103–66, set out as a note under section 38 of this title.

Amendment by section 13443(b)(2) of Pub. L. 103–66 applicable with respect to taxes paid after Dec. 31, 1993, with respect to services performed before, on, or after such date, see section 13443(d) of Pub. L. 103–66, as amended, set out as a note under section 38 of this title.

EFFECTIVE DATE OF 1992 AMENDMENT

Amendment by Pub. L. 102–486 applicable to taxable years ending after Dec. 31, 1992, see section 1914(e) of Pub. L. 102–486, set out as a note under section 38 of this title.

EFFECTIVE DATE OF 1990 AMENDMENT

Amendment by section 11511(b)(2) of Pub. L. 101–508 applicable to costs paid or incurred in taxable years beginning after Dec. 31, 1990, see section 11511(d)(1) of Pub. L. 101–508, set out as an Effective Date note under section 43 of this title.

Amendment by section 11611(b)(2) of Pub. L. 101–508 applicable to expenditures paid or incurred after Nov. 5, 1990, see section 11611(e)(1) of Pub. L. 101–508, set out as a note under section 38 of this title.

EFFECTIVE DATE OF 1988 AMENDMENT

Amendment by Pub. L. 100–647 effective, except as otherwise provided, as if included in the provision of the Tax Reform Act of 1986, Pub. L. 99–514, to which such amendment relates, see section 1019(a) of Pub. L. 100–647, set out as a note under section 1 of this title.

EFFECTIVE DATE OF 1986 AMENDMENT

Amendment by section 231(d)(3)(C)(i) of Pub. L. 99–514 applicable to taxable years beginning after Dec. 31, 1985, see section 231(g) of Pub. L. 99–514, set out as a note under section 41 of this title.

Amendment by section 1846 of Pub. L. 99–514 effective, except as otherwise provided, as if included in the provisions of the Tax Reform Act of 1984, Pub. L. 98–369, div. A, to which such amendment relates, see section 1881 of Pub. L. 99–514, set out as a note under section 48 of this title.

EFFECTIVE DATE

Section applicable to taxable years beginning after Dec. 31, 1983, and to carrybacks from such years, see section 475(a) of Pub. L. 98–369, set out as an Effective Date of 1984 Amendment note under section 21 of this title.

SAVINGS PROVISION

For provisions that nothing in amendment by Pub. L. 115–141 be construed to affect treatment of certain transactions occurring, property acquired, or items of income, loss, deduction, or credit taken into account prior to Mar. 23, 2018, for purposes of determining liability for tax for periods ending after Mar. 23, 2018, see section 401(e) of Pub. L. 115–141, set out as a note under section 23 of this title.

For provisions that nothing in amendment by section 11801(a)(2) of Pub. L. 101–508 be construed to affect treatment of certain transactions occurring, property acquired, or items of income, loss, deduction, or credit taken into account prior to Nov. 5, 1990, for purposes of determining liability for tax for periods ending after Nov. 5, 1990, see section 11821(b) of Pub. L. 101–508, set out as a note under section 45K of this title.

PLAN AMENDMENTS NOT REQUIRED UNTIL JANUARY 1, 1989

For provisions directing that if any amendments made by subtitle A or subtitle C of title XI [§§1101–1147 and 1171–1177] or title XVIII [§§1800–1899A] of Pub. L. 99–514 require an amendment to any plan, such plan amendment shall not be required to be made before the first plan year beginning on or after Jan. 1, 1989, see section 1140 of Pub. L. 99–514, as amended, set out as a note under section 401 of this title.

§40. Alcohol, etc., used as fuel

(a) General rule

For purposes of section 38, the alcohol fuels credit determined under this section for the taxable year is an amount equal to the sum of—

(1) the alcohol mixture credit,

(2) the alcohol credit,

(3) in the case of an eligible small ethanol producer, the small ethanol producer credit, plus

(4) the second generation biofuel producer credit.

(b) Definition of alcohol mixture credit, alcohol credit, and small ethanol producer credit

For purposes of this section, and except as provided in subsection (h)—

(1) Alcohol mixture credit

(A) In general

The alcohol mixture credit of any taxpayer for any taxable year is 60 cents for each gallon of alcohol used by the taxpayer in the production of a qualified mixture.

(B) Qualified mixture

The term "qualified mixture" means a mixture of alcohol and gasoline or of alcohol and a special fuel which—

(i) is sold by the taxpayer producing such mixture to any person for use as a fuel, or

(ii) is used as a fuel by the taxpayer producing such mixture.

(C) Sale or use must be in trade or business, etc.

Alcohol used in the production of a qualified mixture shall be taken into account—

(i) only if the sale or use described in subparagraph (B) is in a trade or business of the taxpayer, and

(ii) for the taxable year in which such sale or use occurs.

(D) Casual off-farm production not eligible

No credit shall be allowed under this section with respect to any casual off-farm production of a qualified mixture.

(2) Alcohol credit

(A) In general

The alcohol credit of any taxpayer for any taxable year is 60 cents for each gallon of alcohol which is not in a mixture with gasoline or a special fuel (other than any denaturant) and which during the taxable year—

(i) is used by the taxpayer as a fuel in a trade or business, or

(ii) is sold by the taxpayer at retail to a person and placed in the fuel tank of such person's vehicle.

(B) User credit not to apply to alcohol sold at retail

No credit shall be allowed under subparagraph (A)(i) with respect to any alcohol which was sold in a retail sale described in subparagraph (A)(ii).

(3) Smaller credit for lower proof alcohol

In the case of any alcohol with a proof which is at least 150 but less than 190, paragraphs (1)(A) and (2)(A) shall be applied by substituting "45 cents" for "60 cents".

(4) Small ethanol producer credit

(A) In general

The small ethanol producer credit of any eligible small ethanol producer for any taxable year is 10 cents for each gallon of qualified ethanol fuel production of such producer.

(B) Qualified ethanol fuel production

For purposes of this paragraph, the term "qualified ethanol fuel production" means any alcohol which is ethanol which is produced by an eligible small ethanol producer, and which during the taxable year—

(i) is sold by such producer to another person—

(I) for use by such other person in the production of a qualified mixture in such other person's trade or business (other than casual off-farm production),

(II) for use by such other person as a fuel in a trade or business, or

(III) who sells such ethanol at retail to another person and places such ethanol in the fuel tank of such other person, or

(ii) is used or sold by such producer for any purpose described in clause (i).

(C) Limitation

The qualified ethanol fuel production of any producer for any taxable year shall not exceed 15,000,000 gallons (determined without regard to any qualified second generation biofuel production).

(D) Additional distillation excluded

The qualified ethanol fuel production of any producer for any taxable year shall not include any alcohol which is purchased by the producer and with respect to which such producer increases the proof of the alcohol by additional distillation.

(5) Adding of denaturants not treated as mixture

The adding of any denaturant to alcohol shall not be treated as the production of a mixture.

(6) Second generation biofuel producer credit

(A) In general

The second generation biofuel producer credit of any taxpayer is an amount equal to the applicable amount for each gallon of qualified second generation biofuel production.

(B) Applicable amount

For purposes of subparagraph (A), the applicable amount means $1.01, except that such amount shall, in the case of second generation biofuel which is alcohol, be reduced by the sum of—

    (i) the amount of the credit in effect for such alcohol under subsection (b)(1) (without regard to subsection (b)(3)) at the time of the qualified second generation biofuel production, plus

    (ii) in the case of ethanol, the amount of the credit in effect under subsection (b)(4) at the time of such production.

(C) Qualified second generation biofuel production

For purposes of this section, the term "qualified second generation biofuel production" means any second generation biofuel which is produced by the taxpayer, and which during the taxable year—

    (i) is sold by the taxpayer to another person—

        (I) for use by such other person in the production of a qualified second generation biofuel mixture in such other person's trade or business (other than casual off-farm production),

        (II) for use by such other person as a fuel in a trade or business, or

        (III) who sells such second generation biofuel at retail to another person and places such second generation biofuel in the fuel tank of such other person, or

    (ii) is used or sold by the taxpayer for any purpose described in clause (i).

The qualified second generation biofuel production of any taxpayer for any taxable year shall not include any alcohol which is purchased by the taxpayer and with respect to which such producer increases the proof of the alcohol by additional distillation.

(D) Qualified second generation biofuel mixture

For purposes of this paragraph, the term "qualified second generation biofuel mixture" means a mixture of second generation biofuel and gasoline or of second generation biofuel and a special fuel which—

    (i) is sold by the person producing such mixture to any person for use as a fuel, or

    (ii) is used as a fuel by the person producing such mixture.

(E) Second generation biofuel

For purposes of this paragraph—

(i) In general

The term "second generation biofuel" means any liquid fuel which—

    (I) is derived by, or from, qualified feedstocks, and

    (II) meets the registration requirements for fuels and fuel additives established by the Environmental Protection Agency under section 211 of the Clean Air Act (42 U.S.C. 7545).

(ii) Exclusion of low-proof alcohol

The term "second generation biofuel" shall not include any alcohol with a proof of less than 150. The determination of the proof of any alcohol shall be made without regard to any added denaturants.

(iii) Exclusion of certain fuels

The term "second generation biofuel" shall not include any fuel if—

    (I) more than 4 percent of such fuel (determined by weight) is any combination of water and sediment,

    (II) the ash content of such fuel is more than 1 percent (determined by weight), or

    (III) such fuel has an acid number greater than 25.

(F) Qualified feedstock

For purposes of this paragraph, the term "qualified feedstock" means—

    (i) any lignocellulosic or hemicellulosic matter that is available on a renewable or recurring basis, and

    (ii) any cultivated algae, cyanobacteria, or lemna.

(G) Special rules for algae

In the case of fuel which is derived by, or from, feedstock described in subparagraph (F)(ii) and which is sold by the taxpayer to another person for refining by such other person into a fuel which meets the requirements of subparagraph (E)(i)(II) and the refined fuel is not excluded under subparagraph (E)(iii)—

    (i) such sale shall be treated as described in subparagraph (C)(i),

    (ii) such fuel shall be treated as meeting the requirements of subparagraph (E)(i)(II) and as not being excluded under subparagraph (E)(iii) in the hands of such taxpayer, and

    (iii) except as provided in this subparagraph, such fuel (and any fuel derived from such fuel) shall not be taken into account under subparagraph (C) with respect to the taxpayer or any other person.

(H) Allocation of second generation biofuel producer credit to patrons of cooperative

Rules similar to the rules under subsection (g)(6) shall apply for purposes of this paragraph.

(I) Registration requirement

No credit shall be determined under this paragraph with respect to any taxpayer unless such taxpayer is registered with the Secretary as a producer of second generation biofuel under section 4101.

(J) Application of paragraph

(i) In general

This paragraph shall apply with respect to qualified second generation biofuel production after December 31, 2008, and before January 1, 2022.

(ii) No carryover to certain years after expiration

If this paragraph ceases to apply for any period by reason of clause (i), rules similar to the rules of subsection (e)(2) shall apply.

(c) Coordination with exemption from excise tax

The amount of the credit determined under this section with respect to any alcohol shall, under regulations prescribed by the Secretary, be properly reduced to take into account any benefit provided with respect to such alcohol solely by reason of the application of section 4041(b)(2), section 6426, or section 6427(e).

(d) Definitions and special rules

For purposes of this section—

(1) Alcohol defined

(A) In general

The term "alcohol" includes methanol and ethanol but does not include—

(i) alcohol produced from petroleum, natural gas, or coal (including peat), or

(ii) alcohol with a proof of less than 150.

(B) Determination of proof

The determination of the proof of any alcohol shall be made without regard to any added denaturants.

(2) Special fuel defined

The term "special fuel" includes any liquid fuel (other than gasoline) which is suitable for use in an internal combustion engine.

(3) Mixture or alcohol not used as a fuel, etc.

(A) Mixtures

If—

(i) any credit was determined under this section with respect to alcohol used in the production of any qualified mixture, and

(ii) any person—

(I) separates the alcohol from the mixture, or

(II) without separation, uses the mixture other than as a fuel,

then there is hereby imposed on such person a tax equal to 60 cents a gallon (45 cents in the case of alcohol with a proof less than 190) for each gallon of alcohol in such mixture.

(B) Alcohol

If—

(i) any credit was determined under this section with respect to the retail sale of any alcohol, and

(ii) any person mixes such alcohol or uses such alcohol other than as a fuel,

then there is hereby imposed on such person a tax equal to 60 cents a gallon (45 cents in the case of alcohol with a proof less than 190) for each gallon of such alcohol.

(C) Small ethanol producer credit

If—

(i) any credit was determined under subsection (a)(3), and

(ii) any person does not use such fuel for a purpose described in subsection (b)(4)(B),

then there is hereby imposed on such person a tax equal to 10 cents a gallon for each gallon of such alcohol.

(D) Second generation biofuel producer credit

If—

(i) any credit is allowed under subsection (a)(4), and

(ii) any person does not use such fuel for a purpose described in subsection (b)(6)(C),

then there is hereby imposed on such person a tax equal to the applicable amount (as defined in subsection (b)(6)(B)) for each gallon of such second generation biofuel.

(E) Applicable laws

All provisions of law, including penalties, shall, insofar as applicable and not inconsistent with this section, apply in respect of any tax imposed under subparagraph (A), (B), (C), or (D) as if such tax were imposed by section 4081 and not by this chapter.

(4) Volume of alcohol

For purposes of determining under subsection (a) the number of gallons of alcohol with respect to which a credit is allowable under subsection (a), the volume of alcohol shall include the volume of any denaturant (including gasoline) which is added under any formulas approved by the Secretary to the extent that such denaturants do not exceed 2 percent of the volume of such alcohol (including denaturants).

(5) Pass-thru in the case of estates and trusts

Under regulations prescribed by the Secretary, rules similar to the rules of subsection (d) of section 52 shall apply.

(6) Special rule for second generation biofuel producer credit

No second generation biofuel producer credit shall be determined under subsection (a) with respect to any second generation biofuel unless such second generation biofuel is produced in the United States and used as a fuel in the United States. For purposes of this subsection, the term "United States" includes any possession of the United States.

(7) Limitation to alcohol with connection to the United States

No credit shall be determined under this section with respect to any alcohol which is produced outside the United States for use as a fuel outside the United States. For purposes of this paragraph, the term "United States" includes any possession of the United States.

(e) Termination

(1) In general

This section shall not apply to any sale or use—

(A) for any period after December 31, 2011, or

(B) for any period before January 1, 2012, during which the rates of tax under section 4081(a)(2)(A) are 4.3 cents per gallon.

(2) No carryovers to certain years after expiration

If this section ceases to apply for any period by reason of paragraph (1), no amount attributable to any sale or use before the first day of such period may be carried under section 39 by reason of this section (treating the amount allowed by reason of this section as the first amount allowed by this subpart) to any taxable year beginning after the 3-taxable-year period beginning with the taxable year in which such first day occurs.

(3) Exception for second generation biofuel producer credit

Paragraph (1) shall not apply to the portion of the credit allowed under this section by reason of subsection (a)(4).

(f) Election to have alcohol fuels credit not apply

(1) In general

A taxpayer may elect to have this section not apply for any taxable year.

(2) Time for making election

An election under paragraph (1) for any taxable year may be made (or revoked) at any time before the expiration of the 3-year period beginning on the last date prescribed by law for filing the return for such taxable year (determined without regard to extensions).

(3) Manner of making election

An election under paragraph (1) (or revocation thereof) shall be made in such manner as the Secretary may by regulations prescribe.

(g) Definitions and special rules for eligible small ethanol producer credit

For purposes of this section—

(1) Eligible small ethanol producer

The term "eligible small ethanol producer" means a person who, at all times during the taxable year, has a productive capacity for alcohol (as defined in subsection (d)(1)(A) without regard to clauses (i) and (ii)) not in excess of 60,000,000 gallons.

(2) Aggregation rule

For purposes of the 15,000,000 gallon limitation under subsection (b)(4)(C) and the 60,000,000 gallon limitation under paragraph (1), all members of the same controlled group of corporations (within the meaning of section 267(f)) and all persons under common control (within the meaning of section 52(b) but determined by treating an interest of more than 50 percent as a controlling interest) shall be treated as 1 person.

(3) Partnership, S corporations, and other pass-thru entities

In the case of a partnership, trust, S corporation, or other pass-thru entity, the limitations contained in subsection (b)(4)(C) and paragraph (1) shall be applied at the entity level and at the partner or similar level.

(4) Allocation

For purposes of this subsection, in the case of a facility in which more than 1 person has an interest, productive capacity shall be allocated among such persons in such manner as the Secretary may prescribe.

(5) Regulations

The Secretary may prescribe such regulations as may be necessary—

(A) to prevent the credit provided for in subsection (a)(3) from directly or indirectly benefiting any person with a direct or indirect productive capacity of more than 60,000,000 gallons of alcohol during the taxable year, or

(B) to prevent any person from directly or indirectly benefiting with respect to more than 15,000,000 gallons during the taxable year.

(6) Allocation of small ethanol producer credit to patrons of cooperative

(A) Election to allocate

(i) In general

In the case of a cooperative organization described in section 1381(a), any portion of the credit determined under subsection (a)(3) for the taxable year may, at the election of the organization, be apportioned pro rata among patrons of the organization on the basis of the quantity or value of business done with or for such patrons for the taxable year.

(ii) Form and effect of election

An election under clause (i) for any taxable year shall be made on a timely filed return for such year. Such election, once made, shall be irrevocable for such taxable year. Such election shall not take effect unless the organization designates the apportionment as such in a written notice mailed to its patrons during the payment period described in section 1382(d).

(B) Treatment of organizations and patrons

(i) Organizations

The amount of the credit not apportioned to patrons pursuant to subparagraph (A) shall be included in the amount determined under subsection (a)(3) for the taxable year of the organization.

(ii) Patrons

The amount of the credit apportioned to patrons pursuant to subparagraph (A) shall be included in the amount determined under such subsection for the first taxable year of each patron ending on or after the last day of the payment period (as defined in section 1382(d)) for the taxable year of the organization or, if earlier, for the taxable year of each patron ending on or after the date on which the patron receives notice from the cooperative of the apportionment.

(iii) Special rules for decrease in credits for taxable year

If the amount of the credit of the organization determined under such subsection for a taxable year is less than the amount of such credit shown on the return of the organization for such year, an amount equal to the excess of—

(I) such reduction, over

(II) the amount not apportioned to such patrons under subparagraph (A) for the taxable year,

shall be treated as an increase in tax imposed by this chapter on the organization. Such increase shall not be treated as tax imposed by this chapter for purposes of determining the amount of any credit under this chapter or for purposes of section 55.

(h) Reduced credit for ethanol blenders

(1) In general

In the case of any alcohol mixture credit or alcohol credit with respect to any sale or use of alcohol which is ethanol during calendar years 2001 through 2011—

(A) subsections (b)(1)(A) and (b)(2)(A) shall be applied by substituting "the blender amount" for "60 cents",

(B) subsection (b)(3) shall be applied by substituting "the low-proof blender amount" for "45 cents" and "the blender amount" for "60 cents", and

(C) subparagraphs (A) and (B) of subsection (d)(3) shall be applied by substituting "the blender amount" for "60 cents" and "the low-proof blender amount" for "45 cents".

(2) Amounts

For purposes of paragraph (1), the blender amount and the low-proof blender amount shall be determined in accordance with the following table:

In the case of any sale or use during calendar year:	The blender amount is:	The low-proof blender amount is:
2001 or 2002	53 cents	39.26 cents
2003 or 2004	52 cents	38.52 cents

2005, 2006, 2007, or 2008	51 cents	37.78 cents
2009 through 2011	45 cents	33.33 cents.

(3) Reduction delayed until annual production or importation of 7,500,000,000 gallons

(A) In general

In the case of any calendar year beginning after 2008, if the Secretary makes a determination described in subparagraph (B) with respect to all preceding calendar years beginning after 2007, the last row in the table in paragraph (2) shall be applied by substituting "51 cents" for "45 cents".

(B) Determination

A determination described in this subparagraph with respect to any calendar year is a determination, in consultation with the Administrator of the Environmental Protection Agency, that an amount less than 7,500,000,000 gallons of ethanol (including cellulosic ethanol) has been produced in or imported into the United States in such year.

(Added Pub. L. 96–223, title II, §232(b)(1), Apr. 2, 1980, 94 Stat. 273, §44E; amended Pub. L. 97–34, title II §207(c)(3), Aug. 13, 1981, 95 Stat. 225; Pub. L. 97–354, §5(a)(2), Oct. 19, 1982, 96 Stat. 1692; Pub. L. 97–424, title V, §511(b)(2), (d)(3), Jan. 6, 1983, 96 Stat. 2170, 2171; renumbered §40 and amended Pub. L. 98–369, div. A, title IV, §§471(c), 474(k), title IX, §§912(c), (f), 913(b), July 18, 1984, 98 Stat. 826, 832, 1007, 1008; Pub. L. 100–203, title X, §10502(d)(1), Dec. 22, 1987, 101 Stat. 1330–444; Pub. L. 101–508, title XI, §11502(a)–(f), Nov. 5, 1990, 104 Stat. 1388–480 to 1388–482; Pub. L. 104–188, title I, §1703(j), Aug. 20, 1996, 110 Stat. 1876; Pub. L. 105–178, title IX, §9003(a)(3), (b)(1), June 9, 1998, 112 Stat. 502; Pub. L. 108–357, title III, §§301(c)(1)–(4), 313(a), Oct. 22, 2004, 118 Stat. 1461, 1467; Pub. L. 109–58, title XIII, §1347(a), (b), Aug. 8, 2005, 119 Stat. 1056; Pub. L. 110–234, title XV, §§15321(a)–(b)(2), (3)(B), (c)–(e), 15331(a), 15332(a), May 22, 2008, 122 Stat. 1512–1516; Pub. L. 110–246, §4(a), title XV, §§15321(a)–(b)(2), (3)(B), (c)–(e), 15331(a), 15332(a), June 18, 2008, 122 Stat. 1664, 2274-2278; Pub. L. 110–343, div. B, title II, §203(a), Oct. 3, 2008, 122 Stat. 3833; Pub. L. 111–152, title I, §1408(a), Mar. 30, 2010, 124 Stat. 1067; Pub. L. 111–240, title II, §2121(a), Sept. 27, 2010, 124 Stat. 2567; Pub. L. 111–312, title VII, §708(a)(1), (2), Dec. 17, 2010, 124 Stat. 3312; Pub. L. 112–240, title IV, §404(a)(1), (2), (b)(1)–(3)(B), Jan. 2, 2013, 126 Stat. 2338, 2339; Pub. L. 113–295, div. A, title I, §152(a), Dec. 19, 2014, 128 Stat. 4021; Pub. L. 114–113, div. Q, title I, §184(a), Dec. 18, 2015, 129 Stat. 3073; Pub. L. 115–123, div. D, title I, §40406(a), Feb. 9, 2018, 132 Stat. 149; Pub. L. 115–141, div. U, title IV, §401(a)(9), Mar. 23, 2018, 132 Stat. 1184; Pub. L. 116–94, div. Q, title I, §122(a), Dec. 20, 2019, 133 Stat. 3231; Pub. L. 116–260, div. EE, title I, §140(a), Dec. 27, 2020, 134 Stat. 3054.)

EDITORIAL NOTES
CODIFICATION

Pub. L. 110–234 and Pub. L. 110–246 made identical amendments to this section. The amendments by Pub. L. 110–234 were repealed by section 4(a) of Pub. L. 110–246.

PRIOR PROVISIONS

A prior section 40, added Pub. L. 92–178, title VI, §601(a), Dec. 10, 1971, 85 Stat. 553; amended Pub. L. 94–455, title XIX, §1906(b)(13)(A), Oct. 4, 1976, 90 Stat. 1834, related to allowance as a credit of expenses of work incentive programs, prior to repeal by Pub. L. 98–369, div. A, title IV, §474(m)(1), July 18, 1984, 98 Stat. 833. Another prior section 40 was renumbered section 37 of this title.

AMENDMENTS

2020—Subsec. (b)(6)(J)(i). Pub. L. 116–260 substituted "January 1, 2022" for "January 1, 2021".

2019—Subsec. (b)(6)(J)(i). Pub. L. 116–94 substituted "January 1, 2021" for "January 1, 2018".

2018—Subsec. (b)(6)(J)(i). Pub. L. 115–123 substituted "January 1, 2018" for "January 1, 2017".

Subsec. (g)(2). Pub. L. 115–141 substituted "Aggregation" for "Aggregration" in heading.

2015—Subsec. (b)(6)(J)(i). Pub. L. 114–113 substituted "January 1, 2017" for "January 1, 2015".

2014—Subsec. (b)(6)(J)(i). Pub. L. 113–295 substituted "January 1, 2015" for "January 1, 2014".

2013—Pub. L. 112–240, §404(b)(3)(A)(i), substituted "second generation biofuel" for "cellulosic biofuel" wherever appearing in text in subsecs. (a)(4), (b)(4)(C), (6), and (d)(3)(D), (6).

Subsec. (b)(6). Pub. L. 112–240, §404(b)(3)(A)(ii), substituted "Second generation" for "Cellulosic" in heading.

Subsec. (b)(6)(C), (D). Pub. L. 112–240, §404(b)(3)(A)(iii), substituted "second generation" for "cellulosic" in heading.

Subsec. (b)(6)(E). Pub. L. 112–240, §404(b)(3)(A)(ii), substituted "Second generation" for "Cellulosic" in heading.

Subsec. (b)(6)(E)(i)(I). Pub. L. 112–240, §404(b)(1), amended subcl. (I) generally. Prior to amendment, subcl. (I) read as follows: "is produced from any lignocellulosic or hemicellulosic matter that is available on a renewable or recurring basis, and".

Subsec. (b)(6)(E)(ii). Pub. L. 112–240, §404(b)(3)(B), substituted "The term 'second generation biofuel' shall not" for "Such term shall not".

Subsec. (b)(6)(F), (G). Pub. L. 112–240, §404(b)(2), added subpars. (F) and (G). Former subpars. (F) and (G) redesignated as (H) and (I), respectively.

Subsec. (b)(6)(H). Pub. L. 112–240, §404(b)(3)(A)(iii), substituted "second generation" for "cellulosic" in heading.

Pub. L. 112–240, §404(b)(2), redesignated subpar. (F) as (H). Former subpar. (H) redesignated (J).

Pub. L. 112–240, §404(a)(1), amended subpar. (H) generally. Prior to amendment, text read as follows: "This paragraph shall apply with respect to qualified cellulosic biofuel production after December 31, 2008, and before January 1, 2013."

Subsec. (b)(6)(I), (J). Pub. L. 112–240, §404(b)(2), redesignated subpars. (G) and (H) as (I) and (J), respectively.

Subsec. (d)(3)(D). Pub. L. 112–240, §404(b)(3)(A)(ii), substituted "Second generation" for "Cellulosic" in heading.

Subsec. (d)(6). Pub. L. 112–240, §404(b)(3)(A)(iii), substituted "second generation" for "cellulosic" in heading.

Subsec. (e)(2). Pub. L. 112–240, §404(a)(2), struck out "or subsection (b)(6)(H)" after "paragraph (1)".

Subsec. (e)(3). Pub. L. 112–240, §404(b)(3)(A)(iii), substituted "second generation" for "cellulosic" in heading.

2010—Subsec. (b)(6)(E)(iii). Pub. L. 111–240, §2121(a)(4), substituted "certain" for "unprocessed" in heading.

Pub. L. 111–152 added cl. (iii).

Subsec. (b)(6)(E)(iii)(III). Pub. L. 111–240, §2121(a)(1)–(3), added subcl. (III).

Subsec. (e)(1)(A). Pub. L. 111–312, §708(a)(1)(A), substituted "December 31, 2011" for "December 31, 2010".

Subsec. (e)(1)(B). Pub. L. 111–312, §708(a)(1)(B), substituted "January 1, 2012" for "January 1, 2011".

Subsec. (h)(1), (2). Pub. L. 111–312, §708(a)(2), substituted "2011" for "2010".

2008—Pub. L. 110–246, §15321(b)(3)(B), inserted ", etc.," after "Alcohol" in section catchline.

Subsec. (a)(4). Pub. L. 110–246, §15321(a), added par. (4).

Subsec. (b)(4)(C). Pub. L. 110–246, §15321(e), inserted "(determined without regard to any qualified cellulosic biofuel production)" after "15,000,000 gallons".

Subsec. (b)(6). Pub. L. 110–246, §15321(b)(1), added par. (6).

Subsec. (d)(3)(C). Pub. L. 110–246, §15321(c)(2)(A), substituted "Small ethanol producer" for "Producer" in heading.

Subsec. (d)(3)(D). Pub. L. 110–246, §15321(c)(1), added subpar. (D). Former subpar. (D) redesignated (E).

Subsec. (d)(3)(E). Pub. L. 110–246, §15321(c)(2)(B), substituted "(C), or (D)" for "or (C)".

Pub. L. 110–246, §15321(c)(1), redesignated subpar. (D) as (E).

Subsec. (d)(4). Pub. L. 110–246, §15332(a), substituted "2 percent" for "5 percent".

Subsec. (d)(6). Pub. L. 110–246, §15321(d), added par. (6).

Subsec. (d)(7). Pub. L. 110–343 added par. (7).

Subsec. (e)(2). Pub. L. 110–246, §15321(b)(2)(A), inserted "or subsection (b)(6)(H)" after "by reason of paragraph (1)".

Subsec. (e)(3). Pub. L. 110–246, §15321(b)(2)(B), added par. (3).

Subsec. (h)(2). Pub. L. 110–246, §15331(a)(1), in table, substituted "2005, 2006, 2007, or 2008" for "2005 through 2010", struck out period after "37.78 cents", and inserted last row reading "2009 through 2010", "45 cents", and "33.33 cents."

Subsec. (h)(3). Pub. L. 110–246, §15331(a)(2), added par. (3).

2005—Subsec. (g)(1), (2), (5)(A). Pub. L. 109–58, §1347(a), substituted "60,000,000" for "30,000,000".

Subsec. (g)(6)(A)(ii). Pub. L. 109–58, §1347(b), inserted at end "Such election shall not take effect unless the organization designates the apportionment as such in a written notice mailed to its patrons during the payment period described in section 1382(d)."

2004—Subsec. (c). Pub. L. 108–357, §301(c)(1), substituted "section 4041(b)(2), section 6426, or section 6427(e)" for "subsection (b)(2), (k), or (m) of section 4041, section 4081(c), or section 4091(c)".

Subsec. (d)(4). Pub. L. 108–357, §301(c)(2), reenacted heading without change and amended text of par. (4) generally, substituting provisions relating to determination of the number of gallons of alcohol with respect to which a credit is allowable under subsec. (a) for provisions relating to determination of the number of gallons of alcohol with respect to which a credit is allowable under subsec. (a) or the percentage of any mixture which consists of alcohol under section 4041(k) or 4081(c).

Subsec. (e)(1)(A). Pub. L. 108–357, §301(c)(3)(A), substituted "2010" for "2007".

Subsec. (e)(1)(B). Pub. L. 108–357, §301(c)(3)(B), substituted "2011" for "2008".

Subsec. (g)(6). Pub. L. 108–357, §313(a), added par. (6).

Subsec. (h)(1). Pub. L. 108–357, §301(c)(4)(A), substituted "2010" for "2007" in introductory provisions.

Subsec. (h)(2). Pub. L. 108–357, §301(c)(4)(B), substituted "through 2010" for ", 2006, or 2007" in table.

1998—Subsec. (e)(1). Pub. L. 105–178, §9003(a)(3), substituted "December 31, 2007" for "December 31, 2000" in subpar. (A) and "January 1, 2008" for "January 1, 2001" in subpar. (B).

Subsec. (h). Pub. L. 105–178, §9003(b)(1), reenacted heading without change and amended text of subsec. (h) generally. Prior to amendment, text read as follows: "In the case of any alcohol mixture credit or alcohol credit with respect to any alcohol which is ethanol—

"(1) subsections (b)(1)(A) and (b)(2)(A) shall be applied by substituting '54 cents' for '60 cents';

"(2) subsection (b)(3) shall be applied by substituting '40 cents' for '45 cents' and '54 cents' for '60 cents'; and

"(3) subparagraphs (A) and (B) of subsection (d)(3) shall be applied by substituting '54 cents' for '60 cents' and '40 cents' for '45 cents'."

1996—Subsec. (e)(1)(B). Pub. L. 104–188 amended subpar. (B) generally. Prior to amendment, subpar. (B) read as follows: "for any period before January 1, 2001, during which the Highway Trust Fund financing rate under section 4081(a)(2) is not in effect."

1990—Subsec. (a)(2). Pub. L. 101–508, §11502(a)(1), substituted ", plus" for period at end.

Subsec. (a)(3). Pub. L. 101–508, §11502(a)(2), added par. (3).

Subsec. (b). Pub. L. 101–508, §11502(e)(2), which directed the insertion of ", and except as provided in subsection (h)" in introductory provisions without specifying the location of such insertion, was executed after "section" to reflect the probable intent of Congress.

Pub. L. 101–508, §11502(b)(3), substituted ", alcohol credit, and small ethanol producer credit" for "and alcohol credit" in heading.

Subsec. (b)(4), (5). Pub. L. 101–508, §11502(b)(1), (2), added par. (4) and redesignated former par. (4) as (5).

Subsec. (d)(3)(C), (D). Pub. L. 101–508, §11502(d)(1), (2), added subpar. (C), redesignated former subpar. (C) as (D), and substituted "subparagraph (A), (B), or (C)" for "subparagraph (A) or (B)".

Subsec. (e). Pub. L. 101–508, §11502(f), amended subsec. (e) generally, substituting present provisions for provisions prohibiting the applicability of this section to any sale or use after Dec. 31, 1992, and prohibiting carryovers to any taxable year beginning after Dec. 31, 1994.

Subsec. (g). Pub. L. 101–508, §11502(e), added subsec. (g).

Subsec. (h). Pub. L. 101–508, §11502(e)(1), added subsec. (h).

1987—Subsec. (c). Pub. L. 100–203 substituted ", section 4081(c), or section 4091(c)" for "or section 4081(c)".

1984—Pub. L. 98–369, §471(c), renumbered section 44E of this title as this section.

Subsec. (a). Pub. L. 98–369, §474(k)(1), substituted "For purposes of section 38, the alcohol fuels credit determined under this section for the taxable year is an amount equal to the sum of" for "There shall be allowed as a credit against the tax imposed by this chapter for the taxable year an amount equal to the sum of" in introductory provisions.

Subsec. (b)(1)(A), (2)(A). Pub. L. 98–369, §912(c)(1), substituted "60 cents" for "50 cents".

Subsec. (b)(3). Pub. L. 98–369, §912(c), substituted "45 cents" for "37.5 cents" and "60 cents" for "50 cents".

Subsec. (c). Pub. L. 98–369, §913(b), substituted "(b)(2), (k), or (m)" for "(b)(2) or (k)".

Pub. L. 98–369, §474(k)(2), substituted "the credit determined under this section" for "the credit allowable under this section".

Subsec. (d)(1)(A)(i). Pub. L. 98–369, §912(f), substituted "coal (including peat)" for "coal".

Subsec. (d)(3)(A). Pub. L. 98–369, §912(c), substituted "60 cents" for "50 cents" and "45 cents" for "37.5 cents".

Subsec. (d)(3)(A)(i). Pub. L. 98–369, §474(k)(3), substituted "credit was determined" for "credit was allowable".

Subsec. (d)(3)(B). Pub. L. 98–369, §912(c), substituted "60 cents" for "50 cents" and "45 cents" for "37.5 cents".

Subsec. (d)(3)(B)(i). Pub. L. 98–369, §474(k)(3), substituted "credit was determined" for "credit was allowable".

Subsec. (e). Pub. L. 98–369, §474(k)(4), redesignated subsec. (f) as (e). Former subsec. (e), which had placed a limitation based on the amount of tax, was struck out.

Subsec. (e)(2). Pub. L. 98–369, §474(k)(5), substituted "section 39 by reason of this section (treating the amount allowed by reason of this section as the first amount allowed by this subpart)" for "subsection (e)(2)".

Subsec. (f). Pub. L. 98–369, §474(k)(6), added subsec. (f). Former subsec. (f) redesignated (e).

1983—Subsec. (b)(1)(A), (2)(A). Pub. L. 97–424, §511(d)(3)(A), substituted "50 cents" for "40 cents".

Subsec. (b)(3). Pub. L. 97–424, §511(d)(3), substituted "50 cents" for "40 cents" and "37.5 cents" for "30 cents".

Subsec. (c). Pub. L. 97–424, §511(b)(2), substituted "subsection (b)(2) or (k) of section 4041 or section 4081(c)" for "section 4041(k) or 4081(c)" after "reason of the application of".

Subsec. (d)(3)(A), (B). Pub. L. 97–424, §511(d)(3), substituted "50 cents" for "40 cents" and "37.5 cents" for "30 cents".

1982—Subsec. (d)(5). Pub. L. 97–354 substituted "Pass-thru in the case of estates and trusts" for "Pass-through in the case of subchapter S corporations, etc." in par. heading, and substituted provisions relating to the applicability of rules similar to rules of subsec. (d) of section 52 for provisions relating to the applicability of rules similar to rules of subsecs. (d) and (e) of section 52.

1981—Subsec. (e)(2)(A). Pub. L. 97–34 substituted "15" for "7" in two places, and "14" for "6" in one place.

STATUTORY NOTES AND RELATED SUBSIDIARIES
EFFECTIVE DATE OF 2020 AMENDMENT

Pub. L. 116–260, div. EE, title I, §140(b), Dec. 27, 2020, 134 Stat. 3054, provided that: "The amendment made by this section [amending this section] shall apply to qualified second generation biofuel production after December 31, 2020."

EFFECTIVE DATE OF 2019 AMENDMENT

Pub. L. 116–94, div. Q, title I, §122(b), Dec. 20, 2019, 133 Stat. 3231, provided that: "The amendment made by this section [amending this section] shall apply to qualified second generation biofuel production after December 31, 2017."

EFFECTIVE DATE OF 2018 AMENDMENT

Pub. L. 115–123, div. D, title I, §40406(b), Feb. 9, 2018, 132 Stat. 149, provided that: "The amendment made by this section [amending this section] shall apply to qualified second generation biofuel production after December 31, 2016."

EFFECTIVE DATE OF 2015 AMENDMENT

Pub. L. 114–113, div. Q, title I, §184(b), Dec. 18, 2015, 129 Stat. 3073, provided that: "The amendment made by this subsection [probably means this section, amending this section] shall apply to qualified second generation biofuel production after December 31, 2014."

EFFECTIVE DATE OF 2014 AMENDMENT

Pub. L. 113–295, div. A, title I, §152(b), Dec. 19, 2014, 128 Stat. 4021, provided that: "The amendment made by this section [amending this section] shall apply to qualified second generation biofuel production after December 31, 2013."

EFFECTIVE DATE OF 2013 AMENDMENT

Pub. L. 112–240, title IV, §404(a)(3), Jan. 2, 2013, 126 Stat. 2338, provided that: "The amendments made by this subsection [amending this section] shall take effect as if included in section 15321(b) of the Heartland, Habitat, and Horticulture Act of 2008 [probably should be Heartland, Habitat, Harvest, and Horticulture Act of 2008, title XV of Pub. L. 110–246]."

Pub. L. 112–240, title IV, §404(b)(4), Jan. 2, 2013, 126 Stat. 2339, provided that: "The amendments made by this subsection [amending this section and section 4101 of this title] shall apply to fuels sold or used after the date of the enactment of this Act [Jan. 2, 2013]."

EFFECTIVE DATE OF 2010 AMENDMENT

Pub. L. 111–312, title VII, §708(a)(3), Dec. 17, 2010, 124 Stat. 3312, provided that: "The amendments made by this subsection [amending this section] shall apply to periods after December 31, 2010."

Pub. L. 111–240, title II, §2121(b), Sept. 27, 2010, 124 Stat. 2567, provided that: "The amendments made by this section [amending this section] shall apply to fuels sold or used on or after January 1, 2010."

Pub. L. 111–152, title I, §1408(b), Mar. 30, 2010, 124 Stat. 1067, provided that: "The amendment made by this section [amending this section] shall apply to fuels sold or used on or after January 1, 2010."

EFFECTIVE DATE OF 2008 AMENDMENT

Pub. L. 110–343, div. B, title II, §203(d), Oct. 3, 2008, 122 Stat. 3834, provided that: "The amendments made by this section [amending this section and sections 40A, 6426, and 6427 of this title] shall apply to claims for credit or payment made on or after May 15, 2008."

Amendment of this section and repeal of Pub. L. 110–234 by Pub. L. 110–246 effective May 22, 2008, the date of enactment of Pub. L. 110–234, except as otherwise provided, see section 4 of Pub. L. 110–246, set out as an Effective Date note under section 8701 of Title 7, Agriculture.

Pub. L. 110–234, title XV, §15321(g), May 22, 2008, 122 Stat. 1514, and Pub. L. 110–246, §4(a), title XV, §15321(g), June 18, 2008, 122 Stat. 1664, 2276, provided that: "The amendments made by this section [amending this section and sections 40A and 4101 of this title] shall apply to fuel produced after December 31, 2008."

[Pub. L. 110–234 and Pub. L. 110–246 enacted identical provisions. Pub. L. 110–234 was repealed by section 4(a) of Pub. L. 110–246, set out as a note under section 8701 of Title 7, Agriculture.]

Pub. L. 110–234, title XV, §15331(c), May 22, 2008, 122 Stat. 1516, and Pub. L. 110–246, §4(a), title XV, §15331(c), June 18, 2008, 122 Stat. 1664, 2278, provided that: "The amendments made by this section [amending this section and section 6426 of this title] shall take effect on the date of the enactment of this Act [June 18, 2008]."

[Pub. L. 110–234 and Pub. L. 110–246 enacted identical provisions. Pub. L. 110–234 was repealed by section 4(a) of Pub. L. 110–246, set out as a note under section 8701 of Title 7, Agriculture.]

Pub. L. 110–234, title XV, §15332(c), May 22, 2008, 122 Stat. 1516, and Pub. L. 110–246, §4(a), title XV, §15332(c), June 18, 2008, 122 Stat. 1664, 2278, provided that: "The amendments made by this section [amending this section and section 6426 of this title] shall apply to fuel sold or used after December 31, 2008."

[Pub. L. 110–234 and Pub. L. 110–246 enacted identical provisions. Pub. L. 110–234 was repealed by section 4(a) of Pub. L. 110–246, set out as a note under section 8701 of Title 7, Agriculture.]

EFFECTIVE DATE OF 2005 AMENDMENT

Pub. L. 109–58, title XIII, §1347(c), Aug. 8, 2005, 119 Stat. 1056, provided that: "The amendments made by this section [amending this section] shall apply to taxable years ending after the date of the enactment of this Act [Aug. 8, 2005]."

EFFECTIVE DATE OF 2004 AMENDMENT

Pub. L. 108–357, title III, §301(d), Oct. 22, 2004, 118 Stat. 1463, provided that:

"(1) In general.—Except as otherwise provided in this subsection, the amendments made by this section [enacting section 6426 of this title and amending this section and sections 4041, 4081, 4083, 4101, 6427, and 9503 of this title] shall apply to fuel sold or used after December 31, 2004.

"(2) Registration requirement.—The amendment made by subsection (b) [amending section 4101 of this title] shall take effect on April 1, 2005.

"(3) Extension of alcohol fuels credit.—The amendments made by paragraphs (3), (4), and (14) of subsection (c) [amending this section] shall take effect on the date of the enactment of this Act [Oct. 22, 2004].

"(4) Repeal of general fund retention of certain alcohol fuels taxes.—The amendments made by subsection (c)(12) [amending section 9503 of this title] shall apply to fuel sold or used after September 30, 2004."

Pub. L. 108–357, title III, §313(b), Oct. 22, 2004, 118 Stat. 1468, provided that: "The amendment made by this section [amending this section] shall apply to taxable years ending after the date of the enactment of this Act [Oct. 22, 2004]."

EFFECTIVE DATE OF 1998 AMENDMENT

Pub. L. 105–178, title IX, §9003(b)(3), June 9, 1998, 112 Stat. 503, provided that: "The amendments made by this subsection [amending this section and sections 4041, 4081, and 4091 of this title] shall take effect on January 1, 2001."

EFFECTIVE DATE OF 1996 AMENDMENT

Amendment by Pub. L. 104–188 effective as if included in the provision of the Revenue Reconciliation Act of 1993, Pub. L. 103–66, §§13001–13444, to which such amendment relates, see section 1703(o) of Pub. L. 104–188, set out as a note under section 39 of this title.

EFFECTIVE DATE OF 1990 AMENDMENT

Pub. L. 101–508, title XI, §11502(h), Nov. 5, 1990, 104 Stat. 1388–482, provided that:

"(1) Except as provided in paragraph (2), the amendments made by this section [amending this section] shall apply to alcohol produced, and sold or used, in taxable years beginning after December 31, 1990.

"(2) The amendments made by subsection (g) [amending provisions not classified to the Code] shall apply to articles entered or withdrawn from warehouse on or after January 1, 1991."

EFFECTIVE DATE OF 1987 AMENDMENT

Pub. L. 100–203, title X, §10502(e), Dec. 22, 1987, 101 Stat. 1330–445, provided that: "The amendments made by this section [enacting sections 4091 to 4093 of this title, amending this section and sections 4041, 4081, 4101, 4221, 6206, 6416, 6421, 6427, 6652, 9502, 9503, and 9508 of this title, and enacting provisions set out as notes under sections 4091 and 9502 of this title] shall apply to sales after March 31, 1988."

EFFECTIVE DATE OF 1984 AMENDMENT

Amendment by section 474(k) of Pub. L. 98–369 applicable to taxable years beginning after Dec. 31, 1983, and to carrybacks from such years, see section 475(a) of Pub. L. 98–369, set out as a note under section 21 of this title.

Pub. L. 98–369, div. A, title IX, §912(g), July 18, 1984, 98 Stat. 1008, provided that: "The amendments made by this section [amending this section and sections 4041, 4081, and 6427 of this title] shall take effect on January 1, 1985."

Amendment by section 913(b) of Pub. L. 98–369 effective Aug. 1, 1984, see section 913(c) of Pub. L. 98–369, set out as a note under section 4041 of this title.

EFFECTIVE DATE OF 1983 AMENDMENT

Amendments by section 511(b)(2), (d)(3) of Pub. L. 97–424 effective Apr. 1, 1983, see section 511(h) of Pub. L. 97–424, set out as a note under section 4041 of this title.

EFFECTIVE DATE OF 1982 AMENDMENT

Amendment by Pub. L. 97–354 applicable to taxable years beginning after Dec. 31, 1982, see section 6(a) of Pub. L. 97–354, set out as an Effective Date note under section 1361 of this title.

EFFECTIVE DATE OF 1981 AMENDMENT

Amendment by Pub. L. 97–34 applicable to unused credit years ending after Sept. 30, 1980, see section 209(c)(2)(C) of Pub. L. 97–34, set out as an Effective Date note under section 168 of this title.

EFFECTIVE DATE

Pub. L. 96–223, title II, §232(h)(1), (4), Apr. 2, 1980, 94 Stat. 281, as amended by Pub. L. 97–448, title II, §202(e), Jan. 12, 1983, 96 Stat. 2396, provided that:

"(1) The amendments made by subsections (b) and (c) [enacting sections 44E [now 40] and 86 of this title and amending sections 55, 381, 383, 4081, and 6096 of this title] shall apply to sales or uses after September 30, 1980, in taxable years ending after such date.

"(4) Notwithstanding paragraph (1), the provisions of section 44E(d)(4)(B) [now 40(d)(4)(B)] of such Code, as added by this section, shall take effect on April 2, 1980."

§40A. Biodiesel and renewable diesel used as fuel

(a) General rule

For purposes of section 38, the biodiesel fuels credit determined under this section for the taxable year is an amount equal to the sum of—

(1) the biodiesel mixture credit, plus

(2) the biodiesel credit, plus

(3) in the case of an eligible small agri-biodiesel producer, the small agri-biodiesel producer credit.

(b) Definition of biodiesel mixture credit, biodiesel credit, and small agri-biodiesel producer credit

For purposes of this section—

(1) Biodiesel mixture credit

(A) In general

The biodiesel mixture credit of any taxpayer for any taxable year is $1.00 for each gallon of biodiesel used by the taxpayer in the production of a qualified biodiesel mixture.

(B) Qualified biodiesel mixture

The term "qualified biodiesel mixture" means a mixture of biodiesel and diesel fuel (as defined in section 4083(a)(3)), determined without regard to any use of kerosene, which—

(i) is sold by the taxpayer producing such mixture to any person for use as a fuel, or

(ii) is used as a fuel by the taxpayer producing such mixture.

(C) Sale or use must be in trade or business, etc.

Biodiesel used in the production of a qualified biodiesel mixture shall be taken into account—

(i) only if the sale or use described in subparagraph (B) is in a trade or business of the taxpayer, and

(ii) for the taxable year in which such sale or use occurs.

(D) Casual off-farm production not eligible

No credit shall be allowed under this section with respect to any casual off-farm production of a qualified biodiesel mixture.

(2) Biodiesel credit

(A) In general

The biodiesel credit of any taxpayer for any taxable year is $1.00 for each gallon of biodiesel which is not in a mixture with diesel fuel and which during the taxable year—

(i) is used by the taxpayer as a fuel in a trade or business, or

(ii) is sold by the taxpayer at retail to a person and placed in the fuel tank of such person's vehicle.

(B) User credit not to apply to biodiesel sold at retail

No credit shall be allowed under subparagraph (A)(i) with respect to any biodiesel which was sold in a retail sale described in subparagraph (A)(ii).

(3) Certification for biodiesel

No credit shall be allowed under paragraph (1) or (2) of subsection (a) unless the taxpayer obtains a certification (in such form and manner as prescribed by the Secretary) from the producer or importer of the biodiesel which identifies the product produced and the percentage of biodiesel and agri-biodiesel in the product.

(4) Small agri-biodiesel producer credit

(A) In general

The small agri-biodiesel producer credit of any eligible small agri-biodiesel producer for any taxable year is 10 cents for each gallon of qualified agri-biodiesel production of such producer.

(B) Qualified agri-biodiesel production

For purposes of this paragraph, the term "qualified agri-biodiesel production" means any agri-biodiesel which is produced by an eligible small agri-biodiesel producer, and which during the taxable year—

(i) is sold by such producer to another person—

(I) for use by such other person in the production of a qualified biodiesel mixture in such other person's trade or business (other than casual off-farm production),

(II) for use by such other person as a fuel in a trade or business, or

(III) who sells such agri-biodiesel at retail to another person and places such agri-biodiesel in the fuel tank of such other person, or

(ii) is used or sold by such producer for any purpose described in clause (i).

(C) Limitation

The qualified agri-biodiesel production of any producer for any taxable year shall not exceed 15,000,000 gallons.

(c) Coordination with credit against excise tax

The amount of the credit determined under this section with respect to any biodiesel shall be properly reduced to take into account any benefit provided with respect to such biodiesel solely by reason of the application of section 6426 or 6427(e).

(d) Definitions and special rules

For purposes of this section—

(1) Biodiesel

The term "biodiesel" means the monoalkyl esters of long chain fatty acids derived from plant or animal matter which meet—

(A) the registration requirements for fuels and fuel additives established by the Environmental Protection Agency under section 211 of the Clean Air Act (42 U.S.C. 7545), and

(B) the requirements of the American Society of Testing and Materials D6751.

Such term shall not include any liquid with respect to which a credit may be determined under section 40.

(2) Agri-biodiesel

The term "agri-biodiesel" means biodiesel derived solely from virgin oils, including esters derived from virgin vegetable oils from corn, soybeans, sunflower seeds, cottonseeds, canola, crambe, rapeseeds, safflowers, flaxseeds, rice bran, mustard seeds, and camelina, and from animal fats.

(3) Mixture or biodiesel not used as a fuel, etc.

(A) Mixtures

If—

(i) any credit was determined under this section with respect to biodiesel used in the production of any qualified biodiesel mixture, and

(ii) any person—

(I) separates the biodiesel from the mixture, or

(II) without separation, uses the mixture other than as a fuel,

then there is hereby imposed on such person a tax equal to the product of the rate applicable under subsection (b)(1)(A) and the number of gallons of such biodiesel in such mixture.

(B) Biodiesel

If—

(i) any credit was determined under this section with respect to the retail sale of any biodiesel, and

(ii) any person mixes such biodiesel or uses such biodiesel other than as a fuel,

then there is hereby imposed on such person a tax equal to the product of the rate applicable under subsection (b)(2)(A) and the number of gallons of such biodiesel.

(C) Producer credit

If—

(i) any credit was determined under subsection (a)(3), and

(ii) any person does not use such fuel for a purpose described in subsection (b)(4)(B),

then there is hereby imposed on such person a tax equal to 10 cents a gallon for each gallon of such agri-biodiesel.

(D) Applicable laws

All provisions of law, including penalties, shall, insofar as applicable and not inconsistent with this section, apply in respect of any tax imposed under subparagraph (A) or (B) as if such tax were imposed by section 4081 and not by this chapter.

(4) Pass-thru in the case of estates and trusts

Under regulations prescribed by the Secretary, rules similar to the rules of subsection (d) of section 52 shall apply.

(5) Limitation to biodiesel with connection to the United States

No credit shall be determined under this section with respect to any biodiesel which is produced outside the United States for use as a fuel outside the United States. For purposes of this paragraph, the term "United States" includes any possession of the United States.

(e) Definitions and special rules for small agri-biodiesel producer credit

For purposes of this section—

(1) Eligible small agri-biodiesel producer

The term "eligible small agri-biodiesel producer" means a person who, at all times during the taxable year, has a productive capacity for agri-biodiesel not in excess of 60,000,000 gallons.

(2) Aggregation rule

For purposes of the 15,000,000 gallon limitation under subsection (b)(4)(C) and the 60,000,000 gallon limitation under paragraph (1), all members of the same controlled group of corporations (within the meaning of section 267(f)) and all persons under common control (within the meaning of section 52(b) but determined by treating an interest of more than 50 percent as a controlling interest) shall be treated as 1 person.

(3) Partnership, S corporation, and other pass-thru entities

In the case of a partnership, trust, S corporation, or other pass-thru entity, the limitations contained in subsection (b)(4)(C) and paragraph (1) shall be applied at the entity level and at the partner or similar level.

(4) Allocation

For purposes of this subsection, in the case of a facility in which more than 1 person has an interest, productive capacity shall be allocated among such persons in such manner as the Secretary may prescribe.

(5) Regulations

The Secretary may prescribe such regulations as may be necessary—

(A) to prevent the credit provided for in subsection (a)(3) from directly or indirectly benefiting any person with a direct or indirect productive capacity of more than 60,000,000 gallons of agri-biodiesel during the taxable year, or

(B) to prevent any person from directly or indirectly benefiting with respect to more than 15,000,000 gallons during the taxable year.

(6) Allocation of small agri-biodiesel credit to patrons of cooperative

(A) Election to allocate

(i) In general

In the case of a cooperative organization described in section 1381(a), any portion of the credit determined under subsection (a)(3) for the taxable year may, at the election of the organization, be apportioned pro rata among patrons of the organization on the basis of the quantity or value of business done with or for such patrons for the taxable year.

(ii) Form and effect of election

An election under clause (i) for any taxable year shall be made on a timely filed return for such year. Such election, once made, shall be irrevocable for such taxable year. Such election shall not take effect unless the organization designates the apportionment as such in a written notice mailed to its patrons during the payment period described in section 1382(d).

(B) Treatment of organizations and patrons

(i) Organizations

The amount of the credit not apportioned to patrons pursuant to subparagraph (A) shall be included in the amount determined under subsection (a)(3) for the taxable year of the organization.

(ii) Patrons

The amount of the credit apportioned to patrons pursuant to subparagraph (A) shall be included in the amount determined under such subsection for the first taxable year of each patron ending on or after the last day of the payment period (as defined in section 1382(d)) for the taxable year of the organization or, if earlier, for the taxable year of each patron ending on or after the date on which the patron receives notice from the cooperative of the apportionment.

(iii) Special rules for decrease in credits for taxable year

If the amount of the credit of the organization determined under such subsection for a taxable year is less than the amount of such credit shown on the return of the organization for such year, an amount equal to the excess of—

(I) such reduction, over

(II) the amount not apportioned to such patrons under subparagraph (A) for the taxable year,

shall be treated as an increase in tax imposed by this chapter on the organization. Such increase shall not be treated as tax imposed by this chapter for purposes of determining the amount of any credit under this chapter or for purposes of section 55.

(f) Renewable diesel

For purposes of this title—

(1) Treatment in the same manner as biodiesel

Except as provided in paragraph (2), renewable diesel shall be treated in the same manner as biodiesel.

(2) Exception

Subsection (b)(4) shall not apply with respect to renewable diesel.

(3) Renewable diesel defined

The term "renewable diesel" means liquid fuel derived from biomass which meets—

(A) the registration requirements for fuels and fuel additives established by the Environmental Protection Agency under section 211 of the Clean Air Act (42 U.S.C. 7545), and

(B) the requirements of the American Society of Testing and Materials D975 or D396, or other equivalent standard approved by the Secretary.

Such term shall not include any liquid with respect to which a credit may be determined under section 40. Such term does not include any fuel derived from coprocessing biomass with a feedstock which is not biomass. For purposes of this paragraph, the term "biomass" has the meaning given such term by section 45K(c)(3).

(4) Certain aviation fuel

(A) In general

Except as provided in the last 3 sentences of paragraph (3), the term "renewable diesel" shall include fuel derived from biomass which meets the requirements of a Department of Defense specification for military jet fuel or an American Society of Testing and Materials specification for aviation turbine fuel.

(B) Application of mixture credits

In the case of fuel which is treated as renewable diesel solely by reason of subparagraph (A), subsection (b)(1) and section 6426(c) shall be applied with respect to such fuel by treating kerosene as though it were diesel fuel.

(g) Termination

This section shall not apply to any sale or use after December 31, 2022.

(Added Pub. L. 108–357, title III, §302(a), Oct. 22, 2004, 118 Stat. 1463; amended Pub. L. 109–58, title XIII, §§1344(a), 1345(a)–(d), 1346(a), (b)(1), Aug. 8, 2005, 119 Stat. 1052–1055; Pub. L. 109–135, title IV, §412(h), Dec. 21, 2005, 119 Stat. 2637; Pub. L. 110–234, title XV, §15321(f), May 22, 2008, 122 Stat. 1514; Pub. L. 110–246, §4(a), title XV, §15321(f), June 18, 2008, 122 Stat. 1664, 2276; Pub. L. 110–343, div. B, title II, §§202(a), (b)(1), (b)(3)–(f), 203(b), Oct. 3, 2008, 122 Stat. 3832, 3833; Pub. L. 111–312, title VII, §701(a), Dec. 17, 2010, 124 Stat. 3310; Pub. L. 112–240, title IV, §405(a), Jan. 2, 2013, 126 Stat. 2340; Pub. L. 113–295, div. A, title I, §153(a), Dec. 19, 2014, 128 Stat. 4021; Pub. L. 114–113, div. Q, title I, §185(a)(1), Dec. 18, 2015, 129 Stat. 3073; Pub. L. 115–123, div. D, title I, §40407(a)(1), Feb. 9, 2018, 132 Stat. 149; Pub. L. 116–94, div. Q, title I, §121(a)(1), Dec. 20, 2019, 133 Stat. 3230.)

EDITORIAL NOTES
CODIFICATION

Pub. L. 110–234 and Pub. L. 110–246 made identical amendments to this section. The amendments by Pub. L. 110–234 were repealed by section 4(a) of Pub. L. 110–246.

AMENDMENTS

2019—Subsec. (g). Pub. L. 116–94 substituted "December 31, 2022" for "December 31, 2017".

2018—Subsec. (g). Pub. L. 115–123 substituted "December 31, 2017" for "December 31, 2016".

2015—Subsec. (g). Pub. L. 114–113 substituted "December 31, 2016" for "December 31, 2014".

2014—Subsec. (g). Pub. L. 113–295 substituted "December 31, 2014" for "December 31, 2013".

2013—Subsec. (g). Pub. L. 112–240 substituted "December 31, 2013" for "December 31, 2011".

2010—Subsec. (g). Pub. L. 111–312 substituted "December 31, 2011" for "December 31, 2009".

2008—Subsec. (b)(1)(A), (2)(A). Pub. L. 110–343, §202(b)(1), substituted "$1.00" for "50 cents".

Subsec. (b)(3) to (5). Pub. L. 110–343, §202(b)(3)(A), redesignated pars. (4) and (5) as (3) and (4), respectively, and struck out heading and text of former par. (3). Text read as follows: "In the case of any biodiesel which is agri-biodiesel, paragraphs (1)(A) and (2)(A) shall be applied by substituting '$1.00' for '50 cents'."

Subsec. (d)(1). Pub. L. 110–246, §15321(f)(1), inserted concluding provisions.

Subsec. (d)(2). Pub. L. 110–343, §202(f), substituted "mustard seeds, and camelina" for "and mustard seeds".

Subsec. (d)(3)(C)(ii). Pub. L. 110–343, §202(b)(3)(D), substituted "subsection (b)(4)(B)" for "subsection (b)(5)(B)".

Subsec. (d)(5). Pub. L. 110–343, §203(b), added par. (5).

Subsec. (e)(2), (3). Pub. L. 110–343, §202(b)(3)(C), substituted "subsection (b)(4)(C)" for "subsection (b)(5)(C)".

Subsec. (f)(2). Pub. L. 110–343, §202(b)(3)(B), amended heading and text of par. (2) generally. Prior to amendment, text read as follows:

"(A) Rate of credit.—Subsections (b)(1)(A) and (b)(2)(A) shall be applied with respect to renewable diesel by substituting '$1.00' for '50 cents'.

"(B) Nonapplication of certain credits.—Subsections (b)(3) and (b)(5) shall not apply with respect to renewable diesel."

Subsec. (f)(3). Pub. L. 110–343, §202(d), in introductory provisions, struck out "(as defined in section 45K(c)(3))" after "derived from biomass" and, in concluding provisions, inserted at end "Such term does not include any fuel derived from coprocessing biomass with a feedstock which is not biomass. For purposes of this paragraph, the term 'biomass' has the meaning given such term by section 45K(c)(3)."

Pub. L. 110–343, §202(c)(1), (2), in introductory provisions, substituted "liquid fuel" for "diesel fuel" and struck out "using a thermal depolymerization process" before "which meets—".

Pub. L. 110–246, §15321(f)(2), inserted concluding provisions.

Subsec. (f)(3)(B). Pub. L. 110–343, §202(c)(3), inserted ", or other equivalent standard approved by the Secretary" before period at end.

Subsec. (f)(4). Pub. L. 110–343, §202(e), added par. (4).

Subsec. (g). Pub. L. 110–343, §202(a), substituted "December 31, 2009" for "December 31, 2008".

2005—Pub. L. 109–58, §1346(b)(1), inserted "and renewable diesel" after "Biodiesel" in section catchline.

Subsec. (a). Pub. L. 109–58, §1345(a), reenacted heading without change and amended text of subsec. (a) generally. Prior to amendment, text read as follows: "For purposes of section 38, the biodiesel fuels credit determined under this section for the taxable year is an amount equal to the sum of—

"(1) the biodiesel mixture credit, plus

"(2) the biodiesel credit."

Subsec. (b). Pub. L. 109–58, §1345(d)(2), substituted ", biodiesel credit, and small agri-biodiesel producer credit" for "and biodiesel credit" in heading.

Subsec. (b)(4). Pub. L. 109–58, §1345(d)(1), substituted "paragraph (1) or (2) of subsection (a)" for "this section".

Subsec. (b)(5). Pub. L. 109–58, §1345(b), added par. (5).

Subsec. (b)(5)(B). Pub. L. 109–135 struck out "(determined without regard to the last sentence of subsection (d)(2))" after "any agri-biodiesel" in introductory provisions.

Subsec. (d)(3)(C), (D). Pub. L. 109–58, §1345(d)(3), added subpar. (C) and redesignated former subpar. (C) as (D). The words following "subsection (b)(5)(B)," in subpar. (C) are shown as a flush provision notwithstanding directory language showing them as part of cl. (ii), to reflect the probable intent of Congress.

Subsec. (e). Pub. L. 109–58, §1345(c), added subsec. (e). The words following "subparagraph (A) for the taxable year," in subsec. (e)(6)(B)(iii) are shown as a flush provision notwithstanding directory language showing them as part of subcl. (II), to reflect the probable intent of Congress. Former subsec. (e) redesignated (f).

Pub. L. 109–58, §1344(a), substituted "2008" for "2006".

Subsec. (f). Pub. L. 109–58, §1346(a), added subsec. (f). Former subsec. (f) redesignated (g).

Pub. L. 109–58, §1345(c), redesignated subsec. (e) as (f).

Subsec. (g). Pub. L. 109–58, §1346(a), redesignated subsec. (f) as (g).

STATUTORY NOTES AND RELATED SUBSIDIARIES

EFFECTIVE DATE OF 2019 AMENDMENT

Pub. L. 116–94, div. Q, title I, §121(a)(2), Dec. 20, 2019, 133 Stat. 3230, provided that: "The amendment made by this subsection [amending this section] shall apply to fuel sold or used after December 31, 2017."

EFFECTIVE DATE OF 2018 AMENDMENT

Pub. L. 115–123, div. D, title I, §40407(a)(2), Feb. 9, 2018, 132 Stat. 149, provided that: "The amendment made by this subsection [amending this section] shall apply to fuel sold or used after December 31, 2016."

EFFECTIVE DATE OF 2015 AMENDMENT

Pub. L. 114–113, div. Q, title I, §185(a)(2), Dec. 18, 2015, 129 Stat. 3073, provided that: "The amendment made by this subsection [amending this section] shall apply to fuel sold or used after December 31, 2014."

EFFECTIVE DATE OF 2014 AMENDMENT

Pub. L. 113–295, div. A, title I, §153(b), Dec. 19, 2014, 128 Stat. 4021, provided that: "The amendment made by this section [amending this section] shall apply to fuel sold or used after December 31, 2013."

EFFECTIVE DATE OF 2013 AMENDMENT

Pub. L. 112–240, title IV, §405(c), Jan. 2, 2013, 126 Stat. 2340, provided that: "The amendments made by this section [amending this section and sections 6426 and 6427 of this title] shall apply to fuel sold or used after December 31, 2011."

EFFECTIVE DATE OF 2010 AMENDMENT

Pub. L. 111–312, title VII, §701(d), Dec. 17, 2010, 124 Stat. 3310, provided that: "The amendments made by this section [amending this section and sections 6426 and 6427 of this title] shall apply to fuel sold or used after December 31, 2009."

EFFECTIVE DATE OF 2008 AMENDMENT

Pub. L. 110–343, div. B, title II, §202(g), Oct. 3, 2008, 122 Stat. 3833, provided that:

"(1) In general.—Except as otherwise provided in this subsection, the amendments made by this section [amending this section and sections 6426 and 6427 of this title] shall apply to fuel produced, and sold or used, after December 31, 2008.

"(2) Coproduction of renewable diesel with petroleum feedstock.—The amendment made by subsection (d) [amending this section] shall apply to fuel produced, and sold or used, after the date of the enactment of this Act [Oct. 3, 2008]."

Amendment by section 203(b) of Pub. L. 110–343 applicable to claims for credit or payment made on or after May 15, 2008, see section 203(d) of Pub. L. 110–343, set out as a note under section 40 of this title.

Amendment of this section and repeal of Pub. L. 110–234 by Pub. L. 110–246 effective May 22, 2008, the date of enactment of Pub. L. 110–234, except as otherwise provided, see section 4 of Pub. L. 110–246, set out as an Effective Date note under section 8701 of Title 7, Agriculture.

Amendment by section 15321(f) of Pub. L. 110–246 applicable to fuel produced after Dec. 31, 2008, see section 15321(g) of Pub. L. 110–246, set out as a note under section 40 of this title.

EFFECTIVE DATE OF 2005 AMENDMENT

Pub. L. 109–58, title XIII, §1344(b), Aug. 8, 2005, 119 Stat. 1052, provided that: "The amendments made by this section [amending this section and sections 6426 and 6427 of this title] shall take effect on the date of the enactment of this Act [Aug. 8, 2005]."

Pub. L. 109–58, title XIII, §1345(e), Aug. 8, 2005, 119 Stat. 1055, provided that: "The amendments made by this section [amending this section] shall apply to taxable years ending after the date of the enactment of this Act [Aug. 8, 2005]."

Pub. L. 109–58, title XIII, §1346(c), Aug. 8, 2005, 119 Stat. 1056, provided that: "The amendment made by subsection (a) [amending this section] shall apply with respect to fuel sold or used after December 31, 2005."

EFFECTIVE DATE

Section applicable to fuel produced, and sold or used, after Dec. 31, 2004, in taxable years ending after such date, see section 302(d) of Pub. L. 108–357, set out as an Effective Date of 2004 Amendment note under section 38 of this title.

§41. Credit for increasing research activities

(a) General rule

For purposes of section 38, the research credit determined under this section for the taxable year shall be an amount equal to the sum of—

(1) 20 percent of the excess (if any) of—

(A) the qualified research expenses for the taxable year, over

(B) the base amount,

(2) 20 percent of the basic research payments determined under subsection (e)(1)(A), and

(3) 20 percent of the amounts paid or incurred by the taxpayer in carrying on any trade or business of the taxpayer during the taxable year (including as contributions) to an energy research consortium for energy research.

(b) Qualified research expenses

For purposes of this section—

(1) Qualified research expenses

The term "qualified research expenses" means the sum of the following amounts which are paid or incurred by the taxpayer during the taxable year in carrying on any trade or business of the taxpayer—

(A) in-house research expenses, and

(B) contract research expenses.

(2) In-house research expenses

(A) In general

The term "in-house research expenses" means—

(i) any wages paid or incurred to an employee for qualified services performed by such employee,

(ii) any amount paid or incurred for supplies used in the conduct of qualified research, and

(iii) under regulations prescribed by the Secretary, any amount paid or incurred to another person for the right to use computers in the conduct of qualified research.

Clause (iii) shall not apply to any amount to the extent that the taxpayer (or any person with whom the taxpayer must aggregate expenditures under subsection (f)(1)) receives or accrues any amount from any other person for the right to use substantially identical personal property.

(B) Qualified services

The term "qualified services" means services consisting of—

(i) engaging in qualified research, or

(ii) engaging in the direct supervision or direct support of research activities which constitute qualified research.

If substantially all of the services performed by an individual for the taxpayer during the taxable year consists of services meeting the requirements of clause (i) or (ii), the term "qualified services" means all of the services performed by such individual for the taxpayer during the taxable year.

(C) Supplies

The term "supplies" means any tangible property other than—

(i) land or improvements to land, and

(ii) property of a character subject to the allowance for depreciation.

(D) Wages

(i) In general

The term "wages" has the meaning given such term by section 3401(a).

(ii) Self-employed individuals and owner-employees

In the case of an employee (within the meaning of section 401(c)(1)), the term "wages" includes the earned income (as defined in section 401(c)(2)) of such employee.

(iii) Exclusion for wages to which work opportunity credit applies

The term "wages" shall not include any amount taken into account in determining the work opportunity credit under section 51(a).

(3) Contract research expenses

(A) In general

The term "contract research expenses" means 65 percent of any amount paid or incurred by the taxpayer to any person (other than an employee of the taxpayer) for qualified research.

(B) Prepaid amounts

If any contract research expenses paid or incurred during any taxable year are attributable to qualified research to be conducted after the close of such taxable year, such amount shall be treated as paid or incurred during the period during which the qualified research is conducted.

(C) Amounts paid to certain research consortia

(i) In general

Subparagraph (A) shall be applied by substituting "75 percent" for "65 percent" with respect to amounts paid or incurred by the taxpayer to a qualified research consortium for qualified research on behalf of the taxpayer and 1 or more unrelated taxpayers. For purposes of the preceding sentence, all persons treated as a single employer under subsection (a) or (b) of section 52 shall be treated as related taxpayers.

(ii) Qualified research consortium

The term "qualified research consortium" means any organization which—

(I) is described in section 501(c)(3) or 501(c)(6) and is exempt from tax under section 501(a),

(II) is organized and operated primarily to conduct scientific research, and

(III) is not a private foundation.

(D) Amounts paid to eligible small businesses, universities, and Federal laboratories

(i) In general

In the case of amounts paid by the taxpayer to—

(I) an eligible small business,

(II) an institution of higher education (as defined in section 3304(f)), or

(III) an organization which is a Federal laboratory,

for qualified research which is energy research, subparagraph (A) shall be applied by substituting "100 percent" for "65 percent".

(ii) Eligible small business

For purposes of this subparagraph, the term "eligible small business" means a small business with respect to which the taxpayer does not own (within the meaning of section 318) 50 percent or more of—

(I) in the case of a corporation, the outstanding stock of the corporation (either by vote or value), and

(II) in the case of a small business which is not a corporation, the capital and profits interests of the small business.

(iii) Small business

For purposes of this subparagraph—

(I) In general

The term "small business" means, with respect to any calendar year, any person if the annual average number of employees employed by such person during either of the 2 preceding calendar years was 500 or fewer. For purposes of the preceding sentence, a preceding calendar year may be taken into account only if the person was in existence throughout the year.

(II) Startups, controlled groups, and predecessors

Rules similar to the rules of subparagraphs (B) and (D) of section 220(c)(4) shall apply for purposes of this clause.

(iv) Federal laboratory

For purposes of this subparagraph, the term "Federal laboratory" has the meaning given such term by section 4(6) of the Stevenson-Wydler Technology Innovation Act of 1980 (15 U.S.C. 3703(6)), as in effect on the date of the enactment of the Energy Tax Incentives Act of 2005.

(4) Trade or business requirement disregarded for in-house research expenses of certain startup ventures

In the case of in-house research expenses, a taxpayer shall be treated as meeting the trade or business requirement of paragraph (1) if, at the time such in-house research expenses are paid or incurred, the principal purpose of the taxpayer in making such expenditures is to use the results of the research in the active conduct of a future trade or business—

(A) of the taxpayer, or

(B) of 1 or more other persons who with the taxpayer are treated as a single taxpayer under subsection (f)(1).

(c) Base amount

(1) In general

The term "base amount" means the product of—

(A) the fixed-base percentage, and

(B) the average annual gross receipts of the taxpayer for the 4 taxable years preceding the taxable year for which the credit is being determined (hereinafter in this subsection referred to as the "credit year").

(2) Minimum base amount

In no event shall the base amount be less than 50 percent of the qualified research expenses for the credit year.

(3) Fixed-base percentage

(A) In general

Except as otherwise provided in this paragraph, the fixed-base percentage is the percentage which the aggregate qualified research expenses of the taxpayer for taxable years beginning after December 31, 1983, and before January 1, 1989, is of the aggregate gross receipts of the taxpayer for such taxable years.

(B) Start-up companies

(i) Taxpayers to which subparagraph applies

The fixed-base percentage shall be determined under this subparagraph if—

(I) the first taxable year in which a taxpayer had both gross receipts and qualified research expenses begins after December 31, 1983, or

(II) there are fewer than 3 taxable years beginning after December 31, 1983, and before January 1, 1989, in which the taxpayer had both gross receipts and qualified research expenses.

(ii) Fixed-base percentage

In a case to which this subparagraph applies, the fixed-base percentage is—

(I) 3 percent for each of the taxpayer's 1st 5 taxable years beginning after December 31, 1993, for which the taxpayer has qualified research expenses,

(II) in the case of the taxpayer's 6th such taxable year, 1/6 of the percentage which the aggregate qualified research expenses of the taxpayer for the 4th and 5th such taxable years is of the aggregate gross receipts of the taxpayer for such years,

(III) in the case of the taxpayer's 7th such taxable year, 1/3 of the percentage which the aggregate qualified research expenses of the taxpayer for the 5th and 6th such taxable years is of the aggregate gross receipts of the taxpayer for such years,

(IV) in the case of the taxpayer's 8th such taxable year, ½ of the percentage which the aggregate qualified research expenses of the taxpayer for the 5th, 6th, and 7th such taxable years is of the aggregate gross receipts of the taxpayer for such years,

(V) in the case of the taxpayer's 9th such taxable year, 2/3 of the percentage which the aggregate qualified research expenses of the taxpayer for the 5th, 6th, 7th, and 8th such taxable years is of the aggregate gross receipts of the taxpayer for such years,

(VI) in the case of the taxpayer's 10th such taxable year, 5/6 of the percentage which the aggregate qualified research expenses of the taxpayer for the 5th, 6th, 7th, 8th, and 9th such taxable years is of the aggregate gross receipts of the taxpayer for such years, and

(VII) for taxable years thereafter, the percentage which the aggregate qualified research expenses for any 5 taxable years selected by the taxpayer from among the 5th through the 10th such taxable years is of the aggregate gross receipts of the taxpayer for such selected years.

(iii) Treatment of de minimis amounts of gross receipts and qualified research expenses

The Secretary may prescribe regulations providing that de minimis amounts of gross receipts and qualified research expenses shall be disregarded under clauses (i) and (ii).

(C) Maximum fixed-base percentage

In no event shall the fixed-base percentage exceed 16 percent.

(D) Rounding

The percentages determined under subparagraphs (A) and (B)(ii) shall be rounded to the nearest 1/100th of 1 percent.

(4) Election of alternative simplified credit

(A) In general

At the election of the taxpayer, the credit determined under subsection (a)(1) shall be equal to 14 percent of so much of the qualified research expenses for the taxable year as exceeds 50 percent of the average qualified research expenses for the 3 taxable years preceding the taxable year for which the credit is being determined.

(B) Special rule in case of no qualified research expenses in any of 3 preceding taxable years

(i) Taxpayers to which subparagraph applies

The credit under this paragraph shall be determined under this subparagraph if the taxpayer has no qualified research expenses in any one of the 3 taxable years preceding the taxable year for which the credit is being determined.

(ii) Credit rate

The credit determined under this subparagraph shall be equal to 6 percent of the qualified research expenses for the taxable year.

(C) Election

An election under this paragraph shall apply to the taxable year for which made and all succeeding taxable years unless revoked with the consent of the Secretary.

(5) Consistent treatment of expenses required

(A) In general

Notwithstanding whether the period for filing a claim for credit or refund has expired for any taxable year taken into account in determining the fixed-base percentage, the qualified research expenses taken into account in computing such percentage shall be determined on a basis consistent with the determination of qualified research expenses for the credit year.

(B) Prevention of distortions

The Secretary may prescribe regulations to prevent distortions in calculating a taxpayer's qualified research expenses or gross receipts caused by a change in accounting methods used by such taxpayer between the current year and a year taken into account in computing such taxpayer's fixed-base percentage.

(6) Gross receipts

For purposes of this subsection, gross receipts for any taxable year shall be reduced by returns and allowances made during the taxable year. In the case of a foreign corporation, there shall be taken into account only gross receipts which are effectively connected with the conduct of a trade or business within the United States, the Commonwealth of Puerto Rico, or any possession of the United States.

(d) Qualified research defined

For purposes of this section—

(1) In general

The term "qualified research" means research—

(A) with respect to which expenditures may be treated as specified research or experimental expenditures under section 174,

(B) which is undertaken for the purpose of discovering information—

(i) which is technological in nature, and

(ii) the application of which is intended to be useful in the development of a new or improved business component of the taxpayer, and

(C) substantially all of the activities of which constitute elements of a process of experimentation for a purpose described in paragraph (3).

Such term does not include any activity described in paragraph (4).

(2) Tests to be applied separately to each business component

For purposes of this subsection—

(A) In general

Paragraph (1) shall be applied separately with respect to each business component of the taxpayer.

(B) Business component defined

The term "business component" means any product, process, computer software, technique, formula, or invention which is to be—

(i) held for sale, lease, or license, or

(ii) used by the taxpayer in a trade or business of the taxpayer.

(C) Special rule for production processes

Any plant process, machinery, or technique for commercial production of a business component shall be treated as a separate business component (and not as part of the business component being produced).

(3) Purposes for which research may qualify for credit

For purposes of paragraph (1)(C)—

(A) In general

Research shall be treated as conducted for a purpose described in this paragraph if it relates to—

(i) a new or improved function,

(ii) performance, or

(iii) reliability or quality.

(B) Certain purposes not qualified

Research shall in no event be treated as conducted for a purpose described in this paragraph if it relates to style, taste, cosmetic, or seasonal design factors.

(4) Activities for which credit not allowed

The term "qualified research" shall not include any of the following:

(A) Research after commercial production

Any research conducted after the beginning of commercial production of the business component.

(B) Adaptation of existing business components

Any research related to the adaptation of an existing business component to a particular customer's requirement or need.

(C) Duplication of existing business component

Any research related to the reproduction of an existing business component (in whole or in part) from a physical examination of the business component itself or from plans, blueprints, detailed specifications, or publicly available information with respect to such business component.

(D) Surveys, studies, etc.

Any—

(i) efficiency survey,

(ii) activity relating to management function or technique,

(iii) market research, testing, or development (including advertising or promotions),

(iv) routine data collection, or

(v) routine or ordinary testing or inspection for quality control.

(E) Computer software

Except to the extent provided in regulations, any research with respect to computer software which is developed by (or for the benefit of) the taxpayer primarily for internal use by the taxpayer, other than for use in—

(i) an activity which constitutes qualified research (determined with regard to this subparagraph), or

(ii) a production process with respect to which the requirements of paragraph (1) are met.

(F) Foreign research

Any research conducted outside the United States, the Commonwealth of Puerto Rico, or any possession of the United States.

(G) Social sciences, etc.

Any research in the social sciences, arts, or humanities.

(H) Funded research

Any research to the extent funded by any grant, contract, or otherwise by another person (or governmental entity).

(e) Credit allowable with respect to certain payments to qualified organizations for basic research

For purposes of this section—

(1) In general

In the case of any taxpayer who makes basic research payments for any taxable year—

(A) the amount of basic research payments taken into account under subsection (a)(2) shall be equal to the excess of—

(i) such basic research payments, over

(ii) the qualified organization base period amount, and

(B) that portion of such basic research payments which does not exceed the qualified organization base period amount shall be treated as contract research expenses for purposes of subsection (a)(1).

(2) Basic research payments defined

For purposes of this subsection—

(A) In general

The term "basic research payment" means, with respect to any taxable year, any amount paid in cash during such taxable year by a corporation to any qualified organization for basic research but only if—

(i) such payment is pursuant to a written agreement between such corporation and such qualified organization, and

(ii) such basic research is to be performed by such qualified organization.

(B) Exception to requirement that research be performed by the organization

In the case of a qualified organization described in subparagraph (C) or (D) of paragraph (6), clause (ii) of subparagraph (A) shall not apply.

(3) Qualified organization base period amount

For purposes of this subsection, the term "qualified organization base period amount" means an amount equal to the sum of—

(A) the minimum basic research amount, plus

(B) the maintenance-of-effort amount.

(4) Minimum basic research amount

For purposes of this subsection—

(A) In general

The term "minimum basic research amount" means an amount equal to the greater of—

(i) 1 percent of the average of the sum of amounts paid or incurred during the base period for—

(I) any in-house research expenses, and

(II) any contract research expenses, or

(ii) the amounts treated as contract research expenses during the base period by reason of this subsection (as in effect during the base period).

(B) Floor amount

Except in the case of a taxpayer which was in existence during a taxable year (other than a short taxable year) in the base period, the minimum basic research amount for any base period shall not be less than 50 percent of the basic research payments for the taxable year for which a determination is being made under this subsection.

(5) Maintenance-of-effort amount

For purposes of this subsection—

(A) In general

The term "maintenance-of-effort amount" means, with respect to any taxable year, an amount equal to the excess (if any) of—

(i) an amount equal to—

(I) the average of the nondesignated university contributions paid by the taxpayer during the base period, multiplied by

(II) the cost-of-living adjustment for the calendar year in which such taxable year begins, over

(ii) the amount of nondesignated university contributions paid by the taxpayer during such taxable year.

(B) Nondesignated university contributions

For purposes of this paragraph, the term "nondesignated university contribution" means any amount paid by a taxpayer to any qualified organization described in paragraph (6)(A)—

(i) for which a deduction was allowable under section 170, and

(ii) which was not taken into account—

(I) in computing the amount of the credit under this section (as in effect during the base period) during any taxable year in the base period, or

(II) as a basic research payment for purposes of this section.

(C) Cost-of-living adjustment defined

(i) In general

The cost-of-living adjustment for any calendar year is the cost-of-living adjustment for such calendar year determined under section 1(f)(3), by substituting "calendar year 1987" for "calendar year 2016" in subparagraph (A)(ii) thereof.

(ii) Special rule where base period ends in a calendar year other than 1983 or 1984

If the base period of any taxpayer does not end in 1983 or 1984, section 1(f)(3)(A)(ii) shall, for purposes of this paragraph, be applied by substituting the calendar year in which such base period ends for 2016. Such substitution shall be in lieu of the substitution under clause (i).

(6) Qualified organization

For purposes of this subsection, the term "qualified organization" means any of the following organizations:

(A) Educational institutions

Any educational organization which—

(i) is an institution of higher education (within the meaning of section 3304(f)), and

(ii) is described in section 170(b)(1)(A)(ii).

(B) Certain scientific research organizations

Any organization not described in subparagraph (A) which—

(i) is described in section 501(c)(3) and is exempt from tax under section 501(a),

(ii) is organized and operated primarily to conduct scientific research, and

(iii) is not a private foundation.

(C) Scientific tax-exempt organizations

Any organization which—

(i) is described in—

(I) section 501(c)(3) (other than a private foundation), or

(II) section 501(c)(6),

(ii) is exempt from tax under section 501(a),

(iii) is organized and operated primarily to promote scientific research by qualified organizations described in subparagraph (A) pursuant to written research agreements, and

(iv) currently expends—

(I) substantially all of its funds, or

(II) substantially all of the basic research payments received by it,

for grants to, or contracts for basic research with, an organization described in subparagraph (A).

(D) Certain grant organizations

Any organization not described in subparagraph (B) or (C) which—

(i) is described in section 501(c)(3) and is exempt from tax under section 501(a) (other than a private foundation),

(ii) is established and maintained by an organization established before July 10, 1981, which meets the requirements of clause (i),

(iii) is organized and operated exclusively for the purpose of making grants to organizations described in subparagraph (A) pursuant to written research agreements for purposes of basic research, and

(iv) makes an election, revocable only with the consent of the Secretary, to be treated as a private foundation for purposes of this title (other than section 4940, relating to excise tax based on investment income).

(7) Definitions and special rules

For purposes of this subsection—

(A) Basic research

The term "basic research" means any original investigation for the advancement of scientific knowledge not having a specific commercial objective, except that such term shall not include—

(i) basic research conducted outside of the United States, and

(ii) basic research in the social sciences, arts, or humanities.

(B) Base period

The term "base period" means the 3-taxable-year period ending with the taxable year immediately preceding the 1st taxable year of the taxpayer beginning after December 31, 1983.

(C) Exclusion from incremental credit calculation

For purposes of determining the amount of credit allowable under subsection (a)(1) for any taxable year, the amount of the basic research payments taken into account under subsection (a)(2)—

(i) shall not be treated as qualified research expenses under subsection (a)(1)(A), and

(ii) shall not be included in the computation of base amount under subsection (a)(1)(B).

(D) Trade or business qualification

For purposes of applying subsection (b)(1) to this subsection, any basic research payments shall be treated as an amount paid in carrying on a trade or business of the taxpayer in the taxable year in which it is paid (without regard to the provisions of subsection (b)(3)(B)).

(E) Certain corporations not eligible

The term "corporation" shall not include—

(i) an S corporation,

(ii) a personal holding company (as defined in section 542), or

(iii) a service organization (as defined in section 414(m)(3)).

(f) Special rules

For purposes of this section—

(1) Aggregation of expenditures

(A) Controlled group of corporations

In determining the amount of the credit under this section—

(i) all members of the same controlled group of corporations shall be treated as a single taxpayer, and

(ii) the credit (if any) allowable by this section to each such member shall be determined on a proportionate basis to its share of the aggregate of the qualified research expenses, basic research payments, and amounts paid or incurred to energy research consortiums, taken into account by such controlled group for purposes of this section.

(B) Common control

Under regulations prescribed by the Secretary, in determining the amount of the credit under this section—

(i) all trades or businesses (whether or not incorporated) which are under common control shall be treated as a single taxpayer, and

(ii) the credit (if any) allowable by this section to each such person shall be determined on a proportionate basis to its share of the aggregate of the qualified research expenses, basic research payments, and amounts paid or incurred to energy research consortiums, taken into account by all such persons under common control for purposes of this section.

The regulations prescribed under this subparagraph shall be based on principles similar to the principles which apply in the case of subparagraph (A).

(2) Allocations

(A) Pass-thru in the case of estates and trusts

Under regulations prescribed by the Secretary, rules similar to the rules of subsection (d) of section 52 shall apply.

(B) Allocation in the case of partnerships

In the case of partnerships, the credit shall be allocated among partners under regulations prescribed by the Secretary.

(3) Adjustments for certain acquisitions, etc.

Under regulations prescribed by the Secretary—

(A) Acquisitions

(i) In general

If a person acquires the major portion of either a trade or business or a separate unit of a trade or business (hereinafter in this paragraph referred to as the "acquired business") of another person (hereinafter in this paragraph referred to as the "predecessor"), then the amount of qualified research expenses paid or incurred by the acquiring person during the measurement period shall be increased by the amount determined under clause (ii), and the gross receipts of the acquiring person for such period shall be increased by the amount determined under clause (iii).

(ii) Amount determined with respect to qualified research expenses

The amount determined under this clause is—

(I) for purposes of applying this section for the taxable year in which such acquisition is made, the acquisition year amount, and

(II) for purposes of applying this section for any taxable year after the taxable year in which such acquisition is made, the qualified research expenses paid or incurred by the predecessor with respect to the acquired business during the measurement period.

(iii) Amount determined with respect to gross receipts

The amount determined under this clause is the amount which would be determined under clause (ii) if "the gross receipts of" were substituted for "the qualified research expenses paid or incurred by" each place it appears in clauses (ii) and (iv).

(iv) Acquisition year amount

For purposes of clause (ii), the acquisition year amount is the amount equal to the product of—

(I) the qualified research expenses paid or incurred by the predecessor with respect to the acquired business during the measurement period, and

(II) the number of days in the period beginning on the date of the acquisition and ending on the last day of the taxable year in which the acquisition is made,

divided by the number of days in the acquiring person's taxable year.

(v) Special rules for coordinating taxable years

In the case of an acquiring person and a predecessor whose taxable years do not begin on the same date—

(I) each reference to a taxable year in clauses (ii) and (iv) shall refer to the appropriate taxable year of the acquiring person,

(II) the qualified research expenses paid or incurred by the predecessor, and the gross receipts of the predecessor, during each taxable year of the predecessor any portion of which is part of the measurement period shall be allocated equally among the days of such taxable year,

(III) the amount of such qualified research expenses taken into account under clauses (ii) and (iv) with respect to a taxable year of the acquiring person shall be equal to the total of the expenses attributable under subclause (II) to the days occurring during such taxable year, and

(IV) the amount of such gross receipts taken into account under clause (iii) with respect to a taxable year of the acquiring person shall be equal to the total of the gross receipts attributable under subclause (II) to the days occurring during such taxable year.

(vi) Measurement period

For purposes of this subparagraph, the term "measurement period" means, with respect to the taxable year of the acquiring person for which the credit is determined, any period of the acquiring person preceding such taxable year which is taken into account for purposes of determining the credit for such year.

(B) Dispositions

If the predecessor furnished to the acquiring person such information as is necessary for the application of subparagraph (A), then, for purposes of applying this section for any taxable year ending after such disposition, the amount of qualified research expenses paid or incurred by, and the gross receipts of, the predecessor during the measurement period (as defined in subparagraph (A)(vi), determined by substituting "predecessor" for "acquiring person" each place it appears) shall be reduced by—

(i) in the case of the taxable year in which such disposition is made, an amount equal to the product of—

(I) the qualified research expenses paid or incurred by, or gross receipts of, the predecessor with respect to the acquired business during the measurement period (as so defined and so determined), and

(II) the number of days in the period beginning on the date of acquisition (as determined for purposes of subparagraph (A)(iv)(II)) and ending on the last day of the taxable year of the predecessor in which the disposition is made,

divided by the number of days in the taxable year of the predecessor, and

(ii) in the case of any taxable year ending after the taxable year in which such disposition is made, the amount described in clause (i)(I).

(C) Certain reimbursements taken into account in determining fixed-base percentage

If during any of the 3 taxable years following the taxable year in which a disposition to which subparagraph (B) applies occurs, the disposing taxpayer (or a person with whom the taxpayer is required to aggregate expenditures under paragraph (1)) reimburses the acquiring person (or a person required to so aggregate expenditures with such person) for research on behalf of the taxpayer, then the amount of qualified research expenses of the taxpayer for the taxable years taken into account in computing the fixed-base percentage shall be increased by the lesser of—

(i) the amount of the decrease under subparagraph (B) which is allocable to taxable years so taken into account, or

(ii) the product of the number of taxable years so taken into account, multiplied by the amount of the reimbursement described in this subparagraph.

(4) Short taxable years

In the case of any short taxable year, qualified research expenses and gross receipts shall be annualized in such circumstances and under such methods as the Secretary may prescribe by regulation.

(5) Controlled group of corporations

The term "controlled group of corporations" has the same meaning given to such term by section 1563(a), except that—

(A) "more than 50 percent" shall be substituted for "at least 80 percent" each place it appears in section 1563(a)(1), and

(B) the determination shall be made without regard to subsections (a)(4) and (e)(3)(C) of section 1563.

(6) Energy research consortium

(A) In general

The term "energy research consortium" means any organization—

(i) which is—

(I) described in section 501(c)(3) and is exempt from tax under section 501(a) and is organized and operated primarily to conduct energy research, or

(II) organized and operated primarily to conduct energy research in the public interest (within the meaning of section 501(c)(3)),

(ii) which is not a private foundation,

(iii) to which at least 5 unrelated persons paid or incurred during the calendar year in which the taxable year of the organization begins amounts (including as contributions) to such organization for energy research, and

(iv) to which no single person paid or incurred (including as contributions) during such calendar year an amount equal to more than 50 percent of the total amounts received by such organization during such calendar year for energy research.

(B) Treatment of persons

All persons treated as a single employer under subsection (a) or (b) of section 52 shall be treated as related persons for purposes of subparagraph (A)(iii) and as a single person for purposes of subparagraph (A)(iv).

(C) Foreign research

For purposes of subsection (a)(3), amounts paid or incurred for any energy research conducted outside the United States, the Commonwealth of Puerto Rico, or any possession of the United States shall not be taken into account.

(D) Denial of double benefit

Any amount taken into account under subsection (a)(3) shall not be taken into account under paragraph (1) or (2) of subsection (a).

(E) Energy research

The term "energy research" does not include any research which is not qualified research.

(g) Special rule for pass-thru of credit

In the case of an individual who—

(1) owns an interest in an unincorporated trade or business,

(2) is a partner in a partnership,

(3) is a beneficiary of an estate or trust, or

(4) is a shareholder in an S corporation,

the amount determined under subsection (a) for any taxable year shall not exceed an amount (separately computed with respect to such person's interest in such trade or business or entity) equal to the amount of tax attributable to that portion of a person's taxable income which is allocable or apportionable to the person's interest in such trade or business or entity. If the amount determined under subsection (a) for any taxable year exceeds the limitation of the preceding sentence, such amount may be carried to other taxable years under the rules of section 39; except that the limitation of the preceding sentence shall be taken into account in lieu of the limitation of section 38(c) in applying section 39.

(h) Treatment of credit for qualified small businesses

(1) In general

At the election of a qualified small business for any taxable year, section 3111(f) shall apply to the payroll tax credit portion of the credit otherwise determined under subsection (a) for the taxable year and such portion shall not be treated (other than for purposes of section 280C) as a credit determined under subsection (a).

(2) Payroll tax credit portion

For purposes of this subsection, the payroll tax credit portion of the credit determined under subsection (a) with respect to any qualified small business for any taxable year is the least of—

(A) the amount specified in the election made under this subsection,

(B) the credit determined under subsection (a) for the taxable year (determined before the application of this subsection), or

(C) in the case of a qualified small business other than a partnership or S corporation, the amount of the business credit carryforward under section 39 carried from the taxable year (determined before the application of this subsection to the taxable year).

(3) Qualified small business

For purposes of this subsection—

(A) In general

The term "qualified small business" means, with respect to any taxable year—

(i) a corporation or partnership, if—

(I) the gross receipts (as determined under the rules of section 448(c)(3), without regard to subparagraph (A) thereof) of such entity for the taxable year is less than $5,000,000, and

(II) such entity did not have gross receipts (as so determined) for any taxable year preceding the 5-taxable-year period ending with such taxable year, and

(ii) any person (other than a corporation or partnership) who meets the requirements of subclauses (I) and (II) of clause (i), determined—

(I) by substituting "person" for "entity" each place it appears, and

(II) by only taking into account the aggregate gross receipts received by such person in carrying on all trades or businesses of such person.

(B) Limitation

Such term shall not include an organization which is exempt from taxation under section 501.

(4) Election

(A) In general

Any election under this subsection for any taxable year—

(i) shall specify the amount of the credit to which such election applies,

(ii) shall be made on or before the due date (including extensions) of—

(I) in the case of a qualified small business which is a partnership, the return required to be filed under section 6031,

(II) in the case of a qualified small business which is an S corporation, the return required to be filed under section 6037, and

(III) in the case of any other qualified small business, the return of tax for the taxable year, and

(iii) may be revoked only with the consent of the Secretary.

(B) Limitations

(i) Amount

The amount specified in any election made under this subsection shall not exceed $250,000.

(ii) Number of taxable years

A person may not make an election under this subsection if such person (or any other person treated as a single taxpayer with such person under paragraph (5)(A)) has made an election under this subsection for 5 or more preceding taxable years.

(C) Special rule for partnerships and S corporations

In the case of a qualified small business which is a partnership or S corporation, the election made under this subsection shall be made at the entity level.

(5) Aggregation rules

(A) In general

Except as provided in subparagraph (B), all persons or entities treated as a single taxpayer under subsection (f)(1) shall be treated as a single taxpayer for purposes of this subsection.

(B) Special rules

For purposes of this subsection and section 3111(f)—

(i) each of the persons treated as a single taxpayer under subparagraph (A) may separately make the election under paragraph (1) for any taxable year, and

(ii) the $250,000 amount under paragraph (4)(B)(i) shall be allocated among all persons treated as a single taxpayer under subparagraph (A) in the same manner as under subparagraph (A)(ii) or (B)(ii) of subsection (f)(1), whichever is applicable.

(6) Regulations

The Secretary shall prescribe such regulations as may be necessary to carry out the purposes of this subsection, including—

(A) regulations to prevent the avoidance of the purposes of the limitations and aggregation rules under this subsection through the use of successor companies or other means,

(B) regulations to minimize compliance and record-keeping burdens under this subsection, and

(C) regulations for recapturing the benefit of credits determined under section 3111(f) in cases where there is a subsequent adjustment to the payroll tax credit portion of the credit determined under subsection (a), including requiring amended income tax returns in the cases where there is such an adjustment.

(Added Pub. L. 97–34, title II, §221(a), Aug. 13, 1981, 95 Stat. 241, §44F; amended Pub. L. 97–354, §5(a)(3), Oct. 19, 1982, 96 Stat. 1692; Pub. L. 97–448, title I, §102(h)(2), Jan. 12, 1983, 96 Stat. 2372; renumbered §30 and amended Pub. L. 98–369, div. A, title IV, §§471(c), 474(i)(1), title VI, §612(e)(1), July 18, 1984, 98 Stat. 826, 831, 912; renumbered §41 and amended Pub. L. 99–514, title II, §231(a)(1), (b), (c), (d)(2), (3)(C)(ii), (e), title XVIII, §1847(b)(1), Oct. 22, 1986, 100 Stat. 2173, 2175, 2178-2180, 2856; Pub. L. 100–647, title I, §1002(h)(1), title IV, §§4007(a), 4008(b)(1), Nov. 10, 1988, 102 Stat. 3370, 3652; Pub. L. 101–239, title VII, §§7110(a)(1), (b), (b)[(c)], 7814(e)(2)(C), Dec. 19, 1989, 103 Stat. 2322, 2323, 2325, 2414; Pub. L. 101–508, title XI, §§11101(d)(1)(C), 11402(a), Nov. 5, 1990, 104 Stat. 1388–405, 1388-473; Pub. L. 102–227, title I, §102(a), Dec. 11, 1991, 105 Stat. 1686; Pub. L. 103–66, title XIII, §§13111(a)(1), 13112(a), (b), 13201(b)(3)(C), Aug. 10, 1993, 107 Stat. 420, 421, 459; Pub. L. 104–188, title I, §§1201(e)(1), (4), 1204(a)–(d), Aug. 20, 1996, 110 Stat. 1772–1774; Pub. L. 105–34, title VI, §601(a), (b)(1), Aug. 5, 1997, 111 Stat. 861; Pub. L. 105–277, div. J, title I, §1001(a), Oct. 21, 1998, 112 Stat. 2681–888; Pub. L. 106–170, title V, §502(a)(1), (b)(1), (c)(1), Dec. 17, 1999, 113 Stat. 1919; Pub. L. 108–311, title III, §301(a)(1), Oct. 4, 2004, 118 Stat. 1178; Pub. L. 109–58, title XIII, §1351(a), (b),

Aug. 8, 2005, 119 Stat. 1056, 1057; Pub. L. 109–135, title IV, §402(l), Dec. 21, 2005, 119 Stat. 2615; Pub. L. 109–432, div. A, title I, §104(a)(1), (b)(1), (c)(1), Dec. 20, 2006, 120 Stat. 2934, 2935; Pub. L. 110–172, §§6(c), 11(e)(2), Dec. 29, 2007, 121 Stat. 2479, 2489; Pub. L. 110–343, div. C, title III, §301(a)(1), (b)–(d), Oct. 3, 2008, 122 Stat. 3865, 3866; Pub. L. 111–312, title VII, §731(a), Dec. 17, 2010, 124 Stat. 3317; Pub. L. 112–240, title III, §301(a)(1), (b), (c), Jan. 2, 2013, 126 Stat. 2326, 2328; Pub. L. 113–295, div. A, title I, §111(a), Dec. 19, 2014, 128 Stat. 4014; Pub. L. 114–113, div. Q, title I, §121(a)(1), (c)(1), Dec. 18, 2015, 129 Stat. 3049; Pub. L. 115–97, title I, §§11002(d)(1)(F), (2), 13206(d)(1), Dec. 22, 2017, 131 Stat. 2060, 2061, 2112; Pub. L. 115–141, div. U, title I, §101(c), title IV, §401(b)(6), Mar. 23, 2018, 132 Stat. 1160, 1202.)

EDITORIAL NOTES
REFERENCES IN TEXT

The date of the enactment of the Energy Tax Incentives Act of 2005, referred to in subsec. (b)(3)(D)(iv), is the date of enactment of title XIII of Pub. L. 109–58, which was approved Aug. 8, 2005.

PRIOR PROVISIONS

A prior section 41, added Pub. L. 97–34, title III, §331(a), Aug. 13, 1981, 95 Stat. 289, §44G; amended Pub. L. 97–448, title I, §103(g)(1), Jan. 12, 1983, 96 Stat. 2379; renumbered §41 and amended Pub. L. 98–369, div. A, title I, §14, title IV, §§471(c), 474(l), 491(e)(2), (3), July 18, 1984, 98 Stat. 505, 826, 833, 852, 853, related to employee stock ownership credit, prior to repeal by Pub. L. 99–514, title XI, §1171(a), Oct. 22, 1986, 100 Stat. 2513, applicable to compensation paid or accrued after Dec. 31, 1986, in taxable years ending after such date, except as otherwise provided, see section 1171(c) of Pub. L. 99–514, set out as an Effective Date of 1986 Amendment note under section 38 of this title. For transition rules relating to such repeal, see section 1177 of Pub. L. 99–514, set out as a Transition Rules note under section 38 of this title.

Another prior section 41 was renumbered section 24 of this title.

AMENDMENTS

2018—Subsec. (c)(4). Pub. L. 115–141, §101(c)(1), (2), redesignated par. (5) as (4) and struck out former par. (4) which related to election of alternative incremental credit.

Subsec. (c)(4)(A). Pub. L. 115–141, §401(b)(6), struck out "(12 percent in the case of taxable years ending before January 1, 2009)" after "14 percent".

Subsec. (c)(4)(C). Pub. L. 115–141, §101(c)(3), struck out at end "An election under this paragraph may not be made for any taxable year to which an election under paragraph (4) applies."

Subsec. (c)(5) to (7). Pub. L. 115–141, §101(c)(2), redesignated pars. (5) to (7) as (4) to (6), respectively.

2017—Subsec. (d)(1)(A). Pub. L. 115–97, §13206(d)(1), substituted "specified research or experimental expenditures under section 174" for "expenses under section 174".

Subsec. (e)(5)(C)(i). Pub. L. 115–97, §11002(d)(1)(F), substituted "for 'calendar year 2016' in subparagraph (A)(ii)" for "for 'calendar year 1992' in subparagraph (B)".

Subsec. (e)(5)(C)(ii). Pub. L. 115–97, §11002(d)(2), substituted "1(f)(3)(A)(ii)" for "1(f)(3)(B)" and "2016" for "1992".

2015—Subsec. (h). Pub. L. 114–113, §121(c)(1), added subsec. (h).

Pub. L. 114–113, §121(a)(1), struck out subsec. (h) which provided the termination date for applicability of this section and the alternative incremental credit and provided the computation for taxable year in which credit terminates.

2014—Subsec. (h)(1). Pub. L. 113–295 substituted "paid or incurred after December 31, 2014." for "paid or incurred—

"(A) after June 30, 1995, and before July 1, 1996, or

"(B) after December 31, 2013."

2013—Subsec. (f)(1)(A)(ii). Pub. L. 112–240, §301(c)(1), substituted "shall be determined on a proportionate basis to its share of the aggregate of the qualified research expenses, basic research payments, and amounts paid or incurred to energy research consortiums, taken into account by such controlled group for purposes of this section" for "shall be its proportionate shares of the qualified research expenses, basic research payments, and amounts paid or incurred to energy research consortiums, giving rise to the credit".

Subsec. (f)(1)(B)(ii). Pub. L. 112–240, §301(c)(2), substituted "shall be determined on a proportionate basis to its share of the aggregate of the qualified research expenses, basic research payments, and amounts paid or incurred to energy research consortiums, taken into account by all such persons under common control for purposes of this section" for "shall be its proportionate shares of the qualified research expenses, basic research payments, and amounts paid or incurred to energy research consortiums, giving rise to the credit".

Subsec. (f)(3)(A). Pub. L. 112–240, §301(b)(1), amended subpar. (A) generally. Prior to amendment, text read as follows: "If, after December 31, 1983, a taxpayer acquires the major portion of a trade or business of another person (hereinafter in this paragraph referred to as the 'predecessor') or the major portion of a separate unit of a trade or business of a predecessor, then, for purposes of applying this section for any taxable year ending after such acquisition, the amount of qualified research expenses paid or incurred by the taxpayer during periods before such acquisition shall be increased by so much of such expenses paid or incurred by the predecessor with respect to the acquired trade or business as is attributable to the portion of such trade or business or separate unit acquired by the taxpayer, and the gross receipts of the taxpayer for such periods shall be increased by so much of the gross receipts of such predecessor with respect to the acquired trade or business as is attributable to such portion."

Subsec. (f)(3)(B). Pub. L. 112–240, §301(b)(2), amended subpar. (B) generally. Prior to amendment, text read as follows: "If, after December 31, 1983—

"(i) a taxpayer disposes of the major portion of any trade or business or the major portion of a separate unit of a trade or business in a transaction to which subparagraph (A) applies, and

"(ii) the taxpayer furnished the acquiring person such information as is necessary for the application of subparagraph (A),

then, for purposes of applying this section for any taxable year ending after such disposition, the amount of qualified research expenses paid or incurred by the taxpayer during periods before such disposition shall be decreased by so much of such expenses as is attributable to the portion of such trade or business or separate unit disposed of by the taxpayer, and the gross receipts of the taxpayer for such periods shall be decreased by so much of the gross receipts as is attributable to such portion."

Subsec. (h)(1)(B). Pub. L. 112–240, §301(a)(1), substituted "December 31, 2013" for "December 31, 2011".

2010—Subsec. (h)(1)(B). Pub. L. 111–312 substituted "December 31, 2011" for "December 31, 2009".

2008—Subsec. (c)(5)(A). Pub. L. 110–343, §301(c), substituted "14 percent (12 percent in the case of taxable years ending before January 1, 2009)" for "12 percent".

Subsec. (h)(1)(B). Pub. L. 110–343, §301(a)(1), substituted "December 31, 2009" for "December 31, 2007".

Subsec. (h)(2). Pub. L. 110–343, §301(d), redesignated par. (3) as (2) related to computation for taxable year in which credit terminates.

Pub. L. 110–343, §301(b), added par. (2). Former par. (2) redesignated (3).

Subsec. (h)(3). Pub. L. 110–343, §301(d), amended par. (3) generally, redesignating it as par. (2) related to computation for taxable year in which credit terminated and amending heading and text generally. Prior to amendment, text read as follows: "In the case of any taxable year with respect to which this section applies to a number of days which is less than the total number of days in such taxable year, the base amount with respect to such taxable year shall be the amount which bears the same ratio to the base amount for such year (determined without regard to this paragraph) as the number of days in such taxable year to which this section applies bears to the total number of days in such taxable year."

Pub. L. 110–343, §301(b), redesignated par. (2) as (3).

2007—Subsec. (a)(3). Pub. L. 110–172, §6(c)(1), inserted "for energy research" before period at end.

Subsec. (f)(1)(A)(ii), (B)(ii). Pub. L. 110–172, §11(e)(2), substituted "qualified research expenses, basic research payments, and amounts paid or incurred to energy research consortiums," for "qualified research expenses and basic research payments".

Subsec. (f)(6)(E). Pub. L. 110–172, §6(c)(2), added subpar. (E).

2006—Subsec. (c)(4)(A)(i). Pub. L. 109–432, §104(b)(1)(A), substituted "3 percent" for "2.65 percent".

Subsec. (c)(4)(A)(ii). Pub. L. 109–432, §104(b)(1)(B), substituted "4 percent" for "3.2 percent".

Subsec. (c)(4)(A)(iii). Pub. L. 109–432, §104(b)(1)(C), substituted "5 percent" for "3.75 percent".

Subsec. (c)(5) to (7). Pub. L. 109–432, §104(c)(1), added par. (5) and redesignated former pars. (5) and (6) as (6) and (7), respectively.

Subsec. (h)(1)(B). Pub. L. 109–432, §104(a)(1), substituted "2007" for "2005".

2005—Subsec. (a)(3). Pub. L. 109–58, §1351(a)(1), added par. (3).

Subsec. (b)(3)(C)(ii). Pub. L. 109–135, §402(l)(2), struck out "(other than an energy research consortium)" after "organization" in introductory provisions.

Pub. L. 109–58, §1351(a)(3), inserted "(other than an energy research consortium)" after "organization" in introductory provisions.

Subsec. (b)(3)(D). Pub. L. 109–58, §1351(b), added subpar. (D).

Subsec. (f)(6). Pub. L. 109–58, §1351(a)(2), added par. (6).

Subsec. (f)(6)(C), (D). Pub. L. 109–135, §402(l)(1), added subpars. (C) and (D).

2004—Subsec. (h)(1)(B). Pub. L. 108–311 substituted "December 31, 2005" for "June 30, 2004".

1999—Subsec. (c)(4)(A)(i). Pub. L. 106–170, §502(b)(1)(A), substituted "2.65 percent" for "1.65 percent".

Subsec. (c)(4)(A)(ii). Pub. L. 106–170, §502(b)(1)(B), substituted "3.2 percent" for "2.2 percent".

Subsec. (c)(4)(A)(iii). Pub. L. 106–170, §502(b)(1)(C), substituted "3.75 percent" for "2.75 percent".

Subsecs. (c)(6), (d)(4)(F). Pub. L. 106–170, §502(c)(1), inserted ", the Commonwealth of Puerto Rico, or any possession of the United States" before period at end.

Subsec. (h)(1). Pub. L. 106–170, §502(a)(1)(B), struck out concluding provisions which read as follows: "Notwithstanding the preceding sentence, in the case of a taxpayer making an election under subsection (c)(4) for its first taxable year beginning after June 30, 1996, and before July 1, 1997, this section shall apply to amounts paid or incurred during the 36-month period beginning with the first month of such year. The 36 months referred to in the preceding sentence shall be reduced by the number of full months after June 1996 (and before the first month of such first taxable year) during which the taxpayer paid or incurred any amount which is taken into account in determining the credit under this section."

Subsec. (h)(1)(B). Pub. L. 106–170, §502(a)(1)(A), substituted "June 30, 2004" for "June 30, 1999".

1998—Subsec. (h)(1). Pub. L. 105–277 substituted "June 30, 1999" for "June 30, 1998" in subpar. (B) and substituted "36-month" for "24-month" and "36 months" for "24 months" in concluding provisions.

1997—Subsec. (c)(4)(B). Pub. L. 105–34, §601(b)(1), amended heading and text of subpar. (B) generally. Prior to amendment, text read as follows: "An election under this paragraph may be made only for the first taxable year of the taxpayer beginning after June 30, 1996. Such an election shall apply to the taxable year for which made and all succeeding taxable years unless revoked with the consent of the Secretary."

Subsec. (h)(1). Pub. L. 105–34, §601(a), substituted "June 30, 1998" for "May 31, 1997" in subpar. (B) and "during the 24-month period beginning with the first month of such year. The 24 months referred to in the preceding sentence shall be reduced by the number of full months after June 1996 (and before the first month of such first taxable year) during which the taxpayer paid or incurred any amount which is taken into account in determining the credit under this section." for "during the first 11 months of such taxable year." in concluding provisions.

1996—Subsec. (b)(2)(D)(iii). Pub. L. 104–188, §1201(e)(1), (4), substituted "work opportunity credit" for "targeted jobs credit" in heading and text.

Subsec. (b)(3)(C). Pub. L. 104–188, §1204(d), added subpar. (C).

Subsec. (c)(3)(B)(i). Pub. L. 104–188, §1204(b), reenacted heading without change and amended text generally. Prior to amendment, text read as follows: "The fixed-base percentage shall be determined under this subparagraph if there are fewer than 3 taxable years beginning after December 31, 1983, and before January 1, 1989, in which the taxpayer had both gross receipts and qualified research expenses."

Subsec. (c)(4) to (6). Pub. L. 104–188, §1204(c), added par. (4) and redesignated former pars. (4) and (5) as (5) and (6), respectively.

Subsec. (h). Pub. L. 104–188, §1204(a), reenacted heading without change and amended text generally. Prior to amendment, text read as follows:

"(1) In general.—This section shall not apply to any amount paid or incurred after June 30, 1995.

"(2) Computation of base amount.—In the case of any taxable year which begins before July 1, 1995, and ends after June 30, 1995, the base amount with respect to such taxable year shall be the amount which bears the same ratio to the base amount for such year (determined without regard to this paragraph) as the number of days in such taxable year before July 1, 1995, bears to the total number of days in such taxable year."

1993—Subsec. (c)(3)(B)(ii). Pub. L. 103–66, §13112(a), amended heading and text of cl. (ii) generally. Prior to amendment, text read as follows: "In a case to which this subparagraph applies, the fixed-base percentage is 3 percent."

Subsec. (c)(3)(B)(iii). Pub. L. 103–66, §13112(b)(1), substituted "clauses (i) and (ii)" for "clause (i)".

Subsec. (c)(3)(D). Pub. L. 103–66, §13112(b)(2), substituted "subparagraphs (A) and (B)(ii)" for "subparagraph (A)".

Subsec. (e)(5)(C). Pub. L. 103–66, §13201(b)(3)(C), substituted "1992" for "1989" in cls. (i) and (ii).

Subsec. (h). Pub. L. 103–66, §13111(a)(1), substituted "June 30, 1995" for "June 30, 1992" in pars. (1) and (2) and "July 1, 1995" for "July 1, 1992" in two places in par. (2).

1991—Subsec. (h). Pub. L. 102–227 substituted "June 30, 1992" for "December 31, 1991" in pars. (1) and (2), and "July 1, 1992" for "January 1, 1992" in two places in par. (2).

1990—Subsec. (e)(5)(C)(i). Pub. L. 101–508, §11101(d)(1)(C)(i), inserted before period at end ", by substituting 'calendar year 1987' for 'calendar year 1989' in subparagraph (B) thereof".

Subsec. (e)(5)(C)(ii). Pub. L. 101–508, §11101(d)(1)(C)(ii), (iii), substituted "1989" for "1987" and inserted at end "Such substitution shall be in lieu of the substitution under clause (i)."

Subsec. (h). Pub. L. 101–508, §11402(a), substituted "December 31, 1991" for "December 31, 1990" wherever appearing and "January 1, 1992" for "January 1, 1991" wherever appearing.

1989—Subsec. (a)(1)(B). Pub. L. 101–239, §7110(b)(2)(A), amended subpar. (B) generally. Prior to amendment, subpar. (B) read as follows: "the base period research expenses, and".

Subsec. (b)(4). Pub. L. 101–239, §7110(b)[(c)], added par. (4).

Subsec. (c). Pub. L. 101–239, §7110(b)(1), substituted "Base amount" for "Base period research expenses" in heading and amended text generally, substituting pars. (1) to (5) for former pars. (1) to (3) which defined "base period research expenses" and "base period" and prescribed minimum base period research expenses.

Subsec. (e)(7)(C)(ii). Pub. L. 101–239, §7110(b)(2)(B), substituted "base amount" for "base period research expenses".

Subsec. (f)(1). Pub. L. 101–239, §7110(b)(2)(C), substituted "proportionate shares of the qualified research expenses and basic research payments" for "proportionate share of the increase in qualified research expenses" in subpars. (A)(ii) and (B)(ii).

Subsec. (f)(3)(A). Pub. L. 101–239, §7110(b)(2)(D), substituted "December 31, 1983" for "June 30, 1980" and inserted before period at end ", and the gross receipts of the taxpayer for such periods shall be increased by so much of the gross receipts of such predecessor with respect to the acquired trade or business as is attributable to such portion".

Subsec. (f)(3)(B). Pub. L. 101–239, §7110(b)(2)(E), substituted "December 31, 1983" for "June 30, 1980" in introductory provisions and inserted before period at end ", and the gross receipts of the taxpayer for such periods shall be decreased by so much of the gross receipts as is attributable to such portion".

Subsec. (f)(3)(C). Pub. L. 101–239, §7110(b)(2)(F), substituted "Certain reimbursements taken into account in determining fixed-base percentage" for "Increase in base period" in heading, "for the taxable years taken into account in computing the fixed-base percentage shall be increased by the lesser of" for "for the base period for such taxable year shall be increased by the lesser of" in introductory provisions, and new cls. (i) and (ii) for former cls. (i) and (ii) which read as follows:

"(i) the amount of the decrease under subparagraph (B) which is allocable to such base period, or

"(ii) the product of the number of years in the base period, multiplied by the amount of the reimbursement described in this subparagraph."

Subsec. (f)(4). Pub. L. 101–239, §7110(b)(2)(G), inserted "and gross receipts" after "qualified research expenses".

Subsec. (h). Pub. L. 101–239, §7814(e)(2)(C), redesignated subsec. (i) as (h) and struck out former subsec. (h) which related to election, time for election, and manner of election by taxpayer to have research credit not apply for a taxable year.

Subsec. (h)(1). Pub. L. 101–239, §7110(a)(1)(A), substituted "December 31, 1990" for "December 31, 1989".

Subsec. (h)(2). Pub. L. 101–239, §7110(a)(1), substituted "January 1, 1991" for "January 1, 1990" in two places and substituted "December 31, 1990" for "December 31, 1989".

Pub. L. 101–239, §7110(b)(2)(H), substituted "base amount" for "base period expenses" in heading and "the base amount with respect to such taxable year shall be the amount which bears the same ratio to the base amount for such year (determined without regard to this paragraph)" for "any amount for any base period with respect to such taxable year shall be the amount which bears the same ratio to such amount for such base period" in text.

Subsec. (i). Pub. L. 101–239, §7814(e)(2)(C), redesignated subsec. (i) as (h).

1988—Subsec. (g). Pub. L. 100–647, §1002(h)(1), inserted at end "If the amount determined under subsection (a) for any taxable year exceeds the limitation of the preceding sentence, such amount may be carried to other taxable years under the rules of section 39; except that the limitation of the preceding sentence shall be taken into account in lieu of the limitation of section 38(c) in applying section 39."

Subsec. (h). Pub. L. 100–647, §4008(b)(1), added subsec. (h). Former subsec. (h) redesignated (i).

Subsec. (i). Pub. L. 100–647, §4008(b)(1), redesignated former subsec. (h) as (i).

Pub. L. 100–647, §4007(a), substituted "1989" and "1990" for "1988" and "1989", respectively, wherever appearing in subsec. (h), prior to redesignation as subsec. (i) by Pub. L. 100–647, §4008(b)(1).

1986—Pub. L. 99–514, §231(d)(2), renumbered section 30 of this title as this section.

Subsec. (a). Pub. L. 99–514, §231(c)(1), amended subsec. (a) generally. Prior to amendment, subsec. (a) read as follows: "There shall be allowed as a credit against the tax imposed by this chapter for the taxable year an amount equal to 25 percent of the excess (if any) of—

"(1) the qualified research expenses for the taxable year, over

"(2) the base period research expenses."

Subsec. (b)(2)(A)(iii). Pub. L. 99–514, §231(e), amended cl. (iii) generally. Prior to amendment, cl. (iii) read as follows: "any amount paid or incurred to another person for the right to use personal property in the conduct of qualified research."

Subsec. (b)(2)(D)(iii). Pub. L. 99–514, §1847(b)(1), substituted "targeted jobs credit" for "new jobs or WIN credit" in heading.

Subsec. (d). Pub. L. 99–514, §231(b), inserted "defined" in heading and amended text generally. Prior to amendment, text read as follows: "For purposes of this section the term 'qualified research' has the same meaning as the term research or experimental has under section 174, except that such term shall not include—

"(1) qualified research conducted outside the United States,

"(2) qualified research in the social sciences or humanities, and

"(3) qualified research to the extent funded by any grant, contract, or otherwise by another person (or any governmental entity)."

Subsec. (e). Pub. L. 99–514, §231(c)(2), amended subsec. (e) generally, substituting "Credit allowable with respect to certain payments to qualified organizations for basic research" for "Credit available with respect to certain basic research by colleges, universities, and certain research organizations" in heading, and restating and expanding provisions of former pars. (1) to (4) into new pars. (1) to (7).

Subsec. (g). Pub. L. 99–514, §231(d)(3)(C)(ii), amended subsec. (g) generally, substituting provisions relating to special rule for pass-thru of credit for provisions relating to limitation on amount of credit for research based on amount of tax liability.

Subsec. (h). Pub. L. 99–514, §231(a)(1), added subsec. (h).

1984—Pub. L. 98–369, §471(c), renumbered section 44F of this title as this section.

Subsec. (b)(2)(D)(iii). Pub. L. 98–369, §474(i)(1)(A), substituted "in determining the targeted jobs credit under section 51(a)" for "in computing the credit under section 40 or 44B".

Subsec. (g)(1)(A). Pub. L. 98–369, §612(e)(1), substituted "section 26(b)" for "section 25(b)".

Pub. L. 98–369, §474(i)(1)(B), amended subpar. (A) generally, substituting "shall not exceed the taxpayer's tax liability for the taxable year (as defined in section 25(b)), reduced by the sum of the credits allowable under subpart A and sections 27, 28, and 29" for "shall not exceed the amount of the tax imposed by this chapter reduced by the sum of the credits allowable under a section of this part having a lower number or letter designation than this section, other than the credits allowable by sections 31, 39, and 43. For purposes of the preceding sentence, the term 'tax imposed by this chapter' shall not include any tax treated as not imposed by this chapter under the last sentence of section 53(a)".

1983—Subsec. (b)(2)(A). Pub. L. 97–448 inserted provision that cl. (iii) would not apply to any amount to the extent that the taxpayer (or any person with whom the taxpayer must aggregate expenditures under subsection (f)(1)) received or accrued any amount from any other person for the right to use substantially identical personal property.

1982—Subsec. (f)(2)(A). Pub. L. 97–354, §5(a)(3)(A), substituted "Pass-thru in the case of estates and trusts" for "Pass-through in the case of subchapter S corporations, etc." in subpar. heading, and substituted provisions relating to the applicability of rules similar to rules of subsec. (d) of section 52 for provisions relating to the applicability of rules similar to rules of subsecs. (d) and (e) of section 52.

Subsec. (g)(1)(B)(iv). Pub. L. 97–354, §5(a)(3)(B), substituted "an S corporation" for "an electing small business corporation (within the meaning of section 1371(b))".

STATUTORY NOTES AND RELATED SUBSIDIARIES
EFFECTIVE DATE OF 2018 AMENDMENT

Amendment by section 101(c) of Pub. L. 115–141 effective as if included in the provision of the Protecting Americans from Tax Hikes Act of 2015, div. Q of Pub. L. 114–113, to which such amendment relates, see section 101(s) of Pub. L. 115–141, set out as a note under section 24 of this title.

EFFECTIVE DATE OF 2017 AMENDMENT

Amendment by section 11002(d)(1)(F), (2) of Pub. L. 115–97 applicable to taxable years beginning after Dec. 31, 2017, see section 11002(e) of Pub. L. 115–97, set out as a note under section 1 of this title.

<u>Pub. L. 115–97, title I, §13206(e), Dec. 22, 2017, 131 Stat. 2113</u>, provided that: "The amendments made by this section [amending this section and sections 174 and 280C of this title] shall apply to amounts paid or incurred in taxable years beginning after December 31, 2021."

EFFECTIVE DATE OF 2015 AMENDMENT

Amendment by section 121(a)(1) of Pub. L. 114–113 applicable to amounts paid or incurred after Dec. 31, 2014, see section 121(d)(1) of Pub. L. 114–113, set out as a note under section 38 of this title.

Amendment by section 121(c)(1) of Pub. L. 114–113 applicable to taxable years beginning after Dec. 31, 2015, see section 121(d)(3) of Pub. L. 114–113, set out as a note under section 38 of this title.

EFFECTIVE DATE OF 2014 AMENDMENT

<u>Pub. L. 113–295, div. A, title I, §111(c), Dec. 19, 2014, 128 Stat. 4014</u>, provided that: "The amendments made by this section [amending this section and section 45C of this title] shall apply to amounts paid or incurred after December 31, 2013."

EFFECTIVE DATE OF 2013 AMENDMENT

<u>Pub. L. 112–240, title III, §301(d), Jan. 2, 2013, 126 Stat. 2328</u>, provided that:

"(1) Extension.—The amendments made by subsection (a) [amending this section and section 45C of this title] shall apply to amounts paid or incurred after December 31, 2011.

"(2) Modifications.—The amendments made by subsections (b) and (c) [amending this section] shall apply to taxable years beginning after December 31, 2011."

EFFECTIVE DATE OF 2010 AMENDMENT

<u>Pub. L. 111–312, title VII, §731(c), Dec. 17, 2010, 124 Stat. 3317</u>, provided that: "The amendments made by this section [amending this section and section 45C of this title] shall apply to amounts paid or incurred after December 31, 2009."

EFFECTIVE DATE OF 2008 AMENDMENT

<u>Pub. L. 110–343, div. C, title III, §301(e), Oct. 3, 2008, 122 Stat. 3866</u>, provided that:

"(1) In general.—Except as provided in paragraph (2), the amendments made by this section [amending this section and section 45C of this title] shall apply to taxable years beginning after December 31, 2007.

"(2) Extension.—The amendments made by subsection (a) [amending this section and section 45C of this title] shall apply to amounts paid or incurred after December 31, 2007."

EFFECTIVE DATE OF 2007 AMENDMENT

Amendment by section 6(c) of Pub. L. 110–172 effective as if included in the provisions of the Energy Policy Act of 2005, Pub. L. 109–58, to which such amendment relates, see section 6(e) of Pub. L. 110–172, set out as a note under section 30C of this title.

<u>Pub. L. 110–172, §11(e)(3), Dec. 29, 2007, 121 Stat. 2489</u>, provided that: "The amendments made by this subsection [amending this section and section 6427 of this title] shall take effect as if included in the provisions of the Energy Policy Act of 2005 [Pub. L. 109–58] to which they relate."

EFFECTIVE DATE OF 2006 AMENDMENT

<u>Pub. L. 109–432, div. A, title I, §104(a)(3), Dec. 20, 2006, 120 Stat. 2934</u>, provided that: "The amendments made by this subsection [amending this section and section 45C of this title] shall apply to amounts paid or incurred after December 31, 2005."

<u>Pub. L. 109–432, div. A, title I, §104(b)(2), (3), Dec. 20, 2006, 120 Stat. 2934</u>, provided that:

"(2) Effective date.—Except as provided in paragraph (3), the amendments made by this subsection [amending this section] shall apply to taxable years ending after December 31, 2006.

"(3) Transition rule.—

"(A) In general.—In the case of a specified transitional taxable year for which an election under section 41(c)(4) of the Internal Revenue Code of 1986 applies, the credit determined under section 41(a)(1) of such Code shall be equal to the sum of—

"(i) the applicable 2006 percentage multiplied by the amount determined under section 41(c)(4)(A) of such Code (as in effect for taxable years ending on December 31, 2006), plus

"(ii) the applicable 2007 percentage multiplied by the amount determined under section 41(c)(4)(A) of such Code (as in effect for taxable years ending on January 1, 2007).

"(B) Definitions.—For purposes of subparagraph (A)—

"(i) Specified transitional taxable year.—The term 'specified transitional taxable year' means any taxable year which ends after December 31, 2006, and which includes such date.

"(ii) Applicable 2006 percentage.—The term 'applicable 2006 percentage' means the number of days in the specified transitional taxable year before January 1, 2007, divided by the number of days in such taxable year.

"(iii) Applicable 2007 percentage.—The term 'applicable 2007 percentage' means the number of days in the specified transitional taxable year after December 31, 2006, divided by the number of days in such taxable year."

<u>Pub. L. 109–432, div. A, title I, §104(c)(2)–(4), Dec. 20, 2006, 120 Stat. 2935</u>, provided that:

"(2) Transition rule for deemed revocation of election of alternative incremental credit.—In the case of an election under section 41(c)(4) of the Internal Revenue Code of 1986 which applies to the taxable year which includes January 1, 2007, such election shall be treated as revoked with the consent of the Secretary of the Treasury if the taxpayer makes an election under section 41(c)(5) of such Code (as added by this subsection) for such year.

"(3) Effective date.—Except as provided in paragraph (4), the amendments made by this subsection [amending this section] shall apply to taxable years ending after December 31, 2006.

"(4) Transition rule for noncalendar taxable years.—

"(A) In general.—In the case of a specified transitional taxable year for which an election under section 41(c)(5) of the Internal Revenue Code of 1986 (as added by this subsection) applies, the credit determined under section 41(a)(1) of such Code shall be equal to the sum of—

"(i) the applicable 2006 percentage multiplied by the amount determined under section 41(a)(1) of such Code (as in effect for taxable years ending on December 31, 2006), plus

"(ii) the applicable 2007 percentage multiplied by the amount determined under section 41(c)(5) of such Code (as in effect for taxable years ending on January 1, 2007).

"(B) Definitions and special rules.—For purposes of subparagraph (A)—

"(i) Definitions.—Terms used in this paragraph which are also used in subsection (b)(3) [set out above] shall have the respective meanings given such terms in such subsection.

"(ii) Dual elections permitted.—Elections under paragraphs (4) and (5) of section 41(c) of such Code may both apply for the specified transitional taxable year.

"(iii) Deferral of deemed election revocation.—Any election under section 41(c)(4) of the Internal Revenue Code of 1986 treated as revoked under paragraph (2) shall be treated as revoked for the taxable year after the specified transitional taxable year."

EFFECTIVE DATE OF 2005 AMENDMENTS

Amendment by Pub. L. 109–135 effective as if included in the provision of the Energy Policy Act of 2005, Pub. L. 109–58, to which such amendment relates, see section 402(m)(1) of Pub. L. 109–135, set out as an Effective and Termination Dates of 2005 Amendments note under section 23 of this title.

Pub. L. 109–58, title XIII, §1351(c), Aug. 8, 2005, 119 Stat. 1058, provided that: "The amendments made by this section [amending this section] shall apply to amounts paid or incurred after the date of the enactment of this Act [Aug. 8, 2005], in taxable years ending after such date."

Effective Date of 2004 Amendment

Pub. L. 108–311, title III, §301(b), Oct. 4, 2004, 118 Stat. 1178, provided that: "The amendments made by this section [amending this section and section 45C of this title] shall apply to amounts paid or incurred after June 30, 2004."

Effective Date of 1999 Amendment

Pub. L. 106–170, title V, §502(a)(3), Dec. 17, 1999, 113 Stat. 1919, provided that: "The amendments made by this subsection [amending this section and section 45C of this title] shall apply to amounts paid or incurred after June 30, 1999."

Pub. L. 106–170, title V, §502(b)(2), Dec. 17, 1999, 113 Stat. 1919, provided that: "The amendments made by this subsection [amending this section] shall apply to taxable years beginning after June 30, 1999."

Pub. L. 106–170, title V, §502(c)(3), Dec. 17, 1999, 113 Stat. 1920, provided that: "The amendments made by this subsection [amending this section and section 280C of this title] shall apply to amounts paid or incurred after June 30, 1999."

Effective Date of 1998 Amendment

Pub. L. 105–277, div. J, title I, §1001(c), Oct. 21, 1998, 112 Stat. 2681–888, provided that: "The amendments made by this section [amending this section and section 45C of this title] shall apply to amounts paid or incurred after June 30, 1998."

Effective Date of 1997 Amendment

Pub. L. 105–34, title VI, §601(c), Aug. 5, 1997, 111 Stat. 862, provided that: "The amendments made by this section [amending this section and section 45C of this title] shall apply to amounts paid or incurred after May 31, 1997."

Effective Date of 1996 Amendment

Amendment by section 1201(e)(1), (4) of Pub. L. 104–188 applicable to individuals who begin work for the employer after Sept. 30, 1996, see section 1201(g) of Pub. L. 104–188, set out as a note under section 38 of this title.

Pub. L. 104–188, title I, §1204(f), Aug. 20, 1996, 110 Stat. 1775, provided that:

"(1) In general.—Except as provided in paragraph (2), the amendments made by this section [amending this section and section 28 [now 45C] of this title] shall apply to taxable years ending after June 30, 1996.

"(2) Subsections (c) and (d).—The amendments made by subsections (c) and (d) [amending this section] shall apply to taxable years beginning after June 30, 1996.

"(3) Estimated tax.—The amendments made by this section shall not be taken into account under section 6654 or 6655 of the Internal Revenue Code of 1986 (relating to failure to pay estimated tax) in determining the amount of any installment required to be paid for a taxable year beginning in 1997."

Effective Date of 1993 Amendment

Amendment by section 13111(a)(1) of Pub. L. 103–66 applicable to taxable years ending after June 30, 1992, see section 13111(c) of Pub. L. 103–66, set out as a note under section 45C of this title.

Pub. L. 103–66, title XIII, §13112(c), Aug. 10, 1993, 107 Stat. 422, provided that: "The amendments made by this section [amending this section] shall apply to taxable years beginning after December 31, 1993."

Amendment by section 13201(b)(3)(C) of Pub. L. 103–66 applicable to taxable years beginning after Dec. 31, 1992, see section 13201(c) of Pub. L. 103–66, set out as a note under section 1 of this title.

Effective Date of 1991 Amendment

Amendment by Pub. L. 102–227 applicable to taxable years ending after Dec. 31, 1991, see section 102(c) of Pub. L. 102–227, set out as a note under section 45C of this title.

Effective Date of 1990 Amendment

Amendment by section 11101(d)(1)(C) of Pub. L. 101–508 applicable to taxable years beginning after Dec. 31, 1990, see section 11101(e) of Pub. L. 101–508, set out as a note under section 1 of this title.

Amendment by section 11402(a) of Pub. L. 101–508 applicable to taxable years beginning after Dec. 31, 1989, see section 11402(c) of Pub. L. 101–508, set out as a note under section 45C of this title.

Effective Date of 1989 Amendment

Pub. L. 101–239, title VII, §7110(e), Dec. 19, 1989, 103 Stat. 2326, provided that: "The amendments made by this section [amending this section and sections 28, 174, 196, and 280C of this title] (other than subsection (a) [amending this section and section 28 of this title]) shall apply to taxable years beginning after December 31, 1989."

Amendment by section 7814(e)(2)(C) of Pub. L. 101–239 effective, except as otherwise provided, as if included in the provision of the Technical and Miscellaneous Revenue Act of 1988, Pub. L. 100–647, to which such amendment relates, see section 7817 of Pub. L. 101–239, set out as a note under section 1 of this title.

Effective Date of 1988 Amendment

Amendment by section 1002(h)(1) of Pub. L. 100–647 effective, except as otherwise provided, as if included in the provision of the Tax Reform Act of 1986, Pub. L. 99–514, to which such amendment relates, see section 1019(a) of Pub. L. 100–647, set out as a note under section 1 of this title.

Pub. L. 100–647, title IV, §4008(d), Nov. 10, 1988, 102 Stat. 3653, provided that: "The amendments made by this section [amending this section and sections 28, 196, 280C, and 6501 of this title] shall apply to taxable years beginning after December 31, 1988."

Effective Date of 1986 Amendment

Pub. L. 99–514, title II, §231(g), Oct. 22, 1986, 100 Stat. 2180, provided that:

"(1) In general.—Except as provided in this subsection (2), the amendments made by this section [amending this section and sections 28, 38, 39, 108, 170, 280C, 381, 936, 6411, and 6511 of this title, renumbering former section 30 of this title as this section, and enacting and amending provisions set out as notes under this section] shall apply to taxable years beginning after December 31, 1985.

"(2) Subsection (a).—The amendments made by subsection (a) [amending this section and provisions set out as a note under this section] shall apply to taxable years ending after December 31, 1985.

"(3) Basic research.—Section 41(a)(2) of the Internal Revenue Code of 1986 (as added by this section), and the amendments made by subsection (c)(2) [amending this section], shall apply to taxable years beginning after December 31, 1986."

Amendment by section 1847(b)(1) of Pub. L. 99–514 effective, except as otherwise provided, as if included in the provisions of the Tax Reform Act of 1984, Pub. L. 98–369, div. A, to which such amendment relates, see section 1881 of Pub. L. 99–514, set out as a note under section 48 of this title.

Effective Date of 1984 Amendment

Amendment by section 474(i)(1) of Pub. L. 98–369 applicable to taxable years beginning after Dec. 31, 1983, and to carrybacks from such years, see section 475(a) of Pub. L. 98–369, set out as a note under section 21 of this title.

Amendment by section 612(e)(1) of Pub. L. 98–369 applicable to interest paid or accrued after Dec. 31, 1984, on indebtedness incurred after Dec. 31, 1984, see section 612(g) of Pub. L. 98–369, set out as an Effective Date note under section 25 of this title.

Pub. L. 97–448, title I, §102(h)(2), Jan. 12, 1983, 96 Stat. 2372, provided that the amendment made by that section is effective only with respect to amounts paid or incurred after March 31, 1982.

EFFECTIVE DATE OF 1982 AMENDMENT

Amendment by Pub. L. 97–354 applicable to taxable years beginning after Dec. 31, 1982, see section 6(a) of Pub. L. 97–354, set out as an Effective Date note under section 1361 of this title.

EFFECTIVE DATE

Pub. L. 97–34, title II, §221(d), Aug. 13, 1981, 95 Stat. 241, as amended by Pub. L. 99–514, §2, title II, §231(a)(2), Oct. 22, 1986, 100 Stat. 2095, 2173, provided that:

"(1) In general.—The amendments made by this section [enacting this section and amending sections 55, 381, 383, 6096, 6411, and 6511 of this title] shall apply to amounts paid or incurred after June 30, 1981.

"(2) Transitional rule.—

"(A) In general.—If, with respect to the first taxable year to which the amendments made by this section apply and which ends in 1981 or 1982, the taxpayer may only take into account qualified research expenses paid or incurred during a portion of such taxable year, the amount of the qualified research expenses taken into account for the base period of such taxable year shall be the amount which bears the same ratio to the total qualified research expenses for such base period as the number of months in such portion of such taxable year bears to the total number of months in such taxable year.

"(B) Definitions.—For purposes of the preceding sentence, the terms 'qualified research expenses' and 'base period' have the meanings given to such terms by section 44F [now 41] of the Internal Revenue Code of 1986 [formerly I.R.C. 1954] (as added by this section)."

SAVINGS PROVISION

For provisions that nothing in amendment by section 401(b)(6) of Pub. L. 115–141 be construed to affect treatment of certain transactions occurring, property acquired, or items of income, loss, deduction, or credit taken into account prior to Mar. 23, 2018, for purposes of determining liability for tax for periods ending after Mar. 23, 2018, see section 401(e) of Pub. L. 115–141, set out as a note under section 23 of this title.

SPECIAL RULE FOR ELECTIONS UNDER EXPIRED PROVISIONS

Pub. L. 109–432, div. A, title I, §123, Dec. 20, 2006, 120 Stat. 2944, provided that:

"(a) Research Credit Elections.—In the case of any taxable year ending after December 31, 2005, and before the date of the enactment of this Act [Dec. 20, 2006], any election under section 41(c)(4) or section 280C(c)(3)(C) [now 280C(c)(2)(C)] of the Internal Revenue Code of 1986 shall be treated as having been timely made for such taxable year if such election is made not later than the later of April 15, 2007, or such time as the Secretary of the Treasury, or his designee, may specify. Such election shall be made in the manner prescribed by such Secretary or designee.

"(b) Other Elections.—Except as otherwise provided by such Secretary or designee, a rule similar to the rule of subsection (a) shall apply with respect to elections under any other expired provision of the Internal Revenue Code of 1986 the applicability of which is extended by reason of the amendments made by this title [amending this section and sections 32, 45A, 45C, 45D, 51, 54, 62, 164, 168, 170, 198, 220, 222, 613A, 1397E, 1400, 1400A to 1400C, 1400F, 1400N, 6103, 7608, 7652, and 9812 of this title, section 1185a of Title 29, Labor, and section 300gg–5 of Title 42, The Public Health and Welfare, and repealing section 51A of this title]."

SPECIAL RULE FOR CREDIT ATTRIBUTABLE TO SUSPENSION PERIODS

Pub. L. 106–170, title V, §502(d), Dec. 17, 1999, 113 Stat. 1920, provided that:

"(1) In general.—For purposes of the Internal Revenue Code of 1986, the credit determined under section 41 of such Code which is otherwise allowable under such Code—

"(A) shall not be taken into account prior to October 1, 2000, to the extent such credit is attributable to the first suspension period; and

"(B) shall not be taken into account prior to October 1, 2001, to the extent such credit is attributable to the second suspension period.

On or after the earliest date that an amount of credit may be taken into account, such amount may be taken into account through the filing of an amended return, an application for expedited refund, an adjustment of estimated taxes, or other means allowed by such Code.

"(2) Suspension periods.—For purposes of this subsection—

"(A) the first suspension period is the period beginning on July 1, 1999, and ending on September 30, 2000; and

"(B) the second suspension period is the period beginning on October 1, 2000, and ending on September 30, 2001.

"(3) Expedited refunds.—

"(A) In general.—If there is an overpayment of tax with respect to a taxable year by reason of paragraph (1), the taxpayer may file an application for a tentative refund of such overpayment. Such application shall be in such manner and form, and contain such information, as the Secretary may prescribe.

"(B) Deadline for applications.—Subparagraph (A) shall apply only to an application filed before the date which is 1 year after the close of the suspension period to which the application relates.

"(C) Allowance of adjustments.—Not later than 90 days after the date on which an application is filed under this paragraph, the Secretary shall—

"(i) review the application;

"(ii) determine the amount of the overpayment; and

"(iii) apply, credit, or refund such overpayment,

in a manner similar to the manner provided in section 6411(b) of such Code.

"(D) Consolidated returns.—The provisions of section 6411(c) of such Code shall apply to an adjustment under this paragraph in such manner as the Secretary may provide.

"(4) Credit attributable to suspension period.—

"(A) In general.—For purposes of this subsection, in the case of a taxable year which includes a portion of the suspension period, the amount of credit determined under section 41 of such Code for such taxable year which is attributable to such period is the amount which bears the same ratio to the amount of credit determined under such section 41 for such taxable year as the number of months in the suspension period which are during such taxable year bears to the number of months in such taxable year.

"(B) Waiver of estimated tax penalties.—No addition to tax shall be made under section 6654 or 6655 of such Code for any period before July 1, 1999, with respect to any underpayment of tax imposed by such Code to the extent such underpayment was created or increased by reason of subparagraph (A).

"(5) Secretary.—For purposes of this subsection, the term 'Secretary' means the Secretary of the Treasury (or such Secretary's delegate)."

SPECIAL RULES FOR TAXABLE YEARS BEGINNING BEFORE OCT. 1, 1990, AND ENDING AFTER SEPT. 30, 1990

Pub. L. 101–239, title VII, §7110(a)(2), Dec. 19, 1989, 103 Stat. 2323, which set forth the method of determining the amount treated as qualified research expenses for taxable years beginning before Oct. 1, 1990, and ending after Sept. 30, 1990, was repealed by Pub. L. 101–508, title XI, §11402(b)(1), Nov. 5, 1990, 104 Stat. 1388–473.

[Pub. L. 104–188, title I, §1702(d)(1), Aug. 20, 1996, 110 Stat. 1870, provided that: "Notwithstanding section 11402(c) of the Revenue Reconciliation Act of 1990 [Pub. L. 101–508, set out as a note under section 45C of this title], the amendment made by section 11402(b)(1) of such Act [repealing section 7110(a)(2) of Pub. L. 101–239, formerly set out as a note above] shall apply to taxable years ending after December 31, 1989."]

§42. Low-income housing credit

(a) In general

For purposes of section 38, the amount of the low-income housing credit determined under this section for any taxable year in the credit period shall be an amount equal to—

(1) the applicable percentage of

(2) the qualified basis of each qualified low-income building.

(b) Applicable percentage: 70 percent present value credit for certain new buildings; 30 percent present value credit for certain other buildings

(1) Determination of applicable percentage

For purposes of this section—

(A) In general

The term "applicable percentage" means, with respect to any building, the appropriate percentage prescribed by the Secretary for the earlier of—

(i) the month in which such building is placed in service, or

(ii) at the election of the taxpayer—

(I) the month in which the taxpayer and the housing credit agency enter into an agreement with respect to such building (which is binding on such agency, the taxpayer, and all successors in interest) as to the housing credit dollar amount to be allocated to such building, or

(II) in the case of any building to which subsection (h)(4)(B) applies, the month in which the tax-exempt obligations are issued.

A month may be elected under clause (ii) only if the election is made not later than the 5th day after the close of such month. Such an election, once made, shall be irrevocable.

(B) Method of prescribing percentages

The percentages prescribed by the Secretary for any month shall be percentages which will yield over a 10-year period amounts of credit under subsection (a) which have a present value equal to—

(i) 70 percent of the qualified basis of a new building which is not federally subsidized for the taxable year, and

(ii) 30 percent of the qualified basis of a building not described in clause (i).

(C) Method of discounting

The present value under subparagraph (B) shall be determined—

(i) as of the last day of the 1st year of the 10-year period referred to in subparagraph (B),

(ii) by using a discount rate equal to 72 percent of the average of the annual Federal mid-term rate and the annual Federal long-term rate applicable under section 1274(d)(1) to the month applicable under clause (i) or (ii) of subparagraph (A) and compounded annually, and

(iii) by assuming that the credit allowable under this section for any year is received on the last day of such year.

(2) Minimum credit rate for non-federally subsidized new buildings

In the case of any new building—

(A) which is placed in service by the taxpayer after the date of the enactment of this paragraph, and

(B) which is not federally subsidized for the taxable year,

the applicable percentage shall not be less than 9 percent.

(3) Minimum credit rate

In the case of any new or existing building to which paragraph (2) does not apply and which is placed in service by the taxpayer after December 31, 2020, the applicable percentage shall not be less than 4 percent.

(4) Cross references

(A) For treatment of certain rehabilitation expenditures as separate new buildings, see subsection (e).

(B) For determination of applicable percentage for increases in qualified basis after the 1st year of the credit period, see subsection (f)(3).

(C) For authority of housing credit agency to limit applicable percentage and qualified basis which may be taken into account under this section with respect to any building, see subsection (h)(7).

(c) Qualified basis; qualified low-income building

For purposes of this section—

(1) Qualified basis

(A) Determination

The qualified basis of any qualified low-income building for any taxable year is an amount equal to—

(i) the applicable fraction (determined as of the close of such taxable year) of

(ii) the eligible basis of such building (determined under subsection (d)(5)).

(B) Applicable fraction

For purposes of subparagraph (A), the term "applicable fraction" means the smaller of the unit fraction or the floor space fraction.

(C) Unit fraction

For purposes of subparagraph (B), the term "unit fraction" means the fraction—

(i) the numerator of which is the number of low-income units in the building, and

(ii) the denominator of which is the number of residential rental units (whether or not occupied) in such building.

(D) Floor space fraction

For purposes of subparagraph (B), the term "floor space fraction" means the fraction—

(i) the numerator of which is the total floor space of the low-income units in such building, and

(ii) the denominator of which is the total floor space of the residential rental units (whether or not occupied) in such building.

(E) Qualified basis to include portion of building used to provide supportive services for homeless

In the case of a qualified low-income building described in subsection (i)(3)(B)(iii), the qualified basis of such building for any taxable year shall be increased by the lesser of—

(i) so much of the eligible basis of such building as is used throughout the year to provide supportive services designed to assist tenants in locating and retaining permanent housing, or

(ii) 20 percent of the qualified basis of such building (determined without regard to this subparagraph).

(2) Qualified low-income building

The term "qualified low-income building" means any building—

(A) which is part of a qualified low-income housing project at all times during the period—

(i) beginning on the 1st day in the compliance period on which such building is part of such a project, and

(ii) ending on the last day of the compliance period with respect to such building, and

(B) to which the amendments made by section 201(a) of the Tax Reform Act of 1986 apply.

(d) Eligible basis

For purposes of this section—

(1) New buildings

The eligible basis of a new building is its adjusted basis as of the close of the 1st taxable year of the credit period.

(2) Existing buildings

(A) In general

The eligible basis of an existing building is—

(i) in the case of a building which meets the requirements of subparagraph (B), its adjusted basis as of the close of the 1st taxable year of the credit period, and

(ii) zero in any other case.

(B) Requirements

A building meets the requirements of this subparagraph if—

(i) the building is acquired by purchase (as defined in section 179(d)(2)),

(ii) there is a period of at least 10 years between the date of its acquisition by the taxpayer and the date the building was last placed in service,

(iii) the building was not previously placed in service by the taxpayer or by any person who was a related person with respect to the taxpayer as of the time previously placed in service, and

(iv) except as provided in subsection (f)(5), a credit is allowable under subsection (a) by reason of subsection (e) with respect to the building.

(C) Adjusted basis

For purposes of subparagraph (A), the adjusted basis of any building shall not include so much of the basis of such building as is determined by reference to the basis of other property held at any time by the person acquiring the building.

(D) Special rules for subparagraph (B)

(i) Special rules for certain transfers

For purposes of determining under subparagraph (B)(ii) when a building was last placed in service, there shall not be taken into account any placement in service—

(I) in connection with the acquisition of the building in a transaction in which the basis of the building in the hands of the person acquiring it is determined in whole or in part by reference to the adjusted basis of such building in the hands of the person from whom acquired,

(II) by a person whose basis in such building is determined under section 1014(a) (relating to property acquired from a decedent),

(III) by any governmental unit or qualified nonprofit organization (as defined in subsection (h)(5)) if the requirements of subparagraph (B)(ii) are met with respect to the placement in service by such unit or organization and all the income from such property is exempt from Federal income taxation,

(IV) by any person who acquired such building by foreclosure (or by instrument in lieu of foreclosure) of any purchase-money security interest held by such person if the requirements of subparagraph (B)(ii) are met with respect to the placement in service by such person and such building is resold within 12 months after the date such building is placed in service by such person after such foreclosure, or

(V) of a single-family residence by any individual who owned and used such residence for no other purpose than as his principal residence.

(ii) Related person

For purposes of subparagraph (B)(iii), a person (hereinafter in this subclause referred to as the "related person") is related to any person if the related person bears a relationship to such person specified in section 267(b) or 707(b)(1), or the related person and such person are engaged in trades or businesses under common control (within the meaning of subsections (a) and (b) of section 52).

(3) Eligible basis reduced where disproportionate standards for units

(A) In general

Except as provided in subparagraph (B), the eligible basis of any building shall be reduced by an amount equal to the portion of the adjusted basis of the building which is attributable to residential rental units in the building which are not low-income units and which are above the average quality standard of the low-income units in the building.

(B) Exception where taxpayer elects to exclude excess costs

(i) In general

Subparagraph (A) shall not apply with respect to a residential rental unit in a building which is not a low-income unit if—

(I) the excess described in clause (ii) with respect to such unit is not greater than 15 percent of the cost described in clause (ii)(II), and

(II) the taxpayer elects to exclude from the eligible basis of such building the excess described in clause (ii) with respect to such unit.

(ii) Excess

The excess described in this clause with respect to any unit is the excess of—

(I) the cost of such unit, over

(II) the amount which would be the cost of such unit if the average cost per square foot of low-income units in the building were substituted for the cost per square foot of such unit.

The Secretary may by regulation provide for the determination of the excess under this clause on a basis other than square foot costs.

(4) Special rules relating to determination of adjusted basis

For purposes of this subsection—

(A) In general

Except as provided in subparagraphs (B) and (C), the adjusted basis of any building shall be determined without regard to the adjusted basis of any property which is not residential rental property.

(B) Basis of property in common areas, etc., included

The adjusted basis of any building shall be determined by taking into account the adjusted basis of property (of a character subject to the allowance for depreciation) used in common areas or provided as comparable amenities to all residential rental units in such building.

(C) Inclusion of basis of property used to provide services for certain nontenants

(i) In general

The adjusted basis of any building located in a qualified census tract (as defined in paragraph (5)(B)(ii)) shall be determined by taking into account the adjusted basis of property (of a character subject to the allowance for depreciation and not otherwise taken into account) used throughout the taxable year in providing any community service facility.

(ii) Limitation

The increase in the adjusted basis of any building which is taken into account by reason of clause (i) shall not exceed the sum of—

(I) 25 percent of so much of the eligible basis of the qualified low-income housing project of which it is a part as does not exceed $15,000,000, plus

(II) 10 percent of so much of the eligible basis of such project as is not taken into account under subclause (I).

For purposes of the preceding sentence, all community service facilities which are part of the same qualified low-income housing project shall be treated as one facility.

(iii) Community service facility

For purposes of this subparagraph, the term "community service facility" means any facility designed to serve primarily individuals whose income is 60 percent or less of area median income (within the meaning of subsection (g)(1)(B)).

(D) No reduction for depreciation

The adjusted basis of any building shall be determined without regard to paragraphs (2) and (3) of section 1016(a).

(5) Special rules for determining eligible basis

(A) Federal grants not taken into account in determining eligible basis

The eligible basis of a building shall not include any costs financed with the proceeds of a federally funded grant.

(B) Increase in credit for buildings in high cost areas

(i) In general

In the case of any building located in a qualified census tract or difficult development area which is designated for purposes of this subparagraph—

(I) in the case of a new building, the eligible basis of such building shall be 130 percent of such basis determined without regard to this subparagraph, and

(II) in the case of an existing building, the rehabilitation expenditures taken into account under subsection (e) shall be 130 percent of such expenditures determined without regard to this subparagraph.

(ii) Qualified census tract

(I) In general

The term "qualified census tract" means any census tract which is designated by the Secretary of Housing and Urban Development and, for the most recent year for which census data are available on household income in such tract, either in which 50 percent or more of the households have an income which is less than 60 percent of the area median gross income for such year or which has a poverty rate of at least 25 percent. If the Secretary of Housing and Urban Development determines that sufficient data for any period are not available to apply this clause on the basis of census tracts, such Secretary shall apply this clause for such period on the basis of enumeration districts.

(II) Limit on MSA's designated

The portion of a metropolitan statistical area which may be designated for purposes of this subparagraph shall not exceed an area having 20 percent of the population of such metropolitan statistical area.

(III) Determination of areas

For purposes of this clause, each metropolitan statistical area shall be treated as a separate area and all nonmetropolitan areas in a State shall be treated as 1 area.

(iii) Difficult development areas

(I) In general

The term "difficult development areas" means any area designated by the Secretary of Housing and Urban Development as an area which has high construction, land, and utility costs relative to area median gross income.

(II) Limit on areas designated

The portions of metropolitan statistical areas which may be designated for purposes of this subparagraph shall not exceed an aggregate area having 20 percent of the population of such metropolitan statistical areas. A comparable rule shall apply to nonmetropolitan areas.

(iv) Special rules and definitions

For purposes of this subparagraph—

(I) population shall be determined on the basis of the most recent decennial census for which data are available,

(II) area median gross income shall be determined in accordance with subsection (g)(4),

(III) the term "metropolitan statistical area" has the same meaning as when used in section 143(k)(2)(B), and

(IV) the term "nonmetropolitan area" means any county (or portion thereof) which is not within a metropolitan statistical area.

(v) Buildings designated by State housing credit agency

Any building which is designated by the State housing credit agency as requiring the increase in credit under this subparagraph in order for such building to be financially feasible as part of a qualified low-income housing project shall be treated for purposes of this subparagraph as located in a difficult development area which is designated for purposes of this subparagraph. The preceding sentence shall not apply to any building if paragraph (1) of subsection (h) does not apply to any portion of the eligible basis of such building by reason of paragraph (4) of such subsection.

(6) Credit allowable for certain buildings acquired during 10-year period described in paragraph (2)(B)(ii)

(A) In general

Paragraph (2)(B)(ii) shall not apply to any federally- or State-assisted building.

(B) Buildings acquired from insured depository institutions in default

On application by the taxpayer, the Secretary may waive paragraph (2)(B)(ii) with respect to any building acquired from an insured depository institution in default (as defined in section 3 of the Federal Deposit Insurance Act) or from a receiver or conservator of such an institution.

(C) Federally- or State-assisted building

For purposes of this paragraph—

(i) Federally-assisted building

The term "federally-assisted building" means any building which is substantially assisted, financed, or operated under section 8 of the United States Housing Act of 1937, section 221(d)(3), 221(d)(4), or 236 of the National Housing Act, section 515 of the Housing Act of 1949, or any other housing program administered by the Department of Housing and Urban Development or by the Rural Housing Service of the Department of Agriculture.

(ii) State-assisted building

The term "State-assisted building" means any building which is substantially assisted, financed, or operated under any State law similar in purposes to any of the laws referred to in clause (i).

(7) Acquisition of building before end of prior compliance period

(A) In general

Under regulations prescribed by the Secretary, in the case of a building described in subparagraph (B) (or interest therein) which is acquired by the taxpayer—

(i) paragraph (2)(B) shall not apply, but

(ii) the credit allowable by reason of subsection (a) to the taxpayer for any period after such acquisition shall be equal to the amount of credit which would have been allowable under subsection (a) for such period to the prior owner referred to in subparagraph (B) had such owner not disposed of the building.

(B) Description of building

A building is described in this subparagraph if—

(i) a credit was allowed by reason of subsection (a) to any prior owner of such building, and

(ii) the taxpayer acquired such building before the end of the compliance period for such building with respect to such prior owner (determined without regard to any disposition by such prior owner).

(e) Rehabilitation expenditures treated as separate new building

(1) In general

Rehabilitation expenditures paid or incurred by the taxpayer with respect to any building shall be treated for purposes of this section as a separate new building.

(2) Rehabilitation expenditures

For purposes of paragraph (1)—

(A) In general

The term "rehabilitation expenditures" means amounts chargeable to capital account and incurred for property (or additions or improvements to property) of a character subject to the allowance for depreciation in connection with the rehabilitation of a building.

(B) Cost of acquisition, etc., not included

Such term does not include the cost of acquiring any building (or interest therein) or any amount not permitted to be taken into account under paragraph (3) or (4) of subsection (d).

(3) Minimum expenditures to qualify

(A) In general

Paragraph (1) shall apply to rehabilitation expenditures with respect to any building only if—

(i) the expenditures are allocable to 1 or more low-income units or substantially benefit such units, and

(ii) the amount of such expenditures during any 24-month period meets the requirements of whichever of the following subclauses requires the greater amount of such expenditures:

(I) The requirement of this subclause is met if such amount is not less than 20 percent of the adjusted basis of the building (determined as of the 1st day of such period and without regard to paragraphs (2) and (3) of section 1016(a)).

(II) The requirement of this subclause is met if the qualified basis attributable to such amount, when divided by the number of low-income units in the building, is $6,000 or more.

(B) Exception from 10 percent rehabilitation

In the case of a building acquired by the taxpayer from a governmental unit, at the election of the taxpayer, subparagraph (A)(ii)(I) shall not apply and the credit under this section for such rehabilitation expenditures shall be determined using the percentage applicable under subsection (b)(2)(B)(ii).

(C) Date of determination

The determination under subparagraph (A) shall be made as of the close of the 1st taxable year in the credit period with respect to such expenditures.

(D) Inflation adjustment

In the case of any expenditures which are treated under paragraph (4) as placed in service during any calendar year after 2009, the $6,000 amount in subparagraph (A)(ii)(II) shall be increased by an amount equal to—

(i) such dollar amount, multiplied by

(ii) the cost-of-living adjustment determined under section 1(f)(3) for such calendar year by substituting "calendar year 2008" for "calendar year 2016" in subparagraph (A)(ii) thereof.

Any increase under the preceding sentence which is not a multiple of $100 shall be rounded to the nearest multiple of $100.

(4) Special rules

For purposes of applying this section with respect to expenditures which are treated as a separate building by reason of this subsection—

(A) such expenditures shall be treated as placed in service at the close of the 24-month period referred to in paragraph (3)(A), and

(B) the applicable fraction under subsection (c)(1) shall be the applicable fraction for the building (without regard to paragraph (1)) with respect to which the expenditures were incurred.

Nothing in subsection (d)(2) shall prevent a credit from being allowed by reason of this subsection.

(5) No double counting

Rehabilitation expenditures may, at the election of the taxpayer, be taken into account under this subsection or subsection (d)(2)(A)(i) but not under both such subsections.

(6) Regulations to apply subsection with respect to group of units in building

The Secretary may prescribe regulations, consistent with the purposes of this subsection, treating a group of units with respect to which rehabilitation expenditures are incurred as a separate new building.

(f) Definition and special rules relating to credit period

(1) Credit period defined

For purposes of this section, the term "credit period" means, with respect to any building, the period of 10 taxable years beginning with—

(A) the taxable year in which the building is placed in service, or

(B) at the election of the taxpayer, the succeeding taxable year,

but only if the building is a qualified low-income building as of the close of the 1st year of such period. The election under subparagraph (B), once made, shall be irrevocable.

(2) Special rule for 1st year of credit period

(A) In general

The credit allowable under subsection (a) with respect to any building for the 1st taxable year of the credit period shall be determined by substituting for the applicable fraction under subsection (c)(1) the fraction—

(i) the numerator of which is the sum of the applicable fractions determined under subsection (c)(1) as of the close of each full month of such year during which such building was in service, and

(ii) the denominator of which is 12.

(B) Disallowed 1st year credit allowed in 11th year

Any reduction by reason of subparagraph (A) in the credit allowable (without regard to subparagraph (A)) for the 1st taxable year of the credit period shall be allowable under subsection (a) for the 1st taxable year following the credit period.

(3) Determination of applicable percentage with respect to increases in qualified basis after 1st year of credit period

(A) In general

In the case of any building which was a qualified low-income building as of the close of the 1st year of the credit period, if—

(i) as of the close of any taxable year in the compliance period (after the 1st year of the credit period) the qualified basis of such building exceeds

(ii) the qualified basis of such building as of the close of the 1st year of the credit period,

the applicable percentage which shall apply under subsection (a) for the taxable year to such excess shall be the percentage equal to 2/3 of the applicable percentage which (after the application of subsection (h)) would but for this paragraph apply to such basis.

(B) 1st year computation applies

A rule similar to the rule of paragraph (2)(A) shall apply to any increase in qualified basis to which subparagraph (A) applies for the 1st year of such increase.

(4) Dispositions of property

If a building (or an interest therein) is disposed of during any year for which credit is allowable under subsection (a), such credit shall be allocated between the parties on the basis of the number of days during such year the building (or interest) was held by each. In any such case, proper adjustments shall be made in the application of subsection (j).

(5) Credit period for existing buildings not to begin before rehabilitation credit allowed

(A) In general

The credit period for an existing building shall not begin before the 1st taxable year of the credit period for rehabilitation expenditures with respect to the building.

(B) Acquisition credit allowed for certain buildings not allowed a rehabilitation credit

(i) In general

In the case of a building described in clause (ii)—

(I) subsection (d)(2)(B)(iv) shall not apply, and

(II) the credit period for such building shall not begin before the taxable year which would be the 1st taxable year of the credit period for rehabilitation expenditures with respect to the building under the modifications described in clause (ii)(II).

(ii) Building described

A building is described in this clause if—

(I) a waiver is granted under subsection (d)(6)(B) with respect to the acquisition of the building, and

(II) a credit would be allowed for rehabilitation expenditures with respect to such building if subsection (e)(3)(A)(ii)(I) did not apply and if the dollar amount in effect under subsection (e)(3)(A)(ii)(II) were two-thirds of such amount.

(g) Qualified low-income housing project

For purposes of this section—

(1) In general

The term "qualified low-income housing project" means any project for residential rental property if the project meets the requirements of subparagraph (A), (B), or (C) whichever is elected by the taxpayer:

(A) 20—50 test

The project meets the requirements of this subparagraph if 20 percent or more of the residential units in such project are both rent-restricted and occupied by individuals whose income is 50 percent or less of area median gross income.

(B) 40—60 test

The project meets the requirements of this subparagraph if 40 percent or more of the residential units in such project are both rent-restricted and occupied by individuals whose income is 60 percent or less of area median gross income.

(C) Average income test

(i) In general

The project meets the minimum requirements of this subparagraph if 40 percent or more (25 percent or more in the case of a project described in section 142(d)(6)) of the residential units in such project are both rent-restricted and occupied by individuals whose income does not exceed the imputed income limitation designated by the taxpayer with respect to the respective unit.

(ii) Special rules relating to income limitation

For purposes of clause (i)—

(I) Designation

The taxpayer shall designate the imputed income limitation of each unit taken into account under such clause.

(II) Average test

The average of the imputed income limitations designated under subclause (I) shall not exceed 60 percent of area median gross income.

(III) 10-percent increments

The designated imputed income limitation of any unit under subclause (I) shall be 20 percent, 30 percent, 40 percent, 50 percent, 60 percent, 70 percent, or 80 percent of area median gross income.

Any election under this paragraph, once made, shall be irrevocable. For purposes of this paragraph, any property shall not be treated as failing to be residential rental property merely because part of the building in which such property is located is used for purposes other than residential rental purposes.

(2) Rent-restricted units

(A) In general

For purposes of paragraph (1), a residential unit is rent-restricted if the gross rent with respect to such unit does not exceed 30 percent of the imputed income limitation applicable to such unit. For purposes of the preceding sentence, the amount of the income limitation under paragraph (1) applicable for any period shall not be less than such limitation applicable for the earliest period the building (which contains the unit) was included in the determination of whether the project is a qualified low-income housing project.

(B) Gross rent

For purposes of subparagraph (A), gross rent—

(i) does not include any payment under section 8 of the United States Housing Act of 1937 or any comparable rental assistance program (with respect to such unit or occupants thereof),

(ii) includes any utility allowance determined by the Secretary after taking into account such determinations under section 8 of the United States Housing Act of 1937,

(iii) does not include any fee for a supportive service which is paid to the owner of the unit (on the basis of the low-income status of the tenant of the unit) by any governmental program of assistance (or by an organization described in section 501(c)(3) and exempt from tax under section 501(a)) if such program (or organization) provides assistance for rent and the amount of assistance provided for rent is not separable from the amount of assistance provided for supportive services, and

(iv) does not include any rental payment to the owner of the unit to the extent such owner pays an equivalent amount to the Farmers' Home Administration under section 515 of the Housing Act of 1949.

For purposes of clause (iii), the term "supportive service" means any service provided under a planned program of services designed to enable residents of a residential rental property to remain independent and avoid placement in a hospital, nursing home, or intermediate care facility for the mentally or physically handicapped. In the case of a single-room occupancy unit or a building described in subsection (i)(3)(B)(iii), such term includes any service provided to assist tenants in locating and retaining permanent housing.

(C) Imputed income limitation applicable to unit

For purposes of this paragraph, the imputed income limitation applicable to a unit is the income limitation which would apply under paragraph (1) to individuals occupying the unit if the number of individuals occupying the unit were as follows:

(i) In the case of a unit which does not have a separate bedroom, 1 individual.

(ii) In the case of a unit which has 1 or more separate bedrooms, 1.5 individuals for each separate bedroom.

In the case of a project with respect to which a credit is allowable by reason of this section and for which financing is provided by a bond described in section 142(a)(7), the imputed income limitation shall apply in lieu of the otherwise applicable income limitation for purposes of applying section 142(d)(4)(B)(ii).

(D) Treatment of units occupied by individuals whose incomes rise above limit

(i) In general

Except as provided in clauses (ii), (iii), and (iv), notwithstanding an increase in the income of the occupants of a low-income unit above the income limitation applicable under paragraph (1), such unit shall continue to be treated as a low-income unit if the income of such occupants initially met such income limitation and such unit continues to be rent-restricted.

(ii) Rental of next available unit in case of 20–50 or 40–60 test

In the case of a project with respect to which the taxpayer elects the requirements of subparagraph (A) or (B) of paragraph (1), if the income of the occupants of the unit increases above 140 percent of the income limitation applicable under paragraph (1), clause (i) shall cease to apply to such unit if any residential rental unit in the building (of a size comparable to, or smaller than, such unit) is occupied by a new resident whose income exceeds such income limitation.

(iii) Rental of next available unit in case of average income test

In the case of a project with respect to which the taxpayer elects the requirements of subparagraph (C) of paragraph (1), if the income of the occupants of the unit increases above 140 percent of the greater of—

(I) 60 percent of area median gross income, or

(II) the imputed income limitation designated with respect to the unit under paragraph (1)(C)(ii)(I),

clause (i) shall cease to apply to any such unit if any residential rental unit in the building (of a size comparable to, or smaller than, such unit) is occupied by a new resident whose income exceeds the limitation described in clause (v).

(iv) Deep rent skewed projects

In the case of a project described in section 142(d)(4)(B), clause (ii) or (iii), whichever is applicable, shall be applied by substituting "170 percent" for "140 percent", and—

(I) in the case of clause (ii), by substituting "any low-income unit in the building is occupied by a new resident whose income exceeds 40 percent of area median gross income" for "any residential rental unit" and all that follows in such clause, and

(II) in the case of clause (iii), by substituting "any low-income unit in the building is occupied by a new resident whose income exceeds the lesser of 40 percent of area median gross income or the imputed income limitation designated with respect to such unit under paragraph (1)(C)(ii)(I)" for "any residential rental unit" and all that follows in such clause.

(v) Limitation described

For purposes of clause (iii), the limitation described in this clause with respect to any unit is—

(I) the imputed income limitation designated with respect to such unit under paragraph (1)(C)(ii)(I), in the case of a unit which was taken into account as a low-income unit prior to becoming vacant, and

(II) the imputed income limitation which would have to be designated with respect to such unit under such paragraph in order for the project to continue to meet the requirements of paragraph (1)(C)(ii)(II), in the case of any other unit.

(E) Units where Federal rental assistance is reduced as tenant's income increases

If the gross rent with respect to a residential unit exceeds the limitation under subparagraph (A) by reason of the fact that the income of the occupants thereof exceeds the income limitation applicable under paragraph (1), such unit shall, nevertheless, be treated as a rent-restricted unit for purposes of paragraph (1) if—

(i) a Federal rental assistance payment described in subparagraph (B)(i) is made with respect to such unit or its occupants, and

(ii) the sum of such payment and the gross rent with respect to such unit does not exceed the sum of the amount of such payment which would be made and the gross rent which would be payable with respect to such unit if—

(I) the income of the occupants thereof did not exceed the income limitation applicable under paragraph (1), and

(II) such units were rent-restricted within the meaning of subparagraph (A).

The preceding sentence shall apply to any unit only if the result described in clause (ii) is required by Federal statute as of the date of the enactment of this subparagraph and as of the date the Federal rental assistance payment is made.

(3) Date for meeting requirements

(A) In general

Except as otherwise provided in this paragraph, a building shall be treated as a qualified low-income building only if the project (of which such building is a part) meets the requirements of paragraph (1) not later than the close of the 1st year of the credit period for such building.

(B) Buildings which rely on later buildings for qualification

(i) In general

In determining whether a building (hereinafter in this subparagraph referred to as the "prior building") is a qualified low-income building, the taxpayer may take into account 1 or more additional buildings placed in service during the 12-month period described in subparagraph (A) with respect to the prior building only if the taxpayer elects to apply clause (ii) with respect to each additional building taken into account.

(ii) Treatment of elected buildings

In the case of a building which the taxpayer elects to take into account under clause (i), the period under subparagraph (A) for such building shall end at the close of the 12-month period applicable to the prior building.

(iii) Date prior building is treated as placed in service

For purposes of determining the credit period and the compliance period for the prior building, the prior building shall be treated for purposes of this section as placed in service on the most recent date any additional building elected by the taxpayer (with respect to such prior building) was placed in service.

(C) Special rule

A building—

(i) other than the 1st building placed in service as part of a project, and

(ii) other than a building which is placed in service during the 12-month period described in subparagraph (A) with respect to a prior building which becomes a qualified low-income building,

shall in no event be treated as a qualified low-income building unless the project is a qualified low-income housing project (without regard to such building) on the date such building is placed in service.

(D) Projects with more than 1 building must be identified

For purposes of this section, a project shall be treated as consisting of only 1 building unless, before the close of the 1st calendar year in the project period (as defined in subsection (h)(1)(F)(ii)), each building which is (or will be) part of such project is identified in such form and manner as the Secretary may provide.

(4) Certain rules made applicable

Paragraphs (2) (other than subparagraph (A) thereof), (3), (4), (5), (6), and (7) of section 142(d), and section 6652(j), shall apply for purposes of determining whether any project is a qualified low-income housing project and whether any unit is a low-income unit; except that, in applying such provisions for such purposes, the term "gross rent" shall have the meaning given such term by paragraph (2)(B) of this subsection.

(5) Election to treat building after compliance period as not part of a project

For purposes of this section, the taxpayer may elect to treat any building as not part of a qualified low-income housing project for any period beginning after the compliance period for such building.

(6) Special rule where de minimis equity contribution

Property shall not be treated as failing to be residential rental property for purposes of this section merely because the occupant of a residential unit in the project pays (on a voluntary basis) to the lessor a de minimis amount to be held toward the purchase by such occupant of a residential unit in such project if—

(A) all amounts so paid are refunded to the occupant on the cessation of his occupancy of a unit in the project, and

(B) the purchase of the unit is not permitted until after the close of the compliance period with respect to the building in which the unit is located.

Any amount paid to the lessor as described in the preceding sentence shall be included in gross rent under paragraph (2) for purposes of determining whether the unit is rent-restricted.

(7) Scattered site projects

Buildings which would (but for their lack of proximity) be treated as a project for purposes of this section shall be so treated if all of the dwelling units in each of the buildings are rent-restricted (within the meaning of paragraph (2)) residential rental units.

(8) Waiver of certain de minimis errors and recertifications

On application by the taxpayer, the Secretary may waive—

(A) any recapture under subsection (j) in the case of any de minimis error in complying with paragraph (1), or

(B) any annual recertification of tenant income for purposes of this subsection, if the entire building is occupied by low-income tenants.

(9) Clarification of general public use requirement

A project does not fail to meet the general public use requirement solely because of occupancy restrictions or preferences that favor tenants—

(A) with special needs,

(B) who are members of a specified group under a Federal program or State program or policy that supports housing for such a specified group, or

(C) who are involved in artistic or literary activities.

(h) Limitation on aggregate credit allowable with respect to projects located in a State

(1) Credit may not exceed credit amount allocated to building

(A) In general

The amount of the credit determined under this section for any taxable year with respect to any building shall not exceed the housing credit dollar amount allocated to such building under this subsection.

(B) Time for making allocation

Except in the case of an allocation which meets the requirements of subparagraph (C), (D), (E), or (F), an allocation shall be taken into account under subparagraph (A) only if it is made not later than the close of the calendar year in which the building is placed in service.

(C) Exception where binding commitment

An allocation meets the requirements of this subparagraph if there is a binding commitment (not later than the close of the calendar year in which the building is placed in service) by the housing credit agency to allocate a specified housing credit dollar amount to such building beginning in a specified later taxable year.

(D) Exception where increase in qualified basis

(i) In general

An allocation meets the requirements of this subparagraph if such allocation is made not later than the close of the calendar year in which ends the taxable year to which it will 1st apply but only to the extent the amount of such allocation does not exceed the limitation under clause (ii).

(ii) Limitation

The limitation under this clause is the amount of credit allowable under this section (without regard to this subsection) for a taxable year with respect to an increase in the qualified basis of the building equal to the excess of—

(I) the qualified basis of such building as of the close of the 1st taxable year to which such allocation will apply, over

(II) the qualified basis of such building as of the close of the 1st taxable year to which the most recent prior housing credit allocation with respect to such building applied.

(iii) Housing credit dollar amount reduced by full allocation

Notwithstanding clause (i), the full amount of the allocation shall be taken into account under paragraph (2).

(E) Exception where 10 percent of cost incurred

(i) In general

An allocation meets the requirements of this subparagraph if such allocation is made with respect to a qualified building which is placed in service not later than the close of the second calendar year following the calendar year in which the allocation is made.

(ii) Qualified building

For purposes of clause (i), the term "qualified building" means any building which is part of a project if the taxpayer's basis in such project (as of the date which is 1 year after the date that the allocation was made) is more than 10 percent of the taxpayer's reasonably expected basis in such project (as of the close of the second calendar year referred to in clause (i)). Such term does not include any existing building unless a credit is allowable under subsection (e) for rehabilitation expenditures paid or incurred by the taxpayer with respect to such building for a taxable year ending during the second calendar year referred to in clause (i) or the prior taxable year.

(F) Allocation of credit on a project basis

(i) In general

In the case of a project which includes (or will include) more than 1 building, an allocation meets the requirements of this subparagraph if—

(I) the allocation is made to the project for a calendar year during the project period,

(II) the allocation only applies to buildings placed in service during or after the calendar year for which the allocation is made, and

(III) the portion of such allocation which is allocated to any building in such project is specified not later than the close of the calendar year in which the building is placed in service.

(ii) Project period

For purposes of clause (i), the term "project period" means the period—

(I) beginning with the 1st calendar year for which an allocation may be made for the 1st building placed in service as part of such project, and

(II) ending with the calendar year the last building is placed in service as part of such project.

(2) Allocated credit amount to apply to all taxable years ending during or after credit allocation year

Any housing credit dollar amount allocated to any building for any calendar year—

(A) shall apply to such building for all taxable years in the compliance period ending during or after such calendar year, and

(B) shall reduce the aggregate housing credit dollar amount of the allocating agency only for such calendar year.

(3) Housing credit dollar amount for agencies

(A) In general

The aggregate housing credit dollar amount which a housing credit agency may allocate for any calendar year is the portion of the State housing credit ceiling allocated under this paragraph for such calendar year to such agency.

(B) State ceiling initially allocated to State housing credit agencies

Except as provided in subparagraphs (D) and (E), the State housing credit ceiling for each calendar year shall be allocated to the housing credit agency of such State. If there is more than 1 housing credit agency of a State, all such agencies shall be treated as a single agency.

(C) State housing credit ceiling

The State housing credit ceiling applicable to any State for any calendar year shall be an amount equal to the sum of—

(i) the unused State housing credit ceiling (if any) of such State for the preceding calendar year,

(ii) the greater of—

(I) $1.75 multiplied by the State population, or

(II) $2,000,000,

(iii) the amount of State housing credit ceiling returned in the calendar year, plus

(iv) the amount (if any) allocated under subparagraph (D) to such State by the Secretary.

For purposes of clause (i), the unused State housing credit ceiling for any calendar year is the excess (if any) of the sum of the amounts described in clauses (ii) through (iv) over the aggregate housing credit dollar amount allocated for such year. For purposes of clause (iii), the amount of State housing credit ceiling returned in the calendar year equals the housing credit dollar amount previously allocated within the State to any project which fails to meet the 10 percent test under paragraph (1)(E)(ii) on a date after the close of the calendar year in which the allocation was made or which does not become a qualified low-income housing project within the period required by this section or the terms of the allocation or to any project with respect to which an allocation is cancelled by mutual consent of the housing credit agency and the allocation recipient.

(D) Unused housing credit carryovers allocated among certain States

(i) In general

The unused housing credit carryover of a State for any calendar year shall be assigned to the Secretary for allocation among qualified States for the succeeding calendar year.

(ii) Unused housing credit carryover

For purposes of this subparagraph, the unused housing credit carryover of a State for any calendar year is the excess (if any) of—

(I) the unused State housing credit ceiling for the year preceding such year, over

(II) the aggregate housing credit dollar amount allocated for such year.

(iii) Formula for allocation of unused housing credit carryovers among qualified States

The amount allocated under this subparagraph to a qualified State for any calendar year shall be the amount determined by the Secretary to bear the same ratio to the aggregate unused housing credit carryovers of all States for the preceding calendar year as such State's population for the calendar year bears to the population of all qualified States for the calendar year. For purposes of the preceding sentence, population shall be determined in accordance with section 146(j).

(iv) Qualified State

For purposes of this subparagraph, the term "qualified State" means, with respect to a calendar year, any State—

(I) which allocated its entire State housing credit ceiling for the preceding calendar year, and

(II) for which a request is made (not later than May 1 of the calendar year) to receive an allocation under clause (iii).

(E) Special rule for States with constitutional home rule cities

For purposes of this subsection—

(i) In general

The aggregate housing credit dollar amount for any constitutional home rule city for any calendar year shall be an amount which bears the same ratio to the State housing credit ceiling for such calendar year as—

(I) the population of such city, bears to

(II) the population of the entire State.

(ii) Coordination with other allocations

In the case of any State which contains 1 or more constitutional home rule cities, for purposes of applying this paragraph with respect to housing credit agencies in such State other than constitutional home rule cities, the State housing credit ceiling for any calendar year shall be reduced by the aggregate housing credit dollar amounts determined for such year for all constitutional home rule cities in such State.

(iii) Constitutional home rule city

For purposes of this paragraph, the term "constitutional home rule city" has the meaning given such term by section 146(d)(3)(C).

(F) State may provide for different allocation

Rules similar to the rules of section 146(e) (other than paragraph (2)(B) thereof) shall apply for purposes of this paragraph.

(G) Population

For purposes of this paragraph, population shall be determined in accordance with section 146(j).

(H) Cost-of-living adjustment

(i) In general

In the case of a calendar year after 2002, the $2,000,000 and $1.75 amounts in subparagraph (C) shall each be increased by an amount equal to—

(I) such dollar amount, multiplied by

(II) the cost-of-living adjustment determined under section 1(f)(3) for such calendar year by substituting "calendar year 2001" for "calendar year 2016" in subparagraph (A)(ii) thereof.

(ii) Rounding

(I) In the case of the $2,000,000 amount, any increase under clause (i) which is not a multiple of $5,000 shall be rounded to the next lowest multiple of $5,000.

(II) In the case of the $1.75 amount, any increase under clause (i) which is not a multiple of 5 cents shall be rounded to the next lowest multiple of 5 cents.

(I) Increase in State housing credit ceiling for 2018, 2019, 2020, and 2021

In the case of calendar years 2018, 2019, 2020, and 2021, each of the dollar amounts in effect under clauses (I) and (II) of subparagraph (C)(ii) for any calendar year (after any increase under subparagraph (H)) shall be increased by multiplying such dollar amount by 1.125.

(4) Credit for buildings financed by tax-exempt bonds subject to volume cap not taken into account

(A) In general

Paragraph (1) shall not apply to the portion of any credit allowable under subsection (a) which is attributable to eligible basis financed by any obligation the interest on which is exempt from tax under section 103 if—

(i) such obligation is taken into account under section 146, and

(ii) principal payments on such financing are applied within a reasonable period to redeem obligations the proceeds of which were used to provide such financing or such financing is refunded as described in section 146(i)(6).

(B) Special rule where 50 percent or more of building is financed with tax-exempt bonds subject to volume cap

For purposes of subparagraph (A), if 50 percent or more of the aggregate basis of any building and the land on which the building is located is financed by any obligation described in subparagraph (A), paragraph (1) shall not apply to any portion of the credit allowable under subsection (a) with respect to such building.

(5) Portion of State ceiling set-aside for certain projects involving qualified nonprofit organizations

(A) In general

Not more than 90 percent of the State housing credit ceiling for any State for any calendar year shall be allocated to projects other than qualified low-income housing projects described in subparagraph (B).

(B) Projects involving qualified nonprofit organizations

For purposes of subparagraph (A), a qualified low-income housing project is described in this subparagraph if a qualified nonprofit organization is to own an interest in the project (directly or through a partnership) and materially participate (within the meaning of section 469(h)) in the development and operation of the project throughout the compliance period.

(C) Qualified nonprofit organization

For purposes of this paragraph, the term "qualified nonprofit organization" means any organization if—

(i) such organization is described in paragraph (3) or (4) of section 501(c) and is exempt from tax under section 501(a),

(ii) such organization is determined by the State housing credit agency not to be affiliated with or controlled by a for-profit organization, and

(iii) 1 of the exempt purposes of such organization includes the fostering of low-income housing.

(D) Treatment of certain subsidiaries

(i) In general

For purposes of this paragraph, a qualified nonprofit organization shall be treated as satisfying the ownership and material participation test of subparagraph (B) if any qualified corporation in which such organization holds stock satisfies such test.

(ii) Qualified corporation

For purposes of clause (i), the term "qualified corporation" means any corporation if 100 percent of the stock of such corporation is held by 1 or more qualified nonprofit organizations at all times during the period such corporation is in existence.

(E) State may not override set-aside

Nothing in subparagraph (F) of paragraph (3) shall be construed to permit a State not to comply with subparagraph (A) of this paragraph.

(6) Buildings eligible for credit only if minimum long-term commitment to low-income housing

(A) In general

No credit shall be allowed by reason of this section with respect to any building for the taxable year unless an extended low-income housing commitment is in effect as of the end of such taxable year.

(B) Extended low-income housing commitment

For purposes of this paragraph, the term "extended low-income housing commitment" means any agreement between the taxpayer and the housing credit agency—

(i) which requires that the applicable fraction (as defined in subsection (c)(1)) for the building for each taxable year in the extended use period will not be less than the applicable fraction specified in such agreement and which prohibits the actions described in subclauses (I) and (II) of subparagraph (E)(ii),

(ii) which allows individuals who meet the income limitation applicable to the building under subsection (g) (whether prospective, present, or former occupants of the building) the right to enforce in any State court the requirement and prohibitions of clause (i),

(iii) which prohibits the disposition to any person of any portion of the building to which such agreement applies unless all of the building to which such agreement applies is disposed of to such person,

(iv) which prohibits the refusal to lease to a holder of a voucher or certificate of eligibility under section 8 of the United States Housing Act of 1937 because of the status of the prospective tenant as such a holder,

(v) which is binding on all successors of the taxpayer, and

(vi) which, with respect to the property, is recorded pursuant to State law as a restrictive covenant.

(C) Allocation of credit may not exceed amount necessary to support commitment

(i) In general

The housing credit dollar amount allocated to any building may not exceed the amount necessary to support the applicable fraction specified in the extended low-income housing commitment for such building, including any increase in such fraction pursuant to the application of subsection (f)(3) if such increase is reflected in an amended low-income housing commitment.

(ii) Buildings financed by tax-exempt bonds

If paragraph (4) applies to any building the amount of credit allowed in any taxable year may not exceed the amount necessary to support the applicable fraction specified in the extended low-income housing commitment for such building. Such commitment may be amended to increase such fraction.

(D) Extended use period

For purposes of this paragraph, the term "extended use period" means the period—

(i) beginning on the 1st day in the compliance period on which such building is part of a qualified low-income housing project, and

(ii) ending on the later of—

(I) the date specified by such agency in such agreement, or

(II) the date which is 15 years after the close of the compliance period.

(E) Exceptions if foreclosure or if no buyer willing to maintain low-income status

(i) In general

The extended use period for any building shall terminate—

(I) on the date the building is acquired by foreclosure (or instrument in lieu of foreclosure) unless the Secretary determines that such acquisition is part of an arrangement with the taxpayer a purpose of which is to terminate such period, or

(II) on the last day of the period specified in subparagraph (I) if the housing credit agency is unable to present during such period a qualified contract for the acquisition of the low-income portion of the building by any person who will continue to operate such portion as a qualified low-income building.

Subclause (II) shall not apply to the extent more stringent requirements are provided in the agreement or in State law.

(ii) Eviction, etc. of existing low-income tenants not permitted

The termination of an extended use period under clause (i) shall not be construed to permit before the close of the 3-year period following such termination—

(I) the eviction or the termination of tenancy (other than for good cause) of an existing tenant of any low-income unit, or

(II) any increase in the gross rent with respect to such unit not otherwise permitted under this section.

(F) Qualified contract

For purposes of subparagraph (E), the term "qualified contract" means a bona fide contract to acquire (within a reasonable period after the contract is entered into) the nonlow-income portion of the building for fair market value and the low-income portion of the building for an amount not less than the applicable fraction (specified in the extended low-income housing commitment) of—

    (i) the sum of—

        (I) the outstanding indebtedness secured by, or with respect to, the building,

        (II) the adjusted investor equity in the building, plus

        (III) other capital contributions not reflected in the amounts described in subclause (I) or (II), reduced by

    (ii) cash distributions from (or available for distribution from) the project.

The Secretary shall prescribe such regulations as may be necessary or appropriate to carry out this paragraph, including regulations to prevent the manipulation of the amount determined under the preceding sentence.

(G) Adjusted investor equity

(i) In general

For purposes of subparagraph (E), the term "adjusted investor equity" means, with respect to any calendar year, the aggregate amount of cash taxpayers invested with respect to the project increased by the amount equal to—

    (I) such amount, multiplied by

    (II) the cost-of-living adjustment for such calendar year, determined under section 1(f)(3) by substituting the base calendar year for "calendar year 2016" in subparagraph (A)(ii) thereof.

An amount shall be taken into account as an investment in the project only to the extent there was an obligation to invest such amount as of the beginning of the credit period and to the extent such amount is reflected in the adjusted basis of the project.

(ii) Cost-of-living increases in excess of 5 percent not taken into account

Under regulations prescribed by the Secretary, if the C-CPI-U for any calendar year (as defined in section 1(f)(6)) exceeds the C-CPI-U for the preceding calendar year by more than 5 percent, the C-CPI-U for the base calendar year shall be increased such that such excess shall never be taken into account under clause (i). In the case of a base calendar year before 2017, the C-CPI-U for such year shall be determined by multiplying the CPI for such year by the amount determined under section 1(f)(3)(B).

(iii) Base calendar year

For purposes of this subparagraph, the term "base calendar year" means the calendar year with or within which the 1st taxable year of the credit period ends.

(H) Low-income portion

For purposes of this paragraph, the low-income portion of a building is the portion of such building equal to the applicable fraction specified in the extended low-income housing commitment for the building.

(I) Period for finding buyer

The period referred to in this subparagraph is the 1-year period beginning on the date (after the 14th year of the compliance period) the taxpayer submits a written request to the housing credit agency to find a person to acquire the taxpayer's interest in the low-income portion of the building.

(J) Effect of noncompliance

If, during a taxable year, there is a determination that an extended low-income housing agreement was not in effect as of the beginning of such year, such determination shall not apply to any period before such year and subparagraph (A) shall be applied without regard to such determination if the failure is corrected within 1 year from the date of the determination.

(K) Projects which consist of more than 1 building

The application of this paragraph to projects which consist of more than 1 building shall be made under regulations prescribed by the Secretary.

(7) Special rules

(A) Building must be located within jurisdiction of credit agency

A housing credit agency may allocate its aggregate housing credit dollar amount only to buildings located in the jurisdiction of the governmental unit of which such agency is a part.

(B) Agency allocations in excess of limit

If the aggregate housing credit dollar amounts allocated by a housing credit agency for any calendar year exceed the portion of the State housing credit ceiling allocated to such agency for such calendar year, the housing credit dollar amounts so allocated shall be reduced (to the extent of such excess) for buildings in the reverse of the order in which the allocations of such amounts were made.

(C) Credit reduced if allocated credit dollar amount is less than credit which would be allowable without regard to placed in service convention, etc.

(i) In general

The amount of the credit determined under this section with respect to any building shall not exceed the clause (ii) percentage of the amount of the credit which would (but for this subparagraph) be determined under this section with respect to such building.

(ii) Determination of percentage

For purposes of clause (i), the clause (ii) percentage with respect to any building is the percentage which—

    (I) the housing credit dollar amount allocated to such building bears to

    (II) the credit amount determined in accordance with clause (iii).

(iii) Determination of credit amount

The credit amount determined in accordance with this clause is the amount of the credit which would (but for this subparagraph) be determined under this section with respect to the building if—

    (I) this section were applied without regard to paragraphs (2)(A) and (3)(B) of subsection (f), and

    (II) subsection (f)(3)(A) were applied without regard to "the percentage equal to 2/3 of".

(D) Housing credit agency to specify applicable percentage and maximum qualified basis

In allocating a housing credit dollar amount to any building, the housing credit agency shall specify the applicable percentage and the maximum qualified basis which may be taken into account under this section with respect to such building. The applicable percentage and maximum qualified basis so specified shall not exceed the applicable percentage and qualified basis determined under this section without regard to this subsection.

(8) Other definitions

For purposes of this subsection—

(A) Housing credit agency

The term "housing credit agency" means any agency authorized to carry out this subsection.

(B) Possessions treated as States

The term "State" includes a possession of the United States.

(i) Definitions and special rules

For purposes of this section—

(1) Compliance period

The term "compliance period" means, with respect to any building, the period of 15 taxable years beginning with the 1st taxable year of the credit period with respect thereto.

(2) Determination of whether building is federally subsidized

(A) In general

Except as otherwise provided in this paragraph, for purposes of subsection (b)(1), a new building shall be treated as federally subsidized for any taxable year if, at any time during such taxable year or any prior taxable year, there is or was outstanding any obligation the interest on which is exempt from tax under section 103 the proceeds of which [1] are or were used (directly or indirectly) with respect to such building or the operation thereof.

(B) Election to reduce eligible basis by proceeds of obligations

A tax-exempt obligation shall not be taken into account under subparagraph (A) if the taxpayer elects to exclude from the eligible basis of the building for purposes of subsection (d) the proceeds of such obligation.

(C) Special rule for subsidized construction financing

Subparagraph (A) shall not apply to any tax-exempt obligation used to provide construction financing for any building if—

(i) such obligation (when issued) identified the building for which the proceeds of such obligation would be used, and

(ii) such obligation is redeemed before such building is placed in service.

(3) Low-income unit

(A) In general

The term "low-income unit" means any unit in a building if—

(i) such unit is rent-restricted (as defined in subsection (g)(2)), and

(ii) the individuals occupying such unit meet the income limitation applicable under subsection (g)(1) to the project of which such building is a part.

(B) Exceptions

(i) In general

A unit shall not be treated as a low-income unit unless the unit is suitable for occupancy and used other than on a transient basis.

(ii) Suitability for occupancy

For purposes of clause (i), the suitability of a unit for occupancy shall be determined under regulations prescribed by the Secretary taking into account local health, safety, and building codes.

(iii) Transitional housing for homeless

For purposes of clause (i), a unit shall be considered to be used other than on a transient basis if the unit contains sleeping accommodations and kitchen and bathroom facilities and is located in a building—

(I) which is used exclusively to facilitate the transition of homeless individuals (within the meaning of section 103 of the McKinney-Vento Homeless Assistance Act (42 U.S.C. 11302), as in effect on the date of the enactment of this clause) to independent living within 24 months, and

(II) in which a governmental entity or qualified nonprofit organization (as defined in subsection (h)(5)) provides such individuals with temporary housing and supportive services designed to assist such individuals in locating and retaining permanent housing.

(iv) Single-room occupancy units

For purposes of clause (i), a single-room occupancy unit shall not be treated as used on a transient basis merely because it is rented on a month-by-month basis.

(C) Special rule for buildings having 4 or fewer units

In the case of any building which has 4 or fewer residential rental units, no unit in such building shall be treated as a low-income unit if the units in such building are owned by—

(i) any individual who occupies a residential unit in such building, or

(ii) any person who is related (as defined in subsection (d)(2)(D)(iii)) to such individual.

(D) Certain students not to disqualify unit

A unit shall not fail to be treated as a low-income unit merely because it is occupied—

(i) by an individual who is—

(I) a student and receiving assistance under title IV of the Social Security Act,

(II) a student who was previously under the care and placement responsibility of the State agency responsible for administering a plan under part B or part E of title IV of the Social Security Act, or

(III) enrolled in a job training program receiving assistance under the Job Training Partnership Act or under other similar Federal, State, or local laws, or

(ii) entirely by full-time students if such students are—

(I) single parents and their children and such parents are not dependents (as defined in section 152, determined without regard to subsections (b)(1), (b)(2), and (d)(1)(B) thereof) of another individual and such children are not dependents (as so defined) of another individual other than a parent of such children, or

(II) married and file a joint return.

(E) Owner-occupied buildings having 4 or fewer units eligible for credit where development plan

(i) In general

Subparagraph (C) shall not apply to the acquisition or rehabilitation of a building pursuant to a development plan of action sponsored by a State or local government or a qualified nonprofit organization (as defined in subsection (h)(5)(C)).

(ii) Limitation on credit

In the case of a building to which clause (i) applies, the applicable fraction shall not exceed 80 percent of the unit fraction.

(iii) Certain unrented units treated as owner-occupied

In the case of a building to which clause (i) applies, any unit which is not rented for 90 days or more shall be treated as occupied by the owner of the building as of the 1st day it is not rented.

(4) New building

The term "new building" means a building the original use of which begins with the taxpayer.

(5) Existing building

The term "existing building" means any building which is not a new building.

(6) Application to estates and trusts

In the case of an estate or trust, the amount of the credit determined under subsection (a) and any increase in tax under subsection (j) shall be apportioned between the estate or trust and the beneficiaries on the basis of the income of the estate or trust allocable to each.

(7) Impact of tenant's right of 1st refusal to acquire property

(A) In general

No Federal income tax benefit shall fail to be allowable to the taxpayer with respect to any qualified low-income building merely by reason of a right of 1st refusal held by the tenants (in cooperative form or otherwise) or resident management corporation of such building or by a qualified nonprofit organization (as defined in subsection (h)(5)(C)) or government agency to purchase the property after the close of the compliance period for a price which is not less than the minimum purchase price determined under subparagraph (B).

(B) Minimum purchase price

For purposes of subparagraph (A), the minimum purchase price under this subparagraph is an amount equal to the sum of—

(i) the principal amount of outstanding indebtedness secured by the building (other than indebtedness incurred within the 5-year period ending on the date of the sale to the tenants), and

(ii) all Federal, State, and local taxes attributable to such sale.

Except in the case of Federal income taxes, there shall not be taken into account under clause (ii) any additional tax attributable to the application of clause (ii).

(8) Treatment of rural projects

For purposes of this section, in the case of any project for residential rental property located in a rural area (as defined in section 520 of the Housing Act of 1949), any income limitation measured by reference to area median gross income shall be measured by reference to the greater of area median gross income or national non-metropolitan median income. The preceding sentence shall not apply with respect to any building if paragraph (1) of section 42(h) does not apply by reason of paragraph (4) thereof to any portion of the credit determined under this section with respect to such building.

(9) Coordination with low-income housing grants

(A) Reduction in State housing credit ceiling for low-income housing grants received in 2009

For purposes of this section, the amounts described in clauses (i) through (iv) of subsection (h)(3)(C) with respect to any State for 2009 shall each be reduced by so much of such amount as is taken into account in determining the amount of any grant to such State under section 1602 of the American Recovery and Reinvestment Tax Act of 2009.

(B) Special rule for basis

Basis of a qualified low-income building shall not be reduced by the amount of any grant described in subparagraph (A).

(j) Recapture of credit

(1) In general

If—

(A) as of the close of any taxable year in the compliance period, the amount of the qualified basis of any building with respect to the taxpayer is less than

(B) the amount of such basis as of the close of the preceding taxable year,

then the taxpayer's tax under this chapter for the taxable year shall be increased by the credit recapture amount.

(2) Credit recapture amount

For purposes of paragraph (1), the credit recapture amount is an amount equal to the sum of—

(A) the aggregate decrease in the credits allowed to the taxpayer under section 38 for all prior taxable years which would have resulted if the accelerated portion of the credit allowable by reason of this section were not allowed for all prior taxable years with respect to the excess of the amount described in paragraph (1)(B) over the amount described in paragraph (1)(A), plus

(B) interest at the overpayment rate established under section 6621 on the amount determined under subparagraph (A) for each prior taxable year for the period beginning on the due date for filing the return for the prior taxable year involved.

No deduction shall be allowed under this chapter for interest described in subparagraph (B).

(3) Accelerated portion of credit

For purposes of paragraph (2), the accelerated portion of the credit for the prior taxable years with respect to any amount of basis is the excess of—

(A) the aggregate credit allowed by reason of this section (without regard to this subsection) for such years with respect to such basis, over

(B) the aggregate credit which would be allowable by reason of this section for such years with respect to such basis if the aggregate credit which would (but for this subsection) have been allowable for the entire compliance period were allowable ratably over 15 years.

(4) Special rules

(A) Tax benefit rule

The tax for the taxable year shall be increased under paragraph (1) only with respect to credits allowed by reason of this section which were used to reduce tax liability. In the case of credits not so used to reduce tax liability, the carryforwards and carrybacks under section 39 shall be appropriately adjusted.

(B) Only basis for which credit allowed taken into account

Qualified basis shall be taken into account under paragraph (1)(B) only to the extent such basis was taken into account in determining the credit under subsection (a) for the preceding taxable year referred to in such paragraph.

(C) No recapture of additional credit allowable by reason of subsection (f)(3)

Paragraph (1) shall apply to a decrease in qualified basis only to the extent such decrease exceeds the amount of qualified basis with respect to which a credit was allowable for the taxable year referred to in paragraph (1)(B) by reason of subsection (f)(3).

(D) No credits against tax

Any increase in tax under this subsection shall not be treated as a tax imposed by this chapter for purposes of determining the amount of any credit under this chapter.

(E) No recapture by reason of casualty loss

The increase in tax under this subsection shall not apply to a reduction in qualified basis by reason of a casualty loss to the extent such loss is restored by reconstruction or replacement within a reasonable period established by the Secretary.

(F) No recapture where de minimis changes in floor space

The Secretary may provide that the increase in tax under this subsection shall not apply with respect to any building if—

(i) such increase results from a de minimis change in the floor space fraction under subsection (c)(1), and

(ii) the building is a qualified low-income building after such change.

(5) Certain partnerships treated as the taxpayer

(A) In general

For purposes of applying this subsection to a partnership to which this paragraph applies—

(i) such partnership shall be treated as the taxpayer to which the credit allowable under subsection (a) was allowed,

(ii) the amount of such credit allowed shall be treated as the amount which would have been allowed to the partnership were such credit allowable to such partnership,

(iii) paragraph (4)(A) shall not apply, and

(iv) the amount of the increase in tax under this subsection for any taxable year shall be allocated among the partners of such partnership in the same manner as such partnership's taxable income for such year is allocated among such partners.

(B) Partnerships to which paragraph applies

This paragraph shall apply to any partnership which has 35 or more partners unless the partnership elects not to have this paragraph apply.

(C) Special rules

(i) Husband and wife treated as 1 partner

For purposes of subparagraph (B)(i), a husband and wife (and their estates) shall be treated as 1 partner.

(ii) Election irrevocable

Any election under subparagraph (B), once made, shall be irrevocable.

(6) No recapture on disposition of building which continues in qualified use

(A) In general

The increase in tax under this subsection shall not apply solely by reason of the disposition of a building (or an interest therein) if it is reasonably expected that such building will continue to be operated as a qualified low-income building for the remaining compliance period with respect to such building.

(B) Statute of limitations

If a building (or an interest therein) is disposed of during any taxable year and there is any reduction in the qualified basis of such building which results in an increase in tax under this subsection for such taxable or any subsequent taxable year, then—

(i) the statutory period for the assessment of any deficiency with respect to such increase in tax shall not expire before the expiration of 3 years from the date the Secretary is notified by the taxpayer (in such manner as the Secretary may prescribe) of such reduction in qualified basis, and

(ii) such deficiency may be assessed before the expiration of such 3-year period notwithstanding the provisions of any other law or rule of law which would otherwise prevent such assessment.

(k) Application of at-risk rules

For purposes of this section—

(1) In general

Except as otherwise provided in this subsection, rules similar to the rules of section 49(a)(1) (other than subparagraphs (D)(ii)(II) and (D)(iv)(I) thereof), section 49(a)(2), and section 49(b)(1) shall apply in determining the qualified basis of any building in the same manner as such sections apply in determining the credit base of property.

(2) Special rules for determining qualified person

For purposes of paragraph (1)—

(A) In general

If the requirements of subparagraphs (B), (C), and (D) are met with respect to any financing borrowed from a qualified nonprofit organization (as defined in subsection (h)(5)), the determination of whether such financing is qualified commercial financing with respect to any qualified low-income building shall be made without regard to whether such organization—

(i) is actively and regularly engaged in the business of lending money, or

(ii) is a person described in section 49(a)(1)(D)(iv)(II).

(B) Financing secured by property

The requirements of this subparagraph are met with respect to any financing if such financing is secured by the qualified low-income building, except that this subparagraph shall not apply in the case of a federally assisted building described in subsection (d)(6)(C) if—

(i) a security interest in such building is not permitted by a Federal agency holding or insuring the mortgage secured by such building, and

(ii) the proceeds from the financing (if any) are applied to acquire or improve such building.

(C) Portion of building attributable to financing

The requirements of this subparagraph are met with respect to any financing for any taxable year in the compliance period if, as of the close of such taxable year, not more than 60 percent of the eligible basis of the qualified low-income building is attributable to such financing (reduced by the principal and interest of any governmental financing which is part of a wrap-around mortgage involving such financing).

(D) Repayment of principal and interest

The requirements of this subparagraph are met with respect to any financing if such financing is fully repaid on or before the earliest of—

(i) the date on which such financing matures,

(ii) the 90th day after the close of the compliance period with respect to the qualified low-income building, or

(iii) the date of its refinancing or the sale of the building to which such financing relates.

In the case of a qualified nonprofit organization which is not described in section 49(a)(1)(D)(iv)(II) with respect to a building, clause (ii) of this subparagraph shall be applied as if the date described therein were the 90th day after the earlier of the date the building ceases to be a qualified low-income building or the date which is 15 years after the close of a compliance period with respect thereto.

(3) Present value of financing

If the rate of interest on any financing described in paragraph (2)(A) is less than the rate which is 1 percentage point below the applicable Federal rate as of the time such financing is incurred, then the qualified basis (to which such financing relates) of the qualified low-income building shall be the present value of the amount of such financing, using as the discount rate such applicable Federal rate. For purposes of the preceding sentence, the rate of interest on any financing shall be determined by treating interest to the extent of government subsidies as not payable.

(4) Failure to fully repay

(A) In general

To the extent that the requirements of paragraph (2)(D) are not met, then the taxpayer's tax under this chapter for the taxable year in which such failure occurs shall be increased by an amount equal to the applicable portion of the credit under this section with respect to such building, increased by an amount of interest for the period—

(i) beginning with the due date for the filing of the return of tax imposed by chapter 1 for the 1st taxable year for which such credit was allowable, and

(ii) ending with the due date for the taxable year in which such failure occurs,

determined by using the underpayment rate and method under section 6621.

(B) Applicable portion

For purposes of subparagraph (A), the term "applicable portion" means the aggregate decrease in the credits allowed to a taxpayer under section 38 for all prior taxable years which would have resulted if the eligible basis of the building were reduced by the amount of financing which does not meet requirements of paragraph (2)(D).

(C) Certain rules to apply

Rules similar to the rules of subparagraphs (A) and (D) of subsection (j)(4) shall apply for purposes of this subsection.

(l) Certifications and other reports to Secretary

(1) Certification with respect to 1st year of credit period

Following the close of the 1st taxable year in the credit period with respect to any qualified low-income building, the taxpayer shall certify to the Secretary (at such time and in such form and in such manner as the Secretary prescribes)—

(A) the taxable year, and calendar year, in which such building was placed in service,

(B) the adjusted basis and eligible basis of such building as of the close of the 1st year of the credit period,

(C) the maximum applicable percentage and qualified basis permitted to be taken into account by the appropriate housing credit agency under subsection (h),

(D) the election made under subsection (g) with respect to the qualified low-income housing project of which such building is a part, and

(E) such other information as the Secretary may require.

In the case of a failure to make the certification required by the preceding sentence on the date prescribed therefor, unless it is shown that such failure is due to reasonable cause and not to willful neglect, no credit shall be allowable by reason of subsection (a) with respect to such building for any taxable year ending before such certification is made.

(2) Annual reports to the Secretary

The Secretary may require taxpayers to submit an information return (at such time and in such form and manner as the Secretary prescribes) for each taxable year setting forth—

(A) the qualified basis for the taxable year of each qualified low-income building of the taxpayer,

(B) the information described in paragraph (1)(C) for the taxable year, and

(C) such other information as the Secretary may require.

The penalty under section 6652(j) shall apply to any failure to submit the return required by the Secretary under the preceding sentence on the date prescribed therefor.

(3) Annual reports from housing credit agencies

Each agency which allocates any housing credit amount to any building for any calendar year shall submit to the Secretary (at such time and in such manner as the Secretary shall prescribe) an annual report specifying—

(A) the amount of housing credit amount allocated to each building for such year,

(B) sufficient information to identify each such building and the taxpayer with respect thereto, and

(C) such other information as the Secretary may require.

The penalty under section 6652(j) shall apply to any failure to submit the report required by the preceding sentence on the date prescribed therefor.

(m) Responsibilities of housing credit agencies

(1) Plans for allocation of credit among projects

(A) In general

Notwithstanding any other provision of this section, the housing credit dollar amount with respect to any building shall be zero unless—

(i) such amount was allocated pursuant to a qualified allocation plan of the housing credit agency which is approved by the governmental unit (in accordance with rules similar to the rules of section 147(f)(2) (other than subparagraph (B)(ii) thereof)) of which such agency is a part,

(ii) such agency notifies the chief executive officer (or the equivalent) of the local jurisdiction within which the building is located of such project and provides such individual a reasonable opportunity to comment on the project,

(iii) a comprehensive market study of the housing needs of low-income individuals in the area to be served by the project is conducted before the credit allocation is made and at the developer's expense by a disinterested party who is approved by such agency, and

(iv) a written explanation is available to the general public for any allocation of a housing credit dollar amount which is not made in accordance with established priorities and selection criteria of the housing credit agency.

(B) Qualified allocation plan

For purposes of this paragraph, the term "qualified allocation plan" means any plan—

(i) which sets forth selection criteria to be used to determine housing priorities of the housing credit agency which are appropriate to local conditions,

(ii) which also gives preference in allocating housing credit dollar amounts among selected projects to—

(I) projects serving the lowest income tenants,

(II) projects obligated to serve qualified tenants for the longest periods, and

(III) projects which are located in qualified census tracts (as defined in subsection (d)(5)(B)(ii)) and the development of which contributes to a concerted community revitalization plan, and

(iii) which provides a procedure that the agency (or an agent or other private contractor of such agency) will follow in monitoring for noncompliance with the provisions of this section and in notifying the Internal Revenue Service of such noncompliance which such agency becomes aware of and in monitoring for noncompliance with habitability standards through regular site visits.

(C) Certain selection criteria must be used

The selection criteria set forth in a qualified allocation plan must include
(i) project location,
(ii) housing needs characteristics,
(iii) project characteristics, including whether the project includes the use of existing housing as part of a community revitalization plan,
(iv) sponsor characteristics,
(v) tenant populations with special housing needs,
(vi) public housing waiting lists,
(vii) tenant populations of individuals with children,
(viii) projects intended for eventual tenant ownership,
(ix) the energy efficiency of the project, and
(x) the historic nature of the project.

(D) Application to bond financed projects

Subsection (h)(4) shall not apply to any project unless the project satisfies the requirements for allocation of a housing credit dollar amount under the qualified allocation plan applicable to the area in which the project is located.

(2) Credit allocated to building not to exceed amount necessary to assure project feasibility

(A) In general

The housing credit dollar amount allocated to a project shall not exceed the amount the housing credit agency determines is necessary for the financial feasibility of the project and its viability as a qualified low-income housing project throughout the credit period.

(B) Agency evaluation

In making the determination under subparagraph (A), the housing credit agency shall consider—
(i) the sources and uses of funds and the total financing planned for the project,
(ii) any proceeds or receipts expected to be generated by reason of tax benefits,
(iii) the percentage of the housing credit dollar amount used for project costs other than the cost of intermediaries, and
(iv) the reasonableness of the developmental and operational costs of the project.

Clause (iii) shall not be applied so as to impede the development of projects in hard-to-develop areas. Such a determination shall not be construed to be a representation or warranty as to the feasibility or viability of the project.

(C) Determination made when credit amount applied for and when building placed in service

(i) In general

A determination under subparagraph (A) shall be made as of each of the following times:
(I) The application for the housing credit dollar amount.
(II) The allocation of the housing credit dollar amount.
(III) The date the building is placed in service.

(ii) Certification as to amount of other subsidies

Prior to each determination under clause (i), the taxpayer shall certify to the housing credit agency the full extent of all Federal, State, and local subsidies which apply (or which the taxpayer expects to apply) with respect to the building.

(D) Application to bond financed projects

Subsection (h)(4) shall not apply to any project unless the governmental unit which issued the bonds (or on behalf of which the bonds were issued) makes a determination under rules similar to the rules of subparagraphs (A) and (B).

(n) Regulations

The Secretary shall prescribe such regulations as may be necessary or appropriate to carry out the purposes of this section, including regulations—
(1) dealing with—
(A) projects which include more than 1 building or only a portion of a building,
(B) buildings which are placed in service in portions,

(2) providing for the application of this section to short taxable years,
(3) preventing the avoidance of the rules of this section, and
(4) providing the opportunity for housing credit agencies to correct administrative errors and omissions with respect to allocations and record keeping within a reasonable period after their discovery, taking into account the availability of regulations and other administrative guidance from the Secretary.

(Added Pub. L. 99–514, title II, §252(a), Oct. 22, 1986, 100 Stat. 2189; amended Pub. L. 99–509, title VIII, §8072(a), Oct. 21, 1986, 100 Stat. 1964; Pub. L. 100–647, title I, §§1002(l)(1)–(25), (32), 1007(g)(3)(B), title IV, §§4003(a), (b)(1), (3), 4004(a), Nov. 10, 1988, 102 Stat. 3373–3381, 3435, 3643, 3644; Pub. L. 101–239, title VII, §§7108(a)(1), (b)–(e)(2), (f)–(m), (n)(2)–(q), 7811(a), 7831(c), 7841(d)(13)–(15), Dec. 19, 1989, 103 Stat. 2306–2321, 2406, 2426, 2429; Pub. L. 101–508, title XI, §§11407(a)(1), (b)(1)–(9), 11701(a)(1)–(3)(A), (4), (5)(A), (6)–(10), 11812(b)(3), 11813(b)(3), Nov. 5, 1990, 104 Stat. 1388–474, 1388-475, 1388-505 to 1388-507, 1388-535, 1388-551; Pub. L. 102–227, title I, §107(a), Dec. 11, 1991, 105 Stat. 1687; Pub. L. 103–66, title XIII, §13142(a)(1), (b)(1)–(5), Aug. 10, 1993, 107 Stat. 437–439; Pub. L. 104–188, title I, §1704(t)(53), (64), Aug. 20, 1996, 110 Stat. 1890; Pub. L. 105–206, title VI, §6004(g)(5), July 22, 1998, 112 Stat. 796; Pub. L. 106–400, §2, Oct. 30, 2000, 114 Stat. 1675; Pub. L. 106–554, §1(a)(7) [title I, §§131(a)–(c), 132–136], Dec. 21, 2000, 114 Stat. 2763, 2763A-610 to 2763A-613; Pub. L. 107–147, title IV, §417(2), (3), Mar. 9, 2002, 116 Stat. 56; Pub. L. 108–311, title II, §207(8), title IV, §408(a)(3), Oct. 4, 2004, 118 Stat. 1177, 1191; Pub. L. 110–142, §6(a), Dec. 20, 2007, 121 Stat. 1806; Pub. L. 110–289, div. C, title I, §§3001–3002(b), 3003(a)–(g), 3004(a)–(g), 3007(b), July 30, 2008, 122 Stat. 2878–2884, 2886; Pub. L. 111–5, div. B, title I, §1404, Feb. 17, 2009, 123 Stat. 352; Pub. L. 112–240, title III, §302(a), Jan. 2, 2013, 126 Stat. 2328; Pub. L. 113–295, div. A, title I, §112(a), title II, §§212(a), 221(a)(7), Dec. 19, 2014, 128 Stat. 4014, 4033, 4038; Pub. L. 114–113, div. Q, title I, §131(a), (b), Dec. 18, 2015, 129 Stat. 3055; Pub. L. 115–97, title I, §11002(d)(1)(G), (3), Dec. 22, 2017, 131 Stat. 2060, 2061; Pub. L. 115–141, div. T, §§102(a), 103(a), (b), div. U, title IV, §401(a)(10)–(13), Mar. 23, 2018, 132 Stat. 1157, 1184, 1185; Pub. L. 116–260, div. EE, title II, §201(a), Dec. 27, 2020, 134 Stat. 3056.)

Inflation Adjusted Items for Certain Years

For inflation adjustment of certain items in this section, see Revenue Procedures listed in a table under section 1 of this title.

Editorial Notes
References in Text

The date of the enactment of this paragraph, referred to in subsec. (b)(2)(A), is the date of enactment of Pub. L. 110–289, which was approved July 30, 2008.

Section 201(a) of the Tax Reform Act of 1986, referred to in subsec. (c)(2)(B), is section 201(a) of Pub. L. 99–514, which amended section 168 of this title generally.

Section 3 of the Federal Deposit Insurance Act, referred to in subsec. (d)(6)(B), is classified to section 1813 of Title 12, Banks and Banking.

Section 8 of the United States Housing Act of 1937, referred to in subsecs. (d)(6)(C)(i), (g)(2)(B), and (h)(6)(B)(iv), is classified to section 1437f of Title 42, The Public Health and Welfare. Section 8(e)(2) of the Act was repealed by Pub. L. 101–625, title II, §289(b)(1), Nov. 28, 1990, 104 Stat. 4128, effective Oct. 1, 1991, but to remain in effect with respect to single room occupancy dwellings as authorized by subchapter IV (§11361 et seq.) of chapter 119 of Title 42. See section 12839(b) of Title 42.

Sections 221(d)(3), (4) and 236 of the National Housing Act, referred to in subsec. (d)(6)(C)(i), are classified to sections 1715l(d)(3), (4) and 1715z–1, respectively, of Title 12, Banks and Banking.

Sections 515, 502(c), and 520 of the Housing Act of 1949, referred to in subsecs. (d)(6)(C)(i), (g)(2)(B)(iv), and (i)(8), are classified to sections 1485, 1472(c), and 1490, respectively, of Title 42, The Public Health and Welfare.

The date of the enactment of this subparagraph, referred to in subsec. (g)(2)(E), is the date of enactment of Pub. L. 100–647, which was approved Nov. 10, 1988.

The date of the enactment of this clause, referred to in subsec. (i)(3)(B)(iii)(I), is date of enactment of Pub. L. 101–239, which was approved Dec. 19, 1989.

The Social Security Act, referred to in subsec. (i)(3)(D)(i)(I), (II), is act Aug. 14, 1935, ch. 531, 49 Stat. 620. Title IV of the Act is classified generally to subchapter IV (§601 et seq.) of chapter 7 of Title 42, The Public Health and Welfare. Parts B and E of title IV of the Act are classified generally to parts B (§620 et seq.) and E (§670 et seq.), respectively, of subchapter IV of chapter 7 of Title 42. For complete classification of this Act to the Code, see section 1305 of Title 42 and Tables.

The Job Training Partnership Act, referred to in subsec. (i)(3)(D)(i)(III), is Pub. L. 97–300, Oct. 13, 1982, 96 Stat. 1322, which was classified generally to chapter 19 (§1501 et seq.) of Title 29, Labor, and was repealed by Pub. L. 105–220, title I, §199(b)(2), (c)(2)(B), Aug. 7, 1998, 112 Stat. 1059, effective July 1, 2000. Pursuant to former section 2940(b) of Title 29, references to a provision of the Job Training Partnership Act, effective Aug. 7, 1998, were deemed to refer to that provision or the corresponding provision of the Workforce Investment Act of 1998, Pub. L. 105–220, Aug. 7, 1998, 112 Stat. 936, and, effective July 1, 2000, were deemed to refer to the corresponding provision of the Workforce Investment Act of 1998. The Workforce Investment Act of 1998 was repealed by Pub. L. 113–128, title V, §511(a), July 22, 2014, 128 Stat. 1705, effective July 1, 2015. Pursuant to section 3361(a) of Title 29, references to a provision of the Workforce Investment Act of 1998 are deemed to refer to the corresponding provision of the Workforce Innovation and Opportunity Act, Pub. L. 113–128, July 22, 2014, 128 Stat. 1425, effective July 1, 2015. For complete classification of the Job Training Partnership Act and the Workforce Investment Act of 1998 to the Code, see Tables. For complete classification of the Workforce Innovation and Opportunity Act to the Code, see Short Title note set out under section 3101 of Title 29 and Tables.

Section 1602 of the American Recovery and Reinvestment Tax Act of 2009, referred to in subsec. (i)(9)(A), is section 1602 of Pub. L. 111–5, which is set out as a note below.

Prior Provisions

A prior section 42, added Pub. L. 94–12, title II, §203(a), Mar. 29, 1975, 89 Stat. 29; amended Pub. L. 94–164, §3(a)(1), Dec. 23, 1975, 89 Stat. 972; Pub. L. 94–455, title IV, §401(a)(2)(A), (B), title V, §503(b)(4), title XIX, §1906(b)(13)(A), Oct. 4, 1976, 90 Stat. 1555, 1562, 1834; Pub. L. 95–30, title I, §101(c), May 23, 1977, 91 Stat. 132, which related to general tax credit allowed to individuals in an amount equal to the greater of (1) 2% of taxable income not exceeding $9,000 or (2) $35 multiplied by each exemption the taxpayer was entitled to, expired Dec. 31, 1978, pursuant to the terms of: (1) Pub. L. 94–12, §209(a) as amended by Pub. L. 94–164, §2(e), set out as an Effective and Termination Dates of 1975 Amendment note under section 56 of this title; (2) Pub. L. 94–164, §3(b), as amended by Pub. L. 94–455, §401(a)(1) and Pub. L. 95–30, §103(a); and (3) Pub. L. 94–455, §401(c), as amended by Pub. L. 95–30, §103(c) and Pub. L. 95–600, title I, §103(b), Nov. 6, 1978, 92 Stat. 2771, set out as an Effective and Termination Dates of 1976 Amendment note under section 32 of this title.

Another prior section 42 was renumbered section 37 of this title.

Amendments

2020—Subsec. (b)(3), (4). Pub. L. 116–260 added par. (3) and redesignated former par. (3) as (4).

2018—Subsec. (d)(4)(C)(i). Pub. L. 115–141, §401(a)(11)(A), substituted "as defined in paragraph (5)(B)(ii)" for "as defined in paragraph (5)(C)".

Subsec. (e)(2)(B). Pub. L. 115–141, §401(a)(10), substituted "etc.," for "etc," in heading.

Subsec. (f)(5)(B)(ii)(I). Pub. L. 115–141, §401(a)(11)(B), substituted "(d)(6)(B)" for "(d)(6)(C)".

Subsec. (g)(1). Pub. L. 115–141, §103(a)(1), substituted "subparagraph (A), (B), or (C)" for "subparagraph (A) or (B)" in introductory provisions.

Subsec. (g)(1)(C). Pub. L. 115–141, §103(a)(2), added subpar. (C).

Subsec. (g)(2)(D)(i). Pub. L. 115–141, §103(b)(1), substituted "clauses (ii), (iii), and (iv)" for "clause (ii)".

Subsec. (g)(2)(D)(ii). Pub. L. 115–141, §103(b)(2), in heading, substituted "Rental of next available unit in case of 20–50 or 40–60 test" for "Next available unit must be rented to low-income tenant if income rises above 140 percent of income limit", and, in text, substituted "In the case of a project with respect to which the taxpayer elects the requirements of subparagraph (A) or (B) of paragraph (1), if" for "If" and struck out at end "In the case of a project described in section 142(d)(4)(B), the preceding sentence shall be applied by substituting '170 percent' for '140 percent' and by substituting 'any low-income unit in the building is occupied by a new resident whose income exceeds 40 percent of area median gross income' for 'any residential unit in the building (of a size comparable to, or smaller than, such unit) is occupied by a new resident whose income exceeds such income limitation'."

Subsec. (g)(2)(D)(iii) to (v). Pub. L. 115–141, §103(b)(3), added cls. (iii) to (v).

Subsec. (h)(3)(I). Pub. L. 115–141, §102(a), amended subpar. (I) generally. Prior to amendment, subpar. (I) related to the increase in State housing credit ceiling for 2008 and 2009.

Subsec. (h)(5)(C)(ii). Pub. L. 115–141, §401(a)(12), substituted ", and" for "; and".

Subsec. (i)(3)(D)(ii)(I). Pub. L. 115–141, §401(a)(13), struck out period at end.

Subsec. (k)(2)(B). Pub. L. 115–141, §401(a)(11)(C)(i), substituted "(d)(6)(C)" for "(d)(6)(B)" in introductory provisions.

Subsec. (k)(2)(B)(ii). Pub. L. 115–141, §401(a)(11)(C)(ii), substituted "building." for "building..".

Subsec. (m)(1)(B)(ii)(III). Pub. L. 115–141, §401(a)(11)(D), substituted "as defined in subsection (d)(5)(B)(ii)" for "as defined in subsection (d)(5)(C)".

2017—Subsecs. (e)(3)(D)(ii), (h)(3)(H)(i)(II). Pub. L. 115–97, §11002(d)(1)(G), substituted "for 'calendar year 2016' in subparagraph (A)(ii)" for "for 'calendar year 1992' in subparagraph (B)".

Subsec. (h)(6)(G)(i)(II). Pub. L. 115–97, §11002(d)(3)(A), substituted "for 'calendar year 2016' in subparagraph (A)(ii) thereof" for "for 'calendar year 1987' ".

Subsec. (h)(6)(G)(ii). Pub. L. 115–97, §11002(d)(3)(B), substituted "if the C-CPI-U for any calendar year (as defined in section 1(f)(6)) exceeds the C-CPI-U for the preceding calendar year by more than 5 percent, the C-CPI-U for the base calendar year shall be increased such that such excess shall never be taken into account under clause (i). In the case of a base calendar year before 2017, the C-CPI-U for such year shall be determined by multiplying the CPI for such year by the amount determined under section 1(f)(3)(B)." for "if the CPI for any calendar year (as defined in section 1(f)(4)) exceeds the CPI for the preceding calendar year by more than 5 percent, the CPI for the base calendar year shall be increased such that such excess shall never be taken into account under clause (i)."

2015—Subsec. (b)(2). Pub. L. 114–113, §131(b), substituted "Minimum" for "Temporary minimum" in heading.

Subsec. (b)(2)(A). Pub. L. 114–113, §131(a), struck out "with respect to housing credit dollar amount allocations made before January 1, 2015" after "paragraph".

2014—Subsec. (b)(1). Pub. L. 113–295, §212(a), substituted "For purposes of this section—" for "For purposes of this section, the term", inserted subpar. (A) designation and heading, and inserted "The term" at beginning of subpar. (A).

Subsec. (b)(2)(A). Pub. L. 113–295, §112(a), substituted "January 1, 2015" for "January 1, 2014".

Subsec. (h)(3)(C)(ii)(I). Pub. L. 113–295, §221(a)(7), struck out "($1.50 for 2001)" after "$1.75".

2013—Subsec. (b)(2)(A). Pub. L. 112–240 substituted "with respect to housing credit dollar amount allocations made before January 1, 2014" for "and before December 31, 2013".

2009—Subsec. (i). Pub. L. 111–5 added par. (9).

2008—Subsec. (b). Pub. L. 110–289, §3002(a), redesignated par. (2) as (1), in heading, substituted "Determination of applicable percentage" for "Buildings placed in service after 1987", in text, substituted "For purposes of this section, the term 'applicable percentage' means, with respect to any building, the appropriate percentage" for "(A) In general.—In the case of any qualified low-income building placed in service by the taxpayer after 1987, the term 'applicable percentage' means the appropriate percentage", "a new building which is not federally subsidized for the taxable year" for "a building described in paragraph (1)(A)", and "a building not described in clause (i)" for "a building described in paragraph (1)(B)", added par. (2), and struck out "For purposes of this section—" after subsec. heading and former par. (1) which related to buildings placed in service during 1987.

Subsec. (c)(2). Pub. L. 110–289, §3004(a), struck out concluding provisions which read as follows: "Such term does not include any building with respect to which moderate rehabilitation assistance is provided, at any time during the compliance period, under section 8(e)(2) of the United States Housing Act of 1937 (other than assistance under the McKinney-Vento Homeless Assistance Act (as in effect on the date of the enactment of this sentence))."

Subsec. (d)(2)(B)(ii). Pub. L. 110–289, §3003(g)(1), substituted "the date the building was last placed in service," for "the later of—

"(I) the date the building was last placed in service, or

"(II) the date of the most recent nonqualified substantial improvement of the building,".

Subsec. (d)(2)(D). Pub. L. 110–289, §3003(e), (g)(2), redesignated cls. (ii) and (iii)(II) as (i) and (ii), respectively, in cl. (ii) struck out at end "For purposes of the preceding sentence, in applying section 267(b) or 707(b)(1), '10 percent' shall be substituted for '50 percent'.", and struck out former cls. (i) and (iii)(I) which related to the term "nonqualified substantial improvement" and application of section 179 for purposes of subpar. (B)(i).

Subsec. (d)(4)(C)(ii). Pub. L. 110–289, §3003(c), substituted "shall not exceed the sum of—" for "shall not exceed 10 percent of the eligible basis of the qualified low-income housing project of which it is a part." and added subcls. (I) and (II).

Subsec. (d)(5)(A). Pub. L. 110–289, §3003(d), amended heading and text of subpar. (A) generally. Prior to amendment, text read as follows: "If, during any taxable year of the compliance period, a grant is made with respect to any building or the operation thereof and any portion of such grant is funded with Federal funds (whether or not includible in gross income), the eligible basis of such building for such taxable year and all succeeding taxable years shall be reduced by the portion of such grant which is so funded."

Subsec. (d)(5)(B), (C). Pub. L. 110–289, §3003(g)(3), redesignated subpar. (C) as (B) and struck out heading and text of former subpar. (B). Text read as follows: "The eligible basis of any building shall not include any portion of its adjusted basis which is attributable to amounts with respect to which an election is made under section 167(k) (as in effect on the day before the date of the enactment of the Revenue Reconciliation Act of 1990)."

Subsec. (d)(5)(C)(v). Pub. L. 110–289, §3003(a), added cl. (v).

Subsec. (d)(6). Pub. L. 110–289, §3003(f), amended par. (6) generally. Prior to amendment, par. (6) consisted of subpars. (A) to (E) relating to general rule for waiver of par. (2)(B)(ii) with respect to any federally-assisted building, definition of "federally-assisted building", waiver for buildings with low-income occupancy, waiver for buildings acquired from insured depository institutions in default, and definition of "appropriate Federal official".

Subsec. (e)(3)(A)(ii)(I). Pub. L. 110–289, §3003(b)(1)(A), substituted "20 percent" for "10 percent".

Subsec. (e)(3)(A)(ii)(II). Pub. L. 110–289, §3003(b)(1)(B), substituted "$6,000" for "$3,000".

Subsec. (e)(3)(D). Pub. L. 110–289, §3003(b)(2), added subpar. (D).

Subsec. (f)(5)(B)(ii)(II). Pub. L. 110–289, §3003(b)(3), substituted "if the dollar amount in effect under subsection (e)(3)(A)(ii)(II) were two-thirds of such amount." for "if subsection (e)(3)(A)(ii)(II) were applied by substituting '$2,000' for '$3,000'."

Subsec. (g)(9). Pub. L. 110–289, §3004(g), added par. (9).

Subsec. (h)(1)(E)(ii). Pub. L. 110–289, §3004(b), substituted "(as of the date which is 1 year after the date that the allocation was made)" for "(as of the later of the date which is 6 months after the date that the allocation was made or the close of the calendar year in which the allocation is made)".

Subsec. (h)(3)(I). Pub. L. 110–289, §3001, added subpar. (I).

Subsec. (h)(4)(A)(ii). Pub. L. 110–289, §3007(b), inserted "or such financing is refunded as described in section 146(i)(6)" before period at end.

Subsec. (i)(2)(A). Pub. L. 110–289, §3002(b)(1), struck out ", or any below market Federal loan," before "the proceeds of which".

Subsec. (i)(2)(B). Pub. L. 110–289, §3002(b)(2)(A), in heading, struck out "balance of loan or" before "proceeds" and in text, struck out "loan or" before "tax-exempt obligation" and substituted "for purposes of subsection (d) the proceeds of such obligation." for "for purposes of subsection (d)—

"(i) in the case of a loan, the principal amount of such loan, and

"(ii) in the case of a tax-exempt obligation, the proceeds of such obligation."

Subsec. (i)(2)(C). Pub. L. 110–289, §3002(b)(2)(B)(i), struck out "or below market Federal loan" after "tax-exempt obligation" in introductory provisions.

Subsec. (i)(2)(C)(i). Pub. L. 110–289, §3002(b)(2)(B)(ii), substituted "(when issued)" for "or loan (when issued or made)" and "the proceeds of such obligation" for "the proceeds of such obligation or loan".

Subsec. (i)(2)(C)(ii). Pub. L. 110–289, §3002(b)(2)(B)(iii), struck out ", and such loan is repaid," after "redeemed".

Subsec. (i)(2)(D), (E). Pub. L. 110–289, §3002(b)(2)(C), struck out subpars. (D) and (E) which related to below market Federal loan and buildings receiving HOME assistance or Native American housing assistance, respectively.

Subsec. (i)(3)(D)(i)(II), (III). Pub. L. 110–289, §3004(e), added subcl. (II) and redesignated former subcl. (II) as (III).

Subsec. (i)(8). Pub. L. 110–289, §3004(f), added par. (8).

Subsec. (j)(6). Pub. L. 110–289, §3004(c), amended par. (6) generally. Prior to amendment, text read as follows: "In the case of a disposition of a building or an interest therein, the taxpayer shall be discharged from liability for any additional tax under this subsection by reason of such disposition if—

"(A) the taxpayer furnishes to the Secretary a bond in an amount satifactory to the Secretary and for the period required by the Secretary, and

"(B) it is reasonably expected that such building will continue to be operated as a qualified low-income building for the remaining compliance period with respect to such building."

Subsec. (m)(1)(C)(ix), (x). Pub. L. 110–289, §3004(d), added cls. (ix) and (x).

2007—Subsec. (i)(3)(D)(ii)(I). Pub. L. 110–142 amended subcl. (I) generally. Prior to amendment, subcl. (I) read as follows: "single parents and their children and such parents and children are not dependents (as defined in section 152, determined without regard to subsections (b)(1), (b)(2), and (d)(1)(B) thereof) of another individual, or".

2004—Subsec. (d)(2)(D)(iii)(I). Pub. L. 108–311, §408(a)(3), substituted "section 179(d)(7)" for "section 179(b)(7)".

Subsec. (i)(3)(D)(ii)(I). Pub. L. 108–311, §207(8), inserted ", determined without regard to subsections (b)(1), (b)(2), and (d)(1)(B) thereof" after "section 152".

2002—Subsec. (h)(3)(C). Pub. L. 107–147, §417(2), substituted "the amounts described in clauses (ii) through (iv) over the aggregate housing credit dollar amount allocated for such year" for "the amounts described in clauses (ii) and (iii) over the aggregate housing credit dollar amount allocated for such year" in concluding provisions.

Subsec. (m)(1)(B)(ii)(II), (III). Pub. L. 107–147, §417(3), struck out second "and" at end of subcl. (II) and inserted "and" at end of subcl. (III).

2000—Subsec. (c)(2). Pub. L. 106–400 substituted "McKinney-Vento Homeless Assistance Act" for "Stewart B. McKinney Homeless Assistance Act" in concluding provisions.

Subsec. (d)(4)(A). Pub. L. 106–554, §1(a)(7) [title I, §134(a)(1)], substituted "subparagraphs (B) and (C)" for "subparagraph (B)".

Subsec. (d)(4)(C), (D). Pub. L. 106–554, §1(a)(7) [title I, §134(a)(2), (3)], added subpar. (C) and redesignated former subpar. (C) as (D).

Subsec. (d)(5)(C)(ii)(I). Pub. L. 106–554, §1(a)(7) [title I, §135(b)], in first sentence, inserted "either" before "in which 50 percent" and "or which has a poverty rate of at least 25 percent" before period at end.

Subsec. (h)(1)(E)(ii). Pub. L. 106–554, §1(a)(7) [title I, §135(a)(1)], in first sentence, substituted "(as of the later of the date which is 6 months after the date that the allocation was made or the close of the calendar year in which the allocation" for "(as of the close of the calendar year in which the allocation".

Subsec. (h)(3)(C). Pub. L. 106–554, §1(a)(7) [title I, §136(b)], which directed the substitution of "clauses (i) through (iv)" for "clauses (i) and (iii)" in the first sentence of concluding provisions, could not be executed because the words "clauses (i) and (iii)" did not appear subsequent to the amendment by Pub. L. 106–554, §1(a)(7) [title I, §131(c)(1)(B)]. See below.

Pub. L. 106–554, §1(a)(7) [title I, §135(a)(2)], in last sentence of concluding provisions, substituted "project which fails to meet the 10 percent test under paragraph (1)(E)(ii) on a date after the close of the calendar year in which the allocation was made or which" for "project which".

Pub. L. 106–554, §1(a)(7) [title I, §131(c)(1)], in first sentence of concluding provisions, substituted "clause (i)" for "clause (ii)" and "clauses (ii)" for "clauses (i)".

Subsec. (h)(3)(C)(i), (ii). Pub. L. 106–554, §1(a)(7) [title I, §131(a)], amended cls. (i) and (ii) generally. Prior to amendment, cls. (i) and (ii) read as follows:

"(i) $1.25 multiplied by the State population,

"(ii) the unused State housing credit ceiling (if any) of such State for the preceding calendar year,".

Subsec. (h)(3)(D)(ii). Pub. L. 106–554, §1(a)(7) [title I, §136(a)], substituted "the excess (if any) of—" for "the excess (if any) of the unused State housing credit ceiling for such year (as defined in subparagraph (C)(i)) over the excess (if any) of—" in introductory provisions, added subcls. (I) and (II), and struck out former subcls. (I) and (II) which read as follows:

"(I) the aggregate housing credit dollar amount allocated for such year, over

"(II) the sum of the amounts described in clauses (ii) and (iii) of subparagraph (C)."

Pub. L. 106–554, §1(a)(7) [title I, §131(c)(2)], substituted "subparagraph (C)(i)" for "subparagraph (C)(ii)" in introductory provisions and "clauses (ii)" for "clauses (i)" in subcl. (II).

Subsec. (h)(3)(H). Pub. L. 106–554, §1(a)(7) [title I, §131(b)], added subpar. (H).

Subsec. (i)(2)(E). Pub. L. 106–554, §1(a)(7) [title I, §134(b)(2)], inserted "or Native American housing assistance" after "HOME assistance" in heading.

Subsec. (i)(2)(E)(i). Pub. L. 106–554, §1(a)(7) [title I, §134(b)(1)], inserted "or the Native American Housing Assistance and Self-Determination Act of 1996 (25 U.S.C. 4101 et seq.) (as in effect on October 1, 1997)" after "this subparagraph)".

Subsec. (i)(3)(B)(iii)(I). Pub. L. 106–400 substituted "McKinney-Vento Homeless Assistance Act" for "Stewart B. McKinney Homeless Assistance Act".

Subsec. (m)(1)(A)(iii), (iv). Pub. L. 106–554, §1(a)(7) [title I, §133(a)], added cls. (iii) and (iv).

Subsec. (m)(1)(B)(ii)(III). Pub. L. 106–554, §1(a)(7) [title I, §132(b)], added subcl. (III).

Subsec. (m)(1)(B)(iii). Pub. L. 106–554, §1(a)(7) [title I, §133(b)], inserted "and in monitoring for noncompliance with habitability standards through regular site visits" before period at end.

Subsec. (m)(1)(C)(iii). Pub. L. 106–554, §1(a)(7) [title I, §132(a)(1)], inserted ", including whether the project includes the use of existing housing as part of a community revitalization plan" before comma at end.

Subsec. (m)(1)(C)(v) to (viii). Pub. L. 106–554, §1(a)(7) [title I, §132(a)(2)], added cls. (v) to (viii) and struck out former cls. (v) to (vii) which read as follows:

"(v) participation of local tax-exempt organizations,

"(vi) tenant populations with special housing needs, and

"(vii) public housing waiting lists."

1998—Subsec. (j)(4)(D). Pub. L. 105–206 substituted "this chapter" for "subpart A, B, D, or G of this part".

1996—Subsec. (c)(2). Pub. L. 104–188, §1704(t)(64), struck out "of 1988" after "Homeless Assistance Act".

Subsec. (d)(5)(B). Pub. L. 104–188, §1704(t)(53), provided that section 11812(b)(3) of Pub. L. 101–508 shall be applied by not executing the amendment therein to the heading of subsec. (d)(5)(B) of this section. See 1990 Amendment note below.

1993—Subsec. (g)(8). Pub. L. 103–66, §13142(b)(3), added par. (8).

Subsec. (h)(6)(B)(iv) to (vi). Pub. L. 103–66, §13142(b)(4), added cl. (iv) and redesignated former cls. (iv) and (v) as (v) and (vi), respectively.

Subsec. (i)(2)(E). Pub. L. 103–66, §13142(b)(5), added subpar. (E).

Subsec. (i)(3)(D). Pub. L. 103–66, §13142(b)(2), amended heading and text of subpar. (D) generally. Prior to amendment, text read as follows: "A unit shall not fail to be treated as a low-income unit merely because it is occupied by an individual who is—

"(i) a student and receiving assistance under title IV of the Social Security Act, or

"(ii) enrolled in a job training program receiving assistance under the Job Training Partnership Act or under other similar Federal, State, or local laws."

Subsec. (m)(2)(B)(iv). Pub. L. 103–66, §13142(b)(1), added cl. (iv).

Subsec. (o). Pub. L. 103–66, §13142(a)(1), struck out subsec. (o) which provided that subsec. (h)(3)(C)(i) would not apply to any amount allocated after June 30, 1992, and that subsec. (h)(4) would not apply to any building placed in service after June 30, 1992, with an exception for bond-financed buildings in progress.

1991—Subsec. (o)(1). Pub. L. 102–227, §107(a)(1), struck out ", for any calendar year after 1991" after "paragraph (2)" in introductory provisions, inserted "to any amount allocated after June 30, 1992" before comma at end of subpar. (A), and substituted "June 30, 1992" for "1991" in subpar. (B).

Subsec. (o)(2). Pub. L. 102–227, §107(a)(2), substituted "July 1, 1992" for "1992" in introductory provisions and subpar. (A), "June 30, 1992" for "December 31, 1991" and "June 30, 1994" for "December 31, 1993" in subpar. (B), and "July 1, 1994" for "January 1, 1994" in subpar. (C).

1990—Subsec. (b)(1). Pub. L. 101–508, §11701(a)(1)(B), struck out at end "A building shall not be treated as described in subparagraph (B) if, at any time during the credit period, moderate rehabilitation assistance is provided with respect to such building under section 8(e)(2) of the United States Housing Act of 1937."

Subsec. (c)(2). Pub. L. 101–508, §11701(a)(1)(A), inserted at end "Such term does not include any building with respect to which moderate rehabilitation assistance is provided, at any time during the compliance period, under section 8(e)(2) of the United States Housing Act of 1937."

Pub. L. 101–508, §11407(b)(5)(A), inserted before period at end of last sentence "(other than assistance under the Stewart B. McKinney Homeless Assistance Act of 1988 (as in effect on the date of the enactment of this sentence))".

Subsec. (d)(2)(D)(i)(I). Pub. L. 101–508, §11812(b)(3), inserted "(as in effect on the day before the date of the enactment of the Revenue Reconciliation Act of 1990)" after "section 167(k)."

Subsec. (d)(2)(D)(ii)(V). Pub. L. 101–508, §11407(b)(8), added subcl. (V).

Subsec. (d)(5)(B). Pub. L. 101–508, §11812(b)(3), which directed the insertion of "(as in effect on the day before the date of the enactment of the Revenue Reconciliation Act of 1990)" after "section 167(k)", was executed to the text, and not the heading, of subpar. (B). See 1996 Amendment note above.

Subsec. (d)(5)(C)(ii)(I). Pub. L. 101–508, §11407(b)(4), inserted at end "If the Secretary of Housing and Urban Development determines that sufficient data for any period are not available to apply this clause on the basis of census tracts, such Secretary shall apply this clause for such period on the basis of enumeration districts."

Pub. L. 101–508, §11701(a)(2)(B), inserted before period at end "for such year".

Pub. L. 101–508, §11701(a)(2)(A), which directed the insertion of "which is designated by the Secretary of Housing and Urban Development and, for the most recent year for which census data are available on household income in such tract," after "census tract", was executed by making the insertion after "any census tract" to reflect the probable intent of Congress.

Subsec. (g)(2)(B)(iv). Pub. L. 101–508, §11407(b)(3), added cl. (iv).

Subsec. (g)(2)(D)(i). Pub. L. 101–508, §11701(a)(3)(A), inserted before period at end "and such unit continues to be rent-restricted".

Subsec. (g)(2)(D)(ii). Pub. L. 101–508, §11701(a)(4), inserted at end "In the case of a project described in section 142(d)(4)(B), the preceding sentence shall be applied by substituting '170 percent' for '140 percent' and by substituting 'any low-income unit in the building is occupied by a new resident whose income exceeds 40 percent of area median gross income' for 'any residential unit in the building (of a size comparable to, or smaller than, such unit) is occupied by a new resident whose income exceeds such income limitation'."

Subsec. (g)(3)(A). Pub. L. 101–508, §11701(a)(5)(A), substituted "the 1st year of the credit period for such building" for "the 12-month period beginning on the date the building is placed in service".

Subsec. (h)(3)(C). Pub. L. 101–508, §11701(a)(6)(A), substituted "the sum of the amounts described in clauses (i) and (iii)" for "the amount described in clause (i)" in second sentence.

Subsec. (h)(3)(D)(ii)(II). Pub. L. 101–508, §11701(a)(6)(B), substituted "the sum of the amounts described in clauses (i) and (iii)" for "the amount described in clause (i)".

Subsec. (h)(5)(B). Pub. L. 101–508, §11407(b)(9)(A), inserted "own an interest in the project (directly or through a partnership) and" after "nonprofit organization is to".

Subsec. (h)(5)(C)(i) to (iii). Pub. L. 101–508, §11407(b)(9)(B), added cl. (ii) and redesignated former cl. (ii) as (iii).

Subsec. (h)(5)(D)(i). Pub. L. 101–508, §11407(b)(9)(C), inserted "ownership and" before "material participation".

Subsec. (h)(6)(B)(i). Pub. L. 101–508, §11701(a)(7)(A), inserted before comma at end "and which prohibits the actions described in subclauses (I) and (II) of subparagraph (E)(ii)".

Subsec. (h)(6)(B)(ii). Pub. L. 101–508, §11701(a)(7)(B), substituted "requirement and prohibitions" for "requirement".

Subsec. (h)(6)(B)(iii) to (v). Pub. L. 101–508, §11701(a)(8)(A), added cl. (iii) and redesignated former cls. (iii) and (iv) as (iv) and (v), respectively.

Subsec. (h)(6)(E)(i)(I). Pub. L. 101–508, §11701(a)(9), inserted before comma "unless the Secretary determines that such acquisition is part of an arrangement with the taxpayer a purpose of which is to terminate such period".

Subsec. (h)(6)(E)(ii)(II). Pub. L. 101–508, §11701(a)(8)(C), inserted before period at end "not otherwise permitted under this section".

Subsec. (h)(6)(F). Pub. L. 101–508, §11701(a)(8)(D), inserted "the nonlow-income portion of the building for fair market value and" before "the low-income portion" in introductory provisions.

Subsec. (h)(6)(J) to (L). Pub. L. 101–508, §11701(a)(8)(B), redesignated subpars. (K) and (L) as (J) and (K), respectively, and struck out former subpar. (J) which related to sales of less than the low-income portions of a building.

Subsec. (i)(3)(D). Pub. L. 101–508, §11407(b)(6), substituted "Certain students" for "Students in government-supported job training programs" in heading and amended text generally. Prior to amendment, text read as follows: "A unit shall not fail to be treated as a low-income unit merely because it is occupied by an individual who is enrolled in a job training program receiving assistance under the Job Training Partnership Act or under other similar Federal, State, or local laws."

Subsec. (i)(7). Pub. L. 101–508, §11701(a)(10), redesignated par. (8) as (7).

Subsec. (i)(7)(A). Pub. L. 101–508, §11407(b)(1), substituted "the tenants (in cooperative form or otherwise) or resident management corporation of such building or by a qualified nonprofit organization (as defined in subsection (h)(5)(C)) or government agency" for "the tenants of such building".

Subsec. (i)(8). Pub. L. 101–508, §11701(a)(10), redesignated par. (8) as (7).

Subsec. (k)(1). Pub. L. 101–508, §11813(b)(3)(A), substituted "49(a)(1)" for "46(c)(8)", "49(a)(2)" for "46(c)(9)", and "49(b)(1)" for "47(d)(1)".

Subsec. (k)(2)(A)(ii), (D). Pub. L. 101–508, §11813(b)(3)(B), substituted "49(a)(1)(D)(iv)(II)" for "46(c)(8)(D)(iv)(II)".

Subsec. (m)(1)(B)(ii) to (iv). Pub. L. 101–508, §11407(b)(7)(B), redesignated cls. (iii) and (iv) as (ii) and (iii), respectively, and struck out former cl. (ii) which read as follows: "which gives the highest priority to those projects as to which the highest percentage of the housing credit dollar amount is to be used for project costs other than the cost of intermediaries unless granting such priority would impede the development of projects in hard-to-develop areas,".

Pub. L. 101–508, §11407(b)(2), amended cl. (iv) generally. Prior to amendment, cl. (iv) read as follows: "which provides a procedure that the agency will follow in notifying the Internal Revenue Service of noncompliance with the provisions of this section which such agency becomes aware of."

Subsec. (m)(2)(B). Pub. L. 101–508, §11407(b)(7)(A), added cl. (iii) and inserted provision that cl. (iii) not be applied so as to impede the development of projects in hard-to-develop areas.

Subsec. (o)(1). Pub. L. 101–508, §11407(a)(1)(A), substituted "1991" for "1990" wherever appearing.

Subsec. (o)(2). Pub. L. 101–508, §11407(a)(1)(B), added par. (2) and struck out former par. (2) which read as follows: "For purposes of paragraph (1)(B), a building shall be treated as placed in service before 1990 if—

"(A) the bonds with respect to such building are issued before 1990,

"(B) such building is constructed, reconstructed, or rehabilitated by the taxpayer,

"(C) more than 10 percent of the reasonably anticipated cost of such construction, reconstruction, or rehabilitation has been incurred as of January 1, 1990, and some of such cost is incurred on or after such date, and

"(D) such building is placed in service before January 1, 1992."

1989—Subsec. (b)(1). Pub. L. 101–239, §7108(h)(5), inserted at end "A building shall not be treated as described in subparagraph (B) if, at any time during the credit period, moderate rehabilitation assistance is provided with respect to such building under section 8(e)(2) of the United States Housing Act of 1937."

Subsec. (b)(3)(C). Pub. L. 101–239, §7108(c)(2), which directed amendment of subpar. (C) by substituting "subsection (h)(7)" for "subsection (h)(6)", was executed by substituting "subsection (h)(7)" for "subsection (h)(6)", as the probable intent of Congress.

Subsec. (c)(1)(E). Pub. L. 101–239, §7108(i)(2), added subpar. (E).

Subsec. (d)(1). Pub. L. 101–239, §7108(l)(1), inserted "as of the close of the 1st taxable year of the credit period" before period at end.

Subsec. (d)(2)(A). Pub. L. 101–239, §7108(l)(2), substituted "subparagraph (B), its adjusted basis as of the close of the 1st taxable year of the credit period, and" for "subparagraph (B), the sum of—

"(I) the portion of its adjusted basis attributable to its acquisition cost, plus

"(II) amounts chargeable to capital account and incurred by the taxpayer (before the close of the 1st taxable year of the credit period for such building) for property (or additions or improvements to property) of a character subject to the allowance for depreciation, and".

Subsec. (d)(2)(B)(iv). Pub. L. 101–239, §7108(d)(1), added cl. (iv).

Subsec. (d)(2)(C). Pub. L. 101–239, §7108(l)(3)(A), substituted "Adjusted basis" for "Acquisition cost" in heading and "adjusted basis" for "cost" in text.

Subsec. (d)(5). Pub. L. 101–239, §7108(l)(3)(B), substituted "Special rules for determining eligible basis" for "Eligible basis determined when building placed in service" in heading.

Subsec. (d)(5)(A). Pub. L. 101–239, §7108(l)(3)(B), redesignated subpar. (B) as (A) and struck out former subpar. (A) which read as follows: "Except as provided in subparagraphs (B) and (C), the eligible basis of any building for the entire compliance period for such building shall be its eligible basis on the date such building is placed in service (increased, in the case of an existing building which meets the requirements of paragraph (2)(B), by the amounts described in paragraph (2)(A)(i)(II))."

Subsec. (d)(5)(B). Pub. L. 101–239, §7108(l)(3)(B), redesignated subpar. (C) as (B). Former subpar. (B) redesignated (A).

Subsec. (d)(5)(C). Pub. L. 101–239, §7108(l)(3)(B), redesignated subpar. (D) as (C). Former subpar. (C) redesignated (B).

Pub. L. 101–239, §7811(a)(1), inserted "section" before "167(k)" in heading.

Subsec. (d)(5)(D). Pub. L. 101–239, §7108(l)(3)(B), redesignated subpar. (D) as (C).

Pub. L. 101–239, §7108(g), added subpar. (D).

Subsec. (d)(6)(A)(i). Pub. L. 101–239, §7841(d)(13), substituted "Farmers Home Administration" for "Farmers' Home Administration".

Subsec. (d)(6)(C) to (E). Pub. L. 101–239, §7108(f), added subpars. (C) and (D) and redesignated former subpar. (C) as (E).

Subsec. (d)(7)(A). Pub. L. 101–239, §7831(c)(6), inserted "(or interest therein)" after "subparagraph (B)" in introductory provisions.

Subsec. (d)(7)(A)(ii). Pub. L. 101–239, §7841(d)(14), substituted "under subsection (a)" for "under sebsection (a)".

Subsec. (e)(2)(A). Pub. L. 101–239, §7841(d)(15), substituted "to capital account" for "to captial account".

Subsec. (e)(3). Pub. L. 101–239, §7108(d)(3), substituted "Minimum expenditures to qualify" for "Average of rehabilitation expenditures must be $2,000 or more" in heading, added subpars. (A) and (B), redesignated former subpar. (B) as (C), and struck out former subpar. (A) which read as follows: "Paragraph (1) shall apply to rehabilitation expenditures with respect to any building only if the qualified basis attributable to such expenditures incurred during any 24-month period, when divided by the low-income units in the building, is $2,000 or more."

Subsec. (e)(5). Pub. L. 101–239, §7108(l)(3)(C), substituted "subsection (d)(2)(A)(i)" for "subsection (d)(2)(A)(i)(II)".

Subsec. (f)(4). Pub. L. 101–239, §7831(c)(4), added par. (4).

Subsec. (f)(5). Pub. L. 101–239, §7108(d)(2), added par. (5).

Subsec. (g)(2)(A). Pub. L. 101–239, §7108(e)(2), inserted at end "For purposes of the preceding sentence, the amount of the income limitation under paragraph (1) applicable for any period shall not be less than such limitation applicable for the earliest period the building (which contains the unit) was included in the determination of whether the project is a qualified low-income housing project."

Pub. L. 101–239, §7108(e)(1)(B), substituted "the imputed income limitation applicable to such unit" for "the income limitation under paragraph (1) applicable to individuals occupying such unit".

Subsec. (g)(2)(B). Pub. L. 101–239, §7108(h)(2), added cl. (iii) and concluding provisions which defined "supportive service".

Subsec. (g)(2)(C) to (E). Pub. L. 101–239, §7108(e)(1)(A), added subpars. (C) and (D) and redesignated former subpar. (C) as (E).

Subsec. (g)(3)(D). Pub. L. 101–239, §7108(m)(3), added subpar. (D).

Subsec. (g)(4). Pub. L. 101–239, §7108(n)(2), struck out "(other than section 142(d)(4)(B)(iii))" after "in applying such provisions".

Subsec. (g)(7). Pub. L. 101–239, §7108(h)(3), added par. (7).

Subsec. (h)(1)(B). Pub. L. 101–239, §7108(m)(2), substituted "(E), or (F)" for "or (E)".

Subsec. (h)(1)(F). Pub. L. 101–239, §7108(m)(1), added subpar. (F).

Subsec. (h)(3)(C) to (G). Pub. L. 101–239, §7108(b)(1), added subpars. (C) and (D), redesignated former subpars. (D) to (F) as (E) to (G), respectively, and struck out former subpar. (C) which read as follows: "The State housing credit ceiling applicable to any State for any calendar year shall be an amount equal to $1.25 multiplied by the State population."

Subsec. (h)(4)(B). Pub. L. 101–239, §7108(j), substituted "50 percent" for "70 percent" in heading and in text.

Subsec. (h)(5)(D)(ii). Pub. L. 101–239, §7811(a)(2), substituted "clause (i)" for "clause (ii)".

Subsec. (h)(5)(E). Pub. L. 101–239, §7108(b)(2)(A), substituted "subparagraph (F)" for "subparagraph (E)".

Subsec. (h)(6). Pub. L. 101–239, §7108(c)(1), added par. (6). Former par. (6) redesignated (7).

Subsec. (h)(6)(B) to (E). Pub. L. 101–239, §7108(b)(2)(B), redesignated subpars. (C) to (E) as (B) to (D), respectively, and struck out former subpar. (B) which provided that the housing credit dollar amount could not be carried over to any other calendar year.

Subsec. (h)(7), (8). Pub. L. 101–239, §7108(c)(1), redesignated pars. (6) and (7) as (7) and (8), respectively.

Subsec. (i)(2)(D). Pub. L. 101–239, §7108(k), inserted at end "Such term shall not include any loan which would be a below market Federal loan solely by reason of assistance provided under section 106, 107, or 108 of the Housing and Community Development Act of 1974 (as in effect on the date of the enactment of this sentence)."

Subsec. (i)(3)(B). Pub. L. 101–239, §7108(i)(1), amended subpar. (B) generally. Prior to amendment, subpar. (B) read as follows: "A unit shall not be treated as a low-income unit unless the unit is suitable for occupancy (as determined under regulations prescribed by the Secretary taking into account local health, safety, and building codes) and used other than on a transient basis. For purposes of the preceding sentence, a single-room occupancy unit shall not be treated as used on a transient basis merely because it is rented on a month-by-month basis."

Pub. L. 101–239, §7831(c)(1), inserted "(as determined under regulations prescribed by the Secretary taking into account local health, safety, and building codes)" after "suitable for occupancy".

Pub. L. 101–239, §7108(h)(1), inserted at end "For purposes of the preceding sentence, a single-room occupancy unit shall not be treated as used on a transient basis merely because it is rented on a month-by-month basis."

Subsec. (i)(3)(D). Pub. L. 101–239, §7831(c)(2), added subpar. (D).

Subsec. (i)(3)(E). Pub. L. 101–239, §7108(h)(4), added subpar. (E).

Subsec. (i)(6). Pub. L. 101–239, §7831(c)(3), added par. (6).

Subsec. (i)(8). Pub. L. 101–239, §7108(q), added par. (8).

Subsec. (k)(2)(D). Pub. L. 101–239, §7108(o), added provision at end relating to the applicability of cl. (ii) to qualified nonprofit organizations not described in section 46(c)(8)(D)(iv)(II) with respect to a building.

Subsec. (l)(1). Pub. L. 101–239, §7108(p), in introductory provisions, substituted "Following" for "Not later than the 90th day following" and inserted "at such time and" before "in such form".

Subsec. (m). Pub. L. 101–239, §7108(o), added subsec. (m). Former subsec. (m) redesignated (n).

Subsec. (m)(4). Pub. L. 101–239, §7831(c)(5), added par. (4).

Subsec. (n). Pub. L. 101–239, §7108(o), redesignated subsec. (m) as (n). Former subsec. (n) redesignated (o).

Pub. L. 101–239, §7108(a)(1), amended subsec. (n) generally. Prior to amendment, subsec. (n) read as follows: "The State housing credit ceiling under subsection (h) shall be zero for any calendar year after 1989 and subsection (h)(4) shall not apply to any building placed in service after 1989."

Subsec. (o). Pub. L. 101–239, §7108(o), redesignated subsec. (n) as (o).

1988—Subsec. (b)(2)(A). Pub. L. 100–647, §1002(l)(1)(A), substituted "for the earlier of—" for "for the month in which such building is placed in service" and added cls. (i) and (ii) and concluding provisions.

Subsec. (b)(2)(C)(ii). Pub. L. 100–647, §1002(l)(1)(B), substituted "the month applicable under clause (i) or (ii) of subparagraph (A)" for "the month in which the building was placed in service".

Subsec. (b)(3). Pub. L. 100–647, §1002(l)(9)(B), amended par. (3) generally. Prior to amendment, par. (3) read as follows: "For treatment of certain rehabilitation expenditures as separate new buildings, see subsection (e)."

Subsec. (c)(2)(A). Pub. L. 100–647, §1002(l)(2)(A), amended subpar. (A) generally. Prior to amendment, subpar. (A) read as follows: "which at all times during the compliance period with respect to such building is part of a qualified low-income housing project, and".

Subsec. (d)(2)(D)(ii). Pub. L. 100–647, §1002(l)(3), substituted "Special rules for certain transfers" for "Special rule for nontaxable exchanges" in heading and amended text generally. Prior to amendment, text read as follows: "For purposes of determining under subparagraph (B)(ii) when a building was last placed in service, there shall not be taken into account any placement in service in connection with the acquisition of the building in a transaction in which the basis of the building in the hands of the person acquiring it is determined in whole or in part by reference to the adjusted basis of such building in the hands of the person from whom aquired [sic]."

Subsec. (d)(3). Pub. L. 100–647, §1002(l)(4), amended par. (3) generally. Prior to amendment, par. (3) read as follows: "The eligible basis of any building shall be reduced by an amount equal to the portion of the adjusted basis of the building which is attributable to residential rental units in the building which are not low-income units and which are above the average quality standard of the low-income units in the building."

Subsec. (d)(5)(A). Pub. L. 100–647, §1002(l)(6)(B), substituted "subparagraphs (B) and (C)" for "subparagraph (B)".

Pub. L. 100–647, §1002(l)(5), inserted "(increased, in the case of an existing building which meets the requirements of paragraph (2)(B), by the amounts described in paragraph (2)(A)(i)(II))" before period at end.

Subsec. (d)(5)(C). Pub. L. 100–647, §1002(l)(6)(A), added subpar. (C).

Subsec. (d)(6)(A)(iii). Pub. L. 100–647, §1002(l)(7), struck out cl. (iii) which related to other circumstances of financial distress.

Subsec. (d)(6)(B)(ii). Pub. L. 100–647, §1002(l)(8), struck out "of 1934" after "Act".

Subsec. (f)(1). Pub. L. 100–647, §1002(l)(2)(B), substituted "beginning with—" for "beginning with" and subpars. (A) and (B) and concluding provisions for "the taxable year in which the building is placed in service or, at the election of the taxpayer, the succeeding taxable year. Such an election, once made, shall be irrevocable."

Subsec. (f)(3). Pub. L. 100–647, §1002(l)(9)(A), amended par. (3) generally. Prior to amendment, par. (3) "Special rule where increase in qualified basis after 1st year of credit period" read as follows:

"(A) Credit increased.—If—

"(i) as of the close of any taxable year in the compliance period (after the 1st year of the credit period) the qualified basis of any building exceeds

"(ii) the qualified basis of such building as of the close of the 1st year of the credit period,

the credit allowable under subsection (a) for the taxable year (determined without regard to this paragraph) shall be increased by an amount equal to the product of such excess and the percentage equal to 2/3 of the applicable percentage for such building.

"(B) 1st year computation applies.—A rule similar to the rule of paragraph (2)(A) shall apply to the additional credit allowable by reason of this paragraph for the 1st year in which such additional credit is allowable."

Subsec. (g)(2)(B)(i). Pub. L. 100–647, §1002(l)(10), struck out "Federal" after "comparable".

Subsec. (g)(2)(C). Pub. L. 100–647, §1002(l)(11), added subpar. (C).

Subsec. (g)(3). Pub. L. 100–647, §1002(l)(12), amended par. (3) generally, substituting subpars. (A) to (C) for former subpars. (A) and (B).

Subsec. (g)(4). Pub. L. 100–647, §1002(l)(13), inserted "; except that, in applying such provisions (other than section 142(d)(4)(B)(iii)) for such purposes, the term 'gross rent' shall have the meaning given such term by paragraph (2)(B) of this subsection" before period at end.

Subsec. (g)(6). Pub. L. 100–647, §1002(l)(32), added par. (6).

Subsec. (h)(1). Pub. L. 100–647, §1002(l)(14)(A), amended par. (1) generally. Prior to amendment, par. (1) read as follows: "No credit shall be allowed by reason of this section for any taxable year with respect to any building in excess of the housing credit dollar amount allocated to such building under this subsection. An allocation shall be taken into account under the preceding sentence only if it occurs not later than the earlier of—

"(A) the 60th day after the close of the taxable year, or

"(B) the close of the calendar year in which such taxable year ends."

Subsec. (h)(1)(B). Pub. L. 100–647, §4003(b)(1), substituted "(C), (D), or (E)" for "(C) or (D)".

Subsec. (h)(1)(E). Pub. L. 100–647, §4003(a), added subpar. (E).

Subsec. (h)(4)(A). Pub. L. 100–647, §1002(l)(15), substituted "if—" for "and which is taken into account under section 146" and added cls. (i) and (ii).

Subsec. (h)(5)(D), (E). Pub. L. 100–647, §1002(l)(16), added subpar. (D) and redesignated former subpar. (D) as (E).

Subsec. (h)(6)(B)(ii). Pub. L. 100–647, §1002(l)(14)(B), struck out cl. (ii) which read as follows:

"(ii) Allocation may not be earlier than year in which building placed in service.—A housing credit agency may allocate its housing credit dollar amount for any calendar year only to buildings placed in service before the close of such calendar year."

Subsec. (h)(6)(D). Pub. L. 100–647, §1002(l)(17), amended subpar. (D) generally. Prior to amendment, subpar. (D) "Credit allowable determined without regard to averaging convention, etc." read as follows: "For purposes of this subsection, the credit allowable under subsection (a) with respect to any building shall be determined—

"(i) without regard to paragraphs (2)(A) and (3)(B) of subsection (f), and

"(ii) by applying subsection (f)(3)(A) without regard to 'the percentage equal to 2/3 of'."

Subsec. (h)(6)(E). Pub. L. 100–647, §1002(l)(18), added subpar. (E).

Subsec. (i)(2)(A). Pub. L. 100–647, §1002(l)(19)(A), inserted "or any prior taxable year" after "such taxable year" and substituted "is or was outstanding" for "is outstanding" and "are or were used" for "are used".

Subsec. (i)(2)(B). Pub. L. 100–647, §1002(l)(19)(B), substituted "balance of loan or proceeds of obligations" for "outstanding balance of loan" in heading and amended text generally. Prior to amendment, text read as follows: "A loan shall not be taken into account under subparagraph (A) if the taxpayer elects to exclude an amount equal to the outstanding balance of such loan from the eligible basis of the building for purposes of subsection (d)."

Subsec. (i)(2)(C). Pub. L. 100–647, §1002(l)(19)(C), added subpar. (C). Former subpar. (C) redesignated (D).

Subsec. (i)(2)(D). Pub. L. 100–647, §1002(l)(19)(C), (D), redesignated former subpar. (C) as (D) and substituted "this paragraph" for "subparagraph (A)".

Subsec. (j)(4)(D). Pub. L. 100–647, §1007(g)(3)(B), substituted "D, or G" for "or D".

Subsec. (j)(4)(F). Pub. L. 100–647, §1002(l)(20), added subpar. (F).

Subsec. (j)(5)(B). Pub. L. 100–647, §4004(a), amended subpar. (B) generally. Prior to amendment, subpar. (B) read as follows: "This paragraph shall apply to any partnership—

"(i) more than ½ the capital interests, and more than ½ the profit interests, in which are owned by a group of 35 or more partners each of whom is a natural person or an estate, and

"(ii) which elects the application of this paragraph."

Subsec. (j)(5)(B)(i). Pub. L. 100–647, §1002(l)(21), amended cl. (i) generally. Prior to amendment, cl. (i) read as follows: "which has 35 or more partners each of whom is a natural person or an estate, and".

Subsec. (j)(6). Pub. L. 100–647, §1002(l)(22), inserted "(or interest therein)" after "disposition of building" in heading, and in text inserted "or an interest therein" after "of a building".

Subsec. (k)(2)(B). Pub. L. 100–647, §1002(l)(23), inserted before period at end ", except that this subparagraph shall not apply in the case of a federally assisted building described in subsection (d)(6)(B) if—" and cls. (i) and (ii).

Subsec. (l). Pub. L. 100–647, §1002(l)(24)(B), substituted "Certifications and other reports to Secretary" for "Certifications to Secretary" in heading.

Subsec. (l)(2), (3). Pub. L. 100–647, §1002(l)(24)(A), added par. (2) and redesignated former par. (2) as (3).

Subsec. (n). Pub. L. 100–647, §4003(b)(3), amended subsec. (n) generally, substituting a single par. for former pars. (1) and (2).

Subsec. (n)(1). Pub. L. 100–647, §1002(l)(25), inserted ", and, except for any building described in paragraph (2)(B), subsection (h)(4) shall not apply to any building placed in service after 1989" after "year after 1989".

1986—Subsec. (k)(1). Pub. L. 99–509 substituted "subparagraphs (D)(ii)(II) and (D)(iv)(I)" for "subparagraph (D)(iv)(I)".

STATUTORY NOTES AND RELATED SUBSIDIARIES
EFFECTIVE DATE OF 2020 AMENDMENT

Pub. L. 116–260, div. EE, title II, §201(b), Dec. 27, 2020, 134 Stat. 3056, provided that: "The amendments made by this section [amending this section] shall apply to—

"(1) any building which receives an allocation of housing credit dollar amount after December 31, 2020, and

"(2) in the case of any building any portion of which is financed with an obligation described in section 42(h)(4)(A), any such building if any such obligation which so finances such building is issued after December 31, 2020."

EFFECTIVE DATE OF 2018 AMENDMENT

Pub. L. 115–141, div. T, §102(b), Mar. 23, 2018, 132 Stat. 1157, provided that: "The amendment made by this section [amending this section] shall apply to calendar years beginning after December 31, 2017."

Pub. L. 115–141, div. T, §103(c), Mar. 23, 2018, 132 Stat. 1159, provided that: "The amendments made by this section [amending this section] shall apply to elections made under section 42(g)(1) of the Internal Revenue Code of 1986 after the date of the enactment of this Act [Mar. 23, 2018]."

EFFECTIVE DATE OF 2017 AMENDMENT

Amendment by Pub. L. 115–97 applicable to taxable years beginning after Dec. 31, 2017, see section 11002(e) of Pub. L. 115–97, set out as a note under section 1 of this title.

EFFECTIVE DATE OF 2015 AMENDMENT

Pub. L. 114–113, div. Q, title I, §131(c), Dec. 18, 2015, 129 Stat. 3055, provided that: "The amendments made by this section [amending this section] shall take effect on January 1, 2015."

EFFECTIVE DATE OF 2014 AMENDMENT

Pub. L. 113–295, div. A, title I, §112(b), Dec. 19, 2014, 128 Stat. 4014, provided that: "The amendment made by this section [amending this section] shall take effect on January 1, 2014."

Pub. L. 113–295, div. A, title II, §212(d), Dec. 19, 2014, 128 Stat. 4033, provided that: "The amendments made by this section [amending this section and sections 121 and 168 of this title] shall take effect as if included in the provisions of the Housing Assistance Tax Act of 2008 [Pub. L. 110–289, div. C] to which they relate."

Amendment by section 221(a)(7) of Pub. L. 113–295 effective Dec. 19, 2014, subject to a savings provision, see section 221(b) of Pub. L. 113–295, set out as a note under section 1 of this title.

EFFECTIVE DATE OF 2013 AMENDMENT

Pub. L. 112–240, title III, §302(b), Jan. 2, 2013, 126 Stat. 2329, provided that: "The amendment made by this section [amending this section] shall take effect on the date of the enactment of this Act [Jan. 2, 2013]."

EFFECTIVE DATE OF 2008 AMENDMENT

Pub. L. 110–289, div. C, title I, §3002(c), July 30, 2008, 122 Stat. 2880, provided that: "The amendments made by this subsection [probably means this section, amending this section] shall apply to buildings placed in service after the date of the enactment of this Act [July 30, 2008]."

Pub. L. 110–289, div. C, title I, §3003(h), July 30, 2008, 122 Stat. 2882, provided that:

"(1) In general.—Except as otherwise provided in paragraph (2), the amendments made by this subsection [probably means this section, amending this section] shall apply to buildings placed in service after the date of the enactment of this Act [July 30, 2008].

"(2) Rehabilitation requirements.—

"(A) In general.—The amendments made by subsection (b) [amending this section] shall apply to buildings with respect to which housing credit dollar amounts are allocated after the date of the enactment of this Act [July 30, 2008].

"(B) Buildings not subject to allocation limits.—To the extent paragraph (1) of section 42(h) of the Internal Revenue Code of 1986 does not apply to any building by reason of paragraph (4) thereof, the amendments made by subsection (b) [amending this section] shall apply [to] buildings financed with bonds issued pursuant to allocations made after the date of the enactment of this Act [July 30, 2008]."

Pub. L. 110–289, div. C, title I, §3004(i), July 30, 2008, 122 Stat. 2884, provided that:

"(1) In general.—Except as otherwise provided in this subsection, the amendments made by this section [amending this section] shall apply to buildings placed in service after the date of the enactment of this Act [July 30, 2008].

"(2) Repeal of bonding requirement on disposition of building.—The amendment made by subsection (c) [amending this section] shall apply to—

"(A) interests in buildings disposed [of] after the date of the enactment of this Act [July 30, 2008], and

"(B) interests in buildings disposed of on or before such date if—

"(i) it is reasonably expected that such building will continue to be operated as a qualified low-income building (within the meaning of section 42 of the Internal Revenue Code of 1986) for the remaining compliance period (within the meaning of such section) with respect to such building, and

"(ii) the taxpayer elects the application of this subparagraph with respect to such disposition.

"(3) Energy efficiency and historic nature taken into account in making allocations.—The amendments made by subsection (d) [amending this section] shall apply to allocations made after December 31, 2008.

"(4) Continued eligibility for students who received foster care assistance.—The amendments made by subsection (e) [amending this section] shall apply to determinations made after the date of the enactment of this Act [July 30, 2008].

"(5) Treatment of rural projects.—The amendment made by subsection (f) [amending this section] shall apply to determinations made after the date of the enactment of this Act [July 30, 2008].

"(6) Clarification of general public use requirement.—The amendment made by subsection (g) [amending this section] shall apply to buildings placed in service before, on, or after the date of the enactment of this Act [July 30, 2008]."

Pub. L. 110–289, div. C, title I, §3007(c), July 30, 2008, 122 Stat. 2886, provided that: "The amendments made by this section [amending this section and section 146 of this title] shall apply to repayments of loans received after the date of the enactment of this Act [July 30, 2008]."

<h3 style="text-align:center">EFFECTIVE DATE OF 2007 AMENDMENT</h3>

Pub. L. 110–142, §6(b), Dec. 20, 2007, 121 Stat. 1806, provided that: "The amendment made by this section [amending this section] shall apply to—

"(1) housing credit amounts allocated before, on, or after the date of the enactment of this Act [Dec. 20, 2007], and

"(2) buildings placed in service before, on, or after such date to the extent paragraph (1) of section 42(h) of the Internal Revenue Code of 1986 does not apply to any building by reason of paragraph (4) thereof."

<h3 style="text-align:center">EFFECTIVE DATE OF 2004 AMENDMENT</h3>

Amendment by section 207(8) of Pub. L. 108–311 applicable to taxable years beginning after Dec. 31, 2004, see section 208 of Pub. L. 108–311, set out as a note under section 2 of this title.

<h3 style="text-align:center">EFFECTIVE DATE OF 2000 AMENDMENT</h3>

Pub. L. 106–554, §1(a)(7) [title I, subtitle D, §131(d)], Dec. 21, 2000, 114 Stat. 2763, 2763A-611, provided that: "The amendments made by this section [amending this section] shall apply to calendar years after 2000."

Pub. L. 106–554, §1(a)(7) [title I, subtitle D, §137], Dec. 21, 2000, 114 Stat. 2763, 2763A-613, provided that: "Except as otherwise provided in this subtitle [amending this section and enacting provisions set out above], the amendments made by this subtitle shall apply to—

"(1) housing credit dollar amounts allocated after December 31, 2000; and

"(2) buildings placed in service after such date to the extent paragraph (1) of section 42(h) of the Internal Revenue Code of 1986 does not apply to any building by reason of paragraph (4) thereof, but only with respect to bonds issued after such date."

<h3 style="text-align:center">EFFECTIVE DATE OF 1998 AMENDMENT</h3>

Amendment by Pub. L. 105–206 effective, except as otherwise provided, as if included in the provisions of the Taxpayer Relief Act of 1997, Pub. L. 105–34, to which such amendment relates, see section 6024 of Pub. L. 105–206, set out as a note under section 1 of this title.

<h3 style="text-align:center">EFFECTIVE DATE OF 1993 AMENDMENT</h3>

Pub. L. 103–66, title XIII, §13142(a)(2), Aug. 10, 1993, 107 Stat. 438, provided that: "The amendment made by paragraph (1) [amending this section] shall apply to periods ending after June 30, 1992."

Pub. L. 103–66, title XIII, §13142(b)(6), Aug. 10, 1993, 107 Stat. 439, as amended by Pub. L. 104–188, title I, §1703(b), Aug. 20, 1996, 110 Stat. 1875, provided that:

"(A) In general.—Except as provided in subparagraphs (B) and (C), the amendments made by this subsection [amending this section] shall apply to—

"(i) determinations under section 42 of the Internal Revenue Code of 1986 with respect to housing credit dollar amounts allocated from State housing credit ceilings after June 30, 1992, or

"(ii) buildings placed in service after June 30, 1992, to the extent paragraph (1) of section 42(h) of such Code does not apply to any building by reason of paragraph (4) thereof, but only with respect to bonds issued after such date.

"(B) Full-time students, waiver authority, and prohibited discrimination.—The amendments made by paragraphs (2), (3), and (4) [amending this section] shall take effect on the date of the enactment of this Act [Aug. 10, 1993].

"(C) HOME assistance.—The amendment made by paragraph (5) [amending this section] shall apply to periods after the date of the enactment of this Act."

<h3 style="text-align:center">EFFECTIVE DATE OF 1991 AMENDMENT</h3>

Pub. L. 102–227, title I, §107(b), Dec. 11, 1991, 105 Stat. 1688, provided that: "The amendments made by this section [amending this section] shall apply to calendar years after 1991."

<h3 style="text-align:center">EFFECTIVE DATE OF 1990 AMENDMENT</h3>

Pub. L. 101–508, title XI, §11407(a)(3), Nov. 5, 1990, 104 Stat. 1388–474, provided that: "The amendments made by this subsection [amending this section and repealing provisions set out below] shall apply to calendar years after 1989."

Pub. L. 101–508, title XI, §11407(b)(10), Nov. 5, 1990, 104 Stat. 1388–476, provided that:

"(A) In general.—Except as otherwise provided in this paragraph, the amendments made by this subsection [amending this section] shall apply to—

"(i) determinations under section 42 of the Internal Revenue Code of 1986 with respect to housing credit dollar amounts allocated from State housing credit ceilings for calendar years after 1990, or

"(ii) buildings placed in service after December 31, 1990, to the extent paragraph (1) of section 42(h) of such Code does not apply to any building by reason of paragraph (4) thereof, but only with respect to bonds issued after such date.

"(B) Tenant rights, etc.—The amendments made by paragraphs (1), (6), (8), and (9) [amending this section] shall take effect on the date of the enactment of this Act [Nov. 5, 1990].

"(C) Monitoring.—The amendment made by paragraph (2) [amending this section] shall take effect on January 1, 1992, and shall apply to buildings placed in service before, on, or after such date.

"(D) Study.—The Inspector General of the Department of Housing and Urban Development and the Secretary of the Treasury shall jointly conduct a study of the effectiveness of the amendment made by paragraph (5) [amending this section] in carrying out the purposes of section 42 of the Internal Revenue Code of 1986. The report of such study shall be submitted not later than January 1, 1993, to the Committee on Ways and Means of the House of Representatives and the Committee on Finance of the Senate."

Pub. L. 101–508, title XI, §11701(a)(3)(B), Nov. 5, 1990, 104 Stat. 1388–506, provided that: "In the case of a building to which (but for this subparagraph) the amendment made by subparagraph (A) [amending this section] does not apply, such amendment shall apply to—

"(i) determinations of qualified basis for taxable years beginning after the date of the enactment of this Act [Nov. 5, 1990], and

"(ii) determinations of qualified basis for taxable years beginning on or before such date except that determinations for such taxable years shall be made without regard to any reduction in gross rent after August 3, 1990, for any period before August 4, 1990."

Pub. L. 101–508, title XI, §11701(n), Nov. 5, 1990, 104 Stat. 1388–513, provided that: "Except as otherwise provided in this section, any amendment made by this section [amending this section and sections 148, 163, 172, 403, 1031, 1253, 2056, 4682, 4975, 4978B and 6038 of this title, and provisions set out as notes under this section and section 2040 of this title] shall take effect as if included in the provision of the Revenue Reconciliation Act of 1989 [Pub. L. 101–239, title VII] to which such amendment relates."

Pub. L. 101–508, title XI, §11812(c), Nov. 5, 1990, 104 Stat. 1388–536, provided that:

"(1) In general.—Except as provided in paragraph (2), the amendments made by this section [amending this section and sections 56, 167, 168, 312, 381, 404, 460, 642, 1016, 1250, and 7701 of this title] shall apply to property placed in service after the date of the enactment of this Act [Nov. 5, 1990].

"(2) Exception.—The amendments made by this section shall not apply to any property to which section 168 of the Internal Revenue Code of 1986 does not apply by reason of subsection (f)(5) thereof.

"(3) Exception for previously grandfather expenditures.—The amendments made by this section shall not apply to rehabilitation expenditures described in section 252(f)(5) of the Tax Reform Act of 1986 [Pub. L. 99–514] (as added by section 1002(l)(31) of the Technical and Miscellaneous Revenue Act of 1988 [see Transitional Rules note below])."

Amendment by section 11813(b)(3) of Pub. L. 101–508 applicable to property placed in service after Dec. 31, 1990, but not applicable to any transition property (as defined in section 49(e) of this title), any property with respect to which qualified progress expenditures were previously taken into account under section 46(d) of this title, and any property described in section 46(b)(2)(C) of this title, as such sections were in effect on Nov. 4, 1990, see section 11813(c) of Pub. L. 101–508, set out as a note under section 45K of this title.

EFFECTIVE DATE OF 1989 AMENDMENT

Pub. L. 101–239, title VII, §7108(r), Dec. 19, 1989, 103 Stat. 2321, as amended by Pub. L. 101–508, title XI, §11701(a)(11), (12), Nov. 5, 1990, 104 Stat. 1388–507; Pub. L. 104–188, title I, §1702(g)(5)(A), Aug. 20, 1996, 110 Stat. 1873, provided that:

"(1) In general.—Except as otherwise provided in this subsection, the amendments made by this section [amending this section and section 142 of this title] shall apply to determinations under section 42 of the Internal Revenue Code of 1986 with respect to housing credit dollar amounts allocated from State housing credit ceilings for calendar years after 1989.

"(2) Buildings not subject to allocation limits.—Except as otherwise provided in this subsection, to the extent paragraph (1) of section 42(h) of such Code does not apply to any building by reason of paragraph (4) thereof, the amendments made by this section shall apply to buildings placed in service after December 31, 1989.

"(3) One-year carryover of unused credit authority, etc.—The amendments made by subsection (b) [amending this section] shall apply to calendar years after 1989, but clauses (ii), (iii), and (iv) of section 42(h)(3)(C) of such Code (as added by this section) shall be applied without regard to allocations for 1989 or any preceding year.

"(4) Additional buildings eligible for waiver of 10-year rule.—The amendments made by subsection (f) [amending this section] shall take effect on the date of the enactment of this Act [Dec. 19, 1989].

"(5) Certifications with respect to 1st year of credit period.—The amendment made by subsection (p) [amending this section] shall apply to taxable years ending on or after December 31, 1989.

"(6) Certain rules which apply to bonds.—Paragraphs (1)(D) and (2)(D) of section 42(m) of such Code, as added by this section, shall apply to obligations issued after December 31, 1989.

"(7) Clarifications.—The amendments made by the following provisions of this section shall apply as if included in the amendments made by section 252 of the Tax Reform Act of 1986 [Pub. L. 99–514, enacting this section and amending sections 38 and 55 of this title]:

"(A) Paragraph (1) of subsection (h) (relating to units rented on a monthly basis) [amending this section].

"(B) Subsection (l) (relating to eligible basis for new buildings to include expenditures before close of 1st year of credit period) [amending this section].

"(8) Guidance on difficult development areas and posting of bond to avoid recapture.—Not later than 180 days after the date of the enactment of this Act [Dec. 19, 1989]—

"(A) the Secretary of Housing and Urban Development shall publish initial guidance on the designation of difficult development areas under section 42(d)(5)(C) of such Code, as added by this section, and

"(B) the Secretary of the Treasury shall publish initial guidance under section 42(j)(6) of such Code (relating to no recapture on disposition of building (or interest therein) where bond posted)."

[Pub. L. 104–188, title I, §1702(g)(5), Aug. 20, 1996, 110 Stat. 1873, provided that:

["(A) Paragraph (11) of section 11701(a) of the Revenue Reconciliation Act of 1990 (and the amendment made by such paragraph) [Pub. L. 101–508, which amended section 7108(r)(2) of Pub. L. 101–239, set out above, by inserting "but only with respect to bonds issued after such date" before the period at the end of such section 7108(r)(2)] are hereby repealed, and section 7108(r)(2) of the Revenue Reconciliation Act of 1989 [Pub. L. 101–239] shall be applied as if such paragraph (and amendment) had never been enacted.

["(B) Subparagraph (A) shall not apply to any building if the owner of such building establishes to the satisfaction of the Secretary of the Treasury or his delegate that such owner reasonably relied on the amendment made by such paragraph (11)."]

Amendment by section 7811(a) of Pub. L. 101–239 effective, except as otherwise provided, as if included in the provision of the Technical and Miscellaneous Revenue Act of 1988, Pub. L. 100–647, to which such amendment relates, see section 7817 of Pub. L. 101–239, set out as a note under section 1 of this title.

Amendment by section 7831(c) of Pub. L. 101–239 effective as if included in the provision of the Tax Reform Act of 1986, Pub. L. 99–514, to which such amendment relates, see section 7831(g) of Pub. L. 101–239, set out as a note under section 1 of this title.

EFFECTIVE DATE OF 1988 AMENDMENT

Amendment by sections 1002(l)(1)–(25), (32) and 1007(g)(3)(B) of Pub. L. 100–647 effective, except as otherwise provided, as if included in the provision of the Tax Reform Act of 1986, Pub. L. 99–514, to which such amendment relates, see section 1019(a) of Pub. L. 100–647, set out as a note under section 1 of this title.

Pub. L. 100–647, title IV, §4003(c), Nov. 10, 1988, 102 Stat. 3644, provided that: "The amendments made by this section [amending this section and provisions set out as a note under section 469 of this title] shall apply to amounts allocated in calendar years after 1987."

Pub. L. 100–647, title IV, §4004(b), Nov. 10, 1988, 102 Stat. 3644, provided that:

"(1) In general.—The amendment made by subsection (a) [amending this section] shall take effect as if included in the amendments made by section 252 of the Reform Act [section 252 of Pub. L. 99–514, enacting this section and amending sections 38 and 55 of this title].

"(2) Period for election.—The period for electing not to have section 42(j)(5) of the 1986 Code apply to any partnership shall not expire before the date which is 6 months after the date of the enactment of this Act [Nov. 10, 1988]."

EFFECTIVE DATE OF 1986 AMENDMENT

Pub. L. 99–509, title VIII, §8072(b), Oct. 21, 1986, 100 Stat. 1964, provided that: "The amendment made by subsection (a) [amending this section] shall take effect as if included in the amendment made by section 252(a) of the Tax Reform Act of 1986 [enacting this section]."

EFFECTIVE DATE

Pub. L. 99–514, title II, §252(e), Oct. 22, 1986, 100 Stat. 2205, provided that:

"(1) In general.—The amendments made by this section [enacting this section and amending sections 38 and 55 of this title] shall apply to buildings placed in service after December 31, 1986, in taxable years ending after such date.

"(2) Special rule for rehabilitation expenditures.—Subsection (e) of section 42 of the Internal Revenue Code of 1986 (as added by this section) shall apply for purposes of paragraph (1)."

SAVINGS PROVISION

For provisions that nothing in amendment by sections 11812(b)(3) and 11813(b)(3) of Pub. L. 101–508 be construed to affect treatment of certain transactions occurring, property acquired, or items of income, loss, deduction, or credit taken into account prior to Nov. 5, 1990, for purposes of determining liability for tax for periods ending after Nov. 5, 1990, see section 11821(b) of Pub. L. 101–508, set out as a note under section 45K of this title.

GRANTS TO STATES FOR LOW-INCOME HOUSING PROJECTS IN LIEU OF LOW-INCOME HOUSING CREDIT ALLOCATIONS FOR 2009

Pub. L. 111–5, div. B, title I, §1602, Feb. 17, 2009, 123 Stat. 362, provided that:

"(a) In General.—The Secretary of the Treasury shall make a grant to the housing credit agency of each State in an amount equal to such State's low-income housing grant election amount.

"(b) Low-Income Housing Grant Election Amount.—For purposes of this section, the term 'low-income housing grant election amount' means, with respect to any State, such amount as the State may elect which does not exceed 85 percent of the product of—

"(1) the sum of—

"(A) 100 percent of the State housing credit ceiling for 2009 which is attributable to amounts described in clauses (i) and (iii) of section 42(h)(3)(C) of the Internal Revenue Code of 1986, and

"(B) 40 percent of the State housing credit ceiling for 2009 which is attributable to amounts described in clauses (ii) and (iv) of such section, multiplied by

"(2) 10.

"(c) Subawards for Low-Income Buildings.—

"(1) In general.—A State housing credit agency receiving a grant under this section shall use such grant to make subawards to finance the construction or acquisition and rehabilitation of qualified low-income buildings. A subaward under this section may be made to finance a qualified low-income building with or without an allocation under section 42 of the Internal Revenue Code of 1986, except that a State housing credit agency may make subawards to finance qualified low-income buildings without an allocation only if it makes a determination that such use will increase the total funds available to the State to build and rehabilitate affordable housing. In complying with such determination requirement, a State housing credit agency shall establish a process in which applicants that are allocated credits are required to demonstrate good faith efforts to obtain investment commitments for such credits before the agency makes such subawards.

"(2) Subawards subject to same requirements as low-income housing credit allocations.—Any such subaward with respect to any qualified low-income building shall be made in the same manner and shall be subject to the same limitations (including rent, income, and use restrictions on such building) as an allocation of housing credit dollar amount allocated by such State housing credit agency under section 42 of the Internal Revenue Code of 1986, except that such subawards shall not be limited by, or otherwise affect (except as provided in subsection (h)(3)(J) of such section [section 42(h)(3) has no subpar. (J)]), the State housing credit ceiling applicable to such agency.

"(3) Compliance and asset management.—The State housing credit agency shall perform asset management functions to ensure compliance with section 42 of the Internal Revenue Code of 1986 and the long-term viability of buildings funded by any subaward under this section. The State housing credit agency may collect reasonable fees from a subaward recipient to cover expenses associated with the performance of its duties under this paragraph. The State housing credit agency may retain an agent or other private contractor to satisfy the requirements of this paragraph.

"(4) Recapture.—The State housing credit agency shall impose conditions or restrictions, including a requirement providing for recapture, on any subaward under this section so as to assure that the building with respect to which such subaward is made remains a qualified low-income building during the compliance period. Any such recapture shall be payable to the Secretary of the Treasury for deposit in the general fund of the Treasury and may be enforced by means of liens or such other methods as the Secretary of the Treasury determines appropriate.

"(d) Return of Unused Grant Funds.—Any grant funds not used to make subawards under this section before January 1, 2011, shall be returned to the Secretary of the Treasury on such date. Any subawards returned to the State housing credit agency on or after such date shall be promptly returned to the Secretary of the Treasury. Any amounts returned to the Secretary of the Treasury under this subsection shall be deposited in the general fund of the Treasury.

"(e) Definitions.—Any term used in this section which is also used in section 42 of the Internal Revenue Code of 1986 shall have the same meaning for purposes of this section as when used in such section 42. Any reference in this section to the Secretary of the Treasury shall be treated as including the Secretary's delegate.

"(f) Appropriations.—There is hereby appropriated to the Secretary of the Treasury such sums as may be necessary to carry out this section."

ELECTION TO DETERMINE RENT LIMITATION BASED ON NUMBER OF BEDROOMS AND DEEP RENT SKEWING

Pub. L. 103–66, title XIII, §13142(c), Aug. 10, 1993, 107 Stat. 439, provided that:

"(1) In the case of a building to which the amendments made by subsection (e)(1) or (n)(2) of section 7108 of the Revenue Reconciliation Act of 1989 [Pub. L. 101–239, amending this section] did not apply, the taxpayer may elect to have such amendments apply to such building if the taxpayer has met the requirements of the procedures described in section 42(m)(1)(B)(iii) of the Internal Revenue Code of 1986.

"(2) In the case of the amendment made by such subsection (e)(1), such election shall apply only with respect to tenants first occupying any unit in the building after the date of the election.

"(3) In the case of the amendment made by such subsection (n)(2), such election shall apply only if rents of low-income tenants in such building do not increase as a result of such election.

"(4) An election under this subsection may be made only during the 180-day period beginning on the date of the enactment of this Act [Aug. 10, 1993] and, once made, shall be irrevocable."

ELECTION TO ACCELERATE CREDIT INTO 1990

Pub. L. 101–508, title XI, §11407(c), Nov. 5, 1990, 104 Stat. 1388–476, provided that:

"(1) In general.—At the election of an individual, the credit determined under section 42 of the Internal Revenue Code of 1986 for the taxpayer's first taxable year ending on or after October 25, 1990, shall be 150 percent of the amount which would (but for this paragraph) be so allowable with respect to investments held by such individual on or before October 25, 1990.

"(2) Reduction in aggregate credit to reflect increased 1990 credit.—The aggregate credit allowable to any person under section 42 of such Code with respect to any investment for taxable years after the first taxable year referred to in paragraph (1) shall be reduced on a pro rata basis by the amount of the increased credit allowable by reason of paragraph (1) with respect to such first taxable year. The preceding sentence shall not be construed to affect whether any taxable year is part of the credit, compliance, or extended use periods.

"(3) Election.—The election under paragraph (1) shall be made at the time and in the manner prescribed by the Secretary of the Treasury or his delegate, and, once made, shall be irrevocable. In the case of a partnership, such election shall be made by the partnership."

EXCEPTION TO TIME PERIOD FOR MEETING PROJECT REQUIREMENTS IN ORDER TO QUALIFY AS LOW-INCOME HOUSING

Pub. L. 101–508, title XI, §11701(a)(5)(B), Nov. 5, 1990, 104 Stat. 1388–506, provided that: "In the case of a building to which the amendment made by subparagraph (A) [amending this section] does not apply, the period specified in section 42(g)(3)(A) of the Internal Revenue Code of 1986 (as in effect before the amendment made by subparagraph (A)) shall not expire before the close of the taxable year following the taxable year in which the building is placed in service."

STATE HOUSING CREDIT CEILING FOR CALENDAR YEAR 1990

Pub. L. 101–239, title VII, §7108(a)(2), Dec. 19, 1989, 103 Stat. 2307, provided that in the case of calendar year 1990, section 42(h)(3)(C)(i) of the Internal Revenue Code of 1986 be applied by substituting "$.9375" for "$1.25", prior to repeal by Pub. L. 101–508, title XI, §11407(a)(2), (3), Nov. 5, 1990, 104 Stat. 1388–474, applicable to calendar years after 1989.

TRANSITIONAL RULES

Pub. L. 99–514, title II, §252(f), Oct. 22, 1986, 100 Stat. 2205, as amended by Pub. L. 100–647, title I, §1002(l)(28)–(31), Nov. 10, 1988, 102 Stat. 3381, provided that:

"(1) Limitation to non-acrs buildings not to apply to certain buildings, etc.—

"(A) In general.—In the case of a building which is part of a project described in subparagraph (B)—

"(i) section 42(c)(2)(B) of the Internal Revenue Code of 1986 (as added by this section) shall not apply,

"(ii) such building shall be treated as not federally subsidized for purposes of section 42(b)(1)(A) of such Code,

"(iii) the eligible basis of such building shall be treated, for purposes of section 42(h)(4)(A) of such Code, as if it were financed by an obligation the interest on which is exempt from tax under section 103 of such Code and which is taken into account under section 146 of such Code, and

"(iv) the amendments made by section 803 [enacting section 263A of this title, amending sections 48, 267, 312, 447, 464, and 471 of this title, and repealing sections 189, 278, and 280 of this title] shall not apply.

"(B) Project described.—A project is described in this subparagraph if—

"(i) an urban development action grant application with respect to such project was submitted on September 13, 1984,

"(ii) a zoning commission map amendment related to such project was granted on July 17, 1985, and

"(iii) the number assigned to such project by the Federal Housing Administration is 023–36602.

"(C) Additional units eligible for credit.—In the case of a building to which subparagraph (A) applies and which is part of a project which meets the requirements of subparagraph (D), for each low-income unit in such building which is occupied by individuals whose income is 30 percent or less of area median gross income, one additional unit (not otherwise a low-income unit) in such building shall be treated as a low-income unit for purposes of such section 42.

"(D) Project described.—A project is described in this subparagraph if—

"(i) rents charged for units in such project are restricted by State regulations,

"(ii) the annual cash flow of such project is restricted by State law,

"(iii) the project is located on land owned by or ground leased from a public housing authority,

"(iv) construction of such project begins on or before December 31, 1986, and units within such project are placed in service on or before June 1, 1990, and

"(v) for a 20-year period, 20 percent or more of the residential units in such project are occupied by individuals whose income is 50 percent or less of area median gross income.

"(E) Maximum additional credit.—The maximum present value of additional credits allowable under section 42 of such Code by reason of subparagraph (C) shall not exceed 25 percent of the eligible basis of the building.

"(2) Additional allocation of housing credit ceiling.—

"(A) In general.—There is hereby allocated to each housing credit agency described in subparagraph (B) an additional housing credit dollar amount determined in accordance with the following table:

"For calendar year:	The additional allocation is:
1987	$3,900,000
1988	$7,600,000
1989	$1,300,000.

"(B) Housing credit agencies described.—The housing credit agencies described in this subparagraph are:

"(i) A corporate governmental agency constituted as a public benefit corporation and established in 1971 under the provisions of Article XII of the Private Housing Finance Law of the State.

"(ii) A city department established on December 20, 1979, pursuant to chapter XVIII of a municipal code of such city for the purpose of supervising and coordinating the formation and execution of projects and programs affecting housing within such city.

"(iii) The State housing finance agency referred to in subparagraph (C), but only with respect to projects described in subparagraph (C).

"(C) Project described.—A project is described in this subparagraph if such project is a qualified low-income housing project which—

"(i) receives financing from a State housing finance agency from the proceeds of bonds issued pursuant to chapter 708 of the Acts of 1966 of such State pursuant to loan commitments from such agency made between May 8, 1984, and July 8, 1986, and

"(ii) is subject to subsidy commitments issued pursuant to a program established under chapter 574 of the Acts of 1983 of such State having award dates from such agency between May 31, 1984, and June 11, 1985.

"(D) Special rules.—

"(i) Any building—

"(I) which is allocated any housing credit dollar amount by a housing credit agency described in clause (iii) of subparagraph (B), and

"(II) which is placed in service after June 30, 1986, and before January 1, 1987,

shall be treated for purposes of the amendments made by this section as placed in service on January 1, 1987.

"(ii) Section 42(c)(2)(B) of the Internal Revenue Code of 1986 shall not apply to any building which is allocated any housing credit dollar amount by any agency described in subparagraph (B).

"(E) All units treated as low income units in certain cases.—In the case of any building—

"(i) which is allocated any housing credit dollar amount by any agency described in subparagraph (B), and

"(ii) which after the application of subparagraph (D)(ii) is a qualified low-income building at all times during any taxable year,

such building shall be treated as described in section 42(b)(1)(B) of such Code and having an applicable fraction for such year of 1. The preceding sentence shall apply to any building only to the extent of the portion of the additional housing credit dollar amount (allocated to such agency under subparagraph (A)) allocated to such building.

"(3) Certain projects placed in service before 1987.—

"(A) In general.—In the case of a building which is part of a project described in subparagraph (B)—

"(i) section 42(c)(2)(B) of such Code shall not apply,

"(ii) such building shall be treated as placed in service during the first calendar year after 1986 and before 1990 in which such building is a qualified low-income building (determined after the application of clause (i)), and

"(iii) for purposes of section 42(h) of such Code, such building shall be treated as having allocated to it a housing credit dollar amount equal to the dollar amount appearing in the clause of subparagraph (B) in which such building is described.

"(B) Project described.—A project is described in this subparagraph if the code number assigned to such project by the Farmers' Home Administration appears in the following table:

"The code number is:	The housing credit dollar amount is:
(i) 49284553664	$16,000
(ii) 4927742022446	$22,000
(iii) 49270742276087	$64,000
(iv) 490270742387293	$48,000
(v) 4927074218234	$32,000
(vi) 49270742274019	$36,000
(vii) 51460742345074	$53,000.

"(C) Determination of adjusted basis.—The adjusted basis of any building to which this paragraph applies for purposes of section 42 of such Code shall be its adjusted basis as of the close of the taxable year ending before the first taxable year of the credit period for such building.

"(D) Certain rules to apply.—Rules similar to the rules of subparagraph (E) of paragraph (2) shall apply for purposes of this paragraph.

"(4) Definitions.—For purposes of this subsection, terms used in such subsection which are also used in section 42 of the Internal Revenue Code of 1986 (as added by this section) shall have the meanings given such terms by such section 42.

"(5) Transitional rule.—In the case of any rehabilitation expenditures incurred with respect to units located in the neighborhood strategy area within the community development block grant program in Ft. Wayne, Indiana—

"(A) the amendments made by this section [enacting this section and amending sections 38 and 55 of this title] shall not apply, and

"(B) paragraph (1) of section 167(k) of the Internal Revenue Code of 1986, shall be applied as if it did not contain the phrase 'and before January 1, 1987'. The number of units to which the preceding sentence applies shall not exceed 150."

¹ *So in original. See 2008 Amendment note below.*

§43. Enhanced oil recovery credit

(a) General rule

For purposes of section 38, the enhanced oil recovery credit for any taxable year is an amount equal to 15 percent of the taxpayer's qualified enhanced oil recovery costs for such taxable year.

(b) Phase-out of credit as crude oil prices increase

(1) In general

The amount of the credit determined under subsection (a) for any taxable year shall be reduced by an amount which bears the same ratio to the amount of such credit (determined without regard to this paragraph) as—

(A) the amount by which the reference price for the calendar year preceding the calendar year in which the taxable year begins exceeds $28, bears to

(B) $6.

(2) Reference price

For purposes of this subsection, the term "reference price" means, with respect to any calendar year, the reference price determined for such calendar year under section 45K(d)(2)(C).

(3) Inflation adjustment

(A) In general

In the case of any taxable year beginning in a calendar year after 1991, there shall be substituted for the $28 amount under paragraph (1)(A) an amount equal to the product of—

(i) $28, multiplied by

(ii) the inflation adjustment factor for such calendar year.

(B) Inflation adjustment factor

The term "inflation adjustment factor" means, with respect to any calendar year, a fraction the numerator of which is the GNP implicit price deflator for the preceding calendar year and the denominator of which is the GNP implicit price deflator for 1990. For purposes of the preceding sentence, the term "GNP implicit price deflator" means the first revision of the implicit price deflator for the gross national product as computed and published by the Secretary of Commerce. Not later than April 1 of any calendar year, the Secretary shall publish the inflation adjustment factor for the preceding calendar year.

(c) Qualified enhanced oil recovery costs

For purposes of this section—

(1) In general

The term "qualified enhanced oil recovery costs" means any of the following:

(A) Any amount paid or incurred during the taxable year for tangible property—

(i) which is an integral part of a qualified enhanced oil recovery project, and

(ii) with respect to which depreciation (or amortization in lieu of depreciation) is allowable under this chapter.

(B) Any intangible drilling and development costs—

(i) which are paid or incurred in connection with a qualified enhanced oil recovery project, and

(ii) with respect to which the taxpayer may make an election under section 263(c) for the taxable year.

(C) Any qualified tertiary injectant expenses (as defined in section 193(b)) which are paid or incurred in connection with a qualified enhanced oil recovery project and for which a deduction is allowable for the taxable year.

(D) Any amount which is paid or incurred during the taxable year to construct a gas treatment plant which—

(i) is located in the area of the United States (within the meaning of section 638(1)) lying north of 64 degrees North latitude,

(ii) prepares Alaska natural gas for transportation through a pipeline with a capacity of at least 2,000,000,000,000 Btu of natural gas per day, and

(iii) produces carbon dioxide which is injected into hydrocarbon-bearing geological formations.

(2) Qualified enhanced oil recovery project

For purposes of this subsection—

(A) In general

The term "qualified enhanced oil recovery project" means any project—

(i) which involves the application (in accordance with sound engineering principles) of 1 or more tertiary recovery methods (as defined in section 193(b)(3)) which can reasonably be expected to result in more than an insignificant increase in the amount of crude oil which will ultimately be recovered,

(ii) which is located within the United States (within the meaning of section 638(1)), and

(iii) with respect to which the first injection of liquids, gases, or other matter commences after December 31, 1990.

(B) Certification

A project shall not be treated as a qualified enhanced oil recovery project unless the operator submits to the Secretary (at such times and in such manner as the Secretary provides) a certification from a petroleum engineer that the project meets (and continues to meet) the requirements of subparagraph (A).

(3) At-risk limitation

For purposes of determining qualified enhanced oil recovery costs, rules similar to the rules of section 49(a)(1), section 49(a)(2), and section 49(b) shall apply.

(4) Special rule for certain gas displacement projects

For purposes of this section, immiscible non-hydrocarbon gas displacement shall be treated as a tertiary recovery method under section 193(b)(3).

(5) Alaska natural gas

For purposes of paragraph (1)(D)—

(A) In general

The term "Alaska natural gas" means natural gas entering the Alaska natural gas pipeline (as defined in section 168(i)(16) (determined without regard to subparagraph (B) thereof)) which is produced from a well—

(i) located in the area of the State of Alaska lying north of 64 degrees North latitude, determined by excluding the area of the Alaska National Wildlife Refuge (including the continental shelf thereof within the meaning of section 638(1)), and

(ii) pursuant to the applicable State and Federal pollution prevention, control, and permit requirements from such area (including the continental shelf thereof within the meaning of section 638(1)).

(B) Natural gas

The term "natural gas" has the meaning given such term by section 613A(e)(2).

(d) Other rules

(1) Disallowance of deduction

Any deduction allowable under this chapter for any costs taken into account in computing the amount of the credit determined under subsection (a) shall be reduced by the amount of such credit attributable to such costs.

(2) Basis adjustments

For purposes of this subtitle, if a credit is determined under this section for any expenditure with respect to any property, the increase in the basis of such property which would (but for this subsection) result from such expenditure shall be reduced by the amount of the credit so allowed.

(e) Election to have credit not apply

(1) In general

A taxpayer may elect to have this section not apply for any taxable year.

(2) Time for making election

An election under paragraph (1) for any taxable year may be made (or revoked) at any time before the expiration of the 3-year period beginning on the last date prescribed by law for filing the return for such taxable year (determined without regard to extensions).

(3) Manner of making election

An election under paragraph (1) (or revocation thereof) shall be made in such manner as the Secretary may by regulations prescribe.

(Added Pub. L. 101–508, title XI, §11511(a), Nov. 5, 1990, 104 Stat. 1388–483; amended Pub. L. 106–554, §1(a)(7) [title III, §317(a)], Dec. 21, 2000, 114 Stat. 2763, 2763A-645; Pub. L. 108–357, title VII, §707(a), (b), Oct. 22, 2004, 118 Stat. 1550; Pub. L. 109–58, title XIII, §1322(a)(3)(B), Aug. 8, 2005, 119 Stat. 1011; Pub. L. 109–135, title IV, §412(i), Dec. 21, 2005, 119 Stat. 2637.)

Inflation Adjusted Items for Certain Tax Years

For inflation adjustment of certain items in this section, see Internal Revenue Notices listed in a table below.

Editorial Notes
Prior Provisions

A prior section 43 was renumbered section 32 of this title.

Another prior section 43 was renumbered section 37 of this title.

Amendments

2005—Subsec. (b)(2). Pub. L. 109–58 substituted "section 45K(d)(2)(C)" for "section 29(d)(2)(C)".

Subsec. (c)(5). Pub. L. 109–135 reenacted heading without change and amended text generally. Prior to amendment, text read as follows: "For purposes of paragraph (1)(D)—

"(1) In general.—The term 'Alaska natural gas' means natural gas entering the Alaska natural gas pipeline (as defined in section 168(i)(16) (determined without regard to subparagraph (B) thereof)) which is produced from a well—

"(A) located in the area of the State of Alaska lying north of 64 degrees North latitude, determined by excluding the area of the Alaska National Wildlife Refuge (including the continental shelf thereof within the meaning of section 638(1)), and

"(B) pursuant to the applicable State and Federal pollution prevention, control, and permit requirements from such area (including the continental shelf thereof within the meaning of section 638(1)).

"(2) Natural gas.—The term 'natural gas' has the meaning given such term by section 613A(e)(2)."

2004—Subsec. (c)(1)(D). Pub. L. 108–357, §707(a), added subpar. (D).

Subsec. (c)(5). Pub. L. 108–357, §707(b), added par. (5).

2000—Subsec. (c)(1)(C). Pub. L. 106–554 inserted "(as defined in section 193(b))" after "expenses" and struck out "under section 193" after "allowable".

STATUTORY NOTES AND RELATED SUBSIDIARIES

EFFECTIVE DATE OF 2005 AMENDMENT

Amendment by Pub. L. 109–58 applicable to credits determined under the Internal Revenue Code of 1986 for taxable years ending after Dec. 31, 2005, see section 1322(c)(1) of Pub. L. 109–58, set out as a note under section 45K of this title.

EFFECTIVE DATE OF 2004 AMENDMENT

Pub. L. 108–357, title VII, §707(c), Oct. 22, 2004, 118 Stat. 1550, provided that: "The amendment made by this section [amending this section] shall apply to costs paid or incurred in taxable years beginning after December 31, 2004."

EFFECTIVE DATE OF 2000 AMENDMENT

Pub. L. 106–554, §1(a)(7) [title III, §317(b)], Dec. 21, 2000, 114 Stat. 2763, 2763A-645, provided that: "The amendment made by this section [amending this section] shall take effect as if included in section 11511 of the Revenue Reconciliation Act of 1990 [Pub. L. 101–508]."

EFFECTIVE DATE

Pub. L. 101–508, title XI, §11511(d), Nov. 5, 1990, 104 Stat. 1388–485, provided that:

"(1) In general.—The amendments made by this section [enacting this section and amending sections 38, 39, 196, and 6501 of this title] shall apply to costs paid or incurred in taxable years beginning after December 31, 1990.

"(2) Special rule for significant expansion of projects.—For purposes of section 43(c)(2)(A)(iii) of the Internal Revenue Code of 1986 (as added by subsection (a)), any significant expansion after December 31, 1990, of a project begun before January 1, 1991, shall be treated as a project with respect to which the first injection commences after December 31, 1990."

INFLATION ADJUSTED ITEMS FOR CERTAIN YEARS

Provisions relating to inflation adjustment of items in this section for certain years were contained in the following:

2021—Internal Revenue Notice 2021–47.
2020—Internal Revenue Notice 2020–31.
2019—Internal Revenue Notice 2019–36.
2018—Internal Revenue Notice 2018–49.
2017—Internal Revenue Notice 2017–25.
2016—Internal Revenue Notice 2016–44.
2015—Internal Revenue Notice 2015–64.
2014—Internal Revenue Notice 2014–64.
2013—Internal Revenue Notice 2013–50.
2012—Internal Revenue Notice 2012–49.
2011—Internal Revenue Notice 2011–57.
2010—Internal Revenue Notice 2010–72.
2009—Internal Revenue Notice 2009–73.
2008—Internal Revenue Notice 2008–72.
2007—Internal Revenue Notice 2007–64.
2006—Internal Revenue Notice 2006–62.
2005—Internal Revenue Notice 2005–56.
2004—Internal Revenue Notice 2004–49.
2003—Internal Revenue Notice 2003–43.
2002—Internal Revenue Notice 2002–53.
2001—Internal Revenue Notice 2001–54.
2000—Internal Revenue Notice 2000–51.
1999—Internal Revenue Notice 99–45.
1998—Internal Revenue Notice 98–41.
1997—Internal Revenue Notice 97–39.
1996—Internal Revenue Notice 96–41.

§44. Expenditures to provide access to disabled individuals

(a) General rule

For purposes of section 38, in the case of an eligible small business, the amount of the disabled access credit determined under this section for any taxable year shall be an amount equal to 50 percent of so much of the eligible access expenditures for the taxable year as exceed $250 but do not exceed $10,250.

(b) Eligible small business

For purposes of this section, the term "eligible small business" means any person if—

(1) either—

(A) the gross receipts of such person for the preceding taxable year did not exceed $1,000,000, or

(B) in the case of a person to which subparagraph (A) does not apply, such person employed not more than 30 full-time employees during the preceding taxable year, and

(2) such person elects the application of this section for the taxable year.

For purposes of paragraph (1)(B), an employee shall be considered full-time if such employee is employed at least 30 hours per week for 20 or more calendar weeks in the taxable year.

(c) Eligible access expenditures

For purposes of this section—

(1) In general

The term "eligible access expenditures" means amounts paid or incurred by an eligible small business for the purpose of enabling such eligible small business to comply with applicable requirements under the Americans With Disabilities Act of 1990 (as in effect on the date of the enactment of this section).

(2) Certain expenditures included

The term "eligible access expenditures" includes amounts paid or incurred—

(A) for the purpose of removing architectural, communication, physical, or transportation barriers which prevent a business from being accessible to, or usable by, individuals with disabilities,

(B) to provide qualified interpreters or other effective methods of making aurally delivered materials available to individuals with hearing impairments,

(C) to provide qualified readers, taped texts, and other effective methods of making visually delivered materials available to individuals with visual impairments,

(D) to acquire or modify equipment or devices for individuals with disabilities, or

(E) to provide other similar services, modifications, materials, or equipment.

(3) Expenditures must be reasonable

Amounts paid or incurred for the purposes described in paragraph (2) shall include only expenditures which are reasonable and shall not include expenditures which are unnecessary to accomplish such purposes.

(4) Expenses in connection with new construction are not eligible

The term "eligible access expenditures" shall not include amounts described in paragraph (2)(A) which are paid or incurred in connection with any facility first placed in service after the date of the enactment of this section.

(5) Expenditures must meet standards

The term "eligible access expenditures" shall not include any amount unless the taxpayer establishes, to the satisfaction of the Secretary, that the resulting removal of any barrier (or the provision of any services, modifications, materials, or equipment) meets the standards promulgated by the Secretary with the concurrence of the Architectural and Transportation Barriers Compliance Board and set forth in regulations prescribed by the Secretary.

(d) Definition of disability; special rules

For purposes of this section—

(1) Disability

The term "disability" has the same meaning as when used in the Americans With Disabilities Act of 1990 (as in effect on the date of the enactment of this section).

(2) Controlled groups

(A) In general

All members of the same controlled group of corporations (within the meaning of section 52(a)) and all persons under common control (within the meaning of section 52(b)) shall be treated as 1 person for purposes of this section.

(B) Dollar limitation

The Secretary shall apportion the dollar limitation under subsection (a) among the members of any group described in subparagraph (A) in such manner as the Secretary shall by regulations prescribe.

(3) Partnerships and S corporations

In the case of a partnership, the limitation under subsection (a) shall apply with respect to the partnership and each partner. A similar rule shall apply in the case of an S corporation and its shareholders.

(4) Short years

The Secretary shall prescribe such adjustments as may be appropriate for purposes of paragraph (1) of subsection (b) if the preceding taxable year is a taxable year of less than 12 months.

(5) Gross receipts

Gross receipts for any taxable year shall be reduced by returns and allowances made during such year.

(6) Treatment of predecessors

The reference to any person in paragraph (1) of subsection (b) shall be treated as including a reference to any predecessor.

(7) Denial of double benefit

In the case of the amount of the credit determined under this section—

(A) no deduction or credit shall be allowed for such amount under any other provision of this chapter, and

(B) no increase in the adjusted basis of any property shall result from such amount.

(e) Regulations

The Secretary shall prescribe regulations necessary to carry out the purposes of this section.

(Added Pub. L. 101–508, title XI, §11611(a), Nov. 5, 1990, 104 Stat. 1388–501.)

EDITORIAL NOTES
REFERENCES IN TEXT

The Americans With Disabilities Act of 1990, referred to in subsecs. (c)(1) and (d)(1) is Pub. L. 101–336, July 26, 1990, 104 Stat. 327, as amended, which is classified principally to chapter 126 (§12101 et seq.) of Title 42, The Public Health and Welfare. For complete classification of this Act to the Code, see Short Title note set out under section 12101 of Title 42 and Tables.

The date of the enactment of this section, referred to in subsecs. (c)(1), (4) and (d)(1), is the date of enactment of Pub. L. 101–508, which was approved Nov. 5, 1990.

PRIOR PROVISIONS

A prior section 44, added Pub. L. 94–12, title II, §208(a), Mar. 29, 1975, 89 Stat. 32; amended Pub. L. 94–45, title IV, §401(a), June 30, 1975, 89 Stat. 243; Pub. L. 94–455, title XIX, §1906(b)(13)(A), Oct. 4, 1976, 90 Stat. 1834, related to purchase of new principal residence, prior to repeal by Pub. L. 98–369, div. A, title IV, §474(m)(1), July 18, 1984, 98 Stat. 833, applicable to taxable years beginning after Dec. 31, 1983, and to carrybacks from such years.

Another prior section 44 was renumbered section 37 of this title.

STATUTORY NOTES AND RELATED SUBSIDIARIES
EFFECTIVE DATE

Section applicable to expenditures paid or incurred after Nov. 5, 1990, see section 11611(e)(1) of Pub. L. 101–508, set out as an Effective Date of 1990 Amendment note under section 38 of this title.

[§44A. Renumbered §21]

[§44B. Repealed. Pub. L. 98–369, div. A, title IV, §474(m)(1), July 18, 1984, 98 Stat. 833]

Section, added Pub. L. 95–30, title II, §202(a), May 23, 1977, 91 Stat. 141; amended Pub. L. 95–600, title III, §321(b)(1), Nov. 6, 1978, 92 Stat. 2834; Pub. L. 96–222, title I, §103(a)(6)(G)(i), (ii), Apr. 1, 1980, 94 Stat. 210, related to credit for employment of certain new employees.

STATUTORY NOTES AND RELATED SUBSIDIARIES
EFFECTIVE DATE OF REPEAL

Repeal applicable to taxable years beginning after Dec. 31, 1983, and to carrybacks from such years, see section 475(a) of Pub. L. 98–369, set out as an Effective Date of 1984 Amendment note under section 21 of this title.

[§44C. Renumbered §23]
[§44D. Renumbered §29]
[§44E. Renumbered §40]
[§44F. Renumbered §30]
[§44G. Renumbered §41]
[§44H. Renumbered §45C]

§45. Electricity produced from certain renewable resources, etc.

(a) General rule

For purposes of section 38, the renewable electricity production credit for any taxable year is an amount equal to the product of—
(1) 1.5 cents, multiplied by
(2) the kilowatt hours of electricity—
(A) produced by the taxpayer—
(i) from qualified energy resources, and
(ii) at a qualified facility during the 10-year period beginning on the date the facility was originally placed in service, and

(B) sold by the taxpayer to an unrelated person during the taxable year.

(b) Limitations and adjustments

(1) Phaseout of credit

The amount of the credit determined under subsection (a) shall be reduced by an amount which bears the same ratio to the amount of the credit (determined without regard to this paragraph) as—
(A) the amount by which the reference price for the calendar year in which the sale occurs exceeds 8 cents, bears to
(B) 3 cents.

(2) Credit and phaseout adjustment based on inflation

The 1.5 cent amount in subsection (a), the 8 cent amount in paragraph (1), the $4.375 amount in subsection (e)(8)(A), the $2 amount in subsection (e)(8)(D)(ii)(I), and in subsection (e)(8)(B)(i) the reference price of fuel used as a feedstock (within the meaning of subsection (c)(7)(A)) in 2002 shall each be adjusted by multiplying such amount by the inflation adjustment factor for the calendar year in which the sale occurs. If any amount as increased under the preceding sentence is not a multiple of 0.1 cent, such amount shall be rounded to the nearest multiple of 0.1 cent.

(3) Credit reduced for grants, tax-exempt bonds, subsidized energy financing, and other credits

The amount of the credit determined under subsection (a) with respect to any project for any taxable year (determined after the application of paragraphs (1) and (2)) shall be reduced by the amount which is the product of the amount so determined for such year and the lesser of ½ or a fraction—
(A) the numerator of which is the sum, for the taxable year and all prior taxable years, of—
(i) grants provided by the United States, a State, or a political subdivision of a State for use in connection with the project,
(ii) proceeds of an issue of State or local government obligations used to provide financing for the project the interest on which is exempt from tax under section 103,
(iii) the aggregate amount of subsidized energy financing provided (directly or indirectly) under a Federal, State, or local program provided in connection with the project, and
(iv) the amount of any other credit allowable with respect to any property which is part of the project, and

(B) the denominator of which is the aggregate amount of additions to the capital account for the project for the taxable year and all prior taxable years.

The amounts under the preceding sentence for any taxable year shall be determined as of the close of the taxable year. This paragraph shall not apply with respect to any facility described in subsection (d)(2)(A)(ii).

(4) Credit rate and period for electricity produced and sold from certain facilities

(A) Credit rate

In the case of electricity produced and sold in any calendar year after 2003 at any qualified facility described in paragraph (3), (5), (6), (7), (9), or (11) of subsection (d), the amount in effect under subsection (a)(1) for such calendar year (determined before the application of the last sentence of paragraph (2) of this subsection) shall be reduced by one-half.

(B) Credit period

(i) In general

Except as provided in clause (ii) or clause (iii), in the case of any facility described in paragraph (3), (4), (5), (6), or (7) of subsection (d), the 5-year period beginning on the date the facility was originally placed in service shall be substituted for the 10-year period in subsection (a)(2)(A)(ii).

(ii) Certain open-loop biomass facilities

In the case of any facility described in subsection (d)(3)(A)(ii) placed in service before the date of the enactment of this paragraph, the 5-year period beginning on January 1, 2005, shall be substituted for the 10-year period in subsection (a)(2)(A)(ii).

(iii) Termination

Clause (i) shall not apply to any facility placed in service after the date of the enactment of this clause.

(5) Phaseout of credit for wind facilities

In the case of any facility using wind to produce electricity, the amount of the credit determined under subsection (a) (determined after the application of paragraphs (1), (2), and (3) and without regard to this paragraph) shall be reduced by—
(A) in the case of any facility the construction of which begins after December 31, 2016, and before January 1, 2018, 20 percent,
(B) in the case of any facility the construction of which begins after December 31, 2017, and before January 1, 2019, 40 percent,
(C) in the case of any facility the construction of which begins after December 31, 2018, and before January 1, 2020, 60 percent, and
(D) in the case of any facility the construction of which begins after December 31, 2019, and before January 1, 2022, 40 percent.

(c) Resources

For purposes of this section:

(1) In general

The term "qualified energy resources" means—
    (A) wind,
    (B) closed-loop biomass,
    (C) open-loop biomass,
    (D) geothermal energy,
    (E) solar energy,
    (F) small irrigation power,
    (G) municipal solid waste,
    (H) qualified hydropower production, and
    (I) marine and hydrokinetic renewable energy.

(2) Closed-loop biomass

The term "closed-loop biomass" means any organic material from a plant which is planted exclusively for purposes of being used at a qualified facility to produce electricity.

(3) Open-loop biomass

(A) In general

The term "open-loop biomass" means—
    (i) any agricultural livestock waste nutrients, or
    (ii) any solid, nonhazardous, cellulosic waste material or any lignin material which is derived from—
        (I) any of the following forest-related resources: mill and harvesting residues, precommercial thinnings, slash, and brush,
        (II) solid wood waste materials, including waste pallets, crates, dunnage, manufacturing and construction wood wastes (other than pressure-treated, chemically-treated, or painted wood wastes), and landscape or right-of-way tree trimmings, but not including municipal solid waste, gas derived from the biodegradation of solid waste, or paper which is commonly recycled, or
        (III) agriculture sources, including orchard tree crops, vineyard, grain, legumes, sugar, and other crop by-products or residues.

Such term shall not include closed-loop biomass or biomass burned in conjunction with fossil fuel (cofiring) beyond such fossil fuel required for startup and flame stabilization.

(B) Agricultural livestock waste nutrients

(i) In general

The term "agricultural livestock waste nutrients" means agricultural livestock manure and litter, including wood shavings, straw, rice hulls, and other bedding material for the disposition of manure.

(ii) Agricultural livestock

The term "agricultural livestock" includes bovine, swine, poultry, and sheep.

(4) Geothermal energy

The term "geothermal energy" means energy derived from a geothermal deposit (within the meaning of section 613(e)(2)).

(5) Small irrigation power

The term "small irrigation power" means power—
    (A) generated without any dam or impoundment of water through an irrigation system canal or ditch, and
    (B) the nameplate capacity rating of which is not less than 150 kilowatts but is less than 5 megawatts.

(6) Municipal solid waste

The term "municipal solid waste" has the meaning given the term "solid waste" under section 1004(27) of the Solid Waste Disposal Act (42 U.S.C. 6903), except that such term does not include paper which is commonly recycled and which has been segregated from other solid waste (as so defined).

(7) Refined coal

(A) In general

The term "refined coal" means a fuel—
    (i) which—
        (I) is a liquid, gaseous, or solid fuel produced from coal (including lignite) or high carbon fly ash, including such fuel used as a feedstock,
        (II) is sold by the taxpayer with the reasonable expectation that it will be used for the purpose of producing steam, and
        (III) is certified by the taxpayer as resulting (when used in the production of steam) in a qualified emission reduction, or

    (ii) which is steel industry fuel.

(B) Qualified emission reduction

The term "qualified emission reduction" means a reduction of at least 20 percent of the emissions of nitrogen oxide and at least 40 percent of the emissions of either sulfur dioxide or mercury released when burning the refined coal (excluding any dilution caused by materials combined or added during the production process), as compared to the emissions released when burning the feedstock coal or comparable coal predominantly available in the marketplace as of January 1, 2003.

(C) Steel industry fuel

(i) In general

The term "steel industry fuel" means a fuel which—
        (I) is produced through a process of liquifying coal waste sludge and distributing it on coal, and
        (II) is used as a feedstock for the manufacture of coke.

(ii) Coal waste sludge

The term "coal waste sludge" means the tar decanter sludge and related byproducts of the coking process, including such materials that have been stored in ground, in tanks and in lagoons, that have been treated as hazardous wastes under applicable Federal environmental rules absent liquefaction and processing with coal into a feedstock for the manufacture of coke.

(8) Qualified hydropower production

(A) In general

The term "qualified hydropower production" means—

(i) in the case of any hydroelectric dam which was placed in service on or before the date of the enactment of this paragraph, the incremental hydropower production for the taxable year, and

(ii) in the case of any nonhydroelectric dam described in subparagraph (C), the hydropower production from the facility for the taxable year.

(B) Determination of incremental hydropower production

(i) In general

For purposes of subparagraph (A), incremental hydropower production for any taxable year shall be equal to the percentage of average annual hydropower production at the facility attributable to the efficiency improvements or additions of capacity placed in service after the date of the enactment of this paragraph, determined by using the same water flow information used to determine an historic average annual hydropower production baseline for such facility. Such percentage and baseline shall be certified by the Federal Energy Regulatory Commission.

(ii) Operational changes disregarded

For purposes of clause (i), the determination of incremental hydropower production shall not be based on any operational changes at such facility not directly associated with the efficiency improvements or additions of capacity.

(C) Nonhydroelectric dam

For purposes of subparagraph (A), a facility is described in this subparagraph if—

(i) the hydroelectric project installed on the nonhydroelectric dam is licensed by the Federal Energy Regulatory Commission and meets all other applicable environmental, licensing, and regulatory requirements,

(ii) the nonhydroelectric dam was placed in service before the date of the enactment of this paragraph and operated for flood control, navigation, or water supply purposes and did not produce hydroelectric power on the date of the enactment of this paragraph, and

(iii) the hydroelectric project is operated so that the water surface elevation at any given location and time that would have occurred in the absence of the hydroelectric project is maintained, subject to any license requirements imposed under applicable law that change the water surface elevation for the purpose of improving environmental quality of the affected waterway.

The Secretary, in consultation with the Federal Energy Regulatory Commission, shall certify if a hydroelectric project licensed at a nonhydroelectric dam meets the criteria in clause (iii). Nothing in this section shall affect the standards under which the Federal Energy Regulatory Commission issues licenses for and regulates hydropower projects under part I of the Federal Power Act.

(9) Indian coal

(A) In general

The term "Indian coal" means coal which is produced from coal reserves which, on June 14, 2005—

(i) were owned by an Indian tribe, or

(ii) were held in trust by the United States for the benefit of an Indian tribe or its members.

(B) Indian tribe

For purposes of this paragraph, the term "Indian tribe" has the meaning given such term by section 7871(c)(3)(E)(ii).

(10) Marine and hydrokinetic renewable energy

(A) In general

The term "marine and hydrokinetic renewable energy" means energy derived from—

(i) waves, tides, and currents in oceans, estuaries, and tidal areas,

(ii) free flowing water in rivers, lakes, and streams,

(iii) free flowing water in an irrigation system, canal, or other man-made channel, including projects that utilize nonmechanical structures to accelerate the flow of water for electric power production purposes, or

(iv) differentials in ocean temperature (ocean thermal energy conversion).

(B) Exceptions

Such term shall not include any energy which is derived from any source which utilizes a dam, diversionary structure (except as provided in subparagraph (A)(iii)), or impoundment for electric power production purposes.

(d) Qualified facilities

For purposes of this section:

(1) Wind facility

In the case of a facility using wind to produce electricity, the term "qualified facility" means any facility owned by the taxpayer which is originally placed in service after December 31, 1993, and the construction of which begins before January 1, 2022. Such term shall not include any facility with respect to which any qualified small wind energy property expenditure (as defined in subsection (d)(4) of section 25D) is taken into account in determining the credit under such section.

(2) Closed-loop biomass facility

(A) In general

In the case of a facility using closed-loop biomass to produce electricity, the term "qualified facility" means any facility—

(i) owned by the taxpayer which is originally placed in service after December 31, 1992, and the construction of which begins before January 1, 2022, or

(ii) owned by the taxpayer which before January 1, 2022, is originally placed in service and modified to use closed-loop biomass to co-fire with coal, with other biomass, or with both, but only if the modification is approved under the Biomass Power for Rural Development Programs or is part of a pilot project of the Commodity Credit Corporation as described in 65 Fed. Reg. 63052.

For purposes of clause (ii), a facility shall be treated as modified before January 1, 2022, if the construction of such modification begins before such date.

(B) Expansion of facility

Such term shall include a new unit placed in service after the date of the enactment of this subparagraph in connection with a facility described in subparagraph (A)(i), but only to the extent of the increased amount of electricity produced at the facility by reason of such new unit.

(C) Special rules

In the case of a qualified facility described in subparagraph (A)(ii)—

(i) the 10-year period referred to in subsection (a) shall be treated as beginning no earlier than the date of the enactment of this clause, and

(ii) if the owner of such facility is not the producer of the electricity, the person eligible for the credit allowable under subsection (a) shall be the lessee or the operator of such facility.

(3) Open-loop biomass facilities

(A) In general

In the case of a facility using open-loop biomass to produce electricity, the term "qualified facility" means any facility owned by the taxpayer which—

    (i) in the case of a facility using agricultural livestock waste nutrients—

        (I) is originally placed in service after the date of the enactment of this subclause and the construction of which begins before January 1, 2022, and

        (II) the nameplate capacity rating of which is not less than 150 kilowatts, and

    (ii) in the case of any other facility, the construction of which begins before January 1, 2022.

(B) Expansion of facility

Such term shall include a new unit placed in service after the date of the enactment of this subparagraph in connection with a facility described in subparagraph (A), but only to the extent of the increased amount of electricity produced at the facility by reason of such new unit.

(C) Credit eligibility

In the case of any facility described in subparagraph (A), if the owner of such facility is not the producer of the electricity, the person eligible for the credit allowable under subsection (a) shall be the lessee or the operator of such facility.

(4) Geothermal or solar energy facility

In the case of a facility using geothermal or solar energy to produce electricity, the term "qualified facility" means any facility owned by the taxpayer which is originally placed in service after the date of the enactment of this paragraph and which—

    (A) in the case of a facility using solar energy, is placed in service before January 1, 2006, or

    (B) in the case of a facility using geothermal energy, the construction of which begins before January 1, 2022.

Such term shall not include any property described in section 48(a)(3) the basis of which is taken into account by the taxpayer for purposes of determining the energy credit under section 48.

(5) Small irrigation power facility

In the case of a facility using small irrigation power to produce electricity, the term "qualified facility" means any facility owned by the taxpayer which is originally placed in service after the date of the enactment of this paragraph and before October 3, 2008.

(6) Landfill gas facilities

In the case of a facility producing electricity from gas derived from the biodegradation of municipal solid waste, the term "qualified facility" means any facility owned by the taxpayer which is originally placed in service after the date of the enactment of this paragraph and the construction of which begins before January 1, 2022.

(7) Trash facilities

In the case of a facility (other than a facility described in paragraph (6)) which uses municipal solid waste to produce electricity, the term "qualified facility" means any facility owned by the taxpayer which is originally placed in service after the date of the enactment of this paragraph and the construction of which begins before January 1, 2022. Such term shall include a new unit placed in service in connection with a facility placed in service on or before the date of the enactment of this paragraph, but only to the extent of the increased amount of electricity produced at the facility by reason of such new unit.

(8) Refined coal production facility

In the case of a facility that produces refined coal, the term "refined coal production facility" means—

    (A) with respect to a facility producing steel industry fuel, any facility (or any modification to a facility) which is placed in service before January 1, 2010, and

    (B) with respect to any other facility producing refined coal, any facility placed in service after the date of the enactment of the American Jobs Creation Act of 2004 and before January 1, 2012.

(9) Qualified hydropower facility

(A) In general

In the case of a facility producing qualified hydroelectric production described in subsection (c)(8), the term "qualified facility" means—

    (i) in the case of any facility producing incremental hydropower production, such facility but only to the extent of its incremental hydropower production attributable to efficiency improvements or additions to capacity described in subsection (c)(8)(B) placed in service after the date of the enactment of this paragraph and before January 1, 2022, and

    (ii) any other facility placed in service after the date of the enactment of this paragraph and the construction of which begins before January 1, 2022.

(B) Credit period

In the case of a qualified facility described in subparagraph (A), the 10-year period referred to in subsection (a) shall be treated as beginning on the date the efficiency improvements or additions to capacity are placed in service.

(C) Special rule

For purposes of subparagraph (A)(i), an efficiency improvement or addition to capacity shall be treated as placed in service before January 1, 2022, if the construction of such improvement or addition begins before such date.

(10) Indian coal production facility

The term "Indian coal production facility" means a facility that produces Indian coal.

(11) Marine and hydrokinetic renewable energy facilities

In the case of a facility producing electricity from marine and hydrokinetic renewable energy, the term "qualified facility" means any facility owned by the taxpayer—

    (A) which has a nameplate capacity rating of at least 150 kilowatts, and

    (B) which is originally placed in service on or after the date of the enactment of this paragraph and the construction of which begins before January 1, 2022.

(e) Definitions and special rules

For purposes of this section—

(1) Only production in the United States taken into account

Sales shall be taken into account under this section only with respect to electricity the production of which is within—

    (A) the United States (within the meaning of section 638(1)), or

    (B) a possession of the United States (within the meaning of section 638(2)).

(2) Computation of inflation adjustment factor and reference price

(A) In general

The Secretary shall, not later than April 1 of each calendar year, determine and publish in the Federal Register the inflation adjustment factor and the reference price for such calendar year in accordance with this paragraph.

(B) Inflation adjustment factor

The term "inflation adjustment factor" means, with respect to a calendar year, a fraction the numerator of which is the GDP implicit price deflator for the preceding calendar year and the denominator of which is the GDP implicit price deflator for the calendar year 1992. The term "GDP implicit price deflator" means the most recent revision of the implicit price deflator for the gross domestic product as computed and published by the Department of Commerce before March 15 of the calendar year.

(C) Reference price

The term "reference price" means, with respect to a calendar year, the Secretary's determination of the annual average contract price per kilowatt hour of electricity generated from the same qualified energy resource and sold in the previous year in the United States. For purposes of the preceding sentence, only contracts entered into after December 31, 1989, shall be taken into account.

(3) Production attributable to the taxpayer

In the case of a facility in which more than 1 person has an ownership interest, except to the extent provided in regulations prescribed by the Secretary, production from the facility shall be allocated among such persons in proportion to their respective ownership interests in the gross sales from such facility.

(4) Related persons

Persons shall be treated as related to each other if such persons would be treated as a single employer under the regulations prescribed under section 52(b). In the case of a corporation which is a member of an affiliated group of corporations filing a consolidated return, such corporation shall be treated as selling electricity to an unrelated person if such electricity is sold to such a person by another member of such group.

(5) Pass-thru in the case of estates and trusts

Under regulations prescribed by the Secretary, rules similar to the rules of subsection (d) of section 52 shall apply.

[(6) Repealed. Pub. L. 109–58, title XIII, §1301(f)(3), Aug. 8, 2005, 119 Stat. 990]

(7) Credit not to apply to electricity sold to utilities under certain contracts

(A) In general

The credit determined under subsection (a) shall not apply to electricity—

(i) produced at a qualified facility described in subsection (d)(1) which is originally placed in service after June 30, 1999, and

(ii) sold to a utility pursuant to a contract originally entered into before January 1, 1987 (whether or not amended or restated after that date).

(B) Exception

Subparagraph (A) shall not apply if—

(i) the prices for energy and capacity from such facility are established pursuant to an amendment to the contract referred to in subparagraph (A)(ii),

(ii) such amendment provides that the prices set forth in the contract which exceed avoided cost prices determined at the time of delivery shall apply only to annual quantities of electricity (prorated for partial years) which do not exceed the greater of—

(I) the average annual quantity of electricity sold to the utility under the contract during calendar years 1994, 1995, 1996, 1997, and 1998, or

(II) the estimate of the annual electricity production set forth in the contract, or, if there is no such estimate, the greatest annual quantity of electricity sold to the utility under the contract in any of the calendar years 1996, 1997, or 1998, and

(iii) such amendment provides that energy and capacity in excess of the limitation in clause (ii) may be—

(I) sold to the utility only at prices that do not exceed avoided cost prices determined at the time of delivery, or

(II) sold to a third party subject to a mutually agreed upon advance notice to the utility.

For purposes of this subparagraph, avoided cost prices shall be determined as provided for in 18 CFR 292.304(d)(1) or any successor regulation.

(8) Refined coal production facilities

(A) Determination of credit amount

In the case of a producer of refined coal, the credit determined under this section (without regard to this paragraph) for any taxable year shall be increased by an amount equal to $4.375 per ton of qualified refined coal—

(i) produced by the taxpayer at a refined coal production facility during the 10-year period beginning on the date the facility was originally placed in service, and

(ii) sold by the taxpayer—

(I) to an unrelated person, and

(II) during such 10-year period and such taxable year.

(B) Phaseout of credit

The amount of the increase determined under subparagraph (A) shall be reduced by an amount which bears the same ratio to the amount of the increase (determined without regard to this subparagraph) as—

(i) the amount by which the reference price of fuel used as a feedstock (within the meaning of subsection (c)(7)(A)) for the calendar year in which the sale occurs exceeds an amount equal to 1.7 multiplied by the reference price for such fuel in 2002, bears to

(ii) $8.75.

(C) Application of rules

Rules similar to the rules of the subsection (b)(3) and paragraphs (1) through (5) of this subsection shall apply for purposes of determining the amount of any increase under this paragraph.

(D) Special rule for steel industry fuel

(i) In general

In the case of a taxpayer who produces steel industry fuel—

(I) this paragraph shall be applied separately with respect to steel industry fuel and other refined coal, and

(II) in applying this paragraph to steel industry fuel, the modifications in clause (ii) shall apply.

(ii) Modifications

(I) Credit amount

Subparagraph (A) shall be applied by substituting "$2 per barrel-of-oil equivalent" for "$4.375 per ton".

(II) Credit period

In lieu of the 10-year period referred to in clauses (i) and (ii)(II) of subparagraph (A), the credit period shall be the period beginning on the later of the date such facility was originally placed in service, the date the modifications described in clause (iii) were placed in service, or October 1, 2008, and ending on the later of December 31, 2009, or the date which is 1 year after the date such facility or the modifications described in clause (iii) were placed in service.

(III) No phaseout

Subparagraph (B) shall not apply.

(iii) Modifications

The modifications described in this clause are modifications to an existing facility which allow such facility to produce steel industry fuel.

(iv) Barrel-of-oil equivalent

For purposes of this subparagraph, a barrel-of-oil equivalent is the amount of steel industry fuel that has a Btu content of 5,800,000 Btus.

(9) Coordination with credit for producing fuel from a nonconventional source

(A) In general

The term "qualified facility" shall not include any facility which produces electricity from gas derived from the biodegradation of municipal solid waste if such biodegradation occurred in a facility (within the meaning of section 45K) the production from which is allowed as a credit under section 45K for the taxable year or any prior taxable year.

(B) Refined coal facilities

(i) In general

The term "refined coal production facility" shall not include any facility the production from which is allowed as a credit under section 45K for the taxable year or any prior taxable year (or under section 29,[1] as in effect on the day before the date of enactment of the Energy Tax Incentives Act of 2005, for any prior taxable year).

(ii) Exception for steel industry coal

In the case of a facility producing steel industry fuel, clause (i) shall not apply to so much of the refined coal produced at such facility as is steel industry fuel.

(10) Indian coal production facilities

(A) Determination of credit amount

In the case of a producer of Indian coal, the credit determined under this section (without regard to this paragraph) for any taxable year shall be increased by an amount equal to the applicable dollar amount per ton of Indian coal—

(i) produced by the taxpayer at an Indian coal production facility during the 16-year period beginning on January 1, 2006, and

(ii) sold by the taxpayer—

(I) to an unrelated person (either directly by the taxpayer or after sale or transfer to one or more related persons), and

(II) during such 16-year period and such taxable year.

(B) Applicable dollar amount

(i) In general

The term "applicable dollar amount" for any taxable year beginning in a calendar year means—

(I) $1.50 in the case of calendar years 2006 through 2009, and

(II) $2.00 in the case of calendar years beginning after 2009.

(ii) Inflation adjustment

In the case of any calendar year after 2006, each of the dollar amounts under clause (i) shall be equal to the product of such dollar amount and the inflation adjustment factor determined under paragraph (2)(B) for the calendar year, except that such paragraph shall be applied by substituting "2005" for "1992".

(C) Application of rules

Rules similar to the rules of the subsection (b)(3) and paragraphs (1), (3), (4), and (5) of this subsection shall apply for purposes of determining the amount of any increase under this paragraph.

(11) Allocation of credit to patrons of agricultural cooperative

(A) Election to allocate

(i) In general

In the case of an eligible cooperative organization, any portion of the credit determined under subsection (a) for the taxable year may, at the election of the organization, be apportioned among patrons of the organization on the basis of the amount of business done by the patrons during the taxable year.

(ii) Form and effect of election

An election under clause (i) for any taxable year shall be made on a timely filed return for such year. Such election, once made, shall be irrevocable for such taxable year. Such election shall not take effect unless the organization designates the apportionment as such in a written notice mailed to its patrons during the payment period described in section 1382(d).

(B) Treatment of organizations and patrons

The amount of the credit apportioned to any patrons under subparagraph (A)—

(i) shall not be included in the amount determined under subsection (a) with respect to the organization for the taxable year, and

(ii) shall be included in the amount determined under subsection (a) for the first taxable year of each patron ending on or after the last day of the payment period (as defined in section 1382(d)) for the taxable year of the organization or, if earlier, for the taxable year of each patron ending on or after the date on which the patron receives notice from the cooperative of the apportionment.

(C) Special rules for decrease in credits for taxable year

If the amount of the credit of a cooperative organization determined under subsection (a) for a taxable year is less than the amount of such credit shown on the return of the cooperative organization for such year, an amount equal to the excess of—

(i) such reduction, over

(ii) the amount not apportioned to such patrons under subparagraph (A) for the taxable year,

shall be treated as an increase in tax imposed by this chapter on the organization. Such increase shall not be treated as tax imposed by this chapter for purposes of determining the amount of any credit under this chapter.

(D) Eligible cooperative defined

For purposes of this section the term "eligible cooperative" means a cooperative organization described in section 1381(a) which is owned more than 50 percent by agricultural producers or by entities owned by agricultural producers. For this purpose an entity owned by an agricultural producer is one that is more than 50 percent owned by agricultural producers.

(Added Pub. L. 102–486, title XIX, §1914(a), Oct. 24, 1992, 106 Stat. 3020; amended Pub. L. 106–170, title V, §507(a)–(c), Dec. 17, 1999, 113 Stat. 1922; Pub. L. 106–554, §1(a)(7) [title III, §319(1)], Dec. 21, 2000, 114 Stat. 2763, 2763A-646; Pub. L. 107–147, title VI, §603(a), Mar. 9, 2002, 116 Stat. 59; Pub. L. 108–311, title III, §313(a), Oct. 4, 2004, 118 Stat. 1181; Pub. L. 108–357, title VII, §710(a)–(d), (f), Oct. 22, 2004, 118 Stat. 1552–1557; Pub. L. 109–58, title XIII, §§1301(a)–(f)(4), 1302(a), 1322(a)(3)(C), Aug. 8, 2005, 119 Stat. 986–990, 1011; Pub. L. 109–135, title IV, §§402(b), 403(t), 412(j), Dec. 21, 2005, 119 Stat. 2610, 2628, 2637; Pub. L. 109–432, div. A, title II, §201, Dec. 20, 2006, 120 Stat. 2944; Pub. L. 110–172, §§7(b), 9(a), Dec. 29, 2007, 121 Stat. 2482, 2484; Pub. L. 110–343, div. B, title I, §§101(a)–(e), 102(a)–(e), 106(c)(3)(B), 108(a)–(d)(1), Oct. 3, 2008, 122 Stat. 3808–3810, 3815, 3819-3821; Pub. L. 111–5, div. B, title I, §1101(a), (b), Feb. 17, 2009, 123 Stat. 319; Pub. L. 111–312, title VII, §702(a), Dec. 17, 2010, 124 Stat. 3311; Pub. L. 112–240, title IV, §§406(a), 407(a), Jan. 2, 2013, 126 Stat. 2340; Pub. L.

113–295, div. A, title I, §§154(a), 155(a), title II, §210(g)(1), Dec. 19, 2014, 128 Stat. 4021, 4032; Pub. L. 114–113, div. P, title III, §301(a), div. Q, title I, §§186(a)–(c), (d)(2), 187(a), Dec. 18, 2015, 129 Stat. 3038, 3073, 3074; Pub. L. 115–123, div. D, title I, §§40408(a), 40409(a), Feb. 9, 2018, 132 Stat. 149, 150; Pub. L. 115–141, div. U, title IV, §401(a)(14)–(16), Mar. 23, 2018, 132 Stat. 1185; Pub. L. 116–94, div. Q, title I, §§127(a), (c)(1), (2)(A), 128(a), Dec. 20, 2019, 133 Stat. 3231, 3232; Pub. L. 116–260, div. EE, title I, §§131(a), (c)(1), 145(a), Dec. 27, 2020, 134 Stat. 3052, 3054.)

INFLATION ADJUSTED ITEMS FOR CERTAIN YEARS

For inflation adjustment of certain items in this section, see Internal Revenue Notices listed in a table below.

EDITORIAL NOTES
REFERENCES IN TEXT

The date of the enactment of this paragraph, the date of the enactment of this clause, the date of the enactment of this subclause, and the date of the enactment of the American Jobs Creation Act of 2004, referred to in subsecs. (b)(4)(B)(ii) and (d)(2)(C)(i), (3)(A)(i), (4) to (8), is the date of enactment of Pub. L. 108–357, which was approved Oct. 22, 2004.

The date of the enactment of this clause and the date of the enactment of this paragraph, referred to in subsecs. (b)(4)(B)(iii), (c)(8), and (d)(9)(A), are the date of enactment of Pub. L. 109–58, which was approved Aug. 8, 2005.

The Federal Power Act, referred to in subsec. (c)(8)(C), is act June 10, 1920, ch. 285, 41 Stat. 1063. Part I of the Act is classified generally to subchapter I (§791a et seq.) of chapter 12 of Title 16, Conservation. For complete classification of this Act to the Code, see section 791a of Title 16 and Tables.

The date of the enactment of this subparagraph and the date of the enactment of this paragraph, referred to in subsec. (d)(2)(B), (3)(B), (11), are the date of enactment of Pub. L. 110–343, which was approved Oct. 3, 2008.

Section 29, referred to in subsec. (e)(9)(B)(i), was redesignated section 45K of this title by Pub. L. 109–58, title XIII, §1322(a)(1), Aug. 8, 2005, 119 Stat. 1011.

The date of enactment of the Energy Tax Incentives Act of 2005, referred to in subsec. (e)(9)(B)(i), is the date of enactment of title XIII of Pub. L. 109–58, which was approved Aug. 8, 2005.

PRIOR PROVISIONS

A prior section 45 was renumbered section 37 of this title.

AMENDMENTS

2020—Subsec. (b)(5)(D). Pub. L. 116–260, §131(c)(1), substituted "January 1, 2022" for "January 1, 2021".

Subsec. (d)(1), (2)(A), (3)(A), (4)(B), (6), (7), (9), (11)(B). Pub. L. 116–260, §131(a), substituted "January 1, 2022" for "January 1, 2021" wherever appearing.

Subsec. (e)(10)(A). Pub. L. 116–260, §145(a), substituted "16-year period" for "15-year period" in two places.

2019—Subsec. (b)(5)(D). Pub. L. 116–94, §127(c)(2)(A), added subpar. (D).

Subsec. (d)(1). Pub. L. 116–94, §127(c)(1), substituted "January 1, 2021" for "January 1, 2020".

Subsec. (d)(2)(A), (3)(A), (4)(B), (6), (7), (9), (11)(B). Pub. L. 116–94, §127(a), substituted "January 1, 2021" for "January 1, 2018" wherever appearing.

Subsec. (e)(10)(A). Pub. L. 116–94, §128(a), substituted "15-year period" for "12-year period" in two places.

2018—Subsec. (c)(6). Pub. L. 115–141, §401(a)(14), substituted "section 1004(27)" for "section 2(27)".

Subsec. (c)(7)(A)(i)(II). Pub. L. 115–141, §401(a)(15), substituted "for the purpose" for "for purpose".

Subsec. (c)(7)(A)(i)(III). Pub. L. 115–141, §401(a)(16), substituted ", or" for period at end.

Subsec. (d). Pub. L. 115–123, §40409(a), substituted "January 1, 2018" for "January 1, 2017" wherever appearing.

Subsec. (e)(10)(A)(i), (ii)(II). Pub. L. 115–123, §40408(a), substituted "12-year period" for "11-year period".

2015—Subsec. (b)(5). Pub. L. 114–113, §301(a)(2), added par. (5).

Subsec. (d)(1). Pub. L. 114–113, §301(a)(1), substituted "January 1, 2020" for "January 1, 2015".

Subsec. (d)(2)(A). Pub. L. 114–113, §187(a)(1), substituted "January 1, 2017" for "January 1, 2015" wherever appearing.

Subsec. (d)(3)(A)(i)(I), (ii). Pub. L. 114–113, §187(a)(2), substituted "January 1, 2017" for "January 1, 2015".

Subsec. (d)(4)(B). Pub. L. 114–113, §187(a)(3), substituted "January 1, 2017" for "January 1, 2015".

Subsec. (d)(6). Pub. L. 114–113, §187(a)(4), substituted "January 1, 2017" for "January 1, 2015".

Subsec. (d)(7). Pub. L. 114–113, §187(a)(5), substituted "January 1, 2017" for "January 1, 2015".

Subsec. (d)(9)(A)(i), (ii), (C). Pub. L. 114–113, §187(a)(6), substituted "January 1, 2017" for "January 1, 2015".

Subsec. (d)(10). Pub. L. 114–113, §186(b), amended par. (10) generally. Prior to amendment, text read as follows: "In the case of a facility that produces Indian coal, the term 'Indian coal production facility' means a facility which is placed in service before January 1, 2009."

Subsec. (d)(11)(B). Pub. L. 114–113, §187(a)(7), substituted "January 1, 2017" for "January 1, 2015".

Subsec. (e)(10)(A)(i). Pub. L. 114–113, §186(a), substituted "11-year period" for "9-year period".

Subsec. (e)(10)(A)(ii)(I). Pub. L. 114–113, §186(c), inserted "(either directly by the taxpayer or after sale or transfer to one or more related persons)" after "unrelated person".

Subsec. (e)(10)(A)(ii)(II). Pub. L. 114–113, §186(a), substituted "11-year period" for "9-year period".

Subsec. (e)(10)(D). Pub. L. 114–113, §186(d)(2), struck out subpar. (D). Text read as follows: "The increase in the credit determined under subsection (a) by reason of this paragraph with respect to any facility shall be treated as a specified credit for purposes of section 38(c)(4)(A) during the 4-year period beginning on the later of January 1, 2006, or the date on which such facility is placed in service by the taxpayer."

2014—Subsec. (b)(2). Pub. L. 113–295, §210(g)(1), substituted "$2 amount" for "$3 amount".

Subsec. (d). Pub. L. 113–295, §155(a), substituted "January 1, 2015" for "January 1, 2014" wherever appearing.

Subsec. (e)(10)(A)(i), (ii)(II). Pub. L. 113–295, §154(a), substituted "9-year period" for "8-year period".

2013—Subsec. (c)(6). Pub. L. 112–240, §407(a)(2), inserted ", except that such term does not include paper which is commonly recycled and which has been segregated from other solid waste (as so defined)" after "(42 U.S.C. 6903)".

Subsec. (d)(1). Pub. L. 112–240, §407(a)(3)(A)(i), substituted "the construction of which begins before January 1, 2014" for "before January 1, 2014".

Pub. L. 112–240, §407(a)(1), substituted "January 1, 2014" for "January 1, 2013".

Subsec. (d)(2)(A). Pub. L. 112–240, §407(a)(3)(B), inserted concluding provisions.

Subsec. (d)(2)(A)(i). Pub. L. 112–240, §407(a)(3)(A)(ii), substituted "the construction of which begins before January 1, 2014" for "before January 1, 2014".

Subsec. (d)(3)(A)(i)(I). Pub. L. 112–240, §407(a)(3)(A)(iii), substituted "the construction of which begins before January 1, 2014" for "before January 1, 2014".

Subsec. (d)(3)(A)(ii). Pub. L. 112–240, §407(a)(3)(C), substituted "the construction of which begins" for "is originally placed in service".

Subsec. (d)(4). Pub. L. 112–240, §407(a)(3)(D)(i), substituted "and which—", subpars. (A) and (B), and concluding provisions for "and before January 1, 2014 (January 1, 2006, in the case of a facility using solar energy). Such term shall not include any property described in section 48(a)(3) the basis of which is taken into account by the taxpayer for purposes of determining the energy credit under section 48."

Subsec. (d)(6). Pub. L. 112–240, §407(a)(3)(A)(iv), substituted "the construction of which begins before January 1, 2014" for "before January 1, 2014".

Subsec. (d)(7). Pub. L. 112–240, §407(a)(3)(A)(v), substituted "the construction of which begins before January 1, 2014" for "before January 1, 2014".

Subsec. (d)(9). Pub. L. 112–240, §407(a)(3)(E), designated introductory provisions as subpar. (A) and inserted heading, redesignated former subpars. (A) and (B) as cls. (i) and (ii), respectively, of subpar. (A), realigned margins, added subpar. (C), and redesignated former subpar. (C) as (B).

Subsec. (d)(9)(B). Pub. L. 112–240, §407(a)(3)(A)(vi), substituted "the construction of which begins before January 1, 2014" for "before January 1, 2014".

Subsec. (d)(11)(B). Pub. L. 112–240, §407(a)(3)(A)(vii), substituted "the construction of which begins before January 1, 2014" for "before January 1, 2014".

Subsec. (e)(10)(A)(i), (ii)(II). Pub. L. 112–240, §406(a), substituted "8-year period" for "7-year period".

2010—Subsec. (d)(8)(B). Pub. L. 111–312 substituted "January 1, 2012" for "January 1, 2010".

2009—Subsec. (d)(1). Pub. L. 111–5, §1101(a)(1), substituted "2013" for "2010".

Subsec. (d)(2)(A)(i), (ii), (3)(A)(i)(I), (ii), (4). Pub. L. 111–5, §1101(a)(2), substituted "2014" for "2011".

Subsec. (d)(5). Pub. L. 111–5, §1101(b), substituted "and before October 3, 2008." for "and before the date of the enactment of paragraph (11)."

Subsec. (d)(6), (7), (9)(A), (B). Pub. L. 111–5, §1101(a)(2), substituted "2014" for "2011".

Subsec. (d)(11)(B). Pub. L. 111–5, §1101(a)(3), substituted "2014" for "2012".

2008—Subsec. (b)(2). Pub. L. 110–343, §108(b)(2), inserted "the $3 amount in subsection (e)(8)(D)(ii)(I)," after "subsection (e)(8)(A),".

Subsec. (b)(4)(A). Pub. L. 110–343, §102(d), substituted "(9), or (11)" for "or (9)".

Subsec. (c)(1)(I). Pub. L. 110–343, §102(a), added subpar. (I).

Subsec. (c)(7)(A). Pub. L. 110–343, §108(a)(1), reenacted heading without change and amended text generally. Prior to amendment, subpar. (A) defined "refined coal".

Subsec. (c)(7)(A)(i). Pub. L. 110–343, §101(b)(1), amended subsec. (c)(7)(A)(i) as amended by Pub. L. 110–348, §108(a)(1), by inserting "and" at end of subcl. (II), substituting period for ", and" at end of subcl. (III), and striking out subcl. (IV) which read as follows: "is produced in such a manner as to result in an increase of at least 50 percent in the market value of the refined coal (excluding any increase caused by materials combined or added during the production process), as compared to the value of the feedstock coal, or".

Subsec. (c)(7)(B). Pub. L. 110–343, §101(b)(2), inserted "at least 40 percent of the emissions of" after "nitrogen oxide and".

Subsec. (c)(7)(C). Pub. L. 110–343, §108(a)(2), added subpar. (C).

Subsec. (c)(8)(C). Pub. L. 110–343, §101(e), reenacted heading without change and amended text generally. Prior to amendment, subpar. (C) described a nonhydroelectric dam facility for purposes of subpar. (A).

Subsec. (c)(10). Pub. L. 110–343, §102(b), added par. (10).

Subsec. (d)(1). Pub. L. 110–343, §106(c)(3)(B), inserted at end "Such term shall not include any facility with respect to which any qualified small wind energy property expenditure (as defined in subsection (d)(4) of section 25D) is taken into account in determining the credit under such section."

Pub. L. 110–343, §101(a)(1), substituted "January 1, 2010" for "January 1, 2009".

Subsec. (d)(2)(A). Pub. L. 110–343, §101(a)(2)(A), substituted "January 1, 2011" for "January 1, 2009" in cls. (i) and (ii).

Subsec. (d)(2)(B), (C). Pub. L. 110–343, §101(d)(2), added subpar. (B) and redesignated former subpar. (B) as (C).

Subsec. (d)(3)(A). Pub. L. 110–343, §101(a)(2)(B), substituted "January 1, 2011" for "January 1, 2009" in cls. (i)(I) and (ii).

Subsec. (d)(3)(B), (C). Pub. L. 110–343, §101(d)(1), added subpar. (B) and redesignated former subpar. (B) as (C).

Subsec. (d)(4). Pub. L. 110–343, §101(a)(2)(C), substituted "January 1, 2011" for "January 1, 2009".

Subsec. (d)(5). Pub. L. 110–343, §102(e), which directed amendment of par. (5) by substituting "the date of the enactment of paragraph (11)" for "January 1, 2012", was executed by making the substitution for "January 1, 2011" to reflect the probable intent of Congress. See below.

Pub. L. 110–343, §101(a)(2)(D), substituted "January 1, 2011" for "January 1, 2009".

Subsec. (d)(6). Pub. L. 110–343, §101(a)(2)(E), substituted "January 1, 2011" for "January 1, 2009".

Subsec. (d)(7). Pub. L. 110–343, §101(c), struck out "combustion" before "facilities" in heading and substituted "facility (other than a facility described in paragraph (6)) which uses" for "facility which burns".

Pub. L. 110–343, §101(a)(2)(F), substituted "January 1, 2011" for "January 1, 2009".

Subsec. (d)(8). Pub. L. 110–343, §108(c), reenacted heading without change and amended text generally. Prior to amendment, text read as follows: "In the case of a facility that produces refined coal, the term 'refined coal production facility' means a facility which is placed in service after the date of the enactment of this paragraph and before January 1, 2010."

Pub. L. 110–343, §101(a)(1), substituted "January 1, 2010" for "January 1, 2009".

Subsec. (d)(9)(A), (B). Pub. L. 110–343, §101(a)(2)(G), substituted "January 1, 2011" for "January 1, 2009".

Subsec. (d)(11). Pub. L. 110–343, §102(c), added par. (11).

Subsec. (e)(8)(D). Pub. L. 110–343, §108(b)(1), added subpar. (D).

Subsec. (e)(9)(B). Pub. L. 110–343, §108(d)(1), designated existing provisions as cl. (i), inserted heading, and added cl. (ii).

2007—Subsec. (c)(3)(A)(ii). Pub. L. 110–172, §7(b)(1), struck out "which is segregated from other waste materials and" after "lignin material".

Subsec. (d)(2)(B)(i) to (iii). Pub. L. 110–172, §7(b)(2), inserted "and" at the end of cl. (i), redesignated cl. (iii) as (ii), and struck out former cl. (ii) which read as follows: "the amount of the credit determined under subsection (a) with respect to the facility shall be an amount equal to the amount determined without regard to this clause multiplied by the ratio of the thermal content of the closed-loop biomass used in such facility to the thermal content of all fuels used in such facility, and".

Subsec. (e)(7)(A)(i). Pub. L. 110–172, §9(a), substituted "originally placed in service" for "placed in service by the taxpayer".

2006—Subsec. (d)(1) to (7), (9). Pub. L. 109–432 substituted "January 1, 2009" for "January 1, 2008" wherever appearing.

2005—Subsec. (b)(4)(A). Pub. L. 109–58, §1301(c)(2), substituted "(7), or (9)" for "or (7)".

Subsec. (b)(4)(B)(i). Pub. L. 109–58, §1301(b)(1), inserted "or clause (iii)" after "clause (ii)".

Subsec. (b)(4)(B)(ii). Pub. L. 109–58, §1301(f)(1), substituted "January 1, 2005," for "the date of the enactment of this Act".

Subsec. (b)(4)(B)(iii). Pub. L. 109–58, §1301(b)(2), added cl. (iii).

Subsec. (c). Pub. L. 109–58, §1301(d)(4), substituted "Resources" for "Qualified energy resources and refined coal" in heading.

Subsec. (c)(1)(H). Pub. L. 109–58, §1301(c)(1), added subpar. (H).

Subsec. (c)(3)(A)(ii). Pub. L. 109–135, §402(b), substituted "lignin material" for "nonhazardous lignin waste material".

Pub. L. 109–58, §1301(f)(2), inserted "or any nonhazardous lignin waste material" after "cellulosic waste material".

Subsec. (c)(7)(A)(i). Pub. L. 109–135, §403(t), struck out "synthetic" after "solid".

Subsec. (c)(8). Pub. L. 109–58, §1301(c)(3), added par. (8).

Subsec. (c)(9). Pub. L. 109–58, §1301(d)(2), added par. (9).

Subsec. (d)(1) to (3). Pub. L. 109–58, §1301(a)(1), substituted "January 1, 2008" for "January 1, 2006" wherever appearing.

Subsec. (d)(4). Pub. L. 109–58, §1301(a)(2), substituted "January 1, 2008 (January 1, 2006, in the case of a facility using solar energy)" for "January 1, 2006".

Subsec. (d)(5), (6). Pub. L. 109–58, §1301(a)(1), substituted "January 1, 2008" for "January 1, 2006".

Subsec. (d)(7). Pub. L. 109–58, §1301(e), inserted at end "Such term shall include a new unit placed in service in connection with a facility placed in service on or before the date of the enactment of this paragraph, but only to the extent of the increased amount of electricity produced at the facility by reason of such new unit."

Pub. L. 109–58, §1301(a)(1), substituted "January 1, 2008" for "January 1, 2006".

Subsec. (d)(8). Pub. L. 109–135, §412(j)(1), substituted "In the case of a facility that produces refined coal, the term" for "The term".

Subsec. (d)(9). Pub. L. 109–58, §1301(c)(4), added par. (9).

Subsec. (d)(10). Pub. L. 109–135, §412(j)(2), substituted "In the case of a facility that produces Indian coal, the term" for "The term".

Pub. L. 109–58, §1301(d)(3), added par. (10).

Subsec. (e)(6). Pub. L. 109–58, §1301(f)(3), struck out heading and text of par. (6). Text read as follows: "In the case of a facility using poultry waste to produce electricity and owned by a governmental unit, the person eligible for the credit under subsection (a) is the lessee or the operator of such facility."

Subsec. (e)(8)(C). Pub. L. 109–58, §1301(f)(4)(B), struck out "and (9)" after "paragraphs (1) through (5)".

Subsec. (e)(9). Pub. L. 109–58, §1322(a)(3)(C)(i), substituted "section 45K" for "section 29" wherever appearing.

Pub. L. 109–58, §1301(f)(4)(A), reenacted heading without change and amended text of par. (9) generally. Prior to amendment, text read as follows: "The term 'qualified facility' shall not include any facility the production from which is allowed as a credit under section 29 for the taxable year or any prior taxable year."

Subsec. (e)(9)(B). Pub. L. 109–58, §1322(a)(3)(C)(ii), inserted "(or under section 29, as in effect on the day before the date of enactment of the Energy Tax Incentives Act of 2005, for any prior taxable year)" before period at end.

Subsec. (e)(10). Pub. L. 109–58, §1301(d)(1), added par. (10).

Subsec. (e)(11). Pub. L. 109–58, §1302(a), added par. (11).

2004—Pub. L. 108–357, §710(b)(3)(B), inserted ", etc" after "resources" in section catchline.

Subsec. (b)(2). Pub. L. 108–357, §710(b)(3)(C), substituted "The 1.5 cent amount in subsection (a), the 8 cent amount in paragraph (1), the $4.375 amount in subsection (e)(8)(A), and in subsection (e)(8)(B)(i) the reference price of fuel used as a feedstock (within the meaning of subsection (c)(7)(A)) in 2002" for "The 1.5 cent amount in subsection (a) and the 8 cent amount in paragraph (1)".

Subsec. (b)(3). Pub. L. 108–357, §710(f), inserted "the lesser of ½ or" before "a fraction" in introductory provisions and "This paragraph shall not apply with respect to any facility described in subsection (d)(2)(A)(ii)" in concluding provisions.

Subsec. (b)(4). Pub. L. 108–357, §710(c), added par. (4).

Subsec. (c). Pub. L. 108–357, §710(a), amended heading and text of subsec. (c) generally. Prior to amendment, subsec. (c) defined "qualified energy resources", "closed-loop biomass", "qualified facility", and "poultry waste" for purposes of this section.

Subsec. (c)(3). Pub. L. 108–311 substituted "January 1, 2006" for "January 1, 2004" in subpars. (A) to (C).

Subsec. (d). Pub. L. 108–357, §710(b)(1), added subsec. (d). Former subsec. (d) redesignated (e).

Subsec. (e). Pub. L. 108–357, §710(b)(1), redesignated subsec. (d) as (e).

Subsec. (e)(7)(A)(i). Pub. L. 108–357, §710(b)(3)(A), substituted "subsection (d)(1)" for "subsection (c)(3)(A)".

Subsec. (e)(8). Pub. L. 108–357, §710(b)(2), added par. (8).

Subsec. (e)(9). Pub. L. 108–357, §710(d), added par. (9).

2002—Subsec. (c)(3). Pub. L. 107–147 substituted "2004" for "2002" in subpars. (A) to (C).

2000—Subsec. (d)(7)(A)(i). Pub. L. 106–554 substituted "subsection (c)(3)(A)" for "paragraph (3)(A)".

1999—Subsec. (c)(1)(C). Pub. L. 106–170, §507(b)(1), added subpar. (C).

Subsec. (c)(3). Pub. L. 106–170, §507(a), reenacted heading without change and amended text generally. Prior to amendment, text read as follows: "The term 'qualified facility' means any facility owned by the taxpayer which is originally placed in service after December 31, 1993 (December 31, 1992, in the case of a facility using closed-loop biomass to produce electricity), and before July 1, 1999."

Subsec. (c)(4). Pub. L. 106–170, §507(b)(2), added par. (4).

Subsec. (d)(6), (7). Pub. L. 106–170, §507(c), added pars. (6) and (7).

STATUTORY NOTES AND RELATED SUBSIDIARIES
EFFECTIVE DATE OF 2020 AMENDMENT

Pub. L. 116–260, div. EE, title I, §131(d), Dec. 27, 2020, 134 Stat. 3052, provided that: "The amendments made by this section [amending this section and section 48 of this title] shall take effect on January 1, 2021."

Pub. L. 116–260, div. EE, title I, §145(b), Dec. 27, 2020, 134 Stat. 3054, provided that: "The amendments made by this section [amending this section] shall apply to coal produced after December 31, 2020."

EFFECTIVE DATE OF 2019 AMENDMENT

Pub. L. 116–94, div. Q, title I, §127(d), Dec. 20, 2019, 133 Stat. 3232, provided that: "The amendments made by this section [amending this section and section 48 of this title] shall take effect on January 1, 2018."

Pub. L. 116–94, div. Q, title I, §128(b), Dec. 20, 2019, 133 Stat. 3232, provided that: "The amendment made by this section [amending this section] shall apply to coal produced after December 31, 2017."

EFFECTIVE DATE OF 2018 AMENDMENT

Pub. L. 115–123, div. D, title I, §40408(b), Feb. 9, 2018, 132 Stat. 149, provided that: "The amendment made by this section [amending this section] shall apply to coal produced after December 31, 2016."

Pub. L. 115–123, div. D, title I, §40409(c), Feb. 9, 2018, 132 Stat. 150, provided that: "The amendment made by this section [amending this section and section 48 of this title] shall take effect on January 1, 2017."

EFFECTIVE DATE OF 2015 AMENDMENT

Pub. L. 114–113, div. P, title III, §301(b), Dec. 18, 2015, 129 Stat. 3038, provided that: "The amendments made by this section [amending this section] shall take effect on January 1, 2015."

Pub. L. 114–113, div. Q, title I, §186(e)(1), (2), Dec. 18, 2015, 129 Stat. 3074, provided that:

"(1) Extension.—The amendments made by subsection (a) [amending this section] shall apply to coal produced after December 31, 2014.

"(2) Modifications.—The amendments made by subsections (b) and (c) [amending this section] shall apply to coal produced and sold after December 31, 2015, in taxable years ending after such date."

Amendment by section 186(d)(2) of Pub. L. 114–113 applicable to credits determined for taxable years beginning after Dec. 31, 2015, see section 186(e)(3) of Pub. L. 114–113, set out as a note under section 38 of this title.

Pub. L. 114–113, div. Q, title I, §187(c), Dec. 18, 2015, 129 Stat. 3074, provided that: "The amendments made by this section [amending this section and section 48 of this title] shall take effect on January 1, 2015."

EFFECTIVE DATE OF 2014 AMENDMENT

Pub. L. 113–295, div. A, title I, §154(b), Dec. 19, 2014, 128 Stat. 4021, provided that: "The amendment made by this section [amending this section] shall apply to coal produced after December 31, 2013."

Pub. L. 113–295, div. A, title I, §155(c), Dec. 19, 2014, 128 Stat. 4021, provided that: "The amendments made by this section [amending this section and section 48 of this title] shall take effect on January 1, 2014."

Pub. L. 113–295, div. A, title II, §210(h), Dec. 19, 2014, 128 Stat. 4032, provided that: "The amendments made by this section [amending this section and sections 45K, 168, 907, 1012, and 6045 of this title and provisions set out as a note under section 9501 of this title] shall take effect as if included in the provisions of the Energy Improvement and Extension Act of 2008 [Pub. L. 110–343, div. B] to which they relate."

EFFECTIVE DATE OF 2013 AMENDMENT

Pub. L. 112–240, title IV, §406(b), Jan. 2, 2013, 126 Stat. 2340, provided that: "The amendment made by this section [amending this section] shall apply to coal produced after December 31, 2012."

Pub. L. 112–240, title IV, §407(d), Jan. 2, 2013, 126 Stat. 2342, provided that:

"(1) In general.—Except as provided in paragraphs (2) and (3), the amendments made by this section [amending this section, section 48 of this title, and provisions set out as a note under section 48 of this title] shall take effect on the date of the enactment of this Act [Jan. 2, 2013].

"(2) Modification to definition of municipal solid waste.—The amendments made by subsection (a)(2) [amending this section] shall apply to electricity produced and sold after the date of the enactment of this Act, in taxable years ending after such date.

"(3) Technical corrections.—The amendments made by subsection (c) [amending section 48 of this title and provisions set out as a note under section 48 of this title] shall apply as if included in the enactment of the provisions of the American Recovery and Reinvestment Act of 2009 [Pub. L. 111–5] to which they relate."

EFFECTIVE DATE OF 2010 AMENDMENT

Pub. L. 111–312, title VII, §702(b), Dec. 17, 2010, 124 Stat. 3311, provided that: "The amendment made by this section [amending this section] shall apply to facilities placed in service after December 31, 2009."

EFFECTIVE DATE OF 2009 AMENDMENT

Pub. L. 111–5, div. B, title I, §1101(c), Feb. 17, 2009, 123 Stat. 319, provided that:

"(1) In general.—The amendments made by subsection (a) [amending this section] shall apply to property placed in service after the date of the enactment of this Act [Feb. 17, 2009].

"(2) Technical amendment.—The amendment made by subsection (b) [amending this section] shall take effect as if included in section 102 of the Energy Improvement and Extension Act of 2008 [Pub. L. 110–343]."

EFFECTIVE DATE OF 2008 AMENDMENT

Pub. L. 110–343, div. B, title I, §101(f), Oct. 3, 2008, 122 Stat. 3810, provided that:

"(1) In general.—Except as otherwise provided in this subsection, the amendments made by this section [amending this section] shall apply to property originally placed in service after December 31, 2008.

"(2) Refined coal.—The amendments made by subsection (b) [amending this section] shall apply to coal produced and sold from facilities placed in service after December 31, 2008.

"(3) Trash facility clarification.—The amendments made by subsection (c) [amending this section] shall apply to electricity produced and sold after the date of the enactment of this Act [Oct. 3, 2008].

"(4) Expansion of biomass facilities.—The amendments made by subsection (d) [amending this section] shall apply to property placed in service after the date of the enactment of this Act."

Pub. L. 110–343, div. B, title I, §102(f), Oct. 3, 2008, 122 Stat. 3811, provided that: "The amendments made by this section [amending this section] shall apply to electricity produced and sold after the date of the enactment of this Act [Oct. 3, 2008], in taxable years ending after such date."

Amendment by section 106(c)(3)(B) of Pub. L. 110–343 applicable to taxable years beginning after Dec. 31, 2007, see section 106(f)(1) of Pub. L. 110–343, set out as an Effective and Termination Dates of 2008 Amendment note under section 23 of this title.

Pub. L. 110–343, div. B, title I, §108(e), Oct. 3, 2008, 122 Stat. 3821, provided that: "The amendments made by this section [amending this section and section 45K of this title] shall apply to fuel produced and sold after September 30, 2008."

EFFECTIVE DATE OF 2007 AMENDMENT

Amendment by section 7(b) of Pub. L. 110–172 effective as if included in the provision of the American Jobs Creation Act of 2004, Pub. L. 108–357, to which such amendment relates, see section 7(e) of Pub. L. 110–172, set out as a note under section 1092 of this title.

Pub. L. 110–172, §9(c), Dec. 29, 2007, 121 Stat. 2484, provided that: "The amendments made by this section [amending this section and section 856 of this title] shall take effect as if included in the provisions of the Tax Relief Extension Act of 1999 [Pub. L. 106–170] to which they relate."

EFFECTIVE DATE OF 2005 AMENDMENTS

Amendment by section 402(b) of Pub. L. 109–135 effective as if included in the provision of the Energy Policy Act of 2005, Pub. L. 109–58, to which such amendment relates, see section 402(m)(1) of Pub. L. 109–135, set out as an Effective and Termination Dates of 2005 Amendments note under section 23 of this title.

Amendment by section 403(t) of Pub. L. 109–135 effective as if included in the provisions of the American Jobs Creation Act of 2004, Pub. L. 108–357, to which such amendment relates, see section 403(nn) of Pub. L. 109–135, set out as a note under section 26 of this title.

Pub. L. 109–58, title XIII, §1301(g), Aug. 8, 2005, 119 Stat. 990, as amended by Pub. L. 110–172, §11(a)(45), Dec. 29, 2007, 121 Stat. 2488, provided that:

"(1) In general.—Except as provided in paragraph (2), the amendments made by this section [amending this section and section 168 of this title and amending provisions set out as a note under this section] shall take effect on the date of the enactment of this Act [Aug. 8, 2005].

"(2) Technical amendments.—The amendments made by subsections (e) and (f) [amending this section and section 168 of this title and amending provisions set out as a note under this section] shall take effect as if included in the amendments made by section 710 of the American Jobs Creation Act of 2004 [Pub. L. 108–357]."

Pub. L. 109–58, title XIII, §1302(c), Aug. 8, 2005, 119 Stat. 991, provided that: "The amendments made by this section [amending this section and section 55 of this title] shall apply to taxable years of cooperative organizations ending after the date of the enactment of this Act [Aug. 8, 2005]."

Amendment by section 1322(a)(3)(C) of Pub. L. 109–58 applicable to credits determined under the Internal Revenue Code of 1986 for taxable years ending after Dec. 31, 2005, see section 1322(c)(1) of Pub. L. 109–58, set out as a note under section 45K of this title.

EFFECTIVE DATE OF 2004 AMENDMENTS

Pub. L. 108–357, title VII, §710(g), Oct. 22, 2004, 118 Stat. 1557, as amended by Pub. L. 109–58, title XIII, §1301(f)(6), Aug. 8, 2005, 119 Stat. 990, provided that:

"(1) In general.—Except as otherwise provided in this subsection, the amendments made by this section [amending this section and section 48 of this title] shall apply to electricity produced and sold after the date of the enactment of this Act [Oct. 22, 2004], in taxable years ending after such date.

"(2) Certain biomass facilities.—With respect to any facility described in section 45(d)(3)(A)(ii) of the Internal Revenue Code of 1986, as added by subsection (b)(1), which is placed in service before the date of the enactment of this Act, the amendments made by this section shall apply to electricity produced and sold after December 31, 2004, in taxable years ending after such date.

"(3) Credit rate and period for new facilities.—The amendments made by subsection (c) [amending this section] shall apply to electricity produced and sold after December 31, 2004, in taxable years ending after such date.

"(4) Nonapplication of amendments to preeffective date poultry waste facilities.—The amendments made by this section shall not apply with respect to any poultry waste facility (within the meaning of section 45(c)(3)(C), as in effect on the day before the date of the enactment of this Act) placed in service before January 1, 2005.

"(5) Refined coal production facilities.—Section 45(e)(8) of the Internal Revenue Code of 1986, as added by this section, shall apply to refined coal produced and sold after the date of the enactment of this Act."

Pub. L. 108–311, title III, §313(b), Oct. 4, 2004, 118 Stat. 1181, provided that: "The amendments made by subsection (a) [amending this section] shall apply to facilities placed in service after December 31, 2003."

Effective Date of 2002 Amendment

Pub. L. 107–147, title VI, §603(b), Mar. 9, 2002, 116 Stat. 59, provided that: "The amendments made by subsection (a) [amending this section] shall apply to facilities placed in service after December 31, 2001."

Effective Date of 1999 Amendment

Pub. L. 106–170, title V, §507(d), Dec. 17, 1999, 113 Stat. 1923, provided that: "The amendments made by this section [amending this section] shall take effect on the date of the enactment of this Act [Dec. 17, 1999]."

Effective Date

Section applicable to taxable years ending after Dec. 31, 1992, see section 1914(e) of Pub. L. 102–486, set out as an Effective Date of 1992 Amendment note under section 38 of this title.

Inflation Adjusted Items for Certain Years

Provisions relating to inflation adjustment of items in this section for certain years were contained in the following:

2021—Internal Revenue Notice 2021–32.
2020—Internal Revenue Notice 2020–38.
2019—Internal Revenue Notice 2019–41, Internal Revenue Notice 2020–9.
2018—Internal Revenue Notice 2018–50, Internal Revenue Notice 2020–9.
2017—Internal Revenue Notice 2017–33,Internal Revenue Notice 2018–36.
2016—Internal Revenue Notice 2016–34.
2015—Internal Revenue Notice 2015–32, Internal Revenue Notice 2016–11.
2014—Internal Revenue Notice 2014–36.
2013—Internal Revenue Notice 2013–33.
2012—Internal Revenue Notice 2012–35.
2011—Internal Revenue Notice 2011–40.
2010—Internal Revenue Notice 2010–37.
2009—Internal Revenue Notice 2009–40.
2008—Internal Revenue Notice 2008–48.
2007—Internal Revenue Notice 2007–40.
2006—Internal Revenue Notice 2006–51.
2005—Internal Revenue Notice 2005–37.
2004—Internal Revenue Notice 2004–29.
2003—Internal Revenue Notice 2003–29.
2002—Internal Revenue Notice 2002–39.
2001—Internal Revenue Notice 2001–33.
2000—Internal Revenue Notice 2000–52.
1999—Internal Revenue Notice 99–26.
1998—Internal Revenue Notice 98–27.
1997—Internal Revenue Notice 97–30.
1996—Internal Revenue Notice 96–25.

¹ See References in Text note below.

§45A. Indian employment credit

(a) Amount of credit

For purposes of section 38, the amount of the Indian employment credit determined under this section with respect to any employer for any taxable year is an amount equal to 20 percent of the excess (if any) of—

(1) the sum of—

(A) the qualified wages paid or incurred during such taxable year, plus

(B) qualified employee health insurance costs paid or incurred during such taxable year, over

(2) the sum of the qualified wages and qualified employee health insurance costs (determined as if this section were in effect) which were paid or incurred by the employer (or any predecessor) during calendar year 1993.

(b) Qualified wages; qualified employee health insurance costs

For purposes of this section—

(1) Qualified wages

(A) In general

The term "qualified wages" means any wages paid or incurred by an employer for services performed by an employee while such employee is a qualified employee.

(B) Coordination with work opportunity credit

The term "qualified wages" shall not include wages attributable to service rendered during the 1-year period beginning with the day the individual begins work for the employer if any portion of such wages is taken into account in determining the credit under section 51. If any portion of wages are taken into account under subsection (e)(1)(A) of section 51, the preceding sentence shall be applied by substituting "2-year period" for "1-year period".

(2) Qualified employee health insurance costs

(A) In general

The term "qualified employee health insurance costs" means any amount paid or incurred by an employer for health insurance to the extent such amount is attributable to coverage provided to any employee while such employee is a qualified employee.

(B) Exception for amounts paid under salary reduction arrangements

No amount paid or incurred for health insurance pursuant to a salary reduction arrangement shall be taken into account under subparagraph (A).

(3) Limitation

The aggregate amount of qualified wages and qualified employee health insurance costs taken into account with respect to any employee for any taxable year (and for the base period under subsection (a)(2)) shall not exceed $20,000.

(c) Qualified employee

For purposes of this section—

(1) In general

Except as otherwise provided in this subsection, the term "qualified employee" means, with respect to any period, any employee of an employer if—

(A) the employee is an enrolled member of an Indian tribe or the spouse of an enrolled member of an Indian tribe,

(B) substantially all of the services performed during such period by such employee for such employer are performed within an Indian reservation, and

(C) the principal place of abode of such employee while performing such services is on or near the reservation in which the services are performed.

(2) Individuals receiving wages in excess of $30,000 not eligible

An employee shall not be treated as a qualified employee for any taxable year of the employer if the total amount of the wages paid or incurred by such employer to such employee during such taxable year (whether or not for services within an Indian reservation) exceeds the amount determined at an annual rate of $30,000.

(3) Inflation adjustment

The Secretary shall adjust the $30,000 amount under paragraph (2) for years beginning after 1994 at the same time and in the same manner as under section 415(d), except that the base period taken into account for purposes of such adjustment shall be the calendar quarter beginning October 1, 1993.

(4) Employment must be trade or business employment

An employee shall be treated as a qualified employee for any taxable year of the employer only if more than 50 percent of the wages paid or incurred by the employer to such employee during such taxable year are for services performed in a trade or business of the employer. Any determination as to whether the preceding sentence applies with respect to any employee for any taxable year shall be made without regard to subsection (e)(2).

(5) Certain employees not eligible

The term "qualified employee" shall not include—

(A) any individual described in subparagraph (A), (B), or (C) of section 51(i)(1),

(B) any 5-percent owner (as defined in section 416(i)(1)(B)), and

(C) any individual if the services performed by such individual for the employer involve the conduct of class I, II, or III gaming as defined in section 4 of the Indian Gaming Regulatory Act (25 U.S.C. 2703), or are performed in a building housing such gaming activity.

(6) Indian tribe defined

The term "Indian tribe" means any Indian tribe, band, nation, pueblo, or other organized group or community, including any Alaska Native village, or regional or village corporation, as defined in, or established pursuant to, the Alaska Native Claims Settlement Act (43 U.S.C. 1601 et seq.) which is recognized as eligible for the special programs and services provided by the United States to Indians because of their status as Indians.

(7) Indian reservation defined

The term "Indian reservation" has the meaning given such term by section 168(j)(6).

(d) Early termination of employment by employer

(1) In general

If the employment of any employee is terminated by the taxpayer before the day 1 year after the day on which such employee began work for the employer—

(A) no wages (or qualified employee health insurance costs) with respect to such employee shall be taken into account under subsection (a) for the taxable year in which such employment is terminated, and

(B) the tax under this chapter for the taxable year in which such employment is terminated shall be increased by the aggregate credits (if any) allowed under section 38(a) for prior taxable years by reason of wages (or qualified employee health insurance costs) taken into account with respect to such employee.

(2) Carrybacks and carryovers adjusted

In the case of any termination of employment to which paragraph (1) applies, the carrybacks and carryovers under section 39 shall be properly adjusted.

(3) Subsection not to apply in certain cases

(A) In general

Paragraph (1) shall not apply to—

(i) a termination of employment of an employee who voluntarily leaves the employment of the taxpayer,

(ii) a termination of employment of an individual who before the close of the period referred to in paragraph (1) becomes disabled to perform the services of such employment unless such disability is removed before the close of such period and the taxpayer fails to offer reemployment to such individual, or

(iii) a termination of employment of an individual if it is determined under the applicable State unemployment compensation law that the termination was due to the misconduct of such individual.

(B) Changes in form of business

For purposes of paragraph (1), the employment relationship between the taxpayer and an employee shall not be treated as terminated—

(i) by a transaction to which section 381(a) applies if the employee continues to be employed by the acquiring corporation, or

(ii) by reason of a mere change in the form of conducting the trade or business of the taxpayer if the employee continues to be employed in such trade or business and the taxpayer retains a substantial interest in such trade or business.

(4) Special rule

Any increase in tax under paragraph (1) shall not be treated as a tax imposed by this chapter for purposes of—

(A) determining the amount of any credit allowable under this chapter, and

(B) determining the amount of the tax imposed by section 55.

(e) Other definitions and special rules

For purposes of this section—

(1) Wages

The term "wages" has the same meaning given to such term in section 51.

(2) Controlled groups

(A) All employers treated as a single employer under section (a) or (b) of section 52 shall be treated as a single employer for purposes of this section.

(B) The credit (if any) determined under this section with respect to each such employer shall be its proportionate share of the wages and qualified employee health insurance costs giving rise to such credit.

(3) Certain other rules made applicable

Rules similar to the rules of section 51(k) and subsections (c), (d), and (e) of section 52 shall apply.

(4) Coordination with nonrevenue laws

Any reference in this section to a provision not contained in this title shall be treated for purposes of this section as a reference to such provision as in effect on the date of the enactment of this paragraph.

(5) Special rule for short taxable years

For any taxable year having less than 12 months, the amount determined under subsection (a)(2) shall be multiplied by a fraction, the numerator of which is the number of days in the taxable year and the denominator of which is 365.

(f) Termination

This section shall not apply to taxable years beginning after December 31, 2021.

(Added Pub. L. 103–66, title XIII, §13322(b), Aug. 10, 1993, 107 Stat. 559; amended Pub. L. 104–188, title I, §1201(e)(1), Aug. 20, 1996, 110 Stat. 1772; Pub. L. 105–206, title VI, §6023(1), July 22, 1998, 112 Stat. 824; Pub. L. 107–147, title VI, §613(a), Mar. 9, 2002, 116 Stat. 61; Pub. L. 108–311, title III, §315, title IV, §404(b)(1), Oct. 4, 2004, 118 Stat. 1181, 1188; Pub. L. 109–432, div. A, title I, §111(a), Dec. 20, 2006, 120 Stat. 2940; Pub. L. 110–343, div. C, title III, §314(a), Oct. 3, 2008, 122 Stat. 3872; Pub. L. 111–312, title VII, §732(a), Dec. 17, 2010, 124 Stat. 3317; Pub. L. 112–240, title III, §304(a), Jan. 2, 2013, 126 Stat. 2329; Pub. L. 113–295, div. A, title I, §114(a), title II, §216(a), Dec. 19, 2014, 128 Stat. 4014, 4034; Pub. L. 114–113, div. Q, title I, §161(a), Dec. 18, 2015, 129 Stat. 3066; Pub. L. 115–123, div. D, title I, §40301(a), Feb. 9, 2018, 132 Stat. 145; Pub. L. 116–94, div. Q, title I, §111(a), Dec. 20, 2019, 133 Stat. 3228; Pub. L. 116–260, div. EE, title I, §135(a), Dec. 27, 2020, 134 Stat. 3053.)

INFLATION ADJUSTED ITEMS FOR CERTAIN YEARS

For inflation adjustment of certain items in this section, see Internal Revenue Notices listed in a table under section 401 of this title.

EDITORIAL NOTES

REFERENCES IN TEXT

The Alaska Native Claims Settlement Act, referred to in subsec. (c)(6), is Pub. L. 92–203, Dec. 18, 1971, 85 Stat. 688, as amended, which is classified generally to chapter 33 (§1601 et seq.) of Title 43, Public Lands. For complete classification of this Act to the Code, see Short Title note set out under section 1601 of Title 43 and Tables.

The date of the enactment of this paragraph, referred to in subsec. (e)(4), is the date of enactment of Pub. L. 103–66, which was approved Aug. 10, 1993.

AMENDMENTS

2020—Subsec. (f). Pub. L. 116–260 substituted "December 31, 2021" for "December 31, 2020".

2019—Subsec. (f). Pub. L. 116–94 substituted "December 31, 2020" for "December 31, 2017".

2018—Subsec. (f). Pub. L. 115–123 substituted "December 31, 2017" for "December 31, 2016".

2015—Subsec. (f). Pub. L. 114–113 substituted "December 31, 2016" for "December 31, 2014".

2014—Subsec. (b)(1)(B). Pub. L. 113–295, §216(a), inserted at end "If any portion of wages are taken into account under subsection (e)(1)(A) of section 51, the preceding sentence shall be applied by substituting '2-year period' for '1-year period'."

Subsec. (f). Pub. L. 113–295, §114(a), substituted "December 31, 2014" for "December 31, 2013".

2013—Subsec. (f). Pub. L. 112–240 substituted "December 31, 2013" for "December 31, 2011".

2010—Subsec. (f). Pub. L. 111–312 substituted "December 31, 2011" for "December 31, 2009".

2008—Subsec. (f). Pub. L. 110–343 substituted "December 31, 2009" for "December 31, 2007".

2006—Subsec. (f). Pub. L. 109–432 substituted "2007" for "2005".

2004—Subsec. (c)(3). Pub. L. 108–311, §404(b)(1), inserted ", except that the base period taken into account for purposes of such adjustment shall be the calendar quarter beginning October 1, 1993" before period at end.

Subsec. (f). Pub. L. 108–311, §315, substituted "December 31, 2005" for "December 31, 2004".

2002—Subsec. (f). Pub. L. 107–147 substituted "December 31, 2004" for "December 31, 2003".

1998—Subsec. (b)(1)(B). Pub. L. 105–206 substituted "work opportunity credit" for "targeted jobs credit" in heading.

1996—Subsec. (b)(1)(B). Pub. L. 104–188, which directed that subsec. (b)(1)(B) of this section be amended in the text by substituting "work opportunity credit" for "targeted jobs credit", could not be executed because the words "targeted jobs credit" did not appear in the text.

STATUTORY NOTES AND RELATED SUBSIDIARIES

EFFECTIVE DATE OF 2020 AMENDMENT

Pub. L. 116–260, div. EE, title I, §135(b), Dec. 27, 2020, 134 Stat. 3053, provided that: "The amendment made by this section [amending this section] shall apply to taxable years beginning after December 31, 2020."

EFFECTIVE DATE OF 2019 AMENDMENT

Pub. L. 116–94, div. Q, title I, §111(b), Dec. 20, 2019, 133 Stat. 3228, provided that: "The amendment made by this section [amending this section] shall apply to taxable years beginning after December 31, 2017."

EFFECTIVE DATE OF 2018 AMENDMENT

Pub. L. 115–123, div. D, title I, §40301(b), Feb. 9, 2018, 132 Stat. 145, provided that: "The amendment made by this section [amending this section] shall apply to taxable years beginning after December 31, 2016."

EFFECTIVE DATE OF 2015 AMENDMENT

Pub. L. 114–113, div. Q, title I, §161(b), Dec. 18, 2015, 129 Stat. 3066, provided that: "The amendment made by this section [amending this section] shall apply to taxable years beginning after December 31, 2014."

EFFECTIVE DATE OF 2014 AMENDMENT

Pub. L. 113–295, div. A, title I, §114(b), Dec. 19, 2014, 128 Stat. 4014, provided that: "The amendment made by this section [amending this section] shall apply to taxable years beginning after December 31, 2013."

Pub. L. 113–295, div. A, title II, §216(b), Dec. 19, 2014, 128 Stat. 4034, provided that: "The amendment made by this section [amending this section] shall take effect as if included in the provision of the Tax Relief and Health Care Act of 2006 [Pub. L. 109–432] to which it relates."

EFFECTIVE DATE OF 2013 AMENDMENT

Pub. L. 112–240, title III, §304(b), Jan. 2, 2013, 126 Stat. 2329, provided that: "The amendment made by this section [amending this section] shall apply to taxable years beginning after December 31, 2011."

EFFECTIVE DATE OF 2010 AMENDMENT

Pub. L. 111–312, title VII, §732(b), Dec. 17, 2010, 124 Stat. 3317, provided that: "The amendment made by this section [amending this section] shall apply to taxable years beginning after December 31, 2009."

EFFECTIVE DATE OF 2008 AMENDMENT

Pub. L. 110–343, div. C, title III, §314(b), Oct. 3, 2008, 122 Stat. 3872, provided that: "The amendment made by this section [amending this section] shall apply to taxable years beginning after December 31, 2007."

EFFECTIVE DATE OF 2006 AMENDMENT

Pub. L. 109–432, div. A, title I, §111(b), Dec. 20, 2006, 120 Stat. 2940, provided that: "The amendment made by this section [amending this section] shall apply to taxable years beginning after December 31, 2005."

EFFECTIVE DATE OF 2004 AMENDMENT

Pub. L. 108–311, title IV, §404(f), Oct. 4, 2004, 118 Stat. 1188, provided that: "The amendments made by this section [amending this section and sections 403, 408, 415, 530, and 4972 of this title] shall take effect as if included in the provisions of the Economic Growth and Tax Relief Reconciliation Act of 2001 [Pub. L. 107–16] to which they relate."

EFFECTIVE DATE OF 1996 AMENDMENT

Amendment by Pub. L. 104–188 applicable to individuals who begin work for the employer after Sept. 30, 1996, see section 1201(g) of Pub. L. 104–188, set out as a note under section 38 of this title.

EFFECTIVE DATE

Section applicable to wages paid or incurred after Dec. 31, 1993, see section 13322(f) of Pub. L. 103–66, set out as an Effective Date of 1993 Amendment note under section 38 of this title.

§45B. Credit for portion of employer social security taxes paid with respect to employee cash tips

(a) General rule

For purposes of section 38, the employer social security credit determined under this section for the taxable year is an amount equal to the excess employer social security tax paid or incurred by the taxpayer during the taxable year.

(b) Excess employer social security tax

For purposes of this section—

(1) In general

The term "excess employer social security tax" means any tax paid by an employer under section 3111 with respect to tips received by an employee during any month, to the extent such tips—

(A) are deemed to have been paid by the employer to the employee pursuant to section 3121(q) (without regard to whether such tips are reported under section 6053), and

(B) exceed the amount by which the wages (excluding tips) paid by the employer to the employee during such month are less than the total amount which would be payable (with respect to such employment) at the minimum wage rate applicable to such individual under section 6(a)(1) of the Fair Labor Standards Act of 1938 (as in effect on January 1, 2007, and determined without regard to section 3(m) of such Act).

(2) Only tips received for food or beverages taken into account

In applying paragraph (1), there shall be taken into account only tips received from customers in connection with the providing, delivering, or serving of food or beverages for consumption if the tipping of employees delivering or serving food or beverages by customers is customary.

(c) Denial of double benefit

No deduction shall be allowed under this chapter for any amount taken into account in determining the credit under this section.

(d) Election not to claim credit

This section shall not apply to a taxpayer for any taxable year if such taxpayer elects to have this section not apply for such taxable year.

(Added Pub. L. 103–66, title XIII, §13443(a), Aug. 10, 1993, 107 Stat. 568; amended Pub. L. 104–188, title I, §1112(a)(1), (b)(1), Aug. 20, 1996, 110 Stat. 1759; Pub. L. 110–28, title VIII, §8213(a), May 25, 2007, 121 Stat. 193.)

EDITORIAL NOTES
REFERENCES IN TEXT

Sections 3(m) and 6(a)(1) of the Fair Labor Standards Act of 1938, referred to in subsec. (b)(1)(B), are classified to sections 203(m) and 206(a)(1), respectively, of Title 29, Labor.

AMENDMENTS

2007—Subsec. (b)(1)(B). Pub. L. 110–28 inserted "as in effect on January 1, 2007, and" before "determined without regard to".

1996—Subsec. (b)(1)(A). Pub. L. 104–188, §1112(a)(1), inserted "(without regard to whether such tips are reported under section 6053)" after "section 3121(q)".

Subsec. (b)(2). Pub. L. 104–188, §1112(b)(1), amended par. (2) generally. Prior to amendment, par. (2) read as follows: "Only tips received at food and beverage establishments taken into account.—In applying paragraph (1), there shall be taken into account only tips received from customers in connection with the provision of food or beverages for consumption on the premises of an establishment with respect to which the tipping of employees serving food or beverages by customers is customary."

STATUTORY NOTES AND RELATED SUBSIDIARIES
EFFECTIVE DATE OF 2007 AMENDMENT

Pub. L. 110–28, title VIII, §8213(b), May 25, 2007, 121 Stat. 193, provided that: "The amendment made by this section [amending this section] shall apply to tips received for services performed after December 31, 2006."

EFFECTIVE DATE OF 1996 AMENDMENT

Pub. L. 104–188, title I, §1112(a)(3), Aug. 20, 1996, 110 Stat. 1759, provided that: "The amendments made by this subsection [amending this section and provisions set out as a note under section 38 of this title] shall take effect as if included in the amendments made by, and the provisions of, section 13443 of the Revenue Reconciliation Act of 1993 [Pub. L. 103–66]."

Pub. L. 104–188, title I, §1112(b)(2), Aug. 20, 1996, 110 Stat. 1759, provided that: "The amendment made by paragraph (1) [amending this section] shall apply to tips received for services performed after December 31, 1996."

EFFECTIVE DATE

Section applicable with respect to taxes paid after Dec. 31, 1993, with respect to services performed before, on, or after such date, see section 13443(d) of Pub. L. 103–66, as amended, set out as an Effective Date of 1993 Amendment note under section 38 of this title.

§45C. Clinical testing expenses for certain drugs for rare diseases or conditions

(a) General rule

For purposes of section 38, the credit determined under this section for the taxable year is an amount equal to 25 percent of the qualified clinical testing expenses for the taxable year.

(b) Qualified clinical testing expenses

For purposes of this section—

(1) Qualified clinical testing expenses

(A) In general

Except as otherwise provided in this paragraph, the term "qualified clinical testing expenses" means the amounts which are paid or incurred by the taxpayer during the taxable year which would be described in subsection (b) of section 41 if such subsection were applied with the modifications set forth in subparagraph (B).

(B) Modifications

For purposes of subparagraph (A), subsection (b) of section 41 shall be applied—

(i) by substituting "clinical testing" for "qualified research" each place it appears in paragraphs (2) and (3) of such subsection, and

(ii) by substituting "100 percent" for "65 percent" in paragraph (3)(A) of such subsection.

(C) Exclusion for amounts funded by grants, etc.

The term "qualified clinical testing expenses" shall not include any amount to the extent such amount is funded by any grant, contract, or otherwise by another person (or any governmental entity).

(2) Clinical testing

(A) In general

The term "clinical testing" means any human clinical testing—

(i) which is carried out under an exemption for a drug being tested for a rare disease or condition under section 505(i) of the Federal Food, Drug, and Cosmetic Act (or regulations issued under such section),

(ii) which occurs—

(I) after the date such drug is designated under section 526 of such Act, and

(II) before the date on which an application with respect to such drug is approved under section 505(b) of such Act or, if the drug is a biological product, before the date on which a license for such drug is issued under section 351 of the Public Health Service Act, and

(iii) which is conducted by or on behalf of the taxpayer to whom the designation under such section 526 applies.

(B) Testing must be related to use for rare disease or condition

Human clinical testing shall be taken into account under subparagraph (A) only to the extent such testing is related to the use of a drug for the rare disease or condition for which it was designated under section 526 of the Federal Food, Drug, and Cosmetic Act.

(c) Coordination with credit for increasing research expenditures

(1) In general

Except as provided in paragraph (2), any qualified clinical testing expenses for a taxable year to which an election under this section applies shall not be taken into account for purposes of determining the credit allowable under section 41 for such taxable year.

(2) Expenses included in determining base period research expenses

Any qualified clinical testing expenses for any taxable year which are qualified research expenses (within the meaning of section 41(b)) shall be taken into account in determining base period research expenses for purposes of applying section 41 to subsequent taxable years.

(d) Definition and special rules

(1) Rare disease or condition

For purposes of this section, the term "rare disease or condition" means any disease or condition which—

(A) affects less than 200,000 persons in the United States, or

(B) affects more than 200,000 persons in the United States but for which there is no reasonable expectation that the cost of developing and making available in the United States a drug for such disease or condition will be recovered from sales in the United States of such drug.

Determinations under the preceding sentence with respect to any drug shall be made on the basis of the facts and circumstances as of the date such drug is designated under section 526 of the Federal Food, Drug, and Cosmetic Act.

(2) Special limitations on foreign testing

No credit shall be allowed under this section with respect to any clinical testing conducted outside the United States unless—

(A) such testing is conducted outside the United States because there is an insufficient testing population in the United States, and

(B) such testing is conducted by a United States person or by any other person who is not related to the taxpayer to whom the designation under section 526 of the Federal Food, Drug, and Cosmetic Act applies.

(3) Certain rules made applicable

Rules similar to the rules of paragraphs (1) and (2) of section 41(f) shall apply for purposes of this section.

(4) Election

This section shall apply to any taxpayer for any taxable year only if such taxpayer elects (at such time and in such manner as the Secretary may by regulations prescribe) to have this section apply for such taxable year.

(Added Pub. L. 97–414, §4(a), Jan. 4, 1983, 96 Stat. 2053, §44H; renumbered §28 and amended Pub. L. 98–369, div. A, title IV, §§471(c), 474(g), title VI, §612(e)(1), July 18, 1984, 98 Stat. 826, 831, 912; Pub. L. 99–514, title II, §§231(d)(3)(A), 232, title VII, §701(c)(2), title XII, §1275(c)(4), title XVIII, §1879(b)(1), (2), Oct. 22, 1986, 100 Stat. 2178, 2180, 2340, 2599, 2905; Pub. L. 100–647, title I, §1018(q)(1), title IV, §4008(c)(1), Nov. 10, 1988, 102 Stat. 3585, 3653; Pub. L. 101–239, title VII, §7110(a)(3), Dec. 19, 1989, 103 Stat. 2323; Pub. L. 101–508, title XI, §§11402(b)(2), 11411, Nov. 5, 1990, 104 Stat. 1388–473, 1388-479; Pub. L. 102–227, title I, §§102(b), 111(a), Dec. 11, 1991, 105 Stat. 1686, 1688; Pub. L. 103–66, title XIII, §13111(a)(2), (b), Aug. 10, 1993, 107 Stat. 420; renumbered §45C and amended Pub. L. 104–188, title I, §§1204(e), 1205(a)(1), (b), (d)(1), (2), Aug. 20, 1996, 110 Stat. 1775, 1776; Pub. L. 105–34, title VI, §§601(b)(2), 604(a), Aug. 5, 1997, 111 Stat. 862, 863; Pub. L. 105–115, title I, §125(b)(2)(O), Nov. 21, 1997, 111 Stat. 2326; Pub. L. 105–277, div. J, title I, §1001(b), Oct. 21, 1998, 112 Stat. 2681–888; Pub. L. 106–170, title V, §502(a)(2), Dec. 17, 1999, 113 Stat. 1919; Pub. L. 108–311, title III, §301(a)(2), Oct. 4, 2004, 118 Stat. 1178; Pub. L. 109–432, div. A, title I, §104(a)(2), Dec. 20, 2006, 120 Stat. 2934; Pub. L. 110–343, div. C, title III, §301(a)(2), Oct. 3, 2008, 122 Stat. 3865; Pub. L. 111–312, title VII, §731(b), Dec. 17, 2010, 124 Stat. 3317; Pub. L. 112–240, title III, §301(a)(2), Jan. 2, 2013, 126 Stat. 2326; Pub. L. 113–295, div. A, title I, §111(b), Dec. 19, 2014, 128 Stat. 4014; Pub. L. 114–113, div. Q, title I, §121(a)(2), Dec. 18, 2015, 129 Stat. 3049; Pub. L. 115–97, title I, §13401(a), Dec. 22, 2017, 131 Stat. 2133; Pub. L. 115–141, div. U, title IV, §401(a)(17), (d)(1)(D)(iii), Mar. 23, 2018, 132 Stat. 1185, 1206.)

EDITORIAL NOTES
REFERENCES IN TEXT

Sections 505(b), (i) and 526 of the Federal Food, Drug, and Cosmetic Act, referred to in subsecs. (b)(2)(A) and (d)(1), (2)(B), are classified to sections 355(b), (i) and 360bb, respectively, of Title 21, Food and Drugs.

Section 351 of the Public Health Service Act, referred to in subsec. (b)(2)(A)(ii)(II), is classified to section 262 of Title 42, The Public Health and Welfare.

AMENDMENTS

2018—Subsec. (b)(2)(A)(ii)(II). Pub. L. 115–141, §401(a)(17), substituted ", and" for "; and".

Subsec. (d)(2). Pub. L. 115–141, §401(d)(1)(D)(iii), struck out subpar. (A) designation and heading, redesignated cls. (i) and (ii) of former subpar. (A) as subpars. (A) and (B), respectively, realigned margins, and struck out former subpar. (B) which related to special limitation for corporations to which former section 936 applied.

2017—Subsec. (a). Pub. L. 115–97 substituted "25 percent" for "50 percent".

2015—Subsec. (b)(1)(D). Pub. L. 114–113 struck out subpar. (D). Text read as follows: "If section 41 is not in effect for any period, such section shall be deemed to remain in effect for such period for purposes of this paragraph."

2014—Subsec. (b)(1)(D). Pub. L. 113–295 amended subpar. (D) generally. Prior to amendment, text read as follows: "For purposes of this paragraph, section 41 shall be deemed to remain in effect for periods after June 30, 1995, and before July 1, 1996, and periods after December 31, 2013."

2013—Subsec. (b)(1)(D). Pub. L. 112–240 substituted "December 31, 2013" for "December 31, 2011".

2010—Subsec. (b)(1)(D). Pub. L. 111–312 substituted "December 31, 2011" for "December 31, 2009".

2008—Subsec. (b)(1)(D). Pub. L. 110–343 substituted "December 31, 2009" for "December 31, 2007".

2006—Subsec. (b)(1)(D). Pub. L. 109–432 substituted "2007" for "2005".

2004—Subsec. (b)(1)(D). Pub. L. 108–311 substituted "December 31, 2005" for "June 30, 2004".

1999—Subsec. (b)(1)(D). Pub. L. 106–170 substituted "June 30, 2004" for "June 30, 1999".

1998—Subsec. (b)(1)(D). Pub. L. 105–277 substituted "June 30, 1999" for "June 30, 1998".

1997—Subsec. (b)(1)(D). Pub. L. 105–34, §601(b)(2), substituted "June 30, 1998" for "May 31, 1997".

Subsec. (b)(2)(A)(ii)(II). Pub. L. 105–115 struck out "or 507" after "505(b)".

Subsec. (e). Pub. L. 105–34, §604(a), struck out subsec. (e) which read as follows:

"(e) Termination.—This section shall not apply to any amount paid or incurred—

"(1) after December 31, 1994, and before July 1, 1996, or

"(2) after May 31, 1997."

1996—Pub. L. 104–188, §1205(a)(1), renumbered section 28 of this title as this section.

Subsec. (a). Pub. L. 104–188, §1205(d)(1), substituted "For purposes of section 38, the credit determined under this section for the taxable year is" for "There shall be allowed as a credit against the tax imposed by this chapter for the taxable year".

Subsec. (b)(1)(D). Pub. L. 104–188, §1204(e), inserted ", and before July 1, 1996, and periods after May 31, 1997" after "June 30, 1995".

Subsec. (d)(2) to (5). Pub. L. 104–188, §1205(d)(2), redesignated pars. (3) to (5) as (2) to (4), respectively, and struck out former par. (2) which read as follows: "Limitation based on amount of tax.—The credit allowed by this section for any taxable year shall not exceed the excess (if any) of—

"(A) the regular tax (reduced by the sum of the credits allowable under subpart A and section 27), over

"(B) the tentative minimum tax for the taxable year."

Subsec. (e). Pub. L. 104–188, §1205(b), amended subsec. (e) generally. Prior to amendment, subsec. (e) read as follows: "Termination.—This section shall not apply to any amount paid or incurred after December 31, 1994."

1993—Subsec. (b)(1)(D). Pub. L. 103–66, §13111(a)(2), substituted "June 30, 1995" for "June 30, 1992".

Subsec. (e). Pub. L. 103–66, §13111(b), substituted "December 31, 1994" for "June 30, 1992".

1991—Subsec. (b)(1)(D). Pub. L. 102–227, §102(b), substituted "June 30, 1992" for "December 31, 1991".

Subsec. (e). Pub. L. 102–227, §111(a), substituted "June 30, 1992" for "December 31, 1991".

1990—Subsec. (b)(1)(D). Pub. L. 101–508, §11402(b)(2), substituted "December 31, 1991" for "December 31, 1990".

Subsec. (e). Pub. L. 101–508, §11411, substituted "December 31, 1991" for "December 31, 1990".

1989—Subsec. (b)(1)(D). Pub. L. 101–239 substituted "1990" for "1989".

1988—Subsec. (b)(1)(D). Pub. L. 100–647, §4008(c)(1), substituted "1989" for "1988".

Subsec. (b)(2)(A)(ii)(II). Pub. L. 100–647, §1018(q)(1), amended subcl. (II) generally. Prior to amendment, subcl. (II) read as follows: "before the date on which an application with respect to such drug is approved under section 505(b) of such Act or, if the drug is a biological product, before the date on which a license for such drug is issued under section 351 of the Public Health Services Act, and".

1986—Subsec. (b)(1). Pub. L. 99–514, §231(d)(3)(A)(i), (iv), substituted "41" for "30" in subpars. (A), (B), and (D), and substituted "1988" for "1985" in subpar. (D).

Subsec. (b)(2)(A)(ii)(I). Pub. L. 99–514, §1879(b)(1)(A), substituted "the date such drug" for "the date of such drug".

Subsec. (b)(2)(A)(ii)(II). Pub. L. 99–514, §1879(b)(1)(B), inserted "or, if the drug is a biological product, before the date on which a license for such drug is issued under section 351 of the Public Health Services Act".

Subsec. (c). Pub. L. 99–514, §231(d)(3)(A)(i), (ii), substituted "41" for "30" in pars. (1) and (2) and "41(b)" for "30(b)" in par. (2).

Subsec. (d)(1). Pub. L. 99–514, §1879(b)(2), amended par. (1) generally. Prior to amendment, par. (1) read as follows: "For purposes of this section, the term 'rare disease or condition' means any disease or condition which occurs so infrequently in the United States that there is no reasonable expectation that the cost of developing and making available in the United States a drug for such disease or condition will be recovered from sales in the United States of such drug. Determinations under the preceding sentence with respect to any drug shall be made on the basis of the facts and circumstances as of the date such drug is designated under section 526 of the Federal Food, Drug, and Cosmetic Act."

Subsec. (d)(2). Pub. L. 99–514, §701(c)(2), amended par. (2) generally. Prior to amendment, par. (2) read as follows: "The credit allowed by this section for any taxable year shall not exceed the taxpayer's tax liability for the taxable year (as defined in section 26(b)), reduced by the sum of the credits allowable under subpart A and section 27."

Subsec. (d)(3)(B). Pub. L. 99–514, §1275(c)(4), struck out "934(b) or" before "936" in heading and amended text generally. Prior to amendment, text read as follows: "No credit shall be allowed under this section with respect to any clinical testing conducted by a corporation to which section 934(b) applies or to which an election under section 936 applies."

Subsec. (d)(4). Pub. L. 99–514, §231(d)(3)(A)(iii), substituted "section 41(f)" for "section 30(f)".

Subsec. (e). Pub. L. 99–514, §232, substituted "1990" for "1987".

1984—Pub. L. 98–369, §471(c), renumbered section 44H of this title as this section.

Subsec. (b)(1)(A), (B), (D). Pub. L. 98–369, §474(g)(1)(A), substituted "section 30" for "section 44F".

Subsec. (c)(1). Pub. L. 98–369, §474(g)(1)(A), substituted "section 30" for "section 44F".

Subsec. (c)(2). Pub. L. 98–369, §474(g)(1)(A), (B), substituted "section 30" for "section 44F" and "section 30(b)" for "section 44F(b)".

Subsec. (d)(2). Pub. L. 98–369, §612(e)(1), substituted "section 26(b)" for "section 25(b)".

Pub. L. 98–369, §474(g)(2), amended par. (2) generally, substituting "shall not exceed the taxpayer's tax liability for the taxable year (as defined in section 25(b), reduced by the sum of the credits allowable under subpart A and section 27" for "shall not exceed the amount of the tax imposed by this chapter for the taxable year reduced by the sum of the credits allowable under a section of this subpart having a lower number or letter designation than this section, other than the credits allowable by sections 31, 39, and 43. For purposes of the preceding sentence, the term 'tax imposed by this chapter' shall not include any tax treated as not imposed by this chapter under the last sentence of section 53(a)".

Subsec. (d)(4). Pub. L. 98–369, §474(g)(1)(C), substituted "section 30(f)" for "section 44F(f)".

STATUTORY NOTES AND RELATED SUBSIDIARIES

EFFECTIVE DATE OF 2017 AMENDMENT

Pub. L. 115–97, title I, §13401(c), Dec. 22, 2017, 131 Stat. 2134, provided that: "The amendments made by this section [amending this section and section 280C of this title] shall apply to taxable years beginning after December 31, 2017."

EFFECTIVE DATE OF 2015 AMENDMENT

Amendment by Pub. L. 114–113 applicable to amounts paid or incurred after Dec. 31, 2014, see section 121(d)(1) of Pub. L. 114–113, set out as a note under section 38 of this title.

EFFECTIVE DATE OF 2014 AMENDMENT

Amendment by Pub. L. 113–295 applicable to amounts paid or incurred after Dec. 31, 2013, see section 111(c) of Pub. L. 113–295, set out as a note under section 41 of this title.

EFFECTIVE DATE OF 2013 AMENDMENT

Amendment by Pub. L. 112–240 applicable to amounts paid or incurred after Dec. 31, 2011, see section 301(d)(1) of Pub. L. 112–240, set out as a note under section 41 of this title.

EFFECTIVE DATE OF 2010 AMENDMENT

Amendment by Pub. L. 111–312 applicable to amounts paid or incurred after Dec. 31, 2009, see section 731(c) of Pub. L. 111–312, set out as a note under section 41 of this title.

EFFECTIVE DATE OF 2008 AMENDMENT

Amendment by Pub. L. 110–343 applicable to amounts paid or incurred after Dec. 31, 2007, see section 301(e)(2) of Pub. L. 110–343, set out as a note under section 41 of this title.

EFFECTIVE DATE OF 2006 AMENDMENT

Amendment by Pub. L. 109–432 applicable to amounts paid or incurred after Dec. 31, 2005, see section 104(a)(3) of Pub. L. 109–432, set out as a note under section 41 of this title.

EFFECTIVE DATE OF 2004 AMENDMENT

Amendment by Pub. L. 108–311 applicable to amounts paid or incurred after June 30, 2004, see section 301(b) of Pub. L. 108–311, set out as a note under section 41 of this title.

EFFECTIVE DATE OF 1999 AMENDMENT

Amendment by Pub. L. 106–170 applicable to amounts paid or incurred after June 30, 1999, see section 502(a)(3) of Pub. L. 106–170, set out as a note under section 41 of this title.

EFFECTIVE DATE OF 1998 AMENDMENT

Amendment by Pub. L. 105–277 applicable to amounts paid or incurred after June 30, 1998, see section 1001(c) of Pub. L. 105–277, set out as a note under section 41 of this title.

EFFECTIVE DATE OF 1997 AMENDMENT

Amendment by section 601(b)(2) of Pub. L. 105–34 applicable to amounts paid or incurred after May 31, 1997, see section 601(c) of Pub. L. 105–34, set out as a note under section 41 of this title.

Pub. L. 105–34, title VI, §604(b), Aug. 5, 1997, 111 Stat. 863, provided that: "The amendment made by subsection (a) [amending this section] shall apply to amounts paid or incurred after May 31, 1997."

EFFECTIVE DATE OF 1996 AMENDMENT

Amendment by section 1204(e) of Pub. L. 104–188 applicable to taxable years ending after June 30, 1996, and not to be taken into account under section 6654 or 6655 of this title in determining amount of any installment required to be paid for a taxable year beginning in 1997, see section 1204(f) of Pub. L. 104–188, set out as a note under section 41 of this title.

Amendment by section 1205(a)(1), (b), (d)(1), (2) of Pub. L. 104–188 applicable to amounts paid or incurred in taxable years ending after June 30, 1996, see section 1205(e) of Pub. L. 104–188, set out as a note under section 45K of this title.

EFFECTIVE DATE OF 1993 AMENDMENT

Pub. L. 103–66, title XIII, §13111(c), Aug. 10, 1993, 107 Stat. 421, provided that: "The amendments made by this section [amending this section and section 41 of this title] shall apply to taxable years ending after June 30, 1992."

EFFECTIVE DATE OF 1991 AMENDMENT

Pub. L. 102–227, title I, §102(c), Dec. 11, 1991, 105 Stat. 1686, provided that: "The amendments made by this section [amending this section and section 41 of this title] shall apply to taxable years ending after December 31, 1991."

Pub. L. 102–227, title I, §111(b), Dec. 11, 1991, 105 Stat. 1689, provided that: "The amendment made by this section [amending this section] shall apply to taxable years ending after December 31, 1991."

EFFECTIVE DATE OF 1990 AMENDMENT

Pub. L. 101–508, title XI, §11402(c), Nov. 5, 1990, 104 Stat. 1388–473, provided that: "The amendments made by this section [amending this section and section 41 of this title and repealing provisions set out as a note under section 41 of this title] shall apply to taxable years beginning after December 31, 1989."

EFFECTIVE DATE OF 1988 AMENDMENT

Amendment by section 1018(q)(1) of Pub. L. 100–647 effective, except as otherwise provided, as if included in the provision of the Tax Reform Act of 1986, Pub. L. 99–514, to which such amendment relates, see section 1019(a) of Pub. L. 100–647, set out as a note under section 1 of this title.

Amendment by section 4008(c)(1) of Pub. L. 100–647 applicable to taxable years beginning after Dec. 31, 1988, see section 4008(d) of Pub. L. 100–647, set out as a note under section 41 of this title.

EFFECTIVE DATE OF 1986 AMENDMENT

Amendment by section 231(d)(3)(A) of Pub. L. 99–514 applicable to taxable years beginning after Dec. 31, 1985, see section 231(g) of Pub. L. 99–514, set out as a note under section 41 of this title.

Amendment by section 701(c)(2) of Pub. L. 99–514 applicable to taxable years beginning after Dec. 31, 1986, with certain exceptions and qualifications, see section 701(f) of Pub. L. 99–514, set out as an Effective Date note under section 55 of this title.

Amendment by section 1275(c)(4) of Pub. L. 99–514 applicable to taxable years beginning after Dec. 31, 1986, with certain exceptions and qualifications, see section 1277 of Pub. L. 99–514, set out as a note under section 931 of this title.

Pub. L. 99–514, title XVIII, §1879(b)(3), Oct. 22, 1986, 100 Stat. 2906, provided that: "The amendments made by this subsection [amending this section] shall apply to amounts paid or incurred after December 31, 1982, in taxable years ending after such date."

EFFECTIVE DATE OF 1984 AMENDMENT

Amendment by section 474(g) of Pub. L. 98–369 applicable to taxable years beginning after Dec. 31, 1983, and to carrybacks from such years, see section 475(a) of Pub. L. 98–369, set out as a note under section 21 of this title.

Amendment by section 612(e)(1) of Pub. L. 98–369, applicable to interest paid or accrued after December 31, 1984, on indebtedness incurred after December 31, 1984, see section 612(g) of Pub. L. 98–369, set out as an Effective Date note under section 25 of this title.

EFFECTIVE DATE

Pub. L. 97–414, §4(d), Jan. 4, 1983, 96 Stat. 2056, provided that: "The amendments made by this section [enacting this section and amending sections 280C and 6096 of this title] shall apply to amounts paid or incurred after December 31, 1982, in taxable years ending after such date."

SAVINGS PROVISION

For provisions that nothing in amendment by section 401(d)(1)(D)(iii) of Pub. L. 115–141 be construed to affect treatment of certain transactions occurring, property acquired, or items of income, loss, deduction, or credit taken into account prior to Mar. 23, 2018, for purposes of determining liability for tax for periods ending after Mar. 23, 2018, see section 401(e) of Pub. L. 115–141, set out as a note under section 23 of this title.

APPLICABILITY OF CERTAIN AMENDMENTS BY PUBLIC LAW 99–514 IN RELATION TO TREATY OBLIGATIONS OF UNITED STATES

For applicability of amendment by section 701(c)(2) of Pub. L. 99–514 notwithstanding any treaty obligation of the United States in effect on Oct. 22, 1986, with provision that for such purposes any amendment by title I of Pub. L. 100–647 be treated as if it had been included in the provision of Pub. L. 99–514 to which such amendment relates, see section 1012(aa)(2), (4) of Pub. L. 100–647, set out as a note under section 861 of this title.

PLAN AMENDMENTS NOT REQUIRED UNTIL JANUARY 1, 1989

For provisions directing that if any amendments made by subtitle A or subtitle C of title XI [§§1101–1147 and 1171–1177] or title XVIII [§§1800–1899A] of Pub. L. 99–514 require an amendment to any plan, such plan amendment shall not be required to be made before the first plan year beginning on or after Jan. 1, 1989, see section 1140 of Pub. L. 99–514, as amended, set out as a note under section 401 of this title.

§45D. New markets tax credit

(a) Allowance of credit

(1) In general

For purposes of section 38, in the case of a taxpayer who holds a qualified equity investment on a credit allowance date of such investment which occurs during the taxable year, the new markets tax credit determined under this section for such taxable year is an amount equal to the applicable percentage of the amount paid to the qualified community development entity for such investment at its original issue.

(2) Applicable percentage

For purposes of paragraph (1), the applicable percentage is—

(A) 5 percent with respect to the first 3 credit allowance dates, and

(B) 6 percent with respect to the remainder of the credit allowance dates.

(3) Credit allowance date

For purposes of paragraph (1), the term "credit allowance date" means, with respect to any qualified equity investment—

(A) the date on which such investment is initially made, and

(B) each of the 6 anniversary dates of such date thereafter.

(b) Qualified equity investment

For purposes of this section—

(1) In general

The term "qualified equity investment" means any equity investment in a qualified community development entity if—

(A) such investment is acquired by the taxpayer at its original issue (directly or through an underwriter) solely in exchange for cash,

(B) substantially all of such cash is used by the qualified community development entity to make qualified low-income community investments, and

(C) such investment is designated for purposes of this section by the qualified community development entity.

Such term shall not include any equity investment issued by a qualified community development entity more than 5 years after the date that such entity receives an allocation under subsection (f). Any allocation not used within such 5-year period may be reallocated by the Secretary under subsection (f).

(2) Limitation

The maximum amount of equity investments issued by a qualified community development entity which may be designated under paragraph (1)(C) by such entity shall not exceed the portion of the limitation amount allocated under subsection (f) to such entity.

(3) Safe harbor for determining use of cash

The requirement of paragraph (1)(B) shall be treated as met if at least 85 percent of the aggregate gross assets of the qualified community development entity are invested in qualified low-income community investments.

(4) Treatment of subsequent purchasers

The term "qualified equity investment" includes any equity investment which would (but for paragraph (1)(A)) be a qualified equity investment in the hands of the taxpayer if such investment was a qualified equity investment in the hands of a prior holder.

(5) Redemptions

A rule similar to the rule of section 1202(c)(3) shall apply for purposes of this subsection.

(6) Equity investment

The term "equity investment" means—

(A) any stock (other than nonqualified preferred stock as defined in section 351(g)(2)) in an entity which is a corporation, and

(B) any capital interest in an entity which is a partnership.

(c) Qualified community development entity

For purposes of this section—

(1) In general

The term "qualified community development entity" means any domestic corporation or partnership if—

(A) the primary mission of the entity is serving, or providing investment capital for, low-income communities or low-income persons,

(B) the entity maintains accountability to residents of low-income communities through their representation on any governing board of the entity or on any advisory board to the entity, and

(C) the entity is certified by the Secretary for purposes of this section as being a qualified community development entity.

(2) Special rules for certain organizations

The requirements of paragraph (1) shall be treated as met by—

(A) any specialized small business investment company (as defined in section 1044(c)(3)),[1] and

(B) any community development financial institution (as defined in section 103 of the Community Development Banking and Financial Institutions Act of 1994 (12 U.S.C. 4702)).

(d) Qualified low-income community investments

For purposes of this section—

(1) In general

The term "qualified low-income community investment" means—

(A) any capital or equity investment in, or loan to, any qualified active low-income community business,

(B) the purchase from another qualified community development entity of any loan made by such entity which is a qualified low-income community investment,

(C) financial counseling and other services specified in regulations prescribed by the Secretary to businesses located in, and residents of, low-income communities, and

(D) any equity investment in, or loan to, any qualified community development entity.

(2) Qualified active low-income community business

(A) In general

For purposes of paragraph (1), the term "qualified active low-income community business" means, with respect to any taxable year, any corporation (including a nonprofit corporation) or partnership if for such year—

(i) at least 50 percent of the total gross income of such entity is derived from the active conduct of a qualified business within any low-income community,

(ii) a substantial portion of the use of the tangible property of such entity (whether owned or leased) is within any low-income community,

(iii) a substantial portion of the services performed for such entity by its employees are performed in any low-income community,

(iv) less than 5 percent of the average of the aggregate unadjusted bases of the property of such entity is attributable to collectibles (as defined in section 408(m)(2)) other than collectibles that are held primarily for sale to customers in the ordinary course of such business, and

(v) less than 5 percent of the average of the aggregate unadjusted bases of the property of such entity is attributable to nonqualified financial property (as defined in section 1397C(e)).

(B) Proprietorship

Such term shall include any business carried on by an individual as a proprietor if such business would meet the requirements of subparagraph (A) were it incorporated.

(C) Portions of business may be qualified active low-income community business

The term "qualified active low-income community business" includes any trades or businesses which would qualify as a qualified active low-income community business if such trades or businesses were separately incorporated.

(3) Qualified business

For purposes of this subsection, the term "qualified business" has the meaning given to such term by section 1397C(d); except that—

(A) in lieu of applying paragraph (2)(B) thereof, the rental to others of real property located in any low-income community shall be treated as a qualified business if there are substantial improvements located on such property, and

(B) paragraph (3) thereof shall not apply.

(e) Low-income community

For purposes of this section—

(1) In general

The term "low-income community" means any population census tract if—

(A) the poverty rate for such tract is at least 20 percent, or

(B)(i) in the case of a tract not located within a metropolitan area, the median family income for such tract does not exceed 80 percent of statewide median family income, or

(ii) in the case of a tract located within a metropolitan area, the median family income for such tract does not exceed 80 percent of the greater of statewide median family income or the metropolitan area median family income.

Subparagraph (B) shall be applied using possessionwide median family income in the case of census tracts located within a possession of the United States.

(2) Targeted populations

The Secretary shall prescribe regulations under which 1 or more targeted populations (within the meaning of section 103(20) of the Riegle Community Development and Regulatory Improvement Act of 1994 (12 U.S.C. 4702(20))) may be treated as low-income communities. Such regulations shall include procedures for determining which entities are qualified active low-income community businesses with respect to such populations.

(3) Areas not within census tracts

In the case of an area which is not tracted for population census tracts, the equivalent county divisions (as defined by the Bureau of the Census for purposes of defining poverty areas) shall be used for purposes of determining poverty rates and median family income.

(4) Tracts with low population

A population census tract with a population of less than 2,000 shall be treated as a low-income community for purposes of this section if such tract—

(A) is within an empowerment zone the designation of which is in effect under section 1391, and

(B) is contiguous to 1 or more low-income communities (determined without regard to this paragraph).

(5) Modification of income requirement for census tracts within high migration rural counties

(A) In general

In the case of a population census tract located within a high migration rural county, paragraph (1)(B)(i) shall be applied by substituting "85 percent" for "80 percent".

(B) High migration rural county

For purposes of this paragraph, the term "high migration rural county" means any county which, during the 20-year period ending with the year in which the most recent census was conducted, has a net out-migration of inhabitants from the county of at least 10 percent of the population of the county at the beginning of such period.

(f) National limitation on amount of investments designated

(1) In general

There is a new markets tax credit limitation for each calendar year. Such limitation is—

(A) $1,000,000,000 for 2001,

(B) $1,500,000,000 for 2002 and 2003,

(C) $2,000,000,000 for 2004 and 2005,

(D) $3,500,000,000 for 2006 and 2007,

(E) $5,000,000,000 for 2008,

(F) $5,000,000,000 for 2009,

(G) $3,500,000,000 for each of calendar years 2010 through 2019, and

(H) $5,000,000,000 for for [2] each of calendar years 2020 through 2025.

(2) Allocation of limitation

The limitation under paragraph (1) shall be allocated by the Secretary among qualified community development entities selected by the Secretary. In making allocations under the preceding sentence, the Secretary shall give priority to any entity—

(A) with a record of having successfully provided capital or technical assistance to disadvantaged businesses or communities, or

(B) which intends to satisfy the requirement under subsection (b)(1)(B) by making qualified low-income community investments in 1 or more businesses in which persons unrelated to such entity (within the meaning of section 267(b) or 707(b)(1)) hold the majority equity interest.

(3) Carryover of unused limitation

If the new markets tax credit limitation for any calendar year exceeds the aggregate amount allocated under paragraph (2) for such year, such limitation for the succeeding calendar year shall be increased by the amount of such excess. No amount may be carried under the preceding sentence to any calendar year after 2030.

(g) Recapture of credit in certain cases

(1) In general

If, at any time during the 7-year period beginning on the date of the original issue of a qualified equity investment in a qualified community development entity, there is a recapture event with respect to such investment, then the tax imposed by this chapter for the taxable year in which such event occurs shall be increased by the credit recapture amount.

(2) Credit recapture amount

For purposes of paragraph (1), the credit recapture amount is an amount equal to the sum of—

(A) the aggregate decrease in the credits allowed to the taxpayer under section 38 for all prior taxable years which would have resulted if no credit had been determined under this section with respect to such investment, plus

(B) interest at the underpayment rate established under section 6621 on the amount determined under subparagraph (A) for each prior taxable year for the period beginning on the due date for filing the return for the prior taxable year involved.

No deduction shall be allowed under this chapter for interest described in subparagraph (B).

(3) Recapture event

For purposes of paragraph (1), there is a recapture event with respect to an equity investment in a qualified community development entity if—

(A) such entity ceases to be a qualified community development entity,

(B) the proceeds of the investment cease to be used as required of subsection (b)(1)(B), or

(C) such investment is redeemed by such entity.

(4) Special rules

(A) Tax benefit rule

The tax for the taxable year shall be increased under paragraph (1) only with respect to credits allowed by reason of this section which were used to reduce tax liability. In the case of credits not so used to reduce tax liability, the carryforwards and carrybacks under section 39 shall be appropriately adjusted.

(B) No credits against tax

Any increase in tax under this subsection shall not be treated as a tax imposed by this chapter for purposes of determining the amount of any credit under this chapter or for purposes of section 55.

(h) Basis reduction

The basis of any qualified equity investment shall be reduced by the amount of any credit determined under this section with respect to such investment. This subsection shall not apply for purposes of section 1202.

(i) Regulations

The Secretary shall prescribe such regulations as may be appropriate to carry out this section, including regulations—

(1) which limit the credit for investments which are directly or indirectly subsidized by other Federal tax benefits (including the credit under section 42 and the exclusion from gross income under section 103),

(2) which prevent the abuse of the purposes of this section,

(3) which provide rules for determining whether the requirement of subsection (b)(1)(B) is treated as met,

(4) which impose appropriate reporting requirements,

(5) which apply the provisions of this section to newly formed entities, and

(6) which ensure that non-metropolitan counties receive a proportional allocation of qualified equity investments.

(Added Pub. L. 106–554, §1(a)(7) [title I, §121(a)], Dec. 21, 2000, 114 Stat. 2763, 2763A-605; amended Pub. L. 108–357, title II, §§221(a), (b), 223(a), Oct. 22, 2004, 118 Stat. 1431, 1432; Pub. L. 109–432, div. A, title I, §102(a), (b), Dec. 20, 2006, 120 Stat. 2934; Pub. L. 110–343, div. C, title III, §302, Oct. 3, 2008, 122 Stat. 3866; Pub. L. 111–5, div. B, title I, §1403(a), Feb. 17, 2009, 123 Stat. 352; Pub. L. 111–312, title VII, §733(a), (b), Dec. 17, 2010, 124 Stat. 3317, 3318; Pub. L. 112–240, title III, §305(a), (b), Jan. 2, 2013, 126 Stat. 2329; Pub. L. 113–295, div. A, title I, §115(a), (b), Dec. 19, 2014, 128 Stat. 4014; Pub. L. 114–113, div. Q, title I, §141(a), (b), Dec. 18, 2015, 129 Stat. 3056; Pub. L. 115–141, div. U, title IV, §401(a)(18), (d)(4)(B)(iii), Mar. 23, 2018, 132 Stat. 1185, 1209; Pub. L. 116–94, div. Q, title I, §141(a), (b), Dec. 20, 2019, 133 Stat. 3234; Pub. L. 116–260, div. EE, title I, §112(a), (b), Dec. 27, 2020, 134 Stat. 3050.)

EDITORIAL NOTES
REFERENCES IN TEXT

Section 1044, referred to in subsec. (c)(2)(A), was repealed by Pub. L. 115–97, title I, §13313(a), Dec. 22, 2017, 131 Stat. 2133.

AMENDMENTS

2020—Subsec. (f)(1)(H). Pub. L. 116–260, §112(a), substituted "for each of calendar years 2020 through 2025" for "2020".

Subsec. (f)(3). Pub. L. 116–260, §112(b), substituted "2030" for "2025".

2019—Subsec. (f)(1)(H). Pub. L. 116–94, §141(a), added subpar. (H).

Subsec. (f)(3). Pub. L. 116–94, §141(b), substituted "2025" for "2024".

2018—Subsec. (f)(1)(F). Pub. L. 115–141, §401(a)(18), inserted ", and" at end.

Subsec. (h). Pub. L. 115–141, §401(d)(4)(B)(iii), substituted "section 1202" for "sections 1202, 1400B, and 1400F".

2015—Subsec. (f)(1)(G). Pub. L. 114–113, §141(a), substituted "for each of calendar years 2010 through 2019" for "for 2010, 2011, 2012, 2013, and 2014".

Subsec. (f)(3). Pub. L. 114–113, §141(b), substituted "2024" for "2019".

2014—Subsec. (f)(1)(G). Pub. L. 113–295, §115(a), substituted "2013, and 2014" for "and 2013".

Subsec. (f)(3). Pub. L. 113–295, §115(b), substituted "2019" for "2018".

2013—Subsec. (f)(1)(G). Pub. L. 112–240, §305(a), substituted "2010, 2011, 2012, and 2013" for "2010 and 2011".

Subsec. (f)(3). Pub. L. 112–240, §305(b), substituted "2018" for "2016".

2010—Subsec. (f)(1)(G). Pub. L. 111–312, §733(a), added subpar. (G).

Subsec. (f)(3). Pub. L. 111–312, §733(b), substituted "2016" for "2014".

2009—Subsec. (f)(1)(D). Pub. L. 111–5, §1403(a)(2), substituted "and 2007," for ", 2007, 2008, and 2009."

Subsec. (f)(1)(E), (F). Pub. L. 111–5, §1403(a)(1), (3), added subpars. (E) and (F).

2008—Subsec. (f)(1)(D). Pub. L. 110–343 substituted "2008, and 2009" for "and 2008".

2006—Subsec. (f)(1)(D). Pub. L. 109–432, §102(a), substituted ", 2007, and 2008" for "and 2007".

Subsec. (i)(6). Pub. L. 109–432, §102(b), added par. (6).

2004—Subsec. (e)(2). Pub. L. 108–357, §221(a), amended heading and text of par. (2) generally, substituting provisions relating to regulations under which 1 or more targeted populations could be treated as low-income communities for provisions authorizing Secretary to designate any area within any census tract as a low-income community if certain conditions were met.

Subsec. (e)(4). Pub. L. 108–357, §221(b), added par. (4).

Subsec. (e)(5). Pub. L. 108–357, §223(a), added par. (5).

STATUTORY NOTES AND RELATED SUBSIDIARIES

EFFECTIVE DATE OF 2020 AMENDMENT

Pub. L. 116–260, div. EE, title I, §112(c), Dec. 27, 2020, 134 Stat. 3050, provided that: "The amendments made by this section [amending this section] shall apply to calendar years beginning after December 31, 2020."

EFFECTIVE DATE OF 2019 AMENDMENT

Pub. L. 116–94, div. Q, title I, §141(c), Dec. 20, 2019, 133 Stat. 3234, provided that: "The amendments made by this section [amending this section] shall apply to calendar years beginning after December 31, 2019."

EFFECTIVE DATE OF 2015 AMENDMENT

Pub. L. 114–113, div. Q, title I, §141(c), Dec. 18, 2015, 129 Stat. 3056, provided that: "The amendments made by this section [amending this section] shall apply to calendar years beginning after December 31, 2014."

EFFECTIVE DATE OF 2014 AMENDMENT

Pub. L. 113–295, div. A, title I, §115(c), Dec. 19, 2014, 128 Stat. 4014, provided that: "The amendments made by this section [amending this section] shall apply to calendar years beginning after December 31, 2013."

EFFECTIVE DATE OF 2013 AMENDMENT

Pub. L. 112–240, title III, §305(c), Jan. 2, 2013, 126 Stat. 2329, provided that: "The amendments made by this section [amending this section] shall apply to calendar years beginning after December 31, 2011."

EFFECTIVE DATE OF 2010 AMENDMENT

Pub. L. 111–312, title VII, §733(c), Dec. 17, 2010, 124 Stat. 3318, provided that: "The amendments made by this section [amending this section] shall apply to calendar years beginning after 2009."

EFFECTIVE DATE OF 2006 AMENDMENT

Pub. L. 109–432, div. A, title I, §102(c), Dec. 20, 2006, 120 Stat. 2934, provided that: "The amendments made by this section [amending this section] shall take effect on the date of the enactment of this Act [Dec. 20, 2006]."

EFFECTIVE DATE OF 2004 AMENDMENT

Pub. L. 108–357, title II, §221(c), Oct. 22, 2004, 118 Stat. 1431, provided that:

"(1) Targeted areas.—The amendment made by subsection (a) [amending this section] shall apply to designations made by the Secretary of the Treasury after the date of the enactment of this Act [Oct. 22, 2004].

"(2) Tracts with low population.—The amendment made by subsection (b) [amending this section] shall apply to investments made after the date of the enactment of this Act [Oct. 22, 2004]."

Pub. L. 108–357, title II, §223(b), Oct. 22, 2004, 118 Stat. 1432, provided that: "The amendment made by this section [amending this section] shall take effect as if included in the amendment made by section 121(a) of the Community Renewal Tax Relief Act of 2000 [Pub. L. 106–554, §1(a)(7) [title I, §121(a)], enacting this section]."

EFFECTIVE DATE

Section applicable to investments made after Dec. 31, 2000, see §1(a)(7) [title I, §121(e)] of Pub. L. 106–554, set out as a Effective Date of 2000 Amendment note under section 38 of this title.

SAVINGS PROVISION

Amendment by section 401(d)(4)(B)(iii) of Pub. L. 115–141 not applicable to certain obligations issued, DC Zone assets acquired, or principal residences acquired before Jan. 1, 2012, see section 401(d)(4)(C) of Pub. L. 115–141, set out as a note under former section 1400 of this title.

For provisions that nothing in amendment by section 401(d)(4)(B)(iii) of Pub. L. 115–141 be construed to affect treatment of certain transactions occurring, property acquired, or items of income, loss, deduction, or credit taken into account prior to Mar. 23, 2018, for purposes of determining liability for tax for periods ending after Mar. 23, 2018, see section 401(e) of Pub. L. 115–141, set out as a note under section 23 of this title.

SPECIAL RULE FOR ALLOCATION OF INCREASED 2008 LIMITATION

Pub. L. 111–5, div. B, title I, §1403(b), Feb. 17, 2009, 123 Stat. 352, provided that: "The amount of the increase in the new markets tax credit limitation for calendar year 2008 by reason of the amendments made by subsection (a) [amending this section] shall be allocated in accordance with section 45D(f)(2) of the Internal Revenue Code of 1986 to qualified community development entities (as defined in section 45D(c) of such Code) which—

"(1) submitted an allocation application with respect to calendar year 2008, and

"(2)(A) did not receive an allocation for such calendar year, or

"(B) received an allocation for such calendar year in an amount less than the amount requested in the allocation application."

GUIDANCE ON ALLOCATION OF NATIONAL LIMITATION

Pub. L. 106–554, §1(a)(7) [title I, §121(f)], Dec. 21, 2000, 114 Stat. 2763, 2763A-610, provided that: "Not later than 120 days after the date of the enactment of this Act [Dec. 21, 2000], the Secretary of the Treasury or the Secretary's delegate shall issue guidance which specifies—

"(1) how entities shall apply for an allocation under section 45D(f)(2) of the Internal Revenue Code of 1986, as added by this section;

"(2) the competitive procedure through which such allocations are made; and

"(3) the actions that such Secretary or delegate shall take to ensure that such allocations are properly made to appropriate entities."

AUDIT AND REPORT

Pub. L. 106–554, §1(a)(7) [title I, §121(g)], Dec. 21, 2000, 114 Stat. 2763, 2763A–610, provided that: "Not later than January 31 of 2004, 2007, and 2010, the Comptroller General of the United States shall, pursuant to an audit of the new markets tax credit program established under section 45D of the Internal Revenue Code of 1986 (as added by subsection (a)), report to Congress on such program, including all qualified community development entities that receive an allocation under the new markets credit under such section."

¹ See References in Text note below.

² So in original.

§45E. Small employer pension plan startup costs

(a) General rule

For purposes of section 38, in the case of an eligible employer, the small employer pension plan startup cost credit determined under this section for any taxable year is an amount equal to 50 percent of the qualified startup costs paid or incurred by the taxpayer during the taxable year.

(b) Dollar limitation

The amount of the credit determined under this section for any taxable year shall not exceed—

(1) for the first credit year and each of the 2 taxable years immediately following the first credit year, the greater of—

(A) $500, or

(B) the lesser of—

(i) $250 for each employee of the eligible employer who is not a highly compensated employee (as defined in section 414(q)) and who is eligible to participate in the eligible employer plan maintained by the eligible employer, or

(ii) $5,000, and

(2) zero for any other taxable year.

(c) Eligible employer

For purposes of this section—

(1) In general

The term "eligible employer" has the meaning given such term by section 408(p)(2)(C)(i).

(2) Requirement for new qualified employer plans

Such term shall not include an employer if, during the 3-taxable year period immediately preceding the 1st taxable year for which the credit under this section is otherwise allowable for a qualified employer plan of the employer, the employer or any member of any controlled group including the employer (or any predecessor of either) established or maintained a qualified employer plan with respect to which contributions were made, or benefits were accrued, for substantially the same employees as are in the qualified employer plan.

(d) Other definitions

For purposes of this section—

(1) Qualified startup costs

(A) In general

The term "qualified startup costs" means any ordinary and necessary expenses of an eligible employer which are paid or incurred in connection with—

(i) the establishment or administration of an eligible employer plan, or

(ii) the retirement-related education of employees with respect to such plan.

(B) Plan must have at least 1 participant

Such term shall not include any expense in connection with a plan that does not have at least 1 employee eligible to participate who is not a highly compensated employee.

(2) Eligible employer plan

The term "eligible employer plan" means a qualified employer plan within the meaning of section 4972(d).

(3) First credit year

The term "first credit year" means—

(A) the taxable year which includes the date that the eligible employer plan to which such costs relate becomes effective, or

(B) at the election of the eligible employer, the taxable year preceding the taxable year referred to in subparagraph (A).

(e) Special rules

For purposes of this section—

(1) Aggregation rules

All persons treated as a single employer under subsection (a) or (b) of section 52, or subsection (m) or (o) of section 414, shall be treated as one person. All eligible employer plans shall be treated as 1 eligible employer plan.

(2) Disallowance of deduction

No deduction shall be allowed for that portion of the qualified startup costs paid or incurred for the taxable year which is equal to the credit determined under subsection (a).

(3) Election not to claim credit

This section shall not apply to a taxpayer for any taxable year if such taxpayer elects to have this section not apply for such taxable year.

(Added Pub. L. 107–16, title VI, §619(a), June 7, 2001, 115 Stat. 108; amended Pub. L. 107–147, title IV, §411(n)(1), Mar. 9, 2002, 116 Stat. 48; Pub. L. 116–94, div. O, title I, §104(a), Dec. 20, 2019, 133 Stat. 3147.)

EDITORIAL NOTES

AMENDMENTS

2019—Subsec. (b)(1). Pub. L. 116–94 amended par. (1) generally. Prior to amendment, par. (1) read as follows: "$500 for the first credit year and each of the 2 taxable years immediately following the first credit year, and".

2002—Subsec. (e)(1). Pub. L. 107–147 substituted "subsection (m)" for "subsection (n)".

STATUTORY NOTES AND RELATED SUBSIDIARIES

EFFECTIVE DATE OF 2019 AMENDMENT

Pub. L. 116–94, div. O, title I, §104(b), Dec. 20, 2019, 133 Stat. 3147, provided that: "The amendment made by this section [amending this section] shall apply to taxable years beginning after December 31, 2019."

EFFECTIVE DATE OF 2002 AMENDMENT

Amendment by Pub. L. 107–147 effective as if included in the provisions of the Economic Growth and Tax Relief Reconciliation Act of 2001, Pub. L. 107–16, to which such amendment relates, see section 411(x) of Pub. L. 107–147, set out as a note under section 25B of this title.

EFFECTIVE DATE

Section applicable to costs paid or incurred in taxable years beginning after Dec. 31, 2001, with respect to qualified employer plans first effective after such date, see section 619(d) of Pub. L. 107–16, as amended, set out as an Effective Date of 2001 Amendment note under section 38 of this title.

§45F. Employer-provided child care credit

(a) In general

For purposes of section 38, the employer-provided child care credit determined under this section for the taxable year is an amount equal to the sum of—

(1) 25 percent of the qualified child care expenditures, and

(2) 10 percent of the qualified child care resource and referral expenditures,

of the taxpayer for such taxable year.

(b) Dollar limitation

The credit allowable under subsection (a) for any taxable year shall not exceed $150,000.

(c) Definitions

For purposes of this section—

(1) Qualified child care expenditure

(A) In general

The term "qualified child care expenditure" means any amount paid or incurred—

(i) to acquire, construct, rehabilitate, or expand property—

(I) which is to be used as part of a qualified child care facility of the taxpayer,

(II) with respect to which a deduction for depreciation (or amortization in lieu of depreciation) is allowable, and

(III) which does not constitute part of the principal residence (within the meaning of section 121) of the taxpayer or any employee of the taxpayer,

(ii) for the operating costs of a qualified child care facility of the taxpayer, including costs related to the training of employees, to scholarship programs, and to the providing of increased compensation to employees with higher levels of child care training, or

(iii) under a contract with a qualified child care facility to provide child care services to employees of the taxpayer.

(B) Fair market value

The term "qualified child care expenditures" shall not include expenses in excess of the fair market value of such care.

(2) Qualified child care facility

(A) In general

The term "qualified child care facility" means a facility—

(i) the principal use of which is to provide child care assistance, and

(ii) which meets the requirements of all applicable laws and regulations of the State or local government in which it is located, including the licensing of the facility as a child care facility.

Clause (i) shall not apply to a facility which is the principal residence (within the meaning of section 121) of the operator of the facility.

(B) Special rules with respect to a taxpayer

A facility shall not be treated as a qualified child care facility with respect to a taxpayer unless—

(i) enrollment in the facility is open to employees of the taxpayer during the taxable year,

(ii) if the facility is the principal trade or business of the taxpayer, at least 30 percent of the enrollees of such facility are dependents of employees of the taxpayer, and

(iii) the use of such facility (or the eligibility to use such facility) does not discriminate in favor of employees of the taxpayer who are highly compensated employees (within the meaning of section 414(q)).

(3) Qualified child care resource and referral expenditure

(A) In general

The term "qualified child care resource and referral expenditure" means any amount paid or incurred under a contract to provide child care resource and referral services to an employee of the taxpayer.

(B) Nondiscrimination

The services shall not be treated as qualified unless the provision of such services (or the eligibility to use such services) does not discriminate in favor of employees of the taxpayer who are highly compensated employees (within the meaning of section 414(q)).

(d) Recapture of acquisition and construction credit

(1) In general

If, as of the close of any taxable year, there is a recapture event with respect to any qualified child care facility of the taxpayer, then the tax of the taxpayer under this chapter for such taxable year shall be increased by an amount equal to the product of—

(A) the applicable recapture percentage, and

(B) the aggregate decrease in the credits allowed under section 38 for all prior taxable years which would have resulted if the qualified child care expenditures of the taxpayer described in subsection (c)(1)(A) with respect to such facility had been zero.

(2) Applicable recapture percentage

(A) In general

For purposes of this subsection, the applicable recapture percentage shall be determined from the following table:

If the recapture event occurs in:	The applicable recapture percentage is:
Years 1—3	100
Year 4	85
Year 5	70
Year 6	55
Year 7	40
Year 8	25
Years 9 and 10	10
Years 11 and thereafter	0.

(B) Years

For purposes of subparagraph (A), year 1 shall begin on the first day of the taxable year in which the qualified child care facility is placed in service by the taxpayer.

(3) Recapture event defined

For purposes of this subsection, the term "recapture event" means—

(A) Cessation of operation

The cessation of the operation of the facility as a qualified child care facility.

(B) Change in ownership

(i) In general

Except as provided in clause (ii), the disposition of a taxpayer's interest in a qualified child care facility with respect to which the credit described in subsection (a) was allowable.

(ii) Agreement to assume recapture liability

Clause (i) shall not apply if the person acquiring such interest in the facility agrees in writing to assume the recapture liability of the person disposing of such interest in effect immediately before such disposition. In the event of such an assumption, the person acquiring the interest in the facility shall be treated as the taxpayer for purposes of assessing any recapture liability (computed as if there had been no change in ownership).

(4) Special rules

(A) Tax benefit rule

The tax for the taxable year shall be increased under paragraph (1) only with respect to credits allowed by reason of this section which were used to reduce tax liability. In the case of credits not so used to reduce tax liability, the carryforwards and carrybacks under section 39 shall be appropriately adjusted.

(B) No credits against tax

Any increase in tax under this subsection shall not be treated as a tax imposed by this chapter for purposes of determining the amount of any credit under this chapter or for purposes of section 55.

(C) No recapture by reason of casualty loss

The increase in tax under this subsection shall not apply to a cessation of operation of the facility as a qualified child care facility by reason of a casualty loss to the extent such loss is restored by reconstruction or replacement within a reasonable period established by the Secretary.

(e) Special rules

For purposes of this section—

(1) Aggregation rules

All persons which are treated as a single employer under subsections (a) and (b) of section 52 shall be treated as a single taxpayer.

(2) Pass-thru in the case of estates and trusts

Under regulations prescribed by the Secretary, rules similar to the rules of subsection (d) of section 52 shall apply.

(3) Allocation in the case of partnerships

In the case of partnerships, the credit shall be allocated among partners under regulations prescribed by the Secretary.

(f) No double benefit

(1) Reduction in basis

For purposes of this subtitle—

(A) In general

If a credit is determined under this section with respect to any property by reason of expenditures described in subsection (c)(1)(A), the basis of such property shall be reduced by the amount of the credit so determined.

(B) Certain dispositions

If, during any taxable year, there is a recapture amount determined with respect to any property the basis of which was reduced under subparagraph (A), the basis of such property (immediately before the event resulting in such recapture) shall be increased by an amount equal to such recapture amount. For purposes of the preceding sentence, the term "recapture amount" means any increase in tax (or adjustment in carrybacks or carryovers) determined under subsection (d).

(2) Other deductions and credits

No deduction or credit shall be allowed under any other provision of this chapter with respect to the amount of the credit determined under this section.

(Added Pub. L. 107–16, title II, §205(a), June 7, 2001, 115 Stat. 50; amended Pub. L. 107–147, title IV, §411(d)(1), Mar. 9, 2002, 116 Stat. 46.)

EDITORIAL NOTES
AMENDMENTS

2002—Subsec. (d)(4)(B). Pub. L. 107–147 substituted "this chapter or for purposes of section 55" for "subpart A, B, or D of this part".

STATUTORY NOTES AND RELATED SUBSIDIARIES
EFFECTIVE DATE OF 2002 AMENDMENT

Amendment by Pub. L. 107–147 effective as if included in the provisions of the Economic Growth and Tax Relief Reconciliation Act of 2001, Pub. L. 107–16, to which such amendment relates, see section 411(x) of Pub. L. 107–147, set out as a note under section 25B of this title.

Section applicable to taxable years beginning after Dec. 31, 2001, see section 205(c) of Pub. L. 107–16, set out as an Effective Date of 2001 Amendment note under section 38 of this title.

§45G. Railroad track maintenance credit

(a) General rule

For purposes of section 38, the railroad track maintenance credit determined under this section for the taxable year is an amount equal to 40 percent (50 percent in the case of any taxable year beginning before January 1, 2023) of the qualified railroad track maintenance expenditures paid or incurred by an eligible taxpayer during the taxable year.

(b) Limitation

(1) In general

The credit allowed under subsection (a) for any taxable year shall not exceed the product of—

(A) $3,500, multiplied by

(B) the sum of—

(i) the number of miles of railroad track owned or leased by the eligible taxpayer as of the close of the taxable year, and

(ii) the number of miles of railroad track assigned for purposes of this subsection to the eligible taxpayer by a Class II or Class III railroad which owns or leases such railroad track as of the close of the taxable year.

(2) Assignments

With respect to any assignment of a mile of railroad track under paragraph (1)(B)(ii)—

(A) such assignment may be made only once per taxable year of the Class II or Class III railroad and shall be treated as made as of the close of such taxable year,

(B) such mile may not be taken into account under this section by such railroad for such taxable year, and

(C) such assignment shall be taken into account for the taxable year of the assignee which includes the date that such assignment is treated as effective.

(c) Eligible taxpayer

For purposes of this section, the term "eligible taxpayer" means—

(1) any Class II or Class III railroad, and

(2) any person who transports property using the rail facilities of a Class II or Class III railroad or who furnishes railroad-related property or services to a Class II or Class III railroad, but only with respect to miles of railroad track assigned to such person by such Class II or Class III railroad for purposes of subsection (b).

(d) Qualified railroad track maintenance expenditures

For purposes of this section, the term "qualified railroad track maintenance expenditures" means gross expenditures (whether or not otherwise chargeable to capital account) for maintaining railroad track (including roadbed, bridges, and related track structures) owned or leased as of January 1, 2015, by a Class II or Class III railroad (determined without regard to any consideration for such expenditures given by the Class II or Class III railroad which made the assignment of such track).

(e) Other definitions and special rules

(1) Class II or Class III railroad

For purposes of this section, the terms "Class II railroad" and "Class III railroad" have the respective meanings given such terms by the Surface Transportation Board.

(2) Controlled groups

Rules similar to the rules of paragraph (1) of section 41(f) shall apply for purposes of this section.

(3) Basis adjustment

For purposes of this subtitle, if a credit is allowed under this section with respect to any railroad track, the basis of such track shall be reduced by the amount of the credit so allowed.

(Added Pub. L. 108–357, title II, §245(a), Oct. 22, 2004, 118 Stat. 1447; amended Pub. L. 109–135, title IV, §403(f), Dec. 21, 2005, 119 Stat. 2623; Pub. L. 109–432, div. A, title IV, §423(a), Dec. 20, 2006, 120 Stat. 2973; Pub. L. 110–343, div. C, title III, §316(a), Oct. 3, 2008, 122 Stat. 3872; Pub. L. 111–312, title VII, §734(a), Dec. 17, 2010, 124 Stat. 3318; Pub. L. 112–240, title III, §306(a), Jan. 2, 2013, 126 Stat. 2329; Pub. L. 113–295, div. A, title I, §116(a), Dec. 19, 2014, 128 Stat. 4014; Pub. L. 114–113, div. Q, title I, §162(a), (b), Dec. 18, 2015, 129 Stat. 3066; Pub. L. 115–123, div. D, title I, §40302(a), Feb. 9, 2018, 132 Stat. 145; Pub. L. 116–94, div. Q, title I, §112(a), Dec. 20, 2019, 133 Stat. 3228; Pub. L. 116–260, div. EE, title I, §105(a), (b), Dec. 27, 2020, 134 Stat. 3041.)

EDITORIAL NOTES

AMENDMENTS

2020—Subsec. (a). Pub. L. 116–260, §105(b), substituted "40 percent (50 percent in the case of any taxable year beginning before January 1, 2023)" for "50 percent".

Subsec. (f). Pub. L. 116–260, §105(a), struck out subsec. (f). Text read as follows: "This section shall apply to qualified railroad track maintenance expenditures paid or incurred during taxable years beginning after December 31, 2004, and before January 1, 2023."

2019—Subsec. (f). Pub. L. 116–94 substituted "January 1, 2023" for "January 1, 2018".

2018—Subsec. (f). Pub. L. 115–123 substituted "January 1, 2018" for "January 1, 2017".

2015—Subsec. (d). Pub. L. 114–113, §162(b), substituted "January 1, 2015" for "January 1, 2005".

Subsec. (f). Pub. L. 114–113, §162(a), substituted "January 1, 2017" for "January 1, 2015".

2014—Subsec. (f). Pub. L. 113–295 substituted "January 1, 2015" for "January 1, 2014".

2013—Subsec. (f). Pub. L. 112–240 substituted "January 1, 2014" for "January 1, 2012".

2010—Subsec. (f). Pub. L. 111–312 substituted "January 1, 2012" for "January 1, 2010".

2008—Subsec. (f). Pub. L. 110–343 substituted "January 1, 2010" for "January 1, 2008".

2006—Subsec. (d). Pub. L. 109–432 inserted "gross" after "means" and "(determined without regard to any consideration for such expenditures given by the Class II or Class III railroad which made the assignment of such track)" before period at end.

2005—Subsec. (b). Pub. L. 109–135, §403(f)(1), reenacted heading without change and amended text generally. Prior to amendment, text read as follows: "The credit allowed under subsection (a) for any taxable year shall not exceed the product of—

"(1) $3,500, and

"(2) the number of miles of railroad track owned or leased by the eligible taxpayer as of the close of the taxable year.

A mile of railroad track may be taken into account by a person other than the owner only if such mile is assigned to such person by the owner for purposes of this subsection. Any mile which is so assigned may not be taken into account by the owner for purposes of this subsection."

Subsec. (c)(2). Pub. L. 109–135, §403(f)(2), amended par. (2) generally. Prior to amendment, par. (2) read as follows: "any person who transports property using the rail facilities of a person described in paragraph (1) or who furnishes railroad-related property or services to such a person."

EFFECTIVE DATE OF 2020 AMENDMENT

Pub. L. 116–260, div. EE, title I, §105(c), Dec. 27, 2020, 134 Stat. 3041, provided that: "The amendments made by this section [amending this section] shall apply to taxable years ending after the date of the enactment of this Act [Dec. 27, 2020]."

EFFECTIVE DATE OF 2019 AMENDMENT

Pub. L. 116–94, div. Q, title I, §112(c), Dec. 20, 2019, 133 Stat. 3229, provided that: "The amendment made by this section [amending this section] shall apply to expenditures paid or incurred during taxable years beginning after December 31, 2017."

EFFECTIVE DATE OF 2018 AMENDMENT

Pub. L. 115–123, div. D, title I, §40302(b), Feb. 9, 2018, 132 Stat. 145, provided that:

"(1) In general.—The amendment made by this section [amending this section] shall apply to expenditures paid or incurred in taxable years beginning after December 31, 2016.

"(2) Safe harbor assignments.—Assignments, including related expenditures paid or incurred, under paragraph (2) of section 45G(b) of the Internal Revenue Code of 1986 for taxable years ending after January 1, 2017, and before January 1, 2018, shall be treated as effective as of the close of such taxable year if made pursuant to a written agreement entered into no later than 90 days following the date of the enactment of this Act [Feb. 9, 2018]."

EFFECTIVE DATE OF 2015 AMENDMENT

Pub. L. 114–113, div. Q, title I, §162(c), Dec. 18, 2015, 129 Stat. 3066, provided that:

"(1) Extension.—The amendment made by subsection (a) [amending this section] shall apply to expenditures paid or incurred in taxable years beginning after December 31, 2014.

"(2) Modification.—The amendment made by subsection (b) [amending this section] shall apply to expenditures paid or incurred in taxable years beginning after December 31, 2015."

EFFECTIVE DATE OF 2014 AMENDMENT

Pub. L. 113–295, div. A, title I, §116(b), Dec. 19, 2014, 128 Stat. 4014, provided that: "The amendment made by this section [amending this section] shall apply to expenditures paid or incurred in taxable years beginning after December 31, 2013."

EFFECTIVE DATE OF 2013 AMENDMENT

Pub. L. 112–240, title III, §306(b), Jan. 2, 2013, 126 Stat. 2329, provided that: "The amendment made by this section [amending this section] shall apply to expenditures paid or incurred in taxable years beginning after December 31, 2011."

EFFECTIVE DATE OF 2010 AMENDMENT

Pub. L. 111–312, title VII, §734(b), Dec. 17, 2010, 124 Stat. 3318, provided that: "The amendment made by this section [amending this section] shall apply to expenditures paid or incurred in taxable years beginning after December 31, 2009."

EFFECTIVE DATE OF 2008 AMENDMENT

Pub. L. 110–343, div. C, title III, §316(c)(1), Oct. 3, 2008, 122 Stat. 3872, provided that: "The amendment made by subsection (a) [amending this section] shall apply to expenditures paid or incurred during taxable years beginning after December 31, 2007."

EFFECTIVE DATE OF 2006 AMENDMENT

Pub. L. 109–432, div. A, title IV, §423(b), Dec. 20, 2006, 120 Stat. 2973, provided that: "The amendment made by this section [amending this section] shall take effect as if included in the amendment made by section 245(a) of the American Jobs Creation Act of 2004 [Pub. L. 108–357]."

EFFECTIVE DATE OF 2005 AMENDMENT

Amendment by Pub. L. 109–135 effective as if included in the provision of the American Jobs Creation Act of 2004, Pub. L. 108–357, to which such amendment relates, see section 403(nn) of Pub. L. 109–135, set out as a note under section 26 of this title.

EFFECTIVE DATE

Section applicable to taxable years beginning after Dec. 31, 2004, see section 245(e) of Pub. L. 108–357, set out as an Effective Date of 2004 Amendment note under section 38 of this title.

SAFE HARBOR ASSIGNMENTS

Pub. L. 116–94, div. Q, title I, §112(b), Dec. 20, 2019, 133 Stat. 3228, provided that: "Any assignment, including related expenditures paid or incurred, under section 45G(b)(2) of the Internal Revenue Code of 1986 for a taxable year beginning on or after January 1, 2018, and ending before January 1, 2020, shall be treated as effective as of the close of such taxable year if made pursuant to a written agreement entered into no later than 90 days following the date of the enactment of this Act [Dec. 20, 2019]."

§45H. Credit for production of low sulfur diesel fuel

(a) In general

For purposes of section 38, the amount of the low sulfur diesel fuel production credit determined under this section with respect to any facility of a small business refiner is an amount equal to 5 cents for each gallon of low sulfur diesel fuel produced during the taxable year by such small business refiner at such facility.

(b) Maximum credit

(1) In general

The aggregate credit determined under subsection (a) for any taxable year with respect to any facility shall not exceed—

(A) 25 percent of the qualified costs incurred by the small business refiner with respect to such facility, reduced by

(B) the aggregate credits determined under this section for all prior taxable years with respect to such facility.

(2) Reduced percentage

In the case of a small business refiner with average daily domestic refinery runs for the 1-year period ending on December 31, 2002, in excess of 155,000 barrels, the number of percentage points described in paragraph (1) shall be reduced (not below zero) by the product of such number (before the application of this paragraph) and the ratio of such excess to 50,000 barrels.

(c) Definitions and special rule

For purposes of this section—

(1) Small business refiner

The term "small business refiner" means, with respect to any taxable year, a refiner of crude oil—

(A) with respect to which not more than 1,500 individuals are engaged in the refinery operations of the business on any day during such taxable year, and

(B) the average daily domestic refinery run or average retained production of which for all facilities of the taxpayer for the 1-year period ending on December 31, 2002, did not exceed 205,000 barrels.

(2) Qualified costs

The term "qualified costs" means, with respect to any facility, those costs paid or incurred during the applicable period for compliance with the applicable EPA regulations with respect to such facility, including expenditures for the construction of new process operation units or the dismantling and reconstruction of existing process units to be used in the production of low sulfur diesel fuel, associated adjacent or offsite equipment (including tankage, catalyst, and power supply), engineering, construction period interest, and sitework.

(3) Applicable EPA regulations

The term "applicable EPA regulations" means the Highway Diesel Fuel Sulfur Control Requirements of the Environmental Protection Agency.

(4) Applicable period

The term "applicable period" means, with respect to any facility, the period beginning on January 1, 2003, and ending on the earlier of the date which is 1 year after the date on which the taxpayer must comply with the applicable EPA regulations with respect to such facility or December 31, 2009.

(5) Low sulfur diesel fuel

The term "low sulfur diesel fuel" means diesel fuel with a sulfur content of 15 parts per million or less.

(d) Special rule for determination of refinery runs

For purposes of this section and section 179B(b), in the calculation of average daily domestic refinery run or retained production, only refineries which on April 1, 2003, were refineries of the refiner or a related person (within the meaning of section 613A(d)(3)), shall be taken into account.

(e) Certification

(1) Required

No credit shall be allowed unless, not later than the date which is 30 months after the first day of the first taxable year in which the low sulfur diesel fuel production credit is determined with respect to a facility, the small business refiner obtains certification from the Secretary, after consultation with the Administrator of the Environmental Protection Agency, that the taxpayer's qualified costs with respect to such facility will result in compliance with the applicable EPA regulations.

(2) Contents of application

An application for certification shall include relevant information regarding unit capacities and operating characteristics sufficient for the Secretary, after consultation with the Administrator of the Environmental Protection Agency, to determine that such qualified costs are necessary for compliance with the applicable EPA regulations.

(3) Review period

Any application shall be reviewed and notice of certification, if applicable, shall be made within 60 days of receipt of such application. In the event the Secretary does not notify the taxpayer of the results of such certification within such period, the taxpayer may presume the certification to be issued until so notified.

(4) Statute of limitations

With respect to the credit allowed under this section—

(A) the statutory period for the assessment of any deficiency attributable to such credit shall not expire before the end of the 3-year period ending on the date that the review period described in paragraph (3) ends with respect to the taxpayer, and

(B) such deficiency may be assessed before the expiration of such 3-year period notwithstanding the provisions of any other law or rule of law which would otherwise prevent such assessment.

(f) Cooperative organizations

(1) Apportionment of credit

(A) In general

In the case of a cooperative organization described in section 1381(a), any portion of the credit determined under subsection (a) for the taxable year may, at the election of the organization, be apportioned among patrons eligible to share in patronage dividends on the basis of the quantity or value of business done with or for such patrons for the taxable year.

(B) Form and effect of election

An election under subparagraph (A) for any taxable year shall be made on a timely filed return for such year. Such election, once made, shall be irrevocable for such taxable year.

(2) Treatment of organizations and patrons

(A) Organizations

The amount of the credit not apportioned to patrons pursuant to paragraph (1) shall be included in the amount determined under subsection (a) for the taxable year of the organization.

(B) Patrons

The amount of the credit apportioned to patrons pursuant to paragraph (1) shall be included in the amount determined under subsection (a) for the first taxable year of each patron ending on or after the last day of the payment period (as defined in section 1382(d)) for the taxable year of the organization or, if earlier, for the taxable year of each patron ending on or after the date on which the patron receives notice from the cooperative of the apportionment.

(3) Special rule

If the amount of a credit which has been apportioned to any patron under this subsection is decreased for any reason—

(A) such amount shall not increase the tax imposed on such patron, and

(B) the tax imposed by this chapter on such organization shall be increased by such amount.

The increase under subparagraph (B) shall not be treated as tax imposed by this chapter for purposes of determining the amount of any credit under this chapter or for purposes of section 55.

(g) Election to not take credit

No credit shall be determined under subsection (a) for the taxable year if the taxpayer elects not to have subsection (a) apply to such taxable year.

(Added Pub. L. 108–357, title III, §339(a), Oct. 22, 2004, 118 Stat. 1481; amended Pub. L. 110–172, §7(a)(1)(A), (2)(A), (3)(A), (B), Dec. 29, 2007, 121 Stat. 2481, 2482; Pub. L. 115–141, div. U, title IV, §401(a)(19), Mar. 23, 2018, 132 Stat. 1185.)

EDITORIAL NOTES
AMENDMENTS
2018—Subsec. (d). Pub. L. 115–141 substituted "purposes of this" for "purposes this".
2007—Subsec. (b)(1)(A). Pub. L. 110–172, §7(a)(3)(A), substituted "qualified costs" for "qualified capital costs".
Subsec. (c)(2). Pub. L. 110–172, §7(a)(3)(B), struck out "capital" before "costs" in heading.
Pub. L. 110–172, §7(a)(3)(A), substituted "qualified costs" for "qualified capital costs".
Subsec. (d). Pub. L. 110–172, §7(a)(1)(A), redesignated subsec. (e) as (d) and struck out heading and text of former subsec. (d). Text read as follows: "For purposes of this subtitle, if a credit is determined under this section for any expenditure with respect to any property, the increase in basis of such property which would (but for this subsection) result from such expenditure shall be reduced by the amount of the credit so determined."
Subsec. (e). Pub. L. 110–172, §7(a)(1)(A), redesignated subsec. (f) as (e). Former subsec. (e) redesignated (d).

Subsec. (e)(1), (2). Pub. L. 110–172, §7(a)(3)(A), substituted "qualified costs" for "qualified capital costs".
Subsec. (f). Pub. L. 110–172, §7(a)(1)(A), redesignated subsec. (g) as (f). Former subsec. (f) redesignated (e).
Subsec. (g). Pub. L. 110–172, §7(a)(2)(A), added subsec. (g). Former subsec. (g) redesignated (f).

STATUTORY NOTES AND RELATED SUBSIDIARIES
EFFECTIVE DATE OF 2007 AMENDMENT
Amendment by Pub. L. 110–172 effective as if included in the provision of the American Jobs Creation Act of 2004, Pub. L. 108–357, to which such amendment relates, see section 7(e) of Pub. L. 110–172, set out as a note under section 1092 of this title.
EFFECTIVE DATE
Section applicable to expenses paid or incurred after Dec. 31, 2002, in taxable years ending after such date, see section 339(f) of Pub. L. 108–357, set out as an Effective Date of 2004 Amendment note under section 38 of this title.

§45I. Credit for producing oil and gas from marginal wells

(a) General rule

For purposes of section 38, the marginal well production credit for any taxable year is an amount equal to the product of—

(1) the credit amount, and

(2) the qualified crude oil production and the qualified natural gas production which is attributable to the taxpayer.

(b) Credit amount

For purposes of this section—

(1) In general

The credit amount is—

(A) $3 per barrel of qualified crude oil production, and

(B) 50 cents per 1,000 cubic feet of qualified natural gas production.

(2) Reduction as oil and gas prices increase

(A) In general

The $3 and 50 cents amounts under paragraph (1) shall each be reduced (but not below zero) by an amount which bears the same ratio to such amount (determined without regard to this paragraph) as—

(i) the excess (if any) of the applicable reference price over $15 ($1.67 for qualified natural gas production), bears to

(ii) $3 ($0.33 for qualified natural gas production).

The applicable reference price for a taxable year is the reference price of the calendar year preceding the calendar year in which the taxable year begins.

(B) Inflation adjustment

In the case of any taxable year beginning in a calendar year after 2005, each of the dollar amounts contained in subparagraph (A) shall be increased to an amount equal to such dollar amount multiplied by the inflation adjustment factor for such calendar year (determined under section 43(b)(3)(B) by substituting "2004" for "1990").

(C) Reference price

For purposes of this paragraph, the term "reference price" means, with respect to any calendar year—

(i) in the case of qualified crude oil production, the reference price determined under section 45K(d)(2)(C), and

(ii) in the case of qualified natural gas production, the Secretary's estimate of the annual average wellhead price per 1,000 cubic feet for all domestic natural gas.

(c) Qualified crude oil and natural gas production

For purposes of this section—

(1) In general

The terms "qualified crude oil production" and "qualified natural gas production" mean domestic crude oil or natural gas which is produced from a qualified marginal well.

(2) Limitation on amount of production which may qualify

(A) In general

Crude oil or natural gas produced during any taxable year from any well shall not be treated as qualified crude oil production or qualified natural gas production to the extent production from the well during the taxable year exceeds 1,095 barrels or barrel-of-oil equivalents (as defined in section 45K(d)(5)).

(B) Proportionate reductions

(i) Short taxable years

In the case of a short taxable year, the limitations under this paragraph shall be proportionately reduced to reflect the ratio which the number of days in such taxable year bears to 365.

(ii) Wells not in production entire year

In the case of a well which is not capable of production during each day of a taxable year, the limitations under this paragraph applicable to the well shall be proportionately reduced to reflect the ratio which the number of days of production bears to the total number of days in the taxable year.

(3) Definitions

(A) Qualified marginal well

The term "qualified marginal well" means a domestic well—

(i) the production from which during the taxable year is treated as marginal production under section 613A(c)(6), or

(ii) which, during the taxable year—

(I) has average daily production of not more than 25 barrel-of-oil equivalents (as so defined), and

(II) produces water at a rate not less than 95 percent of total well effluent.

(B) Crude oil, etc.

The terms "crude oil", "natural gas", "domestic", and "barrel" have the meanings given such terms by section 613A(e).

(d) Other rules

(1) Production attributable to the taxpayer

In the case of a qualified marginal well in which there is more than one owner of operating interests in the well and the crude oil or natural gas production exceeds the limitation under subsection (c)(2), qualifying crude oil production or qualifying natural gas production attributable to the taxpayer shall be determined on the basis of the ratio which taxpayer's revenue interest in the production bears to the aggregate of the revenue interests of all operating interest owners in the production.

(2) Operating interest required

Any credit under this section may be claimed only on production which is attributable to the holder of an operating interest.

(3) Production from nonconventional sources excluded

In the case of production from a qualified marginal well which is eligible for the credit allowed under section 45K for the taxable year, no credit shall be allowable under this section unless the taxpayer elects not to claim the credit under section 45K with respect to the well.

(Added Pub. L. 108–357, title III, §341(a), Oct. 22, 2004, 118 Stat. 1485; amended Pub. L. 109–58, title XIII, §1322(a)(3)(B), (D), Aug. 8, 2005, 119 Stat. 1011; Pub. L. 109–135, title IV, §412(k), Dec. 21, 2005, 119 Stat. 2637.)

Inflation Adjusted Items for Certain Tax Years

For inflation adjustment of certain items in this section, see Internal Revenue Notices listed in a table below.

Editorial Notes
Amendments

2005—Subsec. (a)(2). Pub. L. 109–135 substituted "qualified crude oil production" for "qualified credit oil production".

Subsec. (b)(2)(C)(i). Pub. L. 109–58, §1322(a)(3)(B), substituted "section 45K(d)(2)(C)" for "section 29(d)(2)(C)".

Subsec. (c)(2)(A). Pub. L. 109–58, §1322(a)(3)(D)(i), substituted "section 45K(d)(5))" for "section 29(d)(5))".

Subsec. (d)(3). Pub. L. 109–58, §1322(a)(3)(D)(ii), substituted "section 45K" for "section 29" in two places.

Statutory Notes and Related Subsidiaries
Effective Date of 2005 Amendment

Amendment by Pub. L. 109–58 applicable to credits determined under the Internal Revenue Code of 1986 for taxable years ending after Dec. 31, 2005, see section 1322(c)(1) of Pub. L. 109–58, set out as a note under section 45K of this title.

Effective Date

Section applicable to production in taxable years beginning after Dec. 31, 2004, see section 341(e) of Pub. L. 108–357, set out as an Effective Date of 2004 Amendment note under section 38 of this title.

Inflation Adjusted Items for Certain Years

Provisions relating to inflation adjustment of items in this section for certain years were contained in the following:

2020—Internal Revenue Notice 2021–34.

2019—Internal Revenue Notice 2020–21.

2018—Internal Revenue Notice 2019–37.

2017—Internal Revenue Notice 2018–52.

2016—Internal Revenue Notice 2017–51.

§45J. Credit for production from advanced nuclear power facilities

(a) General rule

For purposes of section 38, the advanced nuclear power facility production credit of any taxpayer for any taxable year is equal to the product of—

(1) 1.8 cents, multiplied by

(2) the kilowatt hours of electricity—

(A) produced by the taxpayer at an advanced nuclear power facility during the 8-year period beginning on the date the facility was originally placed in service, and

(B) sold by the taxpayer to an unrelated person during the taxable year.

(b) National limitation

(1) In general

The amount of credit which would (but for this subsection and subsection (c)) be allowed with respect to any facility for any taxable year shall not exceed the amount which bears the same ratio to such amount of credit as—

(A) the national megawatt capacity limitation allocated to the facility, bears to

(B) the total megawatt nameplate capacity of such facility.

(2) Amount of national limitation

The aggregate amount of national megawatt capacity limitation allocated by the Secretary under paragraph (3) shall not exceed 6,000 megawatts.

(3) Allocation of limitation

The Secretary shall allocate the national megawatt capacity limitation in such manner as the Secretary may prescribe.

(4) Regulations

Not later than 6 months after the date of the enactment of or any amendment to this section, the Secretary shall prescribe such regulations as may be necessary or appropriate to carry out the purposes of this subsection. Such regulations shall provide a certification process under which the Secretary, after consultation with the Secretary of Energy, shall approve and allocate the national megawatt capacity limitation.

(5) Allocation of unutilized limitation

(A) In general

Any unutilized national megawatt capacity limitation shall be allocated by the Secretary under paragraph (3) as rapidly as is practicable after December 31, 2020—

(i) first to facilities placed in service on or before such date to the extent that such facilities did not receive an allocation equal to their full nameplate capacity, and

(ii) then to facilities placed in service after such date in the order in which such facilities are placed in service.

(B) Unutilized national megawatt capacity limitation

The term "unutilized national megawatt capacity limitation" means the excess (if any) of—

(i) 6,000 megawatts, over

(ii) the aggregate amount of national megawatt capacity limitation allocated by the Secretary before January 1, 2021, reduced by any amount of such limitation which was allocated to a facility which was not placed in service before such date.

(C) Coordination with other provisions

In the case of any unutilized national megawatt capacity limitation allocated by the Secretary pursuant to this paragraph—

(i) such allocation shall be treated for purposes of this section in the same manner as an allocation of national megawatt capacity limitation, and

(ii) subsection (d)(1)(B) shall not apply to any facility which receives such allocation.

(c) Other limitations
(1) Annual limitation

The amount of the credit allowable under subsection (a) (after the application of subsection (b)) for any taxable year with respect to any facility shall not exceed an amount which bears the same ratio to $125,000,000 as—

(A) the national megawatt capacity limitation allocated under subsection (b) to the facility, bears to

(B) 1,000.

(2) Phaseout of credit
(A) In general

The amount of the credit determined under subsection (a) shall be reduced by an amount which bears the same ratio to the amount of the credit (determined without regard to this paragraph) as—

(i) the amount by which the reference price (as defined in section 45(e)(2)(C)) for the calendar year in which the sale occurs exceeds 8 cents, bears to

(ii) 3 cents.

(B) Phaseout adjustment based on inflation

The 8 cent amount in subparagraph (A) shall be adjusted by multiplying such amount by the inflation adjustment factor (as defined in section 45(e)(2)(B)) for the calendar year in which the sale occurs. If any amount as increased under the preceding sentence is not a multiple of 0.1 cent, such amount shall be rounded to the nearest multiple of 0.1 cent.

(d) Advanced nuclear power facility

For purposes of this section—

(1) In general

The term "advanced nuclear power facility" means any advanced nuclear facility—

(A) which is owned by the taxpayer and which uses nuclear energy to produce electricity, and

(B) which is placed in service after the date of the enactment of this paragraph and before January 1, 2021.

(2) Advanced nuclear facility

For purposes of paragraph (1), the term "advanced nuclear facility" means any nuclear facility the reactor design for which is approved after December 31, 1993, by the Nuclear Regulatory Commission (and such design or a substantially similar design of comparable capacity was not approved on or before such date).

(e) Transfer of credit by certain public entities
(1) In general

If, with respect to a credit under subsection (a) for any taxable year—

(A) a qualified public entity would be the taxpayer (but for this paragraph), and

(B) such entity elects the application of this paragraph for such taxable year with respect to all (or any portion specified in such election) of such credit,

the eligible project partner specified in such election, and not the qualified public entity, shall be treated as the taxpayer for purposes of this title with respect to such credit (or such portion thereof).

(2) Definitions

For purposes of this subsection—

(A) Qualified public entity

The term "qualified public entity" means—

(i) a Federal, State, or local government entity, or any political subdivision, agency, or instrumentality thereof,

(ii) a mutual or cooperative electric company described in section 501(c)(12) or 1381(a)(2), or

(iii) a not-for-profit electric utility which had or has received a loan or loan guarantee under the Rural Electrification Act of 1936.

(B) Eligible project partner

The term "eligible project partner" means any person who—

(i) is responsible for, or participates in, the design or construction of the advanced nuclear power facility to which the credit under subsection (a) relates,

(ii) participates in the provision of the nuclear steam supply system to such facility,

(iii) participates in the provision of nuclear fuel to such facility,

(iv) is a financial institution providing financing for the construction or operation of such facility, or

(v) has an ownership interest in such facility.

(3) Special rules
(A) Application to partnerships

In the case of a credit under subsection (a) which is determined at the partnership level—

(i) for purposes of paragraph (1)(A), a qualified public entity shall be treated as the taxpayer with respect to such entity's distributive share of such credit, and

(ii) the term "eligible project partner" shall include any partner of the partnership.

(B) Taxable year in which credit taken into account

In the case of any credit (or portion thereof) with respect to which an election is made under paragraph (1), such credit shall be taken into account in the first taxable year of the eligible project partner ending with, or after, the qualified public entity's taxable year with respect to which the credit was determined.

(C) Treatment of transfer under private use rules

For purposes of section 141(b)(1), any benefit derived by an eligible project partner in connection with an election under this subsection shall not be taken into account as a private business use.

(f) Other rules to apply

Rules similar to the rules of paragraphs (1), (3), (4), and (5) of section 45(e) shall apply for purposes of this section.

(Added Pub. L. 109–58, title XIII, §1306(a), Aug. 8, 2005, 119 Stat. 997; amended Pub. L. 109–135, title IV, §402(d), Dec. 21, 2005, 119 Stat. 2610; Pub. L. 110–172, §6(a), Dec. 29, 2007, 121 Stat. 2479; Pub. L. 115–123, div. D, title I, §40501(a), (b)(1), Feb. 9, 2018, 132 Stat. 153.)

The date of the enactment of this section and the date of the enactment of this paragraph, referred to in subsecs. (b)(4) and (d)(1)(B), are the date of enactment of Pub. L. 109–58, which was approved Aug. 8, 2005.

The Rural Electrification Act of 1936, referred to in subsec. (e)(2)(A)(iii), is act May 20, 1936, ch. 432, 49 Stat. 1363, which is classified generally to chapter 31 (§901 et seq.) of Title 7, Agriculture. For complete classification of this Act to the Code, see section 901 of Title 7 and Tables.

2018—Subsec. (b)(4). Pub. L. 115–123, §40501(a)(1), inserted "or any amendment to" after "enactment of".

Subsec. (b)(5). Pub. L. 115–123, §40501(a)(2), added par. (5).

Subsecs. (e), (f). Pub. L. 115–123, §40501(b)(1), added subsec. (e) and redesignated former subsec. (e) as (f).

2007—Subsec. (b)(2). Pub. L. 110–172 reenacted heading without change and amended text generally. Prior to amendment, text read as follows: "The national megawatt capacity limitation shall be 6,000 megawatts."

2005—Subsec. (c)(2). Pub. L. 109–135, §402(d)(1), amended heading and text of par. (2) generally. Prior to amendment, text read as follows: "Rules similar to the rules of section 45(b)(1) shall apply for purposes of this section."

Subsec. (e). Pub. L. 109–135, §402(d)(2), struck out "(2)," after "(1),".

Pub. L. 115–123, div. D, title I, §40501(c), Feb. 9, 2018, 132 Stat. 154, provided that:

"(1) Treatment of unutilized limitation amounts.—The amendment made by subsection (a) [amending this section] shall take effect on the date of the enactment of this Act [Feb. 9, 2018].

"(2) Transfer of credit by certain public entities.—The amendments made by subsection (b) [amending this section and section 501 of this title] shall apply to taxable years beginning after the date of the enactment of this Act."

Amendment by Pub. L. 110–172 effective as if included in the provisions of the Energy Policy Act of 2005, Pub. L. 109–58, to which such amendment relates, see section 6(e) of Pub. L. 110–172, set out as a note under section 30C of this title.

Amendment by Pub. L. 109–135 effective as if included in the provision of the Energy Policy Act of 2005, Pub. L. 109–58, to which such amendment relates, see section 402(m)(1) of Pub. L. 109–135, set out as a note under section 23 of this title.

Section applicable to production in taxable years beginning after Aug. 8, 2005, see section 1306(d) of Pub. L. 109–58, set out as an Effective Date of 2005 Amendment note under section 38 of this title.

§45K. Credit for producing fuel from a nonconventional source

(a) Allowance of credit

For purposes of section 38, the nonconventional source production credit determined under this section for the taxable year is an amount equal to—

(1) $3, multiplied by

(2) the barrel-of-oil equivalent of qualified fuels—

(A) sold by the taxpayer to an unrelated person during the taxable year, and

(B) the production of which is attributable to the taxpayer.

(b) Limitations and adjustments

(1) Phaseout of credit

The amount of the credit allowable under subsection (a) shall be reduced by an amount which bears the same ratio to the amount of the credit (determined without regard to this paragraph) as—

(A) the amount by which the reference price for the calendar year in which the sale occurs exceeds $23.50, bears to

(B) $6.

(2) Credit and phaseout adjustment based on inflation

The $3 amount in subsection (a) and the $23.50 and $6 amounts in paragraph (1) shall each be adjusted by multiplying such amount by the inflation adjustment factor for the calendar year in which the sale occurs. In the case of gas from a tight formation, the $3 amount in subsection (a) shall not be adjusted.

(3) Credit reduced for grants, tax-exempt bonds, and subsidized energy financing

(A) In general

The amount of the credit allowable under subsection (a) with respect to any project for any taxable year (determined after the application of paragraphs (1) and (2)) shall be reduced by the amount which is the product of the amount so determined for such year and a fraction—

(i) the numerator of which is the sum, for the taxable year and all prior taxable years, of—

(I) grants provided by the United States, a State, or a political subdivision of a State for use in connection with the project,

(II) proceeds of any issue of State or local government obligations used to provide financing for the project the interest on which is exempt from tax under section 103, and

(III) the aggregate amount of subsidized energy financing (within the meaning of section 48(a)(4)(C)) provided in connection with the project, and

(ii) the denominator of which is the aggregate amount of additions to the capital account for the project for the taxable year and all prior taxable years.

(B) Amounts determined at close of year

The amounts under subparagraph (A) for any taxable year shall be determined as of the close of the taxable year.

(4) Credit reduced for energy credit

The amount allowable as a credit under subsection (a) with respect to any project for any taxable year (determined after the application of paragraphs (1), (2), and (3)) shall be reduced by the excess of—

(A) the aggregate amount allowed under section 38 for the taxable year or any prior taxable year by reason of the energy percentage with respect to property used in the project, over

(B) the aggregate amount recaptured with respect to the amount described in subparagraph (A)—

(i) under section 49(b) or 50(a) for the taxable year or any prior taxable year, or

(ii) under this paragraph for any prior taxable year.

The amount recaptured under section 49(b) or 50(a) with respect to any property shall be appropriately reduced to take into account any reduction in the credit allowed by this section by reason of the preceding sentence.

(5) Credit reduced for enhanced oil recovery credit

The amount allowable as a credit under subsection (a) with respect to any project for any taxable year (determined after application of paragraphs (1), (2), (3), and (4)) shall be reduced by the excess (if any) of—

(A) the aggregate amount allowed under section 38 for the taxable year and any prior taxable year by reason of any enhanced oil recovery credit determined under section 43 with respect to such project, over

(B) the aggregate amount recaptured with respect to the amount described in subparagraph (A) under this paragraph for any prior taxable year.

(c) Definition of qualified fuels

For purposes of this section—

(1) In general

The term "qualified fuels" means—

(A) oil produced from shale and tar sands,

(B) gas produced from—

(i) geopressured brine, Devonian shale, coal seams, or a tight formation, or

(ii) biomass, and

(C) liquid, gaseous, or solid synthetic fuels produced from coal (including lignite), including such fuels when used as feedstocks.

(2) Gas from geopressured brine, etc.

(A) In general

Except as provided in subparagraph (B), the determination of whether any gas is produced from geopressured brine, Devonian shale, coal seams, or a tight formation shall be made in accordance with section 503 of the Natural Gas Policy Act of 1978 (as in effect before the repeal of such section).

(B) Special rules for gas from tight formations

The term "gas produced from a tight formation" shall only include gas from a tight formation—

(i) which, as of April 20, 1977, was committed or dedicated to interstate commerce (as defined in section 2(18) of the Natural Gas Policy Act of 1978, as in effect on the date of the enactment of this clause), or

(ii) which is produced from a well drilled after such date of enactment.

(3) Biomass

The term "biomass" means any organic material other than—

(A) oil and natural gas (or any product thereof), and

(B) coal (including lignite) or any product thereof.

(d) Other definitions and special rules

For purposes of this section—

(1) Only production within the United States taken into account

Sales shall be taken into account under this section only with respect to qualified fuels the production of which is within—

(A) the United States (within the meaning of section 638(1)), or

(B) a possession of the United States (within the meaning of section 638(2)).

(2) Computation of inflation adjustment factor and reference price

(A) In general

The Secretary shall, not later than April 1 of each calendar year, determine and publish in the Federal Register the inflation adjustment factor and the reference price for the preceding calendar year in accordance with this paragraph.

(B) Inflation adjustment factor

The term "inflation adjustment factor" means, with respect to a calendar year, a fraction the numerator of which is the GNP implicit price deflator for the calendar year and the denominator of which is the GNP implicit price deflator for calendar year 1979. The term "GNP implicit price deflator" means the first revision of the implicit price deflator for the gross national product as computed and published by the Department of Commerce.

(C) Reference price

The term "reference price" means with respect to a calendar year the Secretary's estimate of the annual average wellhead price per barrel for all domestic crude oil the price of which is not subject to regulation by the United States.

(3) Production attributable to the taxpayer

In the case of a property or facility in which more than 1 person has an interest, except to the extent provided in regulations prescribed by the Secretary, production from the property or facility (as the case may be) shall be allocated among such persons in proportion to their respective interests in the gross sales from such property or facility.

(4) Gas from geopressured brine, Devonian shale, coal seams, or a tight formation

The amount of the credit allowable under subsection (a) shall be determined without regard to any production attributable to a property from which gas from Devonian shale, coal seams, geopressured brine, or a tight formation was produced in marketable quantities before January 1, 1980.

(5) Barrel-of-oil equivalent

The term "barrel-of-oil equivalent" with respect to any fuel means that amount of such fuel which has a Btu content of 5.8 million; except that in the case of qualified fuels described in subparagraph (C) of subsection (c)(1), the Btu content shall be determined without regard to any material from a source not described in such subparagraph.

(6) Barrel defined

The term "barrel" means 42 United States gallons.

(7) Related persons

Persons shall be treated as related to each other if such persons would be treated as a single employer under the regulations prescribed under section 52(b). In the case of a corporation which is a member of an affiliated group of corporations filing a consolidated return, such corporation shall be treated as selling qualified fuels to an unrelated person if such fuels are sold to such a person by another member of such group.

(8) Pass-thru in the case of estates and trusts

Under regulations prescribed by the Secretary, rules similar to the rules of subsection (d) of section 52 shall apply.

(e) Application of section

This section shall apply with respect to qualified fuels—

    (1) which are—

        (A) produced from a well drilled after December 31, 1979, and before January 1, 1993, or

        (B) produced in a facility placed in service after December 31, 1979, and before January 1, 1993, and

    (2) which are sold before January 1, 2003.

(f) Extension for certain facilities
(1) In general

In the case of a facility for producing qualified fuels described in subparagraph (B)(ii) or (C) of subsection (c)(1)—

    (A) for purposes of subsection (e)(1)(B), such facility shall be treated as being placed in service before January 1, 1993, if such facility is placed in service before July 1, 1998, pursuant to a binding written contract in effect before January 1, 1997, and

    (B) if such facility is originally placed in service after December 31, 1992, paragraph (2) of subsection (e) shall be applied with respect to such facility by substituting "January 1, 2008" for "January 1, 2003".

(2) Special rule

Paragraph (1) shall not apply to any facility which produces coke or coke gas unless the original use of the facility commences with the taxpayer.

(g) Extension for facilities producing coke or coke gas

Notwithstanding subsection (e)—

(1) In general

In the case of a facility for producing coke or coke gas (other than from petroleum based products) which was placed in service before January 1, 1993, or after June 30, 1998, and before January 1, 2010, this section shall apply with respect to coke and coke gas produced in such facility and sold during the period—

    (A) beginning on the later of January 1, 2006, or the date that such facility is placed in service, and

    (B) ending on the date which is 4 years after the date such period began.

(2) Special rules

In determining the amount of credit allowable under this section solely by reason of this subsection—

(A) Daily limit

The amount of qualified fuels sold during any taxable year which may be taken into account by reason of this subsection with respect to any facility shall not exceed an average barrel-of-oil equivalent of 4,000 barrels per day. Days before the date the facility is placed in service shall not be taken into account in determining such average.

(B) Extension period to commence with unadjusted credit amount

For purposes of applying subsection (b)(2) to the $3 amount in subsection (a), in the case of fuels sold after 2005, subsection (d)(2)(B) shall be applied by substituting "2004" for "1979".

(C) Denial of double benefit

This subsection shall not apply to any facility producing qualified fuels for which a credit was allowed under this section for the taxable year or any preceding taxable year by reason of subsection (f).

(D) Nonapplication of phaseout

Subsection (b)(1) shall not apply.

(E) Coordination with section 45

No credit shall be allowed with respect to any coke or coke gas which is produced using steel industry fuel (as defined in section 45(c)(7)) as feedstock if a credit is allowed to any taxpayer under section 45 with respect to the production of such steel industry fuel.

(Added Pub. L. 96–223, title II, §231(a), Apr. 2, 1980, 94 Stat. 268, §44D; amended Pub. L. 97–34, title VI §611(a), Aug. 13, 1981, 95 Stat. 339; Pub. L. 97–354, §5(a)(1), Oct. 19, 1982, 96 Stat. 1692; Pub. L. 97–448, title II, §202(a), Jan. 12, 1983, 96 Stat. 2396; renumbered §29 and amended Pub. L. 98–369, div. A, title IV, §§471(c), 474(h), title VI, §612(e)(1), title VII, §722(d)(1), (2), July 18, 1984, 98 Stat. 826, 831, 912, 973; Pub. L. 99–514, title VII, §701(c)(3), title XVIII, §1879(c)(1), Oct. 22, 1986, 100 Stat. 2340, 2906; Pub. L. 100–647, title VI, §6302, Nov. 10, 1988, 102 Stat. 3755; Pub. L. 101–508, title XI, §§11501(a), (b)(1), (c)(1), 11813(b)(1), 11816, Nov. 5, 1990, 104 Stat. 1388–479, 1388-550, 1388-558; Pub. L. 102–486, title XIX, §1918, Oct. 24, 1992, 106 Stat. 3025; Pub. L. 104–188, title I, §§1205(d)(3), 1207(a), Aug. 20, 1996, 110 Stat. 1776; renumbered §45K and amended Pub. L. 109–58, title XIII, §§1321(a), 1322(a)(1), (3)(E), (F), (b), Aug. 8, 2005, 119 Stat. 1010–1012; Pub. L. 109–135, title IV, §§402(g), 412(l), Dec. 21, 2005, 119 Stat. 2611, 2637; Pub. L. 109–432, div. A, title II, §211(a), (b), Dec. 20, 2006, 120 Stat. 2947, 2948; Pub. L. 110–343, div. B, title I, §108(d)(2), Oct. 3, 2008, 122 Stat. 3821; Pub. L. 113–295, div. A, title II, §210(a), Dec. 19, 2014, 128 Stat. 4031.)

INFLATION ADJUSTED ITEMS FOR CERTAIN TAX YEARS

For inflation adjustment of certain items in this section, see Internal Revenue Notices listed in a table below.

EDITORIAL NOTES
REFERENCES IN TEXT

Section 503 of the Natural Gas Policy Act of 1978 (as in effect before the repeal of such section), referred to in subsec. (c)(2)(A), was classified to section 3413 of Title 15, Commerce and Trade, prior to repeal by Pub. L. 101–60, §3(b)(5), July 26, 1989, 103 Stat. 159, effective Jan. 1, 1993.

Section 2(18) of the Natural Gas Policy Act of 1978, referred to in subsec. (c)(2)(B)(i), is classified to section 3301(18) of Title 15, Commerce and Trade.

The date of the enactment of this clause, and such date of enactment, referred to in subsec. (c)(2)(B), probably mean the date of enactment of Pub. L. 101–508, which amended subsec. (c)(2)(B) of this section generally, and which was approved Nov. 5, 1990.

AMENDMENTS

2014—Subsec. (g)(2)(E). Pub. L. 113–295 amended subpar. (E) generally. Prior to amendment, text read as follows: "No credit shall be allowed with respect to any qualified fuel which is steel industry fuel (as defined in section 45(c)(7)) if a credit is allowed to the taxpayer for such fuel under section 45."

2008—Subsec. (g)(2)(E). Pub. L. 110–343 added subpar. (E).

2006—Subsec. (g)(1). Pub. L. 109–432, §211(b), inserted "(other than from petroleum based products)" after "producing coke or coke gas" in introductory provisions.

Subsec. (g)(2)(D). Pub. L. 109–432, §211(a), added subpar. (D).

2005—Pub. L. 109–58, §1322(a)(1), renumbered section 29 of this title as this section.

Subsec. (a). Pub. L. 109–135, §402(g), struck out "if the taxpayer elects to have this section apply," after "For purposes of section 38," in introductory provisions.

Pub. L. 109–58, §1322(a)(3)(E), substituted "For purposes of section 38, if the taxpayer elects to have this section apply, the nonconventional source production credit determined under this section for the taxable year is" for "There shall be allowed as a credit against the tax imposed by this chapter for the taxable year" in introductory provisions.

Subsec. (b)(6). Pub. L. 109–58, §1322(a)(3)(F), struck out heading and text of par. (6). Text read as follows: "The credit allowed by subsection (a) for any taxable year shall not exceed the excess (if any) of—

"(A) the regular tax for the taxable year reduced by the sum of the credits allowable under subpart A and section 27, over

"(B) the tentative minimum tax for the taxable year."

Subsec. (c)(2)(A). Pub. L. 109–58, §1322(b)(1)(A), inserted "(as in effect before the repeal of such section)" after "1978".

Subsecs. (e), (f). Pub. L. 109–58, §1322(b)(1)(B), redesignated subsecs. (f) and (g) as (e) and (f), respectively, and struck out former subsec. (e), which related to application of section with the Natural Gas Policy Act of 1978.

Subsec. (g). Pub. L. 109–135, §412(l)(1), substituted "subsection (e)" for "subsection (f)" in introductory provisions.

Pub. L. 109–58, §1322(b)(1)(B), redesignated subsec. (h) as (g).

Subsec. (g)(1)(A). Pub. L. 109–58, §1322(b)(2)(A), substituted "subsection (e)(1)(B)" for "subsection (f)(1)(B)".

Subsec. (g)(1)(B). Pub. L. 109–58, §1322(b)(2)(B), substituted "subsection (e)" for "subsection (f)".

Subsec. (g)(2)(C). Pub. L. 109–135, §412(l)(2), substituted "subsection (f)" for "subsection (g)".

Subsec. (h). Pub. L. 109–58, §1322(b)(1)(B), redesignated subsec. (h) as (g).

Pub. L. 109–58, §1321(a), added subsec. (h).

1996—Subsec. (b)(6)(A). Pub. L. 104–188, §1205(d)(3), substituted "section 27" for "sections 27 and 28".

Subsec. (g)(1)(A). Pub. L. 104–188, §1207(a), substituted "July 1, 1998" for "January 1, 1997" and "January 1, 1997" for "January 1, 1996".

1992—Subsec. (g). Pub. L. 102–486 added subsec. (g).

1990—Subsec. (b)(3)(A)(i)(III). Pub. L. 101–508, §11813(b)(1)(A), substituted "section 48(a)(4)(C)" for "section 48(l)(11)(C)".

Subsec. (b)(4). Pub. L. 101–508, §11813(b)(1)(B), substituted "section 49(b) or 50(a)" for "section 47" in two places.

Subsec. (b)(5), (6). Pub. L. 101–508, §11501(c)(1), added par. (5) and redesignated former par. (5) as (6).

Subsec. (c)(1)(B) to (E). Pub. L. 101–508, §11816(a), inserted "and" at end of subpar. (B), substituted a period for a comma at end of subpar. (C), and struck out subpar. (D) which related to qualifying processed wood fuels, and subpar. (E) which related to steam produced from solid agricultural byproducts (not including timber byproducts).

Subsec. (c)(2)(B). Pub. L. 101–508, §11501(b)(1), amended subpar. (B) generally. Prior to amendment, subpar. (B) read as follows: "The term 'gas produced from a tight formation' shall only include—

"(i) gas the price of which is regulated by the United States, and

"(ii) gas for which the maximum lawful price applicable under the Natural Gas Policy Act of 1978 is at least 150 percent of the then applicable price under section 103 of such Act."

Subsec. (c)(3). Pub. L. 101–508, §11813(b)(1)(C), amended par. (3) generally. Prior to amendment, par. (3) read as follows: "The term 'biomass' means any organic material which is an alternate substance (as defined in section 48(l)(3)(B)) other than coal (including lignite) or any product of such coal."

Subsec. (c)(4). Pub. L. 101–508, §11816(b)(1), struck out par. (4) "Qualifying processed wood fuel" which read as follows:

"(A) In general.—The term 'qualifying processed wood fuel' means any processed solid wood fuel (other than charcoal, fireplace products, or a product used for ornamental or recreational purposes) which has a Btu content per unit of volume or weight, determined without regard to any nonwood elements, which is at least 40 percent greater per unit of volume or weight than the Btu content of the wood from which it is produced (determined immediately before the processing).

"(B) Election.—A taxpayer shall elect, at such time and in such manner as the Secretary by regulations may prescribe, as to whether Btu content per unit shall be determined for purposes of this paragraph on a volume or weight basis. Any such election—

"(i) shall apply to all production from a facility; and

"(ii) shall be effective for the taxable year with respect to which it is made and for all subsequent taxable years and, once made, may be revoked only with the consent of the Secretary."

Subsec. (c)(5). Pub. L. 101–508, §11816(b)(1), struck out par. (5) "Agricultural byproduct steam" which read as follows: "Steam produced from solid agricultural byproducts which is used by the taxpayer in his trade or business shall be treated as having been sold by the taxpayer to an unrelated person on the date on which it is used."

Subsec. (d)(4). Pub. L. 101–508, §11816(b)(2), amended par. (4) generally, striking out "Special rules applicable to" before "Gas" in heading, redesignating former subpar. (A) as par. (4), striking out subpar. (B) which related to the reference price and application of phaseout for Devonian shale, and making minor changes in phraseology.

Subsec. (d)(5), (6). Pub. L. 101–508, §11816(b)(3), (4), redesignated par. (6) as (5), substituted "subparagraph (C)" for "subparagraph (C), (D), or (E)", and struck out former par. (5) which read as follows: "In the case of a facility for the production of—

"(A) qualifying processed wood fuel,

or

"(B) steam from solid agricultural byproducts,

paragraph (1) of subsection (b) shall not apply with respect to the amount of the credit allowable under subsection (a) for fuels sold during the 3-year period beginning on the date the facility is placed in service."

Subsec. (d)(7) to (9). Pub. L. 101–508, §11816(b)(3), redesignated pars. (7) to (9) as (6) to (8), respectively.

Subsec. (f). Pub. L. 101–508, §11816(b)(5), amended subsec. (f) generally, redesignating former par. (1) as subsec. (f), making minor changes in phraseology, substituting par. (2) for former par. (1)(B) which read as follows: "which are sold after December 31, 1979, and before January 1, 2003.", and striking out former par. (2) which related to special rules applicable to qualified processed wood and solid agricultural byproduct steam.

Subsec. (f)(1)(A)(i), (ii). Pub. L. 101–508, §11501(a)(1), substituted "1993" for "1991".

Subsec. (f)(1)(B). Pub. L. 101–508, §11501(a)(2), substituted "2003" for "2001".

1988—Subsec. (f)(1)(A)(i), (ii). Pub. L. 100–647 substituted "1991" for "1990".

1986—Subsec. (b)(5). Pub. L. 99–514, §701(c)(3), amended par. (5) generally. Prior to amendment, par. (5) read as follows: "The credit allowed by subsection (a) for a taxable year shall not exceed the taxpayer's tax liability for the taxable year (as defined in section 26(b)), reduced by the sum of the credits allowable under subpart A and sections 27 and 28."

Subsec. (d)(8). Pub. L. 99–514, §1879(c)(1), inserted provision directing that a corporation which is a member of an affiliated group of corporations filing a consolidated return shall be treated as selling qualified fuels to an unrelated person if such fuels are sold to such person by another member of such group.

1984—Pub. L. 98–369, §471(c), renumbered section 44D of this title as this section.

Subsec. (b)(1)(A). Pub. L. 98–369, §722(d)(1), substituted "in which the sale occurs" for "in which the taxable year begins".

Subsec. (b)(2). Pub. L. 98–369, §722(d)(2), substituted "in which the sale occurs" for "in which a taxable year begins".

Subsec. (b)(5). Pub. L. 98–369, §612(e)(1), substituted "section 26(b)" for "section 25(b)".

Pub. L. 98–369, §474(h), amended par. (5) generally, substituting "shall not exceed the taxpayer's tax liability for the taxable year (as defined in section 25(b)), reduced by the sum of the credits allowable under subpart A and sections 27 and 28" for "shall not exceed the tax imposed by this chapter for such taxable year, reduced by the sum of the credits allowable under a section of this subpart having a lower number or letter designation than this section, other than the credits allowable by sections 31, 39, and 43. For purposes of the preceding sentence, the term 'tax imposed by this chapter' shall not include any tax treated as not imposed by this chapter under the last sentence of section 53(a)".

1983—Subsec. (f)(1)(B), (2)(A)(i). Pub. L. 97–448 substituted "December 31, 1979" for "December 3, 1979".

1982—Subsec. (d)(9). Pub. L. 97–354 substituted "Pass-thru in the case of estates and trusts" for "Pass-through in the case of subchapter S corporations, etc." in par. heading, and substituted provisions relating to the applicability of rules similar to rules of subsec. (d) of section 52 for provisions relating to the applicability of rules similar to rules of subsecs. (d) and (e) of section 52.

1981—Subsec. (e). Pub. L. 97–34 substituted provisions respecting application with the Natural Gas Policy Act of 1978 for prior provision reading "If the taxpayer makes an election under section 107(d) of the Natural Gas Policy Act of 1978 to have subsections (a) and (b) of section 107 of that Act, and subtitle B of title I of that Act, apply with respect to gas described in subsection (c)(1)(B)(i) produced from any well on a property, then the credit allowable by subsection (a) shall not be allowed with respect to any gas produced on that property."

STATUTORY NOTES AND RELATED SUBSIDIARIES

EFFECTIVE DATE OF 2014 AMENDMENT

Amendment by Pub. L. 113–295 effective as if included in the provisions of the Energy Improvement and Extension Act of 2008, Pub. L. 110–343, div. B, to which such amendment relates, see section 210(h) of Pub. L. 113–295, set out as a note under section 45 of this title.

EFFECTIVE DATE OF 2008 AMENDMENT

Amendment by Pub. L. 110–343 applicable to fuel produced and sold after Sept. 30, 2008, see section 108(e) of Pub. L. 110–343, set out as a note under section 45 of this title.

EFFECTIVE DATE OF 2006 AMENDMENT

Pub. L. 109–432, div. A, title II, §211(c), Dec. 20, 2006, 120 Stat. 2948, provided that: "The amendments made by this section [amending this section] shall take effect as if included in section 1321 of the Energy Policy Act of 2005 [Pub. L. 109–58]."

EFFECTIVE DATE OF 2005 AMENDMENTS

Amendment by section 402(g) of Pub. L. 109–135 effective as if included in the provision of the Energy Policy Act of 2005, Pub. L. 109–58, to which such amendment relates, see section 402(m)(1) of Pub. L. 109–135, set out as an Effective and Termination Dates of 2005 Amendments note under section 23 of this title.

Pub. L. 109–58, title XIII, §1321(b), Aug. 8, 2005, 119 Stat. 1011, provided that: "The amendment made by this section [amending this section] shall apply to fuel produced and sold after December 31, 2005, in taxable years ending after such date."

Pub. L. 109–58, title XIII, §1322(c), Aug. 8, 2005, 119 Stat. 1012, provided that:

"(1) In general.—Except as provided in paragraph (2), the amendments made by this section [amending this section and sections 30, 38, 43, 45, 45I, 53, 55, 613A, and 772 of this title and renumbering section 29 of this title as this section] shall apply to credits determined under the Internal Revenue Code of 1986 for taxable years ending after December 31, 2005.

"(2) Subsection (b).—The amendments made by subsection (b) [amending this section] shall take effect on the date of the enactment of this Act [Aug. 8, 2005]."

EFFECTIVE DATE OF 1996 AMENDMENT

Pub. L. 104–188, title I, §1205(e), Aug. 20, 1996, 110 Stat. 1776, provided that: "The amendments made by this section [amending this section and sections 30, 38, 39, 45C, 53, 55, and 280C of this title] shall apply to amounts paid or incurred in taxable years ending after June 30, 1996."

Pub. L. 104–188, title I, §1207(b), Aug. 20, 1996, 110 Stat. 1776, provided that: "The amendment made by this section [amending this section] shall take effect on the date of the enactment of this Act [Aug. 20, 1996]."

EFFECTIVE DATE OF 1990 AMENDMENT

Pub. L. 101–508, title XI, §11501(b)(2), Nov. 5, 1990, 104 Stat. 1388–479, provided that: "The amendment made by paragraph (1) [amending this section] shall apply to gas produced after December 31, 1990."

Pub. L. 101–508, title XI, §11501(c)(2), Nov. 5, 1990, 104 Stat. 1388–480, provided that: "The amendment made by paragraph (1) [amending this section] shall apply to taxable years beginning after December 31, 1990."

Pub. L. 101–508, title XI, §11813(c), Nov. 5, 1990, 104 Stat. 1388–555, provided that:

"(1) In general.—Except as provided in paragraph (2), the amendments made by this section [enacting section 50 of this title and amending this section and sections 38, 42, 46 to 49, 52, 55, 108, 145, 147, 168, 170, 179, 196, 280F, 312, 465, 469, 861, 865, 1016, 1033, 1245, 1274A, 1371, 1388 and 1503 of this title] shall apply to property placed in service after December 31, 1990.

"(2) Exceptions.—The amendments made by this section shall not apply to—

"(A) any transition property (as defined in section 49(e) of the Internal Revenue Code of 1986 (as in effect on the day before the date of the enactment of this Act [Nov. 5, 1990]),

"(B) any property with respect to which qualified progress expenditures were previously taken into account under section 46(d) of such Code (as so in effect), and

"(C) any property described in section 46(b)(2)(C) of such Code (as so in effect)."

Pub. L. 101–508, title XI, §11821(a), Nov. 5, 1990, 104 Stat. 1388–558, provided that: "Except as otherwise provided in this part, the amendments made by this part [part I (§§11801–11821) of subtitle H of title XI of Pub. L. 101–508, see Tables for classification] shall take effect on the date of the enactment of this Act [Nov. 5, 1990]."

EFFECTIVE DATE OF 1986 AMENDMENT

Amendment by section 701(c)(3) of Pub. L. 99–514 applicable to taxable years beginning after Dec. 31, 1986, with certain exceptions and qualifications, see section 701(f) of Pub. L. 99–514, set out as an Effective Date note under section 55 of this title.

Pub. L. 99–514, title XVIII, §1879(c)(2), Oct. 22, 1986, 100 Stat. 2906, provided that: "The amendment made by paragraph (1) [amending this section] shall take effect as if included in the amendments made by section 231 of Public Law 96–223 [see Effective Date note below]."

EFFECTIVE DATE OF 1984 AMENDMENT

Amendment by section 474(h) of Pub. L. 98–369 applicable to taxable years beginning after Dec. 31, 1983, and to carrybacks from such years, see section 475(a) of Pub. L. 98–369, set out as a note under section 21 of this title.

Amendment by section 612(e)(1) of Pub. L. 98–369 applicable to interest paid or accrued after Dec. 31, 1984, on indebtedness incurred after Dec. 31, 1984, see section 612(g) of Pub. L. 98–369, set out as an Effective Date note under section 25 of this title.

Pub. L. 98–369, title VII, §722(d)(3), July 18, 1984, 98 Stat. 974, provided that: "The amendments made by this subsection [amending this section] shall apply to taxable years ending after December 31, 1979."

EFFECTIVE DATE OF 1983 AMENDMENT

Amendment by Pub. L. 97–448 effective, except as otherwise provided, as if it had been included in the provision of the Crude Oil Windfall Profit Tax Act of 1980, Pub. L. 96–223 to which such amendment relates, see section 203(a) of Pub. L. 97–448, set out as a note under section 6652 of this title.

EFFECTIVE DATE OF 1982 AMENDMENT

Amendment by Pub. L. 97–354 applicable to taxable years beginning after Dec. 31, 1982, see section 6(a) of Pub. L. 97–354, set out as an Effective Date note under section 1361 of this title.

EFFECTIVE DATE OF 1981 AMENDMENT

Pub. L. 97–34, title VI, §611(b), Aug. 13, 1981, 95 Stat. 339, provided that: "The amendment made by this section [amending this section] shall apply to taxable years ending after December 31, 1979."

EFFECTIVE DATE

Pub. L. 96–223, title II, §231(c), Apr. 2, 1980, 94 Stat. 272, provided that: "The amendments made by this section [enacting this section and amending section 6096 of this title] shall apply to taxable years ending after December 31, 1979."

SAVINGS PROVISION

Pub. L. 101–508, title XI, §11821(b), Nov. 5, 1990, 104 Stat. 1388–558, provided that: "If—

"(1) any provision amended or repealed by this part [part I (§§11801–11821) of subtitle H of title XI of Pub. L. 101–508, see Tables for classification] applied to—

"(A) any transaction occurring before the date of the enactment of this Act [Nov. 5, 1990],

"(B) any property acquired before such date of enactment, or

"(C) any item of income, loss, deduction, or credit taken into account before such date of enactment, and

"(2) the treatment of such transaction, property, or item under such provision would (without regard to the amendments made by this part) affect liability for tax for periods ending after such date of enactment,

nothing in the amendments made by this part shall be construed to affect the treatment of such transaction, property, or item for purposes of determining liability for tax for periods ending after such date of enactment."

APPLICABILITY OF CERTAIN AMENDMENTS BY PUB. L. 99–514 IN RELATION TO TREATY OBLIGATIONS OF UNITED STATES

For applicability of amendment by section 701(c)(3) of Pub. L. 99–514 notwithstanding any treaty obligation of the United States in effect on Oct. 22, 1986, with provision that for such purposes any amendment by title I of Pub. L. 100–647 be treated as if it had been included in the provision of Pub. L. 99–514 to which such amendment relates, see section 1012(aa)(2), (4) of Pub. L. 100–647, set out as a note under section 861 of this title.

PLAN AMENDMENTS NOT REQUIRED UNTIL JANUARY 1, 1989

For provisions directing that if any amendments made by subtitle A or subtitle C of title XI [§§1101–1147 and 1171–1177] or title XVIII [§§1800–1899A] of Pub. L. 99–514 require an amendment to any plan, such plan amendment shall not be required to be made before the first plan year beginning on or after Jan. 1, 1989, see section 1140 of Pub. L. 99–514, as amended, set out as a note under section 401 of this title.

INFLATION ADJUSTED ITEMS AND REFERENCE PRICE FOR CERTAIN YEARS

Provisions relating to inflation adjustment of items in this section and reference price for certain years were contained in the following:

2020—Internal Revenue Notice 2021–29.
2019—Internal Revenue Notice 2020–28.
2018—Internal Revenue Notice 2019–28.
2017—Internal Revenue Notice 2018–32.
2016—Internal Revenue Notice 2017–24.
2015—Internal Revenue Notice 2016–43.
2014—Internal Revenue Notice 2015–45.
2013—Internal Revenue Notice 2014–25.
2012—Internal Revenue Notice 2013–25.
2011—Internal Revenue Notice 2012–30.
2010—Internal Revenue Notice 2011–30.
2009—Internal Revenue Notice 2010–31.
2008—Internal Revenue Notice 2009–32.
2007—Internal Revenue Notice 2008–44.
2006—Internal Revenue Notice 2007–38.

§45L. New energy efficient home credit

(a) Allowance of credit

(1) In general

For purposes of section 38, in the case of an eligible contractor, the new energy efficient home credit for the taxable year is the applicable amount for each qualified new energy efficient home which is—

(A) constructed by the eligible contractor, and

(B) acquired by a person from such eligible contractor for use as a residence during the taxable year.

(2) Applicable amount

For purposes of paragraph (1), the applicable amount is an amount equal to—

(A) in the case of a dwelling unit described in paragraph (1) or (2) of subsection (c), $2,000, and

(B) in the case of a dwelling unit described in paragraph (3) of subsection (c), $1,000.

(b) Definitions

For purposes of this section—

(1) Eligible contractor

The term "eligible contractor" means—

(A) the person who constructed the qualified new energy efficient home, or

(B) in the case of a qualified new energy efficient home which is a manufactured home, the manufactured home producer of such home.

(2) Qualified new energy efficient home

The term "qualified new energy efficient home" means a dwelling unit—

(A) located in the United States,

(B) the construction of which is substantially completed after the date of the enactment of this section, and

(C) which meets the energy saving requirements of subsection (c).

(3) Construction

The term "construction" includes substantial reconstruction and rehabilitation.

(4) Acquire

The term "acquire" includes purchase.

(c) Energy saving requirements

A dwelling unit meets the energy saving requirements of this subsection if such unit is—

(1) certified—

(A) to have a level of annual heating and cooling energy consumption which is at least 50 percent below the annual level of heating and cooling energy consumption of a comparable dwelling unit—

(i) which is constructed in accordance with the standards of chapter 4 of the 2006 International Energy Conservation Code, as such Code (including supplements) is in effect on January 1, 2006, and

(ii) for which the heating and cooling equipment efficiencies correspond to the minimum allowed under the regulations established by the Department of Energy pursuant to the National Appliance Energy Conservation Act of 1987 and in effect at the time of completion of construction, and

(B) to have building envelope component improvements account for at least 1/5 of such 50 percent,

(2) a manufactured home which conforms to Federal Manufactured Home Construction and Safety Standards (part 3280 of title 24, Code of Federal Regulations) and which meets the requirements of paragraph (1), or

(3) a manufactured home which conforms to Federal Manufactured Home Construction and Safety Standards (part 3280 of title 24, Code of Federal Regulations) and which—

(A) meets the requirements of paragraph (1) applied by substituting "30 percent" for "50 percent" both places it appears therein and by substituting "1/3" for "1/5" in subparagraph (B) thereof, or

(B) meets the requirements established by the Administrator of the Environmental Protection Agency under the Energy Star Labeled Homes program.

(d) Certification

(1) Method of certification

A certification described in subsection (c) shall be made in accordance with guidance prescribed by the Secretary, after consultation with the Secretary of Energy. Such guidance shall specify procedures and methods for calculating energy and cost savings.

(2) Form

Any certification described in subsection (c) shall be made in writing in a manner which specifies in readily verifiable fashion the energy efficient building envelope components and energy efficient heating or cooling equipment installed and their respective rated energy efficiency performance.

(e) Basis adjustment

For purposes of this subtitle, if a credit is allowed under this section in connection with any expenditure for any property, the increase in the basis of such property which would (but for this subsection) result from such expenditure shall be reduced by the amount of the credit so determined.

(f) Coordination with investment credit

For purposes of this section, expenditures taken into account under section 47 or 48(a) shall not be taken into account under this section.

(g) Termination

This section shall not apply to any qualified new energy efficient home acquired after December 31, 2021.

(Added Pub. L. 109–58, title XIII, §1332(a), Aug. 8, 2005, 119 Stat. 1024; amended Pub. L. 109–432, div. A, title II, §205, Dec. 20, 2006, 120 Stat. 2945; Pub. L. 110–172, §11(a)(7), Dec. 29, 2007, 121 Stat. 2485; Pub. L. 110–343, div. B, title III, §304, Oct. 3, 2008, 122 Stat. 3845; Pub. L. 111–312, title VII, §703(a), Dec. 17, 2010, 124 Stat. 3311; Pub. L. 112–240, title IV, §408(a), (b), Jan. 2, 2013, 126 Stat. 2342; Pub. L. 113–295, div. A, title I, §156(a), Dec. 19, 2014, 128 Stat. 4021; Pub. L. 114–113, div. Q, title I, §188(a), Dec. 18, 2015, 129 Stat. 3074; Pub. L. 115–123, div. D, title I, §40410(a), Feb. 9, 2018, 132 Stat. 150; Pub. L. 116–94, div. Q, title I, §129(a), Dec. 20, 2019, 133 Stat. 3232; Pub. L. 116–260, div. EE, title I, §146(a), Dec. 27, 2020, 134 Stat. 3055.)

EDITORIAL NOTES
REFERENCES IN TEXT

The date of the enactment of this section, referred to in subsec. (b)(2)(B), is the date of enactment of Pub. L. 109–58, which was approved Aug. 8, 2005.

The National Appliance Energy Conservation Act of 1987, referred to in subsec. (c)(1)(A)(ii), is Pub. L. 100–12, Mar. 17, 1987, 101 Stat. 103. For complete classification of this Act to the Code, see Short Title of 1987 Amendment note set out under section 6201 of Title 42, The Public Health and Welfare, and Tables.

AMENDMENTS

2020—Subsec. (g). Pub. L. 116–260 substituted "December 31, 2021" for "December 31, 2020".

2019—Subsec. (g). Pub. L. 116–94 substituted "December 31, 2020" for "December 31, 2017".

2018—Subsec. (g). Pub. L. 115–123 substituted "December 31, 2017" for "December 31, 2016".

2015—Subsec. (g). Pub. L. 114–113 substituted "December 31, 2016" for "December 31, 2014".

2014—Subsec. (g). Pub. L. 113–295 substituted "December 31, 2014" for "December 31, 2013".

2013—Subsec. (c)(1)(A)(i). Pub. L. 112–240, §408(b), substituted "2006 International Energy Conservation Code, as such Code (including supplements) is in effect on January 1, 2006" for "2003 International Energy Conservation Code, as such Code (including supplements) is in effect on the date of the enactment of this section".

Subsec. (g). Pub. L. 112–240, §408(a), substituted "December 31, 2013" for "December 31, 2011".

2010—Subsec. (g). Pub. L. 111–312 substituted "December 31, 2011" for "December 31, 2009".

2008—Subsec. (g). Pub. L. 110–343 substituted "December 31, 2009" for "December 31, 2008".

2007—Subsec. (c)(2), (3). Pub. L. 110–172 substituted "part 3280" for "section 3280" in par. (2) and in introductory provisions of par. (3).

2006—Subsec. (g). Pub. L. 109–432 substituted "2008" for "2007".

STATUTORY NOTES AND RELATED SUBSIDIARIES
EFFECTIVE DATE OF 2020 AMENDMENT

Pub. L. 116–260, div. EE, title I, §146(b), Dec. 27, 2020, 134 Stat. 3055, provided that: "The amendment made by this section [amending this section] shall apply to homes acquired after December 31, 2020."

EFFECTIVE DATE OF 2019 AMENDMENT

Pub. L. 116–94, div. Q, title I, §129(b), Dec. 20, 2019, 133 Stat. 3232, provided that: "The amendment made by this section [amending this section] shall apply to homes acquired after December 31, 2017."

Pub. L. 115–123, div. D, title I, §40410(b), Feb. 9, 2018, 132 Stat. 150, provided that: "The amendment made by this section [amending this section] shall apply to homes acquired after December 31, 2016."

EFFECTIVE DATE OF 2015 AMENDMENT

Pub. L. 114–113, div. Q, title I, §188(b), Dec. 18, 2015, 129 Stat. 3074, provided that: "The amendment made by this section [amending this section] shall apply to homes acquired after December 31, 2014."

EFFECTIVE DATE OF 2014 AMENDMENT

Pub. L. 113–295, div. A, title I, §156(b), Dec. 19, 2014, 128 Stat. 4022, provided that: "The amendment made by this section [amending this section] shall apply to homes acquired after December 31, 2013."

EFFECTIVE DATE OF 2013 AMENDMENT

Pub. L. 112–240, title IV, §408(c), Jan. 2, 2013, 126 Stat. 2342, provided that: "The amendments made by this section [amending this section] shall apply to homes acquired after December 31, 2011."

EFFECTIVE DATE OF 2010 AMENDMENT

Pub. L. 111–312, title VII, §703(b), Dec. 17, 2010, 124 Stat. 3311, provided that: "The amendment made by this section [amending this section] shall apply to homes acquired after December 31, 2009."

EFFECTIVE DATE

Section applicable to qualified new energy efficient homes acquired after Dec. 31, 2005, in taxable years ending after such date, see section 1332(f) of Pub. L. 109–58, set out as an Effective Date of 2005 Amendments note under section 38 of this title.

[§45M. Repealed. Pub. L. 115–141, div. U, title IV, §401(d)(2)(A), Mar. 23, 2018, 132 Stat. 1208]

Section, added Pub. L. 109–58, title XIII, §1334(a), Aug. 8, 2005, 119 Stat. 1030; amended Pub. L. 110–343, div. B, title III, §305(a)–(e), Oct. 3, 2008, 122 Stat. 3845–3847; Pub. L. 111–312, title VII, §709(a)–(d), Dec. 17, 2010, 124 Stat. 3312, 3313; Pub. L. 112–240, title IV, §409(a), (b), Jan. 2, 2013, 126 Stat. 2342, provided for an energy efficient appliance credit.

STATUTORY NOTES AND RELATED SUBSIDIARIES
SAVINGS PROVISION

For provisions that nothing in repeal by Pub. L. 115–141 be construed to affect treatment of certain transactions occurring, property acquired, or items of income, loss, deduction, or credit taken into account prior to Mar. 23, 2018, for purposes of determining liability for tax for periods ending after Mar. 23, 2018, see section 401(e) of Pub. L. 115–141, set out as a note under section 23 of this title.

§45N. Mine rescue team training credit

(a) Amount of credit

For purposes of section 38, the mine rescue team training credit determined under this section with respect to each qualified mine rescue team employee of an eligible employer for any taxable year is an amount equal to the lesser of—

(1) 20 percent of the amount paid or incurred by the taxpayer during the taxable year with respect to the training program costs of such qualified mine rescue team employee (including wages of such employee while attending such program), or

(2) $10,000.

(b) Qualified mine rescue team employee

For purposes of this section, the term "qualified mine rescue team employee" means with respect to any taxable year any full-time employee of the taxpayer who is—

(1) a miner eligible for more than 6 months of such taxable year to serve as a mine rescue team member as a result of completing, at a minimum, an initial 20-hour course of instruction as prescribed by the Mine Safety and Health Administration's Office of Educational Policy and Development, or

(2) a miner eligible for more than 6 months of such taxable year to serve as a mine rescue team member by virtue of receiving at least 40 hours of refresher training in such instruction.

(c) Eligible employer

For purposes of this section, the term "eligible employer" means any taxpayer which employs individuals as miners in underground mines in the United States.

(d) Wages

For purposes of this section, the term "wages" has the meaning given to such term by subsection (b) of section 3306 (determined without regard to any dollar limitation contained in such section).

(e) Termination

This section shall not apply to taxable years beginning after December 31, 2021.

(Added Pub. L. 109–432, div. A, title IV, §405(a), Dec. 20, 2006, 120 Stat. 2957; amended Pub. L. 110–343, div. C, title III, §310, Oct. 3, 2008, 122 Stat. 3869; Pub. L. 111–312, title VII, §735(a), Dec. 17, 2010, 124 Stat. 3318; Pub. L. 112–240, title III, §307(a), Jan. 2, 2013, 126 Stat. 2329; Pub. L. 113–295, div. A, title I, §117(a), Dec. 19, 2014, 128 Stat. 4015; Pub. L. 114–113, div. Q, title I, §163(a), Dec. 18, 2015, 129 Stat. 3066; Pub. L. 115–123, div. D, title I, §40303(a), Feb. 9, 2018, 132 Stat. 146; Pub. L. 116–94, div. Q, title I, §113(a), Dec. 20, 2019, 133 Stat. 3229; Pub. L. 116–260, div. EE, title I, §136(a), Dec. 27, 2020, 134 Stat. 3053.)

EDITORIAL NOTES
AMENDMENTS

2020—Subsec. (e). Pub. L. 116–260 substituted "December 31, 2021" for "December 31, 2020".

2019—Subsec. (e). Pub. L. 116–94 substituted "December 31, 2020" for "December 31, 2017".

2018—Subsec. (e). Pub. L. 115–123 substituted "December 31, 2017" for "December 31, 2016".

2015—Subsec. (e). Pub. L. 114–113 substituted "December 31, 2016" for "December 31, 2014".

2014—Subsec. (e). Pub. L. 113–295 substituted "December 31, 2014" for "December 31, 2013".

2013—Subsec. (e). Pub. L. 112–240 substituted "December 31, 2013" for "December 31, 2011".

2010—Subsec. (e). Pub. L. 111–312 substituted "December 31, 2011" for "December 31, 2009".

2008—Subsec. (e). Pub. L. 110–343 substituted "December 31, 2009" for "December 31, 2008".

STATUTORY NOTES AND RELATED SUBSIDIARIES
EFFECTIVE DATE OF 2020 AMENDMENT

Pub. L. 116–260, div. EE, title I, §136(b), Dec. 27, 2020, 134 Stat. 3053, provided that: "The amendment made by this section [amending this section] shall apply to taxable years beginning after December 31, 2020."

EFFECTIVE DATE OF 2019 AMENDMENT

Pub. L. 116–94, div. Q, title I, §113(b), Dec. 20, 2019, 133 Stat. 3229, provided that: "The amendment made by this section [amending this section] shall apply to taxable years beginning after December 31, 2017."

EFFECTIVE DATE OF 2018 AMENDMENT

Pub. L. 115–123, div. D, title I, §40303(b), Feb. 9, 2018, 132 Stat. 146, provided that: "The amendment made by this section [amending this section] shall apply to taxable years beginning after December 31, 2016."

EFFECTIVE DATE OF 2015 AMENDMENT

Pub. L. 114–113, div. Q, title I, §163(b), Dec. 18, 2015, 129 Stat. 3066, provided that: "The amendment made by this section [amending this section] shall apply to taxable years beginning after December 31, 2014."

EFFECTIVE DATE OF 2014 AMENDMENT

Pub. L. 113–295, div. A, title I, §117(b), Dec. 19, 2014, 128 Stat. 4015, provided that: "The amendment made by this section [amending this section] shall apply to taxable years beginning after December 31, 2013."

EFFECTIVE DATE OF 2013 AMENDMENT

Pub. L. 112–240, title III, §307(b), Jan. 2, 2013, 126 Stat. 2329, provided that: "The amendment made by this section [amending this section] shall apply to taxable years beginning after December 31, 2011."

EFFECTIVE DATE OF 2010 AMENDMENT

Pub. L. 111–312, title VII, §735(b), Dec. 17, 2010, 124 Stat. 3318, provided that: "The amendment made by this section [amending this section] shall apply to taxable years beginning after December 31, 2009."

EFFECTIVE DATE

Section applicable to taxable years beginning after Dec. 31, 2005, see section 405(e) of Pub. L. 109–432, set out as an Effective Date of 2006 Amendment note under section 38 of this title.

§450. Agricultural chemicals security credit

(a) In general

For purposes of section 38, in the case of an eligible agricultural business, the agricultural chemicals security credit determined under this section for the taxable year is 30 percent of the qualified security expenditures for the taxable year.

(b) Facility limitation

The amount of the credit determined under subsection (a) with respect to any facility for any taxable year shall not exceed—

(1) $100,000, reduced by

(2) the aggregate amount of credits determined under subsection (a) with respect to such facility for the 5 prior taxable years.

(c) Annual limitation

The amount of the credit determined under subsection (a) with respect to any taxpayer for any taxable year shall not exceed $2,000,000.

(d) Qualified chemical security expenditure

For purposes of this section, the term "qualified chemical security expenditure" means, with respect to any eligible agricultural business for any taxable year, any amount paid or incurred by such business during such taxable year for—

(1) employee security training and background checks,

(2) limitation and prevention of access to controls of specified agricultural chemicals stored at the facility,

(3) tagging, locking tank valves, and chemical additives to prevent the theft of specified agricultural chemicals or to render such chemicals unfit for illegal use,

(4) protection of the perimeter of specified agricultural chemicals,

(5) installation of security lighting, cameras, recording equipment, and intrusion detection sensors,

(6) implementation of measures to increase computer or computer network security,

(7) conducting a security vulnerability assessment,

(8) implementing a site security plan, and

(9) such other measures for the protection of specified agricultural chemicals as the Secretary may identify in regulation.

Amounts described in the preceding sentence shall be taken into account only to the extent that such amounts are paid or incurred for the purpose of protecting specified agricultural chemicals.

(e) Eligible agricultural business

For purposes of this section, the term "eligible agricultural business" means any person in the trade or business of—

(1) selling agricultural products, including specified agricultural chemicals, at retail predominantly to farmers and ranchers, or

(2) manufacturing, formulating, distributing, or aerially applying specified agricultural chemicals.

(f) Specified agricultural chemical

For purposes of this section, the term "specified agricultural chemical" means—

(1) any fertilizer commonly used in agricultural operations which is listed under—

(A) section 302(a)(2) of the Emergency Planning and Community Right-to-Know Act of 1986,

(B) section 101 of part 172 of title 49, Code of Federal Regulations, or

(C) part 126, 127, or 154 of title 33, Code of Federal Regulations, and

(2) any pesticide (as defined in section 2(u) of the Federal Insecticide, Fungicide, and Rodenticide Act), including all active and inert ingredients thereof, which is customarily used on crops grown for food, feed, or fiber.

(g) Controlled groups

Rules similar to the rules of paragraphs (1) and (2) of section 41(f) shall apply for purposes of this section.

(h) Regulations

The Secretary may prescribe such regulations as may be necessary or appropriate to carry out the purposes of this section, including regulations which—

(1) provide for the proper treatment of amounts which are paid or incurred for purpose of protecting any specified agricultural chemical and for other purposes, and

(2) provide for the treatment of related properties as one facility for purposes of subsection (b).

(i) Termination

This section shall not apply to any amount paid or incurred after December 31, 2012.

(Added Pub. L. 110–234, title XV, §15343(a), May 22, 2008, 122 Stat. 1518, and Pub. L. 110–246, §4(a), title XV, §15343(a), June 18, 2008, 122 Stat. 1664, 2280.)

EDITORIAL NOTES

Section 302(a)(2) of the Emergency Planning and Community Right-to-Know Act of 1986, referred to in subsec. (f)(1)(A), is classified to section 11002(a)(2) of Title 42, The Public Health and Welfare.

Section 2(u) of the Federal Insecticide, Fungicide, and Rodenticide Act, referred to in subsec. (f)(2), is classified to section 136(u) of Title 7, Agriculture.

CODIFICATION

Pub. L. 110–234 and Pub. L. 110–246 enacted identical sections. Pub. L. 110–234 was repealed by section 4(a) of Pub. L. 110–246.

STATUTORY NOTES AND RELATED SUBSIDIARIES
EFFECTIVE DATE

Enactment of this section and repeal of Pub. L. 110–234 by Pub. L. 110–246 effective May 22, 2008, the date of enactment of Pub. L. 110–234, except as otherwise provided, see section 4 of Pub. L. 110–246, set out as a note under section 8701 of Title 7, Agriculture.

Section applicable to amounts paid or incurred after June 18, 2008, see section 15343(e) of Pub. L. 110–246, set out as an Effective Date of 2008 Amendment note under section 38 of this title.

§45P. Employer wage credit for employees who are active duty members of the uniformed services

(a) General rule

For purposes of section 38, the differential wage payment credit for any taxable year is an amount equal to 20 percent of the sum of the eligible differential wage payments for each of the qualified employees of the taxpayer during such taxable year.

(b) Definitions

For purposes of this section—

(1) Eligible differential wage payments

The term "eligible differential wage payments" means, with respect to each qualified employee, so much of the differential wage payments (as defined in section 3401(h)(2)) paid to such employee for the taxable year as does not exceed $20,000.

(2) Qualified employee

The term "qualified employee" means a person who has been an employee of the taxpayer for the 91-day period immediately preceding the period for which any differential wage payment is made.

(3) Controlled groups

All persons treated as a single employer under subsection (b), (c), (m), or (o) of section 414 shall be treated as a single employer.

(c) Coordination with other credits

The amount of credit otherwise allowable under this chapter with respect to compensation paid to any employee shall be reduced by the credit determined under this section with respect to such employee.

(d) Disallowance for failure to comply with employment or reemployment rights of members of the reserve components of the Armed Forces of the United States

No credit shall be allowed under subsection (a) to a taxpayer for—

(1) any taxable year, beginning after the date of the enactment of this section, in which the taxpayer is under a final order, judgment, or other process issued or required by a district court of the United States under section 4323 of title 38 of the United States Code with respect to a violation of chapter 43 of such title, and

(2) the 2 succeeding taxable years.

(e) Certain rules to apply

For purposes of this section, rules similar to the rules of subsections (c), (d), and (e) of section 52 shall apply.

(Added Pub. L. 110–245, title I, §111(a), June 17, 2008, 122 Stat. 1634; amended Pub. L. 111–312, title VII, §736(a), Dec. 17, 2010, 124 Stat. 3318; Pub. L. 112–240, title III, §308(a), Jan. 2, 2013, 126 Stat. 2329; Pub. L. 113–295, div. A, title I, §118(a), Dec. 19, 2014, 128 Stat. 4015; Pub. L. 114–113, div. Q, title I, §122(a), (b), Dec. 18, 2015, 129 Stat. 3052.)

EDITORIAL NOTES
REFERENCES IN TEXT

The date of the enactment of this section, referred to in subsec. (d)(1), is the date of the enactment of Pub. L. 110–245, which was approved June 17, 2008.

AMENDMENTS

2015—Subsec. (a). Pub. L. 114–113, §122(b)(1), struck out ", in the case of an eligible small business employer" after "section 38".

Subsec. (b)(3). Pub. L. 114–113, §122(b)(2), amended par. (3) generally. Prior to amendment, par. (3) defined "eligible small business employer".

Subsec. (f). Pub. L. 114–113, §122(a), struck out subsec. (f). Text read as follows: "This section shall not apply to any payments made after December 31, 2014."

2014—Subsec. (f). Pub. L. 113–295 substituted "December 31, 2014" for "December 31, 2013".

2013—Subsec. (f). Pub. L. 112–240 substituted "December 31, 2013" for "December 31, 2011".

2010—Subsec. (f). Pub. L. 111–312 substituted "December 31, 2011" for "December 31, 2009".

STATUTORY NOTES AND RELATED SUBSIDIARIES
EFFECTIVE DATE OF 2015 AMENDMENT

Pub. L. 114–113, div. Q, title I, §122(c), Dec. 18, 2015, 129 Stat. 3052, provided that:

"(1) Extension.—The amendment made by subsection (a) [amending this section] shall apply to payments made after December 31, 2014.

"(2) Modification.—The amendments made by subsection (b) [amending this section] shall apply to taxable years beginning after December 31, 2015."

EFFECTIVE DATE OF 2014 AMENDMENT

Pub. L. 113–295, div. A, title I, §118(b), Dec. 19, 2014, 128 Stat. 4015, provided that: "The amendment made by this section [amending this section] shall apply to payments made after December 31, 2013."

EFFECTIVE DATE OF 2013 AMENDMENT

Pub. L. 112–240, title III, §308(b), Jan. 2, 2013, 126 Stat. 2329, provided that: "The amendment made by this section [amending this section] shall apply to payments made after December 31, 2011."

EFFECTIVE DATE OF 2010 AMENDMENT

Pub. L. 111–312, title VII, §736(b), Dec. 17, 2010, 124 Stat. 3318, provided that: "The amendment made by this section [amending this section] shall apply to payments made after December 31, 2009."

EFFECTIVE DATE

§45Q. Credit for carbon oxide sequestration

(a) General rule

For purposes of section 38, the carbon oxide sequestration credit for any taxable year is an amount equal to the sum of—

(1) $20 per metric ton of qualified carbon oxide which is—

(A) captured by the taxpayer using carbon capture equipment which is originally placed in service at a qualified facility before the date of the enactment of the Bipartisan Budget Act of 2018, and

(B) disposed of by the taxpayer in secure geological storage and not used by the taxpayer as described in paragraph (2)(B),

(2) $10 per metric ton of qualified carbon oxide which is—

(A) captured by the taxpayer using carbon capture equipment which is originally placed in service at a qualified facility before the date of the enactment of the Bipartisan Budget Act of 2018, and

(B)(i) used by the taxpayer as a tertiary injectant in a qualified enhanced oil or natural gas recovery project and disposed of by the taxpayer in secure geological storage, or

(ii) utilized by the taxpayer in a manner described in subsection (f)(5),

(3) the applicable dollar amount (as determined under subsection (b)(1)) per metric ton of qualified carbon oxide which is—

(A) captured by the taxpayer using carbon capture equipment which is originally placed in service at a qualified facility on or after the date of the enactment of the Bipartisan Budget Act of 2018, during the 12-year period beginning on the date the equipment was originally placed in service, and

(B) disposed of by the taxpayer in secure geological storage and not used by the taxpayer as described in paragraph (4)(B), and

(4) the applicable dollar amount (as determined under subsection (b)(1)) per metric ton of qualified carbon oxide which is—

(A) captured by the taxpayer using carbon capture equipment which is originally placed in service at a qualified facility on or after the date of the enactment of the Bipartisan Budget Act of 2018, during the 12-year period beginning on the date the equipment was originally placed in service, and

(B)(i) used by the taxpayer as a tertiary injectant in a qualified enhanced oil or natural gas recovery project and disposed of by the taxpayer in secure geological storage, or

(ii) utilized by the taxpayer in a manner described in subsection (f)(5).

(b) Applicable dollar amount; additional equipment; election

(1) Applicable dollar amount

(A) In general

The applicable dollar amount shall be an amount equal to—

(i) for any taxable year beginning in a calendar year after 2016 and before 2027—

(I) for purposes of paragraph (3) of subsection (a), the dollar amount established by linear interpolation between $22.66 and $50 for each calendar year during such period, and

(II) for purposes of paragraph (4) of such subsection, the dollar amount established by linear interpolation between $12.83 and $35 for each calendar year during such period, and

(ii) for any taxable year beginning in a calendar year after 2026—

(I) for purposes of paragraph (3) of subsection (a), an amount equal to the product of $50 and the inflation adjustment factor for such calendar year determined under section 43(b)(3)(B) for such calendar year, determined by substituting "2025" for "1990", and

(II) for purposes of paragraph (4) of such subsection, an amount equal to the product of $35 and the inflation adjustment factor for such calendar year determined under section 43(b)(3)(B) for such calendar year, determined by substituting "2025" for "1990".

(B) Rounding

The applicable dollar amount determined under subparagraph (A) shall be rounded to the nearest cent.

(2) Installation of additional carbon capture equipment on existing qualified facility

In the case of a qualified facility placed in service before the date of the enactment of the Bipartisan Budget Act of 2018, for which additional carbon capture equipment is placed in service on or after the date of the enactment of such Act, the amount of qualified carbon oxide which is captured by the taxpayer shall be equal to—

(A) for purposes of paragraphs (1)(A) and (2)(A) of subsection (a), the lesser of—

(i) the total amount of qualified carbon oxide captured at such facility for the taxable year, or

(ii) the total amount of the carbon dioxide capture capacity of the carbon capture equipment in service at such facility on the day before the date of the enactment of the Bipartisan Budget Act of 2018, and

(B) for purposes of paragraphs (3)(A) and (4)(A) of such subsection, an amount (not less than zero) equal to the excess of—

(i) the amount described in clause (i) of subparagraph (A), over

(ii) the amount described in clause (ii) of such subparagraph.

(3) Election

For purposes of determining the carbon oxide sequestration credit under this section, a taxpayer may elect to have the dollar amounts applicable under paragraph (1) or (2) of subsection (a) apply in lieu of the dollar amounts applicable under paragraph (3) or (4) of such subsection for each metric ton of qualified carbon oxide which is captured by the taxpayer using carbon capture equipment which is originally placed in service at a qualified facility on or after the date of the enactment of the Bipartisan Budget Act of 2018.

(c) Qualified carbon oxide

For purposes of this section—

(1) In general

The term "qualified carbon oxide" means—

(A) any carbon dioxide which—

(i) is captured from an industrial source by carbon capture equipment which is originally placed in service before the date of the enactment of the Bipartisan Budget Act of 2018,

(ii) would otherwise be released into the atmosphere as industrial emission of greenhouse gas or lead to such release, and

(iii) is measured at the source of capture and verified at the point of disposal, injection, or utilization,

(B) any carbon dioxide or other carbon oxide which—

(i) is captured from an industrial source by carbon capture equipment which is originally placed in service on or after the date of the enactment of the Bipartisan Budget Act of 2018,

(ii) would otherwise be released into the atmosphere as industrial emission of greenhouse gas or lead to such release, and

(iii) is measured at the source of capture and verified at the point of disposal, injection, or utilization, or

(C) in the case of a direct air capture facility, any carbon dioxide which—

(i) is captured directly from the ambient air, and

(ii) is measured at the source of capture and verified at the point of disposal, injection, or utilization.

(2) Recycled carbon oxide

The term "qualified carbon oxide" includes the initial deposit of captured carbon oxide used as a tertiary injectant. Such term does not include carbon oxide that is recaptured, recycled, and re-injected as part of the enhanced oil and natural gas recovery process.

(d) Qualified facility

For purposes of this section, the term "qualified facility" means any industrial facility or direct air capture facility—

(1) the construction of which begins before January 1, 2026, and—

(A) construction of carbon capture equipment begins before such date, or

(B) the original planning and design for such facility includes installation of carbon capture equipment, and

(2) which captures—

(A) in the case of a facility which emits not more than 500,000 metric tons of carbon oxide into the atmosphere during the taxable year, not less than 25,000 metric tons of qualified carbon oxide during the taxable year which is utilized in a manner described in subsection (f)(5),

(B) in the case of an electricity generating facility which is not described in subparagraph (A), not less than 500,000 metric tons of qualified carbon oxide during the taxable year, or

(C) in the case of a direct air capture facility or any facility not described in subparagraph (A) or (B), not less than 100,000 metric tons of qualified carbon oxide during the taxable year.

(e) Definitions

For purposes of this section—

(1) Direct air capture facility

(A) In general

Subject to subparagraph (B), the term "direct air capture facility" means any facility which uses carbon capture equipment to capture carbon dioxide directly from the ambient air.

(B) Exception

The term "direct air capture facility" shall not include any facility which captures carbon dioxide—

(i) which is deliberately released from naturally occurring subsurface springs, or

(ii) using natural photosynthesis.

(2) Qualified enhanced oil or natural gas recovery project

The term "qualified enhanced oil or natural gas recovery project" has the meaning given the term "qualified enhanced oil recovery project" by section 43(c)(2), by substituting "crude oil or natural gas" for "crude oil" in subparagraph (A)(i) thereof.

(3) Tertiary injectant

The term "tertiary injectant" has the same meaning as when used within section 193(b)(1).

(f) Special rules

(1) Only qualified carbon oxide captured and disposed of or used within the united states taken into account

The credit under this section shall apply only with respect to qualified carbon oxide the capture and disposal, use, or utilization of which is within—

(A) the United States (within the meaning of section 638(1)), or

(B) a possession of the United States (within the meaning of section 638(2)).

(2) Secure geological storage

The Secretary, in consultation with the Administrator of the Environmental Protection Agency, the Secretary of Energy, and the Secretary of the Interior, shall establish regulations for determining adequate security measures for the geological storage of qualified carbon oxide under subsection (a) such that the qualified carbon oxide does not escape into the atmosphere. Such term shall include storage at deep saline formations, oil and gas reservoirs, and unminable coal seams under such conditions as the Secretary may determine under such regulations.

(3) Credit attributable to taxpayer

(A) In general

Except as provided in subparagraph (B) or in any regulations prescribed by the Secretary, any credit under this section shall be attributable to—

(i) in the case of qualified carbon oxide captured using carbon capture equipment which is originally placed in service at a qualified facility before the date of the enactment of the Bipartisan Budget Act of 2018, the person that captures and physically or contractually ensures the disposal, utilization, or use as a tertiary injectant of such qualified carbon oxide, and

(ii) in the case of qualified carbon oxide captured using carbon capture equipment which is originally placed in service at a qualified facility on or after the date of the enactment of the Bipartisan Budget Act of 2018, the person that owns the carbon capture equipment and physically or contractually ensures the capture and disposal, utilization, or use as a tertiary injectant of such qualified carbon oxide.

(B) Election

If the person described in subparagraph (A) makes an election under this subparagraph in such time and manner as the Secretary may prescribe by regulations, the credit under this section—

(i) shall be allowable to the person that disposes of the qualified carbon oxide, utilizes the qualified carbon oxide, or uses the qualified carbon oxide as a tertiary injectant, and

(ii) shall not be allowable to the person described in subparagraph (A).

(4) Recapture

The Secretary shall, by regulations, provide for recapturing the benefit of any credit allowable under subsection (a) with respect to any qualified carbon oxide which ceases to be captured, disposed of, or used as a tertiary injectant in a manner consistent with the requirements of this section.

(5) Utilization of qualified carbon oxide

(A) In general

For purposes of this section, utilization of qualified carbon oxide means—

(i) the fixation of such qualified carbon oxide through photosynthesis or chemosynthesis, such as through the growing of algae or bacteria,

(ii) the chemical conversion of such qualified carbon oxide to a material or chemical compound in which such qualified carbon oxide is securely stored, or

(iii) the use of such qualified carbon oxide for any other purpose for which a commercial market exists (with the exception of use as a tertiary injectant in a qualified enhanced oil or natural gas recovery project), as determined by the Secretary.

(B) Measurement

(i) In general

For purposes of determining the amount of qualified carbon oxide utilized by the taxpayer under paragraph (2)(B)(ii) or (4)(B)(ii) of subsection (a), such amount shall be equal to the metric tons of qualified carbon oxide which the taxpayer demonstrates, based upon an analysis of lifecycle greenhouse gas emissions and subject to such requirements as the Secretary, in consultation with the Secretary of Energy and the Administrator of the Environmental Protection Agency, determines appropriate, were—

(I) captured and permanently isolated from the atmosphere, or

(II) displaced from being emitted into the atmosphere,

through use of a process described in subparagraph (A).

(ii) Lifecycle greenhouse gas emissions

For purposes of clause (i), the term "lifecycle greenhouse gas emissions" has the same meaning given such term under subparagraph (H) of section 211(o)(1) of the Clean Air Act (42 U.S.C. 7545(o)(1)), as in effect on the date of the enactment of the Bipartisan Budget Act of 2018, except that "product" shall be substituted for "fuel" each place it appears in such subparagraph.

(6) Election for applicable facilities

(A) In general

For purposes of this section, in the case of an applicable facility, for any taxable year in which such facility captures not less than 500,000 metric tons of qualified carbon oxide during the taxable year, the person described in paragraph (3)(A)(ii) may elect to have such facility, and any carbon capture equipment placed in service at such facility, deemed as having been placed in service on the date of the enactment of the Bipartisan Budget Act of 2018.

(B) Applicable facility

For purposes of this paragraph, the term "applicable facility" means a qualified facility—

(i) which was placed in service before the date of the enactment of the Bipartisan Budget Act of 2018, and

(ii) for which no taxpayer claimed a credit under this section in regards to such facility for any taxable year ending before the date of the enactment of such Act.

(7) Inflation adjustment

In the case of any taxable year beginning in a calendar year after 2009, there shall be substituted for each dollar amount contained in paragraphs (1) and (2) of subsection (a) an amount equal to the product of—

(A) such dollar amount, multiplied by

(B) the inflation adjustment factor for such calendar year determined under section 43(b)(3)(B) for such calendar year, determined by substituting "2008" for "1990".

(3) [1] Credit reduced for certain tax-exempt bonds

The amount of the credit determined under subsection (a) with respect to any project for any taxable year shall be reduced by the amount which is the product of the amount so determined for such year and the lesser of ½ or a fraction—

(A) the numerator of which is the sum, for the taxable year and all prior taxable years, of the proceeds from an issue described in section 142(a)(17) used to provide financing for the project the interest on which is exempt from tax under section 103, and

(B) the denominator of which is the aggregate amount of additions to the capital account for the project for the taxable year and all prior taxable years.

The amounts under the preceding sentence for any taxable year shall be determined as of the close of the taxable year.

(g) Application of section for certain carbon capture equipment

In the case of any carbon capture equipment placed in service before the date of the enactment of the Bipartisan Budget Act of 2018, the credit under this section shall apply with respect to qualified carbon oxide captured using such equipment before the end of the calendar year in which the Secretary, in consultation with the Administrator of the Environmental Protection Agency, certifies that, during the period beginning after October 3, 2008, a total of 75,000,000 metric tons of qualified carbon oxide have been taken into account in accordance with—

(1) subsection (a) of this section, as in effect on the day before the date of the enactment of the Bipartisan Budget Act of 2018, and

(2) paragraphs (1) and (2) of subsection (a) of this section.

(h) Regulations

The Secretary may prescribe such regulations and other guidance as may be necessary or appropriate to carry out this section, including regulations or other guidance to—

(1) ensure proper allocation under subsection (a) for qualified carbon oxide captured by a taxpayer during the taxable year ending after the date of the enactment of the Bipartisan Budget Act of 2018, and

(2) determine whether a facility satisfies the requirements under subsection (d)(1) during such taxable year.

(Added Pub. L. 110–343, div. B, title I, §115(a), Oct. 3, 2008, 122 Stat. 3829; amended Pub. L. 111–5, div. B, title I, §1131(a), (b), Feb. 17, 2009, 123 Stat. 325; Pub. L. 113–295, div. A, title II, §209(j)(1), Dec. 19, 2014, 128 Stat. 4030; Pub. L. 115–123, div. D, title II, §41119(a), Feb. 9, 2018, 132 Stat. 162; Pub. L. 116–260, div. EE, title I, §121, Dec. 27, 2020, 134 Stat. 3051; Pub. L. 117–58, div. H, title IV, §80402(e), Nov. 15, 2021, 135 Stat. 1334.)

INFLATION ADJUSTED ITEMS FOR CERTAIN TAX YEARS

For inflation adjustment of certain items in this section, see Internal Revenue Notices listed in a table below.

EDITORIAL NOTES

The date of the enactment of the Bipartisan Budget Act of 2018 and the date of the enactment of such Act, referred to in text, is the date of enactment of Pub. L. 115–123, which was approved Feb. 9, 2018.

AMENDMENTS

2021—Subsec. (f)(3). Pub. L. 117–58 added par. (3) relating to certain tax-exempt bonds at end of subsec. (f).

2020—Subsec. (d)(1). Pub. L. 116–260 substituted "January 1, 2026" for "January 1, 2024" in introductory provisions.

2018—Pub. L. 115–123 amended section generally. Prior to amendment, section related to credit for carbon dioxide sequestration.

2014—Subsec. (d)(2). Pub. L. 113–295 substituted "Administrator of the Environmental Protection Agency, the Secretary of Energy, and the Secretary of the Interior, shall establish" for "Administrator of the Environmental Protection Agency the Secretary of Energy, and the Secretary of the Interior,, shall establish".

2009—Subsec. (a)(1)(B). Pub. L. 111–5, §1131(b)(2), inserted "and not used by the taxpayer as described in paragraph (2)(B)" after "storage".

Subsec. (a)(2)(C). Pub. L. 111–5, §1131(a), added subpar. (C).

Subsec. (d)(2). Pub. L. 111–5, §1131(b)(1), inserted "the Secretary of Energy, and the Secretary of the Interior," after "Environmental Protection Agency" and substituted "paragraph (1)(B) or (2)(C) of subsection (a)" for "subsection (a)(1)(B)" and ", oil and gas reservoirs, and unminable coal seams" for "and unminable coal seems".

Subsec. (e). Pub. L. 111–5, §1131(b)(3), substituted "taken into account in accordance with subsection (a)" for "captured and disposed of or used as a tertiary injectant".

STATUTORY NOTES AND RELATED SUBSIDIARIES

EFFECTIVE DATE OF 2021 AMENDMENT

Pub. L. 117–58, div. H, title IV, §80402(f), Nov. 15, 2021, 135 Stat. 1334, provided that: "The amendments made by this section [amending this section and sections 141, 142, and 146 of this title] shall apply to obligations issued after December 31, 2021."

EFFECTIVE DATE OF 2018 AMENDMENT

Pub. L. 115–123, div. D, title II, §41119(b), Feb. 9, 2018, 132 Stat. 168, provided that: "The amendment made by this section [amending this section] shall apply to taxable years beginning after December 31, 2017."

EFFECTIVE DATE OF 2014 AMENDMENT

Amendment by Pub. L. 113–295 effective as if included in the provisions of the American Recovery and Reinvestment Tax Act of 2009, Pub. L. 111–5, div. B, title I, to which such amendment relates, see section 209(k) of Pub. L. 113–295, set out as a note under section 24 of this title.

EFFECTIVE DATE OF 2009 AMENDMENT

Pub. L. 111–5, div. B, title I, §1131(c), Feb. 17, 2009, 123 Stat. 325, provided that: "The amendments made by this section [amending this section] shall apply to carbon dioxide captured after the date of the enactment of this Act [Feb. 17, 2009]."

EFFECTIVE DATE

Section applicable to carbon dioxide captured after Oct. 3, 2008, see section 115(d) of Pub. L. 110–343, set out as an Effective Date of 2008 Amendment note under section 38 of this title.

INFLATION ADJUSTED ITEMS FOR CERTAIN YEARS

Provisions relating to inflation adjustment of items in this section for certain years were contained in the following:

2021——Internal Revenue Notice 2021–35.
2020——Internal Revenue Notice 2020–40.
2019——Internal Revenue Notice 2019–31.
2018——Internal Revenue Notice 2018–40.
2017——Internal Revenue Notice 2017–32.
2016——Internal Revenue Notice 2016–53.
2015——Internal Revenue Notice 2015–44.
2014——Internal Revenue Notice 2014–40.
2013——Internal Revenue Notice 2013–34.
2012——Internal Revenue Notice 2012——42.
2011——Internal Revenue Notice 2011–50.
2010——Internal Revenue Notice 2010–75.

¹ *So in original. Probably should be "(8)".*

§45R. Employee health insurance expenses of small employers

(a) General rule

For purposes of section 38, in the case of an eligible small employer, the small employer health insurance credit determined under this section for any taxable year in the credit period is the amount determined under subsection (b).

(b) Health insurance credit amount

Subject to subsection (c), the amount determined under this subsection with respect to any eligible small employer is equal to 50 percent (35 percent in the case of a tax-exempt eligible small employer) of the lesser of—

(1) the aggregate amount of nonelective contributions the employer made on behalf of its employees during the taxable year under the arrangement described in subsection (d)(4) for premiums for qualified health plans offered by the employer to its employees through an Exchange, or

(2) the aggregate amount of nonelective contributions which the employer would have made during the taxable year under the arrangement if each employee taken into account under paragraph (1) had enrolled in a qualified health plan which had a premium equal to the average premium (as determined by the Secretary of Health and Human Services) for the small group market in the rating area in which the employee enrolls for coverage.

(c) Phaseout of credit amount based on number of employees and average wages

The amount of the credit determined under subsection (b) without regard to this subsection shall be reduced (but not below zero) by the sum of the following amounts:

(1) Such amount multiplied by a fraction the numerator of which is the total number of full-time equivalent employees of the employer in excess of 10 and the denominator of which is 15.

(2) Such amount multiplied by a fraction the numerator of which is the average annual wages of the employer in excess of the dollar amount in effect under subsection (d)(3)(B) and the denominator of which is such dollar amount.

(d) Eligible small employer

For purposes of this section—

(1) In general

The term "eligible small employer" means, with respect to any taxable year, an employer—

    (A) which has no more than 25 full-time equivalent employees for the taxable year,

    (B) the average annual wages of which do not exceed an amount equal to twice the dollar amount in effect under paragraph (3)(B) for the taxable year, and

    (C) which has in effect an arrangement described in paragraph (4).

(2) Full-time equivalent employees

(A) In general

The term "full-time equivalent employees" means a number of employees equal to the number determined by dividing—

    (i) the total number of hours of service for which wages were paid by the employer to employees during the taxable year, by

    (ii) 2,080.

Such number shall be rounded to the next lowest whole number if not otherwise a whole number.

(B) Excess hours not counted

If an employee works in excess of 2,080 hours of service during any taxable year, such excess shall not be taken into account under subparagraph (A).

(C) Hours of service

The Secretary, in consultation with the Secretary of Labor, shall prescribe such regulations, rules, and guidance as may be necessary to determine the hours of service of an employee, including rules for the application of this paragraph to employees who are not compensated on an hourly basis.

(3) Average annual wages

(A) In general

The average annual wages of an eligible small employer for any taxable year is the amount determined by dividing—

    (i) the aggregate amount of wages which were paid by the employer to employees during the taxable year, by

    (ii) the number of full-time equivalent employees of the employee determined under paragraph (2) for the taxable year.

Such amount shall be rounded to the next lowest multiple of $1,000 if not otherwise such a multiple.

(B) Dollar amount

For purposes of paragraph (1)(B) and subsection (c)(2)—

(i) 2010, 2011, 2012, and 2013

The dollar amount in effect under this paragraph for taxable years beginning in 2010, 2011, 2012, or 2013 is $25,000.

(ii) Subsequent years

In the case of a taxable year beginning in a calendar year after 2013, the dollar amount in effect under this paragraph shall be equal to $25,000, multiplied by the cost-of-living adjustment under section 1(f)(3) for the calendar year, determined by substituting "calendar year 2012" for "calendar year 2016" in subparagraph (A)(ii) thereof.

(4) Contribution arrangement

An arrangement is described in this paragraph if it requires an eligible small employer to make a nonelective contribution on behalf of each employee who enrolls in a qualified health plan offered to employees by the employer through an exchange in an amount equal to a uniform percentage (not less than 50 percent) of the premium cost of the qualified health plan.

(5) Seasonal worker hours and wages not counted

For purposes of this subsection—

(A) In general

The number of hours of service worked by, and wages paid to, a seasonal worker of an employer shall not be taken into account in determining the full-time equivalent employees and average annual wages of the employer unless the worker works for the employer on more than 120 days during the taxable year.

(B) Definition of seasonal worker

The term "seasonal worker" means a worker who performs labor or services on a seasonal basis as defined by the Secretary of Labor, including workers covered by section 500.20(s)(1) of title 29, Code of Federal Regulations and retail workers employed exclusively during holiday seasons.

(e) Other rules and definitions

For purposes of this section—

(1) Employee

(A) Certain employees excluded

The term "employee" shall not include—

    (i) an employee within the meaning of section 401(c)(1),

    (ii) any 2-percent shareholder (as defined in section 1372(b)) of an eligible small business which is an S corporation,

    (iii) any 5-percent owner (as defined in section 416(i)(1)(B)(i)) of an eligible small business, or

    (iv) any individual who bears any of the relationships described in subparagraphs (A) through (G) of section 152(d)(2) to, or is a dependent described in section 152(d)(2)(H) of, an individual described in clause (i), (ii), or (iii).

(B) Leased employees

The term "employee" shall include a leased employee within the meaning of section 414(n).

(2) Credit period

The term "credit period" means, with respect to any eligible small employer, the 2-consecutive-taxable year period beginning with the 1st taxable year in which the employer (or any predecessor) offers 1 or more qualified health plans to its employees through an Exchange.

(3) Nonelective contribution

The term "nonelective contribution" means an employer contribution other than an employer contribution pursuant to a salary reduction arrangement.

(4) Wages

The term "wages" has the meaning given such term by section 3121(a) (determined without regard to any dollar limitation contained in such section).

(5) Aggregation and other rules made applicable

(A) Aggregation rules

All employers treated as a single employer under subsection (b), (c), (m), or (o) of section 414 shall be treated as a single employer for purposes of this section.

(B) Other rules

Rules similar to the rules of subsections (c), (d), and (e) of section 52 shall apply.

(f) Credit made available to tax-exempt eligible small employers

(1) In general

In the case of a tax-exempt eligible small employer, there shall be treated as a credit allowable under subpart C (and not allowable under this subpart) the lesser of—

(A) the amount of the credit determined under this section with respect to such employer, or

(B) the amount of the payroll taxes of the employer during the calendar year in which the taxable year begins.

(2) Tax-exempt eligible small employer

For purposes of this section, the term "tax-exempt eligible small employer" means an eligible small employer which is any organization described in section 501(c) which is exempt from taxation under section 501(a).

(3) Payroll taxes

For purposes of this subsection—

(A) In general

The term "payroll taxes" means—

(i) amounts required to be withheld from the employees of the tax-exempt eligible small employer under section 3401(a),

(ii) amounts required to be withheld from such employees under section 3101(b), and

(iii) amounts of the taxes imposed on the tax-exempt eligible small employer under section 3111(b).

(B) Special rule

A rule similar to the rule of section 24(d)(2)(C) shall apply for purposes of subparagraph (A).

(g) Application of section for calendar years 2010, 2011, 2012, and 2013

In the case of any taxable year beginning in 2010, 2011, 2012, or 2013, the following modifications to this section shall apply in determining the amount of the credit under subsection (a):

(1) No credit period required

The credit shall be determined without regard to whether the taxable year is in a credit period and for purposes of applying this section to taxable years beginning after 2013, no credit period shall be treated as beginning with a taxable year beginning before 2014.

(2) Amount of credit

The amount of the credit determined under subsection (b) shall be determined—

(A) by substituting "35 percent (25 percent in the case of a tax-exempt eligible small employer)" for "50 percent (35 percent in the case of a tax-exempt eligible small employer)",

(B) by reference to an eligible small employer's nonelective contributions for premiums paid for health insurance coverage (within the meaning of section 9832(b)(1)) of an employee, and

(C) by substituting for the average premium determined under subsection (b)(2) the amount the Secretary of Health and Human Services determines is the average premium for the small group market in the State in which the employer is offering health insurance coverage (or for such area within the State as is specified by the Secretary).

(3) Contribution arrangement

An arrangement shall not fail to meet the requirements of subsection (d)(4) solely because it provides for the offering of insurance outside of an Exchange.

(h) Insurance definitions

Any term used in this section which is also used in the Public Health Service Act or subtitle A of title I of the Patient Protection and Affordable Care Act shall have the meaning given such term by such Act or subtitle.

(i) Regulations

The Secretary shall prescribe such regulations as may be necessary to carry out the provisions of this section, including regulations to prevent the avoidance of the 2-year limit on the credit period through the use of successor entities and the avoidance of the limitations under subsection (c) through the use of multiple entities.

(Added and amended Pub. L. 111–148, title I, §1421(a), title X, §10105(e)(1), (2), Mar. 23, 2010, 124 Stat. 237, 906; Pub. L. 115–97, title I, §11002(d)(1)(H), Dec. 22, 2017, 131 Stat. 2060.)

INFLATION ADJUSTED ITEMS FOR CERTAIN YEARS

For inflation adjustment of certain items in this section, see Revenue Procedures listed in a table under section 1 of this title.

EDITORIAL NOTES
REFERENCES IN TEXT

The Public Health Service Act, referred to in subsec. (h), is act July 1, 1944, ch. 373, 58 Stat. 682, which is classified generally to chapter 6A (§ 201 et seq.) of Title 42, The Public Health and Welfare. For complete classification of this Act to the Code, see Short Title note set out under section 201 of Title 42 and Tables.

The Patient Protection and Affordable Care Act, referred to in subsec. (h), is Pub. L. 111–148, Mar. 23, 2010, 124 Stat. 119. Subtitle A (§§1001 to 1004) of title I of the Act enacted sections 300gg–11 to 300gg–19, 300gg–93, and 300gg–94 of Title 42, The Public Health and Welfare, redesignated sections 300gg–4 to 300gg–7 of Title 42 as sections 300gg–25 to 300gg–28, respectively, of Title 42, and section 300gg–13 of Title 42 as section 300gg–9 of Title 42, amended former sections 300gg–11 and 300gg–12 and sections 300gg–21 to 300gg–23 of Title 42, and enacted provisions set out as a note under section 300gg–11 of Title 42. For complete classification of this Act to the Code, see Short Title note set out under section 18001 of Title 42 and Tables.

AMENDMENTS

2017—Subsec. (d)(3)(B)(ii). Pub. L. 115–97 substituted "for 'calendar year 2016' in subparagraph (A)(ii)" for "for 'calendar year 1992' in subparagraph (B)".

2010—Subsec. (d)(3)(B). Pub. L. 111–148, §10105(e)(1), amended subpar. (B) generally, including dollar amount for taxable years beginning in 2010 in addition to dollar amounts for taxable years beginning in 2011, 2012, and 2013, and subsequent years.

Subsec. (g). Pub. L. 111–148, §10105(e)(2), substituted "2010, 2011" for "2011" in heading and in introductory provisions.

STATUTORY NOTES AND RELATED SUBSIDIARIES
EFFECTIVE DATE OF 2017 AMENDMENT

Amendment by Pub. L. 115–97 applicable to taxable years beginning after Dec. 31, 2017, see section 11002(e) of Pub. L. 115–97, set out as a note under section 1 of this title.

EFFECTIVE DATE OF 2010 AMENDMENT

Pub. L. 111–148, title X, §10105(e)(5), Mar. 23, 2010, 124 Stat. 907, provided that: "The amendments made by this subsection [amending this section, section 280C of this title, and provisions set out as a note under section 38 of this title] shall take effect as if included in the enactment of section 1421 of this Act."

§45S. Employer credit for paid family and medical leave

(a) Establishment of credit

(1) In general

For purposes of section 38, in the case of an eligible employer, the paid family and medical leave credit is an amount equal to the applicable percentage of the amount of wages paid to qualifying employees during any period in which such employees are on family and medical leave.

(2) Applicable percentage

For purposes of paragraph (1), the term "applicable percentage" means 12.5 percent increased (but not above 25 percent) by 0.25 percentage points for each percentage point by which the rate of payment (as described under subsection (c)(1)(B)) exceeds 50 percent.

(b) Limitation

(1) In general

The credit allowed under subsection (a) with respect to any employee for any taxable year shall not exceed an amount equal to the product of the normal hourly wage rate of such employee for each hour (or fraction thereof) of actual services performed for the employer and the number of hours (or fraction thereof) for which family and medical leave is taken.

(2) Non-hourly wage rate

For purposes of paragraph (1), in the case of any employee who is not paid on an hourly wage rate, the wages of such employee shall be prorated to an hourly wage rate under regulations established by the Secretary.

(3) Maximum amount of leave subject to credit

The amount of family and medical leave that may be taken into account with respect to any employee under subsection (a) for any taxable year shall not exceed 12 weeks.

(c) Eligible employer

For purposes of this section—

(1) In general

The term "eligible employer" means any employer who has in place a written policy that meets the following requirements:

(A) The policy provides—

(i) in the case of a qualifying employee who is not a part-time employee (as defined in section 4980E(d)(4)(B)), not less than 2 weeks of annual paid family and medical leave, and

(ii) in the case of a qualifying employee who is a part-time employee, an amount of annual paid family and medical leave that is not less than an amount which bears the same ratio to the amount of annual paid family and medical leave that is provided to a qualifying employee described in clause (i) as—

(I) the number of hours the employee is expected to work during any week, bears to

(II) the number of hours an equivalent qualifying employee described in clause (i) is expected to work during the week.

(B) The policy requires that the rate of payment under the program is not less than 50 percent of the wages normally paid to such employee for services performed for the employer.

(2) Special rule for certain employers

(A) In general

An added employer shall not be treated as an eligible employer unless such employer provides paid family and medical leave in compliance with a written policy which ensures that the employer—

(i) will not interfere with, restrain, or deny the exercise of or the attempt to exercise, any right provided under the policy, and

(ii) will not discharge or in any other manner discriminate against any individual for opposing any practice prohibited by the policy.

(B) Added employer; added employee

For purposes of this paragraph—

(i) Added employee

The term "added employee" means a qualifying employee who is not covered by title I of the Family and Medical Leave Act of 1993, as amended.

(ii) Added employer

The term "added employer" means an eligible employer (determined without regard to this paragraph), whether or not covered by that title I, who offers paid family and medical leave to added employees.

(3) Aggregation rule

All persons which are treated as a single employer under subsections (a) and (b) of section 52 shall be treated as a single taxpayer.

(4) Treatment of benefits mandated or paid for by state or local governments

For purposes of this section, any leave which is paid by a State or local government or required by State or local law shall not be taken into account in determining the amount of paid family and medical leave provided by the employer.

(5) No inference

Nothing in this subsection shall be construed as subjecting an employer to any penalty, liability, or other consequence (other than ineligibility for the credit allowed by reason of subsection (a) or recapturing the benefit of such credit) for failure to comply with the requirements of this subsection.

(d) Qualifying employees

For purposes of this section, the term "qualifying employee" means any employee (as defined in section 3(e) of the Fair Labor Standards Act of 1938, as amended) who—

(1) has been employed by the employer for 1 year or more, and

(2) for the preceding year, had compensation not in excess of an amount equal to 60 percent of the amount applicable for such year under clause (i) of section 414(q)(1)(B).

(e) Family and medical leave

(1) In general

Except as provided in paragraph (2), for purposes of this section, the term "family and medical leave" means leave for any 1 or more of the purposes described under subparagraph (A), (B), (C), (D), or (E) of paragraph (1), or paragraph (3), of section 102(a) of the Family and Medical Leave Act of 1993, as amended, whether the leave is provided under that Act or by a policy of the employer.

(2) Exclusion

If an employer provides paid leave as vacation leave, personal leave, or medical or sick leave (other than leave specifically for 1 or more of the purposes referred to in paragraph (1)), that paid leave shall not be considered to be family and medical leave under paragraph (1).

(3) Definitions

In this subsection, the terms "vacation leave", "personal leave", and "medical or sick leave" mean those 3 types of leave, within the meaning of section 102(d)(2) of that Act.

(f) Determinations made by Secretary of Treasury

For purposes of this section, any determination as to whether an employer or an employee satisfies the applicable requirements for an eligible employer (as described in subsection (c)) or qualifying employee (as described in subsection (d)), respectively, shall be made by the Secretary based on such information, to be provided by the employer, as the Secretary determines to be necessary or appropriate.

(g) Wages

For purposes of this section, the term "wages" has the meaning given such term by subsection (b) of section 3306 (determined without regard to any dollar limitation contained in such section). Such term shall not include any amount taken into account for purposes of determining any other credit allowed under this subpart.

(h) Election to have credit not apply

(1) In general

A taxpayer may elect to have this section not apply for any taxable year.

(2) Other rules

Rules similar to the rules of paragraphs (2) and (3) of section 51(j) shall apply for purposes of this subsection.

(i) Termination

This section shall not apply to wages paid in taxable years beginning after December 31, 2025.

(Added Pub. L. 115–97, title I, §13403(a)(1), Dec. 22, 2017, 131 Stat. 2135; amended Pub. L. 116–94, div. Q, title I, §142(a), Dec. 20, 2019, 133 Stat. 3234; Pub. L. 116–260, div. EE, title I, §119(a), Dec. 27, 2020, 134 Stat. 3051.)

EDITORIAL NOTES
REFERENCES IN TEXT

The Family and Medical Leave Act of 1993 and that Act, referred to in subsecs. (c)(2)(B) and (e)(1), (3), is Pub. L. 103–3, Feb. 5, 1993, 107 Stat. 6. Title I of the Act is classified generally to subchapter I (§2611 et seq.) of chapter 28 of Title 29, Labor. Section 102 of the Act is classified to section 2612 of Title 29. For complete classification of this Act to the Code, see Short Title note set out under section 2601 of Title 29 and Tables.

Section 3(e) of the Fair Labor Standards Act of 1938, referred to in subsec. (d), is classified to section 203(e) of Title 29, Labor.

AMENDMENTS

2020—Subsec. (i). Pub. L. 116–260 substituted "December 31, 2025" for "December 31, 2020".

2019—Subsec. (i). Pub. L. 116–94 substituted "December 31, 2020" for "December 31, 2019".

STATUTORY NOTES AND RELATED SUBSIDIARIES
EFFECTIVE DATE OF 2020 AMENDMENT

Pub. L. 116–260, div. EE, title I, §119(b), Dec. 27, 2020, 134 Stat. 3051, provided that: "The amendment made by this section [amending this section] shall apply to wages paid in taxable years beginning after December 31, 2020."

EFFECTIVE DATE OF 2019 AMENDMENT

Pub. L. 116–94, div. Q, title I, §142(b), Dec. 20, 2019, 133 Stat. 3234, provided that: "The amendment made by this section [amending this section] shall apply to wages paid in taxable years beginning after December 31, 2019."

EFFECTIVE DATE

Section applicable to wages paid in taxable years beginning after Dec. 31, 2017, see section 13403(e) of Pub. L. 115–97, set out as an Effective Date of 2017 Amendment note under section 38 of this title.

§45T. Auto-enrollment option for retirement savings options provided by small employers

(a) In general

For purposes of section 38, in the case of an eligible employer, the retirement auto-enrollment credit determined under this section for any taxable year is an amount equal to—

(1) $500 for any taxable year occurring during the credit period, and

(2) zero for any other taxable year.

(b) Credit period

For purposes of subsection (a)—

(1) In general

The credit period with respect to any eligible employer is the 3-taxable-year period beginning with the first taxable year for which the employer includes an eligible automatic contribution arrangement (as defined in section 414(w)(3)) in a qualified employer plan (as defined in section 4972(d)) sponsored by the employer.

(2) Maintenance of arrangement

No taxable year with respect to an employer shall be treated as occurring within the credit period unless the arrangement described in paragraph (1) is included in the plan for such year.

(c) Eligible employer

For purposes of this section, the term "eligible employer" has the meaning given such term in section 408(p)(2)(C)(i).

(Added Pub. L. 116–94, div. O, title I, §105(a), Dec. 20, 2019, 133 Stat. 3148.)

STATUTORY NOTES AND RELATED SUBSIDIARIES
EFFECTIVE DATE

Section applicable to taxable years beginning after Dec. 31, 2019, see section 105(d) of Pub. L. 116–94, set out as an Effective Date of 2019 Amendment note under section 38 of this title.

Subpart E—Rules for Computing Investment Credit

EDITORIAL NOTES

AMENDMENTS

2018—Pub. L. 115–141, div. U, title IV, §401(d)(3)(A), Mar. 23, 2018, 132 Stat. 1209, struck out item 48D "Qualifying therapeutic discovery project credit".

2010—Pub. L. 111–148, title IX, §9023(d), Mar. 23, 2010, 124 Stat. 881, added item 48D.

2009—Pub. L. 111–5, div. B, title I, §1302(c)(2), Feb. 17, 2009, 123 Stat. 348, added item 48C.

2005—Pub. L. 109–58, title XIII, §1307(c)(2), Aug. 8, 2005, 119 Stat. 1006, added items 48A and 48B.

2004—Pub. L. 108–357, title III, §322(d)(2)(C), Oct. 22, 2004, 118 Stat. 1475, which directed amendment of item 48 by striking out ", reforestation credit", was executed by striking out "; reforestation credit" after "Energy credit" to reflect the probable intent of Congress.

1990—Pub. L. 101–508, title XI, §11813(a), Nov. 5, 1990, 104 Stat. 1388–536, amended heading and analysis generally, substituting in heading "Investment Credit" for "Credit for Investment in Certain Depreciable Property", in item 47 "Rehabilitation Credit" for "Certain dispositions, etc., of section 38 property", in item 48 "Energy credit; reforestation credit" for "Definitions; special rules", in item 49 "At-risk rules" for "Termination of regular percentage", and adding item 50.

1986—Pub. L. 99–514, title II, §211(c), Oct. 22, 1986, 100 Stat. 2168, added item 49.

1984—Pub. L. 98–369, div. A, title IV, §474(n)(1), July 18, 1984, 98 Stat. 833, substituted "E" for "B" as subpart designation.

1978—Pub. L. 95–600, title III, §312(c)(5), Nov. 6, 1978, 92 Stat. 2826, struck out item 49 "Termination for period beginning April 19, 1969, and ending during 1971" and item 50 "Restoration of credit".

1971—Pub. L. 92–178, title I, §101(b)(5), Dec. 10, 1971, 85 Stat. 499, substituted "Termination for period beginning April 19, 1969, and ending during 1971" for "Termination of credit" in item 49 and added item 50.

1969—Pub. L. 91–172, title VII, §703(d), Dec. 30, 1969, 83 Stat. 667, added item 49.

1962—Pub. L. 87–834, §2(b), Oct. 16, 1962, 76 Stat. 963, added subpart B.

§46. Amount of credit

For purposes of section 38, the amount of the investment credit determined under this section for any taxable year shall be the sum of—

(1) the rehabilitation credit,

(2) the energy credit,

(3) the qualifying advanced coal project credit,

(4) the qualifying gasification project credit,

(5) the qualifying advanced energy project credit, and

(6) the qualifying therapeutic discovery project credit.

(Added Pub. L. 87–834, §2(b), Oct. 16, 1962, 76 Stat. 963; amended Pub. L. 88–272, title II, §201(d)(4), Feb. 26, 1964, 78 Stat. 32; Pub. L. 89–384, §1(c)(1), Apr. 8, 1966, 80 Stat. 102; Pub. L. 89–389, §2(b)(5), Apr. 14, 1966, 80 Stat. 114; Pub. L. 89–800, §3, Nov. 8, 1966, 80 Stat. 1514; Pub. L. 90–225, §2(a), Dec. 27, 1967, 81 Stat. 731; Pub. L. 91–172, title III, §301(b)(4), title IV, §401(e)(1), title VII, §703(b), Dec. 30, 1969, 83 Stat. 585, 603, 666; Pub. L. 92–178, title I, §§102(a)(1), (b), 105(a)–(c), 106(a)–(c), 107(a)(1), 108(a), Dec. 10, 1971, 85 Stat. 499, 503, 506, 507; Pub. L. 93–406, title II, §§2001(g)(2)(B), 2002(g)(2), 2005(c)(4), Sept. 2, 1974, 88 Stat. 957, 968, 991; Pub. L. 94–12, title III, §301(a), (b)(1)–(3), 302(a), (b)(1), Mar. 29, 1975, 89 Stat. 36, 37, 40, 43; Pub. L. 94–455, title V, §503(b)(4), title VIII, §§802(a), (b)(1)–(5), 803(a), (b)(1), 805(a), title XVI, §1607(b)(1)(B), title XVII, §1701(b), 1703, title XIX, §§1901(a)(4), (b)(1)(C), 1906(b)(13)(A), title XXI, §2112(a)(2), Oct. 4, 1976, 90 Stat. 1562, 1580-1583, 1596, 1756, 1759, 1761, 1764, 1790, 1834, 1905; Pub. L. 95–600, title I, §141(e), (f)(2), title III, §§311(a), (c), 312(a), (b), (c)(2), 313(a), 316(a), (b)(1), (2), title VII, §703(a)(1), (2), (j)(9), Nov. 6, 1978, 92 Stat. 2794, 2795, 2824-2826, 2829, 2939, 2941; Pub. L. 95–618, title II, §241(a), title III, §301(a), (c)(1), Nov. 9, 1978, 92 Stat. 3192, 3194, 3199; Pub. L. 96–222, title I, §§101(a)(7)(A), (L)(iii)(I), (v)(I), (M)(i), 103(a)(2)(A), (B)(i)–(iii), (3), (4)(A), 107(a)(3)(A), Apr. 1, 1980, 94 Stat. 197, 200, 201, 208, 209, 223; Pub. L. 96–223, title II, §§221(a), 222(e)(2), 223(b)(1), Apr. 2, 1980, 94 Stat. 260, 263, 266; Pub. L. 97–34, title II, §§207(c)(1), 211(a)(1), (b), (d), (e)(1), (2), (f)(1), 212(a)(1), (2), title III, §§302(c)(3), (d)(1), 332(a), Aug. 13, 1981, 95 Stat. 225, 227-229, 235, 236, 272, 274, 296; Pub. L. 97–248, title II, §201(d)(8)(A), formerly §201(c)(8)(A), §§205(b), 265(b)(2)(A)(i), Sept. 3, 1982, 96 Stat. 420, 430, 547, renumbered §201(d)(8)(A), Pub. L. 97–448, title III, §306(a)(1)(A)(i), Jan. 12, 1983, 96 Stat. 2400; Pub. L. 97–354, §5(a)(4)–(6), Oct. 19, 1982, 96 Stat. 1692; Pub. L. 97–424, title V, §§541(b), 546(b), Jan. 6, 1983, 96 Stat. 2192, 2199; Pub. L. 97–448, title I, §102(e)(1), (f)(5), title II, §202(f), Jan. 12, 1983, 96 Stat. 2370, 2372, 2396; Pub. L. 98–21, title I, §122(c)(1), Apr. 20, 1983, 97 Stat. 87; Pub. L. 98–369, div. A, title I, §§16(a), 31(f), 113(b)(2)(B), title IV, §§431(a), (b)(1), (d)(1)–(3), 474(o)(1)–(7), title VII, §713(c)(1)(C), July 18, 1984, 98 Stat. 505, 521, 637, 805, 807, 810, 834-836, 957; Pub. L. 99–514, title II, §§201(d)(7)(B), 251(a), title IV, §421(a), (b), title XVIII, §§1802(a)(6), (8), 1844(a), (b)(3), (5), 1847(b)(11), 1848(a), Oct. 22, 1986, 100 Stat. 2141, 2183, 2229, 2789, 2855, 2857; Pub. L. 100–647, title I, §§1002(a)(4), (15), (17), (25), 1009(a)(1), 1013(a)(44), title IV, §4006, Nov. 10, 1988, 102 Stat. 3353, 3355, 3356, 3445, 3545, 3652; Pub. L. 101–239, title VII, §§7106, 7814(d), Dec. 19, 1989, 103 Stat. 2306, 2413; Pub. L. 101–508, title XI, §§11406, 11813(a), Nov. 5, 1990, 104 Stat. 1388–474, 1388-536; Pub.

L. 108–357, title III, §322(d)(1), Oct. 22, 2004, 118 Stat. 1475; Pub. L. 109–58, title XIII, §1307(a), Aug. 8, 2005, 119 Stat. 999; Pub. L. 111–5, div. B, title I, §1302(a), Feb. 17, 2009, 123 Stat. 345; Pub. L. 111–148, title IX, §9023(b), Mar. 23, 2010, 124 Stat. 880; Pub. L. 113–295, div. A, title II, §220(c), Dec. 19, 2014, 128 Stat. 4035.)

EDITORIAL NOTES
AMENDMENTS

2014—Par. (4). Pub. L. 113–295 inserted a comma at end.

2010—Par. (2). Pub. L. 111–148, §9023(b)(1), inserted a comma at end.

Par. (6). Pub. L. 111–148, §9023(b)(2), (3), added par. (6).

2009—Par. (5). Pub. L. 111–5 added par. (5).

2005—Pub. L. 109–58 struck out "and" at end of par. (1), struck out period at end of par. (2), and added pars. (3) and (4).

2004—Pub. L. 108–357 inserted "and" at end of par. (1), substituted a period for ", and" at end of par. (2), and struck out par. (3) which read as follows: "the reforestation credit."

1990—Pub. L. 101–508, §11813(a), amended section generally, substituting present provisions for provisions relating to amount of investment credit, determination of percentages, qualified investments and qualified progress expenditures, limitations with respect to certain persons, a limitation in the case of certain regulated companies, a 50 percent credit in the case of certain vessels, and special rule for cooperatives.

Subsec. (b)(2)(A). Pub. L. 101–508, §11406, substituted "Dec. 31, 1991" for "Sept. 30, 1990" in table items (viii) C. and (ix) B.

1989—Subsec. (b)(2)(A). Pub. L. 101–239, §7106, substituted "Sept. 30, 1990" for "Dec. 31, 1989" in table items (viii) C., (ix) B., and (x).

Pub. L. 101–239, §7814(d), made technical correction to language of Pub. L. 100–647, §4006, see 1988 Amendment note below.

1988—Subsec. (b)(2)(A). Pub. L. 100–647, §4006, as amended by Pub. L. 101–239, §7814(d), substituted "1989" for "1988" in table items (viii) C., (ix) B., and (x).

Subsec. (c)(5)(B). Pub. L. 100–647, §1013(a)(44), substituted "private activity bonds" for "industrial development bonds" in heading, and in text substituted "a private activity bond (within the meaning of section 141)" for "an industrial development bond (within the meaning of section 103(b)(2))".

Subsec. (c)(7). Pub. L. 100–647, §1002(a)(17), substituted "property to which section 168 applies" for "recovery property" in heading, substituted "property to which section 168 applies" for "recovery property" and "168(e)" for "168(c)" in subpar. (A), substituted "168(e)" for "168(c)" in subpar. (B), and inserted "(as in effect on the day before the date of the enactment of the Tax Reform Act of 1986)" after "section 168(f)(3)(B)" in concluding provisions.

Subsec. (d)(1)(B)(i). Pub. L. 100–647, §1002(a)(25)(A), substituted "property to which section 168 applies" for "recovery property (within the meaning of section 168)".

Subsec. (d)(1)(B)(ii). Pub. L. 100–647, §1002(a)(25)(B), substituted "to which section 168 does not apply" for "which is not recovery property (within the meaning of section 168)".

Subsec. (e)(3). Pub. L. 100–647, §1002(a)(15), substituted "property to which section 168 applies" for "recovery property (within the meaning of section 168)", "class life" for "present class life", and "168(i)(1)" for "168(g)(2)".

Subsec. (e)(4)(B). Pub. L. 100–647, §1002(a)(4)(A), substituted "168(i)(3)" for "168(j)(6)".

Subsec. (e)(4)(C). Pub. L. 100–647, §1009(a)(1), inserted provisions at end which provided that any such election shall terminate effective with respect to the 1st taxable year of the organization making such election which begins after 1986, and which defined "regular investment tax credit property".

Subsec. (e)(4)(D). Pub. L. 100–647, §1002(a)(4)(B), substituted "paragraphs (5) and (6) of section 168(h)" for "paragraphs (8) and (9) of section 168(j)".

Subsec. (e)(4)(E). Pub. L. 100–647, §1002(a)(4)(C), (D), substituted "168(h)" for "168(j)" and "168(h)(2)" for "168(j)(4)".

1986—Subsec. (b)(2)(A). Pub. L. 99–514, §1847(b)(11), substituted "48(l)(3)(A)(viii)" for "48(l)(3)(A)(vii)" in table item (ii).

Pub. L. 99–514, §421(a), inserted table items (viii) to (xi).

Subsec. (b)(2)(E). Pub. L. 99–514, §421(b), added subpar. (E).

Subsec. (b)(4). Pub. L. 99–514, §251(a), in amending par. (4) generally, substituted in subpar. (A) definition of "rehabilitation percentage" for former table specifying specific rehabilitation percentages, reenacted subpar. (B), and struck out subpar. (C) which related to definitions.

Subsec. (c)(8)(D)(v). Pub. L. 99–514, §1844(a), substituted "this subparagraph" for "clause (i)".

Pub. L. 99–514, §201(d)(7)(B), substituted "section 465(b)(3)(C)" for "section 168(e)(4)".

Subsec. (c)(9)(A). Pub. L. 99–514, §1844(b)(3), substituted "an increase in the credit base for" for "additional qualified investment in".

Subsec. (c)(9)(C)(i). Pub. L. 99–514, §1844(b)(5), substituted "any increase in a taxpayer's credit base for any property by reason of this paragraph shall be taken into account as if it were property placed in service by the taxpayer in the taxable year in which the property referred to in subparagraph (A) was first placed in service" for "any increase in a taxpayer's qualified investment in property by reason of this paragraph shall be deemed to be additional qualified investment made by the taxpayer in the year in which the property referred to in subparagraph (A) was first placed in service".

Subsec. (e)(4)(D), (E). Pub. L. 99–514, §1802(a)(6), (8), added subpars. (D) and (E).

Subsec. (f)(9). Pub. L. 99–514, §1848(a), struck out par. (9) which related to a special rule for additional credit.

1984—Subsec. (a). Pub. L. 98–369, §474(o)(1), amended subsec. (a) generally, so as to contain provisions relating to amount of investment credit, which formerly constituted only par. (2)(A)(i), (ii), and (iv) of subsec. (a).

Subsec. (a)(4). Pub. L. 98–369, §713(c)(1)(C), substituted "premature distributions to key employees" for "premature distributions to owner-employees".

Subsec. (b). Pub. L. 98–369, §474(o)(1), amended subsec. (b) generally, substituting provisions relating to determination of percentages for purposes of subsec. (a), for provisions relating to carryback and carryover of unused credits.

Subsec. (c)(7)(A). Pub. L. 98–369, §13(b)(2)(B), inserted "recovery" before first reference to "property".

Subsec. (c)(8). Pub. L. 98–369, §431(a), substituted "Certain nonrecourse financing excluded from credit base" for "Limitation to amount at risk" in heading.

Subsec. (c)(8)(A). Pub. L. 98–369, §431(a), substituted provisions reducing the credit base of any property to which this paragraph applies by the nonqualified nonrecourse financing with respect to such property for provisions relating to limitation of the basis to the amount at risk in the case of new or used section 38 property placed in service during the taxable year by a taxpayer described in section 465(a)(1) and used in connection with an activity with respect to which any loss was subject to limitation under section 465.

Subsec. (c)(8)(B). Pub. L. 98–369, §431(a), substituted provisions relating to the property to which this paragraph applies for provisions defining "at risk" and stating the circumstances under which a taxpayer would be considered to be at risk for purposes of this paragraph.

Subsec. (c)(8)(C). Pub. L. 98–369, §431(a), substituted provisions defining "credit base" for provisions relating to a special rule for partnerships and subchapter S corporations.

Subsec. (c)(8)(D). Pub. L. 98–369, §431(a), substituted provisions defining "nonqualified nonrecourse financing" for provisions defining "qualified person".

Subsec. (c)(8)(D)(i)(I). Pub. L. 98–369, §16(a), repealed amendments made by Pub. L. 97–34, §302(c). See 1981 Amendment note below.

Subsec. (c)(8)(E). Pub. L. 98–369, §431(a), substituted provisions relating to the application of this paragraph to partnerships and subchapter S corporations for provisions defining "related person".

Subsec. (c)(8)(F)(i). Pub. L. 98–369, §431(d)(1), substituted provisions that subpar. (A) shall not apply with respect to qualified energy property for provisions that subpar. (A) would not apply to amounts borrowed with respect to qualified energy property (other than amounts described in subpar. (B)).

Subsec. (c)(8)(F)(ii)(II). Pub. L. 98–369, §474(o)(2), substituted "subsection (b)(2)" for "section 46(a)(2)(C)".

Subsec. (c)(8)(F)(ii)(III). Pub. L. 98–369, §431(d)(2), substituted provisions that qualified energy property means energy property to which (but for this subpar.) subpar. (A) applies and not more than 75 percent of the basis of which is attributable to nonqualified nonrecourse financing for provisions that qualified energy property meant energy property to which (but for this subpar.) subpar. (A) applied and with respect to which the taxpayer was at risk (within the meaning of section 465(b) without regard to par. (5) thereof) in an amount equal to at least 25 percent of the basis of the property.

Subsec. (c)(8)(F)(ii)(IV). Pub. L. 98–369, §431(d)(3), substituted "nonqualified nonrecourse financing" for "nonrecourse financing (other than financing described in section 46(c)(8)(B)(ii))".

Subsec. (c)(9). Pub. L. 98–369, §431(b)(1), substituted provisions relating to subsequent decreases in nonqualified nonrecourse financing with respect to the property for provisions relating to subsequent increases in the taxpayer's amount at risk with respect to the property.

Subsec. (e)(1). Pub. L. 98–369, §474(o)(3)(A), struck out "and the $25,000 amount specified under subparagraphs (A) and (B) of subsection (a)(3)", and substituted "such qualified investment" for "such items", in provisions following subpar. (B).

Subsec. (e)(2). Pub. L. 98–369, §474(o)(3)(B), substituted "qualified investment" for "the items described therein" in introductory provisions.

Subsec. (e)(4). Pub. L. 98–369, §31(b), added par. (4).

Subsec. (f)(1). Pub. L. 98–369, §474(o)(4)(A), substituted "no credit determined under subsection (a) shall be allowed by section 38" for "no credit shall be allowed by section 38" in introductory provisions.

Subsec. (f)(1)(A), (B). Pub. L. 98–369, §474(o)(4)(B), substituted "the credit determined under subsection (a) and allowable by section 38" for "the credit allowable by section 38".

Subsec. (f)(2). Pub. L. 98–369, §474(o)(4)(A), substituted "no credit determined under subsection (a) shall be allowed by section 38" for "no credit shall be allowed by section 38" in introductory provisions.

Subsec. (f)(2)(A), (B). Pub. L. 98–369, §474(o)(4)(B), substituted "the credit determined under subsection (a) and allowable by section 38" for "the credit allowable by section 38".

Subsec. (f)(4)(B). Pub. L. 98–369, §474(o)(4)(C), substituted "the credit determined under subsection (a) and allowed by section 38" for "the credit allowed by section 38" in introductory provisions.

Subsec. (f)(8). Pub. L. 98–369, §474(o)(5), substituted "the credit determined under subsection (a) and allowable under section 38" for "the credit allowable under section 38" in two places, and "(within the meaning of the first sentence of subsection (c)(3)(B))" for "(within the meaning of subsection (a)(7)(C))".

Subsec. (g)(2). Pub. L. 98–369, §474(o)(6), substituted "the limitation of section 38(c)" for "the limitation of subsection (a)(3)".

Subsec. (h)(1). Pub. L. 98–369, §474(o)(7), substituted "the credit determined under subsection (a) and allowable to the organization under section 38" for "the credit allowable to the organization under section 38" and "the limitation contained in section 38(c)" for "the limitation contained in subsection (a)(3)".

1983—Subsec. (a)(2)(C)(i). Pub. L. 97–424, §546(b), added section VII to the table.

Subsec. (a)(2)(C)(iii)(I). Pub. L. 97–448, §202(f), substituted "before January 1, 1983, all engineering studies in connection with the commencement of the construction of the project have been completed and all environmental and construction permits required under Federal, State, or local law in connection with the commencement of the construction of the project have been applied for, and" for "before January 1, 1983, the taxpayer has completed all engineering studies in connection with the commencement of the construction of the project, and has applied for all environmental and construction permits required under Federal, State, or local law in connection with the commencement of the construction of the project, and".

Subsec. (a)(2)(F)(iii)(II). Pub. L. 97–448, §102(f)(5)(A), substituted "a qualified rehabilitated building" for "any building".

Subsec. (a)(2)(F)(iii)(III). Pub. L. 97–448, §102(f)(5)(B), substituted "means a qualified rehabilitated building which meets the requirements of section 48(g)(3)" for "has the meaning given to such term by section 48(g)(3)".

Subsec. (a)(4)(B). Pub. L. 98–21 substituted "relating to credit for the elderly and the permanently and totally disabled" for "relating to credit for the elderly".

Subsec. (c)(7). Pub. L. 97–448, §102(e)(1), substituted "in the case of property other than 3-year property (within the meaning of section 168(c))" for "in the case of 15-year public utility, 10-year, or 5-year property (within the meaning of section 168(c))" in subpar. (A) and, in provisions following subpar. (B), substituted "shall be treated as property which is not 3-year property" for "shall be treated as 5-year property".

Subsec. (f)(10). Pub. L. 97–424, §541(b), added par. (10).

1982—Subsec. (a)(3)(B). Pub. L. 97–248, §205(b)(1), substituted "85 percent" for "the following percentage", substituted a period for the colon, and struck out table of percentages at end of subpar. (B).

Subsec. (a)(4). Pub. L. 97–354, §5(a)(4), substituted "section 1374 (relating to tax on certain capital gains of S corporations)" for "section 1378 (relating to tax on certain capital gains of subchapter S corporations)".

Pub. L. 97–248, §§201(d)(8)(A), formerly 201(c)(8)(A), 265(b)(2)(A), substituted "(relating to corporate minimum tax)" for "(relating to minimum tax for tax preferences)" after "section 56", and inserted "section 72(q)(1) (relating to 5-percent tax on premature distributions under annuity contracts)," after "owner-employees)".

Subsec. (a)(7). Pub. L. 97–248, §205(b)(2), redesignated par. (9) as (7), and, in par. (7)(B), as so redesignated, substituted reference to 85 percent for former reference to the percentage determined under subsec. (a)(3)(B) in cl. (i), struck out former cl. (ii), which provided that pars. (7) and (8) would not apply in certain instances, and redesignated former cl. (iii) as (ii). Former par. (7), which provided for alternative limitations in the case of certain utilities, was struck out.

Subsec. (a)(8). Pub. L. 97–248, §205(b)(2)(A), struck out par. (8) which provided for alternative limitations in the case of certain railroads and airlines.

Subsec. (a)(9). Pub. L. 97–248, §205(b)(2)(A), redesignated par. (9) as (7).

Subsec. (c)(8)(C). Pub. L. 97–354, §5(a)(5), substituted "S corporation" for "electing small business corporation (within the meaning of section 1371(b))".

Subsec. (e)(3). Pub. L. 97–354, §5(a)(6), substituted "an S corporation" for "an electing small business corporation (as defined in section 1371)".

1981—Subsec. (a)(2)(A)(iv). Pub. L. 97–34, §212(a)(1), added cl. (iv).

Subsec. (a)(2)(E). Pub. L. 97–34, §332(a), substituted "December 31, 1982" for "December 31, 1983" in cls. (i) and (ii) and added cl. (iii).

Subsec. (a)(2)(F). Pub. L. 97–34, §212(a)(2), added subpar. (F).

Subsec. (b)(1). Pub. L. 97–34, §207(c)(1), inserted provision after subpar. (D) directing that, in the case of an unused credit for an unused credit year ending after Dec. 31, 1973, this paragraph be applied by substituting "15" for "7" in subpar. (B) and by substituting "18" for "10" and "17" for "9" in second sentence.

Subsec. (c)(2). Pub. L. 97–34, §211(e)(1), inserted references in provisions preceding table to exceptions provided in paragraphs (3), (6), and (7).

Subsec. (c)(6)(A). Pub. L. 97–34, §211(e)(2), substituted "Notwithstanding paragraph (2) or (3)" for "Notwithstanding paragraph (2)" and inserted "or which is recovery property (within the meaning of section 168)," after "3 years or more,".

Subsec. (c)(7). Pub. L. 97–34, §211(a)(1), added par. (7).

Subsec. (c)(8). Pub. L. 97–34, §211(f)(1), added par. (8).

Subsec. (c)(8)(D)(i)(I). Pub. L. 97–34, §302(c)(3), (d)(1), provided that, applicable to taxable years beginning after Dec. 31, 1984, subsection (c)(8)(D)(i)(I) of this section (relating to limitation to amount at risk) is amended by striking out "clause (i), (ii), or (iii) of subparagraph (A) or subparagraph (B) of section 128(c)(2)" and inserting in lieu thereof "subparagraph (A) or (B) of section 128(c)(1)". Section 16(a) of Pub. L. 98–369, repealed section 302(c) of Pub. L. 97–34, and provided that this title shall be applied and administered as if section 302(c), and the amendments made by section 302(c), had not been enacted.

Subsec. (c)(9). Pub. L. 97–34, §211(f)(1), added par. (9).

Subsec. (d)(1). Pub. L. 97–34, §211(b)(1), designated existing provisions as subpar. (A), substituted "an amount equal to the aggregate of the applicable percentage of each qualified progress expenditure for the taxable year" for "an amount equal to his aggregate qualified progress expenditures for the taxable year" in subpar. (A) as so designated, and added subpar. (B).

Subsec. (d)(2)(A)(ii). Pub. L. 97–34, §211(b)(2), struck out "having a useful life of 7 years or more" after "it is reasonable to believe will be new section 38 property".

Subsec. (e)(3). Pub. L. 97–34, §211(d), in provisions following subpar. (B), inserted provision that, for purposes of subpar. (B), in the case of any recovery property (within the meaning of section 168), the useful life be the present class life for such property (as defined in section 168(g)(2)).

1980—Subsec. (a)(2)(A). Pub. L. 96–222, §101(a)(7)(L)(iii)(I), substituted "employee plan" for "ESOP".

Subsec. (a)(2)(C). Pub. L. 96–223, §221(a), revised provisions relating to energy percentage by substituting a tabular format embracing separate coverage for solar, wind, or geothermal property, ocean thermal property, qualified hydroelectric generating property, and biomass property using percentages varying between 10 and 15 percent and covering periods from Oct. 1, 1978, to Dec. 31, 1985, with longer periods for certain long-term projects and certain hydroelectric generating property for provisions that had set the energy percentage at 10 percent for the period beginning Oct. 1, 1978, and ending Dec. 31, 1982, and zero with respect to any other period.

Subsec. (a)(2)(D). Pub. L. 96–223, §222(e)(2), inserted provision that in the case of any qualified hydroelectric generating property which is a fish passageway, the special rule for certain energy property embraced in the first sentence would not apply to any period after 1979 for which the energy percentage for such property is greater than zero.

Subsec. (a)(2)(E). Pub. L. 96–222, §101(a)(7)(L)(v)(I), (M)(i), substituted in heading "employee plan" for "ESOP" and in cls. (i) and (ii) inserted "and ending on" before "December 31, 1983".

Subsec. (a)(9). Pub. L. 96–222, §103(a)(2)(B)(i), redesignated par. (10) as (9). A former par. (9) was previously repealed by section 312(b)(2) of Pub. L. 95–600.

Subsec. (a)(9)(A). Pub. L. 96–223, §223(b)(1)(A), inserted "and" at end of cl. (i), substituted a period for "(other than solar wind energy property), and" at end of cl. (ii), and struck out cl. (iii) which had provided for the application of so much of the credit allowed by section 38 as was attributable to the application of the energy percentage to solar or wind energy property.

Subsec. (a)(9)(B). Pub. L. 96–223. §223(b)(1)(B), struck out "other than solar or wind energy property" after "energy property" in heading.

Pub. L. 96–222, §103(a)(2)(B)(ii), (iii), substituted "paragraph (3)(B) shall be applied by substituting '100 percent' for the percentage determined under the table contained in such paragraph" for "paragraph (3)(C) shall be applied by substituting '100 percent' for '50 percent' " in cl. (i) and "(7) and (8)" for "(7), (8), and (9)" in cl. (ii).

Subsec. (a)(9)(C). Pub. L. 96–223, §223(b)(1)(C), struck out subpar. (C) which related to a refundable credit for solar or wind energy property.

Subsec. (a)(10). Pub. L. 96–222, §103(a)(2)(B)(i), redesignated par. (10) as (9).

Subsec. (c)(5)(B). Pub. L. 96–222, §103(a)(3), inserted provisions requiring that this subparagraph not apply for purposes of applying the energy percentage.

Subsec. (e)(3). Pub. L. 96–222, §103(a)(4)(A), inserted provisions requiring that this paragraph not apply with respect to any property which is treated as section 38 property by reason of section 48(a)(1)(E).

Subsec. (f)(1), (2). Pub. L. 95–600, §312(c)(2), as amended by Pub. L. 96–222, §103(a)(2)(A), substituted " 'described in section 50 (as in effect before its repeal by the Revenue Act of 1978)' " for " 'described in section 50' ".

Subsec. (f)(8). Pub. L. 96–222, §107(a)(3)(A), substituted "subsection (a)(7)(C)" for "subsection (a)(7)(D)".

Subsec. (f)(9). Pub. L. 96–222, §101(a)(7)(A), substituted in provisions preceding subpar. (A) "subparagraph (E) of subsection (a)(2)" for "subparagraph (B) of subsection (a)(2)" and in subpar. (A) "a tax credit employee stock ownership plan which meets the requirements of section 409A" for "an employee ownership plan which meets the requirements of section 301(d) of the Tax Reduction Act of 1975".

1978—Subsec. (a)(2). Pub. L. 95–618, §301(a)(1), among other changes, inserted provisions relating to an alternative energy property tax credit which would pay for a certain percentage of the cost of equipment which uses sources of energy other than oil and gas and of associated pollution control, handling, and preparation equipment.

Subsec. (a)(2)(B). Pub. L. 95–600, §311(a), made 10 percent limitation on investment tax credit permanent.

Subsec. (a)(2)(E). Pub. L. 95–600, §141(e), (f)(2), substituted "December 31, 1983" for "and ending on December 31, 1980" wherever appearing, "section 48(n)(1)(B)" for "section 301(e) of the Tax Reduction Act of 1975" and "section 409A" for "section 301(d) of the Tax Reduction Act of 1975".

Subsec. (a)(3). Pub. L. 95–600, §312(a), increased the present 50 percent tax liability limitation to 90 percent, to be phased in at an additional 10 percentage points per year beginning with taxable years which end in 1979.

Subsec. (a)(7). Pub. L. 95–600, §312(b)(1), in subpar. (A) substituted "the taxable year ending in 1979" for "a taxable year ending after calendar year 1974 and before calendar year 1981", "subparagraph (B)" for "subparagraph (C)", and "for '60 percent' the taxpayer's" for "for 50 percent his" and inserted "the application of this paragraph results in a percentage higher than 60 percent," before "then subparagraph (B)"; in subpar. (B) substituted "70 percent" for "50 percent plus the tentative percentage for such year"; struck out former subpar. (C), which related to the determination of the tentative percentage, and redesignated former subpar. (D) as (C).

Subsec. (a)(8). Pub. L. 95–600, §312(b)(2), in subpar. (A) substituted "the taxable year ending in 1979" for "a taxable year ending after calendar year 1976, and before calendar year 1983", "subparagraph (B)" for "subparagraph (C)", and "for '60 percent' ('70 percent' in the case of a taxable year ending in 1980) the taxpayer's" for "for 50 percent his" and inserted reference to airline property and "the application of this paragraph results in a percentage higher than 60 percent (70 percent in the case of a taxable year ending in 1980)," before "then subparagraph (B)"; in subpar. (B) inserted reference to airline property and substituted "90 percent (80 percent in the case of a taxable year ending in 1980)" for "50 percent plus the tentative percentage for such year"; in subpar. (C) table struck out tentative percentage of 50 for 1977 or 1978, 20 for 1981, and 10 for 1982; and added subpar. (E).

Subsec. (a)(9). Pub. L. 95–600, §312(b)(2), struck out par. (9) which related to the alternative limitation in the case of certain airlines.

Subsec. (a)(10). Pub. L. 95–618, §301(c)(1), added par. (10).

Subsec. (c)(3)(A). Pub. L. 95–618, §301(a)(2)(A), substituted "For the period beginning on January 1, 1981, in the case of any property" for "To the extent that subsection (a)(2)(C) applies to property" and inserted provisions that the preceding sentence not apply for purposes of applying the energy percentage.

Pub. L. 95–600, §311(c)(1), substituted "To the extent that the credit allowed by section 38 with respect to any public utility property is determined at the rate of 7 percent" for "For the period beginning on January 1, 1981".

Subsec. (c)(5). Pub. L. 95–600, §313(a), increased the investment credit available to pollution control facilities which a taxpayer has elected to amortize over a five-year period to a full investment credit from a one-half investment credit.

Subsec. (c)(6). Pub. L. 95–618, §241(a), added par. (6).

Subsec. (e)(1)(C). Pub. L. 95–600, §316(b)(1), struck out subpar. (C) which related to a cooperative organization described in section 1381(a).

Subsec. (e)(2)(C). Pub. L. 95–600, §316(b)(2), struck out subpar. (C) which related to a cooperative organization.

Subsec. (f)(1), (2). Pub. L. 95–600, §312(c)(2), struck out "described in section 50" after "with respect to any property". See 1980 Amendment note above.

Subsec. (f)(8). Pub. L. 95–618, §301(a)(2)(B), substituted ", the Tax Reform Act of 1976, and the Energy Tax Act of 1978" for "and the Tax Reform Act of 1976".

Pub. L. 95–600, §§311(c)(2), 703(a)(1), substituted "subsection (a)(7)(D)" for "subsection (a)(6)(D)" and inserted reference to the Revenue Act of 1978.

Subsec. (g)(5). Pub. L. 95–600, §703(a)(2), substituted "Merchant Marine Act, 1936" for "Merchant Marine Act, 1970".

Subsec. (h). Pub. L. 95–600, §316(a), added subsec. (h).

1976—Subsec. (a)(1). Pub. L. 94–455, §802(a)(2), added par. (1) and struck out former par. (1) which related to the percentage of allowable credit under section 38.

Subsec. (a)(2). Pub. L. 94–455, §802(a)(2), added par. (2). Former par. (2) redesignated (3).

Subsec. (a)(3). Pub. L. 94–455, §802(a)(1), redesignated former par. (2) as (3). Former par. (3) redesignated (4).

Subsec. (a)(4). Pub. L. 94–455, §§503(b)(4), 802(a)(1), (b)(1), 1901(a)(4)(A), (b)(1)(C), as amended by Pub. L. 95–600, §703(j)(9), redesignated former par. (3) as (4), and in par. (4) as so redesignated, redesignated former subpar. (C) as (B) and substituted in provisions preceding subpar. (A) "paragraph (3)" for "paragraph (2)", in subpar. (B) as so redesignated "credit for the elderly" for "retirement income", and in provisions following subpar. (B) "section 408(f)" for "section 408(e)". Former par. (4) redesignated (5).

Subsec. (a)(5). Pub. L. 94–455, §802(a)(1), (b)(1), redesignated former par. (4) as (5) and substituted "paragraph (3)" for "paragraph (2)". Former par. (5) redesignated (6).

Subsec. (a)(6). Pub. L. 94–455, §§802(a)(1), (b)(1), 1906(b)(13)(A), redesignated former par. (5) as (6) and substituted "paragraph (3)" for "paragraph (2)" and struck out "or his delegate" after "Secretary". Former par. (6) redesignated (7).

Subsec. (a)(7). Pub. L. 94–455, §802(a)(1), (b)(1), redesignated former par. (6) as (7) and substituted "paragraph (3)" for "paragraph (2)".

Subsec. (a)(8). Pub. L. 94–455, §1701(b), added par. (8).

Subsec. (a)(9). Pub. L. 94–455, §1703, added par. (9).

Subsec. (b). Pub. L. 94–455, §802(b)(2), among other changes, inserted requirement that tax credits carried over are applied first to the tax liability for that year, after which tax credits earned currently are then applied.

Subsec. (c)(3)(A). Pub. L. 94–455, §802(b)(3), substituted "subsection (a)(2)(C)" for "subsection (a)(1)(C)".

Subsec. (c)(3)(B)(iii). Pub. L. 94–455, §1901(a)(4)(B), substituted "47 U.S.C. 222(a)(5)" for "47 U.S.C., sec. 222(a)(5)".

Subsec. (c)(5). Pub. L. 94–455, §2112(a)(2), added par. (5).

Subsec. (d)(4)(D), (6). Pub. L. 94–455, §1906(b)(13)(A), struck out "or his delegate" after "Secretary".

Subsec. (e)(1)(C). Pub. L. 94–455, §802(b)(4), substituted "subsection (a)(3)" for "subsection (a)(2)".

Subsec. (e)(2). Pub. L. 94–455, §1607(b)(1)(B), substituted in subpar. (B) "857(b)(2)(B)" for "857(b)(2)(C)" and inserted in provisions following subpar. (C) reference to determine without regard to any deduction for capital gains dividends (as defined in section 857(b)(3)(C)) and by excluding any net capital gain.

Subsec. (f)(1)(B), (2), (3). Pub. L. 94–455, §1906(b)(13)(A), struck out "or his delegate" after "Secretary".

Subsec. (f)(4)(A). Pub. L. 94–455, §803(b)(1)(A), (B), substituted "paragraphs (1), (2), and (9)" for "paragraphs (1) and (2)" and "paragraph (1), (2), or (9)" for "paragraph (1) or (2)" wherever appearing.

Subsec. (f)(4)(B)(ii). Pub. L. 94–455, §803(b)(1)(C), substituted "paragraph (2) or the election described in paragraph (9)," for "paragraph (2),".

Subsec. (f)(7). Pub. L. 94–455, §1906(b)(13)(A), struck out "or his delegate" after "Secretary".

Subsec. (f)(8). Pub. L. 94–455, §§802(b)(5), 1906(b)(13)(A), inserted reference to the Tax Reform Act of 1976 and struck out "or his delegate" after "Secretary".

Subsec. (f)(9). Pub. L. 94–455, §803(a), added par. (9).

Subsec. (g). Pub. L. 94–455, §805(a), added subsec. (g).

1975—Subsec. (a)(1). Pub. L. 94–12, §301(a), designated existing provisions as subpar. (A), substituted "Except as otherwise provided in this paragraph, in the case of a property described in subparagraph (D), the" for "The", "10 percent" for "7 percent", and "(as determined under subsections (c) and (d))" for "(as defined in subsection (c))" in subpar. (A) as so designated, and added subpars. (B), (C), and (D).

Subsec. (a)(6). Pub. L. 94–12, §301(b)(2), added par. (6).

Subsec. (c)(3)(A). Pub. L. 94–12, §301(b)(1), substituted "To the extent that subsection (a)(1)(C) applies to property which is public utility property, the" for "In the case of section 38 property which is public utility property, the".

Subsec. (c)(4). Pub. L. 94–12, §302(b)(1), added par. (4).

Subsecs. (d), (e). Pub. L. 94–12, §302(a), added subsec. (d) and redesignated former subsec. (d) as (e). Former subsec. (e) redesignated (f) and amended.

Subsec. (f). Pub. L. 94–12, §§301(b)(3), 302(a), redesignated former subsec. (e) as (f) and in subsec. (f) as so redesignated added par. (8).

1974—Subsec. (a)(3). Pub. L. 93–406 inserted reference to section 402(e) (relating to tax on lump sum distributions), section 72(m)(5)(B) (relating to 10 percent tax on premature distributions to owner-employees), and section 408(e) (relating to additional tax on income from certain retirement accounts).

1971—Subsec. (b)(1). Pub. L. 92–178, §106(b), inserted concluding sentence "In the case of an unused credit for an unused credit year ending before January 1, 1971, which is an investment credit carryover to a taxable year beginning after December 31, 1970 (determined without regard to this sentence), this paragraph shall be applied by substituting '10 taxable years' for '7 taxable years' in subparagraph (B) and by substituting '13 taxable years' for '10 taxable years' and '12 taxable years' for '9 taxable years' in the preceding sentence."

Subsec. (b)(3). Pub. L. 92–178, §106(a), added par. (3).

Subsec. (b)(5). Pub. L. 92–178, §106(c)(1), substituted "Certain taxable years ending in 1969, 1970, or 1971" for "Taxable years beginning after December 31, 1968, and ending after April 18, 1969" in heading; substituted "ending after April 18, 1969, and before January 1, 1972," for "ending after April 18, 1969,"; and provided that "In the case of a taxable year ending after August 15, 1971, and before January 1, 1972, the percentage contained in the preceding sentence shall be increased by 6 percentage points for each month (or portion thereof) in the taxable year after August 15, 1971."

Subsec. (b)(6). Pub. L. 92–178, §106(c)(2), substituted "ending after April 18, 1969, and before January 1, 1971," for "ending after April 18, 1969," and "following the 7th taxable year after the unused credit year" for "following the last taxable year for which such portion may be added under paragraph (1)", respectively.

Subsec. (c)(2). Pub. L. 92–178, §102(a)(1), (b), substituted "3 years", "5 years", and "7 years" for "4 years" (once), "6 years" (twice), and "8 years" (twice), respectively in tables of first sentence and substituted in second sentence "subpart" for "paragraph" and "useful life of any property shall be the useful life used in computing the allowance for depreciation under section 167 for the taxable year in which the property is placed in service" for "useful life of any property shall be determined as of the time such property is placed in service by the taxpayer".

Subsec. (c)(3)(A). Pub. L. 92–178, §105(a), substituted the fraction of "4/7" for "3/7".

Subsec. (c)(3)(B). Pub. L. 92–178, §105(b)(1), (2), struck out cl. (iii) provisions respecting telephone service, redesignated cl. (iv) as (iii), included in cl. (iii) provision of former cl. (iii) respecting telephone service, included other communication services (other than international telegraph service), and defined term "public utility property" to also mean communication property of type used by persons engaged in providing telephone or microwave communication services to which cl. (iii) applies, if such property is used predominantly for communication purposes, respectively.

Subsec. (c)(3)(C). Pub. L. 92–178, §105(b)(3), added subpar. (C).

Subsec. (c)(4). Pub. L. 92–178, §107(a)(1), struck out provisions respecting reduction in basis or cost of certain replacement property.

Subsec. (d)(3). Pub. L. 92–178, §108(a), added par. (3).

Subsec. (e). Pub. L. 92–178, §105(c), added subsec. (e).

1969—Subsec. (a)(3). Pub. L. 91–172, §301(b)(4), inserted "section 56 (relating to minimum tax for tax preference),".

Subsec. (a)(5). Pub. L. 91–172, §401(e)(1), reenacted subsection with minor changes and substituted reference to section 1563(a) for reference to section 1504.

Subsec. (b)(5), (6). Pub. L. 91–172, §703(b), added pars. (5) and (6).

1967—Subsec. (b). Pub. L. 90–225 struck out par. (3) which provided that to the extent that the excess described in par. (1) of this subsection arises by reason of net operating loss carryback, subpar. (A) of par. (1) of this subsection shall not apply.

1966—Subsec. (a)(2). Pub. L. 89–800, §3(a), inserted "for taxable years ending on or before the last day of the suspension period (as defined in section 48(j))," at beginning of subpar. (B), and added subpar. (C) and provisions following subpar. (C) covering the application of subpar. (C) and the reduction of the amount otherwise determined under par. (2) by the credit allowable but for the application of section 48(h)(1).

Subsec. (a)(3). Pub. L. 89–389 inserted reference to tax imposed for the taxable year by section 1378 (relating to tax on certain capital gains of subchapter S corporations) in the list of taxes not to be considered tax imposed by this chapter for purposes of par. (3).

Pub. L. 89–384 added any additional tax imposed for the taxable year by section 1351 (relating to recoveries of foreign expropriation losses) to the list of taxes not to be considered a tax imposed by this chapter for purposes of par. (3).

Subsec. (b)(1). Pub. L. 89–800, §3(b), substituted "7 taxable years" for "5 taxable years" in subpar. (B) and "10 taxable years" and "other 9 taxable years" for "8 taxable years" and "other 7 taxable years", respectively, in text following subpar. (B).

1964—Subsec. (a)(3)(B) to (D). Pub. L. 88–272 struck out subpar. (B) relating to section 34, and redesignated subpars. (C) and (D) as (B) and (C), respectively.

EFFECTIVE DATE OF 2010 AMENDMENT

Pub. L. 111–148, title IX, §9023(f), Mar. 23, 2010, 124 Stat. 883, provided that: "The amendments made by subsections (a) through (d) of this section [enacting section 48D of this title and amending this section and sections 49 and 280C of this title] shall apply to amounts paid or incurred after December 31, 2008, in taxable years beginning after such date."

EFFECTIVE DATE OF 2009 AMENDMENT

Pub. L. 111–5, div. B, title I, §1302(d), Feb. 17, 2009, 123 Stat. 348, provided that: "The amendments made by this section [enacting section 48C of this title and amending this section and section 49 of this title] shall apply to periods after the date of the enactment of this Act [Feb. 17, 2009], under rules similar to the rules of section 48(m) of the Internal Revenue Code of 1986 (as in effect on the day before the date of the enactment of the Revenue Reconciliation Act of 1990 [Nov. 5, 1990])."

EFFECTIVE DATE OF 2005 AMENDMENT

Pub. L. 109–58, title XIII, §1307(d), Aug. 8, 2005, 119 Stat. 1006, provided that: "The amendments made by this section [enacting sections 48A and 48B of this title and amending this section and section 49 of this title] shall apply to periods after the date of the enactment of this Act [Aug. 8, 2005], under rules similar to the rules of section 48(m) of the Internal Revenue Code of 1986 (as in effect on the day before the date of the enactment of the Revenue Reconciliation Act of 1990 [Nov. 5, 1990])."

EFFECTIVE DATE OF 2004 AMENDMENT

Pub. L. 108–357, title III, §322(e), Oct. 22, 2004, 118 Stat. 1476, provided that: "The amendments made by this section [amending this section and sections 48, 50, and 194 of this title] shall apply with respect to expenditures paid or incurred after the date of the enactment of this Act [Oct. 22, 2004]."

EFFECTIVE DATE OF 1990 AMENDMENT

Amendment by section 11813(a) of Pub. L. 101–508 applicable to property placed in service after Dec. 31, 1990, but not applicable to any transition property (as defined in section 49(e) of this title), any property with respect to which qualified progress expenditures were previously taken into account under section 46(d) of this title, and any property described in section 46(b)(2)(C) of this title, as such sections were in effect on Nov. 4, 1990, see section 11813(c) of Pub. L. 101–508, set out as a note under section 45K of this title.

EFFECTIVE DATE OF 1989 AMENDMENT

Amendment by section 7814(d) of Pub. L. 101–239 effective, except as otherwise provided, as if included in the provision of the Technical and Miscellaneous Revenue Act of 1988, Pub. L. 100–647, to which such amendment relates, see section 7817 of Pub. L. 101–239, set out as a note under section 1 of this title.

EFFECTIVE DATE OF 1988 AMENDMENT

Amendment by sections 1002(a)(4), (15), (17), (25), 1009(a)(1), and 1013(a)(44) of Pub. L. 100–647 effective, except as otherwise provided, as if included in the provision of the Tax Reform Act of 1986, Pub. L. 99–514, to which such amendment relates, see section 1019(a) of Pub. L. 100–647, set out as a note under section 1 of this title.

EFFECTIVE DATE OF 1986 AMENDMENT

Amendment by section 201(d)(7)(B) of Pub. L. 99–514 applicable to property placed in service after Dec. 31, 1986, in taxable years ending after such date, with exceptions, see sections 203 and 204 of Pub. L. 99–514, set out as a note under section 168 of this title.

Pub. L. 99–514, title II, §251(d), Oct. 22, 1986, 100 Stat. 2186, as amended by Pub. L. 100–647, title I, §1002(k), Nov. 10, 1988, 102 Stat. 3371, provided that:

"(1) In general.—Except as otherwise provided in this subsection, the amendments made by this section [amending this section and section 48 of this title] shall apply to property placed in service after December 31, 1986, in taxable years ending after such date.

"(2) General transitional rule.—The amendments made by this section and section 201 [amending this section and sections 48, 167, 168, 178, 179, 280F, 291, 312, 465, 467, 514, 751, 1245, 4162, 6111, and 7701 of this title] shall not apply to any property placed in service before January 1, 1994, if such property is placed in service as part of—

"(A) a rehabilitation which was completed pursuant to a written contract which was binding on March 1, 1986, or

"(B) a rehabilitation incurred in connection with property (including any leasehold interest) acquired before March 2, 1986, or acquired on or after such date pursuant to a written contract that was binding on March 1, 1986, if—

"(i) parts 1 and 2 of the Historic Preservation Certification Application were filed with the Department of the Interior (or its designee) before March 2, 1986, or

"(ii) the lesser of $1,000,000 or 5 percent of the cost of the rehabilitation is incurred before March 2, 1986, or is required to be incurred pursuant to a written contract which was binding on March 1, 1986.

"(3) Certain additional rehabilitations.—The amendments made by this section and section 201 [amending this section and sections 48, 167, 168, 178, 179, 280F, 291, 312, 465, 467, 514, 751, 1245, 4162, 6111, and 7701 of this title] shall not apply to—

"(A) the rehabilitation of 8 bathhouses within the Hot Springs National Park or of buildings in the Central Avenue Historic District at such Park,

"(B) the rehabilitation of the Upper Pontalba Building in New Orleans, Louisiana,

"(C) the rehabilitation of at least 60 buildings listed on the National Register at the Frankford Arsenal,

"(D) the rehabilitation of De Baliveriere Arcade, St. Louis Centre, and Drake Apartments in Missouri,

"(E) the rehabilitation of The Tides in Bristol, Rhode Island,

"(F) the rehabilitation and renovation of the Outlet Company building and garage in Providence, Rhode Island,

"(G) the rehabilitation of 10 structures in Harrisburg, Pennsylvania, with respect to which the Harristown Development Corporation was designated redeveloper and received an option to acquire title to the entire project site for $1 on June 27, 1984,

"(H) the rehabilitation of a project involving the renovation of 3 historic structures on the Minneapolis riverfront, with respect to which the developer of the project entered into a redevelopment agreement with a municipality dated January 4, 1985, and industrial development bonds were sold in 3 separate issues in May, July, and October 1985,

"(I) the rehabilitation of a bank's main office facilities of approximately 120,000 square feet, in connection with which the bank's board of directors authorized a $3,300,000 expenditure for the renovation and retrofit on March 20, 1984,

"(J) the rehabilitation of 10 warehouse buildings built between 1906 and 1910 and purchased under a contract dated February 17, 1986,

"(K) the rehabilitation of a facility which is customarily used for conventions and sporting events if an analysis of operations and recommendations of utilization of such facility was prepared by a certified public accounting firm pursuant to an engagement authorized on March 6, 1984, and presented on June 11, 1984, to officials of the city in which such facility is located,

"(L) Mount Vernon Mills in Columbia, South Carolina,

"(M) the Barbara Jordan II Apartments,

"(N) the rehabilitation of the Federal Building and Post Office, 120 Hanover Street, Manchester, New Hampshire,

"(O) the rehabilitation of the Charleston Waterfront project in South Carolina,

"(P) the Hayes Mansion in San Jose, California,

"(Q) the renovation of a facility owned by the National Railroad Passenger Corporation ('Amtrak') for which project Amtrak engaged a development team by letter agreement dated August 23, 1985, as modified by letter agreement dated September 9, 1985,

"(R) the rehabilitation of a structure or its components which is listed in the National Register of Historic Places, is located in Allegheny County, Pennsylvania, will be substantially rehabilitated (as defined in section 48(g)(1)(C) prior to amendment by this Act), prior to December 31, 1989; and was previously utilized as a market and an auto dealership,

"(S) The Bellevue Stratford Hotel in Philadelphia, Pennsylvania,

"(T) the Dixon Mill Housing project in Jersey City, New Jersey,

"(U) Motor Square Garden,

"(V) the Blackstone Apartments, and the Shriver-Johnson building, in Sioux Falls, South Dakota,

"(W) the Holy Name Academy in Spokane, Washington,

"(X) the Nike/Clemson Mill in Exeter, New Hampshire,

"(Y) the Central Bank Building in Grand Rapids, Michigan, and

"(Z) the Heritage Hotel, in the City of Marquette, Michigan.

"(4) Additional rehabilitations.—The amendments made by this section and section 201 [amending sections 46, 48, 167, 168, 178, 179, 280F, 291, 312, 465, 467, 514, 751, 1245, 4162, 6111, and 7701 of this title] shall not apply to—

"(A) the Fort Worth Town Square Project in Texas,

"(B) the American Youth Hostel in New York, New York,

"(C) The Riverwest Loft Development (including all three phases, two of which do not involve rehabilitations),

"(D) the Gaslamp Quarter Historic District in California,

"(E) the Eberhardt & Ober Brewery, in Pennsylvania,

"(F) the Captain's Walk Limited Partnership-Harris Place Development, in Connecticut,

"(G) the Velvet Mills in Connecticut,

"(H) the Roycroft Inn, in New York,

"(I) Old Main Village, in Mankato, Minnesota,

"(J) the Washburn-Crosby A Mill, in Minneapolis, Minnesota,

"(K) the Marble Arcade office building in Lakeland, Florida,

"(L) the Willard Hotel, in Washington, D.C.,

"(M) the H. P. Lau Building in Lincoln, Nebraska,

"(N) the Starks Building, in Louisville, Kentucky,

"(O) the Bellevue High School, in Bellevue, Kentucky,

"(P) the Major Hampden Smith House, in Owensboro, Kentucky,

"(Q) the Doe Run Inn, in Brandenburg, Kentucky,

"(R) the State National Bank, in Frankfort, Kentucky,

"(S) the Captain Jack House, in Fleming, Kentucky,

"(T) the Elizabeth Arlinghaus House, in Covington, Kentucky,

"(U) Limerick Shamrock, in Louisville, Kentucky,

"(V) the Robert Mills Project, in South Carolina,

"(W) the 620 Project, consisting of 3 buildings, in Kentucky,

"(X) the Warrior Hotel, Ltd., the first two floors of the Martin Hotel, and the 105,000 square foot warehouse constructed in 1910, all in Sioux City, Iowa,

"(Y) the waterpark condominium residential project, to the extent of $2 million of expenditures,

"(Z) the Bigelow-Hartford Carpet Mill in Enfield, Connecticut,

"(AA) properties abutting 125th street in New York County from 7th Avenue west to Morningside and the pier area on the Hudson River at the end of such 125th Street,

"(BB) the City of Los Angeles Central Library project pursuant to an agreement dated December 28, 1983,

"(CC) the Warehouse Row project in Chattanooga, Tennessee,

"(DD) any project described in section 204(a)(1)(F) of this Act [26 U.S.C. 168 note],

"(EE) the Wood Street Commons project in Pittsburgh, Pennsylvania,

"(FF) any project described in section 803(d)(6) of this Act [26 U.S.C. 263A note],

"(GG) Union Station, Indianapolis, Indiana,

"(HH) the Mattress Factory project in Pittsburgh, Pennsylvania,

"(II) Union Station in Providence, Rhode Island,

"(JJ) South Pack Plaza, Asheville, North Carolina,

"(KK) Old Louisville Trust Project, Louisville, Kentucky,

"(LL) Stewarts Rehabilitation Project, Louisville, Kentucky,

"(MM) Bernheim Officenter, Louisville, Kentucky,

"(NN) Springville Mill Project, Rockville, Connecticut, and

"(OO) the D.J. Stewart Company Building, State and Main Streets, Rockford, Illinois.

"(5) Reduction in credit for property under transitional rules.—In the case of property placed in service after December 31, 1986, and to which the amendments made by this section [amending this section and sections 47 and 48 of this title] do not apply, subparagraph (A) of section 46(b)(4) of the Internal Revenue Code of 1954 [now 1986] (as in effect before the enactment of this Act) shall be applied—

"(A) by substituting '10 percent' for '15 percent', and

"(B) by substituting '13 percent' for '20 percent'.

"(6) Expensing of rehabilitation expenses for the frankford arsenal.——In the case of any expenditures paid or incurred in connection with improvements (including repairs and maintenance) of the Frankford Arsenal pursuant to a contract and partnership agreement during the 8-year period specified in the contract or agreement, all such expenditures to be made during the period 1986 through and including 1993 shall—

"(A) be treated as made (and allowable as a deduction) during 1986,

"(B) be treated as qualified rehabilitation expenditures made during 1986, and

"(C) be allocated in accordance with the partnership agreement regardless of when the interest in the partnership was acquired, except that—

"(i) if the taxpayer is not the original holder of such interest, no person (other than the taxpayer) had claimed any benefits by reason of this paragraph,

"(ii) no interest under section 6611 of the 1986 Code on any refund of income taxes which is solely attributable to this paragraph shall be paid for the period—

"(I) beginning on the date which is 45 days after the later of April 15, 1987, or the date on which the return for such taxes was filed, and

"(II) ending on the date the taxpayer acquired the interest in the partnership, and

"(iii) if the expenditures to be made under this provision are not paid or incurred before January 1, 1994, then the tax imposed by chapter 1 of such Code for the taxpayer's last taxable year beginning in 1993 shall be increased by the amount of the tax benefits by reason of this paragraph which are attributable to the expenditures not so paid or incurred.

"(7) Special rule.——In the case of the rehabilitation of the Willard Hotel in Washington, D.C., section 205(c)(1)(B)(ii) of the Tax Equity and Fiscal Responsibility Act of 1982 [section 205(c)(1)(B)(ii) of Pub. L. 97–248, set out as a note under section 196 of this title] shall be applied by substituting '1987' for '1986'."

Pub. L. 99–514, title IV, §421(c), Oct. 22, 1986, 100 Stat. 2229, provided that: "The amendments made by this section [amending this section] shall apply to periods beginning after December 31, 1985, under rules similar to rules under section 48(m) of the Internal Revenue Code of 1986."

Amendment by sections 1802(a)(6), (8), 1844(a), (b)(3), (5), 1847(b)(11), 1848(a) of Pub. L. 99–514 effective, except as otherwise provided, as if included in the provisions of the Tax Reform Act of 1984, Pub. L. 98–369, div. A, to which such amendment relates, see section 1881 of Pub. L. 99–514, set out as a note under section 48 of this title.

EFFECTIVE DATE OF 1984 AMENDMENT

Amendment by section 16 of Pub. L. 98–369 applicable to taxable years ending after Dec. 31, 1983, see section 18(a) of Pub. L. 98–369, set out as a note under section 48 of this title.

Amendment by section 31(f) of Pub. L. 98–369 effective, except as otherwise provided in section 31(g) of Pub. L. 98–369, as to property placed in service by the taxpayer after Nov. 5, 1983, in taxable years ending after such date and to property placed in service by the taxpayer on or before Nov. 5, 1983, if the lease to the organization described in section 593 of this title is entered into after Nov. 5, 1983, see section 31(g)(1), (14) of Pub. L. 98–369, set out as a note under section 168 of this title.

Amendment by section 113(b)(2)(B) of Pub. L. 98–369 applicable as if included in the amendments by sections 201(a), 211(a)(1), and 211(f)(1) of Pub. L. 97–34, which amended this section and enacted section 168 of this title, see section 113(c)(2)(B) of Pub. L. 98–369, set out as a note under section 168 of this title.

Pub. L. 98–369, div. A, title IV, §431(e), July 18, 1984, 98 Stat. 810, provided:

"(1) In general.——The amendments made by this section [amending this section and sections 47 and 48 of this title] shall apply to property placed in service after the date of the enactment of this Act [July 18, 1984] in taxable years ending after such date; except that such amendments shall not apply to any property to which the amendments made by section 211(f) of the Economic Recovery Tax Act of 1981 [section 211(f) of Pub. L. 97–34, amending sections 46 and 47 of this title] do not apply.

"(2) Amendments may be elected retroactively.——At the election of the taxpayer, the amendments made by this section shall apply as if included in the amendments made by section 211(f) of the Economic Recovery Tax Act of 1981. Any election made under the preceding sentence shall apply to all property of the taxpayer to which the amendments made by such section 211(f) apply and shall be made at such time and in such manner as the Secretary of the Treasury or his delegate may by regulations prescribe."

Amendment by section 474(o)(1)–(7) of Pub. L. 98–369 applicable to taxable years beginning after Dec. 31, 1983, and to carrybacks from such years, see section 475(a) of Pub. L. 98–369, set out as a note under section 21 of this title.

Amendment by section 713 of Pub. L. 98–369 effective as if included in the provision of Tax Equity and Fiscal Responsibility Act of 1982, Pub. L. 97–248, to which such amendment relates, see section 715 of Pub. L. 98–369, set out as a note under section 31 of this title.

EFFECTIVE DATE OF 1983 AMENDMENT

Amendment by section 122(c)(1) of Pub. L. 98–21 applicable to taxable years beginning after Dec. 31, 1983, except that if an individual's annuity starting date was deferred under section 105(d)(6) of this title as in effect on the day before Apr. 20, 1983, such deferral shall end on the first day of such individual's first taxable year beginning after Dec. 31, 1983, see section 122(d) of Pub. L. 98–21, set out as a note under section 22 of this title.

Amendment by title I of Pub. L. 97–448 effective, except as otherwise provided, as if it had been included in the provision of the Economic Recovery Tax Act of 1981, Pub. L. 97–34, to which such amendment relates, see section 109 of Pub. L. 97–448, set out as a note under section 1 of this title.

Amendment by section 202(f) of Pub. L. 97–448 effective, except as otherwise provided, as if it had been included in the provision of the Crude Oil Windfall Profit Tax Act of 1980, Pub. L. 96–223, to which such amendment relates, see section 203(a) of Pub. L. 97–448, set out as a note under section 6652 of this title.

Pub. L. 97–424, title V, §541(c), Jan. 6, 1983, 96 Stat. 2193, as amended by Pub. L. 99–514, §2, Oct. 22, 1986, 100 Stat. 2095, provided that:

"(1) General rule.——The amendments made by subsections (a) and (b) [amending this section and sections 167 and 168 of this title] shall apply to taxable years beginning after December 31, 1979.

"(2) Special rule for periods beginning before march 1, 1980.——

"(A) In general.——Subject to the provisions of paragraphs (3) and (4), notwithstanding the provisions of sections 167(l) and 46(f) of the Internal Revenue Code of 1986 [formerly I.R.C. 1954] and of any regulations prescribed by the Secretary of the Treasury (or his delegate) under such sections, the use for ratemaking purposes or for reflecting operating results in the taxpayer's regulated books of account, for any period before March 1, 1980, of—

"(i) any estimates or projections relating to the amounts of the taxpayer's tax expense, depreciation expense, deferred tax reserve, credit allowable under section 38 of such code, or rate base, or

"(ii) any adjustments to the taxpayer's rate of return,

shall not be treated as inconsistent with the requirements of subparagraph (G) of such section 167(l)(3) nor inconsistent with the requirements of paragraph (1) or (2) of such section 46(f), where such estimates or projections, or such rate of return adjustments, were included in a qualified order.

"(B) Qualified order defined.——For purposes of this subsection, the term "qualified order" means an order—

"(i) by a public utility commission which was entered before March 13, 1980,

"(ii) which used the estimates, projections, or rate of return adjustments referred to in subparagraph (A) to determine the amount of the rates to be collected by the taxpayer or the amount of a refund with respect to rates previously collected, and

"(iii) which ordered such rates to be collected or refunds to be made (whether or not such order actually was implemented or enforced).

"(3) Limitations on application of paragraph (2).——

"(A) Paragraph (2) not to apply to amounts actually flowed through.——Paragraph (2) shall not apply to the amount of any—

"(i) rate reduction, or

"(ii) refund,

which was actually made pursuant to a qualified order.

"(B) Taxpayer must enter into closing agreement before paragraph (2) applies.—Paragraph (2) shall not apply to any taxpayer unless, before the later of—

"(i) July 1, 1983, or

"(ii) 6 months after the refunds or rate reductions are actually made pursuant to a qualified order.

the taxpayer enters into a closing agreement (within the meaning of section 7121 of the Internal Revenue Code of 1986) which provides for the payment by the taxpayer of the amount of which paragraph (2) does not apply by reason of subparagraph (A).

"(4) Special rules relating to payment of refunds or interest by the united states or the taxpayer.—

"(A) Refund defined.—For purposes of this subsection, the term "refund" shall include any credit allowed by the taxpayer under a qualified order but shall not include interest payable with respect to any refund (or credit) under such order.

"(B) No interest payable by united states.—No interest shall be payable under section 6611 of the Internal Revenue Code of 1986 on any overpayment of tax which is attributable to the application of paragraph (2).

"(C) Payments may be made in two equal installments.—

"(i) In general.—The taxpayer may make any payment required by reason of paragraph (3) in 2 equal installments, the first installment being due on the last date on which a taxpayer may enter into a closing agreement under paragraph (3)(B), and the second payment being due 1 year after the last date for the first payment.

"(ii) Interest payments.—For purposes of section 6601 of such Code, the last date prescribed for payment with respect to any payment required by reason of paragraph (3) shall be the last date on which such payment is due under clause (i).

"(5) No inference.—The application of subparagraph (G) of section 167(l)(3) of the Internal Revenue Code of 1986, and the application of paragraphs (1) and (2) of section 46(f) of such Code, to taxable years beginning before January 1, 1980, shall be determined without any inference drawn from the amendments made by subsections (a) and (b) of this section [amending this section and sections 167 and 168 of this title] or from the rules contained in paragraphs (2), (3), and (4). Nothing in the preceding sentence shall be construed to limit the relief provided by paragraphs (2), (3), and (4)."

Effective Date of 1982 Amendment

Amendment by Pub. L. 97–354 applicable to taxable years beginning after Dec. 31, 1982, see section 6(a) of Pub. L. 97–354, set out as an Effective Date note under section 1361 of this title.

Amendment by section 201(d)(8)(A), formerly section 201(c)(8)(A), of Pub. L. 97–248, applicable to taxable years beginning after Dec. 31, 1982, see section 201(e)(1) of Pub. L. 97–248, set out as a note under section 5 of this title.

Pub. L. 97–248, title II, §205(c)(2), Sept. 3, 1982, 96 Stat. 431, provided that: "The amendments made by subsection (b) [amending this section] shall apply to taxable years beginning after December 31, 1982."

Amendment by section 265(b)(2)(A)(i) of Pub. L. 97–248 applicable to distributions after Dec. 31, 1982, see section 265(c)(2) of Pub. L. 97–248, set out as a note under section 72 of this title.

Effective Date of 1981 Amendment

Amendment by section 207(c)(1) of Pub. L. 97–34 applicable to unused credit years ending after Dec. 31, 1973, see section 209(c)(2)(A) of Pub. L. 97–34, set out as an Effective Date note under section 168 of this title.

Pub. L. 97–34, title II, §211(i), Aug. 13, 1981, 95 Stat. 235, provided that:

"(1) In general.—Except as provided in this subsection, the amendments made by this section [amending this section and sections 47 and 48 of this title] shall apply to property placed in service after December 31, 1980.

"(2) Progress expenditures.—The amendments made by subsection (b) [amending this section] shall apply to progress expenditures made after December 31, 1980.

"(3) Petroleum storage facilities.—The amendments made by subsection (c) [amending this section] shall apply to periods after December 31, 1980, under rules similar to the rules under section 48(m).

"(4) Noncorporate lessors.—The amendments made by subsection (d) [amending this section] shall apply to leases entered into after June 25, 1981.

"(5) At risk rules.—

"(A) In general.—The amendment made by subsection (f) [amending this section and section 47 of this title] shall not apply to—

"(i) property placed in service by the taxpayer on or before February 18, 1981, and

"(ii) property placed in service by the taxpayer after February 18, 1981, where such property is acquired by the taxpayer pursuant to a binding contract entered into on or before that date.

"(B) Binding contract.—For purposes of subparagraph (A)(ii), property acquired pursuant to a binding contract shall, under regulations prescribed by the Secretary, include property acquired in a manner so that it would have qualified as pretermination property under section 49(b) (as in effect before its repeal by the Revenue Act of 1978) [Pub. L. 95–600].

"(6) Leased rolling stock.—The amendment made by subsection (h) [amending section 48 of this title] shall apply to taxable years beginning after December 31, 1980."

Pub. L. 97–34, title II, §212(e), Aug. 13, 1981, 95 Stat. 239, as amended by Pub. L. 97–448, title I, §102(f)(1), Jan. 12, 1983, 96 Stat. 2371; Pub. L. 99–514, §2, Oct. 22, 1986, 100 Stat. 2095, provided that:

"(1) In general.—Except as provided in paragraph (2), the amendments made by this section [amending this section and sections 48, 57, 167, 280B, 642, 1016, 1082, 1245, and 1250 of this title and repealing section 191 of this title] shall apply to expenditures incurred after December 31, 1981, in taxable years ending after such date.

"(2) Transitional rule.—The amendments made by this section shall not apply with respect to any rehabilitation of a building if—

"(A) the physical work on such rehabilitation began before January 1, 1982, and

"(B) such building does not meet the requirements of paragraph (1) of section 48(g) of the Internal Revenue Code of 1986 [formerly I.R.C. 1954] (as amended by this Act [Pub. L. 97–34])."

Pub. L. 97–34, title III, §332(c)(1), Aug. 13, 1981, 95 Stat. 296, provided that: "The amendments made by subsection (a) [amending this section] shall be effective on the date of enactment of this Act [Aug. 13, 1981]."

Effective Date of 1980 Amendment

Amendment by section 222(e)(2) of Pub. L. 96–223 applicable to periods after Dec. 31, 1979, under rules similar to the rules of section 48(m) of this title, see section 222(j)(1) of Pub. L. 96–223, set out as a note under section 48 of this title.

Pub. L. 96–223, title II, §223(b)(3), Apr. 2, 1980, 94 Stat. 266, provided that: "The amendments made by this subsection [amending this section and section 6401 of this title] shall apply to qualified investment for taxable years beginning after December 31, 1979."

Effective Date of 1978 Amendment

Amendment by section 141(e), (f)(2) of Pub. L. 95–600 effective with respect to qualified investment for taxable years beginning after Dec. 31, 1978, see section 141(g)(1) of Pub. L. 95–600, set out as an Effective Date note under section 409 of this title.

Pub. L. 95–600, title III, §312(d), Nov. 6, 1978, 92 Stat. 2826, provided that: "The amendments made by this section [amending this section and sections 48 and 167 of this title and repealing sections 49 and 50 of this title] shall apply to taxable years ending after December 31, 1978."

Pub. L. 95–600, title III, §313(b), Nov. 6, 1978, 92 Stat. 2827, provided that:

"The amendment made by subsection (a) [amending this section] shall apply to—

"(1) property acquired by the taxpayer after December 31, 1978, and

"(2) property the construction, reconstruction, or erection of which was completed by the taxpayer after December 31, 1978 (but only to the extent of the basis thereof attributable to construction, reconstruction, or erection after such date)."

Pub. L. 95–600, title III, §316(c), Nov. 6, 1978, 92 Stat. 2830, provided that: "The amendments made by this section [amending this section and section 1388 of this title] shall apply to taxable years ending after October 31, 1978."

Pub. L. 95–600, title VII, §703(r), Nov. 6, 1978, 92 Stat. 2944, provided that: "Except as otherwise provided, the amendments made by this section [amending this section and sections 48, 103, 447, 453, 501, 801, 911, 995, 996, 999, 1033, 1212, 1375, 1402, 1561, 4041, 4911, 6104, 6427, 6501, 6504, 6511, 7609 of this title and sections 402, 405, 410, and 411 of Title 42, The Public Health and Welfare, enacting provisions set out as notes under sections 103, 311, 443, 501, and 4973 of this title, and amending provisions set out as notes under section 120, 311, 907, 995, 2011, 2501, and 4940 of this title] shall take effect on October 4, 1976."

EFFECTIVE DATE OF 1976 AMENDMENT

Amendment by section 503(b)(4) of Pub. L. 94–455 applicable to taxable years beginning after Dec. 31, 1975, see section 508 of Pub. L. 94–455, set out as a note under section 3 of this title.

Pub. L. 94–455, title VIII, §802(c), Oct. 4, 1976, 90 Stat. 1583, provided that: "The amendments made by this section [amending this section and section 48 of this title and provisions set out below] shall apply to taxable years beginning after December 31, 1975."

Pub. L. 94–455, title VIII, §803(j), Oct. 4, 1976, 90 Stat. 1591, provided that:

"(1) General rule.—Except as provided in paragraph (2), the amendments made by this section [see Tables for classification of section 803 of Pub. L. 94–455] shall apply for taxable years beginning after December 31, 1974.

"(2) Exceptions.—

"(A) Section 301(e) of the Tax Reduction Act of 1975 [set out below], as added by subsection (d), shall apply for taxable years beginning after December 31, 1976.

"(B) The amendments made by subsections (a) and (b)(1) shall apply for taxable years beginning after December 31, 1975.

"(C) The amendments made by subsections (b)(4) and (f) shall apply for years beginning after December 31, 1975."

Pub. L. 94–455, title VIII, §805(b), Oct. 4, 1976, 90 Stat. 1597, as amended by Pub. L. 99–514, §2, Oct. 22, 1986, 100 Stat. 2095, provided that:

"(1) In general.—Except as provided in subparagraph (B), the amendment made by subsection (a) [amending this section] shall apply to taxable years beginning after December 31, 1975, in the case of property placed in service after such date.

"(2) Section 46(g)(4).—Section 46(g)(4) of the Internal Revenue Code of 1986 [formerly I.R.C. 1954] (as added by subsection (a)) shall apply to taxable years beginning after December 31, 1975."

Amendment by section 1607(b)(1)(B) of Pub. L. 94–455 applicable to taxable years ending after Oct. 4, 1976, with certain exceptions, see section 1608(c) of Pub. L. 94–455, set out as a note under section 857 of this title.

Amendment by section 1901(a)(4)(A), (B), (b)(1)(C) of Pub. L. 94–455 applicable with respect to taxable years beginning after Dec. 31, 1976, see section 1901(d) of Pub. L. 94–455, set out as a note under section 2 of this title.

Pub. L. 94–455, title XXI, §2112(d)(1), Oct. 4, 1976, 90 Stat. 1906, provided that: "The amendments made by subsection (a) [amending this section and section 48 of this title] shall apply to—

"(A) property acquired by the taxpayer after December 31, 1976, and

"(B) property the construction, reconstruction, or erection of which was completed by the taxpayer after December 31, 1976, (but only to the extent of the basis thereof attributable to construction, reconstruction, or erection after such date), in taxable years beginning after such date."

EFFECTIVE DATE OF 1975 AMENDMENT

Pub. L. 94–12, title III, §301(b)(4), Mar. 29, 1975, 89 Stat. 38, provided that: "The amendment made by paragraph (1) of this subsection [amending this section] shall apply to property placed in service after January 21, 1975, in taxable years ending after January 21, 1975. The amendments made by paragraphs (2) and (3) [amending this section] shall apply to taxable years ending after December 31, 1974."

Pub. L. 94–12, title III, §305(a), Mar. 29, 1975, 89 Stat. 45, provided that: "The amendments made by section 302 [amending this section and sections 47, 48, and 50B of this title] shall apply to taxable years ending after December 31, 1974."

EFFECTIVE DATE OF 1974 AMENDMENT

Amendment by section 2001(g)(2)(B) of Pub. L. 93–406 applicable to distributions made in taxable years beginning after Dec. 31, 1975, see section 2001(i)(5) of Pub. L. 93–406, set out as a note under section 72 of this title.

Amendment by section 2002(g)(2) of Pub. L. 93–406 effective on Jan. 1, 1975, see section 2002(i)(2) of Pub. L. 93–406, set out as an Effective Date note under section 4973 of this title.

Amendment by section 2005(c)(4) of Pub. L. 93–406 applicable only with respect to distributions or payments made after Dec. 31, 1973, in taxable years beginning after Dec. 31, 1973, see section 2005(d) of Pub. L. 93–406, set out as a note under section 402 of this title.

EFFECTIVE DATE OF 1971 AMENDMENT

Pub. L. 92–178, title I, §102(d)(1), (2), Dec. 10, 1971, 85 Stat. 500, as amended by Pub. L. 99–514, §2, Oct. 22, 1986, 100 Stat. 2095, provided that:

"(1) The amendments made by subsections (a) and (b) [amending this section and section 48 of this title] shall apply to property described in section 50 of the Internal Revenue Code of 1986 [formerly I.R.C. 1954].

"(2) In redetermining qualified investment for purposes of section 47(a) of the Internal Revenue Code of 1986 in the case of any property which ceases to be section 38 property with respect to the taxpayer after August 15, 1971, or which becomes public utility property after such date, section 46(c)(2) of such Code shall be applied as amended by subsection (a)."

Pub. L. 92–178, title I, §105(d), Dec. 10, 1971, 85 Stat. 505, as amended by Pub. L. 99–514, §2, Oct. 22, 1986, 100 Stat. 2095, provided that: "The amendments made by this section [amending this section and enacting provisions set out below] shall apply to property described in section 50 of the Internal Revenue Code of 1986 [formerly I.R.C. 1954]."

Pub. L. 92–178, title I, §106(d), Dec. 10, 1971, 85 Stat. 506, provided that: "The amendments made by subsections (a), (b), and (c)(2) [amending this section] shall apply to taxable years beginning after December 31, 1970. The amendments made by subsection (c)(1) [amending this section] shall apply to taxable years ending after August 15, 1971."

Pub. L. 92–178, title I, §107(a)(2), Dec. 10, 1971, 85 Stat. 507, provided that: "The repeals made by paragraph (1) [amending this section and section 47 of this title] shall apply to casualties and thefts occurring after August 15, 1971."

Pub. L. 92–178, title I, §108(d), Dec. 10, 1971, 85 Stat. 508, provided that: "The amendments made by subsections (a) and (b) [amending this section and section 48 of this title] shall apply to leases entered into after September 22, 1971. The amendment made by subsection (c) [amending section 48 of this title] shall apply to leases entered into after November 8, 1971."

EFFECTIVE DATE OF 1969 AMENDMENT

Amendment by section 301(b)(4) of Pub. L. 91–172 applicable to taxable years ending after Dec. 31, 1969, see section 301(c) of Pub. L. 91–172, set out as a note under section 5 of this title.

Amendment by section 401(e)(1) of Pub. L. 91–172 applicable with respect to taxable years ending on or after Dec. 31, 1970, see section 401(h)(3) of Pub. L. 91–172, set out as a note under section 1561 of this title.

EFFECTIVE DATE OF 1967 AMENDMENT

Pub. L. 90–225, §2(g), Dec. 27, 1967, 81 Stat. 732, provided that: "The amendments made by this section [amending this section and sections 6411, 6501, 6511, 6601, and 6611 of this title] shall apply with respect to investment credit carrybacks attributable to net operating loss carrybacks from taxable years ending after July 31, 1967."

EFFECTIVE DATE OF 1966 AMENDMENT

Pub. L. 89–800, §4, Nov. 8, 1966, 80 Stat. 1514, provided that: "The amendments made by this Act [amending this section and sections 48 and 167 of this title] shall apply to taxable years ending after October 9, 1966, except that the amendments made by section 3(b) [amending this section] shall apply only if the fifth taxable year following the unused credit year ends after December 31, 1966."

Pub. L. 89–389, §2(c), Apr. 14, 1966, 80 Stat. 114, provided that: "The amendments made by this section [enacting section 1378 of this title and amending this section and sections 1372, 1373, and 1375 of this title] shall apply with respect to taxable years of electing small business corporations beginning after the date of enactment of this Act [Apr. 14, 1966], but such amendments shall not apply with respect to sales or exchanges occurring before February 24, 1966."

Amendment by Pub. L. 89–384 applicable with respect to amounts received after December 31, 1964, in respect of foreign expropriation losses (as defined in section 1351(b) of this title) sustained after December 31, 1958, see section 2 of Pub. L. 89–384, set out as an Effective Date note under section 1351 of this title.

EFFECTIVE DATE OF 1964 AMENDMENT

Amendment by Pub. L. 88–272 applicable with respect to dividends received after Dec. 31, 1964, in taxable years ending after such date, see section 201(e) of Pub. L. 88–272, set out as a note under section 22 of this title.

EFFECTIVE DATE

Pub. L. 87–834, §2(h), Oct. 16, 1962, 76 Stat. 973, provided that: "The amendments made by this section [enacting this section and sections 38, 47, 48, and 181 of this title, amending sections 381, 1016, 6501, 6511, 6601, and 6611 of this title, and renumbering former section 38 as section 39 of this title] shall apply with respect to taxable years ending after December 31, 1961."

SAVINGS PROVISION

For provisions that nothing in amendment by section 11813(a) of Pub. L. 101–508 be construed to affect treatment of certain transactions occurring, property acquired, or items of income, loss, deduction, or credit taken into account prior to Nov. 5, 1990, for purposes of determining liability for tax for periods ending after Nov. 5, 1990, see section 11821(b) of Pub. L. 101–508, set out as a note under section 45K of this title.

PLAN AMENDMENTS NOT REQUIRED UNTIL JANUARY 1, 1989

For provisions directing that if any amendments made by subtitle A or subtitle C of title XI [§§1101–1147 and 1171–1177] or title XVIII [§§1800–1899A] of Pub. L. 99–514 require an amendment to any plan, such plan amendment shall not be required to be made before the first plan year beginning on or after Jan. 1, 1989, see section 1140 of Pub. L. 99–514, as amended, set out as a note under section 401 of this title.

CLARIFICATION OF EFFECT OF 1984 AMENDMENT ON INVESTMENT TAX CREDIT

Pub. L. 98–369, title IV, §475(c), July 18, 1984, 98 Stat. 847, provided that: "Nothing in the amendments made by section 474(o) [amending this section and sections 47 and 48 of this title] shall be construed as reducing the amount of any credit allowable for qualified investment in taxable years beginning before January 1, 1984."

REGULATED PUBLIC UTILITIES; SPECIAL TRANSITIONAL RULE

Pub. L. 97–34, title II, §209(d)(2), Aug. 13, 1981, 95 Stat. 227, as amended by Pub. L. 99–514, §2, Oct. 22, 1986, 100 Stat. 2095, provided that: "If, by the terms of the applicable rate order last entered before the date of the enactment of this Act [Aug. 13, 1981] by a regulatory commission having appropriate jurisdiction, a regulated public utility would (but for this provision) fail to meet the requirements of paragraph (1) or (2) of section 46(f) of the Internal Revenue Code of 1986 [formerly I.R.C. 1954] with respect to property for an accounting period ending after December 31, 1980, such regulated public utility shall not fail to meet such requirements if, by the terms of its first rate order determining cost of service with respect to such property which becomes effective after the date of the enactment of this Act and on or before January 1, 1983, such regulated public utility meets such requirements. This provision shall not apply to any rate order which, under the rules in effect before the date of the enactment of this Act was inconsistent with the requirements of paragraph (1) or (2) of section 46(f) of such Code (whichever would have been applicable)."

PLAN REQUIREMENTS FOR TAXPAYERS ELECTING ADDITIONAL CREDITS

Pub. L. 94–12, title III, §301(d)–(f), Mar. 29, 1975, 89 Stat. 38, as amended by Pub. L. 94–455, title VIII, §§802(b)(7), 803(c)–(e), Oct. 4, 1976, 90 Stat. 1583–1588, relating to plan requirements for taxpayers electing additional credit, was repealed by Pub. L. 95–600, title I, §141(f)(1), Nov. 6, 1978, 92 Stat. 2795.

PUBLIC UTILITY PROPERTY SUBJECT TO SUBSEC. (E); PROVISIONS RESPECTING TREATMENT OF INVESTMENT CREDIT BY FEDERAL REGULATORY AGENCIES INAPPLICABLE

Pub. L. 92–178, title I, §105(e), Dec. 10, 1971, 85 Stat. 506, as amended by Pub. L. 99–514, §2, Oct. 22, 1986, 100 Stat. 2095, provided that: "Section 203(e) of the Revenue Act of 1964 [set out as note under section 38 of this title] shall not apply to public utility property to which section 46(e) of the Internal Revenue Code of 1986 [formerly I.R.C. 1954] (as added by subsection (c)) [subsec. (e) of this section] applies."

§47. Rehabilitation credit

(a) General rule

(1) In general

For purposes of section 46, for any taxable year during the 5-year period beginning in the taxable year in which a qualified rehabilitated building is placed in service, the rehabilitation credit for such year is an amount equal to the ratable share for such year.

(2) Ratable share

For purposes of paragraph (1), the ratable share for any taxable year during the period described in such paragraph is the amount equal to 20 percent of the qualified rehabilitation expenditures with respect to the qualified rehabilitated building, as allocated ratably to each year during such period.

(b) When expenditures taken into account

(1) In general

Qualified rehabilitation expenditures with respect to any qualified rehabilitated building shall be taken into account for the taxable year in which such qualified rehabilitated building is placed in service.

(2) Coordination with subsection (d)

The amount which would (but for this paragraph) be taken into account under paragraph (1) with respect to any qualified rehabilitated building shall be reduced (but not below zero) by any amount of qualified rehabilitation expenditures taken into account under subsection (d) by the taxpayer or a predecessor of the taxpayer (or, in the case of a sale and leaseback described in section 50(a)(2)(C), by the lessee), to the extent any amount so taken into account has not been required to be recaptured under section 50(a).

(c) Definitions

For purposes of this section—

(1) Qualified rehabilitated building

(A) In general

The term "qualified rehabilitated building" means any building (and its structural components) if—

(i) such building has been substantially rehabilitated,

(ii) such building was placed in service before the beginning of the rehabilitation,

(iii) such building is a certified historic structure, and

(iv) depreciation (or amortization in lieu of depreciation) is allowable with respect to such building.

(B) Substantially rehabilitated defined

(i) In general

For purposes of subparagraph (A)(i), a building shall be treated as having been substantially rehabilitated only if the qualified rehabilitation expenditures during the 24-month period selected by the taxpayer (at the time and in the manner prescribed by regulation) and ending with or within the taxable year exceed the greater of—

(I) the adjusted basis of such building (and its structural components), or

(II) $5,000.

The adjusted basis of the building (and its structural components) shall be determined as of the beginning of the 1st day of such 24-month period, or of the holding period of the building, whichever is later. For purposes of the preceding sentence, the determination of the beginning of the holding period shall be made without regard to any reconstruction by the taxpayer in connection with the rehabilitation.

(ii) Special rule for phased rehabilitation

In the case of any rehabilitation which may reasonably be expected to be completed in phases set forth in architectural plans and specifications completed before the rehabilitation begins, clause (i) shall be applied by substituting "60-month period" for "24-month period".

(iii) Lessees

The Secretary shall prescribe by regulation rules for applying this subparagraph to lessees.

(C) Reconstruction

Rehabilitation includes reconstruction.

(2) Qualified rehabilitation expenditure defined

(A) In general

The term "qualified rehabilitation expenditure" means any amount properly chargeable to capital account—

(i) for property for which depreciation is allowable under section 168 and which is—

(I) nonresidential real property,

(II) residential rental property,

(III) real property which has a class life of more than 12.5 years, or

(IV) an addition or improvement to property described in subclause (I), (II), or (III), and

(ii) in connection with the rehabilitation of a qualified rehabilitated building.

(B) Certain expenditures not included

The term "qualified rehabilitation expenditure" does not include—

(i) Straight line depreciation must be used

Any expenditure with respect to which the taxpayer does not use the straight line method over a recovery period determined under subsection (c) or (g) of section 168. The preceding sentence shall not apply to any expenditure to the extent the alternative depreciation system of section 168(g) applies to such expenditure by reason of subparagraph (B) or (C) of section 168(g)(1).

(ii) Cost of acquisition

The cost of acquiring any building or interest therein.

(iii) Enlargements

Any expenditure attributable to the enlargement of an existing building.

(iv) Certified historic structure

Any expenditure attributable to the rehabilitation of a qualified rehabilitated building unless the rehabilitation is a certified rehabilitation (within the meaning of subparagraph (C)).

(v) Tax-exempt use property

(I) In general

Any expenditure in connection with the rehabilitation of a building which is allocable to the portion of such property which is (or may reasonably be expected to be) tax-exempt use property (within the meaning of section 168(h), except that "50 percent" shall be substituted for "35 percent" in paragraph (1)(B)(iii) thereof).

(II) Clause not to apply for purposes of paragraph (1)(C)

This clause shall not apply for purposes of determining under paragraph (1)(C) whether a building has been substantially rehabilitated.

(vi) Expenditures of lessee

Any expenditure of a lessee of a building if, on the date the rehabilitation is completed, the remaining term of the lease (determined without regard to any renewal periods) is less than the recovery period determined under section 168(c).

(C) Certified rehabilitation

For purposes of subparagraph (B), the term "certified rehabilitation" means any rehabilitation of a certified historic structure which the Secretary of the Interior has certified to the Secretary as being consistent with the historic character of such property or the district in which such property is located.

(D) Nonresidential real property; residential rental property; class life

For purposes of subparagraph (A), the terms "nonresidential real property," "residential rental property," and "class life" have the respective meanings given such terms by section 168.

(3) Certified historic structure defined

(A) In general

The term "certified historic structure" means any building (and its structural components) which—

(i) is listed in the National Register, or

(ii) is located in a registered historic district and is certified by the Secretary of the Interior to the Secretary as being of historic significance to the district.

(B) Registered historic district

The term "registered historic district" means—

(i) any district listed in the National Register, and

(ii) any district—

(I) which is designated under a statute of the appropriate State or local government, if such statute is certified by the Secretary of the Interior to the Secretary as containing criteria which will substantially achieve the purpose of preserving and rehabilitating buildings of historic significance to the district, and

(II) which is certified by the Secretary of the Interior to the Secretary as meeting substantially all of the requirements for the listing of districts in the National Register.

(d) Progress expenditures

(1) In general

In the case of any building to which this subsection applies, except as provided in paragraph (3)—

(A) if such building is self-rehabilitated property, any qualified rehabilitation expenditure with respect to such building shall be taken into account for the taxable year for which such expenditure is properly chargeable to capital account with respect to such building, and

(B) if such building is not self-rehabilitated property, any qualified rehabilitation expenditure with respect to such building shall be taken into account for the taxable year in which paid.

(2) Property to which subsection applies

(A) In general

This subsection shall apply to any building which is being rehabilitated by or for the taxpayer if—

(i) the normal rehabilitation period for such building is 2 years or more, and

(ii) it is reasonable to expect that such building will be a qualified rehabilitated building in the hands of the taxpayer when it is placed in service.

Clauses (i) and (ii) shall be applied on the basis of facts known as of the close of the taxable year of the taxpayer in which the rehabilitation begins (or, if later, at the close of the first taxable year to which an election under this subsection applies).

(B) Normal rehabilitation period

For purposes of subparagraph (A), the term "normal rehabilitation period" means the period reasonably expected to be required for the rehabilitation of the building—

(i) beginning with the date on which physical work on the rehabilitation begins (or, if later, the first day of the first taxable year to which an election under this subsection applies), and

(ii) ending on the date on which it is expected that the property will be available for placing in service.

(3) Special rules for applying paragraph (1)

For purposes of paragraph (1)—

(A) Component parts, etc.

Property which is to be a component part of, or is otherwise to be included in, any building to which this subsection applies shall be taken into account—

(i) at a time not earlier than the time at which it becomes irrevocably devoted to use in the building, and

(ii) as if (at the time referred to in clause (i)) the taxpayer had expended an amount equal to that portion of the cost to the taxpayer of such component or other property which, for purposes of this subpart, is properly chargeable (during such taxable year) to capital account with respect to such building.

(B) Certain borrowing disregarded

Any amount borrowed directly or indirectly by the taxpayer from the person rehabilitating the property for him shall not be treated as an amount expended for such rehabilitation.

(C) Limitation for buildings which are not self-rehabilitated

(i) In general

In the case of a building which is not self-rehabilitated, the amount taken into account under paragraph (1)(B) for any taxable year shall not exceed the amount which represents the portion of the overall cost to the taxpayer of the rehabilitation which is properly attributable to the portion of the rehabilitation which is completed during such taxable year.

(ii) Carryover of certain amounts

In the case of a building which is not a self-rehabilitated building, if for the taxable year—

(I) the amount which (but for clause (i)) would have been taken into account under paragraph (1)(B) exceeds the limitation of clause (i), then the amount of such excess shall be taken into account under paragraph (1)(B) for the succeeding taxable year, or

(II) the limitation of clause (i) exceeds the amount taken into account under paragraph (1)(B), then the amount of such excess shall increase the limitation of clause (i) for the succeeding taxable year.

(D) Determination of percentage of completion

The determination under subparagraph (C)(i) of the portion of the overall cost to the taxpayer of the rehabilitation which is properly attributable to rehabilitation completed during any taxable year shall be made, under regulations prescribed by the Secretary, on the basis of engineering or architectural estimates or on the basis of cost accounting records. Unless the taxpayer establishes otherwise by clear and convincing evidence, the rehabilitation shall be deemed to be completed not more rapidly than ratably over the normal rehabilitation period.

(E) No progress expenditures for certain prior periods

No qualified rehabilitation expenditures shall be taken into account under this subsection for any period before the first day of the first taxable year to which an election under this subsection applies.

(F) No progress expenditures for property for year it is placed in service, etc.

In the case of any building, no qualified rehabilitation expenditures shall be taken into account under this subsection for the earlier of—

(i) the taxable year in which the building is placed in service, or

(ii) the first taxable year for which recapture is required under section 50(a)(2) with respect to such property,

or for any taxable year thereafter.

(4) Self-rehabilitated building

For purposes of this subsection, the term "self-rehabilitated building" means any building if it is reasonable to believe that more than half of the qualified rehabilitation expenditures for such building will be made directly by the taxpayer.

(5) Election

This subsection shall apply to any taxpayer only if such taxpayer has made an election under this paragraph. Such an election shall apply to the taxable year for which made and all subsequent taxable years. Such an election, once made, may be revoked only with the consent of the Secretary.

(Added Pub. L. 87–834, §2(b), Oct. 16, 1962, 76 Stat. 966; amended Pub. L. 91–172, title VII, §703(c), Dec. 30, 1969, 83 Stat. 666; Pub. L. 91–676, §1, Jan. 12, 1971, 84 Stat. 2060; Pub. L. 92–178, title I, §§102(c), 107(a)(1), (b)(1), Dec. 10, 1971, 85 Stat. 500, 507; Mar. 29, 1975, Pub. L. 94–12, title III, §302(b)(2)(A), (c)(1), (2), 89 Stat. 43, 44; Pub. L. 94–455, title VIII, §804(b), title XIX, §1906(b)(13)(A), Oct. 4, 1976, 90 Stat. 1594, 1834; Pub. L. 95–600, title III, §317(a), Nov. 6, 1978, 92 Stat. 2830; Pub. L. 95–618, title II, §241(b), Nov. 9, 1978, 92 Stat. 3193; Pub. L. 97–34, title II, §211(f)(2), (g), Aug. 13, 1981, 95 Stat. 231, 233; Pub. L. 97–248, title II, §208(a)(2)(B), Sept. 3, 1982, 96 Stat. 435; Pub. L. 97–448, title I, §102(e)(3), Jan. 12, 1983, 96 Stat. 2371; Pub. L. 98–369, div. A, title IV, §§421(b)(7), 431(b)(2), (d)(4), (5), 474(o)(8), (9), July 18, 1984, 98 Stat. 794, 807, 810, 836; Pub. L. 98–443, §9(p), Oct. 4, 1984, 98 Stat. 1708; Pub. L. 99–121, title I, §103(b)(6), Oct. 11, 1985, 99 Stat. 510; Pub. L. 99–514, title XV, §1511(c)(2), title XVIII, §§1802(a)(5)(A), 1844(b)(1), (2), (4), Oct. 22, 1986, 100 Stat. 2744, 2788, 2855; Pub. L. 100–647, title I, §§1002(a)(18), (26)–(28), 1007(g)(3)(A), Nov. 10, 1988, 102 Stat. 3356, 3357, 3435; Pub. L. 101–508, title XI, §11801(c)(8)(A), 11813(a), Nov. 5, 1990, 104 Stat. 1388–524, 1388-536; Pub. L. 110–289, div. C, title I, §3025(a), July 30, 2008, 122 Stat. 2897; Pub. L. 115–97, title I, §13402(a), (b)(1), Dec. 22, 2017, 131 Stat. 2134.)

EDITORIAL NOTES

PRIOR PROVISIONS

Provisions similar to this section were contained in section 48(g) of this title, prior to the general amendment of this subpart by Pub. L. 101–508.

AMENDMENTS

2017—Subsec. (a). Pub. L. 115–97, §13402(a), amended subsec. (a) generally. Prior to amendment, text read as follows: "For purposes of section 46, the rehabilitation credit for any taxable year is the sum of—

"(1) 10 percent of the qualified rehabilitation expenditures with respect to any qualified rehabilitated building other than a certified historic structure, and

"(2) 20 percent of the qualified rehabilitation expenditures with respect to any certified historic structure."

Subsec. (c)(1)(A)(iii). Pub. L. 115–97, §13402(b)(1)(A)(i), amended cl. (iii) generally. Prior to amendment, cl. (iii) read as follows: "in the case of any building other than a certified historic structure, in the rehabilitation process—

"(I) 50 percent or more of the existing external walls of such building are retained in place as external walls,

"(II) 75 percent or more of the existing external walls of such building are retained in place as internal or external walls, and

"(III) 75 percent or more of the existing internal structural framework of such building is retained in place, and".

Subsec. (c)(1)(B) to (D). Pub. L. 115–97, §13402(b)(1)(A)(ii), (iii), redesignated subpars. (C) and (D) as (B) and (C), respectively, and struck out former subpar. (B). Prior to amendment, text of subpar. (B) read as follows: "In the case of a building other than a certified historic structure, a building shall not be a qualified rehabilitated building unless the building was first placed in service before 1936."

Subsec. (c)(2)(B)(iv). Pub. L. 115–97, §13402(b)(1)(B), amended cl. (iv) generally. Prior to amendment, text read as follows: "Any expenditure attributable to the rehabilitation of a certified historic structure or a building in a registered historic district, unless the rehabilitation is a certified rehabilitation (within the meaning of subparagraph (C)). The preceding sentence shall not apply to a building in a registered historic district if—

"(I) such building was not a certified historic structure,

"(II) the Secretary of the Interior certified to the Secretary that such building is not of historic significance to the district, and

"(III) if the certification referred to in subclause (II) occurs after the beginning of the rehabilitation of such building, the taxpayer certifies to the Secretary that, at the beginning of such rehabilitation, he in good faith was not aware of the requirements of subclause (II)."

2008—Subsec. (c)(2)(B)(v)(I). Pub. L. 110–289 substituted "section 168(h), except that '50 percent' shall be substituted for '35 percent' in paragraph (1)(B)(iii) thereof" for "section 168(h)".

1990—Pub. L. 101–508, §11813(a), amended section generally, substituting section catchline for one which read: "Certain dispositions, etc., of section 38 property" and in text substituting present provisions for provisions relating to general rules regarding disposition of section 38 property, nonapplicability of section in certain cases, the treatment of any increase in tax under the section, increases in nonqualified nonrecourse financing, and transfers between spouses or incident to divorce.

Subsec. (b)(1) to (3). Pub. L. 101–508, §11801(c)(8)(A), inserted "or" at end of par. (1), substituted a period for ", or" at end of par. (2), and struck out par. (3) which related to nonapplicability of subsec. (a) in the case of a transfer of section 38 property related to exchanges under final system plan for ConRail.

1988—Subsec. (a)(5)(D). Pub. L. 100–647, §1002(a)(26)(B), struck out at end "If, prior to a disposition to which this subsection applies, any portion of any credit is not allowable with respect to any property by reason of section 168(i)(3), such portion shall be treated (for purposes of this subparagraph) as not having been used to reduce tax liability."

Subsec. (a)(5)(E)(iii). Pub. L. 100–647, §1002(a)(26)(C), substituted "168(e)" for "168(c)".

Subsec. (a)(5)(E)(v). Pub. L. 100–647, §1002(a)(26)(A), added cl. (v).

Subsec. (a)(9)(A). Pub. L. 100–647, §1002(a)(27), substituted "section 168(h)(2)" for "section 168(j)(4)(C)".

Subsec. (c). Pub. L. 100–647, §1007(g)(3)(A), substituted "D, or G" for "or D".

Subsec. (d)(1). Pub. L. 100–647, §1002(a)(18), substituted "section 46(c)(8)(C)" for "section 48(c)(8)(C)".

Subsec. (d)(3)(C)(i). Pub. L. 100–647, §1002(a)(28), substituted "class life (as defined in section 168(i)(1))" for "present class life (as defined in section 168(g)(2))" and "no class life" for "no present class life".

1986—Subsec. (a)(9). Pub. L. 99–514, §1802(a)(5)(A), added par. (9).

Subsec. (d)(1). Pub. L. 99–514, §1844(b)(1), substituted "reducing the credit base (as defined in section 48(c)(8)(C))" for "reducing the qualified investment" and inserted "For purposes of determining the amount of credit subject to the early disposition or cessation rules of subsection (a), the net increase in the amount of the nonqualified nonrecourse financing with respect to the property shall be treated as reducing the property's credit base (and correspondingly reducing the qualified investment in the property) in the year in which the property was first placed in service."

Subsec. (d)(3)(E)(i). Pub. L. 99–514, §1844(b)(4), inserted "reduced by the sum of the credit recapture amounts with respect to such property for all preceding years".

Subsec. (d)(3)(F). Pub. L. 99–514, §1844(b)(2), struck out subpar. (F) which read as follows: "The amount of any increase in tax under subsection (a) with respect to any property to which this paragraph applies shall be determined by reducing the qualified investment with respect to such property by the aggregate credit recapture amounts for all taxable years under this paragraph."

348

Subsec. (d)(3)(G). Pub. L. 99–514, §1511(c)(2), substituted "determined at the underpayment rate established under section 6621" for "determined under section 6621".

1985—Subsec. (a)(5)(B). Pub. L. 99–121 substituted "For property other than 3-year property" for "For 15-year, 10-year, and 5-year property" in table heading.

1984—Subsec. (a)(5)(D), (6). Pub. L. 98–369, §474(o)(8), substituted "under section 39" for "under section 46(b)".

Subsec. (a)(7)(C). Pub. L. 98–443 substituted "Secretary of Transportation" for "Civil Aeronautics Board".

Subsec. (c). Pub. L. 98–369, §474(o)(9), substituted "subpart A, B, or D" for "subpart A".

Subsec. (d). Pub. L. 98–369, §431(b)(2), substituted "Increases in nonqualified nonrecourse financing" for "Property ceasing to be at risk" in heading.

Subsec. (d)(1). Pub. L. 98–369, §431(b)(2), substituted provisions relating to increases in tax liability resulting from increases in nonqualified nonrecourse financing for provisions relating to increases in tax liability resulting from the taxpayer ceasing to be at risk with respect to certain property.

Subsec. (d)(2). Pub. L. 98–369, §431(b)(2), substituted provisions that for purposes of par. (1), transfers of debt, or agreements to transfer, occurring more than one year after the initial borrowing shall not be treated as increasing nonqualified nonrecourse financing with respect to the taxpayer for provisions that for purposes of par. (1), such transfers (or agreements to transfer) by a qualified person to a nonqualified person would not cause the taxpayer to be treated as ceasing to be at risk.

Subsec. (d)(3)(A). Pub. L. 98–369, §431(d)(4), substituted "increasing the amount of nonqualified nonrecourse financing (within the meaning of section 46(c)(8))" for "ceasing to be at risk".

Subsec. (d)(3)(B)(i). Pub. L. 98–369, §431(d)(5), struck out "other than a loan described in section 46(c)(8)(B)(ii)" after "section 46(c)(8)(F)(iv)".

Subsec. (e). Pub. L. 98–369, §421(b)(7), added subsec. (e).

1983—Subsec. (d)(2). Pub. L. 97–448, §102(e)(3)(A), substituted "section 46(c)(8)(D)" and "section 46(c)(8)(B)" for "section 48(c)(8)(D)" and "section 48(c)(8)(B)", respectively.

Subsec. (d)(3)(A). Pub. L. 97–448, §102(e)(3)(B), substituted "section 46(c)(8)(F)" for "section 46(c)(8)(E)".

1982—Subsec. (a)(5)(D). Pub. L. 97–248, §208(a)(2)(B), inserted provision that if, prior to a disposition to which this subsection applies, any portion of any credit is not allowable with respect to any property by reason of section 168(i)(3), such portion shall be treated, for purposes of this subparagraph, as not having been used to reduce tax liability.

1981—Subsec. (a)(3)(D). Pub. L. 97–34, §211(g)(2)(A), inserted provisions relating to disposition, cessation, or change in expected use described in paragraph (5).

Subsec. (a)(5), (6). Pub. L. 97–34, §211(g)(1), (2)(B), added par. (5), redesignated former par. (5) as (6) and substituted "paragraph (1), (3), or (5)" for "paragraph (1) or (3)". Former par. (6) redesignated (7).

Subsec. (a)(7), (8). Pub. L. 97–34, §211(g)(1), (2)(C), redesignated former par. (6) as (7), substituted "paragraph (6)" for "paragraph (5)", and redesignated former par. (7) as (8).

Subsec. (d). Pub. L. 97–34, §211(f)(2), added subsec. (d).

1978—Subsec. (a)(4), (5). Pub. L. 95–618, §241(b)(1), added par. (4), redesignated former par. (4) as (5) and substituted "paragraph (2) or (4)" for "paragraph (2)".

Subsec. (a)(6)(B). Pub. L. 95–618, §241(b)(3), substituted "paragraph (5)" for "paragraph (4)".

Subsec. (b)(3). Pub. L. 95–600, §317(a), added par. (3).

1976—Subsec. (a). Pub. L. 94–455, §1906(b)(13)(A), struck out in introductory provision and in par. (3)(C) "or his delegate" after "Secretary".

Subsec. (a)(7). Pub. L. 94–455, §804(b), added par. (7).

1975—Subsec. (a)(3), (4). Pub. L. 94–12, §302(b)(2)(A), (c)(1), added par. (3), redesignated former par. (3) as (4) and substituted "paragraph (1) or (3)" for "paragraph (1)". A former par. (4), relating to increase or adjustment of tax where property is destroyed by casualty, etc., was repealed by Pub. L. 92–178.

Subsec. (a)(5), (6)(B). Pub. L. 94–12, §302(c)(2), substituted "paragraph (4)" for "paragraph (3)".

1971—Subsec. (a)(4). Pub. L. 92–178, §107(a)(1), struck out par. (4) relating to property destroyed by casualty, etc.

Subsec. (a)(5). Pub. L. 92–178, §107(b)(1), provided for the repeal of par. (5) with the repeal not to apply, however, in the case of certain replacement property. See section 107(b)(2) of Pub. L. 92–178, set out in the Effective Date of 1971 Amendment note below.

Subsec. (a)(6)(A). Pub. L. 92–178, §102(c), substituted "3½ years" for "4 years".

Subsec. (a)(6). Pub. L. 91–676 added par. (6).

1969—Subsec. (a)(5). Pub. L. 91–172, §703(c)(2), added par. (5).

Subsec. (a)(4). Pub. L. 91–172, §703(c)(1), inserted provision making subpars. (B) and (C) inapplicable to any casualty or theft occurring after April 18, 1969.

STATUTORY NOTES AND RELATED SUBSIDIARIES
EFFECTIVE DATE OF 2017 AMENDMENT

Pub. L. 115–97, title I, §13402(c), Dec. 22, 2017, 131 Stat. 2134, provided that:

"(1) In general.—Except as provided in paragraph (2), the amendments made by this section [amending this section and section 145 of this title] shall apply to amounts paid or incurred after December 31, 2017.

"(2) Transition rule.—In the case of qualified rehabilitation expenditures with respect to any building—

"(A) owned or leased by the taxpayer during the entirety of the period after December 31, 2017, and

"(B) with respect to which the 24-month period selected by the taxpayer under clause (i) of section 47(c)(1)(B) of the Internal Revenue Code (as amended by subsection (b)), or the 60-month period applicable under clause (ii) of such section, begins not later than 180 days after the date of the enactment of this Act [Dec. 22, 2017],

the amendments made by this section shall apply to such expenditures paid or incurred after the end of the taxable year in which the 24-month period, or the 60-month period, referred to in subparagraph (B) ends."

EFFECTIVE DATE OF 2008 AMENDMENT

Pub. L. 110–289, div. C, title I, §3025(b), July 30, 2008, 122 Stat. 2897, provided that: "The amendments made by this section [amending this section] shall apply to expenditures properly taken into account for periods after December 31, 2007."

EFFECTIVE DATE OF 1990 AMENDMENT

Amendment by section 11813(a) of Pub. L. 101–508 applicable to property placed in service after Dec. 31, 1990, but not applicable to any transition property (as defined in section 49(e) of this title), any property with respect to which qualified progress expenditures were previously taken into account under section 46(d) of this title, and any property described in section 46(b)(2)(C) of this title, as such sections were in effect on Nov. 4, 1990, see section 11813(c) of Pub. L. 101–508, set out as a note under section 45K of this title.

EFFECTIVE DATE OF 1988 AMENDMENT

Amendment by Pub. L. 100–647 effective, except as otherwise provided, as if included in the provision of the Tax Reform Act of 1986, Pub. L. 99–514, to which such amendment relates, see section 1019(a) of Pub. L. 100–647, set out as a note under section 1 of this title.

EFFECTIVE DATE OF 1986 AMENDMENT

Pub. L. 99–514, title XV, §1511(d), Oct. 22, 1986, 100 Stat. 2746, provided that: "The amendments made by this section [amending this section and sections 48, 167, 644, 852, 4497, 6214, 6332, 6343, 6601, 6602, 6611, 6621, 6654, 6655, and 7426 of this title and sections 1961 and 2411 of Title 28, Judiciary and Judicial Procedure, and enacting provisions set out as a note under section 6621 of this title] shall apply for purposes of determining interest for periods after December 31, 1986."

Amendment by sections 1802(a)(5)(A) and 1844(b)(1), (2), (4) of Pub. L. 99–514 effective, except as otherwise provided, as if included in the provisions of the Tax Reform Act of 1984, Pub. L. 98–369, div. A, to which such amendment relates, see section 1881 of Pub. L. 99–514, set out as a note under section 48 of this title.

Effective Date of 1985 Amendment

Amendment by Pub. L. 99–121 applicable as if included in the amendments made by section 111 of the Tax Reform Act of 1984, Pub. L. 98–369, see section 105(b)(4) of Pub. L. 99–121, set out as a note under section 168 of this title, and section 111(g) of Pub. L. 98–369, set out as an Effective Date of 1984 Amendment note under section 168 of this title.

Effective Date of 1984 Amendment

Amendment by Pub. L. 98–443 effective Jan. 1, 1985, see section 9(v) of Pub. L. 98–443, set out as a note under section 5314 of Title 5, Government Organization and Employees.

Amendment by section 421(b)(7) of Pub. L. 98–369 applicable to transfers after July 18, 1984, in taxable years ending after such date, subject to election to have amendment apply to transfers after 1983 or to transfers pursuant to existing decrees, see section 421(d) of Pub. L. 98–369, set out as an Effective Date note under section 1041 of this title.

Amendment by section 431(b)(2), (d)(4), (5) of Pub. L. 98–369 applicable to property placed in service after July 18, 1984, in taxable years ending after such date, but not applicable to property to which subsec. (d) of this section and section 46(c)(8), (9) of this title, as enacted by section 211(f) of Pub. L. 97–34, do not apply, with the taxpayer having an option to elect retroactive application of amendment by Pub. L. 98–369, see section 431(e) of Pub. L. 98–369, set out as a note under section 46 of this title.

Amendment by section 474(o)(8), (9) of Pub. L. 98–369 applicable to taxable years beginning after Dec. 31, 1983, and to carrybacks from such years, see section 475(a) of Pub. L. 98–369, set out as a note under section 21 of this title.

Effective Date of 1983 Amendment

Amendment by Pub. L. 97–448 effective, except as otherwise provided, as if it had been included in the provision of the Economic Recovery Tax Act of 1981, Pub. L. 97–34, to which such amendment relates, see section 109 of Pub. L. 97–448, set out as a note under section 1 of this title.

Effective Date of 1982 Amendment

Amendment by Pub. L. 97–248 applicable to agreements entered into after July 1, 1982, or to property placed in service after that date, but not to transitional safe harbor lease property, nor to qualified leased property described in section 168(f)(8)(D)(v) of this title which is placed in service before Jan. 1, 1988, or is placed in service after such date pursuant to a binding contract or commitment entered into before April 1, 1983, and solely because of conditions which, as determined by the Secretary of the Treasury or his delegate, are not within the control of the lessor or lessee, see section 208(d)(1), (2)(A), (5) of Pub. L. 97–248, set out as a note under section 168 of this title.

Effective Date of 1981 Amendment

Amendment by section 211(g) of Pub. L. 97–34 applicable to property placed in service after Dec. 31, 1980, see section 211(i)(1) of Pub. L. 97–34, set out in a note under section 46 of this title.

Amendment by section 211(f)(2) of Pub. L. 97–34 not to apply to property placed in service by the taxpayer on or before Feb. 18, 1981, and property placed in service by the taxpayer after Feb. 18, 1981, where such property was acquired by the taxpayer pursuant to a binding contract entered into on or before that date, see section 211(i)(5) of Pub. L. 97–34, set out as a note under section 46 of this title.

Effective Date of 1978 Amendment

Pub. L. 95–600, title III, §317(b), Nov. 6, 1978, 92 Stat. 2830, provided that: "The amendment made by subsection (a) [amending this section] shall apply to taxable years ending after March 31, 1976."

Effective Date of 1976 Amendment

Amendment by section 804(b) of Pub. L. 94–455 applicable to taxable years beginning after Dec. 31, 1974, see section 804(e) of Pub. L. 94–455, set out as a note under section 48 of this title.

Effective Date of 1975 Amendment

Amendment by Pub. L. 94–12 applicable to taxable years ending after Dec. 31, 1974, see section 305(a) of Pub. L. 94–12, set out as a note under section 46 of this title.

Effective Date of 1971 Amendment

In redetermining qualified investment for purposes of subsec. (a) of this section in the case of any property which ceases to be section 38 property with respect to the taxpayer after Aug. 15, 1971, or which becomes public utility property after such date, section 46(c)(2) of this title as amended by section 102(a) of Pub. L. 92–178 as applicable, see section 102(d)(2) of Pub. L. 92–178, set out as a note under section 46 of this title.

Amendment by section 107(a)(1) of Pub. L. 92–178 applicable to casualties and thefts occurring after Aug. 15, 1971, see section 107(a)(2) of Pub. L. 92–178, set out as a note under section 46 of this title.

Pub. L. 92–178, title I, §107(b)(2), Dec. 10, 1971, 85 Stat. 507, as amended by Pub. L. 99–514, §2, Oct. 22, 1986, 100 Stat. 2095, provided that: "The repeal made by paragraph (1) [repealing subsec. (a)(5) of this section] shall not apply if replacement property described in subparagraph (B) of such section 47(a)(5) is not property described in section 50 of the Internal Revenue Code of 1986 [formerly I.R.C. 1954]."

Pub. L. 92–178, title I, §102(d)(3), Dec. 10, 1971, 85 Stat. 500, provided that: "The amendment made by subsection (c) [amending this section] shall apply to leases executed after April 18, 1969."

Pub. L. 91–676, §2, Jan. 12, 1971, 84 Stat. 2060, provided that: "The amendment made by the first section of this Act [amending this section] shall apply to taxable years ending after April 18, 1969."

Effective Date

Section applicable with respect to taxable years ending after Dec. 31, 1961, see section 2(h) of Pub. L. 87–834, set out as a note under section 46 of this title.

Savings Provision

For provisions that nothing in amendment by Pub. L. 101–508 be construed to affect treatment of certain transactions occurring, property acquired, or items of income, loss, deduction, or credit taken into account prior to Nov. 5, 1990, for purposes of determining liability for tax for periods ending after Nov. 5, 1990, see section 11821(b) of Pub. L. 101–508, set out as a note under section 45K of this title.

Plan Amendments Not Required Until January 1, 1989

For provisions directing that if any amendments made by subtitle A or subtitle C of title XI [§§1101–1147 and 1171–1177] or title XVIII [§§1800–1899A] of Pub. L. 99–514 require an amendment to any plan, such plan amendment shall not be required to be made before the first plan year beginning on or after Jan. 1, 1989, see section 1140 of Pub. L. 99–514, as amended, set out as a note under section 401 of this title.

Clarification of Effect of 1984 Amendment on Investment Tax Credit

For provision that nothing in the amendments made by section 474(o) of Pub. L. 98–369, which amended this section, be construed as reducing the investment tax credit in taxable years beginning before Jan. 1, 1984, see section 475(c) of Pub. L. 98–369, set out as a note under section 46 of this title.

TRANSFER OF FUNCTIONS

Functions, powers, and duties of Federal Aviation Agency and of Administrator and other offices and officers thereof transferred by Pub. L. 89–670, Oct. 15, 1966, 80 Stat. 931, to Secretary of Transportation, with functions, powers, and duties of Secretary of Transportation pertaining to aviation safety to be exercised by Federal Aviation Administrator in Department of Transportation, see section 106 of Title 49, Transportation.

§48. Energy credit

(a) Energy credit

(1) In general

For purposes of section 46, except as provided in paragraphs (1)(B), (2)(B), and (3)(B) of subsection (c), the energy credit for any taxable year is the energy percentage of the basis of each energy property placed in service during such taxable year.

(2) Energy percentage

(A) In general

Except as provided in paragraphs (6) and (7), the energy percentage is—

(i) 30 percent in the case of—

(I) qualified fuel cell property,

(II) energy property described in paragraph (3)(A)(i) but only with respect to property the construction of which begins before January 1, 2024,

(III) energy property described in paragraph (3)(A)(ii),

(IV) qualified small wind energy property, and

(V) waste energy recovery property, and

(ii) in the case of any energy property to which clause (i) does not apply, 10 percent.

(B) Coordination with rehabilitation credit

The energy percentage shall not apply to that portion of the basis of any property which is attributable to qualified rehabilitation expenditures.

(3) Energy property

For purposes of this subpart, the term "energy property" means any property—

(A) which is—

(i) equipment which uses solar energy to generate electricity, to heat or cool (or provide hot water for use in) a structure, or to provide solar process heat, excepting property used to generate energy for the purposes of heating a swimming pool,

(ii) equipment which uses solar energy to illuminate the inside of a structure using fiber-optic distributed sunlight but only with respect to property the construction of which begins before January 1, 2024,

(iii) equipment used to produce, distribute, or use energy derived from a geothermal deposit (within the meaning of section 613(e)(2)), but only, in the case of electricity generated by geothermal power, up to (but not including) the electrical transmission stage,

(iv) qualified fuel cell property or qualified microturbine property,

(v) combined heat and power system property,

(vi) qualified small wind energy property,

(vii) equipment which uses the ground or ground water as a thermal energy source to heat a structure or as a thermal energy sink to cool a structure, but only with respect to property the construction of which begins before January 1, 2024, or

(viii) waste energy recovery property,

(B)(i) the construction, reconstruction, or erection of which is completed by the taxpayer, or

(ii) which is acquired by the taxpayer if the original use of such property commences with the taxpayer,

(C) with respect to which depreciation (or amortization in lieu of depreciation) is allowable, and

(D) which meets the performance and quality standards (if any) which—

(i) have been prescribed by the Secretary by regulations (after consultation with the Secretary of Energy), and

(ii) are in effect at the time of the acquisition of the property.

Such term shall not include any property which is part of a facility the production from which is allowed as a credit under section 45 for the taxable year or any prior taxable year.

(4) Special rule for property financed by subsidized energy financing or industrial development bonds

(A) Reduction of basis

For purposes of applying the energy percentage to any property, if such property is financed in whole or in part by—

(i) subsidized energy financing, or

(ii) the proceeds of a private activity bond (within the meaning of section 141) the interest on which is exempt from tax under section 103,

the amount taken into account as the basis of such property shall not exceed the amount which (but for this subparagraph) would be so taken into account multiplied by the fraction determined under subparagraph (B).

(B) Determination of fraction

For purposes of subparagraph (A), the fraction determined under this subparagraph is 1 reduced by a fraction—

(i) the numerator of which is that portion of the basis of the property which is allocable to such financing or proceeds, and

(ii) the denominator of which is the basis of the property.

(C) Subsidized energy financing

For purposes of subparagraph (A), the term "subsidized energy financing" means financing provided under a Federal, State, or local program a principal purpose of which is to provide subsidized financing for projects designed to conserve or produce energy.

(D) Termination

This paragraph shall not apply to periods after December 31, 2008, under rules similar to the rules of section 48(m) (as in effect on the day before the date of the enactment of the Revenue Reconciliation Act of 1990).

(5) Election to treat qualified facilities as energy property

(A) In general

In the case of any qualified property which is part of a qualified investment credit facility—

(i) such property shall be treated as energy property for purposes of this section, and

(ii) the energy percentage with respect to such property shall be 30 percent.

(B) Denial of production credit

No credit shall be allowed under section 45 for any taxable year with respect to any qualified investment credit facility.

(C) Qualified investment credit facility

For purposes of this paragraph, the term "qualified investment credit facility" means any facility—

(i) which is a qualified facility (within the meaning of section 45) described in paragraph (1), (2), (3), (4), (6), (7), (9), or (11) of section 45(d),

(ii) which is placed in service after 2008 and the construction of which begins before January 1, 2022, and

(iii) with respect to which—

(I) no credit has been allowed under section 45, and

(II) the taxpayer makes an irrevocable election to have this paragraph apply.

(D) Qualified property

For purposes of this paragraph, the term "qualified property" means property—

(i) which is—

(I) tangible personal property, or

(II) other tangible property (not including a building or its structural components), but only if such property is used as an integral part of the qualified investment credit facility,

(ii) with respect to which depreciation (or amortization in lieu of depreciation) is allowable,

(iii) which is constructed, reconstructed, erected, or acquired by the taxpayer, and

(iv) the original use of which commences with the taxpayer.

(E) Phaseout of credit for wind facilities

In the case of any facility using wind to produce electricity which is treated as energy property by reason of this paragraph, the amount of the credit determined under this section (determined after the application of paragraphs (1) and (2) and without regard to this subparagraph) shall be reduced by—

(i) in the case of any facility the construction of which begins after December 31, 2016, and before January 1, 2018, 20 percent,

(ii) in the case of any facility the construction of which begins after December 31, 2017, and before January 1, 2019, 40 percent,

(iii) in the case of any facility the construction of which begins after December 31, 2018, and before January 1, 2020, 60 percent, and

(iv) in the case of any facility the construction of which begins after December 31, 2019, and before January 1, 2022, 40 percent.

(F) Qualified offshore wind facilities

(i) In general

In the case of any qualified offshore wind facility—

(I) subparagraph (C)(ii) shall be applied by substituting "January 1, 2026" for "January 1, 2022",

(II) subparagraph (E) shall not apply, and

(III) for purposes of this paragraph, section 45(d)(1) shall be applied by substituting "January 1, 2026" for "January 1, 2022".

(ii) Qualified offshore wind facility

For purposes of this subparagraph, the term "qualified offshore wind facility" means a qualified facility (within the meaning of section 45) described in paragraph (1) of section 45(d) (determined without regard to any date by which the construction of the facility is required to begin) which is located in the inland navigable waters of the United States or in the coastal waters of the United States.

(6) Phaseout for solar energy property

(A) In general

Subject to subparagraph (B), in the case of any energy property described in paragraph (3)(A)(i) the construction of which begins before January 1, 2024, the energy percentage determined under paragraph (2) shall be equal to—

(i) in the case of any property the construction of which begins after December 31, 2019, and before January 1, 2023, 26 percent, and

(ii) in the case of any property the construction of which begins after December 31, 2022, and before January 1, 2024, 22 percent.

(B) Placed in service deadline

In the case of any energy property described in paragraph (3)(A)(i) the construction of which begins before January 1, 2024, and which is not placed in service before January 1, 2026, the energy percentage determined under paragraph (2) shall be equal to 10 percent.

(7) Phaseout for certain other energy property

(A) In general

Subject to subparagraph (B), in the case of any qualified fuel cell property, qualified small wind property, waste energy recovery property, or energy property described in paragraph (3)(A)(ii), the energy percentage determined under paragraph (2) shall be equal to—

(i) in the case of any property the construction of which begins after December 31, 2019, and before January 1, 2023, 26 percent, and

(ii) in the case of any property the construction of which begins after December 31, 2022, and before January 1, 2024, 22 percent.

(B) Placed in service deadline

In the case of any energy property described in subparagraph (A) which is not placed in service before January 1, 2026, the energy percentage determined under paragraph (2) shall be equal to 0 percent.

(b) Certain progress expenditure rules made applicable

Rules similar to the rules of subsections (c)(4) and (d) of section 46 (as in effect on the day before the date of the enactment of the Revenue Reconciliation Act of 1990) shall apply for purposes of subsection (a).

(c) Definitions

For purposes of this section—

(1) Qualified fuel cell property

(A) In general

The term "qualified fuel cell property" means a fuel cell power plant which—

(i) has a nameplate capacity of at least 0.5 kilowatt of electricity using an electrochemical process, and

(ii) has an electricity-only generation efficiency greater than 30 percent.

(B) Limitation

In the case of qualified fuel cell property placed in service during the taxable year, the credit otherwise determined under subsection (a) for such year with respect to such property shall not exceed an amount equal to $1,500 for each 0.5 kilowatt of capacity of such property.

(C) Fuel cell power plant

The term "fuel cell power plant" means an integrated system comprised of a fuel cell stack assembly and associated balance of plant components which converts a fuel into electricity using electrochemical means.

(D) Termination

The term "qualified fuel cell property" shall not include any property the construction of which does not begin before January 1, 2024.

(2) Qualified microturbine property

(A) In general

The term "qualified microturbine property" means a stationary microturbine power plant which—

(i) has a nameplate capacity of less than 2,000 kilowatts, and

(ii) has an electricity-only generation efficiency of not less than 26 percent at International Standard Organization conditions.

(B) Limitation

In the case of qualified microturbine property placed in service during the taxable year, the credit otherwise determined under subsection (a) for such year with respect to such property shall not exceed an amount equal to $200 for each kilowatt of capacity of such property.

(C) Stationary microturbine power plant

The term "stationary microturbine power plant" means an integrated system comprised of a gas turbine engine, a combustor, a recuperator or regenerator, a generator or alternator, and associated balance of plant components which converts a fuel into electricity and thermal energy. Such term also includes all secondary components located between the existing infrastructure for fuel delivery and the existing infrastructure for power distribution, including equipment and controls for meeting relevant power standards, such as voltage, frequency, and power factors.

(D) Termination

The term "qualified microturbine property" shall not include any property the construction of which does not begin before January 1, 2024.

(3) Combined heat and power system property

(A) Combined heat and power system property

The term "combined heat and power system property" means property comprising a system—

(i) which uses the same energy source for the simultaneous or sequential generation of electrical power, mechanical shaft power, or both, in combination with the generation of steam or other forms of useful thermal energy (including heating and cooling applications),

(ii) which produces—

(I) at least 20 percent of its total useful energy in the form of thermal energy which is not used to produce electrical or mechanical power (or combination thereof), and

(II) at least 20 percent of its total useful energy in the form of electrical or mechanical power (or combination thereof),

(iii) the energy efficiency percentage of which exceeds 60 percent, and

(iv) the construction of which begins before January 1, 2024.

(B) Limitation

(i) In general

In the case of combined heat and power system property with an electrical capacity in excess of the applicable capacity placed in service during the taxable year, the credit under subsection (a)(1) (determined without regard to this paragraph) for such year shall be equal to the amount which bears the same ratio to such credit as the applicable capacity bears to the capacity of such property.

(ii) Applicable capacity

For purposes of clause (i), the term "applicable capacity" means 15 megawatts or a mechanical energy capacity of more than 20,000 horsepower or an equivalent combination of electrical and mechanical energy capacities.

(iii) Maximum capacity

The term "combined heat and power system property" shall not include any property comprising a system if such system has a capacity in excess of 50 megawatts or a mechanical energy capacity in excess of 67,000 horsepower or an equivalent combination of electrical and mechanical energy capacities.

(C) Special rules

(i) Energy efficiency percentage

For purposes of this paragraph, the energy efficiency percentage of a system is the fraction—

(I) the numerator of which is the total useful electrical, thermal, and mechanical power produced by the system at normal operating rates, and expected to be consumed in its normal application, and

(II) the denominator of which is the lower heating value of the fuel sources for the system.

(ii) Determinations made on Btu basis

The energy efficiency percentage and the percentages under subparagraph (A)(ii) shall be determined on a Btu basis.

(iii) Input and output property not included

The term "combined heat and power system property" does not include property used to transport the energy source to the facility or to distribute energy produced by the facility.

(D) Systems using biomass

If a system is designed to use biomass (within the meaning of paragraphs (2) and (3) of section 45(c) without regard to the last sentence of paragraph (3)(A)) for at least 90 percent of the energy source—

(i) subparagraph (A)(iii) shall not apply, but

(ii) the amount of credit determined under subsection (a) with respect to such system shall not exceed the amount which bears the same ratio to such amount of credit (determined without regard to this subparagraph) as the energy efficiency percentage of such system bears to 60 percent.

(4) Qualified small wind energy property

(A) In general

The term "qualified small wind energy property" means property which uses a qualifying small wind turbine to generate electricity.

(B) Qualifying small wind turbine

The term "qualifying small wind turbine" means a wind turbine which has a nameplate capacity of not more than 100 kilowatts.

(C) Termination
The term "qualified small wind energy property" shall not include any property the construction of which does not begin before January 1, 2024.

(5) Waste energy recovery property

(A) In general
The term "waste energy recovery property" means property that generates electricity solely from heat from buildings or equipment if the primary purpose of such building or equipment is not the generation of electricity.

(B) Capacity limitation
The term "waste energy recovery property" shall not include any property which has a capacity in excess of 50 megawatts.

(C) No double benefit
Any waste energy recovery property (determined without regard to this subparagraph) which is part of a system which is a combined heat and power system property shall not be treated as waste energy recovery property for purposes of this section unless the taxpayer elects to not treat such system as a combined heat and power system property for purposes of this section.

(D) Termination
The term "waste energy recovery property" shall not include any property the construction of which does not begin before January 1, 2024.

(d) Coordination with Department of Treasury grants
In the case of any property with respect to which the Secretary makes a grant under section 1603 of the American Recovery and Reinvestment Tax Act of 2009—

(1) Denial of production and investment credits
No credit shall be determined under this section or section 45 with respect to such property for the taxable year in which such grant is made or any subsequent taxable year.

(2) Recapture of credits for progress expenditures made before grant
If a credit was determined under this section with respect to such property for any taxable year ending before such grant is made—

(A) the tax imposed under subtitle A on the taxpayer for the taxable year in which such grant is made shall be increased by so much of such credit as was allowed under section 38,

(B) the general business carryforwards under section 39 shall be adjusted so as to recapture the portion of such credit which was not so allowed, and

(C) the amount of such grant shall be determined without regard to any reduction in the basis of such property by reason of such credit.

(3) Treatment of grants
Any such grant—

(A) shall not be includible in the gross income or alternative minimum taxable income of the taxpayer, but

(B) shall be taken into account in determining the basis of the property to which such grant relates, except that the basis of such property shall be reduced under section 50(c) in the same manner as a credit allowed under subsection (a).

(Added Pub. L. 87–834, §2(b), Oct. 16, 1962, 76 Stat. 967; amended Pub. L. 88–272, title II, §203(a)(1), (3)(A), (b), (c), Feb. 26, 1964, 78 Stat. 33, 34; Pub. L. 89–800, §1 Nov. 8, 1966, 80 Stat. 1508; Pub. L. 89–809, title II, §201(a), Nov. 13, 1966, 80 Stat. 1575; Pub. L. 90–26, §§1, 2(a), 3, June 13, 1967, 81 Stat. 57, 58; Pub. L. 91–172, title I, §121(d)(2)(A), title IV, §401(e)(2)–(4), Dec. 30, 1969, 83 Stat. 547, 603; Pub. L. 92–178, title I, §§102(a)(2), 103, 104(a)(1), (b)–(f)(1), (g), 108(b), (c), Dec. 10, 1971, 85 Stat. 499–502, 507; Pub. L. 94–12, title III, §§301(c)(1), 302(c)(3), title VI, §604(a), Mar. 29, 1975, 89 Stat. 38, 44, 65; Pub. L. 94–455, title VIII, §§802(b)(6), 804(a), title X, §1051(h)(1), title XIX, §§1901(a)(5), (b)(11)(A), 1906(b)(13)(A), title XXI, §2112(a)(1), Oct. 4, 1976, 90 Stat. 1583, 1591, 1647, 1764, 1795, 1834, 1905; Pub. L. 95–473, §2(a)(2)(A), Oct. 17, 1978, 92 Stat. 1464; Pub. L. 95–600, title I, §141(b), title III, §§312(c)(1)–(3), 314(a), (b), 315(a)–(c), title VII, §703(a)(3), (4), Nov. 6, 1978, 92 Stat. 2791, 2826–2829, 2939; Pub. L. 95–618, title III, §301(b), (d)(1), (2), Nov. 9, 1978, 92 Stat. 3195, 3199, 3200; Pub. L. 96–222, title I, §§101(a)(7)(G), (H), (L)(i)(I)–(IV), (ii)(III)–(VI), (iii)(II), (III), (v)(II)–(V), (M)(ii), (iii), 103(a)(2)(A), (4)(B), 108(c)(6), Apr. 1, 1980, 94 Stat. 198–201, 208, 209, 228; Pub. L. 96–223, title II, §§221(b), 222(a)–(e)(1), (f)–(i), 223(a)(1), (c)(1), Apr. 2, 1980, 94 Stat. 261–266; Pub. L. 96–451, title III, §302(a), Oct. 14, 1980, 94 Stat. 1991; Pub. L. 96–605, title I, §109(a), title II, §223(a), Dec. 28, 1980, 94 Stat. 3525, 3528; Pub. L. 97–34, title II, §§211(a)(2), (c), (e)(3), (4), (h), 212(a)(3), (b), (c), (d)(2)(A), 213(a), 214(a), (b), title III, §332(b), Aug. 13, 1981, 95 Stat. 227–229, 235, 236, 239, 240, 296; Pub. L. 97–248, title II, §§205(a)(1), (4), (5)(A), 209(c), Sept. 3, 1982, 96 Stat. 427, 429, 447; Pub. L. 97–354, §§3(d), 5(a)(7), (8), Oct. 19, 1982, 96 Stat. 1689, 1692; Pub. L. 97–362, title I, §104(a), Oct. 25, 1982, 96 Stat. 1729; Pub. L. 97–424, title V, §546(a), Jan. 6, 1983, 96 Stat. 2198; Pub. L. 97–448, title I, §102(e)(2)(A), (f)(2), (3), (6), title II, §202(c), title III, §306(a)(3), Jan. 12, 1983, 96 Stat. 2371, 2372, 2396, 2400; Pub. L. 98–369, div. A, title I, §§11, 31(b), (c), 111(e)(8), 113(a)(1), (b)(3), (4), 114(a), title IV, §§431(c), 474(o)(10)–(18), title VII, §§712(b), 721(x)(1), 735(c)(1), title X, §1043(a), July 18, 1984, 98 Stat. 503, 517, 518, 633, 635, 637, 638, 808, 836, 837, 946, 971, 981, 1044; Pub. L. 99–121, title I, §103(b)(5), Oct. 11, 1985, 99 Stat. 510; Pub. L. 99–514, title II, §251(b), (c), title VII, §701(e)(4)(C), title VIII, §803(b)(2)(B), title XII, §§1272(d)(5), 1275(c)(5), title XV, §1511(c)(3), title XVIII, §1802(a)(4)(C), (5)(B), (9)(A), (B), 1809(d)(2), (e), 1847(b)(6), 1879(j)(1), Oct. 22, 1986, 100 Stat. 2184, 2186, 2343, 2355, 2594, 2599, 2745, 2788, 2789, 2821, 2856, 2908; Pub. L. 100–647, title I, §§1002(a)(14), (16)(A), (20), (29), (30), 1013(a)(41), Nov. 10, 1988, 102 Stat. 3355–3357, 3544; Pub. L. 101–508, title XI, §§11801(c)(6)(A), 11813(a), Nov. 5, 1990, 104 Stat. 1388–523, 1388-541; Pub. L. 102–227, title I, §106, Dec. 11, 1991, 105 Stat. 1687; Pub. L. 102–486, title XIX, §1916(a), Oct. 24, 1992, 106 Stat. 3024; Pub. L. 108–357, title III, §322(d)(2)(A), (B), title VII, §710(e), Oct. 22, 2004, 118 Stat. 1475, 1557; Pub. L. 109–58, title XIII, §§1336(a)–(d), 1337(a)–(c), Aug. 8, 2005, 119 Stat. 1036–1038; Pub. L. 109–135, title IV, §412(m), (n), Dec. 21, 2005, 119 Stat. 2638; Pub. L. 109–432, div. A, title II, §207, Dec. 20, 2006, 120 Stat. 2945; Pub. L. 110–172, §11(a)(8), (9), Dec. 29, 2007, 121 Stat. 2485; Pub. L. 110–343, div. B, title I, §§103(a), (c)–(e), 104(a)–(d), 105(a), Oct. 3, 2008, 122 Stat. 3811, 3813, 3814; Pub. L. 111–5, div. B, title I, §§1102(a), 1103(a), (b)(1), 1104, Feb. 17, 2009, 123 Stat. 319–321; Pub. L. 112–240, title IV, §407(b), (c)(1), Jan. 2, 2013, 126 Stat. 2341; Pub. L. 113–295, div. A, title I, §155(b), title II, §209(d), Dec. 19, 2014, 128 Stat. 4021, 4028; Pub. L. 114–113, div. P, title III, §§302(a), (b), 303(a)–(c), div. Q, title I, §187(b), Dec. 18, 2015, 129 Stat. 3038, 3039, 3074; Pub. L. 115–123, div. D, title I, §§40409(b), 40411(a)–(f), Feb. 9, 2018, 132 Stat. 150, 151; Pub. L. 115–141, div. U, title IV, §401(a)(20)–(23), (350), Mar. 23, 2018, 132 Stat. 1185, 1201; Pub. L. 116–94, div. Q, title I, §127(b), (c)(2)(B), Dec. 20, 2019, 133 Stat. 3232; Pub. L. 116–260, div. EE, title I, §§131(b), (c)(2), 132(a), (b), title II, §§203(a)–(d), 204(a), Dec. 27, 2020, 134 Stat. 3052, 3057.)

EDITORIAL NOTES

REFERENCES IN TEXT

The date of the enactment of the Revenue Reconciliation Act of 1990, referred to in subsecs. (a)(4)(D) and (b), is the date of enactment of Pub. L. 101–508, which was approved Nov. 5, 1990.

Section 1603 of the American Recovery and Reinvestment Tax Act of 2009, referred to in subsec. (d), is section 1603 of Pub. L. 111–5, which is set out as a note below.

AMENDMENTS

2020—Subsec. (a)(2)(A)(i)(II). Pub. L. 116–260, §132(a)(1)(A), substituted "January 1, 2024" for "January 1, 2022".

Subsec. (a)(2)(A)(i)(V). Pub. L. 116–260, §203(b), added subcl. (V).

Subsec. (a)(3)(A)(ii), (vii). Pub. L. 116–260, §132(a)(1)(B), substituted "January 1, 2024" for "January 1, 2022".

Subsec. (a)(3)(A)(viii). Pub. L. 116–260, §203(a), added cl. (viii).

Subsec. (a)(5)(C)(ii). Pub. L. 116–260, §131(b), substituted "January 1, 2022" for "January 1, 2021".

Subsec. (a)(5)(E)(iv). Pub. L. 116–260, §131(c)(2), substituted "January 1, 2022" for "January 1, 2021".

Subsec. (a)(5)(F). Pub. L. 116–260, §204(a), added subpar. (F).

Subsec. (a)(6)(A). Pub. L. 116–260, §132(b)(1)(A)(i), substituted "January 1, 2024, the energy percentage" for "January 1, 2022, the energy percentage" in introductory provisions.

Subsec. (a)(6)(A)(i). Pub. L. 116–260, §132(b)(1)(A)(ii), substituted "January 1, 2023" for "January 1, 2021".

Subsec. (a)(6)(A)(ii). Pub. L. 116–260, §132(b)(1)(A)(iii), substituted "after December 31, 2022, and before January 1, 2024" for "after December 31, 2020, and before January 1, 2022".

Subsec. (a)(6)(B). Pub. L. 116–260, §132(b)(1)(B), substituted "begins before January 1, 2024, and which is not placed in service before January 1, 2026" for "begins before January 1, 2022, and which is not placed in service before January 1, 2024".

Subsec. (a)(7). Pub. L. 116–260, §203(c)(2), substituted "certain other" for "fiber-optic solar, qualified fuel cell, and qualified small wind" in heading.

Subsec. (a)(7)(A). Pub. L. 116–260, §203(c)(1), inserted "waste energy recovery property," after "qualified small wind property," in introductory provisions.

Subsec. (a)(7)(A)(i). Pub. L. 116–260, §132(b)(2)(A)(i), substituted "January 1, 2023" for "January 1, 2021".

Subsec. (a)(7)(A)(ii). Pub. L. 116–260, §132(b)(2)(A)(ii), substituted "after December 31, 2022, and before January 1, 2024" for "after December 31, 2020, and before January 1, 2022".

Subsec. (a)(7)(B). Pub. L. 116–260, §132(b)(2)(B), substituted "January 1, 2026" for "January 1, 2024".

Subsec. (c)(1)(D), (2)(D), (3)(A)(iv), (4)(C). Pub. L. 116–260, §132(a)(2), substituted "January 1, 2024" for "January 1, 2022".

Subsec. (c)(5). Pub. L. 116–260, §203(d), added par. (5).

2019—Subsec. (a)(5)(C)(ii). Pub. L. 116–94, §127(b), substituted "January 1, 2021" for "January 1, 2018 (January 1, 2020, in the case of any facility which is described in paragraph (1) of section 45(d))".

Subsec. (a)(5)(E)(iv). Pub. L. 116–94, §127(c)(2)(B), added cl. (iv).

2018—Subsec. (a)(1). Pub. L. 115–141, §401(a)(20), substituted "and (3)(B)" for "(3)(B), and (4)(B)".

Subsec. (a)(2)(A). Pub. L. 115–123, §40411(b)(2), substituted "paragraphs (6) and (7)" for "paragraph (6)" in introductory provisions.

Subsec. (a)(3)(A)(ii), (vii). Pub. L. 115–123, §40411(a), substituted "property the construction of which begins before January 1, 2022" for "periods ending before January 1, 2017".

Subsec. (a)(5)(C)(ii). Pub. L. 115–141, §401(a)(350)(A), made technical amendment to directory language of Pub. L. 114–113, §302(a). See 2015 Amendment note below.

Pub. L. 115–123, §40409(b), substituted "January 1, 2018" for "January 1, 2017".

Subsec. (a)(5)(E). Pub. L. 115–141, §401(a)(350)(B), made technical amendment to directory language of Pub. L. 114–113, §302(b). See 2015 Amendment note below.

Pub. L. 115–123, §40411(b)(3), inserted "which is treated as energy property by reason of this paragraph" after "using wind to produce electricity" in introductory provisions.

Subsec. (a)(6)(B). Pub. L. 115–141, §401(a)(21), substituted "energy property" for "property energy property".

Subsec. (a)(7). Pub. L. 115–123, §40411(b)(1), added par. (7).

Subsec. (c)(1)(D). Pub. L. 115–123, §40411(c), substituted "the construction of which does not begin before January 1, 2022" for "for any period after December 31, 2016".

Subsec. (c)(2)(B). Pub. L. 115–141, §401(a)(22), substituted "equal to $200" for "equal $200".

Subsec. (c)(2)(D). Pub. L. 115–123, §40411(d), substituted "the construction of which does not begin before January 1, 2022" for "for any period after December 31, 2016".

Subsec. (c)(3)(A)(iv). Pub. L. 115–123, §40411(e), substituted "the construction of which begins before January 1, 2022" for "which is placed in service before January 1, 2017".

Subsec. (c)(4)(C). Pub. L. 115–123, §40411(f), substituted "the construction of which does not begin before January 1, 2022" for "for any period after December 31, 2016".

Subsec. (d)(3). Pub. L. 115–141, §401(a)(23)(A), struck out "shall" after "grant" in introductory provisions.

Subsec. (d)(3)(A). Pub. L. 115–141, §401(a)(23)(B), inserted "shall" before "not".

2015—Subsec. (a)(2)(A). Pub. L. 114–113, §303(c), substituted "Except as provided in paragraph (6), the energy percentage" for "The energy percentage" in introductory provisions.

Subsec. (a)(2)(A)(i)(II). Pub. L. 114–113, §303(a), substituted "property the construction of which begins before January 1, 2022" for "periods ending before January 1, 2017".

Subsec. (a)(5)(C)(ii). Pub. L. 114–113, §187(b), substituted "January 1, 2017" for "January 1, 2015".

Pub. L. 114–113, §302(a), as amended by Pub. L. 115–141, §401(a)(350)(A), inserted "(January 1, 2020, in the case of any facility which is described in paragraph (1) of section 45(d))" before ", and".

Subsec. (a)(5)(E). Pub. L. 114–113, §302(b), as amended by Pub. L. 115–141, §401(a)(350)(B), added subpar. (E).

Subsec. (a)(6). Pub. L. 114–113, §303(b), added par. (6).

2014—Subsec. (a)(5)(C)(ii). Pub. L. 113–295, §155(b), substituted "January 1, 2015" for "January 1, 2014".

Subsec. (d)(3)(A). Pub. L. 113–295, §209(d), inserted "or alternative minimum taxable income" after "includible in the gross income".

2013—Subsec. (a)(5)(C). Pub. L. 112–240, §407(b), amended subpar. (C) generally. Prior to amendment, text read as follows: "For purposes of this paragraph, the term 'qualified investment credit facility' means any of the following facilities if no credit has been allowed under section 45 with respect to such facility and the taxpayer makes an irrevocable election to have this paragraph apply to such facility:

"(i) Wind facilities.—Any qualified facility (within the meaning of section 45) described in paragraph (1) of section 45(d) if such facility is placed in service in 2009, 2010, 2011, or 2012.

"(ii) Other facilities.—Any qualified facility (within the meaning of section 45) described in paragraph (2), (3), (4), (6), (7), (9), or (11) of section 45(d) if such facility is placed in service in 2009, 2010, 2011, 2012, or 2013."

Subsec. (a)(5)(D)(iii), (iv). Pub. L. 112–240, §407(c)(1), added cls. (iii) and (iv).

2009—Subsec. (a)(4)(D). Pub. L. 111–5, §1103(b)(1), added subpar. (D).

Subsec. (a)(5). Pub. L. 111–5, §1102(a), added par. (5).

Subsec. (c)(4)(B) to (D). Pub. L. 111–5, §1103(a), redesignated subpars. (C) and (D) as (B) and (C), respectively, and struck out former subpar. (B). Text of former subpar. (B) read as follows: "In the case of qualified small wind energy property placed in service during the taxable year, the credit otherwise determined under subsection (a)(1) for such year with respect to all such property of the taxpayer shall not exceed $4,000."

Subsec. (d). Pub. L. 111–5, §1104, added subsec. (d).

2008—Subsec. (a)(1). Pub. L. 110–343, §104(d), substituted "paragraphs (1)(B), (2)(B), (3)(B), and (4)(B)" for "paragraphs (1)(B), (2)(B), and (3)(B)".

Pub. L. 110–343, §103(c)(3), substituted "paragraphs (1)(B), (2)(B), and (3)(B)" for "paragraphs (1)(B) and (2)(B)".

Subsec. (a)(2)(A)(i)(II). Pub. L. 110–343, §103(a)(1), substituted "January 1, 2017" for "January 1, 2009".

Subsec. (a)(2)(A)(i)(IV). Pub. L. 110–343, §104(b), added subcl. (IV).

Subsec. (a)(3). Pub. L. 110–343, §103(e)(1), in concluding provisions, struck out "The term 'energy property' shall not include any property which is public utility property (as defined in section 46(f)(5) as in effect on the day before the date of the enactment of the Revenue Reconciliation Act of 1990)." before "Such term".

Subsec. (a)(3)(A)(ii). Pub. L. 110–343, §103(a)(1), substituted "January 1, 2017" for "January 1, 2009".

Subsec. (a)(3)(A)(v). Pub. L. 110–343, §103(c)(1), added cl. (v).

Subsec. (a)(3)(A)(vi). Pub. L. 110–343, §104(a), added cl. (vi).

Subsec. (a)(3)(A)(vii). Pub. L. 110–343, §105(a), added cl. (vii).

Subsec. (c). Pub. L. 110–343, §103(c)(2)(A), inserted heading and struck out former heading "Qualified fuel cell property; qualified microturbine property".

Subsec. (c)(1)(B). Pub. L. 110–343, §103(d), substituted "$1,500" for "$500".

Subsec. (c)(1)(D). Pub. L. 110–343, §103(e)(2)(A), redesignated subpar. (E) as (D) and struck out heading and text of former subpar. (D). Text read as follows: "The first sentence of the matter in subsection (a)(3) which follows subparagraph (D) thereof shall not apply to qualified fuel cell property which is used predominantly in the trade or business of the furnishing or sale of telephone service, telegraph service by means of domestic telegraph operations, or other telegraph services (other than international telegraph services)."

Subsec. (c)(1)(E). Pub. L. 110–343, §103(e)(2)(A), redesignated subpar. (E) as (D).

Pub. L. 110–343, §103(a)(2), substituted "December 31, 2016" for "December 31, 2008".

Subsec. (c)(2)(D). Pub. L. 110–343, §103(e)(2)(B), redesignated subpar. (E) as (D) and struck out heading and text of former subpar. (D). Text read as follows: "The first sentence of the matter in subsection (a)(3) which follows subparagraph (D) thereof shall not apply to qualified microturbine property which is used predominantly in the trade or business of the furnishing or sale of telephone service, telegraph service by means of domestic telegraph operations, or other telegraph services (other than international telegraph services)."

Subsec. (c)(2)(E). Pub. L. 110–343, §103(e)(2)(B), redesignated subpar. (E) as (D).

Pub. L. 110–343, §103(a)(3), substituted "December 31, 2016" for "December 31, 2008".

Subsec. (c)(3). Pub. L. 110–343, §103(c)(2)(B), added par. (3).

Subsec. (c)(4). Pub. L. 110–343, §104(c), added par. (4).

2007—Subsec. (c). Pub. L. 110–172, §11(a)(8), substituted "section" for "subsection" in introductory provisions.

Subsec. (c)(1)(B), (2)(B). Pub. L. 110–172, §11(a)(9), substituted "subsection (a)" for "paragraph (1)".

2006—Subsec. (a)(2)(A)(i)(II), (3)(A)(ii). Pub. L. 109–432, §207(1), substituted "January 1, 2009" for "January 1, 2008".

Subsec. (c)(1)(E), (2)(E). Pub. L. 109–432, §207(2), substituted "December 31, 2008" for "December 31, 2007".

2005—Subsec. (a)(1). Pub. L. 109–135, §412(m), substituted "paragraphs (1)(B) and (2)(B) of subsection (c)" for "paragraph (1)(B) or (2)(B) of subsection (d)".

Pub. L. 109–58, §1336(d), inserted "except as provided in paragraph (1)(B) or (2)(B) of subsection (d)," before "the energy credit".

Subsec. (a)(2)(A). Pub. L. 109–58, §1337(a), reenacted heading without change and amended text of subpar. (A) generally. Prior to amendment, text read as follows: "The energy percentage is—

"(i) in the case of qualified fuel cell property, 30 percent, and

"(ii) in the case of any other energy property, 10 percent."

Pub. L. 109–58, §1336(c), reenacted heading without change and amended text of subpar. (A) generally. Prior to amendment, text read as follows: "The energy percentage is 10 percent."

Subsec. (a)(3)(A)(i). Pub. L. 109–58, §1337(c), inserted "excepting property used to generate energy for the purposes of heating a swimming pool," after "solar process heat,".

Subsec. (a)(3)(A)(ii). Pub. L. 109–135, §412(n)(2), struck out "or" at end.

Pub. L. 109–58, §1337(b), added cl. (ii). Former cl. (ii) redesignated (iii) relating to equipment used to produce, distribute, or use energy derived from a geothermal deposit.

Subsec. (a)(3)(A)(iii). Pub. L. 109–58, §1337(b), redesignated cl. (ii) as (iii) relating to equipment used to produce, distribute, or use energy derived from a geothermal deposit.

Pub. L. 109–58, §1336(a), added cl. (iii) relating to qualified fuel cell property or qualified microturbine property.

Subsec. (a)(3)(A)(iv). Pub. L. 109–135, §412(n)(1), redesignated cl. (iii), relating to qualified fuel cell property or qualified microturbine property, as (iv).

Subsec. (c). Pub. L. 109–58, §1336(b), added subsec. (c).

2004—Pub. L. 108–357, §322(d)(2)(B), struck out "; reforestation credit" after "Energy credit" in section catchline.

Subsec. (a)(3). Pub. L. 108–357, §710(e), inserted at end of concluding provisions "Such term shall not include any property which is part of a facility the production from which is allowed as a credit under section 45 for the taxable year or any prior taxable year."

Subsec. (a)(5). Pub. L. 108–357, §322(d)(2)(A)(iii), redesignated subsec. (a)(5) as (b).

Pub. L. 108–357, §322(d)(2)(A)(ii), substituted "subsection (a)" for "this subsection".

Subsec. (b). Pub. L. 108–357, §322(d)(2)(A)(iii), redesignated subsec. (a)(5) as (b).

Pub. L. 108–357, §322(d)(2)(A)(i), struck out heading and text of subsec. (b). Text read as follows:

"(1) In general.—For purposes of section 46, the reforestation credit for any taxable year is 10 percent of the portion of the amortizable basis of any qualified timber property which was acquired during such taxable year and which is taken into account under section 194 (after the application of section 194(b)(1)).

"(2) Definitions.—For purposes of this subpart, the terms 'amortizable basis' and 'qualified timber property' have the respective meanings given to such terms by section 194."

1992—Subsec. (a)(2). Pub. L. 102–486 substituted "The" for "Except as provided in subparagraph (B), the" in subpar. (A), redesignated subpar. (C) as (B), and struck out former subpar. (B) which read as follows: "(B) Termination.—Effective with respect to periods after June 30, 1992, the energy percentage is zero. For purposes of the preceding sentence, rules similar to the rules of section 48(m) (as in effect on the day before the date of the enactment of the Revenue Reconciliation Act of 1990) shall apply."

1991—Subsec. (a)(2)(B). Pub. L. 102–227 substituted "June 30, 1992" for "December 31, 1991".

1990—Pub. L. 101–508, §11813(a), amended section generally, substituting section catchline for one which read: "Definitions; special rules" and in text substituting present provisions for provisions defining section 38 property, new section 38 property, used section 38 property, provisions relating to certain leased property, estates and trusts, special rules for qualified rehabilitated buildings, credit for movie and television films, treatment of energy property, application of certain transitional rules, definitions of certain credits, definition of single purpose agricultural or horticultural structure, basis adjustment to section 38 property, certain section 501(d) organizations, special rules relating to sound recordings, and a cross reference to section 381 of this title.

356

Subsec. (a)(8). Pub. L. 101–508, §11801(c)(6)(A), struck out par. (8) "Amortized property" which read as follows: "Any property with respect to which an election under section 167(k), 184, or 188 applies shall not be treated as section 38 property."

1988—Subsec. (a)(1). Pub. L. 100–647, §1002(a)(29), which directed amendment of par. (1) by substituting "property to which section 168 applies" for "recovery property (within the meaning of section 168)" in penultimate sentence, was executed by making the substitution for "recovery property (within the meaning of section 168)", which results in retaining remaining parenthetical material and closing parenthesis.

Subsec. (a)(5)(A)(ii). Pub. L. 100–647, §1002(a)(14)(A)–(C), substituted "168(h)(2)(C)" for "168(j)(4)(C)", "168(h)(2)(A)(iii)" for "168(j)(4)(A)(iii)", and "168(h)(2)(B)" for "168(j)(4)(B)".

Subsec. (a)(5)(B)(i). Pub. L. 100–647, §1002(a)(14)(D), substituted "168(i)(3)" for "168(j)(6)".

Subsec. (a)(5)(B)(ii). Pub. L. 100–647, §1002(a)(14)(E), substituted "168(h)(1)(C)(ii)" for "168(j)(3)(C)(ii)".

Subsec. (a)(5)(D). Pub. L. 100–647, §1002(a)(14)(F), substituted "paragraphs (5) and (6) of section 168(h)" for "paragraphs (8) and (9) of section 168(j)".

Subsec. (a)(5)(E). Pub. L. 100–647, §1002(a)(14)(G), amended subpar. (E) generally, substituting "provision" for "provisions" and "168(h)" for "168(j)".

Subsec. (l)(2)(C). Pub. L. 100–647, §1002(a)(30), substituted "to which section 168 applies" for "which is recovery property (within the meaning of section 168)".

Subsec. (l)(11)(A)(ii). Pub. L. 100–647, §1013(a)(41), substituted "a private activity bond (within the meaning of section 141)" for "an industrial development bond (within the meaning of section 103(b)(2))".

Subsec. (s). Pub. L. 100–647, §1002(a)(20), redesignated subsec. (s), relating to cross reference, as (t).

Subsec. (s)(9). Pub. L. 100–647, §1002(a)(16)(A), added par. (9).

Subsec. (t). Pub. L. 100–647, §1002(a)(20), redesignated subsec. (s), relating to cross reference, as (t).

1986—Subsec. (a)(2)(B)(vii). Pub. L. 99–514, §§1272(d)(5), 1275(c)(5), struck out "932," after "931," and "or which is entitled to the benefits of section 934(b)" after "in effect under section 936", and substituted "or 933" for ", 933, or 934(c)".

Subsec. (a)(4). Pub. L. 99–514, §1802(a)(9)(A), substituted "514(b)" for "514(c)" and "514(a)" for "514(b)".

Subsec. (a)(5)(B)(iii). Pub. L. 99–514, §1802(a)(5)(B), struck out cl. (iii) which provided that (I) in the case of any aircraft used under a qualifying lease (as defined in section 47(a)(7)(C) and which is leased to a foreign person or entity before January 1, 1990, clause (i) shall be applied by substituting "3 years" for "6 months" and that (II) for purposes of applying section 47(a)(1) and (5)(B) there shall not be taken into account any period of a lease to which subclause (I) applies.

Subsec. (a)(5)(D), (E). Pub. L. 99–514, §1802(a)(4)(C), added subpar. (D) and redesignated former subpar. (D) as (E).

Subsec. (b)(1). Pub. L. 99–514, §1809(e)(1), inserted "Such term includes any section 38 property the reconstruction of which is completed by the taxpayer, but only with respect to that portion of the basis which is properly attributable to such reconstruction."

Subsec. (b)(2). Pub. L. 99–514, §1809(e)(2), in introductory provisions substituted "the first sentence of paragraph (1)" for "paragraph (1)", in subpar. (B) substituted "3 months after" for "3 months of", in closing provisions substituted "used under the leaseback (or lease) referred to in subparagraph (B)" for "used under the lease" and inserted "The preceding sentence shall not apply to any property if the lessee and lessor of such property make an election under this sentence. Such an election, once made, may be revoked only with the consent of the Secretary."

Subsec. (d)(4)(D). Pub. L. 99–514, §701(e)(4)(C), inserted "(as in effect on the day before the date of the enactment of the Tax Reform Act of 1986)".

Subsec. (d)(6)(C)(ii). Pub. L. 99–514, §1511(c)(3), substituted "the underpayment rate" for "the rate" in closing provisions.

Subsec. (g)(1). Pub. L. 99–514, §251(b), amended par. (1) generally, restating in subpars. (A) to (D) provisions relating to qualified rehabilitated buildings which had in subpar. (A) provided general definition of qualified rehabilitated building, in subpar. (B) directed that 30 years must have elapsed since construction, in subpar. (C) provided general definition of substantially rehabilitated with special rule for phased rehabilitation and application of provision to lessees, and in subpar. (D) provided that rehabilitation included reconstruction, and striking out former subpar. (E) which had provided an alternative test for definition of qualified rehabilitated building.

Subsec. (g)(2). Pub. L. 99–514, §251(b), amended par. (2) generally, in subpar. (A) striking out reference to amounts "incurred after December 31, 1981" in introductory provision, and in cl. (i) substituting subcls. (I) to (IV) for "for real property (or additions or improvements to real property) which have a recovery period (within the meaning of section 168) of 19 (15 years in the case of low-income housing) years,", in subpar. (B), in cl. (i), substituting provision relating to use of straight line depreciation for provision relating to use of accelerated methods of depreciation, redesignating former cl. (vi) as (v) and substituting "section 168(h)" for "section 168(j)", redesignating former cl. (v) as (vi) and substituting "less than the recovery period determined under section 168(c)" for "less than 19 years (15 years in the case of low-income housing", restating subpar. (C) without change, and in subpar. (D) substituting provisions defining nonresidential real property, residential rental property and class life for provisions defining low-income housing.

Subsec. (g)(2)(B)(vi)(I). Pub. L. 99–514, §1802(a)(9)(B), substituted "section 168(j)" for "section 168(j)(3)".

Subsec. (g)(3). Pub. L. 99–514, §251(b), in amending par. (3) generally, inserted introductory phrase "For purposes of this subsection—".

Subsec. (g)(4). Pub. L. 99–514, §251(b), in amending subsec. (g) generally, reenacted par. (4) without change.

Subsec. (l)(5). Pub. L. 99–514, §1847(b)(6), substituted "section 23(c)" for "section 44C(c)" and "section 23(c)(4)(A)(viii)" for "section 44C(c)(4)(A)(viii)".

Subsec. (q)(3). Pub. L. 99–514, §251(c), struck out "other than a certified historic structure" after "qualified rehabilitated building".

Subsec. (q)(7). Pub. L. 99–514, §1809(d)(2), renumbered par. (6), relating to special rule for qualified films, as (7).

Subsec. (r). Pub. L. 99–514, §1879(j)(1), added subsec. (r). Former subsec. (r) redesignated (s).

Subsec. (s). Pub. L. 99–514, §1879(j)(1), redesignated former subsec. (r) as (s).

Subsec. (s)(5). Pub. L. 99–514, §803(b)(2)(B), which directed the general amendment of par. (5) of subsec. (r), was executed by amending par. (5) of subsec. (s) to reflect the probable intent of Congress and the intervening redesignation of subsec. (r) as (s) by Pub. L. 99–514, §1879(j)(1), see note above. Prior to amendment, par. (5) read as follows: "For purposes of this subsection, the term 'sound recording' means any sound recording described in section 280(c)(2)."

1985—Subsec. (g)(2)(A)(i), (B)(v). Pub. L. 99–121 substituted "19" for "18".

1984—Subsec. (a)(5). Pub. L. 98–369, §31(b), amended par. (5) generally, to extend its scope to encompass property used by foreign persons or entities and to create an exception for short-term leases by substituting provisions covered by subpars. (A) to (D) for former provisions which had directed that property used by the United States, any State or political subdivision thereof, any international organization, or any agency or instrumentality of any of the foregoing not be treated as section 38 property, that for purposes of that prohibition the International Telecommunications Satellite Consortium, the International Maritime Satellite Organization, and any successor organization of such Consortium or Organization not be treated as an international organization, and that if any qualified rehabilitated building were used by the governmental unit pursuant to a lease, this paragraph would not apply to that portion of the basis of such building attributable to qualified rehabilitation expenditures.

Subsec. (b). Pub. L. 98–369, §114(a), amended subsec. (b) generally, substituting a general definition of "new section 38 property" for definitions which made reference to property constructed, reconstructed or erected after December 31, 1961, and adding pars. (2) and (3).

Subsec. (c)(2)(A). Pub. L. 98–369, §11(a), substituted "$125,000 ($150,000 for taxable years beginning after 1987)" for "$150,000 ($125,000 for taxable years beginning in 1981, 1982, 1983, or 1984)" in first sentence, and "$125,000 (or $150,000)" for "$150,000 (or $125,000)" in two places in second sentence.

Subsec. (c)(2)(B). Pub. L. 98–369, §11(b), substituted "$62,500 ($75,000 for taxable years beginning after 1987)" for "$75,000 ($62,500 for taxable years beginning in 1981, 1982, 1983, or 1984)".

Subsec. (c)(3)(B). Pub. L. 98–369, §474(o)(10), substituted "section 39" for "section 46(b)".

Subsec. (d)(1)(B). Pub. L. 98–369, §474(o)(11), substituted "section 38(c)(3)(B)" for "section 46(a)(6)".

Subsec. (d)(6). Pub. L. 98–369, §431(c), added par. (6).

Subsec. (f)(3). Pub. L. 98–369, §474(o)(12), struck out par. (3) which provided that the $25,000 amount specified under subparagraphs (A) and (B) of section 46(a)(3) applicable to an estate or trust be reduced to an amount which bore the same ratio to $25,000 as the amount of the qualified investment allocated to the estate or trust under paragraph (1) to the entire amount of the qualified investment.

Subsec. (g)(1)(E). Pub. L. 98–369, §1043(a), added subpar. (E).

Subsec. (g)(2)(A)(i). Pub. L. 98–369, §111(e)(8)(A), (B), substituted "real property" for "property" in two places, and "18 (15 years in the case of low-income housing)" for "15".

Subsec. (g)(2)(B)(i). Pub. L. 98–369, §31(c)(2), inserted "The preceding sentence shall not apply to any expenditure to the extent subsection (f)(12) or (j) of section 168 applies to such expenditure."

Subsec. (g)(2)(B)(v). Pub. L. 98–369, §111(e)(8)(C), substituted "18 years (15 years in the case of low-income housing)" for "15 years".

Subsec. (g)(2)(B)(vi). Pub. L. 98–369, §31(c)(1), added cl. (vi).

Subsec. (g)(2)(D). Pub. L. 98–369, §111(e)(8)(D), added subpar. (D).

Subsec. (k)(4). Pub. L. 98–369, §113(b)(3)(B), inserted "or at-risk rules" after "test" in heading.

Subsec. (k)(4)(A). Pub. L. 98–369, §113(b)(3)(A), inserted ", section 46(c)(8), or section 46(c)(9)".

Subsec. (k)(4)(B). Pub. L. 98–369, §113(b)(3)(C), substituted "used" for "issued".

Subsec. (k)(5)(D)(i). Pub. L. 98–369, §721(x)(1), substituted "S corporation" for "electing small business corporation".

Subsec. (l)(1). Pub. L. 98–369, §474(o)(13), substituted "section 46(b)(2)" for "section 46(a)(2)(C)".

Subsec. (l)(16)(B)(i). Pub. L. 98–369, §735(c)(1), substituted "the chassis of which is an automobile bus chassis and the body of which is an automobile bus body" for "the chassis and body of which is exempt under section 4063(a)(6) from the tax imposed by section 4061(a)".

Subsec. (m). Pub. L. 98–369, §474(o)(14), substituted "subsection (b)" for "subsection (a)(2)".

Subsec. (n). Pub. L. 98–369, §474(o)(15), repealed subsec. (n). For continuing applicability of par. (4) of subsec. (n), see section 474(o)(15) of Pub. L. 98–369, set out in Effective Date of 1984 Amendment note below.

Subsec. (o)(3) to (8). Pub. L. 98–369, §474(o)(16), redesignated par. (8) as (3) and struck out former pars. (3) to (7) which defined "employee plan credit", "basic employee plan credit", "matching employee plan credit", "basic employee plan percentage", and "matching employee plan percentage", respectively.

Subsec. (q)(1), (3). Pub. L. 98–369, §474(o)(17)(A), substituted "section 46(a)" for "section 46(a)(2)".

Subsec. (q)(4)(A)(i). Pub. L. 98–369, §474(o)(17), substituted "section 46(a)" for "section 46(a)(2)" and "section 46(b)(1)" for "section 46(a)(2)(B)".

Subsec. (q)(4)(B)(ii). Pub. L. 98–369, §474(o)(17)(B), substituted "section 46(b)(1)" for "section 46(a)(2)(B)".

Subsec. (q)(6). Pub. L. 98–369, §712(b), added par. (6) relating to adjustment in basis of interest in partnership or S corporation.

Pub. L. 98–369, §113(b)(4), added par. (6) relating to special rule for qualified films.

Subsec. (r). Pub. L. 98–369, §113(a)(1), added subsec. (r). Former subsec. (r) redesignated (s).

Pub. L. 98–369, §474(o)(18), substituted "section 381(c)(26)" for "section 381(c)(23)".

Subsec. (s). Pub. L. 98–369, §113(a)(1), redesignated former subsec. (r) as (s).

1983—Subsec. (a)(1)(G). Pub. L. 97–448, §102(e)(2)(A), inserted "(not including a building and its structural components) used in connection" after "storage facility".

Subsec. (a)(10). Pub. L. 97–448, §202(c), amended directory language of Pub. L. 96–223, §223(a)(1), to correct an error, and did not involve any change in text. See 1980 Amendment note below.

Subsec. (g)(1)(C)(i). Pub. L. 97–448, §102(f)(2), (6), substituted "the 24-month period selected by the taxpayer (at the time and in the manner prescribed by regulation) and ending with or within the taxable year" for "the 24-month period ending on the last day of the taxable year" in provisions preceding subcl. (I), substituted "adjusted basis of such building (and its structural components)" for "adjusted basis of such property" both in subcl. (I) and in provision following subcl. (I), and, in provisions following subcl. (II), substituted "holding period of the building" for "holding period of the property" and inserted provision that, for purposes of the preceding sentence, the determination of the beginning of the holding period shall be made without regard to any reconstruction by the taxpayer in connection with the rehabilitation.

Subsec. (g)(5)(A). Pub. L. 97–448, §102(f)(3), substituted "a credit is determined under section 46(a)(2)" for "a credit is allowed under this section" and "the credit so determined" for "the credit so allowed". See 1982 Amendment note for subsec. (g)(5) below and see Effective Date of 1982 and 1983 Amendment notes set out under sections 1 and 196 of this title.

Subsec. (l)(5). Pub. L. 97–424, §546(a)(3), substituted reference to subpar. (N) for reference to subpar. (M) in provision following subparagraphs.

Subsec. (l)(5)(M), (N). Pub. L. 97–424, §546(a)(1), (2), added subpar. (M) and redesignated former subpar. (M) as (N).

Subsec. (q)(3). Pub. L. 97–448, §306(a)(3), substituted "paragraphs (1) and (2) of this subsection and paragraph (5) of subsection (d)" for "paragraphs (1) and (2)".

1982—Subsec. (b). Pub. L. 97–248, §209(c), inserted provision that for purposes of determining whether section 38 property subject to a lease is new section 38 property, such property shall be treated as originally placed in service not earlier than the date such property is used under the lease, but only if such property is leased within 3 months after such property is placed in service.

Subsec. (c)(2)(D). Pub. L. 97–354 substituted "Partnerships and S corporations" for "Partnerships" in subpar. heading, and inserted "A similar rule shall apply in the case of an S corporation and its shareholders".

Subsec. (d)(5). Pub. L. 97–248, §205(a)(4), added par. (5).

Subsec. (e). Pub. L. 97–354, §5(a)(7), struck out subsec. (e) relating to apportionment among shareholders of qualified investments by an electing small business corporation.

Subsec. (g)(5). Pub. L. 97–248, §205(a)(5)(A), struck out par. (5) which, as amended by §102(f)(3) of Pub. L. 97–448, had provided that for purposes of this subtitle, if a credit were determined under section 46(a)(2) for any qualified rehabilitation expenditure in connection with a qualified rehabilitated building other than a certified historic structure, the increase in basis of such property which would (but for this paragraph) have resulted from such expenditure had to be reduced by the amount of the credit so determined, that if during any taxable year there was a recapture amount determined with respect to any qualified rehabilitated building the basis of which was reduced under subpar. (A), the basis of such building (immediately before the event resulting in such recapture), had to be increased by an amount equal to such recapture amount, and that for purposes of this paragraph "recapture amount" was defined as any increase in tax (or adjustment in carrybacks or carryovers) determined under section 47(a)(5). See 1983 Amendment note for subsec. (g)(5) above and see Effective Date of 1982 and 1983 Amendment notes set out under sections 1 and 196 of this title.

Subsec. (k)(5)(D)(i). Pub. L. 97–354, §5(a)(8), substituted "an S corporation" for "an electing small business corporation (within the meaning of section 1371)".

Subsec. (l)(7). Pub. L. 97–362, §104(a), temporarily substituted the qualification that such term does not include equipment for hydrogenation, refining, or other process subsequent to retorting other than hydrogenation or other process which is applied in the vicinity of the property from which the shale was extracted and which is applied to bring the shale oil to a grade and quality suitable for transportation to and processing in a refinery, for the qualification that such equipment did not include equipment for hydrogenation, refining, or other processes subsequent to retorting. See Effective and Termination Dates of 1982 Amendment note below.

Subsecs. (q), (r). Pub. L. 97–248, §205(a)(1), added subsec. (q) and redesignated former subsec. (q) as (r).

1981—Subsec. (a)(1). Pub. L. 97–34, §211(e)(4), in provisions following subpar. (G), substituted "Such term includes only recovery property (within the meaning of section 168 without regard to any useful life) and any other property" for "Such term includes only property".

Subsec. (a)(1)(G). Pub. L. 97–34, §211(c), added subpar. (G).

Subsec. (a)(2)(B)(ii). Pub. L. 97–34, §211(h), designated existing provisions as subcl. (I) and added subcl. (II).

Subsec. (a)(3)(D). Pub. L. 97–34, §212(c), added subpar. (D).

Subsec. (a)(4). Pub. L. 97–34, §214(a), inserted provision that, if any qualified rehabilitated building is used by the tax-exempt organization pursuant to a lease, this paragraph shall not apply to that portion of the basis of such building which is attributable to qualified rehabilitation expenditures.

Subsec. (a)(5). Pub. L. 97–34, §214(b), inserted provision that, if any qualified rehabilitated building is used by the governmental unit pursuant to a lease, this paragraph shall not apply to that portion of the basis of such building which is attributable to qualified rehabilitation expenditures.

Subsec. (a)(8). Pub. L. 97–34, §212(d)(2)(A), substituted "or 188" for "188, or 191".

Subsec. (a)(9). Pub. L. 97–34, §211(a)(2), struck out par. (9) which set out a special rule for the depreciation of railroad track.

Subsec. (c)(2)(A) to (C). Pub. L. 97–34, §213(a), amended subpars. (A) to (C) generally raising in subpar. (A) the existing $100,000 dollar limitation to $125,000 in 1981 and to $150,000 in 1985 and in subpar. (B) the existing $50,000 dollar limitation to $62,500 in 1981 and to $75,000 in 1985.

Subsec. (g). Pub. L. 97–34, §212(b), in amending subsec. (c) generally incorporated the concept of "substantial rehabilitation" into par. (1)(A), substituted "30 years" for "20 years" as the requisite period in par. (1)(B), substituted a definition of "substantially rehabilitated" for former provisions that a major portion could be treated as a separate building in certain cases in par. (1)(C), reenacted par. (1)(D) without change, substituted "December 31, 1981" for "October 31, 1978" in provisions of par. (2)(A) preceding cl. (i), substituted provisions for a recovery period of 15 years for provisions that had provided for a useful life of 5 years or more in cl. (i) of par. (2)(A), reenacted cl. (ii) without change, substituted provisions that accelerated methods of depreciation may not be used for provisions relating to property otherwise section 38 property in cl. (i) of par. (2)(B), reenacted cls. (ii) and (iii) without change, revised the provisions of cl. (iv) relating to certified historic structures, and added cl. (v) relating to expenditures of lessees, added par. (3), redesignated former par. (3) as (4), and added par. (5).

Subsec. (l)(2)(C). Pub. L. 97–34, §211(e)(3), inserted "or which is recovery property (within the meaning of section 168)" after "3 years or more".

Subsec. (n)(1)(A)(i). Pub. L. 97–34, §332(b), substituted "which does not exceed" for "equal to".

Subsec. (o)(8). Pub. L. 97–34, §212(a)(3), added par. (8).

1980—Subsec. (a)(1). Pub. L. 96–451 added subpar. (F) and provision for treatment of the useful life of subpar. (F) property as its normal growing period.

Subsec. (a)(2)(B)(xi). Pub. L. 96–223, §222(i)(2), added cl. (xi).

Subsec. (a)(5). Pub. L. 96–605, §109(a), included the International Maritime Satellite Organization or any successor organization within organizations not to be treated as international organizations.

Subsec. (a)(7)(B). Pub. L. 95–600, §312(c)(2), as amended by Pub. L. 96–222, §103(a)(2)(A), substituted " 'described in section 50 (as in effect before its repeal by the Revenue Act of 1978' " for " 'described in section 50' ".

Subsec. (a)(10)(A). Pub. L. 96–223, §223(a)(1), as amended by Pub. L. 97–448, §202(c), provided that "petroleum or petroleum products" does not include petroleum coke or petroleum pitch.

Subsec. (a)(10)(B). Pub. L. 96–222, §108(c)(6), substituted "5" for "51".

Subsec. (g)(2)(B)(i). Pub. L. 96–222, §103(a)(4)(B), substituted "subsections (a)(1)(E) and (l)" for "subsection (a)(1)(E)".

Subsec. (l)(1). Pub. L. 96–223, §221(b)(1), substituted "For any period for which the energy percentage determined under section 46(a)(2)(C) for any energy property is greater than zero" for "For the period beginning on October 1, 1978, and ending on December 31, 1982" in provisions preceding subpar. (A) and, in subpars. (A) and (B), substituted "such energy property" and "such property" for "any energy property".

Subsec. (l)(2)(A). Pub. L. 96–223, §222(a), added cls. (vii), (viii), and (ix).

Subsec. (l)(3)(A). Pub. L. 96–223, §222(b), (g)(2), struck out "(other than coke or coke gas)" after "solid fuel" in cl. (iii) and, in cl. (v), substituted provisions relating to equipment which converts coal into a substitute for a petroleum or natural gas derived feedstock for the manufacture of chemicals or other products and equipment which converts coal into methanol, ammonia, or hydroprocessed coal liquid or solid for provisions which had related simply to equipment which used coal as feedstock for the manufacture of chemicals or other products other than coke or coke gas, added cl. (ix), and, following cl. (ix), inserted provision that the equipment described in cl. (vii) includes equipment used for the storage of fuel derived from garbage at the site at which such fuel was produced from garbage.

Subsec. (l)(3)(B). Pub. L. 96–223, §222(i)(1)(A), redesignated subpar. (C) as (B). Former subpar. (B), which excluded public utility property from the terms "alternative energy property", "solar or wind energy property", or "recycling equipment", was struck out.

Subsec. (l)(3)(C), (D). Pub. L. 96–223, §222(i)(1)(A), (3), redesignated subpar. (D) as (C) and inserted following cl. (ii) provision that, for the purposes of the preceding sentence, in the case of property which is alternative energy property solely by reason of the amendments made by section 222(b) of the Crude Oil Windfall Profit Tax Act of 1980, "January 1, 1980" was to be substituted for "October 1, 1978". Former subpar. (C) redesignated (B).

Subsec. (l)(4)(C). Pub. L. 96–223, §222(c), added subpar. (C).

Subsec. (l)(5). Pub. L. 96–223, §222(d), added subpar. (L), redesignated former subpar. (L) as (M), and inserted provision that the Secretary shall not specify any property under subpar. (M) unless he determines that such specification meets the requirements of par. (9) of section 44C(c) for specification of items under section 44C(c)(4)(A)(viii).

Subsec. (l)(11). Pub. L. 96–223, §221(b)(2), substituted "one-half of the energy percentage determined under section 46(a)(2)(C)" for "5 percent".

Pub. L. 96–223, §223(c)(1), completely revised par. (11) to incorporate property financed by subsidized energy financing, effective with regard to periods after Dec. 31, 1982. Prior to the revision par. (11) read as follows: "In the case of property which is financed in whole or in part by the proceeds of an industrial development bond (within the meaning of section 103(b)(2)) the interest on which is exempt from tax under section 103, the energy percentage shall be one-half of the energy percentage determined under section 46(a)(2)(C)."

Subsec. (l)(13). Pub. L. 96–223, §222(e)(1), added par. (13).

Subsec. (l)(14). Pub. L. 96–223, §222(f), added par. (14).

Subsec. (l)(15). Pub. L. 96–223, §222(g)(1), added par. (15).

Subsec. (l)(16). Pub. L. 96–223, §222(h), added par. (16).

Subsec. (l)(17). Pub. L. 96–223, §222(i)(1)(B), added par. (17).

Subsec. (n). Pub. L. 96–222, §101(a)(7)(G), (H), (L)(i)(I)–(IV), (ii)(III)–(VI), (iii)(II), (v)(II)–(IV), (M)(ii), amended subsec. (n) generally to reflect the renaming of an investment tax credit ESOP to a tax credit employee stock ownership plan and a leveraged employee stock ownership plan (commonly referred to as an ESOP) to an employee stock ownership plan.

Subsec. (n)(6)(B)(i). Pub. L. 96–605, §223(a), substituted "the date on which the securities are contributed to the plan" for "the due date for filing the return for the taxable year (determined with regard to extensions)".

Subsec. (o). Pub. L. 96–222, §101(a)(7)(L)(iii)(III), (v)(IV), (V), (M)(iii), substituted "employee plan" for "ESOP" wherever appearing and inserted "percentage" after "attributable to the matching employee plan" in par. (5).

1978—Subsec. (a)(1)(A). Pub. L. 95–618, §301(d)(1), inserted "(other than an air conditioning or heating unit)" after "personal property".

Subsec. (a)(1)(D). Pub. L. 95–600, §314(a), added par. (D).

Subsec. (a)(1)(E). Pub. L. 95–600, §315(a), added par. (E).

Subsec. (a)(2)(B)(ii). Pub. L. 95–473, §2(a)(2)(A), substituted "providing transportation subject to subchapter I of chapter 105 of title 49" for "subject to part I of the Interstate Commerce Act".

Subsec. (a)(7)(A). Pub. L. 95–600, §312(c)(3), struck out "(other than pretermination property)" after "Property".

Subsec. (a)(7)(B). Pub. L. 95–600, §312(c)(2), struck out "described in section 50" after "with respect to property". See 1980 Amendment note above.

Subsec. (a)(8). Pub. L. 95–600, §315(c), substituted "188, or 191" for "or 188".

Subsec. (a)(10). Pub. L. 95–618, §301(d)(2), added par. (10).

Subsec. (d)(1)(B). Pub. L. 95–600, §703(a)(3), substituted "section 46(a)(6)" for "section 46(a)(5)".

Subsec. (d)(4)(D). Pub. L. 95–600, §703(a)(4), substituted "section 57(c)(1)(B)" for "section 57(c)(2)".

Subsec. (g). Pub. L. 95–600, §315(b), added subsec. (g).

Subsec. (h). Pub. L. 95–600, §312(c)(1), struck out subsec. (h) which related to suspension of investment credit.

Subsec. (i). Pub. L. 95–600, §312(c)(1), struck out subsec. (i) which related to an exemption from suspension of $20,000 of investment.

Subsec. (j). Pub. L. 95–600, §312(c)(1), struck out subsec. (j) which defined "suspension period".

Subsecs. (l), (m). Pub. L. 95–618, §301(b), added subsecs. (l) and (m) and redesignated former subsec. (l) as (n).

Subsec. (n). Pub. L. 95–618, §301(b), redesignated former subsec. (l) as (n).

Pub. L. 95–600, §141(b), added subsec. (n). Former subsec. (n) redesignated (p).

Subsec. (o). Pub. L. 95–600, §141(b), added subsec. (o).

Subsecs. (p), (q). Pub. L. 95–600, §§141(b), 314(b), added subsec. (p). Former subsec. (n) redesignated (p) and subsequently as (q).

1976—Subsec. (a)(2)(B)(vi). Pub. L. 94–455, §1901(a)(5)(A), substituted "(43 U.S.C. 1331))" for "; 43 U.S.C., sec. 1331)".

Subsec. (a)(2)(B)(vii). Pub. L. 94–455, §1051(h)(1), substituted "(other than a corporation which has an election in effect under section 936 or which is entitled to the benefits of section 934(b))" for "(other than a corporation entitled to the benefits of section 931 or 934(b))".

Subsec. (a)(2)(B)(viii). Pub. L. 94–455, §1901(a)(5)(B), substituted "47 U.S.C. 702" for "47 U.S.C., sec. 702".

Subsec. (a)(8). Pub. L. 94–455, §§1901(b)(11)(A), 2112(a)(1), struck out "169," after "section 167(k),", "187," before "or 188 applies", and provisions relating to the limitation of the applicability of this paragraph on property to which section 169 applies.

Subsecs. (c)(2)(A), (d)(1), (2)(A). Pub. L. 94–455, §1906(b)(13)(A), struck out "or his delegate" after "Secretary".

Subsec. (f). Pub. L. 94–455, §802(b)(6), substituted "section 46(a)(3)" for "section 46(a)(2)".

Subsec. (i)(2). Pub. L. 94–455, §1906(b)(13)(A), struck out "or his delegate" after "Secretary".

Subsecs. (k), (l). Pub. L. 94–455, §804(a), added subsec. (k) and redesignated former subsec. (k) as subsec. (l).

1975—Subsec. (a)(2)(B). Pub. L. 94–12, §604(a), substituted "territorial waters within the northern portion of the Western Hemisphere" for "territorial waters" in cl. (x) and inserted definition of "northern portion of the Western Hemisphere" following cl. (x).

Subsec. (c)(2)(A). Pub. L. 94–12 §301(c)(1)(A), substituted "$100,000" for "$50,000".

Subsec. (c)(2)(B). Pub. L. 94–12, §301(c)(1)(A), (B), substituted "$50,000" for "$25,000" and "$100,000" for "$50,000".

Subsec. (c)(2)(C). Pub. L. 94–12, §301(c)(1)(A), substituted "$100,000" for "$50,000".

Subsec. (d)(1), (2)(A). Pub. L. 94–12, §302(c)(3), substituted "section 46(d)(1)" for "section 46(d)(1)".

1971—Subsec. (a)(1). Pub. L. 92–178, §102(a)(2), substituted "3 years" for "4 years" in second sentence.

Subsec. (a)(1)(B)(ii), (iii). Pub. L. 92–178, §104(a)(1), substituted "research facility" for "research or storage facility" in cl. (ii) and added cl. (iii).

Subsec. (a)(2)(B). Pub. L. 92–178, §104(c)(2), (3), (d), added cls. (viii) to (x), respectively.

Subsec. (a)(3)(C). Pub. L. 92–178, §104(b), added subpar. (C).

Subsec. (a)(5). Pub. L. 92–178, §104(c)(1), inserted "(other than the International Telecommunications Satellite Consortium or any successor organization)" after "international organization".

Subsec. (a)(6). Pub. L. 92–178, §104(e), substituted provisions for treatment of livestock (other than horses) acquired by the taxpayer as section 38 property, with exception provision for reduction of acquisition cost by amount equal to amount realized on sale or other disposition under certain circumstances, and for nontreatment of horses as section 38 property for former provision that livestock shall not be treated as section 38 property.

Subsec. (a)(7) to (9). Pub. L. 92–178, §§103, 104(f)(1), (g), added pars. (7) to (9), respectively.

Subsec. (d). Pub. L. 92–178, §108(b) and (c), substituted "section 46(d)(1)" for "section 46(d)"; and designated as par. (1) the present first sentence, redesignated as subpars. (A) and (B) provisions formerly designated cls. (1) and (2), again substituted "section 46(d)(1)" for "section 46(d)" in par. (1) and inserted "(other than property described in paragraph (4))" in par. (1), added pars. (2) and (4), incorporated provisions of former second, third, and fourth sentences in provisions designated as par. (3), substituted in par. (3) "the lessee shall be treated for all purposes of this subpart as having acquired a fractional portion of such property equal to the fraction determined under paragraph (2)(B) with respect to such property" for "the lessee shall be treated for all purposes of this subpart as having acquired such property", and struck out former fifth and sixth sentences respecting election regarding treatment of leases of suspension period property and section 38 property. See Effective Date of 1971 Amendment note below.

1969—Subsec. (a)(4). Pub. L. 91–172, §121(d)(2)(A), inserted provision relating to the percentage of the basis or cost of debt-financed property that may be considered in computing qualified investment under section 46(c) of this title.

Subsec. (c)(2)(C). Pub. L. 91–172, §401(e)(2), reenacted subpar. (C) with minor changes and substituted reference to controlled group for reference to affiliated group.

Subsec. (c)(3)(C). Pub. L. 91–172, §401(e)(3), substituted definition of controlled group for definition of affiliated group.

Subsec. (d)(2). Pub. L. 91–172, §401(e)(4), substituted reference to a component member of a controlled group for reference to a member of an affiliated group.

1967—Subsec. (a)(2)(B)(i). Pub. L. 90–26, §3, inserted "or is operated under contract with the United States" after "the United States".

Subsec. (h)(2). Pub. L. 90–26, §2(a), limited definition of suspension period property to section 38 property where the physical construction, reconstruction or erection was begun before May 24, 1967, pursuant to an order placed during the suspension period, subject to the proviso that in applying the definition to property the physical construction, reconstruction or erection of which was begun before May 24, 1967, only that portion of the basis properly attributable to construction, reconstruction or erection before May 24, 1967 be taken into account.

Subsec. (j). Pub. L. 90–26, §1, substituted "March 9, 1967" for "December 31, 1967".

1966—Subsec. (a)(2)(B). Pub. L. 89–809 added cl. (vii).

Subsec. (d). Pub. L. 89–800, §1(b), inserted provisions covering the treatment of suspension period property, and the elections to be deemed made in connection therewith.

Subsecs. (h) to (k). Pub. L. 89–800, §1(a), added subsecs. (h) to (j) and redesignated former subsec. (h) as (k).

1964—Subsec. (a)(1)(C). Pub. L. 88–272, §203(c)(2), added subpar. (C).

Subsec. (d). Pub. L. 88–272, §203(a)(3)(A), (b), substituted "except as provided in paragraph (2)" for "if such property was constructed by the lessor (or by a corporation which controls or is controlled by the lessor within the meaning of section 368(c))" in par. (1), "if such property is leased by a corporation which is a member of an affiliated group (within the meaning of section 46(a)(5) to another corporation which is a member of the same affiliated group" for "if paragraph (1) does not apply" in par. (2), and deleted provisions which stated that if a lessor made an election under this subsection, subsec. (g) would not apply with respect to such property, and deductions otherwise allowable under section 162 to the lessee for amounts paid the lessor would be adjusted consistent with subsec. (g).

Subsec. (g). Pub. L. 88–272, §203(a)(1), repealed subsec. (g) which required that the basis of section 38 property be reduced by 7 percent of the qualified investment.

EFFECTIVE DATE OF 2020 AMENDMENT

Amendment by section 131 of Pub. L. 116–260 effective Jan. 1, 2021, see section 131(d) of div. EE of Pub. L. 116–260, set out as a note under section 45 of this title.

Pub. L. 116–260, div. EE, title I, §132(c), Dec. 27, 2020, 134 Stat. 3053, provided that: "The amendments made by this section [amending this section] shall take effect on January 1, 2020."

Pub. L. 116–260, div. EE, title II, §203(e), Dec. 27, 2020, 134 Stat. 3057, provided that: "The amendments made by this section [amending this section] shall apply to periods after December 31, 2020, under rules similar to the rules of section 48(m) as in effect on the day before the date of the enactment of the Revenue Reconciliation Act of 1990 [Nov. 5, 1990]."

Pub. L. 116–260, div. EE, title II, §204(b), Dec. 27, 2020, 134 Stat. 3058, provided that: "The amendment made by this section [amending this section] shall apply to periods after December 31, 2016, under rules similar to the rules of section 48(m) of the Internal Revenue Code of 1986 (as in effect on the day before the date of the enactment of the Revenue Reconciliation Act of 1990 [Nov. 5, 1990])."

EFFECTIVE DATE OF 2019 AMENDMENT

Amendment by Pub. L. 116–94 effective on Jan. 1, 2018, see section 127(d) of Pub. L. 116–94, set out as a note under section 45 of this title.

EFFECTIVE DATE OF 2018 AMENDMENT

Amendment by section 40409(b) of Pub. L. 115–123 effective on Jan. 1, 2017, see section 40409(c) of Pub. L. 115–123, set out as a note under section 45 of this title.

Pub. L. 115–123, div. D, title I, §40411(g), Feb. 9, 2018, 132 Stat. 151, provided that:

"(1) In general.—Except as otherwise provided in this subsection, the amendments made by this section [amending this section] shall apply to periods after December 31, 2016, under rules similar to the rules of section 48(m) of the Internal Revenue Code of 1986 (as in effect on the day before the date of the enactment of the Revenue Reconciliation Act of 1990 [Nov. 5, 1990]).

"(2) Extension of combined heat and power system property.—The amendment made by subsection (e) [amending this section] shall apply to property placed in service after December 31, 2016.

"(3) Phaseouts and terminations.—The amendments made by subsection (b) [amending this section] shall take effect on the date of the enactment of this Act [Feb. 9, 2018]."

EFFECTIVE DATE OF 2015 AMENDMENT

Pub. L. 114–113, div. P, title III, §302(c), Dec. 18, 2015, 129 Stat. 3039, provided that: "The amendments made by this section [amending this section] shall take effect on January 1, 2015."

Pub. L. 114–113, div. P, title III, §303(d), Dec. 18, 2015, 129 Stat. 3039, provided that: "The amendments made by this section [amending this section] shall take effect on the date of the enactment of this Act [Dec. 18, 2015]."

Amendment by section 187(b) of Pub. L. 114–113 effective Jan. 1, 2015, see section 187(c) of Pub. L. 114–113, set out as a note under section 45 of this title.

EFFECTIVE DATE OF 2014 AMENDMENT

Amendment by section 155(b) of Pub. L. 113–295 effective Jan. 1, 2014, see section 155(c) of Pub. L. 113–295, set out as a note under section 45 of this title.

Amendment by section 209(d) of Pub. L. 113–295 effective as if included in the provisions of the American Recovery and Reinvestment Tax Act of 2009, Pub. L. 111–5, div. B, title I, to which such amendment relates, see section 209(k) of Pub. L. 113–295, set out as a note under section 24 of this title.

EFFECTIVE DATE OF 2013 AMENDMENT

Amendment by Pub. L. 112–240 effective on Jan. 2, 2013, and amendment by section 407(c)(1) of Pub. L. 112–240 applicable as if included in the enactment of the provisions of the American Recovery and Reinvestment Act of 2009, Pub. L. 111–5, to which it relates, see section 407(d) of Pub. L. 112–240, set out as a note under section 45 of this title.

EFFECTIVE DATE OF 2009 AMENDMENT

Pub. L. 111–5, div. B, title I, §1102(b), Feb. 17, 2009, 123 Stat. 320, provided that: "The amendments made by this section [amending this section] shall apply to facilities placed in service after December 31, 2008."

Amendment by section 1103(a), (b)(1) of Pub. L. 111–5 applicable to periods after Dec. 31, 2008, under rules similar to the rules of subsec. (m) of this section as in effect on the day before Nov. 5, 1990, see section 1103(c)(1) of Pub. L. 111–5, set out as a note under section 25C of this title.

EFFECTIVE DATE OF 2008 AMENDMENT

Pub. L. 110–343, div. B, title I, §103(f), Oct. 3, 2008, 122 Stat. 3813, provided that:

"(1) In general.—Except as otherwise provided in this subsection, the amendments made by this section [amending this section and section 38 of this title] shall take effect on the date of the enactment of this Act [Oct. 3, 2008].

"(2) Allowance against alternative minimum tax.—The amendments made by subsection (b) [amending section 38 of this title] shall apply to credits determined under section 46 of the Internal Revenue Code of 1986 in taxable years beginning after the date of the enactment of this Act and to carrybacks of such credits.

"(3) Combined heat and power and fuel cell property.—The amendments made by subsections (c) and (d) [amending this section] shall apply to periods after the date of the enactment of this Act, in taxable years ending after such date, under rules similar to the rules of section 48(m) of the Internal Revenue Code of 1986 (as in effect on the day before the date of the enactment of the Revenue Reconciliation Act of 1990 [Nov. 5, 1990]).

"(4) Public utility property.—The amendments made by subsection (e) [amending this section] shall apply to periods after February 13, 2008, in taxable years ending after such date, under rules similar to the rules of section 48(m) of the Internal Revenue Code of 1986 (as in effect on the day before the date of the enactment of the Revenue Reconciliation Act of 1990)."

Pub. L. 110–343, div. B, title I, §104(e), Oct. 3, 2008, 122 Stat. 3814, provided that: "The amendments made by this section [amending this section] shall apply to periods after the date of the enactment of this Act [Oct. 3, 2008], in taxable years ending after such date, under rules similar to the rules of section 48(m) of the Internal Revenue Code of 1986 (as in effect on the day before the date of the enactment of the Revenue Reconciliation Act of 1990 [Nov. 5, 1990])."

Pub. L. 110–343, div. B, title I, §105(b), Oct. 3, 2008, 122 Stat. 3814, provided that: "The amendments made by this section [amending this section] shall apply to periods after the date of the enactment of this Act [Oct. 3, 2008], in taxable years ending after such date, under rules similar to the rules of section 48(m) of the Internal Revenue Code of 1986 (as in effect on the day before the date of the enactment of the Revenue Reconciliation Act of 1990 [Nov. 5, 1990])."

EFFECTIVE DATE OF 2005 AMENDMENT

Pub. L. 109–58, title XIII, §1336(e), Aug. 8, 2005, 119 Stat. 1038, provided that: "The amendments made by this section [amending this section] shall apply to periods after December 31, 2005, in taxable years ending after such date, under rules similar to the rules of section 48(m) of the Internal Revenue Code of 1986 (as in effect on the day before the date of the enactment of the Revenue Reconciliation Act of 1990 [Nov. 5, 1990])."

Pub. L. 109–58, title XIII, §1337(d), Aug. 8, 2005, 119 Stat. 1038, provided that: "The amendments made by this section [amending this section] shall apply to periods after December 31, 2005, in taxable years ending after such date, under rules similar to the rules of section 48(m) of the Internal Revenue Code of 1986 (as in effect on the day before the date of the enactment of the Revenue Reconciliation Act of 1990 [Nov. 5, 1990])."

EFFECTIVE DATE OF 2004 AMENDMENT

Amendment by section 322(d)(2)(A), (B) of Pub. L. 108–357 applicable with respect to expenditures paid or incurred after Oct. 22, 2004, see section 322(e) of Pub. L. 108–357, set out as a note under section 46 of this title.

Amendment by section 710(e) of Pub. L. 108–357 applicable, except as otherwise provided, to electricity produced and sold after Oct. 22, 2004, in taxable years ending after such date, see section 710(g) of Pub. L. 108–357, as amended, set out as a note under section 45 of this title.

EFFECTIVE DATE OF 1992 AMENDMENT

Pub. L. 102–486, title XIX, §1916(b), Oct. 24, 1992, 106 Stat. 3024, provided that: "The amendments made by this section [amending this section] shall take effect on June 30, 1992."

EFFECTIVE DATE OF 1990 AMENDMENT

Amendment by section 11813(a) of Pub. L. 101–508 applicable to property placed in service after Dec. 31, 1990, but not applicable to any transition property (as defined in section 49(e) of this title), any property with respect to which qualified progress expenditures were previously taken into account under section 46(d) of this title, and any property described in section 46(b)(2)(C) of this title, as such sections were in effect on Nov. 4, 1990, see section 11813(c) of Pub. L. 101–508, set out as a note under section 45K of this title.

EFFECTIVE DATE OF 1988 AMENDMENT

Amendment by Pub. L. 100–647 effective, except as otherwise provided, as if included in the provision of the Tax Reform Act of 1986, Pub. L. 99–514, to which such amendment relates, see section 1019(a) of Pub. L. 100–647, set out as a note under section 1 of this title.

EFFECTIVE DATE OF 1986 AMENDMENT

If any interest costs incurred after Dec. 31, 1986, are attributable to costs incurred before Jan. 1, 1987, the amendment by section 803(b)(2)(B) of Pub. L. 99–514 is applicable to such interest costs only to the extent such interest costs are attributable to costs which were required to be capitalized under section 263 of the Internal Revenue Code of 1954 and which would have been taken into account in applying section 189 of the Internal Revenue Code of 1954 (as in effect before its repeal by section 803 of Pub. L. 99–514) or, if applicable, section 266 of such Code, see section 7831(d)(2) of Pub. L. 101–239, set out as an Effective Date note under section 263A of this title.

Amendment by section 251(b), (c) of Pub. L. 99–514 applicable to property placed in service after Dec. 31, 1986, in taxable years ending after such date, except as otherwise provided for certain rehabilitations, see section 251(d) of Pub. L. 99–514, set out as a note under section 46 of this title.

Amendment by section 701(e)(4)(C) of Pub. L. 99–514 applicable to taxable years beginning after Dec. 31, 1986, with certain exceptions and qualifications, see section 701(f) of Pub. L. 99–514, set out as an Effective Date note under section 55 of this title.

Amendment by section 803(b)(2)(B) of Pub. L. 99–514 applicable to costs incurred after Dec. 31, 1986, in taxable years ending after such date, except as otherwise provided, see section 803(d) of Pub. L. 99–514, set out as an Effective Date note under section 263A of this title.

Amendment by sections 1272(d)(5) and 1275(c)(5) of Pub. L. 99–514 applicable to taxable years beginning after Dec. 31, 1986, with certain exceptions and qualifications, see section 1277 of Pub. L. 99–514, set out as a note under section 931 of this title.

Amendment by section 1511(c)(3) of Pub. L. 99–514 applicable for purposes of determining interest for periods after Dec. 31, 1986, see section 1511(d) of Pub. L. 99–514, set out as a note under section 47 of this title.

Pub. L. 99–514, title XVIII, §1879(j)(2), Oct. 22, 1986, 100 Stat. 2909, provided that: "The amendments made by this subsection [amending this section] shall apply to periods after December 31, 1978 (under rules similar to the rules of section 48(m) of the Internal Revenue Code of 1954 [now 1986]), in taxable years ending after such date."

Pub. L. 99–514, title XVIII, §1881, Oct. 22, 1986, 100 Stat. 2914, provided that: "Except as otherwise provided in this subtitle, any amendment made by this subtitle [subtitle A (§§1801–1881) of title XVIII of Pub. L. 99–514, see Tables for classification] shall take effect as if included in the provision of the Tax Reform Act of 1984 [Pub. L. 98–369, div. A] to which such amendment relates."

EFFECTIVE DATE OF 1985 AMENDMENT

Amendment by Pub. L. 99–121 applicable with respect to property placed in service by the taxpayer after May 8, 1985, with specified exceptions, but amendment of subsec. (g)(2)(B)(v) not applicable to leases entered into before May 22, 1985, if the lessee signed the lease before May 17, 1985, see section 105(b)(1), (5) of Pub. L. 99–121, set out as a note under section 168 of this title.

EFFECTIVE DATE OF 1984 AMENDMENT

Pub. L. 98–369, div. A, title I, §18, July 18, 1984, 98 Stat. 506, provided that:

"(a) General Rule.—The amendments made by this part [part I (§§11–18) of subtitle A of title I of div. A of Pub. L. 98–369, amending this section and sections 41, 46, 57, 128, 168, 179, 265, 415, 854, 857, and 911 of this title, enacting provisions set out as a note under section 168 of this title, and amending provisions set out as notes under sections 128 and 168 of this title] shall apply to taxable years ending after December 31, 1983.

"(b) Special Rule for Section 14.—The amendment made by section 14 [amending section 41 of this title] shall not apply in the case of a tax credit employee stock ownership plan if—

"(1) such plan was favorably approved on September 23, 1983, by employees, and

"(2) not later than January 11, 1984, the employer of such employees was 100 percent owned by such plan."

Amendment by section 31(b), (c)(1) of Pub. L. 98–369 effective, except as otherwise provided in section 31(g) of Pub. L. 98–369, as to property placed in service by the taxpayer after May 23, 1983, in taxable years ending after such date and to property placed in service by the taxpayer on or before May 23, 1983, if the lease to the tax-exempt entity is entered into after May 23, 1983, and amendment by section 31(c)(2) of Pub. L. 98–369, to the extent it relates to section 168(f)(12) of this title, effective as if it had been included in the amendments to section 168 of this title by section 216(a) of Pub. L. 97–248, see section 31(g)(1), (12) of Pub. L. 98–369, set out as a note under section 168 of this title.

Amendment by section 111(e)(8) of Pub. L. 98–369 applicable with respect to property placed in service by the taxpayer after Mar. 15, 1984, subject to certain exceptions, see section 111(g) of Pub. L. 98–369, set out as a note under section 168 of this title.

Amendment by section 113(b)(3) of Pub. L. 98–369 applicable as if included in the amendments made by sections 201(a), 211(a)(1), and 211(f)(1) of Pub. L. 97–34, which enacted section 168 and amended section 46 of this title, see section 113(c)(2)(B) of Pub. L. 98–369, set out as a note under section 168 of this title.

Amendment by section 113(b)(4) of Pub. L. 98–369 applicable as if included in the amendments made by section 205(a)(1) of Pub. L. 97–248, see section 113(c)(2)(C) of Pub. L. 98–369, set out as a note under section 168 of this title.

Pub. L. 98–369, div. A, title I, §113(c)(1), July 18, 1984, 98 Stat. 637, provided that: "The amendments made by subsection (a) [amending this section and section 168 of this title] shall apply to property placed in service after March 15, 1984, in taxable years ending after such date."

Pub. L. 98–369, div. A, title I, §114(b), July 18, 1984, 98 Stat. 638, provided that: "The amendment made by this section [amending this section] shall apply to property originally placed in service after April 11, 1984 (determined without regard to such amendment)."

Amendment by section 431(c) of Pub. L. 98–369 applicable to property placed in service after July 18, 1984, in taxable years ending after such date, but not applicable to property to which sections 46(c)(8), (9) and 47(d) of this title, as enacted by section 211(f) of Pub. L. 97–34, do not apply, with the taxpayer having an option to elect retroactive application of amendment by Pub. L. 98–369, see section 431(e) of Pub. L. 98–369, set out as a note under section 46 of this title.

Amendment by section 474(o)(10)–(18) of Pub. L. 98–369 applicable to taxable years beginning after Dec. 31, 1983, and to carrybacks from such years, see section 475(a) of Pub. L. 98–369, set out as a note under section 21 of this title.

Pub. L. 98–369, div. A, title IV, §474(o)(15), July 18, 1984, 98 Stat. 837, as amended by Pub. L. 99–514, §2, Oct. 22, 1986, 100 Stat. 2095, provided that: "Subsection (n) of section 48 (relating to requirements for allowance of employee plan percentage) is hereby repealed; except that paragraph (4) of section 48(n) of the

Internal Revenue Code of 1986 [formerly I.R.C. 1954] (as in effect before its repeal by this paragraph) shall continue to apply in the case of any recapture under section 47(f) of such Code of a credit allowable for a taxable year beginning before January 1, 1984."

Amendment by section 712(b) of Pub. L. 98–369 effective as if included in the provision of the Tax Equity and Fiscal Responsibility Act of 1982, Pub. L. 97–248, to which such amendment relates, see section 715 of Pub. L. 98–369, set out as a note under section 31 of this title.

Amendment by section 721(x)(1) of Pub. L. 98–369 effective as if included in the Subchapter S Revision Act of 1982, Pub. L. 97–354, see section 721(y)(1) of Pub. L. 98–369, set out as a note under section 1361 of this title.

Amendment by section 735(c)(1) of Pub. L. 98–369 effective, except as otherwise provided, as if included in the provisions of the Highway Revenue Act of 1982, title V of Pub. L. 97–424, to which such amendment relates, see section 736 of Pub. L. 98–369, set out as a note under section 4051 of this title.

Pub. L. 98–369, div. A, title X, §1043(b), July 18, 1984, 98 Stat. 1044, provided that: "The amendments made by this section [amending this section] shall apply to expenditures incurred after December 31, 1983, in taxable years ending after such date."

EFFECTIVE DATE OF 1983 AMENDMENT

Amendment by title I of Pub. L. 97–448 effective, except as otherwise provided, as if it had been included in the provision of the Economic Recovery Tax Act of 1981, Pub. L. 97–34, to which such amendment relates, see section 109 of Pub. L. 97–448, set out as a note under section 1 of this title.

Amendment by section 202(c) of Pub. L. 97–448 effective, except as otherwise provided, as if it had been included in the provision of the Crude Oil Windfall Profit Tax Act of 1980, Pub. L. 96–223 to which such amendment relates, see section 203(a) of Pub. L. 97–448, set out as a note under section 6652 of this title.

Amendment by section 306(a)(3) of Pub. L. 97–448 effective as if included in the provisions of the Tax Equity and Fiscal Responsibility Act of 1982, Pub. L. 97–248, to which such amendment relates, see section 311(d) of Pub. L. 97–448, set out as a note under section 31 of this title.

EFFECTIVE AND TERMINATION DATES OF 1982 AMENDMENT

Pub. L. 97–362, title I, §104(b), Oct. 25, 1982, 96 Stat. 1729, as amended by Pub. L. 99–514, §2, Oct. 22, 1986, 100 Stat. 2095, provided that: "The amendment made by this section [amending this section] shall apply to periods beginning after December 31, 1980, and before January 1, 1983, under rules similar to the rules of section 48(m) of the Internal Revenue Code of 1986 [formerly I.R.C. 1954]."

Amendment by Pub. L. 97–354 applicable to taxable years beginning after Dec. 31, 1982, see section 6(a) of Pub. L. 97–354, set out as an Effective Date note under section 1361 of this title.

Amendment by section 205(a)(1), (4), (5)(A) of Pub. L. 97–248, applicable to periods after Dec. 31, 1982, under rules similar to the rules of subsec. (m) of this section, with certain exceptions and qualifications, see section 205(c)(1) of Pub. L. 97–248, set out as an Effective Date note under section 196 of this title.

Amendment by section 209(c) of Pub. L. 97–248 applicable to property placed in service after Dec. 31, 1983, but not to qualified leased property described in section 168(f)(8)(D)(v) of this title which is placed in service before Jan. 1, 1988, or is placed in service after such date pursuant to a binding contract or commitment entered into before April 1, 1983, and solely because of conditions which, as determined by the Secretary of the Treasury or his delegate, are not within the control of the lessor or lessee, see sections 208(d)(5) and 209(d)(2) of Pub. L. 97–248, set out as notes under section 168 of this title.

EFFECTIVE DATE OF 1981 AMENDMENT

Pub. L. 97–34, title II, §213(b), Aug. 13, 1981, 95 Stat. 240, as amended by Pub. L. 97–448, title I, §102(g), Jan. 12, 1983, 96 Stat. 2372, provided that: "The amendment made by this section [amending this section] shall apply to taxable years beginning after December 31, 1980."

Pub. L. 97–34, title II, §214(c), Aug. 13, 1981, 95 Stat. 241, provided that: "The amendments made by this section [amending this section] shall apply to uses after July 29, 1980, in taxable years ending after such date."

Pub. L. 97–34, title III, §332(c)(2), Aug. 13, 1981, 95 Stat. 296, provided that: "The amendment made by subsection (b) [amending this section] shall apply to qualified investments made after December 31, 1981."

Amendment by section 211(a)(2), (e)(3), (4) of Pub. L. 97–34 applicable to property placed in service after Dec. 31, 1980, see section 211(i)(1) of Pub. L. 97–34, set out as a note under section 46 of this title.

Amendment by section 211(c) of Pub. L. 97–34 applicable to periods after Dec. 31, 1980, under rules similar to the rules under subsec. (m) of this section, see section 211(i)(3) of Pub. L. 97–34, set out as a note under section 46 of this title.

Amendment by section 211(h) of Pub. L. 97–34 applicable to taxable years beginning after Dec. 31, 1980, see section 211(i)(6) of Pub. L. 97–34, set out as a note under section 46 of this title.

Amendment by section 212(a)(3), (b), (c), (d)(2)(A) of Pub. L. 97–34 applicable to expenditures incurred after Dec. 31, 1981, in taxable years ending after such date, see section 212(e) of Pub. L. 97–34, set out as a note under section 46 of this title.

EFFECTIVE DATE OF 1980 AMENDMENT

Pub. L. 96–605, title I, §109(b), Dec. 28, 1980, 94 Stat. 3525, provided that: "The amendment made by subsection (a) [amending this section] shall apply to taxable years beginning after December 31, 1979."

Pub. L. 96–605, title II, §223(b), Dec. 28, 1980, 94 Stat. 3528, provided that: "The amendment made by subsection (a) [amending this section] shall apply with respect to taxable years beginning after December 31, 1980."

Pub. L. 96–451, title III, §302(b), Oct. 14, 1980, 94 Stat. 1991, provided that: "The amendments made by this section [amending this section] shall apply with respect to additions to capital account made after December 31, 1979."

Pub. L. 96–223, title II, §222(j), Apr. 2, 1980, 94 Stat. 266, as amended by Pub. L. 99–514, §2, Oct. 22, 1986, 100 Stat. 2095, provided that:

"(1) In general.—Except as provided in paragraph (2), the amendments made by this section [amending this section and section 46 of this title] shall apply to periods after December 31, 1979, under rules similar to the rules of section 48(m) of the Internal Revenue Code of 1986 [formerly I.R.C. 1954].

"(2) Alumina electrolytic cells.—The amendments made by subsection (d)(1) [amending this section] shall apply to periods after September 30, 1978, under rules similar to the rules of section 48(m) of such Code."

Pub. L. 96–223, title II, §223(a)(2), Apr. 2, 1980, 94 Stat. 266, as amended by Pub. L. 99–514, §2, Oct. 22, 1986, 100 Stat. 2095, provided that: "The amendment made by paragraph (1) [amending this section] shall apply to periods after December 31, 1979, under rules similar to the rules of section 48(m) of the Internal Revenue Code of 1986 [formerly I.R.C. 1954]."

Pub. L. 96–223, title II, §223(c)(2), Apr. 2, 1980, 94 Stat. 267, as amended by Pub. L. 99–514, §2, Oct. 22, 1986, 100 Stat. 2095, provided that:

"(A) In general.—Except as provided in subparagraph (B), the amendment made by paragraph (1) [amending this section] shall apply to periods after December 31, 1982, under rules similar to the rules of section 48(m) of the Internal Revenue Code of 1986 [formerly I.R.C. 1954]."

"(B) Earlier application for certain property.—In the case of property which is—

"(i) qualified hydroelectric generating property (described in section 48(l)(2)(A)(vii) of such Code),

"(ii) cogeneration equipment (described in section 48(l)(2)(A)(viii) of such Code),

"(iii) qualified intercity buses (described in section 48(l)(2)(A)(ix) of such Code),

"(iv) ocean thermal property (described in section 48(l)(3)(A)(ix) of such Code), or

"(v) expanded energy credit property,

the amendment made by paragraph (1) shall apply to periods after December 31, 1979, under rules similar to the rules of section 48(m) of the Internal Revenue Code of 1986.

"(C) Expanded energy credit property.—For purposes of subparagraph (B), the term 'expanded energy credit property' means—

"(i) property to which section 48(l)(3)(A) of such Code applies because of the amendments made by paragraphs (1) and (2) of section 222(b) [amending this section],

"(ii) property described in section 48(l)(4)(C) of such Code (relating to solar process heat),

"(iii) property described in section 48(l)(5)(L) of such Code (relating to alumina electrolytic cells), and

"(iv) property described in the last sentence of section 48(l)(3)(A) of such Code (relating to storage equipment for refuse-derived fuel).

"(D) Financing taken into account.—For the purpose of applying the provisions of section 48(l)(11) of such Code in the case of property financed in whole or in part by subsidized energy financing (within the meaning of section 48(l)(11)(C) of such Code), no financing made before January 1, 1980, shall be taken into account. The preceding sentence shall not apply to financing provided from the proceeds of any tax exempt industrial development bond (within the meaning of section 103(b)(2) of such Code)."

Amendment by Pub. L. 96–222 effective, except as otherwise provided, as if it had been included in the provisions of the Revenue Act of 1978, Pub. L. 95–600, to which such amendment relates, see section 201 of Pub. L. 96–222, set out as a note under section 32 of this title.

Pub. L. 96–222, title I, §108(c)(7), Apr. 1, 1980, 94 Stat. 228, provided that: "Any amendment made by this subsection [amending sections 4071, 4221, 6416, and 6421 of this title] shall take effect as if included in the provision of the Energy Tax Act of 1978 [See Short Title of 1978 Amendment note set out under section 1 of this title] to which such amendment relates; except that the amendment made by paragraph (6) [amending this section] shall take effect on the first day of the first calendar month which begins more than 10 days after the date of the enactment of this Act [Apr. 1, 1980]."

EFFECTIVE DATE OF 1978 AMENDMENT

Pub. L. 95–618, title III, §301(d)(4), Nov. 9, 1978, 92 Stat. 3200, provided that:

"(A) In general.—The amendments made by this subsection [amending this section and section 167 of this title] shall apply to property which is placed in service after September 30, 1978.

"(B) Binding contracts.—The amendments made by this subsection [amending this section and section 167 of this title] shall not apply to property which is constructed, reconstructed, erected, or acquired pursuant to a contract which, on October 1, 1978, and at all times thereafter, was binding on the taxpayer."

Amendment by section 141(b) of Pub. L. 95–600 effective with respect to qualified investment for taxable years beginning after Dec. 31, 1978, see section 141(g)(1) of Pub. L. 95–600, set out as an Effective Date note under section 409 of this title.

Amendment by section 312(c)(1), (2), (3) of Pub. L. 95–600 applicable to taxable years ending after Dec. 31, 1978, see section 312(d) of Pub. L. 95–600, set out as a note under section 46 of this title.

Pub. L. 95–600, title III, §314(c), Nov. 6, 1978, 92 Stat. 2828, provided that: "The amendments made by subsections (a) and (b) [amending this section] shall apply to taxable years ending after August 15, 1971."

Pub. L. 95–600, title III, §315(d), Nov. 6, 1978, 92 Stat. 2829, provided that: "The amendments made by this section [amending this section] shall apply to taxable years ending after October 31, 1978; except that the amendment made by subsection (c) shall only apply with respect to property placed in service after such date."

Amendment by section 703(a)(3), (4) of Pub. L. 95–600 effective on Oct. 4, 1976, see section 703(r) of Pub. L. 95–600, set out as a note under section 46 of this title.

EFFECTIVE DATE OF 1976 AMENDMENT

Amendment by section 802(b)(6) of Pub. L. 94–455 applicable to taxable years beginning after Dec. 31, 1975, see section 802(c) of Pub. L. 94–455, set out as a note under section 46 of this title.

Pub. L. 94–455, title VIII, §804(e), Oct. 4, 1976, 90 Stat. 1596, as amended by Pub. L. 99–514, §2, Oct. 22, 1986, 100 Stat. 2095, provided that:

"(1) In general.—The amendments made by subsections (a) and (b) [amending this section and section 47 of this title] shall apply to taxable years beginning after December 31, 1974.

"(2) Election may also apply to property described in section 50(a).—At the election of the taxpayer, made within 1 year after the date of the enactment of this Act [Oct. 4, 1976] in such manner as the Secretary of the Treasury or his delegate may by regulations prescribe, the amendments made by subsections (a) and (b) shall also apply to property which is property described in section 50(a) of the Internal Revenue Code of 1986 [formerly I.R.C. 1954] and which is placed in service in taxable years beginning before January 1, 1975."

Amendment by section 1051(h)(1) of Pub. L. 94–455 applicable to taxable years beginning after Dec. 31, 1975 with certain exceptions, see section 1051(i) of Pub. L. 94–455, set out as a note under section 27 of this title.

Amendment by section 1901(a)(5), (b)(11)(A) of Pub. L. 94–455 applicable with respect to taxable years beginning after Dec. 31, 1976, see section 1901(d) of Pub. L. 94–455, set out as a note under section 2 of this title.

Amendment by section 2112(a) of Pub. L. 94–455 applicable to property acquired by the taxpayer after Dec. 31, 1976, and property, the construction, reconstruction, or erection of which was completed by the taxpayer after Dec. 31, 1976, (but only to the extent of the basis thereof attributable to construction, reconstruction, or erection after such date), in taxable years beginning after such date, see section 2112(d)(1) of Pub. L. 94–455, set out as a note under section 46 of this title.

EFFECTIVE AND TERMINATION DATES OF 1975 AMENDMENT

Pub. L. 94–12, title III, §301(c)(2), Mar. 29, 1975, 89 Stat. 38, as amended by Pub. L. 94–455, title VIII, §801, Oct. 4, 1976, 90 Stat. 1580; Pub. L. 95–600, title III, §311(b), Nov. 6, 1978, 92 Stat. 2824, provided that: "The amendments made by paragraph (1) [amending this section] shall apply only to taxable years beginning after December 31, 1974."

Amendment by section 302(c)(3) of Pub. L. 94–12 applicable to taxable years ending after Dec. 31, 1974, see section 305(a) of Pub. L. 94–12, set out as an Effective Date of 1975 Amendment note under section 46 of this title.

Pub. L. 94–12, title VI, §604(b), Mar. 29, 1975, 89 Stat. 65, as amended by Pub. L. 99–514, §2, Oct. 22, 1986, 100 Stat. 2095, provided that:

"(1) In general.—The amendments made by subsection (a) [amending this section] shall apply to property, the construction, reconstruction, or erection of which was completed after March 18, 1975, or the acquisition of which by the taxpayer occurred after such date.

"(2) Binding contract.—The amendments made by subsection (a) [amending this section] shall not apply to property constructed, reconstructed, erected, or acquired pursuant to a contract which was on April 1, 1974, and at all times thereafter, binding on the taxpayer.

"(3) Certain lease-back transactions, etc.—Where a person who is a party to a binding contract described in paragraph (2) transfers rights in such contract (or in the property to which such contract relates) to another person but a party to such contract retains a right to use the property under a lease with such other person, then to the extent of the transferred rights such other person shall, for purposes of paragraph (2), succeed to the position of the transferor with respect to such binding contract and such property. The preceding sentence shall apply, in any case in which the lessor does not make an election under section 48(d) of the Internal Revenue Code of 1986 [formerly I.R.C. 1954], only if a party to such contract retains a right to use the property under a long-term lease."

EFFECTIVE DATE OF 1971 AMENDMENT

Pub. L. 92–178, title I, §104(h), Dec. 10, 1971, 85 Stat. 503, as amended by Pub. L. 99–514, §2, Oct. 22, 1986, 100 Stat. 2095, provided that: "The amendments made by this section [amending this section and sections 169 and 1245 of this title] (other than by subsections (c)(1), (c)(2), and (g) [amending this section]) shall apply to property described in section 50 of the Internal Revenue Code of 1986 [formerly I.R.C. 1954]. The amendments made by subsections (c)(1), (c)(2), and (g) [amending this section] shall apply to taxable years ending after December 31, 1961."

Amendment by section 108(b), (c) of Pub. L. 92–178, applicable to leases entered into after Sept. 22, 1971, and after Nov. 8, 1971, respectively, see section 108(d) of Pub. L. 92–178, set out as a note under section 46 of this title.

Amendment by section 121(d)(2)(A) of Pub. L. 91–172 applicable to taxable years beginning after Dec. 31, 1969, see section 121(g) of Pub. L. 91–172, set out as a note under section 511 of this title.

Amendment by section 401(e)(2)–(4) of Pub. L. 91–172 applicable with respect to taxable years ending on or after Dec. 31, 1970, see section 401(h)(3) of Pub. L. 91–172, set out as a note under section 1561 of this title.

EFFECTIVE DATE OF 1967 AMENDMENT

Pub. L. 90–26, §4, June 13, 1967, 81 Stat. 58, provided that: "The amendments made by the first three sections of this Act [amending this section and section 167 of this title] shall apply to taxable years ending after March 9, 1967."

EFFECTIVE DATE OF 1966 AMENDMENT

Pub. L. 89–809, title II, §201(b), Nov. 13, 1966, 80 Stat. 1576, as amended by Pub. L. 99–514, §2, Oct. 22, 1986, 100 Stat. 2095, provided that: "The amendments made by subsection (a) [amending this section] shall apply to taxable years ending after December 31, 1965, but only with respect to property placed in service after such date. In applying section 46(b) of the Internal Revenue Code of 1986 [formerly I.R.C. 1954] (relating to carryback and carryover of unused credits), the amount of any investment credit carryback to any taxable year ending on or before December 31, 1965, shall be determined without regard to the amendments made by this section."

Amendment by Pub. L. 89–800 applicable to taxable years ending after Oct. 9, 1966, see section 4 of Pub. L. 89–800, set out as a note under section 46 of this title.

EFFECTIVE DATE OF 1964 AMENDMENT

Pub. L. 88–272, title II, §203(a)(4), Feb. 26, 1964, 78 Stat. 34, provided that: "Paragraphs (1) [amending this section] and (3) [amending this section and section 1016 of this title and repealing section 181 of this title] of this subsection shall apply—

"(A) in the case of property placed in service after December 31, 1963, with respect to taxable years ending after such date, and

"(B) in the case of property placed in service before January 1, 1964, with respect to taxable years beginning after December 31, 1963."

Pub. L. 88–272, title II, §203(f), Feb. 26, 1964, 78 Stat. 35, provided that:

"(1) The amendments made by subsection (b) [amending this section] shall apply with respect to property possession of which is transferred to a lessee on or after the date of enactment of this Act [Feb. 26, 1964].

"(2) The amendments made by subsection (c) [amending this section] shall apply with respect to taxable years ending after June 30, 1963.

"(3) The amendments made by subsection (d) [amending section 1245 of this title] shall apply with respect to dispositions after December 31, 1963, in taxable years ending after such date."

EFFECTIVE DATE

Section applicable with respect to taxable years ending after Dec. 31, 1961, see section 2(h) of Pub. L. 87–834, set out as a note under section 46 of this title.

SAVINGS PROVISION

For provisions that nothing in amendment by Pub. L. 101–508 be construed to affect treatment of certain transactions occurring, property acquired, or items of income, loss, deduction, or credit taken into account prior to Nov. 5, 1990, for purposes of determining liability for tax for periods ending after Nov. 5, 1990, see section 11821(b) of Pub. L. 101–508, set out as a note under section 45K of this title.

TRANSFER OF FUNCTIONS

Functions, powers, and duties of Federal Aviation Agency and of Administrator and other offices and officers thereof transferred by Pub. L. 89–670, Oct. 15, 1966, 80 Stat. 931, to Secretary of Transportation, with functions, powers, and duties of Secretary of Transportation pertaining to aviation safety to be exercised by Federal Aviation Administrator in Department of Transportation, see section 106 of Title 49, Transportation.

GRANTS FOR SPECIFIED ENERGY PROPERTY IN LIEU OF TAX CREDITS

Pub. L. 111–5, div. B, title I, §1603, Feb. 17, 2009, 123 Stat. 364, as amended by Pub. L. 111–312, title VII, §707, Dec. 17, 2010, 124 Stat. 3312; Pub. L. 112–81, div. A, title X, §1096(a), Dec. 31, 2011, 125 Stat. 1608; Pub. L. 112–240, title IV, §407(c)(2), Jan. 2, 2013, 126 Stat. 2342, provided that:

"(a) In General.—Upon application, the Secretary of the Treasury shall, subject to the requirements of this section, provide a grant to each person who places in service specified energy property to reimburse such person for a portion of the expense of such property as provided in subsection (b). No grant shall be made under this section with respect to any property unless such property—

"(1) is originally placed in service by such person during 2009, 2010, or 2011, or

"(2) is originally placed in service by such person after 2011 and before the credit termination date with respect to such property, but only if the construction of such property began during 2009, 2010, or 2011.

"(b) Grant Amount.—

"(1) In general.—The amount of the grant under subsection (a) with respect to any specified energy property shall be the applicable percentage of the basis of such property.

"(2) Applicable percentage.—For purposes of paragraph (1), the term 'applicable percentage' means—

"(A) 30 percent in the case of any property described in paragraphs (1) through (4) of subsection (d), and

"(B) 10 percent in the case of any other property.

"(3) Dollar limitations.—In the case of property described in paragraph (2), (6), or (7) of subsection (d), the amount of any grant under this section with respect to such property shall not exceed the limitation described in section 48(c)(1)(B), 48(c)(2)(B), or 48(c)(3)(B) of the Internal Revenue Code of 1986, respectively, with respect to such property.

"(c) Time for Payment of Grant.—The Secretary of the Treasury shall make payment of any grant under subsection (a) during the 60-day period beginning on the later of—

"(1) the date of the application for such grant, or

"(2) the date the specified energy property for which the grant is being made is placed in service.

"(d) Specified Energy Property.—For purposes of this section, the term 'specified energy property' means any of the following:

"(1) Qualified facilities.—Any qualified property (as defined in section 48(a)(5)(D) of the Internal Revenue Code of 1986) which is part of a qualified facility (within the meaning of section 45 of such Code) described in paragraph (1), (2), (3), (4), (6), (7), (9), or (11) of section 45(d) of such Code.

"(2) Qualified fuel cell property.—Any qualified fuel cell property (as defined in section 48(c)(1) of such Code).

"(3) Solar property.—Any property described in clause (i) or (ii) of section 48(a)(3)(A) of such Code.

"(4) Qualified small wind energy property.—Any qualified small wind energy property (as defined in section 48(c)(4) of such Code).

"(5) Geothermal property.—Any property described in clause (iii) of section 48(a)(3)(A) of such Code.

"(6) Qualified microturbine property.—Any qualified microturbine property (as defined in section 48(c)(2) of such Code).

"(7) Combined heat and power system property.—Any combined heat and power system property (as defined in section 48(c)(3) of such Code).

"(8) Geothermal heat pump property.—Any property described in clause (vii) of section 48(a)(3)(A) of such Code.

Such term shall not include any property unless depreciation (or amortization in lieu of depreciation) is allowable with respect to such property.

"(e) Credit Termination Date.—For purposes of this section, the term 'credit termination date' means—

"(1) in the case of any specified energy property which is part of a facility described in paragraph (1) of section 45(d) of the Internal Revenue Code of 1986, January 1, 2013,

"(2) in the case of any specified energy property which is part of a facility described in paragraph (2), (3), (4), (6), (7), (9), or (11) of section 45(d) of such Code, January 1, 2014, and

"(3) in the case of any specified energy property described in section 48 of such Code, January 1, 2017.

In the case of any property which is described in paragraph (3) and also in another paragraph of this subsection, paragraph (3) shall apply with respect to such property.

"(f) Application of Certain Rules.—In making grants under this section, the Secretary of the Treasury shall apply rules similar to the rules of section 50 of the Internal Revenue Code of 1986 (other than subsection (d)(2) thereof). In applying such rules, if the property is disposed of, or otherwise ceases to be specified energy property, the Secretary of the Treasury shall provide for the recapture of the appropriate percentage of the grant amount in such manner as the Secretary of the Treasury determines appropriate.

"(g) Exception for Certain Non-Taxpayers.—The Secretary of the Treasury shall not make any grant under this section to—

"(1) any Federal, State, or local government (or any political subdivision, agency, or instrumentality thereof),

"(2) any organization described in section 501(c) of the Internal Revenue Code of 1986 and exempt from tax under section 501(a) of such Code,

"(3) any entity referred to in paragraph (4) of [former] section 54(j) of such Code, or

"(4) any partnership or other pass-thru entity any partner (or other holder of an equity or profits interest) of which is described in paragraph (1), (2) or (3).

"(h) Definitions.—Terms used in this section which are also used in section 45 or 48 of the Internal Revenue Code of 1986 shall have the same meaning for purposes of this section as when used in such section 45 or 48. Any reference in this section to the Secretary of the Treasury shall be treated as including the Secretary's delegate.

"(i) Appropriations.—There is hereby appropriated to the Secretary of the Treasury such sums as may be necessary to carry out this section.

"(j) Termination.—The Secretary of the Treasury shall not make any grant to any person under this section unless the application of such person for such grant is received before October 1, 2012."

[Pub. L. 112–81, div. A, title X, §1096(b), Dec. 31, 2011, 125 Stat. 1608, provided that: "The amendment made by this section [amending section 1603 of Pub. L. 111–5, set out above] shall take effect as if included in section 1603 of the American Recovery and Reinvestment Tax Act of 2009 [Pub. L. 111–5]."]

PLAN AMENDMENTS NOT REQUIRED UNTIL JANUARY 1, 1989

For provisions directing that if any amendments made by subtitle A or subtitle C of title XI [§§1101–1147 and 1171–1177] or title XVIII [§§1800–1899A] of Pub. L. 99–514 require an amendment to any plan, such plan amendment shall not be required to be made before the first plan year beginning on or after Jan. 1, 1989, see section 1140 of Pub. L. 99–514, as amended, set out as a note under section 401 of this title.

APPLICABILITY OF CERTAIN AMENDMENTS BY PUB. L. 99–514 IN RELATION TO TREATY OBLIGATIONS OF UNITED STATES

For applicability of amendment by section 701(e)(4)(C) of Pub. L. 99–514 notwithstanding any treaty obligation of the United States in effect on Oct. 22, 1986, with provision that for such purposes any amendment by title I of Pub. L. 100–647 be treated as if it had been included in the provision of Pub. L. 99–514 to which such amendment relates, see section 1012(aa)(2), (4) of Pub. L. 100–647, set out as a note under section 861 of this title.

SPECIAL RULE

Pub. L. 99–514, title XVIII, §1879(j)(3), Oct. 22, 1986, 100 Stat. 2909, provided that: "If refund or credit of any overpayment of tax resulting from the application of this subsection [amending this section] is prevented at any time before the close of the date which is 1 year after the date of the enactment of this Act [Oct. 22, 1986] by operation of any law or rule of law (including res judicata), refund or credit of such overpayment (to the extent attributable to the application of the amendments made by this subsection [amending this section]) may, nevertheless, be made or allowed if claim therefor is filed before the close of such 1-year period."

CLARIFICATION OF EFFECT OF 1984 AMENDMENT ON INVESTMENT TAX CREDIT

For provision that nothing in the amendments made by section 474(o) of Pub. L. 98–369, which amended this section, be construed as reducing the investment tax credit in taxable years beginning before Jan. 1, 1984, see section 475(c) of Pub. L. 98–369, set out as a note under section 46 of this title.

ALTERNATIVE METHODS OF COMPUTING CREDIT FOR PAST PERIODS

Pub. L. 94–455, title VIII, §804(c), Oct. 4, 1976, 90 Stat. 1594, as amended by Pub. L. 99–514, §2, Oct. 22, 1986, 100 Stat. 2095, provided that:

"(1) General rule for determining useful life, predominant foreign use, etc.—In the case of a qualified film (within the meaning of section 48(k)(1)(B) of the Internal Revenue Code of 1986 [formerly I.R.C. 1954]) placed in service in a taxable year beginning before January 1, 1975, with respect to which neither an election under paragraph (2) of this subsection nor an election under subsection (e)(2) applies—

"(A) the applicable percentage under section 46(c)(2) of such Code shall be determined as if the useful life of the film would have expired at the close of the first taxable year by the close of which the aggregate amount allowable as a deduction under section 167 of such Code would equal or exceed 90 percent of the basis of such property (adjusted for any partial dispositions),

"(B) for purposes of section 46(c)(1) of such Code, the basis of the property shall be determined by taking into account the total production costs (within the meaning of section 48(k)(5)(B) of such Code),

"(C) for purposes of section 48(a)(2) of such Code, such film shall be considered to be used predominantly outside the United States in the first taxable year for which 50 percent or more of the gross revenues received or accrued during the taxable year from showing the film were received or accrued from showing the film outside the United States, and

"(D) Section 47(a)(7) of such Code shall apply.

"(2) Election of 40-percent method.—

"(A) In general.—A taxpayer may elect to have this paragraph apply to all qualified films placed in service during taxable years beginning before January 1, 1975 (other than films to which an election under subsection (e)(2) of this section applies).

"(B) Effect of election.—If the taxpayer makes an election under this paragraph, then section 48(k) of the Internal Revenue Code of 1986 shall apply to all qualified films described in subparagraph (A) with the following modifications:

"(i) subparagraph (B) of paragraph (4) shall not apply, but in determining qualified investment under section 46(c)(1) of such Code there shall be used (in lieu of the basis of such property) an amount equal to 40 percent of the aggregate production costs (within the meaning of paragraph (5)(B) of such section 48(k)),

"(ii) paragraph (2) shall be applied by substituting '100 percent' for '66⅔ percent', and

"(iii) paragraph (3) and paragraph (5) (other than subparagraph (B)) shall not apply.

"(C) Rules relating to elections.—An election under this paragraph shall be made not later than the day which is 6 months after the date of the enactment of this Act [Oct. 4, 1976] and shall be made in such manner as the Secretary of the Treasury or his delegate shall by regulations prescribe. Such an election may be revoked only with the consent of the Secretary of the Treasury or his delegate.

"(D) The taxpayer must consent to join in certain proceedings.—No election may be made under this paragraph or subsection (e)(2) by any taxpayer unless he consents, under regulations prescribed by the Secretary of the Treasury or his delegate, to treat the determination of the investment credit allowable on each film subject to an election as a separate cause of action, and to join in any judicial proceeding for determining the person entitled to, and the amount of, the credit allowable under section 38 of the Internal Revenue Code of 1986 with respect to any film covered by such election.

"(3) Election to have credit determined in accordance with previous litigation.—

"(A) In general.——A taxpayer described in subparagraph (B) may elect to have this paragraph apply to all films (whether or not qualified) placed in service in taxable years beginning before January 1, 1975, and with respect to which an election under subsection (e)(2) is not made.

"(B) Who may elect.——A taxpayer may make an election under this paragraph if he has filed an action in any court of competent jurisdiction, before January 1, 1976, for a determination of such taxpayer's rights to the allowance of a credit against tax under section 38 of the Internal Revenue Code of 1986 for any taxable year beginning before January 1, 1975, with respect to any film.

"(C) Effect of election.——If the taxpayer makes an election under this paragraph——

"(i) paragraphs (1) and (2) of this subsection, and subsection (d) shall not apply to any film placed in service by the taxpayer, and

"(ii) subsection 48(k) of the Internal Revenue Code of 1986 shall not apply to any film placed in service by the taxpayer in any taxable year beginning before January 1, 1975, and with respect to which an election under subsection (e)(2) is not made,

and the right of the taxpayer to the allowance of a credit against tax under section 38 of such Code with respect to any film placed in service in any taxable year beginning before January 1, 1975, and as to which an election under subsection (e)(2) is not made, shall be determined as though this section (other than this paragraph) has not been enacted.

"(D) Rules relating to elections.——An election under this paragraph shall be made not later than the day which is 90 days after the date of the enactment of this Act [Oct. 4, 1976], by filing a notification of such election with the national office of the Internal Revenue Service. Such an election, once made, shall be irrevocable."

ENTITLEMENT TO CREDIT

Pub. L. 94–455, title VIII, §804(d), Oct. 4, 1976, 90 Stat. 1596, as amended by Pub. L. 99–514, §2, Oct. 22, 1986, 100 Stat. 2095, provided that: "Paragraph (1) of section 48(k) of the Internal Revenue Code of 1986 [formerly I.R.C. 1954] (relating to entitlement to credit) shall apply to any motion picture film or video tape placed in service in any taxable year beginning before January 1, 1975."

INCREASE IN BASIS OF PROPERTY PLACED IN SERVICE BEFORE JANUARY 1, 1964

Pub. L. 88–272, title II, §203(a)(2), Feb. 26, 1964, 78 Stat. 33, as amended by Pub. L. 99–514, §2, Oct. 22, 1986, 100 Stat. 2095, provided that:

"(A) The basis of any section 38 property (as defined in section 48(a) of the Internal Revenue Code of 1986 [formerly I.R.C. 1954]) placed in service before January 1, 1964, shall be increased, under regulations prescribed by the Secretary of the Treasury or his delegate, by an amount equal to 7 percent of the qualified investment with respect to such property under section 46(c) of the Internal Revenue Code of 1986. If there has been any increase with respect to such property under section 48(g)(2) of such Code, the increase under the preceding sentence shall be appropriately reduced therefor.

"(B) If a lessor made the election provided by section 48(d) of the Internal Revenue Code of 1986 with respect to property placed in service before January 1, 1964——

"(i) subparagraph (A) shall not apply with respect to such property, but

"(ii) under regulations prescribed by the Secretary of the Treasury or his delegate, the deductions otherwise allowable under section 162 of such Code to the lessee for amounts paid to the lessor under the lease (or, if such lessee has purchased such property, the basis of such property) shall be adjusted in a manner consistent with subparagraph (A).

"(C) The adjustments under this paragraph shall be made as of the first day of the taxpayer's first taxable year which begins after December 31, 1963."

§48A. Qualifying advanced coal project credit

(a) In general

For purposes of section 46, the qualifying advanced coal project credit for any taxable year is an amount equal to——

(1) 20 percent of the qualified investment for such taxable year in the case of projects described in subsection (d)(3)(B)(i),

(2) 15 percent of the qualified investment for such taxable year in the case of projects described in subsection (d)(3)(B)(ii), and

(3) 30 percent of the qualified investment for such taxable year in the case of projects described in clause (iii) of subsection (d)(3)(B).

(b) Qualified investment

(1) In general

For purposes of subsection (a), the qualified investment for any taxable year is the basis of eligible property placed in service by the taxpayer during such taxable year which is part of a qualifying advanced coal project——

(A)(i) the construction, reconstruction, or erection of which is completed by the taxpayer, or

(ii) which is acquired by the taxpayer if the original use of such property commences with the taxpayer, and

(B) with respect to which depreciation (or amortization in lieu of depreciation) is allowable.

(2) Special rule for certain subsidized property

Rules similar to section 48(a)(4) (without regard to subparagraph (D) thereof) shall apply for purposes of this section.

(3) Certain qualified progress expenditures rules made applicable

Rules similar to the rules of subsections (c)(4) and (d) of section 46 (as in effect on the day before the enactment of the Revenue Reconciliation Act of 1990) shall apply for purposes of this section.

(c) Definitions

For purposes of this section——

(1) Qualifying advanced coal project

The term "qualifying advanced coal project" means a project which meets the requirements of subsection (e).

(2) Advanced coal-based generation technology

The term "advanced coal-based generation technology" means a technology which meets the requirements of subsection (f).

(3) Eligible property

The term "eligible property" means——

(A) in the case of any qualifying advanced coal project using an integrated gasification combined cycle, any property which is a part of such project and is necessary for the gasification of coal, including any coal handling and gas separation equipment, and

(B) in the case of any other qualifying advanced coal project, any property which is a part of such project.

(4) Coal

The term "coal" means anthracite, bituminous coal, subbituminous coal, lignite, and peat.

(5) Greenhouse gas capture capability

The term "greenhouse gas capture capability" means an integrated gasification combined cycle technology facility capable of adding components which can capture, separate on a long-term basis, isolate, remove, and sequester greenhouse gases which result from the generation of electricity.

(6) Electric generation unit

The term "electric generation unit" means any facility at least 50 percent of the total annual net output of which is electrical power, including an otherwise eligible facility which is used in an industrial application.

(7) Integrated gasification combined cycle

The term "integrated gasification combined cycle" means an electric generation unit which produces electricity by converting coal to synthesis gas which is used to fuel a combined-cycle plant which produces electricity from both a combustion turbine (including a combustion turbine/fuel cell hybrid) and a steam turbine.

(d) Qualifying advanced coal project program

(1) Establishment

Not later than 180 days after the date of enactment of this section, the Secretary, in consultation with the Secretary of Energy, shall establish a qualifying advanced coal project program for the deployment of advanced coal-based generation technologies.

(2) Certification

(A) Application period

Each applicant for certification under this paragraph shall submit an application meeting the requirements of subparagraph (B). An applicant may only submit an application—

(i) for an allocation from the dollar amount specified in clause (i) or (ii) of paragraph (3)(B) during the 3-year period beginning on the date the Secretary establishes the program under paragraph (1), and

(ii) for an allocation from the dollar amount specified in paragraph (3)(B)(iii) during the 3-year period beginning at the earlier of the termination of the period described in clause (i) or the date prescribed by the Secretary.

(B) Requirements for applications for certification

An application under subparagraph (A) shall contain such information as the Secretary may require in order to make a determination to accept or reject an application for certification as meeting the requirements under subsection (e)(1). Any information contained in the application shall be protected as provided in section 552(b)(4) of title 5, United States Code.

(C) Time to act upon applications for certification

The Secretary shall issue a determination as to whether an applicant has met the requirements under subsection (e)(1) within 60 days following the date of submittal of the application for certification.

(D) Time to meet criteria for certification

Each applicant for certification shall have 2 years from the date of acceptance by the Secretary of the application during which to provide to the Secretary evidence that the criteria set forth in subsection (e)(2) have been met.

(E) Period of issuance

An applicant which receives a certification shall have 5 years from the date of issuance of the certification in order to place the project in service and if such project is not placed in service by that time period then the certification shall no longer be valid.

(3) Aggregate credits

(A) In general

The aggregate credits allowed under subsection (a) for projects certified by the Secretary under paragraph (2) may not exceed $2,550,000,000.

(B) Particular projects

Of the dollar amount in subparagraph (A), the Secretary is authorized to certify—

(i) $800,000,000 for integrated gasification combined cycle projects the application for which is submitted during the period described in paragraph (2)(A)(i),

(ii) $500,000,000 for projects which use other advanced coal-based generation technologies the application for which is submitted during the period described in paragraph (2)(A)(i), and

(iii) $1,250,000,000 for advanced coal-based generation technology projects the application for which is submitted during the period described in paragraph (2)(A)(ii).

(4) Review and redistribution

(A) Review

Not later than 6 years after the date of enactment of this section, the Secretary shall review the credits allocated under this section as of the date which is 6 years after the date of enactment of this section.

(B) Redistribution

The Secretary may reallocate credits available under clauses (i) and (ii) of paragraph (3)(B) if the Secretary determines that—

(i) there is an insufficient quantity of qualifying applications for certification pending at the time of the review, or

(ii) any certification made pursuant to paragraph (2) has been revoked pursuant to paragraph (2)(D) because the project subject to the certification has been delayed as a result of third party opposition or litigation to the proposed project.

(C) Reallocation

If the Secretary determines that credits under clause (i) or (ii) of paragraph (3)(B) are available for reallocation pursuant to the requirements set forth in paragraph (2), the Secretary is authorized to conduct an additional program for applications for certification.

(5) Disclosure of allocations

The Secretary shall, upon making a certification under this subsection or section 48B(d), publicly disclose the identity of the applicant and the amount of the credit certified with respect to such applicant.

(e) Qualifying advanced coal projects

(1) Requirements

For purposes of subsection (c)(1), a project shall be considered a qualifying advanced coal project that the Secretary may certify under subsection (d)(2) if the Secretary determines that, at a minimum—

(A) the project uses an advanced coal-based generation technology—

(i) to power a new electric generation unit; or

(ii) to retrofit or repower an existing electric generation unit (including an existing natural gas-fired combined cycle unit);

(B) the fuel input for the project, when completed, is at least 75 percent coal;

(C) the project, consisting of one or more electric generation units at one site, will have a total nameplate generating capacity of at least 400 megawatts;

(D) the applicant provides evidence that a majority of the output of the project is reasonably expected to be acquired or utilized;

(E) the applicant provides evidence of ownership or control of a site of sufficient size to allow the proposed project to be constructed and to operate on a long-term basis;

(F) the project will be located in the United States; and

(G) in the case of any project the application for which is submitted during the period described in subsection (d)(2)(A)(ii), the project includes equipment which separates and sequesters at least 65 percent (70 percent in the case of an application for reallocated credits under subsection (d)(4)) of such project's total carbon dioxide emissions.

(2) Requirements for certification

For the purpose of subsection (d)(2)(D), a project shall be eligible for certification only if the Secretary determines that—

(A) the applicant for certification has received all Federal and State environmental authorizations or reviews necessary to commence construction of the project; and

(B) the applicant for certification, except in the case of a retrofit or repower of an existing electric generation unit, has purchased or entered into a binding contract for the purchase of the main steam turbine or turbines for the project, except that such contract may be contingent upon receipt of a certification under subsection (d)(2).

(3) Priority for certain projects

In determining which qualifying advanced coal projects to certify under subsection (d)(2), the Secretary shall—

(A) certify capacity, in accordance with the procedures set forth in subsection (d), in relatively equal amounts to—

(i) projects using bituminous coal as a primary feedstock,

(ii) projects using subbituminous coal as a primary feedstock, and

(iii) projects using lignite as a primary feedstock,

(B) give high priority to projects which include, as determined by the Secretary—

(i) greenhouse gas capture capability,

(ii) increased by-product utilization,

(iii) applicant participants who have a research partnership with an eligible educational institution (as defined in section 529(e)(5)), and

(iv) other benefits, and

(C) give highest priority to projects with the greatest separation and sequestration percentage of total carbon dioxide emissions.

(f) Advanced coal-based generation technology

(1) In general

For the purpose of this section, an electric generation unit uses advanced coal-based generation technology if—

(A) the unit—

(i) uses integrated gasification combined cycle technology, or

(ii) except as provided in paragraph (3), has a design net heat rate of 8530 Btu/kWh (40 percent efficiency), and

(B) the unit is designed to meet the performance requirements in the following table:

Performance characteristic:	Design level for project:
SO_2 (percent removal)	99 percent
NO_x (emissions)	0.07 lbs/MMBTU
PM* (emissions)	0.015 lbs/MMBTU
Hg (percent removal)	90 percent

For purposes of the performance requirement specified for the removal of SO_2 in the table contained in subparagraph (B), the SO_2 removal design level in the case of a unit designed for the use of feedstock substantially all of which is subbituminous coal shall be 99 percent SO_2 removal or the achievement of an emission level of 0.04 pounds or less of SO_2 per million Btu, determined on a 30-day average.

(2) Design net heat rate

For purposes of this subsection, design net heat rate with respect to an electric generation unit shall—

(A) be measured in Btu per kilowatt hour (higher heating value),

(B) be based on the design annual heat input to the unit and the rated net electrical power, fuels, and chemicals output of the unit (determined without regard to the cogeneration of steam by the unit),

(C) be adjusted for the heat content of the design coal to be used by the unit—

(i) if the heat content is less than 13,500 Btu per pound, but greater than 7,000 Btu per pound, according to the following formula: design net heat rate = unit net heat rate x [1−[((13,500−design coal heat content, Btu per pound)/1,000)* 0.013]], and

(ii) if the heat content is less than or equal to 7,000 Btu per pound, according to the following formula: design net heat rate = unit net heat rate x [1−[((13,500−design coal heat content, Btu per pound)/1,000)* 0.018]], and

(D) be corrected for the site reference conditions of—

(i) elevation above sea level of 500 feet,

(ii) air pressure of 14.4 pounds per square inch absolute,

(iii) temperature, dry bulb of 63°F,

(iv) temperature, wet bulb of 54°F, and

(v) relative humidity of 55 percent.

(3) Existing units

In the case of any electric generation unit in existence on the date of the enactment of this section, such unit uses advanced coal-based generation technology if, in lieu of the requirements under paragraph (1)(A)(ii), such unit achieves a minimum efficiency of 35 percent and an overall thermal design efficiency improvement, compared to the efficiency of the unit as operated, of not less than—

(A) 7 percentage points for coal of more than 9,000 Btu,

(B) 6 percentage points for coal of 7,000 to 9,000 Btu, or

(C) 4 percentage points for coal of less than 7,000 Btu.

(g) Applicability

No use of technology (or level of emission reduction solely by reason of the use of the technology), and no achievement of any emission reduction by the demonstration of any technology or performance level, by or at one or more facilities with respect to which a credit is allowed under this section, shall be considered to indicate that the technology or performance level is—

(1) adequately demonstrated for purposes of section 111 of the Clean Air Act (42 U.S.C. 7411);

(2) achievable for purposes of section 169 of that Act (42 U.S.C. 7479); or

(3) achievable in practice for purposes of section 171 of such Act (42 U.S.C. 7501).

(h) Competitive certification awards modification authority

In implementing this section or section 48B, the Secretary is directed to modify the terms of any competitive certification award and any associated closing agreement where such modification—

(1) is consistent with the objectives of such section,

(2) is requested by the recipient of the competitive certification award, and

(3) involves moving the project site to improve the potential to capture and sequester carbon dioxide emissions, reduce costs of transporting feedstock, and serve a broader customer base,

unless the Secretary determines that the dollar amount of tax credits available to the taxpayer under such section would increase as a result of the modification or such modification would result in such project not being originally certified. In considering any such modification, the Secretary shall consult with other relevant Federal agencies, including the Department of Energy.

(i) Recapture of credit for failure to sequester

The Secretary shall provide for recapturing the benefit of any credit allowable under subsection (a) with respect to any project which fails to attain or maintain the separation and sequestration requirements of subsection (e)(1)(G).

(Added Pub. L. 109–58, title XIII, §1307(b), Aug. 8, 2005, 119 Stat. 999; amended Pub. L. 109–432, div. A, title II, §203(a), Dec. 20, 2006, 120 Stat. 2945; Pub. L. 110–172, §11(a)(10), Dec. 29, 2007, 121 Stat. 2485; Pub. L. 110–234, title XV, §15346(a), May 22, 2008, 122 Stat. 1523; Pub. L. 110–246, §4(a), title XV, §15346(a), June 18, 2008, 122 Stat. 1664, 2285; Pub. L. 110–343, div. B, title I, §111(a)–(d), Oct. 3, 2008, 122 Stat. 3822, 3823; Pub. L. 111–5, div. B, title I, §1103(b)(2)(C), Feb. 17, 2009, 123 Stat. 321.)

Pub. L. 110–234, title XV, §15346(b), May 22, 2008, 122 Stat. 1523, and Pub. L. 110–246, §4(a), title XV, §15346(b), June 18, 2008, 122 Stat. 1664, 2285, provided that: "The amendment made by this section [amending this section] shall take effect on the date of the enactment of this Act [June 18, 2008] and is applicable to all competitive certification awards entered into under section 48A or 48B of the Internal Revenue Code of 1986, whether such awards were issued before, on, or after such date of enactment."

[Pub. L. 110–234 and Pub. L. 110–246 enacted identical provisions. Pub. L. 110–234 was repealed by section 4(a) of Pub. L. 110–246, set out as a note under section 8701 of Title 7, Agriculture.]

EFFECTIVE DATE OF 2006 AMENDMENT

Pub. L. 109–432, div. A, title II, §203(b), Dec. 20, 2006, 120 Stat. 2945, provided that: "The amendment made by this section [amending this section] shall take apply [sic] with respect to applications for certification under section 48A(d)(2) of the Internal Revenue Code of 1986 submitted after October 2, 2006."

EFFECTIVE DATE

Section applicable to periods after Aug. 8, 2005, under rules similar to the rules of section 48(m) of this title, as in effect on the day before Nov. 5, 1990, see section 1307(d) of Pub. L. 109–58, set out as an Effective Date of 2005 Amendment note under section 46 of this title.

§48B. Qualifying gasification project credit

(a) In general

For purposes of section 46, the qualifying gasification project credit for any taxable year is an amount equal to 20 percent (30 percent in the case of credits allocated under subsection (d)(1)(B)) of the qualified investment for such taxable year.

(b) Qualified investment

(1) In general

For purposes of subsection (a), the qualified investment for any taxable year is the basis of eligible property placed in service by the taxpayer during such taxable year which is part of a qualifying gasification project—

(A)(i) the construction, reconstruction, or erection of which is completed by the taxpayer, or

(ii) which is acquired by the taxpayer if the original use of such property commences with the taxpayer, and

(B) with respect to which depreciation (or amortization in lieu of depreciation) is allowable.

(2) Special rule for certain subsidized property

Rules similar to section 48(a)(4) (without regard to subparagraph (D) thereof) shall apply for purposes of this section.

(3) Certain qualified progress expenditures rules made applicable

Rules similar to the rules of subsections (c)(4) and (d) of section 46 (as in effect on the day before the enactment of the Revenue Reconciliation Act of 1990) shall apply for purposes of this section.

(c) Definitions

For purposes of this section—

(1) Qualifying gasification project

The term "qualifying gasification project" means any project which—

(A) employs gasification technology,

(B) will be carried out by an eligible entity, and

(C) any portion of the qualified investment of which is certified under the qualifying gasification program as eligible for credit under this section in an amount (not to exceed $650,000,000) determined by the Secretary.

(2) Gasification technology

The term "gasification technology" means any process which converts a solid or liquid product from coal, petroleum residue, biomass, or other materials which are recovered for their energy or feedstock value into a synthesis gas composed primarily of carbon monoxide and hydrogen for direct use or subsequent chemical or physical conversion.

(3) Eligible property

The term "eligible property" means any property which is a part of a qualifying gasification project and is necessary for the gasification technology of such project.

(4) Biomass

(A) In general

The term "biomass" means any—

(i) agricultural or plant waste,

(ii) byproduct of wood or paper mill operations, including lignin in spent pulping liquors, and

(iii) other products of forestry maintenance.

(B) Exclusion

The term "biomass" does not include paper which is commonly recycled.

(5) Carbon capture capability

The term "carbon capture capability" means a gasification plant design which is determined by the Secretary to reflect reasonable consideration for, and be capable of, accommodating the equipment likely to be necessary to capture carbon dioxide from the gaseous stream, for later use or sequestration, which would otherwise be emitted in the flue gas from a project which uses a nonrenewable fuel.

(6) Coal

The term "coal" means anthracite, bituminous coal, subbituminous coal, lignite, and peat.

(7) Eligible entity

The term "eligible entity" means any person whose application for certification is principally intended for use in a domestic project which employs domestic gasification applications related to—

(A) chemicals,

(B) fertilizers,

(C) glass,

(D) steel,

(E) petroleum residues,

(F) forest products,

(G) agriculture, including feedlots and dairy operations, and

(H) transportation grade liquid fuels.

(8) Petroleum residue

The term "petroleum residue" means the carbonized product of high-boiling hydrocarbon fractions obtained in petroleum processing.

(d) Qualifying gasification project program

(1) In general

Not later than 180 days after the date of the enactment of this section, the Secretary, in consultation with the Secretary of Energy, shall establish a qualifying gasification project program to consider and award certifications for qualified investment eligible for credits under this section to qualifying gasification project sponsors under this section. The total amounts of credit that may be allocated under the program shall not exceed—

(A) $350,000,000, plus

(B) $250,000,000 for qualifying gasification projects that include equipment which separates and sequesters at least 75 percent of such project's total carbon dioxide emissions.

(2) Period of issuance

A certificate of eligibility under paragraph (1) may be issued only during the 10-fiscal year period beginning on October 1, 2005.

(3) Selection criteria

The Secretary shall not make a competitive certification award for qualified investment for credit eligibility under this section unless the recipient has documented to the satisfaction of the Secretary that—

(A) the award recipient is financially viable without the receipt of additional Federal funding associated with the proposed project,

(B) the recipient will provide sufficient information to the Secretary for the Secretary to ensure that the qualified investment is spent efficiently and effectively,

(C) a market exists for the products of the proposed project as evidenced by contracts or written statements of intent from potential customers,

(D) the fuels identified with respect to the gasification technology for such project will comprise at least 90 percent of the fuels required by the project for the production of chemical feedstocks, liquid transportation fuels, or coproduction of electricity,

(E) the award recipient's project team is competent in the construction and operation of the gasification technology proposed, with preference given to those recipients with experience which demonstrates successful and reliable operations of the technology on domestic fuels so identified, and

(F) the award recipient has met other criteria established and published by the Secretary.

(4) Selection priorities

In determining which qualifying gasification projects to certify under this section, the Secretary shall—

(A) give highest priority to projects with the greatest separation and sequestration percentage of total carbon dioxide emissions, and

(B) give high priority to applicant participants who have a research partnership with an eligible educational institution (as defined in section 529(e)(5)).

(e) Denial of double benefit

A credit shall not be allowed under this section for any qualified investment for which a credit is allowed under section 48A.

(f) Recapture of credit for failure to sequester

The Secretary shall provide for recapturing the benefit of any credit allowable under subsection (a) with respect to any project which fails to attain or maintain the separation and sequestration requirements for such project under subsection (d)(1).

(Added Pub. L. 109–58, title XIII, §1307(b), Aug. 8, 2005, 119 Stat. 1004; amended Pub. L. 110–343, div. B, title I, §112(a)–(e), Oct. 3, 2008, 122 Stat. 3824; Pub. L. 111–5, div. B, title I, §1103(b)(2)(D), Feb. 17, 2009, 123 Stat. 321.)

EDITORIAL NOTES
REFERENCES IN TEXT

The enactment of the Revenue Reconciliation Act of 1990, referred to in subsec. (b)(3), is the date of enactment of title XI of Pub. L. 101–508, which was approved Nov. 5, 1990.

The date of the enactment of this section, referred to in subsec. (d)(1), is the date of enactment of Pub. L. 109–58, which was approved Aug. 8, 2005.

AMENDMENTS

2009—Subsec. (b)(2). Pub. L. 111–5 inserted "(without regard to subparagraph (D) thereof)" after "section 48(a)(4)".

2008—Subsec. (a). Pub. L. 110–343, §112(a), inserted "(30 percent in the case of credits allocated under subsection (d)(1)(B))" after "20 percent".

Subsec. (c)(7)(H). Pub. L. 110–343, §112(e), added subpar. (H).

Subsec. (d)(1). Pub. L. 110–343, §112(b), substituted "shall not exceed—" for "shall not exceed $350,000,000 under rules similar to the rules of section 48A(d)(4)." and added subpars. (A) and (B).

Subsec. (d)(4). Pub. L. 110–343, §112(d), added par. (4).

Subsec. (f). Pub. L. 110–343, §112(c), added subsec. (f).

STATUTORY NOTES AND RELATED SUBSIDIARIES
EFFECTIVE DATE OF 2009 AMENDMENT

Amendment by Pub. L. 111–5 applicable to periods after Dec. 31, 2008, under rules similar to the rules of section 48(m) of this title as in effect on the day before Nov. 5, 1990, see section 1103(c)(1) of Pub. L. 111–5, set out as a note under section 25C of this title.

EFFECTIVE DATE OF 2008 AMENDMENT

Pub. L. 110–343, div. B, title I, §112(f), Oct. 3, 2008, 122 Stat. 3824, provided that: "The amendments made by this section [amending this section] shall apply to credits described in section 48B(d)(1)(B) of the Internal Revenue Code of 1986 which are allocated or reallocated after the date of the enactment of this Act [Oct. 3, 2008]."

EFFECTIVE DATE

Section applicable to periods after Aug. 8, 2005, under rules similar to the rules of section 48(m) of this title, as in effect on the day before Nov. 5, 1990, see section 1307(d) of Pub. L. 109–58, set out as an Effective Date of 2005 Amendment note under section 46 of this title.

§48C. Qualifying advanced energy project credit

(a) In general

For purposes of section 46, the qualifying advanced energy project credit for any taxable year is an amount equal to 30 percent of the qualified investment for such taxable year with respect to any qualifying advanced energy project of the taxpayer.

(b) Qualified investment

(1) In general

For purposes of subsection (a), the qualified investment for any taxable year is the basis of eligible property placed in service by the taxpayer during such taxable year which is part of a qualifying advanced energy project.

(2) Certain qualified progress expenditures rules made applicable

Rules similar to the rules of subsections (c)(4) and (d) of section 46 (as in effect on the day before the enactment of the Revenue Reconciliation Act of 1990) shall apply for purposes of this section.

(3) Limitation

The amount which is treated as the qualified investment for all taxable years with respect to any qualifying advanced energy project shall not exceed the amount designated by the Secretary as eligible for the credit under this section.

(c) Definitions

(1) Qualifying advanced energy project

(A) In general

The term "qualifying advanced energy project" means a project—

(i) which re-equips, expands, or establishes a manufacturing facility for the production of—

(I) property designed to be used to produce energy from the sun, wind, geothermal deposits (within the meaning of section 613(e)(2)), or other renewable resources,

(II) fuel cells, microturbines, or an energy storage system for use with electric or hybrid-electric motor vehicles,

(III) electric grids to support the transmission of intermittent sources of renewable energy, including storage of such energy,

(IV) property designed to capture and sequester carbon dioxide emissions,

(V) property designed to refine or blend renewable fuels or to produce energy conservation technologies (including energy-conserving lighting technologies and smart grid technologies),

(VI) new qualified plug-in electric drive motor vehicles (as defined by section 30D) or components which are designed specifically for use with such vehicles, including electric motors, generators, and power control units, or

(VII) other advanced energy property designed to reduce greenhouse gas emissions as may be determined by the Secretary, and

(ii) any portion of the qualified investment of which is certified by the Secretary under subsection (d) as eligible for a credit under this section.

(B) Exception

Such term shall not include any portion of a project for the production of any property which is used in the refining or blending of any transportation fuel (other than renewable fuels).

(2) Eligible property

The term "eligible property" means any property—

(A) which is necessary for the production of property described in paragraph (1)(A)(i),

(B) which is—

(i) tangible personal property, or

(ii) other tangible property (not including a building or its structural components), but only if such property is used as an integral part of the qualified investment credit facility, and

(C) with respect to which depreciation (or amortization in lieu of depreciation) is allowable.

(d) Qualifying advanced energy project program

(1) Establishment

(A) In general

Not later than 180 days after the date of enactment of this section, the Secretary, in consultation with the Secretary of Energy, shall establish a qualifying advanced energy project program to consider and award certifications for qualified investments eligible for credits under this section to qualifying advanced energy project sponsors.

(B) Limitation

The total amount of credits that may be allocated under the program shall not exceed $2,300,000,000.

(2) Certification

(A) Application period

Each applicant for certification under this paragraph shall submit an application containing such information as the Secretary may require during the 2-year period beginning on the date the Secretary establishes the program under paragraph (1).

(B) Time to meet criteria for certification

Each applicant for certification shall have 1 year from the date of acceptance by the Secretary of the application during which to provide to the Secretary evidence that the requirements of the certification have been met.

(C) Period of issuance

An applicant which receives a certification shall have 3 years from the date of issuance of the certification in order to place the project in service and if such project is not placed in service by that time period, then the certification shall no longer be valid.

(3) Selection criteria

In determining which qualifying advanced energy projects to certify under this section, the Secretary—

(A) shall take into consideration only those projects where there is a reasonable expectation of commercial viability, and

(B) shall take into consideration which projects—

(i) will provide the greatest domestic job creation (both direct and indirect) during the credit period,

(ii) will provide the greatest net impact in avoiding or reducing air pollutants or anthropogenic emissions of greenhouse gases,

(iii) have the greatest potential for technological innovation and commercial deployment,

(iv) have the lowest levelized cost of generated or stored energy, or of measured reduction in energy consumption or greenhouse gas emission (based on costs of the full supply chain), and

(v) have the shortest project time from certification to completion.

(4) Review and redistribution

(A) Review

Not later than 4 years after the date of enactment of this section, the Secretary shall review the credits allocated under this section as of such date.

(B) Redistribution

The Secretary may reallocate credits awarded under this section if the Secretary determines that—

(i) there is an insufficient quantity of qualifying applications for certification pending at the time of the review, or

(ii) any certification made pursuant to paragraph (2) has been revoked pursuant to paragraph (2)(B) because the project subject to the certification has been delayed as a result of third party opposition or litigation to the proposed project.

(C) Reallocation

If the Secretary determines that credits under this section are available for reallocation pursuant to the requirements set forth in paragraph (2), the Secretary is authorized to conduct an additional program for applications for certification.

(5) Disclosure of allocations

The Secretary shall, upon making a certification under this subsection, publicly disclose the identity of the applicant and the amount of the credit with respect to such applicant.

(e) Denial of double benefit

A credit shall not be allowed under this section for any qualified investment for which a credit is allowed under section 48, 48A, or 48B.

(Added Pub. L. 111–5, div. B, title I, §1302(b), Feb. 17, 2009, 123 Stat. 345; amended Pub. L. 113–295, div. A, title II, §§209(g), 221(a)(2)(C), Dec. 19, 2014, 128 Stat. 4029, 4037.)

EDITORIAL NOTES
REFERENCES IN TEXT

Subsections (c)(4) and (d) of section 46 (as in effect on the day before the enactment of the Revenue Reconciliation Act of 1990), referred to in subsec. (b)(2), means section 46(c)(4) and (d) as in effect before enactment of Pub. L. 101–508, which amended section 46 generally.

The date of enactment of this section, referred to in subsec. (d)(1)(A), (4)(A), is the date of enactment of Pub. L. 111–5, which was approved Feb. 17, 2009.

AMENDMENTS

2014—Subsec. (b)(3). Pub. L. 113–295, §209(g), inserted "as the qualified investment" after "The amount which is treated".

Subsec. (c)(1)(A)(i)(VI). Pub. L. 113–295, §221(a)(2)(C), struck out ", qualified plug-in electric vehicles (as defined by section 30(d))," before "or components".

STATUTORY NOTES AND RELATED SUBSIDIARIES
EFFECTIVE DATE OF 2014 AMENDMENT

Amendment by section 209(g) of Pub. L. 113–295 effective as if included in the provisions of the American Recovery and Reinvestment Tax Act of 2009, Pub. L. 111–5, div. B, title I, to which such amendment relates, see section 209(k) of Pub. L. 113–295, set out as a note under section 24 of this title.

Amendment by section 221(a)(2)(C) of Pub. L. 113–295 effective Dec. 19, 2014, subject to a savings provision, see section 221(b) of Pub. L. 113–295, set out as a note under section 1 of this title.

EFFECTIVE DATE

Section applicable to periods after Feb. 17, 2009, under rules similar to the rules of section 48(m) of this title as in effect on the day before Nov. 5, 1990, see section 1302(d) of Pub. L. 111–5, set out as an Effective Date of 2009 Amendment note under section 46 of this title.

[§48D. Repealed. Pub. L. 115–141, div. U, title IV, §401(d)(3)(A), Mar. 23, 2018, 132 Stat. 1209]

Section, added Pub. L. 111–148, title IX, §9023(a), Mar. 23, 2010, 124 Stat. 877, provided for a qualifying therapeutic discovery project credit.

STATUTORY NOTES AND RELATED SUBSIDIARIES
SAVINGS PROVISION

Pub. L. 115–141, div. U, title IV, §401(d)(3)(C), Mar. 23, 2018, 132 Stat. 1209, provided that: "In the case of the repeal of section 48D(e)(1) of the Internal Revenue Code of 1986, the amendments made by this paragraph [amending sections 49, 50, and 280C of this title and repealing this section] shall not apply to expenditures made in taxable years beginning before January 1, 2011."

For provisions that nothing in repeal by Pub. L. 115–141 be construed to affect treatment of certain transactions occurring, property acquired, or items of income, loss, deduction, or credit taken into account prior to Mar. 23, 2018, for purposes of determining liability for tax for periods ending after Mar. 23, 2018, see section 401(e) of Pub. L. 115–141, set out as a note under section 23 of this title.

GRANTS FOR QUALIFIED INVESTMENTS IN THERAPEUTIC DISCOVERY PROJECTS IN LIEU OF TAX CREDITS

Pub. L. 111–148, title IX, §9023(e), Mar. 23, 2010, 124 Stat. 881, directed the Secretary of the Treasury to award grants for 50 percent of a qualified investment in a qualifying therapeutic discovery project in 2009 or 2010 in lieu of tax credit allowed under section 48D of this title.

§49. At-risk rules

(a) General rule

(1) Certain nonrecourse financing excluded from credit base

(A) Limitation

The credit base of any property to which this paragraph applies shall be reduced by the nonqualified nonrecourse financing with respect to such credit base (as of the close of the taxable year in which placed in service).

(B) Property to which paragraph applies

This paragraph applies to any property which—

(i) is placed in service during the taxable year by a taxpayer described in section 465(a)(1), and

(ii) is used in connection with an activity with respect to which any loss is subject to limitation under section 465.

(C) Credit base defined

For purposes of this paragraph, the term "credit base" means—

(i) the portion of the basis of any qualified rehabilitated building attributable to qualified rehabilitation expenditures,

(ii) the basis of any energy property,

(iii) the basis of any property which is part of a qualifying advanced coal project under section 48A,

(iv) the basis of any property which is part of a qualifying gasification project under section 48B, and

(v) the basis of any property which is part of a qualifying advanced energy project under section 48C.

(D) Nonqualified nonrecourse financing

(i) In general

For purposes of this paragraph and paragraph (2), the term "nonqualified nonrecourse financing" means any nonrecourse financing which is not qualified commercial financing.

(ii) Qualified commercial financing

For purposes of this paragraph, the term "qualified commercial financing" means any financing with respect to any property if—

(I) such property is acquired by the taxpayer from a person who is not a related person,

(II) the amount of the nonrecourse financing with respect to such property does not exceed 80 percent of the credit base of such property, and

(III) such financing is borrowed from a qualified person or represents a loan from any Federal, State, or local government or instrumentality thereof, or is guaranteed by any Federal, State, or local government.

Such term shall not include any convertible debt.

(iii) Nonrecourse financing

For purposes of this subparagraph, the term "nonrecourse financing" includes—

(I) any amount with respect to which the taxpayer is protected against loss through guarantees, stop-loss agreements, or other similar arrangements, and

(II) except to the extent provided in regulations, any amount borrowed from a person who has an interest (other than as a creditor) in the activity in which the property is used or from a related person to a person (other than the taxpayer) having such an interest.

In the case of amounts borrowed by a corporation from a shareholder, subclause (II) shall not apply to an interest as a shareholder.

(iv) Qualified person

For purposes of this paragraph, the term "qualified person" means any person which is actively and regularly engaged in the business of lending money and which is not—

(I) a related person with respect to the taxpayer,

(II) a person from which the taxpayer acquired the property (or a related person to such person), or

(III) a person who receives a fee with respect to the taxpayer's investment in the property (or a related person to such person).

(v) Related person

For purposes of this subparagraph, the term "related person" has the meaning given such term by section 465(b)(3)(C). Except as otherwise provided in regulations prescribed by the Secretary, the determination of whether a person is a related person shall be made as of the close of the taxable year in which the property is placed in service.

(E) Application to partnerships and S corporations

For purposes of this paragraph and paragraph (2)—

(i) In general

Except as otherwise provided in this subparagraph, in the case of any partnership or S corporation, the determination of whether a partner's or shareholder's allocable share of any financing is nonqualified nonrecourse financing shall be made at the partner or shareholder level.

(ii) Special rule for certain recourse financing of S corporation

A shareholder of an S corporation shall be treated as liable for his allocable share of any financing provided by a qualified person to such corporation if—

(I) such financing is recourse financing (determined at the corporate level), and

(II) such financing is provided with respect to qualified business property of such corporation.

(iii) Qualified business property

For purposes of clause (ii), the term "qualified business property" means any property if—

(I) such property is used by the corporation in the active conduct of a trade or business,

(II) during the entire 12-month period ending on the last day of the taxable year, such corporation had at least 3 full-time employees who were not owner-employees (as defined in section 465(c)(7)(E)(i)) and substantially all the services of whom were services directly related to such trade or business, and

(III) during the entire 12-month period ending on the last day of such taxable year, such corporation had at least 1 full-time employee substantially all of the services of whom were in the active management of the trade or business.

(iv) Determination of allocable share

The determination of any partner's or shareholder's allocable share of any financing shall be made in the same manner as the credit allowable by section 38 with respect to such property.

(F) Special rules for energy property

Rules similar to the rules of subparagraph (F) of section 46(c)(8) (as in effect on the day before the date of the enactment of the Revenue Reconciliation Act of 1990) shall apply for purposes of this paragraph.

(2) Subsequent decreases in nonqualified nonrecourse financing with respect to the property

(A) In general

If, at the close of a taxable year following the taxable year in which the property was placed in service, there is a net decrease in the amount of nonqualified nonrecourse financing with respect to such property, such net decrease shall be taken into account as an increase in the credit base for such property in accordance with subparagraph (C).

(B) Certain transactions not taken into account

For purposes of this paragraph, nonqualified nonrecourse financing shall not be treated as decreased through the surrender or other use of property financed by nonqualified nonrecourse financing.

(C) Manner in which taken into account

(i) Credit determined by reference to taxable year property placed in service

For purposes of determining the amount of credit allowable under section 38 and the amount of credit subject to the early disposition or cessation rules under section 50(a), any increase in a taxpayer's credit base for any property by reason of this paragraph shall be taken into account as if it were property placed in service by the taxpayer in the taxable year in which the property referred to in subparagraph (A) was first placed in service.

(ii) Credit allowed for year of decrease in nonqualified nonrecourse financing

Any credit allowable under this subpart for any increase in qualified investment by reason of this paragraph shall be treated as earned during the taxable year of the decrease in the amount of nonqualified nonrecourse financing.

(b) Increases in nonqualified nonrecourse financing
(1) In general

If, as of the close of the taxable year, there is a net increase with respect to the taxpayer in the amount of nonqualified nonrecourse financing (within the meaning of subsection (a)(1)) with respect to any property to which subsection (a)(1) applied, then the tax under this chapter for such taxable year shall be increased by an amount equal to the aggregate decrease in credits allowed under section 38 for all prior taxable years which would have resulted from reducing the credit base (as defined in subsection (a)(1)(C)) taken into account with respect to such property by the amount of such net increase. For purposes of determining the amount of credit subject to the early disposition or cessation rules of section 50(a), the net increase in the amount of the nonqualified nonrecourse financing with respect to the property shall be treated as reducing the property's credit base in the year in which the property was first placed in service.

(2) Transfers of debt more than 1 year after initial borrowing not treated as increasing nonqualified nonrecourse financing

For purposes of paragraph (1), the amount of nonqualified nonrecourse financing (within the meaning of subsection (a)(1)(D)) with respect to the taxpayer shall not be treated as increased by reason of a transfer of (or agreement to transfer) any evidence of any indebtedness if such transfer occurs (or such agreement is entered into) more than 1 year after the date such indebtedness was incurred.

(3) Special rules for certain energy property

Rules similar to the rules of section 47(d)(3) (as in effect on the day before the date of the enactment of the Revenue Reconciliation Act of 1990) shall apply for purposes of this subsection.

(4) Special rule

Any increase in tax under paragraph (1) shall not be treated as tax imposed by this chapter for purposes of determining the amount of any credit allowable under this chapter.

(Added Pub. L. 99–514, title II, §211(a), Oct. 22, 1986, 100 Stat. 2166; amended Pub. L. 100–647, title I, §1002(e)(1)–(3), (8)(B), Nov. 10, 1988, 102 Stat. 3367, 3369; Pub. L. 101–508, title XI, §11813(a), Nov. 5, 1990, 104 Stat. 1388–543; Pub. L. 105–206, title VI, §6004(g)(6), July 22, 1998, 112 Stat. 796; Pub. L. 109–58, title XIII, §1307(c)(1), Aug. 8, 2005, 119 Stat. 1006; Pub. L. 111–5, div. B, title I, §1302(c)(1), Feb. 17, 2009, 123 Stat. 347; Pub. L. 111–148, title IX, §9023(c)(1), Mar. 23, 2010, 124 Stat. 880; Pub. L. 115–141, div. U, title IV, §401(a)(24), (d)(3)(B)(i), Mar. 23, 2018, 132 Stat. 1185, 1209.)

EDITORIAL NOTES
REFERENCES IN TEXT

The date of the enactment of the Revenue Reconciliation Act of 1990, referred to in subsecs. (a)(1)(F) and (b)(3), is the date of enactment of Pub. L. 101–508, which was approved Nov. 5, 1990.

PRIOR PROVISIONS

A prior section 49, Pub. L. 91–172, title VII, §703(a), Dec. 30, 1969, 83 Stat. 660; Pub. L. 92–178, title I, §101(b)(1)–(4), Dec. 10, 1971, 85 Stat. 498, 499, related to termination of rules for computing credit for investment in certain depreciable property for period beginning Apr. 19, 1969, and ending during 1971, prior to repeal by Pub. L. 95–600, title III, §312(c)(1), Nov. 6, 1978, 92 Stat. 2826, applicable to taxable years ending after Dec. 31, 1978.

AMENDMENTS

2018—Subsec. (a)(1)(C)(vi). Pub. L. 115–141, §401(d)(3)(B)(i), struck out cl. (vi) which read as follows: "the basis of any property to which paragraph (1) of section 48D(e) applies which is part of a qualifying therapeutic discovery project under such section 48D."

Subsec. (a)(1)(D)(iii). Pub. L. 115–141, §401(a)(24), substituted "shareholder" for "share-holder" in concluding provisions.

2010—Subsec. (a)(1)(C)(vi). Pub. L. 111–148 added cl. (vi).

2009—Subsec. (a)(1)(C)(v). Pub. L. 111–5 added cl. (v).

2005—Subsec. (a)(1)(C)(iii), (iv). Pub. L. 109–58 added cls. (iii) and (iv) and struck out former cl. (iii) which read as follows: "the amortizable basis of any qualified timber property."

1998—Subsec. (b)(4). Pub. L. 105–206 substituted "this chapter" for "subpart A, B, D, or G".

1990—Pub. L. 101–508, §11813(a), amended section generally, substituting section catchline for one which read: "Termination of regular percentage" and in text substituting present provisions for provisions relating to the nonapplicability of the regular percentage to any property placed in service after Dec. 31, 1985, for purposes of determining the investment tax credit, exceptions to such rule, the 35 percent reduction in credit for taxable years after 1986, the full basis adjustment in determining investment tax credit, and the definition of transition property and treatment of progress expenditures.

1988—Subsec. (c)(4)(B). Pub. L. 100–647, §1002(e)(2), substituted "years" for "year" in heading and amended text generally. Prior to amendment, text read as follows: "The amount of the reduction of the regular investment credit under paragraph (3)—

"(i) may not be carried back to any taxable year, but

"(ii) shall be added to the carryforwards from the taxable year before applying paragraph (2)."

Subsec. (c)(5)(B)(i). Pub. L. 100–647, §1002(e)(3), amended cl. (i) generally. Prior to amendment, cl. (i) read as follows: "The term 'regular investment credit' has the meaning given such term by section 48(o)".

Subsec. (c)(5)(C). Pub. L. 100–647, §1002(e)(8)(B), struck out subpar. (C) which related to portion of credits attributable to regular investment credit.

Subsec. (d)(1). Pub. L. 100–647, §1002(e)(1), amended par. (1) generally. Prior to amendment, par. (1) read as follows: "In the case of periods after December 31, 1985, section 48(q) (relating to basis adjustment to section 38 property) shall be applied with respect to transaction property—

"(A) by substituting '100 percent' for '50 percent' in paragraph (1), and

"(B) without regard to paragraph (4) thereof (relating to election of reduced credit in lieu of basis adjustment)."

STATUTORY NOTES AND RELATED SUBSIDIARIES
EFFECTIVE DATE OF 2010 AMENDMENT

Amendment by Pub. L. 111–148 applicable to amounts paid or incurred after Dec. 31, 2008, in taxable years beginning after such date, see section 9023(f) of Pub. L. 111–148, set out as a note under section 46 of this title.

EFFECTIVE DATE OF 2009 AMENDMENT

Amendment by Pub. L. 111–5 applicable to periods after Feb. 17, 2009, under rules similar to the rules of section 48(m) of this title as in effect on the day before Nov. 5, 1990, see section 1302(d) of Pub. L. 111–5, set out as a note under section 46 of this title.

EFFECTIVE DATE OF 2005 AMENDMENT

Amendment by Pub. L. 109–58 applicable to periods after Aug. 8, 2005, under rules similar to the rules of section 48(m) of this title, as in effect on the day before Nov. 5, 1990, see section 1307(d) of Pub. L. 109–58, set out as a note under section 46 of this title.

EFFECTIVE DATE OF 1998 AMENDMENT

Amendment by Pub. L. 105–206 effective, except as otherwise provided, as if included in the provisions of the Taxpayer Relief Act of 1997, Pub. L. 105–34, to which such amendment relates, see section 6024 of Pub. L. 105–206, set out as a note under section 1 of this title.

EFFECTIVE DATE OF 1990 AMENDMENT

Amendment by Pub. L. 101–508 applicable to property placed in service after Dec. 31, 1990, but not applicable to any transition property (as defined in section 49(e) of this title), any property with respect to which qualified progress expenditures were previously taken into account under section 46(d) of this title, and any property described in section 46(b)(2)(C) of this title, as such sections were in effect on Nov. 4, 1990, see section 11813(c) of Pub. L. 101–508, set out as a note under section 45K of this title.

EFFECTIVE DATE OF 1988 AMENDMENT

Amendment by section 1002(e)(1)–(3) of Pub. L. 100–647 effective, except as otherwise provided, as if included in the provision of the Tax Reform Act of 1986, Pub. L. 99–514, to which such amendment relates, see section 1019(a) of Pub. L. 100–647, set out as a note under section 1 of this title.

Amendment by section 1002(e)(8)(B) of Pub. L. 100–647 applicable to taxable years beginning after Dec. 31, 1983, and to carrybacks from such years, see section 1002(e)(8)(C) of Pub. L. 100–647, set out as a note under section 38 of this title.

EFFECTIVE DATE OF 1986 AMENDMENT

Pub. L. 99–514, title II, §211(e), Oct. 22, 1986, 100 Stat. 2169, as amended by Pub. L. 100–647, title I, §1002(e)(4)–(7), Nov. 10, 1988, 102 Stat. 3367, 3368, provided that:

"(1) In general.—Except as provided in this subsection, the amendments made by this section [enacting this section and provisions set out below] shall apply to property placed in service after December 31, 1985, in taxable years ending after such date. Section 49(c) of the Internal Revenue Code of 1986 (as added by subsection (a)) shall apply to taxable years ending after June 30, 1987, and to amounts carried to such taxable years.

"(2) Exceptions for certain films.—For purposes of determining whether any property is transition property within the meaning of section 49(e) of the Internal Revenue Code of 1986—

"(A) in the case of any motion picture or television film, construction shall be treated as including production for purposes of section 203(b)(1) of this Act [enacting provisions set out as a note under section 168 of this title], and written contemporary evidence of an agreement (in accordance with industry practice) shall be treated as a written binding contract for such purposes,

"(B) in the case of any television film, a license agreement or agreement for production services between a television network and a producer shall be treated as a binding contract for purposes of section 203(b)(1)(A) of this Act, and

"(C) a motion picture film shall be treated as described in section 203(b)(1)(A) of this Act if—

"(i) funds were raised pursuant to a public offering before September 26, 1985, for the production of such film,

"(ii) 40 percent of the funds raised pursuant to such public offering are being spent on films the production of which commenced before such date, and

"(iii) all of the films funded by such public offering are required to be distributed pursuant to distribution agreements entered into before September 26, 1985.

"(3) Normalization rules.—The provisions of subsection (b) [see Normalization Rules note below] shall apply to any violation of the normalization requirements under paragraph (1) or (2) of section 46(f) of the Internal Revenue Code of 1986 occurring in taxable years ending after December 31, 1985.

"(4) Additional exceptions.—

"(A) Subsections (c) and (d) of section 49 of the Internal Revenue Code of 1986 shall not apply to any continuous caster facility for slabs and blooms which is subject to a lease and which is part of a project the second phase of which is a continuous slab caster which was placed in service before December 31, 1985.

"(B) For purposes of determining whether an automobile manufacturing facility (including equipment and incidental appurtenances) is transition property within the meaning of section 49(e), property with respect to which the Board of Directors of an automobile manufacturer formally approved the plan for the project on January 7, 1985 shall be treated as transition property and subsections (c) and (d) of section 49 of such Code shall not apply to such property, but only with respect to $70,000,000 of regular investment tax credits.

"(C) Any solid waste disposal facility which will process and incinerate solid waste of one or more public or private entities including Dakota County, Minnesota, and with respect to which a bond carryforward from 1985 was elected in an amount equal to $12,500,000 shall be treated as transition property within the meaning of section 49(e) of the Internal Revenue Code of 1986.

"(D) For purposes of section 49 of such Code, the following property shall be treated as transition property:

"(i) 2 catamarans built by a shipbuilder incorporated in the State of Washington in 1964, the contracts for which were signed on April 22, 1986 and November 12, 1985, and 1 barge built by such shipbuilder the contract for which was signed on August 7, 1985.

"(ii) 2 large passenger ocean-going United States flag cruise ships with a passenger rated capacity of up to 250 which are built by the shipbuilder described in clause (i), which are the first such ships built in the United States since 1952, and which were designed at the request of a Pacific Coast cruise line pursuant to a contract entered into in October 1985. This clause shall apply only to that portion of the cost of each ship which does not exceed $40,000,000.

"(iii) Property placed in service during 1986 by Satellite Industries, Inc., with headquarters in Minneapolis, Minnesota, to the extent that the cost of such property does not exceed $1,950,000.

"(E) Subsections (c) and (d) of section 49 of such Code shall not apply to property described in section 204(a)(4) of this Act [enacting provisions set out as a note under section 168 of this title]."

SAVINGS PROVISION

For provisions that amendment made by section 401(d)(3)(B)(i) of Pub. L. 115–141 not apply to expenditures made in taxable years beginning before Jan. 1, 2011, in the case of the repeal of section 48D(e)(1) of this title, see section 401(d)(3)(C) of Pub. L. 115–141, set out as a note under section 48D of this title.

For provisions that nothing in amendment by section 401(d)(3)(B)(i) of Pub. L. 115–141 be construed to affect treatment of certain transactions occurring, property acquired, or items of income, loss, deduction, or credit taken into account prior to Mar. 23, 2018, for purposes of determining liability for tax for periods ending after Mar. 23, 2018, see section 401(e) of Pub. L. 115–141, set out as a note under section 23 of this title.

For provisions that nothing in amendment by Pub. L. 101–508 be construed to affect treatment of certain transactions occurring, property acquired, or items of income, loss, deduction, or credit taken into account prior to Nov. 5, 1990, for purposes of determining liability for tax for periods ending after Nov. 5, 1990, see section 11821(b) of Pub. L. 101–508, set out as a note under section 45K of this title.

NORMALIZATION RULES

Pub. L. 99–514, title II, §211(b), Oct. 22, 1986, 100 Stat. 2168, provided that: "If, for any taxable year beginning after December 31, 1985, the requirements of paragraph (1) or (2) of section 46(f) of the Internal Revenue Code of 1986 are not met with respect to public utility property to which the regular percentage applied for purposes of determining the amount of the investment tax credit—

"(1) all credits for open taxable years as of the time of the final determination referred to in section 46(f)(4)(A) of such Code shall be recaptured, and

"(2) if the amount of the taxpayer's unamortized credits (or the credits not previously restored to rate base) with respect to such property (whether or not for open years) exceeds the amount referred to in paragraph (1), the taxpayer's tax for the taxable year shall be increased by the amount of such excess.

If any portion of the excess described in paragraph (2) is attributable to a credit which is allowable as a carryover to a taxable year beginning after December 31, 1985, in lieu of applying paragraph (2) with respect to such portion, the amount of such carryover shall be reduced by the amount of such portion. Rules similar to the rules of this subsection shall apply in the case of any property with respect to which the requirements of section 46(f)(9) of such Code are met."

EXCEPTION FOR CERTAIN AIRCRAFT USED IN ALASKA

Pub. L. 99–514, title II, §211(d), Oct. 22, 1986, 100 Stat. 2168, provided that:

"(1) The amendments made by subsection (a) [enacting this section and provisions set out above] shall not apply to property originally placed in service after December 29, 1982, and before August 1, 1985, by a corporation incorporated in Alaska on May 21, 1953, and used by it—

"(A) in part, for the transportation of mail for the United States Postal Service in the State of Alaska, and

"(B) in part, to provide air service in the State of Alaska on routes which had previously been served by an air carrier that received compensation from the Civil Aeronautics Board for providing service.

"(2) In the case of property described in subparagraph (A)—

"(A) such property shall be treated as recovery property described in section 208(d)(5) of the Tax Equity and Fiscal Responsibility Act of 1982 ('TEFRA') [section 208(d)(5) of Pub. L. 97–248, enacting provisions set out as a note under section 168 of this title];

"(B) '48 months' shall be substituted for '3 months' each place it appears in applying—

"(i) section 48(b)(2)(B) of the Code [26 U.S.C. 48(b)(2)(B)], and

"(ii) section 168(f)(8)(D) of the Code [26 U.S.C. 168(f)(8)(D)] (as in effect after the amendments made by the Technical Corrections Act of 1982 [Pub. L. 97–448] but before the amendments made by TEFRA); and

"(C) the limitation of section 168(f)(8)(D)(ii)(III) (as then in effect) shall be read by substituting 'the lessee's original cost basis.', for 'the adjusted basis of the lessee at the time of the lease.'

"(3) The aggregate amount of property to which this paragraph shall apply shall not exceed $60,000,000."

§50. Other special rules

(a) Recapture in case of dispositions, etc.

Under regulations prescribed by the Secretary—

(1) Early disposition, etc.

(A) General rule

If, during any taxable year, investment credit property is disposed of, or otherwise ceases to be investment credit property with respect to the taxpayer, before the close of the recapture period, then the tax under this chapter for such taxable year shall be increased by the recapture percentage of the aggregate decrease in the credits allowed under section 38 for all prior taxable years which would have resulted solely from reducing to zero any credit determined under this subpart with respect to such property.

(B) Recapture percentage

For purposes of subparagraph (A), the recapture percentage shall be determined in accordance with the following table:

If the property ceases to be investment credit property within—	The recapture percentage is:
(i) One full year after placed in service	100
(ii) One full year after the close of the period described in clause (i)	80
(iii) One full year after the close of the period described in clause (ii)	60
(iv) One full year after the close of the period described in clause (iii)	40
(v) One full year after the close of the period described in clause (iv)	20

(2) Property ceases to qualify for progress expenditures

(A) In general

If during any taxable year any building to which section 47(d) applied ceases (by reason of sale or other disposition, cancellation or abandonment of contract, or otherwise) to be, with respect to the taxpayer, property which, when placed in service, will be a qualified rehabilitated building, then the tax under this chapter for such taxable year shall be increased by an amount equal to the aggregate decrease in the credits allowed under section 38 for all prior taxable years which would have resulted solely from reducing to zero the credit determined under this subpart with respect to such building.

(B) Certain excess credit recaptured

Any amount which would have been applied as a reduction under paragraph (2) of section 47(b) but for the fact that a reduction under such paragraph cannot reduce the amount taken into account under section 47(b)(1) below zero shall be treated as an amount required to be recaptured under subparagraph (A) for the taxable year during which the building is placed in service.

(C) Certain sales and leasebacks

Under regulations prescribed by the Secretary, a sale by, and leaseback to, a taxpayer who, when the property is placed in service, will be a lessee to whom the rules referred to in subsection (d)(5) apply shall not be treated as a cessation described in subparagraph (A) to the extent that the amount which will be passed through to the lessee under such rules with respect to such property is not less than the qualified rehabilitation expenditures properly taken into account by the lessee under section 47(d) with respect to such property.

(D) Coordination with paragraph (1)

If, after property is placed in service, there is a disposition or other cessation described in paragraph (1), then paragraph (1) shall be applied as if any credit which was allowable by reason of section 47(d) and which has not been required to be recaptured before such disposition, cessation, or change in use were allowable for the taxable year the property was placed in service.

(E) Special rules

Rules similar to the rules of this paragraph shall apply in cases where qualified progress expenditures were taken into account under the rules referred to in section 48(b), 48A(b)(3), 48B(b)(3), or 48C(b)(2).

(3) Carrybacks and carryovers adjusted

In the case of any cessation described in paragraph (1) or (2), the carrybacks and carryovers under section 39 shall be adjusted by reason of such cessation.

(4) Subsection not to apply in certain cases

Paragraphs (1) and (2) shall not apply to—

(A) a transfer by reason of death, or

(B) a transaction to which section 381(a) applies.

For purposes of this subsection, property shall not be treated as ceasing to be investment credit property with respect to the taxpayer by reason of a mere change in the form of conducting the trade or business so long as the property is retained in such trade or business as investment credit property and the taxpayer retains a substantial interest in such trade or business.

(5) Definitions and special rules

(A) Investment credit property

For purposes of this subsection, the term "investment credit property" means any property eligible for a credit determined under this subpart.

(B) Transfer between spouses or incident to divorce

In the case of any transfer described in subsection (a) of section 1041—

(i) the foregoing provisions of this subsection shall not apply, and

(ii) the same tax treatment under this subsection with respect to the transferred property shall apply to the transferee as would have applied to the transferor.

(C) Special rule

Any increase in tax under paragraph (1) or (2) shall not be treated as tax imposed by this chapter for purposes of determining the amount of any credit allowable under this chapter.

(b) Certain property not eligible

No credit shall be determined under this subpart with respect to—

(1) Property used outside United States

(A) In general

Except as provided in subparagraph (B), no credit shall be determined under this subpart with respect to any property which is used predominantly outside the United States.

(B) Exceptions

Subparagraph (A) shall not apply to any property described in section 168(g)(4).

(2) Property used for lodging

No credit shall be determined under this subpart with respect to any property which is used predominantly to furnish lodging or in connection with the furnishing of lodging. The preceding sentence shall not apply to—

(A) nonlodging commercial facilities which are available to persons not using the lodging facilities on the same basis as they are available to persons using the lodging facilities;

(B) property used by a hotel or motel in connection with the trade or business of furnishing lodging where the predominant portion of the accommodations is used by transients;

(C) a certified historic structure to the extent of that portion of the basis which is attributable to qualified rehabilitation expenditures; and

(D) any energy property.

(3) Property used by certain tax-exempt organization

No credit shall be determined under this subpart with respect to any property used by an organization (other than a cooperative described in section 521) which is exempt from the tax imposed by this chapter unless such property is used predominantly in an unrelated trade or business the income of which is subject to tax under section 511. If the property is debt-financed property (as defined in section 514(b)), the amount taken into account for purposes of determining the amount of the credit under this subpart with respect to such property shall be that percentage of the amount (which but for this paragraph would be so taken into account) which is the same percentage as is used under section 514(a), for the year the property is placed in service, in computing the amount of gross income to be taken into account during such taxable year with respect to such property. If any qualified rehabilitated building is used by the tax-exempt organization pursuant to a lease, this paragraph shall not apply for purposes of determining the amount of the rehabilitation credit.

(4) Property used by governmental units or foreign persons or entities

(A) In general

No credit shall be determined under this subpart with respect to any property used—

(i) by the United States, any State or political subdivision thereof, any possession of the United States, or any agency or instrumentality of any of the foregoing, or

(ii) by any foreign person or entity (as defined in section 168(h)(2)(C)), but only with respect to property to which section 168(h)(2)(A)(iii) applies (determined after the application of section 168(h)(2)(B)).

(B) Exception for short-term leases

This paragraph and paragraph (3) shall not apply to any property by reason of use under a lease with a term of less than 6 months (determined under section 168(i)(3)).

(C) Exception for qualified rehabilitated buildings leased to governments, etc.

If any qualified rehabilitated building is leased to a governmental unit (or a foreign person or entity) this paragraph shall not apply for purposes of determining the rehabilitation credit with respect to such building.

(D) Special rules for partnerships, etc.

For purposes of this paragraph and paragraph (3), rules similar to the rules of paragraphs (5) and (6) of section 168(h) shall apply.

(E) Cross reference

For special rules for the application of this paragraph and paragraph (3), see section 168(h).

(c) Basis adjustment to investment credit property

(1) In general

For purposes of this subtitle, if a credit is determined under this subpart with respect to any property, the basis of such property shall be reduced by the amount of the credit so determined.

(2) Certain dispositions

If during any taxable year there is a recapture amount determined with respect to any property the basis of which was reduced under paragraph (1), the basis of such property (immediately before the event resulting in such recapture) shall be increased by an amount equal to such recapture amount. For purposes of the preceding sentence, the term "recapture amount" means any increase in tax (or adjustment in carrybacks or carryovers) determined under subsection (a).

(3) Special rule

In the case of any energy credit—

(A) only 50 percent of such credit shall be taken into account under paragraph (1), and

(B) only 50 percent of any recapture amount attributable to such credit shall be taken into account under paragraph (2).

(4) Recapture of reductions

(A) In general

For purposes of sections 1245 and 1250, any reduction under this subsection shall be treated as a deduction allowed for depreciation.

(B) Special rule for section 1250

For purposes of section 1250(b), the determination of what would have been the depreciation adjustments under the straight line method shall be made as if there had been no reduction under this section.

(5) Adjustment in basis of interest in partnership or S corporation

The adjusted basis of—

(A) a partner's interest in a partnership, and

(B) stock in an S corporation,

shall be appropriately adjusted to take into account adjustments made under this subsection in the basis of property held by the partnership or S corporation (as the case may be).

(d) Certain rules made applicable

For purposes of this subpart, rules similar to the rules of the following provisions (as in effect on the day before the date of the enactment of the Revenue Reconciliation Act of 1990) shall apply:

(1) Section 46(e) (relating to limitations with respect to certain persons).

(2) Section 46(f) (relating to limitation in case of certain regulated companies).

(3) Section 46(h) (relating to special rules for cooperatives).

(4) Paragraphs (2) and (3) of section 48(b) (relating to special rule for sale-leasebacks).

(5) Section 48(d) (relating to certain leased property).

(6) Section 48(f) (relating to estates and trusts).

(7) Section 48(r) (relating to certain 501(d) organizations).

Paragraphs (1)(A), (2)(A), and (4) of the section 46(e) referred to in paragraph (1) of this subsection shall not apply to any taxable year beginning after December 31, 1995.

(Added Pub. L. 101–508, title XI, §11813(a), Nov. 5, 1990, 104 Stat. 1388–546; amended Pub. L. 104–188, title I, §§1616(b)(1), 1702(h)(11), 1704(t)(29), Aug. 20, 1996, 110 Stat. 1856, 1874, 1889; Pub. L. 105–206, title VI, §6004(g)(7), July 22, 1998, 112 Stat. 796; Pub. L. 108–357, title III, §322(d)(2)(D), Oct. 22, 2004, 118 Stat. 1475; Pub. L. 109–135, title IV, §412(o), Dec. 21, 2005, 119 Stat. 2638; Pub. L. 113–295, div. A, title II, §220(d), Dec. 19, 2014, 128 Stat. 4036; Pub. L. 115–141, div. U, title IV, §401(a)(25), (d)(3)(B)(ii), Mar. 23, 2018, 132 Stat. 1185, 1209.)

Editorial Notes
References in Text

The date of the enactment of the Revenue Reconciliation Act of 1990, referred to in subsec. (d), is the date of enactment of Pub. L. 101–508, which was approved Nov. 5, 1990.

Prior Provisions

A prior section 50, Pub. L. 92–178, title I, §101(a), Dec. 10, 1971, 85 Stat. 498, related to restoration of credit for investment in certain depreciable property, prior to repeal by Pub. L. 95–600, title III, §312(c)(1), Nov. 6, 1978, 92 Stat. 2826, applicable to taxable years ending after Dec. 31, 1978.

Amendments

2018—Subsec. (a)(2)(E). Pub. L. 115–141, §401(d)(3)(B)(ii), substituted "or 48C(b)(2)" for "48C(b)(2), or 48D(b)(4)".

Subsec. (b)(2)(A). Pub. L. 115–141, §401(a)(25), substituted semicolon for period at end.

2014—Subsec. (a)(2)(E). Pub. L. 113–295 inserted ", 48A(b)(3), 48B(b)(3), 48C(b)(2), or 48D(b)(4)" after "in section 48(b)".

2005—Subsec. (a)(2)(E). Pub. L. 109–135 substituted "section 48(b)" for "section 48(a)(5)".

2004—Subsec. (c)(3). Pub. L. 108–357 struck out "or reforestation credit" after "energy credit" in introductory provisions.

1998—Subsec. (a)(5)(C). Pub. L. 105–206 substituted "this chapter" for "subpart A, B, D, or G".

1996—Subsec. (a)(2)(C). Pub. L. 104–188, §1704(t)(29), substituted "subsection (d)(5)" for "subsection (c)(4)".

Subsec. (a)(2)(E). Pub. L. 104–188, §1702(h)(11), substituted "48(a)(5)" for "48(a)(5)(A)".

Subsec. (d). Pub. L. 104–188, §1616(b)(1), inserted closing provisions.

Statutory Notes and Related Subsidiaries
Effective Date of 2004 Amendment

Amendment by Pub. L. 108–357 applicable with respect to expenditures paid or incurred after Oct. 22, 2004, see section 322(e) of Pub. L. 108–357, set out as a note under section 46 of this title.

Effective Date of 1998 Amendment

Amendment by Pub. L. 105–206 effective, except as otherwise provided, as if included in the provisions of the Taxpayer Relief Act of 1997, Pub. L. 105–34, to which such amendment relates, see section 6024 of Pub. L. 105–206, set out as a note under section 1 of this title.

Effective Date of 1996 Amendment

Amendment by section 1616(b)(1) of Pub. L. 104–188 applicable to taxable years beginning after Dec. 31, 1995, see section 1616(c) of Pub. L. 104–188, set out as a note under section 593 of this title.

Amendment by section 1702(h)(11) of Pub. L. 104–188 effective, except as otherwise expressly provided, as if included in the provision of the Revenue Reconciliation Act of 1990, Pub. L. 101–508, title XI, to which such amendment relates, see section 1702(i) of Pub. L. 104–188, set out as a note under section 38 of this title.

Effective Date

Section applicable to property placed in service after Dec. 31, 1990, but not applicable to any transition property (as defined in section 49(e) of this title), any property with respect to which qualified progress expenditures were previously taken into account under section 46(d) of this title, and any property described in section 46(b)(2)(C) of this title, as such sections were in effect on Nov. 4, 1990, see section 11813(c) of Pub. L. 101–508, set out as an Effective Date of 1990 Amendment note under section 45K of this title.

Savings Provision

For provisions that amendment made by section 401(d)(3)(B)(ii) of Pub. L. 115–141 not apply to expenditures made in taxable years beginning before Jan. 1, 2011, in the case of the repeal of section 48D(e)(1) of this title, see section 401(d)(3)(C) of Pub. L. 115–141, set out as a note under section 48D of this title.

For provisions that nothing in amendment by section 401(d)(3)(B)(ii) of Pub. L. 115–141 be construed to affect treatment of certain transactions occurring, property acquired, or items of income, loss, deduction, or credit taken into account prior to Mar. 23, 2018, for purposes of determining liability for tax for periods ending after Mar. 23, 2018, see section 401(e) of Pub. L. 115–141, set out as a note under section 23 of this title.

For provisions that nothing in this section be construed to affect treatment of certain transactions occurring, property acquired, or items of income, loss, deduction, or credit taken into account prior to Nov. 5, 1990, for purposes of determining liability for tax for periods ending after Nov. 5, 1990, see section 11821(b) of Pub. L. 101–508, set out as a note under section 45K of this title.

[§§50A, 50B. Repealed. Pub. L. 98–369, div. A, title IV, §474(m)(2), July 18, 1984, 98 Stat. 833]

Section 50A, added Pub. L. 92–178, title VI, §601(b), Dec. 10, 1971, 85 Stat. 554; amended Pub. L. 93–406, title II, §§2001(g)(2)(B), 2002(g)(2), 2005(c)(4), Sept. 2, 1974, 88 Stat. 957, 968, 991; Pub. L. 94–12, title IV, §401(a)(1), (2), Mar. 29, 1975, 89 Stat. 45; Pub. L. 94–401, §4(a), Sept. 7, 1976, 90 Stat. 1217; Pub. L. 94–455, title V, §503(b)(4), title XIX, §§1901(a)(6), (b)(1)(D), 1906(b)(13)(A), title XXI, §2107(a)(1)–(3), (b), (c), Oct. 4, 1976, 90 Stat. 1562, 1765, 1790, 1834, 1903, 1904; Pub. L. 95–600, title III, §322(a)–(c), Nov. 6, 1978, 92 Stat. 2836, 2837; Pub. L. 96–178, §6(c)(1), Jan. 2, 1980, 93 Stat. 1298; Pub. L. 96–222, title I, §103(a)(7)(D)(i), Apr. 1, 1980, 94 Stat. 211; Pub. L. 97–34, title II, §207(c)(1), Aug. 13, 1981, 95 Stat. 225; Pub. L. 97–248, title I, §265(b)(2)(A)(ii), Sept. 3, 1982, 96 Stat. 547; Pub. L. 97–354, §5(a)(9), Oct. 19, 1982, 96 Stat. 1693, provided for a credit for expenses of work incentive programs, for the determination of the amount of that credit, and for the carryover and carryback of unused credit.

Section 50B, added Pub. L. 92–178, title VI, §601(b), Dec. 10, 1971, 85 Stat. 556; amended Pub. L. 94–12, title III, §302(c)(4), title IV, §401(a)(3)–(5), Mar. 29, 1975, 89 Stat. 44, 46; Pub. L. 94–401, §4(b), Sept. 7, 1976, 90 Stat. 1218; Pub. L. 94–455, title XIX, §1906(b)(13)(A), title XXI, §2107(a)(4), (d)–(f), Oct. 4, 1976, 90 Stat. 1834, 1903, 1904; Pub. L. 95–171, §1(e), Nov. 12, 1977, 91 Stat. 1353; Pub. L. 95–600, title III, §322(d), Nov. 6, 1978, 92 Stat. 2837; Pub. L. 96–178, §§3(a)(1), (3), 6(c)(2), (3), Jan. 2, 1980, 93 Stat. 1295, 1298; Pub. L. 96–222, title I, §103(a)(5), (7)(C), (D)(ii), (iii), Apr. 1, 1980, 94 Stat. 209, 211; Pub. L. 96–272, title II, §208(b)(1), (2), June 17, 1980, 94 Stat. 526, 527; Pub. L. 97–34, title II, §261(b)(2)(B)(i), Aug. 13, 1981, 95 Stat. 261; Pub. L. 97–354, §5(a)(10), Oct. 19, 1982, 96 Stat. 1693; Pub. L. 101–239, title VII, §7644, Dec. 19, 1989, 103 Stat. 2381, provided for the definition of terms related to the expenses of work incentive programs, limitations on such expenses, and special rules to be applied in connection with the computation of the credit.

Subsequent to repeal, Pub. L. 101–239, title VII, §7644(a), Dec. 19, 1989, 103 Stat. 2381, provided that:

"(a) In General.—So much of subparagraph (A) of section 50B(h)(1) of the Internal Revenue Code of 1954 (as in effect for taxable years beginning before January 1, 1982) as precedes clause (i) thereof is amended to read as follows:

" '(A) who has been certified (or for whom a written request for certification has been made) on or before the day the individual began work for the taxpayer by the Secretary of Labor or by the appropriate agency of State or local government as—'.

"(b) Effective Date.—The amendment made by subsection (a) shall apply for purposes of credits first claimed after March 11, 1987."

STATUTORY NOTES AND RELATED SUBSIDIARIES
EFFECTIVE DATE OF REPEAL

Repeal applicable to taxable years beginning after Dec. 31, 1983, and to carrybacks from such years, see section 475(a) of Pub. L. 98–369, set out as an Effective Date of 1984 Amendment note under section 21 of this title.

Subpart F—Rules for Computing Work Opportunity Credit

Sec.
51.
Amount of credit.
[51A.
Repealed.]
52.
Special rules.

EDITORIAL NOTES
AMENDMENTS

2006—Pub. L. 109–432, div. A, title I, §105(e)(4)(B), Dec. 20, 2006, 120 Stat. 2937, struck out item 51A "Temporary incentives for employing long-term family assistance recipients".

1997—Pub. L. 105–34, title VIII, §801(b), Aug. 5, 1997, 111 Stat. 871, added item 51A.

1996—Pub. L. 104–188, title I, §1201(e)(2), Aug. 20, 1996, 110 Stat. 1772, substituted "Work Opportunity Credit" for "Targeted Jobs Credit" in subpart heading.

1984—Pub. L. 98–369, div. A, title IV, §474(n)(1), (2), (p)(9), July 18, 1984, 98 Stat. 833, 838, substituted "F" for "D" as subpart designation, substituted "Rules for Computing Targeted Jobs Credit" for "Rules for Computing Credit for Employment of Certain New Employees" in heading, and struck out item 53 "Limitation based on amount of tax".

§51. Amount of credit

(a) Determination of amount

For purposes of section 38, the amount of the work opportunity credit determined under this section for the taxable year shall be equal to 40 percent of the qualified first-year wages for such year.

(b) Qualified wages defined

For purposes of this subpart—

(1) In general

The term "qualified wages" means the wages paid or incurred by the employer during the taxable year to individuals who are members of a targeted group.

(2) Qualified first-year wages

The term "qualified first-year wages" means, with respect to any individual, qualified wages attributable to service rendered during the 1-year period beginning with the day the individual begins work for the employer.

(3) Limitation on wages per year taken into account

The amount of the qualified first-year wages which may be taken into account with respect to any individual shall not exceed $6,000 per year ($12,000 per year in the case of any individual who is a qualified veteran by reason of subsection (d)(3)(A)(ii)(I), $14,000 per year in the case of any individual who is a qualified veteran by reason of subsection (d)(3)(A)(iv), and $24,000 per year in the case of any individual who is a qualified veteran by reason of subsection (d)(3)(A)(ii)(II)).

(c) Wages defined

For purposes of this subpart—

(1) In general

Except as otherwise provided in this subsection and subsection (h)(2), the term "wages" has the meaning given to such term by subsection (b) of section 3306 (determined without regard to any dollar limitation contained in such section).

(2) On-the-job training and work supplementation payments

(A) Exclusion for employers receiving on-the-job training payments

The term "wages" shall not include any amounts paid or incurred by an employer for any period to any individual for whom the employer receives federally funded payments for on-the-job training of such individual for such period.

(B) Reduction for work supplementation payments to employers

The amount of wages which would (but for this subparagraph) be qualified wages under this section for an employer with respect to an individual for a taxable year shall be reduced by an amount equal to the amount of the payments made to such employer (however utilized by such employer) with respect to such individual for such taxable year under a program established under section 482(e) [1] of the Social Security Act.

(3) Payments for services during labor disputes

If—

(A) the principal place of employment of an individual with the employer is at a plant or facility, and

(B) there is a strike or lockout involving employees at such plant or facility,

the term "wages" shall not include any amount paid or incurred by the employer to such individual for services which are the same as, or substantially similar to, those services performed by employees participating in, or affected by, the strike or lockout during the period of such strike or lockout.

(4) Termination

The term "wages" shall not include any amount paid or incurred to an individual who begins work for the employer after December 31, 2025.

(5) Coordination with payroll tax forgiveness

The term "wages" shall not include any amount paid or incurred to a qualified individual (as defined in section 3111(d)(3)) [1] during the 1-year period beginning on the hiring date of such individual by a qualified employer (as defined in section 3111(d)) [1] unless such qualified employer makes an election not to have section 3111(d) [1] apply.

(d) Members of targeted groups

For purposes of this subpart—

(1) In general

An individual is a member of a targeted group if such individual is—

(A) a qualified IV–A recipient,

(B) a qualified veteran,

(C) a qualified ex-felon,

(D) a designated community resident,

(E) a vocational rehabilitation referral,

(F) a qualified summer youth employee,

(G) a qualified supplemental nutrition assistance program benefits recipient,

(H) a qualified SSI recipient,

(I) a long-term family assistance recipient, or

(J) a qualified long-term unemployment recipient.

(2) Qualified IV–A recipient

(A) In general

The term "qualified IV–A recipient" means any individual who is certified by the designated local agency as being a member of a family receiving assistance under a IV–A program for any 9 months during the 18-month period ending on the hiring date.

(B) IV–A program

For purposes of this paragraph, the term "IV–A program" means any program providing assistance under a State program funded under part A of title IV of the Social Security Act and any successor of such program.

(3) Qualified veteran

(A) In general

The term "qualified veteran" means any veteran who is certified by the designated local agency as—

(i) being a member of a family receiving assistance under a supplemental nutrition assistance program under the Food and Nutrition Act of 2008 for at least a 3-month period ending during the 12-month period ending on the hiring date,

(ii) entitled to compensation for a service-connected disability, and—

(I) having a hiring date which is not more that 1 year after having been discharged or released from active duty in the Armed Forces of the United States, or

(II) having aggregate periods of unemployment during the 1-year period ending on the hiring date which equal or exceed 6 months,

(iii) having aggregate periods of unemployment during the 1-year period ending on the hiring date which equal or exceed 4 weeks (but less than 6 months), or

(iv) having aggregate periods of unemployment during the 1-year period ending on the hiring date which equal or exceed 6 months.

(B) Veteran

For purposes of subparagraph (A), the term "veteran" means any individual who is certified by the designated local agency as—

(i)(I) having served on active duty (other than active duty for training) in the Armed Forces of the United States for a period of more than 180 days, or

(II) having been discharged or released from active duty in the Armed Forces of the United States for a service-connected disability, and

(ii) not having any day during the 60-day period ending on the hiring date which was a day of extended active duty in the Armed Forces of the United States.

For purposes of clause (ii), the term "extended active duty" means a period of more than 90 days during which the individual was on active duty (other than active duty for training).

(C) Other definitions

For purposes of subparagraph (A), the terms "compensation" and "service-connected" have the meanings given such terms under section 101 of title 38, United States Code.

(4) Qualified ex-felon

The term "qualified ex-felon" means any individual who is certified by the designated local agency—

(A) as having been convicted of a felony under any statute of the United States or any State, and

(B) as having a hiring date which is not more than 1 year after the last date on which such individual was so convicted or was released from prison.

(5) Designated community residents

(A) In general

The term "designated community resident" means any individual who is certified by the designated local agency—

(i) as having attained age 18 but not age 40 on the hiring date, and

(ii) as having his principal place of abode within an empowerment zone, enterprise community, renewal community, or rural renewal county.

(B) Individual must continue to reside in zone, community, or county

In the case of a designated community resident, the term "qualified wages" shall not include wages paid or incurred for services performed while the individual's principal place of abode is outside an empowerment zone, enterprise community, renewal community, or rural renewal county.

(C) Rural renewal county

For purposes of this paragraph, the term "rural renewal county" means any county which—

(i) is outside a metropolitan statistical area (defined as such by the Office of Management and Budget), and

(ii) during the 5-year periods 1990 through 1994 and 1995 through 1999 had a net population loss.

(6) Vocational rehabilitation referral

The term "vocational rehabilitation referral" means any individual who is certified by the designated local agency as—

(A) having a physical or mental disability which, for such individual, constitutes or results in a substantial handicap to employment, and

(B) having been referred to the employer upon completion of (or while receiving) rehabilitative services pursuant to—

(i) an individualized written plan for employment under a State plan for vocational rehabilitation services approved under the Rehabilitation Act of 1973,

(ii) a program of vocational rehabilitation carried out under chapter 31 of title 38, United States Code, or

(iii) an individual work plan developed and implemented by an employment network pursuant to subsection (g) of section 1148 of the Social Security Act

with respect to which the requirements of such subsection are met.

(7) Qualified summer youth employee

(A) In general

The term "qualified summer youth employee" means any individual—

(i) who performs services for the employer between May 1 and September 15,

(ii) who is certified by the designated local agency as having attained age 16 but not 18 on the hiring date (or if later, on May 1 of the calendar year involved),

(iii) who has not been an employee of the employer during any period prior to the 90-day period described in subparagraph (B)(i), and

(iv) who is certified by the designated local agency as having his principal place of abode within an empowerment zone, enterprise community, or renewal community.

(B) Special rules for determining amount of credit

For purposes of applying this subpart to wages paid or incurred to any qualified summer youth employee—

(i) subsection (b)(2) shall be applied by substituting "any 90-day period between May 1 and September 15" for "the 1-year period beginning with the day the individual begins work for the employer", and

(ii) subsection (b)(3) shall be applied by substituting "$3,000" for "$6,000".

The preceding sentence shall not apply to an individual who, with respect to the same employer, is certified as a member of another targeted group after such individual has been a qualified summer youth employee.

(C) Youth must continue to reside in zone or community

Paragraph (5)(B) shall apply for purposes of subparagraph (A)(iv).

(8) Qualified supplemental nutrition assistance program benefits recipient

(A) In general

The term "qualified supplemental nutrition assistance program benefits recipient" means any individual who is certified by the designated local agency—

(i) as having attained age 18 but not age 40 on the hiring date, and

(ii) as being a member of a family—

(I) receiving assistance under a supplemental nutrition assistance program under the Food and Nutrition Act of 2008 for the 6-month period ending on the hiring date, or

(II) receiving such assistance for at least 3 months of the 5-month period ending on the hiring date, in the case of a member of a family who ceases to be eligible for such assistance under section 6(o) of the Food and Nutrition Act of 2008.

(B) Participation information

Notwithstanding any other provision of law, the Secretary of the Treasury and the Secretary of Agriculture shall enter into an agreement to provide information to designated local agencies with respect to participation in the supplemental nutrition assistance program.

(9) Qualified SSI recipient

The term "qualified SSI recipient" means any individual who is certified by the designated local agency as receiving supplemental security income benefits under title XVI of the Social Security Act (including supplemental security income benefits of the type described in section 1616 of such Act or section 212 of Public Law 93–66) for any month ending within the 60-day period ending on the hiring date.

(10) Long-term family assistance recipient

The term "long-term family assistance recipient" means any individual who is certified by the designated local agency—

(A) as being a member of a family receiving assistance under a IV–A program (as defined in paragraph (2)(B)) for at least the 18-month period ending on the hiring date,

(B)(i) as being a member of a family receiving such assistance for 18 months beginning after August 5, 1997, and

(ii) as having a hiring date which is not more than 2 years after the end of the earliest such 18-month period, or

(C)(i) as being a member of a family which ceased to be eligible for such assistance by reason of any limitation imposed by Federal or State law on the maximum period such assistance is payable to a family, and

(ii) as having a hiring date which is not more than 2 years after the date of such cessation.

(11) Hiring date

The term "hiring date" means the day the individual is hired by the employer.

(12) Designated local agency

The term "designated local agency" means a State employment security agency established in accordance with the Act of June 6, 1933, as amended (29 U.S.C. 49–49n).

(13) Special rules for certifications

(A) In general

An individual shall not be treated as a member of a targeted group unless—

(i) on or before the day on which such individual begins work for the employer, the employer has received a certification from a designated local agency that such individual is a member of a targeted group, or

(ii)(I) on or before the day the individual is offered employment with the employer, a pre-screening notice is completed by the employer with respect to such individual, and

(II) not later than the 28th day after the individual begins work for the employer, the employer submits such notice, signed by the employer and the individual under penalties of perjury, to the designated local agency as part of a written request for such a certification from such agency.

For purposes of this paragraph, the term "pre-screening notice" means a document (in such form as the Secretary shall prescribe) which contains information provided by the individual on the basis of which the employer believes that the individual is a member of a targeted group.

(B) Incorrect certifications

If—

(i) an individual has been certified by a designated local agency as a member of a targeted group, and

(ii) such certification is incorrect because it was based on false information provided by such individual,

the certification shall be revoked and wages paid by the employer after the date on which notice of revocation is received by the employer shall not be treated as qualified wages.

(C) Explanation of denial of request

If a designated local agency denies a request for certification of membership in a targeted group, such agency shall provide to the person making such request a written explanation of the reasons for such denial.

(D) Credit for unemployed veterans

(i) In general

Notwithstanding subparagraph (A), for purposes of paragraph (3)(A)—

(I) a veteran will be treated as certified by the designated local agency as having aggregate periods of unemployment meeting the requirements of clause (ii)(II) or (iv) of such paragraph (whichever is applicable) if such veteran is certified by such agency as being in receipt of unemployment compensation under State or Federal law for not less than 6 months during the 1-year period ending on the hiring date, and

(II) a veteran will be treated as certified by the designated local agency as having aggregate periods of unemployment meeting the requirements of clause (iii) of such paragraph if such veteran is certified by such agency as being in receipt of unemployment compensation under State or Federal law for not less than 4 weeks (but less than 6 months) during the 1-year period ending on the hiring date.

(ii) Regulatory authority

The Secretary may provide alternative methods for certification of a veteran as a qualified veteran described in clause (ii)(II), (iii), or (iv) of paragraph (3)(A), at the Secretary's discretion.

(14) Credit allowed for unemployed veterans and disconnected youth hired in 2009 or 2010

(A) In general

Any unemployed veteran or disconnected youth who begins work for the employer during 2009 or 2010 shall be treated as a member of a targeted group for purposes of this subpart.

(B) Definitions

For purposes of this paragraph—

(i) Unemployed veteran

The term "unemployed veteran" means any veteran (as defined in paragraph (3)(B), determined without regard to clause (ii) thereof) who is certified by the designated local agency as—

(I) having been discharged or released from active duty in the Armed Forces at any time during the 5-year period ending on the hiring date, and

(II) being in receipt of unemployment compensation under State or Federal law for not less than 4 weeks during the 1-year period ending on the hiring date.

(ii) Disconnected youth

The term "disconnected youth" means any individual who is certified by the designated local agency—

(I) as having attained age 16 but not age 25 on the hiring date,

(II) as not regularly attending any secondary, technical, or post-secondary school during the 6-month period preceding the hiring date,

(III) as not regularly employed during such 6-month period, and

(IV) as not readily employable by reason of lacking a sufficient number of basic skills.

(15) Qualified long-term unemployment recipient

The term "qualified long-term unemployment recipient" means any individual who is certified by the designated local agency as being in a period of unemployment which—

(A) is not less than 27 consecutive weeks, and

(B) includes a period in which the individual was receiving unemployment compensation under State or Federal law.

(e) Credit for second-year wages for employment of long-term family assistance recipients

(1) In general

With respect to the employment of a long-term family assistance recipient—

(A) the amount of the work opportunity credit determined under this section for the taxable year shall include 50 percent of the qualified second-year wages for such year, and

(B) in lieu of applying subsection (b)(3), the amount of the qualified first-year wages, and the amount of qualified second-year wages, which may be taken into account with respect to such a recipient shall not exceed $10,000 per year.

(2) Qualified second-year wages

For purposes of this subsection, the term "qualified second-year wages" means qualified wages—

(A) which are paid to a long-term family assistance recipient, and

(B) which are attributable to service rendered during the 1-year period beginning on the day after the last day of the 1-year period with respect to such recipient determined under subsection (b)(2).

(3) Special rules for agricultural and railway labor

If such recipient is an employee to whom subparagraph (A) or (B) of subsection (h)(1) applies, rules similar to the rules of such subparagraphs shall apply except that—

(A) such subparagraph (A) shall be applied by substituting "$10,000" for "$6,000", and

(B) such subparagraph (B) shall be applied by substituting "$833.33" for "$500".

(f) Remuneration must be for trade or business employment

(1) In general

For purposes of this subpart, remuneration paid by an employer to an employee during any taxable year shall be taken into account only if more than one-half of the remuneration so paid is for services performed in a trade or business of the employer.

(2) Special rule for certain determination

Any determination as to whether paragraph (1), or subparagraph (A) or (B) of subsection (h)(1), applies with respect to any employee for any taxable year shall be made without regard to subsections (a) and (b) of section 52.

(g) United States Employment Service to notify employers of availability of credit

The United States Employment Service, in consultation with the Internal Revenue Service, shall take such steps as may be necessary or appropriate to keep employers apprised of the availability of the work opportunity credit determined under this subpart.

(h) Special rules for agricultural labor and railway labor

For purposes of this subpart—

(1) Unemployment insurance wages

(A) Agricultural labor

If the services performed by any employee for an employer during more than one-half of any pay period (within the meaning of section 3306(d)) taken into account with respect to any year constitute agricultural labor (within the meaning of section 3306(k)), the term "unemployment insurance wages" means, with respect to the remuneration paid by the employer to such employee for such year, an amount equal to so much of such remuneration as constitutes "wages" within the meaning of section 3121(a), except that the contribution and benefit base for each calendar year shall be deemed to be $6,000.

(B) Railway labor

If more than one-half of remuneration paid by an employer to an employee during any year is remuneration for service described in section 3306(c)(9), the term "unemployment insurance wages" means, with respect to such employee for such year, an amount equal to so much of the remuneration paid to such employee during such year which would be subject to contributions under section 8(a) of the Railroad Unemployment Insurance Act (45 U.S.C. 358(a)) if the maximum amount subject to such contributions were $500 per month.

(2) Wages

In any case to which subparagraph (A) or (B) of paragraph (1) applies, the term "wages" means unemployment insurance wages (determined without regard to any dollar limitation).

(i) Certain individuals ineligible

(1) Related individuals

No wages shall be taken into account under subsection (a) with respect to an individual who—

(A) bears any of the relationships described in subparagraphs (A) through (G) of section 152(d)(2) to the taxpayer, or, if the taxpayer is a corporation, to an individual who owns, directly or indirectly, more than 50 percent in value of the outstanding stock of the corporation, or, if the taxpayer is an entity other than a corporation, to any individual who owns, directly or indirectly, more than 50 percent of the capital and profits interests in the entity (determined with the application of section 267(c)),

(B) if the taxpayer is an estate or trust, is a grantor, beneficiary, or fiduciary of the estate or trust, or is an individual who bears any of the relationships described in subparagraphs (A) through (G) of section 152(d)(2) to a grantor, beneficiary, or fiduciary of the estate or trust, or

(C) is a dependent (described in section 152(d)(2)(H)) of the taxpayer, or, if the taxpayer is a corporation, of an individual described in subparagraph (A), or, if the taxpayer is an estate or trust, of a grantor, beneficiary, or fiduciary of the estate or trust.

(2) Nonqualifying rehires

No wages shall be taken into account under subsection (a) with respect to any individual if, prior to the hiring date of such individual, such individual had been employed by the employer at any time.

(3) Individuals not meeting minimum employment periods

(A) Reduction of credit for individuals performing fewer than 400 hours of service

In the case of an individual who has performed at least 120 hours, but less than 400 hours, of service for the employer, subsection (a) shall be applied by substituting "25 percent" for "40 percent".

(B) Denial of credit for individuals performing fewer than 120 hours of service

No wages shall be taken into account under subsection (a) with respect to any individual unless such individual has performed at least 120 hours of service for the employer.

(j) Election to have work opportunity credit not apply

(1) In general

A taxpayer may elect to have this section not apply for any taxable year.

(2) Time for making election

An election under paragraph (1) for any taxable year may be made (or revoked) at any time before the expiration of the 3-year period beginning on the last date prescribed by law for filing the return for such taxable year (determined without regard to extensions).

(3) Manner of making election

An election under paragraph (1) (or revocation thereof) shall be made in such manner as the Secretary may by regulations prescribe.

(k) Treatment of successor employers; treatment of employees performing services for other persons

(1) Treatment of successor employers

Under regulations prescribed by the Secretary, in the case of a successor employer referred to in section 3306(b)(1), the determination of the amount of the credit under this section with respect to wages paid by such successor employer shall be made in the same manner as if such wages were paid by the predecessor employer referred to in such section.

(2) Treatment of employees performing services for other persons

No credit shall be determined under this section with respect to remuneration paid by an employer to an employee for services performed by such employee for another person unless the amount reasonably expected to be received by the employer for such services from such other person exceeds the remuneration paid by the employer to such employee for such services.

(Added Pub. L. 95–30, title II, §202(b), May 23, 1977, 91 Stat. 141; amended Pub. L. 95–600, title III, §321(a), Nov. 6, 1978, 92 Stat. 2830; Pub. L. 96–222, title I, §103(a)(6)(A), (E), (F), (G)(iii)–(ix), Apr. 1, 1980, 94 Stat. 209, 210; Pub. L. 97–34, title II, §261(a)–(b)(2)(A), (B)(ii)–(f)(1), Aug. 13, 1981, 95 Stat. 260–262; Pub. L. 97–248, title II, §233(a)–(d), (f), Sept. 3, 1982, 96 Stat. 501, 502; Pub. L. 97–448, title I, §102(l)(1), (3), (4), Jan. 12, 1983, 96 Stat. 2374; Pub. L. 98–369, div. A, title IV, §474(p)(1)–(3), title VII, §712(n), title X, §1041(a), (c)(1)–(4), div. B, title VI, §§2638(b), 2663(j)(5)(A), July 18, 1984, 98 Stat. 837, 955, 1042, 1043, 1144, 1171; Pub. L. 99–514, title XVII, §1701(a)–(c), title XVIII, §1878(f)(1), Oct. 22, 1986, 100 Stat. 2772, 2904; Pub. L. 100–203, title X, §10601(a), Dec. 22, 1987, 101 Stat. 1330–451; Pub. L. 100–485, title II, §202(c)(6), Oct. 13, 1988, 102 Stat. 2378; Pub. L. 100–647, title I, §1017(a), title IV, §4010(a), (c)(1), (d)(1), Nov. 10, 1988, 102 Stat. 3575, 3655; Pub. L. 101–239, title VII, §7103(a), (c)(1), Dec. 19, 1989, 103 Stat. 2305; Pub. L. 101–508, title XI, §11405(a), Nov. 5, 1990, 104 Stat. 1388–473; Pub. L. 102–227, title I, §105(a), Dec. 11, 1991, 105 Stat. 1687; Pub. L. 103–66, title XIII, §§13102(a), 13302(d), Aug. 10, 1993, 107 Stat. 420, 556; Pub. L. 104–188, title I, §1201(a)–(e)(1), (5), (f), Aug. 20, 1996, 110 Stat. 1768–1772; Pub. L. 104–193, title I, §110(l)(1), Aug. 22, 1996, 110 Stat. 2173; Pub. L. 105–33, title V, §5514(a)(1), Aug. 5, 1997, 111 Stat. 620; Pub. L. 105–34, title VI, §603(a)–(d), Aug. 5, 1997, 111 Stat. 862; Pub. L. 105–277, div. J, title I, §1002(a), title IV, §4006(c)(1), Oct. 21, 1998, 112 Stat. 2681–888, 2681-912; Pub. L. 106–170, title V, §505(a), (b), Dec. 17, 1999, 113 Stat. 1921; Pub. L. 106–554, §1(a)(7) [title I, §102(a)–(c), title III, §316(a)], Dec. 21, 2000, 114 Stat. 2763, 2763A-600, 2763A-644; Pub. L. 107–147, title VI, §604(a), Mar. 9, 2002, 116 Stat. 59; Pub. L. 108–311, title II, §207(5), title III, §303(a)(1), Oct. 4, 2004, 118 Stat. 1177, 1179; Pub. L. 109–432, div. A, title I, §105(a)–(e)(3), Dec. 20, 2006, 120 Stat. 2936, 2937; Pub. L. 110–28, title VIII, §8211(a)–(d), May 25, 2007, 121 Stat. 191; Pub. L. 110–234, title IV, §4002(b)(1)(A), (B), (D), (2)(O), May 22, 2008, 122 Stat. 1095–1097; Pub. L. 110–246, §4(a), title IV, §4002(b)(1)(A), (B), (D), (2)(O), June 18, 2008, 122 Stat. 1664, 1857, 1858; Pub. L. 111–5, div. B, title I, §1221(a), Feb. 17, 2009, 123 Stat. 337; Pub. L. 111–147, title I, §101(b), Mar. 18, 2010, 124 Stat. 74; Pub. L. 111–312, title VII, §757(a), Dec. 17, 2010, 124 Stat. 3322; Pub. L. 112–56, title II, §261(a)–(d), Nov. 21, 2011, 125 Stat. 729, 730; Pub. L. 112–240, title III, §309(a), Jan. 2, 2013, 126 Stat. 2329; Pub. L. 113–295, div. A, title I, §119(a), Dec. 19, 2014, 128 Stat. 4015; Pub. L. 114–113, div. Q, title I, §142(a), (b), Dec. 18, 2015, 129 Stat. 3056; Pub. L. 115–141, div. U, title IV, §401(a)(26)–(29), Mar. 23, 2018, 132 Stat. 1185; Pub. L. 116–94, div. Q, title I, §143(a), Dec. 20, 2019, 133 Stat. 3234; Pub. L. 116–260, div. EE, title I, §113(a), Dec. 27, 2020, 134 Stat. 3050.)

Editorial Notes
References in Text

The Social Security Act, referred to in subsecs. (c)(2)(B) and (d)(2)(B), (6)(B)(iii), (9), is act Aug. 14, 1935, ch. 531, 49 Stat. 620, as amended. Part A of title IV of the Act is classified generally to part A (§601 et seq.) of subchapter IV of chapter 7 of Title 42, The Public Health and Welfare. Title XVI of the Act is classified generally to subchapter XVI (§1381 et seq.) of chapter 7 of Title 42. Section 482 of the Act, which was classified to section 682 of Title 42, was repealed by Pub. L. 104–193, title I, §108(e), Aug. 22, 1996, 110 Stat. 2167. Sections 1148(g) and 1616 of the Act are classified to sections 1320b–19(g) and 1382e, respectively, of Title 42. For complete classification of this Act to the Code, see section 1305 of Title 42 and Tables.

Section 3111(d), referred to in subsec. (c)(5), was repealed by Pub. L. 115–141, div. U, title IV, §401(b)(34), Mar. 23, 2018, 132 Stat. 1204.

The Food and Nutrition Act of 2008, referred to in subsec. (d)(3)(A)(i), (8)(A)(ii), is Pub. L. 88–525, Aug. 31, 1964, 78 Stat. 703, which is classified generally to chapter 51 (§2011 et seq.) of Title 7, Agriculture. Section 6(o) of the Act is classified to section 2015(o) of Title 7. For complete classification of this Act to the Code, see Short Title note set out under section 2011 of Title 7 and Tables.

The Rehabilitation Act of 1973, referred to in subsec. (d)(6)(B)(i), is Pub. L. 93–112, Sept. 26, 1973, 87 Stat. 355, as amended, which is classified generally to chapter 16 (§701 et seq.) of Title 29, Labor. For complete classification of this Act to the Code, see Short Title note set out under section 701 of Title 29 and Tables.

Section 212 of Public Law 93–66, referred to in subsec. (d)(9), is set out as a note under section 1382 of Title 42, The Public Health and Welfare.

Act of June 6, 1933, referred to in subsec. (d)(12), is act June 6, 1933, ch. 49, 48 Stat. 113, as amended, popularly known as the Wagner-Peyser Act, which is classified generally to chapter 4B (§49 et seq.) of Title 29, Labor. For complete classification of this Act to the Code, see Short Title note set out under section 49 of Title 29 and Tables.

Codification

Pub. L. 110–234 and Pub. L. 110–246 made identical amendments to this section. The amendments by Pub. L. 110–234 were repealed by section 4(a) of Pub. L. 110–246.

Prior Provisions

A prior section 51, added Pub. L. 90–364, title I, §102(a), June 28, 1968, 82 Stat. 252; amended Pub. L. 91–53, §5(a), Aug. 7, 1969, 83 Stat. 93; Pub. L. 91–172, title III, §301(b)(5), title VII, §701(a), Dec. 30, 1969, 83 Stat. 585, 657, related to the imposition of a tax surcharge, prior to repeal by Pub. L. 94–455, title XIX, §1901(a)(7), Oct. 4, 1976, 90 Stat. 1765.

Amendments

2020—Subsec. (c)(4). Pub. L. 116–260 substituted "December 31, 2025" for "December 31, 2020".

2019—Subsec. (c)(4). Pub. L. 116–94 substituted "December 31, 2020" for "December 31, 2019".

2018—Subsec. (c)(4). Pub. L. 115–141, §401(a)(26), inserted period at end.

Subsec. (d)(3)(A)(ii)(II). Pub. L. 115–141, §401(a)(27), inserted comma at end.

Subsec. (d)(8). Pub. L. 115–141, §401(a)(28), substituted "supplemental nutrition assistance program benefits recipient" for "food stamp recipient" in heading.

Subsec. (i)(1)(A). Pub. L. 115–141, §401(a)(29), substituted "entity" for "entity,".

2015—Subsec. (c)(4). Pub. L. 114–113, §142(a), substituted "December 31, 2019" for "December 31, 2014".

Subsec. (d)(1)(J). Pub. L. 114–113, §142(b)(1), added subpar. (J).

Subsec. (d)(15). Pub. L. 114–113, §142(b)(2), added par. (15).

2014—Subsec. (c)(4). Pub. L. 113–295 substituted "for the employer after December 31, 2014" for "for the employer—

"(A) after December 31, 1994, and before October 1, 1996, or

"(B) after December 31, 2013".

2013—Subsec. (c)(4)(B). Pub. L. 112–240 substituted "after December 31, 2013" for "after—

"(i) December 31, 2012, in the case of a qualified veteran, and

"(ii) December 31, 2011, in the case of any other individual."

2011—Subsec. (b)(3). Pub. L. 112–56, §261(a), substituted "($12,000 per year in the case of any individual who is a qualified veteran by reason of subsection (d)(3)(A)(ii)(I), $14,000 per year in the case of any individual who is a qualified veteran by reason of subsection (d)(3)(A)(iv), and $24,000 per year in the case of any individual who is a qualified veteran by reason of subsection (d)(3)(A)(ii)(II))" for "($12,000 per year in the case of any individual who is a qualified veteran by reason of subsection (d)(3)(A)(ii))".

Subsec. (c)(4)(B). Pub. L. 112–56, §261(d), amended subpar. (B) generally. Prior to amendment, subpar. (B) read as follows: "after December 31, 2011."

Subsec. (d)(3)(A)(iii), (iv). Pub. L. 112–56, §261(b), added cls. (iii) and (iv).

Subsec. (d)(13)(D). Pub. L. 112–56, §261(c), added subpar. (D).

2010—Subsec. (c)(4)(B). Pub. L. 111–312 substituted "December 31, 2011" for "August 31, 2011".

Subsec. (c)(5). Pub. L. 111–147 added par. (5).

2009—Subsec. (d)(14). Pub. L. 111–5 added par. (14).

2008—Subsec. (d)(1)(G). Pub. L. 110–246, §4002(b)(1)(D), (2)(O), substituted "supplemental nutrition assistance program benefits" for "food stamp".

Subsec. (d)(3)(A)(i). Pub. L. 110–246, §4002(b)(1)(A), (B), (2)(O), substituted "Food and Nutrition Act of 2008" for "Food Stamp Act of 1977" and "supplemental nutrition assistance program" for "food stamp program".

Subsec. (d)(8)(A). Pub. L. 110–246, §4002(b)(1)(D), (2)(O), substituted "supplemental nutrition assistance program benefits" for "food stamp" in introductory provisions.

Subsec. (d)(8)(A)(ii)(I). Pub. L. 110–246, §4002(b)(1)(A), (B), (2)(O), substituted "Food and Nutrition Act of 2008" for "Food Stamp Act of 1977" and "supplemental nutrition assistance program" for "food stamp program".

Subsec. (d)(8)(A)(ii)(II). Pub. L. 110–246, §4002(b)(1)(B), (2)(O), substituted "Food and Nutrition Act of 2008" for "Food Stamp Act of 1977".

Subsec. (d)(8)(B). Pub. L. 110–246, §4002(b)(1)(A), (2)(O), substituted "supplemental nutrition assistance program" for "food stamp program".

2007—Subsec. (b)(3). Pub. L. 110–28, §8211(d)(2), substituted "Limitation on" for "Only first $6,000 of" in heading and inserted "($12,000 per year in the case of any individual who is a qualified veteran by reason of subsection (d)(3)(A)(ii))" before period at end.

Subsec. (c)(4)(B). Pub. L. 110–28, §8211(a), substituted "August 31, 2011" for "December 31, 2007".

Subsec. (d)(1)(D). Pub. L. 110–28, §8211(b)(2), amended subpar. (D) generally. Prior to amendment, subpar. (D) read as follows: "a high-risk youth,".

Subsec. (d)(3)(A). Pub. L. 110–28, §8211(d)(1)(A), substituted "agency as—" and cls. (i) and (ii) for "agency as being a member of a family receiving assistance under a food stamp program under the Food Stamp Act of 1977 for at least a 3-month period ending during the 12-month period ending on the hiring date."

Subsec. (d)(3)(C). Pub. L. 110–28, §8211(d)(1)(B), added subpar. (C).

Subsec. (d)(5). Pub. L. 110–28, §8211(b)(1), amended heading and text of par. (5) generally. Prior to amendment, text read as follows:

"(A) In general.—The term 'high-risk youth' means any individual who is certified by the designated local agency—

"(i) as having attained age 18 but not age 25 on the hiring date, and

"(ii) as having his principal place of abode within an empowerment zone, enterprise community, or renewal community.

"(B) Youth must continue to reside in zone or community.—In the case of a high-risk youth, the term 'qualified wages' shall not include wages paid or incurred for services performed while such youth's principal place of abode is outside an empowerment zone, enterprise community, or renewal community."

Subsec. (d)(6)(B)(iii). Pub. L. 110–28, §8211(c), added cl. (iii).

2006—Subsec. (c)(4)(B). Pub. L. 109–432, §105(a), substituted "2007" for "2005".

Subsec. (d)(1)(I). Pub. L. 109–432, §105(e)(1), added subpar. (I).

Subsec. (d)(4). Pub. L. 109–432, §105(b), inserted "and" at end of subpar. (A), substituted a period for ", and" at end of subpar. (B), and struck out subpar. (C) and concluding provisions which read as follows:

"(C) as being a member of a family which had an income during the 6 months immediately preceding the earlier of the month in which such income determination occurs or the month in which the hiring date occurs, which, on an annual basis, would be 70 percent or less of the Bureau of Labor Statistics lower living standard. Any determination under subparagraph (C) shall be valid for the 45-day period beginning on the date such determination is made."

Subsec. (d)(8)(A)(i). Pub. L. 109–432, §105(c), substituted "40" for "25".

Subsec. (d)(10) to (12). Pub. L. 109–432, §105(e)(2), added par. (10) and redesignated former pars. (10) and (11) as (11) and (12), respectively. Former par. (12) redesignated (13).

Subsec. (d)(12)(A)(ii)(II). Pub. L. 109–432, §105(d), substituted "28th day" for "21st day".

Subsec. (d)(13). Pub. L. 109–432, §105(e)(2), redesignated par. (12) as (13).

Subsec. (e). Pub. L. 109–432, §105(e)(3), added subsec. (e).

2004—Subsec. (c)(4)(B). Pub. L. 108–311, §303(a)(1), substituted "2005" for "2003".

Subsec. (i)(1)(A), (B). Pub. L. 108–311, §207(5)(A), substituted "subparagraphs (A) through (G) of section 152(d)(2)" for "paragraphs (1) through (8) of section 152(a)".

Subsec. (i)(1)(C). Pub. L. 108–311, §207(5)(B), substituted "152(d)(2)(H)" for "152(a)(9)".

2002—Subsec. (c)(4)(B). Pub. L. 107–147 substituted "2003" for "2001".

2000—Subsec. (d)(2)(B). Pub. L. 106–554, §1(a)(7) [title III, §316(a)], substituted "program funded" for "plan approved" and struck out "(relating to assistance for needy families with minor children)" after "Social Security Act".

Subsec. (d)(5)(A)(ii). Pub. L. 106–554, §1(a)(7) [title I, §102(a)], substituted "empowerment zone, enterprise community, or renewal community" for "empowerment zone or enterprise community".

Subsec. (d)(5)(B). Pub. L. 106–554, §1(a)(7) [title I, §102(a), (c)], inserted "or community" after "zone" in heading and substituted "empowerment zone, enterprise community, or renewal community" for "empowerment zone or enterprise community" in text.

Subsec. (d)(7)(A)(iv). Pub. L. 106–554, §1(a)(7) [title I, §102(b)], substituted "empowerment zone, enterprise community, or renewal community" for "empowerment zone or enterprise community".

Subsec. (d)(7)(C). Pub. L. 106–554, §1(a)(7) [title I, §102(c)], inserted "or community" after "zone" in heading.

1999—Subsec. (c)(4)(B). Pub. L. 106–170, §505(a), substituted "December 31, 2001" for "June 30, 1999".

Subsec. (i)(2). Pub. L. 106–170, §505(b), struck out "during which he was not a member of a targeted group" before period at end.

1998—Subsec. (c)(4)(B). Pub. L. 105–277, §1002(a), substituted "June 30, 1999" for "June 30, 1998".

Subsec. (d)(6)(B)(i). Pub. L. 105–277, §4006(c)(1), substituted "plan for employment" for "rehabilitation plan".

1997—Subsec. (a). Pub. L. 105–34, §603(d)(1), substituted "40 percent" for "35 percent".

Subsec. (c)(4)(B). Pub. L. 105–34, §603(a), substituted "June 30, 1998" for "September 30, 1997".

Subsec. (d)(1)(H). Pub. L. 105–34, §603(c)(1), added subpar. (H).

Subsec. (d)(2)(A). Pub. L. 105–34, §603(b)(1), substituted "for any 9 months during the 18-month period ending on the hiring date" for "for at least a 9-month period ending during the 9-month period ending on the hiring date".

Subsec. (d)(3)(A). Pub. L. 105–34, §603(b)(2), amended heading and text of subpar. (A) generally. Prior to amendment, text read as follows: "The term 'qualified veteran' means any veteran who is certified by the designated local agency as being—

"(i) a member of a family receiving assistance under a IV–A program (as defined in paragraph (2)(B)) for at least a 9-month period ending during the 12-month period ending on the hiring date, or

387

    "(ii) a member of a family receiving assistance under a food stamp program under the Food Stamp Act of 1977 for at least a 3-month period ending during the 12-month period ending on the hiring date."

Subsec. (d)(9). Pub. L. 105–34, §603(c)(2), added par. (9). Former par. (9) redesignated (10).

Pub. L. 105–33 repealed Pub. L. 104–193, §110(l)(1). See 1996 Amendment note below.

Subsec. (d)(10) to (12). Pub. L. 105–34, §603(c)(2), redesignated pars. (9) to (11) as (10) to (12), respectively.

Subsec. (i)(3). Pub. L. 105–34, §603(d)(2), amended heading and text of par. (3) generally. Prior to amendment, text read as follows: "No wages shall be taken into account under subsection (a) with respect to any individual unless such individual either—

    "(A) is employed by the employer at least 180 days (20 days in the case of a qualified summer youth employee), or

    "(B) has completed at least 400 hours (120 hours in the case of a qualified summer youth employee) of services performed for the employer."

1996—Subsec. (a), (e)(1). Pub. L. 104–188, §1201(a), substituted "work opportunity credit" for "targeted jobs credit" and "35 percent" for "40 percent".

Subsec. (c)(1). Pub. L. 104–188, §1201(f), struck out ", subsection (d)(8)(D)," after "this subsection".

Subsec. (c)(4). Pub. L. 104–188, §1201(d), amended par. (4) generally. Prior to amendment, par. (4) read as follows: "Termination.—The term 'wages' shall not include any amount paid or incurred to an individual who begins work for the employer after December 31, 1994."

Subsec. (d). Pub. L. 104–188, §1201(b), reenacted heading without change and amended text generally, revising and restating as pars. (1) to (11) provisions formerly contained in pars. (1) to (16).

Subsec. (d)(9). Pub. L. 104–193, §110(l)(1), which directed amendment of par. (9) by striking all that follows "agency as" and inserting "being eligible for financial assistance under part A of title IV of the Social Security Act and as having continually received such financial assistance during the 90-day period which immediately precedes the date on which such individual is hired by the employer.", was repealed by Pub. L. 105–33.

Subsec. (g). Pub. L. 104–188, §1201(e)(1), substituted "work opportunity credit" for "targeted jobs credit".

Subsec. (i)(3). Pub. L. 104–188, §1201(c), amended par. (3) generally. Prior to amendment, par. (3) read as follows: "Individuals not meeting minimum employment period.—No wages shall be taken into account under subsection (a) with respect to any individual unless such individual either—

    "(A) is employed by the employer at least 90 days (14 days in the case of an individual described in subsection (d)(12)), or

    "(B) has completed at least 120 hours (20 hours in the case of an individual described in subsection (d)(12)) of services performed for the employer."

Subsec. (j). Pub. L. 104–188, §1201(e)(5), substituted "Work opportunity credit" for "Targeted jobs credit" in heading.

1993—Subsec. (c)(4). Pub. L. 103–66, §13102(a), substituted "December 31, 1994" for "June 30, 1992".

Subsec. (i)(1)(A). Pub. L. 103–66, §13302(d), inserted ", or, if the taxpayer is an entity other than a corporation, to any individual who owns, directly or indirectly, more than 50 percent of the capital and profits interests in the entity," after "of the corporation".

1991—Subsec. (c)(4). Pub. L. 102–227 substituted "June 30, 1992" for "December 31, 1991".

1990—Subsec. (c)(4). Pub. L. 101–508 substituted "December 31, 1991" for "September 30, 1990".

1989—Subsec. (c)(4). Pub. L. 101–239, §7103(a), substituted "September 30, 1990" for "December 31, 1989".

Subsec. (d)(16)(C). Pub. L. 101–239, §7103(c)(1), added subpar. (C).

1988—Subsec. (c)(2)(B). Pub. L. 100–485 substituted "section 482(e)" for "section 414".

Subsec. (c)(4). Pub. L. 100–647, §4010(a), substituted "1989" for "1988".

Subsec. (d)(3)(B). Pub. L. 100–647, §4010(c)(1), substituted "age 23" for "age 25".

Subsec. (d)(12)(B). Pub. L. 100–647, §4010(d)(1), redesignated former cls. (ii) and (iii) as (i) and (ii), respectively, and struck out former cl. (i) which provided that subsection (a) shall be applied by substituting "85 percent" for "40 percent".

Pub. L. 100–647, §1017(a), substituted "subsection (a)" for "subsection (a)(1)" in cl. (i).

1987—Subsec. (c)(3), (4). Pub. L. 100–203 added par. (3) and redesignated former par. (3) as (4).

1986—Subsec. (a). Pub. L. 99–514, §1701(b)(1), amended subsec. (a) generally. Prior to amendment, subsec. (a) read as follows: "For purposes of section 38, the amount of the targeted jobs credit determined under this section for the taxable year shall be the sum of—

    "(1) 50 percent of the qualified first-year wages for such year, and

    "(2) 25 percent of the qualified second-year wages for such year."

Subsec. (b)(3), (4). Pub. L. 99–514, §1701(b)(2)(A), redesignated par. (4) as (3) and struck out ", and the amount of the qualified second-year wages," after "first-year wages" and struck out par. (3) which defined "qualified second-year wages".

Subsec. (c)(3). Pub. L. 99–514, §1701(a), substituted "December 31, 1988" for "December 31, 1985".

Subsec. (d)(12)(B). Pub. L. 99–514, §1701(b)(2)(B), in cl. (i), substituted "40 percent" for "50 percent", struck out cl. (ii) which directed that subsecs. (a)(2) and (b)(3) were not to apply, redesignated cl. (iii) as cl. (ii), redesignated cl. (iv) as cl. (iii), and in cl. (iii) as so redesignated substituted "subsection (b)(3)" for "subsection (b)(4)".

Subsec. (i)(3). Pub. L. 99–514, §1701(c), added par. (3).

Subsec. (k). Pub. L. 99–514, §1878(f)(1), redesignated subsec. (j) added by section 1041(c)(1) of Pub. L. 98–369 and relating to treatment of successor employers, and employees performing services for other persons, as subsec. (k).

1984—Subsec. (a). Pub. L. 98–369, §474(p)(1), substituted "For purposes of section 38, the amount of the targeted jobs credit determined under this section" for "The amount of the credit allowable by section 44B" in introductory provisions.

Subsec. (b)(2). Pub. L. 98–369, §1041(c)(4), struck out "(or, in the case of a vocational rehabilitation referral, the day the individual begins work for the employer on or after the beginning of such individual's rehabilitation plan)" after "begins work for the employer".

Subsec. (c)(2). Pub. L. 98–369, §2638(b), designated existing provisions as subpar. (A), inserted par. (2) heading, and added subpar. (B).

Subsec. (c)(3). Pub. L. 98–369, §1041(a), substituted "December 31, 1985" for "December 31, 1984".

Subsec. (d)(6)(B)(ii). Pub. L. 98–369, §2663(j)(5)(A), substituted "Secretary of Health and Human Services" for "Secretary of Health Education and Welfare".

Subsec. (d)(11). Pub. L. 98–369, §712(n), made determination respecting membership of a qualified summer youth employee or youth participating in a qualified cooperative education program with respect to an employer applicable for purposes of determining whether such individual is a member of another targeted group with respect to such employer.

Subsec. (d)(12)(A)(ii). Pub. L. 98–369, §1041(c)(3), substituted "(or if later, on May 1 of the calendar year involved)" for "(as defined in paragraph (14))".

Subsec. (d)(16)(A). Pub. L. 98–369, §1041(c)(2), inserted "For purposes of the preceding sentence, if on or before the day on which such individual begins work for the employer, such individual has received from a designated local agency (or other agency or organization designated pursuant to a written agreement with such designated local agency) a written preliminary determination that such individual is a member of a targeted group, then 'the fifth day' shall be substituted for 'the day' in such sentence."

Subsec. (g). Pub. L. 98–369, §474(p)(2), substituted "the targeted jobs credit determined under this subpart" for "the credit provided by section 44B".

Subsec. (j). Pub. L. 98–369, §1041(c)(1), added subsec. (j) relating to treatment of successor employers, and employees performing services for other persons.

Pub. L. 98–369, §474(p)(3), added subsec. (j) relating to election to have targeted jobs credit not apply.

1983—Subsec. (d)(8)(D). Pub. L. 97–448, §102(l)(1), substituted "clauses (i), (ii), and (iii) of subparagraph (A)" for "subparagraph (A)".

Subsec. (d)(9)(B). Pub. L. 97–448, §102(l)(3), substituted "section 432(b)(1) or 445" for "section 432(b)(1)".

Subsec. (d)(11). Pub. L. 97–448, §102(l)(4), substituted "the earlier of the month in which such determination occurs or the month in which the hiring date occurs" for "the month in which such determination occurs".

1982—Subsec. (c)(3). Pub. L. 97–248, §233(a), substituted "1984" for "1982".

Subsec. (d)(1)(J). Pub. L. 97–248, §233(b)(3), added subpar. (J).

Subsec. (d)(6)(B)(i)(II). Pub. L. 97–248, §233(d), substituted "consists of money payments or voucher or scrip, and" for "consists of money payments".

Subsec. (d)(10). Pub. L. 97–248, §233(c), inserted provision respecting nonapplicability of paragraph to individuals who begin work for the employer after December 31, 1982.

Subsec. (d)(12) to (15). Pub. L. 97–248, §233(b)(4), (5), added par. (12) and redesignated former pars. (12) to (15) as (13) to (16), respectively.

Subsec. (d)(16). Pub. L. 97–248, §233(b)(4), redesignated former par. (15) as (16).

Pub. L. 97–248, §233(f), substituted "on or before" for "before" in subpar. (A).

1981—Subsec. (c)(3), (4). Pub. L. 97–34, §261(b)(2)(B)(ii), redesignated par. (4) as (3). Former par. (3), which excluded from term "wages" any amount paid or incurred by the employer to an individual with respect to whom the employer claims credit under section 40 of this title, was struck out.

Pub. L. 97–34, §261(a), extended termination date to Dec. 31, 1982, from Dec. 31, 1981, and inserted "to an individual who begins work for the employer" after "paid or incurred".

Subsec. (d)(1)(H), (I). Pub. L. 97–34, §261(b)(1), added subpars. (H) and (I).

Subsec. (d)(3)(A)(ii). Pub. L. 97–34, §261(b)(2)(B)(iii), substituted "paragraph (11)" for "paragraph (9)".

Subsec. (d)(4). Pub. L. 97–34, §261(b)(2)(B)(iii), (3), in subpar. (B) inserted "and" after "States," in subpar. (C) substituted "paragraph (11)" for "paragraph (9)", and struck out "(D) not having attained the age of 35 on the hiring date."

Subsec. (d)(7)(B). Pub. L. 97–34, §261(b)(2)(B)(iii), substituted "paragraph (11)" for "paragraph (9)".

Subsec. (d)(8)(A)(iv). Pub. L. 97–34, §261(b)(4), added cl. (iv).

Subsec. (d)(9), (10). Pub. L. 97–34, §261(b)(2)(A), added pars. (9) and (10) and redesignated former pars. (9) and (10) as (11) and (12), respectively.

Subsec. (d)(11). Pub. L. 97–34, §261(b)(2)(A), (c)(2), redesignated former par. (9) as (11), substituted "70 percent or less" for "less than 70 percent", and provided for validity of any determination for 45-day period beginning on the date the determination is made. Former par. (11) redesignated (13).

Subsec. (d)(12), (13). Pub. L. 97–34, §261(b)(2)(A), redesignated former pars. (10) and (11) as pars. (12) and (13), respectively. Former par. (12) redesignated (14).

Subsec. (d)(14). Pub. L. 97–34, §261(f)(1)(A), substituted as definition for term " 'designated local agency' means a State employment security agency established in accordance with the Act of June 6, 1933, as amended (29 U.S.C. 49–49n)" for " 'designated local agency' means the agency for any locality designated jointly by the Secretary and the Secretary of Labor to perform certification of employees for employers in that locality".

Pub. L. 97–34, §261(b)(2)(A), redesignated former par. (12) as (14).

Subsec. (d)(15). Pub. L. 97–34, §261(c)(1), added par. (15).

Subsec. (e). Pub. L. 97–34, §261(e)(1), struck out subsec. (e) which set forth limitation that qualified first-year wages could not exceed 30 percent of FUTA wages for all employees.

Subsec. (f). Pub. L. 97–34, §261(e)(2), substituted "any taxable year" for "any year" in pars. (1) and (2) and struck out par. (3), defining "year" which is covered in pars. (1) and (2).

Subsec. (g). Pub. L. 97–34, §261(f)(1)(B), substituted "United States Employment Service" for "Secretary of Labor" in heading and text.

Subsec. (i). Pub. L. 97–34, §261(d), added subsec. (i).

1980—Subsec. (c)(1). Pub. L. 96–222, §103(a)(6)(E)(ii), substituted ", subsection (d)(8)(D), and subsection (h)(2)" for "subsection (h)(2)".

Subsec. (c)(2). Pub. L. 96–222, §103(a)(6)(G)(iii), inserted "or incurred" after "amounts paid".

Subsec. (c)(4). Pub. L. 96–222, §103(a)(6)(A), substituted "December 31, 1981" for "December 31, 1980".

Subsec. (d)(1)(E). Pub. L. 96–222, §103(a)(6)(G)(iv), struck out "or" after "recipient,".

Subsec. (d)(4)(A)(i). Pub. L. 96–222, §103(a)(6)(G)(v), substituted "active duty" for "active day".

Subsec. (d)(4)(B). Pub. L. 96–222, §103(a)(6)(G)(vi), substituted "preemployment" for "premployment".

Subsec. (d)(5). Pub. L. 96–222, §103(a)(6)(G)(vii), substituted "preemployment" for "pre-employment".

Subsec. (d)(8)(A). Pub. L. 96–222, §103(a)(6)(F), substituted "age 20" for "age 19".

Subsec. (d)(8)(D). Pub. L. 96–222, §103(a)(6)(E)(i), in heading substituted "Wages" for "Individual must be currently pursuing program" and in text substituted "In the case of remuneration" for "Wages shall be taken into account with respect to a qualified cooperative education program only if the wages are" and inserted ", wages, and unemployment insurance wages, shall be determined without regard to section 3306(c)(10)(C)".

Subsec. (d)(12). Pub. L. 96–222, §103(a)(6)(G)(viii), substituted "employers" for "employer".

Subsec. (e). Pub. L. 96–222, §103(a)(6)(G)(ix), inserted "except as provided in subsection (h)(1)" after "the preceding sentence,".

1978—Pub. L. 95–600 amended section generally and limited allowance of credit to the hiring of seven target groups with high unemployment rates.

STATUTORY NOTES AND RELATED SUBSIDIARIES
EFFECTIVE DATE OF 2020 AMENDMENT
Pub. L. 116–260, div. EE, title I, §113(b), Dec. 27, 2020, 134 Stat. 3050, provided that: "The amendment made by this section [amending this section] shall apply to individuals who begin work for the employer after December 31, 2020."

EFFECTIVE DATE OF 2019 AMENDMENT
Pub. L. 116–94, div. Q, title I, §143(b), Dec. 20, 2019, 133 Stat. 3234, provided that: "The amendment made by this section [amending this section] shall apply to individuals who begin work for the employer after December 31, 2019."

EFFECTIVE DATE OF 2015 AMENDMENT
Pub. L. 114–113, div. Q, title I, §142(c), Dec. 18, 2015, 129 Stat. 3056, provided that:

"(1) Extension.—The amendment made by subsection (a) [amending this section] shall apply to individuals who begin work for the employer after December 31, 2014.

"(2) Modification.—The amendments made by subsection (b) [amending this section] shall apply to individuals who begin work for the employer after December 31, 2015."

EFFECTIVE DATE OF 2014 AMENDMENT
Pub. L. 113–295, div. A, title I, §119(b), Dec. 19, 2014, 128 Stat. 4015, provided that: "The amendment made by this section [amending this section] shall apply to individuals who begin work for the employer after December 31, 2013."

EFFECTIVE DATE OF 2013 AMENDMENT
Pub. L. 112–240, title III, §309(b), Jan. 2, 2013, 126 Stat. 2329, provided that: "The amendment made by this section [amending this section] shall apply to individuals who begin work for the employer after December 31, 2011."

EFFECTIVE DATE OF 2011 AMENDMENT

Pub. L. 112–56, title II, §261(g), Nov. 21, 2011, 125 Stat. 732, provided that: "The amendments made by this section [amending this section and sections 52 and 3111 of this title] shall apply to individuals who begin work for the employer after the date of the enactment of this Act [Nov. 21, 2011]."

EFFECTIVE DATE OF 2010 AMENDMENT

Pub. L. 111–312, title VII, §757(b), Dec. 17, 2010, 124 Stat. 3322, provided that: "The amendment made by this section [amending this section] shall apply to individuals who begin work for the employer after the date of the enactment of this Act [Dec. 17, 2010]."

Pub. L. 111–147, title I, §101(e), Mar. 18, 2010, 124 Stat. 75, provided that:

"(1) In general.—Except as provided in paragraph (2), the amendments made by this subsection [probably should be "section", amending this section and sections 3111 and 3221 of this title] shall apply to wages paid after the date of the enactment of this Act [Mar. 18, 2010].

"(2) Railroad retirement taxes.—The amendments made by subsection (d) [amending section 3221 of this title] shall apply to compensation paid after the date of the enactment of this Act."

EFFECTIVE DATE OF 2009 AMENDMENT

Pub. L. 111–5, div. B, title I, §1221(b), Feb. 17, 2009, 123 Stat. 338, provided that: "The amendments made by this section [amending this section] shall apply to individuals who begin work for the employer after December 31, 2008."

EFFECTIVE DATE OF 2008 AMENDMENT

Amendment of this section and repeal of Pub. L. 110–234 by Pub. L. 110–246 effective May 22, 2008, the date of enactment of Pub. L. 110–234, except as otherwise provided, see section 4 of Pub. L. 110–246, set out as an Effective Date note under section 8701 of Title 7, Agriculture.

Amendment by section 4002(b)(1)(A), (B), (D), (2)(O) of Pub. L. 110–246 effective Oct. 1, 2008, see section 4407 of Pub. L. 110–246, set out as a note under section 1161 of Title 2, The Congress.

EFFECTIVE DATE OF 2007 AMENDMENT

Pub. L. 110–28, title VIII, §8211(e), May 25, 2007, 121 Stat. 192, provided that: "The amendments made by this section [amending this section] shall apply to individuals who begin work for the employer after the date of the enactment of this Act [May 25, 2007]."

EFFECTIVE DATE OF 2006 AMENDMENT

Pub. L. 109–432, div. A, title I, §105(f), Dec. 20, 2006, 120 Stat. 2938, provided that:

"(1) In general.—Except as provided in paragraph (2), the amendments made by this section [amending this section and section 51A of this title and repealing section 51A of this title] shall apply to individuals who begin work for the employer after December 31, 2005.

"(2) Consolidation.—The amendments made by subsections (b), (c), (d), and (e) [amending this section and repealing section 51A of this title] shall apply to individuals who begin work for the employer after December 31, 2006."

EFFECTIVE DATE OF 2004 AMENDMENT

Amendment by section 207(5) of Pub. L. 108–311 applicable to taxable years beginning after Dec. 31, 2004, see section 208 of Pub. L. 108–311, set out as a note under section 2 of this title.

Pub. L. 108–311, title III, §303(b), Oct. 4, 2004, 118 Stat. 1179, provided that:"The amendments made by this section [amending this section and section 51A of this title] shall apply to individuals who begin work for the employer after December 31, 2003."

EFFECTIVE DATE OF 2002 AMENDMENT

Pub. L. 107–147, title VI, §604(b), Mar. 9, 2002, 116 Stat. 59, provided that: "The amendment made by subsection (a) [amending this section] shall apply to individuals who begin work for the employer after December 31, 2001."

EFFECTIVE DATE OF 2000 AMENDMENT

Pub. L. 106–554, §1(a)(7) [title I, §102(d)], Dec. 21, 2000, 114 Stat. 2763, 2763A–600, provided that: "The amendments made by this section [amending this section] shall apply to individuals who begin work for the employer after December 31, 2001."

Pub. L. 106–554, §1(a)(7) [title III, §316(e)], Dec. 21, 2000, 114 Stat. 2763, 2763A–645, provided that: "The amendments made by this section [amending this section and sections 219, 401 and 1361 of this title] shall take effect as if included in the provisions of the Small Business Job Protection Act of 1996 [Pub. L. 104–188] to which they relate."

EFFECTIVE DATE OF 1999 AMENDMENT

Pub. L. 106–170, title V, §505(c), Dec. 17, 1999, 113 Stat. 1921, provided that: "The amendments made by this section [amending this section and section 51A of this title] shall apply to individuals who begin work for the employer after June 30, 1999."

EFFECTIVE DATE OF 1998 AMENDMENT

Pub. L. 105–277, div. J, title I, §1002(b), Oct. 21, 1998, 112 Stat. 2681–888, provided that: "The amendment made by this section [amending this section] shall apply to individuals who begin work for the employer after June 30, 1998."

EFFECTIVE DATE OF 1997 AMENDMENT

Pub. L. 105–34, title VI, §603(e), Aug. 5, 1997, 111 Stat. 863, provided that: "The amendments made by this section [amending this section] shall apply to individuals who begin work for the employer after September 30, 1997."

Pub. L. 105–33, title V, §5518(c), Aug. 5, 1997, 111 Stat. 621, provided that: "The amendments made by section 5514(a) of this Act [amending this section and sections 3304, 6103, 6334, 6402, and 7523 of this title] shall take effect as if the amendments had been included in section 110 of the Personal Responsibility and Work Opportunity Reconciliation Act of 1996 [Pub. L. 104–193] at the time such section 110 became law."

EFFECTIVE DATE OF 1996 AMENDMENT

Amendment by Pub. L. 104–193 effective July 1, 1997, with transition rules relating to State options to accelerate such date, rules relating to claims, actions, and proceedings commenced before such date, rules relating to closing out of accounts for terminated or substantially modified programs and continuance in office of Assistant Secretary for Family Support, and provisions relating to termination of entitlement under AFDC program, see section 116 of Pub. L. 104–193, as amended, set out as an Effective Date note under section 601 of Title 42, The Public Health and Welfare.

Amendment by Pub. L. 104–188 applicable to individuals who begin work for the employer after Sept. 30, 1996, see section 1201(g) of Pub. L. 104–188, set out as a note under section 38 of this title.

EFFECTIVE DATE OF 1993 AMENDMENT

Pub. L. 103–66, title XIII, §13102(b), Aug. 10, 1993, 107 Stat. 420, provided that: "The amendment made by subsection (a) [amending this section] shall apply to individuals who begin work for the employer after June 30, 1992."

EFFECTIVE DATE OF 1991 AMENDMENT

Pub. L. 102–227, title I, §105(b), Dec. 11, 1991, 105 Stat. 1687, provided that: "The amendment made by this section [amending this section] shall apply to individuals who begin work for the employer after December 31, 1991."

EFFECTIVE DATE OF 1990 AMENDMENT

Pub. L. 101–508, title XI, §11405(c), Nov. 5, 1990, 104 Stat. 1388–473, provided that:

"(1) Credit.—The amendment made by subsection (a) [amending this section] shall apply to individuals who begin work for the employer after September 30, 1990.

"(2) Authorization.—The amendment made by subsection (b) [amending provisions set out below] shall apply to fiscal years beginning after 1990."

EFFECTIVE DATE OF 1989 AMENDMENT

Pub. L. 101–239, title VII, §7103(c)(2), Dec. 19, 1989, 103 Stat. 2305, provided that: "The amendment made by paragraph (1) [amending this section] shall apply to individuals who begin work for the employer after December 31, 1989."

EFFECTIVE DATE OF 1988 AMENDMENT

Amendment by section 1017(a) of Pub. L. 100–647 effective, except as otherwise provided, as if included in the provision of the Tax Reform Act of 1986, Pub. L. 99–514, to which such amendment relates, see section 1019(a) of Pub. L. 100–647, set out as a note under section 1 of this title.

Pub. L. 100–647, title IV, §4010(c)(2), Nov. 10, 1988, 102 Stat. 3655, provided that: "The amendment made by paragraph (1) [amending this section] shall apply to individuals who begin work for the employer after December 31, 1988."

Pub. L. 100–647, title IV, §4010(d)(2), Nov. 10, 1988, 102 Stat. 3655, provided that: "The amendment made by paragraph (1) [amending this section] shall apply to individuals who begin work for the employer after December 31, 1988."

Amendment by Pub. L. 100–485 effective Oct. 1, 1990, with provision for earlier effective dates in case of States making certain changes in their State plans and formally notifying the Secretary of Health and Human Services of their desire to become subject to the amendments made by title II of Pub. L. 100–485 on the earlier effective dates, see section 204 of Pub. L. 100–485, set out as a note under section 671 of Title 42, The Public Health and Welfare.

EFFECTIVE DATE OF 1987 AMENDMENT

Pub. L. 100–203, title X, §10601(b), Dec. 22, 1987, 101 Stat. 1330–451, provided that: "The amendment made by subsection (a) [amending this section] shall apply to amounts paid or incurred on or after January 1, 1987, for services rendered on or after such date."

EFFECTIVE DATE OF 1986 AMENDMENT

Pub. L. 99–514, title XVII, §1701(e), Oct. 22, 1986, 100 Stat. 2772, provided that: "The amendments made by this section [amending this section and provisions set out below] shall apply with respect to individuals who begin work for the employer after December 31, 1985."

Amendment by section 1878(f)(1) of Pub. L. 99–514 effective, except as otherwise provided, as if included in the provisions of the Tax Reform Act of 1984, Pub. L. 98–369, div. A, to which such amendment relates, see section 1881 of Pub. L. 99–514, set out as a note under section 48 of this title.

EFFECTIVE DATE OF 1984 AMENDMENT

Amendment by section 474(p)(1)–(3) of Pub. L. 98–369 applicable to taxable years beginning after Dec. 31, 1983, and to carrybacks from such years, see section 475(a) of Pub. L. 98–369, set out as a note under section 21 of this title.

Amendment by section 712 of Pub. L. 98–369 effective as if included in the provision of the Tax Equity and Fiscal Responsibility Act of 1982, Pub. L. 97–248, to which such amendment relates, see section 715 of Pub. L. 98–369, set out as a note under section 31 of this title.

Pub. L. 98–369, div. A, title X, §1041(c)(5), July 18, 1984, 98 Stat. 1043, as amended by Pub. L. 99–514, §2, title XVIII, §1878(f)(2), Oct. 22, 1986, 100 Stat. 2095, 2904, provided that:

"(A) In general.—Except as provided in subparagraph (B), the amendments made by this section [amending this section] shall apply to individuals who begin work for the employer after the date of the enactment of this Act [July 18, 1984].

"(B) Special rule for employees performing services for other persons.—Paragraph (2) of section 51(k) of the Internal Revenue Code of 1986 [formerly I.R.C. 1954] (as added by this subsection) and the amendment made by paragraph (3) of this subsection [amending this section] shall apply to individuals who begin work for the employer after December 31, 1984."

Pub. L. 98–369, div. B, title VI, §2638(c)(2), July 18, 1984, 98 Stat. 1144, provided that: "The amendments made by subsection (b) [amending this section] shall apply with respect to payments made on or after the date of the enactment of this Act [July 18, 1984]."

Amendment by section 2663 of Pub. L. 98–369 effective July 18, 1984, but not to be construed as changing or affecting any right, liability, status or interpretation which existed (under the provisions of law involved) before that date, see section 2664(b) of Pub. L. 98–369, set out as a note under section 401 of Title 42, The Public Health and Welfare.

EFFECTIVE DATE OF 1983 AMENDMENT

Pub. L. 97–448, title I, §102(l)(4), Jan. 12, 1983, 96 Stat. 2374, provided that the amendment made by that section is effective with respect to certifications made after Jan. 12, 1983, with respect to individuals beginning work for an employer after May 11, 1982.

Amendment by title I of Pub. L. 97–448 effective, except as otherwise provided, as if it had been included in the provision of the Economic Recovery Tax Act of 1981, Pub. L. 97–34, to which such amendment relates, see section 109 of Pub. L. 97–448, set out as a note under section 1 of this title.

EFFECTIVE DATE OF 1982 AMENDMENT

Pub. L. 97–248, title II, §233(f), Sept. 3, 1982, 96 Stat. 502, provided that the amendments made by that section are effective only with respect to individuals who begin work for the taxpayer after May 11, 1982.

Pub. L. 97–248, title II, §233(g), Sept. 3, 1982, 96 Stat. 503, provided that:

"(1) Subsection (b).—The amendments made by subsection (b) [amending this section] shall apply to amounts paid or incurred after April 30, 1983, to individuals beginning work for the employer after such date.

"(2) Subsection (d).—The amendments made by subsection (d) [amending this section] shall apply to amounts paid or incurred after July 1, 1982, to individuals beginning work for the employer after such date."

EFFECTIVE DATE OF 1981 AMENDMENT

Pub. L. 97–34, title II, §261(g), Aug. 13, 1981, 95 Stat. 263, as amended by Pub. L. 97–448, title I, §102(l)(2), Jan. 12, 1983, 96 Stat. 2374; Pub. L. 99–514, §2, Oct. 22, 1986, 100 Stat. 2095, provided that:

"(1) Amendments relating to members of targeted groups.—

"(A) In general.—Except as provided in subparagraphs (B), (C), and (D), the amendments made by subsections (b), (c)(2), and (d) [amending this section and section 50B of this title] shall apply to wages paid or incurred with respect to individuals first beginning work for an employer after the date of the enactment of this Act [Aug. 13, 1981] in taxable years ending after such date.

"(B) Eligible work incentive employees.—The amendments made by subsection (b)(2) [amending this section] to the extent relating to the designation of eligible work incentive employees (within the meaning of section 51(d)(9) [now 51(d)(10)] of the Internal Revenue Code of 1986 [formerly I.R.C. 1954]) as members of a targeted group and subsection (b)(2)(B)(ii) [amending this section] shall apply to taxable years beginning after December 31, 1981. In the case of an eligible work incentive employee, subsections (a) and (b) of section 51 of such Code shall be applied for taxable years beginning after December 31, 1981, as if such employees had been members of a targeted group for taxable years beginning before January 1, 1982.

"(C) Cooperative education program participants.—The amendments made by subsection (b)(4) [amending this section] shall apply to wages paid or incurred after December 31, 1981, in taxable years ending after such date.

"(D) Designated local agency.—The amendments made by subsection (f)(1) [amending this section] shall take effect on the date 60 days after the date of the enactment of this act [Aug. 13, 1981].

"(2) Certifications.—

"(A) In general.—The amendment made by subsection (c)(1) [amending this section] shall apply to all individuals whether such individuals began work for their employer before, on, or after the date of the enactment of this Act [Aug. 13, 1981].

"(B) Special rule for individuals who began work for the employer before 45th day before date of enactment.—In the case of any individual (other than an individual described in section 51(d)(8) of the Internal Revenue Code of 1986) who began work for the employer before the date 45 days before the date of the enactment of this Act [Aug. 13, 1981], paragraph (15) of section 51(d) of the Internal Revenue Code of 1986 (as added by subsection (c)(1)) shall be applied by substituting 'July 23, 1981,' for the day on which such individual begins work for the employer.

"(C) Individuals who begin work for employer within 45 days before or after date of enactment.—In the case of any individual (other than an individual described in section 51(d)(8) of the Internal Revenue Code of 1986) who begins work for the employer during the 90-day period beginning with the date 45 days before the date of the enactment of this Act [Aug. 13, 1981], and in the case of an individual described in section 51(d)(8) of such Code who begins work before the end of such 90-day period, paragraph (15) of section 51(d) of such Code (as added by subsection (c)(1)) shall be applied by substituting 'the last day of the 90-day period beginning with the date 45 days before the date of the enactment of this Act' for the day on which such individual begins work for the employer.

"(3) Limitation on qualified first-year wages.—The amendment made by subsection (e) [amending this section] shall apply to taxable years beginning after December 31, 1981."

Effective Date of 1980 Amendment

Pub. L. 96–222, title I, §103(b)(1), Apr. 1, 1980, 94 Stat. 214, provided that: "The amendment made by subsection (a)(5)(F) [probably means subsec. (a)(6)(F), amending this section] shall apply to wages paid or incurred on or after November 27, 1979, in taxable years ending on or after such date."

Amendment by Pub. L. 96–222 effective, except as otherwise provided, as if it had been included in the provisions of the Revenue Act of 1978, Pub. L. 95–600, to which such amendment relates, see section 201 of Pub. L. 96–222, set out as a note under section 32 of this title.

Effective Date of 1978 Amendment

Pub. L. 95–600, title III, §321(d)(1), Nov. 6, 1978, 92 Stat. 2835, provided that: "Except as otherwise provided in this subsection, the amendments made by this section [amending this section and sections 44B, 52, 53, and 6501 of this title] shall apply to amounts paid or incurred after December 31, 1978, in taxable years ending after such date."

Effective Date

Pub. L. 95–30, title II, §202(e), May 23, 1977, 91 Stat. 151, provided that: "The amendments made by this section [enacting this section and sections 44B, 52, 53, and 280C of this title and amending sections 56, 381, 383, 6096, 6411, 6501, 6511, 6601, and 6611 of this title] shall apply to taxable years beginning after December 31, 1976, and to credit carrybacks from such years."

Returning Heroes and Wounded Warriors Work Opportunity Tax Credits; Treatment of Possessions of United States

Pub. L. 112–56, title II, §261(f), Nov. 21, 2011, 125 Stat. 731, provided that:

"(1) Payments to possessions.—

"(A) Mirror code possessions.—The Secretary of the Treasury shall pay to each possession of the United States with a mirror code tax system amounts equal to the loss to that possession by reason of the amendments made by this section [amending this section and sections 52 and 3111 of this title]. Such amounts shall be determined by the Secretary of the Treasury based on information provided by the government of the respective possession of the United States.

"(B) Other possessions.—The Secretary of the Treasury shall pay to each possession of the United States which does not have a mirror code tax system the amount estimated by the Secretary of the Treasury as being equal to the loss to that possession that would have occurred by reason of the amendments made by this section if a mirror code tax system had been in effect in such possession. The preceding sentence shall not apply with respect to any possession of the United States unless such possession establishes to the satisfaction of the Secretary that the possession has implemented (or, at the discretion of the Secretary, will implement) an income tax benefit which is substantially equivalent to the income tax credit in effect after the amendments made by this section.

"(2) Coordination with credit allowed against united states income taxes.—The credit allowed against United States income taxes for any taxable year under the amendments made by this section to section 51 of the Internal Revenue Code of 1986 [26 U.S.C. 51] to any person with respect to any qualified veteran shall be reduced by the amount of any credit (or other tax benefit described in paragraph (1)(B)) allowed to such person against income taxes imposed by the possession of the United States by reason of this subsection with respect to such qualified veteran for such taxable year.

"(3) Definitions and special rules.—

"(A) Possession of the united states.—For purposes of this subsection, the term 'possession of the United States' includes American Samoa, Guam, the Commonwealth of the Northern Mariana Islands, the Commonwealth of Puerto Rico, and the United States Virgin Islands.

"(B) Mirror code tax system.—For purposes of this subsection, the term 'mirror code tax system' means, with respect to any possession of the United States, the income tax system of such possession if the income tax liability of the residents of such possession under such system is determined by reference to the income tax laws of the United States as if such possession were the United States.

"(C) Treatment of payments.—For purposes of section 1324(b)(2) of title 31, United States Code, the payments under this subsection shall be treated in the same manner as a refund due from credit provisions described in such section."

Reference to Plan for Employment

Pub. L. 105–277, div. J, title IV, §4006(c)(1), Oct. 21, 1998, 112 Stat. 2681–912, provided that: "The reference to 'plan for employment' in such clause [26 U.S.C. 51(d)(6)(B)(i)] shall be treated as including a reference to the rehabilitation plan referred to in such clause as in effect before the amendment made by the preceding sentence."

Authorization of Appropriations

Pub. L. 97–34, title II, §261(f)(2), Aug. 13, 1981, 95 Stat. 263, as amended by Pub. L. 97–248, title II, §233(e), Sept. 3, 1982, 96 Stat. 502; Pub. L. 98–369, div. A, title X, §1041(b), July 18, 1984, 98 Stat. 1042; Pub. L. 99–514, title XVII, §1701(d), Oct. 22, 1986, 100 Stat. 2772; Pub. L. 100–647, title IV, §4010(b), Nov. 10, 1988, 102 Stat. 3655; Pub. L. 101–239, title VII, §7103(b), Dec. 19, 1989, 103 Stat. 2305; Pub. L. 101–508, title XI, §11405(b), Nov. 5, 1990, 104 Stat. 1388–473, provided that: "There is authorized to be appropriated for each fiscal year such sums as may be necessary, to carry out the functions described by the amendments made by paragraph (1) [amending this section], except that, of the amounts appropriated pursuant to this paragraph—

"(A) $5,000,000 shall be used to test whether individuals certified as members of targeted groups under section 51 of such Code are eligible for such certification (including the use of statistical sampling techniques), and

"(B) the remainder shall be distributed under performance standards prescribed by the Secretary of Labor.

The Secretary of Labor shall each calendar year beginning with calendar year 1983 report to the Committee on Ways and Means of the House of Representatives and to the Committee on Finance of the Senate with respect to the results of the testing conducted under subparagraph (A) during the preceding calendar year."

[For termination, effective May 15, 2000, of reporting provisions in section 261(f)(2) of Pub. L. 97–34, set out above, see section 3003 of Pub. L. 104–66, as amended, set out as a note under section 1113 of Title 31, Money and Finance, and page 124 of House Document No. 103–7.]

[Amendment by Pub. L. 101–508 applicable to fiscal years beginning after 1990, see section 11405(c)(2) of Pub. L. 101–508, set out as an Effective Date of 1990 Amendment note above.]

Plan Amendments Not Required Until January 1, 1989

For provisions directing that if any amendments made by subtitle A or subtitle C of title XI [§§1101–1147 and 1171–1177] or title XVIII [§§1800–1899A] of Pub. L. 99–514 require an amendment to any plan, such plan amendment shall not be required to be made before the first plan year beginning on or after Jan. 1, 1989, see section 1140 of Pub. L. 99–514, as amended, set out as a note under section 401 of this title.

Pub. L. 95–600, title III, §321(d)(2), Nov. 6, 1978, 92 Stat. 2835, as amended by Pub. L. 96–222, title I, §103(a)(6)(C), (G)(xi), Apr. 1, 1980, 94 Stat. 209, 211; Pub. L. 99–514, §2, Oct. 22, 1986, 100 Stat. 2095, provided that:

"(A) Individual must be hired after september 26, 1978.—In the case of a member of a newly targeted group, for purposes of applying the amendments made by this section—

"(i) such individual shall be taken into account for purposes of the credit allowable by section 44B of the Internal Revenue Code of 1986 [formerly I.R.C. 1954] only if such individual is first hired by the employer after September 26, 1978, and

"(ii) such individual shall be treated for purposes of such credit as having first begun work for the employer not earlier than January 1, 1979.

"(B) Member of newly targeted group defined.—For purposes of subparagraph (A), an individual is a member of a newly targeted group if—

"(i) such individual meets the requirements of paragraph (1) of section 51(d) of such Code, and

"(ii) in the case of an individual meeting the requirements of subparagraph (A) of such paragraph (1), a credit was not claimed for such individual by the taxpayer for a taxable year beginning before January 1, 1979."

Pub. L. 95–600, title III, §321(d)(3), Nov. 6, 1978, 92 Stat. 2836, as amended by Pub. L. 96–222, title I, §103(a)(6)(D), Apr. 1, 1980, 94 Stat. 209; Pub. L. 99–514, §2, Oct. 22, 1986, 100 Stat. 2095, provided that: "In the case of a taxable year which begins in 1978 and ends after December 31, 1978, the amount of the credit determined under section 51 of the Internal Revenue Code of 1986 [formerly I.R.C. 1954] shall be the sum of—

"(A) the amount of the credit which would be so determined without regard to the amendments made by this section, plus

"(B) the amount of the credit which would be so determined by reason of the amendments made by this section."

¹ See References in Text note below.

[§51A. Repealed. Pub. L. 109–432, div. A, title I, §105(e)(4)(A), Dec. 20, 2006, 120 Stat. 2937]

Section, added Pub. L. 105–34, title VIII, §801(a), Aug. 5, 1997, 111 Stat. 869; amended Pub. L. 105–277, div. J, title I, §1003, Oct. 21, 1998, 112 Stat. 2681–888; Pub. L. 106–170, title V, §505(a), Dec. 17, 1999, 113 Stat. 1921; Pub. L. 107–16, title IV, §411(c), June 7, 2001, 115 Stat. 63; Pub. L. 107–147, title IV, §417(4), title VI, §605(a), Mar. 9, 2002, 116 Stat. 56, 60; Pub. L. 108–311, title III, §303(a)(2), Oct. 4, 2004, 118 Stat. 1179; Pub. L. 109–432, div. A, title I, §105(a), Dec. 20, 2006, 120 Stat. 2936, related to temporary incentives for employing long-term family assistance recipients. See section 51(e) of this title.

Repeal applicable to individuals who begin work for the employer after Dec. 31, 2006, see section 105(f)(2) of Pub. L. 109–432, set out as an Effective Date of 2006 Amendment note under section 51 of this title.

§52. Special rules

(a) Controlled group of corporations

For purposes of this subpart, all employees of all corporations which are members of the same controlled group of corporations shall be treated as employed by a single employer. In any such case, the credit (if any) determined under section 51(a) with respect to each such member shall be its proportionate share of the wages giving rise to such credit. For purposes of this subsection, the term "controlled group of corporations" has the meaning given to such term by section 1563(a), except that—

(1) "more than 50 percent" shall be substituted for "at least 80 percent" each place it appears in section 1563(a)(1), and

(2) the determination shall be made without regard to subsections (a)(4) and (e)(3)(C) of section 1563.

(b) Employees of partnerships, proprietorships, etc., which are under common control

For purposes of this subpart, under regulations prescribed by the Secretary—

(1) all employees of trades or business (whether or not incorporated) which are under common control shall be treated as employed by a single employer, and

(2) the credit (if any) determined under section 51(a) with respect to each trade or business shall be its proportionate share of the wages giving rise to such credit.

The regulations prescribed under this subsection shall be based on principles similar to the principles which apply in the case of subsection (a).

(c) Tax-exempt organizations

(1) In general

No credit shall be allowed under section 38 for any work opportunity credit determined under this subpart to any organization (other than a cooperative described in section 521) which is exempt from income tax under this chapter.

(2) Credit made available to qualified tax-exempt organizations employing qualified veterans

For credit against payroll taxes for employment of qualified veterans by qualified tax-exempt organizations, see section 3111(e).

(d) Estates and trusts

In the case of an estate or trust—

(1) the amount of the credit determined under this subpart for any taxable year shall be apportioned between the estate or trust and the beneficiaries on the basis of the income of the estate or trust allocable to each, and

(2) any beneficiary to whom any amount has been apportioned under paragraph (1) shall be allowed, subject to section 38(c), a credit under section 38(a) for such amount.

(e) Limitations with respect to certain persons

Under regulations prescribed by the Secretary, in the case of—

(1) a regulated investment company or a real estate investment trust subject to taxation under subchapter M (section 851 and following), and

(2) a cooperative organization described in section 1381(a),

rules similar to the rules provided in subsections (e) and (h) of section 46 (as in effect on the day before the date of the enactment of the Revenue Reconciliation Act of 1990) shall apply in determining the amount of the credit under this subpart.

(Added Pub. L. 95–30, title II, §202(b), May 23, 1977, 91 Stat. 143; amended Pub. L. 95–600, title III, §321(c)(1), Nov. 6, 1978, 92 Stat. 2835; Pub. L. 96–222, title I, §103(a)(5), Apr. 1, 1980, 94 Stat. 209; Pub. L. 97–354, §5(a)(11), Oct. 19, 1982, 96 Stat. 1693; Pub. L. 98–369, div. A, title IV, §474(p)(4)–(7), July 18, 1984, 98 Stat. 838; Pub. L. 101–508, title XI, §11813(b)(4), Nov. 5, 1990, 104 Stat. 1388–551; Pub. L. 104–188, title I, §1616(b)(2), Aug. 20, 1996, 110 Stat. 1856; Pub. L. 105–34, title XVI, §1601(b), Aug. 5, 1997, 111 Stat. 1087; Pub. L. 112–56, title II, §261(e)(1), Nov. 21, 2011, 125 Stat. 730.)

The date of the enactment of the Revenue Reconciliation Act of 1990, referred to in subsec. (e), is the date of enactment of Pub. L. 101–508, which was approved Nov. 5, 1990.

AMENDMENTS

2011—Subsec. (c). Pub. L. 112–56 designated existing provisions as par. (1), inserted heading, and added par. (2).

1997—Subsec. (c). Pub. L. 105–34 substituted "work opportunity credit" for "targeted jobs credit".

1996—Subsec. (e)(1) to (3). Pub. L. 104–188 redesignated pars. (2) and (3) as (1) and (2), respectively, and struck out former par. (1) which read as follows: "an organization to which section 593 (relating to reserves for losses on loans) applies,".

1990—Subsec. (e). Pub. L. 101–508 substituted "section 46 (as in effect on the day before the date of the enactment of the Revenue Reconciliation Act of 1990)" for "section 46" in concluding provisions.

1984—Subsec. (a). Pub. L. 98–369, §474(p)(4), substituted "the credit (if any) determined under section 51(a) with respect to each such member" for "the credit (if any) allowable by section 44B to each such member".

Subsec. (b)(2). Pub. L. 98–369, §474(p)(5), substituted "the credit (if any) determined under section 51(a)" for "the credit (if any) allowable by section 44B".

Subsec. (c). Pub. L. 98–369, §474(p)(6), substituted "credit shall be allowed under section 38 for any targeted jobs credit determined under this subpart" for "credit shall be allowed under section 44B".

Subsec. (d)(2). Pub. L. 98–369, §474(p)(7), substituted ", subject to section 38(c), a credit under section 38(a)" for ", subject to section 53 a credit under section 44B".

1982—Subsecs. (d) to (f). Pub. L. 97–354 struck out subsec. (d) relating to apportionment of credit among shareholders, and redesignated subsecs. (e) and (f) as (d) and (e), respectively.

1980—Subsec. (f). Pub. L. 96–222 substituted "subsections (e) and (h) of section 46" for "section 46(e)".

1978—Subsecs. (a), (b). Pub. L. 95–600, §321(c)(1)(B), substituted "proportionate share of the wages" for "proportionate contribution to the increase in unemployment insurance wages".

Subsecs. (c), (d). Pub. L. 95–600, §321(c)(1)(A), struck out subsec. (c) which related to dispositions by an employer, and redesignated subsecs. (d) and (f) as (c) and (d), respectively.

Subsec. (e). Pub. L. 95–600, §321(c)(1)(A), (C), redesignated subsec. (g) as (e) and struck out par. (3) which provided that the $100,000 amount specified in section 51(d) applicable to such estate or trust be reduced to an amount which bears the same ratio to $100,000 as the portion of the credit allocable to the estate or trust under paragraph (1) bears to the entire amount of such credit. Former subsec. (e), which related to a change in status from self-employed to employee, was struck out.

Subsecs. (f) to (h). Pub. L. 95–600, §321(c)(1)(A), redesignated subsecs. (f) to (h) as (d) to (f), respectively.

Subsec. (i). Pub. L. 95–600, §321(c)(1)(A)(i), struck out subsec. (i) which related to a $50,000 limitation in the case of married individuals filing separate returns.

Subsec. (j). Pub. L. 95–600, §321(c)(1)(A)(i), struck out subsec. (j) which related to certain short taxable years.

STATUTORY NOTES AND RELATED SUBSIDIARIES

EFFECTIVE DATE OF 2011 AMENDMENT

Amendment by Pub. L. 112–56 applicable to individuals who begin work for the employer after Nov. 21, 2011, see section 261(g) of Pub. L. 112–56, set out as a note under section 51 of this title.

EFFECTIVE DATE OF 1997 AMENDMENT

Amendment by Pub. L. 105–34 effective as if included in the provisions of the Small Business Job Protection Act of 1996, Pub. L. 104–188, to which it relates, see section 1601(j) of Pub. L. 105–34, set out as a note under section 23 of this title.

EFFECTIVE DATE OF 1996 AMENDMENT

Amendment by Pub. L. 104–188 applicable to taxable years beginning after Dec. 31, 1995, see section 1616(c) of Pub. L. 104–188, set out as a note under section 593 of this title.

EFFECTIVE DATE OF 1990 AMENDMENT

Amendment by Pub. L. 101–508 applicable to property placed in service after Dec. 31, 1990, but not applicable to any transition property (as defined in section 49(e) of this title), any property with respect to which qualified progress expenditures were previously taken into account under section 46(d) of this title, and any property described in section 46(b)(2)(C) of this title, as such sections were in effect on Nov. 4, 1990, see section 11813(c) of Pub. L. 101–508, set out as a note under section 45K of this title.

EFFECTIVE DATE OF 1984 AMENDMENT

Amendment by Pub. L. 98–369 applicable to taxable years beginning after Dec. 31, 1983, and to carrybacks from such years, see section 475(a) of Pub. L. 98–369, set out as a note under section 21 of this title.

EFFECTIVE DATE OF 1982 AMENDMENT

Amendment by Pub. L. 97–354 applicable to taxable years beginning after Dec. 31, 1982, see section 6(a) of Pub. L. 97–354, set out as an Effective Date note under section 1361 of this title.

EFFECTIVE DATE OF 1980 AMENDMENT

Amendment by Pub. L. 96–222 effective, except as otherwise provided, as if it had been included in the provisions of the Revenue Act of 1978, Pub. L. 95–600, to which such amendment relates, see section 201 of Pub. L. 96–222, set out as a note under section 32 of this title.

EFFECTIVE DATE OF 1978 AMENDMENT

Amendment by Pub. L. 95–600 applicable to amounts paid or incurred after Dec. 31, 1978, in taxable years ending after such date, see section 321(d)(1) of Pub. L. 95–600, set out as a note under section 51 of this title.

EFFECTIVE DATE

Section applicable to taxable years beginning after Dec. 31, 1976, and to credit carrybacks from such years, see section 202(e) of Pub. L. 95–30, set out as a note under section 51 of this title.

SAVINGS PROVISION

For provisions that nothing in amendment by Pub. L. 101–508 be construed to affect treatment of certain transactions occurring, property acquired, or items of income, loss, deduction, or credit taken into account prior to Nov. 5, 1990, for purposes of determining liability for tax for periods ending after Nov. 5, 1990, see section 11821(b) of Pub. L. 101–508, set out as a note under section 45K of this title.

Subpart G—Credit Against Regular Tax for Prior Year Minimum Tax Liability

§53. Credit for prior year minimum tax liability

(a) Allowance of credit

There shall be allowed as a credit against the tax imposed by this chapter for any taxable year an amount equal to the minimum tax credit for such taxable year.

(b) Minimum tax credit

For purposes of subsection (a), the minimum tax credit for any taxable year is the excess (if any) of—

(1) the adjusted net minimum tax imposed for all prior taxable years beginning after 1986, over

(2) the amount allowable as a credit under subsection (a) for such prior taxable years.

(c) Limitation

The credit allowable under subsection (a) for any taxable year shall not exceed the excess (if any) of—

(1) the regular tax liability of the taxpayer for such taxable year reduced by the sum of the credits allowable under subparts A, B, D, E, and F of this part, over

(2) the tentative minimum tax for the taxable year.

(d) Definitions

For purposes of this section—

(1) Net minimum tax

(A) In general

The term "net minimum tax" means the tax imposed by section 55.

(B) Credit not allowed for exclusion preferences

(i) Adjusted net minimum tax

The adjusted net minimum tax for any taxable year is—

(I) the amount of the net minimum tax for such taxable year, reduced by

(II) the amount which would be the net minimum tax for such taxable year if the only adjustments and items of tax preference taken into account were those specified in clause (ii).

(ii) Specified items

The following are specified in this clause—

(I) the adjustments provided for in subsection (b)(1) of section 56, and

(II) the items of tax preference described in paragraphs (1), (5), and (7) of section 57(a).

(iii) Credit allowable for exclusion preferences of corporations

In the case of a corporation—

(I) the preceding provisions of this subparagraph shall not apply, and

(II) the adjusted net minimum tax for any taxable year is the amount of the net minimum tax for such year.

(2) Tentative minimum tax

The term "tentative minimum tax" has the meaning given to such term by section 55(b), except that in the case of a corporation, the tentative minimum tax shall be treated as zero.

(3) AMT term references

In the case of a corporation, any references in this subsection to section 55, 56, or 57 shall be treated as a reference to such section as in effect before the amendments made by Tax Cuts and Jobs Act.[1]

(e) Portion of credit treated as refundable

(1) In general

In the case of any taxable year of a corporation beginning in 2018 or 2019, the limitation under subsection (c) shall be increased by the AMT refundable credit amount for such year.

(2) AMT refundable credit amount

For purposes of paragraph (1), the AMT refundable credit amount is an amount equal to 50 percent (100 percent in the case of a taxable year beginning in 2019) of the excess (if any) of—

(A) the minimum tax credit determined under subsection (b) for the taxable year, over

(B) the minimum tax credit allowed under subsection (a) for such year (before the application of this subsection for such year).

(3) Credit refundable

For purposes of this title (other than this section), the credit allowed by reason of this subsection shall be treated as a credit allowed under subpart C (and not this subpart).

(4) Short taxable years

In the case of any taxable year of less than 365 days, the AMT refundable credit amount determined under paragraph (2) with respect to such taxable year shall be the amount which bears the same ratio to such amount determined without regard to this paragraph as the number of days in such taxable year bears to 365.

(5) Special rule

In the case of a corporation making an election under this paragraph—

(A) paragraph (1) shall not apply, and

(B) subsection (c) shall not apply to the first taxable year of such corporation beginning in 2018.

(Added Pub. L. 99–514, title VII, §701(b), Oct. 22, 1986, 100 Stat. 2339; amended Pub. L. 100–647, title I, §1007(g)(4), title VI, §6304(a), Nov. 10, 1988, 102 Stat. 3435, 3756; Pub. L. 101–239, title VII, §§7612(a)(1), (2), (b)(1), 7811(d)(2), Dec. 19, 1989, 103 Stat. 2373, 2374, 2408; Pub. L. 102–486, title XIX, §1913(b)(2)(C), Oct. 24, 1992, 106 Stat. 3020; Pub. L. 103–66, title XIII, §§13113(b)(2), 13171(c), Aug. 10, 1993, 107 Stat. 429, 455; Pub. L. 104–188, title I, §§1205(d)(5), 1704(j)(1), Aug. 20, 1996, 110 Stat. 1776, 1881; Pub. L. 108–357, title IV, §421(a)(2), Oct. 22, 2004, 118 Stat. 1514; Pub. L. 109–58, title XIII, §1322(a)(3)(G), Aug. 8, 2005, 119 Stat. 1012; Pub. L. 109–432, div. A, title IV, §402(a), Dec. 20, 2006, 120 Stat. 2953; Pub. L. 110–172, §2(a), Dec. 29, 2007, 121 Stat. 2473; Pub. L. 110–343, div. C, title I, §103(a), (b), Oct. 3, 2008, 122 Stat. 3863; Pub. L. 111–5, div. B, title I, §1142(b)(4), Feb. 17, 2009, 123 Stat. 331; Pub. L. 113–295, div. A, title II, §221(a)(8)(A)(i), Dec. 19, 2014, 128 Stat. 4038; Pub. L. 115–97, title I, §§12001(b)(2), 12002(a), (b), Dec. 22, 2017, 131 Stat. 2092, 2094; Pub. L. 116–136, div. A, title II, §2305(a), (b), Mar. 27, 2020, 134 Stat. 357.)

EDITORIAL NOTES
REFERENCES IN TEXT

The Tax Cuts and Jobs Act, referred to in subsec. (d)(3), probably means title I of Pub. L. 115–97, Dec. 22, 2017, 131 Stat. 2054. Prior versions of the bill that was enacted into law as Pub. L. 115–97 included such Short Title, but it was not enacted as part of title I of Pub. L. 115–97. For complete classification of title I of Pub. L. 115–97 to the Code, see Tables.

PRIOR PROVISIONS

A prior section 53, added Pub. L. 95–30, title II, §202(b), May 23, 1977, 91 Stat. 146; amended Pub. L. 95–600, title III, §321(c)(2), Nov. 6, 1978, 92 Stat. 2835; Pub. L. 97–34, title II, §207(c)(2), Aug. 13, 1981, 95 Stat. 225; Pub. L. 97–248, title II, §201(d)(8)(A), formerly §201(c)(8)(A), and §265(b)(2)(A)(iii), Sept. 3, 1982, 96 Stat. 420, 547, renumbered §201(d)(8)(A), Pub. L. 97–448, title III, §306(a)(1)(A)(i), Jan. 12, 1983, 96 Stat. 2400; 97–354, §5(a)(12), Oct. 19, 1982, 96 Stat. 1693; 97–448, title I, §102(d)(3), Jan. 12, 1983, 96 Stat. 2370; Pub. L. 98–21, title I, §122(c)(1), Apr. 20, 1983, 97 Stat. 87; Pub. L. 98–369, div. A, title VII, §713(c)(1)(C), July 18, 1984, 98 Stat. 957, placed limitations on the amount of credit allowed by former section 44B for employment of certain new employees, prior to repeal by Pub. L. 98–369, div. A, title IV, §474(p)(8), July 18, 1984, 98 Stat. 838, applicable to taxable years beginning after Dec. 31, 1983, and to carrybacks from such years.

Amendments

2020—Subsec. (e)(1). Pub. L. 116–136, §2305(a)(1), substituted "2018 or 2019" for "2018, 2019, 2020, or 2021".

Subsec. (e)(2). Pub. L. 116–136, §2305(a)(2), substituted "2019" for "2021" in introductory provisions.

Subsec. (e)(5). Pub. L. 116–136, §2305(b)(1), added par. (5).

2017—Subsec. (d)(2). Pub. L. 115–97, §12001(b)(2), inserted ", except that in the case of a corporation, the tentative minimum tax shall be treated as zero" before period at end.

Subsec. (d)(3). Pub. L. 115–97, §12002(b), added par. (3).

Subsec. (e). Pub. L. 115–97, §12002(a), added subsec. (e).

2014—Subsecs. (e), (f). Pub. L. 113–295 struck out subsecs. (e) and (f) which related to special rule for individuals with long-term unused credits and treatment of certain underpayments, interest, and penalties attributable to the treatment of incentive stock options, respectively.

2009—Subsec. (d)(1)(B)(iii). Pub. L. 111–5, §1142(b)(4)(A), redesignated cl. (iv) as (iii) and struck out former cl. (iii). Prior to amendment, text read as follows: "The adjusted net minimum tax for the taxable year shall be increased by the amount of the credit not allowed under section 30 solely by reason of the application of section 30(b)(3)(B)."

Subsec. (d)(1)(B)(iii)(II). Pub. L. 111–5, §1142(b)(4)(B), struck out "increased in the manner provided in clause (iii)" before period.

Subsec. (d)(1)(B)(iv). Pub. L. 111–5, §1142(b)(4)(A), redesignated cl. (iv) as (iii).

2008—Subsec. (e)(2). Pub. L. 110–343, §103(a), reenacted heading without change and amended text generally. Prior to amendment, par. (2) defined "AMT refundable credit amount" and provided for phaseout of AMT refundable credit amount based on adjusted gross income.

Subsec. (f). Pub. L. 110–343, §103(b), added subsec. (f).

2007—Subsec. (e)(2)(A). Pub. L. 110–172 reenacted heading without change and amended text generally. Prior to amendment, text read as follows: "The term 'AMT refundable credit amount' means, with respect to any taxable year, the amount equal to the greater of—

      "(i) the lesser of—

          "(I) $5,000, or

          "(II) the amount of long-term unused minimum tax credit for such taxable year, or

      "(ii) 20 percent of the amount of such credit."

2006—Subsec. (e). Pub. L. 109–432 added subsec. (e).

2005—Subsec. (d)(1)(B)(iii). Pub. L. 109–58 struck out "under section 29 (relating to credit for producing fuel from a nonconventional source) solely by reason of the application of section 29(b)(6)(B), or not allowed" before "under section 30".

2004—Subsec. (d)(1)(B)(i)(II). Pub. L. 108–357 struck out "and if section 59(a)(2) did not apply" before period at end.

1996—Subsec. (d)(1)(B)(iii). Pub. L. 104–188, §1205(d)(5)(A), which directed that cl. (iii) be amended by striking out "or not allowed under section 28 solely by reason of the application of section 28(d)(2)(B)," was executed by striking out "not allowed under section 28 solely by reason of the application of section 28(d)(2)(B)," after "29(b)(6)(B),", to reflect the probable intent of Congress.

Subsec. (d)(1)(B)(iv)(II). Pub. L. 104–188, §1704(j)(1), amended subcl. (II) generally. Prior to amendment, subcl. (II) read as follows: "the adjusted net minimum tax for any taxable year is the amount of the net minimum tax for such year increased by the amount of any credit not allowed under section 29 solely by reason of the application of section 29(b)(5)(B) or not allowed under section 28 solely by reason of the application of section 28(d)(2)(B)."

Pub. L. 104–188, §1205(d)(5)(B), which directed that subcl. (II) be amended by striking out "or not allowed under section 28 solely by reason of the application of section 28(d)(2)(B)", could not be executed because the phrase sought to be struck out did not appear in text subsequent to the general amendment of subcl. (II) by Pub. L. 104–188, §1704(j)(1), see above, which, pursuant to section 1701 of Pub. L. 104–188, set out as a note under section 1 of this title, is treated as having been enacted before section 1205(d)(5)(B) of Pub. L. 104–188.

1993—Subsec. (d)(1)(B)(ii)(II). Pub. L. 103–66, §13171(c), substituted "(5), and (7)" for "(5), (6), and (8)".

Pub. L. 103–66, §13113(b)(2), substituted "(6), and (8)" for "and (6)".

1992—Subsec. (d)(1)(B)(iii). Pub. L. 102–486, §1913(b)(2)(C)(i), substituted "section 29(b)(6)(B)," for "section 29(b)(5)(B) or".

Pub. L. 102–486, §1913(b)(2)(C)(ii), inserted before period at end ", or not allowed under section 30 solely by reason of the application of section 30(b)(3)(B)".

1989—Subsec. (d)(1)(B)(i)(II). Pub. L. 101–239, §7811(d)(2), inserted before period at end "and if section 59(a)(2) did not apply".

Subsec. (d)(1)(B)(ii). Pub. L. 101–239, §7612(a)(2), substituted "subsection (b)(1)" for "subsections (b)(1) and (c)(3)" in subcl. (I) and struck out at end "In the case of taxable years beginning after 1989, the adjustments provided in section 56(g) shall be treated as specified in this clause to the extent attributable to items which are excluded from gross income for any taxable year for purposes of the regular tax, or are not deductible for any taxable year under the adjusted current earnings method of section 56(g)."

Subsec. (d)(1)(B)(iii). Pub. L. 101–239, §7612(b)(1), which directed amendment of cl. (iii) by inserting "or not allowed under section 28 solely by reason of the application of section 28(d)(2)(B)" after "section 29(d)(5)(B)", was executed by making the insertion after "section 29(b)(5)(B)", as the probable intent of Congress.

Subsec. (d)(1)(B)(iv). Pub. L. 101–239, §7612(b)(1), which directed amendment of cl. (iv) by inserting "or not allowed under section 28 solely by reason of the application of section 28(d)(2)(B)" after "section 29(d)(5)(B)", was executed by making the insertion after "section 29(b)(5)(B)" in subcl. (II), as the probable intent of Congress.

Pub. L. 101–239, §7612(a)(1), added cl. (iv).

1988—Subsec. (d)(1)(B)(ii). Pub. L. 100–647, §1007(g)(4), substituted "current earnings" for "earnings and profits" in last sentence.

Subsec. (d)(1)(B)(iii). Pub. L. 100–647, §6304(a), added cl. (iii).

Statutory Notes and Related Subsidiaries

Effective Date of 2020 Amendment

Pub. L. 116–136, div. A, title II, §2305(c), Mar. 27, 2020, 134 Stat. 357, provided that: "The amendments made by this section [amending this section] shall apply to taxable years beginning after December 31, 2017."

Effective Date of 2017 Amendment

Amendment by section 12001(b)(2) of Pub. L. 115–97 applicable to taxable years beginning after Dec. 31, 2017, see section 12001(c) of Pub. L. 115–97, set out as a note under section 11 of this title.

Pub. L. 115–97, title I, §12002(d), Dec. 22, 2017, 131 Stat. 2095, provided that:

"(1) In general.—The amendments made by this section [amending this section and section 1374 of this title] shall apply to taxable years beginning after December 31, 2017.

"(2) Conforming amendment.—The amendment made by subsection (c) [amending section 1374 of this title] shall apply to taxable years beginning after December 31, 2021."

EFFECTIVE DATE OF 2014 AMENDMENT

Amendment by Pub. L. 113–295 effective Dec. 19, 2014, subject to a savings provision, see section 221(b) of Pub. L. 113–295, set out as a note under section 1 of this title.

EFFECTIVE DATE OF 2009 AMENDMENT

Amendment by Pub. L. 111–5 applicable to vehicles acquired after Feb. 17, 2009, see section 1142(c) of Pub. L. 111–5, set out as an Effective and Termination Dates of 2009 Amendment note under section 24 of this title.

EFFECTIVE DATE OF 2008 AMENDMENT

Pub. L. 110–343, div. C, title I, §103(c), Oct. 3, 2008, 122 Stat. 3864, provided that:

"(1) In general.—Except as provided in paragraph (2), the amendments made by this section [amending this section] shall apply to taxable years beginning after December 31, 2007.

"(2) Abatement.—Section 53(f)(1), as added by subsection (b), shall take effect on the date of the enactment of this Act [Oct. 3, 2008]."

EFFECTIVE DATE OF 2007 AMENDMENT

Pub. L. 110–172, §2(b), Dec. 29, 2007, 121 Stat. 2474, provided that: "The amendment made by this section [amending this section] shall take effect as if included in the provision of the Tax Relief and Health Care Act of 2006 [Pub. L. 109–432] to which it relates."

EFFECTIVE DATE OF 2006 AMENDMENT

Pub. L. 109–432, div. A, title IV, §402(c), Dec. 20, 2006, 120 Stat. 2954, provided that: "The amendments made by this section [amending this section, section 6211 of this title, and section 1324 of Title 31, Money and Finance] shall apply to taxable years beginning after the date of the enactment of this Act [Dec. 20, 2006]."

EFFECTIVE DATE OF 2005 AMENDMENT

Amendment by Pub. L. 109–58 applicable to credits determined under the Internal Revenue Code of 1986 for taxable years ending after Dec. 31, 2005, see section 1322(c)(1) of Pub. L. 109–58, set out as a note under section 45K of this title.

EFFECTIVE DATE OF 2004 AMENDMENT

Pub. L. 108–357, title IV, §421(b), Oct. 22, 2004, 118 Stat. 1514, provided that: "The amendments made by this section [amending this section and section 59 of this title] shall apply to taxable years beginning after December 31, 2004."

EFFECTIVE DATE OF 1996 AMENDMENT

Amendment by section 1205(d)(5) of Pub. L. 104–188 applicable to amounts paid or incurred in taxable years ending after June 30, 1996, see section 1205(e) of Pub. L. 104–188, set out as a note under section 45K of this title.

Pub. L. 104–188, title I, §1704(j)(1), Aug. 20, 1996, 110 Stat. 1881, provided that the amendment made by that section is effective with respect to taxable years beginning after Dec. 31, 1990.

EFFECTIVE DATE OF 1993 AMENDMENT

Pub. L. 103–66, title XIII, §13113(e), Aug. 10, 1993, 107 Stat. 430, provided that: "The amendments made by this section [enacting section 1202 of this title and amending this section and sections 57, 172, 642, 643, 691, 871, and 6652 of this title] shall apply to stock issued after the date of the enactment of this Act [Aug. 10, 1993]."

Pub. L. 103–66, title XIII, §13171(d), Aug. 10, 1993, 107 Stat. 455, provided that: "The amendments made by this section [amending this section and sections 56 and 57 of this title] shall apply to contributions made after June 30, 1992, except that in the case of any contribution of capital gain property which is not tangible personal property, such amendments shall apply only if the contribution is made after December 31, 1992."

EFFECTIVE DATE OF 1992 AMENDMENT

Pub. L. 104–188, title I, §1702(e)(5), Aug. 20, 1996, 110 Stat. 1870, provided that: "The amendment made by section 1913(b)(2)(C)(i) of the Energy Policy Act of 1992 [Pub. L. 102–486] shall apply to taxable years beginning after December 31, 1990."

Pub. L. 102–486, title XIX, §1913(c), Oct. 24, 1992, 106 Stat. 3020, provided that: "The amendments made by this section [enacting sections 30 and 179A of this title and amending this section and sections 55, 62, and 1016 of this title] shall apply to property placed in service after June 30, 1993."

EFFECTIVE DATE OF 1989 AMENDMENT

Pub. L. 101–239, title VII, §7612(a)(3), Dec. 19, 1989, 103 Stat. 2373, provided that: "The amendments made by this subsection [amending this section] shall apply for purposes of determining the adjusted net minimum tax for taxable years beginning after December 31, 1989."

Pub. L. 101–239, title VII, §7612(b)(2), Dec. 19, 1989, 103 Stat. 2374, provided that: "The amendment made by paragraph (1) [amending this section] shall apply for purposes of determining the amount of the minimum tax credit for taxable years beginning after December 31, 1989; except that, for such purposes, section 53(b)(1) of the Internal Revenue Code of 1986 shall be applied as if such amendment had been in effect for all prior taxable years."

Amendment by section 7811(d)(2) of Pub. L. 101–239 effective, except as otherwise provided, as if included in the provision of the Technical and Miscellaneous Revenue Act of 1988, Pub. L. 100–647, to which such amendment relates, see section 7817 of Pub. L. 101–239, set out as a note under section 1 of this title.

EFFECTIVE DATE OF 1988 AMENDMENT

Amendment by section 1007(g)(4) of Pub. L. 100–647 effective, except as otherwise provided, as if included in the provision of the Tax Reform Act of 1986, Pub. L. 99–514, to which such amendment relates, see section 1019(a) of Pub. L. 100–647, set out as a note under section 1 of this title.

Pub. L. 100–647, title VI, §6304(b), Nov. 10, 1988, 102 Stat. 3756, provided that: "The amendment made by this section [amending this section] shall take effect as if included in the amendments made by section 701 of the Tax Reform Act of 1986 [Pub. L. 99–514]."

EFFECTIVE DATE

Section applicable to taxable years beginning after Dec. 31, 1986, with certain exceptions and qualifications, see section 701(f) of Pub. L. 99–514, set out as an Effective Date of 1986 Amendment note under section 55 of this title.

APPLICABILITY OF CERTAIN AMENDMENTS BY PUB. L. 99–514 IN RELATION TO TREATY OBLIGATIONS OF UNITED STATES

For applicability of amendment by section 701(b) of Pub. L. 99–514 [enacting this section] notwithstanding any treaty obligation of the United States in effect on Oct. 22, 1986, with provision that for such purposes any amendment by title I of Pub. L. 100–647 be treated as if it had been included in the provision of Pub. L. 99–514 to which such amendment relates, see section 1012(aa)(2), (4) of Pub. L. 100–647, set out as a note under section 861 of this title.

CONSTRUCTION

Pub. L. 113–295, div. A, title II, §221(a)(8)(A)(ii), Dec. 19, 2014, 128 Stat. 4038, provided that: "The amendment made by clause (i) striking subsection (f) of section 53 of the Internal Revenue Code of 1986 shall not be construed to allow any tax abated by reason of section 53(f)(1) of such Code (as in effect before such amendment) to be included in the amount determined under section 53(b)(1) of such Code."

SPECIAL RULE

Pub. L. 116–136, div. A, title II, §2305(d), Mar. 27, 2020, 134 Stat. 357, provided that:

"(1) In general.—For purposes of the Internal Revenue Code of 1986, a credit or refund for which an application described in paragraph (2)(A) is filed shall be treated as made under section 6411 of such Code.

"(2) Tentative refund.—

"(A) Application.—A taxpayer may file an application for a tentative refund of any amount for which a refund is due by reason of an election under section 53(e)(5) of the Internal Revenue Code of 1986. Such application shall be in such manner and form as the Secretary of the Treasury (or the Secretary's delegate) may prescribe and shall—

"(i) be verified in the same manner as an application under section 6411(a) of such Code,

"(ii) be filed prior to December 31, 2020, and

"(iii) set forth—

"(I) the amount of the refundable credit claimed under section 53(e) of such Code for such taxable year,

"(II) the amount of the refundable credit claimed under such section for any previously filed return for such taxable year, and

"(III) the amount of the refund claimed.

"(B) Allowance of adjustments.—Within a period of 90 days from the date on which an application is filed under subparagraph (A), the Secretary of the Treasury (or the Secretary's delegate) shall—

"(i) review the application,

"(ii) determine the amount of the overpayment, and

"(iii) apply, credit, or refund such overpayment,

in a manner similar to the manner provided in section 6411(b) of the Internal Revenue Code of 1986.

"(C) Consolidated returns.—The provisions of section 6411(c) of the Internal Revenue Code of 1986 Code shall apply to an adjustment under this paragraph to the same extent and manner as the Secretary of the Treasury (or the Secretary's delegate) may provide."

¹ *So in original. Probably should be "the Tax Cuts and Jobs Act."*

[Subpart H—Repealed]

[§54. Repealed. Pub. L. 115–97, title I, §13404(a), Dec. 22, 2017, 131 Stat. 2138]

Section, added Pub. L. 109–58, title XIII, §1303(a), Aug. 8, 2005, 119 Stat. 992; amended Pub. L. 109–135, title I, §101(b)(1), title IV, §402(c)(1), Dec. 21, 2005, 119 Stat. 2593, 2610; Pub. L. 109–222, title V, §508(d)(3), May 17, 2006, 120 Stat. 362; Pub. L. 109–432, div. A, title I, §107(b)(2), title II, §202(a), Dec. 20, 2006, 120 Stat. 2939, 2944; Pub. L. 110–234, title XV, §15316(c)(1), May 22, 2008, 122 Stat. 1511; Pub. L. 110–246, §4(a), title XV, §15316(c)(1), June 18, 2008, 122 Stat. 1664, 2273; Pub. L. 110–343, div. B, title I, §107(c), Oct. 3, 2008, 122 Stat. 3819; Pub. L. 111–5, div. B, title I, §§1531(c)(3), 1541(b)(1), Feb. 17, 2009, 123 Stat. 360, 362; Pub. L. 115–97, title I, §13404(c)(2), Dec. 22, 2017, 131 Stat. 2138, related to credit to holders of clean renewable energy bonds.

STATUTORY NOTES AND RELATED SUBSIDIARIES
EFFECTIVE DATE OF REPEAL

Pub. L. 115–97, title I, §13404(d), Dec. 22, 2017, 131 Stat. 2138, provided that: "The amendments made by this section [amending this section and sections 6211 and 6401 of this title and repealing this section and sections 54A to 54F, 54AA, 1397E, and 6431 of this title] shall apply to bonds issued after December 31, 2017."

REGULATIONS

Pub. L. 109–58, title XIII, §1303(d), Aug. 8, 2005, 119 Stat. 997, provided that the Secretary of the Treasury was to issue regulations required under former 26 U.S.C. 54 not later than 120 days after Aug. 8, 2005.

[Subpart I—Repealed]

[§§54A to 54F. Repealed. Pub. L. 115–97, title I, §13404(a), Dec. 22, 2017, 131 Stat. 2138]

Section 54A, added Pub. L. 110–234, title XV, §15316(a), May 22, 2008, 122 Stat. 1505, and Pub. L. 110–246, §4(a), title XV, §15316(a), June 18, 2008, 122 Stat. 1664, 2267; amended Pub. L. 110–343, div. B, title I, §107(b)(1), (2), title III, §301(b)(1), (2), div. C, title III, §313(b)(1), (2), Oct. 3, 2008, 122 Stat. 3818, 3819, 3843, 3844, 3872; Pub. L. 111–5, div. B, title I, §§1521(b)(1), (2), 1531(c)(2), 1541(b)(2), Feb. 17, 2009, 123 Stat. 357, 360, 362; Pub. L. 113–295, div. A, title II, §220(e), Dec. 19, 2014, 128 Stat. 4036, related to credit to holders of qualified tax credit bonds.

Section 54B, added Pub. L. 110–234, title XV, §15316(a), May 22, 2008, 122 Stat. 1509, and Pub. L. 110–246, §4(a), title XV, §15316(a), June 18, 2008, 122 Stat. 1664, 2271, related to qualified forestry conservation bonds.

Section 54C, added Pub. L. 110–343, div. B, title I, §107(a), Oct. 3, 2008, 122 Stat. 3817; amended Pub. L. 111–5, div. B, title I, §1111, Feb. 17, 2009, 123 Stat. 322, related to new clean renewable energy bonds.

Section 54D, added Pub. L. 110–343, div. B, title III, §301(a), Oct. 3, 2008, 122 Stat. 3841; amended Pub. L. 111–5, div. B, title I, §1112, Feb. 17, 2009, 123 Stat. 322, related to qualified energy conservation bonds.

Section 54E, added Pub. L. 110–343, div. C, title III, §313(a), Oct. 3, 2008, 122 Stat. 3869; amended Pub. L. 111–5, div. B, title I, §1522(a), Feb. 17, 2009, 123 Stat. 358; Pub. L. 111–312, title VII, §758(a), Dec. 17, 2010, 124 Stat. 3322; Pub. L. 112–240, title III, §310(a), Jan. 2, 2013, 126 Stat. 2330; Pub. L. 113–295, div. A, title I, §120(a), Dec. 19, 2014, 128 Stat. 4015; Pub. L. 114–95, title IX, §9215(uu)(1), Dec. 10, 2015, 129 Stat. 2183; Pub. L. 114–113, div. Q, title I, §164(a), Dec. 18, 2015, 129 Stat. 3066, related to qualified zone academy bonds.

Section 54F, added Pub. L. 111–5, div. B, title I, §1521(a), Feb. 17, 2009, 123 Stat. 355; amended Pub. L. 111–147, title III, §301(b), Mar. 18, 2010, 124 Stat. 78, related to qualified school construction bonds.

STATUTORY NOTES AND RELATED SUBSIDIARIES
EFFECTIVE DATE OF REPEAL

Repeal applicable to bonds issued after Dec. 31, 2017, see section 13404(d) of Pub. L. 115–97, set out as a note under former section 54 of this title.

[Subpart J—Repealed]

[§54AA. Repealed. Pub. L. 115–97, title I, §13404(a), Dec. 22, 2017, 131 Stat. 2138]

Section, added Pub. L. 111–5, div. B, title I, §1531(a), Feb. 17, 2009, 123 Stat. 358, related to build America bonds.

STATUTORY NOTES AND RELATED SUBSIDIARIES
EFFECTIVE DATE OF REPEAL

Repeal applicable to bonds issued after Dec. 31, 2017, see section 13404(d) of Pub. L. 115–97, set out as a note under former section 54 of this title.

TRANSITIONAL COORDINATION WITH STATE LAW

Pub. L. 111–5, div. B, title I, §1531(d), Feb. 17, 2009, 123 Stat. 360, provided that, except as otherwise provided by a State after Feb. 17, 2009, the interest on any build America bond (as defined in former 26 U.S.C. 54AA) and the amount of any credit determined under such section with respect to such bond was to be treated for purposes of the income tax laws of such State as being exempt from Federal income tax.

[PART V—REPEALED]

EDITORIAL NOTES
CODIFICATION

Part V, consisting of a prior section 51, was repealed by Pub. L. 94–455, title XIX, §1901(a)(7), Oct. 4, 1976, 90 Stat. 1765. See Prior Provisions note set out under section 51 of this title.

PART VI—ALTERNATIVE MINIMUM TAX

§55. Alternative minimum tax imposed

(a) General rule

In the case of a taxpayer other than a corporation, there is hereby imposed (in addition to any other tax imposed by this subtitle) a tax equal to the excess (if any) of—
(1) the tentative minimum tax for the taxable year, over
(2) the regular tax for the taxable year.

(b) Tentative minimum tax

For purposes of this part—

(1) Amount of tentative tax

(A) In general

The tentative minimum tax for the taxable year is the sum of—
(i) 26 percent of so much of the taxable excess as does not exceed $175,000, plus
(ii) 28 percent of so much of the taxable excess as exceeds $175,000.

The amount determined under the preceding sentence shall be reduced by the alternative minimum tax foreign tax credit for the taxable year.

(B) Taxable excess

For purposes of this subsection, the term "taxable excess" means so much of the alternative minimum taxable income for the taxable year as exceeds the exemption amount.

(C) Married individual filing separate return

In the case of a married individual filing a separate return, subparagraph (A) shall be applied by substituting 50 percent of the dollar amount otherwise applicable under clause (i) and clause (ii) thereof. For purposes of the preceding sentence, marital status shall be determined under section 7703.

(2) Alternative minimum taxable income

The term "alternative minimum taxable income" means the taxable income of the taxpayer for the taxable year—
(A) determined with the adjustments provided in section 56 and section 58, and
(B) increased by the amount of the items of tax preference described in section 57.

If a taxpayer is subject to the regular tax, such taxpayer shall be subject to the tax imposed by this section (and, if the regular tax is determined by reference to an amount other than taxable income, such amount shall be treated as the taxable income of such taxpayer for purposes of the preceding sentence).

(3) Maximum rate of tax on net capital gain of noncorporate taxpayers

The amount determined under the first sentence of paragraph (1)(A) shall not exceed the sum of—
(A) the amount determined under such first sentence computed at the rates and in the same manner as if this paragraph had not been enacted on the taxable excess reduced by the lesser of—
(i) the net capital gain; or
(ii) the sum of—
(I) the adjusted net capital gain, plus
(II) the unrecaptured section 1250 gain, plus

(B) 0 percent of so much of the adjusted net capital gain (or, if less, taxable excess) as does not exceed an amount equal to the excess described in section 1(h)(1)(B), plus
(C) 15 percent of the lesser of—
(i) so much of the adjusted net capital gain (or, if less, taxable excess) as exceeds the amount on which tax is determined under subparagraph (B), or
(ii) the excess described in section 1(h)(1)(C)(ii), plus

(D) 20 percent of the adjusted net capital gain (or, if less, taxable excess) in excess of the sum of the amounts on which tax is determined under subparagraphs (B) and (C), plus
(E) 25 percent of the amount of taxable excess in excess of the sum of the amounts on which tax is determined under the preceding subparagraphs of this paragraph.

Terms used in this paragraph which are also used in section 1(h) shall have the respective meanings given such terms by section 1(h) but computed with the adjustments under this part.

(c) Regular tax

(1) In general

For purposes of this section, the term "regular tax" means the regular tax liability for the taxable year (as defined in section 26(b)) reduced by the foreign tax credit allowable under section 27(a).[1] Such term shall not include any increase in tax under section 45(e)(11)(C), 49(b) or 50(a) or subsection (j) or (k) of section 42.

(2) Coordination with income averaging for farmers and fishermen

Solely for purposes of this section, section 1301 (relating to averaging of farm and fishing income) shall not apply in computing the regular tax liability.

(3) Cross references

For provisions providing that certain credits are not allowable against the tax imposed by this section, see sections 30C(d)(2) and 38(c).

(d) Exemption amount

For purposes of this section—

(1) Exemption amount for taxpayers other than corporations

In the case of a taxpayer other than a corporation, the term "exemption amount" means—

(A) $78,750 in the case of—
(i) a joint return, or
(ii) a surviving spouse,

(B) $50,600 in the case of an individual who—
(i) is not a married individual, and
(ii) is not a surviving spouse,

(C) 50 percent of the dollar amount applicable under subparagraph (A) in the case of a married individual who files a separate return, and
(D) $22,500 in the case of an estate or trust.

For purposes of this paragraph, the term "surviving spouse" has the meaning given to such term by section 2(a), and marital status shall be determined under section 7703.

(2) Phase-out of exemption amount

The exemption amount of any taxpayer shall be reduced (but not below zero) by an amount equal to 25 percent of the amount by which the alternative minimum taxable income of the taxpayer exceeds—

(A) $150,000 in the case of a taxpayer described in paragraph (1)(A),
(B) $112,500 in the case of a taxpayer described in paragraph (1)(B), and
(C) 50 percent of the dollar amount applicable under subparagraph (A) in the case of a taxpayer described in subparagraph (C) or (D) of paragraph (1).

In the case of a taxpayer described in paragraph (1)(C), alternative minimum taxable income shall be increased by the lesser of (i) 25 percent of the excess of alternative minimum taxable income (determined without regard to this sentence) over the minimum amount of such income (as so determined) for which the exemption amount under paragraph (1)(C) is zero, or (ii) such exemption amount (determined without regard to this paragraph).

(3) Inflation adjustment

(A) In general

In the case of any taxable year beginning in a calendar year after 2012, the amounts described in subparagraph (B) shall each be increased by an amount equal to—
(i) such dollar amount, multiplied by
(ii) the cost-of-living adjustment determined under section 1(f)(3) for the calendar year in which the taxable year begins, determined by substituting "calendar year 2011" for "calendar year 2016" in subparagraph (A)(ii) thereof.

(B) Amounts described

The amounts described in this subparagraph are—
(i) each of the dollar amounts contained in subsection (b)(1)(A),
(ii) each of the dollar amounts contained in subparagraphs (A), (B), and (D) of paragraph (1), and
(iii) each of the dollar amounts in subparagraphs (A) and (B) of paragraph (2).

(C) Rounding

Any increased amount determined under subparagraph (A) shall be rounded to the nearest multiple of $100.

(4) Special rule for taxable years beginning after 2017 and before 2026

(A) In general

In the case of any taxable year beginning after December 31, 2017, and before January 1, 2026—
(i) paragraph (1) shall be applied—
(I) by substituting "$109,400" for "$78,750" in subparagraph (A), and
(II) by substituting "$70,300" for "$50,600" in subparagraph (B),

(ii) paragraph (2) shall be applied—
(I) by substituting "$1,000,000" for "$150,000" in subparagraph (A),
(II) by substituting "50 percent of the dollar amount applicable under subparagraph (A)" for "$112,500" in subparagraph (B), and
(III) in the case of a taxpayer described in paragraph (1)(D), without regard to the substitution under subclause (I), and

(iii) subsection (j) of section 59 shall not apply.

(B) Inflation adjustment

(i) In general

In the case of any taxable year beginning in a calendar year after 2018, the amounts described in clause (ii) shall each be increased by an amount equal to—

(I) such dollar amount, multiplied by

(II) the cost-of-living adjustment determined under section 1(f)(3) for the calendar year in which the taxable year begins, determined by substituting "calendar year 2017" for "calendar year 2016" in subparagraph (A)(ii) thereof.

(ii) Amounts described

The amounts described in this clause are the $109,400 amount in subparagraph (A)(i)(I), the $70,300 amount in subparagraph (A)(i)(II), and the $1,000,000 amount in subparagraph (A)(ii)(I).

(iii) Rounding

Any increased amount determined under clause (i) shall be rounded to the nearest multiple of $100.

(iv) Coordination with current adjustments

In the case of any taxable year to which subparagraph (A) applies, no adjustment shall be made under paragraph (3) to any of the numbers which are substituted under subparagraph (A) and adjusted under this subparagraph.

(Added and amended Pub. L. 99–514, title II, §252(c), title VII, §701(a), Oct. 22, 1986, 100 Stat. 2205, 2321; Pub. L. 100–647, title I, §§1002(l)(27), 1007(a), Nov. 10, 1988, 102 Stat. 3381, 3428; Pub. L. 101–508, title XI, §§11102(a), 11813(b)(5), Nov. 5, 1990, 104 Stat. 1388–406, 1388-551; Pub. L. 102–318, title V, §521(b)(1), July 3, 1992, 106 Stat. 310; Pub. L. 102–486, title XIX, §1913(b)(2)(D), Oct. 24, 1992, 106 Stat. 3020; Pub. L. 103–66, title XIII, §13203(a)–(c)(1), Aug. 10, 1993, 107 Stat. 461, 462; Pub. L. 104–188, title I, §§1205(d)(6), 1401(b)(3), 1601(b)(2)(A), Aug. 20, 1996, 110 Stat. 1776, 1788, 1832; Pub. L. 105–34, title III, §311(b)(1), (2)(A), title IV, §401(a), title XVI, §1601(f)(1)(C), Aug. 5, 1997, 111 Stat. 834, 835, 843, 1090; Pub. L. 105–206, title VI, §§6005(d)(2), 6006(a), July 22, 1998, 112 Stat. 804, 806; Pub. L. 107–16, title VII, §701(a), (b), June 7, 2001, 115 Stat. 148; Pub. L. 108–27, title I, §106(a), title III, §301(a)(1), (2)(B), (b)(2), May 28, 2003, 117 Stat. 755, 758; Pub. L. 108–311, title I, §103(a), title IV, §406(d), Oct. 4, 2004, 118 Stat. 1168, 1189; Pub. L. 108–357, title III, §314(a), Oct. 22, 2004, 118 Stat. 1468; Pub. L. 109–58, title XIII, §§1302(b), 1322(a)(3)(H), 1341(b)(3), 1342(b)(3), Aug. 8, 2005, 119 Stat. 991, 1012, 1049, 1051; Pub. L. 109–135, title IV, §§403(h), 412(p), Dec. 21, 2005, 119 Stat. 2624, 2638; Pub. L. 109–222, title III, §301(a), May 17, 2006, 120 Stat. 353; Pub. L. 110–166, §2(a), Dec. 26, 2007, 121 Stat. 2461; Pub. L. 110–234, title XV, §15311(b), May 22, 2008, 122 Stat. 1503; Pub. L. 110–246, §4(a), title XV, §15311(b), June 18, 2008, 122 Stat. 1664, 2265; Pub. L. 110–343, div. C, title I, §102(a), Oct. 3, 2008, 122 Stat. 3863; Pub. L. 111–5, div. B, title I, §§1012(a), 1142(b)(5), 1144(b)(3), Feb. 17, 2009, 123 Stat. 319, 331, 332; Pub. L. 111–240, title II, §2013(b), Sept. 27, 2010, 124 Stat. 2555; Pub. L. 111–312, title II, §201(a), Dec. 17, 2010, 124 Stat. 3299; Pub. L. 112–240, title I, §§102(b)(2), 104(a), (b), (c)(2)(J), Jan. 2, 2013, 126 Stat. 2319, 2320, 2322; Pub. L. 113–295, div. A, title II, §202(c), Dec. 19, 2014, 128 Stat. 4024; Pub. L. 114–113, div. Q, title III, §334(b), Dec. 18, 2015, 129 Stat. 3108; Pub. L. 115–97, title I, §§11002(d)(1)(I), 12001(a), (b)(3)(A), (B), (4)–(6), 12003(a), Dec. 22, 2017, 131 Stat. 2060, 2092, 2093, 2095; Pub. L. 116–94, div. O, title V, §501(b), Dec. 20, 2019, 133 Stat. 3180.)

INFLATION ADJUSTED ITEMS FOR CERTAIN YEARS

For inflation adjustment of certain items in this section, see Revenue Procedures listed in a table under section 1 of this title.

EDITORIAL NOTES
REFERENCES IN TEXT

Section 27, referred to in subsec. (c)(1), was amended generally by Pub. L. 115–141, div. U, title IV, §401(d)(1)(A), Mar. 23, 2018, 132 Stat. 1206, and as so amended, no longer contains a subsec. (a) designation. Text of section 27 as amended by Pub. L. 115–141 is identical to that of former section 27(a).

CODIFICATION

Pub. L. 110–234 and Pub. L. 110–246 made identical amendments to this section. The amendments by Pub. L. 110–234 were repealed by section 4(a) of Pub. L. 110–246.

PRIOR PROVISIONS

A prior section 55, Pub. L. 95–600, title IV, §421(a), Nov. 6, 1978, 92 Stat. 2871; amended Pub. L. 96–222, title I, §104(a)(4)(A)–(D), (G), (H)(i), (ii), (viii), Apr. 1, 1980, 94 Stat. 215–218; Pub. L. 96–223, title II, §232(b)(2)(A), (c)(2), Apr. 2, 1980, 94 Stat. 276, 277; Pub. L. 96–603, §4(a), (b), Dec. 28, 1980, 94 Stat. 3513, 3514; Pub. L. 97–34, title I, §101(d)(1), title II, §221(b)(1)(A), title III, §331(d)(1)(A), Aug. 13, 1981, 95 Stat. 183, 246, 294; Pub. L. 97–248, title II, §201(a), Sept. 3, 1982, 96 Stat. 411; Pub. L. 97–354, §5(a)(13), Oct. 19, 1982, 96 Stat. 1693; Pub. L. 97–448, title I, §103(g)(2)(E), title III, §§305(c), 306(a)(1)(B), (C), Jan. 12, 1983, 96 Stat. 2379, 2399, 2400; Pub. L. 98–369, div. A, title IV, §§474(q), 491(d)(1), title VI, §612(e)(3), title VII, §711(a)(1), (4), (5), July 18, 1984, 98 Stat. 838, 849, 912, 942, 943; Pub. L. 99–514, title XVIII, §1847(a), Oct. 22, 1986, 100 Stat. 2856, related to alternative minimum tax for taxpayers other than corporations, prior to the general revision of this part by Pub. L. 99–514, §701(a).

AMENDMENTS

2019—Subsec. (d)(4)(A)(iii). Pub. L. 116–94 added cl. (iii).

2017—Subsec. (a). Pub. L. 115–97, §12001(a), substituted "In the case of a taxpayer other than a corporation, there" for "There" in introductory provisions.

Subsec. (b)(1). Pub. L. 115–97, §12001(b)(3)(A), amended par. (1) generally. Prior to amendment, par. (1) related to amount of tentative tax.

Subsec. (b)(3). Pub. L. 115–97, §12001(b)(3)(B), substituted "paragraph (1)(A)" for "paragraph (1)(A)(i)" in introductory provisions.

Subsec. (c)(1). Pub. L. 115–97, §12001(b)(4), struck out ", the section 936 credit allowable under section 27(b), and the Puerto Rico economic activity credit under section 30A" after "section 27(a)".

Subsec. (d)(2). Pub. L. 115–97, §12001(b)(5)(A), redesignated par. (3) as (2) and struck out former par. (2). Prior to amendment, text of par. (2) read as follows: "In the case of a corporation, the term 'exemption amount' means $40,000."

Subsec. (d)(2)(D). Pub. L. 115–97, §12001(b)(5)(B), struck out subpar. (D) which read as follows: "$150,000 in the case of a taxpayer described in paragraph (2)."

Subsec. (d)(3). Pub. L. 115–97, §12001(b)(5)(A), redesignated (2).

Subsec. (d)(3)(B)(i). Pub. L. 115–97, §12001(b)(5)(C)(i), substituted "(b)(1)(A)" for "(b)(1)(A)(i)".

Subsec. (d)(3)(B)(iii). Pub. L. 115–97, §12001(b)(5)(C)(ii), substituted "paragraph (2)" for "paragraph (3)".

Subsec. (d)(4). Pub. L. 115–97, §12003(a), added par. (4). Former par. (4) redesignated (3).

Subsec. (d)(4)(A)(ii). Pub. L. 115–97, §11002(d)(1)(I), substituted "for 'calendar year 2016' in subparagraph (A)(ii)" for "for 'calendar year 1992' in subparagraph (B)".

Subsec. (e). Pub. L. 115–97, §12001(b)(6), struck out subsec. (e) which related to exemption for small corporations.

2015—Subsec. (b)(4). Pub. L. 114–113 struck out par. (4) which related to the maximum rate of tax on qualified timber gain of corporations.

2014—Subsec. (d)(4)(B)(ii). Pub. L. 113–295, §202(c)(1), inserted "subparagraphs (A), (B), and (D) of" before "paragraph (1)".

Subsec. (d)(4)(C). Pub. L. 113–295, §202(c)(2), substituted "increased amount" for "increase".

2013—Subsec. (b)(1)(A)(iii). Pub. L. 112–240, §104(b)(2)(A), substituted "by substituting 50 percent of the dollar amount otherwise applicable under subclause (I) and subclause (II) thereof." for "by substituting '$87,500' for '$175,000' each place it appears."

Subsec. (b)(3)(B). Pub. L. 112–240, §102(c)(2), substituted "0 percent" for "5 percent (0 percent in the case of taxable years beginning after 2007)".

Subsec. (b)(3)(C) to (E). Pub. L. 112–240, §102(b)(2), added subpars. (C) and (D), redesignated former subpar. (D) as (E), and struck out former subpar. (C) which read as follows: "15 percent of the adjusted net capital gain (or, if less, taxable excess) in excess of the amount on which tax is determined under subparagraph (B), plus".

Subsec. (c)(3). Pub. L. 112–240, §104(c)(2)(J), substituted "30C(d)(2)" for "26(a), 30C(d)(2),".

Subsec. (d)(1)(A). Pub. L. 112–240, §104(a)(1)(A), in introductory provisions, substituted "$78,750" for "$45,000 ($72,450 in the case of taxable years beginning in 2010 and $74,450 in the case of taxable years beginning in 2011)".

Subsec. (d)(1)(B). Pub. L. 112–240, §104(a)(1)(B), in introductory provisions, substituted "$50,600" for "$33,750 ($47,450 in the case of taxable years beginning in 2010 and $48,450 in the case of taxable years beginning in 2011)".

Subsec. (d)(1)(C). Pub. L. 112–240, §104(a)(1)(C), substituted "subparagraph (A)" for "paragraph (1)(A)".

Subsec. (d)(3)(A). Pub. L. 112–240, §104(b)(2)(B)(i), struck out "or (2)" after "paragraph (1)(A)".

Subsec. (d)(3)(C), (D). Pub. L. 112–240, §104(b)(2)(B)(ii), (iii), added subpars. (C) and (D) and struck out former subpar. (C) which read as follows: "$75,000 in the case of a taxpayer described in subparagraph (C) or (D) of paragraph (1)."

Subsec. (d)(4). Pub. L. 112–240, §104(b)(1), added par. (4).

2010—Subsec. (d)(1)(A). Pub. L. 111–312, §201(a)(1), substituted "$72,450 in the case of taxable years beginning in 2010 and $74,450 in the case of taxable years beginning in 2011" for "$70,950 in the case of taxable years beginning in 2009".

Subsec. (d)(1)(B). Pub. L. 111–312, §201(a)(2), substituted "$47,450 in the case of taxable years beginning in 2010 and $48,450 in the case of taxable years beginning in 2011" for "$46,700 in the case of taxable years beginning in 2009".

Subsec. (e)(5). Pub. L. 111–240 substituted "38(c)(6)(B)" for "38(c)(3)(B)".

2009—Subsec. (c)(3). Pub. L. 111–5, §1144(b)(3), struck out "30B(g)(2)," after "sections 26(a),".

Pub. L. 111–5, §1142(b)(5), struck out "30(b)(3)," after "sections 26(a),".

Subsec. (d)(1)(A). Pub. L. 111–5, §1012(a)(1), substituted "($70,950 in the case of taxable years beginning in 2009)" for "($69,950 in the case of taxable years beginning in 2008)".

Subsec. (d)(1)(B). Pub. L. 111–5, §1012(a)(2), substituted "($46,700 in the case of taxable years beginning in 2009)" for "($46,200 in the case of taxable years beginning in 2008)".

2008—Subsec. (b)(4). Pub. L. 110–246, §15311(b), added par. (4).

Subsec. (d)(1)(A). Pub. L. 110–343, §102(a)(1), substituted "($69,950 in the case of taxable years beginning in 2008)" for "($66,250 in the case of taxable years beginning in 2007)".

Subsec. (d)(1)(B). Pub. L. 110–343, §102(a)(2), substituted "($46,200 in the case of taxable years beginning in 2008)" for "($44,350 in the case of taxable years beginning in 2007)".

2007—Subsec. (d)(1)(A). Pub. L. 110–166, §2(a)(1), substituted "($66,250 in the case of taxable years beginning in 2007)" for "($62,550 in the case of taxable years beginning in 2006)".

Subsec. (d)(1)(B). Pub. L. 110–166, §2(a)(2), substituted "($44,350 in the case of taxable years beginning in 2007)" for "($42,500 in the case of taxable years beginning in 2006)".

2006—Subsec. (d)(1)(A). Pub. L. 109–222, §301(a)(1), substituted "$62,550 in the case of taxable years beginning in 2006" for "$58,000 in the case of taxable years beginning in 2003, 2004, and 2005".

Subsec. (d)(1)(B). Pub. L. 109–222, §301(a)(2), substituted "$42,500 in the case of taxable years beginning in 2006" for "$40,250 in the case of taxable years beginning in 2003, 2004, and 2005".

2005—Subsec. (c)(1). Pub. L. 109–58, §1302(b), which directed amendment of par. (1) by inserting "45(e)(11)(C)," after "section" in last sentence, was executed by making the insertion after "section" the first place it appeared in last sentence, to reflect the probable intent of Congress.

Subsec. (c)(2). Pub. L. 109–135, §403(h), substituted "regular tax liability" for "regular tax".

Pub. L. 109–58, §1342(b)(3), which directed amendment of par. (2) by inserting "30C(d)(2)," after "30B(g)(2),", was repealed by Pub. L. 109–135, §412(p)(3).

Pub. L. 109–58, §1341(b)(3), which directed amendment of par. (2) by inserting "30B(g)(2)," after "30(b)(2),", was repealed by Pub. L. 109–135, §412(p)(2).

Subsec. (c)(3). Pub. L. 109–135, §412(p)(1), inserted "30B(g)(2), 30C(d)(2)," after "30(b)(3),".

Pub. L. 109–58, §1322(a)(3)(H), struck out "29(b)(6)," after "26(a),".

2004—Subsec. (b)(3)(B). Pub. L. 108–311, §406(d), substituted "an amount equal to the excess described in" for "the amount on which a tax is determined under".

Subsec. (c)(2), (3). Pub. L. 108–357 added par. (2) and redesignated former par. (2) as (3).

Subsec. (d)(1)(A), (B). Pub. L. 108–311, §103(a), substituted "2003, 2004, and 2005" for "2003 and 2004".

2003—Subsec. (b)(3). Pub. L. 108–27, §301(b)(2), struck out first sentence of concluding provisions which read as follows: "In the case of taxable years beginning after December 31, 2000, rules similar to the rules of section 1(h)(2) shall apply for purposes of subparagraphs (B) and (C)."

Subsec. (b)(3)(B). Pub. L. 108–27, §301(a)(1), substituted "5 percent (0 percent in the case of taxable years beginning after 2007)" for "10 percent".

Subsec. (b)(3)(C). Pub. L. 108–27, §301(a)(2)(B), substituted "15 percent" for "20 percent".

Subsec. (d)(1)(A). Pub. L. 108–27, §106(a)(1), substituted "$58,000 in the case of taxable years beginning in 2003 and 2004" for "$49,000 in the case of taxable years beginning in 2001, 2002, 2003, and 2004".

Subsec. (d)(1)(B). Pub. L. 108–27, §106(a)(2), substituted "$40,250 in the case of taxable years beginning in 2003 and 2004" for "$35,750 in the case of taxable years beginning in 2001, 2002, 2003, and 2004".

2001—Subsec. (d)(1)(A). Pub. L. 107–16, §701(a)(1), substituted "$45,000 ($49,000 in the case of taxable years beginning in 2001, 2002, 2003, and 2004)" for "$45,000".

Subsec. (d)(1)(B). Pub. L. 107–16, §701(b)(1), struck out "and" at end.

Pub. L. 107–16, §701(a)(2), substituted "$33,750 ($35,750 in the case of taxable years beginning in 2001, 2002, 2003, and 2004)" for "$33,750".

Subsec. (d)(1)(C), (D). Pub. L. 107–16, §701(b)(1), added subpars. (C) and (D) and struck out former subpar. (C) which read as follows: "$22,500 in the case of—

"(i) a married individual who files a separate return, or

"(ii) an estate or trust."

Subsec. (d)(3). Pub. L. 107–16, §701(b)(3), in concluding provisions, substituted "paragraph (1)(C)" for "paragraph (1)(C)(i)" and "the minimum amount of such income (as so determined) for which the exemption amount under paragraph (1)(C) is zero, or (ii) such exemption amount (determined without regard to this paragraph)" for "$165,000 or (ii) $22,500".

Subsec. (d)(3)(C). Pub. L. 107–16, §701(b)(2), substituted "subparagraph (C) or (D) of paragraph (1)" for "paragraph (1)(C)".

1998—Subsec. (b)(3). Pub. L. 105–206, §6005(d)(2), reenacted par. heading without change and amended text of par. (3) generally. Prior to amendment, text read as follows: "The amount determined under the first sentence of paragraph (1)(A)(i) shall not exceed the sum of—

"(A) the amount determined under such first sentence computed at the rates and in the same manner as if this paragraph had not been enacted on the taxable excess reduced by the lesser of—

"(i) the net capital gain, or

"(ii) the sum of—

"(I) the adjusted net capital gain, plus

"(II) the unrecaptured section 1250 gain, plus

"(B) 25 percent of the lesser of—

    "(i) the unrecaptured section 1250 gain, or

    "(ii) the amount of taxable excess in excess of the sum of—

        "(I) the adjusted net capital gain, plus

        "(II) the amount on which a tax is determined under subparagraph (A), plus

    "(C) 10 percent of so much of the taxpayer's adjusted net capital gain (or, if less, taxable excess) as does not exceed the amount on which a tax is determined under section 1(h)(1)(D), plus

    "(D) 20 percent of the taxpayer's adjusted net capital gain (or, if less, taxable excess) in excess of the amount on which tax is determined under subparagraph (C).

In the case of taxable years beginning after December 31, 2000, rules similar to the rules of section 1(h)(2) shall apply for purposes of subparagraphs (C) and (D). Terms used in this paragraph which are also used in section 1(h) shall have the respective meanings given such terms by section 1(h)."

Subsec. (e)(1). Pub. L. 105–206, §6006(a), reenacted par. heading without change and amended text of par. (1) generally. Prior to amendment, text read as follows: "The tentative minimum tax of a corporation shall be zero for any taxable year if—

    "(A) such corporation met the $5,000,000 gross receipts test of section 448(c) for its first taxable year beginning after December 31, 1996, and

    "(B) such corporation would meet such test for the taxable year and all prior taxable years beginning after such first taxable year if such test were applied by substituting '$7,500,000' for '$5,000,000'."

1997—Subsec. (b)(1)(A)(ii). Pub. L. 105–34, §311(b)(2)(A), substituted "this subsection" for "clause (i)".

Subsec. (b)(3). Pub. L. 105–34, §311(b)(1), added par. (3).

Subsec. (c)(1). Pub. L. 105–34, §1601(f)(1)(C), substituted "Puerto Rico" for "Puerto Rican".

Subsec. (e). Pub. L. 105–34, §401(a), added subsec. (e).

1996—Subsec. (c)(1). Pub. L. 104–188, §1601(b)(2)(A), substituted ", the section 936 credit allowable under section 27(b), and the Puerto Rican economic activity credit under section 30A" for "and the section 936 credit allowable under section 27(b)".

Pub. L. 104–188, §1401(b)(3), struck out "shall not include any tax imposed by section 402(d) and" before "shall not include any increase in tax under section 49(b)".

Subsec. (c)(2). Pub. L. 104–188, §1205(d)(6), struck out "28(d)(2)," after "26(a),".

1993—Subsec. (b)(1). Pub. L. 103–66, §13203(a), amended heading and text of par. (1) generally. Prior to amendment, text read as follows: "The tentative minimum tax for the taxable year is—

    "(A) 20 percent (24 percent in the case of a taxpayer other than a corporation) of so much of the alternative minimum taxable income for the taxable year as exceeds the exemption amount, reduced by

    "(B) the alternative minimum tax foreign tax credit for the taxable year."

Subsec. (d)(1). Pub. L. 103–66, §13203(b), substituted "$45,000" for "$40,000" in subpar. (A), "$33,750" for "$30,000" in subpar. (B), and "$22,500" for "$20,000" in subpar. (C).

Subsec. (d)(3). Pub. L. 103–66, §13203(c)(1), substituted "$165,000 or (ii) $22,500" for "$155,000 or (ii) $20,000" in last sentence.

1992—Subsec. (c)(1). Pub. L. 102–318 substituted "402(d)" for "402(e)".

Subsec. (c)(2). Pub. L. 102–486 substituted "29(b)(6), 30(b)(3)," for "29(b)(5),".

1990—Subsec. (b)(1)(A). Pub. L. 101–508, §11102(a), substituted "24 percent" for "21 percent".

Subsec. (c)(1). Pub. L. 101–508, §11813(b)(5), substituted "section 49(b) or 50(a)" for "section 47".

1988—Subsec. (b)(2). Pub. L. 100–647, §1007(a)(2), inserted at end "If a taxpayer is subject to the regular tax, such taxpayer shall be subject to the tax imposed by this section (and, if the regular tax is determined by reference to an amount other than taxable income, such amount shall be treated as the taxable income of such taxpayer for purposes of the preceding sentence)."

Subsec. (c)(1). Pub. L. 100–647, §1007(a)(1), inserted "and the section 936 credit allowable under section 27(b)" before period at end of first sentence.

Pub. L. 100–647, §1002(l)(27), substituted "subsection (j) or (k) of section 42" for "section 42(j)".

Subsec. (d)(3). Pub. L. 100–647, §1007(a)(3), inserted at end "In the case of a taxpayer described in paragraph (1)(C)(i), alternative minimum taxable income shall be increased by the lesser of (i) 25 percent of the excess of alternative minimum taxable income (determined without regard to this sentence) over $155,000, or (ii) $20,000."

1986—Subsec. (c)(1). Pub. L. 99–514, §252(c), inserted "or section 42(j)".

Statutory Notes and Related Subsidiaries

Effective Date of 2019 Amendment

Amendment by Pub. L. 116–94 applicable to taxable years beginning after Dec. 31, 2017, see section 501(c)(2) of Pub. L. 116–94, set out in a note under section 1 of this title.

Effective Date of 2017 Amendment

Amendment by section 11002(d)(1)(I) of Pub. L. 115–97 applicable to taxable years beginning after Dec. 31, 2017, see section 11002(e) of Pub. L. 115–97, set out as a note under section 1 of this title.

Amendment by section 12001(a), (b)(3)(A), (B), (4)–(6) of Pub. L. 115–97 applicable to taxable years beginning after Dec. 31, 2017, see section 12001(c) of Pub. L. 115–97, set out as a note under section 11 of this title.

Pub. L. 115–97, title I, §12003(b), Dec. 22, 2017, 131 Stat. 2096, provided that: "The amendments made by this section [amending this section] shall apply to taxable years beginning after December 31, 2017."

Effective Date of 2015 Amendment

Pub. L. 114–113, div. Q, title III, §334(c), Dec. 18, 2015, 129 Stat. 3109, provided that: "The amendments made by this section [amending this section and section 1201 of this title] shall apply to taxable years beginning after December 31, 2015."

Effective Date of 2014 Amendment

Pub. L. 113–295, div. A, title II, §202(f), Dec. 19, 2014, 128 Stat. 4024, provided that: "The amendments made by this section [amending this section and sections 168, 642, 911, and 6431 of this title] shall take effect as if included in the provision of the American Taxpayer Relief Act of 2012 [Pub. L. 112–240] to which they relate."

Effective Date of 2013 Amendment

Amendment by section 102(b)(2), (c)(2) of Pub. L. 112–240 applicable to taxable years beginning after Dec. 31, 2012, see section 102(d)(1) of Pub. L. 112–240, set out as a note under section 1 of this title.

Amendment by section 104(a), (b), (c)(2)(J) of Pub. L. 112–240 applicable to taxable years beginning after Dec. 31, 2011, see section 104(d) of Pub. L. 112–240, set out as a note under section 23 of this title.

Effective Date of 2010 Amendment

Pub. L. 111–312, title II, §201(b), Dec. 17, 2010, 124 Stat. 3299, provided that: "The amendments made by this section [amending this section] shall apply to taxable years beginning after December 31, 2009."

EFFECTIVE DATE OF 2009 AMENDMENT

Pub. L. 111–5, div. B, title I, §1012(b), Feb. 17, 2009, 123 Stat. 319, provided that: "The amendments made by this section [amending this section] shall apply to taxable years beginning after December 31, 2008."

Amendment by section 1142(b)(5) of Pub. L. 111–5 applicable to vehicles acquired after Feb. 17, 2009, see section 1142(c) of Pub. L. 111–5, set out as an Effective and Termination Dates of 2009 Amendment note under section 24 of this title.

Amendment by section 1144(b)(3) of Pub. L. 111–5 applicable to taxable years beginning after Dec. 31, 2008, see section 1144(c) of Pub. L. 111–5, set out as an Effective and Termination Dates of 2009 Amendment note under section 24 of this title.

EFFECTIVE DATE OF 2008 AMENDMENT

Pub. L. 110–343, div. C, title I, §102(b), Oct. 3, 2008, 122 Stat. 3863, provided that: "The amendments made by this section [amending this section] shall apply to taxable years beginning after December 31, 2007."

Amendment of this section and repeal of Pub. L. 110–234 by Pub. L. 110–246 effective May 22, 2008, the date of enactment of Pub. L. 110–234, except as otherwise provided, see section 4 of Pub. L. 110–246, set out as an Effective Date note under section 8701 of Title 7, Agriculture.

Pub. L. 110–234, title XV, §15311(d), May 22, 2008, 122 Stat. 1503, and Pub. L. 110–246, §4(a), title XV, §15311(d), June 18, 2008, 122 Stat. 1664, 2265, provided that: "The amendments made by this section [amending this section and sections 857 and 1201 of this title] shall apply to taxable years ending after the date of enactment [June 18, 2008]."

[Pub. L. 110–234 and Pub. L. 110–246 enacted identical provisions. Pub. L. 110–234 was repealed by section 4(a) of Pub. L. 110–246, set out as a note under section 8701 of Title 7, Agriculture.]

EFFECTIVE DATE OF 2007 AMENDMENT

Pub. L. 110–166, §2(b), Dec. 26, 2007, 121 Stat. 2461, provided that: "The amendments made by this section [amending this section] shall apply to taxable years beginning after December 31, 2006."

EFFECTIVE DATE OF 2006 AMENDMENT

Pub. L. 109–222, title III, §301(b), May 17, 2006, 120 Stat. 353, provided that: "The amendments made by this section [amending this section] shall apply to taxable years beginning after December 31, 2005."

EFFECTIVE DATE OF 2005 AMENDMENTS

Amendment by section 403(h) of Pub. L. 109–135 effective as if included in the provision of the American Jobs Creation Act of 2004, Pub. L. 108–357, to which such amendment relates, see section 403(nn) of Pub. L. 109–135, set out as a note under section 26 of this title.

Amendment by section 1302(b) of Pub. L. 109–58 applicable to taxable years of cooperative organizations ending after Aug. 8, 2005, see section 1302(c) of Pub. L. 109–58, set out as a note under section 45 of this title.

Amendment by section 1322(a)(3)(H) of Pub. L. 109–58 applicable to credits determined under the Internal Revenue Code of 1986 for taxable years ending after Dec. 31, 2005, see section 1322(c)(1) of Pub. L. 109–58, set out as a note under section 45K of this title.

Amendment by section 1342(b)(3) of Pub. L. 109–58 applicable to property placed in service after Dec. 31, 2005, in taxable years ending after such date, see section 1342(c) of Pub. L. 109–58, set out as an Effective Date note under section 30C of this title.

Amendment by section 1341(b)(3) of Pub. L. 109–58 applicable to property placed in service after Dec. 31, 2005, in taxable years ending after such date, see section 1341(c) of Pub. L. 109–58, set out as an Effective Date note under section 30B of this title.

EFFECTIVE AND TERMINATION DATES OF 2004 AMENDMENTS

Pub. L. 108–357, title III, §314(c), Oct. 22, 2004, 118 Stat. 1469, provided that: "The amendments made by this section [amending this section and section 1301 of this title] shall apply to taxable years beginning after December 31, 2003."

Pub. L. 108–311, title I, §103(b), Oct. 4, 2004, 118 Stat. 1168, provided that: "The amendments made by this section [amending this section] shall apply to taxable years beginning after December 31, 2004."

Amendment by section 103(a) of Pub. L. 108–311 subject to title IX of the Economic Growth and Tax Relief Reconciliation Act of 2001, Pub. L. 107–16, §901, to the same extent and in the same manner as the provision of such Act to which such amendment relates, see section 105 of Pub. L. 108–311, set out as a note under section 1 of this title. Title IX of Pub. L. 107–16 was repealed by Pub. L. 112–240, title I, §101(a)(1), Jan. 2, 2013, 126 Stat. 2315.

Pub. L. 108–311, title IV, §406(h), Oct. 4, 2004, 118 Stat. 1190, provided that: "The amendments made by this section [amending this section and sections 246, 529, 530, 901, 1259, and 1397E of this title] shall take effect as if included in the provisions of the Taxpayer Relief Act of 1997 [Pub. L. 105–34] to which they relate."

EFFECTIVE AND TERMINATION DATES OF 2003 AMENDMENT

Pub. L. 108–27, title I, §106(b), May 28, 2003, 117 Stat. 755, provided that: "The amendments made by subsection (a) [amending this section] shall apply to taxable years beginning after December 31, 2002."

Amendment by section 106(a) of Pub. L. 108–27 subject to title IX of the Economic Growth and Tax Relief Reconciliation Act of 2001, Pub. L. 107–16, §901, to the same extent and in the same manner as the provision of such Act to which such amendment relates, see section 107 of Pub. L. 108–27, set out as a note under section 1 of this title. Title IX of Pub. L. 107–16 was repealed by Pub. L. 112–240, title I, §101(a)(1), Jan. 2, 2013, 126 Stat. 2315.

Amendment by section 301(a)(1), (2)(B), (b)(2) of Pub. L. 108–27 applicable to taxable years ending on or after May 6, 2003, see section 301(d) of Pub. L. 108–27, set out as a note under section 1 of this title.

EFFECTIVE DATE OF 2001 AMENDMENT

Pub. L. 107–16, title VII, §701(c), June 7, 2001, 115 Stat. 148, provided that: "The amendments made by this section [amending this section] shall apply to taxable years beginning after December 31, 2000."

EFFECTIVE DATE OF 1998 AMENDMENT

Amendment by Pub. L. 105–206 effective, except as otherwise provided, as if included in the provisions of the Taxpayer Relief Act of 1997, Pub. L. 105–34, to which such amendment relates, see section 6024 of Pub. L. 105–206, set out as a note under section 1 of this title.

EFFECTIVE DATE OF 1997 AMENDMENT

Amendment by section 311(b)(1), (2)(A) of Pub. L. 105–34 applicable to taxable years ending after May 6, 1997, see section 311(d) of Pub. L. 105–34, set out as a note under section 1 of this title.

Pub. L. 105–34, title IV, §401(b), Aug. 5, 1997, 111 Stat. 844, provided that: "The amendment made by this section [amending this section] shall apply to taxable years beginning after December 31, 1997."

Amendment by section 1601(f)(1)(C) of Pub. L. 105–34 effective as if included in the provisions of the Small Business Job Protection Act of 1996, Pub. L. 104–188, to which it relates, see section 1601(j) of Pub. L. 105–34, set out as a note under section 23 of this title.

EFFECTIVE DATE OF 1996 AMENDMENT

Amendment by section 1205(d)(6) of Pub. L. 104–188 applicable to amounts paid or incurred in taxable years ending after June 30, 1996, see section 1205(e) of Pub. L. 104–188, set out as a note under section 45K of this title.

Amendment by section 1401(b)(3) of Pub. L. 104–188 applicable to taxable years beginning after Dec. 31, 1999, with retention of certain transition rules, see section 1401(c) of Pub. L. 104–188, set out as a note under section 402 of this title.

Pub. L. 104–188, title I, §1601(c), Aug. 20, 1996, 110 Stat. 1833, provided that:

"(1) In general.—Except as provided in paragraph (2), the amendments made by this section [enacting section 30A of this title and amending this section and sections 56, 59, and 936 of this title] shall apply to taxable years beginning after December 31, 1995.

"(2) Special rule for qualified possession source investment income.—The amendments made by this section shall not apply to qualified possession source investment income received or accrued before July 1, 1996, without regard to the taxable year in which received or accrued.

"(3) Special transition rule for payment of estimated tax installment.—In determining the amount of any installment due under section 6655 of the Internal Revenue Code of 1986 after the date of the enactment of this Act [Aug. 20, 1996] and before October 1, 1996, only ½ of any increase in tax (for the taxable year for which such installment is made) by reason of the amendments made by subsections (a) and (b) [enacting section 30A of this title and amending this section and sections 56, 59, and 936 of this title] shall be taken into account. Any reduction in such installment by reason of the preceding sentence shall be recaptured by increasing the next required installment for such year by the amount of such reduction."

EFFECTIVE DATE OF 1993 AMENDMENT

Pub. L. 103–66, title XIII, §13203(d), Aug. 10, 1993, 107 Stat. 462, provided that: "The amendments made by this section [amending this section and section 897 of this title] shall apply to taxable years beginning after December 31, 1992."

EFFECTIVE DATE OF 1992 AMENDMENT

Amendment by Pub. L. 102–486 applicable to property placed in service after June 30, 1993, see section 1913(c) of Pub. L. 102–486, set out as a note under section 53 of this title.

Amendment by Pub. L. 102–318 applicable to distributions after Dec. 31, 1992, see section 521(e) of Pub. L. 102–318, set out as a note under section 402 of this title.

EFFECTIVE DATE OF 1990 AMENDMENT

Pub. L. 101–508, title XI, §11102(b), Nov. 5, 1990, 104 Stat. 1388–406, provided that: "The amendment made by subsection (a) [amending this section] shall apply to taxable years beginning after December 31, 1990."

Amendment by section 11813(b)(5) of Pub. L. 101–508 applicable to property placed in service after Dec. 31, 1990, but not applicable to any transition property (as defined in section 49(e) of this title), any property with respect to which qualified progress expenditures were previously taken into account under section 46(d) of this title, and any property described in section 46(b)(2)(C) of this title, as such sections were in effect on Nov. 4, 1990, see section 11813(c) of Pub. L. 101–508, set out as a note under section 45K of this title.

EFFECTIVE DATE OF 1988 AMENDMENT

Amendment by section 1002(l)(27) of Pub. L. 100–647 effective, except as otherwise provided, as if included in the provision of the Tax Reform Act of 1986, Pub. L. 99–514, to which such amendment relates, see section 1019(a) of Pub. L. 100–647, set out as a note under section 1 of this title.

Pub. L. 100–647, title I, §1007(a)(3), Nov. 10, 1988, 102 Stat. 3428, provided that the amendment made by that section is effective with respect to taxable years ending after Nov. 10, 1988.

EFFECTIVE DATE OF 1986 AMENDMENT

Amendment by Pub. L. 99–514 applicable to buildings placed in service after Dec. 31, 1986, in taxable years ending after such date, see section 252(e) of Pub. L. 99–514, set out as an Effective Date note under section 42 of this title.

EFFECTIVE DATE

Pub. L. 99–514, title VII, §701(f), Oct. 22, 1986, 100 Stat. 2343, as amended by Pub. L. 100–647, title I, §1007(f)(2), (3), Nov. 10, 1988, 102 Stat. 3433, provided that:

"(1) In general.—Except as otherwise provided in this subsection, the amendments made by this section [enacting this section and sections 53 and 56 to 59 of this title and amending sections 5, 12, 26, 28, 29, 38, 48, 173, 174, 263, 381, 443, 703, 882, 897, 904, 936, 1016, 1363, 1366, 1561, 6154, 6425, and 6655 of this title] shall apply to taxable years beginning after December 31, 1986.

"(2) Adjustment of net operating loss.—

"(A) Individuals.—In the case of a net operating loss of an individual for a taxable year beginning after December 31, 1982, and before January 1, 1987, for purposes of determining the amount of such loss which may be carried to a taxable year beginning after December 31, 1986, for purposes of the minimum tax, such loss shall be adjusted in the manner provided in section 55(d)(2) of the Internal Revenue Code of 1954 [now 1986] as in effect on the day before the date of the enactment of this Act [Oct. 22, 1986].

"(B) Corporations.—If the minimum tax of a corporation was deferred under section 56(b) of the Internal Revenue Code of 1954 [now 1986] (as in effect on the day before the date of the enactment of this Act [Oct. 22, 1986]) for any taxable year beginning before January 1, 1987, and the amount of such tax has not been paid for any taxable year beginning before January 1, 1987, the amount of the net operating loss carryovers of such corporation which may be carried to taxable years beginning after December 31, 1986, for purposes of the minimum tax shall be reduced by the amount of tax preferences a tax on which was so deferred.

"(3) Installment sales.—Section 56(a)(6) of the Internal Revenue Code of 1986 (as amended by this section) shall not apply to any disposition to which the amendments made by section 811 of this Act [enacting section 453C of this title] (relating to allocation of dealer's indebtedness to installment obligations) do not apply by reason of section 811(c)(2) of this Act [enacting provisions set out as a note under section 453C of this title].

"(4) Exception for charitable contributions before august 16, 1986.—Section 57(a)(6) of the Internal Revenue Code of 1986 (as amended by this section) shall not apply to any deduction attributable to contributions made before August 16, 1986.

"(5) Book income.—

"(A) In general.—In the case of a corporation to which this paragraph applies, the amount of any increase for any taxable year under [former] section 56(c)(1)(A) of the Internal Revenue Code of 1986 (as added by this section) shall be reduced (but not below zero) by the excess (if any) of—

"(i) 50 percent of the excess of taxable income for the 5-taxable year period ending with the taxable year preceding the 1st taxable year to which such section applies over the adjusted net book income for such period, over

"(ii) the aggregate amounts taken into account under this paragraph for preceding taxable years.

"(B) Taxpayer to whom paragraph applies.—This paragraph applies to a taxpayer which was incorporated in Delaware on May 31, 1912.

"(C) Terms.—Any term used in this paragraph which is used in section 56 of such Code (as so added) shall have the same meaning as when used in such section.

"(6) Certain public utility.—

"(A) In the case of investment tax credits described in subparagraph (B) or (C), subsection 38(c)(3)(A)(ii) of the Internal Revenue Code of 1986 shall be applied by substituting '25 percent' for '75 percent', and section 38(c)(3)(B) of the Internal Revenue Code of 1986 shall be applied by substituting '75 percent' for '25 percent'.

"(B) If, on September 25, 1985, a regulated electric utility owned an undivided interest, within the range of 1,111 and 1,149, in the 'maximum dependable capacity, net, megawatts electric' of an electric generating unit located in Illinois or Mississippi for which a binding written contract was in effect on December 31, 1980, then any investment tax credit with respect to such unit shall be described in this subparagraph. The aggregate amount of investment tax credits with respect to the unit in Mississippi allowed solely by reason of being described in this subparagraph shall not exceed $141,000,000.

"(C) If, on September 25, 1985, a regulated electric utility owned an undivided interest, within the range of 1,104 and 1,111, in the 'maximum dependable capacity, net, megawatts electric' of an electric generating unit located in Louisiana for which a binding written contract was in effect on December 31, 1980, then any investment tax credit of such electric utility shall be described in this subparagraph. The aggregate amount of investment tax credits allowed solely by reason of being described by this subparagraph shall not exceed $20,000,000.

"(7) Agreement vessel depreciation adjustment.—

"(A) For purposes of part VI of subchapter A of chapter 1 of the Internal Revenue Code of 1986, in the case of a qualified taxpayer, alternative minimum taxable income for the taxable year shall be reduced by an amount equal to the agreement vessel depreciation adjustment.

"(B) For purposes of this paragraph, the agreement vessel depreciation adjustment shall be an amount equal to the depreciation deduction that would have been allowable for such year under section 167 of such Code with respect to agreement vessels placed in service before January 1, 1987, if the basis of such vessels had not been reduced under section 607 of the Merchant Marine Act of 1936 [see 46 U.S.C. 53510], as amended, and if depreciation with respect to such vessel had been computed using the 25-year straight-line method. The aggregate amount by which basis of a qualified taxpayer is treated as not reduced by reason of this subparagraph shall not exceed $100,000,000.

"(C) For purposes of this paragraph, the term 'qualified taxpayer' means a parent corporation incorporated in the State of Delaware on December 1, 1972, and engaged in water transportation, and includes any other corporation which is a member of the affiliated group of which the parent corporation is the common parent. No taxpayer shall be treated as a qualified corporation for any taxable year beginning after December 31, 1991."

SAVINGS PROVISION

For provisions that nothing in amendment by section 11813(b)(5) of Pub. L. 101–508 be construed to affect treatment of certain transactions occurring, property acquired, or items of income, loss, deduction, or credit taken into account prior to Nov. 5, 1990, for purposes of determining liability for tax for periods ending after Nov. 5, 1990, see section 11821(b) of Pub. L. 101–508, set out as a note under section 45K of this title.

TRANSITIONAL PROVISIONS

Pub. L. 100–647, title I, §1007(f)(1), Nov. 10, 1988, 102 Stat. 3433, provided that: "In the case of the taxable year of an estate or trust which begins before January 1, 1987, and ends on or after such date, the items of tax preference apportioned to any beneficiary of such estate or trust under section 58(c) of the Internal Revenue Code of 1954 (as in effect on the day before the date of the enactment of the Tax Reform Act of 1986 [Oct. 22, 1986]) shall be taken into account for purposes of determining the amount of the tax imposed by section 55 of the Internal Revenue Code of 1986 (as amended by the Tax Reform Act of 1986 [Pub. L. 99–514]) on such beneficiary for such beneficiary's taxable year in which such taxable year of the estate or trust ends."

PLAN AMENDMENTS NOT REQUIRED UNTIL JANUARY 1, 1998

For provisions directing that if any amendments made by subtitle D [§§1401–1465] of title I of Pub. L. 104–188 require an amendment to any plan or annuity contract, such amendment shall not be required to be made before the first day of the first plan year beginning on or after Jan. 1, 1998, see section 1465 of Pub. L. 104–188, set out as a note under section 401 of this title.

PLAN AMENDMENTS NOT REQUIRED UNTIL JANUARY 1, 1994

For provisions directing that if any amendments made by subtitle B [§§521–523] of title V of Pub. L. 102–318 require an amendment to any plan, such plan amendment shall not be required to be made before the first plan year beginning on or after Jan. 1, 1994, see section 523 of Pub. L. 102–318, set out as a note under section 401 of this title.

APPLICABILITY OF CERTAIN AMENDMENTS BY PUB. L. 99–514 IN RELATION TO TREATY OBLIGATIONS OF UNITED STATES

For applicability of amendment by section 701(a) of Pub. L. 99–514 [enacting this section] notwithstanding any treaty obligation of the United States in effect on Oct. 22, 1986, with provision that for such purposes any amendment by title I of Pub. L. 100–647 be treated as if it had been included in the provision of Pub. L. 99–514 to which such amendment relates, see section 1012(aa)(2), (4) of Pub. L. 100–647, set out as a note under section 861 of this title.

HIGH INCOME TAXPAYER REPORT

Pub. L. 94–455, title XXI, §2123, Oct. 4, 1976, 90 Stat. 1915, as amended by Pub. L. 98–369, div. A, title IV, §441(b)(1), July 18, 1984, 98 Stat. 815, provided that: "The Secretary of the Treasury shall publish annually information on the amount of tax paid by individual taxpayers with high total incomes. Total income for this purpose is to be calculated and set forth by adding to adjusted gross income any items of tax preference excluded from, or deducted in arriving at, adjusted gross income, and by subtracting any investment expenses incurred in the production of such income to the extent of the investment income. These data are to include the number of such individuals with total income over $200,000 who owe no Federal income tax (after credits) and the deductions, exclusions, or credits used by them to avoid tax."

[Pub. L. 98–369, div. A, title IV, §441(b)(2), July 18, 1984, 98 Stat. 815, provided that: "The amendment made by paragraph (1) [amending section 2123 of Pub. L. 94–455] shall apply to information published after the date of the enactment of this Act [July 18, 1984]."]

¹ See References in Text note below.

§56. Adjustments in computing alternative minimum taxable income

(a) Adjustments applicable to all taxpayers

In determining the amount of the alternative minimum taxable income for any taxable year the following treatment shall apply (in lieu of the treatment applicable for purposes of computing the regular tax):

(1) Depreciation

(A) In general

(i) Property other than certain personal property

Except as provided in clause (ii), the depreciation deduction allowable under section 167 with respect to any tangible property placed in service after December 31, 1986, shall be determined under the alternative system of section 168(g). In the case of property placed in service after December 31, 1998, the preceding sentence shall not apply but clause (ii) shall continue to apply.

(ii) 150-percent declining balance method for certain property

The method of depreciation used shall be—

(I) the 150 percent declining balance method,

(II) switching to the straight line method for the 1st taxable year for which using the straight line method with respect to the adjusted basis as of the beginning of the year will yield a higher allowance.

The preceding sentence shall not apply to any section 1250 property (as defined in section 1250(c)) (and the straight line method shall be used for such section 1250 property) or to any other property if the depreciation deduction determined under section 168 with respect to such other property for purposes of the regular tax is determined by using the straight line method.

(B) Exception for certain property

This paragraph shall not apply to property described in paragraph (1), (2), (3), or (4) of section 168(f), or in section 168(e)(3)(C)(iv).

(C) Coordination with transitional rules

(i) In general

This paragraph shall not apply to property placed in service after December 31, 1986, to which the amendments made by section 201 of the Tax Reform Act of 1986 do not apply by reason of section 203, 204, or 251(d) of such Act.

(ii) Treatment of certain property placed in service before 1987

This paragraph shall apply to any property to which the amendments made by section 201 of the Tax Reform Act of 1986 apply by reason of an election under section 203(a)(1)(B) of such Act without regard to the requirement of subparagraph (A) that the property be placed in service after December 31, 1986.

(D) Normalization rules

With respect to public utility property described in section 168(i)(10), the Secretary shall prescribe the requirements of a normalization method of accounting for this section.

(2) Mining exploration and development costs

(A) In general

With respect to each mine or other natural deposit (other than an oil, gas, or geothermal well) of the taxpayer, the amount allowable as a deduction under section 616(a) or 617(a) (determined without regard to section 291(b)) in computing the regular tax for costs paid or incurred after December 31, 1986, shall be capitalized and amortized ratably over the 10-year period beginning with the taxable year in which the expenditures were made.

(B) Loss allowed

If a loss is sustained with respect to any property described in subparagraph (A), a deduction shall be allowed for the expenditures described in subparagraph (A) for the taxable year in which such loss is sustained in an amount equal to the lesser of—

(i) the amount allowable under section 165(a) for the expenditures if they had remained capitalized, or

(ii) the amount of such expenditures which have not previously been amortized under subparagraph (A).

(3) Treatment of certain long-term contracts

In the case of any long-term contract entered into by the taxpayer on or after March 1, 1986, the taxable income from such contract shall be determined under the percentage of completion method of accounting (as modified by section 460(b)). For purposes of the preceding sentence, in the case of a contract described in section 460(e)(1), the percentage of the contract completed shall be determined under section 460(b)(1) by using the simplified procedures for allocation of costs prescribed under section 460(b)(3). The first sentence of this paragraph shall not apply to any home construction contract (as defined in section 460(e)(6)).[1]

(4) Alternative tax net operating loss deduction

The alternative tax net operating loss deduction shall be allowed in lieu of the net operating loss deduction allowed under section 172.

(5) Pollution control facilities

In the case of any certified pollution control facility placed in service after December 31, 1986, the deduction allowable under section 169 (without regard to section 291) shall be determined under the alternative system of section 168(g). In the case of such a facility placed in service after December 31, 1998, such deduction shall be determined under section 168 using the straight line method.

(6) Adjusted basis

The adjusted basis of any property to which paragraph (1) or (5) applies (or with respect to which there are any expenditures to which paragraph (2) or subsection (b)(2) applies) shall be determined on the basis of the treatment prescribed in paragraph (1), (2), or (5), or subsection (b)(2), whichever applies.

(7) Section 87 not applicable

Section 87 (relating to alcohol fuel credit) shall not apply.

(b) Adjustments applicable to individuals

In determining the amount of the alternative minimum taxable income of any taxpayer (other than a corporation), the following treatment shall apply (in lieu of the treatment applicable for purposes of computing the regular tax):

(1) Limitation on deductions

(A) In general

No deduction shall be allowed—

(i) for any miscellaneous itemized deduction (as defined in section 67(b)), or

(ii) for any taxes described in paragraph (1), (2), or (3) of section 164(a) or clause (ii) of section 164(b)(5)(A).

Clause (ii) shall not apply to any amount allowable in computing adjusted gross income.

(B) Interest

In determining the amount allowable as a deduction for interest, subsections (d) and (h) of section 163 shall apply, except that—

(i) in lieu of the exception under section 163(h)(2)(D), the term "personal interest" shall not include any qualified housing interest (as defined in subsection (e)),

(ii) interest on any specified private activity bond (and any amount treated as interest on a specified private activity bond under section 57(a)(5)(B)), and any deduction referred to in section 57(a)(5)(A), shall be treated as includible in gross income (or as deductible) for purposes of applying section 163(d),

(iii) in lieu of the exception under section 163(d)(3)(B)(i), the term "investment interest" shall not include any qualified housing interest (as defined in subsection (e)), and

(iv) the adjustments of this section and sections 57 and 58 shall apply in determining net investment income under section 163(d).

(C) Treatment of certain recoveries

No recovery of any tax to which subparagraph (A)(ii) applied shall be included in gross income for purposes of determining alternative minimum taxable income.

(D) Standard deduction and deduction for personal exemptions not allowed

The standard deduction under section 63(c), the deduction for personal exemptions under section 151, and the deduction under section 642(b) shall not be allowed.

(E) Section 68 not applicable

Section 68 shall not apply.

(2) Circulation and research and experimental expenditures

(A) In general

The amount allowable as a deduction under section 173 or 174(a) in computing the regular tax for amounts paid or incurred after December 31, 1986, shall be capitalized and—

(i) in the case of circulation expenditures described in section 173, shall be amortized ratably over the 3-year period beginning with the taxable year in which the expenditures were made, or

(ii) in the case of research and experimental expenditures described in section 174(a), shall be amortized ratably over the 10-year period beginning with the taxable year in which the expenditures were made.

(B) Loss allowed

If a loss is sustained with respect to any property described in subparagraph (A), a deduction shall be allowed for the expenditures described in subparagraph (A) for the taxable year in which such loss is sustained in an amount equal to the lesser of—

(i) the amount allowable under section 165(a) for the expenditures if they had remained capitalized, or

(ii) the amount of such expenditures which have not previously been amortized under subparagraph (A).

(C) Exception for certain research and experimental expenditures

If the taxpayer materially participates (within the meaning of section 469(h)) in an activity, this paragraph shall not apply to any amount allowable as a deduction under section 174(a) for expenditures paid or incurred in connection with such activity.

(3) Treatment of incentive stock options

Section 421 shall not apply to the transfer of stock acquired pursuant to the exercise of an incentive stock option (as defined in section 422). Section 422(c)(2) shall apply in any case where the disposition and the inclusion for purposes of this part are within the same taxable year and such section shall not apply in any other case. The adjusted basis of any stock so acquired shall be determined on the basis of the treatment prescribed by this paragraph.

[(c) Repealed. Pub. L. 115–97, title I, §12001(b)(8)(A), Dec. 22, 2017, 131 Stat. 2093]

(d) Alternative tax net operating loss deduction defined

(1) In general

For purposes of subsection (a)(4), the term "alternative tax net operating loss deduction" means the net operating loss deduction allowable for the taxable year under section 172, except that—

(A) the amount of such deduction shall not exceed the sum of—

(i) the lesser of—

(I) the amount of such deduction attributable to net operating losses (other than the deduction described in clause (ii)(I)), or

(II) 90 percent of alternative minimum taxable income determined without regard to such deduction and the deduction under section 199,[1] plus

(ii) the lesser of—

(I) the amount of such deduction attributable to an applicable net operating loss with respect to which an election is made under section 172(b)(1)(H) (as in effect before its repeal by the Tax Increase Prevention Act of 2014), or

(II) alternative minimum taxable income determined without regard to such deduction and the deduction under section 199[1] reduced by the amount determined under clause (i), and

(B) in determining the amount of such deduction—

(i) the net operating loss (within the meaning of section 172(c)) for any loss year shall be adjusted as provided in paragraph (2), and

(ii) appropriate adjustments in the application of section 172(b)(2) shall be made to take into account the limitation of subparagraph (A).

(2) Adjustments to net operating loss computation

(A) Post-1986 loss years

In the case of a loss year beginning after December 31, 1986, the net operating loss for such year under section 172(c) shall—

(i) be determined with the adjustments provided in this section and section 58, and

(ii) be reduced by the items of tax preference determined under section 57 for such year.

An item of tax preference shall be taken into account under clause (ii) only to the extent such item increased the amount of the net operating loss for the taxable year under section 172(c).

(B) Pre-1987 years

In the case of loss years beginning before January 1, 1987, the amount of the net operating loss which may be carried over to taxable years beginning after December 31, 1986, for purposes of paragraph (2), shall be equal to the amount which may be carried from the loss year to the first taxable year of the taxpayer beginning after December 31, 1986.

(e) Qualified housing interest

For purposes of this part—

(1) In general

The term "qualified housing interest" means interest which is qualified residence interest (as defined in section 163(h)(3)) and is paid or accrued during the taxable year on indebtedness which is incurred in acquiring, constructing, or substantially improving any property which—

(A) is the principal residence (within the meaning of section 121) of the taxpayer at the time such interest accrues, or

(B) is a qualified dwelling which is a qualified residence (within the meaning of section 163(h)(4)).

Such term also includes interest on any indebtedness resulting from the refinancing of indebtedness meeting the requirements of the preceding sentence; but only to the extent that the amount of the indebtedness resulting from such refinancing does not exceed the amount of the refinanced indebtedness immediately before the refinancing.

(2) Qualified dwelling

The term "qualified dwelling" means any—

(A) house,

(B) apartment,

(C) condominium, or

(D) mobile home not used on a transient basis (within the meaning of section 7701(a)(19)(C)(v)),

including all structures or other property appurtenant thereto.

(3) Special rule for indebtedness incurred before July 1, 1982

The term "qualified housing interest" includes interest which is qualified residence interest (as defined in section 163(h)(3)) and is paid or accrued on indebtedness which—

(A) was incurred by the taxpayer before July 1, 1982, and

(B) is secured by property which, at the time such indebtedness was incurred, was—

(i) the principal residence (within the meaning of section 121) of the taxpayer, or

(ii) a qualified dwelling used by the taxpayer (or any member of his family (within the meaning of section 267(c)(4))).

(Added Pub. L. 99–514, title VII, §701(a), Oct. 22, 1986, 100 Stat. 2322; amended Pub. L. 100–203, title X, §§10202(d), 10243(a), Dec. 22, 1987, 101 Stat. 1330–392, 1330-423; Pub. L. 100–647, title I, §§1002(a)(12), 1007(b)(1)–(14)(A), (15)–(19), title II, §§2001(c)(3)(A), 2004(b)(2), (3), title V, §5041(b)(4), title VI, §§6079(a)(1), 6303(a), Nov. 10, 1988, 102 Stat. 3355, 3428-3432, 3594, 3599, 3674, 3709, 3755; Pub. L. 101–239, title VII, §§7205(b), 7611(a)–(f)(4), 7612(c)(1), (d)(1), 7811(d)(3), 7815(e)(2), (4), Dec. 19, 1989, 103 Stat. 2335, 2371-2374, 2408, 2419; Pub. L. 101–508, title XI, §§11103(b), 11301(b), 11531(a), (b)(1), 11704(a)(1), 11801(a)(3), (c)(2)(A)–(C), (9)(G), 11812(b)(4), Nov. 5, 1990, 104 Stat. 1388–406, 1388-449, 1388-488, 1388-490, 1388-518, 1388-520, 1388-522, 1388-523, 1388-526, 1388-535; Pub. L. 102–486, title XIX, §1915(a)(2), (b)(2), (c)(1), (2), Oct. 24, 1992, 106 Stat. 3023, 3024; Pub. L. 103–66, title XIII, §§13115(a), 13171(b), 13227(c), Aug. 10, 1993, 107 Stat. 432, 454, 493; Pub. L. 104–188, title I, §§1601(b)(2)(B), (C), 1621(b)(2), 1702(c)(1), (e)(1)(A), (g)(4), (h)(12), 1704(t)(1), (48), Aug. 20, 1996, 110 Stat. 1832, 1833, 1867, 1869, 1870, 1873, 1874, 1887, 1889; Pub. L. 105–34, title III, §312(d)(1), title IV, §§402, 403(a), title XII, §1212(a), Aug. 5, 1997, 111 Stat. 839, 844, 1000; Pub. L. 105–277, div. J, title IV, §4006(c)(2), Oct. 21, 1998, 112 Stat. 2681–912; Pub. L. 106–519, §4(1), Nov. 15, 2000, 114 Stat. 2432; Pub. L. 106–554, §1(a)(7) [title III, §314(d)], Dec. 21, 2000, 114 Stat. 2763, 2763A-643; Pub. L. 107–147, title I, §102(c)(1), title IV, §417(5), Mar. 9, 2002, 116 Stat. 26, 56; Pub. L. 108–173, title XII, §1202(b), Dec. 8, 2003, 117 Stat. 2480; Pub. L. 108–311, title IV, §403(b)(4), Oct. 4, 2004, 118 Stat. 1187; Pub. L. 108–357, title I, §§101(b)(4), 102(b), title II, §248(b)(1), title IV, §422(b), title VIII, §835(b)(1), Oct. 22, 2004, 118 Stat. 1423, 1428, 1457, 1519, 1593; Pub. L. 109–58, title XIII, §1326(d), Aug. 8, 2005, 119 Stat. 1017; Pub. L. 109–135, title IV, §403(a)(14), (r)(2), Dec. 21, 2005, 119 Stat. 2619, 2628; Pub. L. 109–304, §17(e)(1), Oct. 6, 2006, 120 Stat. 1707; Pub. L. 110–172, §11(g)(1), (2), Dec. 29, 2007, 121 Stat. 2489, 2490; Pub. L. 110–289, div. C, title I, §3022(a)(2), July 30, 2008, 122 Stat. 2894; Pub. L. 110–343, div. C, title VII, §§706(b)(3), 708(c), Oct. 3, 2008, 122 Stat. 3922, 3925; Pub. L. 111–5, div. B, title I, §§1008(d), 1503(b), Feb. 17, 2009, 123 Stat. 318, 354; Pub. L. 111–92, §13(b), Nov. 6, 2009, 123 Stat. 2993; Pub. L. 111–148, title IX, §9013(c), Mar. 23, 2010, 124 Stat. 868; Pub. L. 113–295, div. A, title II, §§215(b), 221(a)(9), (25)(B), (30)(C), Dec. 19, 2014, 128 Stat. 4034, 4038, 4040, 4042; Pub. L. 115–97, title I, §§11027(b), 12001(b)(7), (8)(A), Dec. 22, 2017, 131 Stat. 2077, 2093; Pub. L. 115–141, div. U, title IV, §401(b)(7), (8), Mar. 23, 2018, 132 Stat. 1202; Pub. L. 116–94, div. Q, title I, §103(b), Dec. 20, 2019, 133 Stat. 3228.)

REFERENCES IN TEXT

Section 201 of the Tax Reform Act of 1986, referred to in subsecs. (a)(1)(C) and (g)(4)(A)(ii), is section 201 of Pub. L. 99–514, which amended sections 46, 167, 168, 178, 179, 280F, 291, 312, 465, 467, 514, 751, 1245, 4162, 6111, and 7701 of this title.

Sections 203, 204, and 251(d) of such Act, referred to in subsec. (a)(1)(C), are sections 203, 204, and 251(d) of the Tax Reform Act of 1986, Pub. L. 99–514. Sections 203 and 204 are set out as notes under section 168 of this title. Section 251(d) is set out as a note under section 46 of this title.

Section 460(e)(6), referred to in subsec. (a)(3), was redesignated section 460(e)(5) by Pub. L. 115–97, title I, §13102(d)(2), Dec. 22, 2017, 131 Stat. 2104.

Section 199, referred to in subsec. (d)(1)(A)(i)(II), (ii)(II), was repealed by Pub. L. 115–97, title I, §13305(a), Dec. 22, 2017, 131 Stat. 2126.

Section 172(b)(1)(H) (as in effect before its repeal by the Tax Increase Prevention Act of 2014), referred to subsec. (d)(1)(A)(ii)(I), means subpar. (H) of section 172(b)(1) of this title prior to its repeal by Pub. L. 113–295, div. A, title II, §221(a)(30)(A)(i), Dec. 19, 2014, 128 Stat. 4041.

The date of the enactment of the Tax Reform Act of 1986, referred to in subsec. (g)(4)(A)(iii), is the date of enactment of Pub. L. 99–514, which was approved Oct. 22, 1986.

The FSC Repeal and Extraterritorial Income Exclusion Act of 2000, referred to in subsec. (g)(4)(C)(ii)(I), is Pub. L. 106–519, Nov. 15, 2000, 114 Stat. 2423. For complete classification of this Act to the Code, see Short Title of 2000 Amendments note set out under section 1 of this title and Tables.

PRIOR PROVISIONS

A prior section 56, added Pub. L. 91–172, title III, §301(a), Dec. 30, 1969, 83 Stat. 580; amended Pub. L. 91–614, title V, §501(a), Dec. 31, 1970, 84 Stat. 1846; Pub. L. 92–178, title VI, §601(c)(4), (5), Dec. 10, 1971, 85 Stat. 558; Pub. L. 93–406, title II, §§2001(g)(2)(D), 2002(g)(4), 2005(c)(7), Sept. 2, 1974, 88 Stat. 957, 968, 991; Pub. L. 94–12, title II, §§203(b)(2), (3), 208(d)(2), (3), Mar. 29, 1975, 89 Stat. 30, 35; Pub. L. 94–455, title III, §301(a), (b), (c)(4)(B), Oct. 4, 1976, 90 Stat. 1549, 1552; Pub. L. 95–30, title II, §202(d)(2), May 23, 1977, 91 Stat. 148; Pub. L. 95–600, title I, §141(d), Nov. 6, 1978, 92 Stat. 2794; Pub. L. 95–618, title I, §101(b)(2), Nov. 9, 1978, 92 Stat. 3179; Pub. L. 96–222, title I, §101(a)(7)(L)(iii)(IV), Apr. 1, 1980, 94 Stat. 200; Pub. L. 97–34, title III, §331(c)(2), Aug. 13, 1981, 95 Stat. 293; Pub. L. 97–248, title II, §201(d)(1), formerly §201(c)(1), Sept. 3, 1982, 96 Stat. 419, renumbered §201(d)(1), Pub. L. 97–448, title III, §306(a)(1)(A)(i), Jan. 12, 1983, 96 Stat. 2400; Pub. L. 98–369, div. A, title IV, §474(r)(1), July 18, 1984, 98 Stat. 839; Pub. L. 99–514, title XI, §1171(b)(3), Oct. 22, 1986, 100 Stat. 2513, related to a corporate minimum tax, prior to the general revision of this part by Pub. L. 99–514, §701(a).

AMENDMENTS

2019—Subsec. (b)(1)(B) to (F). Pub. L. 116–94 redesignated subpars. (C) to (F) as (B) to (E), respectively, and struck out former subpar. (B). Prior to amendment, text of subpar. (B) read as follows: "In determining the amount allowable as a deduction under section 213, subsection (a) of section 213 shall be applied without regard to subsection (f) of such section. This subparagraph shall not apply to taxable years beginning after December 31, 2016, and ending before January 1, 2019".

2018—Subsec. (b)(1)(E). Pub. L. 115–141, §401(b)(7), struck out at end "The preceding sentence shall not apply to so much of the standard deduction as is determined under subparagraphs (D) and (E) of section 63(c)(1)."

Subsec. (d)(1)(A)(ii)(I). Pub. L. 115–141, §401(b)(8), inserted "(as in effect before its repeal by the Tax Increase Prevention Act of 2014)" after "section 172(b)(1)(H)".

2017—Subsec. (b)(1)(B). Pub. L. 115–97, §11027(b), inserted at end "This subparagraph shall not apply to taxable years beginning after December 31, 2016, and ending before January 1, 2019".

Subsec. (b)(2)(C), (D). Pub. L. 115–97, §12001(b)(7), redesignated subpar. (D) as (C) and struck out former subpar. (C). Prior to amendment, text of subpar. (C) read as follows: "In the case of circulation expenditures described in section 173, the adjustments provided in this paragraph shall apply also to a personal holding company (as defined in section 542)."

Subsec. (c). Pub. L. 115–97, §12001(b)(8)(A), struck out subsec. (c) which related to adjustments applicable to corporations.

Subsec. (g). Pub. L. 115–97, §12001(b)(8)(A), struck out subsec. (g) which related to adjustments based on adjusted current earnings.

2014—Subsec. (b)(1)(C)(ii) to (v). Pub. L. 113–295, §221(a)(25)(B), redesignated cls. (iii) to (v) as (ii) to (iv), respectively, and struck out former cl. (ii) which read as follows: "sections 163(d)(6) and 163(h)(5) (relating to phase-ins) shall not apply,".

Subsec. (d)(3). Pub. L. 113–295, §221(a)(30)(C), struck out par. (3). Text read as follows: "In the case of a taxpayer which has a qualified disaster loss (as defined by section 172(b)(1)(J)) for the taxable year, paragraph (1) shall be applied by increasing the amount determined under subparagraph (A)(ii)(I) thereof by the sum of the carrybacks and carryovers of such loss."

Subsec. (g)(4)(C)(iv). Pub. L. 113–295, §215(b), substituted "an organization to which part I of subchapter T (relating to tax treatment of cooperatives) applies which is engaged in the marketing of agricultural or horticultural products" for "a cooperative described in section 927(a)(4)". See 2007 Amendment note below.

Subsec. (g)(4)(F)(ii). Pub. L. 113–295, §221(a)(9), substituted "Clause (i)" for "In the case of any taxable year beginning after December 31, 1992, clause (i)".

2010—Subsec. (b)(1)(B). Pub. L. 111–148 substituted "without regard to subsection (f) of such section" for "by substituting '10 percent' for '7.5 percent' ".

2009—Subsec. (b)(1)(E). Pub. L. 111–5, §1008(d), substituted "subparagraphs (D) and (E) of section 63(c)(1)" for "section 63(c)(1)(D)".

Subsec. (d)(1)(A)(ii)(I). Pub. L. 111–92 amended subcl. (I) generally. Prior to amendment, subcl. (I) read as follows: "the amount of such deduction attributable to the sum of carrybacks of net operating losses from taxable years ending during 2001 or 2002 and carryovers of net operating losses to taxable years ending during 2001 and 2002, or".

Subsec. (g)(4)(B)(iv). Pub. L. 111–5, §1503(b), added cl. (iv).

2008—Subsec. (b)(1)(E). Pub. L. 110–343, §706(b)(3), inserted at end "The preceding sentence shall not apply to so much of the standard deduction as is determined under section 63(c)(1)(D)."

Subsec. (d)(3). Pub. L. 110–343, §708(c), added par. (3).

Subsec. (g)(4)(B)(iii). Pub. L. 110–289 added cl. (iii).

2007—Subsec. (g)(4)(C)(ii)(I). Pub. L. 110–172, §11(g)(1), substituted "921 (as in effect before its repeal by the FSC Repeal and Extraterritorial Income Exclusion Act of 2000)" for "921".

Subsec. (g)(4)(C)(iv). Pub. L. 110–172, §11(g)(2), which purported to amend subsec. (g)(4)(C)(iv) of this section, but directed the amendment of section 54(g)(4)(C)(iv) of this title, by substituting "an organization to which part I of subchapter T (relating to tax treatment of cooperatives) applies which is engaged in the marketing of agricultural or horticultural products" for "a cooperative described in section 927(a)(4)", was not executed in light of the identical amendment made by Pub. L. 113–295, §215(b), effective as if included in Pub. L. 110–172. See 2014 Amendment note above.

2006—Subsec. (c)(2). Pub. L. 109–304, in introductory provisions, substituted "chapter 535 of title 46, United States Code" for "section 607 of the Merchant Marine Act, 1936 (46 U.S.C. 1177)", and, in subpars. (A) and (B), substituted "such chapter 535" for "such section 607".

2005—Subsec. (a)(1)(B). Pub. L. 109–58 inserted ", or in section 168(e)(3)(C)(iv)" before period at end.

Subsec. (b)(1)(A)(ii). Pub. L. 109–135, §403(r)(2), inserted "or clause (ii) of section 164(b)(5)(A)" before period at end.

Subsec. (d)(1)(A)(i)(II), (ii)(II). Pub. L. 109–135, §403(a)(14), substituted "such deduction and the deduction under section 199" for "such deduction".

2004—Subsec. (d)(1)(A)(i)(I). Pub. L. 108–311, §403(b)(4)(A), struck out "attributable to carryovers" after "other than the deduction".

Subsec. (d)(1)(A)(ii)(I). Pub. L. 108–311, §403(b)(4)(B), substituted "from taxable years" for "for taxable years" and "carryovers" for "carryforwards".

Subsec. (g)(4)(B)(i). Pub. L. 108–357, §248(b)(1), inserted "or 1357" after "section 139A" in concluding provisions.

Pub. L. 108–357, §101(b)(4), struck out "114 or" before "139A" in concluding provisions.

Subsec. (g)(4)(C)(v). Pub. L. 108–357, §102(b), added cl. (v).

Subsec. (g)(4)(C)(vi). Pub. L. 108–357, §422(b), added cl. (vi).

Subsec. (g)(6). Pub. L. 108–357, §835(b)(1), substituted "or REMIC" for "REMIC, or FASIT".

2003—Subsec. (g)(4)(B)(i). Pub. L. 108–173 inserted "or 139A" after "section 114" in concluding provisions.

2002—Subsec. (a)(1)(A)(ii). Pub. L. 107–147, §417(5), substituted "such section 1250" for "such 1250" in concluding provisions.

Subsec. (d)(1)(A). Pub. L. 107–147, §102(c)(1), amended subpar. (A) generally. Prior to amendment, subpar. (A) read as follows: "the amount of such deduction shall not exceed 90 percent of alternate minimum taxable income determined without regard to such deduction, and".

2000—Subsec. (a)(1)(A)(ii). Pub. L. 106–554 inserted "(and the straight line method shall be used for such 1250 property)" before "or to any other property" in concluding provisions.

Subsec. (g)(4)(B)(i). Pub. L. 106–519 inserted "or under section 114" before the period at end of first sentence in concluding provisions.

1998—Subsec. (a)(3). Pub. L. 105–277 substituted "section 460(b)(1)" for "section 460(b)(2)" and "section 460(b)(3)" for "section 460(b)(4)".

1997—Subsec. (a)(1)(A)(i). Pub. L. 105–34, §402(a), inserted at end "In the case of property placed in service after December 31, 1998, the preceding sentence shall not apply but clause (ii) shall continue to apply."

Subsec. (a)(5). Pub. L. 105–34, §402(b), inserted at end "In the case of such a facility placed in service after December 31, 1998, such deduction shall be determined under section 168 using the straight line method."

Subsec. (a)(6) to (8). Pub. L. 105–34, §403(a), redesignated pars. (7) and (8) as (6) and (7), respectively, and struck out former par. (6) which read as follows:

"(6) Installment sales of certain property.—In the case of any disposition after March 1, 1986, of any property described in section 1221(1), income from such disposition shall be determined without regard to the installment method under section 453. This paragraph shall not apply to any disposition with respect to which an election is in effect under section 453(l)(2)(B)."

Subsec. (e)(1)(A), (3)(B)(i). Pub. L. 105–34, §312(d)(1), substituted "section 121" for "section 1034".

Subsec. (g)(4)(B)(i). Pub. L. 105–34, §1212(a), inserted at end of concluding provisions "In the case of any insurance company taxable under section 831(b), this clause shall not apply to any amount not described in section 834(b)."

1996—Subsec. (b)(3). Pub. L. 104–188, §1702(h)(12), provided that the amendment made by section 11801(c)(9)(G)(ii) of Pub. L. 101–508 shall be applied as if it struck "Section 422A(c)(2)" and inserted "Section 422(c)(2)". See 1990 Amendment note below.

Subsec. (d)(1)(B)(ii). Pub. L. 101–508, §1702(e)(1)(A), amended cl. (ii) generally. Prior to amendment, cl. (ii) read as follows: "in the case of taxable years beginning after December 31, 1986, section 172(b)(2) shall be applied by substituting '90 percent of alternative minimum taxable income determined without regard to the alternative tax net operating loss deduction' for 'taxable income' each place it appears."

Subsec. (g)(1), (2)(A). Pub. L. 104–188, §1704(f)(48), provided that section 11801(c)(2)(B) of Pub. L. 101–508 shall be applied as if "section 56(g)" appeared instead of "section 59(g)". See 1990 Amendment note below.

Subsec. (g)(4)(C)(ii)(I). Pub. L. 104–188, §1601(b)(2)(B), inserted "30A," before "936" and substituted ", (i), and (j)" for "and (i)".

Subsec. (g)(4)(C)(ii)(II). Pub. L. 104–188, §1704(t)(1), substituted "of subclause" for "of the subclause".

Subsec. (g)(4)(C)(iii)(VI). Pub. L. 104–188, §1601(b)(2)(C), added subcl. (VI).

Subsec. (g)(4)(D)(iii). Pub. L. 104–188, §1702(g)(4), inserted ", but only with respect to taxable years beginning after December 31, 1989" before period at end.

Subsec. (g)(4)(H) to (J). Pub. L. 104–188, §1702(c)(1), redesignated subpars. (I) and (J) as (H) and (I), respectively.

Subsec. (g)(6). Pub. L. 104–188, §1621(b)(2), substituted "REMIC, or FASIT" for "or REMIC".

1993—Subsec. (g)(4)(A)(i). Pub. L. 103–66, §13115(a), inserted at end "The preceding sentence shall not apply to any property placed in service after December 31, 1993, and the depreciation deduction with respect to such property shall be determined under the rules of subsection (a)(1)(A)."

Subsec. (g)(4)(C)(ii)(I). Pub. L. 103–66, §13227(c)(1), substituted "sections 936 (including subsections (a)(4) and (i) thereof) and 921" for "sections 936 and 921".

Subsec. (g)(4)(C)(iii)(IV), (V). Pub. L. 103–66, §13227(c)(2), added subcls. (IV) and (V).

Subsec. (g)(4)(J). Pub. L. 103–66, §13171(b), added subpar. (J).

1992—Subsec. (d)(1)(A). Pub. L. 102–486, §1915(c)(2), amended subpar. (A) generally. Prior to amendment, subpar. (A) read as follows: "the amount of such deduction shall not exceed the excess (if any) of—

"(i) 90 percent of alternative minimum taxable income determined without regard to such deduction and the deduction under subsection (h), over

"(ii) the deduction under subsection (h), and".

Subsec. (g)(4)(D)(i). Pub. L. 102–486, §1915(b)(2), inserted at end "In the case of a taxpayer other than an integrated oil company (as defined in section 291(b)(4)), in the case of any oil or gas well, this clause shall not apply in the case of amounts paid or incurred in taxable years beginning after December 31, 1992."

Subsec. (g)(4)(F). Pub. L. 102–486, §1915(a)(2), amended subpar. (F) generally. Prior to amendment, subpar. (F) read as follows: "The allowance for depletion with respect to any property placed in service in a taxable year beginning after 1989 shall be cost depletion determined under section 611."

Subsec. (h). Pub. L. 102–486, §1915(c)(1), struck out subsec. (h) which related to adjustment based on energy preferences.

1990—Subsec. (a)(1)(D). Pub. L. 101–508, §11812(b)(4), substituted "section 168(i)(10)" for "section 167(l)(3)(A)".

410

Subsec. (b)(1)(F). Pub. L. 101–508, §11103(b), added subpar. (F).

Subsec. (b)(3). Pub. L. 101–508, §11801(c)(9)(G)(i), substituted "section 422" for "section 422A".

Pub. L. 101–508, §11801(c)(9)(G)(ii), which directed the substitution of "section 422(c)(2)" for "section 422A(c)(2)", was executed by substituting "Section 422(c)(2)" for "Section 422A(c)(2)". See 1996 Amendment note above.

Subsec. (c)(1). Pub. L. 101–508, §11801(c)(2)(A), substituted heading for one which read: "Adjustment for book income or adjusted current earnings" and amended text generally. Prior to amendment, text read as follows:

"(A) Book income adjustment.—For taxable years beginning in 1987, 1988, and 1989, alternative minimum taxable income shall be adjusted as provided under subsection (f).

"(B) Adjusted current earnings.—For taxable years beginning after 1989, alternative minimum taxable income shall be adjusted as provided under subsection (g)."

Subsec. (d)(1)(A). Pub. L. 101–508, §11531(b)(1), amended subpar. (A) generally. Prior to amendment, subpar. (A) read as follows: "the amount of such deduction shall not exceed 90 percent of alternative minimum taxable income determined without regard to such deduction, and".

Subsec. (f). Pub. L. 101–508, §11801(a)(3), struck out subsec. (f) which related to adjustments for book income of corporations with respect to minimum taxable income, adjusted net book income, adjustments for certain taxes, special rules for related corporations for consolidated returns, treatment of dividends, statements covering different periods, special rule for cooperatives, treatment and limitation of taxes on dividends from 936 corporations, rules for Alaska native corporations, special rules for life insurance companies, exclusion of certain income from transfer of stock for debt, secretarial authority to adjust items, applicable financial statements, earnings and profits used, special rules for more than one statement and exception for certain corporations.

Subsec. (g)(1), (2)(A). Pub. L. 101–508, §11801(c)(2)(B), which directed that pars. (1) and (2) "of section 59(g) are each amended by striking 'beginning after 1989' ", was executed to pars. (1) and (2)(A) of subsec. (g) of this section after "any taxable year". See 1996 Amendment note above.

Subsec. (g)(4)(C)(iii). Pub. L. 101–508, §11801(c)(2)(C), substituted heading for one which read: "Special rule for dividends from section 936 companies" and amended text generally. Prior to amendment, text read as follows: "In the case of any dividend received from a corporation eligible for the credit provided by section 936, rules similar to the rules of subparagraph (F) of subsection (f)(1) shall apply, except that '75 percent' shall be substituted for '50 percent' in clause (i) thereof."

Subsec. (g)(4)(D)(ii). Pub. L. 101–508, §11704(a)(1), substituted "years" for "year".

Subsec. (g)(4)(F) to (H). Pub. L. 101–508, §11301(b), redesignated subpars. (G) and (H) as (F) and (G), respectively, and struck out former subpar. (F) which provided that acquisition expenses for life insurance companies be capitalized and amortized in accordance with the treatment generally required under generally accepted accounting principles as if this subparagraph applied to all taxable years.

Subsec. (h). Pub. L. 101–508, §11531(a), added subsec. (h).

1989—Subsec. (a)(3). Pub. L. 101–239, §7815(e)(2)(B), substituted "The first sentence of this paragraph shall not" for "The preceding sentence shall not".

Pub. L. 101–239, §7815(e)(2)(A), made clarifying amendment to directory language of Pub. L. 100–647, §5041(b)(4), see 1988 Amendment note below.

Pub. L. 101–239, §7612(c)(1), struck out "with respect to which the requirements of clauses (i) and (ii) of section 460(e)(1)(B) are met" after "section 460(e)(6))".

Subsec. (b)(2)(D). Pub. L. 101–239, §7612(d)(1), added subpar. (D).

Subsec. (b)(3). Pub. L. 101–239, §7811(d)(3), inserted after first sentence "Section 422A(c)(2) shall apply in any case where the disposition and the inclusion for purposes of this part are within the same taxable year and such section shall not apply in any other case." and substituted "this paragraph" for "the preceding sentence" in last sentence.

Subsec. (g)(4)(A)(i). Pub. L. 101–239, §7611(a)(1)(A), amended cl. (i) generally. Prior to amendment cl. (i) read as follows: "The depreciation deduction with respect to any property placed in service in a taxable year beginning after 1989 shall be determined under whichever of the following methods yields deductions with a smaller present value:

"(I) The alternative system of section 168(g), or

"(II) The method used for book purposes."

Subsec. (g)(4)(A)(iii). Pub. L. 101–239, §7611(a)(2), inserted "and which is placed in service in a taxable year beginning before 1990" after "thereof) applies".

Subsec. (g)(4)(A)(v) to (vii). Pub. L. 101–239, §7611(a)(1)(B), redesignated cl. (vii) as (v), and struck out former cl. (v), which related to use of slower method if used for book purposes, and cl. (vi), which related to election to have cumulative limitation.

Subsec. (g)(4)(B)(i). Pub. L. 101–239, §7611(f)(2), inserted at end "The preceding sentence shall not apply in the case of any amount excluded from gross income under section 108 (or the corresponding provisions of prior law)."

Subsec. (g)(4)(B)(iii). Pub. L. 101–239, §7611(f)(3), repealed cl. (iii) which read as follows: "In the case of any annuity contract, the income on such contract (as determined under section 72(u)(2)) shall be treated as includible in gross income for such year. The preceding sentence shall not apply to any annuity contract which is held under a plan described in section 403(a) or which is described in section 72(u)(3)(C)."

Subsec. (g)(4)(C)(ii). Pub. L. 101–239, §7611(d), amended cl. (ii) generally. Prior to amendment, cl. (ii) read as follows: "Clause (i) shall not apply to any deduction allowable under section 243 or 245 for a 100-percent dividend—

"(I) if the corporation receiving such dividend and the corporation paying such dividend could not be members of the same affiliated group under section 1504 by reason of section 1504(b),

"(II) but only to the extent such dividend is attributable to income of the paying corporation which is subject to tax under this chapter (determined after the application of sections 936 and 921).

For purposes of the preceding sentence, the term '100 percent dividend' means any dividend if the percentage used for purposes of determining the amount allowable as a deduction under section 243 or 245 with respect to such dividend is 100 percent."

Subsec. (g)(4)(C)(iv). Pub. L. 101–239, §7611(e), added cl. (iv).

Subsec. (g)(4)(D). Pub. L. 101–239, §7611(b), amended subpar. (D) generally, in cl. (i), substituting provisions directing that adjustments in section 312(n)(2)(A) be applied, for provisions directing adjustments in section 312(n) be applied, with certain exceptions, in cl. (ii), substituting provisions directing that sections 173 and 248 not apply to expenditures paid or incurred in taxable years beginning after December 31, 1989, for material relating to special rule for intangible drilling costs and mineral exploration and development costs, and adding cls. (iii) and (iv).

Subsec. (g)(4)(D)(i)(IV), (V). Pub. L. 101–239, §7815(e)(4), added subcl. (IV) relating to inapplicability of pars. (6) to (8) and struck out former subcls. (IV) and (V), which read as follows:

"(IV) paragraph (6) shall apply only to contracts entered into on or after March 1, 1986, and

"(V) paragraphs (7) and (8) shall not apply."

Subsec. (g)(4)(G). Pub. L. 101–239, §7611(c), amended subpar. (G) generally. Prior to amendment, subpar. (G) read as follows: "The allowances for depletion with respect to any property placed in service in a taxable year beginning after 1989, shall be determined under whichever of the following methods yields deductions with a smaller present value:

"(i) cost depletion determined under section 611, or

"(ii) the method used for book purposes."

Subsec. (g)(4)(H). Pub. L. 101–239, §7205(b), added cl. (ii) and concluding provision and struck out former cl. (ii) and concluding provision which read as follows:

"(ii)(I) the aggregate adjusted bases of the assets of such corporation (immediately after the change), exceed

"(II) the value of the stock of such corporation (as determined for purposes of section 382), properly adjusted for liabilities and other relevant items,

then the adjusted basis of each asset of such corporation (as of such time) shall be its proportionate share (determined on the basis of respective fair market values) of the amount referred to in clause (ii)(II)."

Subsec. (g)(4)(H)(i). Pub. L. 101–239, §7611(f)(1), substituted "in a taxable year beginning after 1989" for "after the date of the enactment of the Tax Reform Act of 1986".

Subsec. (g)(5)(A). Pub. L. 101–239, §7611(f)(4), redesignated subpar. (B) as (A) and struck out former subpar. (A) which defined "book purposes".

Subsec. (g)(5)(B). Pub. L. 101–239, §7611(f)(4), redesignated subpar. (D) as (B). Former subpar. (B) redesignated (A).

Subsec. (g)(5)(C). Pub. L. 101–239, §7611(f)(4), struck out subpar. (C) which read as follows: "Present value.—Present value shall be determined as of the time the property is placed in service (or, if later, as of the beginning of the first taxable year beginning after 1989) and under regulations prescribed by the Secretary."

Subsec. (g)(5)(D). Pub. L. 101–239, §7611(f)(4), redesignated subpar. (D) as (B).

1988—Subsec. (a)(1)(A)(i). Pub. L. 100–647, §1007(b)(15), substituted "personal" for "real" in heading.

Subsec. (a)(1)(C)(i). Pub. L. 100–647, §1002(a)(12), inserted "by reason of section 203, 204, or 251(d) of such Act" after "do not apply".

Subsec. (a)(3). Pub. L. 100–647, §5041(b)(4), as amended by Pub. L. 101–239, §7815(e)(2)(A), inserted at end "The preceding sentence shall not apply to any home construction contract (as defined in section 460(e)(6)) with respect to which the requirements of clauses (i) and (ii) of section 460(e)(1)(B) are met."

Pub. L. 100–647, §1007(b)(1), inserted at end "For purposes of the preceding sentence, in the case of a contract described in section 460(e)(1), the percentage of the contract completed shall be determined under section 460(b)(2) by using the simplified procedures for allocation of costs prescribed under section 460(b)(4)."

Subsec. (a)(8). Pub. L. 100–647, §1007(b)(19), added par. (8).

Subsec. (b)(1). Pub. L. 100–647, §1007(b)(16), struck out "itemized" after "Limitation on" in heading.

Subsec. (b)(1)(C)(ii). Pub. L. 100–647, §2004(b)(2), substituted "163(h)(5)" for "163(h)(6)".

Subsec. (b)(1)(C)(iii). Pub. L. 100–647, §1007(b)(4), substituted "specified private activity bond" for "specified activity bond" before "under", and "57(a)(5)(B)" for "56(a)(5)(B)".

Subsec. (b)(1)(C)(iv), (v). Pub. L. 100–647, §1007(b)(3), added cls. (iv) and (v).

Subsec. (b)(1)(E). Pub. L. 100–647, §1007(b)(2), substituted "and deduction for personal exemptions not allowed" for "not allowed" in heading and amended text generally. Prior to amendment, text read as follows: "The standard deduction provided in section 63(c) shall not be allowed."

Subsec. (b)(3). Pub. L. 100–647, §1007(b)(14)(A), added par. (3).

Subsec. (c)(1). Pub. L. 100–647, §1007(b)(13)(A), substituted "adjusted current earnings" for "adjusted earnings and profits" in heading.

Subsec. (c)(1)(B). Pub. L. 100–647, §1007(b)(13)(B), substituted "Adjusted current earnings" for "Adjusted earnings and profits" in heading.

Subsec. (d)(2)(A). Pub. L. 100–647, §1007(b)(5), struck out "(other than subsection (a)(6) thereof)" after "for such year" in cl. (ii) and inserted sentence at end providing that an item of tax preference shall be taken into account under clause (ii).

Subsec. (e)(1). Pub. L. 100–647, §2004(b)(3)(A), substituted "improving" for "rehabilitating" in introductory text.

Pub. L. 100–647, §1007(b)(6)(A)(i), inserted "qualified residence interest (as defined in section 163(h)(3)) and is" after "interest which is" in introductory text.

Subsec. (e)(1)(A). Pub. L. 100–647, §2004(b)(3)(B), struck out "or is paid" after "accrues".

Subsec. (e)(1)(B). Pub. L. 100–647, §1007(b)(6)(A)(ii), substituted "section 163(h)(4)" for "section 163(h)(3)".

Subsec. (e)(3). Pub. L. 100–647, §1007(b)(6)(B), substituted "interest which is qualified residence interest (as defined in section 163(h)(3)) and is paid or accrued" for "interest paid or accrued".

Subsec. (f)(2)(B). Pub. L. 100–647, §2001(c)(3)(A), inserted at end "No adjustment shall be made under this subparagraph for the tax imposed by section 59A."

Pub. L. 100–647, §1007(b)(7), inserted "(otherwise eligible for the credit provided by section 901 without regard to section 901(j))" after "any such taxes".

Subsec. (f)(2)(F). Pub. L. 100–647, §1007(b)(11)(A), substituted "Treatment of taxes on dividends from 936 corporations" for "Treatment of dividends from 936 corporations" in heading and amended text generally, substituting cls. (i) to (iii) for former cls. (i) and (ii).

Subsec. (f)(2)(I), (J). Pub. L. 100–647, §6303(a), added subpar. (I) and redesignated former subpar. (I) as (J).

Subsec. (f)(3)(A)(iii). Pub. L. 100–647, §1007(b)(8), inserted "for a substantial nontax purpose" after "an income statement".

Subsec. (f)(3)(B). Pub. L. 100–647, §1007(b)(9), substituted "this subsection" for "paragraph (3)(A)" in penultimate sentence.

Subsec. (f)(3)(C). Pub. L. 100–647, §1007(b)(10), inserted at end "If the taxpayer has 2 or more statements described in the clause (or subclause) with the lowest number designation, the applicable financial statement shall be the one of such statements specified in regulations."

Subsec. (g)(4)(A)(vi), (vii). Pub. L. 100–647, §1007(b)(17), added cls. (vi) and (vii).

Subsec. (g)(4)(B)(iii). Pub. L. 100–647, §6079(a)(1), amended last sentence generally, inserting "which is" after "any annuity contract" and "or which is described in section 72(u)(3)(C)" after "in section 403(a)".

Pub. L. 100–647, §1007(b)(12), inserted at end "The preceding sentence shall not apply to any annuity contract held under a plan described in section 403(a)."

Subsec. (g)(4)(C)(iii). Pub. L. 100–647, §1007(b)(11)(B), substituted "clause (i)" for "clause (ii)(I)".

Subsec. (g)(4)(I). Pub. L. 100–647, §1007(b)(18), added subpar. (I).

1987—Subsec. (a)(6). Pub. L. 100–203, §10202(d), amended par. (6) generally. Prior to amendment, par. (6) read as follows: "In the case of any—

"(A) disposition after March 1, 1986, of property described in section 1221(1), or

"(B) other disposition if an obligation arising from such disposition would be an applicable installment obligation (as defined in section 453C(e)) to which section 453C applies,

income from such disposition shall be determined without regard to the installment method under section 453 or 453A and all payments to be received for the disposition shall be deemed received in the taxable year of the disposition. This paragraph shall not apply to any disposition with respect to which an election is in effect under section 453C(e)(4)."

Subsec. (f)(2)(H), (I). Pub. L. 100–203, §10243(a), added subpar. (H) and redesignated former subpar. (H) as (I).

STATUTORY NOTES AND RELATED SUBSIDIARIES
EFFECTIVE DATE OF 2019 AMENDMENT

Pub. L. 116–94, div. Q, title I, §103(c), Dec. 20, 2019, 133 Stat. 3228, provided that: "The amendments made by this section [amending this section and section 213 of this title] shall apply to taxable years ending after December 31, 2018."

EFFECTIVE DATE OF 2017 AMENDMENT

Pub. L. 115–97, title I, §11027(c), Dec. 22, 2017, 131 Stat. 2077, provided that: "The amendment made by this section [amending this section and section 213 of this title] shall apply to taxable years beginning after December 31, 2016."

Amendment by section 12001(b)(7), (8)(A) of Pub. L. 115–97 applicable to taxable years beginning after Dec. 31, 2017, see section 12001(c) of Pub. L. 115–97, set out as a note under section 11 of this title.

EFFECTIVE DATE OF 2014 AMENDMENT

Pub. L. 113–295, div. A, title II, §215(c), Dec. 19, 2014, 128 Stat. 4034, provided that: "The amendments made by this section [amending this section and section 911 of this title] shall take effect as if included in the provisions of the Tax Technical Corrections Act of 2007 [Pub. L. 110–172] to which they relate."

Amendment by section 221(a)(9), (25)(B), (30)(C) of Pub. L. 113–295 effective Dec. 19, 2014, subject to a savings provision, see section 221(b) of Pub. L. 113–295, set out as a note under section 1 of this title.

EFFECTIVE DATE OF 2010 AMENDMENT

Pub. L. 111–148, title IX, §9013(d), Mar. 23, 2010, 124 Stat. 868, provided that: "The amendments made by this section [amending this section and section 213 of this title] shall apply to taxable years beginning after December 31, 2012."

EFFECTIVE DATE OF 2009 AMENDMENT

Pub. L. 111–92, §13(e), (f), Nov. 6, 2009, 123 Stat. 2994, 2995, as amended by Pub. L. 113–295, div. A, title II, §220(bb), Dec. 19, 2014, 128 Stat. 4037, provided that:

"(e) Effective Dates.—

"(1) In general.—Except as otherwise provided in this subsection, the amendments made by this section [amending this section and sections 172 and 810 of this title] shall apply to net operating losses arising in taxable years ending after December 31, 2007.

"(2) Alternative tax net operating loss deduction.—The amendment made by subsection (b) [amending this section] shall apply to taxable years ending after December 31, 2002.

"(3) Loss from operations of life insurance companies.—The amendment made by subsection (c) [amending section 810 of this title] shall apply to losses from operations arising in taxable years ending after December 31, 2007.

"(4) Transitional rule.—In the case of any net operating loss (or, in the case of a life insurance company, any loss from operations) for a taxable year ending before the date of the enactment of this Act [Nov. 6, 2009]—

"(A) any election made under section 172(b)(3) or [former] 810(b)(3) of the Internal Revenue Code of 1986 with respect to such loss may (notwithstanding such section) be revoked before the due date (including extension of time) for filing the return for the taxpayer's last taxable year beginning in 2009, and

"(B) any application under section 6411(a) of such Code with respect to such loss shall be treated as timely filed if filed before such due date.

"(f) Exception for TARP Recipients.—The amendments made by this section [amending this section and sections 172 and 810 of this title] shall not apply to—

"(1) any taxpayer if—

"(A) the Federal Government acquired before the date of the enactment of this Act [Nov. 6, 2009] an equity interest in the taxpayer pursuant to the Emergency Economic Stabilization Act of 2008 [div. A of Pub. L. 110–343, see Tables for classification],

"(B) the Federal Government acquired before such date of enactment any warrant (or other right) to acquire any equity interest with respect to the taxpayer pursuant to the Emergency Economic Stabilization Act of 2008, or

"(C) such taxpayer receives after such date of enactment funds from the Federal Government in exchange for an interest described in subparagraph (A) or (B) pursuant to a program established under title I of division A of the Emergency Economic Stabilization Act of 2008 [see Tables for classification] (unless such taxpayer is a financial institution (as defined in section 3 of such Act [12 U.S.C. 5202]) and the funds are received pursuant to a program established by the Secretary of the Treasury for the stated purpose of increasing the availability of credit to small businesses using funding made available under such Act [Pub. L. 110–343, see Tables for classification]), or

"(2) the Federal National Mortgage Association and the Federal Home Loan Mortgage Corporation, and

"(3) any taxpayer which at any time in 2008 or 2009 was or is a member of the same affiliated group (as defined in section 1504 of the Internal Revenue Code of 1986, determined without regard to subsection (b) thereof) as a taxpayer described in paragraph (1) or (2)."

Pub. L. 111–5, div. B, title I, §1008(e), Feb. 17, 2009, 123 Stat. 318, provided that: "The amendments made by this section [amending this section and sections 63 and 164 of this title] shall apply to purchases on or after the date of the enactment of this Act [Feb. 17, 2009] in taxable years ending after such date."

Pub. L. 111–5, div. B, title I, §1503(c), Feb. 17, 2009, 123 Stat. 355, provided that: "The amendments made by this section [amending this section and section 57 of this title] shall apply to obligations issued after December 31, 2008."

EFFECTIVE DATE OF 2008 AMENDMENT

Pub. L. 110–343, div. C, title VII, §706(d), Oct. 3, 2008, 122 Stat. 3923, provided that:

"(1) In general.—Except as provided by paragraph (2), the amendments made by this section [amending this section and sections 63, 139, 165, 172, 1033, and 7508A of this title] shall apply to disasters declared in taxable years beginning after December 31, 2007.

"(2) Increase in limitation on individual loss per casualty.—The amendment made by subsection (c) [amending section 165 of this title] shall apply to taxable years beginning after December 31, 2008.

Pub. L. 110–343, div. C, title VII, §708(e), Oct. 3, 2008, 122 Stat. 3925, provided that: "The amendments made by this section [amending this section and section 172 of this title] shall apply to losses arising in taxable years beginning after December 31, 2007, in connection with disasters declared after such date."

Pub. L. 110–289, div. C, title I, §3022(d)(1), July 30, 2008, 122 Stat. 2894, provided that: "The amendments made by subsection (a) [amending this section and section 57 of this title] shall apply to bonds issued after the date of the enactment of this Act [July 30, 2008]."

EFFECTIVE DATE OF 2005 AMENDMENTS

Amendment by Pub. L. 109–135 effective as if included in the provision of the American Jobs Creation Act of 2004, Pub. L. 108–357, to which such amendment relates, see section 403(nn) of Pub. L. 109–135, set out as a note under section 26 of this title.

Pub. L. 109–58, title XIII, §1326(e), Aug. 8, 2005, 119 Stat. 1017, provided that:

"(1) In general.—The amendments made by this section [amending this section and section 168 of this title] shall apply to property placed in service after April 11, 2005.

"(2) Exception.—The amendments made by this section [amending this section and section 168 of this title] shall not apply to any property with respect to which the taxpayer or a related party has entered into a binding contract for the construction thereof on or before April 11, 2005, or, in the case of self-constructed property, has started construction on or before such date."

EFFECTIVE DATE OF 2004 AMENDMENTS

Pub. L. 108–357, title I, §101(c), Oct. 22, 2004, 118 Stat. 1423, provided that: "The amendments made by this section [amending this section and sections 275, 864, 903, and 999 of this title and repealing sections 114 and 941 to 943 of this title] shall apply to transactions after December 31, 2004."

Pub. L. 108–357, title I, §102(e), Oct. 22, 2004, 118 Stat. 1429, as amended by Pub. L. 109–135, title IV, §403(a)(19), Dec. 21, 2005, 119 Stat. 2619, provided that:

"(1) In general.—The amendments made by this section [enacting section 199 of this title and amending this section and sections 86, 135, 137, 219, 221, 222, 246, 469, 613, and 1402 of this title] shall apply to taxable years beginning after December 31, 2004.

"(2) Application to pass-thru entities, etc.—In determining the deduction under [former] section 199 of the Internal Revenue Code of 1986 (as added by this section), items arising from a taxable year of a partnership, S corporation, estate, or trust beginning before January 1, 2005, shall not be taken into account for purposes of subsection (d)(1) of such section."

Pub. L. 108–357, title II, §248(c), Oct. 22, 2004, 118 Stat. 1457, provided that: "The amendments made by this section [enacting subchapter R of this chapter and amending this section] shall apply to taxable years beginning after the date of the enactment of this Act [Oct. 22, 2004]."

Pub. L. 108–357, title IV, §422(d), Oct. 22, 2004, 118 Stat. 1519, provided that: "The amendments made by this section [enacting section 965 of this title and amending this section] shall apply to taxable years ending on or after the date of the enactment of this Act [Oct. 22, 2004]."

Pub. L. 108–357, title VIII, §835(c), Oct. 22, 2004, 118 Stat. 1594, provided that:

"(1) In general.—Except as provided in paragraph (2), the amendments made by this section [amending this section and sections 382, 582, 856, 860G, 1202, and 7701 of this title and repealing part V of subchapter M of this chapter] shall take effect on January 1, 2005.

"(2) Exception for existing fasits.—Paragraph (1) shall not apply to any FASIT in existence on the date of the enactment of this Act [Oct. 22, 2004] to the extent that regular interests issued by the FASIT before such date continue to remain outstanding in accordance with the original terms of issuance."

Pub. L. 108–311, title IV, §403(f), Oct. 4, 2004, 118 Stat. 1188, provided that: "The amendments made by this section [amending this section, sections 137, 168, 172, and 1400L of this title, section 1306 of Title 29, Labor, and provisions set out as a note under this section] shall take effect as if included in the provisions of the Job Creation and Worker Assistance Act of 2002 [Pub. L. 107–147] to which they relate."

EFFECTIVE DATE OF 2003 AMENDMENT

Pub. L. 108–173, title XII, §1202(d), Dec. 8, 2003, 117 Stat. 2480, provided that: "The amendments made by this section [enacting section 139A of this title and amending this section] shall apply to taxable years ending after the date of the enactment of this Act [Dec. 8, 2003]."

EFFECTIVE DATE OF 2002 AMENDMENT

Pub. L. 107–147, title I, §102(c)(2), Mar. 9, 2002, 116 Stat. 26, as amended Pub. L. 108–311, title IV, §403(b)(3), Oct. 4, 2004, 118 Stat. 1187, provided that: "The amendment made by this subsection [amending this section] shall apply to taxable years ending after December 31, 1990."

EFFECTIVE DATE OF 2000 AMENDMENTS

Pub. L. 106–554, §1(a)(7) [title III, §314(g)], Dec. 21, 2000, 114 Stat. 2763, 2763A–643, provided that: "The amendments made by this section [amending this section and sections 403, 414, 415, 3405, 6211 and 7436 of this title and provisions set out as a note under section 1 of this title] shall take effect as if included in the provisions of the Taxpayer Relief [Act] of 1997 [Pub. L. 105–34] to which they relate."

Pub. L. 106–519, §5, Nov. 15, 2000, 114 Stat. 2433, as amended by Pub. L. 109–222, title V, §513(a), May 17, 2006, 120 Stat. 366, provided that:

"(a) In General.—The amendments made by this Act [enacting sections 114 and 941 to 943 of this title, amending this section and sections 275, 864, 903, and 999 of this title, and repealing sections 921 to 927 of this title] shall apply to transactions after September 30, 2000.

"(b) No New FSCs; Termination of Inactive FSCs.—

"(1) No new fscs.—No corporation may elect after September 30, 2000, to be a FSC (as defined in section 922 of the Internal Revenue Code of 1986, as in effect before the amendments made by this Act).

"(2) Termination of inactive fscs.—If a FSC has no foreign trade income (as defined in section 923(b) of such Code, as so in effect) for any period of 5 consecutive taxable years beginning after December 31, 2001, such FSC shall cease to be treated as a FSC for purposes of such Code for any taxable year beginning after such period.

"(c) Transition Period for Existing Foreign Sales Corporations.—

"(1) In general.—In the case of a FSC (as so defined) in existence on September 30, 2000, and at all times thereafter, the amendments made by this Act shall not apply to any transaction in the ordinary course of trade or business involving a FSC which occurs before January 1, 2002.

"(2) Election to have amendments apply earlier.—A taxpayer may elect to have the amendments made by this Act apply to any transaction by a FSC or any related person to which such amendments would apply but for the application of paragraph (1). Such election shall be effective for the taxable year for which made and all subsequent taxable years, and, once made, may be revoked only with the consent of the Secretary of the Treasury.

"(3) Exception for old earnings and profits of certain corporations.—

"(A) In general.—In the case of a foreign corporation to which this paragraph applies—

"(i) earnings and profits of such corporation accumulated in taxable years ending before October 1, 2000, shall not be included in the gross income of the persons holding stock in such corporation by reason of section 943(e)(4)(B)(i); and

"(ii) rules similar to the rules of clauses (ii), (iii), and (iv) of section 953(d)(4)(B) shall apply with respect to such earnings and profits.

The preceding sentence shall not apply to earnings and profits acquired in a transaction after September 30, 2000, to which section 381 applies unless the distributor or transferor corporation was immediately before the transaction a foreign corporation to which this paragraph applies.

"(B) Existing fscs.—This paragraph shall apply to any controlled foreign corporation (as defined in section 957) if—

"(i) such corporation is a FSC (as so defined) in existence on September 30, 2000;

"(ii) such corporation is eligible to make the election under section 943(e) by reason of being described in paragraph (2)(B) of such section; and

"(iii) such corporation makes such election not later than for its first taxable year beginning after December 31, 2001.

"(C) Other corporations.—This paragraph shall apply to any controlled foreign corporation (as defined in section 957), and such corporation shall (notwithstanding any provision of section 943(e)) be treated as an applicable foreign corporation for purposes of section 943(e), if—

"(i) such corporation is in existence on September 30, 2000;

"(ii) as of such date, such corporation is wholly owned (directly or indirectly) by a domestic corporation (determined without regard to any election under section 943(e));

"(iii) for each of the 3 taxable years preceding the first taxable year to which the election under section 943(e) by such controlled foreign corporation applies—

"(I) all of the gross income of such corporation is subpart F income (as defined in section 952), including by reason of section 954(b)(3)(B); and

"(II) in the ordinary course of such corporation's trade or business, such corporation regularly sold (or paid commissions) to a FSC which on September 30, 2000, was a related person to such corporation;

"(iv) such corporation has never made an election under section 922(a)(2) (as in effect before the date of the enactment of this paragraph [Nov. 15, 2000]) to be treated as a FSC; and

"(v) such corporation makes the election under section 943(e) not later than for its first taxable year beginning after December 31, 2001.

The preceding sentence shall cease to apply as of the date that the domestic corporation referred to in clause (ii) ceases to wholly own (directly or indirectly) such controlled foreign corporation.

"(4) Related person.—For purposes of this subsection, the term 'related person' has the meaning given to such term by section 943(b)(3).

"(5) Section references.—Except as otherwise expressly provided, any reference in this subsection to a section or other provision shall be considered to be a reference to a section or other provision of the Internal Revenue Code of 1986, as amended by this Act.

"(d) Special Rules Relating to Leasing Transactions.—

"(1) Sales income.—If foreign trade income in connection with the lease or rental of property described in section 927(a)(1)(B) of such Code (as in effect before the amendments made by this Act) is treated as exempt foreign trade income for purposes of section 921(a) of such Code (as so in effect), such property shall be treated as property described in section 941(c)(1)(B) of such Code (as added by this Act) for purposes of applying section 941(c)(2) of such Code (as so added) to any subsequent transaction involving such property to which the amendments made by this Act apply.

"(2) Limitation on use of gross receipts method.—If any person computed its foreign trade income from any transaction with respect to any property on the basis of a transfer price determined under the method described in section 925(a)(1) of such Code (as in effect before the amendments made by this Act), then the qualifying foreign trade income (as defined in section 941(a) of such Code, as in effect after such amendment) of such person (or any related person) with respect to any other transaction involving such property (and to which the amendments made by this Act apply) shall be zero."

[Pub. L. 109–222, title V, §513(c), May 17, 2006, 120 Stat. 366, provided that: "The amendments made by this section [amending section 5 of Pub. L. 106–519, set out above, and provisions set out as a note under section 114 of this title] shall apply to taxable years beginning after the date of the enactment of this Act [May 17, 2006]."]

Effective Date of 1997 Amendment

Amendment by section 312(d)(1) of Pub. L. 105–34 applicable to sales and exchanges after May 6, 1997, with certain exceptions, see section 312(d) of Pub. L. 105–34, set out as a note under section 121 of this title.

Pub. L. 105–34, title IV, §403(b), Aug. 5, 1997, 111 Stat. 844, provided that:

"(1) In general.—The amendment made by this section [amending this section] shall apply to dispositions in taxable years beginning after December 31, 1987.

"(2) Special rule for 1987.—In the case of taxable years beginning in 1987, the last sentence of section 56(a)(6) of the Internal Revenue Code of 1986 (as in effect for such taxable years) shall be applied by inserting 'or in the case of a taxpayer using the cash receipts and disbursements method of accounting, any disposition described in section 453C(e)(1)(B)(ii)' after 'section 453C(e)(4)'."

Pub. L. 105–34, title XII, §1212(b), Aug. 5, 1997, 111 Stat. 1000, provided that: "The amendment made by subsection (a) [amending this section] shall apply to taxable years beginning after December 31, 1997."

Effective Date of 1996 Amendment

Amendment by section 1601(b)(2)(B), (C) of Pub. L. 104–188 applicable to taxable years beginning after Dec. 31, 1995, except as otherwise provided, see section 1601(c) of Pub. L. 104–188, set out as a note under section 55 of this title.

Amendment by section 1621(b)(2) of Pub. L. 104–188 effective Sept. 1, 1997, see section 1621(d) of Pub. L. 104–188, set out as a note under section 26 of this title.

Amendment by section 1702(c)(1), (e)(1)(A), (g)(4), and (h)(12) of Pub. L. 104–188 effective, except as otherwise expressly provided, as if included in the provision of the Revenue Reconciliation Act of 1990, Pub. L. 101–508, title XI, to which such amendment relates, see section 1702(i) of Pub. L. 104–188, set out as a note under section 38 of this title.

Effective Date of 1993 Amendment

Pub. L. 103–66, title XIII, §13115(b), Aug. 10, 1993, 107 Stat. 432, provided that:

"(1) In general.—Except as provided in paragraph (2), the amendments made by this section [amending this section] shall apply to property placed in service after December 31, 1993.

"(2) Coordination with transitional rules.—The amendments made by this section shall not apply to any property to which paragraph (1) of section 56(a) of the Internal Revenue Code of 1986 does not apply by reason of subparagraph (C)(i) thereof."

Amendment by section 13171(b) of Pub. L. 103–66 applicable to contributions made after June 30, 1992, except that in case of any contribution of capital gain property which is not tangible personal property, such amendment applicable only if the contribution is made after Dec. 31, 1992, see section 13171(d) of Pub. L. 103–66, set out as a note under section 53 of this title.

Pub. L. 103–66, title XIII, §13227(f), Aug. 10, 1993, 107 Stat. 494, provided that: "The amendments made by this section [amending this section and sections 904, 936, and 7652 of this title] shall apply to taxable years beginning after December 31, 1993; except that the amendment made by subsection (e) [amending section 7652 of this title] shall take effect on October 1, 1993."

Effective Date of 1992 Amendment

Pub. L. 102–486, title XIX, §1915(d), Oct. 24, 1992, 106 Stat. 3024, provided that: "The amendments made by this section [amending this section and sections 57, 59, and 59A of this title] shall apply to taxable years beginning after December 31, 1992."

Effective Date of 1990 Amendment

Amendment by section 11103(b) of Pub. L. 101–508 applicable to taxable years beginning after Dec. 31, 1990, see section 11103(e) of Pub. L. 101–508, set out as a note under section 1 of this title.

Pub. L. 101–508, title XI, §11301(d)(2), Nov. 5, 1990, 104 Stat. 1388–449, provided that:

"(A) In general.—The amendment made by subsection (b) [amending this section] shall apply to taxable years beginning on or after September 30, 1990, except that, in the case of a small insurance company, such amendment shall apply to taxable years beginning after December 31, 1989. For purposes of this paragraph, the term 'small insurance company' means any insurance company which meets the requirements of [former] section 806(a)(3) of the Internal Revenue Code of 1986; except that paragraph (2) of [former] section 806(c) of such Code shall not apply.

"(B) Special rules for year which includes september 30, 1990.—In the case of any taxable year which includes September 30, 1990, the amount of acquisition expenses which is required to be capitalized under [former] section 56(g)(4)(F) of the Internal Revenue Code of 1986 (as in effect before the amendment made by subsection (b)) by a company which is not a small insurance company shall be the amount which bears the same ratio to the amount which (but for this subparagraph) would be so required to be capitalized as the number of days in such taxable year before September 30, 1990, bears to the total number of days in such taxable year. A similar reduction shall be made in the amount amortized for such taxable year under such [former] section 56(g)(4)(F)."

Pub. L. 101–508, title XI, §11531(c), Nov. 5, 1990, 104 Stat. 1388–490, provided that: "The amendments made by this section [amending this section and sections 59 and 59A of this title] shall apply to taxable years beginning after December 31, 1990."

Pub. L. 101–508, title XI, §11704(b), Nov. 5, 1990, 104 Stat. 1388–520, provided that: "The amendments made by this section [amending this section, sections 172, 351, 413, 461, 469, 597, 857, 860D, 860G, 892, 927, 936, 1017, 1245, 1441, 2056A, 2642, 3231, 4091, 4093, 5061, 6013, 6038A, 6039D, 6045, 6323, 6332, 6655, 7519, 7522, 7608, and 7701 of this title, and provisions set out as a note under section 231n of Title 45, Railroads] shall take effect on the date of the enactment of this Act."

Amendment by section 11812(b)(4) of Pub. L. 101–508 applicable to property placed in service after Nov. 5, 1990, but not applicable to any property to which section 168 of this title does not apply by reason of subsec. (f)(5) of section 168, and not applicable to rehabilitation expenditures described in section 252(f)(5) of Pub. L. 99–514, see section 11812(c) of Pub. L. 101–508, set out as a note under section 42 of this title.

Effective Date of 1989 Amendment

Pub. L. 101–239, title VII, §7205(c), Dec. 19, 1989, 103 Stat. 2336, provided that:

"(1) In general.—Except as otherwise provided in this subsection, the amendments made by this section [amending this section and section 382 of this title] shall apply to ownership changes and acquisitions after October 2, 1989, in taxable years ending after such date.

"(2) Binding contract.—The amendments made by this section shall not apply to any ownership change or acquisition pursuant to a written binding contract in effect on October 2, 1989, and at all times thereafter before such change or acquisition.

"(3) Bankruptcy proceedings.—In the case of a reorganization described in section 368(a)(1)(G) of the Internal Revenue Code of 1986, or an exchange of debt for stock in a title 11 or similar case (as defined in section 368(a)(3) of such Code), the amendments made by this section shall not apply to any ownership change resulting from such a reorganization or proceeding if a petition in such case was filed with the court before October 3, 1989.

"(4) Subsidiaries of bankrupt parent.—The amendments made by this section shall not apply to any built-in loss of a corporation which is a member (on October 2, 1989) of an affiliated group the common parent of which (on such date) was subject to title 11 or similar case (as defined in section 368(a)(3) of such Code). The preceding sentence shall apply only if the ownership change or acquisition is pursuant to the plan approved in such proceeding and is before the date 2 years after the date on which the petition which commenced such proceeding was filed."

Pub. L. 101–239, title VII, §7611(g), Dec. 19, 1989, 103 Stat. 2373, provided that:

"(1) In general.—Except as otherwise provided in this subsection, the amendments made by this section [amending this section and sections 59 and 312 of this title] shall apply to taxable years beginning after December 31, 1989.

"(2) Intangible drilling costs.—The amendments made by subsection (f)(5) [amending sections 59 and 312 of this title] shall apply to costs paid or incurred in taxable years beginning after December 31, 1989.

"(3) Regulations on earnings and profits rules.—Not later than March 15, 1991, the Secretary of the Treasury or his delegate shall prescribe initial regulations providing guidance as to which items of income are included in adjusted current earnings under [former] section 56(g)(4)(B)(i) of the Internal Revenue Code of 1986 and which items of deduction are disallowed under [former] section 56(g)(4)(C) of such Code."

Pub. L. 101–239, title VII, §7612(c)(2), Dec. 19, 1989, 103 Stat. 2374, provided that: "The amendment made by paragraph (1) [amending this section] shall apply to contracts entered into in taxable years beginning after September 30, 1990."

Pub. L. 101–239, title VII, §7612(d)(2), Dec. 19, 1989, 103 Stat. 2374, provided that: "The amendment made by paragraph (1) [amending this section] shall apply to taxable years beginning after December 31, 1990."

Amendment by sections 7811(d)(3) and 7815(e)(2), (4) of Pub. L. 101–239 effective, except as otherwise provided, as if included in the provision of the Technical and Miscellaneous Revenue Act of 1988, Pub. L. 100–647, to which such amendment relates, see section 7817 of Pub. L. 101–239, set out as a note under section 1 of this title.

Effective Date of 1988 Amendment

Pub. L. 100–647, title I, §1007(b)(14)(C), Nov. 10, 1988, 102 Stat. 3430, provided that: "The amendments made by this paragraph [amending this section and section 57 of this title] shall apply with respect to options exercised after December 31, 1987."

Amendment by sections 1002(a)(12) and 1007(b)(1)–(13), (15)–(19) of Pub. L. 100–647 effective, except as otherwise provided, as if included in the provision of the Tax Reform Act of 1986, Pub. L. 99–514, to which such amendment relates, see section 1019(a) of Pub. L. 100–647, set out as a note under section 1 of this title.

Pub. L. 100–647, title II, §2001(e), Nov. 10, 1988, 102 Stat. 3597, provided that: "Except as otherwise provided in this section, the amendments made by this section [amending this section, sections 59A, 882, 4041, 4081, 4091, 4662, 4672, 6416, 6421, and 6427 of this title, and provisions set out as a note under section 4081 of this title] shall take effect as if included in the provision of the Superfund Revenue Act of 1986 [Pub. L. 99–499, title V] to which it relates."

Pub. L. 100–647, title II, §2004(u), Nov. 10, 1988, 102 Stat. 3610, provided that: "Except as otherwise provided in this section, any amendment made by this section [amending this section, sections 163, 244, 280H, 301, 304, 355, 384, 444, 453, 453A, 469, 514, 811, 812, 816, 842, 904, 1201, 1363, 1503, 1561, 4093, 5113, 5123, 5276, 5881, 6427, 6655, 7519, and 7704 of this title, and provisions set out as notes under sections 21, 219, 243, 301, 304, 444, 453, 1503, and 7704 of this title] shall take effect as if included in the provisions of the Revenue Act of 1987 [Pub. L. 100–203, title X] to which such amendment relates."

Amendment by section 5041(b)(4) of Pub. L. 100–647 applicable to contracts entered into on or after June 21, 1988, but not applicable to any contract resulting from the acceptance of a bid made before June 21, 1988, if the bid could not have been revoked or altered at any time on or after June 21, 1988, and not applicable in the case of a qualified ship contract (as defined in section 10203(b)(2)(B) of Pub. L. 100–203, set out as a note under section 460 of this title), see section 5041(e) of Pub. L. 100–647, set out as a note under section 460 of this title.

Pub. L. 100–647, title VI, §6079(a)(2), Nov. 10, 1988, 102 Stat. 3709, provided that: "The amendment made by paragraph (1) [amending this section] shall take effect as if included in the amendments made by section 701 of the Reform Act [Pub. L. 99–514]."

Pub. L. 100–647, title VI, §6303(b), Nov. 10, 1988, 102 Stat. 3756, provided that: "The amendment made by subsection (a) [amending this section] shall apply to taxable years beginning after December 31, 1986."

Effective Date of 1987 Amendment

Amendment by section 10202(d) of Pub. L. 100–203 applicable to dispositions in taxable years beginning after Dec. 31, 1986, with coordination with Tax Reform Act of 1986, see section 10202(e)(4), (5) of Pub. L. 100–203, set out as a note under section 453 of this title.

Pub. L. 100–203, title X, §10243(b), Dec. 22, 1987, 101 Stat. 1330–424, provided that: "The amendment made by subsection (a) [amending this section] shall apply to taxable years beginning after December 31, 1987."

Effective Date

Section applicable to taxable years beginning after Dec. 31, 1986, with certain exceptions and qualifications, see section 701(f) of Pub. L. 99–514, set out as a note under section 55 of this title.

Savings Provision

For provisions that nothing in amendment by Pub. L. 115–141 be construed to affect treatment of certain transactions occurring, property acquired, or items of income, loss, deduction, or credit taken into account prior to Mar. 23, 2018, for purposes of determining liability for tax for periods ending after Mar. 23, 2018, see section 401(e) of Pub. L. 115–141, set out as a note under section 23 of this title.

For provisions that nothing in amendment by sections 11801 and 11812 of Pub. L. 101–508 be construed to affect treatment of certain transactions occurring, property acquired, or items of income, loss, deduction, or credit taken into account prior to Nov. 5, 1990, for purposes of determining liability for tax for periods ending after Nov. 5, 1990, see section 11821(b) of Pub. L. 101–508, set out as a note under section 45K of this title.

Coordination With Heartland Disaster Relief

Pub. L. 110–343, div. C, title VII, §712, Oct. 3, 2008, 122 Stat. 3929, as amended by Pub. L. 113–295, div. A, title II, §211(c)(3), Dec. 19, 2014, 128 Stat. 4033, provided that: "The amendments made by this subtitle [subtitle B (§§706–712) of title VII of div. C of Pub. L. 110–343, enacting section 198A of this title and amending this section and sections 63, 139, 143, 165, 168, 172, 179, 1033, and 7508A of this title], other than the amendments made by sections 706(a)(2) [amending sections 139, 165, 172, 1033, and 7508A of this title], 710 [amending section 168 of this title], and 711 [amending section 179 of this title], shall not apply to any disaster described in section 702(b)(1)(A) [122 Stat. 3912], or to any expenditure or loss resulting from such disaster."

Application of Former Subsection (g)(1) and (3) to Taxable Years Beginning in 1991 and 1992

Pub. L. 104–188, title I, §1702(e)(1)(B), Aug. 20, 1996, 110 Stat. 1870, provided that: "For purposes of applying [former] sections 56(g)(1) and 56(g)(3) of the Internal Revenue Code of 1986 with respect to taxable years beginning in 1991 and 1992, the reference in such sections to the alternative tax net operating loss deduction shall be treated as including a reference to the deduction under [former] section 56(h) of such Code as in effect before the amendments made by section 1915 of the Energy Policy Act of 1992 [Pub. L. 102–486]."

Installment Sales; Taxable Years Beginning in 1987

Pub. L. 101–239, title VII, §7821(a)(5), Dec. 19, 1989, 103 Stat. 2424, provided that: "In the case of taxable years beginning in 1987, the reference to section 453 contained in section 56(a)(6) of the Internal Revenue Code of 1986 shall be treated as including a reference to section 453A."

For applicability of amendment by section 701(a) of Pub. L. 99—514 [enacting this section] notwithstanding any treaty obligation of the United States in effect on Oct. 22, 1986, with provision that for such purposes any amendment by title I of Pub. L. 100—647 be treated as if it had been included in the provision of Pub. L. 99—514 to which such amendment relates, see section 1012(aa)(2), (4) of Pub. L. 100—647, set out as a note under section 861 of this title.

STUDY OF BOOK AND EARNINGS AND PROFITS ADJUSTMENTS

Pub. L. 99—514, title VII, §702, Oct. 22, 1986, 100 Stat. 2345, required Secretary of the Treasury or his delegate to conduct a study of operation and effect of provisions of section 56(f) and former section 56(g) of the Internal Revenue Code of 1986, prior to repeal by Pub. L. 101—508, title XI, §11832(4), Nov. 5, 1990, 104 Stat. 1388—559.

 ¹ See References in Text note below.

§57. Items of tax preference

(a) General rule

For purposes of this part, the items of tax preference determined under this section are—

(1) Depletion

With respect to each property (as defined in section 614), the excess of the deduction for depletion allowable under section 611 for the taxable year over the adjusted basis of the property at the end of the taxable year (determined without regard to the depletion deduction for the taxable year). This paragraph shall not apply to any deduction for depletion computed in accordance with section 613A(c).

(2) Intangible drilling costs

(A) In general

With respect to all oil, gas, and geothermal properties of the taxpayer, the amount (if any) by which the amount of the excess intangible drilling costs arising in the taxable year is greater than 65 percent of the net income of the taxpayer from oil, gas, and geothermal properties for the taxable year.

(B) Excess intangible drilling costs

For purposes of subparagraph (A), the amount of the excess intangible drilling costs arising in the taxable year is the excess of—

(i) the intangible drilling and development costs paid or incurred in connection with oil, gas, and geothermal wells (other than costs incurred in drilling a nonproductive well) allowable under section 263(c) or 291(b) for the taxable year, over

(ii) the amount which would have been allowable for the taxable year if such costs had been capitalized and straight line recovery of intangibles (as defined in subsection (b)) had been used with respect to such costs.

(C) Net income from oil, gas, and geothermal properties

For purposes of subparagraph (A), the amount of the net income of the taxpayer from oil, gas, and geothermal properties for the taxable year is the excess of—

(i) the aggregate amount of gross income (within the meaning of section 613(a)) from all oil, gas, and geothermal properties of the taxpayer received or accrued by the taxpayer during the taxable year, over

(ii) the amount of any deductions allocable to such properties reduced by the excess described in subparagraph (B) for such taxable year.

(D) Paragraph applied separately with respect to geothermal properties and oil and gas properties

This paragraph shall be applied separately with respect to—

(i) all oil and gas properties which are not described in clause (ii), and

(ii) all properties which are geothermal deposits (as defined in section 613(e)(2)).

(E) Exception for independent producers

In the case of any oil or gas well—

(i) In general

This paragraph shall not apply to any taxpayer which is not an integrated oil company (as defined in section 291(b)(4)).

(ii) Limitation on benefit

The reduction in alternative minimum taxable income by reason of clause (i) for any taxable year shall not exceed 40 percent of the alternative minimum taxable income for such year determined without regard to clause (i) and the alternative tax net operating loss deduction under section 56(a)(4).

[(3) Repealed. Pub. L. 100—647, title I, §1007(b)(14)(B), Nov. 10, 1988, 102 Stat. 3430]

[(4) Repealed. Pub. L. 104—188, title I, §1616(b)(3), Aug. 20, 1996, 110 Stat. 1856]

(5) Tax-exempt interest

(A) In general

Interest on specified private activity bonds reduced by any deduction (not allowable in computing the regular tax) which would have been allowable if such interest were includible in gross income.

(B) Treatment of exempt-interest dividends

Under regulations prescribed by the Secretary, any exempt-interest dividend (as defined in section 852(b)(5)(A)) shall be treated as interest on a specified private activity bond to the extent of its proportionate share of the interest on such bonds received by the company paying such dividend.

(C) Specified private activity bonds

(i) In general

For purposes of this part, the term "specified private activity bond" means any private activity bond (as defined in section 141) which is issued after August 7, 1986, and the interest on which is not includible in gross income under section 103.

(ii) Exception for qualified 501(c)(3) bonds

For purposes of clause (i), the term "private activity bond" shall not include any qualified 501(c)(3) bond (as defined in section 145).

(iii) Exception for certain housing bonds

For purposes of clause (i), the term "private activity bond" shall not include any bond issued after the date of the enactment of this clause if such bond is—

(I) an exempt facility bond issued as part of an issue 95 percent or more of the net proceeds of which are to be used to provide qualified residential rental projects (as defined in section 142(d)),

(II) a qualified mortgage bond (as defined in section 143(a)), or

(III) a qualified veterans' mortgage bond (as defined in section 143(b)).

The preceding sentence shall not apply to any refunding bond unless such preceding sentence applied to the refunded bond (or in the case of a series of refundings, the original bond).

(iv) Exception for refundings

For purposes of clause (i), the term "private activity bond" shall not include any refunding bond (whether a current or advance refunding) if the refunded bond (or in the case of a series of refundings, the original bond) was issued before August 8, 1986.

(v) Certain bonds issued before September 1, 1986

For purposes of this subparagraph, a bond issued before September 1, 1986, shall be treated as issued before August 8, 1986, unless such bond would be a private activity bond if—

(I) paragraphs (1) and (2) of section 141(b) were applied by substituting "25 percent" for "10 percent" each place it appears,

(II) paragraphs (3), (4), and (5) of section 141(b) did not apply, and

(III) subparagraph (B) of section 141(c)(1) did not apply.

(vi) Exception for bonds issued in 2009 and 2010

(I) In general

For purposes of clause (i), the term "private activity bond" shall not include any bond issued after December 31, 2008, and before January 1, 2011.

(II) Treatment of refunding bonds

For purposes of subclause (I), a refunding bond (whether a current or advance refunding) shall be treated as issued on the date of the issuance of the refunded bond (or in the case of a series of refundings, the original bond).

(III) Exception for certain refunding bonds

Subclause (II) shall not apply to any refunding bond which is issued to refund any bond which was issued after December 31, 2003, and before January 1, 2009.

(6) Accelerated depreciation or amortization on certain property placed in service before January 1, 1987

The amounts which would be treated as items of tax preference with respect to the taxpayer under paragraphs (2), (3), (4), and (12) of this subsection (as in effect on the day before the date of the enactment of the Tax Reform Act of 1986). The preceding sentence shall not apply to any property to which section 56(a)(1) or (5) applies.

(7) Exclusion for gains on sale of certain small business stock

An amount equal to 7 percent of the amount excluded from gross income for the taxable year under section 1202.

(b) Straight line recovery of intangibles defined

For purposes of paragraph (2) of subsection (a)—

(1) In general

The term "straight line recovery of intangibles", when used with respect to intangible drilling and development costs for any well, means (except in the case of an election under paragraph (2)) ratable amortization of such costs over the 120-month period beginning with the month in which production from such well begins.

(2) Election

If the taxpayer elects with respect to the intangible drilling and development costs for any well, the term "straight line recovery of intangibles" means any method which would be permitted for purposes of determining cost depletion with respect to such well and which is selected by the taxpayer for purposes of subsection (a)(2). (Added Pub. L. 99–514, title VII, §701(a), Oct. 22, 1986, 100 Stat. 2333; amended Pub. L. 100–647, title I, §1007(b)(14)(B), (c), Nov. 10, 1988, 102 Stat. 3430, 3432; Pub. L. 101–508, title XI, §§11344, 11801(c)(12)(A), 11815(b)(3), Nov. 5, 1990, 104 Stat. 1388–472, 1388-527, 1388-558; Pub. L. 102–227, title I, §112, Dec. 11, 1991, 105 Stat. 1689; Pub. L. 102–486, title XIX, §1915(a)(1), (b)(1), Oct. 24, 1992, 106 Stat. 3023, 3024; Pub. L. 103–66, title XIII, §§13113(b)(1), 13171(a), Aug. 10, 1993, 107 Stat. 429, 454; Pub. L. 104–188, title I, §1616(b)(3), Aug. 20, 1996, 110 Stat. 1856; Pub. L. 105–34, title III, §311(b)(2)(B), Aug. 5, 1997, 111 Stat. 835; Pub. L. 105–206, title VI, §6005(d)(3), July 22, 1998, 112 Stat. 805; Pub. L. 108–27, title III, §301(b)(3), May 28, 2003, 117 Stat. 759; Pub. L. 110–289, div. C, title I, §3022(a)(1), July 30, 2008, 122 Stat. 2893; Pub. L. 111–5, div. B, title I, §1503(a), Feb. 17, 2009, 123 Stat. 354; Pub. L. 113–295, div. A, title II, §221(a)(10), (11), Dec. 19, 2014, 128 Stat. 4038.)

EDITORIAL NOTES

REFERENCES IN TEXT

The date of the enactment of this clause, referred to in subsec. (a)(5)(C)(iii), is the date of enactment of Pub. L. 110–289, which was approved July 30, 2008.

The date of the enactment of the Tax Reform Act of 1986, referred to in subsec. (a)(6), is the date of enactment of Pub. L. 99–514, which was approved Oct. 22, 1986.

PRIOR PROVISIONS

A prior section 57, added Pub. L. 91–172, title III, §301(a), Dec. 30, 1969, 83 Stat. 581; amended Pub. L. 92–178, title III, §§303(b), 304(a)(1), (b)(1), (d), Dec. 10, 1971, 85 Stat. 522–524; Pub. L. 94–455, title III, §301(c)(1)–(4)(A), (C), title XIX, §§1901(b)(33)(A), (B), 1906(b)(13)(A), Oct. 4, 1976, 90 Stat. 1550–1552, 1800, 1834; Pub. L. 95–30, title I, §101(d)(5), title III, §308(a), title IV, §402(a)(5), May 23, 1977, 91 Stat. 133, 153, 155; Pub. L. 95–600, title III, §301(b)(2), title IV, §§402(b)(1), 421(b), title VII, §701(b)(1), (3), (4), (f)(3)(D), Nov. 6, 1978, 92 Stat. 2820, 2868, 2874, 2898, 2899, 2901; Pub. L. 95–618, title IV, §402(b), Nov. 9, 1978, 92 Stat. 3202; Pub. L. 96–222, title I, §§104(a)(4)(E), (F), 107(a)(1)(A), Apr. 1, 1980, 94 Stat. 217, 222; Pub. L. 96–596, §3(a), Dec. 24, 1980, 94 Stat. 3475; Pub. L. 97–34, title I, §121(c)(1), title II, §§205, 212(d)(2)(B), Aug. 13, 1981, 95 Stat. 197, 223, 239; Pub. L. 97–248, title II, §§201(b), 204(b), Sept. 3, 1982, 96 Stat. 416, 426; Pub. L. 97–354, §5(a)(14), (15), Oct. 19, 1982, 96 Stat. 1693; Pub. L. 97–448, title I, §102(b)(1)(A), (3), (4), Jan. 12, 1983, 96 Stat. 2369, 2370; Pub. L. 98–369, div. A, title I, §§16(b), 68(c), 111(e)(5)–(7), title V, §555(a)(2), title VII, §§711(a)(3)(A), 722(a)(1), July 18, 1984, 98 Stat. 505, 588, 633, 897, 942, 972; Pub. L. 99–121, title I, §103(b)(1)(B), (7), Oct. 11, 1985, 99 Stat. 509, 510; Pub. L. 99–272, title XIII, §13208(a), Apr. 7, 1986, 100 Stat. 321; Pub. L. 99–514, title XVIII, §§1804(k)(3)(B)–(D), 1809(a)(3), Oct. 22, 1986, 100 Stat. 2809, 2819, related to items of tax preference, prior to the general revision of this part by Pub. L. 99–514, §701(a).

AMENDMENTS

2014—Subsec. (a)(1). Pub. L. 113–295, §221(a)(10), substituted "This paragraph" for "Effective with respect to taxable years beginning after December 31, 1992, this paragraph".

Subsec. (a)(2)(E)(i). Pub. L. 113–295, §221(a)(11)(A), substituted "This paragraph" for "In the case of any taxable year beginning after December 31, 1992, this paragraph".

Subsec. (a)(2)(E)(ii). Pub. L. 113–295, §221(a)(11)(B), struck out "(30 percent in case of taxable years beginning in 1993)" after "40 percent".

2009—Subsec. (a)(5)(C)(vi). Pub. L. 111–5 added cl. (vi).

2008—Subsec. (a)(5)(C)(iii) to (v). Pub. L. 110–289 added cl. (iii) and redesignated former cls. (iii) and (iv) as (iv) and (v), respectively.

2003—Subsec. (a)(7). Pub. L. 108–27 substituted "7 percent" for "42 percent" after "An amount equal to" and struck out last sentence which read as follows: "In the case of stock the holding period of which begins after December 31, 2000 (determined with the application of the last sentence of section 1(h)(2)(B)), the preceding sentence shall be applied by substituting '28 percent' for '42 percent'."

1998—Subsec. (a)(7). Pub. L. 105–206 inserted at end "In the case of stock the holding period of which begins after December 31, 2000 (determined with the application of the last sentence of section 1(h)(2)(B)), the preceding sentence shall be applied by substituting '28 percent' for '42 percent'."

1997—Subsec. (a)(7). Pub. L. 105–34 substituted "42 percent" for "one-half".

1996—Subsec. (a)(4). Pub. L. 104–188 struck out par. (4) which read as follows: "Reserves for losses on bad debts of financial institutions.—In the case of a financial institution to which section 593 applies, the amount by which the deduction allowable for the taxable year for a reasonable addition to a reserve for bad debts exceeds the amount that would have been allowable had the institution maintained its bad debt reserve for all taxable years on the basis of actual experience."

1993—Subsec. (a)(6), (7). Pub. L. 103–66, §13171(a), redesignated pars. (7) and (8) as (6) and (7), respectively, and struck out heading and text of former par. (6). Text read as follows:

"(A) In general.—The amount by which the deduction allowable under section 170 or 642(c) would be reduced if all capital gain property were taken into account at its adjusted basis.

"(B) Capital gain property.—For purposes of subparagraph (A), the term 'capital gain property' has the meaning given to such term by section 170(b)(1)(C)(iv). Such term shall not include any property to which an election under section 170(b)(1)(C)(iii) applies. In the case of any taxable year beginning in 1991, such term shall not include any tangible personal property. In the case of a contribution made before July 1, 1992, in a taxable year beginning in 1992, such term shall not include any tangible personal property."

Subsec. (a)(8). Pub. L. 103–66, §13171(a), redesignated par. (8) as (7).

Pub. L. 103–66, §13113(b)(1), added par. (8).

1992—Subsec. (a)(1). Pub. L. 102–486, §1915(a)(1), inserted at end "Effective with respect to taxable years beginning after December 31, 1992, this paragraph shall not apply to any deduction for depletion computed in accordance with section 613A(c)."

Subsec. (a)(2)(E). Pub. L. 102–486, §1915(b)(1), added subpar. (E).

1991—Subsec. (a)(6)(B). Pub. L. 102–227 inserted at end "In the case of a contribution made before July 1, 1992, in a taxable year beginning in 1992, such term shall not include any tangible personal property."

1990—Subsec. (a)(2)(D)(ii). Pub. L. 101–508, §11815(b)(3), substituted "section 613(e)(2)" for "section 613(e)(3)".

Subsec. (a)(4). Pub. L. 101–508, §11801(c)(12)(A), struck out "585 or" after "section".

Subsec. (a)(6)(B). Pub. L. 101–508, §11344, inserted at end "In the case of any taxable year beginning in 1991, such term shall not include any tangible personal property."

1988—Subsec. (a)(3). Pub. L. 100–647, §1007(b)(14)(B), struck out par. (3) which related to incentive stock options.

Subsec. (a)(5)(C)(i). Pub. L. 100–647, §1007(c)(2), amended cl. (i) generally. Prior to amendment, cl. (i) read as follows: "For purposes of this part, the term 'specified private activity bonds' means any private activity bond (as defined in section 141) issued after August 7, 1986."

Subsec. (a)(5)(C)(iii). Pub. L. 100–647, §1007(c)(1), inserted "(whether a current or advance refunding)" after "any refunding bond".

Subsec. (a)(6)(A). Pub. L. 100–647, §1007(c)(3), inserted "or 642(c)" after "section 170".

EFFECTIVE DATE OF 2014 AMENDMENT

Amendment by Pub. L. 113–295 effective Dec. 19, 2014, subject to a savings provision, see section 221(b) of Pub. L. 113–295, set out as a note under section 1 of this title.

EFFECTIVE DATE OF 2009 AMENDMENT

Amendment by Pub. L. 111–5 applicable to obligations issued after Dec. 31, 2008, see section 1503(c) of Pub. L. 111–5, set out as a note under section 56 of this title.

EFFECTIVE DATE OF 2008 AMENDMENT

Amendment by Pub. L. 110–289 applicable to bonds issued after July 30, 2008, see section 3022(d)(1) of Pub. L. 110–289, set out as a note under section 56 of this title.

EFFECTIVE DATE OF 2003 AMENDMENT

Amendment by Pub. L. 108–27 applicable to dispositions on or after May 6, 2003, see section 301(d)(3) of Pub. L. 108–27, set out as an Effective and Termination Dates of 2003 Amendment note under section 1 of this title.

EFFECTIVE DATE OF 1998 AMENDMENT

Amendment by Pub. L. 105–206 effective, except as otherwise provided, as if included in the provisions of the Taxpayer Relief Act of 1997, Pub. L. 105–34, to which such amendment relates, see section 6024 of Pub. L. 105–206, set out as a note under section 1 of this title.

EFFECTIVE DATE OF 1997 AMENDMENT

Amendment by Pub. L. 105–34 applicable to taxable years ending after May 6, 1997, see section 311(d) of Pub. L. 105–34, set out as a note under section 1 of this title.

EFFECTIVE DATE OF 1996 AMENDMENT

Amendment by Pub. L. 104–188 applicable to taxable years beginning after Dec. 31, 1995, see section 1616(c) of Pub. L. 104–188, set out as a note under section 593 of this title.

EFFECTIVE DATE OF 1993 AMENDMENT

Amendment by section 13113(b)(1) of Pub. L. 103–66 applicable to stock issued after Aug. 10, 1993, see section 13113(e) of Pub. L. 103–66, set out as a note under section 53 of this title.

Amendment by section 13171(a) of Pub. L. 103–66 applicable to contributions made after June 30, 1992, except that in case of any contribution of capital gain property which is not tangible personal property, such amendment applicable only if the contribution is made after Dec. 31, 1992, see section 13171(d) of Pub. L. 103–66, set out as a note under section 53 of this title.

EFFECTIVE DATE OF 1992 AMENDMENT

Amendment by Pub. L. 102–486 applicable to taxable years beginning after Dec. 31, 1992, see section 1915(d) of Pub. L. 102–486, set out as a note under section 56 of this title.

EFFECTIVE DATE OF 1988 AMENDMENT

Amendment by section 1007(b)(14)(B) of Pub. L. 100–647 applicable with respect to options exercised after Dec. 31, 1987, see section 1007(b)(14)(C) of Pub. L. 100–647, set out as a note under section 56 of this title.

Amendment by section 1007(c) of Pub. L. 100–647 effective, except as otherwise provided, as if included in the provision of the Tax Reform Act of 1986, Pub. L. 99–514, to which such amendment relates, see section 1019(a) of Pub. L. 100–647, set out as a note under section 1 of this title.

EFFECTIVE DATE

Section applicable to taxable years beginning after Dec. 31, 1986, with certain exceptions and qualifications, but subsec. (a)(6) not to apply to any deduction attributable to contributions made before Aug. 16, 1986, see section 701(f) of Pub. L. 99–514, set out as a note under section 55 of this title.

SAVINGS PROVISION

For provisions that nothing in amendment by sections 11801 and 11815 of Pub. L. 101–508 be construed to affect treatment of certain transactions occurring, property acquired, or items of income, loss, deduction, or credit taken into account prior to Nov. 5, 1990, for purposes of determining liability for tax for periods ending after Nov. 5, 1990, see section 11821(b) of Pub. L. 101–508, set out as a note under section 45K of this title.

Pub. L. 100–647, title I, §1007(f)(4), Nov. 10, 1988, 102 Stat. 3433, provided that:

"(A) If any property to which this paragraph applies is placed in service in a taxable year which begins before January 1, 1987, and ends on or after August 1, 1986, the item of tax preference determined under section 57(a) of the Internal Revenue Code of 1954 (as in effect on the day before the date of the enactment of the Tax Reform Act of 1986 [Oct. 22, 1986]) with respect to such property shall be the excess of—

"(i) the amount allowable as a deduction for depreciation or amortization for such taxable year, over

"(ii) the amount which would be determined for such taxable year under the rules of paragraph (1) or (5) (whichever is appropriate) of section 56(a) of the Internal Revenue Code of 1954 (as amended by the Tax Reform Act of 1986 [Pub. L. 99–514]).

"(B) This paragraph shall apply to any property—

"(i) which is described in paragraph (4) or (12) of section 57(a) of the Internal Revenue Code of 1954 (as so in effect), and

"(ii) to which paragraph (1) or (5) of section 56(a) of the Internal Revenue Code of 1986 would apply if the taxable year referred to in subparagraph (A) began after December 31, 1986."

APPLICABILITY OF CERTAIN AMENDMENTS BY PUB. L. 99–514 IN RELATION TO TREATY OBLIGATIONS OF UNITED STATES

For applicability of amendment by section 701(a) of Pub. L. 99–514 [enacting this section] notwithstanding any treaty obligation of the United States in effect on Oct. 22, 1986, with provision that for such purposes any amendment by title I of Pub. L. 100–647 be treated as if it had been included in the provision of Pub. L. 99–514 to which such amendment relates, see section 1012(aa)(2), (4) of Pub. L. 100–647, set out as a note under section 861 of this title.

§58. Denial of certain losses

(a) Denial of farm loss

(1) In general

For purposes of computing the amount of the alternative minimum taxable income for any taxable year of a taxpayer other than a corporation—

(A) Disallowance of farm loss

No loss of the taxpayer for such taxable year from any tax shelter farm activity shall be allowed.

(B) Deduction in succeeding taxable year

Any loss from a tax shelter farm activity disallowed under subparagraph (A) shall be treated as a deduction allocable to such activity in the 1st succeeding taxable year.

(2) Tax shelter farm activity

For purposes of this subsection, the term "tax shelter farm activity" means—

(A) any farming syndicate as defined in section 461(k), and

(B) any other activity consisting of farming which is a passive activity (within the meaning of section 469(c)).

(3) Determination of loss

In determining the amount of the loss from any tax shelter farm activity, the adjustments of sections 56 and 57 shall apply.

(b) Disallowance of passive activity loss

In computing the alternative minimum taxable income of the taxpayer for any taxable year, section 469 shall apply, except that in applying section 469—

(1) the adjustments of sections 56 and 57 shall apply, and

(2) in lieu of applying section 469(j)(7), the passive activity loss of a taxpayer shall be computed without regard to qualified housing interest (as defined in section 56(e)).

(c) Special rules

For purposes of this section—

(1) Special rule for insolvent taxpayers

(A) In general

The amount of losses to which subsection (a) or (b) applies shall be reduced by the amount (if any) by which the taxpayer is insolvent as of the close of the taxable year.

(B) Insolvent

For purposes of this paragraph, the term "insolvent" means the excess of liabilities over the fair market value of assets.

(2) Loss allowed for year of disposition of farm shelter activity

If the taxpayer disposes of his entire interest in any tax shelter farm activity during any taxable year, the amount of the loss attributable to such activity (determined after carryovers under subsection (a)(1)(B)) shall (to the extent otherwise allowable) be allowed for such taxable year in computing alternative minimum taxable income and not treated as a loss from a tax shelter farm activity.

(Added Pub. L. 99–514, title VII, §701(a), Oct. 22, 1986, 100 Stat. 2335; amended Pub. L. 100–203, title X, §10212(b), Dec. 22, 1987, 101 Stat. 1330–406; Pub. L. 100–647, title I, §1007(d), Nov. 10, 1988, 102 Stat. 3432; Pub. L. 113–295, div. A, title II, §221(a)(58)(E), (60)(B), Dec. 19, 2014, 128 Stat. 4047, 4048; Pub. L. 115–97, title I, §12001(b)(9), Dec. 22, 2017, 131 Stat. 2093; Pub. L. 115–141, div. U, title IV, §401(a)(30), Mar. 23, 2018, 132 Stat. 1185.)

EDITORIAL NOTES
PRIOR PROVISIONS

A prior section 58, added Pub. L. 91–172, title III, §301(a), Dec. 30, 1969, 83 Stat. 583; amended Pub. L. 92–178, title III, §308(a), Dec. 10, 1971, 85 Stat. 524; Pub. L. 94–455, title III, §301(d), title XIX, §§1901(b)(40), 1906(b)(13)(A), Oct. 4, 1976, 90 Stat. 1553, 1803, 1834; Pub. L. 95–600, title IV, §§421(c), 423(a), title VII, §701(b)(2), Nov. 6, 1978, 92 Stat. 2875, 2877, 2898; Pub. L. 96–222, title I, §107(a)(1)(C), Apr. 1, 1980, 94 Stat. 222; Pub. L. 97–248, title II, §201(c)(1), §201(d)(3), formerly §201(c)(3), Sept. 3, 1982, 96 Stat. 417, 419, renumbered §201(d)(3), Pub. L. 97–448, title III, §306(a)(1)(A)(i), Jan. 12, 1983, 96 Stat. 2400; Pub. L. 97–354, §§3(c), 5(a)(16), Oct. 19, 1982, 96 Stat. 1688, 1693; Pub. L. 97–448, title I, §102(b)(2), Jan. 12, 1983, 96 Stat. 2369; Pub. L. 98–369, div. A, title VII, §711(a)(2), (3)(B), July 18, 1984, 98 Stat. 942; Pub. L. 99–514, title XVIII, §1875(a), Oct. 22, 1986, 100 Stat. 2894, related to rules for application of minimum tax for tax preferences, prior to the general revision of this part by Pub. L. 99–514, §701(a).

AMENDMENTS

2018—Subsec. (a)(2)(A). Pub. L. 115–141 substituted "461(k)" for "461(j)".

2017—Subsec. (a)(3), (4). Pub. L. 115–97 redesignated par. (4) as (3) and struck out former par. (3). Prior to amendment, text of par. (3) read as follows: "For purposes of paragraph (1), a personal service corporation (within the meaning of section 469(j)(2)) shall be treated as a taxpayer other than a corporation."

2014—Subsec. (a)(2)(A). Pub. L. 113–295, §221(a)(58)(E), substituted "section 461(j)" for "section 464(c)".

Subsec. (b). Pub. L. 113–295, §221(a)(60)(B), inserted "and" at end of par. (1), redesignated par. (3) as (2) and struck out former par. (2) which read as follows: "the provisions of section 469(m) (relating to phase-in of disallowance) shall not apply, and".

1988—Subsec. (a)(2). Pub. L. 100–647, §1007(d)(1), struck out "(as modified by section 461(i)(4)(A))" after "section 464(c)" in subpar. (A) and substituted "section 469(c)" for "section 469(d), without regard to paragraph (1)(B) thereof" in subpar. (B).

Subsec. (a)(3). Pub. L. 100–647, §1007(d)(2), substituted "469(j)(2)" for "469(g)(1)(C)".

Subsec. (a)(4). Pub. L. 100–647, §1007(d)(3), added par. (4).

Subsec. (b). Pub. L. 100–647, §1007(d)(4), added pars. (1) to (3) and struck out former pars. (1) to (3) which read as follows:

"(1) the adjustments of section 56 shall apply,

"(2) any deduction to the extent such deduction is an item of tax preference under section 57(a) shall not be taken into account, and

"(3) the provisions of section 469(m) (relating to phase-in of disallowance) shall not apply."

1987—Subsec. (b)(3). Pub. L. 100–203 substituted "section 469(m)" for "section 469(l)".

STATUTORY NOTES AND RELATED SUBSIDIARIES
EFFECTIVE DATE OF 2017 AMENDMENT

Amendment by Pub. L. 115–97 applicable to taxable years beginning after Dec. 31, 2017, see section 12001(c) of Pub. L. 115–97, set out as a note under section 11 of this title.

EFFECTIVE DATE OF 2014 AMENDMENT

Amendment by Pub. L. 113–295 effective Dec. 19, 2014, subject to a savings provision, see section 221(b) of Pub. L. 113–295, set out as a note under section 1 of this title.

EFFECTIVE DATE OF 1988 AMENDMENT

Amendment by Pub. L. 100–647 effective, except as otherwise provided, as if included in the provision of the Tax Reform Act of 1986, Pub. L. 99–514, to which such amendment relates, see section 1019(a) of Pub. L. 100–647, set out as a note under section 1 of this title.

EFFECTIVE DATE OF 1987 AMENDMENT

Section 10212(c) of Pub. L. 100–203 provided that: "The amendments made by this section [amending this section and sections 163 and 469 of this title] shall take effect as if included in the amendments made by section 501 of the Tax Reform Act of 1986 [section 501 of Pub. L. 99–514, see section 501(c) of Pub. L. 99–514, set out as an Effective Date note under section 469 of this title]."

EFFECTIVE DATE

Section applicable to taxable years beginning after Dec. 31, 1986, with certain exceptions and qualifications, see section 701(f) of Pub. L. 99–514, set out as a note under section 55 of this title.

APPLICABILITY OF 1986 REPEAL

Pub. L. 101–239, title VII, §7811(d)(1)(B), Dec. 19, 1989, 103 Stat. 2408, provided that: "The repeal of section 58(h) of the Internal Revenue Code of 1954 by the Tax Reform Act of 1986 [Pub. L. 99–514] shall be effective only with respect to items of tax preference arising in taxable years beginning after December 31, 1986."

APPLICABILITY OF CERTAIN AMENDMENTS BY PUB. L. 99–514 IN RELATION TO TREATY OBLIGATIONS OF UNITED STATES

For applicability of amendment by section 701(a) of Pub. L. 99–514 [enacting this section] notwithstanding any treaty obligation of the United States in effect on Oct. 22, 1986, with provision that for such purposes any amendment by title I of Pub. L. 100–647 be treated as if it had been included in the provision of Pub. L. 99–514 to which such amendment relates, see section 1012(aa)(2), (4) of Pub. L. 100–647, set out as a note under section 861 of this title.

§59. Other definitions and special rules

(a) Alternative minimum tax foreign tax credit

For purposes of this part—

(1) In general

The alternative minimum tax foreign tax credit for any taxable year shall be the credit which would be determined under section 27 for such taxable year if—

(A) the pre-credit tentative minimum tax were the tax against which such credit was taken for purposes of section 904 for the taxable year and all prior taxable years beginning after December 31, 1986,

(B) section 904 were applied on the basis of alternative minimum taxable income instead of taxable income, and

(C) the determination of whether any income is high-taxed income for purposes of section 904(d)(2) were made on the basis of the applicable rate specified in section 55(b)(1) in lieu of the highest rate of tax specified in section 1.

(2) Pre-credit tentative minimum tax

For purposes of this subsection, the term "pre-credit tentative minimum tax" means the amount determined under the first sentence of section 55(b)(1)(A).

(3) Election to use simplified section 904 limitation

(A) In general

In determining the alternative minimum tax foreign tax credit for any taxable year to which an election under this paragraph applies—

(i) subparagraph (B) of paragraph (1) shall not apply, and

(ii) the limitation of section 904 shall be based on the proportion which—

(I) the taxpayer's taxable income (as determined for purposes of the regular tax) from sources without the United States (but not in excess of the taxpayer's entire alternative minimum taxable income), bears to

(II) the taxpayer's entire alternative minimum taxable income for the taxable year.

(B) Election

(i) In general

An election under this paragraph may be made only for the taxpayer's first taxable year which begins after December 31, 1997, and for which the taxpayer claims an alternative minimum tax foreign tax credit.

(ii) Election revocable only with consent

An election under this paragraph, once made, shall apply to the taxable year for which made and all subsequent taxable years unless revoked with the consent of the Secretary.

[(b) Repealed. Pub. L. 115–97, title I, §12001(b)(10), Dec. 22, 2017, 131 Stat. 2093]

(c) Treatment of estates and trusts

In the case of any estate or trust, the alternative minimum taxable income of such estate or trust and any beneficiary thereof shall be determined by applying part I of subchapter J with the adjustments provided in this part.

(d) Apportionment of differently treated items in case of certain entities

(1) In general

The differently treated items for the taxable year shall be apportioned (in accordance with regulations prescribed by the Secretary)—

(A) Regulated investment companies and real estate investment trusts

In the case of a regulated investment company to which part I of subchapter M applies or a real estate investment company to which part II of subchapter M applies, between such company or trust and shareholders and holders of beneficial interest in such company or trust.

(B) Common trust funds

In the case of a common trust fund (as defined in section 584(a)), pro rata among the participants of such fund.

(2) Differently treated items

For purposes of this section, the term "differently treated item" means any item of tax preference or any other item which is treated differently for purposes of this part than for purposes of computing the regular tax.

(e) Optional 10-year writeoff of certain tax preferences

(1) In general

For purposes of this title, any qualified expenditure to which an election under this paragraph applies shall be allowed as a deduction ratably over the 10-year period (3-year period in the case of circulation expenditures described in section 173) beginning with the taxable year in which such expenditure was made (or, in the case of a qualified expenditure described in paragraph (2)(C), over the 60-month period beginning with the month in which such expenditure was paid or incurred).

(2) Qualified expenditure

For purposes of this subsection, the term "qualified expenditure" means any amount which, but for an election under this subsection, would have been allowable as a deduction (determined without regard to section 291) for the taxable year in which paid or incurred under—

(A) section 173 (relating to circulation expenditures),

(B) section 174(a) (relating to research and experimental expenditures),

(C) section 263(c) (relating to intangible drilling and development expenditures),

(D) section 616(a) (relating to development expenditures), or

(E) section 617(a) (relating to mining exploration expenditures).

(3) Other sections not applicable

Except as provided in this subsection, no deduction shall be allowed under any other section for any qualified expenditure to which an election under this subsection applies.

(4) Election

(A) In general

An election may be made under paragraph (1) with respect to any portion of any qualified expenditure.

(B) Revocable only with consent

Any election under this subsection may be revoked only with the consent of the Secretary.

(C) Partners and shareholders of S corporations

In the case of a partnership, any election under paragraph (1) shall be made separately by each partner with respect to the partner's allocable share of any qualified expenditure. A similar rule shall apply in the case of an S corporation and its shareholders.

(5) Dispositions

(A) Application of section 1254

In the case of any disposition of property to which section 1254 applies (determined without regard to this section), any deduction under paragraph (1) with respect to amounts which are allocable to such property shall, for purposes of section 1254, be treated as a deduction allowable under section 263(c), 616(a), or 617(a), whichever is appropriate.

(B) Application of section 617(d)

In the case of any disposition of mining property to which section 617(d) applies (determined without regard to this subsection), any deduction under paragraph (1) with respect to amounts which are allocable to such property shall, for purposes of section 617(d), be treated as a deduction allowable under section 617(a).

(6) Amounts to which election apply not treated as tax preference

Any portion of any qualified expenditure to which an election under paragraph (1) applies shall not be treated as an item of tax preference under section 57(a) and section 56 shall not apply to such expenditure.

[(f) Repealed. Pub. L. 115–97, title I, §12001(b)(10), Dec. 22, 2017, 131 Stat. 2093]

(g) Tax benefit rule

The Secretary may prescribe regulations under which differently treated items shall be properly adjusted where the tax treatment giving rise to such items will not result in the reduction of the taxpayer's regular tax for the taxable year for which the item is taken into account or for any other taxable year.

(h) Coordination with certain limitations

The limitations of sections 704(d), 465, and 1366(d) (and such other provisions as may be specified in regulations) shall be applied for purposes of computing the alternative minimum taxable income of the taxpayer for the taxable year with the adjustments of sections 56, 57, and 58.

(i) Special rule for amounts treated as tax preference

For purposes of this subtitle (other than this part), any amount shall not fail to be treated as wholly exempt from tax imposed by this subtitle solely by reason of being included in alternative minimum taxable income.

(j) Treatment of unearned income of minor children

(1) In general

In the case of a child to whom section 1(g) applies, the exemption amount for purposes of section 55 shall not exceed the sum of—

(A) such child's earned income (as defined in section 911(d)(2)) for the taxable year, plus

(B) $5,000.

(2) Inflation adjustment

In the case of any taxable year beginning in a calendar year after 1998, the dollar amount in paragraph (1)(B) shall be increased by an amount equal to the product of—

(A) such dollar amount, and

(B) the cost-of-living adjustment determined under section 1(f)(3) for the calendar year in which the taxable year begins, determined by substituting "1997" for "2016" in subparagraph (A)(ii) thereof.

If any increase determined under the preceding sentence is not a multiple of $50, such increase shall be rounded to the nearest multiple of $50.

(Added Pub. L. 99–514, title VII, §701(a), Oct. 22, 1986, 100 Stat. 2336; amended Pub. L. 100–647, title I, §§1007(e), 1014(e)(5)(A), Nov. 10, 1988, 102 Stat. 3432, 3561; Pub. L. 101–239, title VII, §§7611(f)(5)(B), (6), 7612(e)(1), 7811(d)(1)(A), (j)(7), Dec. 19, 1989, 103 Stat. 2373, 2374, 2408, 2412; Pub. L. 101–508, title XI, §§11101(d)(3), 11531(b)(2), 11702(d), 11801(c)(2)(D), Nov. 5, 1990, 104 Stat. 1388–405, 1388–490, 1388–514, 1388–523; Pub. L. 102–486, title XIX, §1915(c)(3), Oct. 24, 1992, 106 Stat. 3024; Pub. L. 104–188, title I, §§1601(b)(2)(D), 1702(a)(1), 1703(e), 1704(m)(3), Aug. 20, 1996, 110 Stat. 1833, 1868, 1875, 1883; Pub. L. 105–34, title X, §1057(a), title XI, §1103(a), title XII, §1201(b)(1), Aug. 5, 1997, 111 Stat. 945, 966, 994; Pub. L. 105–206, title VI, §§6011(a), 6023(2), July 22, 1998, 112 Stat. 817, 824; Pub. L. 108–357, title IV, §421(a)(1), Oct. 22, 2004, 118 Stat. 1514; Pub. L. 115–97, title I, §§11002(d)(4), 12001(b)(3)(C), (10), Dec. 22, 2017, 131 Stat. 2061, 2093; Pub. L. 115–141, div. U, title IV, §401(d)(1)(D)(ii), Mar. 23, 2018, 132 Stat. 1206.)

INFLATION ADJUSTED ITEMS FOR CERTAIN YEARS

For inflation adjustment of certain items in this section, see Revenue Procedures listed in a table under section 1 of this title.

EDITORIAL NOTES
AMENDMENTS

2018—Subsec. (a)(1). Pub. L. 115–141 substituted "27" for "27(a)" in introductory provisions.

2017—Subsec. (a)(1)(C). Pub. L. 115–97, §12001(b)(3)(C)(i), substituted "section 55(b)(1) in lieu of the highest rate of tax specified in section 1" for "subparagraph (A)(i) or (B)(i) of section 55(b)(1) (whichever applies) in lieu of the highest rate of tax specified in section 1 or 11 (whichever applies)".

Subsec. (a)(2). Pub. L. 115–97, §12001(b)(3)(C)(ii), substituted "means the amount determined under the first sentence of section 55(b)(1)(A)." for "means—

"(A) in the case of a taxpayer other than a corporation, the amount determined under the first sentence of section 55(b)(1)(A)(i), or

"(B) in the case of a corporation, the amount determined under section 55(b)(1)(B)(i)."

Subsec. (b). Pub. L. 115–97, §12001(b)(10), struck out subsec. (b). Text read as follows: "In the case of any corporation for which a credit is allowable for the taxable year under section 30A or 936, alternative minimum taxable income shall not include any income with respect to which a credit is determined under section 30A or 936."

Subsec. (f). Pub. L. 115–97, §12001(b)(10), struck out subsec. (f). Text read as follows: "Except as otherwise provided in this part, section 291 (relating to cutback of corporate preferences) shall apply before the application of this part."

Subsec. (j)(2)(B). Pub. L. 115–97, §11002(d)(4), substituted "for '2016' in subparagraph (A)(ii)" for "for '1992' in subparagraph (B)".

2004—Subsec. (a)(2) to (4). Pub. L. 108–357 redesignated pars. (3) and (4) as (2) and (3), respectively, and struck out former par. (2) which related to limitation on alternative minimum tax foreign tax credit and carryback and carryforward of excess.

1998—Subsec. (a)(3), (4). Pub. L. 105–206, §6011(a), redesignated par. (3), relating to election to use simplified section 904 limitation, as (4).

Subsec. (b). Pub. L. 105–206, §6023(2), substituted "credits under section 30A or 936" for "section 936 credit" in heading.

1997—Subsec. (a)(2)(C). Pub. L. 105–34, §1057(a), struck out subpar. (C) which read as follows:

"(C) Exception.—Subparagraph (A) shall not apply to any domestic corporation if—

"(i) more than 50 percent of the stock of such domestic corporation (by vote and value) is owned by United States persons who are not members of an affiliated group (as defined in section 1504 of such Code) which includes such corporation,

"(ii) all of the activities of such corporation are conducted in 1 foreign country with which the United States has an income tax treaty in effect and such treaty provides for the exchange of information between such foreign country and the United States,

"(iii) all of the current earnings and profits of such corporation are distributed at least annually (other than current earnings and profits retained for normal maintenance or capital replacements or improvements of an existing business), and

"(iv) all of such distributions by such corporation to United States persons are used by such persons in a trade or business conducted in the United States."

Subsec. (a)(3). Pub. L. 105–34, §1103(a), added par. (3) relating to election to use simplified section 904 limitation.

Subsec. (j). Pub. L. 105–34, §1201(b)(1), amended subsec. (j) generally, restating limitation on exemption amount, adding provisions for inflation adjustment of such amount, and deleting provisions relating to limitation based on parental minimum tax and unused parental minimum tax exemption.

1996—Subsec. (a)(1)(A). Pub. L. 104–188, §1703(e)(1), substituted "the pre-credit tentative minimum tax" for "the amount determined under section 55(b)(1)(A)".

Subsec. (a)(1)(C). Pub. L. 104–188, §1703(e)(2), substituted "specified in subparagraph (A)(i) or (B)(i) of section 55(b)(1) (whichever applies)" for "specified in section 55(b)(1)(A)".

Subsec. (a)(2)(A)(i). Pub. L. 104–188, §1703(e)(1), substituted "the pre-credit tentative minimum tax" for "the amount determined under section 55(b)(1)(A)".

Subsec. (a)(2)(A)(ii). Pub. L. 104–188, §1703(e)(3), substituted "which would be the pre-credit tentative minimum tax" for "which would be determined under section 55(b)(1)(A)".

Subsec. (a)(3). Pub. L. 104–188, §1703(e)(4), added par. (3).

Subsec. (b). Pub. L. 104–188, §1601(b)(2)(D), substituted "section 30A or 936, alternative minimum taxable income shall not include any income with respect to which a credit is determined under section 30A or 936." for "section 936, alternative minimum taxable income shall not include any amount with respect to which the requirements of subparagraph (A) or (B) of section 936(a)(1) are met."

Subsec. (j)(1)(B). Pub. L. 104–188, §1704(m)(3), substituted "twice the amount in effect for the taxable year under section 63(c)(5)(A)" for "$1,000".

Subsec. (j)(3)(B). Pub. L. 104–188, §1702(a)(1), substituted "section 1(g)(3)(B)" for "section 1(i)(3)(B)".

1992—Subsec. (a)(2)(A)(ii). Pub. L. 102–486 substituted "and section 57(a)(2)(E)" for "and the alternative tax energy preference deduction under section 56(h)".

1990—Subsec. (a)(1)(B) to (D). Pub. L. 101–508, §11801(c)(2)(D), inserted "and" at end of subpar. (B), redesignated subpar. (D) as (C), and struck out former subpar. (C) which read as follows: "for purposes of section 904, any increase in alternative minimum taxable income by reason of section 56(c)(1)(A) (relating to adjustment for book income) shall have the same proportionate source (and character) as alternative minimum taxable income determined without regard to such increase, and".

Subsec. (a)(2)(A)(ii). Pub. L. 101–508, §11531(b)(2), inserted before period at end "and the alternative tax energy preference deduction under section 56(h)".

Subsec. (j). Pub. L. 101–508, §11101(d)(3)(A), substituted "section 1(g)" for "section 1(i)" in pars. (1), (2)(A), (B)(i)(I), (II), (D), and (3).

Subsec. (j)(1)(B). Pub. L. 101–508, §11702(d)(1), inserted "(or, if greater, the child's share of the unused parental minimum tax exemption)" before period at end.

Subsec. (j)(2)(C). Pub. L. 101–508, §11101(d)(3)(B), substituted "section 1(g)(3)(B)" for "section 1(i)(3)(B)".

Subsec. (j)(2)(D). Pub. L. 101–508, §11702(d)(3), substituted "paragraphs (3)(D), (5), and (6)" for "paragraphs (5) and (6)".

Subsec. (j)(3). Pub. L. 101–508, §11702(d)(2), added par. (3).

1989—Subsec. (a)(2)(C). Pub. L. 101–239, §7612(e)(1), added subpar. (C).

Subsec. (e)(1). Pub. L. 101–239, §7611(f)(5)(B), inserted before period at end "(or, in the case of a qualified expenditure described in paragraph (2)(C), over the 60-month period beginning with the month in which such expenditure was paid or incurred)".

Subsec. (g). Pub. L. 101–239, §7811(d)(1)(A), substituted "for the taxable year for which the item is taken into account or for any other taxable year" for "for any taxable year".

Subsec. (i). Pub. L. 101–239, §7611(f)(6), substituted "amounts" for "interest" in heading and "any amount shall" for "interest shall" in text.

Subsec. (j)(2)(D). Pub. L. 101–239, §7811(j)(7), substituted "Other rules" for "Others rules" in heading.

1988—Subsec. (a)(1)(D). Pub. L. 100–647, §1007(e)(3), added subpar. (D).

Subsec. (e)(2). Pub. L. 100–647, §1007(e)(1), inserted "(determined without regard to section 291)" after "as a deduction".

Subsec. (h). Pub. L. 100–647, §1007(e)(2), substituted "taxable year with the adjustments of sections 56, 57, and 58" for "taxable year—
"(1) with the adjustments of section 56, and
"(2) by not taking into account any deduction to the extent such deduction is an item of tax preference under section 57(a)".
Subsec. (i). Pub. L. 100–647, §1007(e)(4), inserted "(other than this part)" after "of this subtitle" and substituted "subtitle" for "title" before "solely".
Subsec. (j). Pub. L. 100–647, §1014(e)(5)(A), added subsec. (j).

Amendment by section 11002(d)(4) of Pub. L. 115–97 applicable to taxable years beginning after Dec. 31, 2017, see section 11002(e) of Pub. L. 115–97, set out as a note under section 1 of this title.

Amendment by section 12001(b)(3)(C), (10) of Pub. L. 115–97 applicable to taxable years beginning after Dec. 31, 2017, see section 12001(c) of Pub. L. 115–97, set out as a note under section 11 of this title.

EFFECTIVE DATE OF 2004 AMENDMENT

Amendment by Pub. L. 108–357 applicable to taxable years beginning after Dec. 31, 2004, see section 421(b) of Pub. L. 108–357, set out as a note under section 53 of this title.

EFFECTIVE DATE OF 1998 AMENDMENT

Amendment by section 6023(2) of Pub. L. 105–206 effective July 22, 1998, see section 6023(32) of Pub. L. 105–206, set out as a note under section 34 of this title.

Amendment by section 6011(a) of Pub. L. 105–206 effective, except as otherwise provided, as if included in the provisions of the Taxpayer Relief Act of 1997, Pub. L. 105–34, to which such amendment relates, see section 6024 of Pub. L. 105–206, set out as a note under section 1 of this title.

EFFECTIVE DATE OF 1997 AMENDMENT

Pub. L. 105–34, title X, §1057(b), Aug. 5, 1997, 111 Stat. 945, provided that: "The amendment made by this section [amending this section] shall apply to taxable years beginning after the date of the enactment of this Act [Aug. 5, 1997]."

Pub. L. 105–34, title XI, §1103(b), Aug. 5, 1997, 111 Stat. 966, provided that: "The amendment made by this section [amending this section] shall apply to taxable years beginning after December 31, 1997."

Pub. L. 105–34, title XII, §1201(c), Aug. 5, 1997, 111 Stat. 994, provided that: "The amendments made by this section [amending this section and sections 63 and 6103 of this title] shall apply to taxable years beginning after December 31, 1997."

EFFECTIVE DATE OF 1996 AMENDMENT

Amendment by section 1601(b)(2)(D) of Pub. L. 104–188 applicable to taxable years beginning after Dec. 31, 1995, except as otherwise provided, see section 1601(c) of Pub. L. 104–188, set out as a note under section 55 of this title.

Amendment by section 1702(a)(1) of Pub. L. 104–188 effective, except as otherwise expressly provided, as if included in the provision of the Revenue Reconciliation Act of 1990, Pub. L. 101–508, title XI, to which such amendment relates, see section 1702(i) of Pub. L. 104–188, set out as a note under section 38 of this title.

Amendment by section 1703(e) of Pub. L. 104–188 effective as if included in the provision of the Revenue Reconciliation Act of 1993, Pub. L. 103–66, §§13001–13444, to which such amendment relates, see section 1703(o) of Pub. L. 104–188, set out as a note under section 39 of this title.

Amendment by section 1704(m)(3) of Pub. L. 104–188 applicable to taxable years beginning after Dec. 31, 1995, see section 1704(m)(4) of Pub. L. 104–188, set out as a note under section 1 of this title.

EFFECTIVE DATE OF 1992 AMENDMENT

Amendment by Pub. L. 102–486 applicable to taxable years beginning after Dec. 31, 1992, see section 1915(d) of Pub. L. 102–486, set out as a note under section 56 of this title.

EFFECTIVE DATE OF 1990 AMENDMENT

Amendment by section 11101(d)(3) of Pub. L. 101–508 applicable to taxable years beginning after Dec. 31, 1990, see section 11101(e) of Pub. L. 101–508, set out as a note under section 1 of this title.

Amendment by section 11531(b)(2) of Pub. L. 101–508 applicable to taxable years beginning after Dec. 31, 1990, see section 11531(c) of Pub. L. 101–508, set out as a note under section 56 of this title.

Pub. L. 101–508, title XI, §11702(j), Nov. 5, 1990, 104 Stat. 1388–516, provided that: "Any amendment made by this section [amending this section and sections 135, 216, 355, 367, 447, 453B, 468B, 2056, 2056A, 2523, 4980B, and 6114 of this title] shall take effect as if included in the provision of the Technical and Miscellaneous Revenue Act of 1988 [Pub. L. 100–647] to which such amendment relates."

EFFECTIVE DATE OF 1989 AMENDMENT

Amendment by section 7611(f)(6) of Pub. L. 101–239 applicable to taxable years beginning after Dec. 31, 1989, see section 7611(g)(1) of Pub. L. 101–239, set out as a note under section 56 of this title.

Amendment by section 7611(f)(5)(B) of Pub. L. 101–239 applicable to costs paid or incurred in taxable years beginning after Dec. 31, 1989, see section 7611(g)(2) of Pub. L. 101–239, set out as a note under section 56 of this title.

Pub. L. 101–239, title VII, §7612(e)(2), Dec. 19, 1989, 103 Stat. 2375, provided that:

"(A) In general.—The amendment made by paragraph (1) [amending this section] shall apply to taxable years beginning after March 31, 1990.

"(B) Special rule for year which includes march 31, 1990.—In the case of any taxable year (of a corporation described in subparagraph (C) of section 59(a)(2) of the Internal Revenue Code of 1986 (as added by paragraph (1))) which begins after December 31, 1989, and includes March 31, 1990, the amount determined under clause (ii) of section 59(a)(2)(A) of such Code shall be an amount which bears the same ratio to the amount which would have been determined under such clause without regard to this subparagraph as the number of days in such taxable year on or before March 31, 1990, bears to the total number of days in such taxable year."

Amendment by section 7811(d)(1)(A), (j)(7) of Pub. L. 101–239 effective, except as otherwise provided, as if included in the provision of the Technical and Miscellaneous Revenue Act of 1988, Pub. L. 100–647, to which such amendment relates, see section 7817 of Pub. L. 101–239, set out as a note under section 1 of this title.

EFFECTIVE DATE OF 1988 AMENDMENT

Amendment by section 1007(e) of Pub. L. 100–647 effective, except as otherwise provided, as if included in the provision of the Tax Reform Act of 1986, Pub. L. 99–514, to which such amendment relates, see section 1019(a) of Pub. L. 100–647, set out as a note under section 1 of this title.

Pub. L. 100–647, title I, §1014(e)(5)(B), Nov. 10, 1988, 102 Stat. 3562, provided that: "The amendment made by subparagraph (A) [amending this section] shall apply to taxable years beginning after December 31, 1988."

EFFECTIVE DATE

Section applicable to taxable years beginning after Dec. 31, 1986, with certain exceptions and qualifications, see section 701(f) of Pub. L. 99–514, set out as a note under section 55 of this title.

SAVINGS PROVISION

For provisions that nothing in amendment by Pub. L. 115–141 be construed to affect treatment of certain transactions occurring, property acquired, or items of income, loss, deduction, or credit taken into account prior to Mar. 23, 2018, for purposes of determining liability for tax for periods ending after Mar. 23, 2018, see section 401(e) of Pub. L. 115–141, set out as a note under section 23 of this title.

For provisions that nothing in amendment by section 11801 of Pub. L. 101–508 be construed to affect treatment of certain transactions occurring, property acquired, or items of income, loss, deduction, or credit taken into account prior to Nov. 5, 1990, for purposes of determining liability for tax for periods ending after Nov. 5, 1990, see section 11821(b) of Pub. L. 101–508, set out as a note under section 45K of this title.

CONSIDERATION OF CERTAIN TAXES TREATED AS PAID OR ACCRUED UNDER SECTION 904(C) IN DETERMINATION OF ALTERNATIVE MINIMUM TAX FOREIGN TAX CREDIT

Pub. L. 100–647, title I, §1007(f)(5), Nov. 10, 1988, 102 Stat. 3434, provided that: "In determining the amount of the alternative minimum tax foreign tax credit under section 59 of the 1986 Code, there shall not be taken into account any taxes paid or accrued in a taxable year beginning after December 31, 1986, which are treated under section 904(c) of the 1986 Code as paid or accrued in a taxable year beginning on or before December 31, 1986."

APPLICABILITY OF CERTAIN AMENDMENTS BY PUB. L. 99–514 IN RELATION TO TREATY OBLIGATIONS OF UNITED STATES

For applicability of amendment by section 701(a) of Pub. L. 99–514 [enacting this section] notwithstanding any treaty obligation of the United States in effect on Oct. 22, 1986, with provision that for such purposes any amendment by title I of Pub. L. 100–647 be treated as if it had been included in the provision of Pub. L. 99–514 to which such amendment relates, see section 1012(aa)(2), (4) of Pub. L. 100–647, set out as a note under section 861 of this title.

PART VII—BASE EROSION AND ANTI-ABUSE TAX

Sec.
59A.
Tax on base erosion payments of taxpayers with substantial gross receipts.

EDITORIAL NOTES
PRIOR PROVISIONS

A prior part VII, Environmental Tax, consisted of section 59A, prior to repeal by Pub. L. 113–295, div. A, title II, §221(a)(12)(A), Dec. 19, 2014, 128 Stat. 4038.

§59A. Tax on base erosion payments of taxpayers with substantial gross receipts

(a) Imposition of tax

There is hereby imposed on each applicable taxpayer for any taxable year a tax equal to the base erosion minimum tax amount for the taxable year. Such tax shall be in addition to any other tax imposed by this subtitle.

(b) Base erosion minimum tax amount

For purposes of this section—

(1) In general

Except as provided in paragraphs (2) and (3), the term "base erosion minimum tax amount" means, with respect to any applicable taxpayer for any taxable year, the excess (if any) of—

(A) an amount equal to 10 percent (5 percent in the case of taxable years beginning in calendar year 2018) of the modified taxable income of such taxpayer for the taxable year, over

(B) an amount equal to the regular tax liability (as defined in section 26(b)) of the taxpayer for the taxable year, reduced (but not below zero) by the excess (if any) of—

(i) the credits allowed under this chapter against such regular tax liability, over

(ii) the sum of—

(I) the credit allowed under section 38 for the taxable year which is properly allocable to the research credit determined under section 41(a), plus

(II) the portion of the applicable section 38 credits not in excess of 80 percent of the lesser of the amount of such credits or the base erosion minimum tax amount (determined without regard to this subclause).

(2) Modifications for taxable years beginning after 2025

In the case of any taxable year beginning after December 31, 2025, paragraph (1) shall be applied—

(A) by substituting "12.5 percent" for "10 percent" in subparagraph (A) thereof, and

(B) by reducing (but not below zero) the regular tax liability (as defined in section 26(b)) for purposes of subparagraph (B) thereof by the aggregate amount of the credits allowed under this chapter against such regular tax liability rather than the excess described in such subparagraph.

(3) Increased rate for certain banks and securities dealers

(A) In general

In the case of a taxpayer described in subparagraph (B) who is an applicable taxpayer for any taxable year, the percentage otherwise in effect under paragraphs (1)(A) and (2)(A) shall each be increased by one percentage point.

(B) Taxpayer described

A taxpayer is described in this subparagraph if such taxpayer is a member of an affiliated group (as defined in section 1504(a)(1)) which includes—

(i) a bank (as defined in section 581), or

(ii) a registered securities dealer under section 15(a) of the Securities Exchange Act of 1934.

(4) Applicable section 38 credits

For purposes of paragraph (1)(B)(ii)(II), the term "applicable section 38 credits" means the credit allowed under section 38 for the taxable year which is properly allocable to—

(A) the low-income housing credit determined under section 42(a),

(B) the renewable electricity production credit determined under section 45(a), and

(C) the investment credit determined under section 46, but only to the extent properly allocable to the energy credit determined under section 48.

(c) Modified taxable income

For purposes of this section—

(1) In general

The term "modified taxable income" means the taxable income of the taxpayer computed under this chapter for the taxable year, determined without regard to—

(A) any base erosion tax benefit with respect to any base erosion payment, or

(B) the base erosion percentage of any net operating loss deduction allowed under section 172 for the taxable year.

(2) Base erosion tax benefit

(A) In general

The term "base erosion tax benefit" means—

(i) any deduction described in subsection (d)(1) which is allowed under this chapter for the taxable year with respect to any base erosion payment,

(ii) in the case of a base erosion payment described in subsection (d)(2), any deduction allowed under this chapter for the taxable year for depreciation (or amortization in lieu of depreciation) with respect to the property acquired with such payment,

(iii) in the case of a base erosion payment described in subsection (d)(3)—

(I) any reduction under section 803(a)(1)(B) in the gross amount of premiums and other consideration on insurance and annuity contracts for premiums and other consideration arising out of indemnity insurance, and

(II) any deduction under section 832(b)(4)(A) from the amount of gross premiums written on insurance contracts during the taxable year for premiums paid for reinsurance, and

(iv) in the case of a base erosion payment described in subsection (d)(4), any reduction in gross receipts with respect to such payment in computing gross income of the taxpayer for the taxable year for purposes of this chapter.

(B) Tax benefits disregarded if tax withheld on base erosion payment
(i) In general

Except as provided in clause (ii), any base erosion tax benefit attributable to any base erosion payment—

(I) on which tax is imposed by section 871 or 881, and

(II) with respect to which tax has been deducted and withheld under section 1441 or 1442,

shall not be taken into account in computing modified taxable income under paragraph (1)(A) or the base erosion percentage under paragraph (4).

(ii) Exception

The amount not taken into account in computing modified taxable income by reason of clause (i) shall be reduced under rules similar to the rules under section 163(j)(5)(B) (as in effect before the date of the enactment of the Tax Cuts and Jobs Act).

(3) Special rules for determining interest for which deduction allowed

For purposes of applying paragraph (1), in the case of a taxpayer to which section 163(j) applies for the taxable year, the reduction in the amount of interest for which a deduction is allowed by reason of such subsection shall be treated as allocable first to interest paid or accrued to persons who are not related parties with respect to the taxpayer and then to such related parties.

(4) Base erosion percentage

For purposes of paragraph (1)(B)—

(A) In general

The term "base erosion percentage" means, for any taxable year, the percentage determined by dividing—

(i) the aggregate amount of base erosion tax benefits of the taxpayer for the taxable year, by

(ii) the sum of—

(I) the aggregate amount of the deductions (including deductions described in clauses (i) and (ii) of paragraph (2)(A)) allowable to the taxpayer under this chapter for the taxable year, plus

(II) the base erosion tax benefits described in clauses (iii) and (iv) of paragraph (2)(A) allowable to the taxpayer for the taxable year.

(B) Certain items not taken into account

The amount under subparagraph (A)(ii) shall be determined by not taking into account—

(i) any deduction allowed under section 172, 245A, or 250 for the taxable year,

(ii) any deduction for amounts paid or accrued for services to which the exception under subsection (d)(5) applies, and

(iii) any deduction for qualified derivative payments which are not treated as a base erosion payment by reason of subsection (h).

(d) Base erosion payment

For purposes of this section—

(1) In general

The term "base erosion payment" means any amount paid or accrued by the taxpayer to a foreign person which is a related party of the taxpayer and with respect to which a deduction is allowable under this chapter.

(2) Purchase of depreciable property

Such term shall also include any amount paid or accrued by the taxpayer to a foreign person which is a related party of the taxpayer in connection with the acquisition by the taxpayer from such person of property of a character subject to the allowance for depreciation (or amortization in lieu of depreciation).

(3) Reinsurance payments

Such term shall also include any premium or other consideration paid or accrued by the taxpayer to a foreign person which is a related party of the taxpayer for any reinsurance payments which are taken into account under sections 803(a)(1)(B) or 832(b)(4)(A).

(4) Certain payments to expatriated entities
(A) In general

Such term shall also include any amount paid or accrued by the taxpayer with respect to a person described in subparagraph (B) which results in a reduction of the gross receipts of the taxpayer.

(B) Person described

A person is described in this subparagraph if such person is a—

(i) surrogate foreign corporation which is a related party of the taxpayer, but only if such person first became a surrogate foreign corporation after November 9, 2017, or

(ii) foreign person which is a member of the same expanded affiliated group as the surrogate foreign corporation.

(C) Definitions

For purposes of this paragraph—

(i) Surrogate foreign corporation

The term "surrogate foreign corporation" has the meaning given such term by section 7874(a)(2)(B) but does not include a foreign corporation treated as a domestic corporation under section 7874(b).

(ii) Expanded affiliated group

The term "expanded affiliated group" has the meaning given such term by section 7874(c)(1).

(5) Exception for certain amounts with respect to services

Paragraph (1) shall not apply to any amount paid or accrued by a taxpayer for services if—

(A) such services are services which meet the requirements for eligibility for use of the services cost method under section 482 (determined without regard to the requirement that the services not contribute significantly to fundamental risks of business success or failure), and

(B) such amount constitutes the total services cost with no markup component.

(e) Applicable taxpayer

For purposes of this section—

(1) In general

The term "applicable taxpayer" means, with respect to any taxable year, a taxpayer—

(A) which is a corporation other than a regulated investment company, a real estate investment trust, or an S corporation,

(B) the average annual gross receipts of which for the 3-taxable-year period ending with the preceding taxable year are at least $500,000,000, and

(C) the base erosion percentage (as determined under subsection (c)(4)) of which for the taxable year is 3 percent (2 percent in the case of a taxpayer described in subsection (b)(3)(B)) or higher.

(2) Gross receipts

(A) Special rule for foreign persons

In the case of a foreign person the gross receipts of which are taken into account for purposes of paragraph (1)(B), only gross receipts which are taken into account in determining income which is effectively connected with the conduct of a trade or business within the United States shall be taken into account. In the case of a taxpayer which is a foreign person, the preceding sentence shall not apply to the gross receipts of any United States person which are aggregated with the taxpayer's gross receipts by reason of paragraph (3).

(B) Other rules made applicable

Rules similar to the rules of subparagraphs (B), (C), and (D) of section 448(c)(3) shall apply in determining gross receipts for purposes of this section.

(3) Aggregation rules

All persons treated as a single employer under subsection (a) of section 52 shall be treated as 1 person for purposes of this subsection and subsection (c)(4), except that in applying section 1563 for purposes of section 52, the exception for foreign corporations under section 1563(b)(2)(C) shall be disregarded.

(f) Foreign person

For purposes of this section, the term "foreign person" has the meaning given such term by section 6038A(c)(3).

(g) Related party

For purposes of this section—

(1) In general

The term "related party" means, with respect to any applicable taxpayer—

(A) any 25-percent owner of the taxpayer,

(B) any person who is related (within the meaning of section 267(b) or 707(b)(1)) to the taxpayer or any 25-percent owner of the taxpayer, and

(C) any other person who is related (within the meaning of section 482) to the taxpayer.

(2) 25-percent owner

The term "25-percent owner" means, with respect to any corporation, any person who owns at least 25 percent of—

(A) the total voting power of all classes of stock of a corporation entitled to vote, or

(B) the total value of all classes of stock of such corporation.

(3) Section 318 to apply

Section 318 shall apply for purposes of paragraphs (1) and (2), except that—

(A) "10 percent" shall be substituted for "50 percent" in section 318(a)(2)(C), and

(B) subparagraphs (A), (B), and (C) of section 318(a)(3) shall not be applied so as to consider a United States person as owning stock which is owned by a person who is not a United States person.

(h) Exception for certain payments made in the ordinary course of trade or business

For purposes of this section—

(1) In general

Except as provided in paragraph (3), any qualified derivative payment shall not be treated as a base erosion payment.

(2) Qualified derivative payment

(A) In general

The term "qualified derivative payment" means any payment made by a taxpayer pursuant to a derivative with respect to which the taxpayer—

(i) recognizes gain or loss as if such derivative were sold for its fair market value on the last business day of the taxable year (and such additional times as required by this title or the taxpayer's method of accounting),

(ii) treats any gain or loss so recognized as ordinary, and

(iii) treats the character of all items of income, deduction, gain, or loss with respect to a payment pursuant to the derivative as ordinary.

(B) Reporting requirement

No payments shall be treated as qualified derivative payments under subparagraph (A) for any taxable year unless the taxpayer includes in the information required to be reported under section 6038B(b)(2) with respect to such taxable year such information as is necessary to identify the payments to be so treated and such other information as the Secretary determines necessary to carry out the provisions of this subsection.

(3) Exceptions for payments otherwise treated as base erosion payments

This subsection shall not apply to any qualified derivative payment if—

(A) the payment would be treated as a base erosion payment if it were not made pursuant to a derivative, including any interest, royalty, or service payment, or

(B) in the case of a contract which has derivative and nonderivative components, the payment is properly allocable to the nonderivative component.

(4) Derivative defined

For purposes of this subsection—

(A) In general

The term "derivative" means any contract (including any option, forward contract, futures contract, short position, swap, or similar contract) the value of which, or any payment or other transfer with respect to which, is (directly or indirectly) determined by reference to one or more of the following:

(i) Any share of stock in a corporation.

(ii) Any evidence of indebtedness.

(iii) Any commodity which is actively traded.

(iv) Any currency.

(v) Any rate, price, amount, index, formula, or algorithm.

Such term shall not include any item described in clauses (i) through (v).

(B) Treatment of American depository receipts and similar instruments

Except as otherwise provided by the Secretary, for purposes of this part, American depository receipts (and similar instruments) with respect to shares of stock in foreign corporations shall be treated as shares of stock in such foreign corporations.

(C) Exception for certain contracts

Such term shall not include any insurance, annuity, or endowment contract issued by an insurance company to which subchapter L applies (or issued by any foreign corporation to which such subchapter would apply if such foreign corporation were a domestic corporation).

(i) Regulations

The Secretary shall prescribe such regulations or other guidance as may be necessary or appropriate to carry out the provisions of this section, including regulations—

(1) providing for such adjustments to the application of this section as are necessary to prevent the avoidance of the purposes of this section, including through—

(A) the use of unrelated persons, conduit transactions, or other intermediaries, or

(B) transactions or arrangements designed, in whole or in part—

(i) to characterize payments otherwise subject to this section as payments not subject to this section, or

(ii) to substitute payments not subject to this section for payments otherwise subject to this section and

(2) for the application of subsection (g), including rules to prevent the avoidance of the exceptions under subsection (g)(3).

(Added Pub. L. 115–97, title I, §14401(a), Dec. 22, 2017, 131 Stat. 2226.)

EDITORIAL NOTES
REFERENCES IN TEXT

Section 15(a) of the Securities Exchange Act of 1934, referred to in subsec. (b)(3)(B)(ii), is classified to section 78o(a) of Title 15, Commerce and Trade.

The date of the enactment of the Tax Cuts and Jobs Act, referred to in subsec. (c)(2)(B)(ii), probably means the date of enactment of title I of Pub. L. 115–97, which was approved Dec. 22, 2017. Prior versions of the bill that was enacted into law as Pub. L. 115–97 included such Short Title, but it was not enacted as part of title I of Pub. L. 115–97.

PRIOR PROVISIONS

A prior section 59A, added Pub. L. 99–499, title V, §516(a), Oct. 17, 1986, 100 Stat. 1770; amended Pub. L. 100–647, title II, §2001(c)(1), (3)(B), Nov. 10, 1988, 102 Stat. 3594; Pub. L. 101–508, title XI, §§11231(a)(1)(A), 11531(b)(3), 11801(c)(2)(E), Nov. 5, 1990, 104 Stat. 1388–444, 1388-490, 1388-523; Pub. L. 102–486, title XIX, §1915(c)(4), Oct. 24, 1992, 106 Stat. 3024, related to environmental tax, prior to repeal by Pub. L. 113–295, div. A, title II, §221(a)(12)(A), Dec. 19, 2014, 128 Stat. 4038.

STATUTORY NOTES AND RELATED SUBSIDIARIES
EFFECTIVE DATE

Section applicable to base erosion payments (as defined in subsec. (d) of this section) paid or accrued in taxable years beginning after Dec. 31, 2017, see section 14401(e) of Pub. L. 115–97, set out as an Effective Date of 2017 Amendment note under section 26 of this title.

[PART VIII—REPEALED]

[§59B. Repealed. Pub. L. 101–234, title I, §102(a), Dec. 13, 1989, 103 Stat. 1980]

Section, added Pub. L. 100–360, title I, §111(a), July 1, 1988, 102 Stat. 690, provided for imposition of a supplemental medicare premium.

STATUTORY NOTES AND RELATED SUBSIDIARIES
EFFECTIVE DATE OF REPEAL

Pub. L. 101–234, title I, §102(d), Dec. 13, 1989, 103 Stat. 1981, provided that:

"(1) In general.—Except as provided in this subsection, the provisions of this section [repealing section 1395i–1a of Title 42, The Public Health and Welfare, enacting provisions set out as notes under section 6050F of this title and section 1395t of Title 42, and repealing provisions set out as a note under section 1395i–1a of Title 42] shall take effect January 1, 1990.

"(2) Repeal of supplemental medicare premium.—The repeal of section 111 of MCCA [Pub. L. 100–360, which enacted this section, amended section 6050F of this title, and enacted provisions set out as notes below] shall apply to taxable years beginning after December 31, 1988."

EFFECTIVE DATE

Pub. L. 100–360, title I, §111(e), July 1, 1988, 102 Stat. 698, which provided that the enactment of this section and the amendment of section 6050F of this title applied to taxable years beginning after December 31, 1988, and that in case of a taxable year beginning in 1989, the premium imposed by this section should not be treated as a tax for purposes of applying section 6654 of this title, was repealed by Pub. L. 101–234, title I, §102(a), Dec. 13, 1989, 103 Stat. 1980.

ANNOUNCEMENT OF SUPPLEMENTAL PREMIUM RATE

Pub. L. 100–360, title I, §111(d), July 1, 1988, 102 Stat. 697, which provided that in the case of calendar year 1993 or any calendar year thereafter (1) not later than July 1 of such calendar year, the Secretary of the Treasury or his delegate was required to make an announcement of the estimated supplemental premium rate under this section for taxable years beginning in the following calendar year, and (2) not later than October 1 of such calendar year, the Secretary of the Treasury or his delegate was required to make an announcement of the actual supplemental premium rate under this section for such taxable years, was repealed by Pub. L. 101–234, title I, §102(a), Dec. 13, 1989, 103 Stat. 1980.

Subchapter B—Computation of Taxable Income

V.

Deductions for personal exemptions.

VI.

Itemized deductions for individuals and corporations.

VII.

Additional itemized deductions for individuals.

VIII.

Special deductions for corporations.

IX.

Items not deductible.

X.

Terminal railroad corporations and their shareholders.

XI.

Special rules relating to corporate preference items.

EDITORIAL NOTES

AMENDMENTS

1982—Pub. L. 97–248, title II, §204(c)(2), Sept. 3, 1982, 96 Stat. 427, added item for part XI.

1977—Pub. L. 95–30, title I, §101(e)(3), May 23, 1977, 91 Stat. 135, substituted "Determination of marital status" for "Standard deduction for individuals" in item for part IV.

1976—Pub. L. 94–455, title XIX, §1901(b)(4)(C), Oct. 4, 1976, 90 Stat. 1793, substituted "taxable income, etc." for "and taxable income." in item for part I.

1962—Pub. L. 87–870, §1(b), Oct. 23, 1962, 76 Stat. 1160, added item for part X.

¹ Part heading amended by Pub. L. 99–514 without corresponding amendment of analysis.

PART I—DEFINITION OF GROSS INCOME, ADJUSTED GROSS INCOME, TAXABLE INCOME, ETC.

EDITORIAL NOTES

AMENDMENTS

1990—Pub. L. 101–508, title XI, §11103(d), Nov. 5, 1990, 104 Stat. 1388–407, added item 68.

1986—Pub. L. 99–514, title I, §132(d), Oct. 22, 1986, 100 Stat. 2116, added item 67.

1984—Pub. L. 98–369, div. A, title IV, §424(b)(2)(C), July 18, 1984, 98 Stat. 803, struck out "where spouses live apart" in item 66.

1980—Pub. L. 96–605, title I, §101(b), Dec. 28, 1980, 94 Stat. 3522, added item 66.

1976—Pub. L. 94–455, title XIX, §1901(b)(4)(A), (B), Oct. 4, 1976, 90 Stat. 1793, substituted "TAXABLE INCOME, ETC." for "AND TAXABLE INCOME" in part heading, and added items 64 and 65.

§61. Gross income defined

(a) General definition

Except as otherwise provided in this subtitle, gross income means all income from whatever source derived, including (but not limited to) the following items:

(1) Compensation for services, including fees, commissions, fringe benefits, and similar items;

(2) Gross income derived from business;

(3) Gains derived from dealings in property;

(4) Interest;

(5) Rents;

(6) Royalties;

(7) Dividends;

(8) Annuities;

(9) Income from life insurance and endowment contracts;

(10) Pensions;

(11) Income from discharge of indebtedness;

(12) Distributive share of partnership gross income;

(13) Income in respect of a decedent; and

(14) Income from an interest in an estate or trust.

(b) Cross references

For items specifically included in gross income, see part II (sec. 71 and following). For items specifically excluded from gross income, see part III (sec. 101 and following).

(Aug. 16, 1954, ch. 736, 68A Stat. 17; Pub. L. 98–369, div. A, title V, §531(c), July 18, 1984, 98 Stat. 884; Pub. L. 115–97, title I, §11051(b)(1)(A), Dec. 22, 2017, 131 Stat. 2089.)

EDITORIAL NOTES
AMENDMENTS

2017—Subsec. (a)(8) to (15). Pub. L. 115–97 redesignated pars. (9) to (15) as (8) to (14), respectively, and struck out former par. (8) which read as follows: "Alimony and separate maintenance payments;".

1984—Subsec. (a)(1). Pub. L. 98–369 inserted reference to fringe benefits.

STATUTORY NOTES AND RELATED SUBSIDIARIES
EFFECTIVE DATE OF 2017 AMENDMENT

Pub. L. 115–97, title I, §11051(c), Dec. 22, 2017, 131 Stat. 2090, provided that: "The amendments made by this section [amending this section and sections 62, 121, 152, 219, 220, 223, 382, 408, 3402, 6724, and 7701 of this title and repealing sections 71, 215, and 682 of this title] shall apply to—

"(1) any divorce or separation instrument (as defined in section 71(b)(2) of the Internal Revenue Code of 1986 as in effect before the date of the enactment of this Act [Dec. 22, 2017]) executed after December 31, 2018, and

"(2) any divorce or separation instrument (as so defined) executed on or before such date and modified after such date if the modification expressly provides that the amendments made by this section apply to such modification."

EFFECTIVE DATE OF 1984 AMENDMENT

Amendment by Pub. L. 98–369 effective Jan. 1, 1985, see section 531(h) of Pub. L. 98–369, set out as an Effective Date note under section 132 of this title.

TERMINATION DATE OF 1978 AMENDMENT

Pub. L. 95–615, §210(a), Nov. 8, 1978, 92 Stat. 3109, provided that: "Title I of this Act [probably means sections 1 to 8 of Pub. L. 95–615, see Short Title of 1978 Amendment note under section 1 of this title] (other than sections 4 and 5 thereof) [amending section 167 of this title, enacting provisions set out as notes under this section and sections 61 and 62 of this title, and amending provisions set out as notes under sections 117, 167, and 382 of this title] shall cease to have effect on the day after the date of the enactment of this Act [Nov. 8, 1978]."

REGULATIONS

Pub. L. 95–427, §1, Oct. 7, 1978, 92 Stat. 996, as amended by Pub. L. 96–167, §1, Dec. 29, 1979, 93 Stat. 1275; Pub. L. 97–34, title VIII, §801, Aug. 13, 1981, 95 Stat. 349; Pub. L. 99–514, §2, Oct. 22, 1986, 100 Stat. 2095, provided that:

"(a) In General.—No fringe benefit regulation shall be issued—

"(1) in final form on or after May 1, 1978, and on or before December 31, 1983, or

"(2) in proposed or final form on or after May 1, 1978, if such regulation has an effective date on or before December 31, 1983.

"(b) Definition of Fringe Benefit Regulation.—For purposes of subsection (a), the term 'fringe benefit regulation' means a regulation providing for the inclusion of any fringe benefit in gross income by reason of section 61 of the Internal Revenue Code of 1986 [formerly I.R.C. 1954]."

Pub. L. 95–615, §3, Nov. 8, 1978, 92 Stat. 3097, as amended by Pub. L. 99–514, §2, Oct. 22, 1986, 100 Stat. 2095, provided that no regulations be issued in final form on or after Oct. 1, 1977, and before July 1, 1978, providing for inclusion of any fringe benefit in gross income by reason of section 61 of the Internal Revenue Code of 1986 [formerly I.R.C. 1954], ceased to have effect on the day after Nov. 8, 1978, pursuant to section 210(a) of that Act.

NO GAIN RECOGNIZED FROM NET GIFTS MADE BEFORE MARCH 4, 1981

Pub. L. 98–369, div. A, title X, §1026, July 18, 1984, 98 Stat. 1031, as amended by Pub. L. 99–514, §2, Oct. 22, 1986, 100 Stat. 2095, provided that:

"(a) In General.—In the case of any transfer of property subject to gift tax made before March 4, 1981, for purposes of subtitle A of the Internal Revenue Code of 1986 [formerly I.R.C. 1954, 26 U.S.C. 1 et seq.], gross income of the donor shall not include any amount attributable to the donee's payment of (or agreement to pay) any gift tax imposed with respect to such gift.

"(b) Gift Tax Defined.——For purposes of subsection (a), the term 'gift tax' means—

"(1) the tax imposed by chapter 12 of such Code [26 U.S.C. 2501 et seq.], and

"(2) any tax imposed by a State (or the District of Columbia) on transfers by gifts.

"(c) Statute of Limitations.——If refund or credit of any overpayment of tax resulting from subsection (a) is prevented on the date of the enactment of this Act [July 18, 1984] (or at any time within 1 year after such date) by the operation of any law or rule of law (including res judicata), refund or credit of such overpayment (to the extent attributable to subsection (a)) may nevertheless be made or allowed if claim therefor is filed within 1 year after the date of the enactment of this Act."

PAYMENT-IN-KIND TAX TREATMENT ACT OF 1983

Pub. L. 98–4, Mar. 11, 1983, 97 Stat. 7, as amended by Pub. L. 98–369, div. A, title X, §1061(a), July 18, 1984, 98 Stat. 1046; Pub. L. 99–514, §2, Oct. 22, 1986, 100 Stat. 2095; Pub. L. 100–647, title VI, §6252(a)(1), Nov. 10, 1988, 102 Stat. 3752, provided that:

"SECTION 1. SHORT TITLE.

"This Act may be cited as the 'Payment-in-Kind Tax Treatment Act of 1983'.

"SEC. 2. INCOME TAX TREATMENT OF AGRICULTURAL COMMODITIES RECEIVED UNDER A 1983 PAYMENT-IN-KIND PROGRAM.

"(a) Income Tax Deferral, Etc.—Except as otherwise provided in this Act, for purposes of the Internal Revenue Code of 1986 [formerly I.R.C. 1954]—

"(1) a qualified taxpayer shall not be treated as having realized income when he receives a commodity under a 1983 payment-in-kind program,

"(2) such commodity shall be treated as if it were produced by such taxpayer, and

"(3) the unadjusted basis of such commodity in the hands of such taxpayer shall be zero.

"(b) Effective Date.—This section shall apply to taxable years ending after December 31, 1982, but only with respect to commodities received for the 1983 crop year.

"SEC. 3. LAND DIVERTED UNDER 1983 PAYMENT-IN-KIND PROGRAM TREATED AS USED IN FARMING BUSINESS, ETC.

"(a) General Rule.—For purposes of the provisions specified in subsection (b), in the case of any land diverted from the production of an agricultural commodity under a 1983 payment-in-kind program—

"(1) such land shall be treated as used during the 1983 crop year by the qualified taxpayer in the active conduct of the trade or business of farming, and

"(2) any qualified taxpayer who materially participates in the diversion and devotion to conservation uses required under a 1983 payment-in-kind program shall be treated as materially participating in the operation of such land during such crop year.

"(b) Provisions to Which Subsection (a) Applies.—The provisions specified in this subsection are—

"(1) section 2032A of the Internal Revenue Code of 1986 (relating to valuation of certain farm, etc., real property),

"(2) section 6166 of such Code (relating to extension of time for payment of estate tax where estate consists largely of interest in closely held business),

"(3) chapter 2 of such Code (relating to tax on self-employment income), and

"(4) title II of the Social Security Act [42 U.S.C. 401 et seq.] (relating to Federal old-age, survivors, and disability insurance benefits).

"SEC. 4. ANTIABUSE RULES.

"(a) General Rule.—In the case of any person, sections 2 and 3 of this Act shall not apply with respect to any land acquired by such person after February 23, 1983, unless such land was acquired in a qualified acquisition.

"(b) Qualified Acquisition.—For purposes of this section, the term 'qualified acquisition' means any acquisition—

"(1) by reason of the death of a qualified transferor,

"(2) by reason of a gift from a qualified transferor, or

"(3) from a qualified transferor who is a member of the family of the person acquiring the land.

"(c) Definitions and Special Rules.—For purposes of this section—

"(1) Qualified transferor.—The term 'qualified transferor' means any person—

"(A) who held the land on February 23, 1983, or

"(B) who acquired the land after February 23, 1983, in a qualified acquisition.

"(2) Member of family.—The term 'member of the family' has the meaning given such term by section 2032A(e)(2) of the Internal Revenue Code of 1986.

"(3) Mere change in form of business.—Subsection (a) shall not apply to any change in ownership by reason of a mere change in the form of conducting the trade or business so long as the land is retained in such trade or business and the person holding the land before such change retains a direct or indirect 80-percent interest in such land.

"(4) Treatment of certain acquisitions of right to the crop.—The acquisition of a direct or indirect interest in 80 percent or more of the crop from any land shall be treated as an acquisition of such land.

"SEC. 5. DEFINITIONS AND SPECIAL RULES.

"(a) General Rule.—For purposes of this Act—

"(1) 1983 payment-in-kind program.—The term '1983 payment-in-kind program' means any program for the 1983 crop year—

"(A) under which the Secretary of Agriculture (or his delegate) makes payments in kind of any agricultural commodity to any person in return for—

"(i) the diversion of farm acreage from the production of an agricultural commodity, and

"(ii) the devotion of such acreage to conservation uses, and

"(B) which the Secretary of Agriculture certifies to the Secretary of the Treasury as being described in subparagraph (A).

"(2) Crop year.—The term '1983 crop year' means the crop year for any crop the planting or harvesting period for which occurs during 1983. The term '1984 crop year' means the crop year for wheat the planting and harvesting period for which occurs during 1984.

"(3) Qualified taxpayer.—The term 'qualified taxpayer' means any producer of agricultural commodities (within the meaning of the 1983 payment-in-kind programs) who receives any agricultural commodity in return for meeting the requirements of clauses (i) and (ii) of paragraph (1)(A).

"(4) Receipt includes right to receive, etc.—A right to receive (or other constructive receipt of) a commodity shall be treated the same as actual receipt of such commodity.

"(5) Amounts received by the taxpayer as reimbursement for storage.—A qualified taxpayer reporting on the cash receipts and disbursements method of accounting shall not be treated as being entitled to receive any amount as reimbursement for storage of commodities received under a 1983 payment-in-kind program until such amount is actually received by the taxpayer.

"(6) Commodity credit loans treated separately.—Subsection (a) of section 2 shall apply to the receipt of any commodity under a 1983 payment-in-kind program separately from, and without taking into account, any related transaction or series of transactions involving the satisfaction of loans from the Commodity Credit Corporation.

"(b) Extension to Wheat Planted and Harvested in 1984.—In the case of wheat—

"(1) any reference in this Act to the 1983 crop year shall include a reference to the 1984 crop year, and

"(2) any reference to the 1983 payment-in-kind program shall include a reference to any program for the 1984 year for wheat which meets the requirements of subparagraphs (A) and (B) of subsection (a)(1).

"(c) Regulations.—The Secretary of the Treasury or his delegate (after consultation with the Secretary of Agriculture) shall prescribe such regulations as may be necessary to carry out the purposes of this Act, including (but not limited to) such regulations as may be necessary to carry out the purposes of this Act where the commodity is received by a cooperative on behalf of the qualified taxpayer."

[Pub. L. 98–369, div. A, title X, §1061(b), July 18, 1984, 98 Stat. 1047, provided that: "The amendments made by this section [amending Pub. L. 98–4 set out above] shall apply with respect to commodities received for the 1984 crop year (as defined in section 5(a)(2) of the Payment-in-Kind Tax Treatment Act of 1983 [Pub. L. 98–4, set out above] as amended by subsection (a)).")

CANCELLATION OF CERTAIN STUDENT LOANS

Pub. L. 94–455, title XXI, §2117, Oct. 4, 1976, 90 Stat. 1911, as amended by Pub. L. 95–600, title I, §162, Nov. 6, 1978, 92 Stat. 2810; Pub. L. 99–514, §2, Oct. 22, 1986, 100 Stat. 2095, provided that no amount be included in gross income of an individual for purposes of 26 U.S.C. 61 by reason of the discharge made before Jan. 1, 1983 of the indebtedness of the individual under a student loan if the discharge was pursuant to a provision of the loan under which the indebtedness of the individual would be discharged if the individual worked for a certain period of time in certain geographical areas or for certain classes of employers.

REGULATIONS RELATING TO TAX TREATMENT OF CERTAIN PREPUBLICATION EXPENDITURES OF PUBLISHERS

Pub. L. 94–455, title XXI, §2119, Oct. 4, 1976, 90 Stat. 1912, as amended by Pub. L. 99–514, §2, Oct. 22, 1986, 100 Stat. 2095, provided that:

"(a) General Rule.—With respect to taxable years beginning on or before the date on which regulations dealing with prepublication expenditures are issued after the date of the enactment of this Act [Oct. 4, 1976], the application of sections 61 (as it relates to cost of goods sold), 162, 174, 263, and 471 of the Internal Revenue Code of 1986 [formerly I.R.C. 1954] to any prepublication expenditure shall be administered—

"(1) without regard to Revenue Ruling 73–395, and

"(2) in the manner in which such sections were applied consistently by the taxpayer to such expenditures before the date of the issuance of such revenue ruling.

"(b) Regulations To Be Prospective Only.—Any regulations issued after the date of the enactment of this Act [Oct. 4, 1976] which deal with the application of sections 61 (as it relates to cost of goods sold), 162, 174, 263, and 471 of the Internal Revenue Code of 1986 to prepublication expenditures shall apply only with respect to taxable years beginning after the date on which such regulations are issued.

"(c) Prepublication Expenditures Defined.—For purposes of this section, the term 'prepublication expenditures' means expenditures paid or incurred by the taxpayer (in connection with his trade or business of publishing) for the writing, editing, compiling, illustrating, designing, or other development or improvement of a book, teaching aid, or similar product."

REIMBURSEMENT OF MOVING EXPENSES OF EMPLOYEES OF CERTAIN CORPORATIONS EXCLUDED FROM GROSS INCOME; CLAIM FOR REFUND OR CREDIT; LIMITATIONS; INTEREST

Pub. L. 86–780, §5, Sept. 14, 1960, 74 Stat. 1013, provided for the exclusion from gross income of any amount received after Dec. 31, 1949, and before Oct. 1, 1955, by employees of certain corporations as reimbursement for moving expenses, and the refund or credit of any overpayments.

§62. Adjusted gross income defined

(a) General rule

For purposes of this subtitle, the term "adjusted gross income" means, in the case of an individual, gross income minus the following deductions:

(1) Trade and business deductions

The deductions allowed by this chapter (other than by part VII of this subchapter) which are attributable to a trade or business carried on by the taxpayer, if such trade or business does not consist of the performance of services by the taxpayer as an employee.

(2) Certain trade and business deductions of employees

(A) Reimbursed expenses of employees

The deductions allowed by part VI (section 161 and following) which consist of expenses paid or incurred by the taxpayer, in connection with the performance by him of services as an employee, under a reimbursement or other expense allowance arrangement with his employer. The fact that the reimbursement may be provided by a third party shall not be determinative of whether or not the preceding sentence applies.

(B) Certain expenses of performing artists

The deductions allowed by section 162 which consist of expenses paid or incurred by a qualified performing artist in connection with the performances by him of services in the performing arts as an employee.

(C) Certain expenses of officials

The deductions allowed by section 162 which consist of expenses paid or incurred with respect to services performed by an official as an employee of a State or a political subdivision thereof in a position compensated in whole or in part on a fee basis.

(D) Certain expenses of elementary and secondary school teachers

The deductions allowed by section 162 which consist of expenses, not in excess of $250, paid or incurred by an eligible educator—

(i) by reason of the participation of the educator in professional development courses related to the curriculum in which the educator provides instruction or to the students for which the educator provides instruction, and

(ii) in connection with books, supplies (other than nonathletic supplies for courses of instruction in health or physical education), computer equipment (including related software and services) and other equipment, and supplementary materials used by the eligible educator in the classroom.

(E) Certain expenses of members of reserve components of the Armed Forces of the United States

The deductions allowed by section 162 which consist of expenses, determined at a rate not in excess of the rates for travel expenses (including per diem in lieu of subsistence) authorized for employees of agencies under subchapter I of chapter 57 of title 5, United States Code, paid or incurred by the taxpayer in connection with the performance of services by such taxpayer as a member of a reserve component of the Armed Forces of the United States for any period during which such individual is more than 100 miles away from home in connection with such services.

(3) Losses from sale or exchange of property

The deductions allowed by part VI (sec. 161 and following) as losses from the sale or exchange of property.

(4) Deductions attributable to rents and royalties

The deductions allowed by part VI (sec. 161 and following), by section 212 (relating to expenses for production of income), and by section 611 (relating to depletion) which are attributable to property held for the production of rents or royalties.

(5) Certain deductions of life tenants and income beneficiaries of property

In the case of a life tenant of property, or an income beneficiary of property held in trust, or an heir, legatee, or devisee of an estate, the deduction for depreciation allowed by section 167 and the deduction allowed by section 611.

(6) Pension, profit-sharing, and annuity plans of self-employed individuals

In the case of an individual who is an employee within the meaning of section 401(c)(1), the deduction allowed by section 404.

(7) Retirement savings

The deduction allowed by section 219 (relating to deduction of certain retirement savings).

[(8) Repealed. Pub. L. 104–188, title I, §1401(b)(4), Aug. 20, 1996, 110 Stat. 1788]

(9) Penalties forfeited because of premature withdrawal of funds from time savings accounts or deposits

The deductions allowed by section 165 for losses incurred in any transaction entered into for profit, though not connected with a trade or business, to the extent that such losses include amounts forfeited to a bank, mutual savings bank, savings and loan association, building and loan association, cooperative bank or homestead association as a penalty for premature withdrawal of funds from a time savings account, certificate of deposit, or similar class of deposit.

[(10) Repealed. Pub. L. 115–97, title I, §11051(b)(2)(A), Dec. 22, 2017, 131 Stat. 2089]

(11) Reforestation expenses

The deduction allowed by section 194.

(12) Certain required repayments of supplemental unemployment compensation benefits

The deduction allowed by section 165 for the repayment to a trust described in paragraph (9) or (17) of section 501(c) of supplemental unemployment compensation benefits received from such trust if such repayment is required because of the receipt of trade readjustment allowances under section 231 or 232 of the Trade Act of 1974 (19 U.S.C. 2291 and 2292).

(13) Jury duty pay remitted to employer

Any deduction allowable under this chapter by reason of an individual remitting any portion of any jury pay to such individual's employer in exchange for payment by the employer of compensation for the period such individual was performing jury duty. For purposes of the preceding sentence, the term "jury pay" means any payment received by the individual for the discharge of jury duty.

[(14) Repealed. Pub. L. 113–295, div. A, title II, §221(a)(34)(C), Dec. 19, 2014, 128 Stat. 4042]

(15) Moving expenses

The deduction allowed by section 217.

(16) Archer MSAs

The deduction allowed by section 220.

(17) Interest on education loans

The deduction allowed by section 221.

[(18) Repealed. Pub. L. 116–260, div. EE, title I, §104(b)(2)(A), Dec. 27, 2020, 134 Stat. 3041]

(19) Health savings accounts

The deduction allowed by section 223.

(20) Costs involving discrimination suits, etc.

Any deduction allowable under this chapter for attorney fees and court costs paid by, or on behalf of, the taxpayer in connection with any action involving a claim of unlawful discrimination (as defined in subsection (e)) or a claim of a violation of subchapter III of chapter 37 of title 31, United States Code, or a claim made under section 1862(b)(3)(A) of the Social Security Act (42 U.S.C. 1395y(b)(3)(A)). The preceding sentence shall not apply to any deduction in excess of the amount includible in the taxpayer's gross income for the taxable year on account of a judgment or settlement (whether by suit or agreement and whether as lump sum or periodic payments) resulting from such claim.

(21) Attorneys' fees relating to awards to whistleblowers

(A) In general

Any deduction allowable under this chapter for attorney fees and court costs paid by, or on behalf of, the taxpayer in connection with any award under—

(i) section 7623(b), or

(ii) in the case of taxable years beginning after December 31, 2017, any action brought under—

(I) section 21F of the Securities Exchange Act of 1934 (15 U.S.C. 78u–6),

(II) a State false claims act, including a State false claims act with qui tam provisions, or

(III) section 23 of the Commodity Exchange Act (7 U.S.C. 26).

(B) May not exceed award

Subparagraph (A) shall not apply to any deduction in excess of the amount includible in the taxpayer's gross income for the taxable year on account of such award.

Nothing in this section shall permit the same item to be deducted more than once. Any deduction allowed by section 199A shall not be treated as a deduction described in any of the preceding paragraphs of this subsection.

(b) Qualified performing artist

(1) In general

For purposes of subsection (a)(2)(B), the term "qualified performing artist" means, with respect to any taxable year, any individual if—

(A) such individual performed services in the performing arts as an employee during the taxable year for at least 2 employers,

(B) the aggregate amount allowable as a deduction under section 162 in connection with the performance of such services exceeds 10 percent of such individual's gross income attributable to the performance of such services, and

(C) the adjusted gross income of such individual for the taxable year (determined without regard to subsection (a)(2)(B)) does not exceed $16,000.

(2) Nominal employer not taken into account

An individual shall not be treated as performing services in the performing arts as an employee for any employer during any taxable year unless the amount received by such individual from such employer for the performance of such services during the taxable year equals or exceeds $200.

(3) Special rules for married couples

(A) In general

Except in the case of a husband and wife who lived apart at all times during the taxable year, if the taxpayer is married at the close of the taxable year, subsection (a)(2)(B) shall apply only if the taxpayer and his spouse file a joint return for the taxable year.

(B) Application of paragraph (1)

In the case of a joint return—

(i) paragraph (1) (other than subparagraph (C) thereof) shall be applied separately with respect to each spouse, but

(ii) paragraph (1)(C) shall be applied with respect to their combined adjusted gross income.

(C) Determination of marital status

For purposes of this subsection, marital status shall be determined under section 7703(a).

(D) Joint return

For purposes of this subsection, the term "joint return" means the joint return of a husband and wife made under section 6013.

(c) Certain arrangements not treated as reimbursement arrangements

For purposes of subsection (a)(2)(A), an arrangement shall in no event be treated as a reimbursement or other expense allowance arrangement if—

(1) such arrangement does not require the employee to substantiate the expenses covered by the arrangement to the person providing the reimbursement, or

(2) such arrangement provides the employee the right to retain any amount in excess of the substantiated expenses covered under the arrangement.

The substantiation requirements of the preceding sentence shall not apply to any expense to the extent that substantiation is not required under section 274(d) for such expense by reason of the regulations prescribed under the 2nd sentence thereof.

(d) Definition; special rules

(1) Eligible educator

(A) In general

For purposes of subsection (a)(2)(D), the term "eligible educator" means, with respect to any taxable year, an individual who is a kindergarten through grade 12 teacher, instructor, counselor, principal, or aide in a school for at least 900 hours during a school year.

(B) School

The term "school" means any school which provides elementary education or secondary education (kindergarten through grade 12), as determined under State law.

(2) Coordination with exclusions

A deduction shall be allowed under subsection (a)(2)(D) for expenses only to the extent the amount of such expenses exceeds the amount excludable under section 135, 529(c)(1), or 530(d)(2) for the taxable year.

(3) Inflation adjustment

In the case of any taxable year beginning after 2015, the $250 amount in subsection (a)(2)(D) shall be increased by an amount equal to—

(A) such dollar amount, multiplied by

(B) the cost-of-living adjustment determined under section 1(f)(3) for the calendar year in which the taxable year begins, determined by substituting "calendar year 2014" for "calendar year 2016" in subparagraph (A)(ii) thereof.

Any increase determined under the preceding sentence shall be rounded to the nearest multiple of $50.

(e) Unlawful discrimination defined

For purposes of subsection (a)(20), the term "unlawful discrimination" means an act that is unlawful under any of the following:

(1) Section 302 of the Civil Rights Act of 1991 (42 U.S.C. 2000e–16b).

(2) Section 201, 202, 203, 204, 205, 206, 207, or 208 of the Congressional Accountability Act of 1995 (2 U.S.C. 1311, 1312, 1313, 1314, 1315, 1316, or 1317).[1]

(3) The National Labor Relations Act (29 U.S.C. 151 et seq.).

(4) The Fair Labor Standards Act of 1938 (29 U.S.C. 201 et seq.).

(5) Section 4 or 15 of the Age Discrimination in Employment Act of 1967 (29 U.S.C. 623 or 633a).

(6) Section 501 or 504 of the Rehabilitation Act of 1973 (29 U.S.C. 791 or 794).

(7) Section 510 of the Employee Retirement Income Security Act of 1974 (29 U.S.C. 1140).

(8) Title IX of the Education Amendments of 1972 (20 U.S.C. 1681 et seq.).

(9) The Employee Polygraph Protection Act of 1988 (29 U.S.C. 2001 et seq.).

(10) The Worker Adjustment and Retraining Notification Act (29 U.S.C. 2102 et seq.).

(11) Section 105 of the Family and Medical Leave Act of 1993 (29 U.S.C. 2615).

(12) Chapter 43 of title 38, United States Code (relating to employment and reemployment rights of members of the uniformed services).

(13) Section 1977, 1979, or 1980 of the Revised Statutes (42 U.S.C. 1981, 1983, or 1985).

(14) Section 703, 704, or 717 of the Civil Rights Act of 1964 (42 U.S.C. 2000e–2, 2000e–3, or 2000e–16).

(15) Section 804, 805, 806, 808, or 818 of the Fair Housing Act (42 U.S.C. 3604, 3605, 3606, 3608, or 3617).

(16) Section 102, 202, 302, or 503 of the Americans with Disabilities Act of 1990 (42 U.S.C. 12112, 12132, 12182, or 12203).

(17) Any provision of Federal law (popularly known as whistleblower protection provisions) prohibiting the discharge of an employee, the discrimination against an employee, or any other form of retaliation or reprisal against an employee for asserting rights or taking other actions permitted under Federal law.

(18) Any provision of Federal, State, or local law, or common law claims permitted under Federal, State, or local law—

(i) providing for the enforcement of civil rights, or

(ii) regulating any aspect of the employment relationship, including claims for wages, compensation, or benefits, or prohibiting the discharge of an employee, the discrimination against an employee, or any other form of retaliation or reprisal against an employee for asserting rights or taking other actions permitted by law.

(Aug. 16, 1954, ch. 736, 68A Stat. 17; Pub. L. 87–792, §7(b), Oct. 10, 1962, 76 Stat. 828; Pub. L. 88–272, title II, §213(b), Feb. 26, 1964, 78 Stat. 52; Pub. L. 91–172, title V, §531(b), Dec. 30, 1969, 83 Stat. 655; Pub. L. 93–406, title II, §§2002(a)(2), 2005(c)(9), Sept. 2, 1974, 88 Stat. 959, 992; Pub. L. 93–483, §6(a), Oct. 26, 1974, 88 Stat. 1458; Pub. L. 94–455, title V, §502(a), title XV, §1501(b)(1), title XIX, §1901(a)(8), (9), Oct. 4, 1976, 90 Stat. 1559, 1735, 1765; Pub. L. 95–615, §203(b), Nov. 8, 1978, 92 Stat. 3106; Pub. L. 96–451, title III, §301(b), Oct. 14, 1980, 94 Stat. 1990; Pub. L. 96–608, §3(a), Dec. 28, 1980, 94 Stat. 3551; Pub. L. 97–34, title I, §§103(b), 112(b)(2), title III, §311(h)(1), Aug. 13, 1981, 95 Stat. 187, 195, 282; Pub. L. 97–354, §5(a)(17), Oct. 19, 1982, 96 Stat. 1693; Pub. L. 98–369, div. A, title IV, §491(d)(2), July 18, 1984, 98 Stat. 849; Pub. L. 99–514, title I, §§131(b)(1), 132(b), (c), title III, §301(b)(1), title XVIII, §1875(c)(3), Oct. 22, 1986, 100 Stat. 2113, 2115, 2116, 2217, 2894; Pub. L. 100–485, title VII, §702(a), Oct. 13, 1988, 102 Stat. 2426; Pub. L. 100–647, title I, §1001(b)(3)(A), title VI, §6007(b), Nov. 10, 1988, 102 Stat. 3349, 3687; Pub. L. 101–508, title XI, §11802(e)(1), Nov. 5, 1990, 104 Stat. 1388–530; Pub. L. 102–318, title V, §521(b)(2), July 3, 1992, 106 Stat. 310; Pub. L. 102–486, title XIX, §1913(a)(2), Oct. 24, 1992, 106 Stat. 3019; Pub. L. 103–66, title XIII, §13213(c)(1), Aug. 10, 1993, 107 Stat. 474; Pub. L. 104–188, title I, §1401(b)(4), Aug. 20, 1996, 110 Stat. 1788; Pub. L. 104–191, title III, §301(b), Aug. 21, 1996, 110 Stat. 2048; Pub. L. 105–34, title II, §202(b), title IX, §975(a), Aug. 5, 1997, 111 Stat. 808, 898; Pub. L. 106–554, §1(a)(7) [title II, §202(b)(1)], Dec. 21, 2000, 114 Stat. 2763, 2763A-629; Pub. L. 107–16, title IV, §431(b), June 7, 2001, 115 Stat. 68; Pub. L. 107–147, title IV, §406(a), (b), Mar. 9, 2002, 116 Stat. 43; Pub. L. 108–121, title I, §109(b), Nov. 11, 2003, 117 Stat. 1341; Pub. L. 108–173, title XII, §1201(b), Dec. 8, 2003, 117 Stat. 2476; Pub. L. 108–311, title III, §307(a), Oct. 4, 2004, 118 Stat. 1179; Pub. L. 108–357, title VII, §703(a), (b), Oct. 22, 2004, 118 Stat. 1546, 1547; Pub. L. 109–135, title IV, §412(q), Dec. 21, 2005, 119 Stat. 2638; Pub. L. 109–432, div. A, title I, §108(a), title IV, §406(a)(3), Dec. 20, 2006, 120 Stat. 2939, 2959; Pub. L. 110–343, div. C, title II, §203(a), Oct. 3, 2008, 122 Stat. 3864; Pub. L. 111–312, title VII, §721(a), Dec. 17, 2010, 124 Stat. 3316; Pub. L. 112–240, title II, §201(a), Jan. 2, 2013, 126 Stat. 2323; Pub. L. 113–295, div. A, title I, §101(a), title II, §221(a)(34)(C), Dec. 19, 2014, 128 Stat. 4012, 4042; Pub. L. 114–113, div. Q, title I, §104(a)–(c), Dec. 18, 2015, 129 Stat. 3045; Pub. L. 115–97, title I, §§11002(d)(1)(J), 11011(b)(1), 11051(b)(2)(A), Dec. 22, 2017, 131 Stat. 2060, 2070, 2089; Pub. L. 115–123, div. D, title II, §41107(a), Feb. 9, 2018, 132 Stat. 158; Pub. L. 115–141, div. T, §101(a)(2)(B), div. U, title IV, §401(a)(31), (32), Mar. 23, 2018, 132 Stat. 1155, 1185, 1186; Pub. L. 116–92, div. A, title XI, §1122(d)(2)(B), Dec. 20, 2019, 133 Stat. 1609; Pub. L. 116–136, div. A, title II, §2204(a), (b), Mar. 27, 2020, 134 Stat. 345; Pub. L. 116–260, div. EE, title I, §104(b)(2)(A), title II, §212(c), Dec. 27, 2020, 134 Stat. 3041, 3068.)

INFLATION ADJUSTED ITEMS FOR CERTAIN YEARS

For inflation adjustment of certain items in this section, see Revenue Procedures listed in a table under section 1 of this title.

EDITORIAL NOTES
REFERENCES IN TEXT

Section 208 of the Congressional Accountability Act of 1995, referred to in subsec. (e)(2), was formerly section 207 of the Act prior to renumbering by Pub. L. 116–92, and is classified to section 1317 of Title 2, The Congress. A new section 207 of the Act was enacted by Pub. L. 116–92 and is classified to section 1316b of Title 2. Pub. L. 116–92 amended list of Act sections in subsec. (e)(2) of this section without corresponding amendment of Code citations, see 2019 Amendment note below.

The National Labor Relations Act, referred to in subsec. (e)(3), is act July 5, 1935, ch. 372, 49 Stat. 449, as amended, which is classified generally to subchapter II (§151 et seq.) of chapter 7 of Title 29, Labor. For complete classification of this Act to the Code, see section 167 of Title 29 and Tables.

The Fair Labor Standards Act of 1938, referred to in subsec. (e)(4), is act June 25, 1938, ch. 676, 52 Stat. 1060, as amended, which is classified generally to chapter 8 (§201 et seq.) of Title 29, Labor. For complete classification of this Act to the Code, see section 201 of Title 29 and Tables.

The Education Amendments of 1972, referred to in subsec. (e)(8), is Pub. L. 92–318, June 23, 1972, 86 Stat. 235, as amended. Title IX of the Act, known as the Patsy Takemoto Mink Equal Opportunity in Education Act, is classified principally to chapter 38 (§1681 et seq.) of Title 20, Education. For complete classification of title IX to the Code, see Short Title note set out under section 1681 of Title 20 and Tables.

The Employee Polygraph Protection Act of 1988, referred to in subsec. (e)(9), is Pub. L. 100–347, June 27, 1988, 102 Stat. 646, as amended, which is classified generally to chapter 22 (§2001 et seq.) of Title 29, Labor. For complete classification of this Act to the Code, see Short Title note set out under section 2001 of Title 29 and Tables.

The Worker Adjustment and Retraining Notification Act, referred to in subsec. (e)(10), is Pub. L. 100–379, Aug. 4, 1988, 102 Stat. 890, as amended, which is classified generally to chapter 23 (§2101 et seq.) of Title 29, Labor. For complete classification of this Act to the Code, see Short Title note set out under section 2101 of Title 29 and Tables.

AMENDMENTS

2020—Subsec. (a)(18). Pub. L. 116–260, §104(b)(2)(A), struck out par. (18). Text read as follows: "The deduction allowed by section 222."

Subsec. (a)(22). Pub. L. 116–260, §212(c)(1), struck out par. (22). Text read as follows: "In the case of taxable years beginning in 2020, the amount (not to exceed $300) of qualified charitable contributions made by an eligible individual during the taxable year."

Pub. L. 116–136, §2204(a), added par. (22).

Subsec. (f). Pub. L. 116–260, §212(c)(2), struck out subsec. (f) which defined terms relating to qualified charitable contributions.

Pub. L. 116–136, §2204(b), added subsec. (f).

2019—Subsec. (e)(2). Pub. L. 116–92 substituted "207, or 208" for "or 207".

2018—Subsec. (a). Pub. L. 115–141, §101(a)(2)(B), substituted "Any deduction" for "The deduction" in concluding provisions.

Subsec. (a)(20). Pub. L. 115–141, §401(a)(31), inserted comma after "United States Code".

Subsec. (a)(21). Pub. L. 115–123 amended par. (21) generally. Prior to amendment, text read as follows: "Any deduction allowable under this chapter for attorney fees and court costs paid by, or on behalf of, the taxpayer in connection with any award under section 7623(b) (relating to awards to whistleblowers). The preceding sentence shall not apply to any deduction in excess of the amount includible in the taxpayer's gross income for the taxable year on account of such award."

Subsec. (e)(1). Pub. L. 115–141, §401(a)(32), substituted "(42 U.S.C. 2000e–16b)" for "(2 U.S.C. 1202)".

2017—Subsec. (a). Pub. L. 115–97, §11011(b)(1), inserted at end of concluding provisions "The deduction allowed by section 199A shall not be treated as a deduction described in any of the preceding paragraphs of this subsection."

Subsec. (a)(10). Pub. L. 115–97, §11051(b)(2)(A), struck out par. (10). Text read as follows: "The deduction allowed by section 215."

Subsec. (d)(3)(B). Pub. L. 115–97, §11002(d)(1)(J), substituted "for 'calendar year 2016' in subparagraph (A)(ii)" for "for 'calendar year 1992' in subparagraph (B)".

2015—Subsec. (a)(2)(D). Pub. L. 114–113, §104(c), substituted "educator—" for "educator in connection with books, supplies (other than nonathletic supplies for courses of instruction in health or physical education), computer equipment (including related software and services) and other equipment, and supplementary materials used by the eligible educator in the classroom." and added cls. (i) and (ii).

Pub. L. 114–113, §104(a), substituted "The deductions" for "In the case of taxable years beginning during 2002, 2003, 2004, 2005, 2006, 2007, 2008, 2009, 2010, 2011, 2012, 2013, or 2014, the deductions".

Subsec. (d)(3). Pub. L. 114–113, §104(b), added par. (3).

2014—Subsec. (a)(2)(D). Pub. L. 113–295, §101(a), substituted "2013, or 2014" for "or 2013".

Subsec. (a)(14). Pub. L. 113–295, §221(a)(34)(C), struck out par. (14). Text read as follows: "The deduction allowed by section 179A."

2013—Subsec. (a)(2)(D). Pub. L. 112–240 substituted "2011, 2012, or 2013" for "or 2011".

2010—Subsec. (a)(2)(D). Pub. L. 111–312 substituted "2009, 2010, or 2011" for "or 2009".

2008—Subsec. (a)(2)(D). Pub. L. 110–343 substituted "2007, 2008, or 2009" for "or 2007".

2006—Subsec. (a)(2)(D). Pub. L. 109–432, §108(a), substituted "2005, 2006, or 2007" for "or 2005".

Subsec. (a)(21). Pub. L. 109–432, §406(a)(3), added par. (21).

2005—Subsec. (a)(19), (20). Pub. L. 109–135, §412(q)(1), redesignated par. (19) relating to costs involving discrimination suits, etc., as par. (20) and moved to follow par. (19) relating to health savings accounts.

Subsec. (e). Pub. L. 109–135, §412(q)(2), substituted "subsection (a)(20)" for "subsection (a)(19)" in introductory provisions.

2004—Subsec. (a)(2)(D). Pub. L. 108–311 substituted ", 2003, 2004, or 2005" for "or 2003".

Subsec. (a)(19). Pub. L. 108–357, §703(a), added par. (19) relating to costs involving discrimination suits, etc.

Subsec. (e). Pub. L. 108–357, §703(b), added subsec. (e).

2003—Subsec. (a)(2)(E). Pub. L. 108–121 added subpar. (E).

Subsec. (a)(19). Pub. L. 108–173 added par. (19).

2002—Subsec. (a)(2)(D). Pub. L. 107–147, §406(a), added subpar. (D).

Subsec. (d). Pub. L. 107–147, §406(b), added subsec. (d).

2001—Subsec. (a)(18). Pub. L. 107–16 added par. (18).

2000—Subsec. (a)(16). Pub. L. 106–554 amended heading and text of par. (16) generally. Prior to amendment, text read as follows: "The deduction allowed by section 220."

1997—Subsec. (a)(2)(C). Pub. L. 105–34, §975(a), added subpar. (C).

Subsec. (a)(17). Pub. L. 105–34, §202(b), added par. (17).

1996—Subsec. (a)(8). Pub. L. 104–188 struck out par. (8) which read as follows: "Certain portion of lump-sum distributions from pension plans taxed under section 402(d).—The deduction allowed by section 402(d)(3)."

Subsec. (a)(16). Pub. L. 104–191 added par. (16).

1993—Subsec. (a)(15). Pub. L. 103–66 added par. (15).

1992—Subsec. (a)(8). Pub. L. 102–318 substituted "402(d)" for "402(e)" in heading and in text.

Subsec. (a)(14). Pub. L. 102–486 added par. (14).

1990—Subsec. (a)(13). Pub. L. 101–508, §11802(e)(1), amended par. (13) generally. Prior to amendment, par. (13) read as follows: "The deduction allowed by section 220."

1988—Subsec. (a)(2)(A). Pub. L. 100–647, §1001(b)(3)(A), inserted at end "The fact that the reimbursement may be provided by a third party shall not be determinative of whether or not the preceding sentence applies."

Subsec. (a)(13). Pub. L. 100–647, §6007(b), added par. (13).

Subsec. (c). Pub. L. 100–485 added subsec. (c).

1986—Subsec. (a). Pub. L. 99–514, §132(b)(2)(A), designated existing provisions as subsec. (a) and added heading.

Subsec. (a)(2). Pub. L. 99–514, §132(b)(1), amended par. (2) generally, substituting "Certain trade" for "Trade" in heading and inserting "of employees" in subpar. (A) heading, substituting provision relating to deduction of certain expenses of performing artists for provision relating to deduction of expenses for travel away from home in subpar. (B), and striking out subpar. (C) relating to deduction of travel expenses and subpar. (D) relating to deduction of expenses of outside salesmen.

Subsec. (a)(3) to (5). Pub. L. 99–514, §301(b)(1), redesignated pars. (4) to (6) as (3) to (5), respectively, and struck out former par. (3) which related to long-term capital gains and read as follows: "The deduction allowed by section 1202."

Subsec. (a)(6). Pub. L. 99–514, §301(b)(1), redesignated par. (7) as (6). Former par. (6) redesignated (5).

Pub. L. 99–514, §1875(c)(3), struck out "to the extent attributable to contributions made on behalf of such individual" after "section 404".

Subsec. (a)(7). Pub. L. 99–514, §301(b)(1), redesignated par. (10) as (7). Former par. (7) redesignated (6).

Subsec. (a)(8). Pub. L. 99–514, §301(b)(1), redesignated par. (11) as (8). Former par. (8) struck out.

Pub. L. 99–514, §132(c), struck out par. (8) which related to moving expense deduction and read as follows: "The deduction allowed by section 217."

Subsec. (a)(9) to (15). Pub. L. 99–514, §301(b)(1), redesignated pars. (12) to (15) as (9) to (12), respectively. Former pars. (10) and (11) redesignated (7) and (8), respectively.

Subsec. (a)(16). Pub. L. 99–514, §131(b)(1), struck out par. (16) which related to deduction for two-earner married couples and read as follows: "The deduction allowed by section 221."

Subsec. (b). Pub. L. 99–514, §132(b)(2)(B), added subsec. (b).

1984—Par. (7). Pub. L. 98–369, §491(d)(2), substituted "and annuity" for "annuity, and bond purchase" in heading, and substituted "the deduction allowed by section 404" for "the deductions allowed by section 404 and section 405(c)" in text.

1983—Par. (9). Pub. L. 97–354 repealed par. (9) relating to the deduction allowed by section 1379(b)(3).

1981—Par. (10). Pub. L. 97–34, §311(h)(1), struck out "and the deduction allowed by section 220 (relating to retirement savings for certain married individuals)" after "retirement savings".

Par. (14). Pub. L. 97–34, §112(b)(2), redesignated par. (15) as (14). Former par. (14), relating to deduction for certain expenses of living abroad, was struck out.

Par. (15). Pub. L. 97–34, §112(b)(2), redesignated par. (16) as (15). Former par. (15) redesignated (14).

Par. (16). Pub. L. 97–34, §§103(b), 112(b)(2), added par. (16). Former par. (16) redesignated (15).

1980—Par. (15). Pub. L. 96–451 added par. (15).

Par. (16). Pub. L. 96–608 added par. (16).

1978—Par. (14). Pub. L. 95–615 added par. (14).

1976—Par. (10). Pub. L. 94–455, §1501(b)(1), inserted reference to the deduction allowed by section 220 (relating to retirement savings for certain married individuals).

Pars. (11), (12). Pub. L. 94–455, §1901(a)(8), (9), redesignated par. (11) relating to penalties forfeited because of premature withdrawal of funds from time savings accounts or deposits, as par. (12), and substituted "trade or business, to the extent" for "trade or business to the extent".

Par. (13). Pub. L. 94–455, §502(a), added par. (13).

1974—Par. (10). Pub. L. 93–406, §2002(a)(2), added par. (10).

Par. (11). Pub. L. 93–483 added par. (11) relating to penalties forfeited because of premature withdrawal of funds from time savings accounts or deposits. Another par. (11) relating to certain portions of lump-sum distributions from pension plans taxed under section 402(e) of this title, was added by Pub. L. 93–406, §2005(c)(9).

1969—Par. (9). Pub. L. 91–172 added par. (9).

1964—Par. (8). Pub. L. 88–272 added par. (8).

1962—Par. (7). Pub. L. 87–792 added par. (7).

Amendment by section 104(b)(2)(A) of Pub. L. 116–260 applicable to taxable years beginning after Dec. 31, 2020, see section 104(c) of div. EE of Pub. L. 116–260, set out as a note under section 25A of this title.

Pub. L. 116–260, div. EE, title II, §212(d), Dec. 27, 2020, 134 Stat. 3068, provided that: "The amendments made by this section [amending this section and sections 63, 170, 6662, and 6751 of this title] shall apply to taxable years beginning after December 31, 2020."

Pub. L. 116–136, div. A, title II, §2204(c), Mar. 27, 2020, 134 Stat. 345, provided that: "The amendments made by this section [amending this section] shall apply to taxable years beginning after December 31, 2019."

Effective Date of 2018 Amendment

Pub. L. 115–141, div. T, §101(d), Mar. 23, 2018, 132 Stat. 1157, provided that:

"(1) In general.—Except as otherwise provided in this subsection, the amendments made by this section [amending this section, sections 63, 172, 199A, 613, and 6662 of this title, and provisions set out as a note under section 74 of this title] shall take effect as if included in section 11011 of Public Law 115–97.

"(2) Application of section 199 to certain qualified payments paid after 2017.—The amendment made by subsection (c) [amending provisions set out as a note under section 74 of this title] shall take effect as if included in section 13305 of Public Law 115–97."

Pub. L. 115–123, div. D, title II, §41107(b), Feb. 9, 2018, 132 Stat. 158, provided that: "The amendment made by this section [amending this section] shall apply to taxable years beginning after December 31, 2017."

Effective Date of 2017 Amendment

Amendment by section 11002(d)(1)(J) of Pub. L. 115–97 applicable to taxable years beginning after Dec. 31, 2017, see section 11002(e) of Pub. L. 115–97, set out as a note under section 1 of this title.

Pub. L. 115–97, title I, §11011(e), Dec. 22, 2017, 131 Stat. 2071, provided that: "The amendments made by this section [enacting section 199A of this title and amending this section and sections 63, 170, 172, 246, 613, 613A, 3402, and 6662 of this title] shall apply to taxable years beginning after December 31, 2017."

Amendment by section 11051(b)(2)(A) of Pub. L. 115–97 applicable to any divorce or separation instrument (as defined in former section 71(b)(2) of this title as in effect before Dec. 22, 2017) executed after Dec. 31, 2018, and to such instruments executed on or before Dec. 31, 2018, and modified after Dec. 31, 2018, if the modification expressly provides that the amendment made by section 11051 of Pub. L. 115–97 applies to such modification, see section 11051(c) of Pub. L. 115–97, set out as a note under section 61 of this title.

Effective Date of 2015 Amendment

Pub. L. 114–113, div. Q, title I, §104(d), Dec. 18, 2015, 129 Stat. 3046, provided that:

"(1) Extension.—The amendment made by subsection (a) [amending this section] shall apply to taxable years beginning after December 31, 2014.

"(2) Modifications.—The amendments made by subsections (b) and (c) [amending this section] shall apply to taxable years beginning after December 31, 2015."

Effective Date of 2014 Amendment

Pub. L. 113–295, div. A, title I, §101(b), Dec. 19, 2014, 128 Stat. 4013, provided that: "The amendment made by this section [amending this section] shall apply to taxable years beginning after December 31, 2013."

Amendment by section 221(a)(34)(C) of Pub. L. 113–295 effective Dec. 19, 2014, subject to a savings provision, see section 221(b) of Pub. L. 113–295, set out as a note under section 1 of this title.

Effective Date of 2013 Amendment

Pub. L. 112–240, title II, §201(b), Jan. 2, 2013, 126 Stat. 2323, provided that: "The amendment made by this section [amending this section] shall apply to taxable years beginning after December 31, 2011."

Effective Date of 2010 Amendment

Pub. L. 111–312, title VII, §721(b), Dec. 17, 2010, 124 Stat. 3316, provided that: "The amendment made by this section [amending this section] shall apply to taxable years beginning after December 31, 2009."

Effective Date of 2008 Amendment

Pub. L. 110–343, div. C, title II, §203(b), Oct. 3, 2008, 122 Stat. 3864, provided that: "The amendment made by subsection (a) [amending this section] shall apply to taxable years beginning after December 31, 2007."

Effective Date of 2006 Amendment

Pub. L. 109–432, div. A, title I, §108(b), Dec. 20, 2006, 120 Stat. 2939, provided that: "The amendment made by this section [amending this section] shall apply to taxable years beginning after December 31, 2005."

Pub. L. 109–432, div. A, title IV, §406(d), Dec. 20, 2006, 120 Stat. 2960, provided that: "The amendments made by subsection (a) [amending this section and sections 7443A and 7623 of this title] shall apply to information provided on or after the date of the enactment of this Act [Dec. 20, 2006]."

Effective Date of 2004 Amendment

Pub. L. 108–357, title VII, §703(c), Oct. 22, 2004, 118 Stat. 1548, provided that: "The amendments made by this section [amending this section] shall apply to fees and costs paid after the date of the enactment of this Act [Oct. 22, 2004] with respect to any judgment or settlement occurring after such date."

Pub. L. 108–311, title III, §307(b), Oct. 4, 2004, 118 Stat. 1179, provided that: "The amendment made by subsection (a) [amending this section] shall apply to expenses paid or incurred in taxable years beginning after December 31, 2003."

EFFECTIVE DATE OF 2003 AMENDMENT

Pub. L. 108–173, title XII, §1201(k), Dec. 8, 2003, 117 Stat. 2479, provided that: "The amendments made by this section [enacting sections 223 and 4980G of this title, amending this section and sections 106, 125, 220, 848, 3231, 3306, 3401, 4973, 4975, 6051, and 6693 of this title, and renumbering former section 223 of this title as 224] shall apply to taxable years beginning after December 31, 2003."

Pub. L. 108–121, title I, §109(c), Nov. 11, 2003, 117 Stat. 1342, provided that: "The amendments made by this section [amending this section and section 162 of this title] shall apply to amounts paid or incurred in taxable years beginning after December 31, 2002."

EFFECTIVE DATE OF 2002 AMENDMENT

Pub. L. 107–147, title IV, §406(c), Mar. 9, 2002, 116 Stat. 44, provided that: "The amendment made by this section [amending this section] shall apply to taxable years beginning after December 31, 2001."

EFFECTIVE DATE OF 2001 AMENDMENT

Pub. L. 107–16, title IV, §431(d), June 7, 2001, 115 Stat. 69, provided that: "The amendments made by this section [enacting section 222 of this title, amending this section and sections 86, 135, 137, 219, 221, and 469 of this title, and renumbering former section 222 of this title as 223] shall apply to payments made in taxable years beginning after December 31, 2001."

EFFECTIVE DATE OF 1997 AMENDMENT

Pub. L. 105–34, title II, §202(e), Aug. 5, 1997, 111 Stat. 809, provided that: "The amendments made by this section [enacting section 221 of this title, amending this section and section 6050S of this title, and renumbering former section 221 of this title as section 222 of this title] shall apply to any qualified education loan (as defined in section 221(e)(1) of the Internal Revenue Code of 1986, as added by this section) incurred on, before, or after the date of the enactment of this Act [Aug. 5, 1997], but only with respect to—

"(1) any loan interest payment due and paid after December 31, 1997, and

"(2) the portion of the 60-month period referred to in section 221(d) of the Internal Revenue Code of 1986 (as added by this section) after December 31, 1997."

Pub. L. 105–34, title IX, §975(b), Aug. 5, 1997, 111 Stat. 898, provided that: "The amendment made by this section [amending this section] shall apply to expenses paid or incurred in taxable years beginning after December 31, 1986."

EFFECTIVE DATE OF 1996 AMENDMENT

Pub. L. 104–191, title III, §301(j), Aug. 21, 1996, 110 Stat. 2052, provided that: "The amendments made by this section [enacting sections 220 and 4980E of this title, amending this section and sections 106, 125, 848, 3231, 3306, 3401, 4973, 4975, 6051, and 6693 of this title, and renumbering section 220 of this title as section 221] shall apply to taxable years beginning after December 31, 1996."

Amendment by Pub. L. 104–188 applicable to taxable years beginning after Dec. 31, 1999, with retention of certain transition rules, see section 1401(c) of Pub. L. 104–188, set out as a note under section 402 of this title.

EFFECTIVE DATE OF 1993 AMENDMENT

Pub. L. 103–66, title XIII, §13213(e), Aug. 10, 1993, 107 Stat. 475, provided that: "The amendments made by this section [amending this section and sections 67, 82, 132, 217, 1001, 1016, and 4977 of this title] shall apply to expenses incurred after December 31, 1993; except that the amendments made by subsection (d) [amending sections 82, 132, and 4977 of this title] shall apply to reimbursements or other payments in respect of expenses incurred after such date."

EFFECTIVE DATE OF 1992 AMENDMENT

Amendment by Pub. L. 102–486 applicable to property placed in service after June 30, 1993, see section 1913(c) of Pub. L. 102–486, set out as a note under section 53 of this title.

Amendment by Pub. L. 102–318 applicable to distributions after Dec. 31, 1992, see section 521(e) of Pub. L. 102–318, set out as a note under section 402 of this title.

EFFECTIVE DATE OF 1988 AMENDMENT

Amendment by section 1001(b)(3)(A) of Pub. L. 100–647 effective, except as otherwise provided, as if included in the provision of the Tax Reform Act of 1986, Pub. L. 99–514, to which such amendment relates, see section 1019(a) of Pub. L. 100–647, set out as a note under section 1 of this title.

Pub. L. 100–647, title VI, §6007(d), Nov. 10, 1988, 102 Stat. 3687, provided that: "The amendments made by this section [enacting section 220 of this title, amending this section, and renumbering former section 220 of this title as section 221 of this title] shall apply as if included in the amendments made by section 132 of the Tax Reform Act of 1986 [Pub. L. 99–514]."

Pub. L. 100–485, title VII, §702(b), Oct. 13, 1988, 102 Stat. 2426, provided that: "The amendment made by subsection (a) [amending this section] shall apply to taxable years beginning after December 31, 1988."

EFFECTIVE DATE OF 1986 AMENDMENT

Amendment by sections 131(b)(1) and 132(b), (c) of Pub. L. 99–514 applicable to taxable years beginning after Dec. 31, 1986, see section 151(a) of Pub. L. 99–514, set out as a note under section 1 of this title.

Pub. L. 99–514, title III, §301(c), Oct. 22, 1986, 100 Stat. 2218, provided that: "The amendments made by this section [amending this section and sections 170, 172, 219, 220, 223, 642, 643, 691, 871, 1211, 1212, and 1402 of this title and repealing section 1202 of this title] shall apply to taxable years beginning after December 31, 1986."

Pub. L. 99–514, title XVIII, §1875(c)(12), Oct. 22, 1986, 100 Stat. 2895, provided that: "The amendments made by paragraphs (3), (4), and (6) [amending this section and sections 219 and 408 of this title] shall take effect as if included in the amendments made by section 238 of the Tax Equity and Fiscal Responsibility Act of 1982 [section 238 of Pub. L. 97–248, see section 241 of Pub. L. 97–248, set out as an Effective Date note under section 416 of this title]."

EFFECTIVE DATE OF 1984 AMENDMENT

Pub. L. 98–369, div. A, title IV, §491(f)(1), July 18, 1984, 98 Stat. 853, provided that: "The amendments and repeals made by subsections (a), (b), and (d) [amending this section, sections 55, 72, 172, 219, 402, 403, 406, 407, 408, 412, 414, 415, 457, 2039, 2517, 3121, 3306, 3401, 4972, 4973, 4975, 6047, 6058, 6104, 6652, 7207, 7476, and 7701 of this title, section 3107 of Title 31, Money and Finance, and section 409 of Title 42, The Public Health and Welfare, and repealing sections 405 and 409 of this title] shall apply to obligations issued after December 31, 1983."

EFFECTIVE DATE OF 1983 AMENDMENT

Par. (9) as in effect before date of repeal by Pub. L. 97–354 to remain in effect for years beginning before Jan. 1, 1984, see section 6(b)(1) of Pub. L. 97–354, set out as an Effective Date note under section 3761 of this title.

EFFECTIVE DATE OF 1981 AMENDMENT

Pub. L. 97–34, title I, §103(d), Aug. 13, 1981, 95 Stat. 188, provided that: "The amendments made by this section [enacting section 219 of this title and amending this section and sections 85 and 105 of this title] shall apply to taxable years beginning after December 31, 1981."

Amendment by sections 112(b)(2) and 311(h)(1) of Pub. L. 97–34 applicable to taxable years beginning after Dec. 31, 1981, see sections 115 and 311(i)(1) of Pub. L. 97–34, set out as notes under sections 911 and 219, respectively, of this title.

EFFECTIVE DATE OF 1980 AMENDMENT

Pub. L. 96–608, §3(b), Dec. 28, 1980, 94 Stat. 3551, provided that: "The amendment made by subsection (a) [amending this section] shall apply to repayments made in taxable years beginning after the date of the enactment of this Act [Dec. 28, 1980]."

Amendment by Pub. L. 96–451 applicable with respect to additions to capital account made after Dec. 31, 1979, see section 301(d) of Pub. L. 96–451, set out as an Effective Date note under section 194 of this title.

Effective Date of 1978 Amendment; Election of Prior Law

Amendment by Pub. L. 95–615 applicable to taxable years beginning after Dec. 31, 1977, with provision for election of prior law, see section 209 of Pub. L. 95–615, set out as a note under section 911 of this title.

Effective Date of 1976 Amendment

Pub. L. 94–455, title V, §502(c), Oct. 4, 1976, 90 Stat. 1559, provided that: "The amendments made by this section [amending this section and section 3402 of this title] shall apply to taxable years beginning after December 31, 1976."

Pub. L. 94–455, title XV, §1501(d), Oct. 4, 1976, 90 Stat. 1737, provided that: "The amendments made by this section [enacting section 220 of this title, amending this section and sections 219, 408, 409, 3401, 4973, and 6047 of this title, and renumbering former section 220 as 221 of this title], other than the amendment made by subsection (b)(3), shall apply to taxable years beginning after December 31, 1976. The amendment made by subsection (b)(3) [amending section 415 of this title] shall apply to years beginning after December 31, 1976."

Amendment by section 1901(a)(8), (9) of Pub. L. 94–455 applicable with respect to taxable years beginning after Dec. 31, 1976, see section 1901(d) of Pub. L. 94–455, set out as a note under section 2 of this title.

Effective Date of 1974 Amendment

Pub. L. 93–483, §6(b), Oct. 26, 1974, 88 Stat. 1459, provided that: "The amendment made by this section [amending this section] applies to taxable years beginning after December 31, 1972."

Amendment by section 2002(a)(2) of Pub. L. 93–406 applicable to taxable years beginning after Dec. 31, 1974, see section 2002(i)(1) of Pub. L. 93–406, set out as an Effective Date note under section 219 of this title.

Amendment by section 2005(c)(9) of Pub. L. 93–406 applicable only with respect to distributions or payments made after Dec. 31, 1973, in taxable years beginning after Dec. 31, 1973, see section 2005(d) of Pub. L. 93–406, set out as a note under section 402 of this title.

Effective Date of 1969 Amendment

Amendment by Pub. L. 91–172 applicable with respect to taxable years of electing small business corporations beginning after Dec. 31, 1970, see section 531(d) of Pub. L. 91–172, set out as an Effective Date note under section 1379 of this title.

Effective Date of 1964 Amendment

Pub. L. 88–272, title II, §213(d), Feb. 26, 1964, 78 Stat. 52, provided that: "The amendments made by subsections (a) [enacting section 217 and redesignating former section 217 as 218] and (b) [amending this section] shall apply to expenses incurred after December 31, 1963, in taxable years ending after such date. The amendment made by subsection (c) [amending section 3401 of this title] shall apply with respect to remuneration paid after the seventh day following the date of the enactment of this Act [Feb. 26, 1964]."

Effective Date of 1962 Amendment

Amendment by Pub. L. 87–792 applicable to taxable years beginning after Dec. 31, 1962, see section 8 of Pub. L. 87–792, set out as a note under section 22 of this title.

Regulations or Guidance Clarifying Application of Educator Expense Tax Deduction

Pub. L. 116–260, div. N, title II, §275, Dec. 27, 2020, 134 Stat. 1978, provided that: "Not later than February 28, 2021, the Secretary of the Treasury (or the Secretary's delegate) shall by regulation or other guidance clarify that personal protective equipment, disinfectant, and other supplies used for the prevention of the spread of COVID–19 are treated as described in section 62(a)(2)(D)(ii) of the Internal Revenue Code of 1986. Such regulations or other guidance shall apply to expenses paid or incurred after March 12, 2020."

Savings Provision

For provisions that nothing in amendment by Pub. L. 101–508 be construed to affect treatment of certain transactions occurring, property acquired, or items of income, loss, deduction, or credit taken into account prior to Nov. 5, 1990, for purposes of determining liability for tax for periods ending after Nov. 5, 1990, see section 11821(b) of Pub. L. 101–508, set out as a note under section 45K of this title.

Plan Amendments Not Required Until January 1, 1998

For provisions directing that if any amendments made by subtitle D [§§1401–1465] of title I of Pub. L. 104–188 require an amendment to any plan or annuity contract, such amendment shall not be required to be made before the first day of the first plan year beginning on or after Jan. 1, 1998, see section 1465 of Pub. L. 104–188, set out as a note under section 401 of this title.

Plan Amendments Not Required Until January 1, 1994

For provisions directing that if any amendments made by subtitle B [§§521–523] of title V of Pub. L. 102–318 require an amendment to any plan, such plan amendment shall not be required to be made before the first plan year beginning on or after Jan. 1, 1994, see section 523 of Pub. L. 102–318, set out as a note under section 401 of this title.

Plan Amendments Not Required Until January 1, 1989

For provisions directing that if any amendments made by subtitle A or subtitle C of title XI [§§1101–1147 and 1171–1177] or title XVIII [§§1800–1899A] of Pub. L. 99–514 require an amendment to any plan, such plan amendment shall not be required to be made before the first plan year beginning on or after Jan. 1, 1989, see section 1140 of Pub. L. 99–514, as amended, set out as a note under section 401 of this title.

Commuting Expenses

Pub. L. 95–427, §2, Oct. 7, 1978, 92 Stat. 996, as amended by Pub. L. 96–167, §2, Dec. 29, 1979, 93 Stat. 1275, provided that with respect to transportation costs paid or incurred after December 31, 1976, and on or before May 31, 1981, the application of sections 62, 162, and 262 and of chapters 21, 23, and 24 of the Internal Revenue Code of 1954 [now 1986] to transportation expenses in traveling between a taxpayer's residence and place of work be determined without regard to Revenue Ruling 76–453 or any other regulation, ruling, or decision reaching the same or similar result, and with full regard to the rules in effect before that Revenue Ruling.

Pub. L. 95–615, §2, Nov. 8, 1978, 92 Stat. 3097, provided that with respect to transportation costs paid or incurred after Dec. 31, 1976, and before Apr. 30, 1978, the application of sections 62, 162, and 262 and chapters 21, 23, and 24 of the Internal Revenue Code of 1954 [now 1986] to transportation expenses in traveling between a taxpayer's residence and place of work be determined without regard to Revenue Ruling 76–453 or any other regulation, ruling or decision reaching the same or similar result, and with full regard to the rules in effect before that Revenue Ruling, and ceased to have effect on the day after Nov. 8, 1978 pursuant to section 210(a) of that Act.

¹ See References in Text note below.

§63. Taxable income defined

(a) In general

Except as provided in subsection (b), for purposes of this subtitle, the term "taxable income" means gross income minus the deductions allowed by this chapter (other than the standard deduction).

(b) Individuals who do not itemize their deductions

In the case of an individual who does not elect to itemize his deductions for the taxable year, for purposes of this subtitle, the term "taxable income" means adjusted gross income, minus—

(1) the standard deduction,

(2) the deduction for personal exemptions provided in section 151,

(3) any deduction provided in section 199A, and

(4) the deduction provided in section 170(p).

(c) Standard deduction

For purposes of this subtitle—

(1) In general

Except as otherwise provided in this subsection, the term "standard deduction" means the sum of—

(A) the basic standard deduction, and

(B) the additional standard deduction.

(2) Basic standard deduction

For purposes of paragraph (1), the basic standard deduction is—

(A) 200 percent of the dollar amount in effect under subparagraph (C) for the taxable year in the case of—

(i) a joint return, or

(ii) a surviving spouse (as defined in section 2(a)),

(B) $4,400 in the case of a head of household (as defined in section 2(b)), or

(C) $3,000 in any other case.

(3) Additional standard deduction for aged and blind

For purposes of paragraph (1), the additional standard deduction is the sum of each additional amount to which the taxpayer is entitled under subsection (f).

(4) Adjustments for inflation

In the case of any taxable year beginning in a calendar year after 1988, each dollar amount contained in paragraph (2)(B), (2)(C), or (5) or subsection (f) shall be increased by an amount equal to—

(A) such dollar amount, multiplied by

(B) the cost-of-living adjustment determined under section 1(f)(3) for the calendar year in which the taxable year begins, by substituting for "calendar year 2016" in subparagraph (A)(ii) thereof—

(i) "calendar year 1987" in the case of the dollar amounts contained in paragraph (2)(B), (2)(C), or (5)(A) or subsection (f), and

(ii) "calendar year 1997" in the case of the dollar amount contained in paragraph (5)(B).

(5) Limitation on basic standard deduction in the case of certain dependents

In the case of an individual with respect to whom a deduction under section 151 is allowable to another taxpayer for a taxable year beginning in the calendar year in which the individual's taxable year begins, the basic standard deduction applicable to such individual for such individual's taxable year shall not exceed the greater of—

(A) $500, or

(B) the sum of $250 and such individual's earned income.

(6) Certain individuals, etc., not eligible for standard deduction

In the case of—

(A) a married individual filing a separate return where either spouse itemizes deductions,

(B) a nonresident alien individual,

(C) an individual making a return under section 443(a)(1) for a period of less than 12 months on account of a change in his annual accounting period, or

(D) an estate or trust, common trust fund, or partnership,

the standard deduction shall be zero.

(7) Special rules for taxable years 2018 through 2025

In the case of a taxable year beginning after December 31, 2017, and before January 1, 2026—

(A) Increase in standard deduction

Paragraph (2) shall be applied—

(i) by substituting "$18,000" for "$4,400" in subparagraph (B), and

(ii) by substituting "$12,000" for "$3,000" in subparagraph (C).

(B) Adjustment for inflation

(i) In general

Paragraph (4) shall not apply to the dollar amounts contained in paragraphs (2)(B) and (2)(C).

(ii) Adjustment of increased amounts

In the case of a taxable year beginning after 2018, the $18,000 and $12,000 amounts in subparagraph (A) shall each be increased by an amount equal to—

(I) such dollar amount, multiplied by

(II) the cost-of-living adjustment determined under section 1(f)(3) for the calendar year in which the taxable year begins, determined by substituting "2017" for "2016" in subparagraph (A)(ii) thereof.

If any increase under this clause is not a multiple of $50, such increase shall be rounded to the next lowest multiple of $50.

(d) Itemized deductions

For purposes of this subtitle, the term "itemized deductions" means the deductions allowable under this chapter other than—

(1) the deductions allowable in arriving at adjusted gross income, and

(2) any deduction referred to in any paragraph of subsection (b).

(e) Election to itemize

(1) In general

Unless an individual makes an election under this subsection for the taxable year, no itemized deduction shall be allowed for the taxable year. For purposes of this subtitle, the determination of whether a deduction is allowable under this chapter shall be made without regard to the preceding sentence.

(2) Time and manner of election

Any election under this subsection shall be made on the taxpayer's return, and the Secretary shall prescribe the manner of signifying such election on the return.

(3) Change of election

Under regulations prescribed by the Secretary, a change of election with respect to itemized deductions for any taxable year may be made after the filing of the return for such year. If the spouse of the taxpayer filed a separate return for any taxable year corresponding to the taxable year of the taxpayer, the change shall not be allowed unless, in accordance with such regulations—

(A) the spouse makes a change of election with respect to itemized deductions, for the taxable year covered in such separate return, consistent with the change of treatment sought by the taxpayer, and

(B) the taxpayer and his spouse consent in writing to the assessment (within such period as may be agreed on with the Secretary) of any deficiency, to the extent attributable to such change of election, even though at the time of the filing of such consent the assessment of such deficiency would otherwise be prevented by the operation of any law or rule of law.

This paragraph shall not apply if the tax liability of the taxpayer's spouse for the taxable year corresponding to the taxable year of the taxpayer has been compromised under section 7122.

(f) Aged or blind additional amounts

(1) Additional amounts for the aged

The taxpayer shall be entitled to an additional amount of $600—

(A) for himself if he has attained age 65 before the close of his taxable year, and

(B) for the spouse of the taxpayer if the spouse has attained age 65 before the close of the taxable year and an additional exemption is allowable to the taxpayer for such spouse under section 151(b).

(2) Additional amount for blind

The taxpayer shall be entitled to an additional amount of $600—

(A) for himself if he is blind at the close of the taxable year, and

(B) for the spouse of the taxpayer if the spouse is blind as of the close of the taxable year and an additional exemption is allowable to the taxpayer for such spouse under section 151(b).

For purposes of subparagraph (B), if the spouse dies during the taxable year the determination of whether such spouse is blind shall be made as of the time of such death.

(3) Higher amount for certain unmarried individuals

In the case of an individual who is not married and is not a surviving spouse, paragraphs (1) and (2) shall be applied by substituting "$750" for "$600".

(4) Blindness defined

For purposes of this subsection, an individual is blind only if his central visual acuity does not exceed 20/200 in the better eye with correcting lenses, or if his visual acuity is greater than 20/200 but is accompanied by a limitation in the fields of vision such that the widest diameter of the visual field subtends an angle no greater than 20 degrees.

(g) Marital status

For purposes of this section, marital status shall be determined under section 7703.

(Aug. 16, 1954, ch. 736, 68A Stat. 18; Pub. L. 95–30, title I, §102(a), May 23, 1977, 91 Stat. 135; Pub. L. 95–600, title I, §101(b), Nov. 6, 1978, 92 Stat. 2769; Pub. L. 97–34, title I, §§104(b), 111(b)(4), 121(b), (c)(2), Aug. 13, 1981, 95 Stat. 189, 194, 196, 197; Pub. L. 99–514, title I, §102(a), title XII, §1272(d)(6), Oct. 22, 1986, 100 Stat. 2099, 2594; Pub. L. 100–647, title I, §1001(b)(1), Nov. 10, 1988, 102 Stat. 3349; Pub. L. 101–508, title XI, §§11101(d)(1)(D), 11801(a)(4), Nov. 5, 1990, 104 Stat. 1388–405, 1388-520; Pub. L. 103–66, title XIII, §13201(b)(3)(D), Aug. 10, 1993, 107 Stat. 459; Pub. L. 105–34, title XII, §1201(a), Aug. 5, 1997, 111 Stat. 993; Pub. L. 107–16, title III, §301(a), (b), (c)(2), June 7, 2001, 115 Stat. 53, 54; Pub. L. 107–147, title IV, §411(e), Mar. 9, 2002, 116 Stat. 46; Pub. L. 108–27, title I, §103(a), May 28, 2003, 117 Stat. 754; Pub. L. 108–311, title I, §101(b), Oct. 4, 2004, 118 Stat. 1167; Pub. L. 110–289, div. C, title I, §3012(a), (b), July 30, 2008, 122 Stat. 2891, 2892; Pub. L. 110–343, div. C, title II, §204(a), title VII, §706(b)(1), (2), Oct. 3, 2008, 122 Stat. 3865, 3922; Pub. L. 111–5, div. B, title I, §1008(c), Feb. 17, 2009, 123 Stat. 318; Pub. L. 113–295, div. A, title II, §221(a)(13), Dec. 19, 2014, 128 Stat. 4039; Pub. L. 115–97, title I, §§11002(d)(1)(K), 11011(b)(2), (3), 11021(a), Dec. 22, 2017, 131 Stat. 2060, 2070, 2072; Pub. L. 115–141, div. T, §101(a)(2)(A), Mar. 23, 2018, 132 Stat. 1155; Pub. L. 116–260, div. EE, title II, §212(b), Dec. 27, 2020, 134 Stat. 3067.)

INFLATION ADJUSTED ITEMS FOR CERTAIN YEARS

For inflation adjustment of certain items in this section, see Revenue Procedures listed in a table under section 1 of this title.

EDITORIAL NOTES
CODIFICATION

Another section 212(b) of div. EE of Pub. L. 116–260 amended sections 6662 and 6751 of this title.

AMENDMENTS

2020—Subsec. (b)(4). Pub. L. 116–260, §212(b)(1), added par. (4).

Subsec. (d)(2), (3). Pub. L. 116–260, §212(b)(2), added par. (2) and struck out former pars. (2) and (3) which read as follows:

"(2) the deduction for personal exemptions provided by section 151, and

"(3) any deduction provided in section 199A."

2018—Subsecs. (b)(3), (d)(3). Pub. L. 115–141 substituted "any deduction" for "the deduction".

2017—Subsec. (b)(3). Pub. L. 115–97, §11011(b)(2), added par. (3).

Subsec. (c)(4)(B). Pub. L. 115–97, §11002(d)(1)(K), substituted "for 'calendar year 2016' in subparagraph (A)(ii)" for "for 'calendar year 1992' in subparagraph (B)" in introductory provisions.

Subsec. (c)(7). Pub. L. 115–97, §11021(a), added par. (7).

Subsec. (d)(3). Pub. L. 115–97, §11011(b)(3), added par. (3).

2014—Subsec. (c)(1). Pub. L. 113–295, §221(a)(13)(A), added subpars. (A) and (B) and struck out former subpars. (A) to (E) which read as follows:

"(A) the basic standard deduction,

"(B) the additional standard deduction,

"(C) in the case of any taxable year beginning in 2008 or 2009, the real property tax deduction,

"(D) the disaster loss deduction, and

"(E) the motor vehicle sales tax deduction."

Subsec. (c)(7) to (9). Pub. L. 113–295, §221(a)(13)(B), struck out pars. (7) to (9) which related to real property tax deduction, disaster loss deduction, and motor vehicle sales tax deduction, respectively.

2009—Subsec. (c)(1)(E). Pub. L. 111–5, §1008(c)(1), added subpar. (E).

Subsec. (c)(9). Pub. L. 111–5, §1008(c)(2), added par. (9).

2008—Subsec. (c)(1)(C). Pub. L. 110–343, §204(a), inserted "or 2009" after "2008".

Pub. L. 110–289, §3012(a), added subpar. (C).

Subsec. (c)(1)(D). Pub. L. 110–343, §706(b)(1), added subpar. (D).

Subsec. (c)(7). Pub. L. 110–289, §3012(b), added par. (7).

Subsec. (c)(8). Pub. L. 110–343, §706(b)(2), added par. (8).

2004—Subsec. (c)(2). Pub. L. 108–311, §101(b)(1), reenacted heading without change and amended text generally, substituting provisions relating to a specific percentage for provisions relating to applicable percentage in subpar. (A), redesignating subpar. (D) as (C), and deleting former subpar. (C) relating to married individuals filing separately.

Subsec. (c)(4). Pub. L. 108–311, §101(b)(2)(A), substituted "(2)(C)" for "(2)(D)" in introductory provisions and in subpar. (B)(i).

Subsec. (c)(7). Pub. L. 108–311, §101(b)(2)(B), struck out par. (7) which related to applicable percentage for purposes of par. (2).

2003—Subsec. (c)(7). Pub. L. 108–27 inserted table item relating to years 2003 and 2004.

2002—Subsec. (c)(2). Pub. L. 107–147, §411(e)(1)(E), inserted "If any amount determined under subparagraph (A) is not a multiple of $50, such amount shall be rounded to the next lowest multiple of $50." at end.

Subsec. (c)(2)(A). Pub. L. 107–147, §411(e)(1)(A), substituted "subparagraph (D)" for "subparagraph (C)".

Subsec. (c)(2)(B). Pub. L. 107–147, §411(e)(1)(B), struck out "or" at end.

Subsec. (c)(2)(C), (D). Pub. L. 107–147, §411(e)(1)(C), (D), added subpar. (C) and redesignated former subpar. (C) as (D).

Subsec. (c)(4). Pub. L. 107–147, §411(e)(2)(C), which directed amendment by striking out the flush sentence at the end added by section 301(c)(2) of Public Law 107–17, was executed by striking out "The preceding sentence shall not apply to the amount referred to in paragraph (2)(A).", which was inserted by section 301(c)(2) of Pub. L. 107–16, to reflect the probable intent of Congress. See 2001 Amendment note below.

Pub. L. 107–147, §411(e)(2)(A), substituted "paragraph (2)(B), (2)(D), or (5)" for "paragraph (2) or (5)" in introductory provisions.

Subsec. (c)(4)(B)(i). Pub. L. 107–147, §411(e)(2)(B), substituted "paragraph (2)(B), (2)(D)," for "paragraph (2)".

2001—Subsec. (c)(2)(A). Pub. L. 107–16, §301(a)(1), substituted "the applicable percentage of the dollar amount in effect under subparagraph (C) for the taxable year" for "$5,000".

Subsec. (c)(2)(B). Pub. L. 107–16, §301(a)(2), inserted "or" at end.

Subsec. (c)(2)(C). Pub. L. 107–16, §301(a)(3), substituted "in any other case." for "in the case of an individual who is not married and who is not a surviving spouse or head of household, or".

Subsec. (c)(2)(D). Pub. L. 107–16, §301(a)(4), struck out subpar. (D) which read as follows: "$2,500 in the case of a married individual filing a separate return."

Subsec. (c)(4). Pub. L. 107–16, §301(c)(2), inserted at end "The preceding sentence shall not apply to the amount referred to in paragraph (2)(A)."

Subsec. (c)(7). Pub. L. 107–16, §301(b), added par. (7).

1997—Subsec. (c)(4). Pub. L. 105–34, §1201(a)(2), in introductory provisions, substituted "(5)" for "(5)(A)" and, in subpar. (B), substituted "by substituting for 'calendar year 1992' in subparagraph (B) thereof—" for "by substituting 'calendar year 1987' for 'calendar year 1992' in subparagraph (B) thereof" and added cls. (i) and (ii).

Subsec. (c)(5)(B). Pub. L. 105–34, §1201(a)(1), substituted "the sum of $250 and such individual's earned income" for "such individual's earned income".

1993—Subsec. (c)(4)(B). Pub. L. 103–66 substituted "1992" for "1989".

1990—Subsec. (c)(4)(B). Pub. L. 101–508, §11101(d)(1)(D), inserted before period at end ", by substituting 'calendar year 1987' for 'calendar year 1989' in subparagraph (B) thereof".

Subsec. (h). Pub. L. 101–508, §11801(a)(4), struck out subsec. (h) "Transitional rule for taxable years beginning in 1987" which read as follows: "In the case of any taxable year beginning in 1987, paragraph (2) of subsection (c) shall be applied—

"(1) by substituting '$3,760' for '$5,000',

"(2) by substituting '$2,540' for '$4,400',

"(3) by substituting '$2,540' for '$3,000', and

"(4) by substituting '$1,880' for '$2,500'.

The preceding sentence shall not apply if the taxpayer is entitled to an additional amount determined under subsection (f) (relating to additional amount for aged and blind) for the taxable year."

1988—Subsec. (c)(5). Pub. L. 100–647 substituted "basic standard deduction" for "standard deduction" in heading and text.

1986—Subsec. (a). Pub. L. 99–514, §102(a), substituted "In general" for "Corporations" in heading and amended text generally. Prior to amendment, text read as follows: "For purposes of this subtitle, in the case of a corporation, the term 'taxable income' means gross income minus the deductions allowed by this chapter."

Subsec. (b). Pub. L. 99–514, §102(a), substituted "Individuals who do not itemize their deductions" for "Individuals" in heading and amended text generally. Prior to amendment, text read as follows: "For purposes of this subtitle, in the case of an individual, the term 'taxable income' means adjusted gross income—

"(1) reduced by the sum of—

"(A) the excess itemized deductions,

"(B) the deductions for personal exemptions provided by section 151, and

"(C) the direct charitable deduction, and

"(2) increased (in the case of an individual for whom an unused zero bracket amount computation is provided by subsection (e)) by the unused zero bracket amount (if any)."

Subsec. (c). Pub. L. 99–514, §102(a), substituted "Standard deduction" for "Excess itemized deductions" in heading and amended text generally. Prior to amendment, text read as follows: "For purposes of this subtitle, the term 'excess itemized deductions' means the excess (if any) of—

"(1) the itemized deductions, over

"(2) the zero bracket amount."

Subsec. (c)(6)(C) to (E). Pub. L. 99–514, §1272(d)(6), redesignated subpars. (D) and (E) as (C) and (D), respectively, and struck out former subpar. (C) which read as follows: "a citizen of the United States entitled to the benefits of section 931 (relating to income from sources within possessions of the United States),".

Subsec. (d). Pub. L. 99–514, §102(a), substituted "Itemized deductions" for "Zero bracket amount" in heading and amended text generally. Prior to amendment, subsec. (d) read as follows: "For purposes of this subtitle, the term 'zero bracket amount' means—

"(1) in the case of an individual to whom subsection (a), (b), (c), or (d) of section 1 applies, the maximum amount of taxable income on which no tax is imposed by the applicable subsection of section 1, or

"(2) zero in any other case."

Subsec. (e). Pub. L. 99–514, §102(a), substituted "Election to itemize" for "Unused zero bracket amount" in heading.

Subsec. (e)(1). Pub. L. 99–514, §102(a), substituted "In general" for "Individuals for whom computation must be made" in heading and amended text generally. Prior to amendment, text read as follows: "A computation for the taxable year shall be made under this subsection for the following individuals:

"(A) a married individual filing a separate return where either spouse itemized deductions,

"(B) a nonresident alien individual,

"(C) a citizen of the United States entitled to the benefits of section 931 (relating to income from sources within possessions of the United States), and

"(D) an individual with respect to whom a deduction under section 151(e) is allowable to another taxpayer for a taxable year beginning in the calendar year in which the individual's taxable year begins."

Subsec. (e)(2). Pub. L. 99–514, §102(a), substituted "Time and manner of election" for "Computation" in heading and amended text generally. Prior to amendment, text read as follows: "For purposes of this subtitle, an individual's unused zero bracket amount for the taxable year is an amount equal to the excess (if any) of—

"(A) the zero bracket amount, over

"(B) the itemized deductions.

In the case of an individual referred to in paragraph (1)(D), if such individual's earned income (as defined in section 911(d)(2)) exceeds the itemized deductions, such earned income shall be substituted for the itemized deductions in subparagraph (B)."

Subsec. (e)(3). Pub. L. 99–514, §102(a), in amending subsec. (e) generally, added par. (3).

Subsec. (f). Pub. L. 99–514, §102(a), substituted "Aged or blind additional amounts" for "Itemized deductions" in heading and amended text generally. Prior to amendment, text read as follows: "For purposes of this subtitle, the term 'itemized deductions' means the deductions allowable by this chapter other than—

"(1) the deductions allowable in arriving at adjusted gross income,

"(2) the deductions for personal exemptions provided by section 151, and

"(3) the direct charitable deduction."

Subsec. (g). Pub. L. 99–514, §102(a), amended subsec. (g) generally, substituting provision that marital status be determined under section 7703 for provisions relating to election to itemize. See subsec. (e).

Subsec. (h). Pub. L. 99–514, §102(a), substituted "Transitional rule for taxable years beginning in 1987" for "Marital status" in heading and amended text generally. Prior to amendment, text read as follows: "For purposes of this section, marital status shall be determined under section 143."

Subsec. (i). Pub. L. 99–514, §102(a), in amending section generally, struck out subsec. (i), "Direct charitable deduction", which read as follows: "For purposes of this section, the term 'direct charitable deduction' means that portion of the amount allowable under section 170(a) which is taken as a direct charitable deduction for the taxable year under section 170(i)."

1981—Subsec. (b)(1)(C). Pub. L. 97–34, §121(b)(1), added subpar. (C).

Subsec. (d). Pub. L. 97–34, §104(b), substituted a blanket reference to individuals to whom subsection (a), (b), (c), or (d) of section 1 applies and the maximum amount of taxable income on which no tax is imposed by the applicable subsection of section 1 for provisions specifically referring to amounts of $3,400 in the case of (A) a joint return under section 6013, or (B) a surviving spouse (as defined in section 2(a)), $2,300 in the case of an individual who is not married and who is not a surviving spouse (as so defined), and $1,700 in the case of a married individual filing a separate return.

Subsec. (e)(2). Pub. L. 97–34, §111(b)(4), substituted "section 911(d)(2)" for "section 911(b)" in provisions following subpar. (B).

Subsec. (f)(3). Pub. L. 97–34, §121(c)(2), added par. (3).

Subsec. (i). Pub. L. 97–34, §121(b)(2), added subsec. (i).

1978—Pub. L. 95–600 substituted "$3,400" for "$3,200" in par. (1), "$2,300" for "$2,200" in par. (2), and "$1,700" for "$1,600" in par. (3).

1977—Pub. L. 95–30 completely revised definition of taxable income from one using the concept of a standard deduction and consisting of subsecs. (a) and (b) entitled, respectively, "General rule" and "Individuals electing standard deduction" to definition using the concepts of zero bracket amounts and excess itemized deductions and consisting of subsecs. (a) to (h) entitled, respectively, "Corporations", "Individuals", "Excess itemized deductions", "Zero bracket amount", "Unused zero bracket amount", "Itemized deductions", "Election to itemize", and "Marital status".

STATUTORY NOTES AND RELATED SUBSIDIARIES
EFFECTIVE DATE OF 2020 AMENDMENT

Amendment by Pub. L. 116–260 applicable to taxable years beginning after Dec. 31, 2020, see section 212(d) of div. EE of Pub. L. 116–260, set out as a note under section 62 of this title.

EFFECTIVE DATE OF 2018 AMENDMENT

Amendment by Pub. L. 115–141 effective as if included in section 11011 of Pub. L. 115–97, see section 101(d) of Pub. L. 115–141, set out as a note under section 62 of this title.

EFFECTIVE DATE OF 2017 AMENDMENT

Amendment by section 11002(d)(1)(K) of Pub. L. 115–97 applicable to taxable years beginning after Dec. 31, 2017, see section 11002(e) of Pub. L. 115–97, set out as a note under section 1 of this title.

Amendment by section 11011(b)(2), (3) of Pub. L. 115–97 applicable to taxable years beginning after Dec. 31, 2017, see section 11011(e) of Pub. L. 115–97, set out as a note under section 62 of this title.

Pub. L. 115–97, title I, §11021(b), Dec. 22, 2017, 131 Stat. 2073, provided that: "The amendment made by this section [amending this section] shall apply to taxable years beginning after December 31, 2017."

EFFECTIVE DATE OF 2014 AMENDMENT

Amendment by Pub. L. 113–295 effective Dec. 19, 2014, subject to a savings provision, see section 221(b) of Pub. L. 113–295, set out as a note under section 1 of this title.

EFFECTIVE DATE OF 2009 AMENDMENT

Amendment by Pub. L. 111–5 applicable to purchases on or after Feb. 17, 2009, in taxable years ending after such date, see section 1008(e) of Pub. L. 111–5, set out as a note under section 56 of this title.

EFFECTIVE DATE OF 2008 AMENDMENT

Pub. L. 110–343, div. C, title II, §204(b), Oct. 3, 2008, 122 Stat. 3865, provided that: "The amendment made by this section [amending this section] shall apply to taxable years beginning after December 31, 2008."

Amendment by section 706(b)(1), (2) of Pub. L. 110–343 applicable to disasters declared in taxable years beginning after Dec. 31, 2007, see section 706(d)(1) of Pub. L. 110–343, set out as a note under section 56 of this title.

Pub. L. 110–289, div. C, title I, §3012(c), July 30, 2008, 122 Stat. 2892, provided that: "The amendments made by this section [amending this section] shall apply to taxable years beginning after December 31, 2007."

EFFECTIVE AND TERMINATION DATES OF 2004 AMENDMENT

Amendment by Pub. L. 108–311 applicable to taxable years beginning after Dec. 31, 2003, see section 101(e) of Pub. L. 108–311, set out as a note under section 1 of this title.

Amendment by Pub. L. 108–311 subject to title IX of the Economic Growth and Tax Relief Reconciliation Act of 2001, Pub. L. 107–16, §901, to the same extent and in the same manner as the provisions of such Act to which such amendments relate, see section 105 of Pub. L. 108–311, set out as a note under section 1 of this title. Title IX of Pub. L. 107–16 was repealed by Pub. L. 112–240, title I, §101(a)(1), Jan. 2, 2013, 126 Stat. 2315.

EFFECTIVE AND TERMINATION DATES OF 2003 AMENDMENT

Pub. L. 108–27, title I, §103(c), May 28, 2003, 117 Stat. 754, provided that: "The amendments made by this section [amending this section and provisions set out as an Effective and Termination Dates of 2001 Amendment note under section 1 of this title] shall apply to taxable years beginning after December 31, 2002."

Amendments by title I of Pub. L. 108–27 subject to title IX of the Economic Growth and Tax Relief Reconciliation Act of 2001, Pub. L. 107–16, §901, to the same extent and in the same manner as the provisions of such Act to which such amendments relate, see section 107 of Pub. L. 108–27, set out as a note under section 1 of this title. Title IX of Pub. L. 107–16 was repealed by Pub. L. 112–240, title I, §101(a)(1), Jan. 2, 2013, 126 Stat. 2315.

EFFECTIVE DATE OF 2002 AMENDMENT

Amendment by Pub. L. 107–147 effective as if included in the provisions of the Economic Growth and Tax Relief Reconciliation Act of 2001, Pub. L. 107–16, to which such amendment relates, see section 411(x) of Pub. L. 107–147, set out as a note under section 25B of this title.

EFFECTIVE DATE OF 2001 AMENDMENT

Amendment by Pub. L. 107–16 applicable to taxable years beginning after Dec. 31, 2002, see section 301(d) of Pub. L. 107–16, set out as an Effective and Termination Dates of 2001 Amendment note under section 1 of this title.

EFFECTIVE DATE OF 1997 AMENDMENT

Amendment by Pub. L. 105–34 applicable to taxable years beginning after Dec. 31, 1997, see section 1201(c) of Pub. L. 105–34, set out as a note under section 59 of this title.

EFFECTIVE DATE OF 1993 AMENDMENT

Amendment by Pub. L. 103–66 applicable to taxable years beginning after Dec. 31, 1992, see section 13201(c) of Pub. L. 103–66, set out as a note under section 1 of this title.

EFFECTIVE DATE OF 1990 AMENDMENT

Amendment by section 11101(d)(1)(D) of Pub. L. 101–508 applicable to taxable years beginning after Dec. 31, 1990, see section 11101(e) of Pub. L. 101–508, set out as a note under section 1 of this title.

EFFECTIVE DATE OF 1988 AMENDMENT

Amendment by Pub. L. 100–647 effective, except as otherwise provided, as if included in the provision of the Tax Reform Act of 1986, Pub. L. 99–514, to which such amendment relates, see section 1019(a) of Pub. L. 100–647, set out as a note under section 1 of this title.

EFFECTIVE DATE OF 1986 AMENDMENT

Amendment by section 102(a) of Pub. L. 99–514 applicable to taxable years beginning after Dec. 31, 1986, see section 151(a) of Pub. L. 99–514, set out as a note under section 1 of this title.

Amendment by section 1272(d)(6) of Pub. L. 99–514 applicable to taxable years beginning after Dec. 31, 1986, with certain exceptions and qualifications, see section 1277 of Pub. L. 99–514, set out as a note under section 931 of this title.

EFFECTIVE DATE OF 1981 AMENDMENT

Amendment by section 104(b) of Pub. L. 97–34 applicable to taxable years beginning after Dec. 31, 1984, see section 104(e) of Pub. L. 97–34, set out as a note under section 1 of this title.

Amendment by section 111(b)(4) of Pub. L. 97–34 applicable with respect to taxable years beginning after Dec. 31, 1981, see section 115 of Pub. L. 97–34, set out as a note under section 911 of this title.

Amendment by section 121(b), (c)(2) of Pub. L. 97–34 applicable to contributions made after Dec. 31, 1981, in taxable years beginning after such date, see section 121(d) of Pub. L. 97–34, set out as a note under section 170 of this title.

EFFECTIVE DATE OF 1978 AMENDMENT

Amendment by Pub. L. 95–600 effective with respect to taxable years beginning after Dec. 31, 1978, see section 101(f)(1) of Pub. L. 95–600, set out as a note under section 1 of this title.

EFFECTIVE DATE OF 1977 AMENDMENT

Amendment by Pub. L. 95–30 applicable to taxable years beginning after Dec. 31, 1976, see section 106(a) of Pub. L. 95–30, set out as a note under section 1 of this title.

SAVINGS PROVISION

For provisions that nothing in amendment by section 11801 of Pub. L. 101–508 be construed to affect treatment of certain transactions occurring, property acquired, or items of income, loss, deduction, or credit taken into account prior to Nov. 5, 1990, for purposes of determining liability for tax for periods ending after Nov. 5, 1990, see section 11821(b) of Pub. L. 101–508, set out as a note under section 45K of this title.

§64. Ordinary income defined

For purposes of this subtitle, the term "ordinary income" includes any gain from the sale or exchange of property which is neither a capital asset nor property described in section 1231(b). Any gain from the sale or exchange of property which is treated or considered, under other provisions of this subtitle, as "ordinary income" shall be treated as gain from the sale or exchange of property which is neither a capital asset nor property described in section 1231(b).

(Added Pub. L. 94–455, title XIX, §1901(a)(10), Oct. 4, 1976, 90 Stat. 1765.)

§65. Ordinary loss defined

For purposes of this subtitle, the term "ordinary loss" includes any loss from the sale or exchange of property which is not a capital asset. Any loss from the sale or exchange of property which is treated or considered, under other provisions of this subtitle, as "ordinary loss" shall be treated as loss from the sale or exchange of property which is not a capital asset.

(Added Pub. L. 94–455, title XIX, §1901(a)(11), Oct. 4, 1976, 90 Stat. 1765.)

§66. Treatment of community income

(a) Treatment of community income where spouses live apart

If—

(1) 2 individuals are married to each other at any time during a calendar year;

(2) such individuals—

(A) live apart at all times during the calendar year, and

(B) do not file a joint return under section 6013 with each other for a taxable year beginning or ending in the calendar year;

(3) one or both of such individuals have earned income for the calendar year which is community income; and

(4) no portion of such earned income is transferred (directly or indirectly) between such individuals before the close of the calendar year,

then, for purposes of this title, any community income of such individuals for the calendar year shall be treated in accordance with the rules provided by section 879(a).

(b) Secretary may disregard community property laws where spouse not notified of community income

The Secretary may disallow the benefits of any community property law to any taxpayer with respect to any income if such taxpayer acted as if solely entitled to such income and failed to notify the taxpayer's spouse before the due date (including extensions) for filing the return for the taxable year in which the income was derived of the nature and amount of such income.

(c) Spouse relieved of liability in certain other cases

Under regulations prescribed by the Secretary, if—

(1) an individual does not file a joint return for any taxable year,

(2) such individual does not include in gross income for such taxable year an item of community income properly includible therein which, in accordance with the rules contained in section 879(a), would be treated as the income of the other spouse,

(3) the individual establishes that he or she did not know of, and had no reason to know of, such item of community income, and

(4) taking into account all facts and circumstances, it is inequitable to include such item of community income in such individual's gross income,

then, for purposes of this title, such item of community income shall be included in the gross income of the other spouse (and not in the gross income of the individual). Under procedures prescribed by the Secretary, if, taking into account all the facts and circumstances, it is inequitable to hold the individual liable for any unpaid tax or any deficiency (or any portion of either) attributable to any item for which relief is not available under the preceding sentence, the Secretary may relieve such individual of such liability.

(d) Definitions

For purposes of this section—

(1) Earned income

The term "earned income" has the meaning given to such term by section 911(d)(2).

(2) Community income

The term "community income" means income which, under applicable community property laws, is treated as community income.

(3) Community property laws

The term "community property laws" means the community property laws of a State, a foreign country, or a possession of the United States.

(Added Pub. L. 96–605, title I, §101(a), Dec. 28, 1980, 94 Stat. 3521; amended Pub. L. 98–369, div. A, title IV, §424(b)(1)–(2)(B), July 18, 1984, 98 Stat. 802, 803; Pub. L. 101–239, title VII, §7841(d)(8), Dec. 19, 1989, 103 Stat. 2428; Pub. L. 105–206, title III, §3201(b), July 22, 1998, 112 Stat. 739.)

EDITORIAL NOTES

AMENDMENTS

1998—Subsec. (c). Pub. L. 105–206 inserted at end "Under procedures prescribed by the Secretary, if, taking into account all the facts and circumstances, it is inequitable to hold the individual liable for any unpaid tax or any deficiency (or any portion of either) attributable to any item for which relief is not available under the preceding sentence, the Secretary may relieve such individual of such liability."

1989—Subsec. (d)(1). Pub. L. 101–239 substituted "section 911(d)(2)" for "section 911(b)".

1984—Pub. L. 98–369, §424(b)(2)(A), struck out "where spouses live apart" in section catchline.

Subsec. (a). Pub. L. 98–369, §424(b)(2)(B), substituted "Treatment of community income where spouses live apart" for "General rule" in heading.

Subsecs. (b) to (d). Pub. L. 98–369, §424(b)(1), added subsecs. (b) and (c) and redesignated former subsec. (b) as (d).

STATUTORY NOTES AND RELATED SUBSIDIARIES

EFFECTIVE DATE OF 1998 AMENDMENT

Amendment by Pub. L. 105–206 applicable to any liability for tax arising after July 22, 1998, and any liability for tax arising on or before such date but remaining unpaid as of such date, see section 3201(g)(1) of Pub. L. 105–206, set out as a note under section 6015 of this title.

EFFECTIVE DATE OF 1984 AMENDMENT

Amendment by Pub. L. 98–369 applicable to all taxable years to which the Internal Revenue Code of 1986 [formerly I.R.C. 1954] applies with corresponding provisions deemed to be included in the Internal Revenue Code of 1939 and applicable to all taxable years to which such Code applies, except subsection (b) of this section is applicable to taxable years beginning after December 31, 1984, see section 424(c) of Pub. L. 98–369, set out as a note under section 6013 of this title.

EFFECTIVE DATE

Pub. L. 96–605, title I, §101(c), Dec. 28, 1980, 94 Stat. 3522, provided that: "The amendments made by this section [enacting this section] shall apply to calendar years beginning after December 31, 1980."

§67. 2-percent floor on miscellaneous itemized deductions

(a) General rule

In the case of an individual, the miscellaneous itemized deductions for any taxable year shall be allowed only to the extent that the aggregate of such deductions exceeds 2 percent of adjusted gross income.

(b) Miscellaneous itemized deductions

For purposes of this section, the term "miscellaneous itemized deductions" means the itemized deductions other than—

(1) the deduction under section 163 (relating to interest),

(2) the deduction under section 164 (relating to taxes),

(3) the deduction under section 165(a) for casualty or theft losses described in paragraph (2) or (3) of section 165(c) or for losses described in section 165(d),

(4) the deductions under section 170 (relating to charitable, etc., contributions and gifts) and section 642(c) (relating to deduction for amounts paid or permanently set aside for a charitable purpose),

(5) the deduction under section 213 (relating to medical, dental, etc., expenses),

(6) any deduction allowable for impairment-related work expenses,

(7) the deduction under section 691(c) (relating to deduction for estate tax in case of income in respect of the decedent),

(8) any deduction allowable in connection with personal property used in a short sale,

(9) the deduction under section 1341 (relating to computation of tax where taxpayer restores substantial amount held under claim of right),

(10) the deduction under section 72(b)(3) (relating to deduction where annuity payments cease before investment recovered),

(11) the deduction under section 171 (relating to deduction for amortizable bond premium), and

(12) the deduction under section 216 (relating to deductions in connection with cooperative housing corporations).

(c) Disallowance of indirect deduction through pass-thru entity

(1) In general

The Secretary shall prescribe regulations which prohibit the indirect deduction through pass-thru entities of amounts which are not allowable as a deduction if paid or incurred directly by an individual and which contain such reporting requirements as may be necessary to carry out the purposes of this subsection.

(2) Treatment of publicly offered regulated investment companies

(A) In general

Paragraph (1) shall not apply with respect to any publicly offered regulated investment company.

(B) Publicly offered regulated investment companies

For purposes of this subsection—

(i) In general

The term "publicly offered regulated investment company" means a regulated investment company the shares of which are—

(I) continuously offered pursuant to a public offering (within the meaning of section 4 of the Securities Act of 1933, as amended (15 U.S.C. 77a to 77aa)),

(II) regularly traded on an established securities market, or

(III) held by or for no fewer than 500 persons at all times during the taxable year.

(ii) Secretary may reduce 500 person requirement

The Secretary may by regulation decrease the minimum shareholder requirement of clause (i)(III) in the case of regulated investment companies which experience a loss of shareholders through net redemptions of their shares.

(3) Treatment of certain other entities

Paragraph (1) shall not apply—

(A) with respect to cooperatives and real estate investment trusts, and

(B) except as provided in regulations, with respect to estates and trusts.

(d) Impairment-related work expenses

For purposes of this section, the term "impairment-related work expenses" means expenses—

(1) of a handicapped individual (as defined in section 190(b)(3)) for attendant care services at the individual's place of employment and other expenses in connection with such place of employment which are necessary for such individual to be able to work, and

(2) with respect to which a deduction is allowable under section 162 (determined without regard to this section).

(e) Determination of adjusted gross income in case of estates and trusts

For purposes of this section, the adjusted gross income of an estate or trust shall be computed in the same manner as in the case of an individual, except that—

(1) the deductions for costs which are paid or incurred in connection with the administration of the estate or trust and which would not have been incurred if the property were not held in such trust or estate, and

(2) the deductions allowable under sections 642(b), 651, and 661,

shall be treated as allowable in arriving at adjusted gross income. Under regulations, appropriate adjustments shall be made in the application of part I of subchapter J of this chapter to take into account the provisions of this section.

(f) Coordination with other limitation

This section shall be applied before the application of the dollar limitation of the second sentence of section 162(a) (relating to trade or business expenses).

(g) Suspension for taxable years 2018 through 2025

Notwithstanding subsection (a), no miscellaneous itemized deduction shall be allowed for any taxable year beginning after December 31, 2017, and before January 1, 2026.

(Added Pub. L. 99–514, title I, §132(a), Oct. 22, 1986, 100 Stat. 2113; amended Pub. L. 100–647, title I, §1001(f), title IV, §4011(a), Nov. 10, 1988, 102 Stat. 3351, 3655; Pub. L. 101–239, title VII, §7814(f), Dec. 19, 1989, 103 Stat. 2414; Pub. L. 103–66, title XIII, §13213(c)(2), Aug. 10, 1993, 107 Stat. 474; Pub. L. 105–277, div. J, title IV, §4004(b)(1), Oct. 21, 1998, 112 Stat. 2681–910; Pub. L. 106–554, §1(a)(7) [title III, §319(2)], Dec. 21, 2000, 114 Stat. 2763, 2763A-646; Pub. L. 115–97, title I, §11045(a), Dec. 22, 2017, 131 Stat. 2088.)

EDITORIAL NOTES

REFERENCES IN TEXT

Section 4 of the Securities Act of 1933, referred to in subsec. (c)(2)(B)(i)(I), is classified to section 77d of Title 15, Commerce and Trade.

AMENDMENTS

2017—Subsec. (g). Pub. L. 115–97 added subsec. (g).

2000—Subsec. (f). Pub. L. 106–554 substituted "the second sentence" for "the last sentence".

1998—Subsec. (b)(3). Pub. L. 105–277 substituted "for casualty or theft losses described in paragraph (2) or (3) of section 165(c) or for losses described in section 165(d)" for "for losses described in subsection (c)(3) or (d) of section 165".

1993—Subsec. (b)(6) to (13). Pub. L. 103–66 redesignated pars. (7) to (13) as (6) to (12), respectively, and struck out former par. (6) which read as follows: "the deduction under section 217 (relating to moving expenses),".

1989—Subsec. (c)(4). Pub. L. 101–239 struck out par. (4) which read as follows: "Termination.—This subsection shall not apply to any taxable year beginning after December 31, 1989."

1988—Subsec. (b)(4). Pub. L. 100–647, §1001(f)(2), substituted "deductions" for "deduction" and inserted before comma at end "and section 642(c) (relating to deduction for amounts paid or permanently set aside for a charitable purpose)".

Subsec. (c). Pub. L. 100–647, §4011(a), amended subsec. (c) generally. Prior to amendment subsec. (c) read as follows: "The Secretary shall prescribe regulations which prohibit the indirect deduction through pass-thru entities of amounts which are not allowable as a deduction if paid or incurred directly by an individual and which contain such reporting requirements as may be necessary to carry out the purposes of this subsection. The preceding sentence shall not apply—

"(1) with respect to cooperatives and real estate investment trusts, and

"(2) except as provided in regulations, with respect to estates and trusts."

Pub. L. 100–647, §1001(f)(4), amended last sentence generally. Prior to amendment, last sentence read as follows: "The preceding sentence shall not apply with respect to estates, trusts, cooperatives, and real estate investment trusts."

Subsec. (e). Pub. L. 100–647, §1001(f)(3), amended subsec. (e) generally. Prior to amendment, subsec. (e) read as follows: "For purposes of this section, the adjusted gross income of an estate or trust shall be computed in the same manner as in the case of an individual, except that the deductions for costs which are paid or incurred in connection with the administration of the estate or trust and would not have been incurred if the property were not held in such trust or estate shall be treated as allowable in arriving at adjusted gross income."

Subsec. (f). Pub. L. 100–647, §1001(f)(1), added subsec. (f).

STATUTORY NOTES AND RELATED SUBSIDIARIES

EFFECTIVE DATE OF 2017 AMENDMENT

Pub. L. 115–97, title I, §11045(b), Dec. 22, 2017, 131 Stat. 2088, provided that: "The amendment made by this section [amending this section] shall apply to taxable years beginning after December 31, 2017."

EFFECTIVE DATE OF 1998 AMENDMENT

Pub. L. 105–277, div. J, title IV, §4004(c)(2), Oct. 21, 1998, 112 Stat. 2681–911, provided that: "The amendment made by subsection (b)(1) [amending this section] shall apply to taxable years beginning after December 31, 1986."

EFFECTIVE DATE OF 1993 AMENDMENT

Amendment by Pub. L. 103–66 applicable to expenses incurred after Dec. 31, 1993, see section 13213(e) of Pub. L. 103–66 set out as a note under section 62 of this title.

EFFECTIVE DATE OF 1989 AMENDMENT

Amendment by Pub. L. 101–239 effective, except as otherwise provided, as if included in the provision of the Technical and Miscellaneous Revenue Act of 1988, Pub. L. 100–647, to which such amendment relates, see section 7817 of Pub. L. 101–239, set out as a note under section 1 of this title.

EFFECTIVE DATE OF 1988 AMENDMENT

Amendment by section 1001(f) of Pub. L. 100–647 effective, except as otherwise provided, as if included in the provision of the Tax Reform Act of 1986, Pub. L. 99–514, to which such amendment relates, see section 1019(a) of Pub. L. 100–647, set out as a note under section 1 of this title.

Pub. L. 100–647, title IV, §4011(b), Nov. 10, 1988, 102 Stat. 3656, provided that: "The amendment made by subsection (a) [amending this section] shall apply to taxable years beginning after December 31, 1987."

EFFECTIVE DATE

Section applicable to taxable years beginning after Dec. 31, 1986, see section 151(a) of Pub. L. 99–514, set out as an Effective Date of 1986 Amendment note under section 1 of this title.

1-YEAR DELAY IN TREATMENT OF PUBLICLY OFFERED REGULATED INVESTMENT COMPANIES UNDER 2-PERCENT FLOOR

Pub. L. 100–203, title X, §10104(a), Dec. 22, 1987, 101 Stat. 1330–386, provided that:

"(1) General rule.—Section 67(c) of the Internal Revenue Code of 1986 to the extent it relates to indirect deductions through a publicly offered regulated investment company shall apply only to taxable years beginning after December 31, 1987.

"(2) Publicly offered regulated investment company defined.—For purposes of this subsection—

"(A) In general.—The term 'publicly offered regulated investment company' means a regulated investment company the shares of which are—

"(i) continuously offered pursuant to a public offering (within the meaning of section 4 of the Securities Act of 1933, as amended (15 U.S.C. 77a to 77aa) [15 U.S.C. 77d]),

"(ii) regularly traded on an established securities market, or

"(iii) held by or for no fewer than 500 persons at all times during the taxable year.

"(B) Secretary may reduce 500 person requirement.—The Secretary of the Treasury or his delegate may by regulation decrease the minimum shareholder requirement of subparagraph (A)(iii) in the case of regulated investment companies which experience a loss of shareholders through net redemptions of their shares."

§68. Overall limitation on itemized deductions

(a) General rule

In the case of an individual whose adjusted gross income exceeds the applicable amount, the amount of the itemized deductions otherwise allowable for the taxable year shall be reduced by the lesser of—

(1) 3 percent of the excess of adjusted gross income over the applicable amount, or

(2) 80 percent of the amount of the itemized deductions otherwise allowable for such taxable year.

(b) Applicable amount

(1) In general

For purposes of this section, the term "applicable amount" means—

(A) $300,000 in the case of a joint return or a surviving spouse (as defined in section 2(a)),

(B) $275,000 in the case of a head of household (as defined in section 2(b)),

(C) $250,000 in the case of an individual who is not married and who is not a surviving spouse or head of household, and

(D) ½ the amount applicable under subparagraph (A) (after adjustment, if any, under paragraph (2)) in the case of a married individual filing a separate return.

For purposes of this paragraph, marital status shall be determined under section 7703.

(2) Inflation adjustment

In the case of any taxable year beginning in calendar years after 2013, each of the dollar amounts under subparagraphs (A), (B), and (C) of paragraph (1) shall be increased by an amount equal to—

(A) such dollar amount, multiplied by

(B) the cost-of-living adjustment determined under section 1(f)(3) for the calendar year in which the taxable year begins, except that section 1(f)(3)(A)(ii) shall be applied by substituting "2012" for "2016".

If any amount after adjustment under the preceding sentence is not a multiple of $50, such amount shall be rounded to the next lowest multiple of $50.

(c) Exception for certain itemized deductions

For purposes of this section, the term "itemized deductions" does not include—

(1) the deduction under section 213 (relating to medical, etc. expenses),

(2) any deduction for investment interest (as defined in section 163(d)), and

(3) the deduction under section 165(a) for casualty or theft losses described in paragraph (2) or (3) of section 165(c) or for losses described in section 165(d).

(d) Coordination with other limitations

This section shall be applied after the application of any other limitation on the allowance of any itemized deduction.

(e) Exception for estates and trusts

This section shall not apply to any estate or trust.

(f) Section not to apply

This section shall not apply to any taxable year beginning after December 31, 2017, and before January 1, 2026.

(Added Pub. L. 101–508, title XI, §11103(a), Nov. 5, 1990, 104 Stat. 1388–406; amended Pub. L. 103–66, title XIII, §§13201(b)(3)(E), 13204, Aug. 10, 1993, 107 Stat. 459, 462; Pub. L. 105–277, div. J, title IV, §4004(b)(2), Oct. 21, 1998, 112 Stat. 2681–911; Pub. L. 107–16, title I, §103(a), June 7, 2001, 115 Stat. 44; Pub. L. 112–240, title I, §101(b)(2)(A), Jan. 2, 2013, 126 Stat. 2316; Pub. L. 115–97, title I, §§11002(d)(2), 11046(a), Dec. 22, 2017, 131 Stat. 2061, 2088; Pub. L. 115–141, div. U, title IV, §401(a)(33), Mar. 23, 2018, 132 Stat. 1186.)

INFLATION ADJUSTED ITEMS FOR CERTAIN YEARS

For inflation adjustment of certain items in this section, see Revenue Procedures listed in a table under section 1 of this title.

EDITORIAL NOTES

AMENDMENTS

2018—Subsec. (b)(2). Pub. L. 115–141 substituted "shall be" for "shall be shall be" in introductory provisions.

2017—Subsec. (b)(2)(B). Pub. L. 115–97, §11002(d)(2), substituted "1(f)(3)(A)(ii)" for "1(f)(3)(B)" and "2016" for "1992".

Subsec. (f). Pub. L. 115–97, §11046(a), added subsec. (f).

2013—Subsec. (b). Pub. L. 112–240, §101(b)(2)(A)(i), added subsec. (b) and struck out former subsec. (b). Prior to amendment, text read as follows:

"(1) In general.—For purposes of this section, the term 'applicable amount' means $100,000 ($50,000 in the case of a separate return by a married individual within the meaning of section 7703).

"(2) Inflation adjustments.—In the case of any taxable year beginning in a calendar year after 1991, each dollar amount contained in paragraph (1) shall be increased by an amount equal to—

"(A) such dollar amount, multiplied by

"(B) the cost-of-living adjustment determined under section 1(f)(3) for the calendar year in which the taxable year begins, by substituting 'calendar year 1990' for 'calendar year 1992' in subparagraph (B) thereof."

Subsecs. (f), (g). Pub. L. 112–240, §101(b)(2)(A)(ii), struck out subsecs. (f) and (g), which related to phaseout of limitation and termination of applicability of section, respectively.

2001—Subsecs. (f), (g). Pub. L. 107—16 added subsecs. (f) and (g).

1998—Subsec. (c)(3). Pub. L. 105–277 substituted "for casualty or theft losses described in paragraph (2) or (3) of section 165(c) or for losses described in section 165(d)" for "for losses described in subsection (c)(3) or (d) of section 165".

1993—Subsec. (b)(2)(B). Pub. L. 103–66, §13201(b)(3)(E), substituted "1992" for "1989".

Subsec. (f). Pub. L. 103–66, §13204, struck out heading and text of subsec. (f). Text read as follows: "This section shall not apply to any taxable year beginning after December 31, 1995."

STATUTORY NOTES AND RELATED SUBSIDIARIES

EFFECTIVE DATE OF 2017 AMENDMENT

Amendment by section 11002(d)(2) of Pub. L. 115–97 applicable to taxable years beginning after Dec. 31, 2017, see section 11002(e) of Pub. L. 115–97, set out as a note under section 1 of this title.

Pub. L. 115–97, title I, §11046(b), Dec. 22, 2017, 131 Stat. 2088, provided that: "The amendments made by this section [amending this section] shall apply to taxable years beginning after December 31, 2017."

EFFECTIVE DATE OF 2013 AMENDMENT

Amendment by Pub. L. 112–240 applicable to taxable years beginning after Dec. 31, 2012, see section 101(b)(3) of Pub. L. 112–240, set out as a note under section 1 of this title.

EFFECTIVE DATE OF 2001 AMENDMENT

Pub. L. 107–16, title I, §103(b), June 7, 2001, 115 Stat. 45, provided that: "The amendment made by this section [amending this section] shall apply to taxable years beginning after December 31, 2005."

EFFECTIVE DATE OF 1998 AMENDMENT

Pub. L. 105–277, div. J, title IV, §4004(c)(3), Oct. 21, 1998, 112 Stat. 2681–911, provided that: "The amendment made by subsection (b)(2) [amending this section] shall apply to taxable years beginning after December 31, 1990."

EFFECTIVE DATE OF 1993 AMENDMENT

Amendment by section 13201(b)(3)(E) of Pub. L. 103–66 applicable to taxable years beginning after Dec. 31, 1992, see section 13201(c) of Pub. L. 103–66, set out as a note under section 1 of this title.

EFFECTIVE DATE

Section applicable to taxable years beginning after Dec. 31, 1990, see section 11103(e) of Pub. L. 101–508, set out as an Effective Date of 1990 Amendment note under section 1 of this title.

PART II—ITEMS SPECIFICALLY INCLUDED IN GROSS INCOME

78.

Dividends received from certain foreign corporations by domestic corporations choosing foreign tax credit.[1]

79.

Group-term life insurance purchased for employees.

80.

Restoration of value of certain securities.

[81.

Repealed.]

82.

Reimbursement of moving expenses.

83.

Property transferred in connection with performance of services.

84.

Transfer of appreciated property to political organizations.

85.

Unemployment compensation.

86.

Social security and tier 1 railroad retirement benefits.

87.

Alcohol and biodiesel fuels credits.

88.

Certain amounts with respect to nuclear decommissioning costs.

[89.

Repealed.]

90.

Illegal Federal irrigation subsidies.

91.

Certain foreign branch losses transferred to specified 10-percent owned foreign corporations.

EDITORIAL NOTES
AMENDMENTS

2017—Pub. L. 115–97, title I, §§11051(b)(1)(B), 14102(d)(2), Dec. 22, 2017, 131 Stat. 2089, 2194, struck out item 71 "Alimony and separate maintenance payments" and added item 91.

2004—Pub. L. 108–357, title III, §302(c)(1)(B), Oct. 22, 2004, 118 Stat. 1465, substituted "and biodiesel fuels credits" for "fuel credit" in item 87.

1989—Pub. L. 101–239, title VII, §7822(c), Dec. 19, 1989, 103 Stat. 2425, substituted "Illegal Federal irrigation" for "Federal irrigation" in item 90.

Pub. L. 101–140, title II, §202(b), Nov. 8, 1989, 103 Stat. 830, struck out item 89 "Benefits provided under certain employee benefit plans".

1987—Pub. L. 100–203, title X, §§10201(b)(6), 10611(b), Dec. 22, 1987, 101 Stat. 1330–387, 1330-452, struck out item 81 "Increase in vacation pay suspense account" and added item 90.

1986—Pub. L. 99–514, title VIII, §805(c)(1)(B), title XI, §1151(j)(1), Oct. 22, 1986, 100 Stat. 2362, 2508, substituted "Increase in vacation pay suspense account" for "Certain increases in suspense accounts" in item 81, and added item 89.

1984—Pub. L. 98–369, div. A, title I, §91(f)(2), July 18, 1984, 98 Stat. 608, added item 88.

1983—Pub. L. 98–21, title I, §121(f)(3), Apr. 20, 1983, 97 Stat. 84, added item 86 and redesignated former item 86 as 87.

1980—Pub. L. 96–223, title II, §232(c)(3), Apr. 2, 1980, 94 Stat. 277, added item 86.

1978—Pub. L. 95–600, title I, §112(c)(1), Nov. 6, 1978, 92 Stat. 2778, added item 85.

1976—Pub. L. 94–455, title XIX, §1901(b)(5), Oct. 4, 1976, 90 Stat. 1793, struck out item 76 "Mortgages made or obligations issued by joint-stock land banks".

1975—Pub. L. 93–625, §§4(c)(2), 13(a)(2), Jan. 3, 1975, 88 Stat. 2111, 2121, substituted "Certain increases in suspense accounts" for "Increases in suspense account under section 166(g)" in item 81, and added item 84.

1969—Pub. L. 91–172, title II, §231(c)(1), title III, §321(c), Dec. 30, 1969, 83 Stat. 579, 591, added items 82, 83.

1966—Pub. L. 89–722, §1(b)(2), Nov. 2, 1966, 80 Stat. 1152, added item 81.

Pub. L. 89–384, §1(b)(2), Apr. 8, 1966, 80 Stat. 102, added item 80.

1964—Pub. L. 88–272, title II, §204(a)(2), Feb. 26, 1964, 78 Stat. 36, added item 79.

1962—Pub. L. 87–834, §9(d)(1), Oct. 16, 1962, 76 Stat. 1001, added item 78.

[1] *Section catchline amended by Pub. L. 115–97 without corresponding amendment of analysis.*

[§71. Repealed. Pub. L. 115–97, title I, §11051(b)(1)(B), Dec. 22, 2017, 131 Stat. 2089]

Section, Aug. 16, 1954, ch. 736, 68A Stat. 19; Pub. L. 98–369, div. A, title IV, §422(a), July 18, 1984, 98 Stat. 795; Pub. L. 99–514, title XVIII, §1843(a)–(c)(1), (d), Oct. 22, 1986, 100 Stat. 2853, 2855, related to inclusion in gross income of amounts received as alimony or separate maintenance payments.

STATUTORY NOTES AND RELATED SUBSIDIARIES
EFFECTIVE DATE OF REPEAL

Repeal applicable to any divorce or separation instrument (as defined in former subsec. (b)(2) of this section as in effect before Dec. 22, 2017) executed after Dec. 31, 2018, and to such instruments executed on or before Dec. 31, 2018, and modified after Dec. 31, 2018, if the modification expressly provides that the amendment made by section 11051 of Pub. L. 115–97 applies to such modification, see section 11051(c) of Pub. L. 115–97, set out as an Effective Date of 2017 Amendment note under section 61 of this title.

§72. Annuities; certain proceeds of endowment and life insurance contracts

(a) General rules for annuities

(1) Income inclusion

Except as otherwise provided in this chapter, gross income includes any amount received as an annuity (whether for a period certain or during one or more lives) under an annuity, endowment, or life insurance contract.

(2) Partial annuitization

If any amount is received as an annuity for a period of 10 years or more or during one or more lives under any portion of an annuity, endowment, or life insurance contract—

(A) such portion shall be treated as a separate contract for purposes of this section,

(B) for purposes of applying subsections (b), (c), and (e), the investment in the contract shall be allocated pro rata between each portion of the contract from which amounts are received as an annuity and the portion of the contract from which amounts are not received as an annuity, and

(C) a separate annuity starting date under subsection (c)(4) shall be determined with respect to each portion of the contract from which amounts are received as an annuity.

(b) Exclusion ratio
(1) In general

Gross income does not include that part of any amount received as an annuity under an annuity, endowment, or life insurance contract which bears the same ratio to such amount as the investment in the contract (as of the annuity starting date) bears to the expected return under the contract (as of such date).

(2) Exclusion limited to investment

The portion of any amount received as an annuity which is excluded from gross income under paragraph (1) shall not exceed the unrecovered investment in the contract immediately before the receipt of such amount.

(3) Deduction where annuity payments cease before entire investment recovered
(A) In general

If—

(i) after the annuity starting date, payments as an annuity under the contract cease by reason of the death of an annuitant, and

(ii) as of the date of such cessation, there is unrecovered investment in the contract,

the amount of such unrecovered investment (in excess of any amount specified in subsection (e)(5) which was not included in gross income) shall be allowed as a deduction to the annuitant for his last taxable year.

(B) Payments to other persons

In the case of any contract which provides for payments meeting the requirements of subparagraphs (B) and (C) of subsection (c)(2), the deduction under subparagraph (A) shall be allowed to the person entitled to such payments for the taxable year in which such payments are received.

(C) Net operating loss deductions provided

For purposes of section 172, a deduction allowed under this paragraph shall be treated as if it were attributable to a trade or business of the taxpayer.

(4) Unrecovered investment

For purposes of this subsection, the unrecovered investment in the contract as of any date is—

(A) the investment in the contract (determined without regard to subsection (c)(2)) as of the annuity starting date, reduced by

(B) the aggregate amount received under the contract on or after such annuity starting date and before the date as of which the determination is being made, to the extent such amount was excludable from gross income under this subtitle.

(c) Definitions
(1) Investment in the contract

For purposes of subsection (b), the investment in the contract as of the annuity starting date is—

(A) the aggregate amount of premiums or other consideration paid for the contract, minus

(B) the aggregate amount received under the contract before such date, to the extent that such amount was excludable from gross income under this subtitle or prior income tax laws.

(2) Adjustment in investment where there is refund feature

If—

(A) the expected return under the contract depends in whole or in part on the life expectancy of one or more individuals;

(B) the contract provides for payments to be made to a beneficiary (or to the estate of an annuitant) on or after the death of the annuitant or annuitants; and

(C) such payments are in the nature of a refund of the consideration paid,

then the value (computed without discount for interest) of such payments on the annuity starting date shall be subtracted from the amount determined under paragraph (1). Such value shall be computed in accordance with actuarial tables prescribed by the Secretary. For purposes of this paragraph and of subsection (e)(2)(A), the term "refund of the consideration paid" includes amounts payable after the death of an annuitant by reason of a provision in the contract for a life annuity with minimum period of payments certain, but (if part of the consideration was contributed by an employer) does not include that part of any payment to a beneficiary (or to the estate of the annuitant) which is not attributable to the consideration paid by the employee for the contract as determined under paragraph (1)(A).

(3) Expected return

For purposes of subsection (b), the expected return under the contract shall be determined as follows:

(A) Life expectancy

If the expected return under the contract, for the period on and after the annuity starting date, depends in whole or in part on the life expectancy of one or more individuals, the expected return shall be computed with reference to actuarial tables prescribed by the Secretary.

(B) Installment payments

If subparagraph (A) does not apply, the expected return is the aggregate of the amounts receivable under the contract as an annuity.

(4) Annuity starting date

For purposes of this section, the annuity starting date in the case of any contract is the first day of the first period for which an amount is received as an annuity under the contract.

(d) Special rules for qualified employer retirement plans
(1) Simplified method of taxing annuity payments
(A) In general

In the case of any amount received as an annuity under a qualified employer retirement plan—

(i) subsection (b) shall not apply, and

(ii) the investment in the contract shall be recovered as provided in this paragraph.

(B) Method of recovering investment in contract

(i) In general

Gross income shall not include so much of any monthly annuity payment under a qualified employer retirement plan as does not exceed the amount obtained by dividing—

(I) the investment in the contract (as of the annuity starting date), by

(II) the number of anticipated payments determined under the table contained in clause (iii) (or, in the case of a contract to which subsection (c)(3)(B) applies, the number of monthly annuity payments under such contract).

(ii) Certain rules made applicable

Rules similar to the rules of paragraphs (2) and (3) of subsection (b) shall apply for purposes of this paragraph.

(iii) Number of anticipated payments

If the annuity is payable over the life of a single individual, the number of anticipated payments shall be determined as follows:

If the age of the annuitant on the annuity starting date is:	The number of anticipated payments is:
Not more than 55	360
More than 55 but not more than 60	310
More than 60 but not more than 65	260
More than 65 but not more than 70	210
More than 70	160.

(iv) Number of anticipated payments where more than one life

If the annuity is payable over the lives of more than 1 individual, the number of anticipated payments shall be determined as follows:

If the combined ages of annuitants are:	The number is:
Not more than 110	410
More than 110 but not more than 120	360
More than 120 but not more than 130	310
More than 130 but not more than 140	260
More than 140	210.

(C) Adjustment for refund feature not applicable

For purposes of this paragraph, investment in the contract shall be determined under subsection (c)(1) without regard to subsection (c)(2).

(D) Special rule where lump sum paid in connection with commencement of annuity payments

If, in connection with the commencement of annuity payments under any qualified employer retirement plan, the taxpayer receives a lump-sum payment—

(i) such payment shall be taxable under subsection (e) as if received before the annuity starting date, and

(ii) the investment in the contract for purposes of this paragraph shall be determined as if such payment had been so received.

(E) Exception

This paragraph shall not apply in any case where the primary annuitant has attained age 75 on the annuity starting date unless there are fewer than 5 years of guaranteed payments under the annuity.

(F) Adjustment where annuity payments not on monthly basis

In any case where the annuity payments are not made on a monthly basis, appropriate adjustments in the application of this paragraph shall be made to take into account the period on the basis of which such payments are made.

(G) Qualified employer retirement plan

For purposes of this paragraph, the term "qualified employer retirement plan" means any plan or contract described in paragraph (1), (2), or (3) of section 4974(c).

(2) Treatment of employee contributions under defined contribution plans

For purposes of this section, employee contributions (and any income allocable thereto) under a defined contribution plan may be treated as a separate contract.

(e) Amounts not received as annuities

(1) Application of subsection

(A) In general

This subsection shall apply to any amount which—

(i) is received under an annuity, endowment, or life insurance contract, and

(ii) is not received as an annuity,

if no provision of this subtitle (other than this subsection) applies with respect to such amount.

(B) Dividends

For purposes of this section, any amount received which is in the nature of a dividend or similar distribution shall be treated as an amount not received as an annuity.

(2) General rule

Any amount to which this subsection applies—

(A) if received on or after the annuity starting date, shall be included in gross income, or

(B) if received before the annuity starting date—

(i) shall be included in gross income to the extent allocable to income on the contract, and

(ii) shall not be included in gross income to the extent allocable to the investment in the contract.

(3) Allocation of amounts to income and investment
For purposes of paragraph (2)(B)—
(A) Allocation to income
Any amount to which this subsection applies shall be treated as allocable to income on the contract to the extent that such amount does not exceed the excess (if any) of—
    (i) the cash value of the contract (determined without regard to any surrender charge) immediately before the amount is received, over
    (ii) the investment in the contract at such time.
(B) Allocation to investment
Any amount to which this subsection applies shall be treated as allocable to investment in the contract to the extent that such amount is not allocated to income under subparagraph (A).

(4) Special rules for application of paragraph (2)(B)
For purposes of paragraph (2)(B)—
(A) Loans treated as distributions
If, during any taxable year, an individual—
    (i) receives (directly or indirectly) any amount as a loan under any contract to which this subsection applies, or
    (ii) assigns or pledges (or agrees to assign or pledge) any portion of the value of any such contract,

such amount or portion shall be treated as received under the contract as an amount not received as an annuity. The preceding sentence shall not apply for purposes of determining investment in the contract, except that the investment in the contract shall be increased by any amount included in gross income by reason of the amount treated as received under the preceding sentence.
(B) Treatment of policyholder dividends
Any amount described in paragraph (1)(B) shall not be included in gross income under paragraph (2)(B)(i) to the extent such amount is retained by the insurer as a premium or other consideration paid for the contract.
(C) Treatment of transfers without adequate consideration
(i) In general
If an individual who holds an annuity contract transfers it without full and adequate consideration, such individual shall be treated as receiving an amount equal to the excess of—
    (I) the cash surrender value of such contract at the time of transfer, over
    (II) the investment in such contract at such time,

under the contract as an amount not received as an annuity.
(ii) Exception for certain transfers between spouses or former spouses
Clause (i) shall not apply to any transfer to which section 1041(a) (relating to transfers of property between spouses or incident to divorce) applies.
(iii) Adjustment to investment in contract of transferee
If under clause (i) an amount is included in the gross income of the transferor of an annuity contract, the investment in the contract of the transferee in such contract shall be increased by the amount so included.

(5) Retention of existing rules in certain cases
(A) In general
In any case to which this paragraph applies—
    (i) paragraphs (2)(B) and (4)(A) shall not apply, and
    (ii) if paragraph (2)(A) does not apply,

the amount shall be included in gross income, but only to the extent it exceeds the investment in the contract.
(B) Existing contracts
This paragraph shall apply to contracts entered into before August 14, 1982. Any amount allocable to investment in the contract after August 13, 1982, shall be treated as from a contract entered into after such date.
(C) Certain life insurance and endowment contracts
Except as provided in paragraph (10) and except to the extent prescribed by the Secretary by regulations, this paragraph shall apply to any amount not received as an annuity which is received under a life insurance or endowment contract.
(D) Contracts under qualified plans
Except as provided in paragraph (8), this paragraph shall apply to any amount received—
    (i) from a trust described in section 401(a) which is exempt from tax under section 501(a),
    (ii) from a contract—
        (I) purchased by a trust described in clause (i),
        (II) purchased as part of a plan described in section 403(a),
        (III) described in section 403(b), or
        (IV) provided for employees of a life insurance company under a plan described in section 818(a)(3), or

    (iii) from an individual retirement account or an individual retirement annuity.

Any dividend described in section 404(k) which is received by a participant or beneficiary shall, for purposes of this subparagraph, be treated as paid under a separate contract to which clause (ii)(I) applies.
(E) Full refunds, surrenders, redemptions, and maturities
This paragraph shall apply to—
    (i) any amount received, whether in a single sum or otherwise, under a contract in full discharge of the obligation under the contract which is in the nature of a refund of the consideration paid for the contract, and
    (ii) any amount received under a contract on its complete surrender, redemption, or maturity.

In the case of any amount to which the preceding sentence applies, the rule of paragraph (2)(A) shall not apply.

(6) Investment in the contract
For purposes of this subsection, the investment in the contract as of any date is—

(A) the aggregate amount of premiums or other consideration paid for the contract before such date, minus

(B) the aggregate amount received under the contract before such date, to the extent that such amount was excludable from gross income under this subtitle or prior income tax laws.

[(7) Repealed. Pub. L. 100–647, title I, §1011A(b)(9)(A), Nov. 10, 1988, 102 Stat. 3474]

(8) Extension of paragraph (2)(b) ¹ to qualified plans

(A) In general
Notwithstanding any other provision of this subsection, in the case of any amount received before the annuity starting date from a trust or contract described in paragraph (5)(D), paragraph (2)(B) shall apply to such amounts.

(B) Allocation of amount received
For purposes of paragraph (2)(B), the amount allocated to the investment in the contract shall be the portion of the amount described in subparagraph (A) which bears the same ratio to such amount as the investment in the contract bears to the account balance. The determination under the preceding sentence shall be made as of the time of the distribution or at such other time as the Secretary may prescribe.

(C) Treatment of forfeitable rights
If an employee does not have a nonforfeitable right to any amount under any trust or contract to which subparagraph (A) applies, such amount shall not be treated as part of the account balance.

(D) Investment in the contract before 1987
In the case of a plan which on May 5, 1986, permitted withdrawal of any employee contributions before separation from service, subparagraph (A) shall apply only to the extent that amounts received before the annuity starting date (when increased by amounts previously received under the contract after December 31, 1986) exceed the investment in the contract as of December 31, 1986.

(9) Extension of paragraph (2)(B) to qualified tuition programs and Coverdell education savings accounts
Notwithstanding any other provision of this subsection, paragraph (2)(B) shall apply to amounts received under a qualified tuition program (as defined in section 529(b)) or under a Coverdell education savings account (as defined in section 530(b)). The rule of paragraph (8)(B) shall apply for purposes of this paragraph.

(10) Treatment of modified endowment contracts

(A) In general
Notwithstanding paragraph (5)(C), in the case of any modified endowment contract (as defined in section 7702A)—

(i) paragraphs (2)(B) and (4)(A) shall apply, and

(ii) in applying paragraph (4)(A), "any person" shall be substituted for "an individual".

(B) Treatment of certain burial contracts
Notwithstanding subparagraph (A), paragraph (4)(A) shall not apply to any assignment (or pledge) of a modified endowment contract if such assignment (or pledge) is solely to cover the payment of expenses referred to in section 7702(e)(2)(C)(iii) and if the maximum death benefit under such contract does not exceed $25,000.

(11) Special rules for certain combination contracts providing long-term care insurance
Notwithstanding paragraphs (2), (5)(C), and (10), in the case of any charge against the cash value of an annuity contract or the cash surrender value of a life insurance contract made as payment for coverage under a qualified long-term care insurance contract which is part of or a rider on such annuity or life insurance contract—

(A) the investment in the contract shall be reduced (but not below zero) by such charge, and

(B) such charge shall not be includible in gross income.

(12) Anti-abuse rules

(A) In general
For purposes of determining the amount includible in gross income under this subsection—

(i) all modified endowment contracts issued by the same company to the same policyholder during any calendar year shall be treated as 1 modified endowment contract, and

(ii) all annuity contracts issued by the same company to the same policyholder during any calendar year shall be treated as 1 annuity contract.

The preceding sentence shall not apply to any contract described in paragraph (5)(D).

(B) Regulatory authority
The Secretary may by regulations prescribe such additional rules as may be necessary or appropriate to prevent avoidance of the purposes of this subsection through serial purchases of contracts or otherwise.

(f) Special rules for computing employees' contributions
In computing, for purposes of subsection (c)(1)(A), the aggregate amount of premiums or other consideration paid for the contract, and for purposes of subsection (e)(6), the aggregate premiums or other consideration paid, amounts contributed by the employer shall be included, but only to the extent that—

(1) such amounts were includible in the gross income of the employee under this subtitle or prior income tax laws; or

(2) if such amounts had been paid directly to the employee at the time they were contributed, they would not have been includible in the gross income of the employee under the law applicable at the time of such contribution.

Paragraph (2) shall not apply to amounts which were contributed by the employer after December 31, 1962, and which would not have been includible in the gross income of the employee by reason of the application of section 911 if such amounts had been paid directly to the employee at the time of contribution. The preceding sentence shall not apply to amounts which were contributed by the employer, as determined under regulations prescribed by the Secretary, to provide pension or annuity credits, to the extent such credits are attributable to services performed before January 1, 1963, and are provided pursuant to pension or annuity plan provisions in existence on March 12, 1962, and on that date applicable to such services, or to the extent such credits are attributable to services performed as a foreign missionary (within the meaning of section 403(b)(2)(D)(iii), as in effect before the enactment of the Economic Growth and Tax Relief Reconciliation Act of 2001).

(g) Rules for transferee where transfer was for value
Where any contract (or any interest therein) is transferred (by assignment or otherwise) for a valuable consideration, to the extent that the contract (or interest therein) does not, in the hands of the transferee, have a basis which is determined by reference to the basis in the hands of the transferor, then—

(1) for purposes of this section, only the actual value of such consideration, plus the amount of the premiums and other consideration paid by the transferee after the transfer, shall be taken into account in computing the aggregate amount of the premiums or other consideration paid for the contract;

(2) for purposes of subsection (c)(1)(B), there shall be taken into account only the aggregate amount received under the contract by the transferee before the annuity starting date, to the extent that such amount was excludable from gross income under this subtitle or prior income tax laws; and

(3) the annuity starting date is the first day of the first period for which the transferee received an amount under the contract as an annuity.

For purposes of this subsection, the term "transferee" includes a beneficiary of, or the estate of, the transferee.

(h) Option to receive annuity in lieu of lump sum

If—

(1) a contract provides for payment of a lump sum in full discharge of an obligation under the contract, subject to an option to receive an annuity in lieu of such lump sum;

(2) the option is exercised within 60 days after the day on which such lump sum first became payable; and

(3) part or all of such lump sum would (but for this subsection) be includible in gross income by reason of subsection (e)(1),

then, for purposes of this subtitle, no part of such lump sum shall be considered as includible in gross income at the time such lump sum first became payable.

[(i) Repealed. Pub. L. 94–455, title XIX, §1951(b)(1)(A), Oct. 4, 1976, 90 Stat. 1836]

(j) Interest

Notwithstanding any other provision of this section, if any amount is held under an agreement to pay interest thereon, the interest payments shall be included in gross income.

[(k) Repealed. Pub. L. 98–369, div. A, title IV, §421(b)(1), July 18, 1984, 98 Stat. 794]

(l) Face-amount certificates

For purposes of this section, the term "endowment contract" includes a face-amount certificate, as defined in section 2(a)(15) of the Investment Company Act of 1940 (15 U.S.C., sec. 80a–2), issued after December 31, 1954.

(m) Special rules applicable to employee annuities and distributions under employee plans

[(1) Repealed. Pub. L. 93–406, title II, §2001(h)(2), Sept. 2, 1974, 88 Stat. 957]

(2) Computation of consideration paid by the employee

In computing—

(A) the aggregate amount of premiums or other consideration paid for the contract for purposes of subsection (c)(1)(A) (relating to the investment in the contract), and

(B) the aggregate premiums or other consideration paid for purposes of subsection (e)(6) (relating to certain amounts not received as an annuity),

any amount allowed as a deduction with respect to the contract under section 404 which was paid while the employee was an employee within the meaning of section 401(c)(1) shall be treated as consideration contributed by the employer, and there shall not be taken into account any portion of the premiums or other consideration for the contract paid while the employee was an owner-employee which is properly allocable (as determined under regulations prescribed by the Secretary) to the cost of life, accident, health, or other insurance.

(3) Life insurance contracts

(A) This paragraph shall apply to any life insurance contract—

(i) purchased as a part of a plan described in section 403(a), or

(ii) purchased by a trust described in section 401(a) which is exempt from tax under section 501(a) if the proceeds of such contract are payable directly or indirectly to a participant in such trust or to a beneficiary of such participant.

(B) Any contribution to a plan described in subparagraph (A)(i) or a trust described in subparagraph (A)(ii) which is allowed as a deduction under section 404, and any income of a trust described in subparagraph (A)(ii), which is determined in accordance with regulations prescribed by the Secretary to have been applied to purchase the life insurance protection under a contract described in subparagraph (A), is includible in the gross income of the participant for the taxable year when so applied.

(C) In the case of the death of an individual insured under a contract described in subparagraph (A), an amount equal to the cash surrender value of the contract immediately before the death of the insured shall be treated as a payment under such plan or a distribution by such trust, and the excess of the amount payable by reason of the death of the insured over such cash surrender value shall not be includible in gross income under this section and shall be treated as provided in section 101.

[(4) Repealed. Pub. L. 97–248, title II, §236(b)(1), Sept. 3, 1982, 96 Stat. 510]

(5) Penalties applicable to certain amounts received by 5-percent owners

(A) This paragraph applies to amounts which are received from a qualified trust described in section 401(a) or under a plan described in section 403(a) at any time by an individual who is, or has been, a 5-percent owner, or by a successor of such an individual, but only to the extent such amounts are determined, under regulations prescribed by the Secretary, to exceed the benefits provided for such individual under the plan formula.

(B) If a person receives an amount to which this paragraph applies, his tax under this chapter for the taxable year in which such amount is received shall be increased by an amount equal to 10 percent of the portion of the amount so received which is includible in his gross income for such taxable year.

(C) For purposes of this paragraph, the term "5-percent owner" means any individual who, at any time during the 5 plan years preceding the plan year ending in the taxable year in which the amount is received, is a 5-percent owner (as defined in section 416(i)(1)(B)).

(6) Owner-employee defined

For purposes of this subsection, the term "owner-employee" has the meaning assigned to it by section 401(c)(3) and includes an individual for whose benefit an individual retirement account or annuity described in section 408(a) or (b) is maintained. For purposes of the preceding sentence, the term "owner-employee" shall include an employee within the meaning of section 401(c)(1).

(7) Meaning of disabled

For purposes of this section, an individual shall be considered to be disabled if he is unable to engage in any substantial gainful activity by reason of any medically determinable physical or mental impairment which can be expected to result in death or to be of long-continued and indefinite duration. An individual shall not be considered to be disabled unless he furnishes proof of the existence thereof in such form and manner as the Secretary may require.

[(8) Repealed. Pub. L. 97–248, title II, §236(b)(1), Sept. 3, 1982, 96 Stat. 510]

[(9) Repealed. Pub. L. 98–369, div. A, title VII, §713(d)(1), July 18, 1984, 98 Stat. 957]

(10) Determination of investment in the contract in the case of qualified domestic relations orders

Under regulations prescribed by the Secretary, in the case of a distribution or payment made to an alternate payee who is the spouse or former spouse of the participant pursuant to a qualified domestic relations order (as defined in section 414(p)), the investment in the contract as of the date prescribed in such regulations shall be allocated on a pro rata basis between the present value of such distribution or payment and the present value of all other benefits payable with respect to the participant to which such order relates.

(n) Annuities under retired serviceman's family protection plan or survivor benefit plan

Subsection (b) shall not apply in the case of amounts received after December 31, 1965, as an annuity under chapter 73 of title 10 of the United States Code, but all such amounts shall be excluded from gross income until there has been so excluded (under section 122(b)(1) or this section, including amounts excluded before January 1, 1966) an amount equal to the consideration for the contract (as defined by section 122(b)(2)), plus any amount treated pursuant to section 101(b)(2)(D) (as in effect on the day before the date of the enactment of the Small Business Job Protection Act of 1996) as additional consideration paid by the employee. Thereafter all amounts so received shall be included in gross income.

(o) Special rules for distributions from qualified plans to which employee made deductible contributions

(1) Treatment of contributions

For purposes of this section and sections 402 and 403, notwithstanding section 414(h), any deductible employee contribution made to a qualified employer plan or government plan shall be treated as an amount contributed by the employer which is not includible in the gross income of the employee.

[(2) Repealed. Pub. L. 100–647, title I, §1011A(c)(8), Nov. 10, 1988, 102 Stat. 3476]

(3) Amounts constructively received

(A) In general

For purposes of this subsection, rules similar to the rules provided by subsection (p) (other than the exception contained in paragraph (2) thereof) shall apply.

(B) Purchase of life insurance

To the extent any amount of accumulated deductible employee contributions of an employee are applied to the purchase of life insurance contracts, such amount shall be treated as distributed to the employee in the year so applied.

(4) Special rule for treatment of rollover amounts

For purposes of sections 402(c), 403(a)(4), 403(b)(8), 408(d)(3), and 457(e)(16), the Secretary shall prescribe regulations providing for such allocations of amounts attributable to accumulated deductible employee contributions, and for such other rules, as may be necessary to insure that such accumulated deductible employee contributions do not become eligible for additional tax benefits (or freed from limitations) through the use of rollovers.

(5) Definitions and special rules

For purposes of this subsection—

(A) Deductible employee contributions

The term "deductible employee contributions" means any qualified voluntary employee contribution (as defined in section 219(e)(2)) made after December 31, 1981, in a taxable year beginning after such date and made for a taxable year beginning before January 1, 1987, and allowable as a deduction under section 219(a) for such taxable year.

(B) Accumulated deductible employee contributions

The term "accumulated deductible employee contributions" means the deductible employee contributions—

(i) increased by the amount of income and gain allocable to such contributions, and

(ii) reduced by the sum of the amount of loss and expense allocable to such contributions and the amounts distributed with respect to the employee which are attributable to such contributions (or income or gain allocable to such contributions).

(C) Qualified employer plan

The term "qualified employer plan" has the meaning given to such term by subsection (p)(3)(A)(i).

(D) Government plan

The term "government plan" has the meaning given such term by subsection (p)(3)(B).

(6) Ordering rules

Unless the plan specifies otherwise, any distribution from such plan shall not be treated as being made from the accumulated deductible employee contributions, until all other amounts to the credit of the employee have been distributed.

(p) Loans treated as distributions

For purposes of this section—

(1) Treatment as distributions

(A) Loans

If during any taxable year a participant or beneficiary receives (directly or indirectly) any amount as a loan from a qualified employer plan, such amount shall be treated as having been received by such individual as a distribution under such plan.

(B) Assignments or pledges

If during any taxable year a participant or beneficiary assigns (or agrees to assign) or pledges (or agrees to pledge) any portion of his interest in a qualified employer plan, such portion shall be treated as having been received by such individual as a loan from such plan.

(2) Exception for certain loans

(A) General rule

Paragraph (1) shall not apply to any loan to the extent that such loan (when added to the outstanding balance of all other loans from such plan whether made on, before, or after August 13, 1982), does not exceed the lesser of—

(i) $50,000, reduced by the excess (if any) of—

(I) the highest outstanding balance of loans from the plan during the 1-year period ending on the day before the date on which such loan was made, over

(II) the outstanding balance of loans from the plan on the date on which such loan was made, or

(ii) the greater of (I) one-half of the present value of the nonforfeitable accrued benefit of the employee under the plan, or (II) $10,000.

For purposes of clause (ii), the present value of the nonforfeitable accrued benefit shall be determined without regard to any accumulated deductible employee contributions (as defined in subsection (o)(5)(B)).

(B) Requirement that loan be repayable within 5 years

(i) In general

Subparagraph (A) shall not apply to any loan unless such loan, by its terms, is required to be repaid within 5 years.

(ii) Exception for home loans

Clause (i) shall not apply to any loan used to acquire any dwelling unit which within a reasonable time is to be used (determined at the time the loan is made) as the principal residence of the participant.

(C) Requirement of level amortization

Except as provided in regulations, this paragraph shall not apply to any loan unless substantially level amortization of such loan (with payments not less frequently than quarterly) is required over the term of the loan.

(D) Prohibition of loans through credit cards and other similar arrangements

Subparagraph (A) shall not apply to any loan which is made through the use of any credit card or any other similar arrangement.

(E) Related employers and related plans

For purposes of this paragraph—

(i) the rules of subsections (b), (c), and (m) of section 414 shall apply, and

(ii) all plans of an employer (determined after the application of such subsections) shall be treated as 1 plan.

(3) Denial of interest deductions in certain cases

(A) In general

No deduction otherwise allowable under this chapter shall be allowed under this chapter for any interest paid or accrued on any loan to which paragraph (1) does not apply by reason of paragraph (2) during the period described in subparagraph (B).

(B) Period to which subparagraph (A) applies

For purposes of subparagraph (A), the period described in this subparagraph is the period—

(i) on or after the 1st day on which the individual to whom the loan is made is a key employee (as defined in section 416(i)), or

(ii) such loan is secured by amounts attributable to elective deferrals described in subparagraph (A) or (C) of section 402(g)(3).

(4) Qualified employer plan, etc.

For purposes of this subsection—

(A) Qualified employer plan

(i) In general

The term "qualified employer plan" means—

(I) a plan described in section 401(a) which includes a trust exempt from tax under section 501(a),

(II) an annuity plan described in section 403(a), and

(III) a plan under which amounts are contributed by an individual's employer for an annuity contract described in section 403(b).

(ii) Special rule

The term "qualified employer plan" shall include any plan which was (or was determined to be) a qualified employer plan or a government plan.

(B) Government plan

The term "government plan" means any plan, whether or not qualified, established and maintained for its employees by the United States, by a State or political subdivision thereof, or by an agency or instrumentality of any of the foregoing.

(5) Special rules for loans, etc., from certain contracts

For purposes of this subsection, any amount received as a loan under a contract purchased under a qualified employer plan (and any assignment or pledge with respect to such a contract) shall be treated as a loan under such employer plan.

(q) 10-percent penalty for premature distributions from annuity contracts

(1) Imposition of penalty

If any taxpayer receives any amount under an annuity contract, the taxpayer's tax under this chapter for the taxable year in which such amount is received shall be increased by an amount equal to 10 percent of the portion of such amount which is includible in gross income.

(2) Subsection not to apply to certain distributions

Paragraph (1) shall not apply to any distribution—

(A) made on or after the date on which the taxpayer attains age 59½,

(B) made on or after the death of the holder (or, where the holder is not an individual, the death of the primary annuitant (as defined in subsection (s)(6)(B))),

(C) attributable to the taxpayer's becoming disabled within the meaning of subsection (m)(7),

(D) which is a part of a series of substantially equal periodic payments (not less frequently than annually) made for the life (or life expectancy) of the taxpayer or the joint lives (or joint life expectancies) of such taxpayer and his designated beneficiary,

(E) from a plan, contract, account, trust, or annuity described in subsection (e)(5)(D),

(F) allocable to investment in the contract before August 14, 1982, or [2]

(G) under a qualified funding asset (within the meaning of section 130(d), but without regard to whether there is a qualified assignment),

(H) to which subsection (t) applies (without regard to paragraph (2) thereof),

(I) under an immediate annuity contract (within the meaning of section 72(u)(4)), or

(J) which is purchased by an employer upon the termination of a plan described in section 401(a) or 403(a) and which is held by the employer until such time as the employee separates from service.

(3) Change in substantially equal payments

If—

(A) paragraph (1) does not apply to a distribution by reason of paragraph (2)(D), and

(B) the series of payments under such paragraph are subsequently modified (other than by reason of death or disability)—

(i) before the close of the 5-year period beginning on the date of the first payment and after the taxpayer attains age 59½, or

(ii) before the taxpayer attains age 59½,

the taxpayer's tax for the 1st taxable year in which such modification occurs shall be increased by an amount, determined under regulations, equal to the tax which (but for paragraph (2)(D)) would have been imposed, plus interest for the deferral period (within the meaning of subsection (t)(4)(B)).

(r) Certain railroad retirement benefits treated as received under employer plans

(1) In general

Notwithstanding any other provision of law, any benefit provided under the Railroad Retirement Act of 1974 (other than a tier 1 railroad retirement benefit) shall be treated for purposes of this title as a benefit provided under an employer plan which meets the requirements of section 401(a).

(2) Tier 2 taxes treated as contributions

(A) In general

For purposes of paragraph (1)—

(i) the tier 2 portion of the tax imposed by section 3201 (relating to tax on employees) shall be treated as an employee contribution,

(ii) the tier 2 portion of the tax imposed by section 3211 (relating to tax on employee representatives) shall be treated as an employee contribution, and

(iii) the tier 2 portion of the tax imposed by section 3221 (relating to tax on employers) shall be treated as an employer contribution.

(B) Tier 2 portion

For purposes of subparagraph (A)—

(i) After 1984

With respect to compensation paid after 1984, the tier 2 portion shall be the taxes imposed by sections 3201(b), 3211(b), and 3221(b).

(ii) After September 30, 1981, and before 1985

With respect to compensation paid before 1985 for services rendered after September 30, 1981, the tier 2 portion shall be—

(I) so much of the tax imposed by section 3201 as is determined at the 2 percent rate, and

(II) so much of the taxes imposed by sections 3211 and 3221 as is determined at the 11.75 percent rate.

With respect to compensation paid for services rendered after December 31, 1983, and before 1985, subclause (I) shall be applied by substituting "2.75 percent" for "2 percent", and subclause (II) shall be applied by substituting "12.75 percent" for "11.75 percent".

(iii) Before October 1, 1981

With respect to compensation paid for services rendered during any period before October 1, 1981, the tier 2 portion shall be the excess (if any) of—

(I) the tax imposed for such period by section 3201, 3211, or 3221, as the case may be (other than any tax imposed with respect to man-hours), over

(II) the tax which would have been imposed by such section for such period had the rates of the comparable taxes imposed by chapter 21 for such period applied under such section.

(C) Contributions not allocable to supplemental annuity or windfall benefits

For purposes of paragraph (1), no amount treated as an employee contribution under this paragraph shall be allocated to—

(i) any supplemental annuity paid under section 2(b) of the Railroad Retirement Act of 1974, or

(ii) any benefit paid under section 3(h), 4(e), or 4(h) of such Act.

(3) Tier 1 railroad retirement benefit

For purposes of paragraph (1), the term "tier 1 railroad retirement benefit" has the meaning given such term by section 86(d)(4).

(s) Required distributions where holder dies before entire interest is distributed

(1) In general

A contract shall not be treated as an annuity contract for purposes of this title unless it provides that—

(A) if any holder of such contract dies on or after the annuity starting date and before the entire interest in such contract has been distributed, the remaining portion of such interest will be distributed at least as rapidly as under the method of distributions being used as of the date of his death, and

(B) if any holder of such contract dies before the annuity starting date, the entire interest in such contract will be distributed within 5 years after the death of such holder.

(2) Exception for certain amounts payable over life of beneficiary

If—

(A) any portion of the holder's interest is payable to (or for the benefit of) a designated beneficiary,

(B) such portion will be distributed (in accordance with regulations) over the life of such designated beneficiary (or over a period not extending beyond the life expectancy of such beneficiary), and

(C) such distributions begin not later than 1 year after the date of the holder's death or such later date as the Secretary may by regulations prescribe,

then for purposes of paragraph (1), the portion referred to in subparagraph (A) shall be treated as distributed on the day on which such distributions begin.

(3) Special rule where surviving spouse beneficiary

If the designated beneficiary referred to in paragraph (2)(A) is the surviving spouse of the holder of the contract, paragraphs (1) and (2) shall be applied by treating such spouse as the holder of such contract.

(4) Designated beneficiary

For purposes of this subsection, the term "designated beneficiary" means any individual designated a beneficiary by the holder of the contract.

(5) Exception for certain annuity contracts

This subsection shall not apply to any annuity contract—

(A) which is provided—

(i) under a plan described in section 401(a) which includes a trust exempt from tax under section 501, or

(ii) under a plan described in section 403(a),

(B) which is described in section 403(b),

(C) which is an individual retirement annuity or provided under an individual retirement account or annuity, or

(D) which is a qualified funding asset (as defined in section 130(d), but without regard to whether there is a qualified assignment).

(6) Special rule where holder is corporation or other non-individual

(A) In general

For purposes of this subsection, if the holder of the contract is not an individual, the primary annuitant shall be treated as the holder of the contract.

(B) Primary annuitant

For purposes of subparagraph (A), the term "primary annuitant" means the individual, the events in the life of whom are of primary importance in affecting the timing or amount of the payout under the contract.

(7) Treatment of changes in primary annuitant where holder of contract is not an individual

For purposes of this subsection, in the case of a holder of an annuity contract which is not an individual, if there is a change in a primary annuitant (as defined in paragraph (6)(B)), such change shall be treated as the death of the holder.

(t) 10-percent additional tax on early distributions from qualified retirement plans

(1) Imposition of additional tax

If any taxpayer receives any amount from a qualified retirement plan (as defined in section 4974(c)), the taxpayer's tax under this chapter for the taxable year in which such amount is received shall be increased by an amount equal to 10 percent of the portion of such amount which is includible in gross income.

(2) Subsection not to apply to certain distributions

Except as provided in paragraphs (3) and (4), paragraph (1) shall not apply to any of the following distributions:

(A) In general

Distributions which are—

(i) made on or after the date on which the employee attains age 59½,

(ii) made to a beneficiary (or to the estate of the employee) on or after the death of the employee,

(iii) attributable to the employee's being disabled within the meaning of subsection (m)(7),

(iv) part of a series of substantially equal periodic payments (not less frequently than annually) made for the life (or life expectancy) of the employee or the joint lives (or joint life expectancies) of such employee and his designated beneficiary,

(v) made to an employee after separation from service after attainment of age 55,

(vi) dividends paid with respect to stock of a corporation which are described in section 404(k),

(vii) made on account of a levy under section 6331 on the qualified retirement plan, or

(viii) payments under a phased retirement annuity under section 8366a(a)(5) [3] or 8412a(a)(5) of title 5, United States Code, or a composite retirement annuity under section 8366a(a)(1) [3] or 8412a(a)(1) of such title.

(B) Medical expenses

Distributions made to the employee (other than distributions described in subparagraph (A), (C), or (D)) to the extent such distributions do not exceed the amount allowable as a deduction under section 213 to the employee for amounts paid during the taxable year for medical care (determined without regard to whether the employee itemizes deductions for such taxable year).

(C) Payments to alternate payees pursuant to qualified domestic relations orders

Any distribution to an alternate payee pursuant to a qualified domestic relations order (within the meaning of section 414(p)(1)).

(D) Distributions to unemployed individuals for health insurance premiums

(i) In general

Distributions from an individual retirement plan to an individual after separation from employment—

(I) if such individual has received unemployment compensation for 12 consecutive weeks under any Federal or State unemployment compensation law by reason of such separation,

(II) if such distributions are made during any taxable year during which such unemployment compensation is paid or the succeeding taxable year, and

(III) to the extent such distributions do not exceed the amount paid during the taxable year for insurance described in section 213(d)(1)(D) with respect to the individual and the individual's spouse and dependents (as defined in section 152, determined without regard to subsections (b)(1), (b)(2), and (d)(1)(B) thereof).

(ii) Distributions after reemployment

Clause (i) shall not apply to any distribution made after the individual has been employed for at least 60 days after the separation from employment to which clause (i) applies.

(iii) Self-employed individuals

To the extent provided in regulations, a self-employed individual shall be treated as meeting the requirements of clause (i)(I) if, under Federal or State law, the individual would have received unemployment compensation but for the fact the individual was self-employed.

(E) Distributions from individual retirement plans for higher education expenses

Distributions to an individual from an individual retirement plan to the extent such distributions do not exceed the qualified higher education expenses (as defined in paragraph (7)) of the taxpayer for the taxable year. Distributions shall not be taken into account under the preceding sentence if such distributions are described in subparagraph (A), (C), or (D) or to the extent paragraph (1) does not apply to such distributions by reason of subparagraph (B).

(F) Distributions from certain plans for first home purchases

Distributions to an individual from an individual retirement plan which are qualified first-time homebuyer distributions (as defined in paragraph (8)). Distributions shall not be taken into account under the preceding sentence if such distributions are described in subparagraph (A), (C), (D), or (E) or to the extent paragraph (1) does not apply to such distributions by reason of subparagraph (B).

(G) Distributions from retirement plans to individuals called to active duty

(i) In general

Any qualified reservist distribution.

(ii) Amount distributed may be repaid

Any individual who receives a qualified reservist distribution may, at any time during the 2-year period beginning on the day after the end of the active duty period, make one or more contributions to an individual retirement plan of such individual in an aggregate amount not to exceed the amount of such distribution. The dollar limitations otherwise applicable to contributions to individual retirement plans shall not apply to any contribution made pursuant to the preceding sentence. No deduction shall be allowed for any contribution pursuant to this clause.

(iii) Qualified reservist distribution

For purposes of this subparagraph, the term "qualified reservist distribution" means any distribution to an individual if—

(I) such distribution is from an individual retirement plan, or from amounts attributable to employer contributions made pursuant to elective deferrals described in subparagraph (A) or (C) of section 402(g)(3) or section 501(c)(18)(D)(iii),

(II) such individual was (by reason of being a member of a reserve component (as defined in section 101 of title 37, United States Code)) ordered or called to active duty for a period in excess of 179 days or for an indefinite period, and

(III) such distribution is made during the period beginning on the date of such order or call and ending at the close of the active duty period.

(iv) Application of subparagraph

This subparagraph applies to individuals ordered or called to active duty after September 11, 2001. In no event shall the 2-year period referred to in clause (ii) end before the date which is 2 years after the date of the enactment of this subparagraph.

(H) Distributions from retirement plans in case of birth of child or adoption

(i) In general

Any qualified birth or adoption distribution.

457

(ii) Limitation

The aggregate amount which may be treated as qualified birth or adoption distributions by any individual with respect to any birth or adoption shall not exceed $5,000.

(iii) Qualified birth or adoption distribution

For purposes of this subparagraph—

(I) In general

The term "qualified birth or adoption distribution" means any distribution from an applicable eligible retirement plan to an individual if made during the 1-year period beginning on the date on which a child of the individual is born or on which the legal adoption by the individual of an eligible adoptee is finalized.

(II) Eligible adoptee

The term "eligible adoptee" means any individual (other than a child of the taxpayer's spouse) who has not attained age 18 or is physically or mentally incapable of self-support.

(iv) Treatment of plan distributions

(I) In general

If a distribution to an individual would (without regard to clause (ii)) be a qualified birth or adoption distribution, a plan shall not be treated as failing to meet any requirement of this title merely because the plan treats the distribution as a qualified birth or adoption distribution, unless the aggregate amount of such distributions from all plans maintained by the employer (and any member of any controlled group which includes the employer) to such individual exceeds $5,000.

(II) Controlled group

For purposes of subclause (I), the term "controlled group" means any group treated as a single employer under subsection (b), (c), (m), or (o) of section 414.

(v) Amount distributed may be repaid

(I) In general

Any individual who receives a qualified birth or adoption distribution may make one or more contributions in an aggregate amount not to exceed the amount of such distribution to an applicable eligible retirement plan of which such individual is a beneficiary and to which a rollover contribution of such distribution could be made under section 402(c), 403(a)(4), 403(b)(8), 408(d)(3), or 457(e)(16), as the case may be.

(II) Limitation on contributions to applicable eligible retirement plans other than IRAs

The aggregate amount of contributions made by an individual under subclause (I) to any applicable eligible retirement plan which is not an individual retirement plan shall not exceed the aggregate amount of qualified birth or adoption distributions which are made from such plan to such individual. Subclause (I) shall not apply to contributions to any applicable eligible retirement plan which is not an individual retirement plan unless the individual is eligible to make contributions (other than those described in subclause (I)) to such applicable eligible retirement plan.

(III) Treatment of repayments of distributions from applicable eligible retirement plans other than IRAs

If a contribution is made under subclause (I) with respect to a qualified birth or adoption distribution from an applicable eligible retirement plan other than an individual retirement plan, then the taxpayer shall, to the extent of the amount of the contribution, be treated as having received such distribution in an eligible rollover distribution (as defined in section 402(c)(4)) and as having transferred the amount to the applicable eligible retirement plan in a direct trustee to trustee transfer within 60 days of the distribution.

(IV) Treatment of repayments for distributions from IRAs

If a contribution is made under subclause (I) with respect to a qualified birth or adoption distribution from an individual retirement plan, then, to the extent of the amount of the contribution, such distribution shall be treated as a distribution described in section 408(d)(3) and as having been transferred to the applicable eligible retirement plan in a direct trustee to trustee transfer within 60 days of the distribution.

(vi) Definition and special rules

For purposes of this subparagraph—

(I) Applicable eligible retirement plan

The term "applicable eligible retirement plan" means an eligible retirement plan (as defined in section 402(c)(8)(B)) other than a defined benefit plan.

(II) Exemption of distributions from trustee to trustee transfer and withholding rules

For purposes of sections 401(a)(31), 402(f), and 3405, a qualified birth or adoption distribution shall not be treated as an eligible rollover distribution.

(III) Taxpayer must include TIN

A distribution shall not be treated as a qualified birth or adoption distribution with respect to any child or eligible adoptee unless the taxpayer includes the name, age, and TIN of such child or eligible adoptee on the taxpayer's return of tax for the taxable year.

(IV) Distributions treated as meeting plan distribution requirements

Any qualified birth or adoption distribution shall be treated as meeting the requirements of sections 401(k)(2)(B)(i), 403(b)(7)(A)(ii), 403(b)(11), and 457(d)(1)(A).

(3) Limitations

(A) Certain exceptions not to apply to individual retirement plans

Subparagraphs (A)(v) and (C) of paragraph (2) shall not apply to distributions from an individual retirement plan.

(B) Periodic payments under qualified plans must begin after separation

Paragraph (2)(A)(iv) shall not apply to any amount paid from a trust described in section 401(a) which is exempt from tax under section 501(a) or from a contract described in section 72(e)(5)(D)(ii) unless the series of payments begins after the employee separates from service.

(4) Change in substantially equal payments

(A) In general

If—

(i) paragraph (1) does not apply to a distribution by reason of paragraph (2)(A)(iv), and

(ii) the series of payments under such paragraph are subsequently modified (other than by reason of death or disability or a distribution to which paragraph (10) applies)—

(I) before the close of the 5-year period beginning with the date of the first payment and after the employee attains age 59½, or

(II) before the employee attains age 59½,

the taxpayer's tax for the 1st taxable year in which such modification occurs shall be increased by an amount, determined under regulations, equal to the tax which (but for paragraph (2)(A)(iv)) would have been imposed, plus interest for the deferral period.

(B) Deferral period

For purposes of this paragraph, the term "deferral period" means the period beginning with the taxable year in which (without regard to paragraph (2)(A)(iv)) the distribution would have been includible in gross income and ending with the taxable year in which the modification described in subparagraph (A) occurs.

(5) Employee

For purposes of this subsection, the term "employee" includes any participant, and in the case of an individual retirement plan, the individual for whose benefit such plan was established.

(6) Special rules for simple retirement accounts

In the case of any amount received from a simple retirement account (within the meaning of section 408(p)) during the 2-year period beginning on the date such individual first participated in any qualified salary reduction arrangement maintained by the individual's employer under section 408(p)(2), paragraph (1) shall be applied by substituting "25 percent" for "10 percent".

(7) Qualified higher education expenses

For purposes of paragraph (2)(E)—

(A) In general

The term "qualified higher education expenses" means qualified higher education expenses (as defined in section 529(e)(3)) for education furnished to—

(i) the taxpayer,

(ii) the taxpayer's spouse, or

(iii) any child (as defined in section 152(f)(1)) or grandchild of the taxpayer or the taxpayer's spouse,

at an eligible educational institution (as defined in section 529(e)(5)).

(B) Coordination with other benefits

The amount of qualified higher education expenses for any taxable year shall be reduced as provided in section 25A(g)(2).

(8) Qualified first-time homebuyer distributions

For purposes of paragraph (2)(F)—

(A) In general

The term "qualified first-time homebuyer distribution" means any payment or distribution received by an individual to the extent such payment or distribution is used by the individual before the close of the 120th day after the day on which such payment or distribution is received to pay qualified acquisition costs with respect to a principal residence of a first-time homebuyer who is such individual, the spouse of such individual, or any child, grandchild, or ancestor of such individual or the individual's spouse.

(B) Lifetime dollar limitation

The aggregate amount of payments or distributions received by an individual which may be treated as qualified first-time homebuyer distributions for any taxable year shall not exceed the excess (if any) of—

(i) $10,000, over

(ii) the aggregate amounts treated as qualified first-time homebuyer distributions with respect to such individual for all prior taxable years.

(C) Qualified acquisition costs

For purposes of this paragraph, the term "qualified acquisition costs" means the costs of acquiring, constructing, or reconstructing a residence. Such term includes any usual or reasonable settlement, financing, or other closing costs.

(D) First-time homebuyer; other definitions

For purposes of this paragraph—

(i) First-time homebuyer

The term "first-time homebuyer" means any individual if—

(I) such individual (and if married, such individual's spouse) had no present ownership interest in a principal residence during the 2-year period ending on the date of acquisition of the principal residence to which this paragraph applies, and

(II) subsection (h) or (k) of section 1034 [4] (as in effect on the day before the date of the enactment of this paragraph) did not suspend the running of any period of time specified in section 1034 [4] (as so in effect) with respect to such individual on the day before the date the distribution is applied pursuant to subparagraph (A).

(ii) Principal residence

The term "principal residence" has the same meaning as when used in section 121.

(iii) Date of acquisition

The term "date of acquisition" means the date—

(I) on which a binding contract to acquire the principal residence to which subparagraph (A) applies is entered into, or

(II) on which construction or reconstruction of such a principal residence is commenced.

(E) Special rule where delay in acquisition

If any distribution from any individual retirement plan fails to meet the requirements of subparagraph (A) solely by reason of a delay or cancellation of the purchase or construction of the residence, the amount of the distribution may be contributed to an individual retirement plan as provided in section 408(d)(3)(A)(i) (determined by substituting "120th day" for "60th day" in such section), except that—

(i) section 408(d)(3)(B) shall not be applied to such contribution, and

(ii) such amount shall not be taken into account in determining whether section 408(d)(3)(B) applies to any other amount.

(9) Special rule for rollovers to section 457 plans

For purposes of this subsection, a distribution from an eligible deferred compensation plan (as defined in section 457(b)) of an eligible employer described in section 457(e)(1)(A) shall be treated as a distribution from a qualified retirement plan described in 4974(c)(1) to the extent that such distribution is attributable to an amount transferred to an eligible deferred compensation plan from a qualified retirement plan (as defined in section 4974(c)).

(10) Distributions to qualified public safety employees in governmental plans

(A) In general

In the case of a distribution to a qualified public safety employee from a governmental plan (within the meaning of section 414(d)), paragraph (2)(A)(v) shall be applied by substituting "age 50" for "age 55".

(B) Qualified public safety employee

For purposes of this paragraph, the term "qualified public safety employee" means—

(i) any employee of a State or political subdivision of a State who provides police protection, firefighting services, or emergency medical services for any area within the jurisdiction of such State or political subdivision, or

(ii) any Federal law enforcement officer described in section 8331(20) or 8401(17) of title 5, United States Code, any Federal customs and border protection officer described in section 8331(31) or 8401(36) of such title, any Federal firefighter described in section 8331(21) or 8401(14) of such title, any air traffic controller described in 8331(30) or 8401(35) of such title, any nuclear materials courier described in section 8331(27) or 8401(33) of such title, any member of the United States Capitol Police, any member of the Supreme Court Police, or any diplomatic security special agent of the Department of State.

(u) Treatment of annuity contracts not held by natural persons
(1) In general

If any annuity contract is held by a person who is not a natural person—

(A) such contract shall not be treated as an annuity contract for purposes of this subtitle (other than subchapter L), and

(B) the income on the contract for any taxable year of the policyholder shall be treated as ordinary income received or accrued by the owner during such taxable year.

For purposes of this paragraph, holding by a trust or other entity as an agent for a natural person shall not be taken into account.

(2) Income on the contract
(A) In general

For purposes of paragraph (1), the term "income on the contract" means, with respect to any taxable year of the policyholder, the excess of—

(i) the sum of the net surrender value of the contract as of the close of the taxable year plus all distributions under the contract received during the taxable year or any prior taxable year, reduced by

(ii) the sum of the amount of net premiums under the contract for the taxable year and prior taxable years and amounts includible in gross income for prior taxable years with respect to such contract under this subsection.

Where necessary to prevent the avoidance of this subsection, the Secretary may substitute "fair market value of the contract" for "net surrender value of the contract" each place it appears in the preceding sentence.

(B) Net premiums

For purposes of this paragraph, the term "net premiums" means the amount of premiums paid under the contract reduced by any policyholder dividends.

(3) Exceptions

This subsection shall not apply to any annuity contract which—

(A) is acquired by the estate of a decedent by reason of the death of the decedent,

(B) is held under a plan described in section 401(a) or 403(a), under a program described in section 403(b), or under an individual retirement plan,

(C) is a qualified funding asset (as defined in section 130(d), but without regard to whether there is a qualified assignment),

(D) is purchased by an employer upon the termination of a plan described in section 401(a) or 403(a) and is held by the employer until all amounts under such contract are distributed to the employee for whom such contract was purchased or the employee's beneficiary, or

(E) is an immediate annuity.

(4) Immediate annuity

For purposes of this subsection, the term "immediate annuity" means an annuity—

(A) which is purchased with a single premium or annuity consideration,

(B) the annuity starting date (as defined in subsection (c)(4)) of which commences no later than 1 year from the date of the purchase of the annuity, and

(C) which provides for a series of substantially equal periodic payments (to be made not less frequently than annually) during the annuity period.

(v) 10-percent additional tax for taxable distributions from modified endowment contracts
(1) Imposition of additional tax

If any taxpayer receives any amount under a modified endowment contract (as defined in section 7702A), the taxpayer's tax under this chapter for the taxable year in which such amount is received shall be increased by an amount equal to 10 percent of the portion of such amount which is includible in gross income.

(2) Subsection not to apply to certain distributions

Paragraph (1) shall not apply to any distribution—

(A) made on or after the date on which the taxpayer attains age 59½,

(B) which is attributable to the taxpayer's becoming disabled (within the meaning of subsection (m)(7)), or

(C) which is part of a series of substantially equal periodic payments (not less frequently than annually) made for the life (or life expectancy) of the taxpayer or the joint lives (or joint life expectancies) of such taxpayer and his beneficiary.

(w) Application of basis rules to nonresident aliens
(1) In general

Notwithstanding any other provision of this section, for purposes of determining the portion of any distribution which is includible in gross income of a distributee who is a citizen or resident of the United States, the investment in the contract shall not include any applicable nontaxable contributions or applicable nontaxable earnings.

(2) Applicable nontaxable contribution

For purposes of this subsection, the term "applicable nontaxable contribution" means any employer or employee contribution—

(A) which was made with respect to compensation—

(i) for labor or personal services performed by an employee who, at the time the labor or services were performed, was a nonresident alien for purposes of the laws of the United States in effect at such time, and

(ii) which is treated as from sources without the United States, and

(B) which was not subject to income tax (and would have been subject to income tax if paid as cash compensation when the services were rendered) under the laws of the United States or any foreign country.

(3) Applicable nontaxable earnings

For purposes of this subsection, the term "applicable nontaxable earnings" means earnings—

(A) which are paid or accrued with respect to any employer or employee contribution which was made with respect to compensation for labor or personal services performed by an employee,

(B) with respect to which the employee was at the time the earnings were paid or accrued a nonresident alien for purposes of the laws of the United States, and

(C) which were not subject to income tax under the laws of the United States or any foreign country.

(4) Regulations

The Secretary shall prescribe such regulations as may be necessary to carry out the provisions of this subsection, including regulations treating contributions and earnings as not subject to tax under the laws of any foreign country where appropriate to carry out the purposes of this subsection.

(x) Cross reference

For limitation on adjustments to basis of annuity contracts sold, see section 1021.

(Aug. 16, 1954, ch. 736, 68A Stat. 20; Pub. L. 87–792, §4(a), (b), Oct. 10, 1962, 76 Stat. 821; Pub. L. 87–834, §11(b), Oct. 16, 1962, 76 Stat. 1005; Pub. L. 88–272, title II, §232(b), Feb. 26, 1964, 78 Stat. 110; Pub. L. 89–44, title VIII, §809(d)(2), June 21, 1965, 79 Stat. 167; Pub. L. 89–97, title I, §106(d)(2), July 30, 1965, 79 Stat. 337; Pub. L. 89–365, §1(b), Mar. 8, 1966, 80 Stat. 32; Pub. L. 91–172, title V, §515(b), Dec. 30, 1969, 83 Stat. 644; Pub. L. 93–406, title II, §§2001(e)(5), (g)(1), (2)(A), (h)(2), (3), 2002(g)(10), 2005(c)(3), 2007(b)(2), Sept. 2, 1974, 88 Stat. 955, 957, 970, 991, 994; Pub. L. 94–455, title XIX, §§1901(a)(12), (13), 1906(b)(13)(A), 1951(b)(1)(A), Oct. 4, 1976, 90 Stat. 1765, 1834, 1836; Pub. L. 97–34, title III, §§311(b)(1), 312(d), (e)(1), Aug. 13, 1981, 95 Stat. 278, 284; Pub. L. 97–248, title II, §§236(a), (b), 237(d), 265(a), (b)(1), Sept. 3, 1982, 96 Stat. 509–511, 544-546; Pub. L. 97–448, title I, §103(c)(3)(B)(i), (6), Jan. 12, 1983, 96 Stat. 2376; Pub. L. 98–76, title III, §224(a), Aug. 12, 1983, 97 Stat. 421; Pub. L. 98–369, div. A, title II, §§211(b)(1), 222(a), (b), title IV, §§421(b)(1), 491(d)(3), (4), title V, §§521(d), 523(a), (b), title VII, §713(b)(1)–(c)(1)(B), (d)(1), July 18, 1984, 98 Stat. 754, 774, 794, 849, 868, 871, 872, 956, 957; Pub. L. 98–397, title II, §204(c)(2), Aug. 23, 1984, 98 Stat. 1448; Pub. L. 99–514, title XI, §§1101(b)(2)(B), (C), 1122(c), 1123(a), (b), (d)(1), 1134(a)–(d), 1135(a), title XVIII, §§1826(a), (b)(1)–(3), (c), (d), 1852(a)(2), (c)(1)–(4), 1854(b)(1), 1898(c)(1)(B), Oct. 22, 1986, 100 Stat. 2413, 2414, 2467, 2472, 2474, 2475, 2483, 2484, 2848-2850, 2864, 2867, 2878, 2951; Pub. L. 100–647, title I, §§1011A(b)(1)(A), (B), (2), (9), (c)(1)–(8), (h), (i), 1018(k), (t)(1)(A), (B), (u)(8), title V, §5012(a), (b)(1), (d), Nov. 10, 1988, 102 Stat. 3472, 3474-3476, 3482, 3583, 3587, 3590, 3661, 3662, 3664; Pub. L. 101–239, title VII, §§7811(m)(4), 7815(a)(3), (5), Dec. 19, 1989, 103 Stat. 2412, 2414; Pub. L. 101–508, title XI, §11802(a), Nov. 5, 1990, 104 Stat. 1388–529; Pub. L. 102–318, title V, §521(b)(3), July 3, 1992, 106 Stat. 310; Pub. L. 104–188, title I, §§1403(a), 1421(b)(4)(A), 1463(a), 1704(l)(1), (t)(2), (77), Aug. 20, 1996, 110 Stat. 1790, 1796, 1824, 1882, 1887, 1891; Pub. L. 104–191, title III, §361(a)–(c), Aug. 21, 1996, 110 Stat. 2071, 2072; Pub. L. 105–34, title II, §203(a), (b), title III, §303(a), (b), title X, §1075(a), (b), Aug. 5, 1997, 111 Stat. 809, 829, 949; Pub. L. 105–206, title III, §3436(a), title VI, §§6004(d)(3)(B), 6005(c)(1), 6023(3), (4), July 22, 1998, 112 Stat. 761, 794, 800, 824; Pub. L. 107–16, title IV, §402(a)(4)(A), (B), title VI, §§632(a)(3)(A), 641(a)(2)(C), (e)(1), June 7, 2001, 115 Stat. 60, 61, 113, 120; Pub. L. 107–22, §1(b)(1)(A), (3)(A), July 26, 2001, 115 Stat. 196, 197; Pub. L. 107–90, title II, §204(e)(2), Dec. 21, 2001, 115 Stat. 893; Pub. L. 108–311, title II, §207(6), (7), title IV, §408(a)(4), (b)(3), Oct. 4, 2004, 118 Stat. 1177, 1191, 1192; Pub. L. 108–357, title VIII, §906(a), Oct. 22, 2004, 118 Stat. 1653; Pub. L. 109–280, title VIII, §§827(a), 828(a), 844(a), Aug. 17, 2006, 120 Stat. 999, 1001, 1010; Pub. L. 110–245, title I, §107(a), June 17, 2008, 122 Stat. 1631; Pub. L. 110–458, title I, §108(e), Dec. 23, 2008, 122 Stat. 5109; Pub. L. 111–240, title II, §2113(a), Sept. 27, 2010, 124 Stat. 2566; Pub. L. 112–141, div. F, title I, §100121(c), July 6, 2012, 126 Stat. 914; Pub. L. 113–295, div. A, title II, §221(a)(14), Dec. 19, 2014, 128 Stat. 4039; Pub. L. 114–26, §2(a)–(c), June 29, 2015, 129 Stat. 319; Pub. L. 114–113, div. Q, title III, §308(a), Dec. 18, 2015, 129 Stat. 3089; Pub. L. 116–94, div. O, title I, §§108(a), 113(a), Dec. 20, 2019, 133 Stat. 3149, 3154.)

EDITORIAL NOTES
REFERENCES IN TEXT

The enactment of the Economic Growth and Tax Relief Reconciliation Act of 2001, referred to in subsec. (f), means the enactment of Pub. L. 107–16, which was approved June 7, 2001.

The date of the enactment of the Small Business Job Protection Act of 1996, referred to in subsec. (n), is the date of enactment of Pub. L. 104–188, which was approved Aug. 20, 1996.

The Railroad Retirement Act of 1974, referred to in subsec. (r)(1), (2)(C)(i), (ii), is act Aug. 29, 1935, ch. 812, as amended generally by Pub. L. 93–445, title I, §101, Oct. 16, 1974, 88 Stat. 1305, which is classified generally to subchapter IV (§231 et seq.) of chapter 9 of Title 45, Railroads. Sections 2(b), 3(h), and 4(e) and (h) of the Act are classified to sections 231a(b), 231b(h), and 231c(e) and (h), respectively, of Title 45. For further details and complete classification of this Act to the Code, see Codification note set out preceding section 231 of Title 45, section 231t of Title 45, and Tables.

The date of the enactment of this subparagraph, referred to in subsec. (t)(2)(G)(iv), is the date of enactment of Pub. L. 109–280, which was approved Aug. 17, 2006.

Section 1034 (as in effect on the day before the date of the enactment of this paragraph), referred to in subsec. (t)(8)(D)(i)(II), means section 1034 of this title as in effect on the day before Aug. 5, 1997. Section 1034 was repealed by Pub. L. 105–34, title III, §312(b), Aug. 5, 1997, 111 Stat. 839.

AMENDMENTS

2019—Subsec. (p)(2)(D), (E). Pub. L. 116–94, §108(a), added subpar. (D) and redesignated former subpar. (D) as (E).

Subsec. (t)(2)(H). Pub. L. 116–94, §113(a), added subpar. (H).

2015—Subsec. (t)(4)(A)(ii). Pub. L. 114–26, §2(c), inserted "or a distribution to which paragraph (10) applies" after "other than by reason of death or disability" in introductory provisions.

Subsec. (t)(10)(A). Pub. L. 114–26, §2(b), struck out "which is a defined benefit plan" after "section 414(d))".

Subsec. (t)(10)(B). Pub. L. 114–26, §2(a), substituted "means—" for "means", designated remainder of existing provisions as cl. (i), and added cl. (ii).

Subsec. (t)(10)(B)(ii). Pub. L. 114–113 substituted "any air traffic controller" for "or any air traffic controller" and inserted before period at end ", any nuclear materials courier described in section 8331(27) or 8401(33) of such title, any member of the United States Capitol Police, any member of the Supreme Court Police, or any diplomatic security special agent of the Department of State".

2014—Subsec. (c)(4). Pub. L. 113–295, §221(a)(14)(A), struck out "; except that if such date was before January 1, 1954, then the annuity starting date is January 1, 1954" before period at end.

Subsec. (g)(3). Pub. L. 113–295, §221(a)(14)(B), struck out "January 1, 1954, or" before "the first day".

Pub. L. 113–295, §221(a)(14)(B), which directed striking out ", whichever is later", was executed by striking out ", whichever is the later" after "as an annuity" to reflect the probable intent of Congress.

2012—Subsec. (t)(2)(A)(viii). Pub. L. 112–141 added cl. (viii).

2010—Subsec. (a). Pub. L. 111–240 amended subsec. (a) generally. Prior to amendment, text read as follows: "Except as otherwise provided in this chapter, gross income includes any amount received as an annuity (whether for a period certain or during one or more lives) under an annuity, endowment, or life insurance contract."

2008—Subsec. (t)(2)(G)(iv). Pub. L. 110–245, which directed amendment by striking out ", and before December 31, 2007" after "September 11, 2001", was executed by striking out ", and on or before December 31, 2007" after "September 11, 2001", to reflect the probable intent of Congress and the intervening amendment by Pub. L. 110–458. See Amendment note and Effective Date of 2008 Amendment note below.

Pub. L. 110–458 inserted "on or" before "before" in first sentence.

2006—Subsec. (e)(11), (12). Pub. L. 109–280, §844(a), added par. (11) and redesignated former par. (11) as (12).

Subsec. (t)(2)(G). Pub. L. 109–280, §827(a), added subpar. (G).

Subsec. (t)(10). Pub. L. 109–280, §828(a), added par. (10).

2004—Subsec. (e)(9). Pub. L. 108–311, §408(b)(3), amended Pub. L. 107–22, §1(b)(3)(A). See 2001 Amendment note below.

Subsec. (f). Pub. L. 108–311, §408(a)(4), substituted "Economic Growth and Tax Relief Reconciliation Act of 2001)" for "Economic Growth and Tax Relief Reconciliation Act of 2001" in concluding provisions.

Subsec. (t)(2)(D)(i)(III). Pub. L. 108–311, §207(6), inserted ", determined without regard to subsections (b)(1), (b)(2), and (d)(1)(B) thereof" after "section 152".

Subsec. (t)(7)(A)(iii). Pub. L. 108–311, §207(7), substituted "152(f)(1)" for "151(c)(3)".

Subsecs. (w), (x). Pub. L. 108–357 added subsec. (w) and redesignated former subsec. (w) as (x).

2001—Subsec. (e)(9). Pub. L. 107–22, §1(b)(3)(A), as amended by Pub. L. 108–311, §408(b)(3), substituted "Coverdell education savings" for "educational individual retirement" in heading.

Pub. L. 107–22, §1(b)(1)(A), substituted "a Coverdell education savings" for "an education individual retirement".

Pub. L. 107–16, §402(a)(4)(A), (B), substituted "qualified tuition" for "qualified State tuition" in heading and text.

Subsec. (f). Pub. L. 107–16, §632(a)(3)(A), substituted "section 403(b)(2)(D)(iii), as in effect before the enactment of the Economic Growth and Tax Relief Reconciliation Act of 2001" for "section 403(b)(2)(D)(iii))" in concluding provisions.

Subsec. (o)(4). Pub. L. 107–16, §641(e)(1), substituted "403(b)(8), 408(d)(3), and 457(e)(16)" for "and 408(d)(3)".

Subsec. (r)(2)(B)(i). Pub. L. 107–90 substituted "3211(b)" for "3211(a)(2)".

Subsec. (t)(9). Pub. L. 107–16, §641(a)(2)(C), added par. (9).

1998—Subsec. (e)(9). Pub. L. 105–206, §6004(d)(3)(B), added par. (9).

Subsec. (n). Pub. L. 105–206, §6023(3), inserted "(as in effect on the day before the date of the enactment of the Small Business Job Protection Act of 1996)" after "section 101(b)(2)(D)".

Subsec. (t)(2)(A)(iv). Pub. L. 105–206, §3436(a), which directed amendment of cl. (iv) by striking out "or" at end, could not be executed because the word "or" did not appear at end.

Subsec. (t)(2)(A)(vii). Pub. L. 105–206, §3436(a), added cl. (vii).

Subsec. (t)(3)(A). Pub. L. 105–206, §6023(4), substituted "(A)(v)" for "(A)(v),".

Subsec. (t)(8)(E). Pub. L. 105–206, §6005(c)(1), in introductory provisions, substituted "120th day" for "120 days" and "60th day" for "60 days".

1997—Subsec. (d)(1)(B)(iii). Pub. L. 105–34, §1075(b), inserted "If the annuity is payable over the life of a single individual, the number of anticipated payments shall be determined as follows:" before table and struck out "primary" after "If the age of the" in table.

Subsec. (d)(1)(B)(iv). Pub. L. 105–34, §1075(a), added cl. (iv).

Subsec. (t)(2)(E). Pub. L. 105–34, §203(a), added subpar. (E).

Subsec. (t)(2)(F). Pub. L. 105–34, §303(a), added subpar. (F).

Subsec. (t)(7). Pub. L. 105–34, §203(b), added par. (7).

Subsec. (t)(8). Pub. L. 105–34, §303(b), added par. (8).

1996—Subsec. (b)(4)(A). Pub. L. 104–188, §1704(l)(1), inserted "(determined without regard to subsection (c)(2))" after "contract".

Subsec. (d). Pub. L. 104–188, §1403(a), amended subsec. (d) generally. Prior to amendment, subsec. (d) read as follows: "Treatment of Employee Contributions Under Defined Contribution Plans as Separate Contracts.—For purposes of this section, employee contributions (and any income allocable thereto) under a defined contribution plan may be treated as a separate contract."

Subsec. (f). Pub. L. 104–188, §1463(a), in closing provisions, inserted before period at end ", or to the extent such credits are attributable to services performed as a foreign missionary (within the meaning of section 403(b)(2)(D)(iii))".

Subsec. (m)(2)(A) to (C). Pub. L. 104–188, §1704(t)(2), inserted "and" at end of subpar. (A), redesignated subpar. (C) as (B), and struck out former subpar. (B) which read as follows: "the consideration for the contract contributed by the employee for purposes of subsection (d)(1) (relating to employee's contributions recoverable in 3 years) and subsection (e)(7) (relating to plans where substantially all contributions are employee contributions), and".

Subsec. (p)(4)(A)(ii). Pub. L. 104–188, §1704(t)(77), amended cl. (ii) generally. Prior to amendment, cl. (ii) read as follows: "Special rules.—The term 'qualified employer plan'—

"(I) shall include any plan which was (or was determined to be) a qualified employer plan or a government plan, but

"(II) shall not include a plan described in subsection (e)(7)."

Subsec. (t)(2)(B). Pub. L. 104–191, §361(c), substituted ", (C), or (D)" for "or (C)".

Subsec. (t)(2)(D). Pub. L. 104–191, §361(b), added subpar. (D).

Subsec. (t)(3)(A). Pub. L. 104–191, §361(a), struck out "(B)," after "Subparagraphs (A)(v),".

Subsec. (t)(6). Pub. L. 104–188, §1421(b)(4)(A), added par. (6).

1992—Subsec. (o)(4). Pub. L. 102–318 substituted "402(c)" for "402(a)(5), 402(a)(7)".

1990—Subsec. (t)(2)(C), (D). Pub. L. 101–508, §11802(a)(1), (2), redesignated subpar. (D) as (C) and struck out former subpar. (C) "Exceptions for distributions from employee stock ownership plans" which read as follows: "Any distribution made before January 1, 1990, to an employee from an employee stock ownership plan (as defined in section 4975(e)(7)) or a tax credit employee stock ownership plan (as defined in section 409) if—

"(i) such distribution is attributable to assets which have been invested in employer securities (within the meaning of section 409(l)) at all times during the 5-plan-year period preceding the plan year in which the distribution is made, and

"(ii) at all times during such period the requirements of sections 401(a)(28) and 409 (as in effect at such times) are met with respect to such employer securities."

Subsec. (t)(3)(A). Pub. L. 101–508, §11802(a)(3), substituted "and (C)" for "(C), and (D)".

1989—Subsec. (e)(11)(A). Pub. L. 101–239, §7815(a)(3), (5), substituted "calendar year" for "12-month period" in cls. (i) and (ii), and inserted at end "The preceding sentence shall not apply to any contract described in paragraph (5)(D)."

Subsec. (q)(2)(B). Pub. L. 101–239, §7811(m)(4), inserted an additional closing parenthesis after "subsection (s)(6)(B))".

1988—Subsec. (d). Pub. L. 100–647, §1011A(b)(2)(A), added subsec. (d).

Subsec. (e)(4)(A). Pub. L. 100–647, §5012(d)(1), inserted at end "The preceding sentence shall not apply for purposes of determining investment in the contract, except that the investment in the contract shall be increased by any amount included in gross income by reason of the amount treated as received under the preceding sentence."

Subsec. (e)(5)(C). Pub. L. 100–647, §5012(a)(2), substituted "Except as provided in paragraph (10) and except to the extent" for "Except to the extent".

Subsec. (e)(5)(D). Pub. L. 100–647, §1011A(b)(9)(B), substituted "paragraph (8)" for "paragraphs (7) and (8)".

Subsec. (e)(7). Pub. L. 100–647, §1011A(b)(9)(A), struck out par. (7) which related to special rules for plans where substantially all contributions are employee contributions.

Subsec. (e)(8)(A). Pub. L. 100–647, §1011A(b)(9)(C), struck out "(other than paragraph (7))" after "this subsection".

Subsec. (e)(9). Pub. L. 100–647, §1011A(b)(2)(B), struck out par. (9) which related to treatment of employee contributions as separate contract.

Subsec. (e)(10). Pub. L. 100–647, §5012(a)(1), added par. (10).

Subsec. (e)(11). Pub. L. 100–647, §5012(d)(2), added par. (11).

Subsec. (f). Pub. L. 100–647, §1011A(b)(1)(A), struck out "for purposes of subsections (d)(1) and (e)(7), the consideration for the contract contributed by the employee," after "contract," in introductory provisions.

Subsec. (n). Pub. L. 100–647, §1011A(b)(1)(B), substituted "Subsection (b)" for "Subsections (b) and (d)".

Subsec. (o)(2). Pub. L. 100–647, §1011A(c)(8), struck out par. (2) which related to additional tax if amount received before age 59½.

Subsec. (p)(3)(A). Pub. L. 100–647, §1011A(h)(1), inserted "to which paragraph (1) does not apply by reason of paragraph (2) during the period" after "loan".

Subsec. (p)(3)(B). Pub. L. 100–647, §1011A(h)(2), substituted "Period" for "Loans" in heading and amended text generally. Prior to amendment, text read as follows: "For purposes of subparagraph (A), a loan is described in this subparagraph—

"(i) if paragraph (1) does not apply to such loan by reason of paragraph (2), and

"(ii) if—

"(I) such loan is made to a key employee (as defined in section 416(i)), or

"(II) such loan is secured by amounts attributable to elective 401(k) or 403(b) deferrals (as defined in section 402(g)(3))."

Subsec. (q)(2)(B). Pub. L. 100–647, §1018(t)(1)(B), substituted "subsection (s)(6)(B))" for "subsection (s)(6)(B)))".

Subsec. (q)(2)(D). Pub. L. 100–647, §1011A(c)(7), inserted "designated" before "beneficiary".

Pub. L. 100–647, §§1011A(c)(4), 1018(u)(8), amended subpar. (D) identically, substituting a comma for period at end.

Subsec. (q)(2)(E). Pub. L. 100–647, §1011A(b)(9)(D), struck out "(determined without regard to subsection (e)(7))" after "subsection (e)(5)(D)".

Subsec. (q)(2)(G). Pub. L. 100–647, §1011A(c)(4), substituted a comma for period at end.

Subsec. (q)(2)(H). Pub. L. 100–647, §1011A(c)(6), added subpar. (H).

Subsec. (q)(3)(B). Pub. L. 100–647, §1011A(c)(5), substituted "taxpayer" for "employee" in cls. (i) and (ii).

Subsec. (s)(5). Pub. L. 100–647, §1018(k)(2), substituted "certain annuity contracts" for "annuity contracts which are part of qualified plans" in heading.

Subsec. (s)(5)(D). Pub. L. 100–647, §1018(k)(1), added subpar. (D).

Subsec. (s)(7). Pub. L. 100–647, §1018(t)(1)(A), substituted "primary annuitant" for "primary annuity".

Subsec. (t)(2)(A)(iv). Pub. L. 100–647, §1011A(c)(7), inserted "designated" before "beneficiary".

Subsec. (t)(2)(A)(v). Pub. L. 100–647, §1011A(c)(1), struck out "on account of early retirement under the plan" after "separation from service".

Subsec. (t)(2)(C). Pub. L. 100–647, §1011A(c)(2), substituted "Exceptions for distributions from employee stock ownership plans" for "Certain plans" in heading and amended text generally. Prior to amendment, text read as follows:

"(i) In general.—Except as provided in clause (ii), any distribution made before January 1, 1990, to an employee from an employee stock ownership plan defined in section 4975(e)(7) to the extent that, on average, a majority of assets in the plan have been invested in employer securities (as defined in section 409(l)) for the 5-plan-year period preceding the plan year in which the distribution is made.

"(ii) Benefits distributed must be invested in employer securities for 5 years.—Clause (i) shall not apply to any distribution which is attributable to assets which have not been invested in employer securities at all times during the period referred to in clause (i)."

Subsec. (t)(3)(A). Pub. L. 100–647, §1011A(c)(3), substituted "(C), and (D)" for "and (C)".

Subsec. (u)(1)(A). Pub. L. 100–647, §1011A(i)(1), inserted "(other than subchapter L)" after "subtitle".

Subsec. (u)(3)(D). Pub. L. 100–647, §1011A(i)(3), substituted "is purchased" for "which is purchased" and "is held" for "which is held".

Pub. L. 100–647, §1011A(i)(2), substituted "until all amounts under such contract are distributed to the employee for whom such contract was purchased or the employee's beneficiary" for "until such time as the employee separates from service".

Subsec. (u)(3)(E). Pub. L. 100–647, §1011A(i)(3), substituted "is" for "which is".

Subsec. (u)(4)(C). Pub. L. 100–647, §1011A(i)(4), added subpar. (C).

Subsecs. (v), (w). Pub. L. 100–647, §5012(b)(1), added subsec. (v) and redesignated former subsec. (v) as (w).

1986—Subsec. (b). Pub. L. 99–514, §1122(c)(2), amended subsec. (b) generally. Prior to amendment, subsec. (b) read as follows: "Gross income does not include that part of any amount received as an annuity under an annuity, endowment, or life insurance contract which bears the same ratio to such amount as the investment in the contract (as of the annuity starting date) bears to the expected return under the contract (as of such date). This subsection shall not apply to any amount to which subsection (d)(1) (relating to certain employee annuities) applies."

Subsec. (d). Pub. L. 99–514, §1122(c)(1), struck out subsec. (d) which related to employee's annuities where the employee's contributions were recoverable in 3 years.

Subsec. (e)(4)(C). Pub. L. 99–514, §1826(b)(3), added subpar. (C).

Subsec. (e)(5)(D). Pub. L. 99–514, §1122(c)(3)(B), substituted "paragraphs (7) and (8)" for "paragraph (7)" in introductory provisions.

Pub. L. 99–514, §1854(b)(1), inserted closing provisions which read as follows: "Any dividend described in section 404(k) which is received by a participant or beneficiary shall, for purposes of this subparagraph, be treated as paid under a separate contract to which clause (ii)(I) applies."

Subsec. (e)(7)(B). Pub. L. 99–514, §1852(c)(1), in introductory provisions substituted "any plan or contract" for "any trust or contract", in cl. (ii) substituted "85 percent or more of" for "85 percent of", and inserted closing provision: "For purposes of clause (ii), deductible employee contributions (as defined in subsection (o)(5)(A)) shall not be taken into account."

Subsec. (e)(8), (9). Pub. L. 99–514, §1122(c)(3)(A), added pars. (8) and (9).

Subsec. (f). Pub. L. 99–514, §1852(c)(3), in introductory provisions, substituted "subsections (d)(1) and (e)(7)" for "subsection (d)(1)" and "subsection (e)(6)" for "subsection (e)(1)(B)".

Subsec. (m)(2)(B). Pub. L. 99–514, §1852(c)(4)(A), inserted "and subsection (e)(7) (relating to plans where substantially all contributions are employee contributions)".

Subsec. (m)(2)(C). Pub. L. 99–514, §1852(c)(4)(B), substituted "subsection (e)(6)" for "subsection (e)(1)(B)".

Subsec. (m)(5). Pub. L. 99–514, §1852(a)(2)(C), which directed that par. (5) be amended by substituting "5-percent owners" for "owner-employees" in heading, was executed by substituting "5-percent owners" for "key employees", to reflect the probable intent of Congress and intervening amendment by section 713(c)(1)(B) of Pub. L. 98–369.

Subsec. (m)(5)(A). Pub. L. 99–514, §1123(d)(1), amended subpar. (A) generally. Prior to amendment, subpar. (A) read as follows: "This subparagraph shall apply—

"(i) to amounts which—

"(I) are received from a qualified trust described in section 401(a) or under a plan described in section 403(a), and

"(II) are received by a 5-percent owner before such owner attains the age of 59½ years, for any reason other than such owner becoming disabled (within the meaning of paragraph (7) of this section), and

"(ii) to amounts which are received from a qualified trust described in section 401(a) or under a plan described in section 403(a) at any time by a 5-percent owner, or by the successor of such owner, but only to the extent that such amounts are determined (under regulations prescribed by the Secretary) to exceed the benefits provided for such individual under the plan formula.

Clause (i) shall not apply to any amount received by an individual in his capacity as a policyholder of an annuity, endowment, or life insurance contract which is in the nature of a dividend or similar distribution and clause (i) shall not apply to amounts attributable to benefits accrued before January 1, 1985."

Pub. L. 99–514, §1852(a)(2)(A), amended subpar. (A) generally. Prior to amendment, subpar. (A) read as follows: "This paragraph shall apply—

"(i) to amounts (other than any amount received by an individual in his capacity as a policyholder of an annuity, endowment, or life insurance contract which is in the nature of a dividend or similar distribution) which are received from a qualified trust described in section 401(a) or under a plan described in section 403(a) and which are received by an individual, who is, or has been, a 5-percent owner, before such individual attains the age of 59½ years, for any reason other than the individual's becoming disabled (within the meaning of paragraph (7) of this subsection), but only to the extent that such amounts are attributable to contributions paid on behalf of such individual (other than contributions made by him as a 5-percent owner) while he was a 5-percent owner, and

"(ii) to amounts which are received from a qualified trust described in section 401(a) or under a plan described in section 403(a) at any time by an individual who is, or has been, a 5-percent owner or by the successor of such individual, but only to the extent that such amounts are determined, under regulations prescribed by the Secretary, to exceed the benefits provided for such individual under the plan formula."

Subsec. (m)(5)(C). Pub. L. 99–514, §1852(a)(2)(B), amended subpar. (C) generally. Prior to amendment, subpar. (C) read as follows: "For purposes of this paragraph, the term '5 percent owner' have the same meanings as when used in section 416."

Subsec. (m)(10). Pub. L. 99–514, §1898(c)(1)(B), inserted "who is the spouse or former spouse of the participant".

Subsec. (o)(5). Pub. L. 99–514, §1101(b)(2)(C), inserted "and made for a taxable year beginning before January 1, 1987," in subpar. (A), substituted "subsection (p)(3)(A)(i)" for "section 219(e)(3)" in subpar. (C), and substituted "subsection (p)(3)(B)" for "section 219(e)(4)" in subpar. (D).

Subsec. (p)(2)(A)(i). Pub. L. 99–514, §1134(a), amended cl. (i) generally. Prior to amendment, cl. (i) read as follows: "$50,000, or".

Subsec. (p)(2)(B)(ii). Pub. L. 99–514, §1134(d), amended cl. (ii) generally. Prior to amendment, cl. (ii) read as follows: "Clause (i) shall not apply to any loan used to acquire, construct, reconstruct, or substantially rehabilitate any dwelling unit which within a reasonable time is to be used (determined at the time the loan is made) as a principal residence of the participant or a member of the family (within the meaning of section 267(c)(4)) of the participant."

Subsec. (p)(2)(C), (D). Pub. L. 99–514, §1134(b), added subpar. (C) and redesignated former subpar. (C) as (D).

Subsec. (p)(3). Pub. L. 99–514, §1134(c), added par. (3) and redesignated former par. (3) as (4).

Pub. L. 99–514, §1101(b)(2)(B), amended par. (3) generally. Prior to amendment, par. (3) read as follows: "For purposes of this subsection, the term 'qualified employer plan' means any plan which was (or was determined to be) a qualified employer plan (as defined in section 219(e)(3) other than a plan described in subsection (e)(7)). For purposes of this subsection, such term includes any government plan (as defined in section 219(e)(4))."

Subsec. (p)(4), (5). Pub. L. 99–514, §1134(c), redesignated former pars. (3) and (4) as (4) and 5, respectively.

Subsec. (q). Pub. L. 99–514, §1123(b)(1)(B), substituted "10-percent" for "5-percent" in heading.

Subsec. (q)(1). Pub. L. 99–514, §1123(b)(1)(A), substituted "10 percent" for "5 percent".

Subsec. (q)(2). Pub. L. 99–514, §1123(b)(3), substituted "Paragraph (1)" for "This subsection" in introductory provisions.

Subsec. (q)(2)(B). Pub. L. 99–514, §1826(c), amended subpar. (B) generally. Prior to amendment, subpar. (B) read as follows: "made to a beneficiary (or to the estate of an annuitant) on or after the death of an annuitant,".

Subsec. (q)(2)(D). Pub. L. 99–514, §1123(b)(2), amended subpar. (D) generally. Prior to amendment, subpar. (D) read as follows: "which is one of a series of substantially equal periodic payments made for the life of a taxpayer or over a period extending for at least 60 months after the annuity starting date,".

Subsec. (q)(2)(E). Pub. L. 99–514, §1852(c)(2), inserted "(determined without regard to subsection (e)(7))".

Subsec. (q)(2)(G). Pub. L. 99–514, §1826(d), added subpar. (G).

Subsec. (q)(2)(I), (J). Pub. L. 99–514, §1123(b)(4), which added subpars. (I) and (J) directed the amendment of subpar. (G) by striking out "or" at the end thereof, and of subpar. (H) by striking out the period at the end thereof, could not be executed to subpars. (G) and (H) because subpar. (G) does not contain "or", and no subpar. (H) was enacted.

Subsec. (q)(3). Pub. L. 99–514, §1123(b)(3), added par. (3).

Subsec. (s)(1). Pub. L. 99–514, §1826(b)(2), substituted "any holder of such contract" for "the holder of such contract" in subpars. (A) and (B).

Subsec. (s)(5). Pub. L. 99–514, §1826(a), added par. (5).

Subsec. (s)(6), (7). Pub. L. 99–514, §1826(b)(1), added pars. (6) and (7).

Subsec. (t). Pub. L. 99–514, §1123(a), added subsec. (t) and redesignated former subsec. (t) as (u).

Subsecs. (u), (v). Pub. L. 99–514, §1135(a), added subsec. (u) and redesignated former subsec. (u) as (v).

1984—Subsec. (e)(5)(D). Pub. L. 98–369, §523(b)(1), substituted "Except as provided in paragraph (7), this" for "This".

Subsec. (e)(5)(D)(ii)(IV). Pub. L. 98–369, §211(b)(1), which directed substitution of "section 818(a)(3)" for "805(d)(3)" in subpar. (D)(i)(IV), was executed to subpar. (D)(ii)(IV) to reflect the probable intent of Congress.

Subsec. (e)(7). Pub. L. 98–369, §523(a), added par. (7).

Subsec. (k). Pub. L. 98–369, §421(b)(1), repealed subsec. (k) relating to payments in discharge of alimony.

Subsec. (m)(5). Pub. L. 98–369, §713(c)(1)(B), substituted "key employees" for "owner-employees" in heading.

Subsec. (m)(5)(A). Pub. L. 98–369, §521(d)(1), (2), substituted "5-percent owner" for "key employee" wherever appearing and struck out "in a top-heavy plan" at end of cl. (i).

Pub. L. 98–369, §713(c)(1)(A), substituted "as a key employee" for "as an owner-employee" in cl. (i).

Subsec. (m)(5)(C). Pub. L. 98–369, §521(d)(3), substituted "the term '5 percent owner' " for "the terms 'key employee' and 'top-heavy plan' ".

Subsec. (m)(9). Pub. L. 98–369, §713(d)(1), repealed par. (9) relating to return of excess contributions before due date of return.

Subsec. (m)(10). Pub. L. 98–397 added par. (10).

Subsec. (o)(1). Pub. L. 98–369, §491(d)(3), substituted "402 and 403" for "402, 403, and 405".

Subsec. (o)(3)(A). Pub. L. 98–369, §713(b)(1)(A), inserted "(other than the exception contained in paragraph (2) thereof)".

Subsec. (o)(4). Pub. L. 98–369, §491(d)(4), substituted "and 408(d)(3)" for "408(d)(3), and 409(b)(3)(C)".

Subsec. (p)(2)(A). Pub. L. 98–369, §713(b)(1)(B), inserted at end "For purposes of clause (ii), the present value of the nonforfeitable accrued benefit shall be determined without regard to any accumulated deductible employee contributions (as defined in subsection (o)(5)(B))."

Subsec. (p)(2)(A)(ii). Pub. L. 98–369, §713(b)(4), substituted as cl. (ii) "the greater of (I) one-half of the present value of the nonforfeitable accrued benefit of the employee under the plan, or (II) $10,000" for "½ of the present value of the nonforfeitable accrued benefit of the employee under the plan (but not less than $10,000)".

Subsec. (p)(3). Pub. L. 98–369, §523(b)(2), inserted "other than a plan described in subsection (e)(7)".

Subsec. (q)(1). Pub. L. 98–369, §222(a), amended par. (1) generally, striking out designation "(A) In general.—" preceding text, substituting "which is includible in gross income" for "includible in gross income which is properly allocable to any investment in the annuity contract made during the 10-year period ending on the date such amount was received by the taxpayer", and striking out former subpar. (B), which had provided that for purposes of subpar. (A), the amount includible in gross income would be allocated to the earliest investment in the contract with respect to which amounts had not been previously fully allocated under this par.

Subsecs. (s), (t). Pub. L. 98–369, §222(b), added subsec. (s) and redesignated former subsec. (s) as (t).

1983—Subsec. (o)(2)(A). Pub. L. 97–448, §103(c)(6), struck out "to which the employee made one or more deductible employee contributions" after "from a qualified employer plan or government plan".

Subsec. (p)(3). Pub. L. 97–448, §103(c)(3)(B)(i), struck out "without regard to subparagraph (D) thereof" after "as defined in section 219(e)(3)".

Subsecs. (r), (s). Pub. L. 98–76 added subsec. (r) and redesignated former subsec. (r) as (s).

1982—Subsec. (e). Pub. L. 97–248, §265(a), in par. (1) substituted provisions relating to the application of this subsection to amounts received under annuity, endowment, or life insurance contracts which are not received as annuities and to amounts received as dividends for provisions which stated a general rule relating to the includability as gross income of amounts that were received under annuity, endowment, or life insurance contracts which were not received as annuities and also stated that for the purposes of this section amounts which were received as dividends would be treated as amounts not received as an annuity, in par. (2) substituted provisions stating a general rule as to the includability as gross income of amounts received before or after the annuity starting date for provisions which set out those amounts which would be treated as amounts not received as an annuity, and added pars. (3) to (6).

Subsec. (m)(4). Pub. L. 97–248, §236(b)(1), struck out par. (4) which related to amounts constructively received with respect to assignments or pledges, and loans on contracts.

Subsec. (m)(5). Pub. L. 97–248, §237(d)(1), (2), in subpar. (A) substituted applicability to key employees for applicability to owner-employees and added subpar. (C).

Subsec. (m)(6). Pub. L. 97–248, §237(d)(3), struck out "except in applying paragraph (5)," after "shall".

Subsec. (m)(8). Pub. L. 97–248, §236(b)(1), struck out par. (8) which related to loans to owner-employees.

Subsec. (o)(3)(A). Pub. L. 97–248, §236(b)(2), substituted reference to subsec. (p) of this section for references to subsec. (m)(4) and (8) of this section.

Subsec. (p). Pub. L. 97–248, §236(a), added subsec. (p). Former subsec. (p) redesignated (q).

Subsec. (q). Pub. L. 97–248, §265(b)(1), added subsec. (q). Former subsec. (q) redesignated (r).

Pub. L. 97–248, §236(a), redesignated former subsec. (p) as (q).

Subsec. (r). Pub. L. 97–248, §§236(a), 265(b)(1), redesignated former subsec. (p) as (r).

1981—Subsec. (m)(6). Pub. L. 97–34, §312(d)(1), expanded definition of "owner-employee" to include an employee within the meaning of section 401(c)(1) except in applying paragraph (5).

Subsec. (m)(8). Pub. L. 97–34, §312(d)(2), added par. (8).

Subsec. (m)(9). Pub. L. 97–34, §312(e)(1), added par. (9).

Subsecs. (o), (p). Pub. L. 97–34, §311(b)(1), added subsec. (o) and redesignated former subsec. (o) as (p).

1976—Subsec. (c)(2), (3)(A). Pub. L. 94–455, §1906(b)(13)(A), struck out "or his delegate" after "Secretary".

Subsec. (d)(1). Pub. L. 94–455, §1901(a)(12), struck out in subpar. (B) "(whether or not before January 1, 1954)" after "beginning on the date", and in provisions following subpar. (B) struck out "(under this paragraph and prior income tax laws)" after "until there has been so excluded".

Subsec. (f). Pub. L. 94–455, §1906(b)(13)(A), struck out "or his delegate" after "Secretary".

Subsec. (i). Pub. L. 94–455, §1951(b)(1)(A), struck out subsec. (i) which related to joint annuities where first annuitant died in 1951, 1952, or 1953.

Subsec. (m)(2), (3). Pub. L. 94–455, §1906(b)(13)(A), struck out "or his delegate" after "Secretary".

Subsec. (m)(4)(A). Pub. L. 94–455, §1901(a)(13), substituted "an individual retirement account" for "an individual retirement amount".

Subsec. (m)(5)(A)(ii), (7). Pub. L. 94–455, §1906(b)(13)(A), struck out "or his delegate" after "Secretary".

1974—Subsec. (m)(1). Pub. L. 93–406, §2001(h)(2), struck out par. (1) which related to certain amounts received before annuity starting date.

Subsec. (m)(4)(A). Pub. L. 93–406, §2002(g)(10)(A), inserted references to an individual retirement amount described in section 408(a) and an individual retirement annuity described in section 408(b).

Subsec. (m)(5)(A). Pub. L. 93–406, §2001(e)(5), (h)(3), substituted "(other than contributions made by him as an owner-employee)" for "(whether or not paid by him)" in cl. (i), and struck out cl. (iii) which had made reference to amounts which were received, by an individual who was or had been, an owner-employee, by reason of the distribution under the provisions of section 401(e)(2)(E) of his entire interest in all qualified trusts described in section 401(a) and in all plans described in section 403(a).

Subsec. (m)(5)(B). Pub. L. 93–406, §2001(g)(1), substituted provisions that if a person receives an amount to which subsec. (m)(5) applies, his tax under this chapter for the taxable year in which such amount is received shall be increased by an amount equal to 10 percent of the portion of the amount so received which is includible in his gross income for such taxable year for provisions that if the aggregate amounts to which subsec. (m)(5) applied received by any person in his taxable year equalled or exceeded $2,500, the increase in his tax for the taxable year in which such amounts were received and attributable to such amounts could not be less than 110 percent of the aggregate increase in taxes, for the taxable year and the 4 immediately preceding taxable years, which would have resulted if such amounts had been included in such person's gross income ratably over such taxable years, with provision for alternate computation if deductions had been allowed under section 404 for contributions paid for a number of prior taxable years less than 4.

Subsec. (m)(5)(C) to (E). Pub. L. 93–406, §2001(g)(2)(A), struck out subpars. (C) to (E) which contained special rules for the application of subsec. (m)(5).

Subsec. (m)(6). Pub. L. 93–406, §2002(g)(10)(B), inserted reference to an individual for whose benefit an individual retirement account or annuity described in section 408(a) or (b) is maintained.

Subsec. (n). Pub. L. 93–406, §§2005(c)(3), 2007(b)(2), redesignated former subsec. (o) as (n) and in heading of subsec. (n) as so redesignated inserted reference to survivor benefit plan. Former subsec. (n), which set out provisions covering the treatment to be accorded total distributions, was struck out.

Subsec. (o). Pub. L. 93–406, §2005(c)(3), redesignated former subsec. (p) as (o). Former subsec. (o) redesignated (n) and amended.

Subsec. (p). Pub. L. 93–406, §2005(c)(3), redesignated subsec. (p) as (o).

1969—Subsec. (n)(1). Pub. L. 91–172, §515(b)(1), altered section to accommodate the insertion into sections 402 and 403 of provisions under which employer contributions to qualified pension, profit sharing, stock bonus, and annuity plans for plan years beginning after 1969 are to be treated as ordinary income when received in a lump sum distribution, but with such amounts to be eligible for a special averaging procedure.

Subsec. (n)(4). Pub. L. 91–172, §515(b)(2), added par. (4).

1966—Subsecs. (o), (p). Pub. L. 89–365 added subsec. (o) and redesignated former subsec. (o) as (p).

1965—Subsec. (m)(5)(A)(i). Pub. L. 89–97, §106(d)(2)(A), substituted "paragraph (7) of this subsection" for "section 213(g)(3)".

Subsec. (m)(7). Pub. L. 89–97, §106(d)(2)(B), added par. (7).

Subsec. (n)(1). Pub. L. 89–97, §106(d)(2)(C), substituted in subpars. (A)(iii) and (B)(iii) "subsection (m)(7)" for "section 213(g)(3)".

Subsec. (n)(3). Pub. L. 89–44 substituted "sections 31 and 39" for "section 31" in sentence following subpar. (B).

1964—Subsec. (e)(3). Pub. L. 88–272 struck out par. (3) which provided for a limit on the tax attributable to the receipt of a lump sum.

1962—Subsec. (d)(2). Pub. L. 87–792, §4(a), designated existing provisions as cl. (A) and added cl. (B).

Subsec. (f). Pub. L. 87–834 inserted sentence providing that par. (2) shall not apply to amounts which were contributed by the employer after Dec. 31, 1962, and which would not have been includible in the gross income of the employee by reason of the application of Section 911 if such amounts had been paid directly to the employee at the time of contribution, and making such sentence inapplicable to amounts which were contributed by the employer, as determined under regulations, to provide pension or annuity credits, to the extent such credits are attributable to services performed before Jan. 1, 1963, and are provided pursuant to pension or annuity plan provisions in existence on Mar. 12, 1962, and on that date applicable to such services.

Subsecs. (m) to (o). Pub. L. 87–792, §4(b), added subsecs. (m) and (n) and redesignated former subsec. (m) as (o).

STATUTORY NOTES AND RELATED SUBSIDIARIES
EFFECTIVE DATE OF 2019 AMENDMENT

Pub. L. 116–94, div. O, title I, §108(b), Dec. 20, 2019, 133 Stat. 3149, provided that: "The amendments made by subsection (a) [amending this section] shall apply to loans made after the date of the enactment of this Act [Dec. 20, 2019]."

Pub. L. 116–94, div. O, title I, §113(b), Dec. 20, 2019, 133 Stat. 3156, provided that: "The amendments made by this section [amending this section] shall apply to distributions made after December 31, 2019."

EFFECTIVE DATE OF 2015 AMENDMENT

Pub. L. 114–113, div. Q, title III, §308(b), Dec. 18, 2015, 129 Stat. 3089, provided that: "The amendments made by this section [amending this section] shall apply to distributions after December 31, 2015."

Pub. L. 114–26, §2(d), June 29, 2015, 129 Stat. 319, provided that: "The amendments made by this section [amending this section] shall apply to distributions after December 31, 2015."

EFFECTIVE DATE OF 2014 AMENDMENT

Amendment by Pub. L. 113–295 effective Dec. 19, 2014, subject to a savings provision, see section 221(b) of Pub. L. 113–295, set out as a note under section 1 of this title.

EFFECTIVE DATE OF 2010 AMENDMENT

Pub. L. 111–240, title II, §2113(b), Sept. 27, 2010, 124 Stat. 2567, provided that: "The amendment made by this section [amending this section] shall apply to amounts received in taxable years beginning after December 31, 2010."

EFFECTIVE DATE OF 2008 AMENDMENT

Pub. L. 110–458, title I, §112, Dec. 23, 2008, 122 Stat. 5113, provided that: "Except as otherwise provided in this subtitle [subtitle A (§§101–112) of title I of Pub. L. 110–458, see Tables for classification], the amendments made by this subtitle shall take effect as if included in the provisions of the 2006 Act [Pub. L. 109–280] to which the amendments relate."

Pub. L. 110–245, title I, §107(b), June 17, 2008, 122 Stat. 1631, provided that: "The amendment made by this section [amending this section] shall apply to individuals ordered or called to active duty on or after December 31, 2007."

EFFECTIVE DATE OF 2006 AMENDMENT

Pub. L. 109–280, title VIII, §827(c), Aug. 17, 2006, 120 Stat. 1001, provided that:

"(1) Effective date.——The amendment made by this section [amending this section and sections 401 and 403 of this title] shall apply to distributions after September 11, 2001.

"(2) Waiver of limitations.——If refund or credit of any overpayment of tax resulting from the amendments made by this section is prevented at any time before the close of the 1-year period beginning on the date of the enactment of this Act [Aug. 17, 2006] by the operation of any law or rule of law (including res judicata), such refund or credit may nevertheless be made or allowed if claim therefor is filed before the close of such period."

Pub. L. 109–280, title VIII, §828(b), Aug. 17, 2006, 120 Stat. 1001, provided that: "The amendment made by this section [amending this section] shall apply to distributions after the date of the enactment of this Act [Aug. 17, 2006]."

Pub. L. 109–280, title VIII, §844(g), Aug. 17, 2006, 120 Stat. 1013, provided that:

"(1) In general.——Except as otherwise provided in this subsection, the amendments made by this section [enacting section 6050U of this title and amending this section and sections 848, 1035, 6724, and 7702B of this title] shall apply to contracts issued after December 31, 1996, but only with respect to taxable years beginning after December 31, 2009.

"(2) Tax-free exchanges.——The amendments made by subsection (b) [amending section 1035 of this title] shall apply with respect to exchanges occurring after December 31, 2009.

"(3) Information reporting.——The amendments made by subsection (d) [enacting section 6050U of this title and amending section 6724 of this title] shall apply to charges made after December 31, 2009.

"(4) Policy acquisition expenses.——The amendment made by subsection (e) [amending section 848 of this title] shall apply to specified policy acquisition expenses determined for taxable years beginning after December 31, 2009.

"(5) Technical amendment.——The amendment made by subsection (f) [amending section 7702B of this title] shall take effect as if included in section 321(a) of the Health Insurance Portability and Accountability Act of 1996 [Pub. L. 104–191]."

EFFECTIVE DATE OF 2004 AMENDMENT

Pub. L. 108–357, title VIII, §906(c), Oct. 22, 2004, 118 Stat. 1654, provided that: "The amendments made by this section [amending this section and section 83 of this title] shall apply to distributions on or after the date of the enactment of this Act [Oct. 22, 2004]."

Amendment by section 207(6), (7) of Pub. L. 108–311 applicable to taxable years beginning after Dec. 31, 2004, see section 208 of Pub. L. 108–311, set out as a note under section 2 of this title.

EFFECTIVE DATE OF 2001 AMENDMENT

Amendment by Pub. L. 107–90 applicable to calendar years beginning after Dec. 31, 2001, see section 204(f) of Pub. L. 107–90, set out as a note under section 24 of this title.

Amendment by Pub. L. 107–22 effective July 26, 2001, see section 1(c) of Pub. L. 107–22, set out as a note under section 26 of this title.

Pub. L. 107–16, title IV, §402(h), June 7, 2001, 115 Stat. 63, provided that: "The amendments made by this section [amending this section and sections 135, 221, 529, 530, 4973, and 6693 of this title] shall apply to taxable years beginning after December 31, 2001."

Pub. L. 107–16, title VI, §632(a)(4), June 7, 2001, 115 Stat. 115, provided that: "The amendments made by this subsection [amending this section and sections 402, 403, 404, 415, and 664 of this title] shall apply to years beginning after December 31, 2001."

Amendment by section 641(a)(2)(C), (e)(1) of Pub. L. 107–16 applicable to distributions after Dec. 31, 2001, see section 641(f)(1) of Pub. L. 107–16, set out as a note under section 402 of this title.

EFFECTIVE DATE OF 1998 AMENDMENT

Pub. L. 105–206, title III, §3436(b), July 22, 1998, 112 Stat. 761, provided that: "The amendments made by this section [amending this section] shall apply to distributions after December 31, 1999."

Amendment by section 6023(3), (4) of Pub. L. 105–206 effective July 22, 1998, see section 6023(32) of Pub. L. 105–206, set out as a note under section 34 of this title.

Amendment by sections 6004(d)(3)(B) and 6005(c)(1) of Pub. L. 105–206 effective, except as otherwise provided, as if included in the provisions of the Taxpayer Relief Act of 1997, Pub. L. 105–34, to which such amendment relates, see section 6024 of Pub. L. 105–206, set out as a note under section 1 of this title.

EFFECTIVE DATE OF 1997 AMENDMENT

Pub. L. 105–34, title II, §203(c), Aug. 5, 1997, 111 Stat. 809, provided that: "The amendments made by this section [amending this section] shall apply to distributions after December 31, 1997, with respect to expenses paid after such date (in taxable years ending after such date), for education furnished in academic periods beginning after such date."

Pub. L. 105–34, title III, §303(c), Aug. 5, 1997, 111 Stat. 831, provided that: "The amendments made by this section [amending this section] shall apply to payments and distributions in taxable years beginning after December 31, 1997."

Pub. L. 105–34, title X, §1075(c), Aug. 5, 1997, 111 Stat. 949, provided that: "The amendments made by this section [amending this section] shall apply with respect to annuity starting dates beginning after December 31, 1997."

EFFECTIVE DATE OF 1996 AMENDMENT

Pub. L. 104–191, title III, §361(d), Aug. 21, 1996, 110 Stat. 2072, provided that: "The amendments made by this section [amending this section] shall apply to distributions after December 31, 1996."

Pub. L. 104–188, title I, §1403(b), Aug. 20, 1996, 110 Stat. 1791, provided that: "The amendment made by this section [amending this section] shall apply in cases where the annuity starting date is after the 90th day after the date of the enactment of this Act [Aug. 20, 1996]."

Pub. L. 104–188, title I, §1421(e), Aug. 20, 1996, 110 Stat. 1800, provided that: "The amendments made by this section [amending this section, sections 219, 280G, 402, 404, 408, 414, 416, 457, 3121, 3306, 3401, 4972, and 6693 of this title, sections 1021 and 1104 of Title 29, Labor, and section 409 of Title 42, The Public Health and Welfare] shall apply to taxable years beginning after December 31, 1996."

Pub. L. 104–188, title I, §1463(b), Aug. 20, 1996, 110 Stat. 1824, provided that: "The amendment made by this section [amending this section] shall apply to taxable years beginning after December 31, 1996."

Pub. L. 104–188, title I, §1704(l)(2), Aug. 20, 1996, 110 Stat. 1882, provided that: "The amendment made by paragraph (1) [amending this section] shall take effect as if included in the amendments made by section 1122(c) of the Tax Reform Act of 1986 [Pub. L. 99–514]."

EFFECTIVE DATE OF 1992 AMENDMENT

Amendment by Pub. L. 102–318 applicable to distributions after Dec. 31, 1992, see section 521(e) of Pub. L. 102–318, set out as a note under section 402 of this title.

EFFECTIVE DATE OF 1989 AMENDMENT

Amendment by Pub. L. 101–239 effective, except as otherwise provided, as if included in the provision of the Technical and Miscellaneous Revenue Act of 1988, Pub. L. 100–647, to which such amendment relates, see section 7817 of Pub. L. 101–239, set out as a note under section 1 of this title.

EFFECTIVE DATE OF 1988 AMENDMENT

Amendment by sections 1011A(b)(1)(A), (B), (2), (9), (c)(1)–(8), (h), (i), and 1018(k), (t)(1)(A), (B), and (u)(8) of Pub. L. 100–647 effective, except as otherwise provided, as if included in the provision of the Tax Reform Act of 1986, Pub. L. 99–514, to which such amendment relates, see section 1019(a) of Pub. L. 100–647, set out as a note under section 1 of this title.

Amendment by section 5012(a), (b)(1), (d) of Pub. L. 100–647 applicable to contracts entered into on or after June 21, 1988, with special rule where death benefit increases by more than $150,000, certain other material changes taken into account, certain exchanges permitted, and special rule in the case of annuity contracts, see section 5012(e) of Pub. L. 100–647, set out as an Effective Date note under section 7702A of this title.

EFFECTIVE DATE OF 1986 AMENDMENT

Pub. L. 99–514, title XI, §1101(c), Oct. 22, 1986, 100 Stat. 2414, provided that: "The amendments made by this section [amending this section and section 219 of this title] shall apply to contributions for taxable years beginning after December 31, 1986."

Amendment by section 1122(c)(1) of Pub. L. 99–514 applicable to individuals whose annuity starting date is after July 1, 1986, amendment by section 1122(c)(2) of Pub. L. 99–514 applicable to individuals whose annuity starting date is after Dec. 31, 1986, and amendment by section 1122(c)(3) of Pub. L. 99–514 applicable to amounts received after July 1, 1986, in the case of any plan not described in section 72(e)(8)(D) of this title, see section 1122(h)(2) of Pub. L. 99–514, set out as a note under section 402 of this title.

Pub. L. 99–514, title XI, §1123(e), Oct. 22, 1986, 100 Stat. 2475, as amended by Pub. L. 100–647, title I, §1011A(c)(11), (12), Nov. 10, 1988, 102 Stat. 3476, provided that:

"(1) In general.—Except as otherwise provided in this subsection, the amendments made by this section [amending this section and sections 403 and 408 of this title] shall apply to taxable years beginning after December 31, 1986.

"(2) Subsection (c).—The amendments made by subsection (c) [amending section 403 of this title] shall apply to years beginning after December 31, 1988, but only with respect to distributions from contracts described in section 403(b) of the Internal Revenue Code of 1986 which are attributable to assets other than assets held as of the close of the last year beginning before January 1, 1989.

"(3) Exception where distribution commences.—The amendments made by this section shall not apply to distributions to any employee from a plan maintained by any employer if—

"(A) as of March 1, 1986, the employee separated from service with the employer,

"(B) as of March 1, 1986, the accrued benefit of the employee was in pay status pursuant to a written election providing a specific schedule for the distribution of the entire accrued benefit of the employee, and

"(C) such distribution is made pursuant to such written election.

"(4) Transition rule.—The amendments made by this section shall not apply with respect to any benefits with respect to which a designation is in effect under section 242(b)(2) of the Tax Equity and Fiscal Responsibility Act of 1982 [section 242(b)(2) of Pub. L. 97–248, formerly set out as an Effective Date of 1982 Amendment note under section 401 of this title].

"(5) Special rule for distributions under an annuity contract.—The amendments made by paragraphs (1), (2), and (3) of subsection (b) [amending this section] shall not apply to any distribution under an annuity contract if—

"(A) as of March 1, 1986, payments were being made under such contract pursuant to a written election providing a specific schedule for the distribution of the taxpayer's interest in such contract, and

"(B) such distribution is made pursuant to such written election."

Pub. L. 99–514, title XI, §1134(e), Oct. 22, 1986, 100 Stat. 2484, provided that: "The amendments made by this section [amending this section] shall apply to loans made, renewed, renegotiated, modified, or extended after December 31, 1986."

Pub. L. 99–514, title XI, §1135(b), Oct. 22, 1986, 100 Stat. 2485, provided that: "The amendment made by subsection (a) [amending this section] shall apply to contributions to annuity contracts after February 28, 1986."

Amendment by sections 1826(a), (d), 1852(a)(2), (c)(1)–(4), and 1854(b)(1) of Pub. L. 99–514 effective, except as otherwise provided, as if included in the provisions of the Tax Reform Act of 1984, Pub. L. 98–369, div. A, to which such amendment relates, see section 1881 of Pub. L. 99–514, set out as a note under section 48 of this title.

Pub. L. 99–514, title XVIII, §1826(b)(4), Oct. 22, 1986, 100 Stat. 2850, provided that: "The amendments made by this subsection [amending this section] shall apply to contracts issued after the date which is 6 months after the date of the enactment of this Act [Oct. 22, 1986] in taxable years ending after such date."

Pub. L. 99–514, title XVIII, §1826(c), Oct. 22, 1986, 100 Stat. 2850, as amended by Pub. L. 100–647, title I, §1018(t)(1)(D), Nov. 10, 1988, 102 Stat. 3587, provided that the amendment made by section 1826(c) of Pub. L. 99–514 is effective with respect to distributions commencing after the date 6 months after Oct. 22, 1986.

Pub. L. 99–514, title XVIII, §1854(b)(6), Oct. 22, 1986, 100 Stat. 2878, provided that: "The amendments made by paragraphs (1) and (2) [amending this section and section 404 of this title] shall not apply to dividends paid before January 1, 1986, if the taxpayer treated such dividends in a manner inconsistent with such amendments on a return filed with the Secretary before the date of the enactment of this Act [Oct. 22, 1986]."

Pub. L. 99–514, title XVIII, §1898(c)(1)(C), Oct. 22, 1986, 100 Stat. 2951, provided that: "The amendments made by this paragraph [amending this section and section 402 of this title] shall apply to payments made after the date of the enactment of this Act [Oct. 22, 1986]."

Amendment by Pub. L. 98–397 effective Jan. 1, 1985, except as otherwise provided, see section 303(d) of Pub. L. 98–397, set out as a note under section 1001 of Title 29, Labor.

Amendment by section 211(b)(1) of Pub. L. 98–369 applicable to taxable years beginning after Dec. 31, 1983, see section 215 of Pub. L. 98–369, set out as an Effective Date note under section 801 of this title.

Pub. L. 98–369, div. A, title II, §222(c), July 18, 1984, 98 Stat. 774, as amended by Pub. L. 99–514, §2, Oct. 22, 1986, 100 Stat. 2095, provided:

"(1) In general.—The amendments made by this section [amending this section] shall apply to contracts issued after the day which is 6 months after the date of the enactment of this Act [July 18, 1984] in taxable years ending after such date.

"(2) Transitional rules for contracts issued before effective date.—In the case of any contract (other than a single premium contract) which is issued on or before the day which is 6 months after the date of the enactment of this Act, for purposes of section 72(q)(1)(A) of the Internal Revenue Code of 1986 [formerly I.R.C. 1954] (as in effect on the day before the date of the enactment of this Act), any investment in such contract which is made during any calendar year shall be treated as having been made on January 1 of such calendar year."

Amendment by section 421(b)(1) of Pub. L. 98–369 applicable to transfers after July 18, 1984, in taxable years ending after such date, subject to election to have repeal apply to transfers after 1983 or to transfers pursuant to existing decrees, see section 421(d) of Pub. L. 98–369, set out as an Effective Date note under section 1041 of this title.

Amendment by section 491(d)(3), (4) of Pub. L. 98–369 applicable to obligations issued after Dec. 31, 1983, see section 491(f)(1) of Pub. L. 98–369, set out as a note under section 62 of this title.

Amendment by section 521(d) of Pub. L. 98–369 applicable to years beginning after Dec. 31, 1984, see section 521(e) of Pub. L. 98–369, set out as a note under section 401 of this title.

Pub. L. 98–369, div. A, title V, §523(c), July 18, 1984, 98 Stat. 872, provided that: "The amendments made by this section [amending this section] shall apply to any amount received or loan made after the 90th day after the date of enactment of this Act [July 18, 1984]."

Amendment by section 713(b)(1), (4), (c)(1)(A), (B) of Pub. L. 98–369 effective as if included in the provision of the Tax Equity and Fiscal Responsibility Act of 1982, Pub. L. 97–248, to which such amendment relates, see section 715 of Pub. L. 98–369, set out as a note under section 31 of this title.

Pub. L. 98–369, div. A, title VII, §713(d)(1), July 18, 1984, 98 Stat. 957, as amended by Pub. L. 99–514, title XVIII, §1875(c)(5), Oct. 22, 1986, 100 Stat. 2895, provided that the amendment made by section 713(d)(1) of Pub. L. 98–369 is effective with respect to contributions made in taxable years beginning after Dec. 31, 1983.

Pub. L. 98–76, title II, §227(b), Aug. 12, 1983, 97 Stat. 426, as amended by Pub. L. 99–514, §2, Oct. 22, 1986, 100 Stat. 2095, provided that:

"(1) In general.—Except as provided in paragraph (2), the amendments made by section 224 [enacting section 6050G of this title, amending this section and section 86 of this title, and enacting provisions set out as a note under section 231n of Title 45, Railroads] shall apply to benefits received after December 31, 1983, in taxable years ending after such date.

"(2) Treatment of certain lump-sum payments received after december 31, 1983.—The amendments made by section 224 shall not apply to any portion of a lump-sum payment received after December 31, 1983, if the generally applicable payment date for such portion was before January 1, 1984.

"(3) No fresh start.—For purposes of determining whether any benefit received after December 31, 1983, is includible in gross income by reason of section 72(r) of the Internal Revenue Code of 1986 [formerly I.R.C. 1954], as added by this Act, the amendments made by section 224 be treated as having been in effect during all periods before 1984."

Pub. L. 97–448, title I, §103(c)(3)(B)(ii), Jan. 12, 1983, 96 Stat. 2376, provided that: "The amendment made by clause (i) [amending this section] shall take effect as if the matter struck out had never been included in such paragraph."

Amendment by title I of Pub. L. 97–448 effective, except as otherwise provided, as if it had been included in the provision of the Economic Recovery Tax Act of 1981, Pub. L. 97–34, to which such amendment relates, see section 109 of Pub. L. 97–448, set out as a note under section 1 of this title.

Pub. L. 97–248, title II, §236(c), Sept. 3, 1982, 96 Stat. 510, as amended by Pub. L. 97–448, title III, §306(a)(11), Jan. 12, 1983, 96 Stat. 2404; Pub. L. 98–369, div. A, title V, §554, title VII, §713(b)(2), July 18, 1984, 98 Stat. 897, 957; Pub. L. 99–514, §2, Oct. 22, 1986, 100 Stat. 2095, provided that:

"(1) In general.—The amendments made by this section [amending this section] shall apply to loans, assignments, and pledges made after August 13, 1982. For purposes of the preceding sentence, the outstanding balance of any loan which is renegotiated, extended, renewed, or revised after such date shall be treated as an amount received as a loan on the date of such renegotiation, extension, renewal, or revision.

"(2) Exception for certain loans used to repay outstanding obligations.—

"(A) In general.—Any qualified refunding loan shall not be treated as a distribution by reason of the amendments made by this section to the extent such loan is repaid before August 14, 1983.

"(B) Qualified refunding loan.—For purposes of subparagraph (A), the term 'qualified refunding loan' means any loan made after August 13, 1982, and before August 14, 1983, to the extent such loan is used to make a required principal payment.

"(C) Required principal payment.—For purposes of subparagraph (B), the term 'required principal payment' means any principal repayment on a loan made under the plan which was outstanding on August 13, 1982, if such repayment is required to be made after August 13, 1982, and before August 14, 1983 or if such loan was payable on demand.

"(D) Special rule for non-key employees.—In the case of a non-key employee (within the meaning of section 416(i)(2) of the Internal Revenue Code of 1986 [formerly I.R.C. 1954]), this paragraph shall be applied by substituting 'January 1, 1985' for 'August 14, 1983' each place it appears.

"(3) Treatment of certain renegotiations.—If—

"(A) the taxpayer after August 13, 1982, and before September 4, 1982, borrows money from a government plan (as defined in section 219(e)(4) of the Internal Revenue Code of 1986),

"(B) under the applicable State law, such loan requires the renegotiation of all outstanding prior loans made to the taxpayer under such plan, and

"(C) the renegotiation described in subparagraph (B) does not change the interest rate on, or extend the duration of, any such outstanding prior loan,

then the renegotiation described in subparagraph (B) shall not be treated as a renegotiation, extension, renewal, or revision for purposes of paragraph (1). If the renegotiation described in subparagraph (B) does not meet the requirements of subparagraph (C) solely because it extends the duration of any such outstanding prior loan, the requirements of subparagraph (C) shall be treated as met with respect to such renegotiation if, before April 1, 1983, such extension is eliminated."

Pub. L. 97–248, title II, §265(c), Sept. 3, 1982, 96 Stat. 547, provided that:

"(1) Subsection (a).—The amendments made by subsection (a) [amending this section] shall take effect on August 13, 1982.

"(2) Subsection (b).—The amendments made by subsection (b) [amending this section and sections 46, 50A, 53, 901, 1302, and 1304 of this title] shall apply to distributions after December 31, 1982."

Amendment by section 237(d) of Pub. L. 97–248 applicable to years beginning after Dec. 31, 1983, see section 241 of Pub. L. 97–248, set out as an Effective Date note under section 416 of this title.

Pub. L. 97–34, title III, §312(f), Aug. 13, 1981, 95 Stat. 285, as amended by Pub. L. 97–448, title I, §103(d)(3), 96 Stat. 2378, provided that:

"(1) In general.—Except as provided in paragraph (2), the amendments made by this section [amending this section and sections 219, 401, 404, 408, 1379, and 4972 of this title] shall apply to taxable years beginning after December 31, 1981.

"(2) Transitional rule.—The amendments made by subsection (d) [amending this section] shall not apply to any loan from a plan to a self-employed individual who is an employee within the meaning of section 401(c)(1) which is outstanding on December 31, 1981. For purposes of the preceding sentence, any loan which is renegotiated, extended, renewed, or revised after such date shall be treated as a new loan."

EFFECTIVE DATE OF 1976 AMENDMENT

Amendment by section 1901(a)(12), (13) of Pub. L. 94–455 applicable with respect to taxable years beginning after Dec. 31, 1976, see section 1901(d) of Pub. L. 94–455, set out as a note under section 2 of this title.

Pub. L. 94–455, title XIX, §1951(d), Oct. 4, 1976, 90 Stat. 1841, provided that: "Except as otherwise expressly provided, the amendments made by this section [see Tables for classification of section 1951 of Pub. L. 94–455] shall apply with respect to taxable years beginning after December 31, 1976."

EFFECTIVE DATE OF 1974 AMENDMENT

Amendment by section 2001(e)(5) of Pub. L. 93–406 applicable to contributions made in taxable years beginning after Dec. 31, 1975, see section 2001(i)(4) of Pub. L. 93–406, set out as a note under section 401 of this title.

Pub. L. 93–406, title II, §2001(i)(5), (6), Sept. 2, 1974, 88 Stat. 958, provided that:

"(5) The amendments made by subsection (g) [amending this section and sections 46, 50A, 56, 404, and 901 of this title] apply to distributions made in taxable years beginning after December 31, 1975.

"(6) The amendments made by subsection (h) [amending this section and section 401 of this title] apply to taxable years ending after the date of enactment of this Act [Sept. 2, 1974]."

Amendment by section 2002(g)(10) of Pub. L. 93–406 effective on Jan. 1, 1975, see section 2002(i)(2) of Pub. L. 93–406, set out as an Effective Date note under section 4973 of this title.

Amendment by section 2005(c)(3) of Pub. L. 93–406, applicable only with respect to distributions or payments made after Dec. 31, 1973, in taxable years beginning after Dec. 31, 1973, see section 2005(d) of Pub. L. 93–406, set out as a note under section 402 of this title.

Amendment by section 2007(b)(2) of Pub. L. 93–406 applicable to taxable years ending on or after Sept. 21, 1972, see section 2007(c) of Pub. L. 93–406, set out as a note under section 122 of this title.

EFFECTIVE DATE OF 1969 AMENDMENT

Amendment by Pub. L. 91–172 applicable to taxable years ending after Dec. 31, 1969, see section 515(d) of Pub. L. 91–172, set out as a note under section 402 of this title.

EFFECTIVE DATE OF 1966 AMENDMENT

Amendment by Pub. L. 89–365 applicable with respect to taxable years ending after Dec. 31, 1965, see section 1(d) of Pub. L. 89–365, set out as an Effective Date note under section 122 of this title.

EFFECTIVE DATE OF 1965 AMENDMENT

Amendment by Pub. L. 89–97 applicable to taxable years beginning after Dec. 31, 1966, see section 106(e) of Pub. L. 89–97, set out as a note under section 213 of this title.

Amendment by Pub. L. 89–44 applicable to taxable years beginning on or after July 1, 1965, see section 809(f) of Pub. L. 89–44, set out as a note under section 6420 of this title.

EFFECTIVE DATE OF 1964 AMENDMENT

Amendment by Pub. L. 88–272 applicable to taxable years beginning after Dec. 31, 1963, see section 232(g) of Pub. L. 88–272, set out as a note under section 5 of this title.

EFFECTIVE DATE OF 1962 AMENDMENT

Pub. L. 87–834, §11(c)(2), Oct. 16, 1962, 76 Stat. 1006, provided that: "The amendment made by subsection (b) [amending this section] shall apply to taxable years ending after December 31, 1962."

Amendment by Pub. L. 87–792 applicable to taxable years beginning after Dec. 31, 1962, see section 8 of Pub. L. 87–792, set out as a note under section 22 of this title.

SAVINGS PROVISION

For provisions that nothing in amendment by Pub. L. 101–508 be construed to affect treatment of certain transactions occurring, property acquired, or items of income, loss, deduction, or credit taken into account prior to Nov. 5, 1990, for purposes of determining liability for tax for periods ending after Nov. 5, 1990, see section 11821(b) of Pub. L. 101–508, set out as a note under section 45K of this title.

Pub. L. 94–455, title XIX, §1951(b)(1)(B), Oct. 4, 1976, 90 Stat. 1836, provided that: "Notwithstanding subparagraph (A) [repealing subsec. (i) of this section], if the provisions of section 72(i) applied to amounts received in taxable years beginning before January 1, 1977, under an annuity contract, then amounts received under such contract on or after such date shall be treated as if such provisions were not repealed."

SPECIAL RULES FOR USE OF RETIREMENT FUNDS

Pub. L. 116–136, div. A, title II, §2202, Mar. 27, 2020, 134 Stat. 340, as amended by Pub. L. 116–260, div. N, title II, §280(a), Dec. 27, 2020, 134 Stat. 1982, provided that:

"(a) Tax-favored Withdrawals From Retirement Plans.—

"(1) In general.—Section 72(t) of the Internal Revenue Code of 1986 shall not apply to any coronavirus-related distribution.

"(2) Aggregate dollar limitation.—

"(A) In general.—For purposes of this subsection, the aggregate amount of distributions received by an individual which may be treated as coronavirus-related distributions for any taxable year shall not exceed $100,000.

"(B) Treatment of plan distributions.—If a distribution to an individual would (without regard to subparagraph (A)) be a coronavirus-related distribution, a plan shall not be treated as violating any requirement of the Internal Revenue Code of 1986 merely because the plan treats such distribution as a coronavirus-related distribution, unless the aggregate amount of such distributions from all plans maintained by the employer (and any member of any controlled group which includes the employer) to such individual exceeds $100,000.

"(C) Controlled group.—For purposes of subparagraph (B), the term 'controlled group' means any group treated as a single employer under subsection (b), (c), (m), or (o) of section 414 of the Internal Revenue Code of 1986.

"(3) Amount distributed may be repaid.—

"(A) In general.—Any individual who receives a coronavirus-related distribution may, at any time during the 3-year period beginning on the day after the date on which such distribution was received, make 1 or more contributions in an aggregate amount not to exceed the amount of such distribution to an eligible retirement plan of which such individual is a beneficiary and to which a rollover contribution of such distribution could be made under section 402(c), 403(a)(4), 403(b)(8), 408(d)(3), or 457(e)(16), of the Internal Revenue Code of 1986, as the case may be.

"(B) Treatment of repayments of distributions from eligible retirement plans other than iras.—For purposes of the Internal Revenue Code of 1986, if a contribution is made pursuant to subparagraph (A) with respect to a coronavirus-related distribution from an eligible retirement plan other than an individual retirement plan, then the taxpayer shall, to the extent of the amount of the contribution, be treated as having received the coronavirus-related distribution in an eligible rollover distribution (as defined in section 402(c)(4) of such Code) and as having transferred the amount to the eligible retirement plan in a direct trustee to trustee transfer within 60 days of the distribution.

"(C) Treatment of repayments of distributions from iras.—For purposes of the Internal Revenue Code of 1986, if a contribution is made pursuant to subparagraph (A) with respect to a coronavirus-related distribution from an individual retirement plan (as defined by section 7701(a)(37) of such Code), then, to the extent of the amount of the contribution, the coronavirus-related distribution shall be treated as a distribution described in section 408(d)(3) of such Code and as having been transferred to the eligible retirement plan in a direct trustee to trustee transfer within 60 days of the distribution.

"(4) Definitions.—For purposes of this subsection—

"(A) Coronavirus-related distribution.—Except as provided in paragraph (2), the term 'coronavirus-related distribution' means any distribution from an eligible retirement plan made—

"(i) on or after January 1, 2020, and before December 31, 2020,

"(ii) to an individual—

"(I) who is diagnosed with the virus SARS–CoV–2 or with coronavirus disease 2019 (COVID–19) by a test approved by the Centers for Disease Control and Prevention,

"(II) whose spouse or dependent (as defined in section 152 of the Internal Revenue Code of 1986) is diagnosed with such virus or disease by such a test, or

"(III) who experiences adverse financial consequences as a result of being quarantined, being furloughed or laid off or having work hours reduced due to such virus or disease, being unable to work due to lack of child care due to such virus or disease, closing or reducing hours of a business owned or operated by the individual due to such virus or disease, or other factors as determined by the Secretary of the Treasury (or the Secretary's delegate).

"(B) Employee certification.—The administrator of an eligible retirement plan may rely on an employee's certification that the employee satisfies the conditions of subparagraph (A)(ii) in determining whether any distribution is a coronavirus-related distribution.

"(C) Eligible retirement plan.—The term 'eligible retirement plan' has the meaning given such term by section 402(c)(8)(B) of the Internal Revenue Code of 1986.

"(5) Income inclusion spread over 3-year period.—

"(A) In general.—In the case of any coronavirus-related distribution, unless the taxpayer elects not to have this paragraph apply for any taxable year, any amount required to be included in gross income for such taxable year shall be so included ratably over the 3-taxable-year period beginning with such taxable year.

"(B) Special rule.—For purposes of subparagraph (A), rules similar to the rules of subparagraph (E) of section 408A(d)(3) of the Internal Revenue Code of 1986 shall apply.

"(6) Special rules.—

"(A) Exemption of distributions from trustee to trustee transfer and withholding rules.—For purposes of sections 401(a)(31), 402(f), and 3405 of the Internal Revenue Code of 1986, coronavirus-related distributions shall not be treated as eligible rollover distributions.

"(B) Coronavirus-related distributions treated as meeting plan distribution requirements.—For purposes of the Internal Revenue Code of 1986, a coronavirus-related distribution shall be treated as meeting the requirements of sections 401(k)(2)(B)(i), 403(b)(7)(A)(i), 403(b)(11), and 457(d)(1)(A) of such Code and section 8433(h)(1) of title 5, United States Code, and, in the case of a money purchase pension plan, a coronavirus-related distribution which is an in-service withdrawal shall be treated as meeting the distribution rules of section 401(a) of the Internal Revenue Code of 1986.

"(b) Loans From Qualified Plans.—

"(1) Increase in limit on loans not treated as distributions.—In the case of any loan from a qualified employer plan (as defined under section 72(p)(4) of the Internal Revenue Code of 1986) to a qualified individual made during the 180-day period beginning on the date of the enactment of this Act [Mar. 27, 2020]—

"(A) clause (i) of section 72(p)(2)(A) of such Code shall be applied by substituting '$100,000' for '$50,000', and

"(B) clause (ii) of such section shall be applied by substituting 'the present value of the nonforfeitable accrued benefit of the employee under the plan' for 'one-half of the present value of the nonforfeitable accrued benefit of the employee under the plan'.

"(2) Delay of repayment.—In the case of a qualified individual with an outstanding loan (on or after the date of the enactment of this Act) from a qualified employer plan (as defined in section 72(p)(4) of the Internal Revenue Code of 1986)—

"(A) if the due date pursuant to subparagraph (B) or (C) of section 72(p)(2) of such Code for any repayment with respect to such loan occurs during the period beginning on the date of the enactment of this Act and ending on December 31, 2020, such due date shall be delayed for 1 year,

"(B) any subsequent repayments with respect to any such loan shall be appropriately adjusted to reflect the delay in the due date under subparagraph (A) and any interest accruing during such delay, and

"(C) in determining the 5-year period and the term of a loan under subparagraph (B) or (C) of section 72(p)(2) of such Code, the period described in subparagraph (A) of this paragraph shall be disregarded.

"(3) Qualified individual.—For purposes of this subsection, the term 'qualified individual' means any individual who is described in subsection (a)(4)(A)(ii).

"(c) Provisions Relating to Plan Amendments.—

"(1) In general.—If this subsection applies to any amendment to any plan or annuity contract—

"(A) such plan or contract shall be treated as being operated in accordance with the terms of the plan during the period described in paragraph (2)(B)(i), and

"(B) except as provided by the Secretary of the Treasury (or the Secretary's delegate), such plan or contract shall not fail to meet the requirements of section 411(d)(6) of the Internal Revenue Code of 1986 and section 204(g) of the Employee Retirement Income Security Act of 1974 [29 U.S.C. 1054(g)] by reason of such amendment.

"(2) Amendments to which subsection applies.—

"(A) In general.—This subsection shall apply to any amendment to any plan or annuity contract which is made—

"(i) pursuant to any provision of this section, or pursuant to any regulation issued by the Secretary of the Treasury or the Secretary of Labor (or the delegate of either such Secretary) under any provision of this section, and

"(ii) on or before the last day of the first plan year beginning on or after January 1, 2022, or such later date as the Secretary of the Treasury (or the Secretary's delegate) may prescribe.

In the case of a governmental plan (as defined in section 414(d) of the Internal Revenue Code of 1986), clause (ii) shall be applied by substituting the date which is 2 years after the date otherwise applied under clause (ii).

"(B) Conditions.—This subsection shall not apply to any amendment unless—

"(i) during the period—

"(I) beginning on the date that this section or the regulation described in subparagraph (A)(i) takes effect (or in the case of a plan or contract amendment not required by this section or such regulation, the effective date specified by the plan), and

"(II) ending on the date described in subparagraph (A)(ii) (or, if earlier, the date the plan or contract amendment is adopted),

the plan or contract is operated as if such plan or contract amendment were in effect, and

"(ii) such plan or contract amendment applies retroactively for such period."

[Pub. L. 116–260, div. N, title II, §280(b), Dec. 27, 2020, 134 Stat. 1982, provided that: "The amendment made by this section [amending section 2202 of Pub. L. 116–136, set out above] shall apply as if included in the enactment of section 2202 of the CARES Act [Pub. L. 116–136, approved Mar. 27, 2020].")

APPLICABILITY OF SUBSECTION (T)

Pub. L. 100–647, title I, §1011A(c)(13), Nov. 10, 1988, 102 Stat. 3476, provided that: "Section 72(t) of the 1986 Code shall apply to any distribution without regard to whether such distribution is made without the consent of the participant pursuant to section 411(a)(11) or section 417(e) of the 1986 Code."

PLAN AMENDMENTS NOT REQUIRED UNTIL JANUARY 1, 1998

For provisions directing that if any amendments made by subtitle D [§§1401–1465] of title I of Pub. L. 104–188 require an amendment to any plan or annuity contract, such amendment shall not be required to be made before the first day of the first plan year beginning on or after Jan. 1, 1998, see section 1465 of Pub. L. 104–188, set out as a note under section 401 of this title.

PLAN AMENDMENTS NOT REQUIRED UNTIL JANUARY 1, 1994

For provisions directing that if any amendments made by subtitle B [§§521–523] of title V of Pub. L. 102–318 require an amendment to any plan, such plan amendment shall not be required to be made before the first plan year beginning on or after Jan. 1, 1994, see section 523 of Pub. L. 102–318, set out as a note under section 401 of this title.

PLAN AMENDMENTS NOT REQUIRED UNTIL JANUARY 1, 1989

For provisions directing that if any amendments made by subtitle A or subtitle C of title XI [§§1101–1147 and 1171–1177] or title XVIII [§§1800–1899A] of Pub. L. 99–514 require an amendment to any plan, such plan amendment shall not be required to be made before the first plan year beginning on or after Jan. 1, 1989, see section 1140 of Pub. L. 99–514, as amended, set out as a note under section 401 of this title.

DEFINITION OF TERMS USED IN TITLE I OF PUB. L. 110–458

Pub. L. 110–458, title I, §100, Dec. 23, 2008, 122 Stat. 5093, provided that: "For purposes of this title [see Tables for classification]:

"(1) Amendment of 1986 code.—The term '1986 Code' means the Internal Revenue Code of 1986.

"(2) Amendment of erisa.—The term 'ERISA' means the Employee Retirement Income Security Act of 1974 [Pub. L. 93–406; see Short Title note under section 1001 of Title 29, Labor].

"(3) 2006 act.—The term '2006 Act' means the Pension Protection Act of 2006 [Pub. L. 109–280; see Short Title of 2006 Amendment note under section 1001 of Title 29, Labor]."

¹ So in original. Probably should be paragraph "(2)(B)".

² So in original. The word "or" probably should not appear.

³ So in original. Probably should refer to section 8336a.

⁴ See References in Text note below.

§73. Services of child

(a) Treatment of amounts received

Amounts received in respect of the services of a child shall be included in his gross income and not in the gross income of the parent, even though such amounts are not received by the child.

(b) Treatment of expenditures

All expenditures by the parent or the child attributable to amounts which are includible in the gross income of the child (and not of the parent) solely by reason of subsection (a) shall be treated as paid or incurred by the child.

(c) Parent defined

For purposes of this section, the term "parent" includes an individual who is entitled to the services of a child by reason of having parental rights and duties in respect of the child.

(d) Cross reference

For assessment of tax against parent in certain cases, see section 6201(c).

(Aug. 16, 1954, ch. 736, 68A Stat. 24.)

§74. Prizes and awards

(a) General rule

Except as otherwise provided in this section or in section 117 (relating to qualified scholarships), gross income includes amounts received as prizes and awards.

(b) Exception for certain prizes and awards transferred to charities

Gross income does not include amounts received as prizes and awards made primarily in recognition of religious, charitable, scientific, educational, artistic, literary, or civic achievement, but only if—

(1) the recipient was selected without any action on his part to enter the contest or proceeding;

(2) the recipient is not required to render substantial future services as a condition to receiving the prize or award; and

(3) the prize or award is transferred by the payor to a governmental unit or organization described in paragraph (1) or (2) of section 170(c) pursuant to a designation made by the recipient.

(c) Exception for certain employee achievement awards

(1) In general

Gross income shall not include the value of an employee achievement award (as defined in section 274(j)) received by the taxpayer if the cost to the employer of the employee achievement award does not exceed the amount allowable as a deduction to the employer for the cost of the employee achievement award.

(2) Excess deduction award

If the cost to the employer of the employee achievement award received by the taxpayer exceeds the amount allowable as a deduction to the employer, then gross income includes the greater of—

(A) an amount equal to the portion of the cost to the employer of the award that is not allowable as a deduction to the employer (but not in excess of the value of the award), or

(B) the amount by which the value of the award exceeds the amount allowable as a deduction to the employer.

The remaining portion of the value of such award shall not be included in the gross income of the recipient.

(3) Treatment of tax-exempt employers

In the case of an employer exempt from taxation under this subtitle, any reference in this subsection to the amount allowable as a deduction to the employer shall be treated as a reference to the amount which would be allowable as a deduction to the employer if the employer were not exempt from taxation under this subtitle.

(4) Cross reference

For provisions excluding certain de minimis fringes from gross income, see section 132(e).

(d) Exception for Olympic and Paralympic medals and prizes

(1) In general

Gross income shall not include the value of any medal awarded in, or any prize money received from the United States Olympic Committee on account of, competition in the Olympic Games or Paralympic Games.

(2) Limitation based on adjusted gross income

(A) In general

Paragraph (1) shall not apply to any taxpayer for any taxable year if the adjusted gross income (determined without regard to this subsection) of such taxpayer for such taxable year exceeds $1,000,000 (half of such amount in the case of a married individual filing a separate return).

(B) Coordination with other limitations

For purposes of sections 85(c), 86, 135, 137, 219, 221, and 469, adjusted gross income shall be determined after the application of paragraph (1) and before the application of subparagraph (A).

(Aug. 16, 1954, ch. 736, 68A Stat. 24; Pub. L. 99–514, title I, §§122(a)(1), 123(b)(1), Oct. 22, 1986, 100 Stat. 2109, 2113; Pub. L. 114–239, §2(a), Oct. 7, 2016, 130 Stat. 973; Pub. L. 115–97, title I, §13305(b)(1), Dec. 22, 2017, 131 Stat. 2126; Pub. L. 116–260, div. EE, title I, §104(b)(2)(B), Dec. 27, 2020, 134 Stat. 3041; Pub. L. 117–2, title IX, §9042(b)(1), Mar. 11, 2021, 135 Stat. 122.)

EDITORIAL NOTES
AMENDMENTS

2021—Subsec. (d)(2)(B). Pub. L. 117–2 inserted "85(c)," before "86".

2020—Subsec. (d)(2)(B). Pub. L. 116–260 struck out "222," after "221,".

2017—Subsec. (d)(2)(B). Pub. L. 115–97 struck out "199," after "137,".

2016—Subsec. (d). Pub. L. 114–239 added subsec. (d).

1986—Subsec. (a). Pub. L. 99–514, §123(b)(1), which directed that subsec. (a) be amended by substituting "(relating to qualified scholarships)" for "(relating to scholarship and fellowship grants)", was executed by making the substitution for "(relating to scholarships and fellowship grants)" to reflect the probable intent of Congress.

Pub. L. 99–514, §122(a)(1)(A), substituted "Except as otherwise provided in this section or" for "Except as provided in subsection (b) and".

Subsec. (b). Pub. L. 99–514, §122(a)(1)(B), (C), inserted "for certain prizes and awards transferred to charities" in heading and added par. (3).

Subsec. (c). Pub. L. 99–514, §122(a)(1)(D), added subsec. (c).

STATUTORY NOTES AND RELATED SUBSIDIARIES
CHANGE OF NAME

References to the United States Olympic Committee deemed to refer to the United States Olympic and Paralympic Committee, see section 220502(c) of Title 36, Patriotic and National Observances, Ceremonies, and Organizations.

EFFECTIVE DATE OF 2021 AMENDMENT

Pub. L. 117–2, title IX, §9042(c), Mar. 11, 2021, 135 Stat. 122, provided that: "The amendments made by this section [amending this section and sections 85, 86, 135, 137, 219, 221, 222, and 469 of this title] shall apply to taxable years beginning after December 31, 2019."

EFFECTIVE DATE OF 2020 AMENDMENT

Amendment by Pub. L. 116–260 applicable to taxable years beginning after Dec. 31, 2020, see section 104(c) of div. EE of Pub. L. 116–260, set out as a note under section 25A of this title.

EFFECTIVE DATE OF 2017 AMENDMENT

Pub. L. 115–97, title I, §13305(c), Dec. 22, 2017, 131 Stat. 2126, as amended by Pub. L. 115–141, div. T, §101(c), Mar. 23, 2018, 132 Stat. 1156, provided that:

"(1) In general.—Except as provided in paragraph (2), the amendments made by this section [amending this section and sections 86, 135, 137, 170, 172, 219, 221, 222, 246, 469, 613, and 613A of this title and repealing section 199 of this title] shall apply to taxable years beginning after December 31, 2017.

"(2) Transition rule for qualified payments of patrons of cooperatives.—

"(A) In general.—The amendments made by this section shall not apply to a qualified payment received by a taxpayer from a specified agricultural or horticultural cooperative in a taxable year of the taxpayer beginning after December 31, 2017, which is attributable to qualified production activities income with respect to which a deduction is allowable to the cooperative under section 199 of the Internal Revenue Code of 1986 (as in effect before the amendments made by this section) for a taxable year of the cooperative beginning before January 1, 2018. Any term used in this subparagraph which is also used in section 199 of such Code (as so in effect) shall have the same meaning as when used in such section.

"(B) Coordination with section 199a.—No deduction shall be allowed under section 199A of such Code for any qualified payment to which subparagraph (A) applies."

[Amendment by Pub. L. 115–141 to section 13305(c) of Pub. L. 115–97, set out above, effective as if included in section 13305 of Pub. L. 115–97, see section 101(d) of Pub. L. 115–141, set out as a note under section 62 of this title.]

EFFECTIVE DATE OF 2016 AMENDMENT

Pub. L. 114–239, §2(b), Oct. 7, 2016, 130 Stat. 973, provided that: "The amendment made by this section [amending this section] shall apply to prizes and awards received after December 31, 2015."

EFFECTIVE DATE OF 1986 AMENDMENT

Amendment by section 122(a)(1) of Pub. L. 99–514 applicable to prizes and awards granted after Dec. 31, 1986, see section 151(c) of Pub. L. 99–514, set out as a note under section 1 of this title.

Amendment by section 123(b)(1) of Pub. L. 99–514 applicable to taxable years beginning after Dec. 31, 1986, but only in the case of scholarships and fellowships granted after Aug. 16, 1986, see section 151(d) of Pub. L. 99–514, set out as a note under section 1 of this title.

APPLICABILITY OF CERTAIN AMENDMENTS BY PUBLIC LAW 99–514 IN RELATION TO TREATY OBLIGATIONS OF UNITED STATES

For nonapplication of amendment by section 123(b)(1) of Pub. L. 99–514 to the extent application of such amendment would be contrary to any treaty obligation of the United States in effect on Oct. 22, 1986, see section 1012(aa)(3) of Pub. L. 100–647, set out as a note under section 861 of this title.

§75. Dealers in tax-exempt securities

(a) Adjustment for bond premium

In computing the gross income of a taxpayer who holds during the taxable year a municipal bond (as defined in subsection (b)(1)) primarily for sale to customers in the ordinary course of his trade or business—

(1) if the gross income of the taxpayer from such trade or business is computed by the use of inventories and his inventories are valued on any basis other than cost, the cost of securities sold (as defined in subsection (b)(2)) during such year shall be reduced by an amount equal to the amortizable bond premium which would be disallowed as a deduction for such year by section 171(a)(2) (relating to deduction for amortizable bond premium) if the definition in section 171(d) of the term "bond" did not exclude such municipal bond; or

(2) if the gross income of the taxpayer from such trade or business is computed without the use of inventories, or by use of inventories valued at cost, and the municipal bond is sold or otherwise disposed of during such year, the adjusted basis (computed without regard to this paragraph) of the municipal bond shall be reduced by the amount of the adjustment which would be required under section 1016(a)(5) (relating to adjustment to basis for amortizable bond premium) if the definition in section 171(d) of the term "bond" did not exclude such municipal bond.

Notwithstanding the provisions of paragraph (1), no reduction to the cost of securities sold during the taxable year shall be made in respect of any obligation described in subsection (b)(1)(A)(ii) which is held by the taxpayer at the close of the taxable year; but in the taxable year in which any such obligation is sold or otherwise disposed of, if such obligation is a municipal bond (as defined in subsection (b)(1)), the cost of securities sold during such year shall be reduced by an amount equal to the adjustment described in paragraph (2), without regard to the fact that the taxpayer values his inventories on any basis other than cost.

(b) Definitions

For purposes of subsection (a)—

(1) The term "municipal bond" means any obligation issued by a government or political subdivision thereof if the interest on such obligation is excludable from gross income; but such term does not include such an obligation if—

(A)(i) it is sold or otherwise disposed of by the taxpayer within 30 days after the date of its acquisition by him, or

(ii) its earliest maturity or call date is a date more than 5 years from the date on which it was acquired by the taxpayer; and

(B) when it is sold or otherwise disposed of by the taxpayer—

(i) in the case of a sale, the amount realized, or

(ii) in the case of any other disposition, its fair market value at the time of such disposition,

is higher than its adjusted basis (computed without regard to this section and section 1016(a)(6)).

Determinations under subparagraph (B) shall be exclusive of interest.

(2) The term "cost of securities sold" means the amount ascertained by subtracting the inventory value of the closing inventory of a taxable year from the sum of—

(A) the inventory value of the opening inventory for such year, and

(B) the cost of securities and other property purchased during such year which would properly be included in the inventory of the taxpayer if on hand at the close of the taxable year.

(Aug. 16, 1954, ch. 736, 68A Stat. 25; Pub. L. 85–866, title I, §2(a), Sept. 2, 1958, 72 Stat. 1606.)

EDITORIAL NOTES
AMENDMENTS

1958—Subsec. (a). Pub. L. 85–866, §2(a)(2), (3), struck out "short-term" each place it appeared, and inserted sentence to provide that no reduction to cost of securities sold during taxable year shall be made in respect of subsec. (b)(1)(A)(ii) obligations held at close of year, and to permit reduction in cost of securities sold in taxable year sold if obligation is municipal bond.

Subsec. (b)(1). Pub. L. 85–866, §2(a)(1), substituted "municipal bond" for "short-term municipal bond", designated former subpars. (A) and (B) as (A)(i) and (ii), respectively, and added subpar. (B).

STATUTORY NOTES AND RELATED SUBSIDIARIES
EFFECTIVE DATE OF 1958 AMENDMENT

Pub. L. 85–866, §2(c), Sept. 2, 1958, 72 Stat. 1607, provided that: "The amendments made by subsections (a) and (b) [amending this section and section 1016 of this title] shall apply with respect to taxable years ending after December 31, 1957, but only with respect to obligations acquired after such date."

[§76. Repealed. Pub. L. 94–455, title XIX, §1901(a)(14), Oct. 4, 1976, 90 Stat. 1765]

Section, act Aug. 16, 1954, ch. 736, 68A Stat. 25, related to inclusion in gross of all income derived from mortgages made, or obligations issued, by a joint-stock land bank.

§77. Commodity credit loans

(a) Election to include loans in income

Amounts received as loans from the Commodity Credit Corporation shall, at the election of the taxpayer, be considered as income and shall be included in gross income for the taxable year in which received.

(b) Effect of election on adjustments for subsequent years

If a taxpayer exercises the election provided for in subsection (a) for any taxable year, then the method of computing income so adopted shall be adhered to with respect to all subsequent taxable years unless with the approval of the Secretary a change to a different method is authorized.

(Aug. 16, 1954, ch. 736, 68A Stat. 25; Pub. L. 94–455, title XIX, §1906(b)(13)(A), Oct. 4, 1976, 90 Stat. 1834.)

EDITORIAL NOTES
AMENDMENTS

1976—Subsec. (b). Pub. L. 94–455 struck out "or his delegate" after "Secretary".

§78. Gross up for deemed paid foreign tax credit

If a domestic corporation chooses to have the benefits of subpart A of part III of subchapter N (relating to foreign tax credit) for any taxable year, an amount equal to the taxes deemed to be paid by such corporation under subsections (a), (b), and (d) of section 960 (determined without regard to the phrase "80 percent of" in subsection (d)(1) thereof) for such taxable year shall be treated for purposes of this title (other than sections 245 and 245A) as a dividend received by such domestic corporation from the foreign corporation.

(Added Pub. L. 87–834, §9(b), Oct. 16, 1962, 76 Stat. 1001; amended Pub. L. 94–455, title X, §1033(b)(1), Oct. 4, 1976, 90 Stat. 1628; Pub. L. 115–97, title I, §14301(c)(1), Dec. 22, 2017, 131 Stat. 2222.)

EDITORIAL NOTES
AMENDMENTS

2017—Pub. L. 115–97 amended section generally. Prior to amendment, text read as follows: "If a domestic corporation chooses to have the benefits of subpart A of part III of subchapter N (relating to foreign tax credit) for any taxable year, an amount equal to the taxes deemed to be paid by such corporation under section 902(a) (relating to credit for corporate stockholder in foreign corporation) or under section 960(a)(1) (relating to taxes paid by foreign corporation) for such taxable year shall be treated for purposes of this title (other than section 245) as a dividend received by such domestic corporation from the foreign corporation."

1976—Pub. L. 94–455 substituted "section 902(a)" for "section 902(a)(1)" and "section 960(a)(1)" for "section 960(a)(1)(C)".

STATUTORY NOTES AND RELATED SUBSIDIARIES
EFFECTIVE DATE OF 2017 AMENDMENT

Pub. L. 115–97, title I, §14301(d), Dec. 22, 2017, 131 Stat. 2225, provided that: "The amendments made by this section [amending this section and sections 245, 535, 545, 814, 865, 901, 904 to 909, 958 to 960, 1291, 1293, and 6038 of this title and repealing section 902 of this title] shall apply to taxable years of foreign corporations beginning after December 31, 2017, and to taxable years of United States shareholders in which or with which such taxable years of foreign corporations end."

EFFECTIVE DATE OF 1976 AMENDMENT

Amendment by Pub. L. 94–455 applicable on different dates depending on the date the distributions were received, see section 1033(c) of Pub. L. 94–455, set out as a note under section 960 of this title.

EFFECTIVE DATE

Pub. L. 87–834, §9(e), Oct. 16, 1962, 76 Stat. 1001, provided that: "The amendments made by this section [enacting this section and amending sections 535, 545, 861, 901, and 902 of this title] shall apply—

"(1) in respect of any distribution received by a domestic corporation after December 31, 1964, and

"(2) in respect of any distribution received by a domestic corporation before January 1, 1965, in a taxable year of such corporation beginning after December 31, 1962, but only to the extent that such distribution is made out of the accumulated profits of a foreign corporation for a taxable year (of such foreign corporation) beginning after December 31, 1962.

For purposes of paragraph (2), a distribution made by a foreign corporation out of its profits which are attributable to a distribution received from a foreign subsidiary to which [former] section 902(b) applies shall be treated as made out of the accumulated profits of a foreign corporation for a taxable year beginning before January 1, 1963, to the extent that such distribution was paid out of the accumulated profits of such foreign subsidiary for a taxable year beginning before January 1, 1963."

§79. Group-term life insurance purchased for employees

(a) General rule

There shall be included in the gross income of an employee for the taxable year an amount equal to the cost of group-term life insurance on his life provided for part or all of such year under a policy (or policies) carried directly or indirectly by his employer (or employers); but only to the extent that such cost exceeds the sum of—

(1) the cost of $50,000 of such insurance, and

(2) the amount (if any) paid by the employee toward the purchase of such insurance.

(b) Exceptions

Subsection (a) shall not apply to—

(1) the cost of group-term life insurance on the life of an individual which is provided under a policy carried directly or indirectly by an employer after such individual has terminated his employment with such employer and is disabled (within the meaning of section 72(m)(7)),

(2) the cost of any portion of the group-term life insurance on the life of an employee provided during part or all of the taxable year of the employee under which—

(A) the employer is directly or indirectly the beneficiary, or

(B) a person described in section 170(c) is the sole beneficiary,

for the entire period during such taxable year for which the employee receives such insurance, and

(3) the cost of any group-term life insurance which is provided under a contract to which section 72(m)(3) applies.

(c) Determination of cost of insurance

For purposes of this section and section 6052, the cost of group-term insurance on the life of an employee provided during any period shall be determined on the basis of uniform premiums (computed on the basis of 5-year age brackets) prescribed by regulations by the Secretary.

(d) Nondiscrimination requirements

(1) In general

In the case of a discriminatory group-term life insurance plan—

(A) subsection (a)(1) shall not apply with respect to any key employee, and

(B) the cost of group-term life insurance on the life of any key employee shall be the greater of—

(i) such cost determined without regard to subsection (c), or

(ii) such cost determined with regard to subsection (c).

(2) Discriminatory group-term life insurance plan

For purposes of this subsection, the term "discriminatory group-term life insurance plan" means any plan of an employer for providing group-term life insurance unless—

(A) the plan does not discriminate in favor of key employees as to eligibility to participate, and

(B) the type and amount of benefits available under the plan do not discriminate in favor of participants who are key employees.

(3) Nondiscriminatory eligibility classification

(A) In general

A plan does not meet requirements of subparagraph (A) of paragraph (2) unless—

(i) such plan benefits 70 percent or more of all employees of the employer,

(ii) at least 85 percent of all employees who are participants under the plan are not key employees,

(iii) such plan benefits such employees as qualify under a classification set up by the employer and found by the Secretary not to be discriminatory in favor of key employees, or

(iv) in the case of a plan which is part of a cafeteria plan, the requirements of section 125 are met.

(B) Exclusion of certain employees

For purposes of subparagraph (A), there may be excluded from consideration—

(i) employees who have not completed 3 years of service;

(ii) part-time or seasonal employees;

(iii) employees not included in the plan who are included in a unit of employees covered by an agreement between employee representatives and one or more employers which the Secretary finds to be a collective bargaining agreement, if the benefits provided under the plan were the subject of good faith bargaining between such employee representatives and such employer or employers; and

(iv) employees who are nonresident aliens and who receive no earned income (within the meaning of section 911(d)(2)) from the employer which constitutes income from sources within the United States (within the meaning of section 861(a)(3)).

(4) Nondiscriminatory benefits

A plan does not meet the requirements of paragraph (2)(B) unless all benefits available to participants who are key employees are available to all other participants.

(5) Special rule

A plan shall not fail to meet the requirements of paragraph (2)(B) merely because the amount of life insurance on behalf of the employees under the plan bears a uniform relationship to the total compensation or the basic or regular rate of compensation of such employees.

(6) Key employee defined

For purposes of this subsection, the term "key employee" has the meaning given to such term by paragraph (1) of section 416(i). Such term also includes any former employee if such employee when he retired or separated from service was a key employee.

(7) Exemption for church plans

(A) In general

This subsection shall not apply to a church plan maintained for church employees.

(B) Definitions

For purposes of subparagraph (A), the terms "church plan" and "church employee" have the meaning given such terms by paragraphs (1) and (3)(B) of section 414(e), respectively, except that—

(i) section 414(e) shall be applied by substituting "section 501(c)(3)" for "section 501" each place it appears, and

(ii) the term "church employee" shall not include an employee of—

(I) an organization described in section 170(b)(1)(A)(ii) above the secondary school level (other than a school for religious training),

(II) an organization described in section 170(b)(1)(A)(iii), and

(III) an organization described in section 501(c)(3), the basis of the exemption for which is substantially similar to the basis for exemption of an organization described in subclause (II).

(8) Treatment of former employees

To the extent provided in regulations, this subsection shall be applied separately with respect to former employees.

(e) Employee includes former employee

For purposes of this section, the term "employee" includes a former employee.

(f) Exception for life insurance purchased in connection with qualified transfer of excess pension assets

Subsection (b)(3) and section 72(m)(3) shall not apply in the case of any cost paid (whether directly or indirectly) with assets held in an applicable life insurance account (as defined in section 420(e)(4)) under a defined benefit plan.

(Added Pub. L. 88–272, title II, §204(a)(1), Feb. 26, 1964, 78 Stat. 36; amended Pub. L. 89–97, title I, §106(d)(3), July 30, 1965, 79 Stat. 337; Pub. L. 94–455, title XIX, §1906(b)(13)(A), Oct. 4, 1976, 90 Stat. 1834; Pub. L. 97–248, title II, §244(a), Sept. 3, 1982, 96 Stat. 523; Pub. L. 98–369, div. A, title II, §223(a), (b), July 18, 1984, 98 Stat. 775; Pub. L. 99–514, title XI, §1151(c)(1), title XVIII, §1827(a)(1), (c), (d), Oct. 22, 1986, 100 Stat. 2503, 2850, 2851; Pub. L. 100–647, title V, §5013(a), Nov. 10, 1988, 102 Stat. 3666; Pub. L. 101–140, title II, §203(a)(1), (b)(1)(A), Nov. 8, 1989, 103 Stat. 830, 831; Pub. L. 101–508, title XI, §11703(e)(1), Nov. 5, 1990, 104 Stat. 1388–517; Pub. L. 112–141, div. D, title II, §40242(d), July 6, 2012, 126 Stat. 861.)

EDITORIAL NOTES
AMENDMENTS

2012—Subsec. (f). Pub. L. 112–141 added subsec. (f).

1990—Subsec. (d)(6). Pub. L. 101–508 substituted "any former employee" for "any retired employee".

1989—Subsec. (d). Pub. L. 101–140, §203(a)(1), amended subsec. (d) to read as if amendments by Pub. L. 99–514, §1151(c)(1), had not been enacted, see 1986 Amendment note below.

Subsec. (d)(7). Pub. L. 101–140, §203(b)(1)(A), amended par. (7) generally. Prior to amendment, par. (7) read as follows: "All employees who are treated as employed by a single employer under subsection (b), (c), or (m) of section 414 shall be treated as employed by a single employer for purposes of this section."

1988—Subsec. (c). Pub. L. 100–647 struck out at end "In the case of an employee who has attained age 64, the cost prescribed shall not exceed the cost with respect to such individual if he were age 63."

1986—Subsec. (d). Pub. L. 99–514, §1151(c)(1), amended subsec. (d) generally, substituting "In the case of a group-term life insurance plan which is a discriminatory employee benefit plan, subsection (a)(1) shall apply only to the extent provided in section 89." for provisions formerly designated as pars. (1)(A) and (B) that in the case of a discriminatory group-term life insurance plan subsec. (a)(1) shall not apply with respect to any key employee and the cost of group-term life insurance on the life of any key employee shall be determined without regard to subsec. (c), and striking out pars. (2) to (7) relating to classifications and eligibility classifications of nondiscriminatory plans.

Subsec. (d)(1)(B). Pub. L. 99–514, §1827(a)(1), amended subpar. (B) generally. Prior to amendment, subpar. (B) read as follows: "the cost of group-term life insurance on the life of any key employee shall be determined without regard to subsection (c)."

Subsec. (d)(6). Pub. L. 99–514, §1827(c), struck out ", except that subparagraph (A)(iv) of such paragraph shall be applied by not taking into account employees described in paragraph (3)(B) who are not participants in the plan" from first sentence and inserted provision that such term also includes any retired employee if such employee when he retired or separated from service was a key employee.

Subsec. (d)(8). Pub. L. 99–514, §1827(d), added par. (8).

1984—Subsec. (b)(1). Pub. L. 98–369, §223(a)(2), struck out "either has reached the retirement age with respect to such employer or" before "is disabled".

Subsec. (d)(1). Pub. L. 98–369, §223(b), designated existing provisions as subpar. (A) and added subpar. (B).

Subsec. (e). Pub. L. 98–369, §223(a)(1), added subsec. (e).

1982—Subsec. (d). Pub. L. 97–248 added subsec. (d).

1976—Subsec. (c). Pub. L. 94–455 struck out "or his delegate" after "Secretary".

1965—Subsec. (b)(1). Pub. L. 89–97 substituted "section 72(m)(7)" for "paragraph (3) of section 213(g), determined without regard to paragraph (4) thereof".

STATUTORY NOTES AND RELATED SUBSIDIARIES
EFFECTIVE DATE OF 2012 AMENDMENT

Amendment by Pub. L. 112–141 applicable to transfers made after July 6, 2012, see section 40242(h) of Pub. L. 112–141, set out as a note under section 420 of this title.

Pub. L. 101–508, title XI, §11703(e)(2), Nov. 5, 1990, 104 Stat. 1388–517, provided that: "The amendment made by paragraph (1) [amending this section] shall apply to employees separating from service after the date of the enactment of this Act [Nov. 5, 1990]."

EFFECTIVE DATE OF 1989 AMENDMENT

Pub. L. 101–140, title II, §203(c), Nov. 8, 1989, 103 Stat. 832, provided that: "The amendments made by this section [amending this section and sections 105, 117, 120, 125, 127, 129, 132, 162, 401, 414, 505, 3121, 3231, 3306, 3401, 4976, and 6652 of this title, section 409 of title 42, The Public Health and Welfare, and provisions set out as notes under sections 89 and 3121 of this title] shall take effect as if included in section 1151 of the Tax Reform Act of 1986 [Pub. L. 99–514, see section 1151(k) set out below]."

EFFECTIVE DATE OF 1988 AMENDMENT

Pub. L. 100–647, title V, §5013(b), Nov. 10, 1988, 102 Stat. 3666, provided that: "The amendment made by subsection (a) [amending this section] shall apply to taxable years beginning after December 31, 1988."

EFFECTIVE DATE OF 1986 AMENDMENT

Pub. L. 99–514, title XI, §1151(k), Oct. 22, 1986, 100 Stat. 2508, as amended by Pub. L. 100–647, title I, §1011B(a)(25), (26), Nov. 10, 1988, 102 Stat. 3486, provided that:

"(1) In general.—The amendments made by this section [enacting section 89 of this title and amending this section and sections 105, 106, 117, 120, 125, 127, 129, 132, 414, 505, 6039D, and 6652 of this title] shall apply to years beginning after the later of—

"(A) December 31, 1987, or

"(B) the earlier of—

"(i) the date which is 3 months after the date on which the Secretary of the Treasury or his delegate issues such regulations as are necessary to carry out the provisions of section 89 of the Internal Revenue Code of 1986 (as added by this section), or

"(ii) December 31, 1988.

Notwithstanding the preceding sentence, the amendments made by subsections (e)(1) and (i)(3)(C) [amending section 414 of this title] shall, to the extent they relate to sections 106, 162(i)(2), and 162(k) of the Internal Revenue Code of 1986, apply to years beginning after 1986.

"(2) Special rule for collective bargaining plan.—In the case of a plan maintained pursuant to 1 or more collective bargaining agreements between employee representatives and 1 or more employers ratified before March 1, 1986, the amendments made by this section [enacting section 89 of this title and amending this section and sections 105, 106, 117, 120, 125, 127, 129, 132, 414, 505, 6039D, and 6652 of this title] shall not apply to employees covered by such an agreement in years beginning before the earlier of—

"(A) the date on which the last of such collective bargaining agreements terminates (determined without regard to any extension thereof after February 28, 1986), or

"(B) January 1, 1991.

A plan shall not be required to take into account employees to which the preceding sentence applies for purposes of applying section 89 of the Internal Revenue Code of 1986 (as added by this section) to employees to which the preceding sentence does not apply for any year preceding the year described in the preceding sentence.

"(3) Exception for certain group-term insurance plans.—In the case of a plan described in section 223(d)(2) of the Tax Reform Act of 1984 [section 232(d)(2) of Pub. L. 98–369, set out as an Effective Date of 1984 Amendment note below], such plan shall be treated as meeting the requirements of section 89 of the Internal Revenue Code of 1986 (as added by this section) with respect to individuals described in section 223(d)(2) of such Act. An employer may elect to disregard such individuals in applying section 89 of such Code (as so added) to other employees of the employer.

"(4) Special rule for church plans.—In the case of a church plan (within the meaning of section 414(e)(3) of the Internal Revenue Code of 1986) maintaining an insured accident and health plan, the amendments made by this section [enacting section 89 of this title and amending this section and sections 105, 106, 117, 120, 125, 127, 129, 132, 414, 505, 6039D, and 6652 of this title] shall apply to years beginning after December 31, 1988.

"(5) Cafeteria plans.—The amendments made by subsection (d)(2) [amending sections 3121 and 3306 of this title and section 409 of Title 42, The Public Health and Welfare] shall apply to taxable years beginning after December 31, 1983.

"(6) Certain plans maintained by educational institutions.—If an educational organization described in section 170(b)(1)(A)(ii) of the Internal Revenue Code of 1986 makes an election under this paragraph with respect to a plan described in section 125(c)(2)(C) of such Code, the amendments made by this section shall apply with respect to such plan for plan years beginning after the date of the enactment of this Act [Oct. 22, 1986]."

Pub. L. 99–514, title XVIII, §1827(a)(2), Oct. 22, 1986, 100 Stat. 2850, provided that: "The amendment made by paragraph (1) [amending this section] shall apply to taxable years ending after the date of the enactment of this Act [Oct. 22, 1986]."

Amendment by section 1827(c), (d) of Pub. L. 99–514 effective, except as otherwise provided, as if included in the provisions of the Tax Reform Act of 1984, Pub. L. 98–369, div. A, to which such amendment relates, see section 1881 of Pub. L. 99–514, set out as a note under section 48 of this title.

EFFECTIVE DATE OF 1984 AMENDMENT

Pub. L. 98–369, div. A, title II, §223(d), July 18, 1984, 98 Stat. 775, as amended by Pub. L. 99–514, §2, title XVIII, §1827(b), Oct. 22, 1986, 100 Stat. 2095, 2850, provided that:

"(1) In general.—Except as provided in paragraph (2), the amendments made by this section [amending this section and section 83 of this title] shall apply to taxable years beginning after December 31, 1983.

"(2) Inclusion of former employees in the case of existing group-term insurance plans.—

"(A) In general.—The amendments made by subsection (a) [amending this section] shall not apply—

"(i) to any group-term life insurance plan of the employer in existence on January 1, 1984, or

"(ii) to any group-term life insurance plan of the employer (or a successor employer) which is a comparable successor to a plan described in clause (i),

but only with respect to an individual who attained age 55 on or before January 1, 1984, and was employed by such employer (or a predecessor employer) at any time during 1983. Such amendments also shall not apply to any employee who retired from employment on or before January 1, 1984, and who, when he retired, was covered by the plan (or a predecessor plan).

"(B) Special rule in the case of discriminatory group-term life insurance plan.—In the case of any plan which, after December 31, 1986, is a discriminatory group-term life insurance plan (as defined in section 79(d) of the Internal Revenue Code of 1986 [formerly I.R.C. 1954]), subparagraph (A) shall not apply in the case of any individual retiring under such plan after December 31, 1986.

"(C) Benefits to certain retired individuals not taken into account for purposes of determining whether plan is discriminatory.—For purposes of determining whether a plan described in subparagraph (A) meets the requirements of section 79(d) of the Internal Revenue Code of 1986 with respect to group-term life insurance for former employees, coverage provided to employees who retired on or before December 31, 1986, may, at the employer's election, be disregarded.

"(D) Comparable successor plans.—For purposes of subparagraph (A), a plan shall not fail to be treated as a comparable successor to a plan described in subparagraph (A)(i) with respect to any employee whose benefits do not increase under the successor plan."

EFFECTIVE DATE OF 1982 AMENDMENT

Pub. L. 97–248, title II, §244(b), Sept. 3, 1982, 96 Stat. 524, provided that: "The amendment made by subsection (a) [amending this section] shall apply to taxable years beginning after December 31, 1983."

EFFECTIVE DATE OF 1965 AMENDMENT

Amendment by Pub. L. 89–97 applicable to taxable years beginning after Dec. 31, 1966, see section 106(e) of Pub. L. 89–97, set out as a note under section 213 of this title.

EFFECTIVE DATE

Pub. L. 88–272, title II, §204(d), Feb. 26, 1964, 78 Stat. 37, as amended by Pub. L. 99–514, §2, Oct. 22, 1986, 100 Stat. 2095, provided that: "The amendments made by subsections (a) [amending this section and section 7701 of this title] and (c) [amending sections 6052 and 6678 of this title] and paragraph (3) of section 6652(a) of the Internal Revenue Code of 1986 [formerly I.R.C. 1954] (as amended by section 221(b)(2) of this Act), shall apply with respect to group-term life insurance provided after December 31, 1963, in taxable years ending after such date. The amendments made by subsection (b) [amending section 3401 of this title] shall apply with respect to remuneration paid after December 31, 1963, in the form of group-term life insurance provided after such date. In applying section 79(b) of the Internal Revenue Code of 1986 (as added by subsection (a)(1) of this section) to a taxable year beginning before May 1, 1964, if paragraph (2)(B) of such section applies with respect to an employee for the period beginning May 1, 1964, and ending with the close of his first taxable year ending after April 30, 1964, such paragraph (2)(B) shall be treated as applying with respect to such employee for the period beginning January 1, 1964, and ending April 30, 1964."

NONENFORCEMENT OF AMENDMENT MADE BY SECTION 1151 OF PUB. L. 99–514 FOR FISCAL YEAR 1990

No monies appropriated by Pub. L. 101–136 to be used to implement or enforce section 1151 of Pub. L. 99–514 or the amendments made by such section, see section 528 of Pub. L. 101–136, set out as a note under section 89 of this title.

PLAN AMENDMENTS NOT REQUIRED UNTIL JANUARY 1, 1989

For provisions directing that if any amendments made by subtitle A or subtitle C of title XI [§§1101–1147 and 1171–1177] or title XVIII [§§1800–1899A] of Pub. L. 99–514 require an amendment to any plan, such plan amendment shall not be required to be made before the first plan year beginning on or after Jan. 1, 1989, see section 1140 of Pub. L. 99–514, as amended, set out as a note under section 401 of this title.

§80. Restoration of value of certain securities

(a) General rule

In the case of a domestic corporation subject to the tax imposed by section 11 or 801, if the value of any security (as defined in section 165(g)(2))—

(1) which became worthless by reason of the expropriation, intervention, seizure, or similar taking by the government of any foreign country, any political subdivision thereof, or any agency or instrumentality of the foregoing of property to which such security was related, and

(2) which was taken into account as a loss from the sale or exchange of a capital asset or with respect to which a deduction for a loss was allowed under section 165,

is restored in whole or in part during any taxable year by reason of any recovery of money or other property in respect of the property to which such security was related, the value so restored (to the extent that, when added to the value so restored during prior taxable years, it does not exceed the amount of the loss described in paragraph (2)) shall, except as provided in subsection (b), be included in gross income for the taxable year in which such restoration occurs.

(b) Reduction for failure to receive tax benefit

The amount otherwise includible in gross income under subsection (a) in respect of any security shall be reduced by an amount equal to the amount (if any) of the loss described in subsection (a)(2) which did not result in a reduction of the taxpayer's tax under this subtitle for any taxable year, determined under regulations prescribed by the Secretary.

(c) Character of income

For purposes of this subtitle—

(1) Except as provided in paragraph (2), the amount included in gross income under this section shall be treated as ordinary income.

(2) If the loss described in subsection (a)(2) was taken into account as a loss from the sale or exchange of a capital asset, the amount included in gross income under this section shall be treated as long-term capital gain.

(d) Treatment under foreign expropriation loss recovery provisions

This section shall not apply to any recovery of a foreign expropriation loss to which section 1351 applies.

(Added Pub. L. 89–384, §1(b)(1), Apr. 8, 1966, 80 Stat. 101; amended Pub. L. 94–455, title XIX, §§1901(b)(3)(K), 1906(b)(13)(A), Oct. 4, 1976, 90 Stat. 1793, 1834; Pub. L. 98–369, div. A, title II, §211(b)(2), July 18, 1984, 98 Stat. 754.)

EDITORIAL NOTES
AMENDMENTS

1984—Subsec. (a). Pub. L. 98–369 substituted "801" for "802".

1976—Subsec. (b). Pub. L. 94–455, §1906(b)(13)(A), struck out "or his delegate" after "Secretary".

Subsec. (c)(1). Pub. L. 94–455, §1901(b)(3)(K), substituted "ordinary income" for "gain from the sale or exchange of property which is neither a capital asset nor property described in section 1231".

STATUTORY NOTES AND RELATED SUBSIDIARIES
EFFECTIVE DATE OF 1984 AMENDMENT

Amendment by Pub. L. 98–369 applicable to taxable years beginning after Dec. 31, 1983, see section 215 of Pub. L. 98–369, set out as an Effective Date note under section 801 of this title.

EFFECTIVE DATE OF 1976 AMENDMENT

Amendment by section 1901(b)(3)(K) of Pub. L. 94–455 applicable with respect to taxable years beginning after Dec. 31, 1976, see section 1901(d) of Pub. L. 94–455, set out as a note under section 2 of this title.

EFFECTIVE DATE

Pub. L. 89–384, §1(b)(3), Apr. 8, 1966, 80 Stat. 102, as amended by Pub. L. 99–514, §2, Oct. 22, 1986, 100 Stat. 2095, provided that: "The amendments made by this subsection [enacting this section] shall apply to taxable years beginning after December 31, 1965, but only with respect to losses described in section 80(a)(2) of the Internal Revenue Code of 1986 [formerly I.R.C. 1954] (as added by paragraph (1) of this subsection) which were sustained after December 31, 1958."

[§81. Repealed. Pub. L. 100–203, title X, §10201(b)(1), Dec. 22, 1987, 101 Stat. 1330–387]

Section, added Pub. L. 89–722, §1(b)(1), Nov. 2, 1966, 80 Stat. 1152; amended Pub. L. 93–625, §4(c)(1), Jan. 3, 1975, 88 Stat. 2111; Pub. L. 94–455, title VI, §605(b), Oct. 4, 1976, 90 Stat. 1575; Pub. L. 99–514, title VIII, §805(c)(1)(A), Oct. 22, 1986, 100 Stat. 2362, included increase in vacation pay suspense account in gross income.

STATUTORY NOTES AND RELATED SUBSIDIARIES

Repeal applicable to taxable years beginning after Dec. 31, 1987, see section 10201(c)(1) of Pub. L. 100–203, set out as an Effective Date of 1987 Amendment note under section 404 of this title.

§82. Reimbursement of moving expenses

Except as provided in section 132(a)(6), there shall be included in gross income (as compensation for services) any amount received or accrued, directly or indirectly, by an individual as a payment for or reimbursement of expenses of moving from one residence to another residence which is attributable to employment or self-employment.

(Added Pub. L. 91–172, title II, §231(b), Dec. 30, 1969, 83 Stat. 579; amended Pub. L. 103–66, title XIII, §13213(d)(3)(A), Aug. 10, 1993, 107 Stat. 474; Pub. L. 115–141, div. U, title IV, §401(a)(34), Mar. 23, 2018, 132 Stat. 1186.)

EDITORIAL NOTES
AMENDMENTS

2018—Pub. L. 115–141 substituted "of moving expenses" for "for expenses of moving" in section catchline.

1993—Pub. L. 103–66 substituted "Except as provided in section 132(a)(6), there shall" for "There shall".

STATUTORY NOTES AND RELATED SUBSIDIARIES
EFFECTIVE DATE OF 1993 AMENDMENT

Amendment by Pub. L. 103–66 applicable to reimbursements or other payments in respect of expenses incurred after Dec. 31, 1993, see section 13213(e) of Pub. L. 103–66, set out as a note under section 62 of this title.

EFFECTIVE DATE

Section applicable to taxable years beginning after December 31, 1969, except that it does not apply to moving expenses paid or incurred before July 1, 1970, in connection with the commencement of work by the taxpayer as an employee at a new principal place of work of which the taxpayer had been notified by his employer on or before December 19, 1969, see section 231(d) of Pub. L. 91–172, set out as an Effective Date of 1969 Amendment note under section 217 of this title.

MOVING EXPENSES OF MEMBERS OF THE UNIFORMED SERVICES

Withholding, reporting, inclusion within adjusted gross income, and deduction for reimbursement for moving expenses of members of the uniformed services, see section 2 of Pub. L. 93–490, Oct. 26, 1974, 88 Stat. 1466, set out as a note under section 217 of this title.

§83. Property transferred in connection with performance of services

(a) General rule

If, in connection with the performance of services, property is transferred to any person other than the person for whom such services are performed, the excess of—

(1) the fair market value of such property (determined without regard to any restriction other than a restriction which by its terms will never lapse) at the first time the rights of the person having the beneficial interest in such property are transferable or are not subject to a substantial risk of forfeiture, whichever occurs earlier, over

(2) the amount (if any) paid for such property,

shall be included in the gross income of the person who performed such services in the first taxable year in which the rights of the person having the beneficial interest in such property are transferable or are not subject to a substantial risk of forfeiture, whichever is applicable. The preceding sentence shall not apply if such person sells or otherwise disposes of such property in an arm's length transaction before his rights in such property become transferable or not subject to a substantial risk of forfeiture.

(b) Election to include in gross income in year of transfer

(1) In general

Any person who performs services in connection with which property is transferred to any person may elect to include in his gross income for the taxable year in which such property is transferred, the excess of—

(A) the fair market value of such property at the time of transfer (determined without regard to any restriction other than a restriction which by its terms will never lapse), over

(B) the amount (if any) paid for such property.

If such election is made, subsection (a) shall not apply with respect to the transfer of such property, and if such property is subsequently forfeited, no deduction shall be allowed in respect of such forfeiture.

(2) Election

An election under paragraph (1) with respect to any transfer of property shall be made in such manner as the Secretary prescribes and shall be made not later than 30 days after the date of such transfer. Such election may not be revoked except with the consent of the Secretary.

(c) Special rules

For purposes of this section—

(1) Substantial risk of forfeiture

The rights of a person in property are subject to a substantial risk of forfeiture if such person's rights to full enjoyment of such property are conditioned upon the future performance of substantial services by any individual.

(2) Transferability of property

The rights of a person in property are transferable only if the rights in such property of any transferee are not subject to a substantial risk of forfeiture.

(3) Sales which may give rise to suit under section 16(b) of the Securities Exchange Act of 1934

So long as the sale of property at a profit could subject a person to suit under section 16(b) of the Securities Exchange Act of 1934, such person's rights in such property are—

(A) subject to a substantial risk of forfeiture, and

(B) not transferable.

(4) For purposes of determining an individual's basis in property transferred in connection with the performance of services, rules similar to the rules of section 72(w) shall apply.

(d) Certain restrictions which will never lapse

(1) Valuation

In the case of property subject to a restriction which by its terms will never lapse, and which allows the transferee to sell such property only at a price determined under a formula, the price so determined shall be deemed to be the fair market value of the property unless established to the contrary by the Secretary, and the burden of proof shall be on the Secretary with respect to such value.

(2) Cancellation

If, in the case of property subject to a restriction which by its terms will never lapse, the restriction is canceled, then, unless the taxpayer establishes—

(A) that such cancellation was not compensatory, and

(B) that the person, if any, who would be allowed a deduction if the cancellation were treated as compensatory, will treat the transaction as not compensatory, as evidenced in such manner as the Secretary shall prescribe by regulations,

the excess of the fair market value of the property (computed without regard to the restrictions) at the time of cancellation over the sum of—

(C) the fair market value of such property (computed by taking the restriction into account) immediately before the cancellation, and

(D) the amount, if any, paid for the cancellation,

shall be treated as compensation for the taxable year in which such cancellation occurs.

(e) Applicability of section

This section shall not apply to—

(1) a transaction to which section 421 applies,

(2) a transfer to or from a trust described in section 401(a) or a transfer under an annuity plan which meets the requirements of section 404(a)(2),

(3) the transfer of an option without a readily ascertainable fair market value,

(4) the transfer of property pursuant to the exercise of an option with a readily ascertainable fair market value at the date of grant, or

(5) group-term life insurance to which section 79 applies.

(f) Holding period

In determining the period for which the taxpayer has held property to which subsection (a) applies, there shall be included only the period beginning at the first time his rights in such property are transferable or are not subject to a substantial risk of forfeiture, whichever occurs earlier.

(g) Certain exchanges

If property to which subsection (a) applies is exchanged for property subject to restrictions and conditions substantially similar to those to which the property given in such exchange was subject, and if section 354, 355, 356, or 1036 (or so much of section 1031 as relates to section 1036) applied to such exchange, or if such exchange was pursuant to the exercise of a conversion privilege—

(1) such exchange shall be disregarded for purposes of subsection (a), and

(2) the property received shall be treated as property to which subsection (a) applies.

(h) Deduction by employer

In the case of a transfer of property to which this section applies or a cancellation of a restriction described in subsection (d), there shall be allowed as a deduction under section 162, to the person for whom were performed the services in connection with which such property was transferred, an amount equal to the amount included under subsection (a), (b), or (d)(2) in the gross income of the person who performed such services. Such deduction shall be allowed for the taxable year of such person in which or with which ends the taxable year in which such amount is included in the gross income of the person who performed such services.

(i) Qualified equity grants

(1) In general

For purposes of this subtitle—

(A) Timing of inclusion

If qualified stock is transferred to a qualified employee who makes an election with respect to such stock under this subsection, subsection (a) shall be applied by including the amount determined under such subsection with respect to such stock in income of the employee in the taxable year determined under subparagraph (B) in lieu of the taxable year described in subsection (a).

(B) Taxable year determined

The taxable year determined under this subparagraph is the taxable year of the employee which includes the earliest of—

(i) the first date such qualified stock becomes transferable (including, solely for purposes of this clause, becoming transferable to the employer),

(ii) the date the employee first becomes an excluded employee,

(iii) the first date on which any stock of the corporation which issued the qualified stock becomes readily tradable on an established securities market (as determined by the Secretary, but not including any market unless such market is recognized as an established securities market by the Secretary for purposes of a provision of this title other than this subsection),

(iv) the date that is 5 years after the first date the rights of the employee in such stock are transferable or are not subject to a substantial risk of forfeiture, whichever occurs earlier, or

(v) the date on which the employee revokes (at such time and in such manner as the Secretary provides) the election under this subsection with respect to such stock.

(2) Qualified stock

(A) In general

For purposes of this subsection, the term "qualified stock" means, with respect to any qualified employee, any stock in a corporation which is the employer of such employee, if—

(i) such stock is received—

(I) in connection with the exercise of an option, or

(II) in settlement of a restricted stock unit, and

(ii) such option or restricted stock unit was granted by the corporation—

(I) in connection with the performance of services as an employee, and

(II) during a calendar year in which such corporation was an eligible corporation.

(B) Limitation

The term "qualified stock" shall not include any stock if the employee may sell such stock to, or otherwise receive cash in lieu of stock from, the corporation at the time that the rights of the employee in such stock first become transferable or not subject to a substantial risk of forfeiture.

(C) Eligible corporation

For purposes of subparagraph (A)(ii)(II)—

(i) In general

The term "eligible corporation" means, with respect to any calendar year, any corporation if—

(I) no stock of such corporation (or any predecessor of such corporation) is readily tradable on an established securities market (as determined under paragraph (1)(B)(iii)) during any preceding calendar year, and

(II) such corporation has a written plan under which, in such calendar year, not less than 80 percent of all employees who provide services to such corporation in the United States (or any possession of the United States) are granted stock options, or are granted restricted stock units, with the same rights and privileges to receive qualified stock.

(ii) Same rights and privileges

For purposes of clause (i)(II)—

(I) except as provided in subclauses (II) and (III), the determination of rights and privileges with respect to stock shall be made in a similar manner as under section 423(b)(5),

(II) employees shall not fail to be treated as having the same rights and privileges to receive qualified stock solely because the number of shares available to all employees is not equal in amount, so long as the number of shares available to each employee is more than a de minimis amount, and

(III) rights and privileges with respect to the exercise of an option shall not be treated as the same as rights and privileges with respect to the settlement of a restricted stock unit.

(iii) Employee

For purposes of clause (i)(II), the term "employee" shall not include any employee described in section 4980E(d)(4) or any excluded employee.

(iv) Special rule for calendar years before 2018

In the case of any calendar year beginning before January 1, 2018, clause (i)(II) shall be applied without regard to whether the rights and privileges with respect to the qualified stock are the same.

(3) Qualified employee; excluded employee

For purposes of this subsection—

(A) In general

The term "qualified employee" means any individual who—

(i) is not an excluded employee, and

(ii) agrees in the election made under this subsection to meet such requirements as are determined by the Secretary to be necessary to ensure that the withholding requirements of the corporation under chapter 24 with respect to the qualified stock are met.

(B) Excluded employee

The term "excluded employee" means, with respect to any corporation, any individual—

(i) who is a 1-percent owner (within the meaning of section 416(i)(1)(B)(ii)) at any time during the calendar year or who was such a 1 percent owner at any time during the 10 preceding calendar years,

(ii) who is or has been at any prior time—

(I) the chief executive officer of such corporation or an individual acting in such a capacity, or

(II) the chief financial officer of such corporation or an individual acting in such a capacity,

(iii) who bears a relationship described in section 318(a)(1) to any individual described in subclause (I) or (II) of clause (ii), or

(iv) who is one of the 4 highest compensated officers of such corporation for the taxable year, or was one of the 4 highest compensated officers of such corporation for any of the 10 preceding taxable years, determined with respect to each such taxable year on the basis of the shareholder disclosure rules for compensation under the Securities Exchange Act of 1934 (as if such rules applied to such corporation).

(4) Election

(A) Time for making election

An election with respect to qualified stock shall be made under this subsection no later than 30 days after the first date the rights of the employee in such stock are transferable or are not subject to a substantial risk of forfeiture, whichever occurs earlier, and shall be made in a manner similar to the manner in which an election is made under subsection (b).

(B) Limitations

No election may be made under this section with respect to any qualified stock if—

(i) the qualified employee has made an election under subsection (b) with respect to such qualified stock,

(ii) any stock of the corporation which issued the qualified stock is readily tradable on an established securities market (as determined under paragraph (1)(B)(iii)) at any time before the election is made, or

(iii) such corporation purchased any of its outstanding stock in the calendar year preceding the calendar year which includes the first date the rights of the employee in such stock are transferable or are not subject to a substantial risk of forfeiture, unless—

(I) not less than 25 percent of the total dollar amount of the stock so purchased is deferral stock, and

(II) the determination of which individuals from whom deferral stock is purchased is made on a reasonable basis.

(C) Definitions and special rules related to limitation on stock redemptions

(i) Deferral stock

For purposes of this paragraph, the term "deferral stock" means stock with respect to which an election is in effect under this subsection.

(ii) Deferral stock with respect to any individual not taken into account if individual holds deferral stock with longer deferral period

Stock purchased by a corporation from any individual shall not be treated as deferral stock for purposes of subparagraph (B)(iii) if such individual (immediately after such purchase) holds any deferral stock with respect to which an election has been in effect under this subsection for a longer period than the election with respect to the stock so purchased.

(iii) Purchase of all outstanding deferral stock

The requirements of subclauses (I) and (II) of subparagraph (B)(iii) shall be treated as met if the stock so purchased includes all of the corporation's outstanding deferral stock.

(iv) Reporting

Any corporation which has outstanding deferral stock as of the beginning of any calendar year and which purchases any of its outstanding stock during such calendar year shall include on its return of tax for the taxable year in which, or with which, such calendar year ends the total dollar amount of its outstanding stock so purchased during such calendar year and such other information as the Secretary requires for purposes of administering this paragraph.

(5) Controlled groups

For purposes of this subsection, all persons treated as a single employer under section 414(b) shall be treated as 1 corporation.

(6) Notice requirement

Any corporation which transfers qualified stock to a qualified employee shall, at the time that (or a reasonable period before) an amount attributable to such stock would (but for this subsection) first be includible in the gross income of such employee—

(A) certify to such employee that such stock is qualified stock, and

(B) notify such employee—

(i) that the employee may be eligible to elect to defer income on such stock under this subsection, and

(ii) that, if the employee makes such an election—

(I) the amount of income recognized at the end of the deferral period will be based on the value of the stock at the time at which the rights of the employee in such stock first become transferable or not subject to substantial risk of forfeiture, notwithstanding whether the value of the stock has declined during the deferral period,

(II) the amount of such income recognized at the end of the deferral period will be subject to withholding under section 3401(i) at the rate determined under section 3402(t), and

(III) the responsibilities of the employee (as determined by the Secretary under paragraph (3)(A)(ii)) with respect to such withholding.

(7) Restricted stock units

This section (other than this subsection), including any election under subsection (b), shall not apply to restricted stock units.

(Added Pub. L. 91–172, title III, §321(a), Dec. 30, 1969, 83 Stat. 588; amended Pub. L. 94–455, title XIX, §§1901(a)(15), 1906(b)(13)(A), Oct. 4, 1976, 90 Stat. 1765, 1834; Pub. L. 97–34, title II, §252(a), Aug. 13, 1981, 95 Stat. 260; Pub. L. 97–448, title I, §102(k)(1), Jan. 12, 1983, 96 Stat. 2374; Pub. L. 98–369, div. A, title II, §223(c), July 18, 1984, 98 Stat. 775; Pub. L. 99–514, title XVIII, §1827(e), Oct. 22, 1986, 100 Stat. 2851; Pub. L. 101–508, title XI, §11801(a)(5), Nov. 5, 1990, 104 Stat. 1388–520; Pub. L. 108–357, title VIII, §906(b), Oct. 22, 2004, 118 Stat. 1654; Pub. L. 115–97, title I, §13603(a), Dec. 22, 2017, 131 Stat. 2159.)

EDITORIAL NOTES

REFERENCES IN TEXT

The Securities Exchange Act of 1934, referred to in subsecs. (c)(3) and (i)(3)(B)(iv), is act June 6, 1934, ch. 404, 48 Stat. 881, which is classified principally to chapter 2B (§78a et seq.) of Title 15, Commerce and Trade. Section 16(b) of the Act is classified to section 78p(b) of Title 15. For complete classification of this Act to the Code, see section 78a of Title 15 and Tables.

AMENDMENTS

2017—Subsec. (i). Pub. L. 115–97 added subsec. (i).

2004—Subsec. (c)(4). Pub. L. 108–357 added par. (4).

1990—Subsec. (i). Pub. L. 101–508 struck out subsec. (i) "Transition rules" which read as follows: "This section shall apply to property transferred after June 30, 1969, except that this section shall not apply to property transferred—

"(1) pursuant to a binding written contract entered into before April 22, 1969,

"(2) upon the exercise of an option granted before April 22, 1969,

"(3) before May 1, 1970, pursuant to a written plan adopted and approved before July 1, 1969,

"(4) before January 1, 1973, upon the exercise of an option granted pursuant to a binding written contract entered into before April 22, 1969, between a corporation and the transferor requiring the transferor to grant options to employees of such corporation (or a subsidiary of such corporation) to purchase a determinable number of shares of stock of such corporation, but only if the transferee was an employee of such corporation (or a subsidiary of such corporation) on or before April 22, 1969, or

"(5) in exchange for (or pursuant to the exercise of a conversion privilege contained in) property transferred before July 1, 1969, or for property to which this section does not apply (by reason of paragraphs (1), (2), (3), or (4)), if section 354, 355, 356, or 1036 (or so much of section 1031 as relates to section 1036) applies, or if gain or loss is not otherwise required to be recognized upon the exercise of such conversion privilege, and if the property received in such exchange is subject to restrictions and conditions substantially similar to those to which the property given in such exchange was subject."

1986—Subsec. (e)(5). Pub. L. 99–514 struck out "the cost of" before "group-life insurance".

1984—Subsec. (e)(5). Pub. L. 98–369 added par. (5).

1983—Subsec. (c)(3). Pub. L. 97–448 substituted "Securities Exchange Act of 1934" for "Securities and Exchange Act of 1934" in heading and text.

1981—Subsec. (c)(3). Pub. L. 97–34 added par. (3).

1976—Subsec. (b)(2). Pub. L. 94–455, §1901(a)(15), struck out "(or, if later, 30 days after the date of the enactment of the Tax Reform Act of 1969)" after "after the date of such transfer", and §1906(b)(13)(A), "or his delegate" after "Secretary" wherever appearing.

Subsec. (d)(1), (2)(B). Pub. L. 94–455, §1906(b)(13)(A), struck out "or his delegate" after "Secretary".

STATUTORY NOTES AND RELATED SUBSIDIARIES

EFFECTIVE DATE OF 2017 AMENDMENT

Pub. L. 115–97, title I, §13603(f), Dec. 22, 2017, 131 Stat. 2164, provided that:

"(1) In general.—Except as provided in paragraph (2), the amendments made by this section [amending this section and sections 409A, 422, 423, 3401, 3402, 6051, and 6652 of this title] shall apply to stock attributable to options exercised, or restricted stock units settled, after December 31, 2017.

"(2) Requirement to provide notice.—The amendments made by subsection (e) [amending section 6652 of this title] shall apply to failures after December 31, 2017."

EFFECTIVE DATE OF 2004 AMENDMENT

Amendment by Pub. L. 108–357 applicable to distributions on or after Oct. 22, 2004, see section 906(c) of Pub. L. 108–357, set out as a note under section 72 of this title.

EFFECTIVE DATE OF 1986 AMENDMENT

Amendment by Pub. L. 99–514 effective, except as otherwise provided, as if included in the provisions of the Tax Reform Act of 1984, Pub. L. 98–369, div. A, to which such amendment relates, see section 1881 of Pub. L. 99–514, set out as a note under section 48 of this title.

EFFECTIVE DATE OF 1984 AMENDMENT

Amendment by Pub. L. 98–369 applicable to taxable years beginning after Dec. 31, 1983, see section 223(d)(1) of Pub. L. 98–369, set out as a note under section 79 of this title.

EFFECTIVE DATE OF 1983 AMENDMENT

Amendment by Pub. L. 97–448 effective, except as otherwise provided, as if it had been included in the provision of the Economic Recovery Tax Act of 1981, Pub. L. 97–34, to which such amendment relates, see section 109 of Pub. L. 97–448, set out as a note under section 1 of this title.

EFFECTIVE DATE OF 1981 AMENDMENT

Pub. L. 97–34, title II, §252(c), Aug. 13, 1981, 95 Stat. 260, as amended by Pub. L. 97–448, title I, §102(k)(2), 96 Stat. 2374, provided that: "The amendment made by subsection (a) [amending this section] and the provisions of subsection (b) [set out below] shall apply to transfers after December 31, 1981."

EFFECTIVE DATE OF 1976 AMENDMENT

Amendment by section 1901(a)(15) of Pub. L. 94–455 applicable with respect to taxable years beginning after Dec. 31, 1976, see section 1901(d) of Pub. L. 94–455, set out as a note under section 2 of this title.

§84. Transfer of appreciated property to political organizations

(a) General rule

If—

    (1) any person transfers property to a political organization, and
    (2) the fair market value of such property exceeds its adjusted basis,

then for purposes of this chapter the transferor shall be treated as having sold such property to the political organization on the date of the transfer, and the transferor shall be treated as having realized an amount equal to the fair market value of such property on such date.

(b) Basis of property

In the case of a transfer of property to a political organization to which subsection (a) applies, the basis of such property in the hands of the political organization shall be the same as it would be in the hands of the transferor, increased by the amount of gain recognized to the transferor by reason of such transfer.

(c) Political organization defined

For purposes of this section, the term "political organization" has the meaning given to such term by section 527(e)(1).

(Added Pub. L. 93–625, §13(a)(1), Jan. 3, 1975, 88 Stat. 2120; amended Pub. L. 115–141, div. U, title IV, §401(a)(35), Mar. 23, 2018, 132 Stat. 1186.)

EDITORIAL NOTES
AMENDMENTS

2018—Pub. L. 115–141 substituted "political organizations" for "political organization" in section catchline.

STATUTORY NOTES AND RELATED SUBSIDIARIES
EFFECTIVE DATE

Pub. L. 93–625, §13(b), Jan. 3, 1975, 88 Stat. 2121, provided that: "The amendments made by subsection (a) [enacting this section] shall apply to transfers made after May 7, 1974, in taxable years ending after such date."

NONRECOGNITION OF GAIN OR LOSS WHERE ORGANIZATION SOLD CONTRIBUTED PROPERTY BEFORE AUGUST 2, 1973

Pub. L. 93–625, §13(c), Jan. 3, 1975, 88 Stat. 2121, provided that in the case of the sale or exchange of property before Aug. 2, 1973, which was acquired by the exempt political organization by contribution, no gain or loss shall be recognized by such organization.

§85. Unemployment compensation

(a) General rule

In the case of an individual, gross income includes unemployment compensation.

(b) Unemployment compensation defined

For purposes of this section, the term "unemployment compensation" means any amount received under a law of the United States or of a State which is in the nature of unemployment compensation.

(c) Special rule for 2020

(1) In general

In the case of any taxable year beginning in 2020, if the adjusted gross income of the taxpayer for such taxable year is less than $150,000, the gross income of such taxpayer shall not include so much of the unemployment compensation received by such taxpayer (or, in the case of a joint return, received by each spouse) as does not exceed $10,200.

(2) Application

For purposes of paragraph (1), the adjusted gross income of the taxpayer shall be determined—

(A) after application of sections 86, 135, 137, 219, 221, 222, and 469, and

(B) without regard to this section.

(Added Pub. L. 95–600, title I, §112(a), Nov. 6, 1978, 92 Stat. 2777; amended Pub. L. 97–34, title I, §103(c)(1), Aug. 13, 1981, 95 Stat. 188; Pub. L. 97–248, title VI, §611(a), Sept. 3, 1982, 96 Stat. 706; Pub. L. 98–21, title I, §§121(f)(1), 122(c)(2), Apr. 20, 1983, 97 Stat. 84, 87; Pub. L. 99–514, title I, §121, Oct. 22, 1986, 100 Stat. 2109; Pub. L. 111–5, div. B, title I, §1007(a), Feb. 17, 2009, 123 Stat. 317; Pub. L. 113–295, div. A, title II, §221(a)(15), Dec. 19, 2014, 128 Stat. 4039; Pub. L. 117–2, title IX, §9042(a), Mar. 11, 2021, 135 Stat. 122.)

EDITORIAL NOTES
AMENDMENTS

2021—Subsec. (c). Pub. L. 117–2 added subsec. (c).

2014—Subsec. (c). Pub. L. 113–295 struck out subsec. (c). Text read as follows: "In the case of any taxable year beginning in 2009, gross income shall not include so much of the unemployment compensation received by an individual as does not exceed $2,400."

2009—Subsec. (c). Pub. L. 111–5 added subsec. (c).

1986—Subsec. (a). Pub. L. 99–514 substituted "General rule" for "In general" in heading and amended text generally. Prior to amendment, text read as follows: "If the sum for the taxable year of the adjusted gross income of the taxpayer (determined without regard to this section, section 86 and section 221) and the unemployment compensation exceeds the base amount, gross income for the taxable year includes unemployment compensation in an amount equal to the lesser of—

"(1) one-half of the amount of the excess of such sum over the base amount, or

"(2) the amount of the unemployment compensation."

Subsecs. (b), (c). Pub. L. 99–514, in amending section generally, redesignated former subsec. (c) as (b) and struck out former subsec. (b), "Base amount defined", which read as follows: "For purposes of this section, the term 'base amount' means—

"(1) except as provided in paragraphs (2) and (3), $12,000,

"(2) $18,000, in the case of a joint return under section 6013, or

"(3) zero, in the case of a taxpayer who—

"(A) is married at the close of the taxable year (within the meaning of section 143) but does not file a joint return for such year, and

"(B) does not live apart from his spouse at all times during the taxable year."

1983—Subsec. (a). Pub. L. 98–21, §122(c)(2), struck out ", section 105(d)," after "section 86".

Pub. L. 98–21, §121(f)(1), inserted "section 86," after "this section,".

1982—Subsec. (b)(1). Pub. L. 97–248, §611(a)(1), substituted "$12,000" for "$20,000".

Subsec. (b)(2). Pub. L. 97–248, §611(a)(2), substituted "$18,000" for "$25,000".

1981—Subsec. (a). Pub. L. 97–34 substituted "this section, section 105(d), and section 221" for "this section and without regard to section 105(d)" in parenthetical provision preceding par. (1).

STATUTORY NOTES AND RELATED SUBSIDIARIES
EFFECTIVE DATE OF 2021 AMENDMENT

Amendment by Pub. L. 117–2 applicable to taxable years beginning after Dec. 31, 2019, see section 9042(c) of Pub. L. 117–2, set out as a note under section 74 of this title.

EFFECTIVE DATE OF 2014 AMENDMENT

Amendment by Pub. L. 113–295 effective Dec. 19, 2014, subject to a savings provision, see section 221(b) of Pub. L. 113–295, set out as a note under section 1 of this title.

§86. Social security and tier 1 railroad retirement benefits

(a) In general

(1) In general

Except as provided in paragraph (2), gross income for the taxable year of any taxpayer described in subsection (b) (notwithstanding section 207 of the Social Security Act) includes social security benefits in an amount equal to the lesser of—

(A) one-half of the social security benefits received during the taxable year, or

(B) one-half of the excess described in subsection (b)(1).

(2) Additional amount

In the case of a taxpayer with respect to whom the amount determined under subsection (b)(1)(A) exceeds the adjusted base amount, the amount included in gross income under this section shall be equal to the lesser of—

(A) the sum of—

(i) 85 percent of such excess, plus

(ii) the lesser of the amount determined under paragraph (1) or an amount equal to one-half of the difference between the adjusted base amount and the base amount of the taxpayer, or

(B) 85 percent of the social security benefits received during the taxable year.

(b) Taxpayers to whom subsection (a) applies

(1) In general

A taxpayer is described in this subsection if—

(A) the sum of—

(i) the modified adjusted gross income of the taxpayer for the taxable year, plus

(ii) one-half of the social security benefits received during the taxable year, exceeds

(B) the base amount.

(2) Modified adjusted gross income

For purposes of this subsection, the term "modified adjusted gross income" means adjusted gross income—

(A) determined without regard to this section and sections 85(c), 135, 137, 221, 911, 931, and 933, and

(B) increased by the amount of interest received or accrued by the taxpayer during the taxable year which is exempt from tax.

(c) Base amount and adjusted base amount

For purposes of this section—

(1) Base amount

The term "base amount" means—

(A) except as otherwise provided in this paragraph, $25,000,

(B) $32,000 in the case of a joint return, and

(C) zero in the case of a taxpayer who—

(i) is married as of the close of the taxable year (within the meaning of section 7703) but does not file a joint return for such year, and

(ii) does not live apart from his spouse at all times during the taxable year.

(2) Adjusted base amount

The term "adjusted base amount" means—

(A) except as otherwise provided in this paragraph, $34,000,

(B) $44,000 in the case of a joint return, and

(C) zero in the case of a taxpayer described in paragraph (1)(C).

(d) Social security benefit

(1) In general

For purposes of this section, the term "social security benefit" means any amount received by the taxpayer by reason of entitlement to—

(A) a monthly benefit under title II of the Social Security Act, or

(B) a tier 1 railroad retirement benefit.

(2) Adjustment for repayments during year

(A) In general

For purposes of this section, the amount of social security benefits received during any taxable year shall be reduced by any repayment made by the taxpayer during the taxable year of a social security benefit previously received by the taxpayer (whether or not such benefit was received during the taxable year).

(B) Denial of deduction

If (but for this subparagraph) any portion of the repayments referred to in subparagraph (A) would have been allowable as a deduction for the taxable year under section 165, such portion shall be allowable as a deduction only to the extent it exceeds the social security benefits received by the taxpayer during the taxable year (and not repaid during such taxable year).

(3) Workmen's compensation benefits substituted for social security benefits

For purposes of this section, if, by reason of section 224 of the Social Security Act (or by reason of section 3(a)(1) of the Railroad Retirement Act of 1974), any social security benefit is reduced by reason of the receipt of a benefit under a workmen's compensation act, the term "social security benefit" includes that portion of such benefit received under the workmen's compensation act which equals such reduction.

(4) Tier 1 railroad retirement benefit

For purposes of paragraph (1), the term "tier 1 railroad retirement benefit" means—

(A) the amount of the annuity under the Railroad Retirement Act of 1974 equal to the amount of the benefit to which the taxpayer would have been entitled under the Social Security Act if all of the service after December 31, 1936, of the employee (on whose employment record the annuity is being paid) had been included in the term "employment" as defined in the Social Security Act, and

(B) a monthly annuity amount under section 3(f)(3) of the Railroad Retirement Act of 1974.

(5) Effect of early delivery of benefit checks

For purposes of subsection (a), in any case where section 708 of the Social Security Act causes social security benefit checks to be delivered before the end of the calendar month for which they are issued, the benefits involved shall be deemed to have been received in the succeeding calendar month.

(e) Limitation on amount included where taxpayer receives lump-sum payment

(1) Limitation

If—

(A) any portion of a lump-sum payment of social security benefits received during the taxable year is attributable to prior taxable years, and

(B) the taxpayer makes an election under this subsection for the taxable year,

then the amount included in gross income under this section for the taxable year by reason of the receipt of such portion shall not exceed the sum of the increases in gross income under this chapter for prior taxable years which would result solely from taking into account such portion in the taxable years to which it is attributable.

(2) Special rules

(A) Year to which benefit attributable

For purposes of this subsection, a social security benefit is attributable to a taxable year if the generally applicable payment date for such benefit occurred during such taxable year.

(B) Election

An election under this subsection shall be made at such time and in such manner as the Secretary shall by regulations prescribe. Such election, once made, may be revoked only with the consent of the Secretary.

(f) Treatment as pension or annuity for certain purposes

For purposes of—

(1) section 22(c)(3)(A) (relating to reduction for amounts received as pension or annuity),

(2) section 32(c)(2) (defining earned income),

(3) section 219(f)(1) (defining compensation), and

(4) section 911(b)(1) (defining foreign earned income),

any social security benefit shall be treated as an amount received as a pension or annuity.

(Added and amended Pub. L. 98–21, title I, §121(a), title III, §335(b)(2)(A), Apr. 20, 1983, 97 Stat. 80, 130; Pub. L. 98–76, title II, §224(d), Aug. 12, 1983, 97 Stat. 424; Pub. L. 98–369, div. A, title IV, §474(r)(2), div. B, title VI, §2661(o)(1), July 18, 1984, 98 Stat. 839, 1158; Pub. L. 99–272, title XII, §12111(b), title XIII, §13204(a), Apr. 7, 1986, 100 Stat. 287, 313; Pub. L. 99–514, title I, §131(b)(2), title XIII, §1301(j)(8), title XVIII, §1847(b)(2), Oct. 22, 1986, 100 Stat. 2113, 2658, 2856; Pub. L. 100–647, title I, §1001(e), title VI, §6009(c)(1), Nov. 10, 1988, 102 Stat. 3351, 3690; Pub. L. 103–66, title XIII, §13215(a), (b), Aug. 10, 1993, 107 Stat. 475, 476; Pub. L. 103–296, title III, §309(d), Aug. 15, 1994, 108 Stat. 1523; Pub. L. 104–188, title I, §§1704(t)(3), 1807(c)(2), Aug. 20, 1996, 110 Stat. 1887, 1902; Pub. L. 105–277, div. J, title IV, §4003(a)(2)(B), Oct. 21, 1998, 112 Stat. 2681–908; Pub. L. 107–16, title IV, §431(c)(1), June 7, 2001, 115 Stat. 68; Pub. L. 108–357, title I, §102(d)(1), Oct. 22, 2004, 118 Stat. 1428; Pub. L. 115–97, title I, §13305(b)(1), Dec. 22, 2017, 131 Stat. 2126; Pub. L. 116–260, div. EE, title I, §104(b)(2)(C), Dec. 27, 2020, 134 Stat. 3041; Pub. L. 117–2, title IX, §9042(b)(2), Mar. 11, 2021, 135 Stat. 122.)

EDITORIAL NOTES
REFERENCES IN TEXT

The Social Security Act, referred to in subsecs. (a)(1) and (d)(1)(A), (3), (4)(A), (5), is act Aug. 14, 1935, ch. 531, 49 Stat. 620, as amended, which is classified generally to chapter 7 (§301 et seq.) of Title 42, The Public Health and Welfare. Title II of the Act is classified generally to subchapter II (§401 et seq.) of Title 42. Sections 207, 224, and 708 of the Act are classified to sections 407, 424a, and 909 of Title 42, respectively. For complete classification of this Act to the Code, see section 1305 of Title 42 and Tables.

The Railroad Retirement Act of 1974, referred to in subsec. (d)(3), (4), is act Aug. 29, 1935, ch. 812, as amended generally by Pub. L. 93–445, title I, §101, Oct. 16, 1974, 88 Stat. 1305, which is classified generally to subchapter IV (§231 et seq.) of chapter 9 of Title 45, Railroads. Section 3(a)(1), (f)(3) of the Act is classified to section 231b(a)(1), (f)(3) of Title 45. For further details and complete classification of this Act to the Code, see Codification note set out preceding section 231 of Title 45, section 231t of Title 45, and Tables.

PRIOR PROVISIONS

A prior section 86 was renumbered section 87 of this title.

AMENDMENTS

2021—Subsec. (b)(2)(A). Pub. L. 117–2 inserted "85(c)," before "135".

2020—Subsec. (b)(2)(A). Pub. L. 116–260 struck out "222," after "221,".

2017—Subsec. (b)(2)(A). Pub. L. 115–97 struck out "199," before "221".

2004—Subsec. (b)(2)(A). Pub. L. 108–357 inserted "199," before "221".

2001—Subsec. (b)(2)(A). Pub. L. 107–16 inserted "222," after "221,".

1998—Subsec. (b)(2)(A). Pub. L. 105–277 inserted "221," after "137,".

1996—Subsec. (b)(2). Pub. L. 104–188, §1704(t)(3), substituted "means adjusted" for "means adusted" in introductory provisions.

Subsec. (b)(2)(A). Pub. L. 104–188, §1807(c)(2), inserted "137," before "911".

1994—Subsec. (d)(1). Pub. L. 103–296 struck out at end "For purposes of the preceding sentence, the amount received by any taxpayer shall be determined as if the Social Security Act did not contain section 203(i) thereof."

1993—Subsec. (a). Pub. L. 103–66, §13215(a), designated existing provisions as par. (1), inserted par. (1) heading, substituted "Except as provided in paragraph (2), gross" for "Gross", redesignated former pars. (1) and (2) as subpars. (A) and (B), respectively, and added par. (2).

Subsec. (c). Pub. L. 103–66, §13215(b), amended heading and text of subsec. (c) generally. Prior to amendment, text read as follows: "For purposes of this section, the term 'base amount' means—

"(1) except as otherwise provided in this subsection, $25,000,

"(2) $32,000, in the case of a joint return, and

"(3) zero, in the case of a taxpayer who—

"(A) is married at the close of the taxable year (within the meaning of section 7703) but does not file a joint return for such year, and

"(B) does not live apart from his spouse at all times during the taxable year."

1988—Subsec. (b)(2)(A). Pub. L. 100–647, §6009(c)(1), inserted "135," before "911".

Subsec. (f)(4), (5). Pub. L. 100–647, §1001(e), redesignated par. (5) as (4) and struck out former par. (4) which read as follows: "section 221(b)(2) (defining earned income), and".

1986—Subsec. (b)(2)(A). Pub. L. 99–514, §131(b)(2), substituted "sections" for "sections 221,".

Subsec. (c)(3)(A). Pub. L. 99–514, §1301(j)(8), substituted "section 7703" for "section 143".

Subsec. (d)(4). Pub. L. 99–272, §13204(a), in amending par. (4) generally, designated existing provisions as introductory clause of par. (4), struck out "a monthly benefit under section 3(a), 3(f)(3), 4(a), or 4(f) of the Railroad Retirement Act of 1974", and added cls. (A) and (B).

Subsec. (d)(5). Pub. L. 99–272, §12111(b), added par. (5).

Subsec. (f)(1). Pub. L. 99–514, §1847(b)(2), substituted "section 22(c)(3)(A)" for "section 37(c)(3)(A)".

1984—Subsec. (f)(1). Pub. L. 98–369, §2661(o)(1), added par. (1). Former par. (1) redesignated par. (2).

Pub. L. 98–369, §474(r)(2), substituted "section 32(c)(2)" for "section 43(c)(2)".

Subsec. (f)(2)–(5). Pub. L. 98–369, §2661(o)(1), redesignated pars. (1) to (4) as (2) to (5), respectively.

1983—Subsec. (a). Pub. L. 98–21, §335(b)(2)(A), inserted "(notwithstanding section 207 of the Social Security Act)".

Subsec. (d)(4). Pub. L. 98–76 inserted "3(f)(3)," after "3(a),".

STATUTORY NOTES AND RELATED SUBSIDIARIES
EFFECTIVE DATE OF 2021 AMENDMENT

Amendment by Pub. L. 117–2 applicable to taxable years beginning after Dec. 31, 2019, see section 9042(c) of Pub. L. 117–2, set out as a note under section 74 of this title.

EFFECTIVE DATE OF 2020 AMENDMENT

Amendment by Pub. L. 116–260 applicable to taxable years beginning after Dec. 31, 2020, see section 104(c) of div. EE of Pub. L. 116–260, set out as a note under section 25A of this title.

EFFECTIVE DATE OF 2017 AMENDMENT

Amendment by Pub. L. 115–97 applicable to taxable years beginning after Dec. 31, 2017, except as provided by transition rule, see section 13305(c) of Pub. L. 115–97, set out as a note under section 74 of this title.

EFFECTIVE DATE OF 2004 AMENDMENT

Amendment by Pub. L. 108–357 applicable to taxable years beginning after Dec. 31, 2004, see section 102(e) of Pub. L. 108–357, set out as a note under section 56 of this title.

EFFECTIVE DATE OF 2001 AMENDMENT

Amendment by Pub. L. 107–16 applicable to payments made in taxable years beginning after Dec. 31, 2001, see section 431(d) of Pub. L. 107–16, set out as a note under section 62 of this title.

EFFECTIVE DATE OF 1998 AMENDMENT

Pub. L. 105–277, div. J, title IV, §4003(l), Oct. 21, 1998, 112 Stat. 2681–910, provided that: "The amendments made by this section [amending this section and sections 135, 137, 163, 172, 219, 221, 264, 351, 368, 469, 954, 2001, 6311, 6404, and 9510 of this title and amending provisions set out as a note under section 7508A of this title] shall take effect as if included in the provisions of the 1997 Act [Pub. L. 105–34] to which they relate."

EFFECTIVE DATE OF 1996 AMENDMENT

Amendment by section 1807(c)(2) of Pub. L. 104–188 applicable to taxable years beginning after Dec. 31, 1996, see section 1807(e) of Pub. L. 104–188, set out as an Effective Date note under section 23 of this title.

EFFECTIVE DATE OF 1994 AMENDMENT

Pub. L. 103–296, title III, §309(e)(2), Aug. 15, 1994, 108 Stat. 1524, provided that: "The amendment made by subsection (d) [amending this section] shall apply with respect to benefits received after December 31, 1995, in taxable years ending after such date."

EFFECTIVE DATE OF 1993 AMENDMENT

Pub. L. 103–66, title XIII, §13215(d), Aug. 10, 1993, 107 Stat. 477, provided that: "The amendments made by subsections (a) and (b) [amending this section] shall apply to taxable years beginning after December 31, 1993."

EFFECTIVE DATE OF 1988 AMENDMENT

Amendment by section 1001(e) of Pub. L. 100–647 effective, except as otherwise provided, as if included in the provision of the Tax Reform Act of 1986, Pub. L. 99–514, to which such amendment relates, see section 1019(a) of Pub. L. 100–647, set out as a note under section 1 of this title.

Pub. L. 100–647, title VI, §6009(d), Nov. 10, 1988, 102 Stat. 3690, provided that: "The amendments made by this section [enacting section 135 of this title, amending this section and sections 219 and 469 of this title, and renumbering former section 135 as section 136 of this title] shall apply to taxable years beginning after December 31, 1989."

EFFECTIVE DATE OF 1986 AMENDMENT

Amendment by section 131(b)(2) of Pub. L. 99–514 applicable to taxable years beginning after Dec. 31, 1986, see section 151(a) of Pub. L. 99–514, set out as a note under section 1 of this title.

Amendment by section 1301(j)(8) of Pub. L. 99–514 applicable to bonds issued after Aug. 15, 1986, except as otherwise provided, see sections 1311–1318 of Pub. L. 99–514, set out as an Effective Date; Transitional Rules note under section 141 of this title.

Amendment by section 1847(b)(2) of Pub. L. 99–514 effective, except as otherwise provided, as if included in the provisions of the Tax Reform Act of 1984, Pub. L. 98–369, div. A, to which such amendment relates, see section 1881 of Pub. L. 99–514, set out as a note under section 48 of this title.

Amendment by section 12111(b) of Pub. L. 99–272 applicable with respect to benefit checks issued for months ending after Apr. 7, 1986, see section 12111(c) of Pub. L. 99–272, set out as a note under section 909 of Title 42, The Public Health and Welfare.

Pub. L. 99–272, title XIII, §13204(b), Apr. 7, 1986, 100 Stat. 313, provided that: "The amendment made by subsection (a) [amending this section] shall apply to any monthly benefit for which the generally applicable payment date is after December 31, 1985."

EFFECTIVE DATE OF 1984 AMENDMENT

Amendment by section 474(r)(2) of Pub. L. 98–369 applicable to taxable years beginning after Dec. 31, 1983, and to carrybacks from such years, see section 475(a) of Pub. L. 98–369, set out as a note under section 21 of this title.

Amendment by section 2661 of Pub. L. 98–369 effective as though included in the enactment of the Social Security Amendments of 1983, Pub. L. 98–21, see section 2664(a) of Pub. L. 98–369, set out as a note under section 401 of Title 42, The Public Health and Welfare.

EFFECTIVE DATE OF 1983 AMENDMENT

Amendment by Pub. L. 98–76 applicable to benefits received after Dec. 31, 1983, in taxable years ending after such date, except for portions of lump-sum payments received after Dec. 31, 1983, if the generally applicable payment date for such portion was before Jan. 1, 1984, see section 227(b) of Pub. L. 98–76 set out as a note under section 72 of this title.

EFFECTIVE DATE

Pub. L. 98–21, title I, §121(g), Apr. 20, 1983, 97 Stat. 84, as amended by Pub. L. 99–514, §2, Oct. 22, 1986, 100 Stat. 2095, provided that:

"(1) In general.—Except as provided in paragraph (2), the amendments made by this section [enacting this section and section 6050F of this title, amending sections 85, 128, 861, 871, 1441, and 6103 of this title and section 3413 of Title 12, Banks and Banking, and enacting provisions set out as a note under section 401 of Title 42, The Public Health and Welfare] shall apply to benefits received after December 31, 1983, in taxable years ending after such date.

"(2) Treatment of certain lump-sum payments received after december 31, 1983.—The amendments made by this section shall not apply to any portion of a lump-sum payment of social security benefits (as defined in section 86(d) of the Internal Revenue Code of 1986 [formerly I.R.C. 1954]) received after December 31, 1983, if the generally applicable payment date for such portion was before January 1, 1984."

PLAN AMENDMENTS NOT REQUIRED UNTIL JANUARY 1, 1989

For provisions directing that if any amendments made by subtitle A or subtitle C of title XI [§§1101–1147 and 1171–1177] or title XVIII [§§1800–1899A] of Pub. L. 99–514 require an amendment to any plan, such plan amendment shall not be required to be made before the first plan year beginning on or after Jan. 1, 1989, see section 1140 of Pub. L. 99–514, as amended, set out as a note under section 401 of this title.

§87. Alcohol and biodiesel fuels credits

Gross income includes—

(1) the amount of the alcohol fuel credit determined with respect to the taxpayer for the taxable year under section 40(a), and

(2) the biodiesel fuels credit determined with respect to the taxpayer for the taxable year under section 40A(a).

(Added Pub. L. 96–223, title II, §232(c)(1), Apr. 2, 1980, 94 Stat. 276, §86; renumbered §87, Pub. L. 98–21, title I, §121(a), Apr. 20, 1983, 97 Stat. 80; amended Pub. L. 98–369, div. A, title IV, §474(r)(3), July 18, 1984, 98 Stat. 839; Pub. L. 108–357, title III, §302(c)(1)(A), Oct. 22, 2004, 118 Stat. 1465.)

EDITORIAL NOTES

AMENDMENTS

2004—Pub. L. 108–357 amended section catchline and text generally. Prior to amendment, text read as follows: "Gross income includes the amount of the alcohol fuel credit determined with respect to the taxpayer for the taxable year under section 40(a)."

1984—Pub. L. 98–369 amended section generally, substituting "the amount of the alcohol fuel credit determined with respect to the taxpayer for the taxable year under section 40(a)" for "an amount equal to the amount of the credit allowable to the taxpayer under section 44E for the taxable year (determined without regard to subsection (e) thereof)".

STATUTORY NOTES AND RELATED SUBSIDIARIES

EFFECTIVE DATE OF 2004 AMENDMENT

Amendment by Pub. L. 108–357 applicable to fuel produced, and sold or used, after Dec. 31, 2004, in taxable years ending after such date, see section 302(d) of Pub. L. 108–357, set out as a note under section 38 of this title.

EFFECTIVE DATE OF 1984 AMENDMENT

Amendment by Pub. L. 98–369 applicable to taxable years beginning after Dec. 31, 1983, and to carrybacks from such years, see section 475(a) of Pub. L. 98–369, set out as a note under section 21 of this title.

EFFECTIVE DATE

Section applicable to sales or uses after Sept. 30, 1980, in taxable years ending after such date, see section 232(h)(1) of Pub. L. 96–223, set out as a note under section 40 of this title.

§88. Certain amounts with respect to nuclear decommissioning costs

In the case of any taxpayer who is required to include the amount of any nuclear decommissioning costs in the taxpayer's cost of service for ratemaking purposes, there shall be includible in the gross income of such taxpayer the amount so included for any taxable year.

(Added Pub. L. 98–369, div. A, title I, §91(f)(1), July 18, 1984, 98 Stat. 607; amended Pub. L. 99–514, title XVIII, §1807(a)(4)(E)(vii), Oct. 22, 1986, 100 Stat. 2813.)

EDITORIAL NOTES
AMENDMENTS

1986—Pub. L. 99–514 substituted "for ratemaking purposes" for "of ratemaking purposes".

STATUTORY NOTES AND RELATED SUBSIDIARIES
EFFECTIVE DATE OF 1986 AMENDMENT

Amendment by Pub. L. 99–514 effective, except as otherwise provided, as if included in the provisions of the Tax Reform Act of 1984, Pub. L. 98–369, div. A, to which such amendment relates, see section 1881 of Pub. L. 99–514, set out as a note under section 48 of this title.

EFFECTIVE DATE

Section effective July 18, 1984, with respect to taxable years ending after such date, see section 91(g)(5) of Pub. L. 98–369, as amended, set out as an Effective Date of 1984 Amendment note under section 461 of this title.

PLAN AMENDMENTS NOT REQUIRED UNTIL JANUARY 1, 1989

For provisions directing that if any amendments made by subtitle A or subtitle C of title XI [§§1101–1147 and 1171–1177] or title XVIII [§§1800–1899A] of Pub. L. 99–514 require an amendment to any plan, such plan amendment shall not be required to be made before the first plan year beginning on or after Jan. 1, 1989, see section 1140 of Pub. L. 99–514, as amended, set out as a note under section 401 of this title.

[§89. Repealed. Pub. L. 101–140, title II, §202(a), Nov. 8, 1989, 103 Stat. 830]

Section, added Pub. L. 99–514, title XI, §1151(a), Oct. 22, 1986, 100 Stat. 2494; amended Pub. L. 100–647, title I, §1011B(a)(1)–(9), (21), (28), (29), (34), title III, §3021(a)(1)(A), (B), (2)(A), (3)–(9), (11)–(13)(A), (b)(2)(B), (3), title VI, §6051(a), Nov. 10, 1988, 102 Stat. 3483–3485, 3487, 3488, 3625-3632, 3695, related to nondiscrimination rules regarding benefits provided under employee benefit plans.

STATUTORY NOTES AND RELATED SUBSIDIARIES
EFFECTIVE DATE OF REPEAL

Pub. L. 101–140, title II, §202(c), Nov. 8, 1989, 103 Stat. 830, provided that: "The amendments made by this section [repealing this section] shall take effect as if included in section 1151 of the Tax Reform Act of 1986 [Pub. L. 99–514, see section 1151(k) set out as a note under section 79 of this title]."

NONENFORCEMENT OF SECTION FOR FISCAL YEAR 1990

Pub. L. 101–136, title V, §528, Nov. 3, 1989, 103 Stat. 816, provided that: "No monies appropriated by this Act [see Tables for classification] may be used to implement or enforce section 1151 of the Tax Reform Act of 1986 or the amendments made by such section [section 1151 of Pub. L. 99–514, which enacted section 89 of this title, amended sections 79, 105, 106, 117, 120, 125, 127, 129, 132, 414, 505, 3121, 3306, 6039D, and 6652 of this title and section 409 of Title 42, The Public Health and Welfare, and enacted provisions set out as a note under section 89 of this title]."

TRANSITIONAL PROVISIONS

Pub. L. 100–647, title III, §3021(c), Nov. 10, 1988, 102 Stat. 3633, provided for the first issue of valuation rules, the interim impact on former employees, the meeting of the written requirement for covered plans in connection with implementation of section 89 of the Code, and the issuance by Nov. 15, 1988, of rules necessary to carry out section 89, prior to repeal by Pub. L. 101–140, title II, §203(a)(7), Nov. 8, 1989, 103 Stat. 831.

PART-TIME EMPLOYEE DEFINED FOR PURPOSES OF SUBSECTION (F)

Pub. L. 100–647, title VI, §6070, Nov. 10, 1988, 102 Stat. 3704, increased the number of employees who would be excluded from consideration under this section during plan years 1989 and 1990, in the case of a plan maintained by an employer which employs fewer than 10 employees on a normal working day during a plan year, prior to repeal by Pub. L. 101–140, title II, §203(a)(7), Nov. 8, 1989, 103 Stat. 831.

§90. Illegal Federal irrigation subsidies

(a) General rule

Gross income shall include an amount equal to any illegal Federal irrigation subsidy received by the taxpayer during the taxable year.

(b) Illegal Federal irrigation subsidy

For purposes of this section—

(1) In general

The term "illegal Federal irrigation subsidy" means the excess (if any) of—

(A) the amount required to be paid for any Federal irrigation water delivered to the taxpayer during the taxpayer year, over

(B) the amount paid for such water.

(2) Federal irrigation water

The term "Federal irrigation water" means any water made available for agricultural purposes from the operation of any reclamation or irrigation project referred to in paragraph (8) of section 202 of the Reclamation Reform Act of 1982.

(c) Denial of deduction

No deduction shall be allowed under this subtitle by reason of any inclusion in gross income under subsection (a).

(Added Pub. L. 100–203, title X, §10611(a), Dec. 22, 1987, 101 Stat. 1330–451.)

EDITORIAL NOTES
REFERENCES IN TEXT

Section 202 of the Reclamation Reform Act of 1982, referred to in subsec. (b)(2), is classified to section 390bb of Title 43, Public Lands.

STATUTORY NOTES AND RELATED SUBSIDIARIES
EFFECTIVE DATE

§91. Certain foreign branch losses transferred to specified 10-percent owned foreign corporations

(a) In general

If a domestic corporation transfers substantially all of the assets of a foreign branch (within the meaning of section 367(a)(3)(C), as in effect before the date of the enactment of the Tax Cuts and Jobs Act) to a specified 10-percent owned foreign corporation (as defined in section 245A) with respect to which it is a United States shareholder after such transfer, such domestic corporation shall include in gross income for the taxable year which includes such transfer an amount equal to the transferred loss amount with respect to such transfer.

(b) Transferred loss amount

For purposes of this section, the term "transferred loss amount" means, with respect to any transfer of substantially all of the assets of a foreign branch, the excess (if any) of—

(1) the sum of losses—

(A) which were incurred by the foreign branch after December 31, 2017, and before the transfer, and

(B) with respect to which a deduction was allowed to the taxpayer, over

(2) the sum of—

(A) any taxable income of such branch for a taxable year after the taxable year in which the loss was incurred and through the close of the taxable year of the transfer, and

(B) any amount which is recognized under section 904(f)(3) on account of the transfer.

(c) Reduction for recognized gains

The transferred loss amount shall be reduced (but not below zero) by the amount of gain recognized by the taxpayer on account of the transfer (other than amounts taken into account under subsection (b)(2)(B)).

(d) Source of income

Amounts included in gross income under this section shall be treated as derived from sources within the United States.

(e) Basis adjustments

Consistent with such regulations or other guidance as the Secretary shall prescribe, proper adjustments shall be made in the adjusted basis of the taxpayer's stock in the specified 10-percent owned foreign corporation to which the transfer is made, and in the transferee's adjusted basis in the property transferred, to reflect amounts included in gross income under this section.

(Added Pub. L. 115–97, title I, §14102(d)(1), Dec. 22, 2017, 131 Stat. 2193.)

EDITORIAL NOTES

REFERENCES IN TEXT

The date of the enactment of the Tax Cuts and Jobs Act, referred to in subsec. (a), probably means the date of enactment of title I of Pub. L. 115–97, which was approved Dec. 22, 2017. Prior versions of the bill that was enacted into law as Pub. L. 115–97 included such Short Title, but it was not enacted as part of title I of Pub. L. 115–97.

STATUTORY NOTES AND RELATED SUBSIDIARIES

EFFECTIVE DATE

Pub. L. 115–97, title I, §14102(d)(3), Dec. 22, 2017, 131 Stat. 2194, provided that: "The amendments made by this subsection [enacting this section] shall apply to transfers after December 31, 2017."

TRANSITION RULE

Pub. L. 115–97, title I, §14102(d)(4), Dec. 22, 2017, 131 Stat. 2194, provided that: "The amount of gain taken into account under section 91(c) of the Internal Revenue Code of 1986, as added by this subsection, shall be reduced by the amount of gain which would be recognized under section 367(a)(3)(C) (determined without regard to the amendments made by subsection (e) [amending section 367 of this title]) with respect to losses incurred before January 1, 2018."

Made in United States
North Haven, CT
06 October 2022

25103949R00267